1001 MOVIES
YOU MUST SEE BEFORE YOU DIE

1001 MOVIES
YOU MUST SEE BEFORE YOU DIE

GENERAL EDITOR

STEVEN JAY SCHNEIDER

CASSELL
ILLUSTRATED

A Quintessence Book

Published in Great Britain by Cassell Illustrated
A division of Octopus Publishing Group Limited
Carmelite House, 50 Victoria Embankment,
London EC4Y 0DZ
www.octopusbooks.co.uk

An Hachette UK Company
www.hachette.co.uk

ISBN-13: 978 1 84403 889 3
QSS.FIL12

A CIP catalogue record for this book is available from the British Library

This book was designed and produced by
Quintessence Editions Ltd.
The Old Brewery, 6 Blundell Street, London N7 9BH
www.1001beforeyoudie.com

Updated Edition
Senior Editor: Elspeth Beidas
Senior Designer: Isabel Eeles
Designer: Dean Martin

Original Edition
Associate Publisher: Laura Price
Project Editor: Catherine Osborne
Researcher: Richard Guthrie
Designers: Ian Hunt, James Lawrence
Creative Director: Richard Dewing

Editorial Director: Ruth Patrick
Publisher: Philip Cooper

Colour reproduction by Colourscan Print Co Pte Ltd., Singapore
Printed in China

Contents

Preface   6

Introduction   8

Film Index and Checklist   12

1900   20

1910   24

1920   33

1930   77

1940   158

1950   245

1960   362

1970   502

1980   653

1990   777

2000   883

2010   915

Contributors   944

Genre Index   946

Director Index   956

Picture Acknowledgments   959

Preface   By Ian Haydn Smith

Cinema's transformation, from a sideshow curiosity at the beginning of the twentieth century, into both an artistic endeavor and a going concern over the ensuing years, witnessed the release of hundreds, then thousands, of films from around the world. Over time, some were recognized for their innovation and importance by critics, while countless others were consumed and enjoyed by audiences. But most films faded into obscurity, often seen by no more than a handful of people beyond those who were involved in their production. It is unknown how many films have been produced since the Lumieres' films premiered at Le Salon Indien du Grand Café in Paris on December 28, 1895. Suffice to say that those featured in this book are a mere drop in a vast cinematic ocean.

1001 Movies You Must See Before You Die was never intended as a "best of" collection—although a brief scan through the contents finds the majority of titles featured in *Sight and Sound's* Critics Top 250 and Directors' Top 100 greatest films poll present here. There are likely to be films here that you hate as much as you love. You may consider some entries to be insufficiently artful or far too rarefied for mass appeal, depending on your taste. Yet every film chosen will provoke a reaction, either good or bad, but never indifferent.

The last decade has seen increased focus and activity in both the preservation and rediscovery of films. In some cases, unearthed footage has offered a chance to re-view an already established classic. The discovery of a complete print of Fritz Lang's *Metropolis*, previously thought lost forever, in a museum in Buenos Aires has allowed audiences the opportunity to enjoy the film in the way that Lang himself envisaged it. (One can only wish the same for Erich von Stroheim's *Greed*, Orson Welles's *The Magnificent Ambersons*, or Sam Peckinpah's *Major Dundee*.) The work of organizations like The World Cinema Fund has also enabled audiences to see a wealth of cinema that had only existed in a precarious state. We can now watch such films as Ahamed El Maanouri's *Trances*, Kim Ki-Young's *The Housemaid*, Ritwik Ghatak's *Titash Ekti Nadir Naam*, and Mário Peixoto's *Limite* in the way their makers would have wished.

Peixoto's sublime 1931 film is one of the new additions to this edition, which is the first extended revision of *1001 Movies You Must See Before You Die* since its original publication in 2003, featuring reviews of fifty movies from all ages that previously did not make the cut. Thanks to the work of film archivists and historians, so many "new" titles have become key works in our understanding of cinema's brief but colorful history. They are included here in the hope that audiences unfamiliar with Yonggang Wu's *The Goddess*, Kent McKenzie's *The Exiles*, Franz Osten's *A Throw of Dice*, Ted Kotcheff's *Wake in Fright*, or Herbert Ponting's *The Great White Silence* will seek them out and enjoy them just as much as better-known titles.

There is also the issue of changing trends and tastes. Not all films survive the test of time. In some cases they have been removed to make way for another title from the same era or by the same director, one which might deserve greater recognition or is simply a better example of a filmmaker's work. Such is the case with Hitchcock's *Sabotage* and *The Lady Vanishes*, Ingmar Bergman's *Winter Light* and *Summer with Monika*, Luis Buñuel's *The Young One* and *The Exterminating Angel*, Orson Welles's *The Stranger* and *F for Fake*, Rogers and Hammerstein's *Seven Brides for Seven Brothers* and *Oklahoma*, Bill Forsythe's *Housekeeping* and *Local Hero*, and David Cronenberg's *Naked Lunch* and *Dead Ringers*. In other instances, films have been included because their initial omission might now seem odd. Who could begrudge Rudolf Valentino in *The Eagle*, *The Adventures of Prince Achmed*, *Mrs Minniver*, *Some Came Running*, *Mary Poppins*, *F for Fake*, *Diva*, *Hana-bi*, or even *The Towering Inferno* being brought into the fold?

In attempting to balance the survey across the entire spectrum of cinema's history, acknowledging the important impact of certain individuals, as well as the films they made or appeared in, it was occasionally necessary to trim the presence of certain figures. *I Walked with a Zombie* is a fine film, but Val Lewton's 1940s productions are already well represented. As for Alfred Hitchcock, there is so much material already available on him, it was decided to reduce his presence slightly. (I hope no one will resent the removal of Hitchcock's flawed psychological thriller *Spellbound* in favor of Henry Hathaway's ludicrously entertaining and under-appreciated drama *Peter Ibbertson*, which André Breton himself described as a "triumph of surrealist thought.")

Some removals were tough. *One Eyed Jacks*, *The Man From Laramie*, *Angel Face*, and *Utu* are fine films. The inclusion of *The Devils*, *The Hired Hand*, *Distant Voices, Still Lives*, and *Sleeping Dogs* is not meant to suggest they are better. Their addition, like all the other titles in this book, both new and old, are a provocation—throwing down the gauntlet for you to choose your own movies to die for.

Ian Haydn Smith is the update editor for the revised tenth anniversary edition of 1001 Movies You Must See Before You Die. *He is a London-based writer and the editor of* Curzon Magazine.

Introduction By Steven Jay Schneider

1001 Movies You Must See Before You Die is, as the title suggests, a book that seeks not just to inform and to prescribe, but also to motivate—to turn its curious readers into ardent viewers and to make it obvious that the pressure is on, that time is short, and that the number of films eminently worth watching has become very long indeed.

Nowadays, "Top 10 Movie" lists survive almost exclusively as annual critics' polls; and talk of "The 100 Greatest Films" tends to be restricted either to specific genres, such as comedy, horror, sci-fi, romance, or the Western, or to particular national cinemas, such as France, China, Italy, Japan, the U.K, or the U.S. All of this points to the impossibility, or at least the irresponsibility, of selecting a number less than (oh let's just say) a grand to work with when it comes to preparing a list of "best," or most valuable, or most important, or most unforgettable movies—a list that aims to do justice and give coverage to the entire history of the medium.

With this latter goal in mind, even 1001 can quickly start to seem like way too small a number. Maybe not so small if silent movies were kept off the list; or avant-garde films; or Middle Eastern films; or animated movies; or documentaries; or shorts. . . . But these strategies of exclusion are in the end all just ways of taking the pressure off, of drawing arbitrary lines in the cinematic sand and refusing to make the heap of difficult decisions necessary to end up with a limited selection of films that treats all the heterogeneous types and traditions comprising motion picture art with equal and all due respect. The book you are holding in your hands takes a great risk in offering up an all-time, all-genre, all-world, must-see films list. But it is a risk well worth taking, and if you make the effort to go and see the films discussed herein, you can be sure to die a happy moviegoer. In short: The more you see, the better off you'll be.

So how to determine which 1001 movies must be seen before dying? How much easier (and less controversial) it would be to come up with 1001 movies that should be avoided at all costs! It is no surprise to learn that film criticism hardly qualifies as an exact science—Roger Ebert's infamous formula "Two thumbs up, way, way up!" notwithstanding—and it is hardly an exaggeration to claim that one person's *Midnight Cowboy* may well be another one's *Ishtar*. Perhaps there are ways of objectively comparing, even ranking, highly codified and historically specific cycles, movements, or subgenres, such as the 1970s Italian thriller—in this case on the basis of the form's aestheticized violence, labyrinthine narratives, and psychological resonance. And maybe it really is legitimate to separate out Hitchcock's indisputable classics (*North By Northwest*, *Rear Window*, *Vertigo*, *Psycho*, *The Birds*, and so on) from what are often held to be the director's weaker efforts (*Torn Curtain*, *Family Plot*, *Topaz*, *The Paradine Case*). But what basis could there possibly be for deciding between Tsai Ming-liang's *What Time Is It There?* and Robert Aldrich's *What Ever Happened to Baby Jane?* Or between George Méliès's *A Trip to the Moon* and Marleen Gorris's *A Question of Silence*? If the goal of this book is indeed to include a little bit of everything, then what is to prevent the resulting list of 1001 films from being just a cinematic smorgasbord—a case of mere variety taking precedence over true value?

Good questions all. The first step in determining the 1001 movies to be included here involved taking a close look at a number of existing "greatest," "top," "favorite," and "best" film lists, and prioritizing titles based on the frequency with which they appeared. This allowed us to identify something like a canon of classics (including modern and contemporary films) that we felt confident warranted a spot in this book on the joint basis of quality and reputation. By no means did every film that turned up on these shorter, occasionally idiosyncratic lists make our cut of 1001, but the exercise at least gave us some key reference points and significantly reduced the unavoidably subjective nature of the selection process.

After we tentatively settled on an initial batch of around 1,300 titles, we proceeded to go through the list again (and again, and again, and again) with the dual—and conflicting—aim of reducing the overall number while still achieving sufficient coverage of the medium's various periods, national cinemas, genres, movements, traditions, and notable auteurs. With respect to the latter, we took the notion of an "auteur" in the loosest possible sense to include not only directors (Woody Allen, Ingmar Bergman, John Cassavetes, Federico Fellini, Jean-Luc Godard, Abbas Kiarostami, Satyajit Ray, among others), but also actors (Humphrey Bogart, Marlene Dietrich, Toshiro Mifune), producers (David O. Selznick, Sam Spiegel, Irving Thalberg), screenwriters (Ernest Lehman, Preston Sturges, Cesare Zavattini), cinematographers (Gregg Toland, Gordon Willis, Freddie Young), composers (Bernard Herrmann, Ennio Morricone, Nino Rota), and others.

We were also mindful of not giving automatic preference—free passes, as it were—to self-consciously "quality" productions or high cinematic art (historical epics, Shakespeare adaptations, Russian formalist experiments) at the expense of ignoring the so-called "low" genres (slapstick comedy, 1930s gangster films, blaxploitation cinema), or even movies that are of somewhat questionable aesthetic merit (*Pink Flamingos*, *Saturday Night Fever*, *The Blair Witch Project*), wholeheartedly populist appeal (*Top Gun*, *Rain Man*, *Big*, *E.T.: The Extra-Terrestrial*), or dubious ideological or ethical value (*The Birth of a Nation*, *Freaks*, *Triumph of the Will*, *Salò or The 120 Days of Sodom*). Instead we endeavored to adjudge each of our candidate selections on their own terms, which meant first figuring out as best we could just what the "terms" in question consisted of—not always an easy or obvious task, as in the case of *Pink Flamingos*, whose infamous tagline read, "An exercise in poor taste"—and then coming up with ways of separating the wheat from the chaff (even when the difference between the two might seem so slight as to be indiscernible or irrelevant).

What's that old saying, something along the lines of "Even if you could have filet mignon every single day, once in a while you're bound to crave a hamburger." The point here is, even if your filmgoing preferences lie heavily on the side of acknowledged world classics (*Citizen Kane*, *Rashomon*, *Raging Bull*, *Battleship Potemkin*) or the treasures of European art cinema (*L'Avventura*, *Hiroshima Mon Amour*, *Last Tango in Paris*), there is sure to come a time when you long to see a movie with a wholly different agenda, whether it's a Hollywood blockbuster (*Jurassic Park*, *The Empire Strikes Back*, *Titanic*), an underground oddity (*Scorpio Rising*, *Flaming Creatures*, *Hold Me While I'm Naked*), or a cult curiosity piece (*El Topo*, *Seconds*, *Slacker*, *Mondo Cane*, *Tetsuo*). As we envisioned it, our main task was to make sure that whatever your cinematic tastes—in general, or on those days when you feel like trying something new—this book would be a menu where every dish is a winner.

Finally, after making the last agonizing cuts that were required to bring the list down to a "mere" 1001, the remaining step was for us to tweak the results based on the feedback and suggestions offered by our esteemed group of contributors, whose collective experience, expertise, and passion for watching, discussing, and writing about motion pictures has ensured that, while no list of all-time-greatest anythings can possibly be perfect (whatever that means) or utterly uncontroversial (and wouldn't that be dull?), the one you have before you is, to be sure, as good as it gets. But it isn't just the list itself that makes this book so special: It is also the specially commissioned entries that accompany each of the 1001 movies included on that list—concise, thoughtful, stimulating essays that seamlessly combine important plot details, insightful commentary, cultural and historical context, and a fair share of trivia besides. (George Lucas was originally set to direct *Apocalypse Now*? Who knew?) Don't be fooled by the ease with which these essays are digested. There is a definite skill—one might even say an art—to writing a profound, engaging piece of only 500 words on a film like *Casablanca*, *The Searchers*, or *The Rules of the Game*, much less 350 words on *Boogie Nights*, *Cries and Whispers*, or *The Night of the Hunter*, or (gasp!) 200 words on *Marketa Lazarova*, *The Pianist*, or *Cleo from 5 to 7*. Somehow, with great aplomb, these authors have managed to pull it off, and brilliantly.

As for my own experience working on this book, I can only say that the pain of having to cross several personal favorites off the list was more than made up for by the pleasures of admiring the resulting medley, of reading so many wonderful film entries by so many wonderful writers on film, and of finding out so much about the history, traditions, and secret treasures of the cinema that I never knew before. Even if you have already seen all 1001 movies discussed and paid tribute to in these pages (congratulations, though I seriously doubt it), I'm sure you will benefit tremendously from reading about them here.

But the clock continues to tick away.... So start reading already, and keep watching!

***

As general editor of *1001 Movies You Must See Before You Die*, I have the honor and the privilege of being able to give thanks in print to all the individuals responsible for ensuring the timely completion and inevitable success of this ambitious, enjoyable, eminently worthwhile project. My sincerest gratitude goes out to Laura Price, Catherine Osborne, and the rest of the remarkably industrious and conscientious staff at Quintet Publishing, a division of the Quarto Group; to Andrew Lockett of the British Film Institute; to the close to sixty contributors from eight different countries who worked under tight deadlines and a slave-driving editor (me) to produce the entertaining and educational film entries that make up this volume; and, as always, to my family, friends, and colleagues, whose support and encouragement continues to be my not-so-secret weapon.

Steven Jay Schneider is a film critic, scholar, and producer, with M.A. degrees in Philosophy and Cinema Studies from Harvard University and New York University, respectively. He is the author and editor of a number of books on movies.

Film Index and Checklist

Use the film index and checklist to look up your favorite films, and keep track of what you have watched. Remember, films with both a foreign and an English language title are listed twice.

- ❏ 12 Angry Men 328
- ❏ 12 Years a Slave 927
- ❏ 2001: A Space Odyssey 484
- ❏ 39 Steps, The 120
- ❏ 400 Blows, The 350
- ❏ 42nd Street 100
- ❏ 8½ 400

A

- ❏ À bout de souffle 370
- ❏ "A" gai waak juk jaap 735
- ❏ À nous la liberté 83
- ❏ Abre los ojos 863
- ❏ Ace in the Hole 253
- ❏ Actor's Revenge, An 413
- ❏ Actress, The 807
- ❏ Adam's Rib 238
- ❏ Adventure, The 369
- ❏ Adventures of Prince Achmed, The 55
- ❏ Adventures of Priscilla, Queen of the Desert, The 827
- ❏ Adventures of Robin Hood, The 140
- ❏ Affair to Remember, An 325
- ❏ African Queen, The 257
- ❏ Age of Gold, The 80
- ❏ Aguirre, der Zorn Gottes 538
- ❏ Aguirre, the Wrath of God 538
- ❏ Ai no corrida 609
- ❏ Aileen Wuornos: The Life and Death of a Serial Killer 897
- ❏ Airplane! 662
- ❏ Akira 754
- ❏ Ali: Fear Eats the Soul 584
- ❏ Alice 752
- ❏ Alien 643
- ❏ Aliens 728
- ❏ All About Eve 248
- ❏ All About My Mother 881
- ❏ All Quiet on the Western Front 79
- ❏ All That Heaven Allows 314
- ❏ All That Jazz 648
- ❏ All the President's Men 602
- ❏ Alphaville 436
- ❏ Alphaville, une étrange aventure de Lemmy Caution 436
- ❏ Amadeus 705
- ❏ Amarcord 570
- ❏ American Beauty 879
- ❏ American Friend, The 615
- ❏ American Graffiti 556
- ❏ American in Paris, An 256

- ❏ American Werewolf in London, An 663
- ❏ Amores perros 888
- ❏ Anatomy of a Murder 356
- ❏ Andalusian Dog, An 69
- ❏ Andrei Rublev 492
- ❏ Andrei Rublyov 492
- ❏ Angels with Dirty Faces 140
- ❏ Angst Essen Seele Auf 584
- ❏ Annie Hall 616
- ❏ Aparajito 333
- ❏ Apartment, The 372
- ❏ Apocalypse Now 646
- ❏ Apur Sansar 359
- ❏ Archangel 783
- ❏ Ariel 752
- ❏ Artist, The 918
- ❏ Artists and Models 301
- ❏ Ascent 609
- ❏ Ashes and Diamonds 342
- ❏ Asphalt Jungle, The 245
- ❏ Astenicheskij sindrom 771
- ❏ Asthenic Syndrome, The 771
- ❏ Atlantic City 655
- ❏ Au hasard Balthazar 452
- ❏ Au revoir les enfants 733
- ❏ Audition 878
- ❏ Autumn Afternoon, An 390
- ❏ Avatar 914
- ❏ Awful Truth, The 138

B

- ❏ Ba wang bie ji 814
- ❏ Bab el hadid 343
- ❏ Babbetes Gaestebud 743
- ❏ Babe 837
- ❏ Babette's Feast 743
- ❏ Back to the Future 711
- ❏ Bad and the Beautiful, The 266
- ❏ Bad Day at Black Rock 305
- ❏ Badkonake sefid 839
- ❏ Badlands 554
- ❏ Baker's Wife, The 141
- ❏ Ballad of Narayama, The 688
- ❏ Balthazar 452
- ❏ Band Wagon, The 271
- ❏ Bank Dick, The 164
- ❏ Barefoot Contessa, The 291
- ❏ Barren Lives 408
- ❏ Barry Lyndon 585
- ❏ Batman 767
- ❏ Battle of Algiers, The 434
- ❏ Battle of San Pietro, The 205
- ❏ Battleship Potemkin, The 51
- ❏ Beau Travail 880
- ❏ Beautiful Troublemaker, The 788
- ❏ Beauty and the Beast 210

- ❏ Before the Revolution 421
- ❏ Being John Malkovich 875
- ❏ Being There 644
- ❏ Beiqing chengshi 776
- ❏ Belle de jour 455
- ❏ Ben-Hur 354
- ❏ Best Years of Our Lives, The 208
- ❏ Beverly Hills Cop 703
- ❏ Bharat Mata 335
- ❏ Bicycle Thief, The 223
- ❏ Big 759
- ❏ Big Chill, The 687
- ❏ Big Heat, The 280
- ❏ Big Parade, The 54
- ❏ Big Red One, The 659
- ❏ Big Short, The 940
- ❏ Big Sleep, The 214
- ❏ Bigamist, The 275
- ❏ Bigger Than Life 320
- ❏ Bird with the Crystal Plumage, The 511
- ❏ Birdman 932
- ❏ Birds, The 402
- ❏ Birth of a Nation, The 24
- ❏ Biruma no tategoto 318
- ❏ Bitter Tea of General Yen, The 102
- ❏ Bitter Tears of Petra von Kant, The 546
- ❏ Black Cat, The 117
- ❏ Black God, White Devil 424
- ❏ Black Narcissus 220
- ❏ Black Orpheus 353
- ❏ Black Swan 915
- ❏ Blackmail 76
- ❏ Blade Runner 675
- ❏ Blair Witch Project, The 874
- ❏ Blazing Saddles 582
- ❏ Blonde Cobra 410
- ❏ Blowup 444
- ❏ Blue Angel, The 78
- ❏ Blue is the Warmest Color 926
- ❏ Blue Kite, The 809
- ❏ Blue Velvet 721
- ❏ Boat, The 665
- ❏ Bob le flambeur 313
- ❏ Bob the Gambler 313
- ❏ Body Heat 667
- ❏ Bonnie and Clyde 473
- ❏ Boogie Nights 860
- ❏ Boudu sauvé des eaux 93
- ❏ Boudu Saved from Drowning 93
- ❏ Bowling for Columbine 894
- ❏ Boyhood 931
- ❏ Boyz 'n the Hood 787
- ❏ Brave-Hearted Will Take the Bride, The 840
- ❏ Braveheart 836
- ❏ Brazil 713
- ❏ Breakfast at Tiffany's 381

- Breakfast Club, The 707
- Breaking Away 642
- Breaking the Waves 858
- Breathless 370
- Bride of Frankenstein 122
- Bridge of Spies 939
- Bridge on the River Kwai, The 334
- Brief Encounter 206
- Brighter Summer Day, A 789
- Brightness 735
- Bring Me the Head of Alfredo Garcia 572
- Bringing Up Baby 142
- Broadcast News 742
- Brokeback Mountain 906
- Broken Blossoms 32
- Bronenosets Potyomkin 51
- Buffalo 66 870
- Bull Durham 748
- Burmese Harp, The 318
- Butch Cassidy and the Sundance Kid 494
- Butcher, The 504

C
- C'era una volta il west 475
- C'est arrivé près de chez vous 808
- Cabaret 539
- Cabin in the Woods, The 920
- Cabinet of Dr. Caligari, The 31
- Cairo Station 343
- Camille 129
- Campanadas a medianoche 437
- Captain Blood 123
- Captains Courageous 137
- Caravaggio 724
- Carmen Jones 295
- Caro diario 833
- Carrie 605
- Casablanca 182
- Cat People 184
- Ceddo 615
- Celebration, The 869
- Celine and Julie Go Boating 583
- Céline et Julie vont en bateau 583
- Chant of Jimmie Blacksmith, The 631
- Chariots of Fire 666
- Chelovek s kinoapparatom 72
- Children of a Lesser God 723
- Children of Paradise, The 204
- Chimes at Midnight 437
- Chinatown 578
- Chinese Ghost Story, A 739
- Chong qing sen lin 834
- Christ Stopped at Eboli 649
- Christmas Story, A 684
- Chronicle of a Summer 387

- Chronique d'un été 387
- Chungking Express 834
- Cidade de deus 895
- Cinema Paradiso 757
- Citizen Kane 166
- City Lights 85
- City of God 895
- City of Sadness, A 776
- Cléo de 5 à 7 389
- Cleo from 5 to 7 389
- Clerks 830
- Clockwork Orange, A 518
- Close Encounters of the Third Kind 610
- Close-Up 779
- Closely Watched Trains 466
- Cloud-Capped Star, The 373
- Clueless 842
- Color of Pomegranates, The 492
- Color Purple, The 719
- Come and See 708
- Come Drink With Me 447
- Conformist, The 503
- Consequences of Love, The 901
- Conte d'hiver 805
- Contempt 409
- Conversation, The 576
- Cook, the Thief, His Wife & Her Lover, The 768
- Cool Hand Luke 457
- Cool World, The 410
- Cow, The 474
- Cranes Are Flying, The 332
- Cria cuervos 598
- Cria! 598
- Cries and Whispers 542
- Crimes and Misdemeanors 766
- Cristo si è fermato a Eboli 649
- Crouching Tiger, Hidden Dragon 890
- Crowd, The 66
- Crumb 822
- Crying Game, The 809
- Csillagosok, katonák 459
- Cyclo 841
- Czlowiek z marmuru 620
- Czlowiek z zelaza 668

D
- Da hong deng long gao gao gua 799
- Da zui xia 447
- Daisies 446
- Dances with Wolves 781
- Dangerous Liaisons 763
- Dao ma zei 732
- Dark Knight, The 912
- Das Boot 665
- Das Kabinett des Doktor Caligari 31

- Das Leben der Anderen 908
- David Holzman's Diary 481
- Dawn of the Dead 634
- Day for Night 561
- Day in the Country, A 132
- Day the Earth Stood Still, The 260
- Daybreak 152
- Days of Heaven 628
- De Man die Zijn Haar Kort Liet Knippen 435
- De Stilte Rond Christine M. 683
- De Vierde Man 690
- Dead Man 846
- Dead Ringers 763
- Dead, The 747
- Dear Diary 833
- Decalogue, The 760
- Decline of the American Empire, The 727
- Deep End 507
- Deer Hunter, The 632
- Deewaar 591
- Defiant Ones, The 338
- Dekalog, Jeden 760
- Delicatessen 797
- Deliverance 537
- Demon, The 428
- Der Amerikanische Freund 615
- Der Blaue Engel 78
- Der Himmel Über Berlin 736
- Der Letzte Mann 42
- Der Untergang 902
- Dersu uzala 573
- Deseret 836
- Destry Rides Again 149
- Det sjunde inseglet 326
- Detour 201
- Deus e o diabo na terra do sol 424
- Deux ou trois chose que je sais d'elle 454
- Devils, The 522
- Diary of a Country Priest 259
- Die Abenteuer des Prinzen Achmed 55
- Die Bitteren Tränen der Petra von Kant 546
- Die Blechtrommel 651
- Die Büchse der Pandora 74
- Die Ehe der Maria Braun 638
- Die Hard 762
- Die xue shuang xiong 770
- Dilwale Dulhania le Jayenge 840
- Diner 676
- Dirty Harry 517
- Discreet Charm of the Bourgeoisie, The 543
- Distant Voices, Still Lives 764
- District 9 913
- Diva 663

❑ Do ma daan 727
❑ Do the Right Thing 772
❑ Docks of New York, The 67
❑ Doctor Zhivago 431
❑ Dodsworth 131
❑ Dog Day Afternoon 591
❑ Dog Star Man 389
❑ Dog's Life, A 396
❑ Don't Look Now 560
❑ Double Indemnity 196
❑ Double Life of Veronique, The 798
❑ Down by Law 726
❑ Downfall 902
❑ Dr. Mabuse, der Spieler 35
❑ Dr. Mabuse, Parts 1 and 2 35
❑ Dr. Strangelove 422
❑ Dracula 86
❑ Draughtsman's Contract, The 684
❑ Drugstore Cowboy 771
❑ Duck Soup 105
❑ Dumbo 175

E
❑ E.T.: The Extra-Terrestrial 670
❑ Eagle, The 48
❑ Ear, The 508
❑ Earth 82
❑ Earth Entranced 468
❑ Easy Rider 497
❑ Eclipse, The 395
❑ Edward Scissorhands 784
❑ El ángel exterminador 397
❑ El espíritu de la colmena 568
❑ El labertino del fauno 907
❑ El norte 690
❑ El Topo 505
❑ Elephant 897
❑ Elephant Man, The 658
❑ Empire Strikes Back, The 654
❑ English Patient, The 856
❑ Enter the Dragon 558
❑ Eraserhead 624
❑ Europa '51 263
❑ Europa Europa 785
❑ Evil Dead, The 671
❑ Exiles, The 382
❑ Exorcist, The 565
❑ Exterminating Angel, The 397
❑ Eyes Without a Face 362

F
❑ F for Fake 566
❑ Fa yeung nin wa 884
❑ Faces 476
❑ Fanny and Alexander 682
❑ Fanny och Alexander 682
❑ Fantasia 159

❑ Fantastic Planet 569
❑ Farewell My Concubine 814
❑ Farewell, My Lovely 198
❑ Fargo 850
❑ Fast Times at Ridgemont High 671
❑ Faster, Pussycat! Kill! Kill! 438
❑ Fat City 547
❑ Fatal Attraction 747
❑ Faustrecht der Freiheit 594
❑ Ferris Bueller's Day Off 728
❑ Festen 869
❑ Field of Dreams 767
❑ Fiends, The 287
❑ Fight Club 878
❑ Fireman's Ball, The 470
❑ Fires Were Started 185
❑ Fish Called Wanda, A 755
❑ Fitzcarraldo 679
❑ Five Easy Pieces 506
❑ Flaming Creatures 404
❑ Floating Weeds 361
❑ Fly, The 729
❑ Foolish Wives 41
❑ Footlight Parade 102
❑ Forbidden Games 262
❑ Forbidden Planet 319
❑ Force of Evil 227
❑ Forrest Gump 831
❑ Four Weddings and a Funeral 830
❑ Fourth Man, The 690
❑ Fox and His Friends 594
❑ Frankenstein 88
❑ Freaks 99
❑ Freedom for Us 83
❑ French Connection, The 528
❑ Frenzy 548
❑ From Here to Eternity 277
❑ Full Metal Jacket 740
❑ Funny Games 862

G
❑ Gaav 474
❑ Gabbeh 852
❑ Gallipoli 666
❑ Gandhi 680
❑ Gangs of New York 893
❑ Garden of the Finzi-Continis, The 517
❑ Gaslight 195
❑ Gegen die Wand 900
❑ General, The 60
❑ Gentlemen Prefer Blondes 281
❑ Gertrud 427
❑ Get Carter 529
❑ Ghostbusters 698
❑ Giant 322
❑ Gigi 338
❑ Gilda 215

❑ Gimme Shelter 516
❑ Giulietta degli spiriti 433
❑ Gladiator 885
❑ Gleaners and I, The 883
❑ Glengarry Glen Ross 805
❑ Glory 768
❑ Goddess, The 113
❑ Godfather, The 544
❑ Godfather: Part II, The 574
❑ Godson, The 464
❑ Gold Diggers of 1933 106
❑ Gold Rush, The 53
❑ Golden Coach, The 269
❑ Golden River 442
❑ Goldfinger 416
❑ Gone with the Wind 150
❑ Good Bye Lenin! 899
❑ Good Morning, Vietnam 743
❑ Good, the Bad, and the Ugly, The 448
❑ Goodbye, Children 733
❑ Goodfellas 778
❑ Gospel According to St. Matthew,
   The 429
❑ Graduate, The 460
❑ Grand Budapest Hotel, The 934
❑ Grand Illusion 134
❑ Grapes of Wrath, The 162
❑ Grave of the Fireflies 758
❑ Gravity 924
❑ Grease 636
❑ Great Beauty, The 925
❑ Great Escape, The 412
❑ Great Expectations 216
❑ Great Train Robbery, The 23
❑ Great White Silence, The 45
❑ Greed 46
❑ Groundhog Day 815
❑ Guling jie shaonian sha ren shijian
   789
❑ Gun Crazy 236
❑ Gunfight at the OK Corral 330
❑ Gunga Din 153
❑ Guys and Dolls 309

H
❑ Hable con ella 896
❑ Halloween 629
❑ Hana-Bi 860
❑ Hannah and Her Sisters 722
❑ Hanyeo 373
❑ Happiness 871
❑ Hard Day's Night, A 425
❑ Harder They Come, The 569
❑ Harold and Maude 526
❑ Haunting, The 414
❑ Häxan 40
❑ Head-On 900
❑ Heartbreak Kid, The 547

- Hearts of Darkness: A Filmmaker's Apocalypse 801
- Heat 843
- Heaven and Earth Magic 392
- Heavenly Creatures 823
- Heiress, The 239
- Henry V 195
- Henry: Portrait of a Serial Killer 782
- High Noon 269
- High Plains Drifter 553
- High School 482
- High Sierra 170
- High Society 323
- Hill 24 Doesn't Answer 304
- Hills Have Eyes, The 626
- Hired Hand, The 522
- Hiroshima mon amour 352
- His Girl Friday 158
- Hitlerjunge Salomon 785
- Hold Me While I'm Naked 442
- Hole, The 366
- Hong gao liang 746
- Hoop Dreams 828
- Horí, má panenko 470
- Horse Thief, The 732
- Hotaru no haka 758
- Hôtel Terminus: Klaus Barbie et son temps 748
- Hotel Terminus: The Life and Times of Klaus Barbie 748
- Hour of the Wolf 483
- House Is Black, The 404
- Housemaid, The 373
- How Green Was My Valley 171
- Hsi yen 817
- Hsia nu 495
- Hsimeng jensheng 810
- Hud 405
- Hurt Locker, The 910
- Hustler, The 385

I
- I Am a Fugitive from a Chain Gang 93
- I Know Where I'm Going! 201
- Ice Storm, The 859
- Ida 928
- Idi i smotri 708
- If…. 480
- Ikiru 267
- Il buono, il brutto, il cattivo 448
- Il conformista 503
- Il deserto rosso 417
- Il gattopardo 406
- Il giardino dei Finzi-Contini 517
- Il vangelo secondo Matteo 429
- In a Lonely Place 253
- In the Heat of the Night 469
- In the Mood for Love 884

- In the Realm of the Senses 609
- In the Year of the Pig 499
- Inception 916
- Incredible Shrinking Man, The 330
- Independence Day 859
- India Song 599
- Intolerance 28
- Invasion of the Body Snatchers 321
- It Happened One Night 115
- It's a Gift 112
- It's a Wonderful Life 212
- Ivan Groznyj I i II 199
- Ivan the Terrible, Parts I and II 199

J
- Jalsaghar 345
- Jaws 600
- Jazz Singer, The 64
- Jeanne Dielman, 23 quai du commerce, 1080 Bruxelles 587
- Jerk, The 652
- Jeux interdits 262
- Jezebel 139
- JFK 791
- Jodai-e Nader Az Simin 919
- Johnny Guitar 296
- Journal d'un curé de campagne 259
- Jules and Jim 398
- Jules et Jim 398
- Juliet of the Spirits 433
- Jungle Book, The 471
- Jurassic Park 818

K
- Keeper of Promises 395
- Kes 498
- Khaneh Siah Ast 404
- Kid Brother, The 65
- Killer of Sheep 623
- Killer, The 770
- Killers, The 211
- Killing Fields, The 703
- Killing of a Chinese Bookie, The 603
- Kind Hearts and Coronets 242
- King Kong 107
- King of Comedy, The 694
- King of New York 780
- Kingdom, The 835
- Kippur 886
- Kiss Me Deadly 308
- Kiss of the Spider Woman 714
- Kjærlighetens kjøtere 848
- Klute 525
- Körkarlen 34
- Koyaanisqatsi 692
- Kramer vs. Kramer 652
- Kumonosu jo 324

L
- L.A. Confidential 861
- L'âge d'or 80
- L'albero degli zoccoli 630
- L'année dernière à Marienbad 388
- L'argent 685
- L'Atalante 116
- L'avventura 369
- L'eclisse 395
- L'uccello dalle piume di cristallo 511
- La Battaglia di Algeri 434
- La belle et la bête 210
- La belle noiseuse 788
- La dolce vita 364
- La double vie de Véronique 798
- La femme du boulanger 141
- La grande bellezza 925
- La grande illusion 134
- La jetée 380
- La maman et la putain 552
- La maschera del demonio 378
- La notte 383
- La notte di San Lorenzo 683
- La nuit américaine 561
- La passion de Jeanne d'Arc 68
- La planète sauvage 569
- La règle du jeu 157
- La roue 42
- La souriante Madame Beudet 35
- La strada 286
- La strategia del ragno 507
- La vie d'Adèle—Chapitres 1 et 2 926
- Ladies Man, The 385
- Ladri di biciclette 223
- Lady Eve, The 169
- Lady from Shanghai, The 230
- Lady Vanishes, The 144
- Ladykillers, The 311
- Lan feng zheng 809
- Land Without Bread 108
- Las hurdes 108
- Last Chants for a Slow Dance 619
- Last Laugh, The 42
- Last Metro, The 655
- Last Picture Show, The 533
- Last Seduction, The 821
- Last Tango in Paris 545
- Last Wave, The 611
- Last Year at Marienbad 388
- Låt den rätte komma in 913
- Laura 191
- Lavender Hill Mob, The 259
- Lawrence of Arabia 393
- Le boucher 504
- Le carosse d'or 269
- Le chagrin et la pitié 521
- Le charme discret de la bourgeoisie 543

❏ Le consequenze dell'amore 901
❏ Le déclin de l'empire américain 727
❏ Le dernier métro 655
❏ Le jour se lève 152
❏ Le mépris 409
❏ Le notti di Cabiria 331
❏ Le roman d'un tricheur 129
❏ Le salaire de la peur 274
❏ Le samouraï 464
❏ Le souffle au coeur 534
❏ Le trou 366
❏ Le voyage dans la Lune 20
❏ Leopard, The 406
❏ Les demoiselles de Rochefort 463
❏ Les diaboliques 287
❏ Les enfants du paradis 204
❏ Les glaneurs et la glaneuse 883
❏ Les maîtres fous 304
❏ Les parapluies de Cherbourg 426
❏ Les quatre cents coups 350
❏ Les roseaux sauvages 821
❏ Les vacances de M. Hulot 272
❏ Les vampires 27
❏ Les yeux sans visage 362
❏ Let the Right One In 913
❏ Letjat zhuravli 332
❏ Letter from an Unknown Woman 224
❏ Leviathan 930
❏ Life and Death of Colonel Blimp, The 187
❏ Life of Émile Zola, The 139
❏ Life of Pi 921
❏ Limite 83
❏ Lincoln 922
❏ Lion King, The 820
❏ Little Big Man 510
❏ Little Caesar 77
❏ Lives of Others, The 909
❏ Local Hero 694
❏ Lola 382
❏ Lola Montès 297
❏ Lola Rennt 868
❏ Lolita 391
❏ Lone Star 857
❏ Long Goodbye, The 557
❏ Look of Silence, The 935
❏ Lord of the Rings, The 892
❏ Los olvidados 252
❏ Lost Weekend, The 203
❏ Louisiana Story 235
❏ Loulou 659
❏ Love Me Tonight 94
❏ Lucía 498

M
❏ M 90
❏ M*A*S*H 512

❏ Ma nuit chez maud 502
❏ Mad Masters, The 304
❏ Mad Max 650
❏ Mad Max: Fury Road 943
❏ Madame de . . . 273
❏ Magnificent Ambersons, The 178
❏ Magnolia 877
❏ Make Way for Tomorrow 133
❏ Maltese Falcon, The 174
❏ Man Bites Dog 808
❏ Man Escaped, A 320
❏ Man in Grey, The 188
❏ Man of Iron 668
❏ Man of Marble 620
❏ Man of the West 339
❏ Man Who Fell to Earth, The 601
❏ Man Who Had His Hair Cut Short, The 435
❏ Man Who Shot Liberty Valance, The 392
❏ Man with a Movie Camera, The 72
❏ Man with the Golden Arm, The 308
❏ Manchurian Candidate, The 399
❏ Manhattan 645
❏ Manhunter 720
❏ Manila in the Claws of Brightness 593
❏ Marketa Lazarová 469
❏ Marnie 420
❏ Marriage of Maria Braun, The 638
❏ Marty 301
❏ Mary Poppins 428
❏ Masculin, féminin 453
❏ Masculine-Feminine 453
❏ Masque of the Red Death, The 421
❏ Matrix, The 882
❏ Matter of Life and Death, A 215
❏ Maynila: Sa mga kuko ng liwanag 593
❏ McCabe and Mrs. Miller 520
❏ Mean Streets 562
❏ Méditerranée 413
❏ Meet Me in St. Louis 192
❏ Még kér a nép 529
❏ Meghe Dhaka Tara 373
❏ Memento 889
❏ Memorias del subdesarrollo 481
❏ Memories of Underdevelopment 481
❏ Meshes of the Afternoon 187
❏ Metropolis 57
❏ Midnight Cowboy 493
❏ Midnight Song 135
❏ Mildred Pierce 200
❏ Mirror, The 577
❏ Mishima: A Life in Four Chapters 709
❏ Modern Times 125
❏ Mon oncle 3 46
❏ Mondo cane 396
❏ Money 685
❏ Monsieur Verdoux 222

❏ Monty Python and the Holy Grail 590
❏ Monty Python's Life of Brian 641
❏ Moolaadé 902
❏ Moonstruck 744
❏ Mortal Storm, The 163
❏ Mother and the Whore, The 552
❏ Mother India 335
❏ Mr. Deeds Goes to Town 127
❏ Mr. Hulot's Holiday 272
❏ Mr. Smith Goes to Washington 145
❏ Mrs. Miniver 181
❏ Mujeres al borde de un ataque de nervios 749
❏ Muppet Movie, The 649
❏ Murder, My Sweet 198
❏ Muriel's Wedding 826
❏ Murmur of the Heart 534
❏ Music Room, The 345
❏ Mutiny on the Bounty 119
❏ My Brilliant Career 637
❏ My Darling Clementine 218
❏ My Fair Lady 417
❏ My Left Foot 769
❏ My Life to Live 390
❏ My Man Godfrey 128
❏ My Night at Maud's 502
❏ My Own Private Idaho 794
❏ My Uncle 346

N
❏ Naked Gun, The 757
❏ Naked Spur, The 275
❏ Nanook of the North 36
❏ Napoléon 65
❏ Narayama bushi-ko 688
❏ Nashville 595
❏ Natural Born Killers 826
❏ Natural, The 698
❏ Neco z alenky 752
❏ Nema-ye nazdik 779
❏ Network 604
❏ Night and Fog 306
❏ Night at the Opera, A 121
❏ Night of the Hunter, The 310
❏ Night of the Living Dead 486
❏ Night of the Shooting Stars, The 683
❏ Night, The 383
❏ Nightmare on Elm Street, A 700
❏ Nights of Cabiria, The 331
❏ Ninotchka 153
❏ No Fear, No Die 777
❏ No Man's Land 893
❏ North by Northwest 349
❏ Nosferatu, a Symphony of Terror 39
❏ Nosferatu, eine Symphonie des Grauens 39
❏ Nosferatu: Phantom der Nacht 639

❑ Nosferatu: Phantom of the Night 639
❑ Nostalgia de la luz 915
❑ Nostalgia for the Light 915
❑ Notorious 219
❑ Now, Voyager 176
❑ Nuit et brouillard 306
❑ Nuovo cinema paradiso 757
❑ Nutty Professor, The 411

O
❑ O pagador de promessas 395
❑ O Thiassos 588
❑ Obchod na korze 430
❑ October 62
❑ Odd Man Out 222
❑ Ôdishon 878
❑ Oklahoma 312
❑ Oktyabr 62
❑ Oldboy 898
❑ Oldeuboi 898
❑ Olympia 143
❑ On the Town 244
❑ On the Waterfront 284
❑ Once Upon a Time in America 695
❑ Once Upon a Time in China 793
❑ Once Upon a Time in the West 475
❑ One and a Two, A 886
❑ One Flew Over the Cuckoo's Nest 592
❑ Onibaba 428
❑ Only Angels Have Wings 148
❑ Open City 207
❑ Open Your Eyes 863
❑ Ordet 300
❑ Ordinary People 653
❑ Orfeu negro 353
❑ Orphans of the Storm 33
❑ Orphée 245
❑ Orpheus 245
❑ Osama 900
❑ Ossessione 190
❑ Ostre sledované vlaky 466
❑ Our Hospitality 41
❑ Out of Africa 709
❑ Out of the Past 221
❑ Outlaw Josey Wales, The 603
❑ Ox-Bow Incident, The 186

P
❑ Paisà 209
❑ Paisan 209
❑ Paleface, The 229
❑ Palm Beach Story, The 176
❑ Pan's Labyrinth 907
❑ Pandora and the Flying Dutchman 256
❑ Pandora's Box 74
❑ Papillon 557
❑ Paranormal Activity 908

❑ Paris, Texas 699
❑ Pasazerka 403
❑ Passage to India, A 702
❑ Passenger 403
❑ Passion of Joan of Arc, The 68
❑ Pat Garrett and Billy the Kid 566
❑ Pather Panchali 298
❑ Paths of Glory 324
❑ Patton 511
❑ Peeping Tom 377
❑ Peking Opera Blues 727
❑ Pépé le Moko 132
❑ Performance 513
❑ Persona 450
❑ Peter Ibbertson 124
❑ Phantom Carriage, The 34
❑ Phantom of the Opera, The 49
❑ Phenix City Story, The 307
❑ Philadelphia 810
❑ Philadelphia Story, The 161
❑ Piano, The 816
❑ Pickpocket 351
❑ Pickup on South Street 270
❑ Picnic at Hanging Rock 599
❑ Pier, The 380
❑ Pierrot Goes Wild 441
❑ Pierrot le fou 441
❑ Pink Flamingos 549
❑ Pinocchio 165
❑ Place in the Sun, A 258
❑ Planet of the Apes 477
❑ Platoon 725
❑ Player, The 803
❑ Playtime 458
❑ Point Blank 462
❑ Poltergeist 672
❑ Popiól i diament 342
❑ Postman Always Rings Twice, The 209
❑ Potomok Chingis-Khana 70
❑ Prapancha Pash 71
❑ Pretty Woman 780
❑ Prima della rivoluzione 421
❑ Princess Bride, The 739
❑ Prizzi's Honor 706
❑ Producers, The 489
❑ Project A, Part II 735
❑ Psycho 374
❑ Public Enemy, The 89
❑ Pulp Fiction 824
❑ Puppetmaster, The 810
❑ Purple Rose of Cairo, The 716

Q
❑ Queen Christina 109
❑ Question of Silence, A 683
❑ Quiet Earth, The 715
❑ Quiet Man, The 261

R
❑ Raging Bull 660
❑ Raiders of the Lost Ark 664
❑ Rain Man 761
❑ Raise the Red Lantern 799
❑ Raising Arizona 734
❑ Ran 710
❑ Rapture, The 788
❑ Rashomon 246
❑ Real Life 642
❑ Rear Window 288
❑ Rebecca 160
❑ Rebel Without a Cause 302
❑ Reckless Moment, The 237
❑ Red and the White, The 459
❑ Red Desert, The 417
❑ Red Psalm 529
❑ Red River 228
❑ Red Shoes, The 233
❑ Red Sorghum 746
❑ Reds 669
❑ Rekopis znaleziony w saragossie 439
❑ Report 453
❑ Repulsion 440
❑ Requiem for a Dream 887
❑ Reservoir Dogs 804
❑ Return of the Jedi 688
❑ Revenant, The 937
❑ Revenge of the Vampire/Black Sunday 378
❑ Ride Lonesome 353
❑ Riget 835
❑ Right Stuff, The 686
❑ Ring 870
❑ Rio Bravo 360
❑ Rio Grande 249
❑ Road, The 286
❑ RoboCop 764
❑ Rocco and His Brothers 367
❑ Rocco e i suoi fratelli 367
❑ Rocky 608
❑ Rocky Horror Picture Show, The 586
❑ Roger & Me 774
❑ Roma, città aperta 207
❑ Roman Holiday 282
❑ Romper Stomper 802
❑ Room with a View, A 720
❑ Rope 231
❑ Rosemary's Baby 478
❑ Rules of the Game, The 157
❑ Run Lola Run 868
❑ Rushmore 869
❑ Russian Ark 894
❑ Russkiy kovcheg 894

S

- S'en fout la mort 777
- Safe 843
- Salò o le centoventi giornate di sodoma 596
- Saló, or the 120 Days of Sodom 596
- Salt of the Earth 297
- Salvador 724
- Sanma No Aji 390
- Sans soleil 687
- Sans toi ni loi 717
- Sanshô dayû 294
- Sanshô the Bailiff 294
- Saragossa Manuscript, The 439
- Såsom i en spegel 386
- Sátántangó 829
- Saturday Night and Sunday Morning 363
- Saturday Night Fever 621
- Satyricon 490
- Saul fia 938
- Saving Private Ryan 866
- Sayat nova 492
- Scarface 693
- Scarface: The Shame of a Nation 98
- Schindler's List 813
- Scorpio Rising 419
- Scream 854
- Se7en 838
- Searchers, The 316
- Seconds 447
- Secret Beyond the Door, The 226
- Secrets & Lies 855
- Sedmikrasky 446
- Sen to chihiro no kamikakushi 892
- Senso 290
- Separation, A 919
- Sergeant York 168
- Serpico 559
- Servant, The 403
- Seven Samurai, The 293
- Seventh Seal, The 326
- Seventh Victim, The 188
- Sex, Lies, and Videotape 775
- Shadow of a Doubt 189
- Shadows 357
- Shadows of Forgotten Ancestors 418
- Shaft 531
- Shame 488
- Shane 283
- Shanghai Express 95
- Shao Lin san shi liu fang 637
- Shaolin Master Killer 637
- Shawshank Redemption, The 833
- She Done Him Wrong 103
- She's Gotta Have It 723
- Shen nu 113
- Sherlock, Jr. 44

- Sherman's March 731
- Shichinin no samurai 293
- Shine 853
- Shining, The 656
- Shoah 718
- Shock Corridor 409
- Shoot the Piano Player 376
- Shop on Main Street, The 430
- Short Cuts 811
- Silence of the Lambs, The 796
- Silver Lode 291
- Singin' in the Rain 264
- Sinnui yauman 739
- Sins of Lola Montes, The 297
- Sixth Sense, The 876
- Skammen 488
- Slacker 792
- Sleeper 563
- Sleeping Dogs 619
- Sleuth 550
- Slumdog Millionaire 911
- Smiles of a Summer Night 312
- Smiling Madame Beudet, The 35
- Smoke 839
- Smultronstället 329
- Snake Pit, The 230
- Snow White and the Seven Dwarfs 136
- Social Network, The 917
- Solaris 540
- Soldaat van Oranje 625
- Soldier of Orange 625
- Solyaris 540
- Some Came Running 347
- Some Like it Hot 348
- Sommaren med Monika 270
- Sommarnattens leende 312
- Son of Saul 938
- Sons of the Desert 109
- Sorrow and the Pity, The 521
- Sound of Music, The 435
- Spartacus 371
- Spider's Stratagem, The 507
- Spirit of the Beehive, The 568
- Spirited Away 892
- Splendor in the Grass 379
- Spoorloos 751
- Spotlight 941
- Spring in a Small Town 227
- Stachka 43
- Stagecoach 146
- Stalker 640
- Stand by Me 731
- Star Is Born, A 287
- Star Wars 612
- Star Wars: The Force Awakens 936
- Steamboat Bill, Jr. 70
- Stella Dallas 135

- Sting, The 551
- Storm over Asia 70
- Story of a Cheat, The 129
- Story of the Late Chrysanthemums, The 158
- Straight Outta Compton 942
- Stranger than Paradise 704
- Strangers on a Train 254
- Straw Dogs 535
- Streetcar Named Desire, A 255
- Strictly Ballroom 802
- Strike 43
- Stroszek 614
- Subarnarekha 442
- Sullivan's Travels 172
- Summer with Monika 270
- Suna no onna 418
- Sunless 687
- Sunrise 58
- Sunset Blvd. 251
- Superfly 551
- Suspiria 618
- Sweet Hereafter, The 863
- Sweet Smell of Success 334
- Sweet Sweetback's Baadasssss Song 532
- Swing Time 126

T

- Ta'm e guilass 865
- Tabu 84
- Tale of the Wind, A 756
- Tale of Winter, A 805
- Tales of Ugetsu 278
- Talk to Her 896
- Tampopo 732
- Tangerine 938
- Targets 487
- Taste of Cherry 865
- Taxi Driver 606
- Ten Commandments, The 315
- Terminator 2: Judgment Day 797
- Terminator, The 697
- Terms of Endearment 689
- Terra em transe 468
- Texas Chain Saw Massacre, The 581
- Thelma & Louise 793
- There Will Be Blood 909
- Thief of Bagdad, The 48
- Thin Blue Line, The 753
- Thin Man, The 118
- Thin Red Line, The 872
- Thing, The 681
- Things to Come 130
- Third Man, The 240
- Thirty-Two Short Films About Glenn Gould 817
- This Is Spinal Tap 701

- Three Colors: Blue 814
- Three Colors: Red 825
- Three Kings 877
- Three Lives and Only One Death 853
- Throne of Blood 324
- Through a Glass Darkly 386
- Through the Olive Trees 832
- Throw of Dice, A 71
- Time to Live and the Time to Die, The 706
- Tin Drum, The 651
- Tini zabutykh predkiv 418
- Tirez sur le pianiste 376
- Titanic 864
- To Be or Not to Be 177
- To Have and Have Not 194
- To Kill a Mockingbird 394
- To Live 267
- Todo sobre mi madre 881
- Tokyo Olympiad 432
- Tokyo Orimpikku 432
- Tokyo Story 276
- Tong nien wang shi 706
- Tongues Untied 798
- Too Early, Too Late 672
- Tootsie 677
- Top Gun 730
- Top Hat 124
- Total Recall 783
- Touch of Evil 337
- Touch of Zen, A 495
- Towering Inferno, The 572
- Toy Story trilogy 844
- Trainspotting 849
- Traveling Players, The 588
- Treasure of the Sierra Madre, The 234
- Tree of Wooden Clogs, The 630
- Trip to the Moon, A 20
- Tristana 502
- Triumph des Willens 111
- Triumph of the Will 111
- Trois couleurs: Bleu 814
- Trois couleurs: Rouge 825
- Trois vies & une seule mort 853
- Trouble in Paradise 96
- Trust 777
- Tsotsi 905
- Turkish Delight 567
- Turks Fruit 567
- Two or Three Things I Know About Her 454
- Two-Lane Blacktop 536

U
- Ucho 508
- Ugetsu monogatari 278
- Ukigusa 361
- Ultimo tango a Parigi 545

- Umberto D 268
- Umbrellas of Cherbourg, The 426
- Un chien andalou 69
- Un condamné à mort s'est échappé ou le vent souffle où il veut 320
- Unbelievable Truth, The 774
- Under the Skin 929
- Underground 840
- Une histoire de vent 756
- Une partie de campagne 132
- Unforgiven 806
- Unknown, The 61
- Untouchables, The 745
- Unvanquished, The 333
- Up in Smoke 635
- Usual Suspects, The 847

V
- Vagabond 717
- Vampire, The 92
- Vampyr 92
- Vanishing, The 751
- Vargtimmen 483
- Vérités et mensonges 566
- Vertigo 341
- Viaggio in Italia 279
- Vidas secas 408
- Videodrome 691
- Vinyl 439
- Viridiana 379
- Viskingar och rop 542
- Vivre sa vie: Film en douze tableaux 390
- Viy 474
- Voskhozhdeniye 609
- Voyage in Italy 279

W
- W.R.: Misterije organizma 523
- W.R.: Mysteries of the Organism 523
- Wadjda 923
- Wages of Fear 274
- Wake in Fright 536
- Walkabout 524
- Wall Street 744
- Wall, The 591
- Wanda 534
- Wanton Countess, The 290
- War Game, The 432
- Wavelength 465
- Wedding Banquet, The 817
- Week End 463
- West Side Story 384
- What Ever Happened to Baby Jane? 399
- Wheel, The 42
- When Harry Met Sally 765
- Whiplash 933

- Whisky Galore! 243
- White Balloon, The 839
- White Heat 237
- Who Framed Roger Rabbit 759
- Who's Afraid of Virginia Woolf? 443
- Wicker Man, The 558
- Wild Bunch, The 501
- Wild Reeds, The 821
- Wild Strawberries 329
- Willy Wonka and the Chocolate Factory 521
- Winchester '73 249
- Wings of Desire 736
- Within Our Gates 33
- Withnail and I 738
- Wizard of Oz, The 154
- Wo hu cang long 890
- Wolf Man, The 169
- Woman in the Dunes 418
- Woman Under the Influence, A 580
- Women on the Verge of a Nervous Breakdown 749
- Wong fei-hung 793
- Woodstock 515
- World of Apu, The 359
- Written on the Wind 319
- Wrong Man, The 323
- Wuthering Heights 144

X
- Xiao cheng zhi chun 227
- Xich lo 841

Y
- Yankee Doodle Dandy 180
- Ye ban ge sheng 135
- Yeelen 735
- Yi yi 886
- Yol 673
- Young and the Damned, The 252
- Young Frankenstein 580
- Young Girls of Rochefort, The 463
- Yuen ling-yuk 807
- Yukinojo henge 413

Z
- Z 489
- Zabriskie Point 512
- Zangiku Monogatari 158
- Zemlya 82
- Zerkalo 577
- Zéro de conduite 106
- Zero for Conduct 106
- Zero Kelvin 848
- Zire darakhatan zeyton 832
- Zu Früh, Zu Spät 672

France (Star) 14m Silent BW
Producer Georges Méliès
Screenplay Georges Méliès, from the novel
De la Terre à la Lune by Jules Verne
Photography Michaut, Lucien Tainguy
Cast Victor André, Bleuette Bernon, Brunnet,
Jeanne d'Alcy, Henri Delannoy, Depierre,
Farjaut, Kelm, Georges Méliès

*"Méliès actually was
a magician . . . And
so he understood the
possibilities of the
motion picture camera."*

Martin Scorsese, 2012

ℹ

The lively Selenites were played
by acrobats from Paris's famous
music hall, the Folies Bergère.

Le voyage dans la lune · Georges Méliès, 1902
A Trip to the Moon

When thinking about *A Trip to the Moon*, one's mind is quickly captured by the original and mythic idea of early filmmaking as an art whose "rules" were established in the very process of its production. This French movie was released in 1902 and represents a revolution for the time, given its length (around fourteen minutes), as compared to the more common two-minute short films then being produced.

A Trip to the Moon directly reflects the theatrical personality of its director, Georges Méliès, whose past as a theater actor and magician influenced the making of the movie. The film boldly experiments with some of the most famous cinematic techniques, such as superimpositions, dissolves, and editing practices that would be widely used later on. Despite the simplicity of its special effects, the film is generally considered the first example of science-fiction cinema. It offers many elements characteristic of the genre—a spaceship, the discovery of a new frontier—and establishes most of its conventions.

The movie opens with a Scientific Congress in which Professor Barbenfouillis (played by Méliès himself) tries to convince his colleagues to take part in a trip to explore the moon. Once his plan is accepted, the expedition is organized and the scientists embark in a space ship. The missile-like vessel lands right in the eye of the moon, which is represented as an anthropomorphic being. Once on the surface, the scientists soon meet the hostile inhabitants, the Selenites, who take them to their King. After discovering that the enemies easily disappear in a cloud of smoke with the simple touch of an umbrella, the French men manage to escape and return to Earth. They fall into the ocean and explore the abyss until they are finally rescued and honored in Paris as heroes.

Méliès's movie deserves a legitimate place among the milestones in world cinema history. Despite its surreal look, *A Trip to the Moon* is an entertaining and groundbreaking film able to combine the tricks of the theater with the infinite possibilities of the cinematic medium. Méliès was an orchestrator more than a director; he also contributed to the movie as a writer, actor, producer, set and costume designer, and cinematographer, creating special effects that were considered spectacular at the time. The first true science-fiction film cannot be missed by a spectator looking for the origin of those conventions that would later influence the entire genre and its most famous entries.

In a more general sense, *A Trip to the Moon* can be regarded as the movie that established the major difference between cinematic fiction and nonfiction. At a time when filmmaking mostly portrayed daily life (such as in the films of the Lumière brothers at the end of the 19th century), Méliès was able to offer a fantasy constructed for pure entertainment. He opened the doors to future film artists by visually expressing his creativity in a way utterly uncommon to movies of the time. **CFe**

No. 201

EDISON FILM
COPYRIGHTED 1903

THE GREAT TRAIN

ROBBERY

U.S. (Edison) 12m Silent BW (hand-colored)
Screenplay Scott Marble, Edwin S. Porter
Photography Edwin S. Porter, Blair Smith
Cast A.C. Abadie, Gilbert M. "Bronco Billy"
Anderson, George Barnes, Walter Cameron,
Frank Hanaway, Morgan Jones, Tom London,
Marie Murray, Mary Snow

"In every respect we consider it absolutely the superior of any moving picture ever made."

Edison Company Catalog, 1904

i

Edwin S. Porter gave future director
D.W. Griffith his first acting role in
Rescued from an Eagle's Nest (1908).

The Great Train Robbery Edwin S. Porter, 1903

Most historians regard *The Great Train Robbery* as the first Western, initiating a genre that, in a few short years, became the most popular in American cinema. Made by the Edison Company in November 1903, *The Great Train Robbery* was the most commercially successful film of the pre-Griffith period of American cinema and spawned a host of imitations.

What is exceptional about Edwin S. Porter's film is the degree of narrative sophistication, given the early date. There are over a dozen separate scenes, each further developing the story. In the opening scene, two masked robbers force a telegraph operator to send a false message so that the train will make an unscheduled stop. In the next scene, bandits board the train. The robbers enter the mail car, and, after a fight, open the safe. In the following scene, two robbers overpower the driver and fireman of the train and throw one of them off. Next, the robbers stop the train and hold up the passengers. One runs away and is shot. The robbers then escape aboard the engine, and in the subsequent scene we see them mount horses and ride off. Meanwhile, the telegraph operator on the train sends a message calling for assistance. In a saloon, a newcomer is being forced to dance at gunpoint, but when the message arrives everyone grabs their rifles and exits. Cut to the robbers pursued by a posse. There is a shoot-out, and the robbers are killed.

There's one extra shot, the best known in the film, showing one of the robbers firing point blank out of the screen. This was, it seems, sometimes shown at the start of the film, sometimes at the end. Either way, it gave the spectator a sense of being directly in the line of fire.

One actor in *The Great Train Robbery* was G.M. Anderson (real name Max Aronson). Among other parts, he played the passenger who is shot. Anderson was shortly to become the first star of Westerns, appearing as Bronco Billy in over a hundred films, beginning in 1907.

In later years some have challenged the claim of *The Great Train Robbery* to be regarded as the first Western, on the grounds that it is not the first or not a Western. It is certainly true that there are earlier films with a Western theme, such as Thomas Edison's *Cripple Creek Bar-Room Scene* (1899), but they do not have the fully developed narrative of Porter's film. It's also true that it has its roots both in stage plays incorporating spectacular railroad scenes, and in other films of daring robberies that weren't Westerns. Nor can its claim to being a true Western be based on authentic locations, because *The Great Train Robbery* was shot on the Delaware and Lackawanna Railroad in New Jersey. But train robberies, since the days of Jesse James, had been part of Western lore, and other iconic elements such as six-shooters, cowboy hats, and horses all serve to give the film a genuine Western feel. **EB**

1903

U.S. (D.W. Griffith & Epoch) 190m Silent BW
Producer D.W. Griffith **Screenplay** Frank E. Woods, D.W. Griffith, from the novel *The Clansman: An Historical Romance of the Ku Klux Klan*, the novel *The Leopard's Spots*, and the play *The Clansman* by Thomas F. Dixon Jr. **Photography** G.W. Bitzer **Music** Joseph Carl Breil, D.W. Griffith **Cast** Lillian Gish, Mae Marsh, Henry B. Walthall, Miriam Cooper, Mary Alden, Ralph Lewis, George Siegmann, Walter Long, Robert Harron, Wallace Reid, Joseph Henabery, Elmer Clifton, Josephine Crowell, Spottiswoode Aitken, George Beranger

"It is the biggest thing I have undertaken, but I shall not be satisfied until I do something else . . . I am, like all other human beings, aiming at perfection."

D.W. Griffith, 1915

i

Griffith's movie was the first film to be screened in the White House—in 1915, for President Woodrow Wilson.

The Birth of a Nation D.W. Griffith, 1915

Simultaneously one of the most revered and most reviled films ever made, D.W. Griffith's *The Birth of a Nation* is important for the very reasons that prompt both of those divergent reactions. In fact, rarely has a film so equally deserved such praise and scorn, which in many ways raises the film's estimation not just in the annals of cinema but as an essential historic artifact (some might say relic).

Though it was based on Thomas Dixon's explicitly racist play *The Clansman: An Historical Romance of the Ku Klux Klan*, by many accounts Griffith was indifferent to the racist bent of the subject matter. Just how complicit that makes him in delivering its ugly message has been cause for almost a century of debate. However, there has been no debate concerning the film's technical and artistic merits. Griffith was, as usual, more interested in the possibilities of the medium than the message, and in this regard he set the standards for modern Hollywood.

Most overtly, *The Birth of a Nation* was the first real historical epic, proving that even in the silent era audiences were willing to sit through a nearly three-hour drama. But with countless artistic innovations, Griffith essentially created contemporary film language, and although elements of *The Birth of a Nation* may now seem quaint or dated, virtually every film is beholden to it in one way, shape, or form. Griffith introduced the use of dramatic close-ups, tracking shots, and other expressive camera movements; parallel action sequences, crosscutting, and other editing techniques; and even the first orchestral score. It's a shame all these groundbreaking elements were attached to a story of such dubious value.

The first half of the film begins before the Civil War, explaining the introduction of slavery to America before jumping into battle. Two families, the northern Stonemans and the southern Camerons, are introduced. The story is told through these two families and often their servants, epitomizing the worst racial stereotypes. As the nation is torn apart by war, the slaves and their abolitionist supporters are seen as the destructive force behind it all. The film's racism grows even worse in its second half, set during Reconstruction and featuring the rise of the Ku Klux Klan, introduced as the picture's would-be heroes. The fact that Griffith jammed a love story in the midst of his recreated race war is absolutely audacious. It's thrilling and disturbing, often at the same time.

The Birth of a Nation is no doubt a powerful piece of propaganda, albeit one with a stomach-churning political message. Only the puritanical Ku Klux Klan can maintain the unity of the nation, it seems to be saying, so is it any wonder that even at the time the film was met with outrage? It was protested by the National Association for the Advancement of Colored People (NAACP), sparked riots, and later forced Griffith himself to answer criticisms with his even more ambitious *Intolerance* (1916). Still, the fact that *The Birth of a Nation* remains respected and studied to this day—despite its subject matter—reveals its lasting importance. **JKl**

LES FILMS MYSTÉRIEUX

LES VAMPIRES • **LES YEUX QUI FASCINENT**

France (Gaumont) 440m Silent BW
Screenplay Louis Feuillade **Music** Robert
Israel **Cast** Musidora, Edouard Mathé, Marcel
Lévesque, Jean Aymé, Fernand Herrmann,
Stacia Napierkowska

*"A film is not a sermon
nor a conference . . .
but a means to entertain
the eyes and the spirit."*

Louis Feuillade, 1920

ℹ️

Feuillade was a highly prolific
movie director, with more than
700 films to his name.

Les vampires Louis Feuillade, 1915

Louis Feuillade's legendary opus has been cited as a landmark movie serial, a precursor of the deep-focus aesthetic later advanced by Jean Renoir and Orson Welles, and a close cousin to the surrealist movement, but its strongest relationship is to the development of the movie thriller. Segmented into ten loosely connected parts that lack cliffhanger endings, vary widely in length, and were released at irregular intervals, *Les vampires* falls somewhere between a film series and a film serial. The convoluted, often inconsistent plot centers on a flamboyant gang of Parisian criminals, the Vampires, and their dauntless opponent, the reporter Philippe Guérande (Edouard Mathé).

The Vampires, masters of disguise who often dress in black hoods and leotards while carrying out their crimes, are led by four successive "Grand Vampires," each killed off in turn, each faithfully served by the vampish Irma Vep (her name an anagram of Vampire), who constitutes the heart and soul not only of the Vampires but also of *Les vampires* itself. Portrayed with voluptuous vitality by Musidora, who became a star as a result, Irma is the film's most attractive character, clearly surpassing the pallid hero Guérande and his hammy comic sidekick Mazamette (Marcel Lévesque). Her charisma undercuts the film's good-versus-evil theme and contributes to its somewhat amoral tone, reinforced by the way the good guys and the bad guys often use the same duplicitous methods and by the disturbingly ferocious slaughter of the Vampires at the end.

Much like the detective story and the haunted-house thriller, *Les vampires* creates a sturdy-looking world of bourgeois order while also undermining it. The thick floors and walls of each château and hotel become porous with trap doors and secret panels. Massive fireplaces serve as thoroughfares for assassins and thieves, who scurry over Paris rooftops and shimmy up and down drainpipes like monkeys. Taxicabs bristle with stowaways on their roofs and disclose false floors to eject fugitives into convenient manholes. At one point, the hero unsuspectingly sticks his head out the window of his upper-story apartment, only to be looped around the neck by a wire snare wielded from below; he is yanked down to the street, bundled into a large basket, and whisked off by a taxi. In another scene, a wall with a fireplace opens up to disgorge a cannon, which slides to the window and lobs shells into a nearby cabaret.

Reinforcing this atmosphere of capricious stability, the plot is built around a series of tour de force reversals, involving deceptive appearances on both sides of the law: "dead" characters come to life, pillars of society (a priest, a judge, a policeman) turn out to be Vampires, and Vampires are revealed to be law enforcers operating in disguise. It is Feuillade's ability to create, on an extensive and imaginative scale, a double world—at once weighty and dreamlike, recognizably familiar and excitingly strange—that is of central importance to the evolution of the movie thriller and marks him as a major pioneer of the form. **MR**

1915

Intolerance D.W. Griffith, 1916

Perhaps in part a retort to those who found fault with the racial politics in *The Birth of a Nation* (1915), D.W. Griffith was equally concerned to argue against film censorship. This was addressed more directly in the pamphlet issued at the time of *Intolerance*'s exhibition, *The Rise and Fall of Free Speech in America*. Griffith's design for this film, which he finalized in the weeks following the release of his earlier epic production, is to juxtapose four stories from different periods of history that illustrate "love's struggle throughout the ages." These include a selection of events from the life of Jesus; a tale from ancient Babylon, whose king is betrayed by those who resent his rejection of religious sectarianism; the story of the St. Bartholomew's Day Massacre of French Protestants by King Charles IX of France on the perfidious advice of his mother; and a modern story in which a young boy, wrongly convicted of the murder of a companion, is rescued from execution at the last minute by the intervention of his beloved, who gains a pardon from the governor. These stories are not presented in series. Instead, Griffith cuts from one to another and often introduces suspenseful crosscutting within the stories as well. This revolutionary structure proved too difficult for most filmgoers at the time, who may also have been put off by *Intolerance*'s length. Griffith may have invested as much as $2 million in the project, but the film never came close to making back its costs, even when recut and released as two features, *The Fall of Babylon* and *The Mother and the Law*.

The enormous sets for the Babylon story, which long afterward remained a Hollywood landmark, were dressed with 3,000 extras. These production values were equaled by the sumptuous costumes and elaborate crowd scenes of the French story. Though others wrote some title cards, Griffith himself was responsible for the complicated script, which he continued to work on as production progressed. His stock company of actors performed admirably in the various roles. Constance Talmadge is particularly effective as the "Mountain Girl" in love with the ill-fated Prince Belshazzar (Alfred Paget) in the Babylon story, as are Mae Marsh and Bobby Harron as the reunited lovers in the modern story.

As in *The Birth of a Nation*, Griffith uses the structures of Victorian melodrama to make his political points. Intolerance is examined through the lens of tragic love, which lends emotional energy and pathos to the narratives. In the Babylonian story, Belshazzar and his beloved Attarea (Seena Owen) commit suicide rather than fall into the hands of the victorious Cyrus the Persian (George Siegmann); in the French story, a young couple, he Catholic and she Protestant, are unable to escape the massacre.

Intolerance is a monument to Griffith's talent for screenwriting, directing actors, designing shots, and editing—a one-of-a-kind masterpiece on a scope and scale never equaled. Meant to persuade, this film exerted more influence on the Soviet revolutionary cinema of Sergei Eisenstein and others than on Griffith's American contemporaries. **RBP**

U.S. (Triangle & Wark) 163m Silent BW
Producer D.W. Griffith **Screenplay** Tod Browning, D.W. Griffith **Photography** G.W. Bitzer, Karl Brown **Music** Joseph Carl Breil, Carl Davis, D.W. Griffith **Cast** Spottiswoode Aitken, Mary Alden, Frank Bennett, Barney Bernard, Monte Blue, Lucille Browne, Tod Browning, William H. Brown, Edmund Burns, William E. Cassidy, Elmer Clifton, Miriam Cooper, Jack Cosgrave, Josephine Crowell, Dore Davidson, Sam De Grasse, Edward Dillon, Pearl Elmore, Lillian Gish, Ruth Handforth, Robert Harron, Joseph Henabery, Chandler House, Lloyd Ingraham, W.E. Lawrence, Ralph Lewis, Vera Lewis, Elmo Lincoln, Walter Long, Mrs. Arthur Mackley, Tully Marshall, Mae Marsh, Marguerite Marsh, John P. McCarthy, A.W. McClure, Seena Owen, Alfred Paget, Eugene Pallette, Georgia Pearce, Billy Quirk, Wallace Reid, Allan Sears, George Siegmann, Maxfield Stanley, Carl Stockdale, Madame Sul-Te-Wan, Constance Talmadge, F.A. Turner, W.S. Van Dyke, Guenther von Ritzau, Erich von Stroheim, George Walsh, Eleanor Washington, Margery Wilson, Tom Wilson

Future director Tod Browning co-wrote and acted in the film, and was Griffth's assistant director.

FILMICHANSPIEL IN 6 AKTEN ...

Das Kabinett des Doktor Caligari
The Cabinet of Dr. Caligari Robert Wiene, 1919

The Cabinet of Dr. Caligari is the keystone of a strain of bizarre, fantastical cinema that flourished in Germany in the 1920s and was linked, somewhat spuriously, with the Expressionist art movement. If much of the development of the movies in the medium's first two decades was directed toward the Lumière-style "window on the world," with fictional or documentary stories presented in an emotionally stirring manner designed to make audiences forget they were watching a film, *Caligari* returns to the mode of Georges Méliès by presenting magical, theatrical effects that exaggerate or caricature reality. Officials perch on ridiculously high stools, shadows are painted on walls and faces, and unrealistic backdrops and performances are stylized to the point of hysteria.

Writers Carl Mayer and Hans Janowitz conceived the film as taking place in its own out-of-joint world, and director Robert Wiene and set designers Hermann Warm, Walter Roehrig, and Walter Reimann put a twist on every scene and even intertitle to insist on this. Controversially, Fritz Lang—at an early stage attached as director—suggested that *Caligari*'s radical style would be too much for audiences to take without "explanation." Lang devised a frame story in which hero Francis (Friedrich Feher) recounts the story—of sinister mesmerist charlatan Dr. Caligari (Werner Krauss), his zombielike somnambulist slave Cesare (Conrad Veidt), and a series of murders in the rickety small town of Holstenwall—and is finally revealed to be an asylum inmate who, in *The Wizard of Oz* (1939) style, has imagined a narrative that incorporates various people in his daily life. This undercuts the antiauthoritarian tone of the film as Dr. Caligari, in the main story an asylum director who has become demented, is revealed as a decent man out to help the hero. However, the asylum set in the frame story is the same "unreal" one seen in the flashback, making the whole film and not just Francis's bracketed story somehow unreliable. Indeed, by revealing its expressionist vision to be that of a madman, the film could even appeal to conservatives who deemed all modernist art as demented.

Wiene, less innovative than most of his collaborators, makes little use of cinematic technique, with the exception of the flashback-within-a-flashback as Krauss is driven mad by superimposed instructions that he "must become Caligari." The film relies on theatrical devices, the camera fixed center stage as the sets are displayed and the actors (especially Veidt) providing any movement or impact. Lang's input served to make the movie a strange species of amphibian: It plays as an art movie to the high-class crowds who appreciate its innovations, but it's also a horror movie with a gimmick. With its sideshow ambience, hypnotic mad scientist villain, and leotard-clad, heroine-abducting monster, *The Cabinet of Dr. Caligari* is a major early entry in the horror genre, introducing images, themes, and characters that became fundamental to the likes of Tod Browning's *Dracula* and James Whale's *Frankenstein* (both 1931). **KN**

Germany (Decla-Bioscop) 71m Silent BW (tinted) **Producer** Rudolf Meinert, Erich Pommer **Screenplay** Hans Janowitz, Carl Mayer **Photography** Willy Hameister **Music** Alfredo Antonini, Giuseppe Becce, Timothy Brock, Richard Marriott, Peter Schirmann, Rainer Viertlböck **Cast** Werner Krauss, Conrad Veidt, Friedrich Feher, Lil Dagover, Hans Heinrich von Twardowski, Rudolf Lettinger, Rudolf Klein-Rogge

> *"Wiene was prepared to treat costume like décor, and he used nearly impasto makeup to suggest ghostly spirit."*
>
> **David Thomson, critic, 2008**

i

The sets for the movie were made out of paper, with the shadows painted on them.

1919

Broken Blossoms D.W. Griffith, 1919

The Birth of a Nation and *Intolerance* are, rightly, Griffith's most renowned films, remembered for their remarkable manipulations of story and editing. But another of his films, 1919's *Broken Blossoms*, has always stood out as among his very best, and it is surely his most beautiful.

Along with William Beaudine's glorious Mary Pickford vehicle *Sparrows*, *Broken Blossoms* exemplifies what was known in Hollywood as the "soft style." This was the ultimate in glamour photography: Cinematographers used every available device—powder makeup, specialized lighting instruments, oil smeared on the lens, even immense sheets of diaphanous gauze hanging from the studio ceiling—to soften, highlight, and otherwise accentuate the beauty of their stars. In *Broken Blossoms*, the face of the immortal Lillian Gish literally glows with a lovely, unearthly luminescence, outshining all other elements on the screen.

The beauty of *Broken Blossoms* must be experienced, for it is truly stunning. Gish and her costar, the excellent Richard Barthelmess, glide hauntedly through a London landscape defined by fog, eerie alleyway lights, and arcane, "Orientalist" sets. The film's simple story of forbidden love is complemented perfectly by the gorgeous, mysterious production design, created by Joseph Stringer. No other film looks like *Broken Blossoms*.

The collaboration between Griffith and Gish is one of American cinema's most fruitful: the two also worked together on *Intolerance*, *The Birth of a Nation*, *Orphans of the Storm*, and *Way Down East*, in addition to dozens of shorts. Surely this director–actor collaboration ranks with Scorsese–De Niro, Kurosawa–Mifune, and Leone–Eastwood; indeed, it is the standard by which all others should be judged. Griffith finds a perfect balance between the story's mundanity and the production's seedy lavishness (much of the film takes place in opium dens and dockside dives). It is the tension between the everyday and the extraordinary that drives on *Broken Blossoms*, securing its place in film history. **EdeS**

U.S. (D.W. Griffith) 90m Silent BW (tinted screen) **Producer** D.W. Griffith **Screenplay** Thomas Burke, D.W. Griffith **Photography** G.W. Bitzer **Music** D.W. Griffith **Cast** Lillian Gish, Richard Barthelmess, Donald Crisp, Arthur Howard, Edward Peil Sr., George Beranger, Norman Selby

"Her beauty so long hidden shines out like a poem."

Intertitle

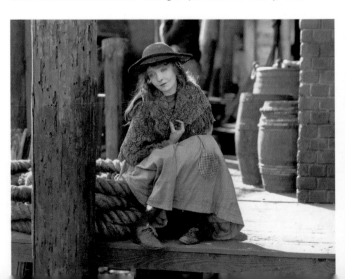

Broken Blossoms was the first movie release from United Artists, of which Griffith was a founder.

Within Our Gates Oscar Micheaux, 1920

U.S. (Micheaux) 79m Silent BW
Producer Oscar Micheaux
Screenplay Oscar Micheaux, Gene DeAnna
Music Philip Carli **Cast** Evelyn Preer, Flo
Clements, James D. Ruffin, Jack Chenault,
William Smith, Charles D. Lucas, Bernice
Ladd, Mrs. Evelyn, William Stark, Mattie
Edwards, Ralph Johnson, E.G. Tatum, Grant
Edwards, Grant Gorman, Leigh Whipper

Successful author, publisher, homesteader, and filmmaker Oscar Micheaux is widely considered the father of African American cinema; only his second effort, *Within Our Gates* is one of forty films Micheaux wrote, directed, and independently produced between 1919 and 1948. Besides its gripping narrative and artistic merits, *Within Our Gates* has immense historical value as the earliest surviving feature by an African American director. Powerful, controversial, and still haunting in its depiction of the atrocities committed by white Americans against blacks during this era, the film remains, in the words of one critic, "a powerful and enlightening cultural document [that] is no less relevant today than it was in 1920."

Within Our Gates follows Sylvia Landry (Evelyn Preer), a Southern black teacher who travels north in an effort to raise money for her school. But this is only one of several stories that Micheaux weaves together in his gripping look at the physical, psychological, and economic repression of African Americans. The film was repeatedly edited by the censors, who found the rape and lynching scenes too provocative after the 1919 Chicago race riots. Lost for seventy years, *Within Our Gates* was rediscovered at the Filmoteca Espanola in Madrid and restored soon after. **SJS**

Orphans of the Storm D.W. Griffith, 1921

U.S. (D.W. Griffith) 150m Silent BW
Producer D.W. Griffith **Screenplay** D.W.
Griffith, from the play *The Two Orphans* by
Eugène Cormon and Adolphe d'Ennery
Photography Paul H. Allen, G W Bitzer,
Hendrik Sartov **Music** Louis F. Gottschalk,
William F. Peters **Cast** Lillian Gish, Dorothy
Gish, Joseph Schildkraut, Frank Losee,
Katherine Emmet, Morgan Wallace, Lucille
La Verne, Sheldon Lewis, Frank Puglia,
Creighton Hale, Leslie King, Monte Blue,
Sidney Herbert, Lee Kohlmar, Marcia Harris

The last of D.W. Griffith's sweeping historical melodramas, *Orphans of the Storm* tells the story of two young girls caught in the turmoil of the French Revolution. Lillian and Dorothy Gish are Henriette and Louise Girard, two babies who become "sisters" when Henriette's impoverished father, thinking of abandoning his daughter in a church, finds Louise and, moved by pity, brings both girls home to raise. Unfortunately, they are left orphaned at an early age when their parents die of the plague. Louise is left blind by the disease, and so the girls make their way to Paris in search of a cure. There they are separated. Henriette, kidnapped by the henchmen of an evil aristocrat, is befriended by a handsome nobleman, Vaudrey (Joseph Schildkraut). Louise is rescued by a kind young man after she falls into the River Seine but, brought to his house, she is put to work by the man's cruel brother. Adventures follow, including imprisonment in the Bastille, being condemned to death during the Reign of Terror, and being saved from the guillotine by the politician Danton (Monte Blue), whose speech advocating the end of such bloodshed is one of the film's most impassioned moments.

Although *Orphans of the Storm* is based on a play that had been successful in the preceding decade, Griffith wrote the script during shooting. Despite the resulting complications, the film is a masterpiece of beautiful staging and acting, with the Gish sisters giving what are perhaps the finest performances of their careers. **RBP**

1921

Körkarlen Victor Sjöström, 1921
The Phantom Carriage

The Phantom Carriage not only cemented the fame of director-screenwriter-actor Victor Sjöström and Swedish silent cinema, but also had a well-documented, artistic influence on many great directors and producers. The best-known element of the film is the representation of the spiritual world as a tormented limbo between heaven and earth. The scene in which the protagonist—the hateful and self-destructive alcoholic David Holm (Sjöström)—wakes up at the chime of midnight on New Year's Eve only to stare at his own corpse, knowing that he is condemned to hell, is one of the most quoted scenes in cinema history.

Made in a simple but time-consuming and meticulously staged series of double exposures, the filmmaker, his photographer, and a lab manager created a three-dimensional illusion of a ghostly world that went beyond anything previously seen at the cinema. More important, perhaps, was the film's complex but readily accessible narration via a series of flashbacks—and even flashbacks within flashbacks—that elevated this gritty tale of poverty and degradation to poetic excellence.

Looking back at Sjöström's career, *The Phantom Carriage* is a theological and philosophical extension of the social themes introduced in his controversial breakthrough *Ingeborg Holm* (1913). Both films depict the step-by-step destruction of human dignity in a cold and heartless society, driving its victims into brutality and insanity. The connection is stressed by the presence of Hilda Borgström, unforgettable as Ingeborg Holm and now in the role of a tortured wife—another desperate Mrs. Holm. She is yet again playing a compassionate but poor mother on her way to suicide or a life in the mental asylum.

The religious naïveté at the heart of Selma Lagerlöf's faithfully adapted novel might draw occasional laughter from a secular audience some eighty years later, but the subdued, "realist" acting and the dark fate of the main characters—which almost comes to its logical conclusion, save for a melodramatic finale—never fails to impress. **MT**

Sweden (Svensk AB) 93m Silent BW
Producer Charles Magnusson
Screenplay Victor Sjöström, from novel by Selma Lagerlöf **Photography** Julius Jaenzon
Cast Victor Sjöström, Hilda Borgström, Tore Svennberg, Astrid Holm, Concordia Selander, Lisa Lundholm, Tor Weijden, Einar Axelsson, Olof Ås, Nils Ahrén, Simon Lindstrand, Nils Elffors, Algot Gunnarsson, Hildur Lithman, John Ekman

"I was deeply shaken by that film ... I was struck by its enormous cinematographic power."

Ingmar Bergman, 1981

i

As part of his research for the film, Sjöström disguised himself and spent time in the slums of Stockholm.

La souriante Madame Beudet Germaine Dulac, 1922

France (Colisée) 54m Silent BW
Screenplay Denys Amiel, André Obey
Photography Maurice Forster, Paul Parguel
Cast Alexandre Arquillière, Germaine
Dermoz, Jean d'Yd, Madeleine Guitty

Germaine Dulac's celebrated film is one of the earliest examples of both feminist and experimental cinema. The plot depicts the life of a bored housewife trapped in a bourgeois marriage. The most captivating aspect of *The Smiling Madame Beudet*, however, is composed of elaborate dream sequences in which the eponymous housewife (Germaine Dermoz) fantasizes a life outside her monotonous existence. Using radical special effects and editing techniques, Dulac incorporates early avant-garde aesthetics to offset the vivid feminine power of Madame Beudet's imaginary life against the dullness of the one she shares with her husband (Alexandre Arquillière). When the complex visual elaboration of her potential liberation through fantasy—the only thing that can put a smile on her face—is cut short by the appearance of her husband in her daydreams, she is left with only one possible solution: kill him.

Dulac not only addresses the oppressive alienation of women within patriarchy but, more importantly, uses the medium of film to offer viewers a radical and subjective female perspective. This led to her picture's inclusion in the first Festival of Women's Films in New York in 1972. **CO**

1922

Dr. Mabuse, der Spieler Fritz Lang, 1922
Dr. Mabuse, Parts I and II

Germany (Uco-Film, Ullstein,
Universum) 95m (part 1), 100m (part 2),
Silent BW Producer Erich Pommer
Screenplay Norbert Jacques, Fritz Lang,
Thea von Harbou Photography Carl
Hoffmann Music Konrad Elfers Cast Rudolf
Klein-Rogge, Alfred Abel, Aud Egede Nissen,
Gertrude Welcker, Bernhard Goetzke, Robert
Forster-Larrinaga, Paul Richter II, Hans
Adalbert Schlettow, Georg John, Grete
Berger, Julius Falkenstein, Lydia Potechina,
Anita Berber, Paul Biensfeldt, Karl Platen

A major commercial success in Germany in 1922, *Dr. Mabuse* was intended not merely as flamboyant thriller but as pointed editorial, using the figure of the master-of-disguise supercriminal to embody the real evils of its era.

The subtitles of each of the film's two parts, harping on about "our time," underline the point made obvious in the opening act, in which Mabuse's gang steals a Swiss–Dutch trade agreement—not to make use of the secret information, but to create a momentary stock market panic that allows Mabuse (Rudolf Klein-Rogge), in disguise as a cartoon plutocrat with top hat and fur coat, to make a fast fortune. He also employs a band of blind men as forgers, contributing to the feeling that German audiences at the time had that money was worthless.

The film's eponymous villain shuffles photographs as if they were a deck of cards, selecting his identity for the day from various disguises, but it is nearly two hours before his "real" name is confirmed. In Part II, he appears as a one-armed stage illusionist and finally loses his grip on the fragile core of his identity to become a ranting madman, tormented by the hollow-cheeked specters of those he has killed and, in a moment that still startles, by the creaking-to-life of vast, grotesque statues and bits of machinery in his final lair. Director Fritz Lang, and others, would return to Mabuse, still embodying the ills of the age—notably in the early talkie *Das Testament des Dr. Mabuse* (1933) and the 1961 high-tech surveillance melodrama *The Thousand Eyes of Dr. Mabuse*. **KN**

U.S. (Les Frères Revillon, Pathé) 79m
Silent BW **Producer** Robert J. Flaherty
Screenplay Robert J. Flaherty
Photography Robert J. Flaherty
Music Stanley Silverman **Cast** Nanook,
Nyla, Cunayou, Allee, Allegoo, Berry
Kroeger (narrator—1939 re-release)

"Beside this film the usual photoplay, the so-called 'dramatic' work of the screen, becomes as thin and blank as the celluloid on which it is printed."

The New York Times, 1922

ℹ

The film was rejected by five distributors before Pathé finally agreed to take it on.

Nanook of the North Robert J. Flaherty, 1922

The history of "documentary" filmmaking—an approach generally thought to involve a filmmaker's recording of an unmediated reality—begins really with the invention of the cinema itself, but for better or worse the nickname "father of the documentary" has generally been bestowed on Robert J. Flaherty. Raised near the U.S.–Canadian border, Flaherty loved exploring the far-off wilderness from an early age, and after his studies went to work as a mineral prospector in Canada's Far North. Before one of his trips, someone suggested he bring along a movie camera; over the next few years, Flaherty would film hours of material of both the land and its inhabitants, which in 1916 he began showing in private screenings in Toronto. The response was enthusiastic, but just as he was about to ship his footage to the United States, he dropped a cigarette ash and his entire negative—30,000 feet—burst into flames. Flaherty took years to raise enough money to go back north and shoot again; when he finally succeeded (thanks to Revillon Frères, a French furrier), he decided to focus his efforts on filming one Nanook, a celebrated Inuit hunter. Based on his memory of the best of what he had shot before, Flaherty fashioned the events to be included in the new film, including things Nanook commonly did, some things he never did, and some things he used to do but hadn't done in a while. The result was the deeply influential, but endlessly debated, *Nanook of the North*.

A series of vignettes that detail the life of Nanook and his family over a few weeks, Flaherty's film is a kind of romantic ode to human courage and fortitude in the face of an overwhelming and essentially hostile Nature. Despite Nanook getting pride of place in the title, many audiences are left with the memory of the arbitrary fury of the arctic landscape. Indeed, the film received a powerful (if tragic) publicity boost when it was revealed that Nanook and his family had indeed perished in a raging snowstorm not long after the film was completed, giving *Nanook of the North*'s extraordinary and already powerful final sequence—in which the family looks for shelter from a storm—a terrible poignancy.

Many contemporary film students are critical of the picture because so much of it seems staged for the camera—several times you can practically hear Flaherty barking out directions to Nanook and the others—but the film's many defenders over the years, such as André Bazin, wisely pointed out that Flaherty's most remarkable achievement here is the way he seemed to capture the texture of their daily lives. The details of the walrus hunt, such as whether or when a gun was used, seem less important than Flaherty's decision to simply follow in long shot Nanook's slow crawl toward his prey; if Nanook's beaming face as he warms his son's hands is part of an act, then he was simply one of the great screen performers in history. Call it what you will—documentary, fiction, or some hybrid—*Nanook of the North* remains one of the few films that completely deserves its description as a classic. **RP**

Nosferatu, eine Symphonie des Grauens
Nosferatu, a Symphony of Terror F.W. Murnau, 1922

Bram Stoker's *Dracula* inspired one of the most impressive of all silent features. The source material and the medium seem almost eerily meant for each other. Stoker's novel, largely written in the form of a series of letters, is light on traditional dialogue and heavy on description, perfect for the primarily visual storytelling of silent films. It is fitting that a story of the eternal conflict between light and darkness should be matched to a format consisting almost entirely of the interplay of light and darkness.

Director F.W. Murnau had already established himself as a star of the German Expressionist movement when he decided to adapt the Stoker novel, renamed *Nosferatu* after legal threats from Stoker's estate. In fact, the finished film barely evaded a court order that all copies be destroyed, but in the end little of Stoker's novel was ultimately altered, save the names of the characters, and indeed the success of *Nosferatu* led to dozens of subsequent (and mostly officially sanctioned) *Dracula* adaptations.

Yet *Nosferatu*, even so many years later, stands apart from most *Dracula* films. One key difference is the striking presence of star Max Schreck, whose surname translates to "fear." Schreck plays the eponymous vampire with an almost savage simplicity. His rodent-like, sinister creature of the night is little different from the rats at his command, lurching instinctively toward any sight of blood with barely disguised lust.

This explains the terror of Hutter (Gustav von Wangenheim), who has traveled to the isolated castle of Count Orlok (Schreck) high in the Carpathian Mountains to help the strange man settle some legal matters. The mere mention of Orlok silences the townsfolk with fear, and Hutter's suspicions deepen when he discovers that the stagecoach taking him to the castle has no driver. Orlok himself offers little solace. He keeps odd hours and leaves Hutter locked in a tower. Fearing for his life—and specifically the bloodlust of his captor—he escapes and returns to Bremen, Germany. But Orlok follows, setting his sights not on Hutter but on his innocent wife, Ellen (Greta Schröder): "Your wife has a beautiful neck," comments Orlok to Hutter. Just as her connection with Hutter helps rescue him from Orlok's clutches, Ellen discovers that it is also up to her to lure the demonic creature to his (permanent) demise: to be vaporized by the rays of the morning sun.

With *Nosferatu*, Murnau created some of cinema's most lasting and haunting imagery: Count Orlok creeping through his castle, striking chilling shadows while he's stalking Hutter; Orlok rising stiffly from his coffin; the Count, caught in a beam of sunlight, cringing in terror before fading from view. He also introduced several vampire myths that fill not just other *Dracula* films but permeate popular culture as well. **JKl**

Germany (Iofa-Atelier Berlin-Johannisthal, Prana-Film) 94m Silent BW **Director** F.W. Murnau **Screenplay** Henrik Galeen **Photography** Günther Krampf, Fritz Arno Wagner **Music** James Bernard (restored version) **Cast** Max Schreck, Alexander Granach, Gustav von Wangenheim, Greta Schröder, Georg H. Schnell, Ruth Landshoff, John Gottowt, Gustav Botz, Max Nemetz, Wolfgang Heinz, Guido Herzfeld, Albert Venohr, Hardy von Francois

i

The 2000 film *Shadow of the Vampire* is set around the making of *Nosferatu*, and depicts Schreck as a real vampire.

Denmark / Sweden (Aljosha, Svensk)
87m Silent BW **Screenplay** Benjamin
Christensen **Photography** Johan
Ankerstjerne **Music** Launy Grøndahl (1922),
Emil Reesen (1941 version) **Cast** Elisabeth
Christensen, Astrid Holm, Karen Winther,
Maren Pedersen, Ella La Cour, Emmy
Schønfeld, Kate Fabian, Oscar Stribolt, Clara
Pontoppidan, Else Vermehren, Alice
O'Fredericks, Johannes Andersen, Elith Pio,
Aage Hertel, Ib Schønberg

*"We no longer burn
our old and poor.
But do they not often
suffer bitterly?"*

Intertitle

Häxan Benjamin Christensen, 1923

Pioneering Danish filmmaker Benjamin Christensen's notorious 1922 "documentary" *Häxan* is a bizarre silent-film oddity that explores the nature of witchcraft and diabolism from ancient Persia through then-modern times using various cinematic approaches, from still images to models to vivid, dramatic reenactments. It is a hard film to pin down, and it defies any boundaries of genre, especially those of the documentary film, which in the early 1920s was still amorphous and undefined. Part earnest academic exercise in correlating ancient fears with misunderstandings about mental illness and part salacious horror movie, *Häxan* is a truly unique work that still holds the power to unnerve, even in today's jaded era.

To visualize his subject matter, Christensen fills the frames with every frightening image he can conjure out of the historical records, often freely blending fact and fantasy. We see a haggard old witch pull a severed, decomposing hand out of a bundle of sticks. There are shocking moments in which we witness a woman give birth to two enormous demons, see a witches' sabbath, and endure tortures by inquisition judges. We watch an endless parade of demons of all shapes and sizes, some of whom look more or less human, whereas others are almost fully animal—pigs, twisted birds, cats, and the like.

Christensen was certainly a cinematic visionary, and he had a keen notion of the powerful effects of mise-en-scène. Although *Häxan* is often cited as a key forerunner of such modern devil-possession films as *The Exorcist* (1973), it also brings to mind Tobe Hooper's effective use of props and background detail in *The Texas Chain Saw Massacre* (1974) to create an enveloping atmosphere of potential violence. *Häxan* is a film that needs to be viewed more than once to gain a full appreciation of the set design and decoration—the eerie use of props, claustrophobic sets, and chiaroscuro lighting to set the tone. It is no surprise that the Surrealists were so fond of the film and that its life was extended in the late 1960s, when it was reissued as a midnight movie with narration by none other than William S. Burroughs. **JKe**

i

Benjamin Christensen himself
plays the part of the Devil
in the movie.

Foolish Wives Erich von Stroheim, 1923

U.S. (Universal) 85m Silent BW
Screenplay Marian Ainslee, Walter Anthony, Erich von Stroheim Photography William H. Daniels, Ben F. Reynolds Music Sigmund Romberg Cast Rudolph Christians, Miss DuPont, Maude George, Mae Busch, Erich von Stroheim, Dale Fuller, Al Edmundsen, Cesare Gravina, Malvina Polo, Louis K. Webb, Mrs. Kent, C.J. Allen, Edward Reinach

Greed is Stroheim's most famous film, but *Foolish Wives* is his masterpiece. Like *Greed*, it was heavily reedited, but what remains (especially after a major 1972 restoration) is a more accomplished work. He himself stars as the unscrupulous Count Karamzin, a Monte Carlo-based pseudoaristocrat who sets out to seduce the neglected wife of an American diplomat.

This witty, ruthlessly objective film confirms its director as the cinema's first great ironist. Karamzin is skewered with sardonic relish—brazenly insincere, thoroughly indiscriminate in his taste in women, and, when the chips are down, contemptibly cowardly—but he and his decadent colleagues are so much more entertaining than the virtuous American hubby and his commonplace spouse. The film's tone of cool, lively detachment is enhanced by its exhaustive elaboration of the world around the characters, articulating space through visual strategies (such as layered depth, peripheral motions, and multiple setups) that make us intensely aware of the entire 360-degree field of each scene. Stroheim stacks the deck by placing his dull, flat Americans in dull, flat spaces; otherwise, there's hardly a shot that doesn't dazzle the eye with rich, shimmering interplay of detail, lighting, gesture, and movement. **MR**

1923

Our Hospitality John G. Blystone & Buster Keaton, 1923

U.S. (Joseph M. Schenck) 74m Silent BW
Producer Joseph M. Schenck
Screenplay Clyde Bruckman, Jean C. Havez Photography Gordon Jennings, Elgin Lessley Cast Joe Roberts, Ralph Bushman, Craig Ward, Monte Collins, Joe Keaton, Kitty Bradbury, Natalie Talmadge, Buster Keaton Jr., Buster Keaton

Arguably as great a film as the better-known *The General* (1927), *Our Hospitality*—Buster Keaton's masterly satire of traditional Southern manners—kicks off with a beautifully staged dramatic prologue that establishes the absurdly murderous parameters of the age-old feud between two families. By the time the main story takes over, Buster's Willie McKay is a twenty-something innocent, raised in New York but returning (thanks to a wondrously funny odyssey involving a primitive train) to his familial town, where his courtship of a girl met en route—the daughter, as it happens, of the clan still sworn to spilling his blood—places him in deadly peril, even though Southern hospitality dictates his enemies treat him properly as long as he's in their home.

Much of the humor thereafter derives from a darkly ironic situation whereby Willie determines to remain a guest of his would-be killers while they smilingly try to ensure his departure. Keaton's wit relies not on individual gags but on a firm grasp of character, predicament, period, place, and camera framing (see how he keeps the camera moving after he's fallen off the ludicrous bicycle it has been tracking alongside); the result is not only very funny, but also dramatically substantial and suspenseful—nowhere more so than in the justly celebrated sequence when Willie saves his beloved from plunging over a waterfall. Never was Keaton's sense of timing so miraculous, and his ability to elicit laughter and excitement simultaneously so gloriously evident. **GA**

La roue Abel Gance, 1923
The Wheel

France (Abel Gance) 273m
Silent BW **Producer** Abel Gance,
Charles Pathé **Screenplay** Abel Gance
Photography Gaston Brun, Marc Bujard,
Léonce-Henri Burel, Maurice Duverger
Music Arthur Honegger **Cast** Severin-Mars,
Ivy Close, Gabriel de Gravone, Pierre
Magnier, Gil Clary, Max Maxudian,
Georges Térof

Abel Gance's *The Wheel* opens with a spectacular fast-cut train crash, as revolutionary to spectators in 1922 as the Lumières' train arriving in a station in 1895. Railwayman Sisif (Severin-Mars) saves Norma (Ivy Close) from the crash and brings her up as his daughter. Both he and his son Elie (Gabriel de Gravone) fall in love with her, so Sisif marries her off to a rich man. She and Elie eventually fall in love; both her husband and Elie die after a struggle. Sisif goes blind and dies, after being tended by Norma.

The Wheel's melodramatic plot was combined with wide-ranging literary references, including Greek tragedy, as is suggested by Sisif's name (Sisyphus) and his blindness associated with incestuous desire (Oedipus). These "pretensions" were seen by intellectuals to conflict with the film's extraordinary cinematographic techniques (such as the accelerating montage sequences based on musical rhythms), which related the film to avant-garde preoccupations with a "pure" cinema and Cubist concerns with machines as the emblem of modernity. The film's contradictions are admirably brought together in the central metaphor of the title: the wheel of fate (Sisif/Sisyphus ends up driving the funicular railway up and down Mont Blanc), the wheel of desire, and the wheel of the film itself with its many cyclical patterns. **PP**

Der Letzte Mann F.W. Murnau, 1924
The Last Laugh

Germany (Universum, UFA) 77m Silent BW
Producer Erich Pommer **Screenplay** Carl
Mayer **Photography** Robert Baberske, Karl
Freund **Music** Giuseppe Becce, Timothy
Brock, Peter Schirmann **Cast** Emil Jannings,
Maly Delschaft, Max Hiller, Emilie Kurz, Max
Unterkircher, Olaf Storm, Hermann Vallentin,
Georg John, Emmy Wyda

Despite a ludicrously unconvincing happy ending grafted on at the insistence of UFA, F.W. Murnau's *The Last Laugh* remains a very impressive attempt to tell a story without the use of intertitles. The plot itself is nothing special—a hotel doorman, humiliated by his loss in status when he is demoted to bathroom attendant because of his advancing years, sinks so low that he is tempted to steal back his beloved uniform (the symbol of his professional pride). In some respects the film is merely a vehicle for one of Emil Jannings's typically grandstand performances.

Above and beyond this somewhat pathetic parable exists one of Murnau's typically eloquent explorations of cinematic space: the camera prowls around with astonishing fluidity, articulating the protagonist's relationship with the world as it follows him around the hotel, the city streets, and his home in the slums. Some of the camera work is "subjective," as when his drunken perceptions are rendered by optical distortion; at other times, it is the camera's mobility that is evocative, as when it passes through the revolving doors that serve as a symbol of destiny. The dazzling technique on display may, in fact, be rather too grand for the simple story of one old man, yet there is no denying the virtuosity either of Murnau's mise-en-scène or of Karl Freund's camera work. **GA**

U.S.S.R. (Goskino, Proletkult) 82m Silent BW
Producer Boris Mikhin **Screenplay** Grigori
Aleksandrov, Sergei M. Eisenstein
Photography Vasili Khvatov, Vladimir Popov,
Eduard Tisse **Cast** Grigori Aleksandrov,
Aleksandr Antonov, Yudif Glizer, Mikhail
Gomorov, I. Ivanov, Ivan Klyukvin, Anatoli
Kuznetsov, M. Mamin, Maksim Shtraukh,
Vladimir Uralsky, Vera Yanukova, Boris Yurtsev

> "Without organization
> of the masses, the
> proletariat is nothing.
> Organized, it is
> everything."
>
> **Lenin, intertitle**

Stachka Sergei M. Eisenstein, 1924
Strike

Eisenstein was a revolutionary in every sense, forging a radical new breed of montage-based cinema from an unprecedented merger of Marxist philosophy, Constructivist aesthetics, and his fascination with the visual contrasts, conflicts, and contradictions built into the dynamics of film itself.

Strike was intended as one installment in a series of works about the rise of Marxist–Leninist rule. Censorship by the new Soviet government thwarted many of Eisenstein's dreams in ensuing years, and this series never got beyond its initial production. Nonetheless, the feverishly energetic *Strike* stands on its own as a tour de force of expressive propaganda and the laboratory in which seminal ideas for his later silent masterpieces—*The Battleship Potemkin* (1925), *October* (1927), and *Old and New* (1928)—were first tested and refined.

Strike depicts a labor uprising in a Russian factory, where workers are goaded toward rebellion by the owners' greed and dishonesty. We see simmering unrest among the laborers, an act of treachery that pushes them into action, the excitement of their mutiny followed by the hardships of prolonged unemployment, and finally the counterstrike of the factory owners, abetted by troops. The film ends with an electrifying example of what Eisenstein called "intellectual montage," intercutting the massacre of strikers with images of animals being slain in a slaughterhouse.

The acting in *Strike* is as unconventional as its editing techniques, mixing naturalistic portrayals of the workers with stylized portrayals of the owners and their spies. The film illustrates Soviet theories of "typage," calling for actors who physically resemble the character types they play, and the "collective hero," whereby a story's protagonist is not a single individual but rather all the people standing on the correct side of history.

Strike's political imperatives have dated; its visual power has not. "I don't believe in the kino-eye," Eisenstein once remarked, referring to a catchword of colleague and rival Dziga Vertov. "I believe in the kino-fist." That hard-hitting philosophy galvanizes every sequence of this unique film. **DS**

i

Strike was Eisenstein's first full-length feature. He had made a short, *Dnevnik Glumova* (*Dnevnik's Diary*), in 1923.

1924

U.S. (Buster Keaton) 44m Silent BW
Producer Joseph M. Schenck, Buster Keaton
Screenplay Clyde Bruckman, Jean C. Havez
Photography Byron Houck Elgin Lessley
Music Myles Boisen, Sheldon Brown, Beth
Custer, Steve Kirk, Nik Phelps **Cast** Buster
Keaton, Kathryn McGuire, Joe Keaton,
Erwin Connelly, Ward Crane

*"[Keaton] kind of said,
'Never play a crazy
scene with anything
but reality.' He was
always intensely and
desperately true."*

Mel Brooks, 1997

Sherlock, Jr. Roscoe "Fatty" Arbuckle & Buster Keaton, 1924

Sherlock, Jr. is Buster Keaton's shortest feature film, yet it is a remarkable achievement, possessing a tightly integrated plot, stunning athleticism (Keaton did all his own stunts, unknowingly breaking his neck during one of them), artistic virtuosity, and an avant-garde exploration of the dichotomy of reality versus illusion. He plays a projectionist and detective wannabe falsely accused of stealing from his girlfriend's father. Framed by a rival suitor (Ward Crane), the young man is banished from the girl's home. Dejected, he falls asleep on the job. In his dream state, he transcends into the screen (in a brilliant sequence of optical effects), where he is the dapper Sherlock, Jr.—the world's second greatest detective.

Unbelievable stunts and complicated gags move this 44-minute film along at a fever pitch. At first, the cinematic reality refuses to accept this new protagonist and the tension between the two worlds is magnificently presented via a montage of spatial shifts that land our bewildered hero in a lion's den, amid roaring waves, and in a snowdrift. Gradually, he assimilates fully into the film world. In the mise-en-abyme storyline, the villain (also played by Ward Crane) is trying to kill the hero in vain, before Sherlock, Jr. solves the mystery of the stolen pearls.

Sherlock, Jr. not only features the stunts for which Keaton is famous, but also poses a number of issues. From a social perspective, it is a commentary on the fantasies about upward mobility in American society. On a psychological plane, it introduces the motif of the double striving for fulfillment in imaginary spaces, as the protagonist is unable to achieve it in reality. Above all, the film is a reflection on the nature of art, a theme that resurfaces in *The Cameraman* (1928), when Keaton's focus shifts from medium to spectator.

Keaton's films remain interesting today, in part due to the director-star's almost otherworldly stoicism (compared to Chaplin's pathos), and in part due to their occasionally surreal nature (admired by Luis Buñuel and Federico García Lorca) and their delving into the nature of cinema and existence. Chuck Jones, Woody Allen, Wes Craven, and Steven Spielberg are among the filmmakers to pay tribute to his mischief. **RDe**

ℹ
It took Keaton four months to learn all the trick shots that he performed during the pool game in the film.

The Great White Silence Herbert G. Ponting, 1924

G.B. (Gaumont British) 108m BW
Producer Herbert G. Ponting
Screenplay Herbert G. Ponting
Photography Herbert G. Ponting
Music Simon Fisher Turner (2010
restoration) Cast Robert Falcon Scott,
Herbert G. Ponting

Herbert Ponting's footage of Captain Scott's ill-fated attempt to lead the first team to the South Pole was never intended as a film. It was the director's skill as a photographer that guaranteed him passage on the *Terra Nova*. His Images were to be the centerpiece of Scott's lecture series, which would travel the world and recoup some costs from the expedition. But with the death of Scott and his team, Ponting returned to Britain and devoted the rest of his life to celebrating the heroism of these pioneers.

The director had assembled a detailed record of daily life on the ship, as Scott—a fleeting presence throughout the film—and his men prepared for their epic journey. With time to kill during preparations, Ponting filmed Ross Island, the mission's base camp, often going to extraordinary lengths—and great personal danger—to capture the most arresting images. Once Scott embarked on his mission, which dominates the last section of the film, Ponting blends life as it continues on Ross Island with animated sequences, mapping the group's final journey.

The completed film was unsuccessful commercially, even when released with a soundtrack, as *90° South* (1933). In 2011, the British Film Institute released a restoration of the film, featuring an atmospheric score by Simon Fisher Turner. This pristine version highlights Ponting's incredible achievement in capturing the glory and the danger of those individuals who defined the "Heroic Age of Antarctic Exploration." **IHS**

i

Herbert Ponting was the first known photographer to take a cinematograph to the Antarctic.

Greed Erich von Stroheim, 1924

The first movie ever shot entirely on location, *Greed* is notorious as much for the story behind its making as for its considerable artistic power. Director Erich von Stroheim wanted to make the most realistic movie possible with his adaptation of Frank Norris's novel *McTeague*, about the rise and violently murderous fall of working-class San Francisco dentist John "Mac" McTeague. But his creation, originally commissioned by the director-friendly Goldwyn Company, was destroyed when the studio became Metro-Goldwyn-Mayer (MGM), with Stroheim's nemesis, Irving Thalberg, as the new General Manager.

MGM wanted a commercial film, and Stroheim wanted an experiment in cinematic realism. During the two-year shoot, he rented an apartment on Laguna Street in San Francisco that became the set for Mac's (Gibson Gowland) dental parlors. Many of the scenes there were shot entirely with natural light. Stroheim also insisted that his actors live in the apartment to help them get into character. When it came time to shoot the film's final climactic moments in Death Valley, Stroheim shipped his whole crew out to the 120°F desert location, where the cameras became so overheated they had to be wrapped with iced towels.

The director's first cut was nearly nine hours long. It was a painstaking reenactment of Norris's novel, which itself was a recreation of an actual crime that took place during the early 1880s. After a quack doctor helps Mac escape the Northern California mining town of his childhood, he becomes a dentist in San Francisco. There he meets Trina (Zasu Pitts), who he falls in love with during a memorably creepy tooth-drilling scene. His best friend and rival for Trina's affections is Marcus (Jean Hersholt), who grants Mac permission to marry Trina but changes his mind after she wins a lottery. Using his connections in local government, Marcus manages to put Mac out of business and send his former friend into a freefall of back-breaking day labor, drunkenness, and wife beating.

Trina turns to her lottery winnings as a source of satisfaction, hoarding her thousands in gold coins while she and Mac starve. One of *Greed*'s most famous scenes has Trina climbing into bed with her money, caressing it, and rolling around with erotic abandon. Shortly thereafter Mac murders her, steals the money, and heads out to Death Valley where his life comes to a bitter end when Marcus hunts him down.

Only a small handful of people ever saw the original nine-hour version of *Greed*. After a friend helped Stroheim cut the picture down to eighteen reels, or about four hours, the studios took it away from him and handed it over to a low-ranking editor who reduced it to 140 minutes. This version of the film, which Stroheim called "a mutilation of my sincere work at the hands of the MGM executives," is nevertheless stark, captivating, and genuinely disturbing. In 1999, film restorer Rick Schmidlin released a four-hour version of *Greed* that was reconstructed from original production stills and Stroheim's shooting script. **AN**

U.S. (MGM) 140m Silent BW
Producer Louis B. Mayer
Screenplay Joseph Farnham, June Mathis, from the novel *McTeague* by Frank Norris
Photography William H. Daniels, Ben F. Reynolds **Cast** Zasu Pitts, Gibson Gowland, Jean Hersholt, Dale Fuller, Tempe Pigott, Sylvia Ashton, Chester Conklin, Frank Hayes, Joan Standing

"The most important picture yet produced in America . . . When the 'movies' can produce a Greed they can no longer be sneered at."

New York Herald Tribune, 1924

i

Jean Hersholt lost 27 pounds and developed a fever while filming in Death Valley.

The Thief of Bagdad Raoul Walsh, 1924

U.S. (Douglas Fairbanks) 155m Silent BW (tinted) **Producer** Douglas Fairbanks **Screenplay** Douglas Fairbanks, Lotta Woods **Photography** Arthur Edeson **Music** Mortimer Wilson **Cast** Douglas Fairbanks, Snitz Edwards, Charles Belcher, Julanne Johnston, Sojin, Anna May Wong, Brandon Hurst, Tote Du Crow, Noble Johnson

The Thief of Bagdad marked the culmination of Douglas Fairbanks's career as the ultimate hero of swashbuckling costume spectacles. It is also one of the most visually breathtaking movies ever made, a unique and integral conception by a genius of film design, William Cameron Menzies. Building his mythical Bagdad on a six-and-a-half-acre site (the biggest in Hollywood history), Menzies created a shimmering, magical world, as insubstantial yet as real and haunting as a dream, with its reflective floors, soaring minarets, flying carpets, ferocious dragons, and winged horses.

As Ahmed the Thief in quest of his Princess, Fairbanks—bare chested and with clinging silken garments—explored a new sensuous eroticism in his screen persona and found an appropriate costar in Anna May Wong, as the Mongol slave girl. Although the nominal director was the gifted and able Raoul Walsh, the overall concept for *The Thief of Bagdad* was Fairbanks's own, as producer, writer, star, stuntman, and showman of unbounded ambition. (Side note: the uncredited Persian Prince in the film is played by a woman, Mathilde Comont.) **DR**

The Eagle Clarence Brown, 1925

U.S. (United Artists) 80m BW **Producer** John W. Considine Jnr., Joseph M. Schenck **Screenplay** George Marion Jr., from story by Alexander Pushkin **Photography** George Barnes, Devereaux Jennings **Music** Lee Erwin, Michael Hoffman, Carl Davis (1985 restoration) **Cast** Rudolph Valentino, Vilma Bánky, louise Dresser, Albert Conti, James A. Marcus, George Nichols, Carrie Clark Ward

Rudolph Valentino will best be remembered as one of cinema's first heartthrobs. His swarthy looks seduced millions and his premature death, at the age of thirty-one, prompted scenes of pandemonium. He is perhaps less remembered for his comic skills, which are on display in *The Eagle*. In the place of brooding romance is an engaging romp, often parodying the star's persona, with Valentino game enough to play along.

He plays Vladimir Dobrovsky, a Cossack serving in the Russian army, whose act of bravery in stopping a runaway carriage and saving its pretty occupant (Vilma Bánky) attracts the attention of the ageing Czarina (Louise Dresser). She attempts to seduce Dobrovsky, who runs away, escaping to his country home only to discover it has been overrun by a villainous braggart. The man's daughter is the very woman Dobrovsky had saved. Donning the disguise of the Black Eagle in order to terrorize the man who took his father's land, and a French tutor so that he can be close to the villain's daughter, Dobrovsky finds himself torn between his heart and his family's honor.

Director Clarence Brown employs a number of visual flourishes, including an elegant tracking shot over a vast banquet of food, which elevates the quality of the film. Although the narrative is uneven—the family's honor is never really restored and the Czarina is perhaps a little too forgiving—*The Eagle* is nevertheless a light-hearted frolic whose balance of comedy and drama foreshadows later action films such as *The Adventures of Robin Hood* (1938) and *The Mark of Zorro* (1940). **IHS**

The Phantom of the Opera
Rupert Julian & Lon Chaney, 1925

U.S. (Universal Pictures) 93m Silent
BW / Color (2-strip Technicolor)
Producer Carl Laemmle **Screenplay** Gaston
Leroux **Photography** Milton Bridenbecker,
Virgil Miller, Charles Van Enger **Music** Gustav
Hinrichs (1925 version), David Broekman,
Sam Perry, William Schiller (1929 version)
Cast Lon Chaney, Mary Philbin, Norman
Kerry, Arthur Edmund Carewe, Gibson
Gowland, John St. Polis, Snitz Edwards

ℹ

Chaney later revealed that the faces
of wounded World War I veterans
had inspired his makeup.

This 1925 silent remains the closest adaption of Gaston Leroux's trash masterpiece of the same name, a novel that has a terrific setting and a great central figure but a plot that creaks at every turn. The film is a strange combination of plodding direction (mostly from Rupert Julian, though other hands intervened) and incredible Universal Pictures set design, so that stick-figure characters—weedy hero Norman Kerry is especially annoying—pose in front of incredibly impressive tableaux.

The Phantom of the Opera delivers a series of masterly moments that cover up its rickety structure: the masked ball (a brief Technicolor sequence), where the Phantom shows up dressed as Edgar Allan Poe's Red Death; the chandelier dropping, where the Phantom lets the audience know what he thinks of the current diva; various trips into the magical underworld beneath the Paris Opera House; and—best of all—the unmasking, in which the tragic villain's disfigured skullface is first seen (so shocking that even the camera is terrified, going briefly out of focus).

The reason this film is a classic is that it enshrines one of the greatest bits of melodramatic acting in the silent cinema—Lon Chaney's impeccably dressed, lovelorn, violent ghoul genius. Favorite intertitle: "You are dancing on the tombs of tortured men!" **KN**

U.S.S.R. (Goskino, Mosfilm)
75m Silent BW **Producer** Jacob Bliokh
Screenplay Nina Agadzhanova, Sergei M.
Eisenstein **Photography** Vladimir Popov,
Eduard Tisse **Music** Nikolai Kryukov,
Edmund Meisel, Dmitri Shostakovich
Cast Aleksandr Antonov, Vladimir Barsky,
Grigori Aleksandrov, Mikhail Gomorov, Ivan
Bobrov, Beatrice Vitoldi, N. Poltavseva,
Julia Eisenstein

*"Its virtuoso technique
remains dazzling and
is at the service of a
revolutionary fervor we
can still experience."*

Philip French,
The Observer, 2011

𝒊

The film was banned in the UK
until 1954 for "Bolshevik propaganda"
and "incitement to class hatred."

Bronenosets Potyomkin
The Battleship Potemkin
Grigori Aleksandrov & Sergei M. Eisenstein, 1925

The Battleship Potemkin—such a famous film! Sergei Eisenstein's legendary second feature was to become not just a point of ideological conflict between the East and the West, the Left and the Right, but a must-see film for every cinema lover. Decades of censorship and militant support, countless words analyzing its structure, its symbolism, its sources and effects, and thousands of visual quotations have all served to make it very difficult for us to see the story behind the film. Eisenstein's *The Battleship Potemkin* may not be historically accurate, but his legendary vision of oppression and rebellion, individual and collective action, and its artistic ambition to work simultaneously with bodies, light, trivial objects, symbols, faces, movement, geometrical forms, and more is a unique keyboard. As a true artist of film, Eisenstein manages to elaborate a magnificent and touching myth.

It should be kept in mind, however, that this aesthetic sensibility was endowed with political significance as well: the "changing of the world by conscious men" that had been dreamed of in those times and was known by the term "Revolution." But even without an awareness of what it meant, or—better—without a precise awareness of what it eventually turned into, the wind of an epic adventure still blows on the screen here and makes it move. Whatever else one chooses to call it, this adventure is the unique impulse that drives the people of Odessa toward liberty, the sailors of the eponymous battleship to battle against hunger and humiliation, and the filmmaker himself to invent new cinematic forms and rhythms.

The Battleship Potemkin has been seen too often in excerpted form, or on the basis of its most famous scenes and sequences. It may come as somewhat of a surprise to find how powerful it is to see the film in its entirety—that is, as a dramatic and touching story—rather than treating it as a priceless jewelry box from which to remove individual pieces on occasion.

Such a renewed, innocent approach to the film will bring back a real sense of being to those icons that have become familiar to us all: the out of control baby carriage on the steps; the face of the dead sailor under the tent at the end of the pier; the worm-ridden meat in the sailors' rations; the leather boots; the iron guns pointed toward bodies and faces; the glasses of a blind political, military, and religious power waiting in the void. Then, before it all becomes ideological interpretation, the stone lion coming alive to roar with anger and a desire to live will become a metaphor for the film itself—and for the high and daring idea of cinema it was bearing—escaping from its monumental status to be found, alive and fresh once again, by every new pair of eyes that looks upon it. **J-MF**

The Gold Rush Charles Chaplin, 1925

The Gold Rush affirmed Charles Chaplin's belief that tragedy and comedy are never far apart. His unlikely dual inspiration came from viewing some stereoscope slides of the privations of prospectors in the Klondyke Gold Rush of 1896–98, and reading a book about the Donner Party Disaster of 1846, when a party of immigrants, snowbound in the Sierra Nevada, were reduced to eating their own moccasins and the corpses of their dead comrades. Out of these grim and unlikely themes, Chaplin created high comedy. The familiar Little Tramp becomes a gold prospector, joining the mass of brave optimists to face all the hazards of cold, starvation, solitude, and the occasional incursion of a grizzly bear.

The film was in every respect the most elaborate undertaking of Chaplin's career. For two weeks the unit shot on location at Truckee in the snow country of the Sierra Nevada. Here Chaplin faithfully recreated the historic image of the prospectors struggling up the Chilkoot Pass. Some 600 extras, many drawn from the vagrants and derelicts of Sacramento, were brought by train to clamber up the 2,300-foot pass dug through the mountain snow. For the main shooting, the unit returned to the Hollywood studio, where a remarkably convincing miniature mountain range was created out of timber, chicken wire, burlap, plaster, salt, and flour. In addition, the studio technicians devised exquisite models to produce the special effects that Chaplin required, like the miners' hut, which is blown by the tempest to teeter on the edge of a precipice, for one of cinema's most sustained sequences of comic suspense. Often it is impossible to detect the shifts in the film from model to full-size set.

The Gold Rush abounds with now-classic comedy scenes. The historic horrors of the starving 19th-century pioneers inspired the sequence in which the Little Tramp and his partner Big Jim (Mack Swain) are snowbound and ravenous. The Little Tramp cooks his boot, with all the airs of a gourmet. In the eyes of the delirious Big Jim, he is intermittently transformed into an oven-worthy chicken—a triumph both for the cameramen, who had to effect the elaborate trick work entirely in the camera, and for Chaplin, who magically assumes the characteristics of a bird.

The lone prospector's dream of hosting a New Year's dinner for the beautiful dance-hall girl (Georgia Hale, who replaced sixteen-year-old Lita Grey when Lita became pregnant and married Chaplin) provides the opportunity for another famous Chaplin set piece: the dance of the rolls. The gag had been seen in films before, but Chaplin gives unique personality to the dancing legs created out of forks and bread rolls.

Today, *The Gold Rush* appears as one of Chaplin's most perfectly accomplished films. Though his affections for his own work changed over time, to the end of his life he would frequently declare that this film was the one by which he would most wish to be remembered. **DR**

U.S. (Charles Chaplin)
72m Silent BW **Producer** Charles
Chaplin **Screenplay** Charles Chaplin
Photography Roland Totheroh **Music** Max
Terr (1942 version) **Cast** Charles Chaplin,
Mack Swain, Tom Murray, Henry Bergman,
Malcolm Waite, Georgia Hale

> *"Back of it all—back of the funny clothes, the mustache, and the big feet—I wanted to produce something that would stir people."*
>
> **Charlie Chaplin, 1925**

i

The boot Chaplin "eats" was licorice. Repeated takes saw him hospitalized to have his stomach pumped.

The Big Parade King Vidor, 1925

U.S. (MGM) 141m Silent BW (tinted sequences) **Producer** Irving Thalberg **Screenplay** Harry Behn, Joseph Farnham **Photography** John Arnold **Music** William Axt, Maurice Baron, David Mendoza **Cast** John Gilbert, Renée Adorée, Hobart Bosworth, Claire McDowell, Claire Adams, Robert Ober, Tom O'Brien, Karl Dane, Rosita Marstini, George Beranger, Frank Currier

"Waiting! Orders! Mud! Blood! Stinking stiffs! What the hell do we get out of this war anyway! "

Jim (John Gilbert)

Based on a story by Laurence Stallings, who wrote the Broadway smash *What Price Glory?*, King Vidor's epic film about the American experience of World War I traces the adventures of three soldiers from different backgrounds who find themselves in France. Rich boy Jim (John Gilbert), whose fiancée had encouraged him to enlist, meets a beautiful French woman (Renée Adorée) in the village where their unit has been assigned lodging. In one of *The Big Parade*'s most tender scenes, she clutches the boot he has left with her as the soldiers make their way to the front. Once they arrive at the trenches, the battle of Belleau Wood commences. Attacking a machine gun nest, Jim's two buddies are killed and he is wounded. Seeking refuge in a shell hole, he discovers a dying German soldier already occupying it, and the two share a cigarette. Eventually, he is found and then taken to a field hospital. His attempts to reach the farmhouse fail as he falls unconscious.

Back in America, Jim is reunited with his family but is bitterly unhappy because he has lost a leg. His fiancée, in any case, has now fallen in love with his brother. Finally, Jim accepts his mother's advice and returns to France, where in the film's most moving scene he locates his lost love as she is helping her mother plow the fields. With its expert mixture of physical comedy (particularly in the French farmhouse scenes) and well-staged action, *The Big Parade* proved an immense success—a testimony to producer Irving Thalberg's oversight of the project—and counts as one of the triumphs of the late silent era.

Gilbert gives a fine performance as Jim, showing the box-office appeal that made him one of the era's biggest stars, and Adorée is appropriately appealing as his love interest. Because it shows the horrors of war, *The Big Parade* has often been thought of as a pacifist tract, but in truth its politics are muted. As Thalberg wanted, the film is much more of a comedy romance, with the war serving as the means through which Jim becomes a man and discovers the kind of life he really wants to live. **RBP**

ℹ

The Big Parade is one of the highest-grossing silent films ever, second only to *The Birth of a Nation* (1915).

Die Abenteuer des Prinzen Achmed
The Adventures of Prince Achmed Lotte Reiniger, 1926

Germany (Comenius-Film
GMBH) 66m BW / (tinted and toned)
Animator Lotte Reiniger
Producer Carl Koch **Screenplay** Lotte
Reiniger **Photography** Carl Koch
Collaborators Walter Ruttmann, Bertold
Bartosch, Alexander Kardan, Walter Türk
Music Wolfgang Zeller

Lotte Reiniger's enchanting *The Adventures of Prince Achmed* is often cited as the first feature-length animation. The film weaves together tales from *The Arabian Nights*, following Prince Achmed as he sets out on a perilous journey on a magical flying horse. He eventually lands on the islands of Waq Waq, where he falls in love with the beautiful fairy Princess Peri Banu.

Reiniger's characters move gracefully in and out of the shadows, magically disappearing and morphing shape through her skilled stop-time animation. The detail of the cutouts is beautifully complemented by the Islamic patterns on the inter-title cards, designed by Edmund Dulac, and the shimmering backgrounds by Walter Ruttmann. Its dizzying action sequences and romantic sensibility give the film a colorful rhythmic style, influenced by Reiniger's circle of avant-garde artist friends.

Reiniger's use of silhouette is as magical as her world of sorcerers, genies, and fairies. Produced over an arduous three years, the film resulted in the invention of many new techniques, including a multi-plane animation stand, which gives the illusion of depth to images. It is a method whose creation is often mistakenly attributed to Walt Disney.

ℹ

Reiniger's silhouette technique
was created entirely from intricate
paper and lead cutouts.

A popular film that imaginatively retells a classic fairytale, *The Adventures of Prince Achmed* is nevertheless firmly entrenched in the avant-garde. It is, in every way, a pioneering work whose timelessness lies in its skill and achievement. **LK**

Metropolis Fritz Lang, 1927

Originally clocking in at over two hours, Fritz Lang's *Metropolis* is the first science-fiction epic, with huge sets, thousands of extras, then-state-of-the-art special effects, lots of sex and violence, a heavy-handed moral, big acting, a streak of Germanic gothicism, and groundbreaking fantasy sequences. Funded by UFA, Germany's giant film studio, it was controversial in its day and proved a box-office disaster that nearly ruined the studio.

The plot is simple, with Freder Fredersen (Gustav Fröhlich), pampered son of the Master of Metropolis (Alfred Abel), learning of the wretched lives of the multitude of workers who keep the super-city going. Freder comes to understand the way things work by the saintly Maria (Brigitte Helm), a pacifist who constantly preaches mediation in industrial disputes, as well as by secretly working a hellish ten-hour shift at one of the grinding machines. The Master consults with mad engineer Rotwang (Rudolf Klein-Rogge), who has created a feminoid robot he reshapes to be an evil double of Maria and unleashes on the city. The robotrix goes from dancing naked in a decadent nightspot to inciting a destructive riot, which allows Lang to get the most value out of the huge factory sets by blowing them up and/or flooding them, but Freder and the real Maria save the day by rescuing the city's children from a flood. Society is reunited when Maria decrees that the heart (Freder) must mediate between the brain (the Master) and the hands (the workers).

Shortly after its premiere, the film was pulled from distribution and reedited against Lang's wishes: this truncated, simplified form remained best known, even in the colorized Giorgio Moroder remix of the 1980s, until the twenty-first century, when a partial restoration—with tactful linking titles to fill in the scenes that remain irretrievably missing—made it much closer to Lang's original vision. This version not only adds many scenes that went unseen for decades, but also restores their original order and puts in the proper intertitles. Previously rated as a spectacular but simplistic science-fiction film, this new-old version reveals that the futuristic setting isn't intended as prophetic but mythical, with elements of 1920s architecture, industry, design, and politics mingled with the medieval and the Biblical to produce images of striking strangeness: a futuristic robot burned at the stake, a steel-handed mad scientist who is also a fifteenth-century alchemist, the trudging workers of a vast factory plodding into the jaws of a machine that is also the ancient god Moloch. Fröhlich's performance as the hero who represents the heart is still wildly overdone, but Klein-Rogge's engineer Rotwang, Abel's Master of Metropolis, and especially Helm in the dual role of saintly savior and metal femme fatale are astonishing. By restoring a great deal of story delving into the mixed motivations of the characters, the wild plot now makes more sense, and we can see it is as much a twisted family drama as an epic of repression, revolution, and reconciliation. **KN**

Germany (Universum/UFA) 120m Silent BW
Producer Erich Pommer **Screenplay** Fritz Lang, Thea von Harbou **Photography** Karl Freund, Günther Rittau **Music** Gottfried Huppertz **Cast** Alfred Abel, Gustav Fröhlich, Brigitte Helm, Rudolf Klein-Rogge, Fritz Rasp, Theodor Loos, Heinrich George

"The clothing of a robot in human flesh provides as great a thrill as anyone could wish."

Iris Barry,
The Spectator, 1927

i

Gustav Fröhlich began the film as an extra; he was given the role of Freder after the original actor was fired.

1927

57

Sunrise F.W. Murnau, 1927

U.S. (Fox) 97m Silent BW
Producer William Fox
Screenplay Hermann Sudermann,
Carl Mayer **Photography** Charles Rosher,
Karl Struss **Music** Timothy Brock, Hugo
Riesenfeld **Cast** George O'Brien, Janet
Gaynor, Margaret Livingston, Bodil Rosing,
J. Farrell MacDonald, Ralph Sipperly, Jane
Winton, Arthur Housman, Eddie Boland,
Barry Norton **Oscars** William Fox (unique
and artistic picture), Janet Gaynor (actress),
Charles Rosher, Karl Struss (photography)
Oscar nomination Rochus Gliese
(art direction)

"The motion picture camera—for so long tethered by sheer bulk and naïveté—had with Sunrise finally learned to fly."

Todd Ludy, critic

🛈

It is rumored that George O'Brien was
made to wear lead boots in order to
feel the weight of his character's guilt.

Trivia buffs might note that, although many history books often cite *Wings* (1927) as the first Best Picture recipient at the Academy Awards, the honor actually went to two films: William Wellman's *Wings*, for "production," and F.W. Murnau's *Sunrise*, for "unique and artistic production." If the latter category sounds more impressive than the former, that explains (in part at least) why *Sunrise*, and not *Wings*, remains one of the most revered films of all time. William Fox initially drew Murnau to America with the promise of a big budget and total creative freedom, and the fact that Murnau made the most of it with this stunning masterpiece ratified his peerless reputation as a cinematic genius.

Sunrise itself is deceptively simple. Subtitled somewhat enigmatically *A Song of Two Humans*, the film focuses on a country-dwelling married couple whose lives are disrupted by a temptress from the city. But Murnau draws waves of emotion from what could have been a rote melodrama, further enhanced by a bevy of groundbreaking filmmaking techniques. Most notable is the use of sound effects, pushing silent cinema one step closer to the talkie era—an achievement unfairly overshadowed by *The Jazz Singer*, released later in 1927. Murnau also creatively manipulates the use and effect of title cards (three years earlier, he had directed the title-free *The Last Laugh*).

The most striking aspect of *Sunrise* is its camera work. Working with a pair of cinematographers, Charles Rosher and Karl Struss, Murnau borrowed from his own experience in the German Expressionist movement as well as from the pastoral portraits of the Dutch masters, particularly Jan Vermeer. Linked with graceful and inventive camera movements and accented with in-camera tricks (such as multiple exposures), each scene of *Sunrise* looks like a masterful still photograph.

The simplicity of its story lends *Sunrise* a formidable dramatic weight. George O'Brien, pondering the murder of his wife, Janet Gaynor, is racked with guilt, and his wife responds with appropriate terror once his intentions become obvious. The boat trip leading to her intended demise is fraught with both suspense and an odd sense of sadness, as the good O'Brien struggles to bring his monstrous thoughts to their fruition. Margaret Livingston, as the urban seductress, in many ways seems like the feminine equivalent of Murnau's vampire Count Orlok (from the 1922 film *Nosferatu*), relentlessly preying on poor O'Brien's soul. In one scene he is even beset by spectral images of her, surrounding him, clutching at him, and provoking him with her murderous desires.

Alas, the film was a box-office flop, and Murnau died in a car accident a few years later. But *Sunrise* remains a benchmark by which all other films should be measured, a pinnacle of craft whose sophistication belies the resources at the time. Its shadow looms over several great works, from Orson Welles's *Citizen Kane* (1941) to Jean Cocteau's *Beauty and the Beast* (1946), yet at the same time its own brilliance is inimitable. **JKl**

The General Clyde Bruckman & Buster Keaton, 1927

Keaton made several films that may be counted among the finest (and funniest) in cinema's entire comic output, but none is as strong a contender to the title of the greatest comedy ever made as this timeless masterpiece. It isn't merely the constant stream of great gags, nor the way they derive wholly from situation and character rather than existing in isolation from the film's drama. What makes *The General* so extraordinary is that it is superlative on every level: in terms of its humor, suspense, historical reconstruction, character study, visual beauty, and technical precision. One might even argue that it comes as close to flawless perfection as any feature ever made, comic or otherwise.

Much of the pleasure derives from the narrative itself, inspired by a book about the real-life exploits of a group of Northern soldiers who, during the Civil War, disguised themselves as Southerners to steal a train, which they drove north to rejoin their Unionist comrades until they were caught and executed. Keaton, understandably given that he was making a comedy, dropped the executions and changed the heroic perspective to that of a Southerner, Johnny Gray, a railway driver who stoically, if somewhat absurdly, goes in solo pursuit of Unionist spies when they steal both his engine—"The General"—and, inside it, Annabelle Lee (Marion Mack), the other love of his life. The film's first half follows Johnny's rejection by the army with his chase after the train, which he recaptures behind enemy lines; the second half depicts his flight (with Annabelle) from the Union troops to his hometown, where—after handing over the Girl, The General, and a real Northern army general inadvertently brought along for the ride—he is acclaimed as a hero.

This symmetrical story line is both formally pleasing and the source of suspense and gags; but the voyage also lends the film an epic tone that, combined with Keaton's meticulous historical detail, transforms it into perhaps the finest Civil War movie ever made. Then, finally, there is Buster's Johnny: unsmiling yet beautiful in his brave, faintly ridiculous determination—the epitome of this serio-comic masterpiece, and as deeply human a hero as the cinema has given us. **GA**

U.S. (Buster Keaton, United Artists)
75m Silent BW (Sepiatone)
Producer Buster Keaton, Joseph M. Schenck
Screenplay Al Boasberg, Clyde Bruckman
Photography Bert Haines, Devereaux
Jennings **Music** Robert Israel, William P.
Perry **Cast** Marion Mack, Charles Smith,
Richard Allen, Glen Cavender, Jim Farley,
Frederick Vroom, Joe Keaton, Mike Donlin,
Tom Nawn, Buster Keaton

"No other comedian could do as much with the deadpan."

James Agee,
LIFE magazine, 1966

ℹ

The famous shot of the enemy train falling through a bridge was the costliest scene of the silent movie era.

The Unknown Tod Browning, 1927

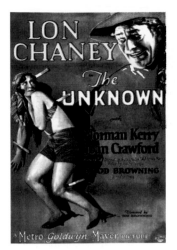

U.S. (MGM) 65m Silent BW
Screenplay Tod Browning, Waldemar
Young **Photography** Merritt B. Gerstad
Cast Lon Chaney, Norman Kerry, Joan
Crawford, Nick De Ruiz, John George,
Frank Lanning, Polly Moran

*"Hands! Men's hands!
How I hate them!"*

Nanon Zanzi
(Joan Crawford)

Best known for directing Bela Lugosi in the 1931 Universal horror classic *Dracula*, and most notorious for his 1932 oddity *Freaks*, circus performer-turned-filmmaker Tod Browning's all-around greatest film is *The Unknown*. It is an under-appreciated silent-era gem starring the writer-director's favorite actor and "Man of a Thousand Faces," Lon Chaney.

Greatly admired for the pain he would endure playing physically disabled antagonists, Chaney here outdoes himself as Alonzo, a criminal with an extra thumb on one hand who seeks to avoid capture by pretending to be an armless knife thrower in a circus. The armless gig at first has an additional benefit, as Alonzo's beautiful assistant, Nanon (Joan Crawford in one of her earliest leads), daughter of the circus owner, cannot stand being embraced by men—in particular Alonzo's main rival for her affections, strongman Malabar the Mighty (Norman Kerry).

After Nanon's father accidentally sees his arms, Alonzo murders him in order to keep the secret from getting out. Nanon, meanwhile, catches a glimpse of the killer's double thumb without seeing his face. Obsessed with Nanon, and distraught over the possibility that she will discover his true identity, Alonzo has his arms surgically amputated. But in one of *The Unknown*'s most delicious and disturbing ironies, when Alonzo returns to the circus he finds that Nanon has gotten over her phobia of being held and has fallen head over heels for Malabar.

Seeking poetic justice (or just plain revenge) for this cruel twist of fate, the now truly armless Alonzo attempts to rig Malabar's latest circus act—in which the strongman ties his arms to a pair of horses, each one pulling in the opposite direction—so that his rival will end up armless as well. However, his scheme is foiled, and Alonzo himself gets killed saving Nanon from being trampled by one of the horses.

Drawing a remarkable and haunting performance from Chaney and filling the plot with twists and unforgettable characters, Browning here creates a chilling masterpiece of psychological (and psychosexual) drama. As Michael Koller writes, "*The Unknown* is a truly horrifying film that takes us into the darkest recesses of the human psyche." **SJS**

1927

i

Browning's plot was inspired by an event that occurred during his own circus days.

Oktyabr Grigori Aleksandrov & Sergei M. Eisenstein, 1927
October

In 1926, Sergei M. Eisenstein went to Germany to present his new film, *The Battleship Potemkin*. He left a promising young filmmaker, but he came back an international cultural superstar. A series of major film productions was being planned to commemorate the tenth anniversary of the Bolshevik victory. Eisenstein eagerly accepted the challenge of presenting on-screen the revolutionary process in Russia—literally, how the country went from the Czar's abdication and Aleksandr Kerensky's "Provisional Government" to the first victories of Lenin and his followers.

No expense was spared. Massive crowd scenes were organized, and city traffic was diverted so Eisenstein could shoot in the very sites where the depicted incident occurred. Contrary to popular belief, the film contains not one meter of documentary footage. Every shot was a re-creation. Working feverishly, Eisenstein finished just in time for the anniversary celebrations, but the reactions, official and otherwise, were less than enthusiastic. Many found the film confusing and difficult to follow. Others wondered why the role of Lenin was so greatly reduced. (The actor playing him, Vasili Nikandrov, appears only a handful of times on-screen.) Several critics who had supported *Potemkin* suggested that Eisenstein go back to the editing room and keep working.

There is no denying that *October* is a masterpiece, but figuring out what kind is a real challenge. As a means of "explaining" the revolution, the film is simply ineffective. For many audiences, sitting through it is a real chore. The characterizations are all paper thin, and anyone with a smattering of historical knowledge can see right through its propaganda. Yet what is perhaps most powerful and touching about *October* is simply its level of ambition. Eisenstein was surely the cinema's most remarkable personality for the first fifty years of its existence, impossibly erudite, with an unlimited belief in cinema's potential. He imagined that cinema could represent "visual thinking"—not just arguments, but the process by which the mind constructs arguments. Photographic images, the raw material of cinema, had to be "neutralized" into sensations and stimuli so that a film could reveal concepts and not just people or things. The real engine that would drive the cinema machine as Eisenstein saw it was montage, editing—the "mystical" interaction that occurs when two separate pieces of film are joined together.

October is the purest, most cogent example of Eisenstein's theory and practice of cinema. There are several absolutely breathtaking sequences: the toppling of the Czar's statue, the raising of the bridge, and especially the "For God and Country" sequence. Evidence of the cold engineer that Eisenstein originally trained to be might be found in the cathedral-like intricacy of its editing. However, scratch below the film's surface and you can feel the exhilaration—and the touch of madness—of an artist on the threshold of what he believes will be a brave new world. **RP**

U.S.S.R. (Sovkino) 95m Silent BW
Screenplay Grigori Aleksandrov, Sergei M. Eisenstein **Photography** Vladimir Nilsen, Vladimir Popov, Eduard Tisse **Music** Alfredo Antonini, Edmund Meisel **Cast** Vladimir Popov, Vasili Nikandrov, Layaschenko, Chibisov, Boris Livanov, Mikholyev, N. Podvoisky, Smelsky, Eduard Tisse

"How I should like to make such a powerful failure."

Vsevolod Pudovkin, director, 1928

i

More people were injured reenacting the storming of the Winter Palace than were hurt in the actual takeover.

The Jazz Singer Alan Crosland, 1927

Throughout film history, certain movies have been the center of special attention, if not for their aesthetics, then for their role in the development of cinema as we know it. Alan Crosland's *The Jazz Singer* is undoubtedly one of the films that has marked the path of motion pictures as both an art form and a profitable industry. Released in 1927 by Warner Brothers and starring Al Jolson, one of the best-known vocal artists at the time, *The Jazz Singer* is unanimously considered the first feature-length sound movie. Although limited to musical performances and a few dialogues following and preceding such performances, the use of sound introduced innovative changes in the industry, destined to revolutionize Hollywood as hardly any other movie has done.

In its blend of vaudeville and melodrama, the plot is relatively simple. Jakie (Jolson) is the only teenage son of the devoted Cantor Rabinowitz (Warner Oland), who encourages his child to follow the same path of generations of Cantors in the family. Although profoundly influenced by his Jewish roots, Jakie's passion is jazz and he dreams about an audience inspired by his voice. After a family friend confesses to Cantor Rabinowitz to having seen Jakie singing in a café, the furious father punishes his son, causing him to run away from the family house and from his heartbroken mother, Sara (Eugenie Besserer). Years later Jakie, aka Jack Robin, comes back as an affirmed jazz singer looking for reconciliation. Finding his father still harsh and now sick, Jack is forced to make a decision between his career as a blackface entertainer and his Jewish identity.

A milestone in film history representing a decisive step toward a new type of cinema and a new type of entertainment, *The Jazz Singer* is more than just the first "talkie." As Michael Rogin, the famed political scientist, has argued, *The Jazz Singer* can be cited as a typical example of Jewish transformation in U.S. society: the racial assimilation into white America, the religious conversion to less strict spiritual dogma, and the entrepreneurial integration into the American motion picture industry during the time of the coming of sound. **CFe**

U.S. (Warner Bros.) 88m BW
Screenplay Alfred A. Cohn, Jack Jarmuth
Photography Hal Mohr **Music** Ernie Erdman, James V. Monaco, Louis Silvers, Irving Berlin **Cast** Al Jolson, May McAvoy, Warner Oland, Eugenie Besserer, Otto Lederer, Bobby Gordon, Richard Tucker, Cantor Joseff Rosenblatt **Oscar** Alfred A. Cohn, Jack Jarmuth (honorary award for pioneering talking pictures)
Oscar nomination Alfred A. Cohn (screenplay)

> *"Wait a minute, wait a minute, you ain't heard nothin' yet!"*
>
> **Jack Robin (Al Jolson)**

ⓘ

George Jessel, star of the stage version, was offered the lead in the film but refused over a pay dispute.

Napoléon Abel Gance, 1927

France / Italy / Germany / Spain / Sweden / Czechoslovakia (Gance, Soc. générale) 378m (original) Silent BW (some color) **Producer** Robert A. Harris **Screenplay** Abel Gance **Photography** Jules Kruger, Joseph-Louis Mundwiller, Torpkoff **Music** Arthur Honegger **Cast** Albert Dieudonné, Vladimir Roudenko, Edmond Van Daële, Alexandre Koubitzky, Antonin Artaud, Abel Gance, Gina Manès, Suzanne Bianchetti, Marguerite Gance, Yvette Dieudonné, Philippe Hériat, Pierre Batcheff, Eugénie Buffet, Acho Chakatouny, Nicolas Koline

At 333 minutes in its longest extant version, Abel Gance's 1927 biopic is an epic on a scale to satisfy its subject. Although it follows Bonaparte from his school days in 1780 through to his triumphant Italian campaign of 1796, by contemporary standards the film lacks depth. For Gance, Napoléon (played by the appropriately named Albert Dieudonné) was a "man of destiny," not pyschology. His paean to the French Emperor has something in common with Sergei Eisenstein's *Alexander Nevsky* (1938), both thrilling pieces of cinema in the service of nationalist propaganda.

If Gance is more of an innovator than an artist, it's a measure of his brilliance that *Napoléon* still brims with energy and invention today. None of his contemporaries—not even Murnau—used the camera with such inspiration. Gance thought nothing of strapping cameramen to horses; he even mounted a camera on the guillotine. In one brilliant sequence, he captures the revolutionary spirit of a rousing (silent) rendition of "La Marseilles" by swinging the camera above the set as if it were on a trapeze. His most spectacular coup, though, is "Polyvision," a split-screen effect that called for three projectors to create a triptych—nearly three decades before the advent of Cinerama. **TCh**

The Kid Brother J.A. Howe & Ted Wilde, 1927

U.S. (Paramount, Harold Lloyd) 84m Silent BW **Producer** Jesse L. Lasky, Harold Lloyd, Adolph Zukor **Screenplay** Thomas J. Crizer, Howard J. Green, John Grey, Lex Neal, Ted Wilde **Photography** Walter Lundin **Cast** Harold Lloyd, Jobyna Ralston, Walter James, Leo Willis, Olin Francis, Constantine Romanoff, Eddie Boland, Frank Lanning, Ralph Yearsley

Harold Lloyd is often regarded as the "third genius" of silent American comedy, his 1920s' work often more successful with the public than that of Buster Keaton, and even Charlie Chaplin. Lloyd's screen persona is routinely noted for its "speedy," can-do optimism and his films singled out for the audacious, often dangerous stunts and acrobatic feats that they contain. *The Kid Brother*, Lloyd's second feature for Paramount, is often considered to be the bespectacled comic's best and most holistic film. In many ways it deliberately turns its back on the 1920s, returning somewhat to the rural "idyll" of the 1922 film *Grandma's Boy*.

The film's two most startling sequences illustrate the combination of delicate and rugged athleticism that marks Lloyd's best work. In the first scene, Lloyd is shown climbing a tall tree to attain a slightly longer look at the woman he has just met (and fallen for). This sequence shows the meticulous and technically adventurous aspects of Lloyd's cinema—an elevator was built to accommodate the ascending camera—and the ways they are intricately connected to elements of character and situation (also demonstrating Lloyd's masterly use of props). The second sequence features a fight between Lloyd and his chief antagonist, and is remarkable for its sustained ferocity and precise staging. Both sequences show Lloyd's character transcending his seeming limitations, moving beyond appearances, and traveling that common trajectory from mama's boy to triumphant "average" American. **AD**

The Crowd King Vidor, 1928

"You've got to be good in that town if you want to beat the crowd." So says young John on his first sight of New York City, the thrilling metropolis where he's sure his special qualities will raise him high above the common herd.

Things work out differently for the hero of *The Crowd*, who shouldn't really be called a hero, because director King Vidor's intention was to portray a man so painfully ordinary that he could seem a randomly selected sample from the movie's eponymous urban multitude. He begins the story as a newborn baby indistinguishable from any other, and ends it as a New York bourgeois man indistinguishable from any other. In between, he undergoes experiences so humdrum that only a studio as adventurous as MGM under Irving G. Thalberg's regime would have considered it the stuff of Hollywood drama at all.

Nor would it have been if Vidor hadn't given it such stunningly imaginative treatment. From the stylized scene where John learns of his father's untimely death—filmed in a stairwell with forced perspective, borrowing from German film expressionism—to the closing shot of John and his wife, Mary, the generically named protagonists of this generically titled film, engulfed in an unthinking throng of moviegoers who mirror their herdlike selves, as unerringly as they mirror our own.

Vidor was riding high in Hollywood when he made *The Crowd*, fresh from the success of *The Big Parade* two years earlier. To play Mary he chose the attractive star Eleanor Boardman, who also happened to be his wife; but for John he took a chance on the little-tested James Murray, whose erratic career ended in suicide less than a decade later.

Although both are brilliant, Murray shines brightest under Vidor's expert guidance; for evidence, see the sequence when an unthinkable tragedy strikes the couple before their horrified eyes, uniting inspired acting with split-second editing and absolutely perfect camera work to produce one of the most unforgettable moments in all of silent cinema. It's a scene that stands leagues above the crowd in a movie that does the same from start to finish. **DS**

U.S. (MGM) 104m Silent BW **Producer** Irving Thalberg **Screenplay** King Vidor & John V.A. Weaver **Photography** Henry Sharp **Cast** Eleanor Boardman, James Murray, Bert Roach, Estelle Clark, Daniel G. Tomlinson, Dell Henderson, Lucy Beaumont, Freddie Burke Frederick, Alice Mildred Puter **Oscar nominations** Irving Thalberg (best picture—unique and artistic picture), King Vidor (director)

"Look at that crowd! The poor slobs . . . all in the same rut!"

John Sims (James Murray)

i

King Vidor filmed many scenes in the streets of New York City, using real crowds instead of extras.

The Docks of New York Josef von Sternberg, 1928

U.S. (Famous Players-Lasky, Paramount)
76m Silent BW **Producer** J.G. Bachmann
Screenplay Jules Furthman, from the story
The Dock Walloper by John Monk Saunders
Photography Harold Rosson **Cast** George
Bancroft, Betty Compson, Olga Baclanova,
Clyde Cook, Mitchell Lewis, Gustav von
Seyffertitz, Guy Oliver, May Foster,
Lillian Worth

Despite nowadays being hailed as a silent classic, the film was a box-office disappointment on its release.

The last full year of Hollywood's silent era, 1928, produced some of its greatest masterpieces. Like other movies from that year, Josef von Sternberg's *The Docks of New York* is a film of consummate economy and refinement. The plot is minimal and the characters few, leaving more room for the film's maximal elaboration of atmosphere and gesture.

Sternberg's waterfront romance contains two main sections: night and morning. Night is a luminous shadowland of mist, smoke, pools of light, and rippling reflections. In this enchanted realm, hulking stoker Bill (George Bancroft) fishes suicidal tramp Mae (Betty Compson) out of the drink. The couple end up at a saloon where they talk each other into a spur-of-the-moment marriage. The cold, clear light of morning brings desertion, disillusion, and a change of heart, as Bill impulsively jumps ship and returns to take the rap for a stolen dress he had given to Mae.

The restraint and care of the performances—Bancroft's guarded nonchalance, the deliberate grace with which he moves his massive body, and Compson's languid weariness and the delicate balance between hurt and hope in her upturned eyes—maintain a constantly rippling veil of speculation over the main characters' inner thoughts and feelings. Sternberg, by all accounts (including his own) was the iciest of directors, yet he created several of the cinema's most moving testaments to the power of love to make fools of us all. *The Docks of New York* is one of them, made all the more convincing by the self-deprecating reticence with which it reveals its foolish heart. **MR**

La passion de Jeanne d'Arc Carl Theodor Dreyer, 1928
The Passion of Joan of Arc

Carl Dreyer's 1928 masterpiece—his last silent film, and the greatest of all Joan of Arc films—is the work of his that brought him worldwide fame, although, like the majority of his later pictures, it was strictly a *succès d'estime* and fared poorly at the box office. A print of the original version—lost for half a century—was rediscovered in a Norwegian mental asylum in the 1980s. Other prints had perished in a warehouse fire, and the two versions subsequently circulated consisted of outtakes.

All of Dreyer's films were based on works of fiction or plays, with the exception of *The Passion of Joan of Arc*, which was essentially based on the official transcripts of the proceedings of Joan's trial—albeit highly selective and radically compressed portions of that trial. It was made only eight years after Joan was canonized in France and ten years after the end of World War I, both of which were central to Dreyer's interpretation. The helmets worn by the occupying British in 1431 resemble those in the recent war, and 1928 audiences saw the film as a historical "documentary" rather like the later films of Peter Watkins.

Joan is played by Renée Falconetti, a stage actress Dreyer discovered in a boulevard comedy, and following his instructions, she played the part without makeup. She and her interlocutors are filmed almost exclusively in close-ups. Though hers is one of the key performances in the history of movies, she never made another film. Antonin Artaud also appears in his most memorable screen role, as the sympathetic brother Jean Massieu.

Dreyer's radical approach to constructing space and the slow intensity of his mobile camera style make this a "difficult" film in the sense that, like all great films, it reinvents the world from the ground up. *The Passion of Joan of Arc* is also painful in a way that all Dreyer's tragedies are, but it will continue to live long after most commercial movies have vanished from memory. **JRos**

France (Société générale) 110m Silent BW
Screenplay Joseph Delteil, Carl Theodor Dreyer **Photography** Rudolph Maté
Cast Renée Falconetti, Eugene Silvain, André Berley, Maurice Schutz, Antonin Artaud, Michel Simon, Jean d'Yd, Louis Ravet, Armand Lurville, Jacques Arnna, Alexandre Mihalesco, Léon Larive

"[Renée Falconetti's portrayal of Joan of Arc] may be the finest performance ever recorded on film."

Pauline Kael, critic, 1982

ℹ️ The huge Rouen Castle set was built as a single, interconnecting structure rather than as individual locations.

Un chien andalou Luis Buñuel, 1928
An Andalusian Dog

France 16m Silent BW
Producer Luis Buñuel Screenplay Luis
Buñuel, Salvador Dalí Photography Albert
Duverger Cast Pierre Batcheff, Simone
Mareuil, Luis Buñuel, Salvador Dalí

The directorial debut of Luis Buñuel, collaborating with artist Salvador Dalí, is etched into our consciousness of film history because of one image above all: a razor slicing open an eyeball. What is this: shock tactic, symbol of a modernist "vision," male aggression toward woman? For Jean Vigo—who hailed *An Andalusian Dog* for its "social consciousness"—Buñuel's associative montage raised a philosophical query: "Is it more dreadful than the spectacle of a cloud veiling a full moon?" One thing is certain: The image kicks off a classic surrealist parable of Eros ever denied, ever frustrated by institutions and mores.

Too often—because of its heavy influence on rock video—*An Andalusian Dog* has been reduced to, and recycled as, a collection of disconnected, striking, incongruous images: dead horse on a piano, ants in a hand. But this overlooks what gives the work its cohering force: the fact that, in many ways, Buñuel scrupulously respects certain conventions of classical continuity and linkage, creating a certain disquieting narrative sense among these fragments from the unconscious. This is a dialectic of surface rationality versus deep, churning forces from the Id that Buñuel would continue exploring to the very end of his career. **AM**

i

According to Buñuel, the eyeball used in the notorious eye-slitting scene belonged to a dead calf.

Steamboat Bill, Jr. Charles Reisner & Buster Keaton, 1928

U.S. (Buster Keaton) 71m Silent BW
Producer Joseph M. Schenck
Screenplay Carl Harbaugh
Photography Bert Haines, Devereaux
Jennings **Cast** Buster Keaton, Tom
McGuire, Ernest Torrence, Tom Lewis,
Marion Byron

Even more than the formally experimental *Sherlock, Jr.* (1924), this film, along with *Our Hospitality* (1923) and *The General* (1927), reveals just how great a director Buster Keaton was, over and above his considerable talents as a comedian. In *Steamboat Bill, Jr.*, by means of his customarily unintrusive but always expert placing of the camera, we get a real feeling for the small Mississippi riverside town where city slicker and college graduate Willie turns up to see his beleaguered steamboat-proprietor father. Dad, a rough-and-ready type, is dismayed by his son's somewhat foolish ways and is even less happy when the boy falls for the daughter of a wealthy rival determined to blow Bill, Sr., out of the water.

Needless to say, Willie finally gets to prove his mettle during a climactic typhoon that destroys the town in an extended sequence of virtuoso stunts, meticulously staged action sequences, and superbly paced suspense, but not before much fun has been had with notions of acceptable/unacceptable masculine behavior. One scene in particular, in which father and son shop for hats (played straight to camera as if it were a mirror), is not only hilarious but a prime example of Keaton's very "modern" and playful awareness of his comic persona. Magic. **GA**

Potomok Chingis-Khana Vsevolod Pudovkin, 1928
Storm Over Asia

U.S.S.R. (Mezhrabpomfilm) 93m Silent BW
Screenplay Osip Brik, I. Novokshenov
Photography Anatoli Golovnya **Cast** Valéry
Inkijinoff, I. Dedintsev, Aleksandr Chistyakov,
Viktor Tsoppi, F. Ivanov, V. Pro, Boris Barnet,
K. Gurnyak, I. Inkishanov, L. Belinskaya,
Anel Sudakevich

Within a month of completing *1927: The End of St. Petersburg*, Vsevolod Pudovkin was at work on this epic fable, apparently inspired both by I. Novokshonov's original story of a herdsman who will rise to become a great leader, and by the prospect of shooting in virgin territory, exotic Outer Mongolia. Pudovkin's State Film School classmate Valéry Inkijinoff plays the unnamed hero, a Mongol who learns to distrust capitalists when a Western fur trader cheats him out of a rare silver fox pelt. The year is 1918, and the Mongol falls in with Socialist partisans fighting against the imperialist British occupying army. Captured, he is condemned to be shot (for recognizing the word "Moscow"), but his life is saved when an ancient talisman is found on his person, a document that proclaims the bearer to be a direct descendant of Genghis Khan. The British install him as a puppet king, but he escapes to lead his people to a fantastic victory.

A curious mix of rip-roaring adventure filmmaking, Soviet socialist propaganda, and ethnographic documentary, *Storm Over Asia* is never less than entertaining. It is distinguished by Pudovkin's epic compositional sense, evident in the cavalry column fanning out to fill the horizon and some striking, cubist-like montage sequences—as well as for its sardonic satire of Buddhist ritual and Western betrayal of faith. **TCh**

Prapancha Pash Franz Osten, 1929
A Throw of Dice

Germany (Universum/UFA) 74m BW
Producer Himansu Rai Screenplay Niranjan
Pal Photography Emil Schünemann
Music Will Schmidt Gentner, Nitin Sawhney
(restored version) Cast Seeta Devi, Himansu
Rai, Charu Roy, Modhu Bose, Sarada Gupta,
Tincory Chakrabarty, Lala Bijoykishen

A German production in collaboration with the actor-producer Himansu Rai, filmed entirely on location in India and based on an episode from the Mahabharata, *A Throw of Dice* is a magnificent and alluring epic. Osten's most critically acclaimed film, it was his third collaboration with Rai, after *The Light of Asia* (1925), about the life of Buddha, and *Shiraz* (1928), which dramatizes events around the building of the Taj Mahal.

Two kings vie for the hand of young Sunita (Seeta Devi). She is enamored of Ranjit (Charu Roy), who is no less besotted with her. Sohan (Himansu Rai) sees her as a way to gain more power. Knowing Ranjit to be addicted to gambling, Sohan uses a set of loaded dice to win Sunita's hand and, eventually, his rival's kingdom. Only when Sunita discovers the dice is Ranjit able to muster the forces to overthrow Sohan.

One of *A Throw of the Dice*'s most striking elements is the naturalism of the performances, particularly compared with the declamatory style of much Western acting at that time. Also noteworthy are Osten and cinematographer Emil Schünemann's stunning visuals, which capture the beauty of India's landscape and its grand palaces along the Ganges.

The film was restored in time for the sixtieth anniversary of India's independence. Featuring an atmospheric score by Nitin Sawhney, accentuating the unbridled romanticism of Osten's drama, it now ranks as one of the pinnacles of early cinema. **IHS**

i

The movie's huge cast included 10,000 extras, 1,000 horses, and scores of elephants and tigers.

Chelovek s kinoapparatom Dziga Vertov, 1929
The Man with a Movie Camera

U.S.S.R. (VUFKU) 80m Silent BW
Screenplay Dziga Vertov
Photography Dziga Vertov

"I am kino-eye, I am a mechanical eye, I, a machine, show you the world as only I can see it."

Dziga Vertov, 1923

Dziga Vertov (Denis Kaufman) began his career with newsreels, filming the Red Army as it fought during the Russian Civil War (1918–21) and screening the footage for audiences in villages and towns who boarded the "agit-trains." The experience helped Vertov formulate his ideas about cinema, ideas shared by a group of like-minded young filmmakers who called themselves Kino-glaz (Cine-Eye). The group's principles—the "honesty" of documentary as compared with fiction film, the "perfection" of the cinematic eye compared with the human eye—inform Vertov's most extraordinary picture, the dazzling *The Man with a Movie Camera*.

In this film Vertov combines radical politics with revolutionary aesthetics to exhilarating, even giddy effect. The two components of filmmaking—camera and editing—function as equal (and gendered) partners. Vertov's male cameraman (his brother Mikhail Kaufman) records a day in the life of the modern city—what Vertov called "life caught unawares"—while his female editor (wife Elizaveta Svilova) cuts and splices the footage, thus reformulating that life. By the end, Vertov has exploited every available device of filming and editing—slow motion, animation, multiple images, split-screen, zooms and reverse zooms, blurring focus, and freeze-frames—to create a textbook of film technique as well as a hymn to the new Soviet state.

The camera begins to roll as the city gradually awakens, its buses and trams emerging from their night-hangars and its empty streets gradually filling, and continues by tracking denizens of the city (mostly Moscow but with extensive footage shot in Kiev, Yalta, and Odessa) through their routines of work and play. A lifetime is compressed into that day, as the camera peers between a woman's legs to watch a baby emerge, espies children entranced by a street conjuror, and tracks an ambulance carrying an accident victim. New rituals supplant old as couples marry, separate, and divorce in a registry office instead of a church.

Vertov gives visual form to Marxist principles in a stunning montage that follows the transformation of handwork into mechanized labor and that lauds the speed, efficiency, and the joy of assembly-line labor. Workers use their new-found leisure to socialize in state-subsidized clubs and beer halls, to play music and chess, to swim and sunbathe, pole-vault and kick soccer balls. Moscow's "ordinary people" become stars of their own lives as they see themselves on-screen. By the time Vertov bids an explosive farewell to the old by splitting the Bolshoi Theater in half, he has made his case for the revolutionary potential of cinema.

Ultimately, Vertov could not accommodate to Socialist Realism, and his career faltered. With *The Man with a Movie Camera*, however, he achieved his goal: a non-linear narrative form for cinema, a glorious tribute to everything that moviemaking can be. **JW**

𝑖
The twenty-four-hour day depicted in the movie was filmed over a period of three years.

Die Büchse der Pandora Georg Wilhelm Pabst, 1929
Pandora's Box

A lasting masterpiece from G.W. Pabst, adapted from Frank Wedekind's "Lulu" plays, *Pandora's Box* is remembered for the creation of an archetypal character in Lulu (Louise Brooks), an innocent temptress whose forthright sexuality winds up ruining the lives of everyone around her. Though Pabst was criticized for casting a foreigner in a role that was considered emblematically German, the main reason the film is remembered is the performance of American star Brooks. So powerful and sexual a presence that she never managed to make a transition from silent flapper parts to the talkie roles she deserved in a Hollywood dominated by Shirley Temple, Brooks is the definitive gamine vamp.

Presented in distinct theatrical "acts," the story picks up Lulu in a bourgeois Berlin drawing room, where she is the adored mistress of widowed newspaper publisher Peter Schön (Fritz Kortner), friendly with her lover's grown-up son Alwa (Franz Lederer) and even with the gnomish pimp Schigolch (Carl Goetz), who is either her father or her first lover. When Schön announces that he is remarrying, Lulu seems to be passed on to a nightclub strongman (Krafft-Raschig) but, provoked when Schön tells his son that "one does not marry" a woman like her, sets up an incident backstage at the music hall where she is dancing that breaks off the editor's engagement and prompts her lover to marry her, though he knows that it will be the death of him.

Though her husband in effect commits suicide, Lulu is convicted of his murder. On the run with Alwa, Schigolch, and her lesbian admirer Countess Geschwitz (Alice Roberte), she makes it to an opium-hazed gambling boat on the Seine—where she is almost sold to an Egyptian brothel and Alwa is humiliatingly caught cheating—then finally to a Christmassy London, where she is stalked by Jack the Ripper (Gustav Diessl). Pabst surrounds Brooks with startling secondary characters and dizzying settings, but it is the actress's vibrant, erotic, scary, and heartbreaking personality that resonates with modern audiences. Her mix of image and attitude is so strong and fresh that she makes Madonna look like Phyllis Diller, and her acting style is strikingly unmannered for the silent era. Her performance is also remarkably honest: never playing for easy sentiment, the audience is forced to recognize how destructive Lulu is even as we fall under her spell.

The original plays are set in 1888, the year of the Ripper murders, yet Pabst imagines a fantastical but contemporary setting, which seems to begin with the 1920s modernity of Berlin and then travels back in time to a foggy London for a death scene that is the cinema's first great insight into the mind-set of a serial killer. Lulu, turned streetwalker so that Schigolch can afford a last Christmas pudding, charms the reticent Jack, who throws aside his knife and genuinely tries not to kill again but is ultimately overwhelmed by the urge to stab. **KN**

Germany (Nero-Film) 97m Silent BW
Producer Seymour Nebenzal
Screenplay Joseph Fleisler, Georg Wilhelm Pabst, from the plays *Erdgeist* and *Die Büchse der Pandora* by Frank Wedekind
Photography Günther Krampf **Cast** Louise Brooks, Fritz Kortner, Francis Lederer, Carl Goetz, Krafft-Raschig, Alice Roberte, Gustav Diessl

"Louise Brooks regards us from the screen as if the screen were not there; she casts away the artifice of film and invites us to play with her."

Roger Ebert, critic, 1998

i

The sharp, bobbed haircut that Brooks models in the film is known as a "Louise Brooks" or "Lulu" to this day.

Blackmail Alfred Hitchcock, 1929

G.B. (BIP, Gainsborough) 96m BW
Producer John Maxwell **Screenplay** Alfred
Hitchcock, from play by Charles Bennett
Photography Jack E. Cox **Music** James
Campbell, Reg Connelly **Cast** Anny Ondra,
Sara Allgood, Charles Paton, John Longden,
Donald Calthrop, Cyril Ritchard,
Hannah Jones, Harvey Braban,
Ex-Detective Sergeant Bishop

"Dialogue should simply be ... something that comes out of the mouths of people whose eyes tell the story in visual terms."

Alfred Hitchcock, 1962

Though Alfred Hitchcock laid down many of the themes he would later return to and staked his claim as master of the suspense genre with the silent *The Lodger* (1927), this 1929 picture sealed his reputation and set him on the road to a remarkable career. *Blackmail* began as a silent movie but was rethought in midshoot as Britain's first all-talkie; that this decision was made shows how ambitious Hitchcock was, but also that his talents were obvious enough for paymaster producers to fund technical innovations. One of Hitchcock's greatest tricks was to be both avant-garde and commercial at the same time: here he uses newfangled technology in the service of a melodrama that may be psychologically acute but still succeeds in delivering thrills (and titillation).

Alice White (Anny Ondra) quarrels with her policeman boyfriend Frank (John Longden) and impulsively accompanies a lecherous artist (Cyril Ritchard) to his apartment. When the heel tries to rape her, she stabs him in self-defense and gets away, though a breakfast-table conversation with her family becomes a reminder of the trauma as the word "knife" keeps stabbing at her and the sight of a bread knife nearly sends her into hysterics. Whereas other directors converting to talkies were working hard to ensure that every line of dialogue was perfectly crisp, Hitchcock monkeys around with the soundtrack in this scene so that most of the conversation becomes an inaudible babble—the better to highlight the crystal-clear key word. This may be the moment when the talkies stopped just talking and singing and the real potential of sound as an addition to the director's arsenal became apparent.

Stuck with an already-cast Czech actress whose English wasn't up to standard, Hitchcock also experimented with dubbing, having Joan Barry off-camera reading the lines as Ondra mouthed them, an unusual (and rarely repeated) approach that allows for a successful synthesis of performance. Ondra is a remarkably fresh, engaging presence and turns the trick of making her innocent killer sympathetic while the slimy creep who blackmails her is painted as the real villain. **KN**

i

The movie was released in both silent and sound versions, as not all cinemas were equipped for sound.

Little Caesar Mervyn LeRoy, 1930

Genre can be used to read history and interpret moments in time. Accordingly, Mervyn LeRoy's *Little Caesar* helped to define the gangster movie while serving as an allegory of production circumstances because it was produced during the Great Depression. Within the film is inscribed a wholesale paranoia about individual achievement in the face of economic devastation. Leavening this theme alongside the demands of social conformity during the early 1930s means that LeRoy's screen classic is far more than the simple sum of its parts.

Caesar "Rico" Bandello (Edward G. Robinson) is a small-stakes thief with a partner named Joe (Douglas Fairbanks Jr.). Recognizing a dead-end future, they move to the heart of Chicago, where Joe becomes an entertainer and falls in love with a dancer named Olga (Glenda Farrell). In contrast, Rico gets a taste of the "life" and enjoys it. Possessing a psychotic ruthlessness, he gradually looms as the new power on-scene before finally succumbing to an ill-tempered ego and the police. Gut shot and dying beneath an ad for Joe and Olga's dinner act, Rico sputters some final words of self-determination, underlining how he won't ever be caught because he lived according to the terms of his own ambition.

For audiences, Rico's killer was undoubtedly a clear call of recent tensions about the state of the world at the time. Limited by the feature film's structure, but not dulled by censorial practice in the days before the Production Code Administration, *Little Caesar* offers a scornful look at free enterprise taken to an extreme. Seen through the long view of history and the focus on ill-gotten gains, it's a perfect corollary for Wall Street's collapse, itself the result of poor regulation, mass speculation, and hysteria manipulated to benefit the few at the expense of the many.

Acting out to get a bigger piece of the pie, Rico expresses the wish for acceptance and the drive toward success in an otherwise indifferent world. Simultaneously terrorizing innocents and devastating the society he desires to control, he ends up illuminating the demands of power with homicidal shadows in this, a seminal film of the early sound era. **GC-Q**

1930

U.S. (First National) 79m BW
Producer Hal B. Wallis, Darryl F. Zanuck
Screenplay Francis Edward Faragoh, Robert N. Lee, from novel by W.R. Burnett
Photography Tony Gaudio **Music** Erno Rapee **Cast** Edward G. Robinson, Douglas Fairbanks Jr., Glenda Farrell, William Collier Jr., Sidney Blackmer, Ralph Ince, Thomas E. Jackson, Stanley Fields, Maurice Black, George E. Stone, Armand Kaliz, Nicholas Bela
Oscar nomination Francis Edward Faragoh, Robert N. Lee (screenplay)

"Mervin LeRoy was ... responsible for some of the finest motion pictures ever [made]."

President and Mrs. Reagan, 1987

ⓘ

Clark Gable was LeRoy's first choice for Rico, but he was vetoed by producer Darryl F. Zanuck over Gable's ear size.

Der Blaue Engel Josef von Sternberg, 1930
The Blue Angel

How appropriate that the film that launched Marlene Dietrich's stardom (although it was far from her first role) should begin with a woman cleaning a window behind which is Dietrich's poster as Lola Lola—and then measuring herself up against this idealized image. In this equation, it is the unglamorous reality of the street (or later, the stage) that is more on the mind of director Josef von Sternberg than that illusory ideal—setting the pattern for the pitiless logic of *The Blue Angel*.

The films Sternberg would go on to make with Dietrich in Hollywood are lush, baroque, often camp affairs. *The Blue Angel*—filmed simultaneously in somewhat different English- and German-language versions—shows the director still in his Expressionist phase, tailoring a dark, heavy style to emphasize Emil Jannings's powerful histrionics. Jannings plays Professor Immanuel Rath, a respected schoolteacher who falls under the spell of Lola after he goes into the den of iniquity known as "The Blue Angel" to investigate the unhealthy obsession of his male students.

Taken from Heinrich Mann's novel, it is a tale of decline, of downward mobility. In the course of the story, Rath will be reduced to a barely human clown—echoing the previous clown who functions as one of several ironic doubles for the doomed hero. Sternberg stresses, with exemplary and systematic rigor, the verticality of the film's spatial relations: Rath is always in a low position looking up at the image of Lola (as when she throws her underpants down on his head), unless—in a parody of his authoritative position—he is put on display in the highest, cheapest seats by the theater's sinister manager.

Lola is a classic femme fatale in so far as she lures men and then moves on when she tires of them—and, along the way, enjoys treating them like slaves. Yet there is also, for a time, a tender, loyal side in her relationship with Rath; when she reprises the famous "Falling in Love Again" we can almost accept her passive acceptance of her vagabond romantic destiny ("I know I'm not to blame"). **AM**

Germany (Universum Film A.G.)
99m BW **Language** German / English
Producer Erich Pommerr **Screenplay** Carl Zuckmayer, from the novel *Professor Unrat* by Heinrich Mann **Music** Frederick Hollander **Photography** Günther Rittau
Cast Emil Jannings, Marlene Dietrich, Kurt Gerron, Rosa Valetti, Hans Albers, Reinhold Bernt, Eduard von Winterstein, Hans Roth, Rolf Müller, Roland Varno, Carl Balhaus, Robert Klein-Lörk, Charles Puffy, Wilhelm Diegelmann, Gerhard Bienert

"A decidedly interesting picture with exceptionally fine performances."

Mordaunt Hall,
The New York Times, 1930

i

Leni Riefenstahl claimed to have been considered for the role of Lola, but the truth of this is debatable.

All Quiet on the Western Front Lewis Milestone, 1930

U.S. (Universal Pictures)
131m BW **Language** English / French
Producer Carl Laemmle Jr. **Screenplay** Erich
Maria Remarque, Maxwell Anderson
Photography Arthur Edeson, Karl Freund
Music David Broekman, Sam Perry, Heinz
Roemheld **Cast** Louis Wolheim, Lew Ayres,
John Wray, Arnold Lucy, Ben Alexander,
Scott Kolk, Owen Davis Jr., Walter Rogers,
William Bakewell, Russell Gleason, Richard
Alexander, Harold Goodwin, Slim
Summerville, G. Pat Collins, Beryl Mercer
Oscars Carl Laemmle Jr. (best picture), Lewis
Milestone (director) **Oscar nominations**
George Abbott, Maxwell Anderson, Del
Andrews (screenplay), Arthur Edeson
(photography)

i

Future director Fred Zinnemann
worked for six weeks as an extra on
the film, before getting fired.

Undiminished by time (and restored in 1998), this classic antiwar film, adapted from Erich Maria Remarque's novel, is a landmark for its vivid depiction of the tragedy of World War I from a German soldier's point of view, for its technically inventive, spectacular battle scenes (at the dawn of sound in film), and for its prescient denunciation of fanatic nationalism and militarism. Lew Ayres, only twenty-one years old, became an international star for his beautifully natural performance as the schoolboy eager to serve but disillusioned by the futility and horror of war. The final shot—a close-up of his hand reaching out to a butterfly, quivering as a gunshot cracks and falling still in death—is an amazingly poignant image.

All Quiet on the Western Front was only the third film to win the Academy Award for Best Picture, and war veteran Lewis Milestone received his second Oscar for direction. Interestingly, German censors passed the film despite violent protests by Nazi groups. In a cruel irony, Ayers's career was all but ruined by public condemnation of his stand as a conscientious objector in World War II, despite his heroic service as a medic rather than a combatant. A 1979 TV remake was strong, if far less remarkable than the original. **AE**

L'âge d'or Luis Buñuel, 1930
The Age of Gold

France (Corinth) 60m BW
Language French Producer Le Vicomte de
Noailles Photography Albert Duverger
Screenplay Luis Buñuel, Salvador Dalí
Music Georges Van Parys Cast Gaston
Modot, Lya Lys, Caridad de Laberdesque,
Max Ernst, Josep Llorens Artigas, Lionel
Salem, Germaine Noizet, Duchange,
Bonaventura Ibáñez

"The sexual instinct and the sense of death form the substance of the film. It is a romantic film performed in full Surrealist frenzy."

Luis Buñuel, 1983

i

The movie's producer, Le Vicomte de
Noailles, commissioned a film every
year as a birthday gift to his wife.

In 1928, two young Spaniards in Paris—twenty-eight-year-old Luis Buñuel and twenty-four-year-old Salvador Dalí—conceived an authentically Surrealist short film, *Un Chien Andalou*. Shot in two weeks, the film shocked, startled, and delighted the intelligentsia; and it encouraged the Vicomte de Noailles to give them the money to finance a feature film. Dalí, however, quickly left the project (though his name remains on the credit titles), and the resulting film, *The Age of Gold*, must be assumed to be Buñuel's alone.

The Age of Gold is driven by the Surrealist notion of *l'amour fou*, and—somewhat denying Surrealist principles—has its own episodic story progression. It opens with a documentary on scorpions—actually a 1912 film to which Buñuel has added a scientific commentary. A group of starving bandits struggle out of their hut while four bishops perform strange rituals on a beach. A fade returns to the bishops now reduced to skeletons. Boats bring a crowd of distinguished individuals to honor the bishops' memory, but their ceremony is interrupted by sexual cries from a man and a woman. The man is arrested and dragged through the streets. Subsequent sequences are set in the home of the woman and at an elegant party in the grounds of a villa, where their amours are resumed but variously interrupted. Scenes of Surrealist frenzy lead into the final sequence as the Marquis de Sade's libertines depart from their orgies at the Château de Sellini. Their leader is clearly portrayed as Jesus.

Not surprisingly, the film aroused ferocious emotions between the Surrealists and right-wing organizations; the League of Patriots and the Anti-Jewish League organized demonstrations that resulted in serious damage to the theater, police prohibition of further shows, and violent political and critical polemics. Notably, Henry Miller wrote extensively on the film and its creator: "Either you are made like the rest of civilized humanity, or you are proud and whole like Buñuel. And if you are whole and proud, then you are an anarchist, and throw bombs."

Following Surrealist tenets of "not making art," Buñuel demanded from his gifted cameraman Albert Duverger plain, simply lit visuals. He also rejected de Noailles's request that Stravinsky should compose the music, instead creating mischievous juxtapositions of his scabrous images, romantic symphonies (Wagner, Schubert, Debussy), and the harsh ceremonial drums of his native Calanda, Spain.

The Age of Gold has bequeathed some of the cinema's most unforgettable images: the mummified bishops; the painter Max Ernst as a frail, dying bandit; the cow on the bed of an elegant haute bourgeois villa; Lya Lys sucking the toe of a statue; the manic face of Gaston Modot; and the angelic Jesus and his gleefully exhausted fellow libertines on the castle drawbridge. It is a film that exists out of time, retaining its power to stir and shock into the twenty-first century and beyond. **DR**

Zemlya Aleksandr Dovzhenko, 1930
Earth

U.S.S.R. (Wufku) 75m Silent BW
Screenplay Aleksandr Dovzhenko
Photography Daniil Demutsky
Music Lev Revutsky (restored version)
Cast Stepan Shkurat, Semyon Svashenko,
Yuliya Solntseva, Yelena Maksimova, Nikolai
Nademsky, I. Franko, Arkhip, Pyotr Masokha,
V. Mikhajlov, Pavel Petrik, P. Umanets,
E. Bondina, L. Lyashenko, M. Matsyutsia,
Nikolai Mikhajlov

Aleksandr Dovzhenko's *Earth* is arguably the single greatest achievement of the ever-more-impressive Soviet silent cinema. A modernist who drew deep inspiration from folk art—not unlike his contemporaries Marc Chagall and Sholem Aleichem—Dovzhenko's ode to the beginning of collectivization in the Ukraine is a riot of delirious imagery of swaying wheat fields, ripening fruits, and stampeding horses. The arrival of a tractor is greeted with joy by the peasants, who begin to imagine new lives for themselves, but surviving *kulaks* (landowners) conspire to assassinate the inspiring young head of the Party's village committee. His death, though, only makes the villagers stronger in their resolve; in a mind-boggling finale Dovzhenko brings together themes of birth, death, harvest, progress, and solidarity as the dead man is reunited with the land he loved so well.

No summary, however, can really do justice to the extraordinary sensuality of the film, a quality not much appreciated by the Soviet censors. Among the choice bits removed from earlier released versions is a scene in which, in a symbol of communion, the village men urinate in the tractor's radiator, and a shot in which men draw strength and comfort by putting their hands inside the blouses of the women at their sides. Anyone looking for the origins of Andrei Tarkovsky's cinema must start with *Earth*. **RP**

i

Dovzenkho drew on his own life for the story; the character of Semyon was based on his grandfather.

À nous la liberté René Clair, 1931
Freedom for Us

France (Sonores Tobis) 104m BW
Language French Producer Frank
Clifford Screenplay René Clair
Photography Georges Périnal
Music Georges Auric Cast Raymond
Cordy, Henri Marchand, Paul Ollivier, André
Michaud, Rolla France, Germaine Aussey,
Léon Lorin, William Burke, Vincent Hyspa,
Jacques Shelly

Two conmen, Louis (Raymond Cordy) and Emile (Henri Marchand), plan their escape from prison. Upon breaking out, Emile is recaptured but Louis runs free and builds an empire on the assembly-line principle. Eventually Emile is paroled and heads to Louis's factory. Within its walls he becomes smitten with a secretary named Jeanne (Rolla France) and asks his old friend for help. According to the rules of comeuppance, Louis is then threatened with discovery as an escaped felon, after which the two men earn lasting freedom as hobos on the road.

Unlike Charlie Chaplin's *Modern Times*, a film later sued for plagiarism by Tobis, the production company of *À Nous la Liberté*, Rene Clair's film is an exaltation of industrial society. Opening on an assembly line and closing in a mechanized factory, the fears often associated with modernization are wholly absent here. Instead, these are substituted with values of loyalty and the comedy of circumstance.

Interestingly, much of the humor in *À Nous la Liberté* stems from carefully manipulated screen space and sequence. First the assembly line hiccups. Then a worker forgets his place, disrupts another worker, angers his boss, and so on. It's a formula freed from dialogue and adopted directly from the silent cinema as a transitional vehicle into the talkies. **GC-Q**

Limite Mario Peixoto, 1931

Brazil (Cinédia) 114m BW
Producer Mario Peixoto Screenplay Mario
Peixoto Photography Edgar Brasil
Cast Olga Breno, Tatiana Rey, Raul Schnoor,
Brutus Pedreira, Carmen Santos, Mario
Peixoto, Edgar Crasil, Iolanda Bernardes

David Bowie chose it as one of his favorite films. Orson Welles watched it in the 1940s. And it was screened for Marie Falconetti, Carl Theodor Dreyer's Joan of Arc. *Limite* is a cult film, but how and why?

The conventional wisdom is that Brazilian cinema started in the 1950s. But two decades earlier, in 1930, aged just twenty-one, Mario Peixoto made this extraordinary film. A man and a woman are handcuffed together—shades of Alfred Hitchcock. But where Hitch would race such a couple through a thriller story, Peixoto, woozy with the influence of the French Avant-Garde, makes something more dreamlike.

The whole film seems to drift, languorously. Special camera mounts were made so that ropes could haul the image into the air to make it soar. Peixoto talked about the "camera-brain," and it's hard not to connect some of his visual ideas to the literary ideas of Virginia Woolf or the movies of French impressionist Germaine Dulac. Past mixes with present. The people, whose clothes are ragged and who seem immensely sad, remember recent events. Story is downplayed, but feeling, perception, looking, and subjectivity animate this film. *Limite* was restored by Martin Scorsese's World Cinema Foundation and, when the restoration was shown in Cannes, its slow rhythms seemed like an elegy, or Derek Jarman's *The Angelic Conversation* (1987). **MC**

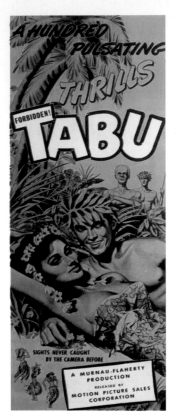

Tabu F.W. Murnau, 1931

Tabu is the last film of F.W. Murnau, who was probably the greatest of all silent directors. He didn't live long enough to make sound films, dying in an auto accident a few days after work on the musical score for this masterpiece was completed and a week before the film's New York premiere. Filmed entirely in the South Seas in 1929 with a nonprofessional cast and gorgeous cinematography by Floyd Crosby, *Tabu* began as a collaboration with the great documentarist Robert Flaherty, who still rightly shares credit for the story. Clearly, though, the German romanticism of Murnau predominates, above all in the heroic poses of the islanders and the fateful diagonals in the compositions. As we now know, Flaherty was ultimately squeezed out of the project because Murnau, who had all the financial control, was not temperamentally suited to sharing directorial credit. This unfortunately has not prevented many commentators from continuing to miscredit Flaherty as a codirector.

Part of Murnau's greatness was his capacity to encompass studio artifice—in such large productions as *The Last Laugh* (1924), *Faust* (1926), and *Sunrise* (1927)—as well as documentary naturalism in *Burning Soil* (1922), *Nosferatu* (1922), and *Tabu*. This versatility bridges both his German and American work. *Tabu*, shot in natural locations and strictly speaking neither German nor American, exhibits facets of both of these talents. The simple plot—the two "chapters" of the film are titled "Paradise" and "Paradise Lost"—is an erotic love story involving a young woman who becomes sexually taboo when she is selected by an elder, one of Murnau's most chilling harbingers of doom, to replace a sacred maiden who has just died. An additional theme is the corrupting power of "civilization"—money in particular—on the innocent hedonism of the islanders. Murnau himself was in flight from the Hollywood studios when he made the picture, although Paramount wound up releasing it in 1931.

However dated some of *Tabu*'s ethnographic idealism may seem today, the film's breathtaking beauty and artistry make it indispensable viewing, and the exquisite tragic ending—conceived musically and rhythmically as a gradually decelerating diminuendo—is one of the pinnacles of silent cinema. **JRos**

U.S. (Murnau-Flaherty, Paramount)
84m Silent BW **Producer** F.W. Murnau
Screenplay Robert J. Flaherty, F.W. Murnau
Photography Floyd Crosby **Music** Hugo
Riesenfeld, W. Franke Harling, Milan Roder,
Chopin, Smetana **Cast** Reri, Matahi, Hitu,
Jean, Jules, Ah Kong, Anne Chevalier
Oscar Floyd Crosby (photography)

"An exceptionally sensuous play of light, rhythm, and composition."

Time Out Film Guide

i

Leading lady Anne Chevalier was discovered in a cocktail bar while Murnau was scouting locations.

City Lights Charles Chaplin, 1931

U.S. (Charles Chaplin) 87m Silent
BW **Producer** Charles Chaplin
Screenplay Charles Chaplin
Photography Gordon Pollock, Roland
Totheroh, Mark Marklatt **Music** Charles
Chaplin, José Padilla **Cast** Virginia Cherrill,
Florence Lee, Harry Myers, Al Ernest Garcia,
Hank Mann, Charles Chaplin

Convinced that speech would mar the beauty of cinema, its greatest mime exponent, Charlie Chaplin, agonized over the introduction of sound technology and determined to ignore it, against all advice. Presented as "a comedy romance in pantomime," his defiantly silent 1931 film *City Lights* was in every way a triumph, its heartrending melodrama and hilarity withstanding audiences' craving for talkies. Nevertheless, after shooting the film, Chaplin incorporated sound effects and composed and conducted his own score, as he would continue to do in his later pictures.

The Little Tramp is touched by a blind flower seller (graceful Virginia Cherrill) and saves an eccentric millionaire from suicide. His gentle wooing of the girl and his determination to restore her sight propel him into a variety of jobs that go awry—like the memorable "fixed" boxing bout—while his on-off relationship with the drunken, unpredictable tycoon provides a parallel string of zany situations. As ever in Chaplin's silent films, there is a deftly choreographed comedic eating scene—here a party streamer entwined in the oblivious Charlie's spaghetti—and a slapstick misadventure with the law. Beautifully acted, this quite perfect balancing act between laughter and eloquent pathos culminates in a deeply moving finish. One of the real, landmark greats. **AE**

i

Chaplin and Cherrill's offscreen relationship was very hostile—at one point he even fired her.

Dracula Tod Browning, 1931

"Better Than 'The Bat'"
N.Y. MERKEL-TRIBUNE

DRACULA
THE WORLD FAMOUS VAMPIRE THRILLER

U.S. (Universal) 75m BW
Language English / Hungarian
Producer E.M. Asher, Tod Browning, Carl Laemmle Jr. **Screenplay** Garrett Fort, from play by John L. Balderston and Hamilton Deane **Photography** Karl Freund **Music** Schubert, Tchaikovsky, Wagner **Cast** Bela Lugosi, Helen Chandler, David Manners, Dwight Frye, Edward Van Sloan, Herbert Bunston, Frances Dade, Joan Standing, Charles K. Gerrard, Tod Browning, Michael Visaroff

"Bela Lugosi creates one of the most unique and powerful roles of the screen."

The Film Daily, 1931

i

Within forty-eight hours of its opening at New York's Roxy Theater, *Dracula* sold around 50,000 tickets.

Although Bram Stoker's seminal 1897 vampire novel had been filmed by F.W. Murnau in 1922 as *Nosferatu* and director Tod Browning had cast Lon Chaney as a bogus vampire in the silent *London After Midnight*, this early talkie was the true beginning of the horror film as a distinct genre and the vampire movie as its most popular subgenre.

Cinematographer Karl Freund had a solid grounding in German Expressionist shadowmaking, whereas Browning was the carnival barker king of American grotesquerie, so the film represents a synthesis of the two major strains of silent chills. Like such major American horror properties as *The Cat and the Canary* and *The Bat*, this Dracula comes to the screen not from the pages of classic gothic literature but directly from the stage: the primary sources of the screenplay are a pair of theatrical takes on Stoker's novel, from Hamilton Deane and John L. Balderston. The break-out star of the new genre was Bela Lugosi, who had played Dracula on Broadway and was finally cast in the film after the early death of Browning's favored star, Chaney. It may be that the loss of Chaney took some of the spark out of Browning's direction, which is actually less inspired than George Melford's work on the simultaneously shot (on the same sets, no less) Spanish version—though the latter suffers from the lack of an iconic Dracula and the fact that it represents exactly the shooting script, whereas the English-language Dracula was considerably tightened by an edit that took out twenty minutes of flab.

Prehistoric in technique and stuck with a drawing-room-centered script, Browning's film nevertheless retains much of its creaky, sinister power, spotlighting (literally, via tiny pinlights aimed at his evil eyes) Lugosi's star-making turn as the vampire, squeezing Hungarian menace out of every syllable of phrases such as "Cheeldren of the naight, leesten to thaim" or "I nevair dreenk vine!" The film opens magnificently, with a snatch of *Swan Lake* and a rickety stagecoach taking us and estate agent Renfield (Dwight Frye) to Lugosi's cobwebbed and vermin-haunted castle. Dracula strides through a curtain of cobwebs, the vampire twitching with bloodlust as his guest cuts his finger while carving bread, and three soulless vampire brides descend upon the unwary visitor.

Once the story hops disappointingly over a dangerous sea voyage and the Count relocates to London, Lugosi calms down. But Edward Van Sloan is staunch as the vampire-killing Professor Abraham Van Helsing, the forgotten Helen Chandler is fraily charming as the bled-dry and semivampirized heroine Mina, and Frye steals every scene that isn't nailed down when Renfield transforms into a fly-eating, giggling maniac. Castle Dracula, with its five-story Gothic windows, is the art direction highlight, but the London scenes offer an impressive staircase and catacombs for Dracula's English lair. Browning falters at the last, however, with a weak climax in which the Count is defeated far too easily, his death conveyed by an offscreen groan as he is impaled. **KN**

Frankenstein James Whale, 1931

Frankenstein is the single most important horror film ever made. James Whale hacked out of Mary Shelley's unwieldy novel a fable of an overreaching scientist and his abused, childlike outcast of a monster. Though Colin Clive's neurotic Frankenstein and Dwight Frye's hunchbacked dwarf assistant are definitive, the career breakout of the film is William Henry Pratt, a forty-two-year-old Englishman who turned his back on a privileged upbringing and emigrated to become a truck driver in Canada and a small-time actor in the United States.

Universal's makeup genius Jack Pierce devised the flattop, the neck terminals, the heavy eyelids, and the elongated, scarred hands, while Whale outfitted the creature with a shabby suit like those worn by the ex-soldier hoboes then riding the rails and added the clumping asphalt-spreader's boots. But it was Pratt who turned the Monster from a snarling bogeyman into a yearning, sympathetic, classic character whose misdeeds are accidental (drowning a little girl) or justified (hanging the dwarf who has tortured him with fire). In the opening credits, the Monster is billed as being played by "?"; only at the end of the film were audiences told it was a fellow by the name of Boris Karloff—Pratt's stage handle—who had terrified, moved, and inspired them.

Frankenstein claims a number of wondrous theatrical set pieces: the "creation," with lightning crackling around the tower and the Monster raised to the angry heavens on an operating table; the Monster's first appearance (seen from behind, he turns to show us his face and the camera stutters toward him); the heartbreaking sequence with the little girl who doesn't float; the primal attack on the heroine in her boudoir on her wedding day (a rare bit taken from the book); and the pursuit of the Monster by a mob of peasants with flaming torches, winding up in the old mill where creator and creation confront each other in one of the earliest horror movie inferno finales. The Universal horror cycle runs the gamut from perfection through pastiche and pulp to parody, but *Frankenstein* remains chilly and invigorating, the cornerstone of its entire genre. **KN**

U.S. (Universal) 71m BW **Producer** E.M. Asher, Carl Laemmle Jr. **Screenplay** John L. Balderston, Francis Edward Faragoh, Garrett Fort, from play by Peggy Webling and novel by Mary Shelley **Photography** Arthur Edeson, Paul Ivano **Music** Bernhard Kaun **Cast** Colin Clive, Mae Clarke, John Boles, Boris Karloff, Edward Van Sloan, Frederick Kerr, Dwight Frye, Lionel Belmore, Marilyn Harris

"There is no denying that it is . . . the most effective thing of its kind. Beside it Dracula *is tame."*

Mordaunt Hall,
***The New York Times*, 1931**

ℹ

Bela Lugosi was originally set to play the Monster, but turned down the role as he did not want a silent part.

The Public Enemy William A. Wellman, 1931

U.S. (Warner Bros.) 83m BW **Producer** Darryl F. Zanuck **Screenplay** Harvey F. Thew, from story by John Bright & Kubec Glasmon **Photography** Devereaux Jennings **Music** David Mendoza **Cast** James Cagney, Edward Woods, Jean Harlow, Joan Blondell, Beryl Mercer, Donald Cook, Mae Clarke, Mia Marvin, Leslie Fenton, Robert Emmett O'Connor, Murray Kinnell, Snitz Edwards, Rita Flynn, Frank Coghlan Jr., Frankie Darro **Oscar nomination** John Bright, Kubec Glasmon (screenplay)

William Wellman's melodramatic chronicle of the rise and fall of gangster Tom Powers (James Cagney) is the greatest of the early 1930s gangster films. The genre's sometime sympathetic portrayal of ruthless criminals eager for the American dream of success at the deliberate and unlawful cost of others prompted the institution of the Production Code Administration to supervise the dubious moral value in Hollywood films.

Raised in Chicago slums, Powers turns to crime at an early age, graduating as a young man to armed robbery and the murder of a policeman. Later, he becomes involved in bootlegging, making real money for the first time. Though his brother and mother plead with him to go straight, Tom rises in the gang, but after being wounded in a battle with rivals, he agrees to rejoin his family. He is taken from the hospital and murdered, his body dumped on the doorstep of his family home.

With its simplistic moralism, the plot of *The Public Enemy* has dated poorly. But Cagney remains powerful and energetic as Powers, dominating the screen in every scene and setting the pattern for all gangster films to come, including *The Godfather* series. Wellman directs the film with a strong visual sense, designing memorable scenes such as one in which Powers, in a sudden fit of anger, shoves a grapefruit into girlfriend Kitty's face. **RBP**

The scene of the machine gun attack on Tom Powers and his best friend Matt Doyle actually used real bullets.

M Fritz Lang, 1931

EIN
FRITZ LANG
FILM
DER NERO

Germany (Nero-Film AG) 117m BW
Language German **Producer** Seymour
Nebenzal **Screenplay** Egon Jacobson, Fritz
Lang **Photography** Fritz Arno Wagner
Music Edvard Grieg **Cast** Peter Lorre, Ellen
Widmann, Inge Landgut, Otto Wernicke,
Theodor Loos, Gustaf Gründgens, Friedrich
Gnaß, Fritz Odemar, Paul Kemp, Theo Lingen,
Rudolf Blümner, Georg John, Franz Stein,
Ernst Stahl-Nachbaur, Gerhard Bienert

*"So many things have
been written about M . . .
and it plays constantly . . .
if a film survives so long
then there may be a right
to call it a piece of art."*

Fritz Lang, 1967

ℹ

Real criminals were used as extras in
the film, twenty-five of whom were
arrested during shooting.

In the early 1930s, MGM's production genius Irving Thalberg assembled all his writers and directors for a screening of Fritz Lang's thriller *M*, then criticized them en masse for not making films as innovative, exciting, profound, and commercial as this. Of course, Thalberg admitted, if anyone had pitched a story about a serial killer of children who is ultimately a tragic victim and accuses all strata of society of a corruption deeper than his psychosis, they would have been kicked off the lot.

Whereas Hollywood first saw sound pictures as best suited to all-singing musicals and all-talking theatrical adaptations, a generation of European filmmakers understood their potential for thrills and psychological effects. Inspired perhaps by the theme of Alfred Hitchcock's 1927 silent *The Lodger* and the techniques of his 1929 talkie *Blackmail*, Lang—who had ended his silent film career with *Metropolis* (1927) and *Woman in the Moon* (1929), both at the time considered costly flops—set out to reestablish himself as a popular artist. Nevertheless, *M* is an unusual piece of storytelling, presenting a series of montage-like scenes (often with voice-over narration, a new device) that add up to a portrait of a German city in terror. The cause of the uproar is Franz Becker (Peter Lorre), a pudgy young man who compulsively whistles an air from Edvard Grieg's "Hall of the Mountain King" as he approaches the children he murders (and, it is implied, molests). His crimes are conveyed by striking, pathetic images like a lost balloon floating against telephone wires or an abandoned ball. Establishing conventions still being used by serial-killer movies, Lang and scenarist Thea von Harbou intercut the pathetic life of the murderer with the frenzy of the police investigation into the outrageous crimes, and pay attention to such side issues as press coverage of the killings, vigilante action, and the political pressure that comes down from the politicians and hinders as much as encourages the police. In a cynical touch, the police crack down on all criminal activities in order to catch the killer, prompting the shadow society of professional crooks to track him down themselves.

In the powerful finale, Becker is put on trial by the underworld and pleads his case on the surprisingly moving grounds that his accusers have only chosen to commit crimes, whereas he is compelled to commit them. Though the film establishes Inspector Karl "Fatty" Lohmann (Otto Wernicke)—who would return to take on Lang's eponymous archfiend (Rudolf Klein-Rogge) in *The Testament of Dr. Mabuse* (1933)—and black-gloved criminal kingpin Schranker (Gustaf Gründgens) as traditional cop-and-crook antagonists, Lorre's desperate, clear-eyed, animal-like impulse murderer is the final voice of *M*, forcing his persecutors (and us) to look into themselves for the seeds of a psychosis that equals his own. Creatively emphasizing the technological developments in film sound, Lang has the killer heard before he is seen (allegedly, the director dubbed Lorre's whistling) and identified by a blind witness. **KN**

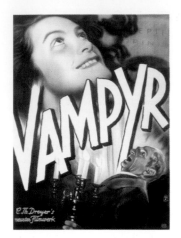

Vampyr Carl Theodor Dreyer, 1932
The Vampire

The greatness of Carl Theodor Dreyer's first sound film derives partly from its handling of the vampire theme in terms of sexuality and eroticism, and partly from its highly distinctive, dreamy look, but it also has something to do with the director's radical recasting of narrative form. Synopsizing the film not only betrays but also misrepresents it: While never less than mesmerizing, it confounds conventions for establishing point of view and continuity and invents a narrative language all its own. Some of the moods and images conveyed by this language are truly uncanny: the long voyage of a coffin from the apparent viewpoint of the corpse inside; a dance of ghostly shadows inside a barn; a female vampire's expression of carnal desire for her fragile sister; an evil doctor's mysterious death by suffocation in a flour mill; and a protracted dream sequence that manages to dovetail eerily into the narrative proper.

Germany (Tobis Klangfilm) 83m BW
Language German **Producer** Carl Theodor
Dreyer, Julian West **Screenplay** Carl
Theodor Dreyer, Christen Jul, from the short
story "Carmilla" by Sheridan Le Fanu
Photography Rudolph Maté, Louis Née
Music Wolfgang Zeller **Cast** Julian West,
Maurice Schutz, Rena Mandel, Sybille
Schmitz, Jan Hieronimko, Henriette Gérard,
Albert Bras, N. Babanini, Jane Mora

Financed and produced by a Dutch cinephile, Baron Nicolas de Gunzburg—who was cast in the leading role of David Gray under the pseudonym of Julian West—*Vampyr* was freely adapted from a short story by Sheridan Le Fanu, "Carmilla," that appeared in his collection *Through a Glass Darkly* (not a novel, as stated erroneously in the film's credits). Like most of Dreyer's other sound features, it flopped commercially when it came out, then went on to become somewhat of a horror and fantasy (as well as art movie) staple, despite never fitting snugly or unambiguously in any of these generic categories.

"I just wanted to make a film different from all other films. I wanted . . . to break new ground for the cinema."

Carl Theodor Dreyer, 1932

The remarkable soundtrack, created entirely in a studio, in contrast to the images, which were all filmed on location, is an essential part of the film's voluptuous and haunting otherworldliness. *Vampyr* was originally released by Dreyer in four separate versions—French, English, German, and Danish. Most circulating prints now contain portions of two or three of these versions, although the dialogue is pretty sparse. If you've never seen a Dreyer film and wonder why many critics regard him as possibly the greatest of all filmmakers, this chilling horror fantasy is the perfect place to begin to understand. **JRos**

i

The movie's dreamlike photography
was apparently achieved by placing
a gauze filter over the camera lens.

I Am a Fugitive from a Chain Gang
Mervyn LeRoy, 1932

U.S. (Vitaphone, Warner Bros.) 93m BW
Producer Hal B. Wallis Screenplay Howard J.
Green, from memoir by Robert E. Burns
Photography Sol Polito Music Leo F.
Forbstein, Bernhard Kaun Cast Paul Muni,
Glenda Farrell, Helen Vinson, Noel Francis,
Preston Foster, Allen Jenkins, Berton
Churchill, Edward Ellis, David Landau, Hale
Hamilton, Sally Blane, Louise Carter, Willard
Robertson, Robert McWade, Robert Warwick
Oscar nominations Hal B. Wallis
(best picture), Paul Muni (actor),
Nathan Levinson (sound)

The grandpappy of prison movies, Mervyn LeRoy's searing indictment of penal practices common in its day was, with its titanic performance from Paul Muni (in a neat reversal from his thuggish role as Scarface the same year), arguably the finest of the hard-hitting social-protest dramas Warner Brothers specialized in during the 1930s.

Based on an autobiographical story by Robert E. Burns, *I Am a Fugitive from a Chain Gang* vividly depicts an innocent man brutalized and criminalized as a down-on-his-luck World War I veteran who is railroaded into shackles and hard labor in the Deep South. Having broken out once to make a decent new life, he is betrayed, escapes again, and is condemned to life as a broken fugitive. Rock splitting, sadistic guards, escapes (including the seminal pursuit by baying bloodhounds through a swamp), solitary confinement—the vocabulary of the behind-bars genre was laid down here. Worth seeing just to appreciate how often it has been referenced, the film is dated but still powerfully disturbing down to the famously haunting last line. As Muni's fugitive, Jim, slips away into the night, his lover plaintively calls out, "How do you live?" From the darkness comes the tragically ironic whisper, "I steal." **AE**

1932

Boudu sauvé des eaux Jean Renoir, 1932
Boudu Saved from Drowning

France (Pathé, Sirius) 90m BW
Language French Producer Jean Gehret,
Michel Simon Screenplay Jean Renoir,
Albert Valentin, from play by René Fauchois
Photography Léonce-Henri Burel, Marcel
Lucien Music Léo Daniderff, Raphael,
Johann Strauss Cast Michel Simon, Charles
Granval, Marcelle Hainia, Severine Lerczinska,
Jean Gehret, Max Dalban, Jean Dasté, Jane
Pierson, Georges D'Arnoux, Régine Lutèce,
Jacques Becker

Renoir had already made eleven films before being selected to direct *Boudu Saved from Drowning* by Michel Simon, who had decided to produce this adaptation of a play by René Fauchois. The pair had worked together three times previously and were both rising personalities with a sense of freedom and a desire to explore unknown territories.

So, like a monstrous Aphrodite, Simon's Boudu the tramp was reborn from the water, brought back to a life he wanted to leave by the kindness and generosity of the Lestingois family. Of course, comparisons with Charlie Chaplin's character come to mind here, and the two tramps have a lot in common—the survivor's sense of life, the amoral relationship with society's rules, the focus on rich versus poor, and the urge for sex. But it is the differences between the two that reveal the power of the recipe above, about the film's connection and rupture with vaudeville, and about the body and diction of Simon.

As Boudu, Simon's voice and physical presence work together as an eruption of carnality, a dissonant yet mesmerizing cello disturbing the happy quartet of the nice home filled with nice people. Boudu's ultimate return to the archaic spring is not only the smiling twist of an epicurean tale but also a troubling assessment of the hypothesis of a continuity between the oldest past and a future toward which the river flows. **J-MF**

Love Me Tonight Rouben Mamoulian, 1932

As with so many of the sadly underrated Rouben Mamoulian's finest films, the delightful thing about this variation on the romantic Ruritanian musical is the way he manages to debunk, through a combination of irreverent humor and technical innovation, the traditions of the very genre he is simultaneously helping to establish and expand. Here he contrives to outstrip the achievements of the then-widely-acclaimed masters of the form—Ernst Lubitsch and René Clair—without seeming to make an effort; he makes the whole thing feel wonderfully relaxed, good-natured, and somehow perfect. True, he is helped to no end by having Richard Rodgers and Lorenz Hart's witty yet melodious songs to work with; but it's the unforced sense of sophisticated fun coexisting with real cinematic invention that reveal the Mamoulian touch.

Jeannette MacDonald and Maurice Chevalier must also take credit for playing their respective romantic leads—the haughty but bored (and, let it be said, sexually frustrated) princess holed up in a musty chateau, and the visiting tailor ("the best in Paris") sufficiently aroused by her to forget his lowly status—with emotional commitment and an engagingly delicate parodic irony. The supporting cast is top-notch, too: Myrna Loy, Charles Ruggles, Charles Butterworth, and the inimitable Sir C. Aubrey Smith (the last three especially delightful when improbably enlisted to sing, solo, verses of "Mimi") are merely the most memorable. But what is really impressive about Love Me Tonight is how music, dance, dialogue, performance, decor, lighting, camera work, editing, and special effects are all combined to create a cogent whole in which each element serves narrative, characterization, and theme. The "Isn't It Romantic?" sequence, for example, which starts with Chevalier and a client in Paris, and proceeds with the song being passed via various minor characters (including, at one point, a whole platoon of soldiers!) to arrive finally at the lonely MacDonald's boudoir—the first link between the future lovers, who have yet to meet—is impressive; so, too, is the final, climactic chase sequence (as exhilaratingly constructed as anything by the Soviets and with far more wit). In short, an enormously entertaining masterpiece. **GA**

U.S. (Paramount) 104m BW
Producer Rouben Mamoulian
Screenplay Samuel Hoffenstein, Waldemar Young, George Marion Jr. from the play *Tailor in the Château* by Paul Armont and Lepold Marchand **Photography** Victor Milner **Music** Richard Rodgers, John Leipold **Cast** Maurice Chevalier, Jeanette MacDonald, Charles Ruggles, Charles Butterworth, Myrna Loy, C. Aubrey Smith, Elizabeth Patterson, Ethel Griffies, Blanche Frederici, Joseph Cawthorn, Robert Greig, Bert Roach

"A musical comedy frolic, whimsical in its aim and deliciously carried out in its pattern, in its playing, and in its direction."

Variety, 1932

i
Mamoulian waited for the songs to be written before finishing the script, so that they integrated with the plot.

Shanghai Express Josef von Sternberg, 1932

In the seven films he made with her, Josef von Sternberg took his obsession with Marlene Dietrich to ever more extreme lengths of intensity and stylization, until both star and story were all but subsumed in a welter of spectacle and design. Coming at the midpoint of the cycle, *Shanghai Express* holds the elements in near-perfect balance.

Sternberg loved to treat his films as controlled experiments in the play of light and shadow, so a plot whose action is largely confined to the eponymous train suited him perfectly. The story, such as it is, concerns a train journey from Peking to Shanghai, interrupted by a bandit attack. But the subject of the film is Dietrich's face, on which it plays an endless series of variations: veiled, shadowed, wreathed with smoke, nestling in furs or feathers, framed in intricate patterns of black on white. Dietrich herself, as the "notorious China coaster," Shanghai Lily, remains enigmatic, her eyes hooded and watchful, as Sternberg—and his regular cinematographer, Lee Garmes—use her face as an exquisite screen on which to project the appropriate emotions.

The setting of *Shanghai Express*, constructed in the studio artifice that Sternberg always preferred, is an elaborately conceived and utterly fictitious China, embodied in the film's opening sequence: a huge, dazzlingly white locomotive steams out of Peking Station and straight down the middle of a narrow street seething with lampshade-hatted coolies, street vendors, children, and animals. Years later, Sternberg visited China for the first time and was gratified to discover that the reality differed completely.

Clive Brook as Lily's ex-lover, a British army captain, plays the kind of staunchly traditional Englishman beside whose stiff upper lip steel-reinforced concrete would seem flabby, and Anna May Wong is no less enjoyably cartoonish as the embodiment of feline Eastern guile. But the film belongs to Sternberg and Dietrich, and the strange fetishistic chemistry between them. Together they created something deliriously unique in cinema; apart they were never quite able to recapture the same magic. **PK**

U.S. (Paramount) 84m BW
Languages English / French / Cantonese / German **Screenplay** Jules Furthman **Photography** Lee Garmes **Music** W. Franke Harling **Cast** Marlene Dietrich, Clive Brook, Anna May Wong, Warner Oland, Eugene Pallette, Lawrence Grant, Louise Closser Hale, Gustav von Seyffertitz, Emile Chautard **Oscar** Lee Garmes (photography) **Oscar nominations** (best picture), Josef von Sternberg (director)

1932

"It is an exciting ride they take in Shanghai Express *... by all odds the best picture Josef von Sternberg has directed."*

Mordaunt Hall,
The New York Times, **1932**

ℹ
China initially banned the movie, and demanded its withdrawal from worldwide circulation.

U.S. (Paramount) 83m BW
Producer Ernst Lubitsch **Screenplay** Grover Jones, from the play *The Honest Finder* by Aladar Laszlo **Photography** Victor Milner **Music** W. Franke Harling **Cast** Miriam Hopkins, Kay Francis, Herbert Marshall, Charles Ruggles, Edward Everett Horton, C. Aubrey Smith, Robert Greig

"It comes as close to perfection as anything I have ever seen in the movies."

Dwight Macdonald, critic, 1933

i

Although Miriam Hopkins was given top billing, she was actually paid the least money of the three stars.

Trouble in Paradise Ernst Lubitsch, 1932

After his emigration from Europe and arrival in Hollywood at the tail end of the silent era, Ernst Lubitsch quickly established himself as a master of the technical with an ear for comedic pacing. Admirers called his particular talents the "Lubitsch Touch," but Lubitsch didn't work with any set formula or system. Rather, he brought from Europe a sophisticated sensibility that sent gentle shock waves through Hollywood, changing the tone of American comedies and leading to the rise of the "screwball" antics of Howard Hawks and Billy Wilder, both of whom revered him.

But that same sophistication kept Lubitsch from veering precipitously toward slapstick or more overt physical humor. That famed "Lubitsch Touch" indicated his deft method of delivering sexual politics with a barely discernible wink, and that meant a clever way with words and stories to subvert, surmount, or gently prod the relatively prudish (though still pre-Hays Code) American standards.

The most carnal and clever aspects of the "Lubitsch Touch" are firmly on display from the first frame of *Trouble in Paradise*, one of the director's first sound features. The title appears initially only in parts, so that for a moment the words "Trouble in . . ." linger over a shot of a bed. By the time the word ". . . Paradise" finally pops up, Lubitsch has already made clear what he meant by "Trouble in Paradise": The film may as well be titled "Trouble in Bed." Of course, *Trouble in Paradise* is only indirectly about sex, but that is typically the case with romantic comedies, of which Lubitsch was a significant pioneer.

Herbert Marshall and Miriam Hopkins are a match made in heaven. Playing expert thieves and con artists Lily (Hopkins) and Gaston Monescu (Marshall), their courtship consists of robbing each other blind one fateful night in Venice. Over dinner they trade tentative praise, revealing stolen personal items in lieu of more traditional flirtation. Theirs is a romance built on deception, an ironic aphrodisiac, and they don't think anything of the other's chosen profession. "Baron, you are a crook," asserts Lily, "May I have the salt?" Life is good until the pair set their eyes on heiress Madame Mariette Colet (Kay Francis). Lily sees a big bank account, but Gaston sees more. He tries to seduce his way into her safe, but finds his feelings for the heiress keep getting in the way.

The film's plot machinations are needed to toss the characters together, but *Trouble in Paradise* is less concerned with the big con than it is with companionship. Gaston initially wants Madame Colet's money, but all the lonely heiress wants is Gaston, and soon the two become lovers, much to Lily's chagrin. But *Trouble in Paradise* is nowhere near as predictable as it seems. Love is something that can't be stolen or bought, which explains the quandary of Lubitsch's compulsively criminal lead characters. As much as Gaston and Lily covet Madame Colet's fortune, even at the cost of their relationship, they realize their uniquely larcenous dispositions make them particularly well suited for one another. **JKl**

Scarface: The Shame of a Nation

Howard Hawks, 1932

Introducing one of cinema history's most notorious, Machiavellian monsters in the perverted Horatio Alger myth that lies at the heart of every gangster film, *Scarface: The Shame of a Nation* stands as the peak of its genre. And it's a telling sign that Brian De Palma's 1983 version of the film, despite all the accolades accorded it, does nothing to diminish the power of Howard Hawks's original. On the contrary, like Shakespeare at his best, the film's seductive combination of fascination and revulsion with its corrupted protagonist and his equally corrupted world makes up the very fabric of the drama.

Completed before Hollywood's conservative Production Code became more rigidly enforced in 1934, ex-journalist Ben Hecht's screenplay uses the Al Capone legend as source material—staging recreations of the St. Valentine's Day Massacre and the murder of Big Jim Colosimo—to show Prohibition-era Chicago as a modern-day Sodom and Gomorrah. Amorality is rampant: Cops are brutal and on the take, journalists are cynical muckrakers. In contrast, the Capone-like protagonist Tony "Scarface" Camonte (Paul Muni) is at least frank in his greedy quest for power and the almighty dollar.

The ultimate irony of *Scarface* is that everything goes well as long as Tony treats his killing spree as purely business. The moment his emotions come into play, he's doomed. Much can be made of the strange twist in the plot when Tony starts losing control because of his violent jealousy concerning the love affair between his sister, Cesca (Ann Dvorak) and his best friend, Guino Rinaldo (George Raft). This could stem from incestuous feelings for his sister, or indicate a repressed homosexual bond with his friend. Hawks effectively underlines Tony's road to ruin with heavy symbolism, achieved via expressive lighting and street signs. The gangster is initially seen as a Nosferatu-like silhouette on the wall as he commits his first murder. At the end, his final showdown is marked by cross-shaped shadows and his dead body lying in the gutter under a travel sign that reads, ironically, "The world is yours." **MT**

U.S. (Caddo, United Artists) 99m BW
Producer Howard Hawks, Howard Hughes
Screenplay Ben Hecht, Fred Pasley, Seton I. Miller, John Lee Mahin, W.R. Burnett, Seton I. Miller, from novel by Armitage Trail
Music Shelton Brooks, W.C. Handy
Photography Lee Garmes, L. William O'Connell **Cast** Paul Muni, Ann Dvorak, Karen Morley, Osgood Perkins, C. Henry Gordon, George Raft, Vince Barnett, Boris Karloff, Purnell Pratt, Tully Marshall, Inez Palange, Edwin Maxwell

"Scarface is one of Howard Hawks's undisputed masterpieces and a landmark in the screen depiction of crime and violence."

Emanuel Levy, critic, 2007

i

Al Capone was rumored to have liked the film so much that he owned a print of it.

THE STORY OF THE LOVE LIFE OF THE SIDESHOW

U.S. (MGM) 64m BW **Producer** Tod Browning **Screenplay** Clarence Aaron "Tod"- Robbins, from his novel *Spurs* **Photography** Merritt B. Gerstad **Cast** Wallace Ford, Leila Hyams, Olga Baclanova, Roscoe Ates, Henry Victor, Harry Earles, Daisy Earles, Rose Dione, Daisy Hilton, Violet Hilton, Schlitze, Josephine Joseph, Johnny Eck, Frances O'Connor, Peter Robinson

"Calling it a mere 'masterpiece of shock cinema'... seriously underplay[s] the film's blistering humanity."

Ed Gonzalez,
Slant Magazine, 2003

Freaks Tod Browning, 1932

From its beginning as a horror movie exceeding all expectations (via Dwain Esper's exploitation of it under such dubious and misleading titles as *Forbidden Love, Monster Show*, and *Nature's Mistakes*), to its revival as an avant-garde film in the tradition of Luis Buñuel and Alain Robbe-Grillet, Tod Browning's *Freaks* has been classed as everything from horror to art house to documentary (because of the movie's use of "real freaks"). Nevertheless, despite its originality of conception and design, and its startling ability to both move and frighten audiences, *Freaks* has remained to this day an underappreciated film.

Freaks opens with a carnival barker addressing some curious spectators. After the crowd catches sight of the female sideshow freak nearby, several women scream and the barker starts telling her story. Cleopatra (Olga Baclanova), a beautiful trapeze artist with the carnival, is adored by a midget named Hans (Harry Earles). But Cleopatra is having an affair with Hercules (Henry Victor), the Strong Man, and the couple devise a plot to get their hands on Hans's recently inherited fortune: Cleopatra will marry the midget she despises and then poison him. During an unforgettable wedding ceremony-cum initiation ritual, Cleopatra rebuffs the assembled freaks, teasing them mercilessly and calling them "dirty" and "slimy." Back in her wagon she poisons Hans's drink, but her plan is foiled and she is attacked by the freaks, who have banded together to exact a brutal revenge. Finally returning to the carnival barker in the present, we now see the result of the freaks' attack on Cleopatra: she has been turned into a legless, half-blind stump—a squawking chicken woman. A final scene, tacked on later as the studio insisted on a happy ending, shows Hans living like a millionaire, reconciled with his midget ex-girlfriend Frieda (Daisy Earles).

But no mere plot summary can do justice to this alarming yet profound movie, which truly must be seen to be believed. It is a supreme oddity (freak?) of world cinema considered by many to be the most remarkable film in the career of a director whose credits include the original version of *Dracula* (1931). **BH**

42nd Street Lloyd Bacon, 1933

"Sawyer, you're going out a youngster, but you've got to come back a star!" The grandmother of backstage musicals is still a tuneful charmer (verified by its adaptation into a Broadway hit fifty years later), but it also occupies a special place in film history, for several appealing reasons.

42nd Street's plot became one of the best-loved bores of showbiz lore. Fresh-faced dancer Peggy Sawyer (Ruby Keeler), newly arrived in New York during the Depression, lands a job in the chorus of a musical called *Pretty Lady*. The show's temperamental star, Dorothy Brock (Bebe Daniels), injures her ankle the night before the show opens, so "real little trouper" Peggy steps into the lead and, with the fate of the company riding on her, bravely goes out there and wows 'em. The script is a cherishable and disarming mix of naïveté, smart toughness, and sassy repartee.

Fleshing out the drama is a cast of characters who became archetypes: the stressed and ailing director (Warner Baxter, whose bullying and pep talks to his company are classic); the harassed dance director (George E. Stone); the saucy, wisecracking chorus girls (Una Merkel and Ginger Rogers); the puppyish juvenile (Dick Powell); and the well-heeled, lecherous backer (Guy Kibbee) with designs on the leading lady, who strings him along while conducting a clandestine romance with a down-on-his-luck vaudevillian (George Brent). The winning cast is a remarkable ensemble. The wonderful Baxter had won the Best Actor Oscar for *In Old Arizona*'s dashing bandito hero, The Cisco Kid. Daniels was a top star of silent pictures who could also sing. Brent was another established romantic lead. Billed beneath them, half a dozen actors were already popular faces, including Rogers, soon to be teamed with Fred Astaire. Dick Powell, baby-faced and peppy, was among those whose careers were launched by *42nd Street*. The big discovery in her film debut was Ruby Keeler, Broadway darling and wife of Al Jolson. She wasn't much of a singer but was adorable, sweetly vivacious, and a tap-dancing treat.

Generally, Warner Brothers films were renowned for realism. But to boost their musical fortunes, Mervyn LeRoy (who developed this project before illness made him defer directing to Lloyd Bacon) brought in songwriters Al Dubin and Harry Warren, who became chief tunesmiths for Warner Brothers. LeRoy also insisted on inventive dance director Busby Berkeley, who had enlivened several musical comedies for Sam Goldwyn. He made much out of the snappy songs, including "Shuffle off to Buffalo," "Young and Healthy," and "You're Beginning to be a Habit with Me." For the show-stopping title song finale, Berkeley created an immortal production number in which Ruby—dancing atop a taxi—swaying Manhattan skyscrapers, and scantily clad beauties arranged in geometric patterns shot from high overhead form a sensational rhythmic kaleidoscope. After seeing what he was up to, Warner Brothers contracted Berkeley and gave him carte blanche, initiating a long run of dazzling dance confections that brightened the decade and remain a highlight in screen musicals. **AE**

1933

U.S. (Warner Bros.) 89m BW **Producer** Hal B. Wallis, Darryl F. Zanuck **Screenplay** Rian James, James Seymour, from novel by Bradford Ropes **Photography** Sol Polito **Music** Harry Warren **Cast** Warner Baxter, Bebe Daniels, George Brent, Ruby Keeler, Guy Kibbee, Una Merkel, Ginger Rogers, Ned Sparks, Dick Powell, Allen Jenkins, Edward J. Nugent, Robert McWade, George E. Stone **Oscar nominations** Hal B. Wallis, Darryl F. Zanuck (best picture), Nathan Levinson (sound)

"'Anytime Annie'? Say, who could forget 'er? She only said 'No' once, and THEN she didn't hear the question!"

**Andy Lee
(George E. Stone)**

ℹ

Warner Bros. was near bankruptcy at the time of *42nd Street,* but the success of the film saved it.

Footlight Parade Lloyd Bacon, 1933

U.S. (Warner Bros.) 104m BW
Producer Robert Lord **Screenplay** Manuel
Seff, James Seymour **Photography** George
Barnes **Music** Al Dubin, Sammy Fain, Irving
Kahal, Harry Warren, Walter Donaldson,
Gus Kahn **Cast** James Cagney, Joan
Blondell, Ruby Keeler, Dick Powell, Frank
McHugh, Ruth Donnelly, Guy Kibbee, Hugh
Herbert, Claire Dodd, Gordon Westcott,
Arthur Hohl, Renee Whitney, Barbara Rogers,
Paul Porcasi, Philip Faversham

The greatest of all Depression-era musicals, *Footlight Parade* is really two films in one. The first is a fast, funny backstage story about frantic efforts to stage live musical interludes at movie houses, with James Cagney in top form as a hard-driving producer too preoccupied to appreciate his adoring secretary (Joan Blondell). The second is a climactic juggernaut of three consecutive Busby Berkeley spectacles, the rigor of whose design is matched by their uninhibited imagery.

I will pass too quickly over "Honeymoon Hotel," which takes a wholesomely naughty tour through an establishment devoted to conjugal bliss, and "Shanghai Lil," which transforms rakish oriental decadence into rousing New Deal morale boosting, in order to concentrate on "By a Waterfall." This aquatic rhapsody, featuring the glistening bodies and geometric group formations displayed by a bevy of water nymphs, pushes its central tension between form and flesh further and further until it reaches an abstract outer space where depth collapses. The distinction between air and water dissolves and human bodies mutate into elemental cell-like units. You can have the "Star Gate" climax of *2001: A Space Odyssey*; when it comes to consciousness-expanding cinematic trips, I'll take a plunge into Berkeley's "Waterfall." **MR**

The Bitter Tea of General Yen Frank Capra, 1933

U.S. (Columbia) 88m BW
Language English / Mandarin /
French **Producer** Walter Wanger
Screenplay Edward E. Paramore Jr., Grace
Zaring Stone **Photography** Joseph Walker
Music W. Franke Harling **Cast** Barbara
Stanwyck, Nils Asther, Toshia Mori, Walter
Connolly, Gavin Gordon, Lucien Littlefield,
Richard Loo, Helen Jerome Eddy,
Emmett Corrigan

Frank Capra's atypical melodrama concerns an American missionary (Barbara Stanwyck) in Shanghai—a prim New England type named Megan Davis, engaged to another missionary, her childhood sweetheart. During an outbreak of civil war, she's taken prisoner by a Chinese warlord named Yen (Nils Asther). The unlikely love story that ensues is not only Capra's unsung masterpiece but also one of the great Hollywood love stories of the 1930s: subtle, delicate, moody, mystical, and passionate. Joseph Walker shot it through filters and with textured shadows that suggest the work of Josef von Sternberg; Edward Paramore wrote the script, adapted from a story by Grace Zaring Stone. Oddly enough, this perverse and beautiful film was chosen to open Radio City Music Hall in 1933. It was not one of Capra's commercial successes, but it arguably beats the rest of his films by miles, and both Stanwyck and Asther are extraordinary.

Among the film's highlights is a remarkable dream sequence in which Megan's bedroom is broken into by a Yellow Peril monster whom one assumes is Yen, and then Megan is saved by a masked man in western clothes, whom one assumes is her fiancé. But when she removes the mask, it turns out to be Yen, who is standing beside her when she wakes. No less memorable is the exquisite final sequence—which might be interpreted as a Hollywood brand of pop Buddhism, though it's rendered with sweetness and delicacy. **JRos**

She Done Him Wrong Lowell Sherman, 1933

In the early 1930s, Hollywood—beset with financial difficulties and production problems related to the conversion to sound cinema—turned to stage performers of proven popularity to lure customers back to the theaters. Among the most notable of these was Mae West, whose play Diamond Lil (which she wrote as a kind of showcase of her several talents) was immensely successful on Broadway and elsewhere. West proved a happy choice for Paramount because her unique brand of sophisticated if bawdy humor easily translated on screen; her first film, Night After Night (1932), was a big hit with audiences. West's antics, especially her famous double entendres and sleazy style, offended religious conservatives of the time and hastened the foundation of the Breen Office in 1934 to enforce the Production Code (promulgated, but widely ignored, in the early 1930s). West's post-1934 films, although interesting, never recaptured the appeal of her earlier work, of which She Done Him Wrong—the screen adaptation of Diamond Lil—is the most notable example, even garnering an Academy Award nomination.

West plays a "saloon keeper" in New York's Bowery who is involved with various criminals in the neighborhood. As Lady Lou, West is pursued by two local entrepreneurs and her fiancé is just released from jail, but she is hardly in need of a man as she inhabits lavish quarters above her establishment, replete with servants and an impressive collection of diamond jewelry. Lou, however, is smitten by her new neighbor, the head of the Salvation Army mission (Cary Grant). Her initial appraisal of the younger man's attractiveness is part of Hollywood legend. To Grant she utters the famous line "Why don't you come up sometime, see me." As a demonstration of her affection (and power), she uses some of her considerable hoard of diamonds to purchase his mission and make him a present of it. In the end, Grant is revealed as a detective who promptly takes all the crooks into custody, but "imprisons" Lou quite differently—with a wedding ring. A classic Hollywood comedy, full of naughtiness and good humor. **RBP**

U.S. (Paramount) 66m BW Producer William LeBaron **Screenplay** Mae West, Harry Thew, John Bright, from the play *Diamond Lil* by Mae West **Photography** Charles Lang **Music** Ralph Rainger, Shelton Brooks, John Leipold, Stephan Pasternacki **Cast** Mae West, Cary Grant, Owen Moore, Gilbert Roland, Noah Beery, David Landau, Rafaela Ottiano, Dewey Robinson, Rochelle Hudson, Tammany Young, Fuzzy Knight, Grace La Rue, Robert Homans, Louise Beavers **Oscar nomination** William LeBaron (best picture)

1933

> "Listen, when women go wrong, men go right after them."
>
> **Lady Lou (Mae West)**

ℹ️

She Done Him Wrong remains the shortest picture to be nominated for a Best Picture Academy Award.

Duck Soup Leo McCarey, 1933

U.S. (Paramount) 70m BW
Producer Herman J. Mankiewicz
Screenplay Bert Kalmar, Harry Ruby
Photography Henry Sharp Music Bert
Kalmar, John Leipold, Harry Ruby
Cast Groucho Marx, Harpo Marx, Chico
Marx, Zeppo Marx, Margaret Dumont,
Raquel Torres, Louis Calhern, Edmund
Breese, Leonid Kinskey, Charles Middleton,
Edgar Kennedy

"Maybe you can suggest something. As a matter of fact, you do suggest something. To me, you suggest a baboon."

**Rufus T. Firefly
(Groucho Marx)**

Groucho wears a total of five different uniforms during the movie's battle scene.

Released in 1933, this madcap comedy is the crowning glory of the comic team of the Marx Brothers, a New York phenomenon who honed their performing skills through vaudeville and went on to take Broadway with a series of comedies including *The Cocoanuts* and *Animal Crackers*. More than original performers, their timing was perfect in more ways than one: sound technology was taking over films just as they peaked on the stages of New York and looked for new audiences to conquer.

Among the five films made in Paramount's New York studios by the brothers—Groucho, Harpo, Chico, and Zeppo—*Duck Soup* is the last to feature all of them (Zeppo, the youngest brother and the group's straight man, went on to be an agent and inventor). It's crammed with visual and verbal gags, most of which are as fresh and funny today as they were in 1933. As with so many classics, *Duck Soup* enjoyed less-than-vigorous box-office traffic. In fact, Paramount canceled the Marx Brothers' contract soon afterward, causing them to head west to Hollywood and MGM, where *A Night at the Opera* and *A Day at the Races* were made.

Duck Soup is only 70 minutes long, but it packs in a seemingly endless string of virtually anything that might get a laugh, from jabs at Paul Revere and snide asides about then-current musicals to unexpected use of stock footage and astonishingly inventive physical sketches like the "three-hat routine," perfected by the brothers on stage over the years, and the famous mirror sequence. This routine—imitated by comics ever since—features Groucho, dressed in nightgown, nightcap, mustache, and cigar, meeting "himself" (Harpo as an identical image) in a doorway.

The plot, as such, involves Groucho as the dictator of the state of Freedonia—Rufus T. Firefly. His patron is the wealthy Mrs. Teasdale, played with ineffable dignity and grace under pressure by Margaret Dumont, the perfect outrageous foil and the subject of most of Groucho's forcefully memorable putdowns. If the physical gags and Groucho's dialogue style were their own, the scripts had expert input from many terrific comedy writers, among them S.J. Perelman. More than a great physical comedy act, the Marx Brothers were comedians lucky enough to have witty dialogue and keen observation, another reason why *Duck Soup* has survived whereas the films of, say, the Ritz Brothers remain unrevered.

Sylvanian Ambassador Trintino (Louis Calhern) wants Freedonia for his own and so pays Harpo and Chico to be his intelligence agents. This slender plot line is strong enough to support some of the best comedy sequences ever filmed, and offensive enough to some to count as Surrealist satire. Benito Mussolini banned the film in Italy because he took Groucho's role as a personal attack; nothing could have pleased the brothers more. Again, before the film's release, a small city in New York called Fredonia complained about the use of its name as well as the additional "e"; the response from the Marx Brothers camp was reassuringly predictable: "Change the name of your town, it's hurting our picture." **KK**

1933

Zéro de conduite Jean Vigo, 1933
Zero for Conduct

France (Argui-Film) 41m BW
Language French **Producer** Jacques-Louis Nounez, Jean Vigo **Screenplay** Jean Vigo **Photography** Boris Kaufman **Music** Maurice Jaubert **Cast** Jean Dasté, Robert le Flon, Du Verron, Delphin, Léon Larive, Mme. Emile, Louis De Gonzague-Frick, Raphaël Diligent, Louis Lefebvre, Gilbert Pruchon, Coco Golstein, Gérard de Bédarieux

"Young Devils at College," the subtitle of *Zero for Conduct*, suggests a mild romp in the *Carry On* vein, but Jean Vigo's classic short film means business. At stake in this vignette of childhood rebellion against an oppressive school institution is nothing less than a veritable Surrealist manifesto—one whose cosmic dimension is assured by the final shot in which its young devils, triumphant on a rooftop, appear ready to take flight.

This is a terrific movie to spring on students unprepared for what they will see: full frontal nudity, scatological and body-obsessed humor, antireligious blasphemy, and insistent homoeroticism. But it transcends the simple duality of youth versus authority (unlike its loose remake, the 1968 film *If....*) via its vision of inescapable, polymorphous perversity: Even the stuffiest teachers here are twisted, secretly wild at heart.

The hearty provocation happens as much on the level of form as content: the experiments with slow-motion, animation, and trick photography are prodigious and wondrous. Vigo had absorbed the avant-gardism of Luis Buñuel and René Clair, but he also invented a unique aesthetic form: the "aquarium shot," a claustrophobic space in which strange apparitions are produced from every available corner and pocket—cinema as a magic act. **AM**

Gold Diggers of 1933 Mervyn LeRoy, 1933

U.S. (Warner Bros.) 96m BW
Producer Robert Lord, Jack L. Warner, Raymond Griffith **Screenplay** David Boehm, Erwin S. Gelsey **Photography** Sol Polito **Music** Harry Warren **Cast** Warren William, Joan Blondell, Aline MacMahon, Ruby Keeler, Dick Powell, Guy Kibbee, Ned Sparks, Ginger Rogers **Oscar nomination** Nathan Levinson (sound)

Of the series of classic early 1930s Warner Brothers musicals featuring numbers by Busby Berkeley, *Gold Diggers of 1933* is the one that most strongly evokes the Great Depression. The bawdy, wisecracking screenplay centers on struggling Broadway showgirls who do what's necessary—including the use of "gold-digging" techniques on rich suckers—to keep the wolf from the door. The film's latter stages are dominated by three spectacular Berkeley numbers: the racy "Pettin' in the Park," elegant "Shadow Waltz," and topical "Remember My Forgotten Man."

An ironic disparity between onstage opulence and offstage economic crisis is established in the "We're in the Money" curtain-raiser, when a peppy paean to prosperity being rehearsed by coin-covered chorines is broken up by the show's creditors. The opening number's correlation of sex and money foreshadows the climactic "Remember My Forgotten Man," in which a streetwalker (Joan Blondell) laments the common man's closely linked losses of earning power and sexual virility, in poignant contrast to his forgotten World War I military glory. With its partisan references to the controversial 1932 Bonus March of jobless veterans and its vivid tableaux connecting war, emasculation, and unemployment, "Remember My Forgotten Man" is one of Hollywood's hardest-hitting political statements of the 1930s. **MR**

King Kong Merian C. Cooper & Ernest B. Schoedsack, 1933

U.S. (RKO) 100m BW **Producer** Merian C. Cooper, Ernest B. Schoedsack, David O. Selznick **Screenplay** James Ashmore Creelman, Ruth Rose, Edgar Wallace **Photography** Edward Linden, J.O. Taylor, Vernon L. Walker, Kenneth Peach **Music** Max Steiner **Cast** Fay Wray, Robert Armstrong, Bruce Cabot, Frank Reicher, Sam Hardy, Noble Johnson, Steve Clemente, James Flavin

"Taxi! Follow that ape!"

**Jack Driscoll
(Bruce Cabot)**

The undisputed champ of all monster movies—and an early Hollywood high-water mark for special effects work—*King Kong* remains one of the most lasting and beloved motion picture masterpieces. Essentially a simian take on the *Beauty and the Beast* fable, told without the transformative happy ending and on a gargantuan scale, Merian C. Cooper and Ernest B. Schoedsack's film fuses groundbreaking model work and emotional resonance to a degree rarely replicated by the literally hundreds of imitators that inevitably followed in its wake.

The story essentially plays out like that age-old conflict between city and nature. An expedition team arrives on the ominously named Skull Island, attracted by the promise that a giant prehistoric gorilla, feared and worshipped by the natives, might be brought home to New York and exploited as a must-see attraction. But mighty Kong doesn't take well to being caged and escapes on a destructive spree through the Big Apple.

The scenes set on Skull Island remain impressive even to this day, from Kong's magnificent first appearance to the number of other prehistoric creatures he and the expedition face in protecting or seeking, respectively, the abducted Ann Darrow (Fay Wray). Indeed, Kong is intimidated by Ann's beauty, and when he inevitably flees captivity and roams through New York City, the first thing he does is capture the young woman and retain her as his prisoner of love. Straddling the Empire State Building and swatting away pesky airplanes, King would ultimately rather sacrifice his own life than hurt Ann, which gives the film its famous, touching sign-off: "'Twas beauty killed the beast."

That the giant ape shifts from feared antagonist to sympathetic protagonist, with the former of course the perspective of his pursuers, shows the success of Willis O'Brian's intricate and expressive stop-animation work (future stop-animation savant Ray Harryhausen worked as his assistant). Although it is a B-movie at heart, *King Kong* set Hollywood's special effects fetish on fast forward, and a case could be made that thanks to *Kong*, many of today's films focus far more on flash than story. But unlike contemporary special effects exercises, the majesty of *Kong* is destined to endure, thanks in no small part to the "performance" of its giant lead. **JKl**

1933

i

Kong's roar was created by combining the roars of a lion and tiger, then running them backward.

Las Hurdes Luis Buñuel, 1933
Land Without Bread

Spain (Ramón Acín) 27m BW
Language Spanish Producer Ramón Acín,
Luis Buñuel Screenplay Luis Buñuel, Rafael
Sánchez Ventura Photography Eli Lotar
Music Brahms Cast Abel Jacquin (voice)

An extraordinarily powerful yet wholly unsentimental account of poverty, disease, malnutrition, and ignorance allowed to exist in a supposedly civilized Christian nation, Luis Buñuel's documentary *Land Without Bread* was shot in the remote mountainous region of Las Hurdes—a small area just north of Extremadura, less than 60 miles (100 kilometers) south of the glories of the university city of Salamanca—in 1932. Physical, psychic, and social ills are all calmly observed by a dispassionate camera, Buñuel realizing that the images would speak volumes for themselves. Nonetheless, he juxtaposed shots of the riches to be found in Catholic churches and, it was learned later, was not above shooting a goat or smearing an ailing ass with honey (to attract a lethal swarm of bees) to emphasize his argument.

But what does all this have to do with a Surrealist? The horrors are not only on view, but they're also the stuff of nightmare; Buñuel also seems all too aware that the only true release from the Hurdanos's cruel sufferings (unless State and Church intervene, at least) is death itself, and certainly many of the actions taken to alleviate their hunger and pain seem informed by a perverse desire for extinction. Cruel, cool, strangely beautiful, and as pungent as sulfur. **GA**

i

Buñuel's friend Ramón Acín promised to fund the film if he won the lottery—two months later he did.

Sons of the Desert William A. Seiter, 1933

U.S. (Hal Roach, MGM) 68m BW
Producer Hal Roach **Screenplay** Frank
Craven **Photography** Kenneth Peach
Music William Axt, George M. Cohan,
Marvin Hatley, Paul Marquardt, O'Donnell-
Heath, Leroy Shield **Cast** Stan Laurel, Oliver
Hardy, Charley Chase, Mae Busch, Dorothy
Christy, Lucien Littlefield, John Elliott,
William Gillespie, John Merton

Essentially a remake of the duo's 1930 film *Be Big*, this full-length Stan Laurel and Oliver Hardy comedy was their fourth feature, and arguably their best. Although other Laurel and Hardy films are, subjectively at least, equal to this one, they tend to inhabit atypical worlds—the fairyland of *Babes in Toyland* (1934), for example, or the western fantasy of *Way Out West* (1937). Although *Sons of the Desert* may be one of Laurel and Hardy's most conventional comedies, it best represents the strange domestic hell the duo inhabit in their finest work, a childlike world full of domineering wives, clandestine fun sessions, and illicit smoking and drinking.

Centering around a trip to Hawaii with the Freemason-like fraternity of the title, and Stan and Ollie's attempts to conceal this jaunt from their wives, *Sons of the Desert* takes a basic farce plot and turns it into a vehicle for motion picture comedy's greatest double act. Superb supporting performances, most notably from Mae Busch as Mrs. Hardy and comedian-director Charley Chase as a drunken version of himself, along with capable direction from William A. Seiter (whose other notable comedy was the Marx Brothers' workmanlike *Room Service* in 1938), also make *Sons of the Desert*—unusually for an eighty-year-old film comedy—utterly watchable today. **KK**

Queen Christina Rouben Mamoulian, 1933

U.S. (MGM) 97m BW **Producer** Walter
Wanger **Screenplay** S.N. Behrman, H.M.
Harwood **Photography** William H. Daniels
Music Herbert Stothart **Cast** Greta Garbo,
John Gilbert, Ian Keith, Lewis Stone,
Elizabeth Young, C. Aubrey Smith, Reginald
Owen, Georges Renavent, David Torrence,
Gustav von Seyffertitz, Ferdinand Munier
Venice Film Festival Rouben Mamoulian
(Mussolini Cup nomination)

Rouben Mamoulian's re-creation of the seventeenth-century Swedish court provides Greta Garbo with a perfect vehicle to dominate the screen. The historical Christina, daughter of Gustavus Adolphus, was a reclusive aesthete who eventually abdicated in order to have a life of her own and change her Lutheranism for Catholicism. Garbo's version, by way of contrast, is an alluring mixture of masculine and feminine qualities. Learned and resolute, she is also sexually experienced, even aggressive, yet committed to her independence.

The plot (which seems to have borrowed a good deal from screen versions of England's Elizabeth I) centers on her counselors' demand that she marry Charles of France, which angers her and her "consort," the burly Count Magnus (Ian Keith). Fleeing the court—and the restrictions placed on her as a woman—Christina dresses like a man and encounters, by chance, the Spanish ambassador, Antonio (John Gilbert, whom Garbo was romancing at the time). What follows are comic scenes of sexual disguise, as Christina begins to fall deeply in love with Antonio, and deep eroticism. When Antonio is killed protecting her honor, Christina abdicates, achieving the solitude that, because of her rank and personal qualities, seems her fate from the beginning. Garbo's performance in the role is inspired, helped by the glamorizing touch of Mamoulian's camera. Well-conceived art design, editing, and music make *Queen Christina* sensational viewing. **RBP**

Triumph des Willens Leni Riefenstahl, 1934
Triumph of the Will

It was Adolf Hitler himself who commissioned dancer and actress-turned-filmmaker Leni Riefenstahl to make a grand, celebratory record of the sixth Nazi Party Congress held in September 1934 at Nuremberg—the medieval Bavarian showplace where, with deliberate irony, a court of Allied victors would convene in 1945–46 to judge war criminals of the Third Reich. Hitler also gave her the film's title. Riefenstahl was a careerist as well as a creative talent and, her postwar protestations to the contrary, there is evidence (not only here but in her photojournalistic coverage of the invasion of Poland and in her later use of concentration camp inmates as "extras") that her enthusiasm for fascism was crafty, if debatably, naïve. But any discussion of motivation cannot diminish the devastating impact of *Triumph of the Will*. This is an awesome spectacle, vulgar but mythic, and technically an overwhelming, assured accomplishment.

Nuremberg was as carefully prepared as if it were a massive soundstage housing a series of elaborate sets. Riefenstahl ordered new bridges and accesses constructed in the city center, and lighting towers and camera tracks built, all of which was carried out to her exact specifications. Deploying thirty cameras and 120 technicians, Riefenstahl brilliantly fulfilled her Nuremberg brief—to glorify the might of the Nazi state and tighten its grip on the hearts and minds of Germany—with breathtaking imagery on a spectacularly sinister, epic scale, creating an infamous masterpiece still regarded as the most powerful propaganda film ever made.

The documentary—which after six months' editing into a carefully selected two hours represents about three percent of the footage shot—opens with Hitler's arrival by plane, his descent from the clouds given the character of a Wagnerian hero's entrance, with his head in a halo of sunlight. The Führer's acclamation by saluting multitudes is central to this presentation of his political philosophy as world theater, lending him a disturbing charisma despite the posturing and stridency so familiar from news archives, historical drama, and masterly parody, like Charlie Chaplin's in *The Great Dictator* (1940). Setting him off are a kaleidoscope of astonishing images: vigorous young men disporting, torchlit processions, swastika-brandishing ritual, militaristic display, thousands of well-drilled children pledging themselves to the Movement, and a continuous folkloric parade concluding with the Nazi anthem, the Horst Wessel Song.

Triumph of the Will is an unsubtle but innovative demonstration of technique, from ingenious camera angles and striking composition to the relentless pace of its canny editing. After World War II, Riefenstahl was imprisoned for four years by the Americans and the French for her role in the Nazi propaganda machine over her insistence that she made "pure historical film, film vérité." Repeated attempts to revive her career were unsuccessful. Later she discovered underwater photography and demonstrated that she still had an artist's eye. **AE**

Germany (Leni Riefenstahl, NSDAP-Reichsleitung) 114m BW
Language German **Producer** Leni Riefenstahl **Screenplay** Leni Riefenstahl, Walter Ruttmann **Photography** Sepp Allgeier, Karl Attenberger, Werner Bohne, Walter Frentz, Willy Zielke **Music** Herbert Windt **Cast** Adolf Hitler, Max Amann, Martin Bormann, Walter Buch, Walter Darré, Otto Dietrich, Sepp Dietrich, Hans Frank, Josef Goebbels, Hermann Göring, Jakob Grimminger, Rudolf Hess, Reinhard Heydrich, Konstantin Hierl, Heinrich Himmler, Robert Ley, Viktor Lutze, Erich Raeder, Fritz Reinhardt, Alfred Rosenberg, Hjalmar Schacht, Franz Xaver Schwarz, Julius Streicher, Fritz Todt, Werner von Blomberg, Hans Georg von Friedeburg, Gerd von Rundstedt, Baldur von Schirach, Adolf Wagner

> *"It reflects the truth that was then in 1934, history. It is therefore a documentary."*
>
> **Leni Riefenstahl, 1964**

i

A British propaganda film later set footage of Hitler and troops from this film to the song "The Lambeth Walk."

1934

It's a Gift Norman Z. McLeod, 1934

Undoubtedly the finest of all of W.C. Fields's comedies, *It's a Gift* may not offer the inspired insanity of such waywardly surreal gems as *Never Give a Sucker an Even Break* (1941) or the unforgettable short *The Fatal Glass of Beer* (1933), but it is certainly the most coherent and most consistently funny of his features.

Despite having been cobbled together from old revue sketches and scenes from earlier movies like *It's the Old Army Game* (1926), Norman Z. McLeod's *It's a Gift* actually provides something resembling a proper story. Harold Bissonette (Fields) is so tired of the constant pressures of family life and running a general store that he secretly buys, with his hard-earned savings, the Californian orange grove of his dreams, and sets off with his family (all vocally horrified by what he's done, naturally), only to discover that their purchase is nothing like the palace pictured in the advertisement. That said, of course, this "plot" is simply an excuse for another of Fields's marvelously misanthropic essays on the perils and pitfalls of parenthood, marriage, neighbors, and Prohibition, allowing him free rein to court our sympathy for an old curmudgeon who feels himself maltreated by virtually the entire world.

It is particularly difficult to select highlights from such a supremely even series of set pieces, but the catastrophically destructive visit to Fields's shop paid by the feeble, deaf, blind, and uncommonly belligerent Mr. Muckle (Charles Sellon) must rank as some kind of peak in politically incorrect hilarity. The protagonist's forlorn attempt to sleep on the porch—despite noisy neighbors, a nagging wife (the inimitable Kathleen Howard), a murderous screwdriver wielded by Baby LeRoy, a rolling coconut, a broken hammock, a rifle, and a quite crazily cheery insurance salesman in search of one Karl LaFong ("Capital K, small A, small R")—is quite simply as brilliant and nightmarish a portrait of ordinary life as deadpan Hollywood comedy ever got. Mind you, the shaving sequence is pretty great, too. Oh, and then there's the dinner with the family. Sheer genius. **GA**

U.S. (Paramount) 73m BW **Producer** William LeBaron **Screenplay** Jack Cunningham, W.C. Fields **Photography** Henry Sharp **Music** Lew Brown, Buddy G. DeSylva, Ray Henderson, Al Jolson, John Leipold **Cast** W.C. Fields, Kathleen Howard, Jean Rouverol, Julian Madison, Tommy Bupp, Baby LeRoy, Tammany Young, Morgan Wallace, Charles Sellon, Josephine Whittell, T. Roy Barnes, Diana Lewis, Spencer Charters, Guy Usher, Dell Henderson

Harold: *"She ran right in front of the car!"*

Amelia: *"It's a statue, you idiot."*

Harold (W.C. Fields) and Amelia (Kathleen Howard)

ℹ

None of W.C. Fields's movies were ever nominated for an Academy Award.

Shen nu Wu Yonggang, 1934
The Goddess

China (Lianhua Film Company) 85m BW
Producer Minwei Tian Screenplay Wu
Yonggang Photography Weilie Hong
Cast Ruan Lingyu, Jian Tian,
Zhizhi Zhang, Li Keng

Who is the greatest actor of the 1930s? Katherine Hepburn? James Cagney? How about a less well-known name, Ruan Lingyu? Here she is in *The Goddess*, a silent Chinese film made in Shanghai. In such a golden decade for cinema, why should we be interested in Ruan and this film? Because each opens up a world of cinema with which we're unfamiliar.

The Goddess is probably the first sympathetic portrayal of a prostitute in cinema. Ruan plays her with weary body language. She sells herself to pay for her son's education, but the school finds out and she's shunned. Director Wu Yonggang uses a beautiful tracking shot along a long row of other mothers to show how they whisper their disapproval from one to another. This was typical of Shanghaiese cinema of the 1930s: innovative, humanistic, leftist, female-centered, and subtly realist, more than a decade before Italian Neorealism.

Such films were hugely popular; Ruan became "the Chinese Greta Garbo," a name that captures her mystery but not her believability. Ordinary women loved her. But tabloid gossip hounded her, and she committed suicide at the age of twenty-four. Her funeral made news around the world. And then she, like poetic, realist Chinese cinema of the 1930s, was quietly forgotten, at least in the West. In our Lazarus era, when old movies are coming back to life, *The Goddess* is a must-see. **MC**

ℹ

Shen Nu translates as "goddess," but it was also slang for "prostitute." Both meanings apply to Ruan's character.

It Happened One Night Frank Capra, 1934

Peter (Clark Gable) is a tough-talking journalist; Ellie (Claudette Colbert) is a "dizzy dame" on the run from home and her father. The two meet while on the road and are forced, reluctantly, to collaborate. He's the salt of the earth, she's a rich kid, and each exploits the other—for him, she means a big newspaper story, for her, he's a way to help her get to New York and a forbidden fiancé. In the course of the story, they move from antagonism to love. It could be one of a hundred routine, American romantic comedies of the 1930s or 1940s.

But, make no mistake, Frank Capra's *It Happened One Night*—the first of only three movies to win all five major Academy Awards, preceding *One Flew Over the Cuckoo's Nest* (1975) and *Silence of the Lambs* (1991)—is movie magic. This has something to do with how it conjures an entire milieu: a "people's America" filled with unlikely rogues and soft-hearted citizens, always ready to share a story and a song, or simply exhibit their lovable eccentricities. But the film is also careful to explore exceptions to its basic rule: Ellie's father, Andrews (Walter Connolly), turns out to be a pretty swell chap, just as the talkative bus passenger Shapeley (Roscoe Karns) ends up a weasel.

Capra was expert at cleverly weaving a story from altogether familiar and ordinary motifs: eating, verbal slang ("ah, nuts"), snoring, washing, dressing and undressing. True to the romantic comedy formula, identities are momentarily dissolved whenever a masquerade is necessary or able to be exploited for secret entertainment—although, whenever Peter and Ellie pretend to be husband and wife, more serious possibilities and destinies do suggest themselves.

It Happened One Night is a distant predecessor of today's "trash comedies," such as those by the Farrelly Brothers. Ass jokes abound and the pretensions and privileges of the wealthy are mercilessly mocked, while Colbert's famous, bare legs stop traffic. And then there is the sexual tension angle: Working patiently through four nights of Peter and Ellie together, the entire film hinges on the symbolism of the "walls of Jericho" finally toppling—the ridding of the blanket that stands, weakly and tremblingly, as the barrier to the consummation of their growing love.

Critics can't rhapsodize over Capra's powers of montage or mise-en-scène; style was a functional, conventional matter for him. But he did have a perfect sense of script (in both overall structure and small details), and a brilliant rapport with his charismatic actors. Gable and Colbert help to truly equalize this one-upmanship battle of the sexes, diluting that ideological thrust of the script that suggests that proletarian guys should teach spoiled gals a thing or two about real life. In the infectious interplay of these stars—in their mutual willingness to play, to laugh, to be vulnerable, to take a joke as good they give it—we encounter an ideal that has been well and truly lost in contemporary, mainstream cinema: fighting reciprocity between the sexes. **AM**

U.S. (Columbia) 105m BW
Producer Frank Capra, Harry Cohn
Screenplay Samuel Hopkins Adams, Robert Riskin **Photography** Joseph Walker
Music Howard Jackson, Louis Silvers
Cast Clark Gable, Claudette Colbert, Walter Connolly, Roscoe Karns, Jameson Thomas, Alan Hale, Arthur Hoyt, Blanche Frederici, Charles C. Wilson **Oscars** Frank Capra, Harry Cohn (best picture), Frank Capra (director), Robert Riskin (screenplay), Clark Gable (actor), Claudette Colbert (actress) **Venice Film Festival** Frank Capra nomination (Mussolini Cup)

> "As buoyant and elegant as bubbles in a glass of champagne."
>
> **Peter Bradshaw,**
> **The Guardian, 2010**

🛈

Gable won his only Oscar for the film but gave the award to a child, saying that it was the winning that counted.

France (Gaumont-Franco Film-Aubert) 89m
BW **Language** French **Producer** Jacques-
Louis Nounez **Screenplay** Jean Guinée,
Albert Riéra **Photography** Jean-Paul
Alphen, Louis Berger, Boris Kaufman
Music Maurice Jaubert **Cast** Michel Simon,
Dita Parlo, Jean Dasté, Gilles Margaritis, Louis
Lefebvre, Maurice Gilles, Raphaël Diligent

*"As Truffaut has said,
in filming prosaic words
and acts, Vigo effortlessly
achieved poetry."*

Derek Malcolm, critic, 1999

ℹ️

L'Atalante was to be Vigo's last film.
He died from tuberculosis later that
year, at the age of twenty-nine.

L'Atalante Jean Vigo, 1934

Heretical as it may be to say it in these enlightened times of gender politics, Jean Vigo's masterpiece *L'Atalante* is the cinema's greatest ode to heterosexual passion. One simply cannot enter into its rapturous poetry without surrendering to the romantic series of oppositions between the sexes, comparisons rigorously installed at every possible level—spiritual, physical, erotic, and emotional. It is only this thrill of absolute "otherness" that can allow both the agony of nonalignment between lovers and the sublimity of their eventual fusion.

This is far removed from the typical romance of the time. As Vigo once memorably complained, it takes "two pairs of lips and three thousand meters of film to come together, and almost as many to come unstuck again." Like Stanley Kubrick's *Eyes Wide Shut* (1999), *L'Atalante* casts the immortal love story within an adventure tale: man (Jean Dasté as Jean) the seafaring adventurer, woman (Dita Parlo as Juliette) the city-craving settler. The seductive temptations and drifts that temporarily split them up are forecast in a charged moment of almost metaphysical agony: In thick fog, Jean stumbles blindly over the boat's barge until he finds his bride and envelops her in an embrace at once angry and relieved, inspiring them instantly to head below deck to make love.

Between these poles of man and woman, however, there is Père Jules (Michel Simon), master of the boat. It is surely the mark of Vigo's greatness as an artist that his imagination could project itself fully into both the heterosexual ideal and the fluid identity of this inspired madman. Jules is a multiple being, man and woman, child and adult, friend and lover, without boundaries—at one point even visually doubled as he wrestles himself. He is a living text covered with extravagant tattoos; he is the cinematic apparatus itself, able to produce sound from records with his magically electrified finger. Jules is Vigo's Surrealist sensibility incarnated by Simon, an astonishingly anarchic, instinctual performer.

Vigo develops and deepens the formal explorations of his previous film *Zero for Conduct* (1933). From silent, burlesque cinema and René Clair he borrows a parade gag for his prologue: stuffed shirts at the couple's funeral filing past the camera, gradually becoming faster until they are an unruly, disheveled mob. Aboard the boat, Vigo finds his beloved "aquarium spaces": enclosed rooms filled with cats, oddities, and wonders (as in Jules's cabin devoted to exotic bric-a-brac). On deck, he uses ghostly, nocturnal lighting. Unifying the film is a superb rhythmic and expressive tone.

Vigo's death at the age of twenty-nine was a tragic loss. But *L'Atalante* crowns his legacy—and is there any scene in cinema sexier than the magnificent, Eisensteinian montage of Jean's and Juliette's bodies, far apart, matched in postures of mutual arousal, an act of love made possible only through the soulful language of film? **AM**

The Black Cat Edgar G. Ulmer, 1934

U.S. (Universal) 65m BW **Producer** Carl Laemmle Jr. **Screenplay** Edgar G. Ulmer, from the story *House of Doom* by Edgar Allan Poe **Photography** John J. Mescall **Music** James Huntley, Heinz Roemheld **Music** Tchaikovsky, Liszt **Cast** Boris Karloff, Bela Lugosi, David Manners, Julie Bishop, Lucille Lund, Egon Brecher, Harry Cording, Henry Armetta, Albert Conti

The first screen teaming of the great monster stars of the 1930s, Boris Karloff (top-billed simply as "KARLOFF") and Bela Lugosi, *The Black Cat* is at once the most perverse and the artiest of the original run of Universal horror pictures, informed by the strange sensibilities of director Edgar G. Ulmer—beginning to seesaw between high art and poverty row—and poetic pulp screenwriter Peter Ruric.

Based on Edgar Allan Poe's story only in concept, *The Black Cat* feels like the last German Expressionist horror film, with a tale of diabolism, revenge, necrophilia, betrayal, and bad manners set in a modernist castle (a rare instance of up-to-date Gothic) built by widow's-peaked Satanist-cum-architect Hjalmar Poelzig (Karloff) atop the mass grave of the soldiers he betrayed to the enemy during World War I. Horror-style honeymooners David Manners and Jacqueline Wells are almost comically out of their depth, the templates for Brad and Janet in *The Rocky Horror Picture Show* (1975), as unwilling houseguests caught between Poelzig, who has his mistresses preserved like waxworks in cases in the cellar, and the vengeance-obsessed Vitus Werdegast (Lugosi), who winds up the odd chess-game plot by skinning the villain alive before the castle is blown up. Deliberately outrageous but also a tease, Karloff's elegantly delivered rituals are all commonplace clichés ("cum granulo salis") delivered in a lisping Latin. **KN**

ℹ

The line "cum granulo salis," uttered as part of a dark incantation, translates as "with a grain of salt."

The Thin Man W.S. Van Dyke, 1934

The chemistry between Myrna Loy and William Powell was so potent in the 1934 film *Manhattan Melodrama* that its director, W.S. Van Dyke, cast the two again in the same year. As Nick and Nora Charles, they are unique in the history of cinema. The first popular husband-and-wife detective team, they not only love each other, but they like each other, too, without being insipid, disrespectful, or dull.

The Thin Man's plot is a messy one. Nick Charles is officially a retired detective, but he takes a personal interest in the disappearance of a crotchety inventor—the "thin man" of the title—whose daughter (Maureen O'Sullivan) is Nick's long-time acquaintance. The inventor's safety is thrown into further doubt when complications arise involving his suspicious mistress, grasping ex-wife, and her money-hungry husband (Cesar Romero). With the addition of multifarious mobsters, cops, and molls, it seems the whole criminal world turns up at the Charles's luxurious hotel suite at one time or another.

Trying to make sense of the story gets in the way of what is genuinely important—the snappy banter full of covetable lines between the rich, sophisticated Nora and her sharp lush of a husband. Nick disarms an unwanted guest one night; the incident is reported in the morning news. "I was shot twice in the *Tribune*," says Nick. "I read you were shot five times in the tabloids," says Nora. "It's not true. He didn't come anywhere near my tabloids." Nick may seem like an alcoholic, but he springs back and forth from relaxed giddiness to active sobriety in the wink of an eye. The couple's prodigious boozing seems to have little effect on their actions; it's more of an elegant prop—a vital element for a country just coming out of the Great Depression.

Taken from a novel written in the same year by Dashiell Hammett, Nick and Nora were supposedly modeled on Hammett's relationship with playwright Lillian Hellman. Shot in fourteen days, this sparkling screwball detective story earned over $2 million and was nominated for four Academy Awards. Not surprisingly, popularity spawned four more movies as well as a radio and television series, and was the inspiration behind TV shows such as *McMillian & Wife* and *Hart to Hart*. **KK**

U.S. (Cosmopolitan, MGM) 93m BW
Producer Hunt Stromberg
Photography James Wong Howe
Screenplay Albert Hackett, from novel by
Dashiell Hammett **Music** William Axt
Cast William Powell, Myrna Loy, Maureen
O'Sullivan, Nat Pendleton, Minna Gombell,
Porter Hall, Henry Wadsworth, William Henry,
Harold Huber, Cesar Romero, Natalie
Moorhead, Edward Brophy, Edward Ellis,
Cyril Thornton **Oscar nominations** Hunt
Stromberg (best picture), W.S. Van Dyke
(director), Frances Goodrich, (screenplay),
Albert Hackett (screenplay),
William Powell (actor)

"Waiter, will you serve the nuts? I mean, will you serve the guests the nuts?"

Nora (Myrna Loy)

i

The movie was released just five months after Hammett's novel was first published.

Mutiny on the Bounty Frank Lloyd, 1935

U.S. (MGM) 132m BW **Producer** Albert
Lewin, Irving Thalberg **Screenplay** Talbot
Jennings, Jules Furthman, from book by
Charles Nordhoff and James Hall
Photography Arthur Edeson **Music** Herbert
Stothart, Walter Jurmann, Gus Kahn,
Bronislau **Cast** Charles Laughton, Clark
Gable, Franchot Tone, Herbert Mundin,
Eddie Quillan, Dudley Digges, Donald Crisp,
Henry Stephenson, Francis Lister, Spring
Byington, Movita, Mamo Clark, Byron Russell,
Percy Waram, David Torrence **Oscar** Albert
Lewin, Irving Thalberg (best picture)
Oscar nominations Frank Lloyd (director),
Jules Furthman, Talbot Jennings, Carey
Wilson (screenplay), Clark Gable, Franchot
Tone, Charles Laughton (actor), Margaret
Booth (editing), Nat W. Finston (music)

🛈

Charles Laughton was terrified of
water and suffered from seasickness
for most of the location shooting.

Epitomizing the classic Hollywood spirit, Frank Lloyd's *Mutiny on the
Bounty* is a masterwork of studio moviemaking. The film's spare-no-
expense canvas, travelogue quality, and moral center result in an
adventure tale of remarkable beauty. Of course this overlooks an acting
style long since left behind. Then there's an American cast imbuing this
British cautionary tale with Depression-era optimism. Still, these minor
criticisms serve to support how well produced the film is when
considering MGM's house style that simultaneously emphasized profits,
escapism, and the broadest possible entertainment.

Set in the late eighteenth century, when the British Empire crested
across the decks of its navy, the crew of the ship *Bounty* mutinies after
months of mistreatment. Led by Fletcher Christian (Clark Gable), they put
their cruel captain, Captain Bligh (Charles Laughton), to sea, only for him
to find his way back to port in an effort nothing short of amazing. Into his
wake sails the *Bounty* for the South Pacific, beset by various complications.

Gable appears without his mustache, and Laughton's bee-stung lips
flutter with harsh discipline. In between are a number of nominal
subplots, though in the end the film is perhaps most memorable as an
early high-water mark for the art of production design. **GC-Q**

The 39 Steps Alfred Hitchcock, 1935

After several tentative early steps and a few small breakthroughs, *The 39 Steps* was the first clear creative peak in Alfred Hitchcock's British period and arguably marked the first fully successful film in the director's rapidly deepening oeuvre—starting at the end of the silent era, by the time of *The 39 Steps* he had already directed eighteen films. After the picture's financial and critical success, Hitchcock further solidified his reputation as a master filmmaker by embarking on a nearly unparalleled streak of compelling and entertaining thrillers that would stretch for several decades. And, indeed, many of his most popular films—*North by Northwest* (1959), for one—clearly have their roots in this early highlight.

Among its many noteworthy achievements, *The 39 Steps* introduced one key Hitchcock first: the notion of the innocent bystander accused, pursued, or punished for a crime he didn't commit. (The theme was one the director would return to again and again, most overtly in his 1956 film *The Wrong Man*.) Richard Hannay (Robert Donat), a Canadian on vacation in England, meets a woman who is later murdered under mysterious circumstances. It seems he has stumbled into a spy plot involving something called "the 39 Steps," and he feels that with this knowledge only he can save the day. Handcuffed to an unwilling female accomplice (Madeleine Carroll), Hannay must simultaneously evade capture by the police and an archvillain with a missing finger in hot pursuit and reveal the titular mystery before it's too late.

In traditional Hitchcock fashion, the revelation of what "the 39 Steps" actually are—and indeed the entire spy plot—is almost peripheral to the flirtatious interplay between the two leads. Literally chained to one another in a teasing mockery of marriage, Donat and Carroll pack their quarrelsome exchanges with little innuendoes—when the chase leaves time for a breather, of course—morphing the espionage thriller into the unlikeliest of love stories. The film, like their relationship, plays out in a rush, a nonstop string of action sequences and chase scenes punctuated by witty dialogue and riveting suspense. **JKl**

G.B. (Gaumont British) 86m BW
Producer Michael Balcon, Ivor Montagu
Screenplay Charles Bennett, from novel by
John Buchan **Photography** Bernard
Knowles **Music** Jack Beaver, Hubert Bath
Cast Robert Donat, Madeleine Carroll, Lucie
Mannheim, Godfrey Tearle, Peggy Ashcroft,
John Laurie, Helen Haye, Frank Cellier, Wylie
Watson, Gus McNaughton, Jerry Verno,
Peggy Simpson

*"For all you know,
I may murder
a woman a week."*

**Richard Hannay
(Robert Donat)**

ℹ

Hitchcock appears fleetingly about
seven minutes in, discarding a
cigarette pack as a bus draws up.

A Night at the Opera Sam Wood, 1935

U.S. (MGM) 96m BW **Language** English /
Italian **Producer** Irving Thalberg
Screenplay James Kevin McGuinness,
George S. Kaufman **Photography** Merritt B.
Gerstad **Music** Nacio Herb Brown, Walter
Jurmann, Bronislau Kaper, Herbert Stothart
Cast Groucho Marx, Chico Marx, Harpo
Marx, Kitty Carlisle, Allan Jones, Walter Woolf
King, Sig Ruman, Margaret Dumont, Edward
Keane, Robert Emmett O'Connor

I was very young, not much more than ten years old, when I walked into a cinema in France to watch *A Night at The Opera*—or, more precisely, was sent there by some adult who knew as little as I did about the Marx Brothers. At my age, reading the subtitles was still rather difficult, especially when this jumping character with a mustache and a cigar was shouting words to the audience like a crazy machine gun. Since then I have had the pleasure of seeing *A Night at the Opera* again, several times, along with the rest of the Marx Brothers' work. I am aware of both the continuity and the variations in their movies, and have been amazed by the brilliance of their performances. But I still feel the incredible power of invention and transgression conveyed by this particular film.

More than the central scenes, like the crowd gathering in the ship cabin, *A Night at the Opera* remains such a strong and dazzling comedy thanks to its most elementary moments—a single word or gesture performed with an incredible sense of rhythm. There is much to say about the way the transgressive weapons of the three brothers initiate a crisis in the spectacle of an opera. Groucho's overflow of words and distortion of his body, Harpo's unnatural silence and childlike power of destruction, and Chico's virtuosity and "foreign ethos" all serve to disturb an opera based on a loathing of art, greed, and corruption. These elements do exist, and they are definitely interesting, but they come after this more obvious characteristic: *A Night at the Opera* was, and remains, a damn funny film. **J-MF**

A Night at the Opera was the first Marx Brothers film to be made without Zeppo Marx.

Bride of Frankenstein James Whale, 1935

Universal Studios had to wait nearly four years before James Whale accepted the offer to direct the follow-up to his 1931 box-office success, *Frankenstein*. But it turned out to be worth the wait: under the director's nearly complete control (producer Carl Laemmle Jr., was vacationing in Europe during most of the production), *Bride of Frankenstein* is a surprising mix of terror and comedy in many ways superior to the original film.

Despite Boris Karloff's reluctance, it was decided that the Monster should now be able to pronounce a few chosen words. His humanization here makes him more complete and faithful to Mary Shelley's novel, and his desperate search for a friendly companion could hardly be more touching. Though it was played down at the censors' request, the Monster is mostly depicted in *Bride of Frankenstein* as a Christlike figure who is led to kill because of his circumstances and the fear he inspires in society. Even the monstrous mate intended just for him is repulsed at first glance by his physical aspect. Without a doubt, Elsa Lanchester's bride remains to this day one of the most astonishing creatures ever seen on-screen: her appearance—in a sort of grotesque version of a marriage ceremony—is still a highlight of the horror genre, what with her mummified body, her swan-like hissing, and her black-and-white-streaked Egyptian hairdo.

Bride of Frankenstein's plot relies heavily on sharp contrasts that make the spectator jump from terror to pathos or comedy. Whale's sense of humor—often described as camp—is mainly brought out by Minnie (Una O'Connor), the household maid, along with the outrageously effeminate acting of Ernest Thesiger, who plays the devilish Dr. Pretorius.

The immense interest in *Bride of Frankenstein* also stems from its portrayal of sexual relations, a portrayal that is considered by many to be at least potentially transgressive. The introduction of a second mad scientist (Pretorius), who forces Colin Clive's Henry Frankenstein to give life again, emphasizes one of the fundamental and disturbing implications of Shelley's myth: (pro)creation as something achieved by men alone. Four years later, Whale's masterpiece itself gave birth to a "son," but the father of the bride would have nothing to do with it. **FL**

U.S. (Universal) 75m BW
Producer Carl Laemmle Jr., James Whale
Screenplay William Hurlbut, John L. Balderston **Photography** John J. Mescall
Music Franz Waxman **Cast** Boris Karloff, Colin Clive, Valerie Hobson, Elsa Lanchester, Ernest Thesiger, Gavin Gordon, Douglas Walton, Una O'Connor, E.E. Clive, Lucien Prival, O.P. Heggie, Dwight Frye, Reginald Barlow, Mary Gordon, Anne Darling
Oscar nomination Gilbert Kurland (sound)

"I've been cursed for delving into the mysteries of life!"

Dr. Henry Frankenstein (Colin Clive)

i

To play the Bride, the five-foot-four-inch Lanchester wore stilts to boost her height to a towering seven foot.

Captain Blood Michael Curtiz, 1935

U.S. (Cosmopolitan, First National, Warner Bros.) 119m BW **Language** English / French **Producer** Harry Joe Brown, Gordon Hollingshead, Hal B. Wallis **Screenplay** Casey Robinson, from novel by Rafael Sabatini **Photography** Ernest Haller, Hal Mohr **Music** Erich Wolfgang Korngold, Liszt **Cast** Errol Flynn, Olivia de Havilland, Lionel Atwill, Basil Rathbone, Ross Alexander, Guy Kibbee, Henry Stephenson, Robert Barrat, Hobart Cavanaugh, Donald Meek, Jessie Ralph, Forrester Harvey, Frank McGlynn Sr., Holmes Herbert, David Torrence **Oscar nominations** Hal B. Wallis, Harry Joe Brown, Gordon Hollingshead (best picture), Michael Curtiz (director), Casey Robinson (screenplay), Leo F. Forbstein (music), Nathan Levinson (sound)

Flynn worked with director Michael Curtiz on twelve adventure films, but the two men disliked each other.

A quintessential swashbuckling adventure directed by expert Michael Curtiz, *Captain Blood* made divinely attractive Australian Errol Flynn a star overnight. His animal magnetism hugely impressed Jack Warner, who handed him this break when Robert Donat disdained the role. The film marks the first pairing in a string of winning romantic costume pictures of Flynn with Olivia de Havilland, whose genteel prettiness was a charming foil for his exuberance and athletic sex appeal.

Flynn plays an honorable seventeenth-century Irish doctor, Peter Blood, unjustly sentenced to deportation to and slavery in the Caribbean, where he aims insolent barbs and suggestive glances at dainty mistress Arabella Bishop (de Havilland). Leading an escape he turns pirate, the vengeful scourge of the bounding main, and forms an uneasy alliance with dastardly French buccaneer Captain Levasseur (Basil Rathbone). Relations become strained when they fall out over booty and the captive beauty, Arabella, resulting in a duel to the death in the first of their famously thrilling screen sword fights. *Captain Blood* has everything you could want in a swashbuckler—sea battles and flashing blades, a dashing hero, an imperiled but plucky heroine, cutthroats, plumed hats, wrongs righted, fellows swinging like gymnasts from masts, and a rousing score by Erich Wolfgang Korngold. It is great fun. **AE**

Top Hat Mark Sandrich, 1935

U.S. (RKO) 101m BW **Producer** Pandro S. Berman **Screenplay** Allan Scott, Dwight Taylor **Photography** David Abel **Music** Irving Berlin, Max Steiner **Cast** Fred Astaire, Ginger Rogers, Edward Everett Horton, Erik Rhodes, Eric Blore, Helen Broderick **Oscar nominations** Pandro S. Berman (best picture), Carroll Clark, Van Nest Polglase (art direction), Irving Berlin (music), Hermes Pan (dance)

There is no clear-cut classic among the Fred Astaire–Ginger Rogers musicals of the mid-1930s—all are mostly marvelous with crucial flaws—but *Top Hat* probably comes the closest. Its plot follows the series' basic formula: Fred instantly falls for Ginger, but a silly misunderstanding (here, she mistakes him for his married friend) stokes her hostility until the final moments.

The director is the underrated Mark Sandrich, whose impeccably superficial touch maximizes the swanky, syncopated slickness so essential to the series. The film's most famous number is "Top Hat," featuring fancy canework among Fred and a chorus of top-hatted gents, but the heart of *Top Hat* is its two great romantic duets, "Isn't It a Lovely Day" and "Cheek to Cheek," the first set on a London bandstand during a thunderstorm, the second beside the sparkling canals of RKO's goofily glossy Art Deco version of Venice. Such dances, with their progression from resistance to surrender, are Fred's main weapon in winning over Ginger, but it would be a mistake to read this process as simple sexual conquest. As Ginger's suppressed amusement makes clear, the two characters approach their respective roles of hot-to-trot and hard-to-get with playful irony, collaborating to prolong and intensify a deliciously elegant erotic game. **MR**

Peter Ibbertson Henry Hathaway, 1935

U.S. (Paramount Pictures) 88m BW **Producer** Louis D. Lighton **Screenplay** Vincent Lawrence, Waldemar Young **Photography** Charles Lang **Music** Ernst Toch **Cast** Gary Cooper, Ann Harding, John Halliday, Ida Lupino, Douglass Dumbrille, Virginia Weidler, Dickie Moore, Doris Lloyd, Gilbert Emery, Donald Meek, Christian Rub, Elisa Buchanan **Oscar nominations** Irvin Talbot (Score)

Henry Hathaway's romantic drama remains one of the more bizarre American productions of the 1930s. A tale of love stymied by class divisions, it might have been just another studio potboiler, was it not for the curious twist facing the lovers in the film's final act.

Gogo and Mimsey are childhood sweethearts who are separated when the boy's mother dies. Despatched to England, Gogo grows up as Peter Ibbertson (Gary Cooper). A trained architect, Peter is hired to design a building for the Duke of Towers but instead embarks on an affair with his wife, only to find out that Mary (Ann Harding) is really Mimsey. The Duke discovers them together and, following a struggle, is killed by Peter in self-defense. A court sentences him to life in prison. But bars cannot separate Peter and Mary, who are reunited every night in their dreams.

Salvador Dalí may have made the biggest splash of any surrealist artist in Hollywood when he worked on Hitchcock's *Spellbound* (1945), but Hathaway's film best channels the spirit of the movement. The early scenes are solid, with the leads convincing as a couple who were meant to be together. But there is no indication of the magnificent extended dream sequence that will follow Peter's incarceration. Described by André Breton as "a triumph of surrealist thought," *Peter Ibbertson*'s unashamedly romantic sweep and sheer loopiness has few equals. **IHS**

Modern Times Charles Chaplin, 1936

Modern Times was the last film in which Chaplin portrayed the character of the Little Tramp, which he had created in 1914 and which had brought him universal fame and affection. In the years between, the world had changed. When the Little Tramp was born, the nineteenth century was still close. In 1936, in the aftermath of the Great Depression, he confronted anxieties that are not so different from those of the twenty-first century— poverty, unemployment, strikes and strike breakers, political intolerance, economic inequalities, the tyranny of the machine, and narcotics.

These were problems with which Chaplin had become acutely preoccupied in the course of an eighteen-month world tour in 1931–32, when he had observed the rise of nationalism and the social effects of the Depression, unemployment, and automation. In 1931, he declared to a newspaper interviewer, "Unemployment is the vital question. . . . Machinery should benefit mankind. It should not spell tragedy and throw it out of work." Exposing these problems to the searchlight of comedy, Chaplin transforms the Little Tramp into one of the millions working in factories throughout the world. He is first seen as a worker driven crazy by his monotonous, inhuman job on a conveyor belt and being used as a guinea pig to test a machine to feed workers as they perform their tasks. Exceptionally, the Little Tramp finds a companion in his battle with this new world—a young girl (Paulette Goddard) whose father has been killed in a strike and who joins forces with Chaplin. The two are neither rebels nor victims, wrote Chaplin, but "the only two live spirits in a world of automatons."

Conceived in four "acts," each one equivalent to one of his old two-reel comedies, *Modern Times* shows Chaplin still at his unrivaled peak as a creator of visual comedy. By the time *Modern Times* was released, talking pictures had been established for almost a decade. Chaplin considered using dialogue and even prepared a script, but he finally recognized that the Little Tramp depended on silent pantomime. At one moment, though, his voice is heard, when, hired as a singing waiter, he improvises the song in a wonderful, mock-Italian gibberish. **DR**

U.S. (Charles Chaplin, United Artists)
87m BW **Producer** Charles Chaplin
Screenplay Charles Chaplin
Photography Ira H. Morgan, Roland Totheroh **Music** Charles Chaplin
Cast Charles Chaplin, Paulette Goddard, Henry Bergman, Tiny Sandford, Chester Conklin, Hank Mann, Stanley Blystone, Al Ernest Garcia, Richard Alexander, Cecil Reynolds, Mira McKinney, Murdock MacQuarrie, Wilfred Lucas, Edward LeSaint, Fred Malatesta

> "*In* Modern Times *Chaplin proves again what the whole world already acknowledges —that he is the greatest artist of the silent screen.*"

The Guardian, 1936

ℹ️

In the film, human voices are only ever heard through mechanical objects, such as radios or phonographs.

Swing Time George Stevens, 1936

A song-and-dance fantasia, George Stevens's *Swing Time* is an audiovisual spectacle organized around a backstage musical. Certainly a high-water mark for the mid-1930s, the film is equally a tease of things to come in the combination of Fred Astaire and Ginger Rogers.

Assembled by legendary RKO producer Pandro S. Berman, *Swing Time* is the story of Lucky Garnett (Fred Astaire), a well-regarded hoofer engaged to the pleasant, though uninspiring, Margaret Watson (Betty Furness). When he's forced to secure a large dowry to continue with his betrothal, their matrimonial plans are put on hold so he can seek his fortune in New York City. Once there, he meets Penny (Ginger Rogers), his true love, and thereafter the film more or less works through various disturbances before allowing them to fall into one another's arms.

Naturally, there are several scenes of mistaken intent, a few nontragic plot turns, and a happy ending, despite brief periods of sorrow and hand-wringing. Yet the purpose of the film is undeniably the presentation of its musical numbers, several of which form part of the generic canon. Jerome Kern wrote the music, while Dorothy Fields provided most of the lyrics. Their combined efforts form the soundtrack's foundation, although the sheer energy, verve, and happy distraction of Astaire and Rogers is what makes every number shine with the addition of movement and tap shoes.

Highlights include Lucky's two solos in "The Way You Look Tonight," a nightclub standard, and "Never Gonna Dance," a sorrowfully ironic song given the actor's well-recognized talent for walking on air. Two duets expand the big-screen canvas in "Waltz in Swing Time" with Astaire and Rogers and, of course, their famous performance of "A Fine Romance." But the showstopper of the picture may well be "Bojangles of Harlem." Here, Lucky begins his performance from within an accompanying chorus while dressed in blackface. Definitely a nod to his training and heritage, if also an antiquated, possibly offensive bit of cultural history, the number builds to a climax of Astaire dancing in triplicate with rear-projection versions of himself. **GC-Q**

U.S. (RKO) 103m BW **Producer** Pandro S. Berman **Screenplay** Erwin Gelsey, Howard Lindsay, Allan Scott, from the story "Portrait of John Garnett" by Elwin Gelsey **Photography** David Abel **Music** Jerome Kern, Dorothy Fields **Cast** Fred Astaire, Ginger Rogers, Victor Moore, Helen Broderick, Eric Blore, Betty Furness, Georges Metaxa **Oscar** Jerome Kern, Dorothy Fields (music) **Oscar nomination** Hermes Pan (dance)

"My talent is gambling, Pop. Hoofing is all right, but there's no future in it."

**John "Lucky" Garnett
(Fred Astaire) to "Pop" Cardetti
(Victor Moore)**

i

"Never Gonna Dance" took nearly fifty takes to nail. Rogers's feet were bleeding by the end.

Mr. Deeds Goes to Town Frank Capra, 1936

U.S. (Columbia) 115m BW **Producer** Frank
Capra **Screenplay** Clarence Budington
Kelland, Robert Riskin **Photography** Joseph
Walker **Music** Howard Jackson **Cast** Gary
Cooper, Jean Arthur, George Bancroft, Lionel
Stander, Douglass Dumbrille, Raymond
Walburn, H.B. Warner, Ruth Donnelly, Walter
Catlett, John Wray **Oscar** Frank Capra
(director) **Oscar nominations** Frank Capra
(best picture), Robert Riskin (screenplay),
Gary Cooper (actor), John P. Livadary (sound)

i

Jean Arthur didn't actually get to see
the film until 1972, when she viewed
it with Frank Capra at a film festival.

Mr. Deeds Goes to Town is the film that invented the screwball comedy
and solidified director Frank Capra's vision of American life, with a support
of small-town, traditional values against self-serving city sophistication.

Longfellow Deeds (Gary Cooper) is a poet from rural Vermont whose
life changes, and not for the better, when he suddenly inherits the estate
of his multimillionaire uncle, whose New York lawyers (used to skimming
funds for their own use) try to convince him to keep them on the payroll.
But after several misadventures and a trip to Manhattan, Deeds is
convinced that the money will do him no good and tries to give it away,
intending to endow a rural commune for displaced farmers. The lawyers
immediately take him to court, claiming he is insane, for no one in their
right mind would give away so much money. Crucial to Deeds's eventual
deliverance is Babe Bennett (Jean Arthur), a wisecracking reporter who
first exploits the hick's naïveté in order to write scathing exclusives about
the "Cinderella Man." Babe is transformed by Deeds's idealism, however,
and her testimony sways the court in the poor man's favor.

Filled with bright comic moments (Deeds playing the tuba to clear
his mind, feeding donuts to horses), *Mr. Deeds Goes to Town* is a hymn
to antimaterialism and the simple country life in the best manner of
Henry David Thoreau. **RBP**

My Man Godfrey Gregory La Cava, 1936

As one of the masters of sophisticated salon comedies, Gregory La Cava might not have had the most aching social consciousness in 1930s Hollywood. But he had a knack for satire with a social and political edge that is clearly visible in films such as *Gabriel over the White House* (1933), *She Married Her Boss* (1935), and especially *My Man Godfrey*, his most memorable work. Made at the end of the Depression era, this screwball classic deals with poor bum Godfrey (William Powell) being hired as a butler as part of a high-society party game on Park Avenue. Some hundred snappy lines later he has taken complete control over the rich people's house, charmed the beautiful Irene (Carole Lombard), exposed her birdbrained mother's boy toy (well, he is called "protégé" because of the Production Code) as a con man, and helped her grumpy father avoid bankruptcy and prison for fraud.

Not surprisingly, it is revealed that Godfrey himself had only been slumming as a hobo when the rich party found him, and so he can marry the socialite of his dreams. However, by then the upper class have been paraded in front of the camera as a bunch of narcissistic, infantile idiots. No doubt this was one reason for the film's great success with a mass audience in those days. *My Man Godfrey* loses some of its bite in the second half, when the fairy-tale ingredient takes over and ends the film on a silly note: that money is not everything! But even then it manages to captivate its audience by the sheer intelligence of its witty screenplay penned by novelist Eric Hatch and Morrie Ryskind. It has the true mark of a great film by not having a single bad line or weak character. La Cava's pacing is sometimes strikingly fast, delivering machine-gun tongue dueling in virtually every scene and applying a narrative economy so effortless that the film could serve as a prototype for classic Hollywood cinema. Though it premiered nearly seventy years ago, *My Man Godfrey* still holds up in a remarkable way and could easily be remade for any audience. **MT**

U.S. (Universal) 94m BW **Producer** Gregory La Cava, Charles R. Rogers **Screenplay** Eric Hatch, Morrie Ryskind, from novel by Eric Hatch **Photography** Ted Tetzlaff **Music** Charles Previn, Rudy Schrager **Cast** William Powell, Carole Lombard, Alice Brady, Gail Patrick, Eugene Pallette, Alan Mowbray, Jean Dixon, Molly, Mischa Auer, Carlo, Robert Light, Pat Flaherty **Oscar nominations** Gregory La Cava (director), Eric Hatch, Morrie Ryskind (screenplay), William Powell (actor), Mischa Auer (actor in support role), Carole Lombard (actress), Alice Brady (actress in support role)

> *"Tommy, there's a very peculiar mental process called thinking—you wouldn't know much about that . . ."*

Godfrey (William Powell)

ℹ️

Powell and Lombard were married for two years. They divorced three years before shooting this movie together.

Le roman d'un tricheur
Sacha Guitry, 1936
The Story of a Cheat

France (Cinéas) 85m BW
Language French Producer Serge
Sandberg Screenplay Sacha Guitry
Photography Marcel Lucien Music Adolphe
Borchard Cast Sacha Guitry, Marguerite
Moreno, Jacqueline Delubac, Roger
Duchesne, Rosine Deréan, Elmire Vautier,
Serge Grave, Pauline Carton, Fréhel, Pierre
Labry, Pierre Assy, Henri Pfeifer,
Gaston Dupray

Widely regarded as Sacha Guitry's masterpiece (though it has competition in 1937's *Pearls of the Crown*), this 1936 tour de force can be regarded as a kind of concerto for the writer-director-performer's special brand of brittle cleverness. After a credits sequence that introduces us to the film's cast and crew, *The Story of a Cheat* settles into a flashback account of how the title hero (played by Guitry himself) learned to benefit from cheating over the course of his life.

A notoriously anticinematic moviemaker whose first love was theater, Guitry nevertheless had a flair for cinematic antics when it came to adapting his plays (or in this case his novel *Memoires d'un Tricheur*) to film. *The Story of a Cheat* registers as a rather lively and stylishly inventive silent movie, with Guitry's character serving as offscreen lecturer. François Truffaut was sufficiently impressed to dub Guitry a French brother of Ernst Lubitsch, though Guitry clearly differs from this master of continental romance in the way his own personality invariably overwhelms that of his characters. **JS**

1936

Camille
George Cukor, 1936

U.S. (MGM) 109m BW Producer David
Lewis, Bernard H. Hyman Screenplay Zoe
Akins, from the novel and play *La Dame aux
camélias* by Alexandre Dumas, fils
Photography William H. Daniels, Karl Freund
Music Herbert Stothart, Edward Ward
Cast Greta Garbo, Robert Taylor, Lionel
Barrymore, Elizabeth Allan, Jessie Ralph,
Henry Daniell, Lenore Ulric, Laura Hope
Crews, Rex O'Malley Oscar nomination
Greta Garbo (actress)

George Cukor's *Camille* is one of the triumphs of early sound cinema, a showcase of superb acting from principals Greta Garbo and Robert Taylor, with able support from studio stalwarts Lionel Barrymore and Henry Daniell. Cukor evokes just enough of mid-nineteenth-century Paris to render affecting the melodramatic stylization of what is perhaps the most famous popular play ever written, adapted for the stage by Alexandre Dumas, fils, from his sensational novel. With its witty and suggestive dialogue, the script makes the novelist's characters come alive for an American audience of another era.

Marguerite Gautier (Garbo), called Camille because of her love for the camellia, is a "courtesan" who falls in love with her "companion," Armand Duval (Taylor), scion of an influential family. Their relationship, which can never be legitimized because of her dubious background, must come to an end and does so in two famous scenes that actresses have always relished. First, Armand's father persuades Camille that she must give him up so that he can pursue a diplomatic career. Heartbroken, she dismisses Armand with the lie that he no longer interests her. Armand returns later to find her on her deathbed, where she expires while he weeps uncontrollably. The Breen Office, charged with the task of enforcing the industry's then-reactionary Production Code, must also have been moved by this story of prohibited and tragic love, requiring only a scene in which the romantic pair, technically "illicit," vow their undying love to one another. **RBP**

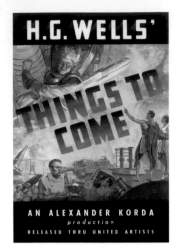

G.B. (London) 100m BW
Producer Alexander Korda **Screenplay** H.G.
Wells from his novel *The Shape of Things to
Come* **Photography** Georges Périnal
Music Arthur Bliss **Cast** Raymond Massey,
Edward Chapman, Ralph Richardson,
Margaretta Scott, Cedric Hardwicke, Maurice
Braddell, Sophie Stewart, Derrick De Marney,
Ann Todd, Pearl Argyle, Kenneth Villiers,
Ivan Brandt, Anne McLaren,
Patricia Hilliard, Charles Carson

*"If we don't end war,
war will end us."*

John Cabal
(Raymond Massey)

Things to Come William Cameron Menzies, 1936

William Cameron Menzies' screen version of H.G. Wells's speculations about the world's future after a disastrous second World War destroys European civilization is perhaps the first true science-fiction film. Only Fritz Lang's *Metropolis* (1927) anticipates its envisioning of the future as a result of technological change and resulting political evolution, but Lang's film doesn't offer a similarly detailed analysis of the new course history might take. In fact, few science-fiction movies are as concerned as is *Things to Come* with a rigorously historical approach to fictionalized prophecy, and this is perhaps because Wells himself penned the screenplay, based on ideas found in his popular tome *The Outline of History*.

Neither Wells nor Menzies took much interest in character-driven narrative (the main characters all represent important ideas), and so the film has seemed distant and uninvolving to many, an effect exacerbated by the fact that the story covers a full century of history. The second European war lasts twenty-five years and manages to destroy most of the world, which regresses to something like the cutthroat feudalism of the early Middle Ages. But human progress is inevitable, thanks to the fact that the intellectual and rational element in man always proves superior to the innate human urge toward self-destruction. *Things to Come* thus offers a more optimistic twist on Freud's understanding of the conflict between Eros and Thanatos, love and death, in human affairs.

The film's later sequences, as in *Metropolis*, are dominated by a vision of the city of the future. It was in his handling of these architectural and art-design aspects of the film that Menzies made his most significant and telling contribution. Despite its episodic narrative, *Things to Come* is visually spectacular, a predecessor of other science-fiction films that imagine the urban future, including Ridley Scott's *Blade Runner* (1982).

Despite the presence of well-known actors, what is most memorable about this unusual film is its engagement with a philosophy of history and of human nature. It captures the anxieties and hopes of 1930s Britain perfectly, chillingly forecasting the blitz that would descend upon London only four years after its release. **RBP**

i

The most costly British production of its time, *Things to Come* flopped at the box office.

Dodsworth William Wyler, 1936

U.S. (Samuel Goldwyn) 101m BW
Producer Samuel Goldwyn, Merritt Hulburd
Screenplay Sidney Howard, from novel by
Sinclair Lewis **Photography** Rudolph Maté
Cast Walter Huston, Ruth Chatterton, Paul
Lukas, Mary Astor, David Niven, Gregory
Gaye, Maria Ouspenskaya, Odette Myrtil,
Spring Byington, Harlan Briggs, Kathryn
Marlowe, John Payne **Oscar** Richard Day
(art direction) **Oscar nominations** Samuel
Goldwyn, Merritt Hulburd (best picture),
William Wyler (director), Sidney Howard
(screenplay), Walter Huston (actor),
Maria Ouspenskaya (actress in support role),
Oscar Lagerstrom (sound)

William Wyler's compelling adaptation of Sinclair Lewis's novel about the dissolution of a wealthy American couple's marriage represents the height of intelligent Hollywood filmmaking. Walter Huston plays the title character, an automobile mogul, who, after selling his business, must face the challenges of an opulent retirement and decides to take a grand tour of Europe with his wife, Fran (Ruth Chatterton). They leave the United States to discover continental culture and refinement. In Europe, the two discover that each wants something different from life, though in their own ways both want to stave off old age. Fran becomes involved in flirtations with playboys who roam the periphery of the rich and fashionable set. She becomes increasingly impatient with Dodsworth's stubbornly American, provincial ways. Dodsworth cannot reconcile with Fran and desperately fears becoming useless. On the journey they meet Edith Cortright (Mary Astor), an American expatriate who has found a new way to live and remain vibrant, and who can offer Dodsworth a solution.

The most remarkable aspects of the film are its moral complexity and its bittersweet tone. Wyler takes care not to portray Fran wholly as the villain; we are made to understand and sympathize with both husband and wife. Some of the most poignant moments of *Dodsworth* take place when Fran sees the illusory life that she has been trying to create fall apart around her. At a time when mainstream American filmmaking all seems to be aimed at the tastes of fourteen-year-old boys, *Dodsworth* is a welcome reminder that Hollywood once made films for adults. **RH**

i

Astor, who was going through a much-publicized divorce, sometimes slept on the set to evade the press.

Une partie de campagne Jean Renoir, 1936
A Day in the Country

France (Pantheon) 40m BW
Language French Director Jean Renoir
Producer Pierre Braunberger
Screenplay Jean Renoir, from story by Guy de Maupassant Photography Jean Bourgoin, Claude Renoir Music Joseph Kosma Cast Sylvia Bataille, Georges St. Saens, Jane Marken, André Gabriello, Jacques B. Brunius, Paul Temps, Gabrielle Fontan, Jean Renoir, Marguerite Renoir

One of the most powerful and unsettling devices in film fiction is the "years later" epilogue, which usually takes us, with wistful sadness, from the concentrated time of a story in which everything was briefly possible, to the singular destiny that ensued. At the end of Jean Renoir's *A Day in the Country*, Henriette (Sylvia Bataille) is seen unhappily married to the man with whom she was betrothed at the start, the gormless clerk Anatole (Paul Temps). But in between these points, nothing is so fixed or certain.

Adapted from the story of the same name by Guy de Maupassant, the film was unfinished in the form originally envisaged by Renoir. It stands, however, as a self-sufficient gem. Its central action is devoted to the illicit pairing off of two local adventurers, Rodolphe (Jacques Borel) and Henri (Georges D'Arnoux), with Henriette and her mother, Juliette (Jeanne Marken). Renoir constructs a superb diagram of contrasts between these characters: Rodolphe and Juliette are lusty and frivolous, while Henri and Henriette are overwhelmed by grave emotion. So what started, in Henriette's words, as "a sort of vague desire" that calls forth both the beauty and harshness of nature, ends badly, as the "years pass, with Sundays as melancholy as Mondays." **AM**

Pépé le Moko Julien Duvivier, 1937

France (Paris) 90m BW Language French
Producer Raymond Hakim, Robert Hakim
Screenplay Jacques Constant, Julien Duvivier Photography Marc Fossard, Jules Kruger Music Vincent Scotto, Mohamed Ygerbuchen Cast Jean Gabin, Mireille Balin, Gabriel Gabrio, Lucas Gridoux, Gilbert Gil, Line Noro, Saturnin Fabre, Fernand Charpin, Marcel Dalio, Charles Granval, Gaston Modot, René Bergeron, Paul Escoffier, Roger Legris, Jean Témerson

Pépé le Moko was the film that consolidated Jean Gabin's stardom and defined his on-screen persona as a tough, streetwise character, outwardly cynical but with an underlying romantic streak that will cause his downfall. As Pépé, an expatriate French hood who has become top dog in the Casbah (the Arab quarter of Algiers), he relishes his power but yearns nostalgically for Paris. When a beautiful French tourist (Mireille Balin), the embodiment of his longed-for homeland, catches his eye, the temptation becomes too great. But once outside the Casbah he's vulnerable because there a tireless policeman (Lucas Gridoux) lies in wait.

Director Julien Duvivier's skill at evoking atmosphere creates a vivid (if romanticized) vision of the Casbah, an exotic labyrinth of twisting alleyways full of pungent detail. Borrowing motifs from the classic Hollywood gangster movies, but seasoning them with doomy Gallic romanticism, *Pépé le Moko* prefigures film noir. Images of bars, grilles, and fences recur throughout the film, underlining Pépé's entrapment within his little fiefdom. The movie is pervaded by a mood of longing, of lost youthful dreams, and of desires that can never be fulfilled. This fatalism led to its being banned during the war by the Vichy regime, but its warm reception after this temporary absence only confirmed its status as a classic. **PK**

1937

Make Way for Tomorrow Leo McCarey, 1937

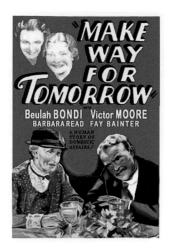

In this one-of-a-kind masterpiece by one of the greatest American directors, Victor Moore and Beulah Bondi play Bark and Lucy Cooper, an elderly couple faced with financial disaster and forced to throw themselves on the mercy of their middle-aged children. The children's first step is to separate the two of them so that the inconvenience of hosting them can be divided. Gradually, the old people's self-confidence and dignity are eroded, until they submit to an arrangement whereby one of them will stay in a nursing home in New York, and the other will go to California.

Leo McCarey's direction in *Make Way for Tomorrow* is beyond praise. All of the actors are expansive and natural, and the generosity McCarey shows toward his characters is unstinting. He demonstrates an exquisite sense of when to cut from his central couple to reveal the attitudes of others, without suggesting either that their compassion is condescending or that their indifference is wicked, and without forcing our tears or rage (which would be a way of forfeiting them). There is nothing contrived about McCarey's handling of the story, and thus no escaping its poignancy.

Two examples will suffice to indicate the film's extraordinary discretion. During the painful sequence in which Lucy's presence inadvertently interferes with her daughter-in-law's attempt to host a bridge party, Lucy receives a phone call from Bark. Because she talks loudly on the phone—one of several annoying traits that McCarey and screenwriter Viña Delmar don't hesitate to give the elderly couple—the guests pause in their games to listen. Their reactions (not emphasized, but merely shown) mix annoyance, discomfort, and sorrow.

The last section of the film, dealing with the couple's brief reuniting and impromptu last idyll in Manhattan, is sublime. McCarey keeps us aware of the sympathy of outsiders (a car salesman, a coat-check girl, a hotel manager, a bandleader), but never imposes their reactions on us through superfluous reverse shots. Meanwhile, Lucy and Bark are constantly shown together in the same compositions. In its passionate commitment to their private universe, *Make Way for Tomorrow* is truly, deeply moving. **CFu**

U.S. (Paramount) 91m BW
Producer Leo McCarey, Adolph Zukor
Screenplay Viña Delmar, from the novel *The Years Are So Long* by Josephine Lawrence **Photography** William C. Mellor
Music George Antheil, Victor Young, Sam Coslow, Leo Robin, Jean Schwartz
Cast Victor Moore, Beulah Bondi, Fay Bainter, Thomas Mitchell, Porter Hall, Barbara Read, Maurice Moscovitch, Elisabeth Risdon, Minna Gombell, Ray Mayer, Ralph Remley, Louise Beavers, Louis Jean Heydt, Gene Morgan

> *"Thanks, but you gave this to me for the wrong picture."*

Leo McCarey, accepting his Oscar for *The Awful Truth*, 1937

1937

i

Beulah Bondi (b.1889) was younger than Elizabeth Risdon (b.1887), who played her daughter Cora.

La grande illusion Jean Renoir, 1937
Grand Illusion

France (R.A.C.) 114m BW
Language French / German / English
Producer Albert Pinkovitch, Frank Rollmer
Screenplay Jean Renoir, Charles Spaak
Photography Christian Matras
Music Joseph Kosma **Cast** Jean Gabin, Dita
Parlo, Pierre Fresnay, Erich von Stroheim,
Julien Carette, Georges Péclet, Werner
Florian, Jean Dasté, Sylvain Itkine, Gaston
Modot, Marcel Dalio **Oscar nomination**
Frank Rollmer, Albert Pinkovitch
(best picture) **Venice Film Festival**
Jean Renoir (overall artistic contribution),
Jean Renoir (Mussolini Cup nomination)

*"The theater's too
deep for me. I prefer
bicycling."*

**Lieutenant Maréchal
(Jean Gabin)**

Sometimes it takes the horrors of war to reveal the things we all have in common. That humanistic irony is the central conceit of Jean Renoir's masterpiece *La Grand Illusion*, a film set during World War I that finds levity and fraternity in a German POW camp. Lieutenant Maréchal (Jean Gabin) and Captain de Boeldieu (Pierre Fresnay) are two French officers making the best of their situation with their men, under the watchful eye of the polite German commandant von Rauffenstein (Erich von Stroheim). They've developed a mirror image of aristocratic society based on honor and order, a system of mutual respect and protocol based on years of tradition.

But it's only an oasis—or, more specifically, a mirage—in the midst of devastating conflict, hence the title of the film: The grand illusion is that somehow class and upbringing sets these officers above the commonness of war, when in fact bullets don't know one bloodline from another. They tirelessly dig an escape tunnel without considering that once they return to freedom, the false camaraderie encouraged by incarceration will once again revert to the harsh realities of life.

One of the most poignant aspects of *La Grand Illusion* is the feeling that the central characters understand this truth all too well yet subconsciously wish things could be different. You can sense that von Stroheim's melancholy commandant really wishes he were socializing with the French officers under different, less severe circumstances. In the POW camp, Rosenthal (Marcel Dalio) is one of the guys. On the outside, he's just a Jew, a jarring reminder of the imminent evils of World War II. In fact, the Germans later banned *La Grand Illusion* during their eventual occupation of France, so effective was its ever timely humanistic vision. That Renoir's remarkable film, with all its memorable characters, thought-provoking themes, and engaging dialogue, could have been lost forever because of its political viewpoint is a pointed reminder of the power of cinema and the ability of fiction to convey the kind of profound truths and moral guidelines that we use and need to direct our lives. **JKl**

1937

ℹ️
In the movie, Gabin wears the
uniform that Renoir had worn as
an aviator during World War I.

Stella Dallas King Vidor, 1937

U.S. (Samuel Goldwyn) 105m BW
Producer Samuel Goldwyn, Merritt Hulburd
Screenplay Joe Bigelow, Harry Wagstaff
Gribble, Sarah Y. Mason, Gertrude Purcell,
Victor Heerman, from novel by Olive Higgins
Prouty Photography Rudolph Maté
Music Alfred Newman Cast Barbara
Stanwyck, John Boles, Anne Shirley, Barbara
O'Neil, Alan Hale, Marjorie Main, George
Walcott, Ann Shoemaker, Tim Holt, Nella
Walker, Bruce Satterlee, Jimmy Butler, Jack
Egger, Dickie Jones Oscars Barbara
Stanwyck (actress), Anne Shirley (actress in
support role)

Stella Dallas offers a lively portrait of a working-class woman strong enough to sacrifice herself for her daughter's advancement. Olive Higgins Prouty's novel had been filmed successfully in 1925. But unlike Henry King's silent version, Vidor's has the advantage of Barbara Stanwyck in the title role.

Stanwyck plays Stella as a resilient, glamorous, intelligent woman. It's easy to understand why well-to-do Stephen Dallas (John Boles) finds her attractive. Not long after the birth of their daughter Laurel (Anne Shirley), however, he wants to return to his former girlfriend. Stella raises Laurel on her own, but as a teenager Laurel finds herself attracted to her father's more affluent lifestyle and wants to live with him. Stella relents, forcing her daughter to leave by pretending to be drunk and no longer interested in the young woman's company. Laurel decamps to her father's house and is soon married to a socialite at a huge wedding that her mother glimpses, tears streaming down her face, through a window from the street. Never again will she cross the social divide separating her from Laurel. A moving and heartfelt story, under Vidor's able direction *Stella Dallas* never descends into mawkish sentimentality. **RBP**

Ye ban ge sheng Ma-Xu Weibang, 1937
Midnight Song

China (Xinhua) 123m BW
Language Mandarin Director Ma-Xu
Weibang Producer Shankun Zhang
Screenplay Weibang Ma-Xu
Photography Boqing Xue, Xingsan Yu
Music Xinghai Xian (song) Cast Menqhe Gu,
Ping Hu, Shan Jin, Chao Shi

Gaston Leroux's 1919 novel *The Phantom of the Opera* gave rise to a score of films. Ma-Xu Weibang's *Midnight Song* is unarguably one of the most inspired. It establishes its dark and eerie mood from the start, with the arrival of a touring opera company at a dilapidated theater, which they learn has been empty and crumbling since the apparent death there of the great opera star Song Danping, ten years before. The company's young star is rehearsing alone in the theater when he hears a beautiful voice, which coaches him through his song. It is the fugitive Song Danping, now dreadfully disfigured, who relates his tragic story, shown in flashback. His physical state was inflicted on him on the orders of an evil feudal lord, angry at Song's love for his daughter. Since then he has hidden in the theater, awaiting a singer who can assume his mantle and perform his great operatic creation. The young singer is chosen and also made envoy to Song's lost love, Li Xiaoxia, whose mind has broken from sorrow. The difference from Western versions of Leroux is that the Phantom, instead of being a lurking menace, becomes a sympathetic, benevolent protagonist.

All this is staged in richly atmospheric settings, with a masterly use of light and shadow clearly inspired by German Expressionist cinema. An important element in the film's immense popularity were the songs, which have remained popular standards in China. In 1941, Ma-Xu was obliged to make a sequel, *Midnight Song II*, and the film has also inspired two Hong Kong remakes, *Mid-Nightmare* (1962) and *The Phantom Lover* (1995). **DR**

1937

Snow White and the Seven Dwarfs

William Cottrell, David Hand, Wilfred Jackson, Larry Morey, Perce Pearce, & Ben Sharpsteen, 1937

Snow White and the Seven Dwarfs begins with a slow zoom to a huge castle, where the wicked Queen queries her magic mirror with the immortal words, "Magic mirror, on the wall, who's the fairest one of all?" The answer, of course, is her virginal rival, Snow White, soon to be the target of her vanity. Like the classic Brothers Grimm story *Snow White* is based on, you are instantly pulled into this magical and sometime scary world. Yet at the time Hollywood considered Walt Disney's first foray into full-length feature animation something of a folly. Who would sit through a ninety-minute animated film?

Needless to say, *Snow White* answered that rhetorical question by becoming one of the biggest hits in the history of cinema, solidifying Disney's claim as the world's foremost animation studio. Walt Disney had already broken the cartoon sound barrier with *Steamboat Willy* in 1928, and a few years later brought animation into vivid color. *Snow White* was merely the next step forward both artistically as well as financially: feature films meant more box-office sales.

Using the Brothers Grimm story as inspiration, Disney unleashed his team of animators on the material, giving them a great deal of freedom in the development of such a creative breakthrough. The film is peppered with gags but also filled with emotion, comprising a soaring combination of beautiful images and strong, enduring songs like "Whistle While You Work" and "Some Day My Prince Will Come." *Snow White*, incidentally, also marked the first commercially released soundtrack.

There is no way to overestimate the effect of *Snow White*. It not only permanently established Disney as one of the foremost studios in the world but also advanced the state of animation to such a degree that it wasn't really until the advent of computer animation that anyone arguably pushed the form further. A creative triumph, *Snow White* inspired hundreds of imitators, gave birth to an empire, and remains to this day the default template for nearly all animated features. **JKl**

U.S. (Walt Disney) 83m Technicolor
Producer Walt Disney **Screenplay** Ted Sears, Richard Creedon **Photography** Maxwell Morgan **Music** Frank Churchill, Leigh Harline, Paul J. Smith **Cast** Roy Atwell, Stuart Buchanan, Adriana Caselotti, Eddie Collins, Pinto Colvig, Marion Darlington, Billy Gilbert, Otis Harlan, Lucille La Verne, James MacDonald, Scotty Mattraw, Moroni Olsen, Harry Stockwell **Oscar** (honorary award—one statuette, seven miniature statuettes) **Oscar nomination** Frank Churchill, Leigh Harline, Paul J. Smith (music)

"Ah, here it is! 'The Victim of the Sleeping Death can be revived only by Love's First Kiss.' 'Love's First Kiss.' Bah! No fear of that. "

Queen
(voiced by Lucille La Verne)

[*i*]

Sergei Eisenstein once stated that he felt *Snow White* to be the greatest movie ever produced.

Captains Courageous Victor Fleming, 1937

U.S. (MGM) 115m BW Producer Louis D. Lighton Screenplay Marc Connelly, John Lee Mahin, Dale Van Every, from novel by Rudyard Kipling Photography Harold Rosson Music Franz Waxman Cast Freddie Bartholomew, Spencer Tracy, Lionel Barrymore, Melvyn Douglas, Charley Grapewin, Mickey Rooney, John Carradine, Oscar O'Shea, Jack La Rue, Walter Kingsford, Donald Briggs, Sam McDaniel, Bill Burrud Oscar Spencer Tracy (actor) Oscar nominations Louis D. Lighton (best picture), Marc Connelly, John Lee Mahin, Dale Van Every (screenplay), Elmo Veron (editing)

i

Tracy's "Portuguese" impression was based on a Yiddish accent he had used in his early days in the theater.

Rudyard Kipling, who died in 1936, did not live long enough to see three of his books adapted for the screen the following year, including Victor Fleming's rousing childhood epic *Captains Courageous*. Freddie Bartholomew stars as Harvey Cheyne, a spoiled rich kid who, after drinking six ice cream sodas, falls off the ocean liner on which he and his father (Melvyn Douglas) are traveling. He has the good fortune to be picked up by a fishing boat out of Gloucester, whose crew, including the good-natured Manuel Fidello (Spencer Tracy), is unimpressed by his wealth and "position." Humiliated, Harvey is left to his own resources, but under Manuel's careful tutelage he learns the value of hard work and real accomplishment. Before they can return to port, however, Manuel dies in an accident. In port, Harvey is met by his father yet wants to stay with the fishermen, but after a moving memorial for his dead friend, father and son are reconciled.

Child star Bartholomew is excellent in a role that requires him to be both obnoxious and irresistible. And Spencer Tracy, his hair curled and face brown with makeup, does an excellent imitation of a Portuguese sailor. With humor, pathos, and an interesting moral, this is one of the best children's movies Hollywood ever produced. **RBP**

137

The Awful Truth Leo McCarey, 1937

U.S. (Columbia) 91m BW **Producer** Leo
McCarey, Everett Riskin **Screenplay** Viña
Delmar, from play by Arthur Richman
Photography Joseph Walker **Music** Ben
Oakland, George Parrish **Cast** Irene Dunne,
Cary Grant, Ralph Bellamy, Alexander D'Arcy,
Cecil Cunningham, Molly Lamont, Esther
Dale, Joyce Compton, Robert Allen, Robert
Warwick, Mary Forbes **Oscar** Leo McCarey
(director) **Oscar nominations** Leo McCarey,
Everett Riskin (best picture), Viña Delmar
(screenplay), Irene Dunne (actress),
Ralph Bellamy (actor in support role),
Al Clark (editing)

*"In the spring, a young
man's fancy lightly
turns to what he's been
thinking about all winter."*

Jerry Warriner
(Cary Grant)

The terrier—"Mr. Smith"—was Skippy,
who played Asta, the pet of Nick and
Nora Charles in the *Thin Man* series.

The legend of Leo McCarey's *The Awful Truth* is that it was largely improvised from day to day. This legend is perfectly in tune with the ethos of the film itself, in which spontaneity, playfulness, the ability to laugh at one's own "act" (as well as to see it with the eye of the person who is seeing right through you at that moment) are so central to its glorious, warm sense of humor as well as its exploration of how to make marriage work.

But the script structure, however it was arrived at, is satisfying. It starts with a rupture: Jerry (Cary Grant) and Lucy (Irene Dunne), believing they have caught each other in infidelities, lies, and—worst of all—a lack of trust, decide to divorce. It takes half the film, covering Lucy's flirtation with Dan (Ralph Bellamy), for her to realize she still loves Jerry. But then it's his turn to hook up with someone, a "madcap heiress." Once all these bets are off, the story becomes a road movie leading to a cabin in the woods—with two beds, and thirty minutes left before the divorce decree becomes final.

McCarey perfects every ingredient of the romantic comedy here, from the opposition of New Yorkers and Southerners, to the role of games, songs, and dances as ways of sorting out the characters' affections and allegiances. Full of splendid minor characters and inspired bits of business, *The Awful Truth* also has a heartbreakingly serious moment when Jerry and Lucy remember their unofficial marriage vow ("This comes from the heart, I'll always adore you").

Of all the great movies, this may be the one that most resists description in words. This has much to do with its small jokes of subtle verbal delivery, where ordinary phrases are transformed by timing, rhythm, and tone, from Lucy's defensively repeated "had better go" and Jerry's stumbling on "Tulsa" to Dan's exasperated "Mom!" via the black servant's reaction to Jerry's fake tan: "You're looking weellll." Above all, the film is a monument to the sheer, magical lovability of its stars. **AM**

138

The Life of Émile Zola William Dieterle, 1937

U.S. (Warner Bros.) 116m BW
Producer Henry Blanke Screenplay Norman
Reilly Raine, Heinz Herald, Geza Herczeg,
from book by Matthew Josephson
Photography Tony Gaudio Music Max
Steiner Cast Paul Muni, Gale Sondergaard,
Joseph Schildkraut, Gloria Holden, Donald
Crisp, Erin O'Brien-Moore, John Litel, Henry
O'Neill, Morris Carnovsky, Louis Calhern,
Ralph Morgan, Robert Barrat Oscars Henry
Blanke (best picture), Heinz Herald, Geza
Herczeg, Norman Reilly Raine (screenplay),
Joseph Schildkraut (actor in support role)
Oscar nominations William Dieterle
(director), Heinz Herald, Geza Herczeg
(screenplay), Paul Muni (actor), Anton Grot
(art direction), Russell Saunders (assistant
director), Max Steiner (music), Nathan
Levinson (sound)

William Dieterle's *The Life of Émile Zola* was a follow-up to his highly successful biopic *The Story of Louis Pasteur* (1935), with actor Paul Muni in another story about a Frenchman of principle and enlightenment overcoming prejudice. At the beginning Zola struggles to establish himself as a writer, until the publication of *Nana*, his sensational novel about a prostitute. Success follows success, and Zola is set to enjoy a prosperous old age when he is visited by the wife of Alfred Dreyfus, a French army officer falsely accused of spying for the Germans and sent to Devil's Island. Zola's conscience is pricked and, in a big set piece tailor-made for Muni, he reads out his famous article "J'Accuse" to a newspaper editor. In a typical Warner Brothers montage sequence, the newspaper staff gather around to listen, presses spew out the article, and people rush to buy the paper.

The film won an Oscar for Best Picture and its underlying seriousness is impressive. Yet though Dreyfus was the victim of anti-Semitic prejudice, not once in *The Life of Émile Zola* is the word "Jew" uttered. Evidently, Warner Brothers feared that in 1937, with the rising tide of anti-Semitism in Europe, pictures about anti Jewish feeling would inflame the very prejudices they were designed to expose. **EB**

1938

Jezebel William Wyler, 1938

U.S. (First National, Warner Bros.) 103m BW
Producer Henry Blanke, Hal B. Wallis, William
Wyler Screenplay Clements Ripley, Abem
Finkel, John Huston, Robert Buckner, from
play by Owen Davis Photography Ernest
Haller Music Al Dubin, Max Steiner, Harry
Warren Cast Bette Davis, Henry Fonda,
George Brent, Margaret Lindsay, Donald
Crisp, Fay Bainter, Richard Cromwell, Henry
O'Neill, Spring Byington, John Litel, Gordon
Oliver, Janet Shaw, Theresa Harris, Margaret
Early, Irving Pichel Oscar Bette Davis
(actress) Oscar nominations Hal B. Wallis,
Henry Blanke (best picture), Fay Bainter
(actress), Ernest Haller (photography),
Max Steiner (music)

Hollywood's second most famous portrayal of a spoiled Southern belle, *Jezebel* offered Bette Davis the perfect vehicle to display her acting talents in a breakthrough role. Davis plays Julie Marsden, who is the most sought-after debutante in 1850s New Orleans, a society ruled by rigid codes of behavior that the young woman finds confining. Engaged to Preston Dillard (Henry Fonda), Julie does not sever her relationship to Buck Cantrell (George Brent), an honorable Southern gentleman and the story's most sympathetic figure. Soon after, Preston leaves New Orleans to travel north, where he works; when he comes back to the city, he is married to another woman. In her petulance, Julie causes a duel in which Buck is killed, and she becomes a pariah, even to her own family. But then she redeems herself through heroic self-sacrifice during a yellow fever outbreak, when she accompanies the desperately ill Preston to the miserable island where victims of the disease are confined.

William Wyler makes use of a lavish budget and meticulous art design in this intriguing evocation of the period. Much more of a character study than *Gone with the Wind* (1939), *Jezebel* also avoids the "plantation myth" so prominent in that film. Its New Orleans is a decadent place, ruled by a planter class intent on its jealous sense of honor. **RBP**

The Adventures of Robin Hood

Michael Curtiz & William Keighley, 1938

U.S. (First National, Warner Bros.) 102m Technicolor **Producer** Henry Blanke, Hal B. Wallis **Screenplay** Norman Reilly Raine, Seton I. Miller **Photography** Tony Gaudio, Sol Polito **Music** Erich Wolfgang Korngold **Cast** Errol Flynn, Olivia de Havilland, Basil Rathbone, Claude Rains, Patric Knowles, Eugene Pallette, Alan Hale, Melville Cooper, Ian Hunter, Una O'Connor, Herbert Mundin, Montagu Love, Leonard Willey, Robert Noble, Kenneth Hunter **Oscars** Carl Jules Weyl (art direction), Ralph Dawson (editing), Erich Wolfgang Korngold (music) **Oscar nomination** Hal B. Wallis, Henry Blanke (best picture)

Whether considered as a swashbuckler, a costume romance, or a mockery of history, *The Adventures of Robin Hood* is simply the best production of its kind ever made. With King Richard on the Crusades, the kingdom is ruled by his rotten brother John, played by Claude Rains as a waspish tyrant who overhears groans from a torture chamber and muses, "Ah, more complaints about the new taxes from our Saxon friends." John's less amusing but more deadly sidekick, Sir Guy of Gisbourne, is incarnated with razor-profiled malice by the unmatchably ruthless Basil Rathbone.

The fairest lady in the land is Marian, an impossibly lovely Olivia de Havilland in Technicolor flesh tones. But it's dispossessed outlaw Robin of Locksley who brings life to this court of intrigue, with Errol Flynn's jaunty goatee and Tasmanian twinkle making Robin a rare hero who can be a light-hearted trickster one moment but spin on a knife-point to become a determined rebel ("Norman or Saxon, what's that matter? It's injustice I hate, not the Normans.") and a balcony-climbing romantic.

It is truly amazing how fast-paced and jam-packed this movie is: the story is as complicated as a Shakespearean comedy; there's a real delight in the sword-clashing and arrow-shooting battles, and it ends as all stories should—with good triumphant and lovers united. **KN**

Angels with Dirty Faces Michael Curtiz, 1938

U.S. (First National) 97m BW **Producer** Samuel Bischoff **Screenplay** Rowland Brown, John Wexley, Warren Duff **Photography** Sol Polito **Music** Max Steiner **Cast** James Cagney, Pat O'Brien, Humphrey Bogart, Ann Sheridan, George Bancroft, Billy Halop, Bobby Jordan, Leo Gorcey, Gabriel Dell, Huntz Hall, Bernard Punsly, Joe Downing, Edward Pawley, Adrian Morris, Frankie Burke **Oscar nominations** Michael Curtiz (director), Rowland Brown (screenplay), James Cagney (actor)

Michael Curtiz's films preach social responsibility, and *Angels with Dirty Faces* is his most powerful sermon. Rocky and Jerry, two pals from a tough New York neighborhood, grow up to be a notorious gangster (James Cagney) and crusading priest (Pat O'Brien), respectively. A gang of teenagers idolize Rocky, until Father Jerry urges his condemned friend to "go yellow" at his execution. In keeping with its didactic mission, the film's visual and performing styles are emphatic and crisp to the point of caricature. In fact, Cagney's performance here, all cocky swagger and hitched-up shoulders, provided the primary model for impressionists such as Frank Gorshin and Rich Little.

Curtiz may be a moralizer, but he is not a facile one. Rocky's final capitulation is a tough pill to swallow, and the director does not sugarcoat it. Rocky is a charismatic rebel, and Father Jerry is a sanctimonious nag, but the film leaves little doubt which choice serves the greater good. The harrowing climax, a nightmare of gruesome details and expressionist shadows as Rocky is dragged whimpering to the electric chair, still has the power to enrage viewers who do not share the film's stern moral viewpoint, but, for Father Mike, such attitudes are sentimental at best and irresponsible at worst. Amen. **MR**

1938

La femme du boulanger
Marcel Pagnol, 1938

The Baker's Wife

Orson Welles thought that Raimu was one of the greatest actors of his time; *The Baker's Wife* proves him right. Directed by Marcel Pagnol from a short story by Jean Giono, this is the tale of Aimable Castanier, a middle-aged baker (Raimu) in a small Provençal village. When his young wife Aurélie (Ginette Leclerc) deserts him for a handsome shepherd, the distraught baker stops baking and without bread the village comes to a halt. Catholic priest, left-wing teacher, lord of the manor, and all the villagers forget their old feuds and gang up to bring back the errant wife. Life resumes happily.

From such simple material Pagnol fashioned a comic gem and a humanist masterpiece. With his regular troupe of actors—Raimu, Fernand Charpin, Robert Vattier, and others—Pagnol animates a galaxy of characters that is both funny and touching. His light touch and the actors' talents transcend the crude stereotypes (womanizing aristocrat, pedantic teacher, cantankerous old maid, cuckolded husband), creating a world in which each has his or her own clearly defined role. Giono and Pagnol's Provence is conservative and patriarchal (the wife does not have much of a say), but it is a world in which shared fundamental values—here represented by bread, both a Christian and pagan symbol—cement social cohesiveness.

Raimu's towering performance effortlessly alternates comic theatricality with minimalist realism, turning his comic cuckold into a tragic hero. Raimu, from the South of France himself, was a superlative stage actor, at ease with the florid language and emphatic delivery of the Marseilles vernacular. His filmic modernity, however, came from his ability to switch within seconds to understated moments, giving them extraordinary emotional impact, as illustrated by the film's most famous scene. As the repentant wife returns, Raimu welcomes her back as if nothing had happened and instead takes it out on a surrogate, the straying female cat "Pomponnette," in the most vivid and affecting terms. In this moment of contrived high comedy I defy anyone to remain dry-eyed. It may be called *The Baker's Wife*, but it is definitely Raimu's film. **GV**

France (Marcel Pagnol) 133m BW
Language French **Producer** Leon Bourrely, Charles Pons **Screenplay** Marcel Pagnol, from the novel *Jean le Bleu* by Jean Giono **Photography** Georges Benoît **Music** Vincent Scotto **Cast** Raimu, Ginette Leclerc, Robert Vattier, Robert Bassac, Fernand Charpin, Edouard Delmont, Charles Blavette, Marcel Maupi, Maximilienne, Alida Rouffe, Odette Roger, Charles Moulin, Yvette Fournier, Charblay, Julien Maffre

1938

> "We had to use the studio . . . Raimu could not play a long scene outside. The wind bothered him. A real tree bothered him."
>
> **Marcel Pagnol, 1965**

ℹ

Joan Crawford was Pagnol's original choice for the part of Aurélie, but declined because of her poor French.

Bringing Up Baby Howard Hawks, 1938

Bringing Up Baby, the definitive screwball comedy, was the first film Howard Hawks made in a six-picture contract with RKO in 1937. Unpromisingly based on a short story about a young couple and their tamed leopard, the shoot went forty days over schedule and over budget. It earned so little upon its release in 1938 that Hawks was fired from RKO and Katherine Hepburn had to buy herself out of her own contract. Ahead of its time, its amazing breakneck pace and disarmingly witty dialogue set new standards for all such comedies thereafter.

At his whimsical best, Cary Grant is Dr. David Huxley, a handsome and easily distracted paleontologist who spends his days piecing together a brontosaurus skeleton while he is taken apart by his nagging fiancée. With one more bone to go before the four-year museum project will be complete, Huxley manages to bumble an important meeting on the golf course with a wealthy potential patron. There, Huxley meets Susan Vance (Hepburn). As beautiful and scatterbrained as he is, she steals his golf ball; after that, Huxley's world never snaps back into place. Trying anything to keep him from marrying another girl, Vance uses Baby, the house-trained pet leopard sent to her by her brother in South America, as a worthy Huxley diversion. By the time the family dog buries Huxley's precious dinosaur bone, the couple is headed to jail.

The laughs in *Bringing Up Baby* are real, almost completely disguising its deft analyses of 1930s-style gender expectations, sex, and marriage. So suspicious was the censor of the script's deeper and possibly sexual meanings that Huxley's quest to find his "lost bone" was queried as a reference to lost masculinity. The scene where Huxley dons Vance's feathery feminine bathrobe didn't help dissuade that notion, containing as it does one of the first popular appearances of the word "gay" being used to mean something other than "extremely happy." The critics may have hated it, the audiences may have stayed away, and Oscar didn't smile upon it at the time, but *Bringing Up Baby* has had the last laugh on all its detractors. It remains one of the true masterpieces of celluloid wit. **KK**

U.S. (RKO) 102m BW **Producer** Howard Hawks, Cliff Reid **Screenplay** Hagar Wilde, Dudley Nichols **Photography** Russell Metty **Music** Roy Webb **Cast** Katharine Hepburn, Cary Grant, Charles Ruggles, Walter Catlett, Barry Fitzgerald, May Robson, Fritz Feld, Leona Roberts, George Irving, Tala Birell, Virginia Walker, John Kelly

> *"When a man is wrestling a leopard in the middle of a pond, he's in no position to run."*
>
> **Dr. David Huxley
> (Cary Grant)**

i

Huxley was partly based on silent-film star Harold Lloyd, and sometimes sports Lloyd-style thick glasses.

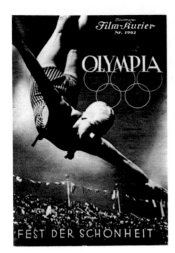

Olympia Leni Riefenstahl, 1938
Olympia 1. Teil: Fest der Völker
Part 1: Festival of the Nations
Olympia 2. Teil: Fest der Schönheit
Part 2: Festival of Beauty

Germany (IOC, Olympia Film, Tobis)
118 m and 107m BW **Language** German
Producer Leni Riefenstahl **Screenplay** Leni
Riefenstahl **Photography** Wilfried Basse,
Werner Bundhausen, Leo De Lafrue, Walter
Frentz, Hans Karl Gottschalk, Willy Hameister,
Walter Hege, Carl Junghans, Albert Kling,
Ernst Kunstmann, Guzzi Lantschner, Otto
Lantschner, Kurt Neubert, Erich
Nitzschmann, Hans Scheib, Hugo O. Schulze,
Károly Vass, Willy Zielke, Andor von Barsy,
Franz von Friedl, Heinz von Jaworsky, Hugo
von Kaweczynski, Alexander von Lagorio
Music Herbert Windt, Walter Gronostay
Cast David Albritton, Jack Beresford, Henri
de Baillet-Latour, Philip Edwards, Donald
Finlay, Wilhelm Frick, Josef Goebbels,
Hermann Göring, Ernest Harper, Rudolf Hess,
Adolf Hitler, Cornelius Johnson, Theodor
Lewald, Luz Long, John Lovelock, Ralph
Metcalfe, Seung-yong Nam, Henri Nannen,
Dorothy Odam, Martinus Osendarp, Jesse
Owens, Leni Riefenstahl, Julius Schaub,
Fritz Schilgen, Kee-chung Sohn, Julius
Streicher, Forrest Towns, Werner von
Blomberg, August von Mackensen,
Glenn Morris, Conrad von Wangenheim
Venice Film Festival Leni Riefenstahl
(Mussolini Cup—best film)

ℹ

Olympia premiered in Germany
on the occasion of Adolf Hitler's
forty-ninth birthday.

Leni Riefenstahl's epic documentary of the 1936 Olympic Games in Berlin is sometimes criticized for its politics. Sponsored by Hitler, the film does contain sequences that seem to support the notion of "Aryan" superiority. Still, the filmmaker did receive a gold medal for her efforts from the Olympic Committee in 1948, long after Hitler's dream of a thousand-year Reich had disintegrated. This is not to deny that *Olympia* is a piece of propaganda; Riefenstahl would never have received the funding and support needed if the result had not been politically useful. In many ways, though, Olympia transcends politics. Overall, it is more a hymn of praise to athletic prowess and to the poetry of the human body in motion.

Riefenstahl's aesthetic interest in physical form and motion and her feat in making this documentary have never been duplicated. Filming the games and supervising the immense task of postproduction would take a Herculean effort today. In the late 1930s, the job was done with primitive equipment. Despite its overtly political message, the film is an artistic triumph, evidence not only of Riefenstahl's personal talent and vision, but also of the energies and expertise of her hundreds of assistants.

Huge preparation was necessary. Steel camera towers were built in the stadium, platforms made for tracking shots, and Germany scoured for the best talent. Nearly 250 hours of film was shot, and the task of editing was personally supervised by Riefenstahl. The final version is masterfully paced, with sublime matched cuts and just enough variation in repetitive events to sustain visual interest. Riefenstahl's protestations of political innocence may be unconvincing, but *Olympia* does have another and more enduring side. Simply put, it is the most moving cinematic record of human sport and physical competition ever produced. **RBP**

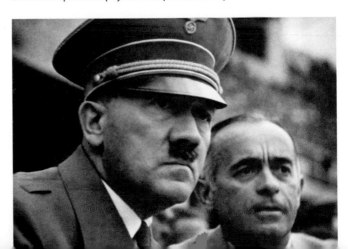

The Lady Vanishes Alfred Hitchcock, 1938

G.B. (Gainsborough Pictures) 96m BW **Producer** Edward Black **Screenplay** Sidney Gilliat, Frank Launder, from novel by Ethel Lina White **Photography** Jack E. Cox **Music** Louis Levey, Charles Williams **Cast** Margaret Lockwood, Michael Redgrave, Paul Lukas, Dame May Whitty, Cecil Parker, Linden Travers, Naunton Wayne, Basil Radford, Mary Clare, Emile Boreo, Googie Withers, Sally Stewart, Philip Leaver

The Lady Vanishes ranks alongside *The Thirty-Nine Steps* (1935) as one of Hitchcock's best British sound films. Aided in no small part by a sparkling script that is mined for all its comic value by a sterling ensemble of British actors, Hitchcock produced a gem of a trans-European thriller.

When the elderly Miss Froy (Dame May Whitty) suddenly disappears on a train traveling across continental Europe, beautiful young heiress Iris (Margaret Lockwood) suspects foul play. Engaging the help of Gilbert (Michael Redgrave), a musicologist apparently oblivious to his traveling companion's beauty, Iris uncovers the real identity of the missing woman and a plot that will throw Europe into the chaos of war.

As with Hitchcock's greatest adventures, the details of what is at stake are always less interesting than the journey to uncover them. The chemistry between the leads is palpable, allowing us to savor the thaw between them as they realize the seemingly insurmountable forces they face. But Launder and Gilliat's script truly shines in bringing to life every character, no matter how minor; best are Charters (Basil Radford) and Caldicott (Naunton Wayne), two cricket-obsessed fanatics.

The action rattles along at a fair pace, and although it lacks the memorable scenes of his Richard Hannay adventure, the success of *The Lady Vanishes* secured Hitchcock a lucrative Hollywood contract. **IHS**

Wuthering Heights William Wyler, 1939

U.S. (Samuel Goldwyn) 103m BW **Producer** Samuel Goldwyn **Screenplay** Charles MacArthur, from novel by Emily Brontë **Photography** Gregg Toland **Music** Alfred Newman **Cast** Merle Oberon, Laurence Olivier, David Niven, Flora Robson, Donald Crisp, Geraldine Fitzgerald, Hugh Williams, Leo G. Carroll, Miles Mander, Cecil Kellaway, Cecil Humphreys, Sarita Wooton, Rex Downing, Douglas Scott **Oscar** Gregg Toland (photography) **Oscar nominations** Samuel Goldwyn (best picture), William Wyler (director), Ben Hecht, Charles MacArthur (screenplay), Laurence Olivier (actor), Geraldine Fitzgerald (actress in support role), Alfred Newman (music), James Basevi (art direction)

William Wyler's film version of Emily Brontë's *Wuthering Heights* is unsurpassed as a gothic tale of inextinguishable passion, thwarted by social circumstance and mischance. A lonely traveler, Dr. Kenneth (Donald Crisp), making his way across the moors of northern England, spends the night at Wuthering Heights, where an aged servant tells him the tragic story of Heathcliff (Laurence Olivier), the house's current owner. A gypsy waif, he had been adopted by the Earnshaws and raised with their own two children. Heathcliff is the constant companion of young Cathy (Merle Oberon), whose snobbish brother Hindley (Hugh Williams) scorns him. Wealthy neighbor Edgar Linton (David Niven) falls in love with Cathy, and she dismisses Heathcliff, who goes to America. Cathy forgets him and ends up marrying Edgar. Heathcliff returns to England a rich man but, furious at Cathy's betrayal, marries Edgar's sister (Geraldine Fitzgerald), mistreating the poor woman as a means of getting revenge. Cathy is miserable with Edgar and falls ill, but before she dies the former lovers are briefly united.

Heathcliff's speech about the life they will live together is one of the most poignant moments in any Hollywood film. It is the acting of Olivier and Oberon as the doomed lovers, framed against the forbidding wildness of the studio-crafted moors, that makes the film most memorable. **RBP**

Mr. Smith Goes to Washington Frank Capra, 1939

Frank Capra's hymn of praise to the American system of government was considered so incisive in its indictment of special-interest corruption that some in Washington thought *Mr. Smith Goes to Washington* should not be released into a world on the verge of war. To show that the system works, however, Capra must demonstrate how it can correct itself. Republicanism (not democracy) is saved in the film by the heroic efforts of a stubborn idealist, who, in the best tradition of the Jeffersonian individualism for which he is named, refuses to go along with party bosses, who plot his ruin. Ashamed, the smooth-talking machine politician assigned to discredit him publicly confesses the plot.

Jimmy Stewart is perfect as Jefferson Smith, whose chief qualification is that he is hopelessly unsophisticated, a man who spends all his time mentoring a troop of young "rangers." But this rube is neither stupid nor lacking in courage. Smith first convinces the cynical woman (Jean Arthur) charged with looking after him of his virtue and his keen sense. And then, after unintentionally creating trouble by proposing a national boys' camp on the precise site that the "machine" hopes to use for its pork barrel project, he defends himself against false charges in a filibuster that goes on for many hours and leaves him barely able to speak or stand. Crucial in Smith's passage from irrelevance through disgrace to vindication is the part played by Senator Joseph Paine (Claude Rains). As opposed to the crudely venal political boss Jim Taylor (Edward Arnold), Paine is a man who believes in the American system but who has been seduced by a politics of compromise and deal making. Smith can only be rescued by Paine's conversion. Smith's deliverance is also made possible by the peculiarly American institution of the filibuster, which permits the individual—symbolically enough, not the group—unlimited free speech according to established rules. Smith can thereby exert a power against the group that would condemn him, insuring his vindication.

Capra's film is full of memorable moments, the most moving of which is the montage sequence tracing the newly arrived senator's tour of Washington monuments, including the Lincoln Memorial. **RBP**

U.S. (Columbia) 125m BW **Producer** Frank Capra **Screenplay** Lewis R. Foster, Sidney Buchman **Photography** Joseph Walker **Music** Dimitri Tiomkin **Cast** Jean Arthur, James Stewart, Claude Rains, Edward Arnold, Guy Kibbee, Thomas Mitchell, Eugene Pallette, Beulah Bondi, H.B. Warner, Harry Carey, Astrid Allwyn, Ruth Donnelly, Grant Mitchell, Porter Hall, Pierre Watkin **Oscar** Lewis R. Foster (screenplay) **Oscar nominations** Frank Capra (best picture), Frank Capra (director), Sidney Buchman (screenplay), James Stewart (actor), Claude Rains (actor in support role), Harry Carey (actor in support role), Lionel Banks (art direction), Gene Havlick, Al Clark (editing), Dimitri Tiomkin (music), John P. Livadary (sound)

1939

> *"Great principles don't get lost once they come to light. They're right here; you just have to see them again!"*
>
> **Jefferson Smith**
> **(James Stewart)**

ℹ

James Stewart used bicarbonate of soda and mercuric chloride to dry out his throat and make his voice hoarse.

Stagecoach John Ford, 1939

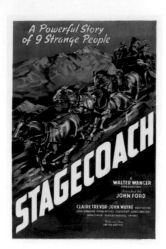

A Powerful Story of 9 Strange People

STAGECOACH

WALTER WANGER PRODUCTION

Directed by JOHN FORD

CLAIRE TREVOR · JOHN WAYNE

U.S. (Walter Wanger) 96m BW
Producer Walter Wanger, John Ford
Screenplay Ernest Haycox, Dudley Nichols
Photography Bert Glennon **Music** Louis Gruenberg, Richard Hageman, Franke Harling, John Leipold, Leo Shuken
Cast Claire Trevor, John Wayne, Andy Devine, John Carradine, Thomas Mitchell, Louise Platt, George Bancroft, Donald Meek, Berton Churchill, Tim Holt, Tom Tyler
Oscars Thomas Mitchell (actor in support role), Richard Hageman, W. Franke Harling, John Leipold, Leo Shuken (music) **Oscar nominations** Walter Wanger (best picture), John Ford (director), Bert Glennon (photography), Alexander Toluboff (art direction), Otho Lovering, Dorothy Spencer (editing)

*"If there's anything
I don't like, it's driving
a stagecoach through
Apache country."*

Buck (Andy Devine)

ℹ️

The film's healthy performance at the box office helped to reestablish the Western genre.

The 1930s wasn't a great decade for the Western. After a few expensive flops such as *The Big Trail* (1930) and *Cimarron* (1931), the major studios largely abandoned the genre to Poverty Row producers making cheap B-movies. John Ford hadn't made a Western for a dozen years when he cast John Wayne and Claire Trevor in a story about a stagecoach ride through dangerous Indian territory. In trying to sell it to producer David O. Selznick, Ford described *Stagecoach* as a "classic Western," a cut above the B-Westerns that Wayne himself had been making. One thing this meant was giving it more appeal to women in the audience. So Ford and screenwriter Dudley Nichols added to the original story by Ernest Haycox a more developed love story and the birth of a baby. But this wasn't enough for Selznick, who looked down his nose and passed on the project.

Not that *Stagecoach* stints on the genre's more traditional satisfactions. The last part of the film packs in plenty of action, including a gunfight between Wayne and the Plummer gang and a stirring Indian attack as the stagecoach careers across the flat desert. The sequence was enriched by some superlative stunt work by Yakima Canutt, who, playing one of the Apache attackers, leaps onto one of the stage's horses, is shot, and has to fall between the horses' hooves and under the wheels.

This was Wayne's second chance at major stardom after the failure of *The Big Trail*, and he took it with both hands. From his first entrance, standing in the desert waving down the stage, he cuts an impressive figure as the Ringo Kid, who has busted out of jail in order to be revenged on the Plummers, killers of his father and brother. But Wayne's appearance is delayed while Ford explores the characters of the other travelers on the coach. Each is deftly and memorably sketched in: Dallas (Claire Trevor), the girl who is no better than she should be, and who is run out of town together with drunken Doc Boone (Thomas Mitchell) by the puritanical ladies of the Law and Order League; Peacock (Donald Meek), a timid whiskey salesman; Hatfield (John Carradine), a Southern gambler; Mrs. Mallory (Louise Platt), the pregnant wife of a cavalry officer; and Gatewood (Berton Churchill), a banker who is making off with the assets. On the outside of the coach are Buck (Andy Devine), the portly driver, and Curly (George Bancroft), the local sheriff. The interaction between this oddly assorted group allows Ford to explore a cherished theme, the superior moral qualities of those whom "respectable" society disdains.

Stagecoach was the first film Ford shot in Monument Valley, a landscape of towering sandstone buttes on the border between Utah and Arizona. As the tiny coach makes its way through the vastness of the desert, the frailty of its occupants is doubly emphasized as the camera tracks toward a group of Indians observing its progress. Ford makes no attempt to present the Indians as individuals; they are merely a force of nature. **EB**

Only Angels Have Wings Howard Hawks, 1939

Howard Hawks turned his attention to the manly cameraderie of dangerous professions (especially aviation) in earlier action pictures such as *The Dawn Patrol* (1930), *The Crowd Roars* (1932), and *Ceiling Zero* (1936). But this 1939 drama marks a transformation of his style, imprinting a personal stamp on a melodramatic genre to set the heroic-comic-romantic tone he would later pursue in *To Have and Have Not* (1944), *Rio Bravo* (1959), and *El Dorado* (1966). Note the community sing-alongs, the in-group banter, the shared domestic chores, the nicknames and gossip, the wryly amusing streak of prissiness among tough guys, and the veneer of cynicism that masks honest sentiment.

There are remarkable, exciting, stunt-heavy flying sequences in *Only Angels Have Wings*, especially a very dangerous landing and takeoff on a high Andean plateau, but the meat of the film is on the ground, observing the cohesion of a disparate group that clusters around white-hat hero Geoff Carter (Cary Grant). Striding a head taller than his crew and looking every inch the star, Geoff runs an airmail service in South America, inspiring a group of traumatized veterans, fresh kids, and deadbeats to hop over the Andes in outmoded airplanes. Showgirl Bonnie Lee (Jean Arthur) is stranded at the airfield; at first appalled by the ostensibly macho attitudes of the pilots when one of their number is killed in a needless accident, she gradually comes to understand their sensitive side, eventually joining Geoff in a spirited rendition of "The Peanut Vendor."

At heart a tough soap opera, the film has a group of "damaged" people showing their worth in crises and cuts between funny, sassy, sexy dialogue exchanges on the ground and still-effective aerial action scenes. It also has a great supporting cast of familiar faces—Richard Barthelmess (trying to live down a reputation for cowardice because he bailed out of a crashing plane and left his engineer behind), Thomas Mitchell (an aging sidekick covering up his increasing blindness), Noah Beery Jr., Sig Rumann, and Rita Hayworth (as the sort of woman men shouldn't mess with but usually do). Catchphrases include "Calling Barranca" and "Who's Joe?" **KN**

U.S. (Columbia) 121m
BW **Producer** Howard Hawks
Screenplay Jules Furthman, Howard
Hawks **Photography** Joseph Walker
Music Dimitri Tiomkin, Manuel Álvarez
Maciste **Cast** Cary Grant, Jean Arthur,
Richard Barthelmess, Rita Hayworth, Thomas
Mitchell, Allyn Joslyn, Sig Ruman, Victor
Kilian, John Carroll, Don "Red" Barry, Noah
Beery Jr., Manuel Maciste, Milisa Sierra, Lucio
Villegas, Pat Flaherty **Oscar nominations**
Joseph Walker (photography), Roy Davidson,
Roy Davidson (special visual effects),
Edwin C. Hahn (special sound effects)

i

Ruman's line "Include me out!" was one of the famous malapropisms of Hollywood producer Sam Goldwyn.

Destry Rides Again George Marshall, 1939

U.S. (Universal) 94m BW **Producer** Islin Auster, Joe Pasternak **Screenplay** Felix Jackson, from novel by Max Brand **Photography** Hal Mohr **Music** Frederick Hollander, Frank Skinner, Ralph Freed **Cast** Marlene Dietrich, James Stewart, Mischa Auer, Charles Winninger, Brian Donlevy, Allen Jenkins, Warren Hymer, Irene Hervey, Una Merkel, Billy Gilbert, Samuel S. Hinds, Jack Carson, Tom Fadden, Virginia Brissac, Edmund MacDonald

Like most comedy Westerns, George Marshall's *Destry Rides Again* is a satire on the conventions of manly heroism. Destry (played by James Stewart in his best "aw, shucks" manner), sheriff of the unruly town of Bottleneck, prefers milk to whiskey and refuses to carry a gun. This gives him a special appeal for saloon girl Frenchy, with Marlene Dietrich belatedly reprising the role that made her famous in *The Blue Angel*. (1930). Dietrich sings a couple of rousing numbers in the Last Chance Saloon, including the celebrated "See What the Boys in the Back Room Will Have." In another reversal of stereotype, the usual "fight in the saloon" scene takes place between two women, as Frenchy and Lily Belle (Una Merkel) engage in an unladylike wrestling match.

Frenchy transfers her affections from gambler Kent (Brian Donlevy) to Destry, then leads the women of the town in a final rout of the bad guys, before throwing herself in front of Destry to take a bullet meant to kill him. It's an amusing tale handled with a deft touch, very different in spirit from the original novel by Max Brand, the most prolific of all Western fiction writers, which was first filmed in 1932 with Tom Mix in the title role, and then again in 1954 with Audie Murphy. **EB**

i

Stewart and Dietrich had an affair that lasted for the duration of the film's production.

Gone with the Wind Victor Fleming & George Cukor, 1939

Margaret Mitchell's Civil War best seller was snapped up by megalomaniac producer David O. Selznick, who resisted Mitchell's suggestion that he cast Basil Rathbone as Rhett Butler in favor of the fans' only choice, Clark Gable. After a nationwide talent search and a Hollywood catfight involving every potential leading lady in town, Selznick hired British Vivien Leigh to play Southern belle Scarlett O'Hara. Insistent from the start that every detail be sumptuous, Selznick then wore out at least three directors (Sam Wood, George Cukor, and Victor Fleming), set fire to the surviving King Kong sets to stage the burning of Atlanta, hired enough extras to refight the Civil War, and sat back to watch the Oscars and acclaim roll in.

Conceived from the outset as the ultimate Hollywood movie, *Gone with the Wind* became the benchmark for popular epic cinema for decades to come. Though the film is monumental enough to be beyond criticism, most of its really great scenes come in the first half, which was substantially directed by Cukor, who brought his skilled touch with character and nuance to the material with a great epic sweep. Fleming, meanwhile, best known for directing macho action, somehow wound up handling the soapier stretches as the leads' marriage falters through postbellum ups and downs far less compelling than the war-torn, cross-purposes romance that got them together.

The motor of the plot is the vacillating heart of Scarlett, whom Leigh plays first as flighty then flinty; she is so infatuated with gentlemanly Ashley Wilkes (Leslie Howard) that she marries several lesser (and doomed) milksops when he opts for the more conventionally feminine (and doomed) Melanie (Olivia de Havilland). Rhett Butler, a pragmatist rather than an idealist, enters the picture and she is drawn to him as the war overturns the Southern way of life, marrying him after she has sworn never to go hungry again and to do anything it takes to keep Tara, her father's plantation, going despite the depradations of Yankees and carpetbaggers. Only when Rhett rejects her does she realize she truly loves him, prompting the classic have-it-both-ways ending in which he walks out ("Frankly, my dear, I don't give a damn") and she swears to win him back ("Tomorrow is another day").

Like *The Birth of a Nation* (1915), *Gone with the Wind* tidies up a lot of complex history, showing only happy devoted slaves and depicting Ashley's postwar involvement in a hooded Klan organization as a heroic (if doomed) endeavor. But the sweep of the movie is near irresistible, and Selznick's set pieces are among the most emblematic in cinema history: the pullback from Scarlett as she walks among the wounded to fill the screen with injured soldiers in gray, the dash through the blazes as Atlanta burns, and Rhett carrying Scarlett upstairs into sexual shadows. Dressed up with gorgeous 1939 Technicolor, pastel-pretty for the dresses and blazing red for the passions, and a thunderous score, *Gone with the Wind* still has a fair claim to be considered the last word in Hollywood filmmaking. **KN**

U.S. (Selznick) 222m Technicolor
Producer David O. Selznick
Screenplay Sidney Howard, from novel by Margaret Mitchell **Photography** Ernest Haller, Ray Rennahan, Lee Garmes **Music** Max Steiner **Cast** Clark Gable, Vivien Leigh, Leslie Howard, Olivia de Havilland, Thomas Mitchell, Barbara O'Neil, Evelyn Keyes, Ann Rutherford, George Reeves, Fred Crane, Hattie McDaniel, Oscar Polk, Butterfly McQueen, Victor Jory, Everett Brown **Oscars** William Cameron Menzies (honorary award—use of color), David O. Selznick (best picture), Victor Fleming (director), Sidney Howard (screenplay), Vivien Leigh (actress), Hattie McDaniel (actress in support role), Lyle R. Wheeler (art direction), Ernest Haller Ray Rennahan (photography), Hal C. Kern, James E. Newcom (editing), Don Musgrave (technical achievement award) **Oscar nominations** Clark Gable (actor), Olivia de Havilland (actress in support role), Max Steiner (music), Thomas T. Moulton (sound), Jack Cosgrove, Fred Albin, Arthur Johns (special effects)

i

The film saw Hattie McDaniel become the first African-American person to win an Academy Award.

Le jour se lève Marcel Carné, 1939
Daybreak

Although it was not the first film to use dissolves to signal flashbacks, Marcel Carné's *Daybreak* was deemed so innovative in 1939 that the producers insisted on a pretitle card to dispel any confusion: "A man has committed murder. Locked, trapped in a room, he recalls how he became a murderer." The murderer is François (Jean Gabin), a common factory worker who has been lured into murder by the victim, an amoral and manipulative vaudeville entertainer by the name of Valentin (Jules Berry). Their fate is bound up with two women: the earthy, sensual Clara (Arletty), who leaves Valentin to take up with François, and the pure, idealized Françoise (Jacqueline Laurent), whom François loves, but who has been corrupted by her association with the other man.

Among the remarkable series of classic films to spring from the collaboration between Carné and screenwriter Jacques Prévert (the others include *Port of Shadows* [1938], *The Devil's Envoys* [1942], and, preeminently, *Children of Paradise* [1945]), *Daybreak* is arguably the most influential. Certainly it rehearses ideas the team would return to in *Children of Paradise*. Although *Daybreak* wears its allegorical themes lightly, François clearly stands for the French working man, and the film gives voice to the despair that overtook the supporters of the Popular Front in the late 1930s as the state swept aside progressive socialist reforms and the specter of fascism loomed. When one friend yells from the crowd gathered outside his building that there's still hope, François retorts, "It's over, there isn't a François anymore. . . . There isn't anything anymore."

The film's doom-laden sense of existential alienation and austere, claustrophobic atmosphere clearly anticipated the mood and form of American film noir. In fact, RKO remade the film with Henry Fonda and Vincent Price as *The Long Night* in 1946 (the studio attempted to destroy all prints of the original but mercifully failed). Similarly, Gabin's rough-hewn romantic predates American counterparts like John Garfield and Humphrey Bogart as an iconic working-class hero. *Daybreak* stands as probably the masterpiece of French poetic realism. **TCh**

France (Sigma, Vauban) 93m BW
Language French **Screenplay** Jacques Prévert, Jacques Viot **Photography** Philippe Agostini, André Bac, Albert Viguier, Curt Courant **Music** Maurice Jaubert **Cast** Jean Gabin, Jules Berry, Arletty, Mady Berry, René Génin, Arthur Devère, René Bergeron, Bernard Blier, Marcel Pérès, Germaine Lix, Gabrielle Fontan, Jacques Baumer, Jacqueline Laurent **Venice Film Festival** Marcel Carné (Mussolini Cup—best film nomination)

"Sure, I'm a killer, but killers are a dime a dozen! They're everywhere! "

François (Jean Gabin)

i

Prévert, a noted poet, wrote the lyrics for the much-loved standard "Les Feuilles Mortes" ("Autumn Leaves").

Gunga Din George Stevens, 1939

U.S. (RKO) 117m BW **Producer** George Stevens **Screenplay** Ben Hecht, from poem by Rudyard Kipling **Photography** Joseph H. August **Music** Alfred Newman **Cast** Cary Grant, Victor McLaglen, Douglas Fairbanks Jr., Sam Jaffe, Eduardo Ciannelli, Joan Fontaine, Montagu Love, Robert Coote, Abner Biberman, Lumsden Hare **Oscar nomination** Joseph H. August (photography)

Classic Hollywood's purest adventure story, *Gunga Din* derives, strangely enough, from a Rudyard Kipling poem, which furnished writers Ben Hecht and Charles MacArthur with only atmosphere and the minor character of its title.

The most famous entry in a series of 1930s productions that praise British shouldering of the white man's burden, *Gunga Din* tells the story of three professional soldiers (Cary Grant, Douglas Fairbanks Jr., and Victor McLaglen) in the "Imperial Lancers." At first the trio seems about to break up, with one man on the verge of marriage—a fate worse than death in this world of exclusive male values. Fortunately, a terrible threat to the community soon arises in the form of a fanatic sect of ritual murderers, the Thuggees. Two set-piece battles follow, expertly staged by Stevens. At the film's climax, the three sergeants are locked in a standoff with the Thuggees, whose evil leader has used them to lure the regiment into a trap. But Gunga Din (Sam Jaffe) rises as if from the dead to sound his bugle and warn the troop, who then slaughter the fanatics. The trio are reunited with their regiment to celebrate the heroism of their fallen companion.

Made on what was a huge budget for the time, *Gunga Din* is a spectacular visual treat, one of the most impressive action films ever made—the buddy film to end all buddy films. **RBP**

Ninotchka Ernst Lubitsch, 1939

U.S. (Loew's, MGM) 110m BW **Producer** Ernst Lubitsch **Screenplay** Melchior Lengyel, Charles Brackett **Photography** William H. Daniels **Music** Werner R. Heymann **Cast** Greta Garbo, Melvyn Douglas, Ina Claire, Bela Lugosi, Sig Ruman, Felix Bressart, Alexander Granach, Gregory Gaye, Rolfe Sedan, Edwin Maxwell, Richard Carle **Oscar nominations** Sidney Franklin (best picture), Melchior Lengyel, Charles Brackett, Walter Reisch, Billy Wilder (screenplay), Greta Garbo (actress)

Ernst Lubitsch's most charming and humorous comedy of European manners features Greta Garbo in a rare comic role. Set in Paris during the 1920s, *Ninotchka*'s plot revolves around the attempt of the Soviet government to recover priceless jewels from the exiled Grand Duchess Swana (Ina Claire). Three bumbling bureaucrats fail at this mission and find themselves seduced by the luxuries and freedoms of Western society. So it is up to Ninotchka (Garbo) to regain the treasure by dealing with the lover of the Grand Duchess, the smooth and handsome Leon (Melvyn Douglas).

In the end, Ninotchka is able to get the jewels only by returning to Moscow and breaking with Leon, who soon follows her to Russia. Though they are in love, she refuses to betray her country, and Leon must use subterfuge to have her travel to Istanbul, where he meets her and they decide to marry. The film's political themes are hardly serious but serve as the background for one comic shtick after another, most memorably perhaps Ninotchka's attempt—in a fancy Paris nightclub—to get the ladies room attendants to go on strike. Douglas is perfect as the enamored and self-indulgent Leon, but this is Garbo's picture and her last great screen role. **RBP**

1939

U.S. (MGM) 101m BW / Technicolor
Producer Mervyn LeRoy, Arthur Freed
Screenplay Noel Langley, Florence Ryerson,
Edgar Allan Woolf, from the novel *The
Wonderful Wizard of Oz* by L. Frank Baum
Photography Harold Rosson **Music** Harold
Arlen, E.Y. Harburg, George Bassman, George
E. Stoll, Herbert Stothart **Cast** Judy Garland,
Frank Morgan, Ray Bolger, Bert Lahr, Jack
Haley, Billie Burke, Margaret Hamilton,
Charley Grapewin, Pat Walshe, Clara
Blandick, Terry the dog, The Singer Midgets
Oscars Herbert Stothart (music), Harold
Arlen, E.Y. Harburg (song) **Oscar
nominations** Mervyn LeRoy (best picture),
Harold Rosson (photography), Cedric
Gibbons, William A. Horning (art direction),
A. Arnold Gillespie (special visual effects),
Douglas Shearer (special sound effects)
Cannes Film Festival Victor Fleming
(Golden Palm nomination)

*"A delightful piece of
wonder-working."*

**Frank S. Nugent,
The New York Times, 1939**

i

The role of the Wizard
was originally envisaged
for comedian W.C. Fields.

The Wizard of Oz Victor Fleming, 1939

Based on *The Wonderful Wizard of Oz*, the turn-of-the-century children's novel by L. Frank Baum, this evergreen classic is one of the great film fairy tales, also a first-rate musical and the vehicle that turned Judy Garland from a talented child performer into a lasting and iconic movie star. Not hugely profitable on its first release, perhaps because it was such an expensive production, *The Wizard of Oz* has become beloved by successive generations. Like *It's a Wonderful Life* (1946), its popularity was boosted in the 1950s by annual Christmas television screenings, which established it as among the most beloved of all movies.

Along with her little dog Toto, Garland's Dorothy Gale (breasts strapped down to make her seem younger) is whisked out of a sepia Kansas by a tornado and dumped in the ravishing Technicolor Land of Oz, where she squashes a witch under her house, is gifted by Glinda the Good (Billie Burke) with the dead hag's magic ruby slippers, and takes off down the Yellow Brick Road to the Emerald City in order to find her way back to the farm from which she once wished she could escape. The "no place like home" theme, a screenwriter's convenience to keep all the characters focused on their quests, has always seemed like a slight cop-out (why would anyone want to leave the wonders of Oz and go back to Kansas?). It never quite squares with the spoilsport interpretation of the whole film as a delirious dream in which Dorothy has recast everyone she knows as her Land of Oz friends and enemies.

The film has many splendors: a superb Harold Arlen–E.Y. Harburg score (ranging from the wistful "Over the Rainbow" through the infectious jollity of "Off to See the Wizard" and "Ding-Dong, the Witch Is Dead" to the classic comedy of "If I Only Had a Brain"), incredible MGM set design, hundreds of squeaky Munchkins and flying monkeys, the "horse of a different color" gag, and perfect performances all round. There are also a number of unforgettable stand-out moments: Ray Bolger's Scarecrow being dismembered while Jack Haley's Tin Man laments, "Well, that's you all over"; Bert Lahr's Cowardly Lion trying to be threatening ("I'll fight you with one paw tied behind my back"); Wicked Witch Margaret Hamilton's fate under a bucket of water ("I'm melting, I'm melting!"); Frank Morgan emerging from behind the curtain ("I'm a very good man, it's just that I'm a very bad wizard").

Like its 1939 MGM stablemate *Gone with the Wind*, *The Wizard of Oz* bears a director's credit for solid pro Victor Fleming but is actually a triumph of the producer's art, with Mervyn LeRoy pulling together all the diverse elements of a hardly smooth shoot. Buddy Ebsen was cast as the Scarecrow then switched to playing the Tin Man until he turned out to be allergic to the makeup; a whole "Jitterbug" number was dropped and hidden until it showed up in *That's Entertainment!* (1974); and the midgets cast as the Munchkins reputedly ran riot. Best line: "Hearts will never be practical until they can be made unbreakable." **KN**

La DISTRIBUTION PARISIENNE DE FILMS présente

LA RÈGLE DU JEU
de JEAN RENOIR

NORA GREGOR . PAULETTE DUBOST . MILA PARELY . DALIO
CARETTE . ROLAND TOUTAIN . GASTON MODOT . PIERRE MAGNIER
JEAN RENOIR

France (Les Nouvelles Editions
Françaises) 110m BW **Language** French
Producer Claude Renoir **Screenplay** Carl
Koch, Jean Renoir **Photography** Jean-Paul
Alphen, Jean Bachelet, Jacques Lemare,
Alain Renoir **Music** Roger Désormières
Cast Nora Gregor, Paulette Dubost, Mila
Parély, Odette Talazac, Claire Gérard, Anne
Mayen, Lise Elina, Marcel Dalio, Julien
Carette, Roland Toutain, Gaston Modot,
Jean Renoir, Pierre Magnier, Eddy Debray,
Pierre Nay

*"That's also part
of the times, today
everyone lies."*

**André Jurieux
(Roland Toutain)**

i

The film aroused violent reactions at
its opening—some of the audience
attempted to set the cinema on fire.

La règle du jeu Jean Renoir, 1939
The Rules of the Game

After the great success of *The Grand Illusion* (1937) and *La Bête Humaine* (1938), Jean Renoir, together with his brother Claude and three friends, founded his own production company, Les Nouvelles Editions Françaises. The NEF's first announced project was an updating of Pierre de Marivaux's *Les Caprices de Marianne*; asked to describe what his film would be like, Renoir answered, "An exact description of the bourgeoisie of our time." This is the film that was eventually titled *The Rules of the Game*.

After completing a transatlantic flight in record time, aviator André Jurieux (Roland Toutain) announces over the radio his disappointment that a certain someone isn't at the airport to greet him. That "someone" is Christine (Nora Gregor), an Austrian married to mechanical bird collector Robert de la Cheyniest (Marcel Dalio). Octave (played by Renoir himself), friend and confidant of both André and Christine, convinces Robert to invite André out to a hunting party at his lavish estate La Colinière as a way of saving face; for his part, Robert hopes having André around might distract Christine while he settles accounts with his longtime mistress Geneviève (Mila Parély). That is what's happening among the "masters." Turning to the "servants," there's Lisette (Paulette Dubost), maid to Christine and married to Schumacher (Gaston Modot), groundskeeper at La Colinière, who catches the eye of Marceau (Julien Carette), a poacher who gets hired by Robert as a house servant. Renoir's screenplay brings the various amorous adventures of the masters and servants together, heading finally to the "accidental" shooting of André, sacrificed so that a corrupt social order can remain intact.

A cinematic style favoring deep spaces and a highly mobile camera here reaches its perfection, as Renoir underlines the theatrical atmosphere that dominates both onstage and off. Most of the performances are flawless: Dalio as Robert, Carette as Marceau, Dubost as Lisette, and Modot as Schumacher. Reviewers over the years have quibbled over Gregor's performance as Christine, wondering why so many men in the film are smitten with her—but perhaps that's the point. Boldly, Renoir cast himself as Octave, a devastating portrait of a man who fills in the emptiness of his own life by serving as the intermediary for the affairs of others.

A commercial disaster when first released in the summer of 1939, *The Rules of the Game* was cut and recut but to no avail; soon after the war began that fall, it was banned as a danger to public morale. In the late 1940s and 1950s, its legend was kept alive by André Bazin and his disciples at *Cahiers du Cinéma*, who claimed that alongside *Citizen Kane* (1941), *Rules* had been the harbinger of modern cinema, yet it was known only in a shortened version (88 minutes). In 1956, it was reconstructed to almost its original length (113 minutes, but it's still missing a scene), presented at the Venice Film Festival in 1959, and the rest is film history, with *The Rules of the Game* finally celebrated internationally as the masterpiece it is. **RP**

Zangiku monogatari Kenji Mizoguchi, 1939
The Story of the Late Chrysanthemums

Japan (Shochiku) 143m BW
Language Japanese Screenplay Matsutarô Kawaguchi, Yoshikata Yoda, from novel by Shôfû Muramatsu Photography Yozô Fuji, Minoru Miki Music Shirô Fukai, Senji Itô Cast Shôtarô Hanayagi, Kôkichi Takada, Gonjurô Kawarazaki, Kakuko Mori, Tokusaburo Arashi, Yôko Umemura

In the nineteenth century, a lazy and untalented Kabuki actor born into a famous family falls in love with his brother's wet nurse. Opposed to their match, his family casts her out of the house. He follows her, and she devotes her life to helping him improve his art, ruining her health in the process. In the end, she dies at home while he, having at last achieved recognition as an actor, leads his troupe on a triumphal boat procession through Osaka.

The Story of the Late Chrysanthemums is one of the essential Kenji Mizoguchi films, a work of dazzling elegance and formal rigor and a powerful attack on the social structures that impose the roles of sacrificial victims upon women. Mizoguchi's long takes move the narrative slowly, enfolding the inexorable logic of events within larger and more complex structures. The film allows time for reflection and interiorization, as the characters, recognizing their places in the patterns of power, react to events with fear, horror, sadness, or revolt. The narrative, with its emphasis on metaphorical journeys—the migrations of the acting troupe and the hero's path to artistic excellence—allows Mizoguchi to create a double metaphorical filter. For him, cinema and theater are machines for the distillation of beauty and the achievement of tragic understanding. **CFu**

His Girl Friday Howard Hawks, 1940

U.S. (Columbia) 92m BW Producer Howard Hawks Screenplay Ben Hecht, Charles MacArthur Photography Joseph Walker Music Sidney Cutner, Felix Mills Cast Cary Grant, Rosalind Russell, Ralph Bellamy, Gene Lockhart, Porter Hall, Ernest Truex, Cliff Edwards, Clarence Kolb, Roscoe Karns, Frank Jenks, Regis Toomey, Abner Biberman, Frank Orth, Helen Mack, John Qualen

Ben Hecht and Charles MacArthur's classic newspaper play *The Front Page* had been filmed successfully before and would be again after this sparkling 1939 version, scripted by Hecht and Charles Lederer. But astute and witty director Howard Hawks delights in the simple twist that was a stroke of genius—turning ace reporter Hildy Johnson into a woman. Voilà, *His Girl Friday* became the fastest-talking battle of the sexes in history of romantic screwball comedy.

Scintillating Rosalind Russell is the wisecracking star reporter her editor and ex-husband (Cary Grant as the unscrupulous and aggressively charming Walter Burns) can't lose in the middle of a hot murder story. When she announces that she's quitting to marry a meek square (Ralph Bellamy), Walter's incredulity and dismay launch him into conniving overdrive. As wily Walter calculates, Hildy can't resist a last big story and is shortly up to her absurd hat in a jailhouse break and corruption exposé. Grant and Russell engage in dizzying verbal play of machine-gun speed in a plot that reaches farcical heights, with a great character ensemble of gum-chewing, smoke-wreathed, poker-playing hacks acting as their cynical chorus. Theatrical and stylish, *His Girl Friday* is unrivaled for comic timing and snappy repartee. **AE**

1940

Fantasia Ben Sharpsteen (supervisor), 1940

U.S. (Walt Disney) 120m Technicolor
Producer Walt Disney, Ben Sharpsteen
Screenplay Joe Grant, Dick Huemer
Photography James Wong Howe, Maxwell
Morgan **Music** Bach, Beethoven, Dukas,
Mussorgsky, Schubert, Stravinsky,
Tchaikovsky **Cast** Leopold Stokowski
(conductor, the Philadelphia Orchestra),
Deems Taylor (narrator), Julietta Novis
(soloist) **Oscars** Walt Disney, William E.
Garity, J.N.A. Hawkins (honorary award),
Leopold Stokowski and associates
(honorary award)

"A creation so thoroughly delightful and exciting in its novelty that one's senses are captivated by it, one's imagination is deliciously inspired."

The New York Times, 1940

Although now commonplace, creating images to interpret music was revolutionary when this audacious milestone in animation and stereophonic audio recording was conceived and executed by the Walt Disney studio to universal acclaim and astonishment. Graced by the eminent symphonic star Leopold Stokowski conducting the Philadelphia Orchestra, *Fantasia*'s eight wide-ranging sequences comprise a concert with ambitious, amusing, portentous, and experimental cartoons accompanying pieces by Tchaikovsky, Mussorgsky, Schubert, and others.

Even on IMAX screens, the exhibition scene of choice for the most recent of Disney's several anniversary restorations, rerecordings, and rereleases of their prized 1940 animation landmark, *Fantasia* can be disappointing because it is still a remorselessly kitsch experience, however impressive and groundbreaking an achievement. Baby boomers who enjoyed it on hallucinogenics in their youths are probably the audience fondest of it now. But there are some magical sequences that endure, as befits a film made by sixty animators working under no less than eleven directors (supervised by Ben Sharpsteen).

Most watchable are the abstractions ahead of their time to Bach, in which the multichannel sound is perfectly synchronized to the drawings and seems to soar out of the screen. Mickey Mouse, never more delightful than as the Sorcerer's Apprentice desperately trying to halt the self-replicating brooms he has conjured up to do his chores, the dancing Chinese mushrooms, a darling chorus line of eyelash-batting pachyderms, the hippos in ballet tutus cavorting daintily and fleeing caped alligators to "The Dance of the Hours"—all still a hoot. Together these make for a sweet hour of greatness. In between are sequences that have not aged as well. The capering fairies who are nude but tastefully free from sexual organs, the seemingly interminable decline of the dinosaurs to Stravinsky's *Rite of Spring*, and the vulgar absurdity to which Beethoven's *Pastorale* has been subjected (centaurs flirtatiously pursuing coy, suspiciously pubescent-looking centaurettes who are coiffed in the style of Joan Crawford) all take some beating for incredulity value. **AE**

ℹ️

Mickey Mouse's image was updated for *Fantasia*. His eyes now had pupils for the first time.

Rebecca Alfred Hitchcock, 1940

It is somewhat surprising that despite Alfred Hitchcock's long, fruitful career, and despite several subsequent nominations, only *Rebecca*, his first American film, earned him an Academy Award for Best Picture. Then again, that may say more about the persuasive power of producer David O. Selznick. Hot from the success of the 1939 film *Gone with the Wind*, Selznick seized the opportunity to work with Hitchcock, pairing the director with Daphne Du Maurier's gothic ghost story.

Working with a big budget, Hitchcock transformed the Manderley mansion into a character unto itself—later the inspiration for the imposing Xanadu in *Citizen Kane* (1941). The palatial seaside estate is the atmospheric setting for the strained romance between Joan Fontaine and Laurence Olivier. He's a wealthy widower wooing the innocent Fontaine, and she never questions her good fortune in finding such a loving man. They marry after a whirlwind romance, but as their relationship deepens, Fontaine is haunted more and more by the spirit of his dead wife—Rebecca. Is the haunting merely a figment of her imagination, or the fruits of paranoia, or is a more nefarious force at work? And what, if anything, does the suspicious servant Mrs. Danvers (Judith Anderson), who always seems to be hovering near the nerve-wracked Fontaine, have to do with the strange goings-on?

Rebecca marked Hitchcock's auspicious arrival in America. All his artistic traits were used to full effect: there's the murky, mysterious earlier history, the barely contained suspicions, the fairy-tale romance doomed by the encroaching past, and, of course, the looming specter of foul play. *Rebecca* does lack some of Hitchcock's trademark playfulness, and the sense of humor is missed; the absence of levity is due in no small part to the unremittingly gloomy, gothic nature of Du Maurier's melodramatic novel. Innocent Fontaine is nearly driven to madness by the lingering secrets of Manderley, but Hitchcock is more than happy to let the tension build and build toward the haunting conclusion. **JKl**

U.S. (Selznick) 130m BW **Producer** David O. Selznick **Screenplay** Philip MacDonald, from novel by Daphne Du Maurier **Photography** George Barnes **Music** Franz Waxman **Cast** Laurence Olivier, Joan Fontaine, George Sanders, Judith Anderson, Gladys Cooper, Nigel Bruce, Reginald Denny, C. Aubrey Smith, Melville Cooper, Florence Bates, Leonard Carey, Leo G. Carroll, Edward Fielding, Lumsden Hare, Forrester Harvey **Oscars** David O. Selznick (best picture), George Barnes (photography) **Oscar nominations** Alfred Hitchcock (director), Robert E. Sherwood, Joan Harrison (screenplay), Laurence Olivier (actor), Joan Fontaine (actress), Judith Anderson (actress in support role), Lyle R. Wheeler (art direction), Hal C. Kern (editing), Jack Cosgrove, Arthur Johns (special effects), Franz Waxman (music)

*"Do you think
the dead come back
and watch the living?"*

**Mrs. Danvers (Judith Anderson)
to The Second Mrs. de Winter
(Joan Fontaine)**

i

Ironically, at the Oscars *Rebecca* triumphed over Hitchcock's final British picture, *Foreign Correspondent*.

The Philadelphia Story George Cukor, 1940

U.S. (MGM) 112m BW **Producer** Joseph L. Mankiewicz **Screenplay** Donald Ogden Stewart, from play by Philip Barry **Photography** Joseph Ruttenberg **Music** Franz Waxman **Cast** Cary Grant, Katharine Hepburn, James Stewart, Ruth Hussey, John Howard, Roland Young, John Halliday, Mary Nash, Virginia Weidler, Henry Daniell, Lionel Pape, Rex Evans **Oscars** Donald Ogden Stewart (screenplay), James Stewart (actor) **Oscar nominations** Joseph L. Mankiewicz (best picture), George Cukor (director), Katharine Hepburn (actress), Ruth Hussey (actress in support role)

i

The play was subsequently remade, with additional musical numbers, as *High Society* (1956).

George Cukor's 1940 adaptation of Philip Barry's theatrical farce is the uncontested classic of all sophisticated slapstick comedies. Katharine Hepburn had starred in the play on Broadway and it is said that playwright Phillip Barry based the leading female character on her reputation at the time. Having left RKO on less than ideal terms, the public saw Hepburn as bossy and unfeminine—not the womanly ideal for the late 1930s.

In the opening scene, now famous for its virtually dialogue-free fury, heiress Tracy Lord (Hepburn) watches her recently divorced playboy husband Dexter Haven (Cary Grant) put a few of his belongings in the car, snapping a golf club over her thigh in anger. Trying to prove that she is not impossible to love, Tracy plans to marry a respectable if colorless man at the family mansion when Dexter returns with two reporters in tow, Mike Connor (James Stewart) and Liz Imbrie (Ruth Hussey), specifically to ruin the wedding. Never more luminous, Hepburn outdoes herself in a role which demands impeccable comic timing as well as true vulnerability.

Hepburn owned the rights to the project, which she then wisely sold to MGM on condition that she recap her leading role as well as choose the director and cast. She had wanted Clark Gable as Dexter and Spencer Tracy as Mike, but because of scheduling clashes neither were available. Cukor managed to make Hepburn's negative public image work for her through her character, eliciting feelings of sorrow for a beautiful woman so misunderstood. The film was an enormous success, with an award-winning screenplay that matched comedy with social commentary. **KK**

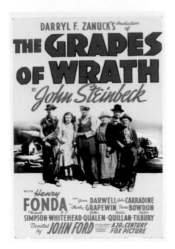

The Grapes of Wrath John Ford, 1940

Few American pictures in the 1930s got to grips with the suffering and dislocation of the Great Depression. Hollywood largely left it to other media to document the national disaster. John Steinbeck's novel *The Grapes of Wrath*, first published in 1939, was based on solid research, following dispossessed farming families from Oklahoma as they journeyed to the orchards of California in search of casual labor.

Despite objections from the conservative financiers who controlled the studio, Darryl Zanuck bought the book for 20th Century Fox. He knew that John Ford was the right man to direct it, with his feeling for the American people and their history. Ford also identified what was most heartbreaking about the plight of the Joad family—not their acute poverty, but the psychological trauma of being uprooted from their home, of being cast out on the road, rootless. In a memorable scene Ma Joad (Jane Darwell) burns the possessions she can't take with her the night before they must abandon their farm.

For his hero, Tom Joad, Ford cast Henry Fonda, who had just appeared in Ford's *Young Mr. Lincoln* (1939) and *Drums Along the Mohawk* (1939), two other pieces of Americana. Members of the unofficial John Ford Stock Company to appear included Russell Simpson as Pa Joad, John Qualen as their friend Muley, and John Carradine as an itinerant preacher. And for his cameraman Ford made an inspired choice. Gregg Toland captured brilliantly the documentary look of the pictures that had been taken of the dustbowl tragedy by government-employed photographers such as Dorothea Lange. Nowhere is this better seen than in a sequence where the Joads drive into a squatters camp, the camera dwelling on the grim faces of the occupants and on the run-down shacks where they live.

Though *The Grapes of Wrath* does not shirk from showing the enormity of its subjects' plight, there is a significant departure from the novel. In Steinbeck's book the Joads first find easier conditions in a government-run camp, but by the end are reduced to starvation wages. In the film, they find the camp later on, thus making their progress an upward curve, marked by Ma's final speech: "We're the people. . . . We'll go on forever." **EB**

U.S. (Fox) 128m BW
Producer Nunnally Johnson, Darryl F. Zanuck **Screenplay** Nunnally Johnson, from novel by John Steinbeck **Photography** Gregg Toland **Cast** Henry Fonda, Jane Darwell, John Carradine, Charley Grapewin, Dorris Bowdon, Russell Simpson, O.Z. Whitehead, John Qualen, Eddie Quillan, Zeffie Tilbury, Frank Sully, Frank Darien, Darryl Hickman, Shirley Mills, Roger Imhof **Oscars** John Ford (director), Jane Darwell (actress in support role) **Oscar nominations** Darryl F. Zanuck, Nunnally Johnson (best picture), Nunnally Johnson (screenplay), Henry Fonda (actor), Robert L. Simpson (editing), Edmund H. Hansen (sound)

> *"Seems like the government's got more interest in a dead man than a live one."*

Tom Joad (Henry Fonda)

i

Tom Joad's last speech was recited at Henry Fonda's funeral in 1982.

The Mortal Storm Frank Borzage, 1940

One of the few anti-Nazi films Hollywood made before Pearl Harbor—detailed and passionate in its condemnation of Nazism—Frank Borzage's *The Mortal Storm* opens on the day Adolf Hitler becomes Chancellor of Germany. The day also happens to be the sixtieth birthday of Professor Viktor Roth (Frank Morgan), a beloved science professor at a university in southern Germany. The film shows the consolidation of Nazi Germany through the destruction of the "non-Aryan" Roth and his family: his wife, his two Aryan stepsons, who become rabid Nazis, and his actual daughter, Freya (Margaret Sullavan).

Borzage portrays Nazism as a form of insanity, to which many men (only one woman as far as we see) succumb as if by contagion or by natural predisposition (the film makes no analysis of the socioeconomic roots of Nazism) but with which, in some individuals, a residual humanity comes into conflict. The magnificent final scene locates this conflict within the character played by Robert Stack. Alone in his stepfather's house, he walks through its empty rooms. The camera tracks past him, exploring the shadowy space, the soundtrack filled with dialogue from earlier scenes; we hear the young man's footsteps as he goes out of the house.

The Mortal Storm is one of American cinema's great love stories. Borzage's poignant and subtle handling of the relationship between Freya and Martin (James Stewart) is in keeping with the director's career long commitment to the transcendent power of love—an idealism to which the admirable performances of Sullavan and Stewart are uncompromisingly faithful. Just before the lovers' trek to the mountainous pass across the Austrian border, Martin's mother (Maria Ouspenskaya) has them celebrate their union by drinking from a ceremonial wine cup. This scene is one of the most luminous in all Borzage's work.

Uncredited coproducer Victor Saville said he directed much of the film, a claim that has been widely repeated but contradicted by several key cast and crew members. There can be no doubt that *The Mortal Storm* is fully representative of the style, philosophy, and concerns of Frank Borzage. **CFu**

U.S. (Loew's, MGM) 100m
BW **Producer** Frank Borzage
Screenplay George Froeschel, Hans Rameau, Claudine West, from novel by Phyllis Bottome **Photography** William H. Daniels **Music** Bronislau Kaper, Eugene Zador **Cast** Margaret Sullavan, James Stewart, Robert Young, Frank Morgan, Robert Stack, Bonita Granville, Irene Rich, William T. Orr, Maria Ouspenskaya, Gene Reynolds, Russell Hicks, William Edmunds, Esther Dale, Dan Dailey, Granville Bates

> "Hollywood has turned its camera eye upon the most tragic human drama of our age."
>
> *The New York Times*, 1940

1940

i

Unsurprisingly, its uncompromising message saw the film—and all MGM movies—banned in Nazi Germany.

The Bank Dick Edward F. Cline, 1940

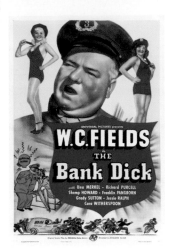

U.S. (Matty Fox, Universal) 74m BW
Producer Jack J. Gross **Screenplay** W.C.
Fields **Photography** Milton R. Krasner
Music Charles Previn **Cast** W.C. Fields, Cora
Witherspoon, Una Merkel, Evelyn Del Rio,
Jessie Ralph, Franklin Pangborn, Shemp
Howard, Dick Purcell, Grady Sutton, Russell
Hicks, Pierre Watkin, Al Hill, George Moran,
Bill Wolfe, Jack Norton

*"Don't be a luddy-duddy!
Don't be a mooncalf!
Don't be a jabbernowl!
You're not those, are you?"*

**Egbert Sousé
(W.C. Fields)**

The Bank Dick was written by W.C. Fields under the name "Mahatma Kane Jeeves," which suggests something of his ambitions, and directed by amiable traffic cop Eddie Cline, whose job was to clear the way so Fields could cut loose with all his multiple idiosyncrasies, As usual, the star is cast as a mild-mannered but resentful bumbler who wants only to be left in peace but is nagged by an unreasonable world into making the effort to respond to various impolite intruders into his happy doze.

Egbert Sousé, a put-upon bumbler who would like nothing more than to spend his life in bars getting quietly drunk, is constantly harassed into making something of himself by his frightful wife (Cora Witherspoon), ghastly mother-in-law (Jessie Relph), obnoxious teenage daughter (Una Merkel), her chinless boob fiancé (Grady Sutton), and his own bratty younger child. When he accidentally foils a bank robbery by blundering into the crook, he is given the job of uniformed security guard and allowed to cause trouble in a succession of absolutely perfect routines that pit him against snooty officials (Franklin Pangborn as a bank inspector driven to distraction), hard-bitten crooks (one would-be robber is dragged off on a hilarious road chase sequence on a par with any silent slapstick), and offensive customers.

Like all the best Fields films (*It's a Gift* [1934], *Never Give a Sucker an Even Break* [1941]), the premise here is just an excuse for a succession of vaudeville-like sketches in which he is pitted against a partner too eccentric to be classed as a straight man but also too vicious to be a victim. Some of the routines in *The Bank Dick*, such as when Sousé somehow finds himself in the director's chair while a movie is being shot, stray far afield from the bank. But the marbled, pompous halls of commerce and capital, with glad-handing moneybags who receive their comeuppance as Sousé somehow becomes rich and "reformed," are an ideal setting for mischief and anarchy. Fields was a rare comedian who could be funny while strangling a small child, and this seventy-five-minute gem is among his masterpieces. **KN**

i

In the film, Sousé's youngest daughter is named after Fields's three sisters: Elsie Mae Adel.

Pinocchio Hamilton Luske & Ben Sharpsteen, 1940

U.S. (Walt Disney) 88m Technicolor
Producer Walt Disney Screenplay Aurelius
Battaglia, from novel by Carlo Collodi
Music Leigh Harline, Paul J. Smith,
Ned Washington Cast (voices) Dickie Jones,
Don Brodie, Walter Catlett, Frankie Darro,
Cliff Edwards, Charles Judels, Christian Rub,
Evelyn Venable Oscars Leigh Harline,
Paul J. Smith, Ned Washington (best original
score), Leigh Harline, Ned Washington
(best original song)

Some of the darker elements of Carlo Collodi's original Italian fable were, of course, discarded once Disney had the story. But only some. The lasting appeal of the animated Pinocchio shows that not all of the alterations the studio made to the story of a wooden puppet brought to life were necessarily for the worse, and several of the story's most frightening details remain prominent. The classic still features plenty of horror as Pinocchio faces the perils of peer pressure that distract him from his goal of becoming a real boy. Guided (but not always led) by his insect "conscience" Jiminy Cricket, Pinocchio must learn not just responsibility but also courage and love during his innocently roguish quest for life.

As Disney's second feature (after *Snow White*), *Pinocchio* showed the then-uncharted world of animation to be rife with possibility, resulting in such enchanting and ethereal creations as the luminous Blue Fairy, and such amazing sequences as the escape from cursed Pleasure Island and the thrilling encounter with the fittingly named Monstro the Whale. Add to these such now standard songs as "When You Wish Upon a Star," and is it any wonder *Pinocchio* has remained a towering standard by which so many animated films are judged? **JKl**

i

All the lines by Mel Blanc (who later voiced Bugs Bunny, among many others) were cut, save some hiccups.

Citizen Kane Orson Welles, 1941

From 1962 until 2012, *Sight & Sound* magazine's oft-cited critics' poll of the greatest films ever made placed *Citizen Kane*, Orson Welles's remarkable debut film, at the top of the list. By 1998, the American Film Institute called it the greatest movie of all time. It also garnered Best Picture awards from the New York Film Critics Circle and the National Board of Review, and won an Oscar for its screenplay. The legend of *Citizen Kane* has partly been fueled by the fact that Welles was only twenty-four when he made the film, but also from the obvious comparisons between the titular character and newspaper magnate William Randolph Hearst, who moved heaven and earth to stop the picture from being made—and then, when he could not stop it from being distributed, tried to discredit it. But beyond the ridiculous hype of any single film being "the greatest movie of all time," *Citizen Kane* is of tremendous interest and importance, for a number of reasons.

The film tells a great story: Charles Foster Kane (played brilliantly by Welles himself) is born poor, but strikes it rich through a gold mine bequeathed to his mother. As a young man he begins to assemble a populist newspaper and radio empire, eventually marrying the niece of an American president and running for governor. But any ambition he has for real power is stymied. As Kane becomes alienated from his power, he becomes increasingly abusive to the women in his life, first his wife, then his mistress. He dies, almost alone, in his reconstructed but unfinished castle, longing for the simplicity of his childhood. Firmly within the traditions of New Deal populism, *Citizen Kane* extols the very American perspective that money cannot buy happiness, but in a highly prosaic, almost Dickensian way.

More significantly, *Citizen Kane* begins with Kane's death, and the enigmatic final word he utters: "Rosebud." A group of intrepid newsreel reporters try to discover the meaning of this last word and interview several of Kane's acquaintances. Not only is the film told in flashback, but each character only knows the man from a certain perspective, which is presented in due course. The film's narrative complexity, without ever violating classical Hollywood narrative continuity and causality, is a remarkable tour de force, responsible in large part for critic Pauline Kael's accusation that the film's true genius lay not in the hands of wunderkind Welles, but in those of screenwriter Herman J. Mankiewicz.

The film's real power, though, lies in its cinematography: Gregg Toland developed a technique for deep-focus photography, wherein the extreme foreground, central middle-ground, and background were all in focus at the same time, allowing the eye to focus on any part of the image. This technique was criticized at the time for calling attention to itself, in direct violation of the codes of classical Hollywood cinematography, wherein good photography was assumed to be invisible. Even by today's different standards, *Citizen Kane*'s cinematography is striking and unforgettable. **MK**

U.S. (Mercury, RKO) 119m BW
Producer Orson Welles, Richard Baer, George Schaefer **Screenplay** Herman J. Mankiewicz, Orson Welles **Photography** Gregg Toland **Music** Bernard Herrmann, Charlie Barnet, Pepe Guízar **Cast** Orson Welles, Joseph Cotten, Dorothy Comingore, Agnes Moorehead, Ruth Warrick, Ray Collins, Erskine Sanford, Everett Sloane, William Alland, Paul Stewart, George Coulouris, Fortunio Bonanova, Gus Schilling, Philip Van Zandt, Georgia Backus, Harry Shannon **Oscar** Herman J. Mankiewicz, Orson Welles (screenplay) **Oscar nominations** Orson Welles (best picture), Orson Welles (director), Orson Welles (actor), Perry Ferguson, Van Nest Polglase, A. Roland Fields, Darrell Silvera (art direction), Gregg Toland (photography), Robert Wise (editing), Bernard Herrmann (music), John Aalberg (sound)

"I always gagged on the silver spoon."

Charles Foster Kane (Orson Welles)

ℹ️

Each time the film's title was announced during the Academy Awards in 1942, it was booed.

Sergeant York Howard Hawks, 1941

U.S. (Warner Bros.) 134m BW
Producer Howard Hawks, Jesse L. Lasky, Hal
B. Wallis **Screenplay** Harry Chandlee, Abem
Finkel **Photography** Sol Polito **Music** Max
Steiner **Cast** Gary Cooper, Walter Brennan,
Joan Leslie, George Tobias, Stanley Ridges,
Margaret Wycherly, Ward Bond, Noah
Beery Jr., June Lockhart **Oscars** Gary Cooper
(actor), William Holmes (editing) **Oscar
nominations** Jesse L. Lasky, Hal B. Wallis
(best picture), Howard Hawks (director),
Harry Chandlee, Abem Finkel, John Huston,
Howard Koch (screenplay), Walter Brennan
(actor in support role), Margaret Wycherly
(actress in support role), Sol Polito
(photography), John Hughes, Fred M.
MacLean (art direction), Max Steiner (music),
Nathan Levinson (sound)

i

Alvin York refused to give permission
for the film to be made unless Gary
Cooper was the actor to play him.

Howard Hawks's *Sergeant York* celebrates the good fight of World War I just as the United States was preparing for World War II. A bellicose subtext is everywhere apparent, yet it is easily assimilated into the moral framework of the film's eponymous lead.

Alvin York, as characterized by Gary Cooper, speaks with a down-home slang, the country bumpkin. His transformation from a spirited Tennessee farmer into a Christian pacifist and finally into a doughboy hero celebrates an array of Hollywood conventions, including sacred mothers and fair-minded leaders. Hackneyed? Yes. But this gem's importance rests in making Cooper a star, if not also in fairly depicting trench warfare only a few months before Pearl Harbor.

That no greater context for World War I is offered here is precisely the point. Sergeant York is narrowly concerned with courage and sacrifice. Anything more would undermine its portrait positing the defense of freedom as an ultimate goal. Simultaneously loving biblical virtue and skilled gunplay, the movie revels in camaraderie, chaste romance, and dueling fisticuffs. In short, it's a Hawksian world here perfectly transposed into a biopic long on small-town values and short on the violent conflict that made the real-life Alvin York famous. **GC-Q**

The Lady Eve
Preston Sturges, 1941

U.S. (Paramount) 97m BW **Producer** Paul Jones **Screenplay** Monckton Hoffe, Preston Sturges **Photography** Victor Milner **Music** Clara Edwards, Sigmund Krumgold **Cast** Barbara Stanwyck, Henry Fonda, Charles Coburn, Eugene Pallette, William Demarest, Eric Blore, Melville Cooper, Martha O'Driscoll, Janet Beecher, Robert Greig, Dora Clement, Luis Alberni **Oscar nomination** Monckton Hoffe (screenplay)

The Lady Eve is a classic screwball comedy and a quintessential Preston Sturges film, reflecting the writer-director's view of romance as the greatest con game of all. The script abounds in superb lines, the dialogue is fast-paced and witty, and the plot offers a clever variation on the familiar battle-of-the-sexes motif.

The film begins on a cruise ship, where resourceful and sophisticated temptress Jean Harrington (Barbara Stanwyck) tries to seduce the guileless snake-lover Charles "Hopsie" Pike (Henry Fonda) in order to con him out of his fortune built on "Pike's Ale." In a highly implausible but delightful plot twist, the action then shifts to Hopsie's Connecticut mansion, where Jean reappears as an English heiress, Lady Eve Sidwich. She seduces Hopsie again and makes him marry her with the intention of dumping him afterward as retribution for having deserted her earlier. In the end, however, her scheming backfires when she truly falls in love with him.

Sturges somehow manages to get away with quite a lot in *The Lady Eve*. Weaving in numerous references to the biblical story of the Fall, he emphasizes sexuality in a way that few filmmakers at the time would have even dared. *The Lady Eve* was remade in 1956 as (the considerably inferior) *The Birds and the Bees*, starring Mitzi Gaynor and David Niven. **RDe**

1941

The Wolf Man
George Waggner, 1941

U.S. (Universal) 70m BW **Producer** Jack J. Gross, George Waggner **Screenplay** Curt Siodmak **Photography** Joseph A. Valentine **Music** Charles Previn, Hans J. Salter, Frank Skinner **Cast** Claude Rains, Warren William, Ralph Bellamy, Patric Knowles, Bela Lugosi, Maria Ouspenskaya, Evelyn Ankers, J.M. Kerrigan, Fay Helm, Lon Chaney Jr., Forrester Harvey

The figure of the wolf man—that bipedal, cinematic version of the werewolf archetype, dramatically embodying the Jekyll/Hyde (superego/id) dichotomy present in us all—first took center stage in Universal's *Werewolf of London* (1935), starring Henry Hull in a role reprised decades later by Jack Nicholson in *Wolf* (1994). Shortly thereafter, Curt Siodmak finished the screenplay for what was to be Universal Pictures' latest horror classic—following *Dracula* (1931), *Frankenstein* (1931), and *The Mummy* (1932)—*The Wolf Man*. In what still remains the most recognizable and cherished version of the myth, Lon Chaney Jr., stars as Lawrence Talbot, an American-educated Welshman who wants nothing more than to be cured of his irrepressible (when the moon is full) lycanthropy.

Makeup king Jack Pierce devised an elaborate yak-hair costume for Chaney that would come to serve as the template for countless Halloween masks. What distinguishes Siodmark's story from previous werewolf tales was the coded emphasis on repressed sexual energy as the motivating force behind Talbot's full-moon transformations. As the gypsy Maleva (Maria Ouspenskaya) explains, "Even a man that is pure in heart, and says his prayers by night, may become a wolf when the wolfbane blooms and the autumn moon is bright." The success of this picture led to four more Chaney-driven Wolf Man films in the 1940s alone. Dozens of imitators, updates, takeoffs, and spoofs have followed. **SJS**

High Sierra Raoul Walsh, 1941

High Sierra is a landmark of the gangster genre, a career turning point for Humphrey Bogart, and a model of action-film existentialism by Raoul Walsh. Like Walsh's earlier *The Roaring Twenties* (1939), *High Sierra* is an elegiac gangster film, unusual in this Production Code-ruled period for its sympathetic portrayal of the gangster as an outdated outcast. Old-timer Roy Earle (Bogart), the nobly named hero, towers above the punks and hypocrites he encounters on both sides of the law as he leads an ill-fated hotel heist, foolishly pursues a respectable girl (Joan Leslie), and briefly finds more suitable companionship with a fellow outcast (Ida Lupino).

In contrast to such contemporaries as John Ford, Howard Hawks, Frank Capra, and Michael Curtiz, who stress the value of the community or group, Walsh in this period gave more weight to his heroes' egotism, nonconformity, and antisocial qualities. *High Sierra*'s view of straight-and-narrow society is scathing, peaking in the scene in which Roy is rejected by his vapid middle-class princess in favor of her smug conformist boyfriend.

After a decade of playing squares and punks, Bogart got his most substantial role yet in *High Sierra*. In *The Maltese Falcon*, his other important film of 1941, Bogart is expansive, smart-alecky, domineering. In *High Sierra*, Bogart's subtler performance creates a distinctively different persona: moody, withdrawn, and tense, his shoulders hunched and his gestures cramped to emphasize the character's insular nature. Even in Roy's intimate scenes with his soulmate Marie (Lupino), Walsh places objects and barriers between the lovers to underline their essential isolation.

High Sierra begins and ends with the lofty peak of Mount Whitney, which appears throughout the film, its siren presence beckoning the hero to his lonely destiny. Another underworld character says to Roy, "You remember what Johnny Dillinger said about guys like you and him? He said you were just rushing toward death. Yeah, that's it: just rushing toward death!" The great car-chase scene in which the cops pursue Roy up the fatal mountain—a spectacular payoff of the entire film's tight, kinetic style—translates those words into the dynamic visual language of action cinema at its height. **MR**

U.S. (Warner Bros.) 100m BW **Producer** Mark Hellinger, Hal B. Wallis **Screenplay** John Huston, from novel by W.R. Burnett **Photography** Tony Gaudio **Music** Adolph Deutsch **Cast** Ida Lupino, Humphrey Bogart, Alan Curtis, Arthur Kennedy, Joan Leslie, Henry Hull, Henry Travers, Jerome Cowan, Minna Gombell, Barton MacLane, Elisabeth Risdon, Cornel Wilde, Donald MacBride, Paul Harvey, Isabel Jewell

> "*I wouldn't give you two cents for a dame without a temper.*"
>
> **Roy Earle**
> **(Humphrey Bogart)**

ℹ️

In the movie, Bogart's own dog, "Zero," played the part of his character's dog, "Pard."

1941

How Green Was My Valley John Ford, 1941

U.S. (Fox) 118 min BW
Producer Darryl F. Zanuck **Screenplay** Philip
Dunne, from novel by Richard Llewellyn
Photography Arthur C. Miller **Music** Alfred
Newman **Cast** Walter Pidgeon, Maureen
O'Hara, Anna Lee, Donald Crisp, Roddy
McDowall, John Loder, Sara Allgood, Barry
Fitzgerald, Patric Knowles, Morton Lowry,
Arthur Shields, Ann E. Todd, Frederick
Worlock, Richard Fraser, Evan S. Evans
Oscars Darryl F. Zanuck (best picture), John
Ford (director), Donald Crisp (actor in
support role), Richard Day, Nathan Juran,
Thomas Little (art direction), Arthur C. Miller
(photography) **Oscar nominations** Philip
Dunne (screenplay), Sara Allgood (actress in
support role), James B. Clark (editing), Alfred
Newman (music), Edmund H. Hansen (sound)

Though John Ford was most famous, of course, for making Westerns, he also had a fondness for all things Irish. Not that this Oscar-winning version of Richard Llewellyn's novel was transported across the Irish Sea from its setting in the Welsh coal-mining valleys; rather, the film is imbued with the same kind of fulsome nostalgia for the eccentric satisfactions of family life in the old country that distinguished the 1952 film *The Quiet Man*. Ford's Wales, in fact, is just as much a country of the mind as was his beloved Ireland (at least in terms of how it was depicted on screen or invoked in words). This explains why Richard Day's beautifully designed mining village, for all the painstaking detail applied to its construction on the Fox backlot, feels like a dream of archetypal Welshness rather than any real village.

That, however, is wholly appropriate to the mood of nostalgia that fuels *How Green Was My Valley* from start to finish. The story is narrated by a man reflecting on his now-distant childhood, when as the youngest son (Roddy McDowall) of the Morgan family, he would see his father (Donald Crisp) and four brothers traipse daily up the hill on the way to the pit. What he recalls are not just the hardships—the perilous working conditions, the threat of poverty, cold, and hunger—and the tragic deaths but also the warm, loving sense of community that reigned in the lives both of the family and of the village as a whole. But that happy togetherness was forever lost when wage cuts brought strikes and conflict between the kindly but traditional patriarch and the (marginally) more militant sons: a conflict that resulted in the boys going off to find better-paid work in the Promised Land of—where else?—America.

The entire film is colored by bittersweet remembrance: by the loss of family, childhood innocence, one's country, and a stern but fair father. It's true Ford idealizes the world he depicts, but that is what makes it so effective. Yes, the film is a tearjerker, it is clichéd (the miners never seem to stop singing), and the accents are an odd mix from all around the United Kingdom and Ireland—but aren't dreams ever thus? **GA**

"You cannot conquer injustice with more injustice."

**Mr. Gruffydd
(Walter Pidgeon)**

ℹ️

The film won the Best Picture Academy Award at the 1942 Oscars, triumphing over *Citizen Kane*.

Sullivan's Travels Preston Sturges, 1941

U.S. (Paramount) 90m BW
Producer Paul Jones, Buddy G. DeSylva,
Preston Sturges **Screenplay** Preston Sturges
Photography John F. Seitz **Music** Charles
Bradshaw, Leo Shuken **Cast** Joel McCrea,
Veronica Lake, Robert Warwick, William
Demarest, Franklin Pangborn, Porter Hall,
Byron Foulger, Margaret Hayes, Robert Greig,
Eric Blore, Torben Meyer, Victor Potel, Richard
Webb, Charles R. Moore, Almira Sessions

*"There's a lot to be said
for making people laugh.
Did you know that that's
all some people have?"*

**John L. Sullivan
(Joel McCrea)**

i

Veronica Lake was between
six and eight months
pregnant during filming.

As one of American cinema's earliest auteurs and cutting a distinctly modern figure (his mother's best friend was Isadora Duncan; he spent his youth criss-crossing the Atlantic; a "kiss-proof" lipstick and ticker-tape machine were among his patented inventions), Preston Sturges was responsible for an explosion of now-classic films in the 1940s. These films are known for their sophisticated verbal wit, uproarious physical comedy, and their affectionate portrayal of eccentric, scene-stealing supporting characters. But Sturges's work is also consistent in its exploration of the possibilities and prospects of upward—and occasionally downward—mobility. In what may be his finest, most complex film, *Sullivan's Travels*, Sturges brilliantly mixes broad humor with sharp-edged cultural commentary, once again—as in *The Great McGinty* (1940), *Christmas in July* (1940), and *The Lady Eve* (1941)—revealing social identity to be a highly unstable proposition, capable of hyperbolic transformation through such prosaic means as disguise, confusion, and self-deception.

John L. Sullivan (Joel McCrea) is a can't-miss Hollywood director who specializes in lightweight entertainment, exemplified by broad comedies such as the 1939 film *Ants in Your Pants*. Naïve and sheltered by a solicitous staff who have no interest in seeing their meal ticket change genres or become overly ambitious in his cinematic pursuits, Sully nonetheless sets his sights on directing an epic social commentary picture about tough times in Depression-era America, to be entitled *O Brother, Where Art Thou?* (a fictional title eventually used by the Coen Brothers for their own 2000 film, in clever tribute to Sturges). To research his topic, which involves such unpleasant issues as suffering, deprivation, and racial inequality, Sully insists on disguising himself as a hobo and making his way across the country to experience "real life" firsthand.

Once on the road, assorted adventures, meetings (notably with Veronica Lake's down-on-her-luck ingenue), and mishaps—some hilarious, others surprisingly poignant—transpire before Sully eventually comes to terms with his true calling as a lowbrow moviemaker with a gift for making people laugh. The lesson here is that strained seriousness and forced profundity have far less benefit for the masses than good old-fashioned humor, with its power to help people forget their troubles, if only for a while.

That *Sullivan's Travels* possesses an autobiographical dimension is impossible to deny, with Sturges affirming the value of what he himself did best—making smart comedies with the power to lift viewers' spirits—while ripping apart the pretentiousness of Hollywood's more sober and "socially committed" filmmakers. Personal statements aside, however, the tour de force script brings together a remarkable range of genres, including slapstick, action, melodrama, social documentary, romance, musical, and prison movie. Though it failed to garner a single Oscar nomination, *Sullivan's Travels* is the most remarkable film in the career of one of America's greatest filmmakers. **SJS**

The Maltese Falcon John Huston, 1941

By 1941, Dashiell Hammett's great private-eye novel had been acceptably filmed twice, under its own title in 1931 with Ricardo Cortez as Sam Spade and as *Satan Met a Lady* in 1935 with Warren William as the Spade character (and the falcon McGuffin turned into the Horn of Roland). John Huston, having served an apprenticeship as a writer, selected the book from Warner Brothers' catalogue of properties and was so confident in the strength of his material that his script essentially consists of a transcription of Hammett's dialogue. He was fortunate enough to have a letter-perfect cast down to the smallest bit parts, and the restraint not to go over the top. This debut feature has little of the razzle-dazzle of the same year's *Citizen Kane*, announcing the arrival not of an enfant terrible but of a consummate professional.

Often considered a cornerstone of film noir, *The Maltese Falcon* is sparing in its use of symbolic shadows—which are withheld until the elevator door casts jail-bar shapes across the face of the duplicitous heroine at the end—and takes place almost entirely in anonymously tidy hotel rooms and offices worlds away from the seedy glamor of *The Big Sleep* (1946) or *Murder, My Sweet* (1944). Humphrey Bogart, graduating from bad-guy roles to tough romantic heroes, is San Francisco private eye Sam Spade. A sharp-suited businessman, he is out to bring in the murderer of his partner and thwart a group of treacherous adventurers who have become so caught up in the search for the fabulous jeweled bird of the title that they make the fatal mistake of assuming everyone is as corrupt and greedy as they are. Mary Astor might at first glance seem a little matronly for a femme fatale, but her strange primness in tight suits and tighter hairstyle is weirdly apt for a woman who always has a backup lie in place. Sydney Greenstreet's talkative, obese, self-delighted Kaspar Gutman and Peter Lorre's polite, sad, scented, whiny Joel Cairo are screen immortals, a Bing and Bob or Laurel and Hardy of crime, with perennial loser/fall guy Elisha Cook Jr. as the angry little gunman Wilmer who is doomed always to be on the outside of the deal.

Hammett's reputation rests on his addition of a certain social realism to the American mystery story, with private eyes who are solid professionals rather than supersleuths. He was also addicted to plots as twisted and bizarre as Jacobean drama: *The Maltese Falcon* climaxes not only with the hysterical punchline that the black bird everyone has been scheming and killing to possess is actually a fraud, but also with the classic moment when the detective admits that he loves the murderess but is still going to let her get hauled off to jail. Whereas other great Hollywood directors pursue their own visions, Huston continued to be at his best—from *The Treasure of the Sierra Madre* (1948) through to *The Asphalt Jungle* (1950), *Fat City* (1972) *Wise Blood* (1979), and *The Dead* (1987)—when making faithful adaptations of minor classic novels. **KN**

U.S. (First National, Warner Bros.) 101m BW
Producer Henry Blanke, Hal B. Wallis
Screenplay John Huston, from novel by Dashiell Hammett **Photography** Arthur Edeson **Music** Adolph Deutsch
Cast Humphrey Bogart, Mary Astor, Gladys George, Peter Lorre, Barton MacLane, Lee Patrick, Sydney Greenstreet, Ward Bond, Jerome Cowan, Elisha Cook Jr., James Burke, Murray Alper, John Hamilton **Oscar nominations** Hal B. Wallis (best picture), John Huston (screenplay), Sydney Greenstreet (actor in supporting role)

"People lose teeth talking like that. If you want to hang around, you'll be polite."

**Sam Spade
(Humphrey Bogart)**

ℹ

It took three days to shoot the final scene between Humphrey Bogart and Mary Astor.

Dumbo Ben Sharpsteen, 1941

U.S. (Walt Disney) 64m Technicolor
Producer Walt Disney Screenplay Otto
Englander, from book by Helen Aberson
Music Frank Churchill, Oliver Wallace
Cast (voices) Herman Bing, Billy Bletcher,
Edward Brophy, Jim Carmichael, Hall
Johnson Choir, Cliff Edwards, Verna Felton,
Noreen Gammill, Sterling Holloway,
Malcolm Hutton, Harold Manley, John
McLeish, Tony Neil, Dorothy Scott, Sarah
Selby, Billy Sheets, Charles Stubbs, Margaret
Wright Oscar Frank Churchill, Oliver
Wallace (scoring of a musical picture)
Oscar nomination Frank Churchill, Ned
Washington (best original song) Cannes
Film Festival Walt Disney (Prix du meilleur
dessin animé—best animation design)

i

Dumbo and *Snow White* (1937)
were the only two pre-1943
Disney films to make a profit.

Even today, Walt Disney's animation mills regularly turn to traditional fairy tales and familiar folk favorites for inspiration. But Disney's fourth animated feature, *Dumbo*, like the immediately subsequent *Bambi* (1942), was derived from a relatively low-profile book, which apparently freed the animators from more standard-issue prince-rescues-princess romanticism.

Dumbo is still awash in sentimentality, but the anthropomorphized leads—Dumbo, the outcast baby circus elephant whose giant ears and clumsiness make him the object of ridicule, and Timothy, his worldly rodent companion—lend themselves to some joyfully chaotic action as well as some creatively rendered circus sequences. Yet two scenes during Dumbo's quest for self-worth stand out above all the rest: the protopsychedelic pink elephant hallucination and the tender, wrenching meeting between Dumbo and his wrongfully "jailed" mother. Animation has rarely been as inventive, moving, and alive as in these two segments, which are paired with equally memorable songs. Dumbo's eventual triumph over adversity, as well as his reunion with his mother, may be telegraphed from the start, but the film's emotional arc is so carefully constructed that the jump-through-the-hoops challenges faced by the put-upon elephant only enhance the heart-warming conclusion. **JKl**

The Palm Beach Story Preston Sturges, 1942

U.S. (Paramount) 88m BW **Producer** Paul Jones **Screenplay** Preston Sturges **Photography** Victor Milner **Music** Victor Young **Cast** Claudette Colbert, Joel McCrea, Mary Astor, Rudy Vallée, Sig Arno, Robert Warwick, Arthur Stuart Hull, Torben Meyer, Jimmy Conlin, Victor Potel, William Demarest, Jack Norton, Robert Greig, Roscoe Ates, Dewey Robinson, Robert Dudley

Rudy Vallée turns in his best performance as a gentle, puny millionaire named John D. Hackensacker III in this tender and scalding 1942 screwball comedy. Claudette Colbert plays Geraldine, the wife of Thomas Jeffers (Joel McCrea), an ambitious but penniless architectural engineer; she takes off for Florida and winds up being wooed by Hackensacker. When Thomas shows up, she persuades him to pose as her brother. Also on hand are such indelible Sturges creations as the Weenie King (Robert Dudley), the madly destructive Ale and Quail Club, Hackensacker's acerbic sister (Mary Astor), her European boyfriend of obscure nationality, and many Sturges regulars.

The Hackensacker character may be the closest thing to a parodic self-portrait in the Sturges canon. The part was written for Vallée after Sturges saw him in a film musical, noticed that the audience laughed every time he opened his mouth, and concluded that the man was hilarious without even knowing it. This unawareness played a major role in Sturges's conception of comedy, extending to the gullibility of viewers as well as characters. The frantic opening "gives away" the plot's surprise ending before the audience can begin to grasp what's going on. As critic James Harvey aptly noted, "In this movie, whenever reality becomes a problem—on the way to Penn Station, for example, when a cab driver played by Frank Faylen agrees to take Colbert there for nothing—it's simply revoked." **JRos**

Now, Voyager Irving Rapper, 1942

U.S. (Warner Bros.) 117m BW **Producer** Hal B. Wallis **Screenplay** Casey Robinson, from novel by Olive Higgins Prouty **Photography** Sol Polito **Music** Max Steiner **Cast** Bette Davis, Paul Henreid, Claude Rains, Gladys Cooper, Bonita Granville, John Loder, Ilka Chase, Lee Patrick, Franklin Pangborn, Katharine Alexander, James Rennie, Mary Wickes **Oscar** Max Steiner (music) **Oscar nominations** Bette Davis (actress), Gladys Cooper (actress in support role)

The enduring popularity of Irving Rapper's Now, Voyager derives from the film's unembarrassed emotional crescendos, its star power, and particularly the pleasure—however perverse—we get from seeing Bette Davis's transformation from ugly duckling to swan (she was nominated for an Academy Award for her performance).

One of the classic American melodramas and the model "makeover" movie, Now, Voyager tells the elaborate story of spinster Charlotte Vale (Davis), the impossibly frumpy daughter (her heavy eyebrows and glasses tell it all) of an oppressive Boston matriarch. Psychiatrist Dr. Jaquith (Claude Rains) rescues Charlotte by sending her to a sanitarium, where her cure is signaled by the doctor's dramatic breaking of her eyeglasses (what "normal" woman needs them?) and her reemergence (set to a dramatic Max Steiner score) as movie star Bette Davis: gorgeous from plucked brows to two-toned pumps. This newly hatched butterfly goes on a cruise and falls in love with Jerry Durrance (Paul Henreid), a married man; their romance is told largely through the expressive use of cigarettes, which imply the sex that is not seen on-screen. The plot spirals wonderfully out from there, ending with the decision not to pursue more than friendship with Charlotte's famous, if cryptic, lines: "Oh, Jerry, don't let's ask for the moon. We have the stars." **MO**

To Be or Not to Be Ernst Lubitsch, 1942

"What he did to Shakespeare, we are now doing to Poland," jokes a German colonel about a hammy thespian in Ernst Lubitsch's outrageous wartime black comedy. In an age when nothing is too sacred or serious to be lampooned, it is difficult to imagine the controversy that originally surrounded Lubitsch's sparklingly witty, screamingly funny screwball anti-Nazi farce.

Lubitsch was a German Jew who settled in the United States in the 1920s and made a string of smashing, inimitably stylish comedies. Even so, he was dubious when Melchior Lengyel, who conceived Lubitsch's *Ninotchka* (1939), pitched his concept about an acting troupe who impersonate members of the Gestapo to save Polish resistants. But eventually the director felt—and hoped—that Americans would be more concerned about Poland if he could arouse their sympathy through laughter by applying the celebrated Lubitsch Touch (with a sophisticated screenplay by Edwin Justus Mayer) to the Nazis and their adversaries.

Comic Jack Benny in his finest hour plays Josef Tura, vain actor-manager of a theater company, forever at odds with his flirtatious wife and leading lady Maria, played by delicious Carole Lombard (who took the part over the misgivings of husband Clark Gable and was tragically killed before the film's release). After a battle-of-the-sexes setup, the Turas have bigger things to worry about—like the invasion of Poland—and they become embroiled in espionage. The tone shifts with a betrayal and shifts again when Tura's bickering troupe puts aside their differences and devise an audacious masquerade to extract Maria and her Resistance hero admirer (Robert Stack) from Gestapo headquarters.

It has often been remarked that this is Lubitsch's funniest film because it is his most serious—proven by Mel Brooks's 1983 remake, which featured amusing mugging but missed the urgency of desperate deeds in a dangerous time. Sardonic laughs (like Tom Dugan's fiendish Hitler impersonation) do not obscure the substance of the satire, the film's insight into the evil ordinary men are capable of when they get a taste of power, or its engaging message that even egotistical actors can do something swell when they act like human beings. **AE**

U.S. (Romaine) 99m BW
Producer Alexander Korda, Ernst Lubitsch **Screenplay** Melchior Lengyel, Edwin Justus Mayer **Photography** Rudolph Maté **Music** Werner R. Heymann, Miklós Rózsa **Cast** Carole Lombard, Jack Benny, Robert Stack, Felix Bressart, Lionel Atwill, Stanley Ridges, Sig Ruman, Tom Dugan, Charles Halton, George Lynn, Henry Victor, Maude Eburne, Halliwell Hobbes, Miles Mander **Oscar nomination** Werner R. Heymann (music)

> "You're the greatest actor in the world. Everybody knows that, including you."
>
> **Maria Tura (Carole Lombard) to Josef Tura (Jack Benny)**

1942

i
After Lombard's death in an airplane crash, her line "What can happen on a plane?" was cut from the movie.

The Magnificent Ambersons

Orson Welles & Fred Fleck, 1942

U.S. (Mercury, RKO) 88m BW
Producer Jack Moss, George Schaefer,
Orson Welles **Screenplay** Orson Welles,
from novel by Booth Tarkington
Photography Stanley Cortez **Music** Bernard
Herrmann, Roy Webb **Cast** Joseph Cotten,
Dolores Costello, Anne Baxter, Tim Holt,
Agnes Moorehead, Ray Collins, Erskine
Sanford, Richard Bennett, Orson Welles
(narrator) **Oscar nominations** Orson Welles
(best picture), Agnes Moorehead (actress in
support role), Stanley Cortez (photography),
Albert S. D'Agostino, A. Roland Fields,
Darrell Silvera (art direction)

_**i**_

After his score was cut, composer
Bernard Herrmann insisted his name
be removed from the credits.

The unprecedented deal with RKO Pictures that Orson Welles signed in 1940 for two films allowed total creative freedom, but within strict budgets. *The Magnificent Ambersons* is the second movie made under that contract, undertaken after the completion of *Citizen Kane* (1941) but before the wrath of William Randolph Hearst and Welles's own unreliable genius "wrecked" his career as a Hollywood filmmaker. Welles's desire to bring Booth Tarkington's novel *The Ambersons* to the big screen was a more personal project for him than *Kane*: He had already completed an adaptation of the novel with the Mercury Theatre, which was broadcast on radio.

Rooted in the turn-of-the-century world of the haute bourgeoisie that Welles remembered from his own childhood, *The Magnificent Ambersons* is the story of George Amberson Minafer (Tim Holt), the talented but unlikable offspring of an aristocratic family who receives the comeuppance everyone wants for him. Apart from all the other parallels, Welles's suppressed first name was George. As this must have seemed not only autobiographical but, at the stage the film was being made, horribly prophetic, it is to Welles's credit that his ego let him cast Holt, a juvenile cowboy taking a rare serious role (as he would again only in 1948's *The Treasure of the Sierra Madre*), as the lead.

The first seventy minutes are a revelation of creative genius, more than equaling *Kane*. The film opens with a charming but pointed lecture on male fashions, narrated by Welles and displayed by Joseph Cotten, then recreates precisely the cluttered, stuffy, lively, strange world of the Ambersons that is gradually torn apart by the twentieth century—symbolized, presciently, by the motor car—and its own hidden weaknesses. Working with cinematographer Stanley Cortez rather than Gregg Toland, Welles crafts a film that is as visually striking as *Kane*, but that also manages a warmer, melancholy nostalgia for sleigh rides and cartes de visite even as it shows how the iniquities of a class-bound society constrain decent folk to lifelong misery. Enterprising Eugene (Cotten) loses his wellborn love, Isabel (Costello), to a clod from a prominent family but is unable to separate himself from the magnificence of the Ambersons, even as the march of time reduces it to pathetic shreds.

While *Citizen Kane* is all set pieces, *The Magnificent Ambersons* is seamless: Typical is a ballroom sequence in which the camera whirls through the dancers, picking up snatches of plot and dialogue, following a large cast, surrendering to music and history. It's a tragedy that Welles's original cut was taken away (admittedly, while he was enjoying himself in Brazil and not returning calls) and cut down. In the last ten minutes, the cast adopts fixed expressions as they struggle through a happy ending stuck on by someone else (probably editor Robert Wise), though Alfonso Arau's 2002 remake, which sticks to Welles's original scripted ending, found little favor: The magic was obviously unrepeatable. **KN**

1942

Yankee Doodle Dandy Michael Curtiz, 1942

How terribly easy it would be from a postmodern, politically correct, and sophisticated perspective to regard *Yankee Doodle Dandy* as jingoistic propaganda. Indeed, this flag-waving musical extravaganza biopic, detailing the life of patriotic Irish-American song-and-dance man George M. Cohan (the first performer to be awarded the Congressional Medal of Honor), gushes with sentimental, simplistic musical numbers invariably characterized by Cohan's trademark stiff-kneed, effervescent, brash dancing style and championing through their lyrics the most stolid American institutions: "Grand Old Flag," "Give My Regards to Broadway," "Over There," and the title song, to name a few. The film is a flashback—told by a modest Cohan to FDR—that ends with a self-conscious advertisement for intervention: "I wouldn't worry about this country if I were you. We've got this thing licked. Where else in the world could a plain guy like me come in and talk things over with the head man?"

But such a cynical reading would fail grossly to miss something surprising and touching and grand that runs through *Yankee Doodle Dandy* like a clear river, and that is James Cagney's magnificent sincerity in the title role. This is evident in his way of embarrassedly smiling to punctuate his thoughts, in his soft and civilized speaking voice; in the astonishing virtuosity of his dancing, which is persuasive and original in style, unrelentingly athletic while also being childish, playful, and beautifully meaningless; and in something we rarely see onscreen anymore since alienated distance has overtaken Hollywood performance, and that is Cagney's complete and loving belief in everything he does. Michael Curtiz's direction never overplays him, and James Wong Howe's lush black-and-white cinematography never fails to show every nuance of his posture and expression in articulate light. And when his hoofer father (Walter Huston) is falling away into death, with Georgie at his bedside, Cagney gives in to a rush of honest feeling that carries him into tears. So much, in fact, do we care for this man we forget we are watching a performance. Cagney has become Cohan. Even more, he has become the optimistic spirit of the screen. **MP**

U.S. (Warner Bros.) 126m BW **Producer** William Cagney, Hal B. Wallis, Jack L. Warner **Screenplay** Robert Buckner, Edmund Joseph **Photography** James Wong Howe **Music** George M. Cohan, Ray Heindorf, Heinz Roemheld **Cast** James Cagney, Joan Leslie, Walter Huston, Richard Whorf, Irene Manning, George Tobias, Rosemary DeCamp, Jeanne Cagney, Frances Langford, George Barbier, S.Z. Sakall, Walter Catlett, Douglas Croft, Eddie Foy Jr., Minor Watson **Oscars** James Cagney (actor), Ray Heindorf, Heinz Roemheld (music), Nathan Levinson (sound) **Oscar nominations** Jack L. Warner, Hal B. Wallis, William Cagney (best picture), Michael Curtiz (director), Robert Buckner (screenplay), Walter Huston (actor in support role), George Amy (editing)

"My mother thanks you, my father thanks you, my sister thanks you, and I thank you."

**George M. Cohan
(James Cagney)**

i

Cagney maintained that Fred Astaire was originally considered for the role of Cohan but turned it down.

Mrs. Miniver William Wyler, 1942

U.S. (MGM) 128m BW **Producer** Sidney A Franklin **Screenplay** Arthur Wimperis, George Froeschel, James Hilton, Claudine West **Photography** Joseph Ruttenberg **Music** Herbert Stothart **Cast** Greer Garson, Walter Pidgeon, Teresa Wright, Dame May Whitty, Reginald Owen, Henry Travers, Richard Ney, Henry Wilcoxon, Helmut Dantine **Oscar** Sidney A Franklin (best picture), William Wyler (director), Arthur Wimperis, George Froeschel, James Hilton, Claudine West (screenplay), Joseph Ruttenberg (photography), Greer Garson (actress), Teresa Wright (supporting actress) **Oscar nominations** Harold F Kress (editing), Douglas Shearer (sound), A Arnold Gillespie, Warren Newcombe (effects), Walter Pidgeon (actor), Henry Travers (supporting actor), Dame May Whitty (supporting actress)

ℹ

Greer Garson's Oscar acceptance speech ran in excess of five minutes—the longest in Oscar history.

Of all the Hollywood movies made during World War II in support of America's allies, *Mrs. Miniver* remains the best known. Dated, sentimental, hopelessly over-idealized in its depiction of a phony rose-garden England, it still exerts surprising emotional impact. Based on a series of newspaper sketches by Jan Struther, it presents a supposedly archetypal English middle-class family living in a quaintly idyllic Kent village. Into this cozy world erupts the war: food rationing, bombing raids, and sudden death. The villagers, forgetting any previous differences, unite against the common foe. The Minivers' son, formerly a hot-headed left-wing student, joins the Royal Air Force as a fighter pilot; Mr. Miniver (Walter Pidgeon) takes his small boat to Dunkirk to rescue British troops; and Mrs. Miniver (Greer Garson) copes heroically through it all.

At the end of the film the vicar preaches a defiant Churchillian sermon in the bombed-out village church. The congregation launches into "Onward Christian Soldiers," the camera lifts to gaze through the shattered roof—and four flights of Spitfires hurtle overhead as "Land of Hope and Glory" swells on the soundtrack.

Mrs. Miniver earned William Wyler his first Best Director Oscar—plus five more, including Best Picture. President Roosevelt was so taken with the vicar's sermon that he had it printed on leaflets to be dropped over German-occupied territories. And the film's effectiveness as propaganda was acknowledged by no less an authority than Dr. Joseph Goebbels. **PK**

U.S. (Warner Bros.) 102m BW
Language English / French / German
Producer Hal B. Wallis, Jack L. Warner
Screenplay Murray Burnett, Joan Alison
Photography Arthur Edeson **Music** M.K. Jerome, Jack Scholl, Max Steiner
Cast Humphrey Bogart, Ingrid Bergman, Paul Henreid, Claude Rains, Conrad Veidt, Sydney Greenstreet, Peter Lorre, S.Z. Sakall, Madeleine LeBeau, Dooley Wilson, Joy Page, John Qualen, Leonid Kinskey, Curt Bois
Oscars Hal B. Wallis (best picture), Michael Curtiz (director), Julius J. Epstein, Philip G. Epstein, Howard Koch (screenplay)
Oscar nominations Humphrey Bogart (actor), Claude Rains (actor in support role), Arthur Edeson (photography), Owen Marks (editing), Max Steiner (music)

"Kiss me. Kiss me as if it were the last time."

**Ilsa Lund
(Ingrid Bergman)**

ℹ️

The set for the Paris train station was originally featured in *Now, Voyager*, produced earlier the same year.

Casablanca Michael Curtiz, 1942

The most beloved Best Picture Oscar winner of all, this romantic war melodrama epitomizes the 1940s craze for studio-bound exotica, with the Warner Bros. lot transformed into a fantastical North Africa that has far more resonance than any mere real place possibly could. *Casablanca* also offers more cult performers, quotable lines, instant clichés, and Hollywood chutzpah than any other film of the movies' golden age.

Humphrey Bogart's Rick ("Of all the gin joints. . ."), in white dinner jacket or belted trenchcoat, and Ingrid Bergman's Ilsa ("I know that I'll never have the strength to leave you again"), a vision in creations more suited to a studio floor than a desert city, moon over each other in a café-casino as that haunting tune ("As Time Goes By") tinkles in the background, transporting them back to a simpler life before the war soured everything. But the best performance comes from Claude Rains as cynical-but-romantic police chief Renault ("Round up the usual suspects"), a wry observer of life's absurdities who is at once an opportunist survivor and the film's truest romantic—fully deserving of the famous final moments ("Louis, I think this is the beginning of a beautiful friendship") that show it is he, not Ilsa, who is the fitting partner for Rick's newly-dedicated-to-freedom hero.

Also memorable in an enormous supporting cast: Paul Henreid's Czech patriot Victor Laszlo, leading the scum of the continent in a rousing rendition of "La Marseillaise" that drowns out the Nazi sing-along and restores even the most ardent collaborationists and parasites to patriotic fervor; Peter Lorre's hustler Ugarte, shyly admitting that he trusts Rick because the man despises him; Conrad Veidt's heel-clicking Nazi villain Major Strasser, reaching to make a phone call he'll never complete; Dooley Wilson's loyal Sam, stroking the piano and exchanging looks with the leads; S.Z. Sakall's blubbery majordomo Carl, a displaced Austro-Hungarian sweating despite the ceiling fan; and Sydney Greenstreet's unlikely Arab-Italian entrepreneur Ferrari, squatting befezzed on what looks like a magic carpet. Even the extras are brilliantly cast, adding to the lively, seductive, populated feel of a movie that, more than any other, its fans have wanted to inhabit—an impulse that fuels Woody Allen's charming homage in *Play It Again, Sam* (1972).

Curtiz tells a complicated, gimmicky story, weighted down with exposition and structured around a midpoint Paris flashback that breaks most screenwriting rules, with so little fuss and so much confidence that the whole assembly seems seamless, though it was apparently rewritten from day to day so that Bergman did not know until the shooting of the final scene whether she would fly off with Henreid or stick around with Bogie. Cult greatness came about through its attitude, but also its rare sense of the incomplete: Made before the war was over, it dares to leave its characters literally up in the air or out in the desert, leaving its audience to wonder what happened to these people (whose petty problems don't amount to "a hill of beans") during the next few turbulent years. **KN**

U.S. (RKO) 73m BW **Producer** Val Lewton, Lou L. Ostrow **Screenplay** DeWitt Bodeen **Photography** Nicholas Musuraca **Music** Roy Webb **Cast** Simone Simon, Kent Smith, Tom Conway, Jane Randolph, Jack Holt

*"I like the dark.
It's friendly."*

**Irena Dubrovna
(Simone Simon)**

Cat People Jacques Tourneur, 1942

The Val Lewton/RKO-produced horror films of the 1940s are a high point of the horror genre, films renowned for a subtle aura of dread rather than gross special effects. *Cat People*, directed by Jacques Tourneur, presents the tragic tale of Irena the cat-woman, who fears she will destroy those she loves most.

Ollie Reed (Kent Smith) spots sweet and sexy Irena Dubrovna (Simone Simon) sketching the black panther at the zoo. Their whirlwind romance leads to marriage, but signs of trouble show up early. Irena seems obsessed with the big cats and listens to their cries ("like a woman") in the night. But when Ollie takes a cute kitten home to her, it hisses and spits. "Strange," the pet store owner tells Ollie, "cats can always tell if there's something not right about a person." What's wrong with Irena remains fundamentally ambiguous, and that is a strength of this film. Is she a repressed young woman afraid to consummate her marriage, as her psychiatrist (Tom Conway) implies, or heir to the evil Satan-worshipping witches of her home village back in Serbia? Irena fears that strong passions of lust, jealousy, or anger will unleash the murderous panther within her. These passions do run amuck: In one scene she destroys her amorous shrink, and in other scary sequences she stalks her rival Alice (Jane Randolph), who works with Ollie and also loves him.

Cat People will not scare the pants off you, but neither does it overdo the sexual angle as did the ludicrous Paul Schrader remake of 1982, with its bondage scenes and graphic violence. It is creepily effective, particularly in its use of light and shadows. In a justly famous scene, Irena follows Alice to a swimming pool, forcing her to tread water in panic while mysterious sounds erupt and shadows flicker across reflections of watery light.

Alice is likable as "the new kind of other woman"—smart, independent, decent, and caring. Ollie is probably too bland to merit the love of such wonderful women. It is Irena who remains central and lingers in the viewer's mind, one of horror's most sympathetic monsters (like Boris Karloff as the Frankenstein creature). Simon is charming—a bit "off" with her catlike visage, sweet, sad, and unwillingly dangerous. **CFr**

i

The meager budget ($150,000) forced the crew to reuse sets from *The Magnificent Ambersons* (1942).

Fires Were Started Humphrey Jennings, 1943

G.B. (Crown) 80m BW **Producer** Ian Dalrymple **Screenplay** Humphrey Jennings **Photography** C.M. Pennington-Richards **Music** William Alwyn **Cast** Philip Dickson, George Gravett, Fred Griffiths, Johnny Houghton, Loris Rey

Humphrey Jennings's wartime classic was previewed in a longer version with a more attention-grabbing title, *I Was a Fireman*, which was oddly unsuitable for its resolutely collectivist vision of blitzed Britain. In 1942, *Fires Were Started* was considered a "documentary" and set against the commercial tradition of filmmaking, hailed as more authentic than an Ealing fiction film on the same subject, *The Bells Go Down* (also 1943). Now, its use of nonprofessional actors who happened to be real firemen playing fictionally named characters in an archetypal story of a day on shift and a fire at night under a full moon ("a bomber's moon") looks far more like Neorealism or even straight off-Hollywood filmmaking. There is some newsreel stock footage, but the fire station is a set and the fire consists of physical effects.

Among the cast are Fred Griffiths, who went pro and became a familiar character actor, and—in the role of the ad exec newbie who is shown the ropes—William Sansom, who became a writer of interestingly creepy short fiction. It's the epitome of Angus Calder's "Myth of the Blitz," with a cross-class, even multicultural (we see an East End Chinaman) group knuckling down to get the job done.

The fiery finale, in which a blaze is controlled before it sets light to a munitions ship, delivers action and suspense. But Jennings seems less stirred by it than the acutely observed buildup in which he catches the men singing round the piano, playing pool, training, doing menial work-related tasks, and generally acting like real people. **KN**

i

Humphrey Jennings was one of the organizers of the 1936 International Surrealist Exhibition in London.

The Ox-Bow Incident William A. Wellman, 1943

A key film in the history of the Western, *The Ox-Bow Incident* was one of many made in the 1940s that showed that the Western—previously a genre with low cultural prestige—could take on important issues. In a small Nevada town in 1885, a rumor spreads that a local rancher has been killed by rustlers. While the sheriff is out of town, a lynch mob is formed and captures three passing strangers. Despite their protestations of innocence, the men are hanged, only for the perpetrators to discover the rancher is not dead and the real rustlers have been apprehended.

This concise little film (only seventy-five minutes long) packs a good deal of star power. Henry Fonda is a local cowboy, shown initially as a thoughtless saloon brawler, who eventually stands up against the mob. The three victims are played by Dana Andrews, a patently innocent family man; Anthony Quinn, a Mexican drifter; and Francis Ford, brother of the more illustrious John, a senile old man. Frank Conroy is excellent as a blustering ex-Confederate major who bullies his son into helping with the hanging, and Jane Darwell, notable as Ma Joad in John Ford's *The Grapes of Wrath* three years earlier, is a merciless old cattlewoman.

The Ox-Bow Incident makes a powerful plea for the rule of law as the basis of civilization. Besides Fonda, the only townspeople who resist the mob hysteria are a storekeeper (Harry Davenport) and a black preacher (Leigh Whipper), who has more reason than most to protest, having seen his own brother lynched. At the end, when the truth has sunk in, Fonda shames the mob by reading out a letter written by Andrews's character to his wife.

Darryl Zanuck, head of 20th Century Fox at the time, insisted the film be cheaply shot on studio sets; in fact, the confined spaces give *The Ox-Bow Incident* a greater intensity than it might have derived from expansive Western landscapes. The script is based on a highly accomplished first novel by Walter Van Tilburg Clark, a Nevadan whose later novel, *Track of the Cat*, was also filmed by William Wellman. **EB**

U.S. (Fox) 75m BW **Producer** Lamar Trotti **Screenplay** Lamar Trotti, from novel by Walter Van Tilburg Clark **Photography** Arthur C. Miller **Music** Cyril J. Mockridge **Cast** Henry Fonda, Dana Andrews, Mary Beth Hughes, Anthony Quinn, William Eythe, Harry Morgan, Jane Darwell, Matt Briggs, Harry Davenport, Frank Conroy, Marc Lawrence, Paul Hurst, Victor Kilian, Chris-Pin Martin, Leigh Whipper, Willard Robertson **Oscar nomination** Lamar Trotti (best picture)

"The Ox-Bow Incident is all buildup . . . It's like watching a long fuse burn."

Terrence Rafferty,
***The New York Times*, 2012**

i

Henry Fonda regarded *The Ox-Bow Incident* as one of his favorite films that he had ever made.

The Life and Death of Colonel Blimp

Michael Powell & Emeric Pressburger, 1943

G.B. (Independent, Archers) 163m Technicolor **Producer** Michael Powell, Emeric Pressburger, Richard Vernon **Screenplay** Michael Powell, Emeric Pressburger **Photography** Georges Périnal **Music** Allan Gray **Cast** James McKechnie, Neville Mapp, Vincent Holman, Roger Livesey, David Hutcheson, Spencer Trevor, Roland Culver, James Knight, Deborah Kerr, Dennis Arundell, David Ward, Jan Van Loewen, Valentine Dyall, Carl Jaffe, Albert Lieven

Clive Wynne-Candy (Roger Livesey) is a veteran of both the Boer War and World War I, twice retired, who believes that all of life's conflicts can be met with honor and decorum. He doesn't realize that the world has changed around him, and that his old-fashioned dictums of behavior may no longer apply in the World War II arena, yet with the stubbornness of a good soldier he holds firm to his beliefs and hurtles forward.

Michael Powell and Emeric Pressburger made *The Life and Death of Colonel Blimp* at the height of World War II, when London was being bombed nightly by the Germans. A comedy of manners may not appear the best way to address current events, but the Powell–Pressburger team once again comes through, delicately revealing the horrible truth of modern warfare with grace and humor. It doesn't hurt that they tell the story through three romances, as Livesey woos the ever-luminous Deborah Kerr (in three different roles) over the years. It all adds up to one of the most ambitious and impressive achievements of not just Powell and Pressburger but in all of British cinema. **JKl**

1943

Meshes of the Afternoon

Maya Deren & Alexander Hammid, 1943

U.S. 18m Silent BW **Screenplay** Maya Deren **Photography** Alexander Hammid **Music** Teiji Ito (added 1952) **Cast** Maya Deren, Alexander Hammid

A famous image from *Meshes of the Afternoon* shows its auteur and star, Maya Deren, at a window, tree leaves reflected in the glass; she looks out wistfully, hands on the pane. This image has since appeared many times, but it remains a vivid, dreamy, terrifying picture of women's confinement.

Meshes comes from a branch of the American avant-garde taken with the surrealist journey of a figure through an ever-changing dreamscape. Deren, working from her own fantasies and shooting in her own home, made an intuitive leap that has given the film its lasting resonance. Her vision of Los Angeles links this impulse with an atmosphere that is proto-film noir in its use of architecture and interior design, not to mention its atmosphere of dread and menace. This was one of the first films to make the indelible link between a woman's gothic experience of coming unglued and the sunny spaces of home. For Deren, it is the domestic everyday that lays the meshes that ensnare and traumatize women.

Deren's extraordinary body language in *Meshes* marries choreography to ordinary rituals, another combination that influenced women's cinema for decades. She used her movements as a way to trigger montage, to suggest rhythmic forms and create pictorial shapes: In this flux of dream projections, she is the only anchor. Yet, for all her movement, the last shot of *Meshes* reveals that this modern heroine has probably not even moved from her lounge chair. But what she has imagined manages to destroy her; this is the tale of a death drive, of a dream that kills. **AM**

The Seventh Victim Mark Robson, 1943

U.S. (RKO) 71m BW Producer Val Lewton
Screenplay DeWitt Bodeen, Charles O'Neal
Photography Nicholas Musuraca Music Roy
Webb Cast Tom Conway, Jean Brooks, Isabel
Jewell, Kim Hunter, Evelyn Brent, Erford
Gage, Ben Bard, Hugh Beaumont, Chef
Milani, Marguerita Sylva

Perhaps the best of the run of terrific RKO horror films produced by Val Lewton in the 1940s, *The Seventh Victim* is a strikingly modern, poetically doom-laden picture. Naive orphan Mary Gibson (Kim Hunter) comes to Manhattan in search of her strange elder sister Jacqueline (Jean Brooks, with a memorable Cleopatra wig) and learns she was mixed up with a sect of chic diabolists who now want to drive her to suicide for betraying their cult.

Director Mark Robson stages several remarkable suspense sequences—two Satanists trying to get rid of a corpse in a crowded subway train, Brooks's pursuit through the city by sinister figures and her own neuroses—and indulges in weirdly arty touches that take the horror film away from traditional witchcraft toward something very like existential angst. *The Seventh Victim* is full of things that must have been startling in 1943 and are still unusual now: a gaggle of varied lesbian characters (not all unsympathetic), a heroine who comes to seem as calculating as the villains, and a desperate finish that contrasts a dying woman (Elizabeth Russell) dressed up to go out on the town for the last time with the end-of-her-tether Jacqueline as she shuts herself up in a grim rented room to hang herself. **KN**

The Man in Grey Leslie Arliss, 1943

G.B. (Gainsborough) 116m B/W
Producer Edward Black
Screenplay Leslie Arliss, Margaret Kennedy
Photography Arthur Crabtree Music Cedric
Mallabey Cast Margaret Lockwood, James
Mason, Phyllis Calvert, Stewart Granger,
Helen Haye, Raymond Lovell, Nora
Swinburne, Martita Hunt, Jane Gill-Davis,
Amy Veness, Stuart Lindsell, Diana King,
Beatrice Varley

English cinema is perhaps best known for realist dramas, but an important second tradition is the costume melodrama, of which *The Man in Grey* is probably the finest example and one of the more popular films Gainsborough Studios ever made. The plot is fairly forgettable, involving two young women whose lives interestingly intersect. Clarissa (Phyllis Calvert) marries the cruelly indifferent Marquis of Rohan (James Mason), but her friend Hesther (Margaret Lockwood) introduces her to another rogue, the bold and immoral Rokeby (Stewart Granger). Soon the pair have switched partners, but all ends badly as Clarissa dies miserably and the crazed Marquis beats Hesther to death.

The plot, however, derived from a subliterary novel by Lady Eleanor Smith, is not the main focus of director Leslie Arliss's efforts. Calvert and Lockwood turn in suitably intense performances as the contrasting blonde- and dark-haired leads, and Mason is effectively reptilian as the Marquis. But the real star of the film is its art design. Regency period England is faithfully resurrected, with its ornate interior decor and European furniture, and its elaborate and elegant dress for actors and actresses alike. The sumptuous look of *The Man in Grey* provides a perfect contrast to its exploration of the dark underside of aristocratic life, with the story's gothic elements eliciting a suitable frisson from the absorbed viewer. **RBP**

Shadow of a Doubt Alfred Hitchcock, 1943

When interviewed by admirer and famous acolyte François Truffaut, Alfred Hitchcock referred to *Shadow of a Doubt* as his favorite film. Tellingly, it's also one of his least flashy works, a quiet character study set in the heart of suburbia. Although the heart of his suburbia is still rotten with murder and deceit, Hitchcock emphasizes traditional suspense beats over intricate set pieces, stocking the story with just as much uneasy humor as tension.

Charlie (Teresa Wright) is elated when her uncle and namesake Charlie (played to smarmy perfection by Joseph Cotten) comes to visit her and her mother. She soon suspects her revered Uncle Charlie is actually a serial killer, "the Merry Widow Murderer," on the run from his latest killing. Once on to her suspicions, her Uncle Charlie doesn't seem interested in leaving behind any loose ends, but the younger Charlie doesn't know how to reconcile her affection for her uncle with her fears.

Hitchcock actually shot *Shadow of a Doubt* on location, in the small town of Santa Rosa, California, the better to tear apart the flimsy façade and expose the bland, safe suburbs for the hotbed of secrets it no doubt is. The script, written by Thornton Wilder with input from Hitchcock's wife Alma Reville, takes perverse glee in destroying preconceived notions of quiet, small-town life. The film is also peppered with numerous references to twins and the duality of good and evil, paralleling the trustful and innocent Charlie with her dangerous and deceitful uncle.

Dimitri Tiomkin's score keeps the suspense ratcheted up, particularly his use of Franz Lehar's "Merry Widow" waltz—the signifier of Uncle Charlie's guilt and the haunting motif that represents the horrific inclinations he can barely disguise or suppress. A pair of nosy neighbors also offer a running commentary, discussing the various means and methods by which a murder might be committed and then covered up. That a real murderer lurks right next door provides dollops of ironic humor. The neighbors continue to ruminate on various homicidal scenarios as Charlie races to settle her conflicted feelings for her Uncle Charlie before he permanently does it for her. **JKl**

U.S. (Skirball, Universal) 108m BW
Producer Jack H. Skirball
Screenplay Gordon McDonell, Thornton Wilder **Photography** Joseph A. Valentine
Music Dimitri Tiomkin **Cast** Teresa Wright, Joseph Cotten, Macdonald Carey, Henry Travers, Patricia Collinge, Hume Cronyn, Wallace Ford, Edna May Wonacott, Charles Bates, Irving Bacon, Clarence Muse, Janet Shaw, Estelle Jewell **Oscar nomination** Gordon McDonell (screenplay)

> "All villains are not black and all heroes are not white. There are grays everywhere."
>
> **Alfred Hitchcock, 1963**

1943

ℹ️

"Shadow of a Doubt" was only meant to be a temporary title for the movie until a better one could be found.

Ossessione Luchino Visconti, 1943

Italy (ICI) 142m BW **Language** Italian
Producer Libero Solaroli
Screenplay Luchino Visconti, Mario Alicata
Photography Domenico Scala, Aldo Tonti
Music Giuseppe Rosati **Cast** Clara Calamai,
Massimo Girotti, Dhia Cristiani, Elio
Marcuzzo, Vittorio Duse, Michele Riccardini,
Juan de Landa

"Comparing . . .
Ossessione with
Garnett['s] Postman is
to stand a production
of Traviata next to a
McDonald's television
commercial."

Vincent Canby,
The New York Times, 1976

One of the great speculative games one can play with cinema history centers on Luchino Visconti's *Ossessione*: What if this had been the picture that heralded the arrival of an exciting new film movement from Italy, and not Roberto Rossellini's *Open City* in 1945? It would have indeed been interesting, but alas we'll never know; because Visconti's screenplay was clearly lifted from James M. Cain's *The Postman Always Rings Twice*, Cain and his publishers kept it off American screens until 1976, when it had its much belated premiere at the New York Film Festival. Cain had just died and probably never saw it—a pity, because he would have discovered the best cinematic adaptation of his work.

Massimo Girotti is Gino Costa, a sweaty, T-shirt-clad drifter who lands a job in a roadside café run by portly opera buff Bragana (Juan de Landa). Bragana has a wife, Giovanna (the luminous Clara Calamai, Rossellini's first choice for the Anna Magnani role in *Open City*), and it isn't long before Gino and Giovanna are in each others arms, making plans to get away. Adhering closely to Cain's storyline, Visconti is aided by the sheer physical chemistry between Calamai and Girotti; all of Cain's descriptions of burning flesh and animal lust are rendered in *Ossessione* with an almost frightening intensity. Consequently, the whole economic imperative for the eventual murder takes somewhat of a backseat here. Visconti also doesn't avoid the obviously homoerotic overtones of Gino's relationship with "lo Spagnolo" (Elio Marcuzzo), a Spanish street performer with whom he goes on the road for a while, rather remarkable when one considers the film was made under the Fascist regime.

One scene that surely would have delighted Cain, himself the son of an opera singer, is Bragana's performance in a local opera competition. A gruff and unapproachable figure—a far cry from Cecil Kellaway's bumbling fool in Tay Garnett's 1946 Hollywood version of the novel—he suddenly comes alive as he bursts into an aria, bringing the assembled listeners to their feet. *Ossessione* could have been the great example of the union of American film noir and Italian Neorealism; instead, it remains something like the ancestral missing link for both movements. **RP**

i

The Fascists destroyed the original
negative; all prints since have been
made from a copy that Visconti saved.

Laura Otto Preminger & Rouben Mamoulian, 1944

U.S. (Fox) 88m BW **Producer** Otto Preminger **Screenplay** Jay Dratler, Samuel Hoffenstein, Elizabeth Reinhardt, from novel by Vera Caspary **Photography** Joseph LaShelle, Lucien Ballard **Music** David Raksin **Cast** Gene Tierney, Dana Andrews, Clifton Webb, Vincent Price, Judith Anderson, Cy Kendall, Grant Mitchell **Oscar** Joseph LaShelle (photography) **Oscar nominations** Clifton Webb (actor in support role), Otto Preminger (director), Jay Dratler, Samuel Hoffenstein, Elizabeth Reinhardt (screenplay), Lyle R. Wheeler, Leland Fuller, Thomas Little (art direction)

The portrait of Gene Tierney as Laura can also be spotted in *On the Riviera* (1951) and *Woman's World* (1954).

Men adore her. Women admire her. Yet alluring young designer Laura Hunt (Gene Tierney) doesn't take center stage in *Laura*, any more than her chilly socialite friend Ann (Judith Anderson), her duplicitous suitor Shelby (Vincent Price), or hard-boiled detective Mark McPherson (Dana Andrews), who, searching for her murderer, falls in love with her ghost. But viciously smarmy author-broadcaster Waldo Lydecker (Clifton Webb) utterly fascinates, adopting Laura as his protégée, making her famous, then fixating upon her life like a spider who has her in its web.

If Otto Preminger's *Laura* intrigues in its jarring mélange of styles—noir psychodrama, melodrama, and crime thriller—then in brief moments of portraiture it becomes monumental. Particularly notable scenes include Ann explaining to Laura why it should be she who has Shelby ("We're both losers") and the romantic tryst at the police station when, turning off the glaring third-degree lights, Mark sees Laura's true radiance. But paramount is Lydecker's poisonous poise when he regales Laura with Shelby's faults. "I'll call him," she says anxiously. "He's not there," Waldo acidly retorts, "He's dining with Ann, didn't you know?" More than doting upon her life, he is inhabiting it, perhaps narrative cinema's first example of a man who wishes he were a woman. **MP**

Meet Me in St. Louis Vincente Minnelli, 1944

A little girl named Tootie (Margaret O'Brien), crying and angry, breaks domestic rank and runs out to the snow. Once there, she sets to destroying her beloved snowmen—a symbol of everything that is stable and reassuring in her familial existence—with a vigor and venom that is extremely disquieting. Who would ever have thought that Judy Garland singing "Have Yourself a Merry Little Christmas" could have such a devastating effect on a child's delicate psyche—or, indeed, on ours?

Vincente Minnelli's *Meet Me in St. Louis* is one of the most unusual and highly charged musicals in Hollywood history. It blends the two genres at which Minnelli was most adept—musical and melodrama—and even, in its darkest moments (such as a sequence devoted to Halloween terrors), edges toward being a horror movie. It is also a film that, then as now, offers itself up to be read in starkly contrasting ways: either as a perfectly innocent and naïve celebration of traditional family values, or else a brooding meditation on everything that tears the family unit apart from within. Put another way, is it comforting, "safety valve" entertainment that admits to just enough that is problematic in order to smooth out and reinforce the status quo, or is it—almost despite itself—a subversive gesture at the heart of the Hollywood system, a howl of unrepressed rage like Tootie's slaughter of imaginary snow people?

Yes, this is the same film in which Garland moons and croons "The Boy Next Door" and—in a showstopping highlight—sways with a pack of colorful passengers as she belts out "The Trolley Song" ("Zing, zing, zing went my heartstrings. . . ."). Minnelli's project is quietly ambitious: not merely to tell the story of a lovably "average" family—and the challenges it stoically faces—but to also sketch the history of a bold new twentieth-century society defined by events such as the World's Fair.

Minnelli's artistic sensibility—his sexuality is either an open question or an open secret, depending on which Hollywood history you consult—responded well to female yearning and male anxiety, and an excess of both makes this musical unfailingly melodramatic. Patriarchy comes in the cuddly, grumpy form of Leon Ames, valiantly trying to assert his authority in the face of an overwhelmingly female household. The parade of boyfriends for the girls have likewise to be prodded, manipulated, and informed of their rightful, mating destiny.

As for the aesthetic challenges of the musical, Minnelli and his collaborators went a long way toward integrating singing and dancing into a whimsical, fairy tale flow of incidents. Songs begin as throwaway phrases, spoken or hummed out in the street or at the door; they suddenly die away as a plot intrigue kicks in. Beneath the elegant display of filmic style, and the civilized veneer of manners, it is only Tootie who can express emotions that are savage and untamed—as her "exotica" duet with Judy, "Under the Bamboo Tree," jovially indicates. **AM**

U.S. (MGM) 113m Technicolor
Producer Roger Edens, Arthur Freed
Screenplay Irving Brecher, Fred F. Finklehoffe, from novel by Sally Benson
Photography George J. Folsey **Music** Ralph Blane, Hugh Martin, Nacio Herb Brown, Arthur Freed, George E. Stoll **Cast** Judy Garland, Margaret O'Brien, Mary Astor, Lucille Bremer, Leon Ames, Tom Drake, Marjorie Main, Harry Davenport, June Lockhart, Henry H. Daniels Jr., Joan Carroll, Hugh Marlowe, Robert Sully, Chill Wills, Gary Gray, Dorothy Raye **Oscar nominations** Irving Brecher, Fred F. Finklehoffe (screenplay), George J. Folsey (photography), George E. Stoll (music), Ralph Blane, Hugh Martin (song)

"I want to make this into the most delightful piece of Americana ever."

Arthur Freed, *Meet Me in St. Louis* producer, 1944

🛈

The seven-year-old Margaret O'Brien was awarded a special Juvenile Oscar for her role as Tootie.

To Have and Have Not Howard Hawks, 1944

Coscripted by two Nobel Prize–winners, Ernest Hemingway and William Faulkner, allegedly from Hemingway's book of the same title, *To Have and Have Not* was mainly improvised by director Howard Hawks and his peerless cast. One of a run of films made after Humphrey Bogart's triumph in *Casablanca* (1942), this even more romantic picture offers a central love affair that threatens to edge World War II offscreen. Hawks, who discovered Lauren Bacall before Bogart did, eventually felt betrayed by his stars' marriage, but he also in great part created the characters the couple wound up playing in real life.

Set in Vichy, Martinique, as opposed to the novel's Cuba, *To Have and Have Not* once again has Bogart's Yankee ex-pat caught up with the Free French and finally committing to the allied cause. The real-life electricity sparking between Bogie and a debuting Bacall, as the girl who drifts into his life and takes over, leads to a sassy, upbeat ending that sends you home with a greater glow even than the wistful resignation of *Casablanca*. Unlike Rick (Bogart) and Ilsa (Ingrid Bergman) in the earlier film, who choose the greater good over love, Harry and Slim rescue each other from isolationism and are able to maintain their relationship because they are willing to work together to win the war. Hawks would have no patience with a woman who saw her job solely in terms of making a happy home life for the hero and so makes Bacall's Slim as intrepid and daring as Bogart's Harry—not just a love interest, but a partner.

Hawks packs every scene in *To Have and Have Not* with relishable business: hilarious but sexy love talk between the stars ("You do know how to whistle?"); comedy relief sidekick Walter Brennan asking, "Was you ever stung by a dead bee?"; Hoagy Carmichael singing "Hong Kong Blues" and accompanying a husky Bacall (or is it Andy Williams's voice?) on "How Little We Know?"; and Bogie snarling at various petty officials and nasty fascists with the genuine voice of a democratic wiseguy who won't put up with any totalitarian nonsense. When John Huston didn't have an ending for his 1948 Bogart–Bacall thriller *Key Largo*, Hawks gave him the shootout-on-a-boat finish of Hemingway's novel that he had never got around to including in this film. **KN**

U.S. (Warner Bros.) 100m BW
Producer Howard Hawks, Jack L. Warner
Screenplay Jules Furthman, from novel by Ernest Hemingway **Photography** Sidney Hickox **Music** Hoagy Carmichael, William Lava, Franz Waxman **Cast** Humphrey Bogart, Walter Brennan, Lauren Bacall, Dolores Moran, Hoagy Carmichael, Sheldon Leonard, Walter Szurovy, Marcel Dalio, Walter Sande, Dan Seymour, Aldo Nadi

"The best of the picture has no plot at all, but is a leisurely series of mating duels between Humphrey Bogart . . . and . . . Lauren Bacall."

James Agee,
The Nation, 1944

🛈

The movie transpired after Hawks bet Hemingway that he could make a film out of Hemingway's "worst book."

Gaslight George Cukor, 1944

U.S. (MGM) 114m BW **Producer** Arthur Hornblow Jr. **Screenplay** John Van Druten, Walter Reisch, John L. Balderston, from the play *Angel Street* by Patrick Hamilton **Photography** Joseph Ruttenberg **Music** Bronislau Kaper **Cast** Charles Boyer, Ingrid Bergman, Joseph Cotten, Dame May Whitty, Angela Lansbury, Barbara Everest, Emil Rameau, Edmund Breon, Halliwell Hobbes, Tom Stevenson, Heather Thatcher, Lawrence Grossmith **Oscars** Ingrid Bergman (actress), Cedric Gibbons, William Ferrari, Edwin B. Willis, Paul Huldschinsky (art direction) **Oscar nominations** Arthur Hornblow Jr. (best picture), John L. Balderston, Walter Reisch, John Van Druten (screenplay), Charles Boyer (actor), Angela Lansbury (actress in support role), Joseph Ruttenberg (photography)

George Cukor's Hollywood version of an earlier British gothic romance is heavy on threatening atmosphere, with a spine-chilling thriller plot. Paula Alquist (Ingrid Bergman) finds herself wooed by the attractive, if strangely possessive, Gregory Anton (Charles Boyer), who seems more interested in the London house Paula owns than in the rather timid woman herself. It turns out that Anton is a clever thief who, some ten years before, had killed Paula's aunt in a failed attempt to steal her fabulously valuable jewels. As he systematically ransacks Paula's house by night, he does his best to convince her, and others, that she is losing her mind. His intention is to put her entirely under his power so that he can have a free hand searching the house. Anton's plot, however, is discovered by Brian Cameron (Joseph Cotten), who, falling in love with the woman he sees mistreated and threatened, intervenes just in time to save her from worse.

While *Gaslight*'s plot is somewhat thin, Cukor draws fine performances from an ensemble cast, including newcomer Angela Lansbury as a saucy servant who, like everything and everyone else in the house, seems to be plotting against its ostensible mistress. With its evocation of persecution and paranoia, Gaslight makes an elegant period-piece companion to the film noir series then featured by Hollywood. **RBP**

1944

Henry V Laurence Olivier, 1944

G.B. (Two Cities) 135m Technicolor **Language** English / French **Producer** Dallas Bower, Filippo Del Giudice, Laurence Olivier **Screenplay** Dallas Bower, Alan Dent, from play by William Shakespeare **Photography** Jack Hildyard, Robert Krasker **Music** William Walton **Cast** Felix Aylmer, Leslie Banks, Robert Helpmann, Vernon Greeves, Gerald Case, Griffith Jones, Morland Graham, Nicholas Hannen, Michael Warre, Laurence Olivier, Ralph Truman, Ernest Thesiger, Roy Emerton, Robert Newton, Freda Jackson **Oscar** Laurence Olivier (honorary award) **Oscar nominations** Laurence Olivier (best picture), Laurence Olivier (actor), Paul Sheriff, Carmen Dillon (art direction), William Walton (music)

Henry V was regarded by the British government as ideal patriotic wartime propaganda, and Laurence Olivier, serving in the Fleet Air Arm, was released to star in it and—after William Wyler had turned it down—to direct it as well. Aiming to preserve both Shakespeare's innately theatrical artifice and the protocinematic sweep of his imagination, Olivier hit on the device of framing the film within a production in the Globe Theatre itself. As *Henry V* opens, the camera soars over a detailed miniature of Elizabethan London, down into the bustle of the Globe audience, and into a high-flown stage performance—only to expand exhilaratingly into cinematic space as the action moves toward France.

Throughout, the film plays with different levels of stylization, from the scenes at the French court—which borrow the exquisite colors and naïve perspectives of medieval miniature paintings—to the realism of the battle scenes, inspired in their exuberant dynamism by Sergei Eisenstein's *Aleksandr Nevsky* (1938). The rhythm of Shakespeare's text, discreetly trimmed to fit the war effort—the three English traitors are dropped, for a start—is buoyed up by the vigor of Olivier's barnstorming performance and William Walton's sweeping score. *Henry V* is the first Shakespeare film that succeeds in being at once truly Shakespearean and wholly cinematic. **PK**

U.S. (Paramount) 107m BW
Producer Joseph Sistrom Screenplay Billy
Wilder, Raymond Chandler, from the novel
Double Indemnity in Three of a Kind by James
M. Cain Photography John F. Seitz
Music Miklós Rózsa Cast Fred MacMurray,
Barbara Stanwyck, Edward G. Robinson,
Porter Hall, Jean Heather, Tom Powers, Byron
Barr, Richard Gaines, Fortunio Bonanova,
John Philliber Oscar nominations Joseph
Sistrom (best picture), Billy Wilder (director),
Raymond Chandler, Billy Wilder (screenplay),
Barbara Stanwyck (actress), John F. Seitz
(photography), Miklós Rózsa (music),
Loren L. Ryder (sound)

"Since Double Indemnity, *the two most important words in motion pictures are 'Billy' and 'Wilder.'"*

Alfred Hitchcock, 1944

🛈

A remake of *Double Indemnity* was proposed in the 1970s, with Robert Redford in the Fred MacMurray role.

Double Indemnity Billy Wilder, 1944

Adapted by director Billy Wilder and author Raymond Chandler from the hard-boiled novel by James M. Cain, *Double Indemnity* is the archetypal film noir, the tale of a desperate dame and a greedy man, of murder for sordid profit and sudden, violent betrayal. Yet it has a weird, evocative romanticism ("How could I have known that murder can sometimes smell like honeysuckle?") and pays off, extraordinarily for 1944, with a confession not only of murder but also of love between two men. The last line, addressed by dying Fred MacMurray to heartbroken Edward G. Robinson, is "I love you, too."

A wounded man staggers by night into a Los Angeles insurance company office, and settles down at his desk to dictate confessional notes on "the Dietrichson claim." He introduces himself as "Walter Neff, insurance salesman, thirty-five years old, unmarried, no visible scars—until a while ago, that is." MacMurray spent his whole career, first at Paramount then at Disney and finally in sitcoms, as a genial nice guy, always smiling, always folksy; twice (his other change-of-pace, also for Wilder, is *The Apartment*) he crawled behind his smile and marvelously played a complete heel, his cleft chin sweaty and in need of a shave, his smooth salesman's talk a cover for lechery, larceny, and murderous intent. The bait that tempts this average nobody off the straight and narrow comes fresh from a sunbath, barely wrapped in a towel, flashing an ankle bracelet. Calling at a fake Spanish mansion on Los Feliz Boulevard about an auto policy renewal, Neff encounters Mrs. Phyllis Dietrichson (Barbara Stanwyck) and can't resist putting verbal moves on her. Neff backs off when she innocently asks if it's possible to insure her older husband (Tom Powers) against accidental death without him knowing about it. Neff mulls it over and, after an embrace in his apartment, agrees to pitch in with the murder plan.

The couple trick Mr. D into signing up for a policy that pays off double if death occurs on a train, then arrange it so his broken-necked corpse is found on the railroad tracks. Enter Barton Keyes (Robinson), a claims investigator of Columbo-like tenacity whose only blind spot is his devotion to Neff. Keyes fusses around the case, ruling out suicide in a brilliant speech about the unlikeliness of suicide by jumping from a train, homing in on the gamey blonde as a murderess, and rooting around for her partner in crime. Keyes doesn't even have to do much work, because postkilling pressures are already splitting Neff and Phyllis apart, as they try not to panic during meets in a local supermarket and come to suspect each other of additional double crosses. In that stifling, shadowed mansion, with "Tangerine" on the radio and honeysuckle in the air, the lovers riddle each other with bullets, and Neff staggers away to confess. Keyes joins him in the office and sadly catches the end of the story. Neff asks for four hours so he can head for Mexico, but Keyes knows, "You'll never make the border. You'll never even make the elevator." **KN**

Murder, My Sweet Edward Dmytryk, 1944
Farewell, My Lovely

U.S. (RKO) 95m BW **Producer** Sid Rogell, Adrian Scott **Screenplay** John Paxton, from the novel *Farewell, My Lovely* by Raymond Chandler **Photography** Harry J. Wild **Music** Roy Webb **Cast** Dick Powell, Claire Trevor, Anne Shirley, Otto Kruger, Mike Mazurki, Miles Mander, Douglas Walton, Donald Douglas, Ralf Harolde, Esther Howard

"Murder, My Sweet remains the purest version of Chandler on film."

Glenn Erickson,
critic, 2004

The first screen adaptation of Raymond Chandler's second novel, *Farewell, My Lovely* was *The Falcon Takes Over*, a 1942 quickie in which Chandler's private eye, Philip Marlowe, was replaced by George Sanders's gentleman sleuth. When Chandler's reputation rose, RKO found it no longer had to pay for the film rights to mount this more faithful adaptation, in which ex-crooner Dick Powell surprised audiences with his wry toughness and bruised romanticism as the first proper screen incarnation of Marlowe. The title change came about because it was assumed that audiences would mistake it for a schmaltzy wartime romance, though the novel's title was retained in Britain, where Chandler was already a respected figure.

The book was one of several Marlowe novels Chandler wrought by cannibalizing several earlier, cruder novellas, which explains why it has several plot threads that turn out to intersect via the odd, unlikely coincidence. *Murder, My Sweet* opens with Marlowe blinded and interrogated by the cops, allowing for the retention of much of Chandler's first-person commentary, as flashbacks take the hero through a puzzle that begins with ex-con "Moose" Malloy (Mike Mazurki) hiring Marlowe to track down the ex-girlfriend who sold him out but with whom he is still smitten. The story takes a left turn when he is also retained by slinky society vamp Helen Grayle (Claire Trevor) to get back some stolen jade and see off a blackmailing "psychic consultant" (Otto Kruger).

No other film so perfectly encapsulates the pleasures of film noir, as director Edward Dmytryk deploys shadows, rain, drug-induced hallucinations ("a black pool opened up"), and sudden bursts of violence within a cobweb of plot traps, slimy master crooks, worthless femmes fatales, gorilla-brained thugs, weary cops, and quack doctors. Powell's Marlowe, striking a match on Cupid's marble bottom and playing hopscotch on the tiled floor of a millionaire's mansion, is closer to Chandler's tone of boyish insolence than better-known readings of the role by Humphrey Bogart or Robert Mitchum. **KN**

i

Dick Powell's portrayal of Philip Marlowe was reportedly applauded by Raymond Chandler himself.

Ivan Groznyj I i II Sergei M. Eisenstein, 1944
Ivan the Terrible, Parts I and II

U.S.S.R. (Alma Ata) 100m BW
Language Russian Producer Sergei M.
Eisenstein Screenplay Sergei M. Eisenstein
Photography Andrei Moskvin, Eduard Tisse
Music Sergei Prokofiev Cast Nikolai
Cherkasov, Lyudmila Tselikovskaya,
Serafima Birman, Mikhail Nazvanov, Mikhail
Zharov, Amvrosi Buchma, Mikhail Kuznetsov,
Pavel Kadochnikov, Andrei Abrikosov,
Aleksandr Mgebrov, Maksim Mikhajlov,
Vsevolod Pudovkin

Ivan the Terrible recounts the rise and fall of one of Russia's most famous Czars, Ivan IV. It was conveived as a trilogy, the filming for which began in the early 1940s upon Stalin's request. Eisenstein could only complete parts I and II, however, because of his premature death. Part I came out in 1945, whereas Part II underwent governmental censorship: Stalin saw in it a critique of his own despotism and banned the movie. Part II was finally released in 1958 after both Eisenstein's and Stalin's deaths.

Part I focuses on Ivan's (Nikolai Cherkasov) establishment of power and shows the favor of the peasants. Part II narrates the schemes of the Boyars in their attempt to assassinate Ivan and reveals the progressive cruelty of the Czar, who creates his own police to keep the country under control. Ivan discovers the plots against him and defeats his enemies by killing them. The acting is particularly staged: Eisenstein makes strong use of extreme close-ups and seems more interested with the characters' reactions to the events than with the events themselves.

Alexander Nevsky (1938) and *Ivan the Terrible* are Eisenstein's only non-silent films. If one compares the latter to his silent movies of the 1920s, not only can a change in style be detected, but also a change in the very themes narrated. Eisenstein here renounces the depiction of the proletarian struggles at the heart of his previous films, turning instead to an epic story, one connected to a "safe" past that does not involve manifest critiques of contemporary political events. **CFe**

i

In Part II, a curiosity can be found in the use of two color scenes in a movie that is mostly black and white.

Mildred Pierce Michael Curtiz, 1945

U.S. (Warner Bros.) 111m BW **Producer** Jerry Wald, Jack L. Warner **Screenplay** Ranald MacDougall, from novel by James M. Cain **Photography** Ernest Haller **Music** Max Steiner **Cast** Joan Crawford, Jack Carson, Zachary Scott, Eve Arden, Ann Blyth, Bruce Bennett, Lee Patrick, Moroni Olsen, Veda Ann Borg, Jo Ann Marlowe **Oscar** Joan Crawford (actress) **Oscar nominations** Jerry Wald (best picture), Ranald MacDougall (screenplay), Eve Arden (actress in support role), Ann Blyth (actress in support role), Ernest Haller (photography)

"Joan Crawford reaches a peak of her acting career in this pic."

Variety magazine, 1945

Gunshots crack in the night and a dying man gasps "Mildred!" In a flashback classic that goes back to the genesis of obsession and murder, the mink-clad confessor Mildred Pierce (Joan Crawford in the Oscar-winning role that revived the forty-one-year-old fading star's stalled career) explains in a police interrogation how she toiled her way from housewife, waitress, and pie baker to prosperous restaurateur in order to fulfill her daughter Veda's (Ann Blyth) demands for the finer things. When they are both fatefully drawn in by a smooth, duplicitous cad (Zachary Scott), the possessive Mildred's smothering, neurotic indulgence and the ungrateful Veda's precocious appetites inevitably boil over in sexual betrayal and rage.

A definitive 1940s women's picture and a seething domestic soap opera, Michael Curtiz's film, adapted by Ranald MacDougall from a breathtakingly perverse novel by James M. Cain (of *Double Indemnity* and *The Postman Always Rings Twice* fame), is also a superbly nasty noir, one that plays havoc with the era's ideals of maternal devotion and mom's apple pie. Mildred is admirable for her hard work and self-sacrifice. She is smart, ambitious, and driven, qualities respected and rewarded in the American ethic. But gradually, as she detaches from her decent but unsuccessful husband (Bruce Bennett), and as she favors the insolent Veda over her sweeter younger daughter, putting the child's death behind her with no evident afterthought, we begin to sense an unhealthy, even pathological, aspect to Mildred's compulsion.

Throbbing melodrama doesn't come with more conviction. Even to those usually turned off by the tough, square-shouldered Crawford, her intense, no-holds-barred performance as Mildred is tragically twisted and compelling. Blyth, only seventeen, is sneeringly sensational as the disdainful femme fatale. A director who imposed his personality on films in every genre, Curtiz's masterly deployment of his actors (sterling support players such as Eve Arden, Jack Carson, and Lee Patrick) and the disparate technical elements—*Gone with the Wind*'s Oscar-winning cinematographer Ernest Haller's expressive shifts from sunny suburbia to shadowy nightmare, and Max Steiner's dramatic score—are intoxicating. **AE**

i

In 2012, Joan Crawford's Best Actress Oscar for *Mildred Pierce* was sold at auction for $426,732.

1945

Detour Edgar G. Ulmer, 1945

U.S. (PRC) 67m BW
Producer Leon Fromkess, Martin Mooney
Screenplay Martin Goldsmith, from his
novel Photography Benjam H. Kline
Music Leo Erdody, Clarence Gaskill, Jimmy
McHugh Cast Tom Neal, Ann Savage,
Claudia Drake, Edmund MacDonald, Tim
Ryan, Esther Howard, Pat Gleason

"Fate or some mysterious force can put the finger on you or me for no good reason at all." One of the greatest of all B-movies, *Detour* makes no attempt to rise above its budget and brief shooting schedule, instead reveling in its cheapness, presenting a world somewhere between pulp fiction and existentialism where life has low production values and a short running time.

A grubby jazz musician (Tom Neal) hitchhikes across country, descending into an on-the-road hell as a driver drops dead, incriminating him. He hooks up with a trampy woman (Ann Savage) who leads him to degradation and murder, climaxing in an unforgettable tussle in a tawdry motel room in which a telephone cord gets tangled up around the woman's neck.

Edgar G. Ulmer, a German Expressionist toiling along Poverty Row, was a more pretentious filmmaker than his admirers will admit, but this is the one genuine masterpiece from his time in the Z-trenches. The unknown stars (real-life loser Neal later did time for murder) are resolutely unglamorous, and the studio sets, anonymous roadsides, and back-projected landscapes conjure up a world spiraling out of control—one where the coincidence-driven plotting of a thrown-together B-picture script can suggest the malign hand of merciless destiny. **KN**

1945

I Know Where I'm Going!
Michael Powell & Emeric Pressburger, 1945

G.B. (Rank, The Archers) 92m BW
Language English / Gaelic
Producer George R. Busby, Michael Powell,
Emeric Pressburger Screenplay Michael
Powell & Emeric Pressburger
Photography Erwin Hillier Music Allan Gray
Cast Wendy Hiller, Roger Livesey, George
Carney, Pamela Brown, Walter Hudd, Captain
Duncan MacKenzie, Ian Sadler, Finlay Currie,
Murdo Morrison, Margot Fitzsimmons,
Captain C.W.R. Knight, Donald Strachan,
John Rae, Duncan McIntyre, Jean Cadell

I Know Where I'm Going! stands tall as one of the most perfect of the run of delirious masterpieces made by the team of Michael Powell and Emeric Pressburger in the 1940s. Joan Webster (Wendy Hiller), very sexy in smart suits, is the practical postwar English miss who travels to the Hebrides to marry a millionaire old enough to be her father. But when bad weather postpones the final leg of her journey, she finds her determined gold-digging sidetracked by an island-load of strange Scots who arrange for her to be diverted into the arms of her predestined lover Torquil MacNeil (Roger Livesey), the local penniless squire and war hero.

Aside from being the only filmmakers who could get away with naming a romantic hero "Torquil," Powell and Pressburger go against the cynical vision of conniving, drunken Scots islanders found in Ealing Studio's 1949 *Whisky Galore!*, presenting a crew who are just as devious but working for good ends. Joan's urban toughness is quickly overwhelmed with lots of Celtic legend involving the local whirlpool, which represents the gods and allows for an exciting rescue-at-sea finale. In a large supporting cast, Pamela Brown is especially memorable as the spookily alluring local girl, Catriona Potts. **KN**

The Lost Weekend Billy Wilder, 1945

Before *The Lost Weekend*, drunkards in Hollywood movies were mostly figures of fun, indeed of farce—lovable buffoons reeling around uttering slurred witticisms and making hopeless passes at pretty girls. Billy Wilder and his regular coscreenwriter, Charles Brackett, dared to do something different, creating American cinema's first adult, intelligent, unsparing look at the grim degradation of alcoholism. Even today, some of the scenes are almost too painful to watch.

Ray Milland, in a career-defining role that netted him an Oscar, plays a New York writer, Don Birnam, struggling with and finally succumbing to his craving over the space of one long, parched summer weekend in the city. Just as he had done with Fred MacMurray in *Double Indemnity* (1944), Wilder ferrets out and avidly exploits the insecurity behind Milland's bland screen persona. Rather than letting us stand back and judge in detached compassion, Wilder pulls us along with Birnam on his downward trajectory. We're obliged to accompany him as he sheds all his remaining moral scruples, showing himself ready to lie, cheat, and steal to get money for drink, until with awful inevitability he ends up in the hell of a public hospital's alcoholics ward, screaming in horror at the hallucinations of delirium tremens.

Parts of the film were shot on Manhattan locations, and Wilder makes the most of the dry, sun-bleached streets, shot by his director of photography John F. Seitz to look bleak and tawdry, as if through Birnam's bleary, self-loathing gaze. In one unforgettable sequence, the writer, reduced to trying to hock his typewriter to raise funds for booze, traipses the dusty length of Third Avenue dragging the heavy machine—only to realize that it's Yom Kippur and all the pawnshops are closed. Even more harrowing is the scene in a smart nightclub where Birman succumbs to temptation and tries to filch money from a woman's handbag—only to be caught and humiliatingly thrown out while the club pianist leads the clientele in a chorus of "Somebody stole her purse" (to the tune of "Somebody Stole My Gal"). And Miklós Rózsa's score makes masterly use of the theremin, that early electronic instrument whose eerie, swooping tone perfectly conjures up Birnam's woozy, out-of-control vision of the world.

The strictures of the Hays Code imposed a happy ending, though Wilder and Brackett managed to sidestep anything too mindlessly reassuring. Even so, Paramount was convinced the movie was doomed to failure, with an alarmed liquor industry offering the studio $5 million to bury the film altogether. Prohibitionists, on the other hand, were up in arms, claiming the film would encourage drinking. In any event, *The Lost Weekend* was a major critical and commercial hit. "It was after this picture," Wilder noted, "that people started taking me seriously." No subsequent film on alcoholism, or any other form of addiction, has been able to avoid a nod to *The Lost Weekend*. **PK**

1945

U.S. (Paramount) 101m BW
Producer Charles Brackett
Screenplay Charles Brackett, Billy Wilder, from novel by Charles R. Jackson
Photography John F. Seitz **Music** Miklós Rózsa **Cast** Ray Milland, Jane Wyman, Phillip Terry, Howard Da Silva, Doris Dowling, Frank Faylen, Mary Young, Anita Sharp-Bolster, Lillian Fontaine, Frank Orth, Lewis L. Russell, Clarence Muse **Oscars** Charles Brackett (best picture), Billy Wilder (director), Charles Brackett, Billy Wilder (screenplay), Ray Milland (actor) **Oscar nominations** John F. Seitz (photography), Doane Harrison (editing), Miklós Rózsa (music) **Cannes Film Festival** Billy Wilder (Grand Prize of the Festival), Ray Milland (actor)

"What I'm trying to say is, I'm not a drinker. I'm a drunk."

**Don Birnam
(Ray Milland)**

i

The reaction to the first preview of *The Lost Weekend* was not good—the audience laughed and called it boring.

Les enfants du paradis Marcel Carné, 1945
The Children of Paradise

France (Pathé) 190m BW
Language French **Producer** Raymond Borderie, Fred Orain **Screenplay** Jacques Prévert **Photography** Marc Fossard, Roger Hubert **Music** Joseph Kosma, Maurice Thiriet **Cast** Arletty, Jean-Louis Barrault, Pierre Brasseur, Marcel Herrand, Pierre Renoir, María Casares, Gaston Modot, Fabien Loris, Marcel Pérès, Palau, Etienne Decroux, Jane Marken, Marcelle Monthil, Louis Florencie, Habib Benglia, Rognoni **Oscar nomination** Jacques Prévert (screenplay)

"Marcel Carné, a true master practitioner, has led the cast with . . . a skill that can not be disputed."

Léon Moussinac,
***La Marseillaise*, 1945**

ℹ

The film's title is a reference to the poor people who could only afford to sit up in "the gods" at the theater.

Ever since its triumphant premiere in the newly liberated France of 1945, *The Children of Paradise* has maintained its place as one of the greatest French films of all time. It represents the high point of the genre often called "poetic realism" and also of the partnership that perfected that genre—that of screenwriter Jacques Prévert and director Marcel Carné. They made an oddly assorted couple: Prévert gregarious, passionate, highly committed politically, one of the finest popular French poets of the century; Carné remote, fastidious, withdrawn, a cool perfectionist. Yet together they created cinematic magic that neither man could equal after they parted. *The Children of Paradise* was their last great success.

The film was some eighteen months in production and involved building the largest studio set in the history of French cinema—the quarter-mile of street frontage representing the "Boulevard du Crime," the theater district of Paris in the 1830s and 1840s. This would have been a daunting enterprise at the best of times; in wartime France, under the conditions of the Occupation, it was little short of heroic. Transport, materials, costumes, and film stock were all scarce. The Italian coproducers pulled out when Italy capitulated. The original French producer had to withdraw when he came under investigation by the Nazis. One lead actor, a prominent pro-Nazi, fled to Germany after D-Day and had to be replaced at the last minute. Alexandre Trauner, the set designer, and the composer Joseph Kosma, who were both Jewish, were obliged to work in hiding and transmit their ideas through intermediaries.

Despite all this, *Children* is a consummate achievement with all the richness and complexity of a great nineteenth-century novel. The crowd scenes deploy their 1,500 extras in riotous profusion, cramming every corner of the screen with lively detail. A defiant affirmation of French theatrical culture at a time when the nation was conquered and occupied, the film offers a meditation on the nature of masquerade, fantasy, and representation. All dialogue is heightened, all actions masterfully staged. The three lead male characters are all performers—Lemaître, the great romantic actor (Pierre Brasseur); Debureau, the supreme mime artiste (Jean-Louis Barrault); and Lacenaire, the failed playwright turned dandyish master criminal (Marcel Herrand). All are real historical personages. The woman they all love, the *grande horizontale* Garance (Arletty in her greatest screen role), is fiction—less a real woman than an icon of the eternal feminine, elusive and infinitely desirable.

Though it runs over three hours, *Children* never seems a minute too long. A celebration of theater as the great popular art of the nineteenth century, it mixes farce, romance, melodrama, and tragedy. Carné was a supreme director of actors, and the film offers a feast of great French screen acting, along with wit, grace, passion, and an all-pervading sense of transience—the melancholy that underlies all Romantic art. **PK**

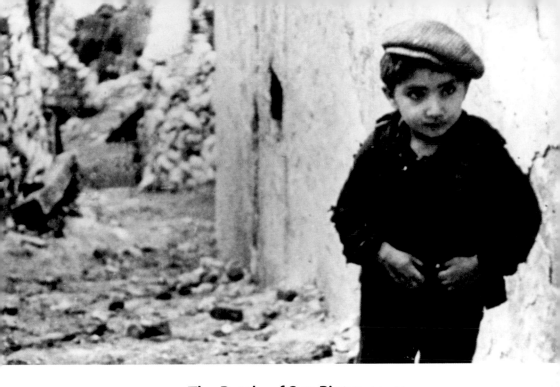

The Battle of San Pietro John Huston, 1945

U.S. (U.S. Army) 33m BW
Producer Frank Capra Screenplay John
Huston Photography Jules Buck
Music Dimitri Tiomkin
Cast John Huston (narrator)

Made for the U.S. Army as a propaganda film, John Huston's *The Battle of San Pietro* remains the best war documentary ever made, despite changes made to remove some material thought to be too disturbing for civilian viewers. The picture details the taking of an Italian hill town from tenacious and well-entrenched German defenders, a battle that cost American units more than a thousand casualties.

While the inconclusiveness of the struggle implicitly indicts a flawed American strategy (despite the director's flag-waving voice-over), Huston's main purpose was to portray the experience of war seen from the viewpoint of those who fight it and have no concern about larger calculations of loss or gain. Huston's crew captures the horror and confusion of combat: the wounding of American soldiers; the pain and suffering of civilians; the boredom and campaigning for troops far from home; the inevitable cost of "victory," measured in the huge number of body bags loaded onto trucks; and the rows and rows of temporary graves dug to accommodate them.

The film was eventually released to the American public only after final victory in Europe, too late to play any role in influencing opinion about the war. *The Battle of San Pietro* is Huston's tribute to the brave men he lived among, as well as a poignant, graphic treatment of battle and its consequences, with some stock footage and staged scenes not detracting from the overall effect of authenticity and objectivity. **RBP**

John Huston was a captain in the army when the movie was filmed; he was later promoted to major.

G.B. (Cineguild, Rank) 86m BW
Producer Noel Coward, Anthony
Havelock-Allan, Ronald Neame
Screenplay Anthony Havelock-Allan,
David Lean, from the play *Still Life* by Noel
Coward **Photography** Robert Krasker
Music Rachmaninov **Cast** Celia Johnson,
Trevor Howard, Stanley Holloway, Joyce
Carey, Cyril Raymond, Everley Gregg,
Marjorie Mars **Oscar nominations** David
Lean (director), Anthony Havelock-Allan,
David Lean, Ronald Neame (screenplay),
Celia Johnson (actress) **Cannes Film
Festival** David Lean (Grand Prize of
the Festival)

*"It's awfully easy to lie
when you know that
you're trusted implicitly."*

Laura Jesson
(Celia Johnson)

i

Noel Coward makes a small cameo
in *Brief Encounter* as the voice of
the station announcer.

Brief Encounter David Lean, 1945

The imposing epics of David Lean's later years sometimes threaten to overshadow the director's relatively modest early works, but to focus too much on the sheer spectacle of *Lawrence of Arabia* or *Doctor Zhivago* would be to overlook some of Lean's greatest accomplishments. After all, only a filmmaker of the highest order could direct *Lawrence of Arabia*, and that same mastery of the form is on display in Lean's formative films.

Lean had already directed three adaptations of Noel Coward's work when he began *Brief Encounter*, based on Coward's one-act play *Still Life*. But the play's brevity forced Lean to expand the material, and in the process he expanded his own film vocabulary as well. Told in flashback, *Brief Encounter* follows the platonic love affair between housewife Laura (Celia Johnson) and doctor Alec (Trevor Howard), who meet fortuitously in a train station. There's obviously a connection between the two, but they know their romance can't go beyond a few furtive lunch meetings.

In crafting one of the most effective tearjerkers in cinema history, Lean made a number of formal advances that quickly established him as more than just someone riding the coattails of Noel Coward. For starters, Lean took the story out of the train station, adding more details to the doomed affair. And he exploited all the cinematic tools at his disposal; the lighting, for example, approaches the severe look of Lean's subsequent Dickens adaptations, making the symbolic most of the dark, smoky station. He also makes good use of sound effects (particularly that of a speeding train), as well as music, incorporating Rachmaninoff's Piano Concerto No. 2 as the film's running theme.

But most importantly, Lean includes frequent close-ups of Johnson's eyes, which tell a better story than most scripts. She and Howard are superlative in this saddest of stories, their every movement steeped in meaning and the sterling dialogue laced with deep emotions. A passing glance, the brush of a finger across a hand, and a shared laugh are virtually all these ill-fated lovers are allowed, and Johnson and Howard beautifully convey this sad realization. **JKl**

Roma, città aperta Roberto Rossellini, 1945
Open City

Considered the initiator of an aesthetic revolution in film, Roberto Rossellini's *Open City* was the first major work of Italian Neorealism, and it managed to explode the conventions of the Mussolinian "cinema of white telephones" that was fashionable in Italy at the beginning of the 1940s. This film about the Italian Resistance was scripted in the days of the underground battle against the Nazis. Recalling Sergei Eisenstein's formula of the "choral film," it tells of a group of patriots hiding in the apartment of a lithographer named Francesco (Francesco Grandjaquet). The communist who leads the group, Manfredi (Marcello Pagliero), is chased by the Gestapo and is finally captured and executed. Francesco's wife, Pina (Anna Magnani), and a sympathetic priest, Don Pietro (Aldo Fabrizi), die, too, trying to help Manfredi escape. But it is the solidarity of Rome as a city that anticipates a final victory against the invaders.

The scarcity of technical and financial resources available to Rossellini proved to be a virtue of *Open City*, which was shot in a documentary style. Showing real people in real locations, the film brought some fresh air to the existing Western cinema. The freedom of the camera movements and the authenticity of the characters, allied to a new way of storytelling, were among the qualities that made *Open City* the revelation of the 1946 Cannes Film Festival, where it was awarded the *Palme d'Or*. Neorealism quickly became an aesthetic model for directors interested in a vivid description of history and society.

One of the most amazing things about *Open City* is the approach Rossellini takes to each character's drama. Some of the film's heroes will forever remain in the hearts of viewers. Who can forget the sight of a pregnant Pina running through bullets or the kind priest shot before the frightened eyes of the children? Although it may veer toward the melodramatic, the story is just as moving today as it was then. And it should come as no surprise to learn that, after this role, Magnani became one of the greatest actresses of the Italian screen. **DD**

Italy (Excelsa, Minerva) 100m BW
Language Italian / German
Producer Giuseppe Amato. Ferruccio De Martino, Roberto Rossellini
Photography Ubaldo Arata
Screenplay Sergio Amidei, Federico Fellini
Music Renzo Rossellini Cast Aldo Fabrizi, Anna Magnani, Marcello Pagliero, Maria Michi, Harry Feist Oscar nomination Sergio Amidei, Federico Fellini (screenplay)
Cannes Film Festival Roberto Rossellini (Grand Prize of the Festival)

1945

"One makes films in order to become a better human being."

Roberto Rossellini, 1973

i
Rossellini used real German POWs as extras in the movie to add to its realistic feel.

The Best Years of Our Lives William Wyler, 1946

This domestic epic about three World War II veterans returning to civilian life, 172 minutes long and winner of nine Oscars, isn't considered hip nowadays. Critics as sharp as Manny Farber and Robert Warshow were pretty contemptuous of it when it came out—although seemingly from opposite political viewpoints. Farber saw it as liberal hogwash from a conservative angle, whereas Warshow skewered it more from a Marxist perspective. Its director, William Wyler, and the literary source, MacKinlay Kantor's novel, are far from fashionable today. The veteran in the cast, Harold Russell, who lost his hands in the war, occasioned outraged reflections from Warshow about challenged masculinity and even sick jokes from humorist Terry Southern many years later. For all that, it is one of the best American movies about returning soldiers ever made—certainly the most moving and the most deeply felt. It bears witness to its times and contemporaries like few other Hollywood features, and Gregg Toland's deep-focus cinematography is incredible.

Part of what is so unusual about The Best Years of Our Lives as a Hollywood picture is its sense of class distinctions—the way that the separate fates and careers of veterans who are well-to-do (March), middle-class (Russell), and working-class (Andrews) are juxtaposed. Admittedly, the fact that they all meet one another at a bar presided over by Hoagy Carmichael is something of a sentimental contrivance, yet the relative blurring of class lines in the armed services that carries over briefly into civilian life has its plausible side as well. Similarly, the limitations of Russell as an actor have been held against the picture, yet the fact that we accept him as the real disabled veteran that he was seems far more important, documentary truth in this case superseding the interests of fiction. The scenes between him and his (fictional) fiancée, as they both struggle to adjust to their reconfigured relationship, are wrenching in their tenderness as well as their honesty, with few passages in American cinema to equal them. **JRos**

U.S. (Samuel Goldwyn) 172m BW **Producer** Samuel Goldwyn **Screenplay** Robert E. Sherwood, from the novel Glory for Me by MacKinlay Kantor **Photography** Gregg Toland **Music** Hugo Friedhofer **Cast** Myrna Loy, Fredric March, Dana Andrews, Teresa Wright, Virginia Mayo, Cathy O'Donnell, Hoagy Carmichael, Harold Russell, Gladys George, Roman Bohnen, Ray Collins, Minna Gombell, Walter Baldwin, Steve Cochran, Dorothy Adams **Oscars** Harold Russell (honorary award), Samuel Goldwyn (best picture), William Wyler (director), Robert E. Sherwood (screenplay), Fredric March (actor), Harold Russell (actor), Daniel Mandell (editing), Hugo Friedhofer (music) **Oscar nomination** Gordon Sawyer (sound)

> "I've seen nothing, I should have stayed at home and found out what was really going on."
>
> **Al Stephenson (Fredric March)**

i

The movie went on to become the biggest box-office hit in the USA since Gone With the Wind (1939).

Paisà Roberto Rossellini, 1946
Paisan

Italy (Foreign Film, OFI) 120m BW
Language Italian / English / German
Director Roberto Rossellini Producer Mario
Conti, Rod E. Geiger, Roberto Rossellini
Screenplay Sergio Amidei, Federico Fellini
Photography Otello Martelli Music Renzo
Rossellini Cast Carmela Sazlo, Robert Van
Loon, Benjam Emmanuel, Harold Wagner,
Merlin Berth, Dots Johnson, Alfonsino Pasca,
Maria Michi, Gar Moore, Harriet Medin,
Renzo Avanzo, William Tubbs, Dale
Edmonds, Cigolani, Allen Dan Oscar
nomination Alfred Hayes, Federico Fellini,
Sergio Amidei, Marcello Pagliero, Roberto
Rossellini (screenplay)

Anyone approaching *Paisan* without foreknowledge of its status as a Neorealist masterpiece could be forgiven for giving up early on: stock footage of the American campaign in Italy, Hollywood-style music, bad actors barking military commands. It is only by the end of the first of six self-contained episodes that Roberto Rossellini's off-hand style has begun to weave its stark magic—soon after a bullet abruptly kills off a soldier telling his life story, we see the corpse of his companion, killed by the Germans and dismissed, unknowingly, by the surviving Americans as a "dirty Iti."

Rossellini's chronicle of 1943–46 is marked by devastation, brutality, and incomprehension at all levels. An American does not realize that a prostitute is the woman he loved six months earlier; a street-urchin befriends a drunken, black soldier and steals his shoes the instant he falls asleep; the film's final, unforgettably bleak image shows the merciless execution of a line of partisans. Rossellini develops a structure to match this succession of events, based on startling plot ellipses, cross-purpose dialogues in multiple languages, and a rigorously unsentimental presentation of horrors. *Paisan* locates the telling traces of personal life within the nightmare of war's history. **AM**

1946

The Postman Always Rings Twice Tay Garnett, 1946

U.S. (MGM) 113m BW
Producer Carey Wilson Screenplay Harry
Ruskin, from novel by James M. Cain
Photography Sidney Wagner Music George
Bassman Cast Lana Turner, John Garfield,
Cecil Kellaway, Hume Cronyn, Leon Ames,
Audrey Totter, Alan Reed, Jeff York

Lana Turner was never more attractive than in her role as Cora Smith, who marries an unattractive older man (Cecil Kellaway) as an escape from poverty but, deeply dissatisfied, gives in to her attraction for a young drifter, Frank Chambers (John Garfield). As in many film noir features, the doomed couple's affair hinges on a crime: the murder of Cora's husband. Aided by a shyster lawyer, the pair are exonerated. Yet they fail to find happiness as Cora is killed in a car accident and Frank is executed for this "crime."

Director Tay Garnett's tight framing emphasizes the imprisonment of the fatal lovers, and the film's gloomy and forbidding mise-en-scène is the perfect setting for their grim story. With white costuming and glamorizing lighting, Turner becomes the visual center of the story, which was based on the James M. Cain novel published a decade earlier. Cora is no ordinary femme fatale. Her feelings for Frank are genuine, not artful manipulation.

The Postman Always Rings Twice reflects the Depression culture of the 1930s, with most of the scenes played in a barely respectable roadside diner, a potent image of rootlessness and limited opportunity. The flashback narrative suits the omnipresent pessimism of the noir series, of which this is one of the most justly celebrated examples. **RBP**

France (DisCina) 96m BW
Language French Producer André Paulvé
Screenplay Jean Cocteau, Jeanne-Marie
Leprince de Beaumont Photography Henri
Alekan Music Georges Auric Cast Jean
Marais, Josette Day, Mila Parély, Nane
Germon, Michel Auclair, Raoul Marco,
Marcel André

*"You will never see me,
except each evening at
7:00, when you will dine,
and I will come to the
great hall. And never
look into my eyes."*

**The Beast (Jean Marais)
to Beauty (Josette Day)**

It took Jean Marais a total
of five hours each day just
to have his makeup applied.

La belle et la bête Jean Cocteau, 1946
Beauty and the Beast

Cocteau never called himself a filmmaker per se. He considered himself a poet; film was just one of many art forms he delved into throughout his career. Yet even if he thought himself a poet rather than a "mere" filmmaker, his visionary rendition of this classic folktale certainly proved the two titles were not mutually exclusive. Moreover, the fact that of all his projects, the dreamlike *Beauty and the Beast* remains his most beloved work reveals not only both his immense versatility and talent but also the endurance and mass acceptance of film over all his other preferred formats.

Indeed, Cocteau approached *Beauty and the Beast*—only his second feature film—fully cognizant of the medium's broad reach and fueled by an agenda. On the one hand, his peers were looking to him to put French filmmaking back on the map after the massive cultural setback of the German occupation; *Beauty and the Beast* was to be a de facto national statement of purpose from France's artistic community. On the other hand, Cocteau was also being egged on by the critics, who accused the artist of elitism and of being out of touch with the public's tastes. Could he ever produce a mainstream work that would be embraced by the people?

Cocteau approached the centuries-old Beauty and the Beast fable as an outlet for his most outlandish and fantastic creative impulses. In fact, the relatively straightforward framework of the story encouraged such experimentation. When her father is held captive by a beast (Jean Marais) in a remote castle, daughter Beauty (Josette Day) volunteers to take his place. But the Beast's bargain is more than it seems: he tells Beauty he wants to marry her, and Beauty must look past the appearance and to the good heart of her hairy suitor before making her decision.

Cocteau sets their courtship in a magical castle—the proving ground for a number of beautiful effects. Beauty doesn't just walk through the halls, she glides. Candles are lodged not in traditional holders but grasped by humanoid arms affixed to the walls. Mirrors are transformed to liquid portals, flames flicker and extinguish with a mind of their own, and statues come to life. The castle works both as a metaphor for the creative process personified as well as an excuse for numerous Freudian images. Because Beauty can't really consummate her relationship with the Beast until he is transformed, Cocteau has her fondling knives and traveling down long corridors as a means of revealing her subconscious desires.

But Cocteau's greatest achievement was making the monstrous Beast convincing as well as appealing. With Marais buried under elaborate makeup, the Beast's goodness must be conveyed through his actions and deeds, thus revealing the humanity both literally and figuratively beneath the fur and fangs. In fact, so successful is Marais's portrayal that at the film's premiere, when the Beast is finally transformed into a blandly handsome Prince and he and Beauty live happily ever after, actress Greta Garbo famously exclaimed, "Give me back my Beast!" **JKl**

The Killers Robert Siodmak, 1946

U.S. (Mark Hellinger, Universal)
105m BW **Producer** Mark Hellinger
Screenplay Anthony Veiller, from story by
Ernest Hemingway **Photography** Elwood
Bredell **Music** Miklós Rózsa **Cast** Burt
Lancaster, Ava Gardner, Edmond O'Brien,
Albert Dekker, Sam Levene, Vince Barnett,
Virginia Christine, Jack Lambert, Charles D.
Brown, Donald MacBride, Charles McGraw,
William Conrad **Oscar nominations** Robert
Siodmak (director), Anthony Veiller
(screenplay), Arthur Hilton (editing),
Miklós Rózsa (music)

ℹ

Miklós Rózsa's musical motif for *The Killers* was later developed to become the theme for the TV series *Dragnet*.

The first ten minutes of Robert Siodmak's classic film noir reproduces Hemingway's brief 1927 story almost verbatim: Two hit men barge into a sleepy burg to gun down the unresisting recluse Swede (Burt Lancaster). Extrapolating imaginatively, screenwriters Anthony Veiller and John Huston invent Riordan (Edmond O'Brien), a zealous insurance investigator who uncovers Swede's past: an ex-pug mixed up with a shady dame (Ava Gardner), a payroll heist, and a double cross.

Citizen Kane (1941) fractured its narrative into flashbacks related by different narrators; *The Killers* takes the idea a step further by scrambling the flashbacks' temporal order. The process of piecing together this jigsaw reinforces a reciprocal link between the spectator and Riordan. As he delves into Swede's past, the restless company-man Riordan gets the thrill of vicariously living a film noir life without paying the usual consequences. The relationship between Riordan and Swede's illicit world becomes analogous to that between the spectator and the film—a concept crystallized when, just before the showdown, Riordan sits silhouetted in the foreground as if he were in the front row of a movie theater. *The Killers* is not only a superior film noir but also a commentary on why we enjoy film noir, as an escape from humdrum security into danger and doom, but only at a safe distance. **MR**

It's a Wonderful Life Frank Capra, 1946

After celebrating the common man in such 1930s classics as *It Happened One Night* (1934), *Mr. Deeds Goes to Town* (1936), and *You Can't Take It with You* (1938), Frank Capra's first postwar film revels unashamedly in the goodness of ordinary folks as well as the value of humble dreams, even if they don't come true. Based on *The Greatest Gift*, a short story written on a Christmas card by Philip Van Doren Stern, the film's vital leading role of a young man saddled with responsibility was almost turned down by war-weary James Stewart. Released in 1946 to mixed reviews, the film was nevertheless nominated for five Academy Awards (including Best Picture and Best Actor), but it didn't win in any category. Whether it was a film that required frequent viewing to be fully appreciated or that simply had been made at the wrong time is now a moot point. By the 1960s, the film's copyright expired, which opened the floodgates for a "public domain" version to be circulated for cheap and frequent television broadcast. Repeated heavily around the holiday season, it became a mainstay of wholesome family viewing. As an emotional touchstone for several generations, public broadcasting stations in the 1970s cemented the film's reputation of quality by scheduling it against the commercial networks' crass and materialistic holiday fare.

Gangling, good-hearted George Bailey (Stewart) grows up in tiny Bedford Falls, Connecticut, but dreams of traveling the world. Duty, though, steps in again and again to crush George's dream. The loss of his freedom is only softened by George's marriage to local beauty Mary (Donna Reed) and later by his young family and his own sense of homey philanthropy in helping the working people of Bedford Falls afford their own homes. Finally, forced to take over the family savings and loan, which is threatened with foreclosure by the greedy town banker Mr. Potter (Lionel Barrymore was rarely more disagreeable), George becomes so overburdened that he attempts suicide by jumping off the local bridge. But a miracle happens: an angel named Clarence (Henry Travers) is sent from heaven to show George what the town would have become if George had had his wish and hadn't lived at all. If and only if George is convinced of his own value will his suicide be undone, the town be returned to normal, and Clarence, a second-class angel, get his wings.

It's a Wonderful Life remains a holiday favorite for its uplifting message tempered by a foreboding notion of "what if." Viewed on a big screen without holiday distractions, the film is actually more of a delightfully shrewd screwball comedy packed with fast, incisive observations on love, sex, and society. The high quality of the banter especially points to uncredited script input from Dorothy Parker, Dalton Trumbo, and Clifford Odets. The movie was a favorite of Capra and Stewart, both of whom expressed extreme dismay when it became an early victim of the colorization craze. **KK**

U.S. (Liberty, RKO) 130m BW
Producer Frank Capra **Screenplay** Philip Van Doren Stern, Frances Goodrich **Photography** Joseph Biroc, Joseph Walker, Victor Milner **Music** Dimitri Tiomkin, Leigh Harline, Leith Stevens, Dave Torbett, Roy Webb **Cast** James Stewart, Donna Reed, Lionel Barrymore, Thomas Mitchell, Henry Travers, Beulah Bondi, Frank Faylen, Ward Bond, Gloria Grahame, H.B. Warner, Frank Albertson, Todd Karns, Samuel S. Hinds, Mary Treen, Virginia Patton **Oscar nominations** Frank Capra (best picture), Frank Capra (director), James Stewart (actor), William Hornbeck (editing), John Aalberg (sound)

"You see, George, you've really had a wonderful life. Don't you see what a mistake it would be to just throw it away?"

Clarence (Henry Travers) to George Bailey (James Stewart)

i

The film was shot during a major heatwave—James Stewart is clearly sweating in several scenes.

The Big Sleep Howard Hawks, 1946

Supposedly when director Howard Hawks asked novelist Raymond Chandler to explain the numerous double crosses, twists, and surprises revealed throughout his book *The Big Sleep*, the writer famously and honestly replied, "I have no idea." That isn't to say the various twists and turns are not important to *The Big Sleep*, or even that their presence in the book is just arbitrary confusion. Rather, Chandler's notoriously muddled "whodunit" merely complicates an already complicated tale of Los Angeles corruption, further tainting a nearly endless list of seedy characters.

It should therefore come as no surprise that Hawks gently shifted the focus of his adaptation from sleuthing to the sleuth, in this case Humphrey Bogart as hard-boiled private investigator Philip Marlowe. Taking advantage of the success of the 1944 film *To Have and Have Not*, Hawks reunited Bogart with Lauren Bacall and played up their palpable chemistry. When they're on the screen together, the detective story fades to the background (they were married six months after shooting ended). Hawks exploited that sexual tension, adding extra scenes with the two actors and stressing the innuendo-laced dialogue, particularly racy (especially an exchange about horses and saddles) in light of the era's Production Code.

And what of the whodunit? Thankfully, the central investigation, confusing though it may be, is still a joy to watch. Marlowe acts as our Virgil-like guide as he descends into Hollywood's darkest and dirtiest corners, unraveling a murder/blackmail plot that involves pornographers, nymphomaniacs, and a bevy of hired hoods who barely have time to reveal more plot points (and red herrings) before getting plugged.

The Big Sleep is a reference to death, and indeed death pervades the movie. This is a film noir masterpiece missing several standard film noir tenets. There are numerous femme fatales, but no flashbacks; chiaroscuro lighting, but no voice-over. More important, Bogart's Marlowe seems not lost in a world of lies and deception but utterly confident and in control at all times. He's a droll antihero, cool in the face of cruelty, unfazed in the face of wanton sleaze, and always appreciative of a pretty face. **JKl**

U.S. (First National, Warner) 114m BW **Producer** Howard Hawks, Jack L. Warner **Screenplay** William Faulkner, from novel by Raymond Chandler **Photography** Sidney Hickox **Music** Max Steiner **Cast** Humphrey Bogart, Lauren Bacall, John Ridgely, Martha Vickers, Dorothy Malone, Peggy Knudsen, Regis Toomey, Charles Waldron, Charles D. Brown, Bob Steele, Elisha Cook Jr., Louis Jean Heydt

> *"You know what he'll do when he comes back? Beat my teeth out, then kick me in the stomach for mumbling."*
>
> **Philip Marlowe**
> **(Humphrey Bogart)**

ℹ️
Bogart's automobile in *The Big Sleep* is the same one that he has in *High Sierra* (1941).

Gilda Charles Vidor, 1946

U.S. (Columbia) 110m BW **Producer** Virginia Van Upp **Screenplay** Jo Eisinger, E.A. Ellington **Photography** Rudolph Maté **Music** Doris Fisher, Allan Roberts, Hugo Friedhofer **Cast** Rita Hayworth, Glenn Ford, George Macready, Joseph Calleia, Steven Geray, Joe Sawyer, Gerald Mohr, Robert E. Scott, Ludwig Donath, Donald Douglas

"Statistics show there are more women in the world than anything else," snaps cynical hero Johnny Farrell (Glenn Ford), adding, with peculiar loathing, "except insects!" And yet this misogyny coexists in director Charles Vidor's film with the exquisite Gilda (Rita Hayworth) herself. A character who is at once a total blank and a masterful ironist, whose signature tune "Put the Blame on Mame"—to which she performs a supremely exotic striptease involving only the removal of her elbow-length velvet gloves—is a pointed exposé of the way women are made to seem responsible for the havoc wreaked by men who become obsessed with them.

Johnny, a hardboiled gambler who looks suavely uncomfortable in his dinner jacket, becomes manager of a casino in Buenos Aires, working for Ballin Mundson (George Macready), a frozen-faced mastermind who wields a sword cane, enjoys spying on his customers and associates from a control room in the gambling joint, and forms the apex of a three-way love triangle that triggers the plot. Ford and Hayworth, limited but engaging and photogenic actors, have definitive performances drawn out of them like teeth, and Macready has the time of his life as the complex villain. As the posters claim, "there never was a woman like Gilda!" **KN**

A Matter of Life and Death
Michael Powell & Emeric Pressburger, 1946

G.B. (The Archers, Independent, Rank) 104m BW / Technicolor **Producer** George R. Busby, Michael Powell, Emeric Pressburger **Screenplay** Michael Powell, Emeric Pressburger **Photography** Jack Cardiff **Music** Allan Gray **Cast** David Niven, Kim Hunter, Robert Coote, Kathleen Byron, Richard Attenborough, Bonar Colleano, Joan Maude, Marius Goring, Roger Livesey, Robert Atkins, Bob Roberts, Edwin Max, Betty Potter, Abraham Sofaer, Raymond Massey

Michael Powell and Emeric Pressburger's 1946 fantasy, *A Matter of Life and Death* (renamed *Stairway To Heaven* for the U.S. market), was intended as a propaganda film to ameliorate strained relations between Britain and America. The movie outstrips its original purpose, however, ending up a lasting tale of romance and human goodness that is both visually exciting and verbally amusing.

Ready to jump from his burning airplane to certain death, a World War II pilot (David Niven) falls in love with the voice of an American radio operator (Kim Hunter). He awakes on a beach, believing he is in heaven. Finding that he is alive, he seizes the opportunity to fall in love with the American girl in person. But the powers above have made an error, and Heavenly Conductor 71 (Marius Goring) is sent to tell him the truth and take him to heaven where he belongs. The outstanding set design by Alfred Junge raises this film above its already impressive sentiments and nimble script, which switches with ease between earth (filmed in Technicolor) and the ethereal black and white of heaven. Along with its use of freeze-frames and breathtaking set decor in the great beyond, the camera includes a behind-the-eyeball shot of which Salvador Dalí would approve. **KK**

Great Expectations David Lean, 1946

G.B. (Cineguild, Rank) 118m BW
Producer Anthony Havelock-Allan, Ronald Neame **Screenplay** Anthony Havelock-Allan, David Lean, Ronald Neame, from novel by Charles Dickens **Photography** Guy Green **Music** Walter Goehr, Kenneth Pakeman **Cast** John Mills, Anthony Wager, Valerie Hobson, Jean Simmons, Bernard Miles, Francis L. Sullivan, Finlay Currie, Martita Hunt, Alec Guinness, Ivor Barnard, Freda Jackson, Eileen Erskine, George Hayes, Hay Petrie, John Forrest **Oscars** John Bryan, Wilfred Shingleton (art direction), Guy Green (photography) **Oscar nominations** Ronald Neame (best picture), David Lean (director), David Lean, Ronald Neame, Anthony Havelock-Allan (screenplay)

"I have come back, Miss Havisham! I have come back—to let in the sunlight!"

Pip (John Mills)

ℹ

The film became the first British movie to secure an Academy Award for photography.

Filmed in 1946 in the wake of the successes *Brief Encounter* and *Blithe Spirit* (both 1945), *Great Expectations* was David Lean's first adaptation of Charles Dickens's novels; *Oliver Twist* was to follow in 1948. Taking on the literary masterpiece as a cinematic task in every sense of the word, Lean explores and exploits the broad emotional horizon of the story and makes it a sweeping, mesmeric visual journey as well. The result is the finest literary adaptation ever filmed, as well as one of the best British films ever made.

Great Expectations shares elements with many horror films, opening on a broad marsh, which leads to a lonely, neglected, cemetery. This opening scene was so vital that Lean, who had exact ideas about how the film should look, replaced the original cinematographer, Robert Krasker, with Guy Green. Here, the young hero Pip is threatened by a fierce and desperate escaped convict named Magwitch (Finlay Currie) who demands food and a file with which to remove his chains. Later, Pip is brought to the decrepit mansion of the equally decrepit and embittered Miss Havisham (Martita Hunt). Jilted at her wedding breakfast many years before, Miss Havisham still wears the remnants of her bridal gown and lingers around the dusty, rotting, and rodent-infested remains of that fateful dinner. Her macabre plan centers on making her ward, the young and beautiful Estella (Jean Simmons), into a one-woman avenger against all men. This includes Pip, who has fallen in love with her. His situation changes when a mysterious benefactor finances Pip's move to London and his becoming a gentleman of means. Sharing a flat with Herbert Pocket (Alec Guinness in his first important role), the adult Pip (John Mills) becomes a snob, believing that Miss Havisham is his benefactor and that Estella is to be his wife. Any reader accustomed to Dickens knows better.

Some have argued that Mills at thirty-eight was far too old to play a character who is twenty going on twenty-one, as dictated by the novel. However, the fact is Pip needs only to be a witness to the drama played out around him rather than an active participant in his own destiny. Lean, who spent seven years as a film editor before directing his first feature, knew this well and so surrounds Mills with a solid yet colorful supporting cast. Some scenes are pure delight, such as Pip's visit to the house of Wemmick (Ivor Barnard), his lawyer's assistant, where our hero meets Wemmick's elderly and slightly senile father called "Aged P.," shorthand for "aged parent" and a term still used by some to refer to their own. Although not essential for the plot, the scene is memorably heartwarming and amusing, bringing with it a great dollop of Dickensian appeal.

Despite its age, *Great Expectations* has not lost any of its grandeur or poignancy. Rated number five on the British Film Institute's list of all-time greatest British movies, it earned Academy Awards for Best Art Direction and Best Black-and-White Cinematography. In scope, vision, and coherence, this remains the supreme film based on Dickens's work. **KK**

My Darling Clementine John Ford, 1946

U.S. (Fox) 97m BW **Producer** Samuel G. Engel, Darryl F. Zanuck **Photography** Joseph MacDonald **Screenplay** Samuel G. Engel, Sam Hellman **Music** Cyril J. Mockridge **Cast** Henry Fonda, Linda Darnell, Victor Mature, Cathy Downs, Walter Brennan, Tim Holt, Ward Bond, Alan Mowbray, John Ireland, Roy Roberts, Jane Darwell, Grant Withers, J. Farrell MacDonald, Russell Simpson

"I've heard a lot about you, too, Doc . . . In fact, a man could almost follow your trail goin' from graveyard to graveyard."

Wyatt Earp (Henry Fonda) to Doc Holliday (Victor Mature)

Ford's gunfight at the OK Corral drew on Wyatt Earp's version of events—as a young man, Ford had known Earp.

Though *Gunfight at the OK Corral* (1957), *Hour of the Gun* (1967), *Doc* (1971), *Tombstone* (1993), and *Wyatt Earp* (1994) are all more "historically accurate" (for what that's worth), John Ford's romantic, balladlike take on the old, old story remains the Wyatt Earp–Doc Holliday–OK Corral movie.

Peaceable cattleman Wyatt (Henry Fonda) rides into the nightmarish helltown of Tombstone and turns down the job of Marshal even though he's the only man who dares intervene to end the rampage of a drunken Indian. When rustlers murder one of his brothers, he holds a Fordian conversation with the youth's gravestone before facing up to responsibilities and pinning on the badge. In cleaning up the wide-open town, Earp makes the community safe for the ordinary church-going, square-dancing folks who have been hiding in the shadows while the place was overrun by the fiendish Old Man Clanton (Walter Brennan) and his gang of killer sons. However, for all the splendors of Monument Valley (the familiar landscape augmented by picturesque cactus) and Fonda's tight-lipped moral integrity, there is a downside to a crusade won only at the cost of the life of Doc Holliday (Victor Mature), a noble outlaw washed away along with the bad elements by bullets and consumption. This dark theme will later resurface in *The Man Who Shot Liberty Valance* (1962), Ford's disillusioned revision of the town-taming Western.

Mature has a reputation for woodenness, but his turn here as the consumptive surgeon-gunman is heartrending and a bitterly witty turn. Fonda's hero unbends slowly, emerging with stick insect-like grace in one of Ford's trademark community dance scenes and memorably depicted in perfect balance on the porch, chair on two legs, one boot against a post. As always with the Fordian West, the action thrills represented by the elaborate last-reel gunfight are leavened by comic elements: a Shakespearean drunk who needs to be prompted by Doc in the middle of "To Be or Not to Be" and romantic complications with the luminous Chihuaha (Linda Darnell) and the schoolmarm Clementine (Cathy Downs). However, the tone is as often wistful or awestruck by the beauties of the landscape as it is cheer-along shoot-'em-up Saturday matinee material. **KN**

Notorious Alfred Hitchcock, 1946

CARY
GRANT
INGRID
BERGMAN
ALFRED HITCHCOCK'S
Notorious!
CLAUDE RAINS
LOUIS CALHERN · MADAME LEOPOLDINE KONSTANTIN
Directed by **ALFRED HITCHCOCK**
Written by BEN HECHT

U.S. (RKO, Vanguard)
101m BW **Language** English / French
Producer Alfred Hitchcock **Screenplay** Ben
Hecht **Photography** Ted Tetzlaff **Music** Roy
Webb **Cast** Cary Grant, Ingrid Bergman,
Claude Rains, Louis Calhern, Leopoldine
Konstantin, Reinhold Schünzel, Moroni
Olsen, Ivan Triesault, Alex Minotis **Oscar
nominations** Ben Hecht (screenplay),
Claude Rains (actor in support role)

"This is truly my favorite Hitchcock picture . . . In my opinion, Notorious *is the very quintessence of Hitchcock."*

François Truffaut, 1983

Though producer David O. Selznick reunited the winning team of director Alfred Hitchcock, star Ingrid Bergman, and writer Ben Hecht from Hitchcock's psychoanalytical drama *Spellbound* (1945), and oversaw (with his customary blizzard of memos) the development of this classy, romantic spy story, he eventually sold the whole package to RKO and let Hitchcock produce it himself. Even David Thomson, Selznick's biographer, admits that the film is as good as it is because Selznick wasn't there to ruin it.

Toward the end of World War II, suave spymaster T. R. Devlin (Cary Grant) recruits loose-living Alicia Huberman (Bergman), the estranged daughter of a convicted traitor, to infiltrate a group of Nazi exiles in Argentina. Having fallen for the man who has rescued her from a life of trampy uselessness, Alicia is agonized when she feels Devlin is pimping her for the cause, and she is driven to take her mission to extremes by marrying the almost-fatherly fascist Alexander Sebastian (Claude Rains). Inside Sebastian's chilly, luxurious mansion, Alicia earns the hatred of the true power among the evil exiles, Sebastian's smothering monster mother (Madame Konstantin), who is the sort of creature Mrs. Bates might have been if left alive. At a party, with a classic suspense mechanism in the dwindling supply of champagne that will eventually lead to a servant venturing into the wine cellar where the angelic Alicia and the devilish Devlin are snooping, Hitchcock produces his most elegant and yet topical detail: wine bottles full of uranium being used to create a Nazi A-bomb. The payoff is an agonizing moment of discovery when Sebastian is duped into believing that his wife is only unfaithful as opposed to a spy.

Notorious's intense triangle drama constantly forces you to change your feelings about the three leads, with Rains even showing a bizarre heroism in the finale. The film is also a sumptuous romance, with Grant and Bergman sharing what was, at that point, the screen's longest close-up kiss. Gorgeously shot by Ted Tetzlaff in luminous monochrome, with the stars looking (and acting) their best, this last reel was extremely unnerving as the monstrous mother supervises Alicia's slow poisoning. **KN**

i
Leopoldine ("Madame") Konstantin was just four years older than Claude Rains, who played her screen son.

1946

Black Narcissus Michael Powell & Emeric Pressburger, 1946

DEBORAH KERR
SABU · DAVID FARRAR
FLORA ROBSON
IN

Black Narcissus
IN TECHNICOLOR

ESMOND KNIGHT
JEAN SIMMONS
and
KATHLEEN BYRON

Written, produced
and directed by
MICHAEL POWELL and
EMERIC PRESSBURGER

Adapted from the novel
by Rumer Godden

A production of THE ARCHERS

G.B. (Independent, Rank, The Archers) 100m Technicolor **Producer** George R. Busby, Michael Powell, Emeric Pressburger **Screenplay** Michael Powell, Emeric Pressburger, from novel by Rumer Godden **Photography** Jack Cardiff **Music** Brian Easdale **Cast** Deborah Kerr, Sabu, David Farrar, Flora Robson, Esmond Knight, Jean Simmons, Kathleen Byron, Jenny Laird, Judith Furse, May Hallatt, Eddie Whaley Jr., Shaun Noble, Nancy Roberts, Ley On **Oscars** Alfred Junge (art direction), Jack Cardiff (photography)

"You'd like the General, Sister—he's also a superior being."

Mr. Dean (David Farrar) to Sister Clodagh (Deborah Kerr)

ℹ️

The ambience of Jack Cardiff's Oscar-winning photography was inspired by the paintings of Johannes Vermeer.

Film historian David Thomson probably understates the case when he refers to *Black Narcissus* as "that rare thing, an erotic English film about the fantasies of nuns." Based very closely on Rumer Godden's 1939 novel, the picture follows a small group of sisters who are gifted with a building high up in the Himalayas that they attempt to turn into a convent school-cum-hospital. The drafty building was once a harem and is still adorned with explicit murals, while a cackling ayah left over from the times of licentiousness gleefully predicts that the sisters will succumb to the place's atmosphere.

On one level, *Black Narcissus* is a matter-of-fact account of the failings of empire: These sensible Christians arrive with good intentions but are in an absurd situation, teaching only pupils who are paid by the local maharajah to attend lessons that mean nothing to them, and doctoring only minor cases—since if they should try and fail to save a patient, the hospital will be abandoned as if cursed. Directors Powell and Pressburger see the humor in the nuns' frustrations, observing a culture clash without dismissing either the rational or primitive point of view, relishing the irony that it is the most religious characters who are the most sensible here (when they should be prone to all manner of unfounded beliefs), and the godless ones who are most inclined to superstition.

Sister Clodagh (Deborah Kerr), promoted too young, tries to keep the mission together like an inexperienced officer in a war movie, thrown together with the smoldering, disreputable Mr. Dean (David Farrar) and thus exciting the eventually homicidal jealousy of the most repressed of the nuns, Sister Ruth (Kathleen Byron). As the obsessions begin to bite, the film becomes more surreal, with the studio-bound exotica glowing under Jack Cardiff's vivid Technicolor cinematography and Kerr and Byron trembling under their wimples as the passionate nuns. Among the most startling moments in British cinema is the "revelation" of Sister Ruth stripped of her habit, in a mail-order dress and blood-red lipstick, transformed into a harpie who tries to push Clodagh over a precipice as she sounds the convent bell. A nearly grown-up Sabu (Mowgli in the 1942 *Jungle Book*) and a young Jean Simmons (with a jeweled snail on her nose) play the sensual innocents who set a bad example. **KN**

Out of the Past Jacques Tourneur, 1947

U.S. (RKO) 97m BW **Producer** Warren
Duff **Screenplay** Daniel Mainwaring,
from his novel *Build My Gallows High*
Photography Nicholas Musuraca
Music Roy Webb **Cast** Robert Mitchum,
Jane Greer, Kirk Douglas, Rhonda Fleming,
Richard Webb, Steve Brodie, Virginia Huston,
Paul Valentine, Dickie Moore, Ken Niles

Out of the Past, adapted from Daniel Mainwaring's novel *Build My Gallows High*, may be the masterpiece of film noir. All the elements are there: the woman who lies, but is so beautiful that one could forgive almost anything, or at least die at her side (Kathy Moffat, played by Jane Greer). The bitter past that rises up again and destroys the main character. The private eye (Jeff Markham—Robert Mitchum), a man of wit and know-how who makes the mistake of giving in to his passion—more than once. Mitchum perfectly embodies this figure. Like Humphrey Bogart, he possesses a calm interiority that expresses independence and confidence. As one character says of him, "He just sits and stays inside himself." But unlike the cautious Bogart, Mitchum literally slouches into his role as Jeff, his heavy relaxation making his vulnerability not only believable but tragic.

Is Kathy's passion for Jeff real? In spite of her inability to endure difficulties for his sake and her fatalistic attitude about love, does she really love him? For that matter, is Jeff's ardor for her sincere? Although he phones the police to convert their final getaway into an ambush, is he surrendering to her allure once again? This is the question that Jeff's small-town girlfriend Ann (Virginia Huston) asks The Kid (Dickie Moore), Jeff's deaf-mute companion, at the film's end. The Kid nods yes. Is he telling the truth? We feel that this gesture will free Ann from any future entanglement with Jeff's fatal world, but does that mean it's a lie? *Out of the Past*, like film noir in general, leaves us with the enigmas of fatal desires, the ambiguities of loves laced with fear. **TG**

i

Robert Mitchum was fourth choice for the lead role, after Humphrey Bogart, John Garfield, and Dick Powell.

Monsieur Verdoux Charles Chaplin, 1947

U.S. (Charles Chaplin, United Artists) 124m BW **Producer** Charles Chaplin **Screenplay** Charles Chaplin **Photography** Roland Totheroh **Music** Charles Chaplin **Cast** Charles Chaplin, Mady Correll, Allison Roddan, Robert Lewis, Audrey Betz, Martha Raye, Ada May, Isobel Elsom, Marjorie Bennett, Helene Heigh, Margaret Hoffman, Marilyn Nash, Irving Bacon, Edwin Mills, Virginia Brissac **Oscar nomination** Charles Chaplin (screenplay)

Charles Chaplin bought the idea for his blackest comedy (for $5,000) from Orson Welles, who had originally planned a dramatized documentary about the legendary French serial wife killer Henri Desiré Landru. Chaplin gave the story a new and acute sociosatirical edge, in response to the then-growing political paranoia of the Cold War years. Verdoux (Chaplin), the suave and charming little bourgeois, only adopts his lucrative profession of marrying and murdering rich widows when economic depression removes the possibility of his earning an honest living as a bank clerk. Finally brought to justice, his defense is that although private murder is condemned, public killing—in the form of war—is glorified: "One murder makes a villain—millions a hero. Numbers sanctify." These were not popular sentiments in 1946 America, and Chaplin found himself more and more the target of the political right—a witch hunt that led to his decision to give up his residency in the United States in 1953.

Verdoux, accompanied by his jaunty little theme tune (Chaplin as usual was his own composer), is a rich and vivid character. The tight economies of the postwar period obliged Chaplin to work more quickly and with much more planning than on any previous films. The result is one of his most tightly constructed narratives, which he unselfconsciously considered "the cleverest and most brilliant film of my career." **DR**

Odd Man Out Carol Reed, 1947

G.B. (Two Cities) 116m BW **Producer** Carol Reed, Phil C. Samuel **Screenplay** R.C. Sherriff, from novel by F.L. Green **Photography** Robert Krasker **Music** William Alwyn **Cast** James Mason, Robert Newton, Cyril Cusack, Peter Judge, William Hartnell, Fay Compton, Denis O'Dea, W.G. Fay, Maureen Delaney, Elwyn Brook-Jones, Robert Beatty, Dan O'Herlihy, Kitty Kirwan, Beryl Measor, Roy Irving **Oscar nomination** Fergus McDonnell (editing)

Carol Reed's chronicle of an Irish republican soldier plays like an expressionist fever dream. James Mason, as Johnny McQueen, plays the leader of an anti-British group that plans a robbery that will help to fund their cause. On the night of the crime, Johnny kills a man and is shot himself, and must run from the authorities who set up a dragnet across the city to catch him and his associates. The entire film takes place during the rest of this night as Johnny seeks refuge and his girlfriend Kathleen (Kathleen Ryan) tries to find him.

Johnny discovers that people he trusted or thought were sympathetic to his cause will not stick their necks out for him. He is forced to keep moving and is passed along from one person to the next; each has a reason not to help him or to use him for their own aims. As his wound worsens, Johnny becomes deliriously philosophical and begins to understand that he is fundamentally alone in the world. The film's score and shadowy black-and-white photography add to the overall sense of moral uncertainty. The way in which *Odd Man Out* bursts the seams of the political thriller genre and becomes a moving, thoughtful, and powerful meditation on social existence will continue to astonish moviegoers for all time. **RH**

1947

Ladri di biciclette Vittorio De Sica, 1948
The Bicycle Thief

Italy (De Sica) 93m BW **Language** Italian
Producer Giuseppe Amato, Vittorio De Sica
Screenplay Cesare Zavattini, Oreste Biancoli,
Suso d'Amico, Vittorio De Sica, Adolfo Franci,
Gerardo Guerrieri, from novel by Luigi
Bartolini **Photography** Carlo Montuori
Music Alessandro Cicognini **Cast** Lamberto
Maggiorani, Enzo Staiola, Lianella Carell,
Gino Saltamerenda, Vittorio Antonucci,
Giulio Chiari, Elena Altieri, Carlo Jachino,
Michele Sakara, Emma Druetti, Fausto
Guerzoni **Oscar** Giuseppe Amato, Vittorio
De Sica (honorary award—best foreign
language film) **Oscar nomination** Cesare
Zavattini (screenplay)

"You live and you suffer."

**Antonio Ricci
(Lamberto Maggiorani)**

Antonio Ricci (Lamberto Maggiorani), an unemployed worker in postwar Rome, finds a job putting up movie posters after his wife pawns the family's bedsheets to get his bicycle out of hock. But right after he starts work the bike is stolen, and with his little boy Bruno (Enzo Staiola) in tow he crisscrosses the city trying to recover it, encountering various aspects of Roman society, including some of the more acute class differences, in the process.

This masterpiece—the Italian title translates as "bicycle thieves"—is one of the key works of Italian Neorealism. French critic André Bazin also recognized it as one of the great communist films. The fact that it received the 1949 Oscar for Best Foreign Language Film suggests that it wasn't perceived that way in the United States at the time. Ironically, the only thing American censors cared about was a scene in which the little boy urinates on the street. For some followers of auteur theory the film lost some of its power because it didn't derive from a single creative intelligence. A collaboration between screenwriter Cesare Zavattini, director Vittorio De Sica, nonprofessional actors, and many others, the production is so charged with a common purpose that there is little point in even trying to separate achievements.

The Bicycle Thief contains what is possibly the greatest depiction of a relationship between a father and son in the history of cinema, full of subtle fluctuations and evolving gradations between the two characters in terms of respect and trust, and it's an awesome heartbreaker. It also has its moments of Chaplinesque comedy—the contrasting behavior of two little boys having lunch at the same restaurant. Set alongside a film like *Life Is Beautiful* (1997), it provides some notion of how much mainstream world cinema and its relation to reality has been infantilized over the past half century. **JRos**

ℹ
Future director Sergio Leone served as an (uncredited) assistant on the film and appears, briefly, as a priest.

Letter from an Unknown Woman Max Ophüls, 1948

U.S. (Rampart, Universal) 86m BW
Producer John Houseman
Screenplay Howard Koch, Stefan Zweig,
from the novel *Brief einer Unbekannten* by
Stefan Zweig **Photography** Franz Planer
Music Daniele Amfitheatrof **Cast** Joan
Fontaine, Louis Jourdan, Mady Christians,
Marcel Journet, Art Smith, Carol Yorke,
Howard Freeman, John Good, Leo B. Pessin,
Erskine Sanford, Otto Waldis, Sonja Bryden

> "Letter from an
> Unknown Woman
> provides a luxurious
> swathe of emotion . . . the
> action of the film, on the
> cusp of melodrama, is
> fashioned to perfection."
>
> Peter Bradshaw,
> *The Guardian*, 2010

ℹ

Universal had already filmed a
version of Zweig's story in 1933,
titled *Only Yesterday*.

Stefan Brand (Louis Jourdan), a concert pianist and gentleman dandy in turn-of-the-century Vienna, arrives home after yet another evening of dissipation. His mute servant hands him a letter. It is from a woman, and its first words well and truly halt him in his tracks: "By the time you read this, I will be dead. . . ."

What unfolds from this extraordinary opening has more than a fair claim to being not only the best film of director Max Ophüls, and a supreme achievement in the often unfairly maligned genre of melodrama, but also one of the greatest films in world cinema history. It is, in its own terms, one of the few movies that deserve to be rated as perfect, right down to the smallest detail.

Superbly adapted from Stefan Zweig's novella by Howard Koch, this is the apotheosis of "doomed love" fiction. Flashing back to trace the hopeless infatuation of young Lisa Berndl (Joan Fontaine) for Stefan, Ophüls gives us a vivid, heartbreaking portrait of a love that should never have been: Her naïve romanticization of artistic men mismatched with his indifferent objectification of available women adds up to gloomy tragedy. Ophüls's intuitive grasp of the inequity of gender roles in 20th-century Western society is breathtaking.

Ophüls constructs a most exquisitely poised work. While encouraging us to identify with Lisa's longing, and the dreams of a whole society fed by its popular culture, *Letter from an Unknown Woman* at the same time provides a trenchant and devastating critique of the myth and ideology of romantic love. Our understanding of the tale hinges on its delicate shifts in mood and viewpoint.

Relentlessly and hypnotically, Ophüls strips away the veils of illusion that envelop Lisa. Either the staging reveals the banal conditions of reality that underwrite these flights of fantasy, or the camera suggests—in subtle positionings and movements slightly detached from the story's world—a knowing perspective that eludes the characters.

The film is a triumph not just of meaningful, expressive style, but of purposive narrative structure. With poignant voice-over narration from Lisa, decades are bridged and key years artfully skipped thanks to a patterning of significant details arranged as motifs, concentrated in repeated gestures (such as the giving of a flower), lines of dialogue (references to passing time are ubiquitous), and key objects (the staircase leading to Stefan's apartment). By the time Ophüls reaches a Hollywood staple—the ghostlike apparition of young Lisa at last conjured in Stefan's memory—the cliché is gloriously transcended, and tears overcome even those modern viewers who resist such old-fashioned "soaps."

Letter from an Unknown Woman is an inexhaustibly rich film, one that has drawn myriad film lovers to try to unravel its themes, patterns, suggestions, and ironies. But no amount of close analysis can ever extinguish the rich, tearing emotion that this masterpiece elicits. **AM**

1948

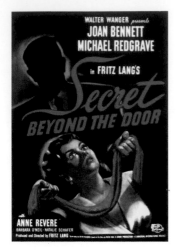

U.S. (Diana) 99m B/W **Producer** Fritz Lang, Walter Wanger **Screenplay** Rufus King, Silvia Richards **Photography** Stanley Cortez **Music** Miklós Rózsa **Cast** Joan Bennett, Michael Redgrave, Anne Revere, Barbara O'Neil, Natalie Schafer, Anabel Shaw, Rosa Rey, James Seay, Mark Dennis, Paul Cavanagh

"It's a pretty silly yarn … But Mr. Lang is still a director who knows how to turn the obvious, such as locked doors and silent chambers and roving spotlights, into strangely tingling stuff."

Bosley Crowther,
The New York Times, 1948

i

The surreal credit titles for *Secret Beyond the Door* were executed at the Disney Studio.

The Secret Beyond the Door Fritz Lang, 1948

Fritz Lang fans often divide on whether they prefer the certified, highbrow classics like *M* (1931), *Metropolis* (1926), and *The Big Heat* (1953), or the stranger, more cryptic and perverse films in his oeuvre that plumb less reputable areas of pop culture, such as *Rancho Notorious* (1952) and *Moonfleet* (1955). *Secret Beyond the Door* scrapes by in some accounts as a respectable film noir, but it is the beguiling mixture of many genres—women's melodrama, Freudian case study, serial killer mystery, and allegory of the artistic/creative process—that makes it such a special and haunting oddity in the director's career.

The film partakes of Hollywood's "Female Gothic" cycle, exploring the fraught attachment of a woman (here, Joan Bennett) to a man (Michael Redgrave) who is all at once enigmatic, seductive, and (as the plot unravels) potentially life threatening. As in Hitchcock's *Rebecca* (1940), which inspired Lang, the heroine enters a home of strangers, brimming with past, unspoken traumas, and sick, subterranean relationships.

Lang fixes the frankly sadomasochistic ambiguities of this plot (What is the true nature of the male beast, sensitivity or aggression? What does the woman really want from him, anyway, love or death?) into a startlingly novel context: Redgrave is a tormented-genius architect who has built a house of "felicitous rooms," each the reconstructed scene of a grisly, patently psychosexual murder.

Secret Beyond the Door joins a special group of 1940s films, including Jean Renoir's *The Woman on the Beach* (1947) and the Val Lewton production *The Seventh Victim* (1943), whose potent, dreamlike aura is virtually guaranteed by their B-movie sparseness and free-association plotting—as well as, here, a voiceover narration that disorientatingly shifts from Bennett to Redgrave and back again. Heretical it may be for a card-carrying auteurist to suggest, but the cuts imposed by Universal on Lang's initial edit probably enhanced this dreamlike quality. The end result may be short on rational links and explanations, but *s* is one of the precious occasions when Lang—aided immeasurably by Stanley Cortez's baroque cinematography and Miklós Rózsa's lush score—managed to add a richly poetic dimension to his familiar fatalism. **AM**

Force of Evil Abraham Polonsky, 1948

U.S. (Enterprise, MGM) 78m BW
Producer Bob Roberts
Screenplay Abraham Polonsky, Ira Wolfert,
from the novel *Tucker's People* by Ira Wolfert
Photography George Barnes **Music** David
Raksin **Cast** John Garfield, Thomas Gomez,
Marie Windsor, Howland Chamberlain,
Roy Roberts, Paul Fix, Stanley Prager, Barry
Kelley, Paul McVey, Beatrice Pearson,
Fred O. Sommers

Like *The Night of the Hunter* (1955), *Force of Evil* is a unique event in the history of American cinema. Its director, Abraham Polonsky, made two subsequent movies much later and scripted others, but this is the sole film in which the full extent of his promising brilliance shined, before being snuffed out by the McCarthy-era blacklist.

Force of Evil sits uncomfortably within the film noir genre, despite the presence of a star (John Garfield) associated with hard-boiled, streetwise movies. It is above all a film of poetry, carried by a "blank verse" voiceover and a highly stylized singsong dialogue, which are among the most astounding and radical innovations of 1940s cinema, anticipating Malick's *Badlands* (1973).

This is a story of amorality, guilt, and redemption, dramatized through the near-Biblical device of betrayal between brothers. Polonsky breaks up the fatalistic gloom of the piece (its final image of a descent to a corpse among garbage is chilling) with a touching and very modern love story between Garfield and Beatrice Pearson.

The film is stylized down to the smallest detail in line with its poetic ambition: to liberate sound, image, and performance and have all three interact in an intoxicating polyphony. **AM**

Xiao cheng zhi chun Fei Mu, 1948
Spring in a Small Town

China 85m BW **Language** Mandarin
Screenplay Li Tianji **Photography** Li
Shengwei **Music** Huang Yijun **Cast** Cui
Chaoming, Li Wei, Shi Yu, Wei Wei,
Zhang Hongmei

If one mark of a great film is its ability to introduce characters in an economical way, Fei Mu's *Spring in a Small Town* projects its greatness instantly. Deftly and poignantly, the film unveils to us five figures: "The Wife" (Wei Wei), lonely and weary of daily chores; "The Husband" (Shi Yu), a sickly melancholic; "The Sister" (Zhang Hongmei), youthfully vivacious; Lao Huang, "The Servant" (Cui Chaoming), ever watchful; and "The Visitor" (Li Wei), strolling into this town (and out of the past) to become the catalyst for change.

Sparingly, the film builds its postwar drama: the desires, hopes, dreams, and hurts that play among these characters caught in the arrangement of bodies in the frame, a choreography of furtive looks, and sudden gestures of resistance or resignation. But there is also a modernist element: The wife's voiceover narration, which poetically reiterates what is plainly visible, covers events she has not witnessed, and puts sad realities into brutal words.

This masterpiece of Chinese cinema has only recently received the worldwide recognition it deserves, influencing Wong Kar-Wai's *In the Mood for Love* (2001) and occasioning a respectful remake (2002). *Spring in a Small Town* stands among cinema's finest, richest, and most moving melodramas. **AM**

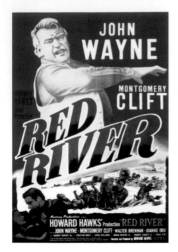

Red River Howard Hawks & Arthur Rosson, 1948

A Western remake of *Mutiny on the Bounty* (1935), this is a considerably deeper film than its source, presenting the Bligh–Christian relationship in terms of a father–son conflict. Star John Wayne—one of the most beautiful male leads of the 1930s, playing older than his real age with authentic and prescient crustiness—is interestingly matched by Hawks against the photogenic Montgomery Clift, epitome of a kind of sensitive, manly neurosis that would come in fashion in the next decade.

After a long prologue set during the aftermath of an 1851 Indian attack, in which we see how bereft Tom Dunson (Wayne) and orphaned Matthew Garth (Clift) combine their herds to form a cattle empire, we pick up the Red River D in a post–Civil War economic depression. Leading a cattle drive up into Missouri, the inflexible Dunson becomes more and more tyrannical, prompting Matt to rebel and steer the herd West by a safer route to Abilene. Dunson admires the kid's guts, but nevertheless swears to track him down and shoot him dead, leading to one of the most emotional climaxes in the genre as the men who love each other face off among milling cattle in the Abilene streets.

Hawks, the great film chronicler of macho pursuits, here stages the definitive cow opera, putting all other cattle-drive Westerns in the shade with beautiful, lyrical, exciting sequences of stampeding, rough weather, cowboying, and Indian skirmishes. The leads are at their best, with Wayne astonishingly matching Clift for subtlety, and you get sterling support from Walter Brennan as the toothless coot, John Ireland as a lanky gunslinger, and Joanne Dru as a pioneer gal who can take an arrow in the shoulder without hardly flinching. Though known for his Westerns, Hawks made surprisingly few films in the genre. This seems like an affectionate tribute to John Ford, mixed in with a certain I-can-do-that-too attitude, as Hawks casts several members of his peer's stock company: Harry Carey Senior and Junior, Hank Worden, even Wayne himself. Hawks uses a Fordian approach to the dangerous splendors of the Western landscape along with a Ford-like folk song–based score from Dimitri Tiomkin. **KN**

1948

U.S. (Charles K. Feldman, Monterey) 133m BW **Producer** Charles K. Feldman, Howard Hawks **Screenplay** Borden Chase, Charles Schnee **Photography** Russell Harlan **Music** Dimitri Tiomkin **Cast** John Wayne, Montgomery Clift, Joanne Dru, Walter Brennan, Coleen Gray, Harry Carey, John Ireland, Noah Beery Jr., Harry Carey Jr., Chief Yowlachie, Paul Fix, Hank Worden, Mickey Kuhn, Ray Hyke, Wally Wales **Oscar nominations** Borden Chase (screenplay), Christian Nyby (editing)

> *"I didn't think the big son-of-a-bitch could act!"*

Howard Hawks, quoting John Ford's reaction to John Wayne's performance in *Red River*, 1976

ℹ️

Footage from *Red River* was used in Wayne's last film, *The Shootist* (1976), to depict his character's backstory.

The Paleface Norman Z. McLeod, 1948

U.S. (Paramount) 91m Technicolor
Producer Robert L. Welch
Screenplay Edmund L. Hartmann, Frank
Tashlin Photography Ray Rennahan
Music Ray Evans, Jay Livingston, Victor
Young Cast Bob Hope, Jane Russell, Robert
Armstrong, Iris Adrian, Bobby Watson, Jackie
Searl, Joseph Vitale, Charles Trowbridge,
Clem Bevans, Jeff York, Stanley Andrews,
Wade Crosby, Chief Yowlachie, Iron Eyes
Cody, John Maxwell Oscar Jay Livingston,
Ray Evans (song)

Jane Russell plays Calamity Jane, recruited by the U.S. government to help track down a gang of renegade whites who are selling guns to the Indians. In order to pose as an emigrant on a wagon train going West, she marries Painless Peter Potter, an incompetent and cowardly dentist she encounters in a bathhouse—one doesn't look for plausibility in such material! As Painless, Bob Hope has a wonderful time, letting forth a fusillade of jokes. Much of the humor in *The Paleface* is along predictable lines, with Indians inhaling the dentist's laughing gas and Hope performing all manner of unheroics, leading to his being mistaken for a courageous Indian fighter. Hope is of course madly attracted to Russell— "You've got just the kind of mouth I like to work on." There's a running joke about the endlessly postponed consummation of the marriage as Russell gets on with the job of defeating the bad guys.

Painless and Calamity are captured and taken to an Indian camp, where Indians are played both by Chief Yowlachie (a genuine Native American) and by Iron Eyes Cody (an Italian-American who passed as a Native American). The comedy at their expense, though hardly politically correct, is too silly to give serious offense.

Hope gives a pleasing rendition of the song "Buttons and Bows," written by Victor Young, which won an Oscar. It's a plea for girls to go back East and wear pretty clothes, but Russell looks equally fetching in satin dresses and buckskin pants. **EB**

ℹ

The movie's sequel, *Son of Paleface* (1952), was directed by the writer of *The Paleface*, Frank Tashlin.

The Snake Pit   Anatole Litvak, 1948

U.S. (Fox) 108m BW Producer Robert
Bassler, Anatole Litvak, Darryl F. Zanuck
Screenplay Millen Brand, Frank Partos, from
novel by Mary Jane Ward Photography Leo
Tover Music Alfred Newman Cast Olivia de
Havilland, Mark Stevens, Leo Genn, Celeste
Holm, Glenn Langan, Helen Craig, Leif
Erickson, Beulah Bondi, Lee Patrick, Howard
Freeman, Natalie Schafer, Ruth Donnelly,
Katherine Locke, Frank Conroy, Minna
Gombell Oscar nominations Robert Bassler,
Anatole Litvak (best picture), Anatole Litvak
(director), Frank Partos, Millen Brand
(screenplay), Olivia de Havilland (actress),
Alfred Newman (music)

Among the more impressive products of Hollywood's postwar turn toward greater realism is Anatole Litvak's brutally honest treatment of mental illness and its cure in the modern sanitarium, whose horrors include the overcrowded ward where the incurables are warehoused—the "snake pit" of the film's title. The Snake Pit offers a more balanced view of mental disturbance than many more recent films, including the often praised One Flew over the Cuckoo's Nest (1976).

Virginia Cunningham (Olivia de Havilland) seems at first a hopeless psychotic, but with treatment from a sympathetic doctor, Mark Kik (Leo Genn), she is able to undergo a "talking cure." Flashbacks show a childhood in which she is denied not only her mother's love but also attention from her father, who died when Virginia was very young. Virginia also suffers the death of the man she loves, for which she believes she is responsible. Under Dr. Kik's care, she graduates to the "best" ward, only to be bullied there by a tyrannical nurse. Virginia's subsequent misbehavior lands her in the "snake pit," but this horrifying experience proves strangely therapeutic. Finally she wins release, at last understanding how her feelings of guilt are irrational.

Memorable is how the film shows the terror that Virginia's illness makes her suffer. The Snake Pit's optimistic realism contrasts with the pseudo-Freudian solutions of other movies of the period, including Hitchcock's Spellbound (1945). **RBP**

The Lady from Shanghai   Orson Welles, 1948

U.S. (Columbia, Mercury) 87m BW
Language English / Cantonese
Producer William Castle, Orson Welles,
Richard Wilson Screenplay Orson Welles,
from the novel If I Die Before I Wake by
Sherwood King Photography Charles
Lawton Jr. Music Doris Fisher, Allan Roberts,
Heinz Roemheld Cast Rita Hayworth, Orson
Welles, Everett Sloane, Glenn Anders, Ted
de Corsia, Erskine Sanford, Gus Schilling,
Carl Frank, Louis Merrill, Evelyn Ellis,
Harry Shannon

Having proved with The Stranger (1946) that he could make a "regular" film if he wanted to, Orson Welles here returns to the film noir genre, picking up almost at random a pulp novel (Sherwood King's If I Die Before I Wake) and delivering something so rich and strange it was guaranteed to irk Columbia head Harry Cohn. Simply by shearing Rita Hayworth's trademarked long hair and dying her crop blonde, Welles deliberately devalued a studio asset who happened to be his ex-wife, and that was even before it emerged that she was playing not the sympathetic bombshell of Gilda (1946) but a villainess so nasty that even her undoubted sex appeal becomes repulsive.

With a variable Irish accent, Welles is a seaman hired by a crippled lawyer (Everett Sloane, lizardy and scary) to crew his yacht and perhaps also (as in the anecdote preserved by Welles as The Immortal Story [1968]) to service his beautiful wife. A murder takes place, followed by a trial in which everyone acts unethically at best, and the crazy kaleidoscope is shattered by a finale involving a shoot-out in a hall of mirrors. The Lady from Shanghai is a broken mirror of a film, with shards of genius that can never be put together into anything that makes sense. **KN**

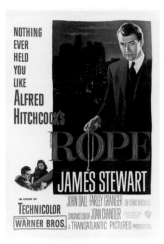

U.S. (Transatlantic, Warner Bros.) 80m
Technicolor **Producer** Sidney Bernstein
Screenplay Hume Cronyn, Arthur Laurents,
from the play *Rope's End* by Patrick Hamilton
Photography William V. Skall, Joseph A.
Valentine **Music** David Buttolph **Cast** James
Stewart, John Dall, Farley Granger, Cedric
Hardwicke, Constance Collier, Douglas Dick,
Edith Evanson, Dick Hogan, Joan Chandler

*"I got this crazy idea,
maybe I could do
[the whole film] in one
shot . . . when I look
back, of course, it's
quite nonsensical."*

Alfred Hitchcock, 1962

Rope Alfred Hitchcock, 1948

Though he owed his fame to showmanship and thrills, Alfred Hitchcock was always among the most experimental of commercial filmmakers. With a strong source in a play by Patrick Hamilton (of *Gaslight* [1944] fame) based on the Leopold and Loeb case, more conventionally dramatized in the 1959 film *Compulsion*, *Rope* calls attention to its theatrical one-set backdrop by consisting of reel-long takes spliced together almost invisibly so that the film appears to unspool unedited. Given that, in 1948, many film audiences had barely registered that movies consisted of brief snippets cut together for dramatic effect—most films about filmmaking even now seem to suggest that scenes are shot as if they were happening in live theater—it may well be that Hitchcock was most interested in addressing his fellow professionals, demonstrating an alternate manner of telling a film story in much the way that the later Dogme95 movement or *The Blair Witch Project* (1999) set out to do.

Apart from the technical challenges of having the camera follow characters around a large New York apartment, telling a story in "real time," *Rope* has quite a bit of intrinsic interest as two cohabiting bachelors (John Dall and Farley Granger) try to get away with a casual murder to prove an obscure point. At once an intense psychological drama and a black comedy in the vein of *Arsenic and Old Lace* (1944), the film delivers cat-and-mouse conflict as the killers invite professorial Jimmy Stewart around to impress him with their cleverness, flirting in more than one way with revelation.

The technique is less of a distraction than it might be, allowing Stewart and Dall to face off in a great battle of murderous camp and moral rectitude; it may be that all the attention paid to the long takes made the censors overlook the unusually frank depiction of a quasi-gay relationship between the murderers—it's never addressed in the dialogue but there is only one bedroom in the apartment they share. Granger's shakiness isn't helped by the merciless length of the takes, but Dall and Stewart rise to the occasion, challenged to deliver sustained, theater-style performances in the more intimate medium of film. **KN**

i

The film was shot in ten takes,
ranging from four-and-a-half to
just over ten minutes long.

The Red Shoes Michael Powell & Emeric Pressburger, 1948

The 1948 Michael Powell–Emeric Pressburger production has been beloved by generations of girls who want to grow up to be ballerinas, though its message to them is decidedly double-edged. In a dazzling twist on the old showbiz star-is-born story, winsome, willful, talented debutante-cum-dancer Victoria Page (Moira Shearer) falls under the spell of Svengali-cum-Rasputin-cum-Diaghilev impresario Boris Lermontov (Anton Walbrook). She neglects her private life (a romance with composer Marius Goring) in favor of a passionate and almost unhealthy devotion to Art, with a beautifully choreographed tragic ending in the offing. After the departure of prima ballerina Boronskaja (Ludmilla Tchérina), whom Lermontov drops when she wants to get married, Vicky makes her starring debut in an especially created ballet version of the Hans Christian Andersen story of the girl whose shoes keep her dancing until she drops dead. This spurs the filmmakers—augmented by choreographer-dancer Robert Helpmann, costar Léonide Massine, and conductor Sir Thomas Beecham—to a twenty-minute fantasy dance sequence that set a trend for such stylized high-culture interludes in musicals, but manages far better than any of the imitators to retell in miniature the larger story of the film while still being credible as a performance piece in its own right.

Of course, Vicky's offstage life sadly follows that of Andersen's heroine, climaxing in a balletic leap in front of a train and the unforgettable tribute performance in which her devastated costars dance the Red Shoes ballet again with only the shoes to stand in for the star. Shearer, tiny and astonishing in her screen debut, is a powerful presence who can stand up to the full force of Walbrook's overwhelming performance, convincing both as the ingenue dancing in a cramped hall with a third-rate company and as the great star adored by the whole world. The heroine is surrounded with weird fairy-tale backdrops for the daringly lush ballet, but production designer Hein Heckroth, art director Arthur Lawson, and cinematographer Jack Cardiff work as hard to make the supposedly normal offstage scenes as rich and strange as the theatrical highlights.

Walbrook coos and hisses Mephistophelean lines with a self-delight that's impossible not to share, manipulating all about him with ease but still tragically alone in his monk-like devotion to the ballet. The Red Shoes is a rare musical to capture the magic of theatrical performance without neglecting the agonizing effort necessary to create such transports of delight. Its gossipy insider feel went a great way toward making ballet accessible outside its supposed high-class audience, contrasting the eager expectation of the musical students crowded into the highest (cheapest) seats with the offhand take-it-for-granted patronage of the well-dressed swine in the stalls before whom the artistic pearls are cast. Wrapped up with gorgeous sparkly color, off-the-beaten-track classical music selections, and a sinister edge that perfectly catches the ambiguity of traditional as opposed to Disney fairy tales, this is a masterpiece. **KN**

G.B. (Independent, Rank, The Archers) 133m Technicolor **Producer** George R. Busby, Michael Powell, Emeric Pressburger **Screenplay** Emeric Pressburger, Michael Powell, Keith Winter, from story by Hans Christian Andersen **Photography** Jack Cardiff **Music** Brian Easdale **Cast** Anton Walbrook, Marius Goring, Moira Shearer, Robert Helpmann, Léonide Massine, Albert Bassermann, Ludmilla Tchérina, Esmond Knight **Oscars** Hein Heckroth, Arthur Lawson (art direction), Brian Easdale (music) **Oscar nominations** Michael Powell, Emeric Pressburger (best picture), Emeric Pressburger (screenplay), Reginald Mills (editing)

"The film is voluptuous in its beauty and passionate in its storytelling. You don't watch it, you bathe in it."

Roger Ebert, critic, 2005

i

It took Powell and Pressburger a year to convince Moira Shearer to agree to star in the movie.

1948

U.S. (Warner Bros.) 126m BW
Producer Henry Blanke, Jack L. Warner
Screenplay John Huston, B. Traven, from
novel by B. Traven **Photography** Ted D.
McCord **Music** Ruddy Kaye, Max Steiner
Cast Humphrey Bogart, Walter Huston,
Tim Holt, Bruce Bennett, Barton MacLane,
Alfonso Bedoya, Arturo Soto Rangel,
Manuel Dondé, José Torvay, Margarito Luna
Oscars John Huston (director) (screenplay),
Walter Huston (actor in support role)
Oscar nominations Henry Blanke
(best picture)

"Treasure of Sierra
Madre *is one of the*
best things Hollywood
has done since it
learned to talk."

Time Magazine, 1948

The Treasure of the Sierra Madre John Huston, 1948

The failed quest, fueled by ambition and frustrated by greed and internal dissension, was John Huston's favorite plot, appealing to the mixture of romantic and cynic that made up his character. From *The Maltese Falcon* (1941) to *The Man Who Would Be King* (1975), he played repeated variations on this theme—but *The Treasure of the Sierra Madre* presents it in something close to its archetypal form. Three ill-assorted American drifters in Mexico join forces to prospect for gold, find it, and—inevitably—in the end, snatch defeat from the jaws of victory and lose it again. Huston, always a great adaptor of literature for the screen, drew his story from a novel by the mysterious and reclusive writer B. Traven and, as ever, treated his source material with respect and affection, preserving much of Traven's laconic dialogue and sardonic outlook.

Despite the studio's opposition—because location filming, at least for A-list Hollywood productions, was rare in those days—Huston insisted on shooting almost entirely on location in Mexico, near an isolated village some 140 miles north of the capital. His intransigence paid off. The film's texture exudes the dusty aridity of the Mexican landscape, so that watching it you can almost taste the grit between your teeth; and the actors, exiled from the comfortable environment of the studio and having to contend with the elements, were pushed into giving taut, edgy performances. This fitted *Treasure*'s theme: how people react under pressure. Whereas the old prospector (played by the director's father Walter Huston) and the naive youngster (cowboy-movie actor Tim Holt) hang on to their principles in the face of adversity and the temptation of gold, the paranoid Fred C. Dobbs (Humphrey Bogart in one of his most memorably unsettling roles) cracks up and succumbs.

Huston's determination to shoot *Treasure* the way he wanted paid off for the studio too. Jack Warner initially detested the film, but it brought Warner Brothers not only a box-office smash hit but triumphs at the Academy Awards. Huston won Oscars for Best Director and Best Screenplay, while his father picked up the Best Supporting Actor Oscar. It was the first and—so far—only time a father-and-son team had won at the Awards. **PK**

i

The reclusive Traven sent his friend Hal
Croves to be an advisor on set; many
believed that Croves was in fact Traven.

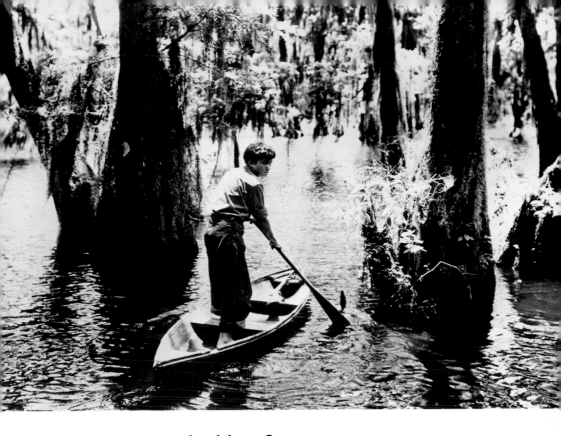

Louisiana Story Robert J. Flaherty, 1948

U.S. (Robert Flaherty) 78m BW
Language English / French
Producer Robert J. Flaherty
Screenplay Frances H. Flaherty, Robert J.
Flaherty Photography Richard Leacock
Music Virgil Thomson Cast Joseph
Boudreaux, Lionel Le Blanc, E.
Bienvenu, Frank Hardy, C.P. Guedry
Oscar nomination Frances H. Flaherty,
Robert J. Flaherty (screenplay)

🛈

The film was re-released in 1952 as
Cajun, and was shown as a second
feature with Armand Denis's *Watusi*.

For his last film, *Louisiana Story*, the great documentarian Robert J. Flaherty accepted sponsorship from Standard Oil to make a movie about oil prospecting in the Louisiana bayous. The funding came without strings, but even so Flaherty maybe soft-pedaled his depiction of the oil company a little, showing it as a benign force causing no damage to the unspoiled wilderness. But a hint of naïveté isn't entirely out of place; events in the bayou, and the arrival of the oilmen, are shown us through the eyes of a twelve-year-old boy (Joseph Boudreaux). The haunted, waterlogged landscape becomes a magical place, full of dark foliage and exotic wildlife, where an oil derrick gliding majestically up a waterway seems as mythical and unfathomable as the werewolves and mermaids the boy believes in.

Dialogue is minimal—partly because the director, as usual, was working with local people, not professional actors—and Flaherty relies mainly on his charged, lyrical images and Virgil Thomson's score to carry the narrative. Thomson's music, drawing ingeniously on original Cajun themes, was awarded a Pulitzer Prize—the first film score to win this honor. In *Louisiana Story*, as in all his finest work, Flaherty celebrates the beauty, danger, and fascination of the wild places of the earth. **PK**

U.S. (King, Pioneer) 86m BW
Producer Frank King, Maurice King
Screenplay MacKinlay Kantor, Millard
Kaufman **Photography** Russell Harlan
Music Victor Young **Cast** Peggy Cummins,
John Dall, Berry Kroeger, Morris Carnovsky,
Anabel Shaw, Harry Lewis, Nedrick Young,
Russ Tamblyn, Ross Elliott

*"We go together,
Annie. I don't know
why. Maybe like guns
and ammunition
go together."*

Bart Tare (John Dall)

🛈

The distributors changed the title to
Deadly Is the Female in 1950, but it
was changed back a few months later.

Gun Crazy Joseph H. Lewis, 1949

Joseph H. Lewis's cult gem *Gun Crazy* (a.k.a. *Deadly Is the Female*) is something of a test case in contemporary debates on the meaning of the critically disputed term film noir. Based loosely on the story of infamous 1930s bandits Bonnie Parker and Clyde Barrow (the screenplay was developed by MacKinlay Kantor and blacklisted writer Dalton Trumbo, the latter here credited as Millard Kaufman to conceal the fact that he was one of the Hollywood Ten), this tale of rural love-on-the-run appears to have little in common with the hard-boiled nocturnal urban underworld that more often defines the noir tradition. But set alongside the similar story of star-crossed lovers in *They Live by Night* (1948), as well as films that featured down-on-their-luck honest laborers—*Desperate* (1947), *Thieves' Highway* (1949), and *The Sound of Fury* (1951)—*Gun Crazy* shares the noir theme of the rootless, marginal man (prevalent during the Depression and a continuing source of anxiety in the years following World War II), which also characterizes canonical noirs such as *The Postman Always Rings Twice* (1946) and *Detour* (1945), both fatalistic tales of drifters.

From an early age, Bart Tare (John Dall) has been obsessed with firearms. After leaving the army, he meets and instantly falls in love with the stunningly beautiful Annie Laurie Starr (Peggy Cummins), who shares his gun fetishism, having been the sharp-shooting main attraction in a traveling tent show. They set out on a series of robberies that, before their death at the law's hands, culminates in the holdup of the pay department in a meatpacking plant.

At the formal level, claims for *Gun Crazy*'s exceptional status among the plethora of B-movies are more than justified in virtue of the film's aesthetic innovations within low-budget restraints—the long single-shot scene of a bank robbery, the chase through the abattoir—and in Cummins's peerless characterization of a psychotic femme fatale. This timeless tale of *amour fou* was a major influence on Jean-Luc Godard's French New Wave classic *Breathless* (1960). **PS**

The Reckless Moment Max Ophüls, 1949

U.S. (Columbia) 82m BW
Producer Walter Wanger Screenplay Mel
Dinelli, Henry Garson Photography Burnett
Guffey Music Hans J. Salter Cast James
Mason, Joan Bennett, Geraldine Brooks,
Henry O'Neill, Shepperd Strudwick,
David Blair, Roy Roberts

The Reckless Moment is an unusual film noir in that it reverses the sexes in a replay of the familiar story (as in *Double Indemnity* [1944] and *Scarlet Street* [1945]) of an innocent who gets involved with a seductive no-good and is embroiled in crime. Here, class and respectability assume the status usually accorded to sex and money as housewife Lucia Harper (Joan Bennett) loses her grip on suburbia when the sleazy specimen (Shepperd Strudwick) who has been seeing her daughter (Geraldine Brooks) is semiaccidentally killed under suspicious circumstances, and she moves his corpse to make things look better.

Lucia's nemesis is played by James Mason, oddly but effectively cast as an Irish lowlife, who starts out blackmailing her but begins, disturbingly, to make sincere romantic overtures. The focus of the film then changes as the criminal is driven to make a sacrifice that will restore the heroine's life but also suggests that Bennett—who, after all, was the tramp in *Scarlet Street*—may have unwittingly been manipulating him to her advantage all along. Viennese director Max Ophüls is more interested in irony and emotion than crime and drama, which gives this a uniquely nerve-fraying feel, and he nudges the lead actors into revelatory, unusual performances. **KN**

1949

White Heat Raoul Walsh, 1949

U.S. (Warner Bros.) 114m BW
Producer Louis F. Edelman
Screenplay Virginia Kellogg, Ivan Goff, Ben
Roberts Photography Sidney Hickox
Music Max Steiner Cast James Cagney,
Virginia Mayo, Edmond O'Brien,
Margaret Wycherly, Steve Cochran,
John Archer, Wally Cassell, Fred Clark
Oscar nomination Virginia Kellogg
(screenplay)

"Do you know what to do?" barks Cody (James Cagney) at his sidekick at the start of a daring train robbery. When the guy starts replying, Cody cuts him off: "Just do it, stop gabbing!" This headlong, action-only attitude sums up the drive of Raoul Walsh's films, which (as Peter Lloyd once remarked) "take the pulse of an individual energy" and embed it within a "demented trajectory out of which is born the construction of a rhythm." Few films are as taut, sustained, and economical in their telling as *White Heat*.

Walsh is a relentlessly linear, forward-moving director whose work harkens back to silent cinema—as in that exciting car-meets-train opener. But he also explores the intriguing, complicating possibilities of twentieth-century psychology. On the job, Cody kills ruthlessly. Once holed up like a caged animal with his gang—as he will later be imprisoned—his psychopathology begins to emerge: indifference to others' suffering, fixation on a tough mom, and searing migraines that send him berserk.

Cody, as immortalized in Cagney's blistering, powerhouse performance, embodies the ultimate contradiction that often brings down movie gangsters: fantastic egotism and dreams of invincibility ("Look, Ma, top of the world!") undermined by all-too-human dependencies and vulnerabilities. **AM**

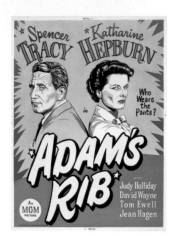

Adam's Rib George Cukor, 1949

This choice battle-of-the-sexes comedy has been an inspiration for countless other films and television series about combative but sexually combustible couples. Of the nine movies legendary partners Spencer Tracy and Katharine Hepburn made together between 1942 and 1967, *Adam's Rib* is arguably the best, still crackling with witty dialogue, spirited discussion of double standards and sexual stereotypes, and wonderful performances. The screenplay was written by Tracy and Hepburn's great pals, the married team of Ruth Gordon (the actress who won an Oscar in *Rosemary's Baby*) and Garson Kanin. The true story that sparked the project was that of husband-and-wife lawyers William and Dorothy Whitney, who represented Mr. and Mrs. Raymond Massey in their divorce, then divorced each other and married their respective clients.

It doesn't quite come to that in *Adam's Rib*. When sweet, ditsy blonde Doris Attinger—played by sensationally funny Judy Holliday making her debut in the role that launched her meteoric career—is charged with the attempted murder of her two-timing husband Warren (Tom Ewell), proto-feminist attorney Amanda "Pinkie" Bonner (Hepburn) agrees to defend her. But Amanda's husband, Adam "Pinky" Bonner (Tracy), is the prosecuting attorney, and their courtroom battle quickly extends into the bedroom, hostilities aggravated by the attentions shown Amanda by smitten songwriter Kip (David Wayne), who composes "Farewell, Amanda" in her honor (a song written by Cole Porter).

Director George Cukor, recognizing the inherent theatricality of courtroom situations, deliberately keeps the proceedings stagy after the comedy-suspense opening sequence of Doris tailing Warren from work to the tryst with his floozy mistress, Beryl (Jean Hagen), and the inept shooting. The film's long single takes give Hepburn free rein for her outrageously crafty showboating in court and allow Tracy to work up his indignation at her tactics and principles. Highlights include brainy Amanda's early questioning of dimwitted Doris, and the spectacle of Adam tearfully getting in touch with his feminine side to get back into his wife's good graces. Although some of the arguments may seem quaint today, the sophistication is undiminished. **AE**

U.S. (MGM) 101m BW **Producer** Lawrence Weingarten **Screenplay** Ruth Gordon, Garson Kanin **Photography** George J. Folsey **Music** Cole Porter, Miklós Rózsa **Cast** Spencer Tracy, Katharine Hepburn, Judy Holliday, Tom Ewell, Francis Attinger, David Wayne, Jean Hagen, Hope Emerson, Eve March, Clarence Kolb, Emerson Treacy, Polly Moran, Will Wright, Elizabeth Flournoy **Oscar nomination** Ruth Gordon, Garson Kanin (screenplay)

"A boy sows a wild oat or two, the whole world winks. A girl does the same—scandal."

Amanda Bonner (Katharine Hepburn)

ℹ

Adam's Rib was adapted as a short-lived television sitcom in 1973, with Ken Howard and Blythe Danner.

The Heiress William Wyler, 1949

U.S. (Paramount) 115m BW
Producer Lester Koenig, Robert Wyler,
William Wyler **Screenplay** Augustus Goetz,
Ruth Goetz, from the novel *Washington
Square* by Henry James **Photography** Leo
Tover **Music** Aaron Copland **Cast** Olivia de
Havilland, Montgomery Clift, Ralph
Richardson, Miriam Hopkins, Vanessa Brown,
Betty Linley, Ray Collins, Mona Freeman,
Selena Royle, Paul Lees, Harry Antrim,
Russ Conway, David Thursby **Oscars** Olivia
de Havilland (actress), John Meehan, Harry
Horner, Emile Kuri (art direction), Edith Head,
Gile Steele (costume), Aaron Copland
(music) **Oscar nominations** William Wyler
(best picture), William Wyler (director),
Ralph Richardson (actor in support role),
Leo Tover (photography)

i

Montgomery Clift was so unhappy
with his performance in *The Heiress*
that he walked out of the premiere.

"How can you be so cruel?" asks her aunt. "I have been taught by masters," comes the icy reply. William Wyler's unforgettable adaptation of Henry James's novel *Washington Square* (pointlessly remade in 1997) revolves around indelible performances, intensified by the director's trademark demanding long takes and meticulous mastery of mood, lighting, and camera technique. Olivia de Havilland, who received her second Academy Award for her performance, is heart-stopping as the dreadfully plain, painfully gauche girl marked as a spinster despite the fortune she will inherit from the cold, caustic father (Ralph Richardson), who regards her as an embarrassment.

Then beautiful, fortune-hunting wastrel Morris Townsend (Montgomery Clift) courts her, as insincere as he is irresistible. Over the insulting objections of her father and with the connivance of her foolishly romantic aunt (Miriam Hopkins), Catherine plots an elopement; when her lover decides to take his chances elsewhere, she undergoes a steely transformation. After the naive Catherine realizes that she has been jilted, de Havilland's slow, exhausted ascent up the stairs is forever haunting. Her final ascent upstairs, in bitter triumph as her returned suitor pounds desperately at the door, is no less affecting. The class of the entire production is underlined by Aaron Copland's evocative original score, also an Oscar winner. **AE**

The Third Man Carol Reed, 1949

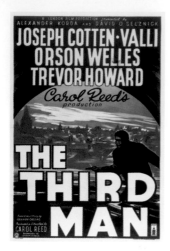

G.B. (British Lion, London) 104m BW
Language English / German
Producer Hugh Perceval, Carol Reed
Screenplay Graham Greene, Alexander
Korda **Photography** Robert Krasker
Music Henry Love, Anton Karas
Cast Joseph Cotten, Alida Valli, Orson Welles,
Trevor Howard, Paul Hörbiger, Ernst Deutsch,
Erich Ponto, Siegfried Breuer, Hedwig
Bleibtreu, Bernard Lee, Wilfrid Hyde-White
Oscar Robert Krasker (photography)
Oscar nominations Carol Reed (director),
Oswald Hafenrichter (editing)

*"I remember William
Wyler, after seeing the
film, made me the gift
of a spirit level. 'Carol,'
he said, 'next time you
make a picture, just put
it on top of the camera,
will you!'"*

Carol Reed, 1972

ℹ

For the movie's U.S. release, Carol
Reed's opening voice-over was
replaced with one by Joseph Cotten.

Written for the screen by Graham Greene, Carol Reed's *The Third Man* effectively transfers the urban nightmare world of Hollywood film noir of the 1940s to a European setting. Picking up the messy aftermath of the war and providing a five-years-on follow-up to the works of British thriller writers and European exile filmmakers, it shows the postwar consequences of movements expressed in early Hitchcock films (*The Lady Vanishes* [1938] and *Secret Agent* [1936]), midperiod Fritz Lang (the Greene-derived *Ministry of Fear* [1944]), the Geoffrey Household–inspired *Man Hunt* (1941), and Eric Ambler adaptations like *Journey into Fear* (1942) and *The Mask of Dimitrios* (1944). Occupied Vienna, divided between four military powers and plagued by black-marketing scoundrels, is as fantastical a setting as any devised for studio exoticism, but Reed and his crew were able to shoot on location, amid rubble and glitz, capturing a world of fear that was all too real.

Into this realm of corruption comes American innocent Holly Martins (Joseph Cotten). A writer of pulp Westerns, he was somehow asked to deliver a serious literary lecture to a cultural group. Only the military police sergeant (Bernard Lee) at the back of the hall has ever read any of his work. Holly is shocked to learn that his boyhood friend Harry Lime (Orson Welles) has recently met a mysterious death and is suspected of involvement in a dastardly racket. Holly gets mixed up with one of Harry's girlfriends (Alida Valli) and a succession of sinister eccentrics, in search of the "third man" who was seen carrying Lime's body away. Harry, as everyone except Holly knows, turns out to have faked his own death to get away from policeman Calloway (Trevor Howard).

After all these years, it isn't exactly a surprise, but the moment of revelation as Welles's Harry is caught by the beam of a streetlight as a cat nuzzles his shoes is still magic. Anton Karras's haunting and unforgettable zither theme "plung-ka-plungs" on the soundtrack, and Welles spins a virtual cameo into one of the screen's greatest charming villains. *The Third Man*'s most famous speech—the "cuckoo clock" anecdote, delivered up above the "little dots" on the Vienna Ferris Wheel—was written by Welles on the spur of the moment as an addition to Greene's script, filling out the character and perhaps securing the picture's lasting greatness.

A rare British film that is as accomplished technically as the best of classic Hollywood—Reed never did anything as masterly again—*The Third Man* is an outstanding mix of political thriller, weird romance, gothic mystery, and black-and-white romantic agony. Welles, who is truly brilliant for five minutes, has hogged all the press, but it's a perfectly acted film, with wonderful work from Cotten as the bewildered and disappointed hero and the luminous beauty of Italian star Valli as the heroine by default. It's a film that constantly shimmers, in its nocturnal cityscapes, its glowing haunted faces, and the gushing waters of the sewers in which Lime is finally flushed away. **KN**

Kind Hearts and Coronets Robert Hamer, 1949

Among the earliest of the Ealing comedies produced by Sir Michael Balcon's West London hothouse of comedic creativity, and a prime example of their distinctively British humor, *Kind Hearts and Coronets* is without equal for grace and savoir faire in black comedy. It is sophisticated, deliciously sly, and resolved with another Ealing trademark, the smart sting in the tale.

Eight members of the snobbish, wealthy, and aristocratic D'Ascoyne family stand between their bitter, coolly self-possessed poor relation Louis Mazzini (suave Dennis Price) and a dukedom, provoking him to mass murder in Robert Hamer's audaciously elegant black comedy of class. The film was adapted by Hamer and John Dighton from a pungent novel of society decadence, *Israel Rank*, by Roy Horniman, but it was also arguably influenced by Charlie Chaplin's more controversial *Monsieur Verdoux* (1947). In his inexorable, unscrupulous rise, Price's Machiavellian Mazzini becomes fatefully entangled with two different women: Edith D'Ascoyne (Valerie Hobson), the touchingly gracious widow of one of his victims, and Sibella, the fabulously eccentric, dangerously feline sex kitten played by Ealing favorite Joan Greenwood.

All eight of the clearly inbred, dotty D'Ascoynes—including the hatchet-faced suffragette Lady Agatha who is shot down in a balloon, the bluff general condemned to short-lived enjoyment of an explosive pot of caviar, and the insane admiral who does Mazzini's job for him by going down with his ship—are famously played by Ealing's man of a thousand faces, unrecognizable from one film to the next (and in this case from one scene to the next), the delightful Alec Guinness.

Hamer's all-too-brief directorial heyday peaked with *Kind Hearts and Coronets*. He had come to the film with a valuable background as an editor and found a balance between the smart dialogue and pithy, satiric visual vignettes. The slick black-and-white work of wartime news cameraman-turned-cinematographer Douglas Slocombe led to a much longer and prolific career: he shot many classic British films of the 1960s and, later, such international hits as the *Indiana Jones* trilogy. **AE**

G.B. (Ealing Studios) 106m BW
Producer Michael Balcon, Michael Relph
Screenplay Robert Hamer, Roy Horniman,
John Dighton, from the novel *Israel Rank* by
Roy Horniman **Photography** Douglas
Slocombe **Music** Ernest Irving **Cast** Dennis
Price, Valerie Hobson, Joan Greenwood, Alec
Guinness, Audrey Fildes, Miles Malleson,
Clive Morton, John Penrose, Cecil Ramage,
Hugh Griffith, John Salew, Eric Messiter, Lyn
Evans, Barbara Leake, Peggy Ann Clifford
Venice Film Festival Robert Hamer
(Golden Lion nomination)

> *"It is so difficult to make a neat job of killing people with whom one is not on friendly terms."*
>
> **Louis Mazzini**
> **(Dennis Price)**

i

The movie's title is derived from a line in Lord Alfred Tennyson's 1842 poem *Lady Clara Vere de Vere*.

Whisky Galore! Alexander Mackendrick, 1949

Along with *Passport to Pimlico* and *Kind Hearts and Coronets* (both also 1949), *Whisky Galore!* was in the first vintage of celebrated postwar comedies from Britain's Ealing Studios under producer Sir Michael Balcon. Universally admired, the film was key in establishing the distinctive, self-deprecating, and understated satiric tone of those following, as well as the theme of defiant little people triumphing over those more powerful.

Alexander "Sandy" Mackendrick's influential culture-clash comedy, shot beautifully on location on Barra in the Outer Hebrides in the style of a mock documentary, sees the sanctimonious, by-the-book, and teetotaling English Home Guard captain Basil Radford hunt for a foundered ship's "salvaged" cargo of malt whisky. Intended for America, the cargo is seized by thirsty islanders deprived by wartime, and Radford is well and truly foiled by the wily natives of Todday, who run rings around him and the Excise men. The story, immortalized by writer Compton MacKenzie, was inspired by the true "disappearance" of 50,000 cases of whisky after a cargo ship was wrecked off the Isle of Eriskay.

Whisky Galore! is more dated than some of the other Ealing comedies, though the quaint charm is countered by the film's hectic hilarity, the affectionate and astute social observation, the authenticity of Hebridean life, and the delightful performances. Ealing's leading English enchantress Joan Greenwood is superb as the canny publican Macroon's (Wylie Watson) flirtatious daughter, as are the mainly genuine Scots players like James Robertson Justice, Gordon Jackson, and the droll narrator, Finlay Currie. The universal appeal of the film's antiauthoritarian humor lies in its idealization of a remote, isolated village world full of eccentrics, cards, pretty lasses, and gutsy, commonsensical folk pricking the balloons of the pompous and bureaucratic types opposing them.

The Scottish (though American-born) Mackendrick, director of three of Ealing's most sparkling gems (the other two being *The Man in the White Suit* [1951] and *The Ladykillers* [1955]) would prove equally impressive directing drama later in his career, after his move to America, notably with the 1957 film *Sweet Smell of Success*. **AE**

G.B. (Ealing Studios, Rank) 82m BW
Language English / Gaelic
Producer Michael Balcon, Monja Danischewsky **Screenplay** Angus MacPhail and Compton MacKenzie, from novel by Compton MacKenzie **Photography** Gerald Gibbs **Music** Ernest Irving **Cast** Basil Radford, Catherine Lacey, Bruce Seton, Joan Greenwood, Wylie Watson, Gabrielle Blunt, Gordon Jackson, Jean Cadell, James Robertson Justice, Morland Graham, John Gregson, James Woodburn, James Anderson, Jameson Clark, Duncan Macrae

1949

> *"This wee comedy dram warms the heart as surely as a blended malt."*
>
> Jamie Russell,
> *Total Film*, 2011

i

Whisky Galore! author Compton MacKenzie appears in the film as the SS *Cabinet Minister*'s captain.

On the Town Stanley Donen & Gene Kelly, 1949

U.S. (MGM) 98m Technicolor
Producer Roger Edens, Arthur Freed
Screenplay Adolph Green and
Betty Comden, from their play
Photography Harold Rosson **Music** Leonard
Bernstein, Saul Chaplin, Roger Edens
Cast Gene Kelly, Frank Sinatra, Betty Garrett,
Ann Miller, Jules Munshin, Vera-Ellen,
Florence Bates, Alice Pearce, George Meader,
Judy Holliday **Oscar** Roger Edens,
Lennie Hayton (music)

*"New York, New York, a
wonderful town!"*

**Gabey, Chip, and Ozzie
(Gene Kelly, Frank Sinatra, and
Jules Munshin), singing**

Two sailors, Gabey (Gene Kelly) and Chip (Frank Sinatra), in the company of cab driver Brunhilde (Betty Garrett), burst into an art school's life-modeling session. They gasp at the sight of a naked woman, glimpsed from the back. The model turns: She is merely wearing a backless dress. Then our trio rushes out through the swinging doors they entered through: revealed are a third sailor, Ozzie (Jules Munshin), and his anthropologist girlfriend Claire (Ann Miller), furtively kissing.

The lightly subversive fun of *On the Town* is contained in this elaborate gag. It is basically about a hunt for casual sex: Three sailors, on twenty-four-hour leave, want to get laid. Of course, on the surface, the film attempts to disavow this base impulse—there is, after all, Gabey's love for the sweet, innocent "Miss Turnstiles," Ivy (Vera-Ellen)—but the proof is everywhere: in cultural references (surrealist art; a museum devoted to "homo erectus"), double entendres (Brunhilde: "He wanted to see the sights, and I showed him plenty"), and above all in the high energy of the song-and-dance numbers, into which all eroticism is artfully sublimated—though there's nothing particularly hidden in Miller's bravura performance of "Prehistoric Man!"

On the Town hangs many, varied delights on its simple but driving "lifetime in a day" premise, codirectors Kelly and Stanley Donen still some years away from their ideal of the dramatically integrated musical. Once the sailors split up, the film becomes especially busy, ranging from low burlesque ("You Can Count On Me") to high ballet, the latter via the Sinatra–Garret duet "Come Up to My Place," a highlight of Leonard Bernstein's jazzy score. Proceedings make room for all manner of reveries (Gabey's zany imagining of Ivy as a gal for all seasons), digressions, and gags.

The left-wing aspect of Kelly's life and career is often overlooked. *On the Town* has, lurking under its surface alongside that sex drive, a political aspiration: This "city symphony" (taking advantage of some terrific location photography) is truly an ode to the joys and woes of ordinary workers, cramming experiences into the cracks of a punishing schedule. **AM**

i

Frank Sinatra had to wear special padding around his buttocks to fill out the seat of his sailor uniform.

Orphée Jean Cocteau, 1950
Orpheus

France (André Paulve, Palais Royal) 112m BW **Language** French **Producer** André Paulvé **Screenplay** Jean Cocteau **Photography** Nicolas Hayer **Music** Georges Auric **Cast** Jean Marais, François Périer, María Casarès, Marie Déa, Henri Crémieux, Juliette Gréco, Roger Blin, Edouard Dermithe, Maurice Carnege, René Worms, Raymond Faure, Pierre Bertin, Jacques Varennes, Claude Mauriac

"It is the privilege of legends to be timeless," notes the narrator at the outset. And so it has proved for Jean Cocteau's fantasy film *Orpheus*, an infinitely strange and beguiling allegory that is also a kind of coded autobiography. Orphée (played by Cocteau's lover, Jean Marais) is an acclaimed poet who has fallen out of fashion. After a despised rival is knocked over by two uniformed motorcyclists, he becomes fascinated with the Princess Death (María Casarès), but when his neglected wife Eurydice (Marie Déa) dies, Orphée follows into the underworld to reclaim her.

Looked at simply as a special-effects movie, this is still a landmark film for Cocteau's ingenious use of reverse motion and back projection. Mirrors are the doors to the other side ("Look at a mirror for a lifetime you will see Death at work"), though only poets can move through them at will. Purgatory is a slow-motion limbo where the laws of physics are suspended. Although the enigmatic narrative is occasionally confusing (it doesn't help that Orphée and Cocteau alike seem more taken with Death than with Eurydice), the film's poetic imagination is spellbinding. **TCh**

1950

The Asphalt Jungle John Huston, 1950

U.S. (MGM) 112m BW **Producer** Arthur Hornblow Jr. **Screenplay** W.R. Burnett, Ben Maddow, John Huston, from novel by W.R. Burnett **Photography** Harold Rosson **Music** Miklós Rózsa **Cast** Sterling Hayden, Louis Calhern, Jean Hagen, James Whitmore, Sam Jaffe, John McIntire, Commissioner Hardy, Marc Lawrence, Barry Kelley, Anthony Caruso, Teresa Celli, Marilyn Monroe, William "Wee Willie" Davis, Dorothy Tree, Brad Dexter, John Maxwell **Oscar nominations** John Huston (director), Ben Maddow, John Huston (screenplay), Sam Jaffe (actor in support role), Harold Rosson (photography)

Perhaps the most finely detailed "caper" film Hollywood ever produced, John Huston's study of a jewelry store robbery shows the business relationships between career criminals of different kinds—from a mastermind plotter to the "box man" who breaks into the safe, to the "muscle" needed to handle the guards. Such crime is merely "a left-handed form of endeavor," suggests the "respectable" businessman who is to fence the proceeds.

The Asphalt Jungle concentrates not only on the robbery but also on the personal lives of the gang members, who are individualized with notable touches of dialogue and visual style. Huston expertly handles a fine ensemble of actors, including Marilyn Monroe—who plays an old man's dizzy-headed mistress in one of her most important early roles. As in most Huston films, the thematic emphasis is on the joys and sorrows of male bonding, with the criminals' inevitable defeat by the law—and their own weaknesses—rendered almost heroic. The gang leader Doc Riedenschneider (Sam Jaffe) is captured because he lingers in a café watching a beautiful young girl dance, and tough guy Dix (Sterling Hayden) bleeds to death as he tries to return to the country and the horses he loves. Such melodramatic elements contrast interestingly with the film's otherwise grim portrayal of alienation, betrayal, and sociopathy. **RBP**

Rashomon Akira Kurosawa, 1950

Three travelers collect under a ruined temple during a storm. Woodcutter (Takashi Shimura), Priest (Minoru Chiaki), and Commoner (Kichijiro Ueda) build a fire and wonder about a troubling story. So begins the story-within-a-story about a married couple and bandit who meet on a forest road. Woodcutter later finds the husband's corpse and testifies before a police commission investigating what happened. The explanation so horrifies Priest and entertains Commoner it occupies them through the storm with four depictions of a crime.

Plotted with competing points-of-view in flashback style, framed with a fluid, moving camera, and shot under a canopy of dappled light, *Rashomon* details unreliable perspectives. The veracity of on-screen characters and depicted actions are therefore rendered false and misleading. Facts are submitted into evidence but immediately questioned. Disagreement among the overlapping stories of husband, wife, and bandit complicate straightforward reportage. In short, every narrator is untrustworthy, along with the overall film.

Nothing less than an epistemological nightmare, Akira Kurosawa's Oscar winner still concludes with an infusion of moral goodness. Although *Rashomon* implicitly explores the lost possibility of renewal and redemption, its central theme about discovering truth as a distinction between good and evil is upheld through simple acts of kindness and sacrifice.

As the forest road is explored from the perspective of the bandit Tajomaru (Toshirô Mifune), he is characterized as a hellion. After seeing Masako (Machiko Kyô), he ravishes her into willing submission before cutting loose her samurai husband Takehiro (Masayuki Mori) so the two men can fight until the latter is killed. From Masako's point of view, she is raped, shamed, then rebuffed by her husband, and submitting to hysterical rage she kills him. Agreeing only that he was killed, Takehiro speaks through a medium (Fumiko Honma) explaining how his wife equalled Tajomaru's passion before demanding his death at the hands of the bandit. Seeing no good result in murder, Tajomaru flees, as does Masako, leaving Takehiro behind to commit suicide.

Each story is told in a self-serving way. Tajomaru is therefore a ruthless criminal, Masako a set-upon innocent, and Takehiro a proud warrior. All true, it seems, until Woodcutter explains what he saw from the shadows. His perspective affirms the wife's shallowness, the bandit's false bravado, and the husband's cowardice. It also conceals his own complicity in the crime until Commoner draws this out, dismissing the search for truth.

Kurosawa ends the bleak tale on a positive note. An abandoned baby is discovered beneath the temple ruin. Woodcutter intoduces the idea of human goodness by taking it upon himself in redemption to care for the orphan. A consistent conclusion, given *Rashomon*'s formal schizophrenia in a brilliant narrative structure—Kurosawa's first masterwork. **GC-Q**

Japan (Daiei) 88m BW **Language** Japanese **Producer** Minoru Jingo, Masaichi Nagata **Screenplay** Ryunosuke Akutagawa, Akira Kurosawa, Shinobu Hashimoto, from the stories Rashomon and In a Grove by Ryunosuke Akutagawa **Photography** Kazuo Miyagawa **Music** Fumio Hayasaka **Cast** Toshirô Mifune, Machiko Kyô, Masayuki Mori, Takashi Shimura, Minoru Chiaki, Kichijiro Ueda, Fumiko Honma, Daisuke Katô **Oscar** Akira Kurosawa (honorary award) **Oscar nomination** So Matsuyama, H. Motsumoto (art direction) **Venice Film Festival** Akira Kurosawa (Golden Lion), Akira Kurosawa (Italian film critics award)

> *"It's human to lie. Most of the time we can't even be honest with ourselves."*
>
> **Commoner (Kichijiro Ueda)**

i

The film is one of the earliest productions to feature hand-held camera footage.

All About Eve Joseph L. Mankiewicz, 1950

U.S. (Fox) 138m BW **Producer** Darryl F. Zanuck **Screenplay** Joseph L. Mankiewicz, from the story "The Wisdom of Eve" by Mary Orr **Photography** Milton R. Krasner **Music** Alfred Newman **Cast** Bette Davis, Anne Baxter, George Sanders, Celeste Holm, Gary Merrill, Hugh Marlowe, Gregory Ratoff, Barbara Bates, Marilyn Monroe, Thelma Ritter, Walter Hampden, Randy Stuart, Craig Hill, Leland Harris, Barbara White **Oscars** Darryl F. Zanuck (best picture), Joseph L. Mankiewicz (director), Joseph L. Mankiewicz (screenplay), George Sanders (actor in support role), Edith Head, Charles Le Maire (costume) **Oscar nominations** Anne Baxter, Bette Davis (actress), Celeste Holm, Thelma Ritter (actress in support role), Lyle R. Wheeler, George W. Davis, Thomas Little, Walter M. Scott (art direction), Milton R. Krasner (photography), Barbara McLean (editing), Alfred Newman (music) **Cannes Film Festival** Joseph L. Mankiewicz (special jury prize), Bette Davis (actress)

Considered one of the sharpest and darkest films ever made about show business, Joseph L. Mankiewicz's 1950 drama was taken from a 1946 *Cosmopolitan* magazine short story called "The Wisdom of Eve." Avoided by other studios for four years, the combination of Mankiewicz's cynical, witty screenplay, and a high-caliber cast transformed the story into an enormous cinematic success. *All About Eve* was nominated for a then-record fourteen Academy Awards and won six, including Best Picture and Best Supporting Actor (for George Sanders), as well as Best Director and Best Screenplay awards for Mankiewicz. Nominations went to Bette Davis, Anne Baxter, Celeste Holm, and Thelma Ritter, thus holding the record for most female acting nominations in a single film.

Opening with an acceptance speech given by gracious young actress Eve Harrington (Anne Baxter), the film pans over the audience. Addison DeWitt (Sanders) begins a narration which goes back in time to the real tale of how such success was achieved. Bette Davis is Margo Channing, an aging, forty-year-old Broadway actress who befriends Eve, a young fan apparently plagued by a hard life. Margo's dresser Birdie (Ritter) is the first to see through Eve's sob story, saying, "What a story! Everything but the bloodhounds snappin' at her rear end." Eve repays Margo's trust by worming into her idol's professional and personal life with more than a few lies. Eve goes on to deceive Margo's best friend (Holm), beguile her loyal but devious critic (Sanders), and vainly attempt to steal away her fiancé Bill (Gary Merrill, Davis's real-life husband). In a brief but dazzling cameo, Marilyn Monroe appears on the arm of DeWitt at Margo's party, the same party where Margo utters the now famous line, "Fasten your seat belts. It's going to be a bumpy night."

Having also won an Oscar in 1949 for *A Letter to Three Wives*, some see Mankiewicz's victory in *All About Eve* as final vindication of his talent in comparison to brother Herman, who won the Best Original Screenplay Oscar for *Citizen Kane*. That debate aside, *All About Eve* is widely considered to be the crowning achievement in Davis's lengthy career; its only flaw is Baxter, who seems to be nothing but pure ambition in womanly form. **KK**

i

Actor Eddie Fisher's sole scene was eventually cut, but his name still appears in the credits for the cast.

Winchester '73 Anthony Mann, 1950

U.S. (Universal) 92m BW **Producer** Aaron Rosenberg **Screenplay** Borden Chase, Stuart N. Lake, Robert L. Richards, from story by Stuart N. Lake **Photography** William H. Daniels **Music** Walter Scharf **Cast** James Stewart, Shelley Winters, Dan Duryea, Stephen McNally, Millard Mitchell, Charles Drake, John McIntire, Will Geer, Jay C. Flippen, Rock Hudson, John Alexander, Steve Brodie, James Millican, Abner Biberman, Tony Curtis

The first of eight collaborations between director Anthony Mann and actor James Stewart, *Winchester '73* sets the tone for this legendary partnership. The Westerns these two men made together are unusually bitter and starkly beautiful, with fascinating overtones of moral uncertainty.

Winchester '73 revolves around a high-powered rifle that changes hands repeatedly. Each man who comes into possession of it is changed in some way—sometimes for good, sometimes for bad. It all comes to a head in a shooting contest, for which the prize is the titular rifle itself.

The cast is extremely strong. Shelley Winters is excellent, and the supporting players include such versatile character actors as Millard Mitchell, Stephen McNally, Will Geer, and the incomparable Dan Duryea. (See if you can spot a young Tony Curtis, and Rock Hudson as an Indian brave!)

Now regarded as an actor of unusual versatility, Stewart was, at the time of the film's production, concerned about perceptions regarding his limited breadth. His character, Lin McAdam, is an unusual hero—somewhat tentative, even if he is the film's moral center. Stewart's performances for Mann would get increasingly complex and cynical in films like *The Man from Laramie* (1955) and *The Naked Spur* (1953) proving beyond a doubt that this master of the craft could adeptly handle any role that came his way. **EdeS**

Rio Grande John Ford, 1950

U.S. (Argosy, Republic) 105m BW **Producer** Merian C. Cooper, John Ford, Herbert J. Yates **Screenplay** James Warner Bellah, James Kevin McGuinness, from the story "Mission With No Record" by James Warner Bellah **Photography** Bert Glennon **Music** Dale Evans, Stan Jones, Tex Owens, Victor Young **Cast** John Wayne, Maureen O'Hara, Ben Johnson, Claude Jarman Jr., Harry Carey Jr., Chill Wills, J. Carrol Naish, Victor McLaglen, Grant Withers, Peter Ortiz, Steve Pendleton, Karolyn Grimes, Alberto Morin, Stan Jones, Fred Kennedy

The last installment of John Ford's "Cavalry Trilogy"—*Fort Apache* (1948) and *She Wore a Yellow Ribbon* (1949) being the other two—*Rio Grande* is a minor work, albeit a key one, allegedly undertaken to secure financing for the director's personal project, *The Quiet Man* (1952). It's less revisionary, mythmaking, or elegiac than the previous Cavalry films, offering a mix of soapsuds, barracks larking, and hard-riding action.

Crusty Yankee Captain Kirby York (John Wayne, not quite recreating his Kirby York of *Fort Apache*) reconciles with estranged Southern wife Kathleen (Maureen O'Hara)—whose mansion he burned down during the Civil War—in order to share the raising of their raw recruit son (Claude Jarman Jr.). The son becomes a man under his father's influence without losing his mother's sensitivity. York leads his men in pursuit of Indian raiders who have snuck up from Mexico with kidnap in mind, suggesting the embryo of Ford and Wayne's masterpiece, *The Searchers* (1956). This is a less neurotic, more action-oriented quest and a rare Ford movie that unquestioningly adopts a goodies versus baddies view of the Indian wars.

Ben Johnson shows off his rodeo skills and great riding stunt work, and the Sons of the Pioneers add to the folkloric feel with appropriate ballads, though "Bold Fenian Men" is an unlikely favorite out West in the 1870s. **KN**

Sunset Blvd. Billy Wilder, 1950

U.S. (Paramount) 110m BW **Producer** Charles Brackett **Screenplay** Charles Brackett, Billy Wilder, D.M. Marshman, Jr., from the story "A Can of Beans" by Charles Brackett and Billy Wilder **Photography** John F. Seitz **Music** Jay Livingston, Franz Waxman **Cast** William Holden, Gloria Swanson, Erich von Stroheim, Nancy Olson, Fred Clark, I loyd Gough, Jack Webb, Franklyn Farnum, Larry J. Blake, Charles Dayton, Cecil B. DeMille, Hedda Hopper, Buster Keaton, Anna Q. Nilsson, H.B. Warner **Oscars** Charles Brackett, Billy Wilder, D.M. Marshman, Jr. (screenplay), Hans Dreier, John Meehan, Sam Comer, Ray Moyer (art direction), Franz Waxman (music) **Oscar nominations** Charles Brackett (best picture), Billy Wilder (director), William Holden (actor), Gloria Swanson (actress), Erich von Stroheim (actor in support role), Nancy Olson (actress in support role), John F. Seitz (photography), Doane Harrison, Arthur P. Schmidt (editing)

"We didn't need dialogue. We had faces!"

Norma (Gloria Swanson)

ℹ️

Mae West, Mary Pickford, and Pola Negri were all offered the role as Norma Desmond before Swanson.

Unemployed screenwriter Joe Gillis (William Holden), floating dead in a swimming pool, recounts his doomed personal and professional involvement with megalomaniac silent-movie queen Norma Desmond (Gloria Swanson). A flapper vampire whose attempts to stay youthful into her fifties paradoxically make her seem a thousand years old, Norma lives in a decaying mansion on Sunset Boulevard, holding a midnight funeral for her pet monkey ("He must have been a very important chimp," muses Joe), scrawling an unproducible script, and dreaming of an impossible comeback ("I hate that word! It's a return!") as Salome. In attendance is a sinister butler (Erich von Stroheim) who used to be her favored director and, incidentally, her first husband.

Usually not given to ostentatious visuals, Wilder is encouraged by this scenario to create compositions that evoke the lair of the Phantom of the Opera and Charles Foster Kane's Xanadu, a huge close-up of white-gloved hands playing a wheezy pipe organ as the trapped gigolo flutters in the background. Wilder's acidic, yet nostalgic, traipse through the film industry's haunted house is a picture that can be endlessly rewatched, even after its influence has seeped into the horror genre (Robert Aldrich's *What Ever Happened to Baby Jane?* [1962]) and spun off an Andrew Lloyd Webber stage adaptation—combining strange affection for has-been Norma and never-was Joe with a somewhat sadistic use of such ravaged and frozen silent faces as Buster Keaton, H. B. Warner, and Anna Q. Nilsson.

One of *Sunset Blvd.*'s unstressed ironies is that although Norma can't get away with her insanity ("No one leaves a star!"), the industry allows and indeed encourages everyone else to act like a monster: Cecil B. DeMille (playing himself) gently reminds Norma that the picture business has changed, but Wilder concludes his scene by having the camera note his polished riding boots and absurdly outdated on-set strut. Although they recognized their chances for one last blaze of glory, Swanson (who took the role after Mary Pickford turned it down) and von Stroheim (who is forced to watch an extract from *Queen Kelly*, an unfinished 1920s disaster he directed Swanson in) understood the cruelty of Wilder's vision and the way he made monsters of all of them. It's a hard and cynical film, which struggles with its doomed but sweet "normal" love affair: In the end, Norma is as terrified that Joe is writing a script ("Untitled Love Story") with D-girl Nancy Olson as she is that he will leave her for a younger rival. Swanson ("I am big, it's the pictures that got small") is vibrant in her madness, climaxing with a moment of unforgettable horror-glamor as she vamps toward a newsreel cameraman during her arrest for murder and declares that she is ready for her close-up, even as Wilder pulls back to frame her in a long shot that emphasizes her isolation in insanity as the big carnival of a celebrity murder scandal begins. This points the way to Wilder's *Ace in the Hole* (1951) and a culture of media-exploited crime that remains horribly alive more than half a century on. **KN**

Los olvidados Luis Buñuel, 1950
The Young and the Damned

Although *Los olvidados* invokes many conventions of social-problem films, it goes far beyond them. Set in the slums of Mexico City, Luis Buñuel's scathing masterpiece centers on two doomed boys: Pedro (Alfonso Mejía), who struggles to be good, and the older, incorrigible Jaibo (Roberto Cobo), who keeps popping up like a demon brother to lead Pedro astray. Critical of Italian Neorealism, Buñuel demanded that the concept of realism be expanded to include such essentials as dream, poetry, and irrationality—represented by Pedro's nightmare, in which tangled threads of guilt and wish fulfillment resolve into the sensational image of a slab of raw meat offered by the hungry boy's mother, and by Jaibo's dying vision, in which the angel of death appears as a mangy dog leading him down a dark road.

Other lost souls in Buñuel's city of the damned include the nasty blind beggar, Carmelo (Miguel Inclán); the abandoned boy, Ojitos (Mário Ramírez), enslaved by Carmelo; the nymphet Meche (Alma Delia Fuentes), whose bare thighs are splashed with milk in one of the film's many provocative images; and the virtuous Julián (Javier Amézcua), quickly slaughtered by Jaibo. Borrowing a tag line from *Nashville* (1975), one could say that the final essential character is you, the hypocrite spectator. A crucial factor that elevates *Los olvidados* above other social-problem films is its aggressive discomfiting of the viewer—most startlingly when Pedro, sulking in a reform school, hurls an egg at the camera.

In less spectacular but still striking ways, *Los olvidados* discourages the spectator from settling into the position of noble sensitivity commonly cultivated by liberal message films. For one thing, the tone is too caustic, distancing, and contradictory—as when the pathetic spectacle of blind Carmelo beaten by Jaibo's gang is capped with a derisive shot of a gawking chicken. In addition, Buñuel neatly sidesteps a veritable catalog of message-film cop-outs, including the use of a surrogate figure to guide our feelings and the concentration on special cases to ameliorate the larger problem. *Los olvidados* has been criticized for callousness and a lack of constructive solutions, but Buñuel is an artist, not a legislator, and the compassion of this remarkably honest film might be difficult to recognize only because it isn't cushioned with sentimentality. **MR**

Mexico (Ultramar) 85m BW
Language Spanish **Producer** Óscar Dancigers, Sergio Kogan, Jaime A. Menasce **Screenplay** Luis Alcoriza, Luis Buñuel **Photography** Gabriel Figueroa **Music** Rodolfo Halffter, Gustavo Pittaluga **Cast** Alfonso Mejía, Estela Inda, Miguel Inclán, Roberto Cobo, Alma Delia Fuentes, Francisco Jambrina, Jesús Navarro, Efraín Arauz, Sergio Villarreal, Jorge Pérez, Javier Amézcua, Mário Ramírez **Cannes Film Festival** Luis Buñuel (director)

"Neorealist reality is incomplete, conventional, and above all rational."

Luis Buñuel, 1953

1950

ℹ️

So stormy was the reaction to the film's initial run in Mexico City that it was withdrawn after just three days.

In a Lonely Place Nicholas Ray, 1950

U.S. (Columbia, Santana) 94m BW
Producer Henry S. Kesler, Robert Lord
Screenplay Dorothy B. Hughes, Edmund H.
North, Andrew Solt, from novel by Dorothy
B. Hughes **Photography** Burnett Guffey
Music George Antheil **Cast** Humphrey
Bogart, Gloria Grahame, Frank Lovejoy, Carl
Benton Reid, Art Smith, Jeff Donnell, Martha
Stewart, Robert Warwick, Morris Ankrum,
William Ching, Steven Geray, Hadda Brooks

In a Lonely Place qualifies as a masterpiece on many grounds: as the single best film of cult director Nicholas Ray; as a uniquely romantic and doom-haunted noir drama; as a showcase for personal best performances by Humphrey Bogart and Gloria Grahame; and as one of the most insightful films about Hollywood.

Short-fused screenwriter Dix Steele (Bogart) is suspected of an especially vicious murder, but his next-door neighbor Laurel Gray (Grahame) can give him an alibi. This leads the pair into a passionate affair that is undermined as Laurel becomes terrified by Dix's violent streak, coming to wonder if he really did commit the murder. After years of playing romantic tough guys, Bogart here gets deeper inside his own persona, revealing the neurotic edge that might have made Sam Spade or Rick Blaine unstable and becoming absolutely terrifying in the sequences where he explodes in fist-frenzy at the deserving and undeserving alike.

The film's downbeat subject matter is rendered exhilarating by Ray's dark visuals and a streak of almost surrealist poetry. Dorothy B. Hughes's fine novel is interestingly adapted: In the book, Steele really does turn out to be the murderer, but the screenplay is actually bleaker in that finally what matters isn't that he's innocent but that he easily could not be. **KN**

1951

Ace in the Hole Billy Wilder, 1951

U.S. (Paramount) 111m BW
Language English / Latin **Producer** William
Schorr, Billy Wilder **Screenplay** Walter
Newman, Lesser Samuels, Billy Wilder
Photography Charles Lang **Music** Hugo
Friedhofer **Cast** Kirk Douglas, Jan Sterling,
Robert Arthur, Porter Hall, Frank Cady,
Richard Benedict, Ray Teal, Frank Jaquet
Oscar nomination Billy Wilder, Lesser
Samuels, Walter Newman (screenplay)
Venice Film Festival Billy Wilder
(international award and Golden
Lion nomination)

Ace in the Hole is noted for two things: It's the only collaboration between Kirk Douglas and Billy Wilder, and it's one of the angriest and most bitter films ever to come out of the Hollywood studio system.

Douglas plays Chuck Tatum, a cynical, arrogant reporter exiled to a small-town newspaper in New Mexico after getting fired from several big-city papers. When he goes out to cover a story about a prospector (Richard Benedict) trapped under a rockslide, he sees his chance to make it back to the big time. He manipulates the sheriff into delaying the rescue efforts with the promise of luring tourists, thrill seekers, and onlookers coming to be a part of this stirring human interest story. Tatum whips up the media frenzy, positions himself as the sole reporter with the scoop, and escalates the event into a carnival. Even the hapless prospector's wife (Jan Sterling), a self-serving poster child for High Maintenance, is drawn into Tatum's spin as she proves his match in venal self-interest. And everything goes as you would expect—horribly, horribly badly.

The anger lingers far beyond the story's end, and Wilder's trademark verbal zingers barely sugarcoat the story's bitter core, which indicts us all. Poignant and thoughtful. **AT**

YOU'LL BE IN THE GRIP OF LOVE'S STRANGEST TRIP!

ALFRED HITCHCOCK'S
Strangers on a Train

FARLEY **GRANGER** RUTH **ROMAN** ROBERT **WALKER**

U.S. (Warner Bros.) 101m BW **Producer** Alfred Hitchcock **Screenplay** Raymond Chandler, Whitfield Cook, Czenzi Ormonde, from novel by Patricia Highsmith **Photography** Robert Burks **Music** Dimitri Tiomkin **Cast** Farley Granger, Ruth Roman, Robert Walker, Leo G. Carroll, Patricia Hitchcock, Kasey Rogers, Marion Lorne, Jonathan Hale, Howard St. John, John Brown, Norma Varden, Robert Gist **Oscar nomination** Robert Burks (photography)

> "My theory is that everyone is a potential murderer."
>
> **Bruno Anthony (Robert Walker)**

Strangers on a Train Alfred Hitchcock, 1951

Is there any wonder why Alfred Hitchcock was drawn to author Patricia Highsmith's *Strangers on a Train*? Her first novel, *Strangers*, includes elements found in virtually all of Hitchcock's films: a fascination with murder, mix-ups, and barely suppressed homosexual urges. Needless to say, it didn't take long for the director to purchase the rights and get to work, and with a great screenplay from Raymond Chandler—with a touch-up by Ben Hecht, among others—the film turned out to be one of Hitchcock's most effective.

Strangers on a Train begins innocently enough. Guy Haines (Farley Granger), a successful tennis player, literally bumps into fellow train passenger Bruno Anthony (Robert Walker), an eccentric and excitable stranger. Both have someone in their lives they'd rather be without. Guy wants his wife out of the picture and Bruno his domineering father, so Bruno devises the "perfect" murder to solve both men's problems: They'll simply swap victims. Guy brushes off the crazy idea, but soon Bruno is blackmailing him into fulfilling his part of the bargain.

Almost a black comedy, *Strangers on a Train* also works as a bizarre courtship ritual, in which Granger plays the straight man to Walker's flamboyant lunatic. As usual, Hitchcock takes particular glee in exploiting the plight of his protagonist. The dialogue sparkles as Walker tightens the screws around Granger, leading to what could be the most suspenseful tennis game in movie history. But this being Hitchcock, the thrilling conclusion takes place on a moving carousel, with Granger and Walker wrestling as the out-of-control ride spins faster and faster.

It's a jarring finale to what is largely an internalized film about madness, blackmail, and guilt, yet Hitchcock pulls it off brilliantly. As the campy charm of Walker leads to more overtly murderous impulses, his stature as a villain grows, and he can only be dispatched in a manner that does justice to his larger-than-life personality. Indeed, Walker (in his last role) dominates the film. He's the ego unleashed, the flashy flip side to the more repressed insanity Hitchcock would explore nine years later in *Psycho*. **JK**

🛈

Hitchcock's signature cameo (he boards a train with a double bass) was directed by his daughter, Patricia.

U.S. (Charles K. Feldman, Warner Bros.) 122m
BW Producer Charles K. Feldman
Screenplay Tennessee Williams, Oscar Saul,
from play by Tennessee Williams
Photography Harry Stradling Sr. Music Alex
North Cast Vivien Leigh, Marlon Brando, Kim
Hunter, Karl Malden, Rudy Bond, Nick Dennis,
Peg Hillias, Wright King, Richard Garrick, Ann
Dere, Edna Thomas, Mickey Kuhn
Oscars Vivien Leigh (actress), Karl Malden
(actor in support role), Kim Hunter (actress in
support role), Richard Day, George James
Hopkins (art direction) Oscar nominations
Charles K. Feldman (best picture), Elia Kazan
(director), Tennessee Williams (screenplay),
Marlon Brando (actor), Harry Stradling Sr.
(photography), Lucinda Ballard (costume),
Alex North (music), Nathan Levinson (sound)

A Streetcar Named Desire Elia Kazan, 1951

Although Tennessee Williams's play was meant to be all about the desperate, poetic heroism of Blanche DuBois, Marlon Brando's uncouth, sweaty animal magnetism opposite Vivien Leigh's frail, faded belle commanded the screen, just as it had electrified Broadway theatergoers opposite Jessica Tandy's Blanche four years earlier (a production also directed by Elia Kazan). Brando's brooding naturalism, his earthy sexuality, and his howls of "Stell-ahhhh!" remain a nearly impossible act to follow for the actors who have subsequently assayed the brutish Stanley Kowalski.

Kazan's screen version—also scripted by Williams but subjected to censorship of some frank content—won three of the four acting Oscars for Leigh, who had also played Blanche in London's West End production, directed by her husband, Sir Laurence Olivier. Oscars were also won by supporting actors Kim Hunter and Karl Malden, but Brando was beaten to the post by Humphrey Bogart (for *The African Queen*). Nevertheless, his impact in *Streetcar* placed him at the forefront of modern screen actors, the most famous and influential exponent of the Actors Studio's "Method."

Having lost the long-in-decline family estate to back taxes and her reputation while seeking oblivion or solace, Blanche arrives in New Orleans to stay with her pregnant sister, Stella, and churlish brother-in-law, Stanley, in their cramped, sweltering apartment. Stanley, convinced that Blanche is holding out on a mythical inheritance, is driven wild by the neurotic woman, pathetically clinging to her refinement and delusions. Under Stanley's resentful bullying, Blanche's last hopes are brutally destroyed, and she retreats into a psychotic state.

Although it was Kazan's seventh feature film, *Streetcar* is theatrical rather than cinematic. Its power emanates from the performances, particularly the absorbing duel between the poignant, ethereal, stagey Leigh and the explosive, instinctive Brando, who are as different in their acting approaches as Blanche and Stanley are in personality. Kazan, who was a cofounder of the Actors Studio in 1947 and still a force in American theater at the time, was showing little interest in the visual possibilities of the medium, but his way with actors is amply apparent here. **AE**

"I have always depended on the kindness of strangers."

Blanche DuBois

(Vivien Leigh)

i

The set had movable walls that closed in progressively, reflecting Blanche's increasing desperation.

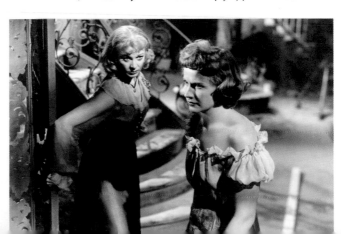

An American in Paris Vincente Minnelli, 1951

U.S. (MGM) 113m Technicolor
Language English / French **Producer** Roger
Edens, Arthur Freed **Screenplay** Alan Jay
Lerner **Photography** John Alton, Alfred
Gilks **Music** Saul Chaplin **Cast** Gene Kelly,
Jerry Mulligan, Leslie Caron, Lise Bouvier,
Oscar Levant, Adam Cook, Georges Guétary,
Henri Baurel, Nina Foch, Milo Roberts
Oscars Arthur Freed (best picture), Alan Jay
Lerner (screenplay), Cedric Gibbons, E.
Preston Ames, Edwin B. Willis, F. Keogh
Gleason (art direction), Alfred Gilks, John
Alton (photography), Orry-Kelly, Walter
Plunkett, Irene Sharaff (costume), Johnny
Green, Saul Chaplin (music) **Oscar
nominations** Vincente Minnelli (director),
Adrienne Fazan (editing)

Vincente Minnelli's joyous musical won six Academy Awards—including
Best Picture (over supposed favorites *A Streetcar Named Desire* and *A Place
in the Sun*)—as well as a special citation for choreographer-star Gene
Kelly and the Thalberg Memorial Award for MGM producer Arthur Freed.
An American in Paris was an original for the screen, conceived by Freed
as a vehicle for Kelly and constructed around a clutch of George Gershwin's
most popular songs (including "I Got Rhythm" and "'S Wonderful").

Penniless artist Kelly brings his athletic exuberance to a sanitized
Montmartre, tap dances with urchins, falls for gamine muse Leslie
Caron, and vies for her with suave French singer Georges Guétary.
Meanwhile, jealous patron Nina Foch seethes, all dryly observed by the
composer pal played by pianist and Gershwin exponent Oscar Levant.
Sending up the penchant of Lost Generation Americans for immersing
themselves in a little culture française, Minnelli fills the film with vitality,
romance, and a riot of color. The sensational, innovative highlight is
Kelly's original eighteen-minute ballet to the title music, staged through
sets in the style of French artists, notably Toulouse Lautrec, and the
blissfully romantic Kelly Caron "Our Love Is Here To Stay" dance number
on the banks of the river Seine. **AE**

Pandora and the Flying Dutchman
Albert Lewin, 1951

G.B. (Dorkay, Romulus) 122m
Technicolor **Language** English / Spanish
Producer Joseph Kaufman, Albert Lewin
Screenplay Albert Lewin **Photography** Jack
Cardiff **Music** Alan Rawsthorne **Cast** James
Mason, Ava Gardner, Nigel Patrick, Sheila
Sim, Harold Warrender, Mario Cabré, Marius
Goring, John Laurie, Pamela Mason, Patricia
Raine, Margarita D'Alvarez, La Pillina,
Abraham Sofaer, Francisco Igual, Guillermo
Beltrán

Once dismissed as pretentious and preposterous, the reputation of this
magical romantic fantasy has steadily grown over the years. Set in the
early 1930s in a town called Esperanza ("Hope") on "the Mediterranean
coast of Spain," where idle rich exiles mingle with working fisherfolk,
Pandora and the Flying Dutchman begins with the discovery of two
drowned corpses, hands locked together. In flashback, Pandora Reynolds
(Ava Gardner), an American singer who specializes in driving men to
death and distraction, meets her predestined match in Hendrick Van
Der Zee (James Mason), captain and sole crew of a luxury yacht; he turns
out to be the Flying Dutchman, cursed to sail the seas until he finds a
woman willing to die for him.

Producer, director, and writer Albert Lewin, one of Hollywood's few
open intellectuals, was a man of ostentatious literary leanings (his films
are littered with quoted poetry, to the point that Pandora makes an
offhand remark about how everything people say to her sounds like a
quotation) and fantastical romanticism (all his pictures are about
impossible loves that find perfect moments between curses). Shot in
dark-hued but ravishing Technicolor by Jack Cardiff, the film is a tribute
to the beauty of Ava Gardner, with footnotes about the brooding
intensity of James Mason. **KN**

The African Queen John Huston, 1951

John Huston's 1951 classic is one of Hollywood's most impressive, entertaining, and compelling adventure stories. Based on C.S. Forester's 1935 novel of the same name, *The African Queen* narrates the unlikely love affair between tramp steamer captain Charlie Allnut (Humphrey Bogart) and puritanical missionary spinster Rose Sayer (Katharine Hepburn). Rose can barely tolerate Charlie, but fate throws them together. Caught amid the violence of the impending World War I, Rose must escape downriver with Charlie in his battered tugboat. However, a German warship blocks their exit route, and Rose launches a plan to rig Charlie's cargo with explosive materials to thwart the Germans and make their escape.

The adventure tale is secondary to the rocky relationship between Charlie and Rose, and *The African Queen*'s more interesting allegory plays out in their love story. Rose's prim, repressed British spinster is seduced by Charlie's unshaven, gin-swigging American masculinity. Although set in 1914, the film's post–World War II subtext of the United States's emergence as a primary international player as the influence of traditional colonial powers waned is unmistakable.

Hepburn and Bogart are tremendously enjoyable as the leads. Both veteran, grizzled stars using their trademark gestures and tics to full effect, they suffuse the film with a light, comic air that does not diminish the action. The chemistry between them is perfect, and the movement from polar opposites to comrades and lovers plays out effortlessly and convincingly, although they are at their most entertaining when they are at each other's throats. The color photography and truly astounding location shots of the jungle all add to *The African Queen*'s tremendous appeal. Bogart won his only Oscar for the film; Huston (for direction and writing), Hepburn, and screenwriter James Agee were also nominated. Yet this description and the many subsequent accolades that the film has received cannot capture all of its magic. Even after repeat viewings, it never fails to impart a good feeling, and of the many wonderful films summarized in this book, it truly is a must-see. **RH**

G.B. (Horizon, Romulus) 105m Technicolor
Language English / German / Swahili
Screenplay James Agee, John Huston, from novel by C.S. Forester **Cast** Humphrey Bogart, Katharine Hepburn, Robert Morley, Peter Bull, Theodore Bikel, Walter Gotell, Peter Swanwick, Richard Marner **Oscar** Humphrey Bogart (actor) **Oscar nominations** John Huston (director), James Agee, John Huston (screenplay), Katharine Hepburn (actress)

"I ain't sorry for you no more, ya crazy, psalm-singing, skinny old maid!"

Charlie Allnut (Humphrey Bogart) to Rose Sayer (Katharine Hepburn)

1951

i
Bogart's character was originally a cockney. The part was rewritten, as he couldn't do the accent.

A Place in the Sun George Stevens, 1951

In adapting Theodore Dreiser's *An American Tragedy*, George Stevens was faced with the difficulty of making the novelist's grimly naturalist tale of class warfare interesting to a 1950s audience more eager for entertainment than political instruction. His solution was to emphasize the erotic longings of George Eastman (Montgomery Clift) for the beautiful Angela Vickers (Elizabeth Taylor). George is stuck in a dead-end job at a Chicago hotel when he meets his wealthy uncle for the first time. Seeing a chance to escape the impoverished, intensely religious environment he grew up in, he quits his job and hitchhikes across the country to work at the man's factory in upstate New York. But George, dominated by feelings of deprivation and exclusion, shows neither the drive nor the initiative to work his way up. In fact, he is so weak that he has barely begun work at the factory when he violates one of its cardinal rules. Dating a fellow employee, he ends up impregnating the poor, desperate woman, in whom he has already lost interest.

U.S. (Paramount) 122m BW **Producer** Ivan Moffat, George Stevens **Screenplay** Harry Brown, Theodore Dreiser, Patrick Kearney, Michael Wilson, from the novel *An American Tragedy* by Theodore Dreiser and the play *A Place* in the Sun by Patrick Kearney **Photography** William C. Mellor **Music** Franz Waxman **Cast** Montgomery Clift, Elizabeth Taylor, Shelley Winters, Anne Revere, Keefe Brasselle, Fred Clark, Raymond Burr, Herbert Heyes, Shepperd Strudwick, Frieda Inescort, Kathryn Givney, Walter Sande, Ted de Corsia, John Ridgely, Lois Chartrand **Oscars** George Stevens (director), Michael Wilson, Harry Brown (screenplay), William C. Mellor (cinematography BW), Edith Head (costume), William Hornbeck (editing), Franz Waxman (music) **Oscar nominations** George Stevens (best picture), Montgomery Clift (actor), Shelley Winters (actress)

A Place in the Sun became one of classic Hollywood's most touching and tragic romances, a result of Stevens's careful coaching of the principals and his artful manipulation of two contrasting styles. George's fairy-tale encounter with the innocent Angela is dominated by intimate camerawork, especially juxtaposed close-ups composed in soft focus. Scenes in the factory, with his first girlfriend, Alice (Shelley Winters), and later in the courtroom, are photographed in a film noir style, emphasizing chiaroscuro lighting and unbalanced compositions that express the threat circumstances pose to George's desire for his "place in the sun."

Pregnant, Alice threatens to expose George to his family if he doesn't marry her; he is saved only because the town hall is closed for a holiday when the couple arrives. George suggests a lake outing in a small boat; his intention is that there should be an "accident" and that Alice will drown. He cannot go through with the murder, but then Alice, frightened, tips over the boat. She drowns because he doesn't try to save her, and George pays with his life for his indifference. Stevens, however, makes him more memorable as a tragic lover than as a socio-political object lesson. **BP**

"And I used to think I was complicated."

Angela Vickers (Elizabeth Taylor) to George Eastman (Montgomery Clift)

ⓘ

George's mother was played by Anne Revere, a descendant of American Revolutionary hero Paul Revere.

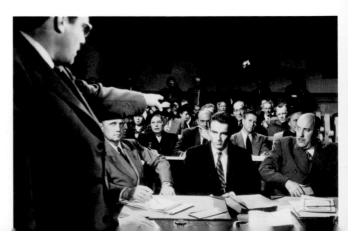

The Lavender Hill Mob Charles Crichton, 1951

G.B. (Ealing Studios, Rank) 78m BW
Producer Michael Balcon, Michael
Truman Screenplay T.E.B. Clarke
Photography Douglas Slocombe
Music Georges Auric Cast Alec Guinness,
Stanley Holloway, Sid James, Alfie Bass,
Marjorie Fielding, Edie Martin, John Salew,
Ronald Adam, Arthur Hambling, Gibb
McLaughlin, John Gregson, Clive Morton,
Sydney Tafler, Marie Burke, Audrey Hepburn
Oscar T.F.B. Clarke (screenplay)
Oscar nomination Alec Guinness (actor)

Along with the 1955 film *The Ladykillers*, also a stickup caper, *The Lavender Hill Mob* is the laugh-out-loud funniest of the celebrated Ealing comedies produced by Sir Michael Balcon and internationally beloved for their irreverent, ironic, inimitably British humor. Peerless Alec Guinness plays the bespectacled, insignificant bank clerk who has it in mind to finance a high-living retirement as recompense for a career being taken for granted. He plans a daring gold bullion robbery with souvenir maker Stanley Holloway and inept career burglars Sid James and Alfie Bass in one-time policeman T.F.B. "Tibby" Clarke's Oscar-winning screenplay.

The film is a master class in neat plotting and incident, served superbly by Charles Crichton's exhilarating direction, particularly of the loot snafu at the Eiffel Tower (Guinness and Holloway hurtling down the spiral stairs in vain pursuit of the English schoolgirls who have innocently purchased erroneously switched, solid gold models of the Parisian landmark) and the riotous chase climax (in which, at one point, a singing Welsh policeman grabs a ride on the running board of the aghast fleeing duo's car). Check out young Audrey Hepburn in the opening scene in Rio, where a benevolent, dapper Guinness tells his story to an interested party. **AE**

Journal d'un curé de campagne
Diary of a Country Priest Robert Bresson, 1951

France (UGC) 110m BW Language French
Screenplay Robert Bresson, from novel by
Georges Bernanos Producer Léon Carré,
Robert Sussfeld Photography Léonce-Henri
Burel Music Jean-Jacques Grunenwald
Cast Claude Laydu, Léon Arvel, Antoine
Balpêtré, Jean Danet, Jeanne Étiévant,
André Guibert, Bernard Hubrenne, Nicole
Ladmiral, Martine Lemaire, Nicole Maurey,
Louise (Mme. Louise) Martial Morange,
Jean Riveyre, Gaston Séverin, Gilberte
Terbois, Marie-Monique Arkell
Venice Film Festival Robert Bresson
(international award, Italian film
critics award, OCIC award, Golden
Lion nomination)

One of the cinema's greatest artists was searching for inspiration, and he found it in the *Diary of a Country Priest*. With imagination, courage, and rigor, Robert Bresson discovered that filmmaking did not require big budgets, stars, or special effects. The cinema could tell any story, provoke any emotion, open itself to all the material and immaterial, private and collective themes through the most elementary uses of its true nature.

Georges Bernanos's novel tells the tale of a young priest living in the countryside dealing with the difficulties of everyday life and the interrogation of his actions and his faith. Bernanos refuses to leave either believers or atheists in peace, opening up chasms in the concrete world. Bresson's adaptation of the *Diary of a Country Priest* is a humble achievement, one that shows what the Christian message is based on—a message that the cinema is designed to translate into images and sounds: the word made into flesh.

Cinema is the concrete and communal accomplishment of the Mystery of Incarnation. Bresson's film demonstrates that everything can become possible: joking with death, writing on the screen, playing with desire, watching the insights of the psyche, generating fascination for life in rural France in the mid-twentieth century, and confronting religious questions. **J-MF**

FROM OUT OF SPACE....
A WARNING AND AN ULTIMATUM!

THE DAY THE EARTH STOOD STILL

MICHAEL RENNIE · PATRICIA NEAL · HUGH MARLOWE

JULIAN BLAUSTEIN · ROBERT WISE · EDMUND H. NORTH

The Day the Earth Stood Still Robert Wise, 1951

Robert Wise's 1951 science-fiction drama based on *Farewell to the Master*, a short story by Harry Bates, hit a nerve with nuclear-war weary and politician-wary audiences of the time. Opening almost as a documentary, it spreads a chilling antiwar message via spectacular special effects and memorable characterizations. More than a B-movie, it is the first popular adult science-fiction film to send out a real message about humanity.

An alien emissary called Klaatu (Michael Rennie) lands in Washington, D.C., to deliver the message that war on Earth must stop. His spacecraft surrounded by guns and tanks, Klaatu is accidentally injured and whisked away to a military hospital, leaving only Gort (Lock Martin), a seven-foot-tall robot, to guard the craft. Faceless, speechless, and possessing a deadly laserlike ray, Gort is invincible. The only way to get him to stop defending the spacecraft is by uttering, "Gort, Klaatu barada niktoh," a sentence learned by heart by virtually every child who has seen the film.

Klaatu escapes from the hospital and meets Helen (Patricia Neal) and her son Bobby (Billy Gray). It is the beautiful, intelligent Helen who must disarm the deadly Gort. To prove his power and lend weight to his message of peace, Klaatu devises a plan to stop all mechanical movement in the world (with the exception of airplanes and hospitals).

The role of Klaatu was originally intended for Claude Rains but a scheduling conflict opened the part for Rennie, whose angular face and calm demeanor lend a remote, gentle superiority to the character. Neal, a symbol of feminine bravery, sums up the best of what humanity has to offer. Gort was played by Lock Martin, a 7'7" usher at Los Angeles' Graumann's Chinese Theater. Burdened by the heavy suit, Martin needed extra help to hold Neal in his arms, and in some scenes assisting wires are easily seen. To make the spacecraft appear seamless, the door crevice was puttied in and painted with silver. The putty tore open, allowing the door to suddenly appear without visual warning. Never bettered, *The Day the Earth Stood Still* is a classic on many fronts, not the least for its antiwar message and clever visual effects as well as Bernard Herrmann's haunting use of the theremin, an early electronic instrument. **KK**

U.S. (Fox) 92m BW **Producer** Julian Blaustein
Screenplay Harry Bates, Edmund H. North, from the story "Farewell to the Master" by Harry Bates **Photography** Leo Tover **Music** Bernard Herrmann **Cast** Michael Rennie, Patricia Neal, Hugh Marlowe, Sam Jaffe, Billy Gray, Frances Bavier, Lock Martin

"Your choice is simple. Join us and live in peace, or pursue your present course and face obliteration."

Klaatu (Michael Rennie)

1951

i

Lock Martin could only stay in the heavy Gort suit for around half an hour at a time while filming.

The Quiet Man John Ford, 1952

U.S. (Argosy, Republic) 129m Technicolor
Language English / Gaelic **Producer** Merian
C. Cooper, G.B. Forbes, John Ford, L.T. Rosso
Screenplay Frank S. Nugent, Maurice Walsh,
from the story "Green Rushes" by Maurice
Walsh **Photography** Winton C. Hoch
Music Victor Young **Cast** John Wayne,
Maureen O'Hara, Barry Fitzgerald, Ward
Bond, Victor McLaglen, Mildred Natwick,
Francis Ford, Eileen Crowe, May Craig, Arthur
Shields, Charles B. Fitzsimons, James Lilburn,
Sean McClory, Jack MacGowran, Joseph
O'Dea **Oscars** John Ford (director), Winton
C. Hoch, Archie Stout (photography)
Oscar nominations John Ford, Merian C.
Cooper (best picture), Frank S. Nugent
(screenplay), Victor McLaglen (actor in
support role), Frank Hotaling, John McCarthy
Jr., Charles S. Thompson (art direction),
Daniel J. Bloomberg (sound) **Venice Film
Festival** John Ford (international award,
OCIC award, Golden Lion nomination)

ℹ️

The Quiet Man was filmed in County
Galway, from where Ford's family
had emigrated to the United States.

Director John Ford is most famous for his celebrations of American history and culture, but he also made a number of films that explored his Celtic roots, of which *The Quiet Man* is perhaps the most successful. A mixture of drama and comedy, the film traces the homecoming of Irish-American Sean Thornton (John Wayne) to the "old sod," where he begins a passionate and stormy relationship with Mary Kate Danaher (Maureen O'Hara). *The Quiet Man* features plenty of Ford-style action, climaxing in ex-boxer Sean's fistfight with Mary's brother Will (Victor McLaglen) over his refusal to grant the American Mary's hand.

The battle ends with both men getting too drunk (during pauses in the action) to continue; they end as friends and, ultimately, family. Yet the film is not really about masculine values. Mary is much more than the simple object of their contention. Though she wants Sean, Mary refuses to go against her brother to marry him. Marrying Sean under these circumstances would be an insult to her. Later, when Will witholds her dowry—which represents her independent worth—Mary refuses to sleep with Sean before it is paid. The concluding boxing match settles both questions, however, and the couple is thereby reconciled.

Under Ford's astute direction, *The Quiet Man* plays off the conventional quaintness of the village against the beautiful natural scenery, resulting in a film that is serious enough to be affecting, but enough of a fantasy to be uproariously funny. **BP**

Jeux interdits René Clément, 1952
Forbidden Games

A good many films have heightened the absurdities and cruelties of human life by depicting them through the eyes of children, but few have done so more effectively, or more poignantly, than René Clément's finest film, *Forbidden Games*. The setting, as with much of Clément's best work, is World War II: A five-year-old girl, Paulette (Brigitte Fossey), is orphaned when her parents, fleeing Paris, are killed in an aerial attack. Grudgingly taken in by a peasant family, she forms a bond with the younger son, eleven-year-old Michel (Georges Poujouly), and the two create a secret world that reflects the death they see all around them. Collecting the corpses of animals and insects, they perform solemn rites over them and bury them in a disused barn, muttering half-understood phrases from the Catholic burial service. These, the "forbidden games" of the title, outrage the adults who discover them, and the children—distressed and bewildered—are torn apart.

Clément made his name with a dramatized documentary, *The Battle of the Rails* (1946), about the operations of the Resistance on the French rail network. Accordingly, the opening of *Forbidden Games* carries a powerfully realistic charge as German fighter planes bomb and machine-gun a straggling column of refugees. The sequence of the attack is all the more horrifying for relying entirely on natural sound effects, with no added music, and for taking place amid the soft summer warmth of the French countryside. But after this the film grows more stylized. On the one hand is the adult world of the peasants, seen through the puzzled, fascinated eyes of the children—the petty feuds and bickering are caricatured, with lip service paid to religion while lives are ruled by greed and malice. By contrast, the children are observed with tenderness and sympathy as they construct their hidden fantasy world, and their final, enforced separation is heartrending.

From his lead child actors, Clément draws remarkably expressive and convincing performances, free from cuteness; there's an instinctive grace in the boy's gentleness toward his young friend. Narciso Yepes contributes a lyrical solo guitar score, expressive in its simplicity. **PK**

France (Silver) 102m BW **Language** French **Producer** Robert Dorfmann **Screenplay** François Boyer, Jean Aurenche, Pierre Bost, René Clément, from the novel *Les Jeux Inconnus* by François Boyer **Photography** Robert Juillard **Music** Narciso Yepes **Cast** Georges Poujouly, Brigitte Fossey, Amédée, Laurence Badie, Madeleine Barbulée, Suzanne Courtal, Lucien Hubert, Jacques Marin, Pierre Merovée, Violette Monnier, Denise Péronne, Fernande Roy, Louis Saintève, André Wasle **Oscar** France (honorary award—best foreign language film) **Oscar nomination** François Boyer (screenplay) **Venice Film Festival** René Clément (Golden Lion)

> "I watched the film thirty-two times. I knew everything from memory."

Narciso Yepes, score composer, 1982

ⓘ

Though its authorship is disputed, Yepes said he based the music on a piece he wrote when he was seven.

Europa '51 Roberto Rossellini, 1952

Italy (Ponti-De Laurentiis) 113m BW
Language Italian Producer Dino
De Laurentiis, Roberto Rossellini
Screenplay Sandro De Feo, Mario
Pannunzio, Ivo Perilli, Brunello Rondi,
Roberto Rossellini Photography Aldo
Tonti Music Renzo Rossellini Cast Ingrid
Bergman, Alexander Knox, Ettore Giannini,
Giulietta Masina, Teresa Pellati, Sandro
Franchina, William Tubbs, Alfred Brown
Venice Film Festival Roberto Rossellini
(international award, Golden
Lion nomination)

Europa '51 contains the most unpredictable mixture of ingredients one can think of: a Scandinavian actress-turned-Hollywood movie star; the father of Italian Neorealism; a statement on the social conditions of cities in postwar Europe; a metaphysical meditation about the nature of good and evil and the inalienable right to self-determination; the opposition of the bourgeoisie and popular classes; the death of a child; the betrayal and redemption of a mother… mamma mia! But then the movie begins. It's simple, elegant, deeply moving, and incredibly alive.

In *Stromboli* (1950), Rossellini had turned Ingrid Bergman into a puppet submitting to the hand of God and the hand of her director (and lover). No such thing this time; only the daring invention—by the same filmmaker and star—of a fusion of the melodrama and the auteur film.

Each situation in *Europa '51* is composed of conventional stuff, and every scene is unexpected, filled with a disturbing sense of reality, of secret connections with real life. And it all takes places without any overly dramatic effect, without any kind of boasting—but, on the contrary, with an incredible modesty (by a director and an actress who were anything but humble) in the way the story is told, shot, and acted.

Europa '51 reaches a level of essential humanism rarely achieved in the cinema—and never by using heavy means. As Bergman's character, Irene Girard, walks through all the obstacles on her way to being called a saint by the people, the film itself walks its way through, escaping from all the sins it seems to have had to endure. A "saintly" film? Why not? **J-MF**

🛈

Composer Renzo Rossellini was the brother of the director, and the uncle of actress Isabella Rossellini.

MGM's *TECHNICOLOR MUSICAL TREASURE!*

GENE KELLY
DONALD O'CONNOR
DEBBIE REYNOLDS

JEAN HAGEN · MILLARD MITCHELL · CYD CHARISSE
BETTY COMDEN · ADOLPH GREEN
ARTHUR FREED · NACIO HERB BROWN · GENE KELLY · STANLEY DONEN · ARTHUR FREED

U.S. (MGM) 103m
Technicolor **Producer** Arthur Freed
Screenplay Betty Comden, Adolph Green
Photography Harold Rosson **Music** Nacio
Herb Brown, Lennie Hayton **Cast** Gene
Kelly, Donald O'Connor, Debbie Reynolds,
Jean Hagen, Millard Mitchell, Cyd
Charisse, Douglas Fowley, Rita Moreno
Oscar nominations Jean Hagen (actress in
support role), Lennie Hayton (music)

*"Gene was not afraid
of competition. If you
could be better than
he was, he loved it."*

Donald O'Connor, 2002

🛈

The title song's first on-screen use was
in *The Hollywood Revue of 1929*. It was
later in *A Clockwork Orange* (1971).

Singin' in the Rain Stanley Donen & Gene Kelly, 1952

Some films are held in high esteem for their artistic breakthroughs or stunning acting debuts. Others are revered simply for being the best of a kind. *Singin' in the Rain* falls into this latter category. It isn't a pioneer in any real sense of the word, nor does it greatly advance the language of film, but few other pictures have so effortlessly and wonderfully encapsulated everything good about the movies: the joyous highs, the pitiful lows, and the perfect, perpetual seesaw between the two.

It is wholly appropriate that the greatest of all Hollywood musicals should be in essence about sound itself. Or at least the arrival of sound. The year is 1927, and Don Lockwood (Gene Kelly) is a celebrated silent film star. In the middle of shooting another swashbuckler with his on-screen partner, Lina Lamont (Jean Hagan), the studio learns of the imminent debut of *The Jazz Singer* and shuts the production down. The only way for the film to compete is to transform it into a musical, but there are two problems: Don can barely stand his leading lady, Lina, and her thick New York accent will never work in the new era of sound films. The solution? Dub Lamont's horrible singing voice with that of ingénue Kathy (Debbie Reynolds) and hope that the public never finds out. But that stop-gap measure leads to yet another problem: Don has fallen in love with Kathy, which throws off his working relationship with Lina.

Codirected by Kelly and Stanley Donen (who had helmed 1949's *On the Town*), *Singin' in the Rain* features several great song-and-dance numbers, particularly Donald O'Connor's "Make 'Em Laugh" routine and Kelly's famous solo turn during the title song. Kelly, wearing a dark suit and a fedora, swings from a light pole and stomps ecstatically in puddles, so enamored is he of the new love in his life. The name of that classic song, remarked Donen, "seems like a wonderful title for the movie. But, at the time, the only reason to call it *Singin' in the Rain* was because the number turned out so well."

Oddly enough, several of the songs from *Singin' in the Rain* were actually recycled from MGM's music vaults, but Kelly and crew breathe such new life into them that they are now inextricably linked to this film. The screenplay, by Adolph Green and Betty Comden, is fleet and funny, parodying the rocky transition from silent films to talkies with the rapid wit only a generation of writing for the latter could foster.

Singin' in the Rain was nominated for two Oscars and a BAFTA award, while Kelly and Donen were nominated for Outstanding Directorial Achievement by the Directors Guild of America, and O'Connor secured a Golden Globe for Best Motion Picture Actor. But its enduring appeal is based not on trophies, but on joyful sequences and charismatic stars. Thank the repertoire circuit in part for crowning *Singin' in the Rain* as king of all musicals, thank numerous film critics and groups for placing it on the top ten list, but most of all thank Donen and Kelly for making it. The world of movies is a better place with *Singin' in the Rain* in it. **JKl**

The Bad and the Beautiful Vincente Minnelli, 1952

Still the best Hollywood-on-Hollywood movie, *The Bad and the Beautiful* is loosely based on the career of David O. Selznick, detouring to take in a few insider anecdotes about Val Lewton, Orson Welles, Raymond Chandler, Diana Barrymore, Alfred Hitchcock, and Irving Thalberg. Also note the silent but influential wife of the British director (played by Hitchcock regular Leo G. Carroll).

Three people with good cause to hate producer Jonathan Shields (Kirk Douglas) are gathered to take a phone call from Paris in which the washed-up Shields will pitch a new project. In flashbacks, they cover his up-from-Poverty Row career, remembering why they loathe him so much. Director Fred Amiel (Barry Sullivan) is an early partner who is inspired by Shields to make something of a cheap monster picture called *The Doom of the Cat Man* (think *Cat People*), but then shut out of his dream project, a hilariously "significant" Mexican project called *The Faraway Mountain*. Georgia Lorrison (Lana Turner), drunken trampy daughter of a John Barrymore-style hellraising star, is hauled out of the gutter and turned into a movie goddess, then dumped for an available slut (the wonderfully wry Elaine Stewart) on the night of the premiere. Least likely to forgive is professorial screenwriter James Lee Bartlow (Dick Powell), whose flighty, flirty distraction of a wife (Academy Award winner Gloria Grahame) Shields passes on to "Latin lover" Victor "Gaucho" Ribera (Gilbert Roland), who gets her killed in a plane crash.

No one can match Douglas as an ambitious megalomaniac, and this teeth-clenched, dimple-thrusting portrait is among his best work. The gossipy screenplay (another Oscar winner for Charles Schnee) is served wonderfully by director Vincente Minnelli's lush melodramatics and David Raksin's seductive score. In sixty years, the film has taken on more tragic-comic resonance as Selznick's reputation has nosedived— Shields's conviction that he is making great art worth sacrificing other people's lives for is all the more unsettling in that Minnelli allows glimpses of exactly the sort of bloated, self-important spectacle that now plays less well than more modest efforts. **KN**

U.S. (Loew's, MGM) 118m BW
Producer John Houseman
Screenplay George Bradshaw, Charles Schnee **Photography** Robert Surtees
Music David Raksin **Cast** Lana Turner, Kirk Douglas, Walter Pidgeon, Dick Powell, Barry Sullivan, Gloria Grahame, Gilbert Roland, Leo G. Carroll, Vanessa Brown, Paul Stewart, Sammy White, Elaine Stewart, Ivan Triesault
Oscars Charles Schnee (screenplay), Gloria Grahame (actress in support role), Cedric Gibbons, Edward C. Carfagno, Edwin B. Willis, F. Keogh Gleason (art direction), Robert Surtees (photography), Helen Rose (costume) **Oscar nomination** Kirk Douglas (actor)

i

Minnelli always wanted Kirk Douglas for the lead, but MGM head Dore Schary first approached Clark Gable.

Ikiru Akira Kurosawa, 1952
To Live

Japan (Toho) 143m BW Language
Japanese Producer Sojiro Motoki
Screenplay Shinobu Hashimoto, Akira
Kurosawa, Hideo Oguni Photography
Asakazu Nakai Music Fumio Hayasaka Cast
Takashi Shimura, Shinichi Himori, Haruo
Tanaka, Minoru Chiaki, Miki Odagiri, Bokuzen
Hidari, Minosuke Yamada, Kamatari Fujiwara,
Makoto Kobori, Nobuo Kaneko, Nobuo
Nakamura, Atsushi Watanabe, Isao Kimura,
Masao Shimizu, Yunosuke Ito Berlin
International Film Festival Akira Kurosawa
(special prize of the senate of Berlin)

Although best known for his samurai epics (*The Seven Samurai*, *Yojimbo*), Akira Kurosawa was not principally concerned with blood and guts—though arguably no other director has so thoroughly explored the potential of violent imagery on screen. Kurosawa was cinema's greatest humanist, and nowhere is this more evident than in *Ikiru*.

The film centers on Kenji Watanabe (Takashi Shimura), a bureaucrat whose greatest achievement—one he takes quite seriously—is that he hasn't missed a day of work in thirty years. This all changes when he learns he has cancer and has only a short time to live. In the last months of his life, Watanabe reconsiders his achievements (none) and priorities (none), and decides that it is not too late for him to change the world for the better. He devotes all his energies to the construction of a public park—a small gesture that nevertheless takes on great significance. Shimura gives the performance of his life: Moving with the look of a truly harrowed man, it is impossible not to feel Watanabe's pain.

Though full of sadness, *Ikiru* is ultimately spiritually uplifting. This was Kurosawa's point—to achieve anything like satisfaction or happiness, one must suffer. But suffering, too, is a part of life, and it can be used for good. *Ikiru* is immensely life-affirming, even if it is about death and sorrow. Kurosawa's gift was to show how these moods are not contradictory, but united as part of the cycle of life. His sincere belief that small things make a difference is both refreshing and touching. **EdeS**

i

Co-writer Hideo Oginu originally envisaged the Watanabe character as a gangster, not a bureaucrat.

Umberto D. Vittorio De Sica, 1952

This heart-wrenching film of a retired bureaucrat (Carlo Battisti) and his dog, Flike, will stay with you forever. Having made the Neorealist classic *The Bicycle Thief* (1948), director Vittorio De Sica and screenwriter Cesare Zavattini return to similar subject matter and method in *Umberto D*. Their technique is to structure the film around an emotionally charged and compelling personal story that reveals, in its telling, the general social conditions in which the story is set.

Umberto D. is shot on the streets of Rome, and the major parts are played by nonprofessional actors, adding to the film's immediacy and authenticity. One major criticism of Neorealism is that the melodramatic treatment of the small story dilutes the larger social message and claim to realism made by the film in question. With its unapologetic tragic story of an old man's despair and love for his pet, and its pointed observations of social injustice, *Umberto D.* provides the perfect opportunity for the viewer to consider this question.

Battisti, a retired professor, plays the title character with an understated sense of both dignity and resignation concerning his situation. Living on an insufficient pension, Umberto can barely afford his rented room, where he is at the mercy of his callous landlady, who wants to get rid of him. He shares the food he gets at a local charity with his dog, Flike, who is his sole companion and source of solace. As things get worse and worse for Umberto, he is on several occasions forced to choose between his own life and that of Flike. In one of the film's central sequences, Flike gets lost and Umberto fears that he will be destroyed at the city pound. As in *The Bicycle Thief*, the suspense built up around the ever-more-desperate search rivals a Hitchcock thriller. A pet who gives joy to a joyless existence is shown to be capable of generating the same interest and excitement as a set of blueprints for a secret weapon or a cache of stolen jewels in a more fantastic scenario. Here, De Sica leaves us wondering whether Umberto's love for his dog, who depends on him alone, is redemptory or futile. **RH**

Italy (Amato, De Sica, Rizzoli) 91m BW
Language Italian Producer Giuseppe Amato, Vittorio De Sica, Angelo Rizzolli Screenplay Cesare Zavattini Photography Aldo Graziati Music Alessandro Cicognini Cast Carlo Battisti, Maria-Pia Casilio, Lina Gennari, Ileana Simova, Elena Rea, Memmo Carotenuto Oscar nomination Cesare Zavattini (Best Writing)

"It's hard to think of a more remarkable tribute to the resilience of the human spirit than the one Umberto D. *puts on the screen."*

Kenneth Turan,
Los Angeles Times, 2002

i

De Sica was also an accomplished actor and was Oscar nominated for his role in *A Farewell to Arms* (1957).

High Noon Fred Zinnemann, 1952

U.S. (Stanley Kramer) 85m BW
Producer Carl Foreman, Stanley Kramer
Screenplay John W. Cunningham, Carl
Foreman, from the story "The Tin Star" by
John W. Cunningham **Photography** Floyd
Crosby **Music** Dimitri Tiomkin **Cast** Gary
Cooper, Thomas Mitchell, Lloyd Bridges, Katy
Jurado, Grace Kelly, Otto Kruger, Lon Chaney
Jr., Harry Morgan, Ian MacDonald, Eve
McVeagh, Morgan Farley, Harry Shannon, Lee
Van Cleef, Robert J. Wilke, Sheb Wooley
Oscars Gary Cooper (actor), Elmo Williams,
Harry W. Gerstad (editing), Dimitri Tiomkin
(music), Dimitri Tiomkin, Ned Washington
(song) **Oscar nominations** Stanley Kramer
(best picture), Fred Zinnemann (director), Carl
Foreman (screenplay)

One Sunday morning in the tamed western town of Hadleyville, New Mexico, as Marshal Will Kane (Gary Cooper) is about to marry a peace-loving Quaker (Grace Kelly), news arrives that Frank Miller (Ian MacDonald)—the psycho Kane previously put away—has been pardoned and is due in on the 12 P.M. train. As Miller's most vicious accomplices (including a harmonica-sucking Lee Van Cleef) loiter at the station, the Marshal appeals for help. But the townspeople (colleagues, friends, dignitaries) refuse to risk their lives and stand by him against the outlaw who wants not only revenge but to run Hadleyville again.

Various clocks reveal that it's getting near noontime; everyone urges Kane to leave town, but the Cooper-style hero must face his responsibilities. *High Noon* plays out in real time, the deadline ticking closer and closer as the ballad theme song ("Do Not Forsake Me Oh My Darling") insists on the situation, with those the Marshal assumes will help him falling like ninepins. In a finale that remains potent even in these days of one-man-against-an-army action movies, he is left almost alone against four villains. Fred Zinnemann's film is at once a great suspense Western and a stark allegory of the climate of fear and suspicion prevailing during the McCarthy era. **KN**

1953

Le carrosse d'or Jean Renoir, 1953
The Golden Coach

Italy / France (Hoche, Panaria) 103m
Technicolor **Producer** Francesco Alliata,
Renzo Avanzo **Screenplay** Renzo Avanzo,
Jack Kirkland, Ginette Doynel, Giulio
Macchi, Jean Renoir, from the play *Le
Carrosse du Saint-Sacrement* by Prosper
Mérimée **Photography** Claude Renoir
Original music Antonio Vivaldi **Cast** Anna
Magnani, Odoardo Spadaro, Nada Fiorelli,
Dante, Duncan Lamont, George Higgins,
Ralph Truman, Gisella Mathews, Raf De La
Torre, Elena Altieri, Paul Campbell, Riccardo
Rioli, William Tubbs, Jean Debucourt

The first in Jean Renoir's loose "theater" trilogy (with *French Cancan* [1955] and *Elena and Her Men* [1956]), this Italian–French co-production features an Anglo-Italian cast led by the indefatigable Anna Magnani. In the English-language version, she laments the difficulty of acting in a foreign language in her inimitably thick Italian accent. She plays Camilla, Columbine in a *commedia dell'arte* troupe that arrives in eighteenth-century Peru. Instead of streets paved with gold, they find no pavement at all—they even have to build the theater they're due to play at.

"What do they make of the new world?"

"It'll be nice when they finish it."

Despite Camilla's first impressions, she is soon being courted by three eligible suitors, one of them the Spanish viceroy (Duncan Lamont), who presents her with the golden coach of the title. Alas, for an actor, sincerity in life is no guarantee of a happy ending. The movie's surface frivolity and farcical plotting camouflage a mature, even melancholy film about the fraught relations between love, art, and life. François Truffaut called it "the noblest and most refined film ever made . . . It is all breeding and politeness, grace, and freshness . . . a film about theater in the theater." Antonio Vivaldi provides the soundtrack and Renoir's brother Claude the exquisite color cinematography. **TCh**

Sommaren med Monika Ingmar Bergman, 1953
Summer with Monika

Sweden (Svensk Filmindustri) 96m BW
Screenplay Ingmar Bergman, PA Fogelström
Photography Gunnar Fischer Music Erik
Nordgren, Filip Olsson Cast Harriet
Andersson, Lars Ekborg, John Harryson, Lars
Skarstedt, Dagmar Ebbesen, Naemi Briese,
Åke Fridell, Gösta Eriksson, Sigge Fürst

Nowhere in all of Ingmar Bergman's films is sensual joy more overwhelming than in the long, island-set section at the heart of *Summer with Monika*—not just in the eroticism between lovers Monika (Harriet Andersson) and Harry (Lars Ekborg), but in the natural world of Ornö, the island in the Stockholm archipelago where they play out their newfound infatuation. Much of this passion derives from real life—Bergman had just discovered the twenty-year-old Andersson, and almost as soon as shooting started the pair embarked on an affair. The film is virtually a love poem to Andersson; she was to become one of Bergman's favorite actresses, appearing in eight of his films.

The joyous light of this summer idyll (vividly conveyed by Gunnar Fischer's lyrical photography) is all the more poignant for the urban gloom of the scenes that precede and follow it. Reverting to the poetic, realism-influenced style of his early work, Bergman shows us the squalid life Monika's escaping from: the cramped apartment, the brutal father, the mother hollowed out with child rearing. But when she and Harry return to Stockholm and set up home together, with her pregnant, the drabness settles in again. The ending is ambiguous: Is Monika slipping into a world of prostitution, or asserting her independence? Her defiant gaze, straight into the camera, could be read either way. **PK**

Pickup on South Street Samuel Fuller, 1953

U.S. (Fox) 80m BW Producer Jules Schermer
Screenplay Samuel Fuller, from story by
Dwight Taylor Photography Joseph
MacDonald Music Leigh Harline
Cast Richard Widmark, Jean Peters, Thelma
Ritter, Murvyn Vye, Richard Kiley, Willis
Bouchey, Jerry O'Sullivan, Harry Carter,
George E. Stone, George Eldredge, Stuart
Randall, Frank Kumagai, Victor Perry, Emmett
Lynn, Parley Baer Oscar nomination Thelma
Ritter (actress in support role)
Venice Film Festival Samuel Fuller
nomination (Golden Lion)

A minor phenomenon of the early Cold War, the anticommunist spy film genre produced one masterpiece, *Pickup on South Street*. The plot revolves around a pickpocket who must choose between patriotism and profit after he swipes a top secret microfilm. *Pickup* transcends its subgenre through its dynamic style and vivid depiction of New York lowlife. Samuel Fuller displays a prodigious range of stylistic invention, finding fresh visual concepts for nearly every scene. The key ingredient is the close-up, with the camera shoved in the actors' faces so aggressively you can almost see their breath fogging the lens. These copious close-ups signal the film's placement of the intimate over the ideological, its endorsement of actions motivated not by abstractions but by love, loyalty, and guilt on the closest personal level.

The main actors never did better work: cocky cynic Richard Widmark, bighearted bimbo Jean Peters, sweaty rat Richard Kiley, and, especially, unapologetic stoolie Thelma Ritter. The most powerful scene depicts a weary Ritter facing obliteration by gunman Kiley. In a film so devoted to the personal, it is fitting that her greatest fear is not death itself but an unmarked grave. As she says in one of the script's many punchy lines, "If I was to be buried in Potter's Field, it would just about kill me!" **MR**

The Band Wagon Vincente Minnelli, 1953

Like *Singin' in the Rain*, Vincente Minnelli's *The Band Wagon* is a musical that affectionately reflects upon the history of its genre—in order to pioneer a new, "integrated" style based on character and plot while also enjoying the benefits of the old, "revue" style. It cleverly does so by making Fred Astaire a dinosaur in a modern, showbiz milieu and giving him a trial wherein he must grapple with the overbearing vision of an Orson Welles–like director (Jack Buchanan) and ultimately affirm his worth as an old-fashioned but adaptable "hoofer" in a dynamic hit show.

Like most musicals, *The Band Wagon* is about compromise. The characters symbolize the extremes of lowbrow and highbrow culture: Tony Hunter (Astaire) versus his reluctant leading lady, Gabrielle Gerard (Cyd Charisse) from ballet. But when push comes to shove, such cultural divisions break down easily: Tony turns out to be a fine art connoisseur, and Gaby will belt out "I See a New Sun" on stage like a song-and-dance trouper. This aesthetic melding is also a literal romance, clinched by the immortal pas de deux in Central Park, "Dancing in the Dark."

Mainly, however, *The Band Wagon* is a delightfully colorful "montage of attractions"—starting with the high-energy comedic contributions of Nanette Fabray and Oscar Levant, alter egos for the writers Betty Comden and Adolph Green. Minnelli gets to show off many kinds of mise-en-scène: playing on décor and architecture in the scene where Buchanan pitches his "Faust" while characters in three adjoining rooms eavesdrop; fluidly moving a group of performers through switches in mood in the indelible "That's Entertainment"; enjoying the purely theatrical novelty of the kooky number "Triplets."

But the ultimate spectacle is the eleven-minute "Girl Hunt: A Murder Mystery in Jazz," a film noir parody (in vibrant color), in which Michael Kidd's choreography explodes in stylized arabesques of familiar gestures (shooting, smoking, fighting) and the stars turn on their glamour, whether in erotic display (Charisse) or the simple joy of walking (Astaire). **AM**

U.S. (MGM) 111m Technicolor
Producer Arthur Freed **Screenplay** Betty Comden, Adolph Green **Photography** Harry Jackson **Music** Arthur Schwartz (songs)
Cast Fred Astaire, Cyd Charisse, Oscar Levant, Nanette Fabray, Jack Buchanan, James Mitchell, Robert Gist
Oscar nominations Betty Comden, Adolph Green (screenplay), Mary Ann Nyberg (costume), Adolph Deutsch (music)

"Of all the many musicals Fred Astaire was in, the very best for my money is [The Band Wagon]."

Peter Bogdanovich, 2010

i

The movie was inspired by Arthur Askey and Richard Murdoch's British radio show of the same name.

1953

France (Cady Films, Specta Films) 114m BW
Language French **Producer** Fred Orain
Screenplay Jacques Tati, Henri Marquet,
Pierre Aubert, Jacques Lagrange
Photography Jacques Mercanton, Jean
Moussselle **Music** Alain Romans
Cast Nathalie Pascaud, Michèle Rolla,
Raymond Carl, Lucien Frégis, Valentine
Camax **Oscar nomination** Jacques Tati,
Henri Marquet (screenplay)

"The central character is an unforgettable amalgam of bafflement at the modern world, eagerness to please, and just the right amount of eccentricity."

Simon O'Hagan,
The Independent on Sunday, 2003

i

Jacques Tati would go on to reprise
the role of the gangly, awkward
Mr. Hulot in another four features.

Les vacances de M. Hulot Jacques Tati, 1953
Mr. Hulot's Holiday

This enduring classic of French cinema revealed Jacques Tati, in only his second feature as a director, to be one of the medium's most inventive and original stylists. A virtually plotless and wordless succession of incidents occurring at a beachside resort, the film milks laughter from the most seemingly banal minutiae of everyday life. Alongside the elaborately staged events—such as a pack of travelers racing from one train platform to the next as incomprehensibly distorted loudspeaker messages blare—there are many droll, lovely moments where nothing much is happening at all. People just sit, eat, read, and stare, determined to be in vacation mode at all times. The stoic silliness of it all is infectious.

Tati understood as finely as Alfred Hitchcock that mise-en-scène is not something to be imposed by filmmakers but discovered within the rituals of everyday life: how close people sit to each other in a dining room; the codes governing when people are allowed to look at one another; all the rules of etiquette and public deportment in play during the free-but-structured time of the French vacation period.

The film rigorously controls the comic timing, spatial setups, and post-synchronized sounds of its brilliantly conceived gags—even the oft-repeated noise of a spring door is funny, due to the way Tati "musicalizes" it. He takes familiar gag forms—like the Keatonesque manner in which the hero imitates an exercise freak—and then makes them strange through the way he shoots and cuts the action, often quickly switching attention to another gag beginning nearby.

Although in his later films Tati deliberately restricted his own on-screen appearances, here his eponymous Hulot is a major source of charm and hilarity—and there is even the poignant trace of a tentative but missed love intrigue. Forever hesitating before entering any space, forever apologizing and politely greeting everyone present once he does, Hulot cannot fail to trigger some calamity with his overanxious movements—resulting in the cinema's most inspired display of fireworks. **AM**

Madame de . . . Max Ophüls, 1953

France / Italy (Franco London, Indus, Rizzoli) 105m BW **Language** French **Producer** Ralph Baum **Screenplay** Marcel Achard, Max Ophüls, Annette Wademant, from the novel *Madame de* by Louise de Vilmorin **Photography** Christian Matras **Music** Oscar Straus, Georges Van Parys **Cast** Charles Boyer, Danielle Darrieux, Vittorio De Sica, Jean Debucourt, Jean Galland, Mireille Perrey, Paul Azaïs, Josselin Hubert Noël, Lia Di Leo **Oscar nomination** Georges Annenkov, Rosine Delamare (costume)

i

Apart from the central theme of the earrings, the film's plot differs greatly from de Vilmorin's source novel.

Few films establish so much, with such economy, as the sublime *Madame de . . . .* Louise (Danielle Darrieux) is "Madame de . . ." because she is anonymous, typical of her privileged class; it is only the earrings we see in the opening frames—about to be pawned—that launch her into a drama. From the first image of Louise in a mirror, amid her material possessions, director Max Ophüls does not let us overlook the underpinnings of this wealthy world: the flows of money and debt, the servants on call, the etiquette of preparation before public appearances.

At the opera, where all is show, we meet Louise's husband, André (Charles Boyer), "debonair" as long as he can control the affairs that define this "sophisticated" marriage. By the third time the earrings come back into André's hands—and Louise has fallen dangerously in love with Donati (Vittorio De Sica)—what could have easily been a cute conceit comes to articulate all the fine distinctions of plot and theme. For Louise, who lives in denial about the conditions that enable her supposed freedom, the earrings are a token of her love with Donati; for André, they are a sign of the power he wields over other people's destinies.

Madame de . . . is by turns brutal, compassionate, and moving. Ophüls delineates this world with Brechtian precision, yet he never discounts the significance of stifled, individual yearnings. Even as the characters writhe in their metaphoric prisons or shut traps on each other, their passions touch us: supremely, when André closes the windows on Louise like a jailer as he declares, half whispering in secret, "I love you." **AM**

Le salaire de la peur Henri-Georges Clouzot, 1953
Wages of Fear

France / Italy (CICC, Filmsonor, Fono, Vera) 141m BW **Language** French / English / Spanish / German **Producer** Raymond Borderie, Henri-Georges Clouzot, Louis Wipf **Screenplay** Henri-Georges Clouzot, Jérôme Géronimi, from novel by Georges Arnaud **Photography** Armand Thirard **Music** Georges Auric **Cast** Yves Montand, Charles Vanel, Peter van Eyck, Antonio Centa, Darling Légitimus, Luis De Lima, Jo Dest, Darío Moreno, Faustini, Seguna, William Tubbs, Véra Clouzot, Folco Lulli, Jeronimo Mitchell **Berlin International Film Festival** Henri-Georges Clouzot (Golden Bear) **Cannes Film Festival** Henri-Georges Clouzot (grand prize of the festival), Charles Vanel (special mention—acting)

i

The town segment at the start of the movie was at one point cut because of its political sentiment.

A withering depiction of greed and the corrupting influence of capitalism disguised as an adventure film, Henri-Georges Clouzot's *Wages of Fear* is possibly the most tension-filled movie ever made. Set in South America, two teams compete to transport a truckload of nitroglycerin along a three-hundred mile mountain pass to the site of an oil refinery fire so that the oil company can then blow the pipeline and put out the blaze. The catch? Notoriously unstable and sensitive, the nitro cargo will blow the drivers to bits if they're not exceedingly careful.

With sadistic invention, Clouzot throws as many obstacles as he can in the way of the two trucks as they race (at a snail's pace) through the bumpy mountain pass. It isn't the promise of glory that sets each pair of drivers on such a dangerous task, but the promise of cash, and as the film proceeds you begin to wonder how far they will go for the money.

Vitally, Clouzot precedes the action with a long segment set in a slum of a South American crossroads, where wanderers and vagabonds end up after they have nowhere else to go, and where we learn that the rogues willing to risk their lives for money are almost not worth knowing. Their suicidal actions are driven by selfishness and desperation, traits exploited by the opportunistic corporation. Indeed, full of distrust and dislike, the mercenaries pose as much of a threat to one another as the truckloads of explosives do to them all. It's a lose-lose situation, as the finish line promises financial reward at the cost of spiritual ruin. **JKl**

The Bigamist Ida Lupino, 1953

U.S. (Filmmakers) 80m BW **Producer** Collier Young **Screenplay** Larry Marcus, Lou Schor, Collier Young **Photography** George E. Diskant **Music** Leith Stevens **Cast** Joan Fontaine, Edmund Gwenn, Ida Lupino, Edmond O'Brien, Kenneth Tobey, Jane Darwell, Peggy Maley

This haunting film is one of several out-of-nowhere masterpieces directed during a too-brief period by Ida Lupino, considered "the poor man's Bette Davis" when she was a hard-boiled Warner Brothers star in the 1940s. Edmond O'Brien stars as Harry Graham, a refrigerator salesman who, from shambling clumsily through life, ends up with two wives, Eve (Joan Fontaine) and Phyllis (Lupino), each unaware of the other's existence. Lupino's understated direction enfolds the characters with discreet, helpless pity.

Such drama as there is in *The Bigamist* is born from the sadness of three people: Harry's loneliness, Eve's sorrow over her father's death and her inability to conceive a child, and Phyllis's reluctance to have Harry acknowledge her because she doesn't want to be a burden to him. The whole film is the crystallization of this collective sadness in terms of environment (San Francisco and Los Angeles as the settings of Harry's dual life), deportment (Harry's numbed, pained passivity; Phyllis's hard-bitten isolation; Eve's desperate and pathetic attempt to be both the perfect wife and the perfect business partner), and, above all, the looks shared or half-avoided between people. In the shattering final courtroom scene, the orchestration of these looks achieves a combination of ambiguity and intensity that recalls both Carl Dreyer and Nicholas Ray. **CFu**

The Naked Spur Anthony Mann, 1953

U.S. (Loew's, MGM) 91m Technicolor **Producer** William H. Wright **Screenplay** Sam Rolfe, Harold Jack Bloom **Photography** William C. Mellor **Music** Bronislau Kaper **Cast** James Stewart, Janet Leigh, Robert Ryan, Ralph Meeker, Millard Mitchell **Oscar nomination** Sam Rolfe, Harold Jack Bloom (screenplay)

The third of the remarkable series of Westerns director Anthony Mann made with James Stewart in the 1950s, *The Naked Spur* has Stewart as Howard Kemp, an embittered bounty hunter trying to earn money to buy back the ranch he lost when his wife was unfaithful to him during the Civil War. Along the trail he falls in with Jesse (Millard Mitchell), an elderly prospector, and Anderson (Ralph Meeker), a renegade army officer. Eventually, Stewart gets his man, a sardonic killer named Ben (Robert Ryan), but Kemp's troubles are just beginning. The arduous journey through the wilderness to bring Ben to justice tests Kemp to the limits.

What makes this an exceptional film is, first, the tautly scripted and finely acted exploration of the tensions between the characters: Kemp and Ben each strive to gain psychological supremacy, with Ben using his girlfriend Lina (Janet Leigh) as bait as he senses Kemp's vulnerability beneath the tough exterior. James Stewart gives a brilliant portrayal of a man on the edge of hysteria. Second, Mann has a wonderful way with mountain scenery, using the arduous nature of the terrain as a physical counterpoint to the characters' inner turmoil. Virtually the entire film was shot on location. **EB**

Tokyo Story Yasujiro Ozu, 1953

"Isn't life disappointing?" asks a teenage girl of her widowed sister-in-law at her mother's funeral. "Yes," comes the answer—with a smile. This brief exchange, near the close of Yasujiro Ozu's masterpiece *Tokyo Story*, typifies the unsentimental mood of calm acceptance that distinguishes his work. The performances, setting (the middle-class home the girl has shared with, until now, both of her elderly parents), and dialogue are wholly naturalistic in tone, and never for a moment seem as if they've been arranged as part of some grand climax; yet by the time the words are uttered, they carry enormous emotional and philosophical weight.

Ozu's films were marvelously understated, deceptively simple affairs, mostly depicting the everyday domestic and professional rituals of middle-class Japanese life with an idiosyncratic lack of emphasis (dramatic or stylistic) that might mislead the inattentive into believing them banal. Here, all that happens is that the old folks leave their youngest daughter at home in the provinces to visit their other children in Tokyo; they've never been to the capital, but make the effort in the knowledge that time is running short. But the kids have their own families now and shunt their parents around, barely disguising their need to get on with their busy lives in postwar Japan. Only their daughter-in-law, who lost her husband in the war, seems to have enough time for them. Not that they'd complain, any more than she would.

All this is observed, as was Ozu's custom, with a static camera placed a couple of feet off the ground; there is only one shot in the film that moves—and even then it tracks with inconspicuous slowness. So how does Ozu hold our attention, when what we see or hear is so uninflected by what most viewers consider dramatic or unusual? It all comes down to the contemplative quality of his gaze, implying that any human activity, however "unimportant," is worthy of our attention. In contrast to his own particular (and particularly illuminating) cinematic style, his characters' experiences, emotions, and thoughts are as "universal" as anything in the movies—a paradox that has rightly enshrined this film's reputation as one of the greatest ever made. **GA**

Japan (Shochiku) 136m BW
Language Japanese **Producer** Takeshi Yamamoto **Screenplay** Kôgo Noda, Yasujiro Ozu **Photography** Yuharu Atsuta **Music** Kojun Saitô **Cast** Chishu Ryu, Chieko Higashiyama, Setsuko Hara, Haruko Sugimura, Sô Yamamura, Kuniko Miyake, Kyôko Kagawa, Eijirô Tono, Nobuo Nakamura, Shirô Osaka, Hisao Toake, Teruko Nagaoka, Mutsuko Sakura, Toyoko Takahashi, Toru Abe

"Ozu is not only a great director but a great teacher, and, after you know his films, a friend."

Roger Ebert, critic, 2003

ⓘ

Co-writer Kôga Noda noted that the writing of *Tokyo Story* took 103 days and forty-three bottles of sake.

From Here to Eternity Fred Zinnemann, 1953

Notwithstanding the famously iconic scene of Burt Lancaster and Deborah Kerr rolling and smooching in the Hawaiian surf, Fred Zinnemann's version of James Jones's best seller about life on a U.S. Army base in 1941 immediately prior to the Japanese attack on Pearl Harbor is a somewhat modified affair. Although the language, the sex, and the violence may have been toned down, the focus on adultery, prostitution, corruption, and sadistic bullying ensured that *From Here to Eternity* was welcomed as an unusually adult Hollywood movie worthy of eight Oscars. With the passing of time, the film's sensationalist elements have come to feel less daring, and it's the vivid performances of its starry cast that now stick in the memory. Lancaster is the principled but pragmatic Sergeant Warden. Montgomery Clift is Prewitt, the bugler new to the barracks (whose conscientious refusal to box for his platoon's team provokes prejudicial treatment by the officers), and Frank Sinatra is his friend Maggio, picked on by obnoxious stockade sergeant Fatso (a memorable Ernest Borgnine). Inevitably, perhaps, in this deeply "masculine" study of rugged courage and individual honor in conflict with the conformist expectations of the community at large, the actresses fare less well. English rose Kerr is just slightly self-conscious as a sultry American adulteress, and Donna Reed plays a dancehall whore passed off as a hostess.

Zinnemann probably wasn't quite right to direct such fare. A rather meticulous craftsman who progressed from modest but reasonably efficient fillers to rather self-consciously "significant" films, he was here at what would prove a turning point in his career. The Oscars meant he could go on to more conspicuous "quality" films, but this movie might have benefited from a less cautiously "realistic" touch. After all, it's really a melodrama, and a touch of lurid expressionism would not have gone amiss. That said, the film is good on the dynamics of bullying, on officers conveniently turning a blind eye to misdemeanors, and on the prejudices that infect any closed group. Plus, he did get those sturdy performances out of his actors. And after that roll in the surf, barracks life would never seem the same again. **GA**

U.S. (Columbia) 118m BW
Producer Buddy Adler **Screenplay** James Jones, Daniel Taradash, from novel by James Jones **Photography** Burnett Guffey **Music** George Duning, James Jones, Fred Karger, Robert Wells **Cast** Burt Lancaster, Montgomery Clift, Deborah Kerr, Donna Reed, Frank Sinatra, Philip Ober, Mickey Shaughnessy, Harry Bellaver, Ernest Borgnine, Jack Warden, John Dennis, Merle Travis, Tim Ryan, Arthur Keegan, Barbara Morrison **Oscars** Buddy Adler (best picture), Fred Zinnemann (director), Daniel Taradash (screenplay), Frank Sinatra (actor in support role), Donna Reed (actress in support role), Burnett Guffey (photography), William A. Lyon (editing), John P. Livadary (sound) **Oscar nominations** Montgomery Clift (actor), Burt Lancaster (actor), Deborah Kerr (actress), Jean Louis (costume design, BW), Morris Stoloff, George Duning (music)

"*Nobody ever lies about being lonely.*"

**Robert E. Lee "Prew" Prewitt
(Montgomery Clift)**

i

The scene in which Prew meets Maggio and Lorene in the bar was actually Frank Sinatra's screen test.

Ugetsu monogatari Kenji Mizoguchi, 1953
Tales of Ugetsu

In the mid-1950s, when the international circuit of film festivals got underway, the cineastes of the West finally discovered what their Japanese counterparts had known for years: This Kenji Mizoguchi fellow was really something special. *Ugetsu monogatari* (literally, *The Story of Ugetsu*; commonly known simply as *Ugetsu*) was the film on which the international gaze focused. Though it is not necessarily Mizoguchi's best (that honor could just as easily go to the profoundly moving 1939 film *The Story of the Late Chrysanthemums*), it is the one for which he is still best known in Europe and America, and surely one of the great masterpieces of world cinema.

Mizoguchi had been writing and directing films since the 1920s, but we have no one, really, to blame for the fact that his work went largely unseen in the West, because Japan's was an insular film market. But when *Ugetsu* did hit Western shores, it hit hard; critics from Europe and the United States alike praised it vigorously, heralding it as the bellwether of an entirely new way of filmmaking. They may have been correct. But what is it that makes *Ugetsu* so remarkable?

Key to the film is the mixing of the real and the supernatural, a theme that infiltrates Mizoguchi's framing and his actors' performances at every turn. The master pulls us from one realm of existence into the other—sometimes with warning, sometimes without. Mizoguchi's control over his film's tone is precise; the aura of unearthliness and unholiness never quite dissipates.

But this is no ordinary ghost story. *Ugetsu* uses the real/supernatural split to explore issues of love, honor, responsibility, and family; each one of these themes is touched in some way by the ghost world Mizoguchi carefully maps atop the familiar world, and not one of them emerges unchanged. The foolish men and the long-suffering women of *Ugetsu* all go through wrenching transformations brought about by the interaction of the supernatural with the real.

Ugetsu is troubling, perplexing, and beautiful. Mostly, though, it is truly humbling: To watch it is to be in the presence of greatness. **EdeS**

Japan (Daiei) 94m BW
Language Japanese **Producer** Masaichi Nagata **Screenplay** Matsutarô Kawaguchi, Akinari Ueda, Yoshikata Yoda, from stories "*Asaji Ga Yado*" and "*Jasei No In*" by Akinari Ueda **Photography** Kazuo Miyagawa **Music** Fumio Hayasaka, Tamekichi Mochizuki, Ichirô Saitô **Cast** Masayuki Mori, Machiko Kyô, Kinuyo Tanaka, Eitarô Ozawa, Ikio Sawamura, Mitsuko Mito, Kikue Môri, Ryosuke Kagawa, Eigoro Onoe, Saburo Date, Sugisaku Aoyama, Reiko Kondo Shozo Nanbu, Kozabuno Ramon, Ichirô Amano **Oscar nomination** Kusune Kainosho (costume) **Venice Film Festival** Kenji Mizoguchi (Silver Lion, Golden Lion nomination)

> *"One of the greatest of all films."*
>
> **Roger Ebert, critic, 2004**

i

Mizoguchi was famous for his "scroll shots," which panned across the landscape like a scroll painting.

France / Italy (Titanus, Italia, Junior, Ariane, S.E.C., SCG, Sveva) 100m BW
Language English / Italian Producer Adolfo Fossataro, Alfredo Guarini, Roberto Rossellini Screenplay Vitaliano Brancati, Roberto Rossellini Photography Enzo Serafin Music Renzo Rossellini Cast Ingrid Bergman, George Sanders, Leslie Daniels, Natalia Ray, Maria Mauban, Anna Proclemer, Jackie Frost, Paul Müller

"After eight years of marriage, it seems like we don't know anything about each other."

Alex Joyce
(George Sanders)

Viaggio in Italia Roberto Rossellini, 1953
Voyage in Italy

French director Jacques Rivette once wrote that Roberto Rossellini's *Voyage in Italy* "opens a breach [that] all cinema, on pain of death, must pass through." This is evident from the first shots, sudden and raw—a shaky, forward-driving view down a road into Naples; a glimpse of the landscape going by; and finally two stars, Ingrid Bergman and George Sanders, shipwrecked far from Hollywood in a plotless, not-quite-picaresque road-movie cruise in which they express the deepest levels of character through terse banalities and simple, mundane gestures.

Nowadays, critics talk about the "comedy of remarriage," a genre in which couples put their union to the test and, after many complications, reaffirm it. *Voyage in Italy* is that rarer thing: a drama of remarriage, where the spark of revitalization must be found within the undramatic flow of daily togetherness. The Joyces, Alex (Sanders) and Katherine (Bergman), bored and resentful of each other, are in a state of suspension. Being on vacation leaves them disquieted by the foreign culture that surrounds them. The food is different, sleep beckons at odd hours, and there are encounters with strangers who offer distraction or temptation.

And then there is the landscape, the cities of Naples, Capri, and Pompei. *Voyage in Italy* typifies the radical turn in Rossellini's work of the 1950s: no longer "social issue" Neorealism, but an inner, emotional realism, prefiguring Michelangelo Antonioni and especially the Jean-Luc Godard of *Contempt* (1963). But there is still a sense of documentary reality in the views Katherine sees from her car, in the churches, catacombs, mud pools, and archaeological excavations. This insistent environment adds context, history, and even mythology to the personal, marital story. It brings the past to bear upon the present, prompting the characters to endlessly recall formative moments. And it places this one small crisis into a great cosmic cycle of birth, death, and rebirth.

Little is explained in *Voyage in Italy*, but everything is felt: This is a film that can proudly end—just before yet another shot of a passing crowd—with a sweeping crane shot and the age-old declaration "I love you." **AM**

ℹ️ Martin Scorsese paid homage to the movie in the title of his 1999 documentary, *My Voyage in Italy*.

U.S. (Paramount) 118m Technicolor
Producer Ivan Moffat, George Stevens
Screenplay A.B. Guthrie Jr., from story by
Jack Schaefer **Photography** Loyal Griggs
Music Victor Young **Cast** Alan Ladd. Jean
Arthur, Van Heflin, Brandon De Wilde, Jack
Palance, Ben Johnson, Edgar Buchanan,
Emile Meyer, Elisha Cook Jr., Douglas
Spencer, John Dierkes, Ellen Corby, Paul
McVey, John Miller, Edith Evanson
Oscar Loyal Griggs (photography)
Oscar nominations George Stevens (best
picture), George Stevens (director), A.B.
Guthrie Jr. (screenplay), Brandon De Wilde
(actor in support role), Jack Palance
(actor in support role)

"Shane *is in a class by
itself . . . if I was making a
list of the best American
movies,* Shane *would
be on it.*"

Woody Allen, 2001

i

The scene where Alan Ladd practices
shooting in front of Brandon De
Wilde took 119 takes to complete.

Shane George Stevens, 1953

Shane is not the most glorious Western (that honor must go to *El Dorado*
[1967]), nor the most masculine (that would be *Red River* [1948]), most
authentic (*McCabe & Mrs. Miller* [1971]), strangest (*Johnny Guitar* [1954]),
or most dramatic (*Stagecoach* [1939]). But it is surely the most iconic, the
Western that burns itself into our memory, the Western no one who sees
it will ever forget. Everything in the film, in fact, is a pure image: the hero
in white buckskin who happens to ride into town (Alan Ladd); the
conniving rancher (Emile Meyer) with his mangy, ill-mannered cowboys;
the humble homesteader (Van Heflin) with his doting, dutiful,
domesticating wife (Jean Arthur) and twinkle-eyed son (Brandon De
Wilde); the taciturn, cautious, aging bartender and owner of the general
store (Paul McVey); the timid Swedish settler (Douglas Spencer); and the
dark, sinuous, slimy personification of Evil Incarnate, Wilson the hired
gun (Jack Palance, dressed in black from head to toe). Indeed, the
characters alone are the story.

The rancher wants the homesteader's land. Shane settles in with the
homesteader to help him protect it, in the process charming the tidy
wife—perhaps a little too much—and the goggle-eyed boy completely
out of his childhood. Wilson is imported to clean out the settlers, and,
but for the intervention of Shane—gun to gun, eye to eye, nobility vs.
evil—he would surely succeed. But Good triumphs, so very deeply,
indeed, that Shane comes to see his own effect on this charming little
family, mounts his obedient steed, and rides away at film's end into a
sunset that outshines all sunsets. After him runs little Joey, crying out,
"Shane! I love you, Shane!"

Shot at Jackson Hole, and before the days of widescreen and Dolby
Stereo, *Shane* is studded with iconic visions. The purple Grand Tetons in
the background, a deer grazing in a mirroring pool while the boy takes
pot shots at it with his toy rifle, the filthy sneer on the rancher's face
when Starrett (Heflin) refuses to give up his land, the look in Palance's
eyes when he guns the gunless Frank "Stonewall" Torrey (Elisha Cook Jr.)
down in the mud. Director George Stevens makes the mud tactile, like
melted chocolate.

For two images alone this film is worth seeing again and again. They
testify, if not to history, then to cinema. When Wilson struts onto the
wooden sidewalk with his spurred boots ringing, the town dog is shown
up close, creeping away with its tail between its legs. And after Shane
has met the Starretts and accepted their invitation to dinner, he feasts
on an apple pie. This is the apple pie to end apple pies (the pie that
taught Martha Stewart): steaming, golden, latticed, voluminous, lifted
out of the oven by a pretty gal in blue gingham and served up with good
black coffee. It is apple pie like this that made the American West, we
may well think; not guns, not cattle, not the dreamy far-sighted gaze
toward the next horizon. **MP**

Gentlemen Prefer Blondes Howard Hawks, 1953

It is not the most famous number in *Gentlemen Prefer Blondes*, but the song "When Love Goes Wrong" captures what is most infectious about this garish, hilariously camp musical. Dorothy (Jane Russell) and Lorelei (Marilyn Monroe) mope at an outdoor Parisian café about the difficulty of sustaining romances with men. As a crowd gathers, the two women warm to the increasingly expansive rhythm of their lament, which soon has them out of their seats, striding and strutting with bystanders in the style of choreographer Jack Cole. And then the commotion winds down: The music thins, the crowd disperses, and our heroines are gliding away in a cab—from banality to ecstasy and back again, beautifully.

Typical of the 1950s, *Gentlemen Prefer Blondes* is an acerbic comedy about gold digging, unafraid to mix sentimental dreams with brittle sarcasm, glamorous magic with a materialist sense of what a girl must do to get by—a set of merry contradictions immortalized in Monroe's oft-imitated "Diamonds Are a Girl's Best Friend."

The film is (as theorists say) a palimpsest, picking up and discarding at whim bits of Anita Loos's novel, its Broadway adaptation, songs by the teams of Leo Robin–Jule Styne and Hoagy Carmichael–Harold Adamson, and, above all, the possibilities accruing to its two powerhouse stars. Russell's persona brings together raunchiness and practicality; Monroe is a potent mixture of slinky eroticism and childlike guilelessness, laced with a hint of savvy manipulation. The comic high point comes when the roles swap for Dorothy's brash courtroom imitation of Lorelei.

Howard Hawks is generally regarded as a very classical, restrained director, but here he veers toward the crazy, spectacularly vulgar comedies of Frank Tashlin—a connection clinched by the presence of that wonderfully grotesque child George Winslow. The excess and oddity of certain set pieces (such as Russell's deathless serenade addressed to indifferent musclemen, "Ain't There Anyone Here for Love?"), and their frequently tangential relation to the nominal plot, are all part of what makes the film so enjoyable to a contemporary audience. **AM**

U.S. (Fox) 91m Technicolor **Producer** Sol C. Siegel **Screenplay** Charles Lederer, from novel by Anita Loos and play by Joseph Fields and Anita Loos **Photography** Harry J. Wild **Music** Harold Adamson, Hoagy Carmichael, Leo Robin, Jule Styne **Cast** Jane Russell, Marilyn Monroe, Charles Coburn, Elliott Reid, Tommy Noonan, George Winslow, Marcel Dalio, Taylor Holmes, Norma Varden, Howard Wendell, Steven Geray, Henri Letondal, Leo Mostovoy, Alex Frazer, George Davis

"*[Gentlemen Prefer Blondes is] an impossible object—a CinemaScope of the mind, a capitalist Potemkin.*"

Jonathan Rosenbaum, critic, 1985

i

A silent film of *Gentlemen Prefer Blondes* was made in 1928, but no copies exist and it is considered lost.

1953

U.S. (Paramount) 118m BW
Producer Robert Wyler, William Wyler
Screenplay Ian McLellan Hunter,
John Dighton **Music** Georges Auric
Photography Henri Alekan, Franz Planer **Cast**
Gregory Peck, Audrey Hepburn, Eddie Albert,
Hartley Power, Harcourt Williams, Margaret
Rawlings, Tullio Carminati, Paolo Carlini,
Claudio Ermelli, Paola Borboni, Alfredo Rizzo,
Laura Solari, Gorella Gori, Heinz Hindrich,
John Horne **Oscars** Audrey Hepburn
(actress), Edith Head (costume), Ian McLellan
Hunter (Dalton Trumbo) (best writing, motion
picture story) **Oscar nominations** William
Wyler (best picture), William Wyler (director),
Ian McLellan Hunter (Dalton Trumbo), John
Dighton (screenplay, writing), Eddie Albert
(actor in support role), Hal Pereira, Walter H.
Tyler (art direction), Franz Planer, Henri Alekan
(photography), Robert Swink (editing)

*"I've never been alone
with a man before,
even with my dress on.
With my dress off, it's
most unusual."*

**Princess Ann
(Audrey Hepburn)**

ℹ️

Frank Capra had the project initially;
he wanted Elizabeth Taylor and Cary
Grant in Hepburn and Peck's roles.

Roman Holiday William Wyler, 1953

If the filmmakers knew exactly what they had on their hands at the time, they might have retitled *Roman Holiday* as *A Star is Born*. Audrey Hepburn had only appeared in a few European roles and in a Broadway production of *Gigi* when she was cast as a princess in William Wyler's film. Needless to say, the role fit, *Roman Holiday* was a hit, and Hepburn was catapulted to the top of Tinseltown royalty. She was the Cinderella story made real by the magic of Hollywood.

Roman Holiday itself actually presents the flip side to the Cinderella fable. Hepburn's Princess Ann is tired of the pomp and circumstance of her official duties. One night she slips out from under her handlers' control and, under the guise of an everyday girl, encounters American journalist Joe Bradley (Gregory Peck). He recognizes the princess as the possible scoop of his career, but as he gets to know her better he feels terrible about taking advantage of her innocence. As the two tour the city, they realize they're falling in love, but the realities of their respective situations may make such a relationship impossible. So they enjoy the city and all its charms, knowing that this short time they spend together may be the last.

Peck and Hepburn are excellent as the two mismatched lovers, and Eddie Albert is perfect as Peck's eager tagalong cameraman. Wyler, one of Hollywood's most reliable directors, shot the film on location in Rome, and the city's landmarks help enhance the already magical story. Just as essential is the enjoyable script, which proved controversial because it was penned by blacklisted writer Dalton Trumbo. It was literally decades before Trumbo finally got the credit he deserved for helping to craft such a wonderful film.

The rest of the crew didn't need to wait nearly as long—*Roman Holiday* earned a whopping ten Academy Award nominations, including a win for the relatively unknown Hepburn. She'd be cast as the ingenue many more times over in her career, but it was this film that officially and auspiciously marked her arrival. **JKl**

The Big Heat Fritz Lang, 1953

U.S. (Columbia) 89m BW
Producer Robert Arthur **Screenplay** Sydney
Boehm, from novel by William P. McGivern
Photography Charles Lang **Music** Daniele
Amfitheatrof, Arthur Morton **Cast** Glenn
Ford, Gloria Grahame, Jocelyn Brando,
Alexander Scourby, Lee Marvin, Jeanette
Nolan, Peter Whitney, Willis Bouchey, Robert
Burton, Adam Williams, Howard Wendell,
Chris Alcaide, Michael Granger, Dorothy
Green, Carolyn Jones

*"Lang [gives] the story
a narrative drive as
efficient and powerful
as a handgun."*

Time Out Film Guide

Like Fritz Lang's 1952 Western *Rancho Notorious*, *The Big Heat* is a ballad of "hate, murder, and revenge": It opens with a close-up of a gun about to be used by corrupt cop Tom Duncan to commit suicide and proceeds rapidly through jolting horrors that malform the characters. Cop Dave Bannion (Glenn Ford) turns from family man to obsessive when his wife (Jocelyn Brando) is blown up by a car bomb meant for him. Moll Debby (Gloria Grahame) is embittered when her thug boyfriend Vince (Lee Marvin) disfigures her with a faceful of hot coffee and takes up Bannion's quest. In a crucial development, the embittered hero still can't commit cold-blooded murder, and so a double has to step in to pull the last thread that allows justice to be done: The big heat that brings down crime boss Lagana (Alexander Scourby) is precipitated when Debby confronts and murders her "sister under the mink," the crooked cop's grasping widow.

Grounded more in political reality than most of Lang's noirs, thanks to the hard-hitting detail of William P. McGivern's novel and Sydney Boehm's script, *The Big Heat* is one of a 1950s cycle of syndicate-runs-the-town crime exposés—others include *The Phenix City Story* (1955) and *The Captive City* (1952). Lang's direction is still indebted to expressionism here, with sets that reflect the characters' overriding personality traits: the cold luxury of the Duncan house, bought with dirty money; the tasteless wealth of Lagana's mansion, with its hideous portrait of the mobster's sainted mother and jiving teenage party; the penthouse moderne of Vince and Debby, where the police commissioner plays cards with killers; the cramped, poor-but-honest apartment of the Bannion family; and the hotel room where Bannion ends up, his life pared down to the need for vengeance. The finale is hardly comforting: After the fall of the crime syndicate, the hero returns to his desk in the Homicide Department. The welcome of workmates—expressed, of course, by an offer of coffee—is curtailed, and the end title appears over Bannion putting on his hat and coat to go out and deal with "a hit and run over on South Street." **KN**

i

Jocelyn Brando, who played
Bannion's wife Katie, was the older
sister of Marlon Brando.

On the Waterfront Elia Kazan, 1954

"I coulda had class. I coulda been a contender. I coulda been somebody, instead of a bum, which is what I am, let's face it." One of the all-time great American films, *On the Waterfront* exploded on a country shaken by the betrayals and paranoia of the anticommunist scare. Searing and tender, it ushered into Hollywood a new kind of hard-hitting social realism, not least because it was filled with indelible performances from a number of New York theater's hot postwar generation of naturalistic and Method actors.

Slow-witted but sensitive Terry Malloy (Marlon Brando, never more beautiful), a failed boxer turned longshoreman and errand boy for corrupt union boss Johnny Friendly (Lee J. Cobb), is disturbed by his unwitting role in the murder of a disaffected docker. His guilt is exacerbated when he falls in love with the dead man's sister, Edie Doyle (Eva Marie Saint in her film debut), but his illuminating crisis is his realization that he, too, has been sold out—most heartbreakingly by his older, smarter brother Charley (Rod Steiger), who is Friendly's sharp lawyer and right-hand man. After Edie shames the initially ineffectual parish priest (Karl Malden) into leading the crusade against harbor union racketeering, Friendly's intimidation turns more deadly. Terry painfully defies the code of silence and testifies at a congressional commission. Despite doing the right thing, Terry is ostracized for "ratting" by the waterfront community and is beaten to a pulp in the dockyard before his fearful comrades fall in behind him, breaking Friendly's hold on their lives and labor.

The film was most visibly inspired by "Crime on the Waterfront," a series of newspaper articles by Malcolm Johnson exposing racketeering in the New York/New Jersey dockyards. Playwright Arthur Miller began working on a screenplay at the behest of director Elia Kazan. But when Kazan testified before the House Un-American Activities Committee, Miller broke with him. Kazan turned to a fellow "friendly witness," writer Budd Schulberg. Both men's reputations suffered permanent damage and *On the Waterfront* is frequently labeled their apology or defense. Kazan admitted he identified with Terry Malloy's conflict of loyalties. Wherever one's sympathies lie, the painful real-life background invested the film with a gut-wrenching, truthful emotional center for the realism of its subject and setting and for the naturalism of its performances (complemented by Leonard Bernstein's evocative score).

Terry confronting Charley in the back of a cab is the most often cited classic scene, but there are many other unforgettable moments: Brando fiddling with Saint's little glove, putting it on his own hand; Terry discovering that all his lovingly cared for pigeons have been killed by the neighborhood boy who admired him; Terry beating down Edie's door and forcing an admission of love as they slide down to the floor in a desperate kiss. Decades later, it endures as an unflinching contemplation of betrayal. **AE**

U.S. (Columbia, Horizon) 108m BW
Producer Sam Spiegel **Screenplay** Malcolm
Johnson, Budd Schulberg, from articles by
Malcolm Johnson **Photography** Boris
Kaufman **Music** Leonard Bernstein
Cast Marlon Brando, Karl Malden, Lee J.
Cobb, Rod Steiger, Pat Henning, Leif
Erickson, James Westerfield, Tony Galento,
Tami Mauriello, John F. Hamilton, John
Heldabrand, Rudy Bond, Don Blackman,
Arthur Keegan, Abe Simon **Oscars** Sam
Spiegel (best picture), Elia Kazan (director),
Budd Schulberg (screenplay), Marlon Brando
(actor), Eva Marie Saint (actress in support
role), Richard Day (art direction), Boris
Kaufman (photography), Gene Milford
(editing) **Oscar nominations** Lee J. Cobb
(actor in support role), Karl Malden (actor
in support role), Rod Steiger (actor in
support role), Leonard Bernstein (music)
Venice Film Festival Elia Kazan (OCIC award,
Silver Lion, Italian film critics award, Golden
Lion nomination)

*"Brando and Kazan
... changed American
movie acting forever."*

Roger Ebert, critic, 1999

ℹ️

On the Waterfront is the only film
that wasn't a musical for which
Leonard Bernstein wrote the score.

La strada Federico Fellini, 1954
The Road

The Road is Federico Fellini's fourth film, and it is the one that made his international reputation. Starring Anthony Quinn as Zampanò the Strongman and the director's wife, Giulietta Masina, as the waif Gelsomina, it is a story of love and jealousy set in the circus, a milieu to which Fellini returns time and again. Zampanò does a hackneyed routine of bursting out of chains wrapped around his chest. He needs an assistant, and so he buys Gelsomina from her mother to accompany him on the road. She acts as a clown, her gestures reminiscent of Charlie Chaplin. When they join a traveling circus, Gelsomina is temporarily fascinated by an acrobat, the Fool, played by Richard Baseheart. Although he treats her badly, Zampanò becomes jealous of the Fool and his actions lead the film to its powerful conclusion.

The Road is told in a fabulist style that begins to move away from the postwar Neorealism of much of Italian cinema, a movement with which Fellini was intimately involved as a screenwriter. Although it is shot on location, it could take place in the present day or it could be 100 years ago. Zampanò and Gelsomina are archetypes, simple characters driven by the most elemental emotions and desires. The action of the film plays out as though it is predetermined and these characters must act as they do, which makes the story tragic. Masina's moving portrayal of the abused but plucky Gelsomina would define her screen persona in several later Fellini films, and in much of her other work as an actress. Quinn is equally unforgettable as the brutish strongman, incapable of understanding his own feelings toward Gelsomina. Both actors highlight the disjuncture between their characters' performances and the realities of their lives.

Throughout his work, Fellini was fascinated by the tension between a character's theatrical facade and his or her unexplored, messy interior life. *The Road* won the Academy Award for Best Foreign Language Film and is probably the director's most accessible and well-loved picture. Snobs and sophisticates should not hold that against this complex and moving film, which continues to provide new insights and ideas on each subsequent viewing. **RH**

Italy (Ponti–De Laurentiis) 94m BW **Language** Italian **Producer** Dino De Laurentiis, Carlo Ponti **Screenplay** Federico Fellini, Tullio Pinelli **Photography** Otello Martelli, Carlo Carlini **Music** Nino Rota **Cast** Anthony Quinn, Giulietta Masina, Richard Baseheart, Aldo Silvani, Marcella Rovere, Livia Venturini **Oscar** Italy (best foreign language film) **Oscar nomination** Federico Fellini, Tullio Pinelli (screenplay) **Venice Film Festival** Federico Fellini (Silver Lion, Golden Lion nomination)

"La strada *is really the complete catalog of my entire mythological world.*"

Federico Fellini, 1965

i

According to Fellini, Walt Disney expressed an interest in making an animated film about Gelsomina.

Les diaboliques Henri-Georges Clouzot, 1954
The Fiends

France (Filmsonor, Vera) 114m BW
Language French Producer Henri-Georges
Clouzot Screenplay Henri-Georges Clouzot,
Jérôme Géronimi, Frédéric Grendel, René
Masson from the novel Celle qui n'était
plus by Pierre Boileau and Thomas Narcejac
Photography Armand Thirard
Music Georges Van Parys Cast Simone
Signoret, Véra Clouzot, Paul Meurisse,
Charles Vanel, Jean Brochard, Pierre Larquey,
Michel Serrault, Thérèse Dorny, Noël
Roquevert, Yves-Marie Maurin, Georges
Poujouly, Georges Chamarat, Jacques
Varennes, Robert Dalban, Jean Lefebvre

In a run-down, provincial public school, murderous passions seethe just below the surface. The put-upon, weak-hearted wife (Véra Clouzot) and mysteriously sensual girlfriend (Simone Signoret) of a sadistic headmaster (Paul Meurisse) murder him, dumping the corpse in the weeded-over swimming pool. When the pool is drained, the body is missing and the women start to lose their minds, especially when a pupil claims to have seen a ghost. Soon, the women too are seeing things, and something ghastly shows up in the bath.

A major international hit in 1954, Les Diaboliques has lost little of its power to disturb, though dozens of films (like Deathtrap [1982] and Hush ... Hush, Sweet Charlotte [1964]) have borrowed its tricky storyline and made familiar the most shocking moments. Henri-Georges Clouzot directs with a gray cruelty that combines a nastily tangled storyline worthy of Hitchcock (the Master is rumored to have made Psycho to reclaim the King of Suspense crown he lost briefly to Clouzot) with three strong central performances and a marvelously seedy setting. The film has scenes of physical horror (one trick with contact lenses is unforgettably creepy), but Clouzot also sets the flesh creeping with incidences of ordinary nastiness, as when Meurisse forces his wife to eat a disgusting school dinner. **KN**

1954

A Star Is Born George Cukor, 1954

U.S. (Transcona, Warner Bros.) 181m
Technicolor Producer Vern Alves, Sidney
Luft Screenplay Moss Hart, from the 1937
screenplay by Alan Campbell and Dorothy
Parker, story by William A.Wellman
Photography Sam Leavitt Music Harold
Arlen, Ray Heindorf Cast Judy Garland,
James Mason, Jack Carson, Charles Bickford,
Tommy Noonan, Lucy Marlow, Amanda
Blake, Irving Bacon, Hazel Shermet
Oscar nominations James Mason (actor),
Judy Garland (actress), Malcolm C. Bert,
Gene Allen, Irene Sharaff, George James
Hopkins (art direction), Jean Louis Mary, Ann
Nyberg, Irene Sharaff (costume), Ray
Heindorf (music), Harold Arlen,
Ira Gershwin (song)

A Star Is Born is George Cukor's musical remake of William Wellman's 1937 film. It is the very best of four films (Cukor also directed What Price Hollywood? [1932], considered the source of A Star Is Born) about a marriage doomed by the meteoric rise to stardom of the younger wife and the self-destruction of the falling idol/mentor she loves. William Wellman's 1937 movie starring Fredric March and Janet Gaynor is still a moving drama; the 1976 rock version with Barbra Streisand and Kris Kristofferson is memorable only for Streisand's singing. But Cukor's musical, in which Judy Garland (in a triumphant comeback) and James Mason are both terrific, broke new ground in the musical genre by propelling dramatic narrative with songs—signally in Garland's tortured "The Man that Got Away" and the show-stopping production number "Born in a Trunk." Not to be outdone, Mason's Norman Maine is spellbinding in his drunken display at the Academy Awards.

Part Hollywood satire—amusingly in the studio transformation of plain Esther Blodgett into glamorous Vicky Lester, acidly in the publicity machine entrapping Esther and Norman—the film is a beautiful blend of music, wit, and romantic tragedy, done with compelling conviction. In 1983, more than twenty minutes of previously cut footage was restored, including two numbers written for Garland by Harold Arlen and Ira Gershwin. **AE**

Rear Window Alfred Hitchcock, 1954

U.S. (Paramount, Patron) 112m Technicolor
Producer Alfred Hitchcock **Screenplay** John
Michael Hayes, from the story "It Had To
Be Murder" by Cornell Woolrich
Photography Robert Burks **Music** Franz
Waxman **Cast** James Stewart, Grace Kelly,
Wendell Corey, Thelma Ritter, Raymond Burr,
Judith Evelyn, Ross Bagdasarian, Georgine
Darcy, Sara Berner, Frank Cady, Jesslyn Fax,
Rand Harper, Irene Winston, Havis
Davenport **Oscar nominations** Alfred
Hitchcock (director), John Michael Hayes
(screenplay), Robert Burks (photography),
Loren L. Ryder (sound)

"I wonder if it's ethical to watch a man with binoculars and a long-focus lens. Do you suppose it's ethical even if you prove he didn't commit a crime?"

**L.B. "Jeff" Jeffries
(James Stewart)**

i

All the apartments in the tenement
building set had electricity and
running water, and could be lived in.

The apotheosis of all his simmering and barely suppressed psychosexual fixations, Alfred Hitchcock's *Rear Window* is also probably (with the possible exception of the 1958 film *Vertigo*) the most successful merger of entertainment, intrigue, and psychology of the director's remarkable career. A fascinating study of obsession and voyeurism—*Rear Window* combines a perfect cast, a perfect screenplay, and particularly a perfect set for a movie—that's even better than the sum of its parts.

For maximum freedom, Hitchcock constructed an intricate replication of a crowded and constantly bustling New York City tenement building and its equally busy courtyard. Each window offers a glimpse into another life and in effect tells another story. In one unit, a composer hunches over his piano struggling with his latest work. In another, a dancer practices compulsively. One apartment houses a lonely woman, unlucky in love, and another an amorous newlywed couple.

L.B. "Jeff" Jeffries (James Stewart) is a successful photojournalist sidelined with a broken leg. Stuck in a wheelchair all day, he has nothing better to do than spy on his neighbors. Or at least that's what he claims, because his fashion model girlfriend (and would-be wife) Lisa (played by a surprisingly carnal Grace Kelly in one of her final roles before retiring) and his cranky caretaker Stella (Thelma Ritter) perceptively observe that he's merely addicted to the thrill of voyeurism.

The notion of anyone able to keep their eyes off a character as beautiful and luminous as Lisa is hard to believe, until Jeff begins to suspect one of his neighbors (a glowering Raymond Burr) of murdering his wife. Soon enough, Jeff has dragged Lisa and Stella into the mystery, obsessively studying Burr's character's behavior for signs of his guilt. But as Jeff's furtive investigation advances, so do the ongoing stories of all of his other neighbors, oblivious to the nefarious plot possibly unfolding literally right next door.

Rear Window, the film, is constructed every bit as thoroughly as its elaborate set. Watching it is like watching a living, breathing ecosystem, with the added thrill of a murder mystery thrown in for good measure. Hitchcock relishes the film's particularly postmodern scenario: we, the viewers, are entranced by the actions of these characters, who are in turn entranced by the actions of still other characters. It's a vicious circle of obsession laced with black humor and a dash of sexiness.

Indeed, although the nosey Jeff may discover a murder in his urban hamlet, it's the numerous romances transpiring in the other units that first draw his attention to the courtyard peep show. It's wholly ironic that his obsessions with the love lives of his neighbors prevent him from acknowledging the romantic interest of Lisa. In fact, the bachelor in Jeff looks to his neighbors as an excuse to ward off her advances. It is only when his actions put her in danger that he finally understands that what he has in front of him is better than anything he can see out the window. **JKl**

Senso Luchino Visconti, 1954
The Wanton Countess

Senso was Count Luchino Visconti's third film, and his first in color. Set in Venice and Verona in the 1860s, on the verge of Giuseppe Garibaldi's expulsion of the Austrians and the creation of the modern Italian state, it marked a complete departure from the working-class milieu of the director's earlier films, *Ossessione* (1942) and *La Terra Trema* (1948). Nevertheless, *Senso*'s overt theatricality is not so different from the extravagant passions of *Ossessione*, and it is no less "authentic" for its sumptuous aristocratic setting.

Alida Valli is the Countess Livia Sepieri, a Garibaldi supporter who intercedes on her cousin's behalf when he suicidally challenges an Austrian officer to a duel. Lt. Franz Mahler (Farley Granger) characteristically ducks out of the fight. A handsome, unprincipled charmer, Mahler seduces the Countess, who will recklessly betray her husband, her honor, and even her country for his love.

With screenplay credits for both Tennessee Williams and Paul Bowles—among six writers in total—*Senso* is a distinctly high-class melodrama. An actress who was past her prime, eyes flashing, teeth bared, Valli seems barely able to credit her own actions as she flings caution to the wind and stakes everything on a feckless character who makes no bones about his own cowardice. (The film was actually retitled *The Wanton Countess* for its belated U.S release.) Farley Granger is even better, especially in the big climactic scene where he thoroughly lets rip with his self-loathing. Similarly unbalanced, sadomasochistic relationships recur in Visconti's later films, especially *The Damned* (1969) and *Death in Venice* (1971), but neither quite matched the ferocity displayed here.

Senso begins at the opera, and Anton Bruckner's score punctuates every dramatic turning point with an operatic thundercrack. "I like opera very much, but not when it happens off-stage," the Countess remarks, as she tries to dissuade Mahler from taking up her cousin's challenge. Italy's most renowned director of operas, Visconti clearly believed otherwise. **TCh**

Italy (Lux) 117m Technicolor
Language English / Italian
Producer Domenico Forges Davanzati
Screenplay Carlo Alianello, Giorgio Bassani, Paul Bowles, Suso Cecchi d'Amico, Giorgio Prosperi, Luchino Visconti, Tennessee Williams, from novella by Camillo Boito
Photography Aldo Graziati, Robert Krasker
Music Anton Bruckner **Cast** Alida Valli, Farley Granger, Heinz Moog, Rina Morelli, Christian Marquand, Sergio Fantoni, Tino Bianchi, Ernst Nadherny, Tonio Selwart, Marcella Mariani, Massimo Girotti
Venice Film Festival Luchino Visconti (Golden Lion nomination)

"An extraordinary film by Visconti, another Neorealist masterpiece."

Martin Scorsese, 2012

🛈

Visconti apparently insisted on daily fresh cut flowers for every room on set, even if they weren't filming there.

Silver Lode
Allan Dwan, 1954

U.S. (Pinecrest) 81m Technicolor
Producer Benedict Bogeaus
Screenplay Karen DeWolf
Photography John Alton **Music** Louis
Forbes **Cast** John Payne, Lizabeth Scott,
Dan Duryea, Dolores Moran, Emile Meyer,
Robert Warwick, John Hudson,
Harry Carey Jr., Alan Hale Jr.

In this gripping Western, John Payne stars as Dan Ballard, a respected and well-liked rancher in the small town where he has lived for the past two years. During the town's Fourth of July celebration, four strangers ride into town, led by a belligerent and unpleasant thug (Dan Duryea) who claims to be a U.S. Marshal with a warrant for Ballard's arrest for murder. Over the course of the action (which is equivalent in span to the film's running time), the townspeople turn against Ballard, eventually forming a mob to hunt him down as he labors to prove his innocence.

Silver Lode is the Allan Dwan film par excellence: concise, plain, inventive, fluid, ironic, unspectacular-but-beautiful. No Western, probably, has more shots through windows (Dwan likes to stage scenes in depth and to emphasize situations in which characters observe each other), and few make such splendid use of the familiar architecture and decor of the Hollywood Western town. In a single stunning shot, Dwan's camera tracks with Payne as he runs four blocks across town. Thanks to the director's visual assurance (and the lighting genius of John Alton), *Silver Lode* is one of the best of the American cinema's many underrated Westerns. **CFu**

1954

The Barefoot Contessa
Joseph L. Mankiewicz, 1954

U.S. / Italy (Figaro, Rizzoli-Haggiag) 128m
Technicolor **Producer** Franco Magli
Screenplay Joseph L. Mankiewicz
Photography Jack Cardiff **Music** Mario
Nascimbene **Cast** Humphrey Bogart, Ava
Gardner, Edmond O'Brien, Marius Goring,
Valentina Cortese, Rossano Brazzi, Elizabeth
Sellars, Warren Stevens, Franco Interlenghi,
Mari Aldon, Alberto Rabagliati, Enzo Staiola,
Maria Zanoli, Renato Chiantoni, Bill Fraser
Oscar Edmond O'Brien (actor in support
role) **Oscar nomination** Joseph L.
Mankiewicz (screenplay)

The surface appeal of *The Barefoot Contessa* is obvious: Ava Gardner at her most glamorous as the rags-to-riches star Maria Vargas alongside Humphrey Bogart at his most acerbic yet tender as filmmaker Harry Dawes; the flood of quotable dialogue ("It's never too late to develop character"); and the intriguing allusions to real-life celebrities, including Rita Hayward and Howard Hughes. But there is much more going on.

The film owes much to *Citizen Kane* (1941), especially the mosaic structure, which offers various points of view on a character—ultimately affirming only that person's inscrutability. From the initial "springboard" situation of Maria's funeral, eight flashbacks proceed from four narrators. Long before *Pulp Fiction* (1994), Joseph Mankiewicz contrives a sequence that shows Maria's transition from Bravano (Marius Goring) to Vincenzo (Rossano Brazzi) from two viewpoints.

Even more intricate is the film's journey through three social worlds— Hollywood show business, the French leisure set, and Italian aristocracy— that register as uncanny variations on each other, each one enclosed, decadent, and dying. Significantly, this suite of decay echoes the presentation of the theater world in Mankiewicz's 1950 classic, *All About Eve*. While his films are sometimes justly criticized as stagey and word-bound, the richness and coherence of *The Barefoot Contessa* come from its metaphor of theatrical spectacle. Mankiewicz's signature touch is the "frieze," where the plot stops and a narrator fills us in on the character and background of each "player" at a table. **AM**

Shichinin no samurai Akira Kurosawa, 1954
The Seven Samurai

Akira Kurosawa is the Japanese director best known around the world. His thrilling, compellingly humane epic *The Seven Samurai* is his most enduringly popular, most widely seen masterpiece. Its rousing, if less profound, gunslinging Hollywood remake, *The Magnificent Seven* (1960), is the most successful of the several Western pictures modeled on Kurosawa's work—including the 1964 film *The Outrage*, a reworking of *Rashomon* (1950), and the landmark spaghetti Western *A Fistful of Dollars* (1964), lifted wholesale by Sergio Leone from *Yojimbo* (1961). The entertaining cultural crossover is delightful testimony to cinema's universal vocabulary and appeal. Kurosawa was inspired by the Westerns of John Ford and made a bold departure from the limited traditions of the typical Japanese *jidai-geki*, historical costume pictures with the emphasis on swordfights in a medieval Japan depicted as a fantasy land. *The Seven Samurai* is packed with a blur of astounding action, comic incident, misadventure, social drama, beautiful character development, and the conflict between duty and desire, all treated with immaculate care for realism.

A poor village of farmers, at the mercy of bandits who return every year to rape, kill, and steal, take the radical decision to fight back by hiring *ronin* (itinerant, masterless samurai) to save them. Because they are able to offer only meager portions of rice in payment, the nervous emissaries who set out in search of swords for hire are lucky to encounter Kambei (Takashi Shimura), an honorable, compassionate man resigned to doing what a man's gotta do, despite knowing he will gain nothing from doing it. Very much the hero figure, he recruits five other wanderers willing to fight for food or fun, including a good-natured old friend, a dewy-eyed young disciple, and a master swordsman of few words. Hot-headed, impulsive, clownish young Kikuchiyo (Toshirô Mifune) is rejected by the seasoned men, but the peasant masquerading as a samurai tags along anyway, frantic to prove himself and impress Kambei. The villagers treat them with mistrust but gradually bonds form, a love affair blossoms, the children are drawn to their heroes, and Kambei organizes a spirited resistance that astonishes, enrages, and ultimately overcomes the invaders.

The film is tireless, fast moving, and economical, eliminating unnecessary exposition. It evokes mystery and sustains a sense of apprehension—with quick shots and short cuts making up the peasants' search for potential protectors and putting their case to Kambei. There are many scenes of overwhelming visual and emotional power—a dying woman drags herself from a burning mill and hands her baby to Kikuchiyo, who sits down in the stream in shock, sobbing and crying, "This baby, it's me. The same thing happened to me," the mill wheel, aflame, turning behind him. But the greatest moment of the film is the resolution: the three survivors survey their comrades' graves as the forgetful villagers below turn all their attention to their joyful rice-planting ritual. **AE**

Japan (Toho) 155m BW
Language Japanese **Producer** Sojiro Motoki **Screenplay** Shinobu Hashimoto, Akira Kurosawa, Hideo Oguni **Music** Fumio Hayasaka **Photography** Asakazu Nakai **Cast** Takashi Shimura, Toshirô Mifune, Yoshio Inaba, Seiji Miyaguchi, Minoru Chiaki, Daisuke Katô, Isao Kimura, Keiko Tsushima, Yukiko Shimazaki, Kamatari Fujiwara, Yoshio Kosugi, Bokuzen Hidari, Yoshio Tsuchiya, Kokuten Kodo, Jiro Kumagai **Oscar nominations** So Matsuyama (art direction), Kôhei Ezaki (costume) **Venice Film Festival** Akira Kurosawa (Silver Lion, Golden Lion nomination)

> "Seven Samurai *is long; it is brutal; it is not always easy to follow. But it is magnificent.*"
>
> Dilys Powell,
> *Sunday Times*, 1955

ℹ
George Lucas was greatly influenced by Kurosawa, and many nods to *The Seven Samurai* appear in *Star Wars*.

1954

Sanshô dayû Kenji Mizoguchi, 1954
Sanshô the Bailiff

"Without compassion, a man is no longer human." So states Taira (Masao Shimizu), a governor in medieval Japan being sent into exile because of his liberal policies, to his young son Zushiô. Together with his mother Tamaki (the great Kinuyo Tanaka) and his sister Anju, Zushiô flees from his family's estate; betrayed by a priestess, Zushiô and Anju are sent off to the enormous slave-labor compound run by the notoriously cruel Sanshô (Eitarô Shindô), while their mother is kidnapped into prostitution on a distant island. Thus begins one of the great emotional and philosophical journeys ever made for the cinema. Possibly the high point in an unbroken string of masterpieces made by Kenji Mizoguchi shortly before his death, Sanshô the Bailiff features the perfection of a signature visual style—made up predominantly by long, complexly staged shots paced by gliding camera movements—that Mizoguchi had already begun to develop in the 1930s.

After this harrowing opening, the story jumps ahead several years. The adult Zushiô (Yoshiaki Hanayagi), strong but emotionally dead, has become one of Sanshô's most reliable henchmen; with unblinking cruelty, he carries out orders to torture and maim. One day Zushiô is ordered to leave an old, ailing woman outside the compound's walls to die; Anju (Kyôko Kagawa) follows him ostensibly to help, but then a minor accident—the two fall down when trying to break off a tree branch—conjures up a childhood memory of their time together before being enslaved. Suddenly Zushiô realizes how horrible he has become; he and Anju decide to run away, but fearing they'll be caught if they stay together, Anju sacrifices herself so her brother may escape.

Zushiô does escape and eventually is able to reclaim his family's noble standing. He returns, now as an official, to Sanshô's compound; dismissing Sanshô, he turns the compound over to its inmates, who burn it down in a scene of orgiastic frenzy. Abandoning his official post, Zushiô goes off to find his mother. Years before, he and Anju had heard a story about an old, lame prostitute on an island who constantly sang a lament about her lost children; he goes to the island and, on a lonely stretch of beach, is reunited with his mother. He breaks down, asking forgiveness for the evil he's done; on the contrary, his mother assures him, his father would have been proud that his son lived so faithfully by his teachings.

If at this point you're not a sobbing mass, there's simply a hole in your soul. Mizoguchi's worldview is pitch black: violence, betrayal, and wanton cruelty are the order of the day. Yet although one can't change this, one can protest by simply staying true to an ideal. The battle between good and evil is finally a battle within oneself, and in the film's magnificent final sequence, as mother and son huddle together sobbing, one feels that the love between them is the most powerful force in the universe; even if that love can't conquer the world, it can transcend it. **RP**

Japan (Daiei) 120m BW
Language Japanese **Producer** Masaichi Nagata **Screenplay** Yahiro Fuji, Ogai Mori, Yoshikata Yoda, from story by Ogai Mori **Photography** Kazuo Miyagawa **Music** Fumio Hayasaka, Tamekichi Mochizuki, Kanahichi Odera **Cast** Kinuyo Tanaka, Yoshiaki Hanayagi, Kyôko Kagawa, Eitarô Shindô, Akitake Kôno, Masao Shimizu, Ken Mitsuda, Kazukimi Okuni, Yôko Kosono, Noriko Tachibana, Ichirô Sugai, Teruko Omi, Masahiko Kato, Keiko Enami, Bontarô Akemi **Venice Film Festival** Kenji Mizoguchi (Silver Lion, Golden Lion nomination)

> "The Bailiff *is a film of breathtaking visual beauty.*"
>
> **Roger Greenspun,**
> *The New York Times,* **1969**

ℹ

In 1990 director Terence Malick was commissioned to write a stage play version of Sanshô the Bailiff.

Carmen Jones Otto Preminger, 1954

U.S. (Fox, Carlyle) 105m Color
Producer Otto Preminger Screenplay Harry
Kleiner, from the novel *Carmen* by Prosper
Mérimée Photography Sam Leavitt
Music Georges Bizet, Oscar Hammerstein
Cast Harry Belafonte, Dorothy Dandridge,
Pearl Bailey, Olga James, Joe Adams, Brock
Peters, Roy Glenn, Nick Stewart, Diahann
Carroll, LeVern Hutcherson, Marilyn Horne,
Marvin Hayes Oscar nominations Dorothy
Dandridge (actress), Herschel Burke Gilbert
(music) Berlin International Film Festival
Otto Preminger (Bronze Bear)

ℹ

After watching Dorothy Dandridge's
screen test, Preminger delcared that
it was the best that he had ever seen.

The legendarily beautiful and troubled African-American actress Dorothy Dandridge, like so many sex symbols, was a martyr to her beauty in life, while in death she lies buried beneath her own mythology. *Carmen Jones* is the substance behind the hype, a potent explanation of her appeal and hold on the imagination so long after her death.

Based on Bizet's opera *Carmen*, *Carmen Jones* is the story of a hungry, ambitious young woman (Dandridge) whose narcissism and greed lead to the destruction of Joe (Harry Belafonte), a good man who loves her dearly. Surprisingly, both Dandridge and Belafonte (who were singers in their own right) were dubbed by Marilyn Horne and LeVern Hutcherson respectively. Yet filled with classic songs (the lyrics and book are by the legendary Oscar Hammerstein II) and a first-rate supporting cast that includes Pearl Bailey and a young Diahann Carroll, the film is packed with sensational musical numbers (mostly shot in single takes by director Otto Preminger) that are integral to the film. But as impeccable as craft, crew, and supporting cast are, this is Dandridge's vehicle all the way. Her Carmen is one of the fieriest, most viscerally devastating sex goddesses ever caught on film—her cool feline strut, curvaceous body, blazing eyes, and mixture of lust and contempt for the men caught in her snare add up to a creature that's otherworldly. It's a powerhouse performance that elevates an excellent film into the realm of classic. **EH**

Johnny Guitar Nicholas Ray, 1954

U.S. (Republic) 110m Trucolor
Producer Herbert J. Yates **Screenplay** Philip
Yordan, from novel by Roy Chanslor
Photography Harry Stradling Sr.
Music Victor Young **Cast** Joan Crawford,
Sterling Hayden, Mercedes McCambridge,
Scott Brady, Ward Bond, Ben Cooper, Ernest
Borgnine, John Carradine, Royal Dano,
Frank Ferguson, Paul Fix, Rhys Williams,
Ian MacDonald

i

Like their characters, Joan Crawford
and Mercedes McCambridge were
fierce rivals off-camera.

The melodrama of *Johnny Guitar* is so over-the-top that some will find it laughable. Others will fall under the spell of its hypnotic power. Joan Crawford plays Vienna, the owner of a saloon that stands on land valued by the railroad. Mercedes McCambridge is Emma Small, the black-clad spinster daughter of a big landowner who lusts after the Dancing Kid (Scott Brady), who in turn wants Vienna, who has another man in her past: Johnny Guitar, played by Sterling Hayden. Driven crazy by frustrated desire, Emma leads a lynch mob to burn down Vienna's saloon and hang the Kid. But Vienna stands firm. At the end there's a shoot-out between Emma and Vienna, the kind of reversal of convention that has led some critics to claim the film for feminism. It's also been read as an anti-McCarthy allegory, against mob hysteria and for those who make a stand on principle.

Whatever its ultimate meaning, the film, financed by the minor studio Republic, is boldly baroque in its use of strong colors, its bravura acting style (with Crawford in particular outstanding), and in the haunting beauty of its theme song, sung by the great Peggy Lee. If you can't take this much artifice, perhaps you'd be safer watching documentaries. **EB**

Salt of the Earth Herbert J. Biberman, 1954

U.S. (Independent, Intl Union of Mine, Mill & Smelter Workers) 94m BW **Producer** Adolfo Barela, Sonja Dahl Biberman, Paul Jarrico **Screenplay** Michael Biberman, Michael Wilson **Photography** Stanley Meredith, Leonard Stark **Music** Sol Kaplan **Cast** Rosaura Revueltas, Will Geer, David Wolfe, Mervin Williams, David Sarvis, Juan Chacón, Henrietta Williams, Ernesto Velázquez, Ángela Sánchez, Joe T. Morales, Clorinda Alderette, Charles Coleman, Virginia Jencks, Clinton Jencks, Victor Torres

This rarely screened classic is the only major American independent feature made by communists. A fictional story about the Mexican-American zinc miners in New Mexico striking against their Anglo management, *Salt of the Earth* was informed by feminist attitudes that are quite uncharacteristic of the period. The film was inspired by the blacklisting of director Herbert Biberman, screenwriter Michael Wilson, producer and former screenwriter Paul Jarrico, and composer Sol Kaplan. As Jarrico later reasoned, because they'd been drummed out of Hollywood for being subversives, they'd commit a "crime to fit the punishment" by making a subversive film. The results are leftist propaganda of a high order, powerful and intelligent even when the film registers in spots as naive or dated.

Basically kept out of American theaters until 1965, *Salt of the Earth* was widely shown and honored in Europe, but it has never received the recognition it deserves Stateside. Regrettably, its best-known critical discussion in the United States is a Pauline Kael broadside in which the film is ridiculed as "propaganda." As accurate as Kael is about some of *Salt of the Earth*'s left-wing clichés, she indiscriminately takes some of her examples from the original script rather than the film itself, and gives no hint as to why it could remain so vital half a century later. **JRos**

Lola Montès Max Ophüls, 1955
The Sins of Lola Montes

France / West Germany (Florida Films, Gamma Film, Oska-Film, Union-Film) 110m Eastmancolor **Language** French / English / German **Producer** Albert Caraco **Screenplay** Max Ophüls, Annette Wademant, Jacques Natanson, from the novel *La Vie Extraordinaire de Lola Montès* by Cécil Saint-Laurent **Photography** Christian Matras **Music** Georges Auric **Cast** Martine Carol, Peter Ustinov, Anton Walbrook, Henri Guisol, Lise Delamare, Paulette Dubost, Oskar Werner, Jean Galland, Will Quadflieg, Héléna Manson, Germaine Delbat, Carl Esmond, Jacques Fayet, Friedrich Domin, Werner Finck

German-born, naturalized French, Viennese by lifelong sensibility, Max Ophüls was ideally suited to film the life of Lola Montès, one of the great cosmopolitan femmes fatales. Montès, dancer and courtesan extraordinaire, cut a swathe of scandal through Europe in the mid-nineteenth century, numbering among her many lovers Franz Liszt and the King of Bavaria.

Ophüls's film, his last (and his only one in color), is no conventional biopic. Instead, he mounts a lavish baroque extravaganza, part circus, part pageant, packed with flashbacks, and sends his famously mobile camera scaling around the elaborate decor. In the title role, Martine Carol gives a sullen, emotionally glazed performance, and Anton Walbrook's pensive king all but steals the movie. But for all her limitations, Carol fits Ophüls's conception. As always, his concern is the gulf between the ideal of love and its flawed, disenchanted reality. His Lola is merely a passive blank onto which men project their fantasies; her final destiny, as a circus sideshow attraction selling kisses for a dollar, reduces her profession to its most brutal logic. *The Sins of Lola Montes*, a classic film maudit, was butchered by its distributors and long available only in a truncated version, but a recent restoration allows us to appreciate Ophüls's swan song in its full poignant splendor. **PK**

India (Government of West Bengal) 115m BW **Language** Bengali **Screenplay** Satyajit Ray, from novel by Bibhutibhushan Bandyopadhyay **Photography** Subrata Mitra **Music** Ravi Shankar **Cast** Kanu Bannerjee, Karuna Bannerjee, Subir Bannerjee, Uma Das Gupta, Chunibala Devi, Runki Banerjee, Reba Devi, Aparna Devi, Haren Banerjee, Tulsi Chakraborty, Nibhanani Devi, Roma Ganguli, Binoy Mukherjee, Harimohan Nag, Kshirod Roy, Rama Gangopadhaya **Cannes Film Festival** Satyajit Ray (human document award, OCIC award—special mention)

"*[Pather Panchali] blindsides the viewer by showing a child's perspective on the world.*"

Stuart Jeffries,
Guardian, 2010

ℹ

Satyajit Ray read the novel of *Pather Panchali* in 1943, while drawing the illustrations for a new edition of it.

Pather Panchali Satyajit Ray, 1955

Based on a classic novel by the Bengali writer Bibhutibhusan Bandyopadhyay, *Pather Panchali*, Satyajit Ray's first film, was eventually to form part of a trilogy together with *Aparajito* (1957) and *The World of Apu* (1959). Ray, who was working in a Calcutta advertising agency at the time, had great difficulty in raising the money to make his film. Eventually he borrowed enough to begin shooting, in the hopes that the footage would persuade backers to help him complete it. Though filming initially began in October 1952, it was not until early in 1955 that *Pather Panchali* was at last finished.

Apu (Subir Bannerjee) is a little boy growing up in a remote country village in Bengal. His parents are poor and can hardly provide food enough for Apu and his older sister Durga (Uma Das Gupta), let alone the aged woman known as Auntie (Chunibala Devi) who lives with them. In an early scene, Durga has stolen some mangoes, which she gives to Auntie, but the children's mother, Sarbajaya (Karuna Bannerjee), scolds her. Later, Durga is accused by a more wealthy neighbor of stealing a necklace. Sarbajaya, shamed by the allegation, throws Durga out of the house. We see not only the distress of mother and daughter but Apu's response too, as he implicitly sides with his sister.

These minor moments of drama are punctuated by greater tragedies. One of the best-known scenes in the film comes when the children quarrel and Durga has once more been scolded by her mother. She runs away across the fields, with Apu following. We see black smoke rising and then a train. Apu and Durga run toward it, excited by this vision of something from the wide world beyond their village. On the way back, chattering together, their quarrel made up, they encounter Auntie sitting in a bamboo grove. When Durga touches her, she keels over. She is dying.

The father, Harihar (Kanu Bannerjee), leaves for the city to try and make some money. While he is away, Durga catches pneumonia and dies. Unaware, the father returns, flushed with success and carrying gifts for his family, including a sari for Durga. Sarbajaya breaks down and weeps. Harihar collapses in grief. We observe Apu listening to his father's cries.

Eventually Harihar decides to take the remainder of his family back to the city. In a telling moment, while helping clear the house Apu finds a necklace hidden in a bowl. So Durga did steal it after all; the knowledge makes Apu's grief more poignant. Apu throws the necklace into a pond, where the weeds close over it.

Ray's mise-en-scène has great delicacy, capable of expressing both strong emotion and lyrical delight. Few will forget the sequence in which Apu and Durga hear the sound of the traveling sweets seller. Although they have no money to buy, they trot along behind him, followed in turn by a curious dog; the little procession is reflected in a pool of water.

Helped by Ravi Shankar's marvelous music, *Pather Panchali* achieved worldwide success, and earned Ray recognition at the 1956 Cannes Film Festival. **EB**

Ordet Carl Theodor Dreyer, 1955

An extraordinary work, and arguably the finest achievement of this great filmmaker, Carl Theodor Dreyer's adaptation of Kaj Munk's play is a cinematic rarity in that, with the simplest of means and no special effects whatsoever, it manages to persuade the viewer that a miracle can happen.

Ordet concerns the Borgens, a farming family, loving and close but also beset by tensions arising from a number of disagreements and misfortunes—notably the wayward behavior of one of the grown-up brothers, seemingly insane due to excessive travails while studying religious thought. Not everyone thinks that Johannes (Preben Lerdorff Rye) is crazy, however, and when Inger (Birgitte Federspiel), another brother's wife, dies, her child asks him to bring her mother back—which, at the end of the film, he appears to do. In fact, Dreyer leaves it to the spectator to decide whether her revival is a matter of mere scientific inability to understand the improbable or of strength of faith, but the scene is remarkably powerful, precisely because he refuses both to explain and to rev up the film's dramatic engines; the scene convinces thanks to its own air of tranquility and that of everything preceding it.

Indeed, this is in many respects the most "realistic" or "naturalistic" of films dealing with the power of faith, love, and the supernatural; Dreyer eschews any kind of trickery. Although Henning Bendtsen's pared-down yet beautiful black-and-white images do endow the Borgens's cottage and pastures with a lustrous quality, Dreyer's quiet rhythms, long takes, and deceptively simple mise-en-scène may suggest that the movie is a straightforward chamber drama about ordinary farming folk. Only Johannes's wheedling voice appears at all unusual, and he, after all, is not quite right in the head. Wherein lies *Ordet*'s greatness: by the time the "miracle" occurs, the film has earned our respect for its integrity—we understand the people on-screen because their actions, emotions, thoughts, and doubts are like our own. And when Inger opens her eyes once more, we probably feel much as they do: astonishment, happiness, and genuine wonder. For even if *Ordet* fails to convert us to religious belief, we have, at least, witnessed cinematic art of the highest order. **GA**

Denmark (Palladium) 126m BW
Language Danish **Producer** Carl Theodor Dreyer, Erik Nielsen, Tage Nielsen
Screenplay Kaj Munk, from his play
Photography Henning Bendtsen
Music Poul Schierbeck, Sylvia Schierbeck
Cast Hanne Agesen, Kirsten Andreasen, Sylvia Eckhausen, Birgitte Federspiel, Ejner Federspiel, Emil Hass Christensen, Cay Kristiansen, Preben Lerdorff Rye, Henrik Malberg, Gerda Nielsen, Ann Elisabeth Rud, Ove Rud, Susanne Rud, Henry Skjær, Edith Trane **Venice Film Festival** Carl Theodor Dreyer (Golden Lion)

"A strange, wondrous, and shocking work. Once seen, it's unlikely to leave you."

Dave Calhoun,
Time Out London, 2012

i

The movie consists of 114 shots, each averaging around a minute, and only three close-ups.

Marty Delbert Mann, 1955

U.S. (Hecht, Hill & Lancaster, Steven)
91m BW **Producer** Harold Hecht
Screenplay Paddy Chayefsky
Photography Joseph LaShelle
Music George Bassman, Harry Warren, Roy
Webb **Cast** Ernest Borgnine, Betsy Blair,
Esther Minciotti, Augusta Ciolli, Joe
Mantell, Karen Steele, Jerry Paris
Oscars Harold Hecht (best picture),
Delbert Mann (director), Paddy Chayefsky
(screenplay), Ernest Borgnine (actor)
Oscar nominations Joe Mantell (actor in
pport role), Betsy Blair (actress in
pport role), Ted Haworth, Walter M.
Simonds, Robert Priestley (art direction),
Joseph LaShelle (photography) **Cannes Film
Festival** Delbert Mann (Golden Palm and
OCIC award)

During the golden age of American television, Paddy Chayefsky wrote the teleplay *Marty*. It was notable for its focus on the ordinary life of an unmarried butcher. Chayefsky then translated the script for the big screen with Ernest Borgnine as the star. Thereafter, Marty Pilletti became a cause célèbre for seizing happiness outside the mold of mid-1950s conformity and consensus.

Tagged "It's the love story of an unsung hero!" *Marty* thrilled audiences in its tale of a man who lives at home with his mother, the classic Italian matriarch. Trolling singles spots with his best friend Angie (Joe Mantell), Marty meets Clara (Betsy Blair) and they begin a ritual courtship. Angie quickly becomes jealous, and Mrs. Pilletti (Esther Minciotti) confounds matters with nightmares of abandonment, but Marty finally pursues Clara because he likes her.

Described thus, *Marty* suggests a yawn fest. But as a portrait of the times, especially of postwar neuroses about domestic tranquility, the film is rich with sociological value. Current cultural politics aside, the struggle for lonely people to find acceptance and love is without doubt a powerful theme. Giving the film buoyancy, this motive also sings the praises of the everyday and the beautiful, one and the same. **GC-Q**

1955

Artists and Models Frank Tashlin, 1955

U.S. (Paramount) 109m Technicolor
Producer Paul Nathan, Hal B. Wallis
Screenplay Don McGuire, Frank Tashlin,
from the story *Rock-A-Bye Baby* by Michael
Davidson and Norman Lessine
Photography Daniel L. Fapp **Music** Harry
Warren **Cast** Dean Martin, Jerry Lewis,
Shirley MacLaine, Dorothy Malone, Eddie
Mayehoff, Eva Gabor, Anita Ekberg, George
Winslow, Jack Elam, Herbert Rudley, Richard
Shannon, Richard Webb, Alan Lee,
Otto Waldis

Like Douglas Sirk's melodramas, Frank Tashlin's crazy comedies exaggerate to the point of subversion the popular values of the American 1950s. Tashlin's terrain was the media-sphere of advertising, TV, movies, and showbiz: By gleefully embracing and slyly satirizing this "plastic" arena of clichés and stereotypes, he anticipated Pop Art.

Artists and Models, which provided the Dean Martin–Jerry Lewis duo with its finest screen hour, is a dizzily self-reflexive play on movie illusion. Eugene Fullstack (Lewis) is a comic book addict whose colorful dreams are transcribed—and secretly sold—by Rick Todd (Martin). They are mirrored by two women, sultry graphic artist Abby (Dorothy Malone) and ditzy Bessie (Shirley MacLaine). Tashlin's endlessly inventive game of permutation and combination between these four characters builds to a great piece of burlesque mayhem: Eugene and Bessie's delirious détournement of the kitsch romantic ballad, "Innamorata."

With a plot that launches without warning into an international espionage intrigue (enter Eva Gabor), and a splendid musical demonstration of image-and-sound artifice ("When You Pretend"), it is only fitting that the strategies of *Artists and Models* are echoed in the merry modernisms of Jacques Rivette (*Celine and Julie Go Boating* [1974]), P.T. Anderson (*Punch-Drunk Love* [2002]), and Australia's Yahoo Serious (*Mr. Accident* [2000]). **AM**

Rebel Without a Cause Nicholas Ray, 1955

Too often, this acknowledged classic is unwittingly damned with faint praise as being the finest of the three features in which James Dean starred during his tragically short life. *Rebel* remains by far the best 1950s film dealing with the then-new phenomenon of teenage delinquency. It is also a key work from Nicholas Ray, an enormously talented and distinctive director who, sadly, remains as underrated now as he was when he worked in Hollywood.

Dean's Jim Stark gives voice to the agonizing confusion and alienation felt by so many of Ray's protagonists. From his first film, *They Live By Night* (1949), the director had repeatedly treated the lonely predicament of America's outsiders, showing himself especially sympathetic to the vulnerable young who looked for guidance from an older generation no wiser or happier than themselves. Jim feels let down by his family, his teachers, the cops, and most of his peers. The constant quest for kicks is as irresponsible (albeit less culpable, given their youth) as the adults' refusal to confront moral dilemmas. Together with other lost souls, Judy (Natalie Wood) and Plato (Sal Mineo), Jim tries to establish his own alternative family, one based on mutual understanding. Small wonder that the trio, brought together by the absurd, unnecessary death of a friend driven by boredom to test his worth in a cliff top "chickee run," and united by idealistic notions of "sincerity," lives in a derelict dreamhouse in the Los Angeles hills, well away from other people.

Ray's response to the question of how to depict his young dreamers' romantic idealism is admirably and exhilaratingly physical. The film was originally slated for black and white, but Ray persuaded Warners to let him shoot in color. The often luridly expressionist hues and Ray's typically fraught CinemaScope compositions evoke the feverish nature of adolescent experience. Similarly, Ray uses architecture and setting, particularly the difference between public and private space, to heighten our understanding of the characters' emotions. The darkness inside a planetarium becomes a space to indulge in private jokes, refuge, and reverie, even contemplation of the individual's place in the cosmos. The terrace outside is later transformed by a lofty camera position into a sunlit arena where a bullfight-like knife fight is played out with appropriately histrionic gestures. Ray understands how, especially when young, we view our lives as drama. His immaculate sense of color, composition, cutting, lighting, and performance enhances the importance of the action.

Not just Dean's style but his whole body gives dramatic life to the turmoil within. Seeing Dean's Jim is witnessing a character being born, growing from moment to moment before our eyes. That, of course, is fitting for *Rebel*'s subject matter, but it also complements Ray's direction in terms of how its acute physicality expresses the tormented vitality within. How sad, then, that the projects Ray and Dean planned to work on together never came to fruition. One great film had to suffice. **GA**

U.S. (Warner Bros.) 111m
Warnercolor **Producer** David Weisbart
Screenplay Nicholas Ray, Irving Shulman, Stewart Stern **Music** Leonard Rosenman
Cast James Dean, Natalie Wood, Sal Mineo, Jim Backus, Ann Doran, Corey Allen, William Hopper, Rochelle Hudson, Dennis Hopper, Edward Platt, Steffi Sidney, Marietta Canty, Virginia Brissac, Beverly Long, Ian Wolfe
Oscar nominations Nicholas Ray (screenplay), Sal Mineo (actor in support role), Natalie Wood (actress in support role)

"You're tearing me apart!"

**Jim Stark
(James Dean)**

i

T-shirt sales soared after James Dean wore one in the movie, as they were suddenly seen as cool and rebellious.

Les maîtres fous Jean Rouch, 1955
The Mad Masters

France (Pléiade) 36m Color
Language French Photography Jean
Rouch Cast Jean Rouch (narrator)

In 1954, ethnographic filmmaker Jean Rouch was invited by a group of Hauka in the West African city of Accra to document their yearly religious ritual. Over the course of this ceremony, the Hauka went into a trancelike state and were possessed by spirits representing the Western colonialists (the engineer, the wife of the doctor, the cruel major, and so on).

Though only thirty-six minutes long, the imagery in *The Mad Masters* is striking and frequently alarming: possessed men, their eyes rolling, foaming at the mouth, burning their bodies with torches. Indeed, Peter Brook's 1966 film *Marat/Sade* would reference the histrionics and made-up language here captured on camera by Rouch.

But as the director himself has noted, for the Hauka possession by spirits was truth, not art. While the film never fully explains the meaning behind the ritual, Rouch's narration hints that participation in this religious ceremony results in a kind of catharsis, one that gives the Hauka—mostly rural migrant laborers—the strength needed to maintain their self-respect and continue working under harsh and oppressive conditions. As one scholar observes, the most intriguing issue raised by *The Mad Masters* concerns the complex relation of the Hauka sect to their experience of colonialism. One of the masterpieces of ethnographic cinema. **SJS**

Hill 24 Doesn't Answer Thorold Dickinson, 1955

Israel (Israel Motion Picture, Sik'or)
101m BW Language English / Hebrew
Producer Thorold Dickinson, Peter Frye, Zvi
Kolitz, Jack Padwa Screenplay Peter Frye,
Zvi Kolitz Photography Gerald Gibbs
Music Paul Ben Chayim Cast Edward
Mulhare, Michael Wager, Margalit Oved, Arik
Lavi, Michael Shillo, Haya Harareet, Eric
Greene, Stanley Preston, Haim Eynav,
Zalman Lebiush, Azaria Rapaport

Made by British director Thorold Dickinson, who had come to Israel to make a documentary on the army (*The Red Background*), *Hill 24 Doesn't Answer* was the first film of the national period to achieve an international success. Dickinson, who was influenced by the documentary/fiction films made in Britain during World War II, uses time-tested techniques of that genre (explanatory maps, an authoritative voice-over) to tell the story of a small Israeli unit defending a strategic hill position near Jerusalem against Arab attack in the 1948 war.

In the manner of David Lean's *In Which We Serve*, Dickinson spends little time on the action itself, which becomes the framework for telling the stories of the four main characters: an American Jew, an Irishman, a native-born Israeli, and a Sephardic Jew. All die in the successful defense of the position, which is thereby assured, after the visit of a U.N. observer, as belonging to Israeli. Flashbacks detail the reasons why each soldier has chosen to fight. The film is fervently pro-Zionist, with Druse and British characters presented sympathetically and the Arabs as an anonymous, hostile, destructive force, whose reasons for attack are never made clear. Despite the obvious propaganda, Dickinson's film is a small-scale masterpiece, an intriguing examination of motivation and heroism in the midst of deadly ideological struggle. **BP**

Bad Day at Black Rock John Sturges, 1955

U.S. (MGM) 81m Eastmancolor
Producer Herman Hoffman, Dore Schary
Screenplay Howard Breslin, Don
McGuire, Millard Kaufman, from the story
"Bad Day at Hondo" by Howard Breslin
Photography William C. Mellor
Music André Previn Cast Spencer Tracy,
Robert Ryan, Anne Francis, Dean Jagger, Walter
Brennan, John Ericson, Ernest Borgnine, Lee
Marvin, Russell Collins, Walter Sande Oscar
nominations John Sturges (director), Millard
Kaufman (screenplay), Spencer Tracy (actor)
Venice Film Festival Spencer Tracy (actor),
tied with cast of Bolshaya semya

*"You're not only wrong.
You're wrong at the top
of your voice."*

**John J. Macreedy
(Spencer Tracy)**

It's 1945, just after World War II, and John J. Macreedy (Spencer Tracy) is a one-armed ex-army man who steps off the train in Black Rock, a remote California desert town. We don't know what he's come for, nor do the inhabitants. But they are hostile, and it soon becomes clear that they are hiding something. Director John Sturges slowly tightens the tension as Macreedy digs deeper into the town's secret, while the inhabitants cut the phone wires and disable a car in which he tries to leave.

Set in an arid western landscape, to which the film's CinemaScope ratio gives full value, and shot in color, mostly in blinding sunlight, *Bad Day at Black Rock* is sandwiched between a number of notable Sturges Westerns, including *Escape from Fort Bravo* (1953) and *Gunfight at the OK Corral* (1957). Yet despite its look, *Black Rock* is really more of a film noir, with its story of dark secrets in the past. There's little physical action and hardly any gunplay, though one scene is memorable, when Macreedy is finally provoked to fight by the brutish Coley Trimble (Ernest Borgnine). The one-armed man reveals a repertoire of karate chops and punches that fell his opponent like a slaughtered ox.

Macreedy faces an impressive lineup of heavies here, including ringleader Reno Smith (Robert Ryan, whose hysteria is never far below the surface), and Lee Marvin in one of his most menacing roles as Hector David. Macreedy has to rely for help on the community's weaker members: the reclusive Doc (Walter Brennan) and the drunken, cowardly sheriff (Dean Jagger). Eventually Macreedy manages to invest them with a little of his courage and they help him make a break, but ultimately he is forced to rely on his own ingenuity.

The town's dirty secret proves to be the murder of a Japanese-American in the days following Pearl Harbor. The film was produced by Dore Schary, who tried to stand up to blacklisting and whose regime at MGM was marked by a number of liberal productions. *Bad Day at Black Rock* is a good example, a taut, expertly acted and directed thriller that pushes a fairly straightforward message about racial tolerance. But whatever its good intentions, it's Tracy whom we remember most. Few actors could project basic goodness so well, without a trace of sanctimoniousness. **EB**

1955

ℹ

Bad Day at Black Rock is one of the most frequently shown films at the screening room in the White House.

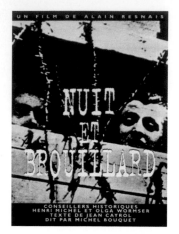

Nuit et brouillard Alain Resnais, 1955
Night and Fog

Documentation of man's inhumanity to man is as old as history itself. Even so, little prepared the world for the atrocities of the Holocaust, a concerted series of events so horrific that it still boggles the mind. Aware how the passage of time has a way of diluting memories, however powerful, filmmaker Alain Resnais (who later rose to prominence as the director of such features as *Hiroshima Mon Amour* [1959]) decided to capture the Nazi atrocities on camera, if not for posterity then certainly as a lasting reminder of what we are capable of doing to one another.

The first film to truly address the Holocaust at a time when World War II still produced raw feelings, especially in Europe, *Night and Fog* juxtaposed black-and-white archival footage of concentration camps and their victims with pastoral color footage of the buildings and locations ten years later. Revealing the depths of distrust and denial that existed even a decade after the fall of the Third Reich, Resnais used footage from France, Belgium, and Poland, but conspicuously not from Germany. He showed that many of the people involved in the death camps either didn't know how to deal with their own guilt and complicity or didn't want to.

Denial is the driving point of *Night and Fog*. Resnais includes footage of the dead being bulldozed into mass graves, corpses hung on barbed wire fences, emaciated faces frozen in fear, skeletal nude bodies being paraded out for humiliation, and anonymous trains and trucks shipping who knows what to who knows where. He documents the gas chambers and crematoriums, as well as the Nazi's gruesome attempts to find a use for the discarded possessions, bones, skin, and bodies of their victims.

Resnais, in his own footage, notes that these death camps existed not in isolated outposts but frequently nearby major cities, hinting that everything that transpired happened with at least some degree of complicity on the part of civilians. Yet even the Nazis in charge of the camps deny culpability. One after the other, each claims, "I am not responsible." But if not them, asks the film, then who?

Night and Fog is more concerned with attributing collective blame than with pointing fingers at any specific figure. Even so soon after the war, Resnais realized that the fleeting nature of memory risked erasure of the Nazi horrors. "A crematorium may look as pretty as a picture postcard," notes the narrator. "Today tourists are photographed standing in front of them." Working from a script by Holocaust survivor Jean Cayrol and enlisting an oddly meandering score by Hanns Eisler (a Marxist and German exile who was also deported from America during Hollywood's own communist purge), Resnais lets the accumulated images of death and terror serve as a vivid rebuttal to any who would ever again turn their backs on such atrocities. If the brief but powerful *Night and Fog* does ultimately parallel the pithy form of a postcard, it is a postcard offering a perpetually valid message—evil can always resurface. **JKl**

France (Argos) 32m BW / Color
Language French **Producer** Anatole Dauman, Samy Halfon, Philippe Lifchitz **Screenplay** Jean Cayrol **Photography** Ghislain Cloquet, Sacha Vierny **Music** Hanns Eisler **Cast** Michel Bouquet, Reinhard Heydrich, Heinrich Himmler, Adolf Hitler, Julius Streicher

"The achievement of Resnais's film is to find a tone appropriate to the desolating enormity of what took place."

Time Out Film Guide

ℹ

The title refers to the way that people who resisted the Nazi occupiers would vanish "into the night and fog."

The Phenix City Story Phil Karlson, 1955

U.S. (Allied Artists) 100m BW
Producer Samuel Bischoff, David Diamond
Screenplay Daniel Mainwaring, Crane
Wilbur **Photography** Harry Neumann
Music Harry Sukman **Cast** John McIntire,
Richard Kiley, Kathryn Grant, Edward
Andrews, Lenka Peterson, Biff McGuire,
Truman Smith, Joan Carson, Kathy Marlowe,
John Larch, Allen Nourse, Helen Martin, Otto
Hulett, George Mitchell, Ma Beachie

Decent citizens fight a bloody war to drive out the vice racket that has earned their Alabama town the title of "Sin City, U.S.A." Based on fact and shot on location, Phil Karlson's *The Phenix City Story* relates to such postwar trends as the semidocumentary, the corrupt city exposé, and the syndicate gangster movie, but none of these labels accounts for the film's extraordinary visceral power.

Although its graphic violence was virtually unprecedented in Hollywood, what makes this low-budget shocker truly innovative is its recognition that new content calls for new form. *The Phenix City Story* is a purposefully ugly movie, full of ugly rednecks, ugly juke joints, ugly camera angles (in the sense that they flout the conventions of "good" composition), and ugly, unaestheticized violence. A little girl's glassy-eyed corpse is heaved onto a suburban lawn, a crippled old man is shot point-blank in the mouth, the townspeople are bloodied and blasted with battlefield-like regularity. The atrocities are either shoved abruptly in our faces or kept at a bewildering distance, as if they were overwhelming the picture's capacity to represent them properly. Many movies since have portrayed more explicit and elaborate violence, but few have conveyed violence's chaotic force with such intelligent crudeness. **MR**

🛈

Karlson also directed *The Scarface Mob* (1959), the TV movie that launched *The Untouchables* TV series.

The Man with the Golden Arm Otto Preminger, 1955

U.S. (Carlyle Productions, Otto Preminger Films) 119m BW **Producer** Otto Preminger **Screenplay** Walter Newman, Lewis Meltzer, from novel by Nelson Algren **Photography** Sam Leavitt **Music** Elmer Berstein **Cast** Frank Sinatra, Eleanore Parker, Kim Novak, Arnold Stang, Darren McGavin, Robert Strauss, John Conte, Doro Merande, George E. Stone, George Matthews, Leonid Kinskey, Emile Meyer **Oscar nominations** Frank Sinatra (actor), Joseph C. Wright, Darrell Silvera (art direction), Elmer Bernstein (score)

Few directors took so many risks within mainstream Hollywood as Otto Preminger. He had already released a film lacking an MPAA certificate with *The Moon is Blue* in 1953. However, it was his take on Nelson Algren's frank account of drug addiction that saw him at his boldest.

Sinatra plays Frankie Machine, an ex-con and heroin addict who wants to start life anew. His wife (Eleanor Parker) fakes her disability in order to ensure Frankie stays with her, while his old employer (Robert Strauss) wants him to return to dealing cards and his pusher (Darren McGavin) is keen to have him back on heroin. Only Molly (Kim Novak), an old flame, offers him any respite from his woes. But as his need for a fix increases, the world seems to close in on Frankie, eclipsing any hope of redemption.

Just two years after his career was resuscitated by a recording contract with Capitol Records and an Oscar for *From Here to Eternity* (1953), Frank Sinatra is on blistering form as Frankie. He conjures up a tragic figure whose attempts to better himself always seem destined to fail. Algren felt the adaptation bore little resemblance to his novel. True, Frankie is more sympathetic on-screen than he is on the page, but Preminger's unwillingness to pull any punches and the film's edgy score accentuate the impact of his addiction. The film would pave the way for an increasingly graphic representation of drug addiction on the screen. **IHS**

Kiss Me Deadly Robert Aldrich, 1955

U.S. (Parklane) 106m BW **Producer** Robert Aldrich **Screenplay** Mickey Spillane, A.I. Bezzerides, from novel by Mickey Spillane **Photography** Ernest Laszlo **Music** Frank De Vol **Cast** Ralph Meeker, Albert Dekker, Paul Stewart, Juano Hernandez, Wesley Addy, Marian Carr, Marjorie Bennett, Maxine Cooper, Fortunio Bonanova, Cloris Leachman, Gaby Rodgers, Robert Cornthwaite, Nick Dennis, Jack Lambert, Jack Elam

Kiss Me Deadly is a thick-ear masterpiece, wrenched by director Robert Aldrich and screenwriter A.I. Bezzerides from Mickey Spillane's trash novel, shot through with poetry ("Remember Me" by Christina Rosetti), unspeakable violence (the kicking naked legs of a woman tortured vaginally with a pair of pliers), hopped-up street talk ("3D-Pow! Va-va-voom!"), strange characters, and fringe-fantastical elements.

After credits that roll the wrong way and a nighttime drive, the desperate Christina Bailey (Cloris Leachman), naked under a trenchcoat, flags down thuggish private eye Mike Hammer (Ralph Meeker) and drags him into a plot involving spies, hoodlums, cops, a mastermind so erudite that he can only speak in metaphors when warning a dim-bulb blonde not to tamper with something deadly enough to kill everyone in range, codeword-dropping secret agents ("Los Alamos . . . Trinity . . . Manhattan Project") and a suitcase containing "the big whatsit" (a box of fissionable treasure that might be either pure plutonium or the head of Medusa). Meeker's nasty hero (note his smile as he tortures innocent witnesses by breaking irreplaceable opera records or slamming hands in drawers) sucker punches his way through a cast of perverts and sluts, then (at least in some prints) goes up with a mushroom cloud that rises from a beach house at the 1950s apocalypse of a finish. **KN**

U.S. (Samuel Goldwyn) 150m Eastmancolor
Producer Samuel Goldwyn Screenplay
Joseph L. Mankiewicz from play by Jo
Swerling and Abe Burrows and the story
"The Idyll of Miss Sarah Brown" by Damon
Runyon Photography Harry Stradling Sr.
Music Jay Blackton, Frank Loesser
Cast Marlon Brando, Jean Simmons, Frank
Sinatra, Vivian Blaine, Robert Keith, Stubby
Kaye, B.S. Pulley, Johnny Silver, Sheldon
Leonard, Danny Dayton, George E. Stone,
Regis Toomey, Kathryn Givney, Veda Ann
Borg, Mary Alan Hokanson Oscar
nominations Oliver Smith, Joseph C. Wright,
Howard Bristol (art direction), Harry Stradling
Sr. (photography), Irene Sharaff (costume),
Jay Blackton, Cyril J. Mockridge (music)

*"I am not putting the
knock on dolls. It's just
that they are something
to have around only
when they come in handy
. . . like cough drops."*

Sky Masterson
(Marlon Brando)

i

The audio for each of Brando's
muscial numbers in the movies is
constructed from multiple takes.

Guys and Dolls   Joseph L. Mankiewicz, 1955

Hollywood's stereotyping of national cultures regularly gives offense, but who can resist the glimpse of Havana, Cuba, in a central scene of *Guys and Dolls*? Suave gambler Sky Masterson (Marlon Brando) has talked prim, Salvation Army member Sarah Brown (Jean Simmons) into taking a plane and dining with him. As she gets drunk and succumbs to her reckless impulses, she is enflamed by the primal, Latin American drama unfolding around her: her instant rival, an exotic dancer, trying to seduce Sky. Soon the whole room is swept up in a hilarious dance of drunken passions.

The scene offers a magnificent example of Michael Kidd's revolutionary choreography for film. Normal, everyday gestures, such as walking or pointing, are by degrees stylized, made angular and rhythmic, until the point of full-blown dance. The actions of individuals are woven into group patterns. And, above all, the staging incorporates movements that are deliberately ungainly, awkward, and seemingly amateur.

Guys and Dolls is really two films in one, divided up for its dual male stars—and indeed, there is an over-the-table dialogue between Brando and Frank Sinatra that anticipates the Al Pacino–Robert De Niro encounter forty years later in *Heat* (1995). The Nathan Detroit (Sinatra) half is more indebted to writer-director Joseph Mankiewicz's source, Damon Runyan's tales of lovable, streetwise crooks (every "ethnic" tic of New York speech and behavior lovingly exaggerated). Nathan has a long-suffering dame, Adelaide (Vivian Blaine), which leads to amusing material about their fraught path to the altar, such as "Adelaide's Lament" in Frank Loesser's colorful score.

Although the more conventionally polished, show-stopping group numbers like "Luck Be a Lady" and "Sit Down, You're Rockin' the Boat" are the ones Broadway devotees remember best, it is in the more romantic, Sky–Sarah half that the film really soars. The songs "If I Were a Bell" and "I'll Know When My Love Comes Along" are glorious swellings of amorous emotion, and Mankiewicz surrounds them with a wonderful mise-en-scène of comings and goings, attractions and repulsions between these two admirable bodies. **AM**

The Night of the Hunter Charles Laughton, 1955

U.S. (Paul Gregory, United Artists) 93m BW
Producer Paul Gregory **Screenplay** James
Agee, from novel by Davis Grubb
Photography Stanley Cortez **Music** Walter
Schumann **Cast** Robert Mitchum, Shelley
Winters, Lillian Gish, James Gleason, Evelyn
Varden, Peter Graves, Don Beddoe, Billy
Chapin, Sally Jane Bruce, Gloria Castillo

"Despite its peculiar overtones of humor, this is one of the most frightening movies ever made."

Pauline Kael,
The New Yorker, 1983

Based on a slim, stark novel by Davis Grubb, Charles Laughton's sole film as a director is a Depression-set fable of psychosis and faith, strikingly sinister and yet deeply humane. Told mostly from the point of view of children, the story is like a fairy tale in its simplicity, and yet seethes with adult complications. The trigger is a stash of money stolen by hard-up bandit Ben Harper (Peter Graves) and entrusted to his children John (Billy Chapin) and Pearl (Sally Jane Bruce), which makes Ben's desperate widow Willa (Shelley Winters) an object of attraction for one of the screen's most unforgettable villains. "Reverend" Harry Powell (Robert Mitchum), in black-and-white clerical garb with a puritan flat hat that curls into a set of demonic-looking horns, is associated with the Bible and a switchblade; with the words "love" and "hate" tattooed on his knuckles, his sermon consists of an allegorical talk about these forces locked in conflict illustrated as he arm wrestles with himself. Powell's wooing of Willa is high pressure, fooling the woman (who ends up serenely drowned) but not the children, who flee after the murder, the money stashed in the little girl's doll.

Mitchum, usually associated with cynical heroes, here plays a sincerely committed villain, moonlighting as a serial killer of loose women but sexually obsessed with the money he feels he needs to fund his bloody crusade. The nocturnal escape down river, shot in expressionist monochrome, is a magical sequence, with close-ups of strange-looking swampland flora and fauna. With Evil/Hate so powerfully conveyed, *The Night of the Hunter* needs an equally strong force to represent Good/Love. Laughton managed to get silent star Lillian Gish to come out of semiretirement to play Rachel, a kindly woman whose farm is open to the many underage runaways who come down the path. Like the snake in Eden, Powell threatens Rachel's idyll, working his seamy charm on one of the older girls to find a way onto the farm. In a remarkable siege finale, Mitchum's menacing drone of an edited hymn ("Leanin'") is joined and completed by Gish, who knows the full lyric ("Lean on Jesus") and adds her voice to his, banishing his darkness aurally before he is actually defeated. **KN**

i

Laughton did not like the two child actors, and they received most of their direction from Mitchum.

The Ladykillers Alexander Mackendrick, 1955

G.B. (Ealing Studios, Rank) 97m Technicolor
Producer Michael Balcon, Seth Holt
Screenplay William Rose **Photography** Otto
Heller **Music** Tristram Cary **Cast** Alec
Guinness, Cecil Parker, Herbert Lom, Peter
Sellers, Danny Green, Jack Warner, Katie
Johnson, Philip Stainton, Frankie Howerd
Oscar nomination William Rose (screenplay)

Alexander Mackendrick's final Ealing film (and also his darkest), made before he went to Hollywood and gave us the memorably bilious *Sweet Smell of Success* (1957), is a deliciously black comedy of English manners. A gang of thieves, hiding out disguised as a music quintet in the genteel Edwardian home of innocent and very, very proper little old lady Katie Johnson, decide they must murder her after she finds out about their recent robbery and insists they return the loot. The trouble is, the honor among these particular thieves is skewed, and although they can't quite bring themselves to kill off the sweet old thing, they have no such reservations with regard to one another.

Essentially, then, *The Ladykillers* is a farcical variation on the classic heist-gone-wrong theme, fascinating both for its deft characterizations (the gang comprise a devious mastermind, a bluff military type, an Italianate hit man, a spivvish "Teddy boy," and an intellectually challenged muscle man) and for its suggestion that postwar Britain, overly reverential toward an earlier age, was so divided as to be unable to move forward into the modern era. Otto Heller's color camera work and Jim Morahan's production design serve to reinforce the sense of a society trapped in the past. **GA**

i

The Coen brothers remade *The Ladykillers* in 2004, with Tom Hanks in the Alec Guiness role.

Oklahoma! Fred Zinneman, 1955

U.S. (20th Century Fox) 145m Color
Producer Arthur Hornblow
Screenplay Sonya Levien, William Ludwig,
based on a play by Lynn Riggs
Photography Robert Surtees Music Oscar
Hammerstein II, Richard Rodgers
Cast Gordon MacRae, Gloria Grahame, Gene
Nelson, Charlotte Greenwood, Shirley Jones,
Eddie Albert, James Whitmore, Rod Steiger,
Barbara Lawrence, Jay C Flippen, Roy
Barcroft, James Mitchell Oscars Robert
Russell Bennett, Jay Blackton, Adolph
Deutsch (scoring of a musical picture), Fred
Hynes (sound) Oscar nominations Robert
Surtees (cinematography), Gene Ruggiero,
George Boemier (editing)

Based on a 1943 Broadway stage show by Richard Rodgers and Oscar Hammerstein II, Oklahoma! is a lively, colorful, full-blooded musical set among pioneer folk in the eponymous American state. Unfolding at the turn of the last century, on the eve of Oklahoma achieving full statehood, the film stars Gordon MacRae as cowboy Curly McLain, who falls in love with Shirley Jones's farm girl Laurey Williams. Combining the boy-meets-girl plotline of the romantic musical with the wide vistas of the best Westerns—mostly shot in Arizona rather than Oklahoma—the movie was a prestige studio production.

The first musical directed by Fred Zinneman, a director hitherto better known for serious drama, Oklahoma! is generally a buoyant and joyous experience. Rod Steiger is the exception, whose appearance as Judd, Curly's bitter rival for Laurey's affections, gives the film a surprisingly dark and menacing layer. But it is the songs, such as "Oh What a Beautiful Morning," and accompanying dance numbers (choreographed by Agnes de Mille, who worked on the original Broadway show) that most impress. One of the last gasps from the halcyon days of the Hollywood musical, Oklahoma! remains a sterling example of the genre. **EL**

Sommarnattens leende Ingmar Bergman, 1955
Smiles of a Summer Night

Sweden (Svensk) 108m BW
Language Swedish Producer Allan
Ekelund Screenplay Ingmar Bergman
Photography Gunnar Fischer Music Erik
Nordgren Cast Ulla Jacobsson, Eva
Dahlbeck, Harriet Andersson, Margit
Carlqvist, Gunnar Björnstrand, Jarl Kulle,
Åke Fridell, Björn Bjelfvenstam, Naima
Wifstrand, Jullan Kindahl, Gull Natorp,
Birgitta Valberg, Bibi Andersson Cannes
Film Festival Ingmar Bergman (poetic
humor award)

This first international success by Ingmar Bergman might, in retrospect, look like an anomaly in his career. In interviews Bergman often claimed he had no talent for comedy, and his later work in the genre—The Devil's Eye (1960) and All These Women (1964)—would seem to confirm this sentiment. However, with Waiting Women (1952) and especially A Lesson in Love (1954), he found a successful formula for witty, sophisticated comedies featuring the two excellent actors Gunnar Björnstrand and Eva Dahlbeck (lovingly referred to by the director as "The Battleship Femininity") as a middle-aged couple playfully tormenting each other.

Smiles of a Summer Night is a variation of this formula, transposed into a nineteenth-century moral comedy and with a theatrical plot heavily influenced by Shakespeare's A Midsummer Night's Dream. Here, the Björnstrand character is a middle-aged philistine and Dahlbeck's an aging actress. Both are vain and self-important, living in separate relationships that have proved to be even more frustrating than their own former liaison. Egged on by an aphrodisiac wine and the magical twilight of a midsummer night, their—and their spouses'—true feelings are revealed. Everybody finds his/her true mate. But this new equilibrium of bourgeois complacency was later to be disrupted by Bergman with a vengeance in his hellish visions of marriage and midlife crisis in Scenes from a Marriage (1973) and From the Life of the Marionettes (1980). **MT**

Bob le flambeur Jean-Pierre Melville, 1955
Bob the Gambler

Bob the Gambler, Jean-Pierre Melville's fourth feature, belongs to a very specific moment in history, and in the history of cinema. It is the milestone of a subtle turning point, and it maintains the flavor of this moment. Previously there was European cinema and American cinema. There was classic cinema and modern cinema. There were gangster films and comedies and daily chronicles. There was a guy, still rather young for a director, who at age thirty-nine, with one or two lives already behind him, had made a ghostly war film of incredible intensity (*The Silence of the Sea* [1949]), an adaptation from a Jean Cocteau novel (*Les Enfants Terribles* [1950]), and a lame melodrama (*When You Read This Letter* [1953]). Later, he would become the uncle of the New Wave, the French master of film noir, the director who paved the road for Sergio Leone, John Woo, and many others, the owner of a studio (quickly ruined), and the ultimate dandy of European filmmaking. But at the moment in question, Melville was working out the modernity of the second half of the twentieth century using the tools of the first half. *Bob the Gambler* is nostalgic and burlesque, yet filled with compassion and an accurate and respectful attention to places, objects, words, and the dreams everyone is entitled to live with.

Casino attacks, large-shouldered gangsters, macho talk, cars running fast in the dark, betrayal—sure! The film is a matter of human material, an inflection of voices, a remembrance of golden ages that never existed. It is often said that great films are universal and for all time. But *Bob the Gambler* is great for precisely the opposite reason: It belongs to its time and place, more or less consciously elaborating from that toward a completely different future. Although its ironic plot is important, the film's essence lies in its beauty and melancholy. Certainly, the world has gone on since *Bob the Gambler*. But something was captured in this film, like in a glass snow globe, for us to look back on and remember. And there is nothing sad in that. **J-MF**

France (OGC, Play Art, Cyme) 98m BW
Language French **Producer** Jean-Pierre Melville **Screenplay** Auguste Le Breton, Jean-Pierre Melville **Photography** Henri Decaë **Music** Eddie Barclay **Cast** Isabelle Corey, Daniel Cauchy, Roger Duchesne, Guy Decomble, André Garet, Gérard Buhr, Claude Cerval, Colette Fleury, René Havard, Simone Paris, Howard Vernon, Henry Allaume, Germaine Amiel, Yvette Amirante, Dominique Antoine

*"I was born with an
ace in my palm."*

Bob (Roger Duchesne)

i
Stanley Kubrick once said that he decided to give up making crime films after seeing *Bob the Gambler*.

All That Heaven Allows Douglas Sirk, 1955

U.S. (Universal) 89m Technicolor
Producer Ross Hunter **Screenplay** Peg
Fenwick, Edna L. Lee, Harry Lee, from story
by Edna L. Lee **Photography** Russell Metty
Music Frank Skinner **Cast** Jane Wyman,
Rock Hudson, Agnes Moorehead, Conrad
Nagel, Virginia Grey, Gloria Talbott, William
Reynolds, Charles Drake, Hayden Rorke,
Jacqueline deWit, Leigh Snowden, Donald
Curtis, Alex Gerry, Nestor Paiva, Forrest Lewis

*"The one thing that
Mr Sirk gave me was
confidence ... I, when
I started out, was
quite insecure ... He
said, 'You can do it.'"*

Rock Hudson, 1980

i

Although the plot focuses on their
age difference, Wyman was only
eight years older than Hudson.

On one level, Douglas Sirk's *All That Heaven Allows* is like a fabulous, ironic piece of performance art, the relic of a specifically mid-twentieth-century genre that degenerated into television soap opera. But the emotional core of the film's distant lives is timelessly compelling. This is arguably the finest example of the plush 1950s Technicolor melodramas, and the most classic one made at Universal by Danish-born Sirk (formerly Detlef Sierck), a leftist theater-director-turned-filmmaker of some stature who fled with his Jewish wife from Nazi Germany to Hollywood. Back to square one as an unknown émigré, he applied distinctive taste to seemingly undemanding, trite assignments. His European sophistication and formal visual style elevated absurd and maudlin stories into deliriously entertaining heightened reality and multiple-hanky domestic dramas, including *Magnificent Obsession* (1954), *Written on the Wind* (1956), *The Tarnished Angels* (1958), and *Imitation of Life* (1959).

In *All That Heaven Allows*, pleasant middle-class widow Cary Scott (Jane Wyman), estranged from her selfish grown children and facing social ostracism from her shallow country club set, falls in love with young gardener Ron Kirby (Rock Hudson—a favorite of Sirk's who also appears as Wyman's leading man in *Magnificent Obsession*). Her distant son Ned (William Reynolds) is preoccupied with his career, and spoiled college-girl daughter Kay (Gloria Talbott) is embarrassed her mother is a woman with needs. Their idea of a great gift to fill mom's time is a TV set. Love wins out, but only after being tested by cruel gossip, tearful sacrificial separation, and a life-threatening crisis. These are all traditional staples of vintage women's pictures, but Sirk presents them with an eye for darker impulses beneath the suburban wholesomeness idealized in 1950s America, and with a subtle handling of its repressed insecurities.

Along with *Imitation of Life*, *All That Heaven Allows* was a touchstone for Todd Haynes's bold, sumptuous homage melodrama *Far From Heaven* (2002). It also provided the source of Rainer Werner Fassbinder's racially charged reworking further down the socioeconomic scale. *Ali: Fear Eats the Soul* (1974) features a poor German widow, exposed to prejudice and derision when she falls in love with the much younger Ali, a kind, equally lonely North African immigrant. Costume design from *All That Heaven Allows* even found its way into the period homage French farce *Eight Women* (2002), with Catherine Deneuve's daughter arriving home for the holidays in a replica of Gloria Talbott's beanie hat and ensemble.

Hunky Hudson, who did much of his best work with Sirk, is perfectly sincere as the rugged but sensitive young outdoorsman in whom Wyman's soulful homemaker finds liberating warmth and empathy. The picture looks good enough to eat, with wonderful color, compositions, lighting, art direction, costumes, and cinematography. But the style serves the content superbly—observation of human nature with high gloss making heavenly romantic melodrama. **AE**

The Ten Commandments Cecil B. DeMille, 1956

U.S. (Cecil B. DeMille, Paramount) 220m
Technicolor **Producer** Cecil B. DeMille,
Henry Wilcoxon **Screenplay** Aeneas
MacKenzie, Jesse Lasky Jr., Jack Gariss,
Fredric M. Frank, from the novels *Pillar of Fire*
by J.H. Ingraham, *On Eagle's Wing* by A.E.
Southon, and *Prince of Egypt* by Dorothy
Clarke Wilson **Photography** Loyal Griggs
Music Elmer Bernstein **Cast** Charlton
Heston, Yul Brynner, Anne Baxter, Edward G.
Robinson, Yvonne De Carlo, Debra Paget,
John Derek, Cedric Hardwicke, Nina Foch
Oscar John P. Fulton (special effects) **Oscar
nominations** Cecil B. DeMille (best picture),
Hal Pereira, Walter H. Tyler, Albert Nozaki,
Sam Comer, Ray Moyer (art direction), Loyal
Griggs (photography), Edith Head, Ralph
Jester, John Jensen, Dorothy Jeakins, Arnold
Friberg (costume), Anne Bauchens (editing),
Loren L. Ryder (sound recording)

🛈

The (uncredited) voice of God at
the burning bush was provided
by Charlton Heston.

With a running time of nearly four hours, Cecil B. DeMille's last feature and most extravagant blockbuster is full of absurdities and vulgarities, but the color is ravishing, and DeMille's form of showmanship, which includes his own narration, never falters. Charlton Heston might be said to achieve his apotheosis as Moses and most of the others in the cast are comparably mythic.

Simultaneously ludicrous and splendid, this epic is driven by the sort of personal conviction rarely found in subsequent Hollywood monoliths. To read it properly, one has to see it as an ideological, spiritual manifesto relating specifically to how DeMille viewed the Cold War world in 1956. Thus, when he appears in front of a gold-tasseled curtain to introduce the film, his main point isn't simply his use of ancient sources such as Philo and Josephus to recount the thirty years of Moses's life omitted in the Bible, but also to declare that "The theme of this picture is whether man should be ruled by God's laws or... by the whims of a dictator like Ramses." By "dictator," he's clearly thinking of a Mao Tse-tung figure, which the orientalism suggested by Yul Brynner as Ramses makes clear.

The film has sometimes been rereleased in a stretched, anamorphic widescreen format, which means the top and bottom of every frame is cropped. There may be some form of divine retribution at work here; DeMille was a notorious foot fetishist, and thanks to this studio trick, many of his foreground players have been deprived of their feet. **JRos**

The Searchers John Ford, 1956

The Searchers opens on a shot of a desert landscape seen from inside a house. Someone is approaching on horseback. It is Ethan Edwards (John Wayne), returned from the Civil War to his brother's ranch in Texas. From a series of looks and gestures we realize that Ethan is in love with his brother's wife, Martha (Dorothy Jordan). The next day he departs with a party of Texas Rangers in pursuit of Indians who have stolen some cattle. While he's away Comanches attack the ranch, killing Ethan's brother and sister-in-law and capturing their two daughters. For the remainder of the film, in actions set over a period of five years, Ethan and his part-Indian companion Martin (Jeffrey Hunter) crisscross the West in search of the girls.

How did John Ford turn this simple story into one of the greatest of all Westerns? First, there's the setting. Ford shot many Westerns in Monument Valley, an isolated region on the border between Utah and Arizona. The eroded red sandstone rocks are an awesome spectacle, and Ford's unerring eye for composition invests them with a special aura. The sheer size of the landscape makes the human figures seem especially vulnerable, and the life of the Texan settlers precarious. How could anyone scratch a living in such a barren wilderness?

At the heart of the story, though, is the figure of Ethan Edwards. As played by Wayne, Ethan is a colossus, overwhelming and indomitable. But he has a tragic flaw. Ethan is eaten up with hatred of the Indians, and it becomes clear that his quest is driven by an implacable racism. His intention, as Martin discerns, is not to rescue Debbie (Natalie Wood), his surviving niece, but to murder her. In Ethan's view she has become contaminated through contact with her Comanche captors. Slowly we realize that the Comanche chief Scar (Henry Brandon) functions as a kind of mirror image of Ethan. In raping Martha before he kills her, Scar has performed a horrific travesty of the act that Ethan secretly dreamed of committing. Ethan's urge to kill both Scar and Debbie thus arises from his need to obliterate his own illegitimate desires.

The true genius of *The Searchers* is in its being able to keep the audience's sympathy for Ethan, despite the evident fact that he is a murderous racist. In doing so, it elicits a far more complex and productive response than that of more obviously liberal films in this vein, such as *Broken Arrow* (1950). Instead of preaching a message, Ford leads us into the complexities of the American experience of racial difference.

Along the way there are many other pleasures, including a marvelous score by Max Steiner and comedy from stalwarts of the John Ford Stock Company such as Harry Carey Jr., Ken Curtis, Hank Worden, and Ward Bond. Vera Miles is excellent as Martin's girlfriend Laurie, whose mother is played by Olive Carey, widow of Ford's first Western star, Harry Carey.

In 1992, *The Searchers* was voted the fifth greatest movie of all time in a poll of international critics conducted by *Sight & Sound* magazine. That's quite an accolade, but Ford's picture lives up to it. **EB**

U.S. (Whitney, Warner Bros.) 120m
Technicolor **Producer** Merian C. Cooper,
Patrick Ford, C.V. Whitney **Screenplay** Frank
S. Nugent, from novel by Alan Le May
Photography Winton C. Hoch **Music** Stan
Jones, Max Steiner **Cast** John Wayne, Jeffrey
Hunter, Vera Miles, Ward Bond, Natalie Wood,
John Qualen, Olive Carey, Henry Brandon,
Ken Curtis, Harry Carey Jr., Antonio Moreno,
Hank Worden, Beulah Archuletta, Walter Coy,
Dorothy Jordan

"The Searchers is a picture that you keep looking at, over and over again, and you find more meaning in it, you find more identification with it, you find more levels . . . It's so rich, it's so rich."

Martin Scorsese, 1993

i

Jeffrey Hunter played Captain Kirk's predecessor, Christopher Pike, in the 1965 pilot episode of *Star Trek*.

Biruma no tategoto Kon Ichikawa, 1956
The Burmese Harp

Although Akira Kurosawa may be the most famous Japanese filmmaker in the West, his contemporary Kon Ichikawa has displayed equal artistry in literally dozens of films, among them *The Burmese Harp*, his elegy for lost innocence. Opening at the end of World War II, Captain Inouye (Rentaro Mikuni) leads his platoon into Burma with a mix of discipline and musical instruction. Trained to fight and to sing, the soldiers are an odd assortment of conscripts who eventually collide with Armistice Day.

Held in a British internment camp awaiting repatriation, they hear rumors about an isolated group of Japanese refusing to surrender. As Inouye's harp player and the center of his platoon's spiritual life, Mizushima (Shôji Yasui) volunteers to talk down the soldiers rather than let them die in an artillery barrage. Unimpressed with his entreaties, the entrenched force is killed and Mizushima assumed lost, but for the rumors his platoon clings to about his survival.

What follows is a touching journey as Mizushima awakens from the attack, injured and afraid. Aided by peasants, he begins making his way back to Inouye but gradually realizes a higher purpose. Garbed as a Buddhist monk he sets about burying the war dead strewn across Southeast Asia without funerary attention or final messages home. He recognizes the need to mourn, but also how the peace will be based on mutual care and personal loyalty, and so forsakes his old life to walk the earth bringing small labors to bear where they're needed. He subsequently crosses paths with Inouye on several occasions but finally explains his cause as a lasting tribute to the dead, both innocent and guilty, good and evil, because it's upon their backs the future will rise.

A breath of warm sentiment inserted over a macabre scenario, *The Burmese Harp* retains every bit of dignity associated with gentility and kindness. Burma itself becomes a passive supporting character, but the idea of a spiritual renewal, presented without dogma or propagandistic impulses, proves a likable epilogue to the horrors of World War II in this, Ichikawa's early masterpiece. **GC-Q**

Japan (Nikkatsu) 116m BW
Language Japanese **Producer** Masayuki Takaki **Screenplay** Natto Wada, from novel by Michio Takeyama **Photography** Minoru Yokoyama **Music** Akira Ifukube **Cast** Rentaro Mikuni, Shôji Yasui, Jun Hamamura, Taketoshi Naitô, Ko Nishimura, Hiroshi Tsuchikata, Sanpei Mine, Yoshiaki Kato, Sojiro Amano, Yôji Nagahama, Eiji Nakamura, Shojiro Ogasawara, Tomoko Tonai, Tatsuya Mihashi, Yunosuke Ito **Oscar nomination** Japan (best foreign language film) **Venice Film Festival** Kon Ichikawa (OCIC award—honorable mention, Golden Lion nomination)

"For young people today, the hero is a wonderful man, an ideal Japanese."

Kon Ichikawa, 2000

i

The Burmese Harp was scored by Akira Ifukube, most famous for Godzilla's 1954 movie debut, *Gojira*.

Forbidden Planet Fred M. Wilcox, 1956

U.S. (MGM) 98m Eastmancolor
Producer Nicholas Nayfack
Screenplay Irving Block, Allen Adler, Cyril
Hume Photography George J. Folsey
Music Bebe Barron, Louis Barron Cast Walter
Pidgeon, Anne Francis, Leslie Nielsen, Robby
the Robot, Warren Stevens, Jack Kelly,
Richard Anderson, Earl Holliman, George
Wallace, Robert Dix, Jimmy Thompson,
James Drury, Harry Harvey Jr., Roger McGee,
Peter MillerOscar nomination A. Arnold
Gillespie, Irving G. Ries, Wesley C. Miller
(special effects)

This superior 1950s sci-fi gem by director Fred M. Wilcox, ambitiously shot in widescreen CinemaScope, owes nothing to the period's paranoid McCarthyite preoccupation with hostile invaders from outer space but a great deal to the plot of William Shakespeare's *The Tempest* and the sophisticated psychological premise that the most dangerous monsters are those lurking in the primitive impulses of the subconscious mind.

Commander John J. Adams (Leslie Nielsen) leads a mission to the planet Altair 4, to discover what became of an expedition from Earth of which nothing has been heard for decades. It finds the only survivors are brilliant, arrogant scientist Edward Morbius (Walter Pidgeon) and his seductively miniskirted, child-of-nature daughter Altaira (Anne Francis), attended by one of film's best-loved metallic characters, the versatile and obliging Robby the Robot. Doctor Morbius has found the awesome remains of the ancient, annihilated Krell civilization, and dabbling with its technological wonders brings destruction down upon them all.

Outstanding effects (including the unleashed "monsters from the id"), the awesome Krell underground complex, and Louis and Bebe Barron's eerie, groundbreaking score of electronic tones are among the treats in a much-referenced picture that inspired many later speculative fictions of technology running away with its users. **AE**

Written on the Wind Douglas Sirk, 1956

U.S. (Universal) 99m Technicolor
Producer Albert Zugsmith Screenplay
George Zuckerman, from novel by Robert
Wilder Photography Russell Metty
Music Frank Skinner, Victor Young Cast Rock
Hudson, Lauren Bacall, Robert Stack,
Dorothy Malone, Robert Keith, Grant
Williams, Robert J. Wilke, Edward Platt, Harry
Shannon, John Larch, Joseph Granby, Roy
Glenn, Sam, Maidie Norman, William
Schallert, Joanne Jordan Oscar Dorothy
Malone (actress in support role) Oscar
nominations Robert Stack (actor in support
role), Victor Young, Sammy Cahn (song)

Robert Stack, in a drunken rage, smashes a bottle of booze against the wall. Lauren Bacall, at her bedroom curtain, faints. Gunshots, death, tears. And on the soundtrack, a male chorus begins singing: "Our night of stolen bliss was written on the wind." From its first moments, this is the Hollywood melodrama that encapsulates all others, in an electric, condensed, powerfully lyrical fashion.

Written on the Wind is about the twisted, fatal connections between sex, power, and money. Characters are arranged into inverted mirror images of each other, good facing evil—but everyone, ultimately, inhabits a complex, contradictory position in the impossible scheme of things. Dorothy Malone—marvelous as the quintessential bad girl who drinks, smokes, loves jazz, picks up guys at oil derricks, and sends her father plummeting down the stairs—is particularly riveting.

Few films are at once as visceral and insightful as *Written on the Wind*—a soap opera with passion, seriousness, and intelligence. Director Douglas Sirk specialized in films like *All That Heaven Allows* (1955) that were once dismissed by highbrows and lowbrows alike as "women's weepies." When they were finally rediscovered in the early 1970s at film festivals around the world, the audaciousness and true subversiveness of his work were appreciated for the first time. **AM**

Un condamné à mort s'est échappé ou Le vent souffle où il veut

A Man Escaped Robert Bresson, 1956

France (Gaumont, Nouvelles Éditions) 99m BW **Language** French **Producer** Alain Poiré, Jean Thuillier **Screenplay** Robert Bresson, from memoir by André Devigny **Photography** Léonce-Henri Burel **Music** Wolfgang Amadeus Mozart **Cast** François Leterrier, Charles Le Clainche, Maurice Beerblock, Roland Monod, Jacques Ertaud, Jean Paul Delhumeau, Roger Treherne, Jean Philippe Delamarre, César Gattegno, Jacques Oerlemans, Klaus Detlef Grevenhorst, Leonhard Schmidt **Cannes Film Festival** Robert Bresson (director)

If anyone needs to be won over to the joys and rewards of minimalism in cinema, *A Man Escaped* is the best place to start. Much of it shows Fontaine (François Leterrier) alone in his cell, making contact with fellow prisoners and slowly chipping his way to freedom.

Like all of Robert Bresson's films, this one illustrates the director's long-developed theories of the "cinematograph": nonprofessionals giving strictly de-dramatized performances; enormous emphasis on offscreen sound and the information it carries; music held off until a final, glorious moment. And like the other great prison films of French cinema—Jacques Becker's *Le trou* (1960) and Jean Genet's *Un chant d'amour* (1950)—*A Man Escaped* offers a remarkably potent allegory of human suffering and the drive to liberation. At the same time, it delivers a taut form of suspense to rival the best of Alfred Hitchcock.

For many years, *A Man Escaped* was appreciated for its existential and spiritual dimensions: man's solitude, the fragility of communication with others, the gift of God's grace. More recently, Its political dimension has been foregrounded, as a reflection of Bresson's experience in the French Resistance—thus giving his entire career, with its themes of subjection and "souls in torment," a socially grounded urgency. **AM**

Bigger Than Life Nicholas Ray, 1956

U.S. (Fox) 95m DeLuxe **Producer** James Mason **Screenplay** Cyril Hume, Richard Maibaum, from article by Burton Roueche **Photography** Joseph MacDonald **Music** David Raksin **Cast** James Mason, Barbara Rush, Walter Matthau, Robert F. Simon, Christopher Olsen, Roland Winters, Rusty Lane, Rachel Stephens, Kipp Hamilton **Venice Film Festival nomination** Nicholas Ray (Golden Lion)

Though best known for *Rebel Without a Cause* (1955), Nicholas Ray's finest film is a brilliant expressionist melodrama that used the then-topical controversy over the discovery and deployment of the "wonder-drug" cortisone (a type of steroid) to mount a devastating critique on materialistic, middle-class conformism in the postwar era.

The brooding James Mason (who also produced) is perfectly cast as a small-town teacher beset by worries about money and middle age who, having been prescribed steroids, becomes addicted to the sense of well-being that they bring. This turns him into an irascibly neurotic, megalomaniac tyrant to his wife, son, and everyone around him.

The drug, however, is merely the catalyst that ignites the loathing he feels for himself and the staid, complacently unquestioning world in which he is trapped. Indeed, his despair goes so deep that when, finally, he decides he must save his son from the depravities of humanity by killing him, and his wife (Barbara Rush) reminds him that God stopped Abraham from killing Isaac, Mason simply responds: "God was wrong."

A profoundly radical Hollywood movie, then, distinguished not only by its distaste for suburban notions of "normality" but by the beautifully nightmarish clarity of its intensely colored CinemaScope imagery. **GA**

Invasion of the Body Snatchers Don Siegel, 1956

One of the most popular and paranoid films from the golden age of American science-fiction cinema, *Invasion of the Body Snatchers* is both an ambivalent Cold War allegory and an extraterrestrial terror tale.

Despite its B-movie feel, Siegel's film—based on a novel by Jack Finney—is less concerned with subscribing to generic sci-fi convention than with dramatizing the dangers of social conformity and the threat of invasion coming both from outside and inside one's own community. But the absence of any manifest monsters—partly due to economic considerations, the theme of "body snatching" plants and doppelganger drones served as a creative cost-cutting tactic—is more than made up for by the uncanny depiction of "ordinary life" that may no longer be so ordinary. As critic Kim Newman writes, "Rather than rubbery claws, animated dinosaurs, and alien death rays, the film finds horror in an uncle mowing the lawn, an abandoned roadside vegetable stall, a bar all but empty of patrons, a mother putting a plant in baby's playpen, or a crowd purposefully gathering in a town square at 7:45 on a Saturday morning."

When Dr. Miles Bennell (Kevin McCarthy) returns home to his small California town of Santa Mira from a medical convention, he is confronted by strange reports from several of his patients, who insist that their seemingly benign relatives are in fact imposters. After some initial skepticism, Miles is convinced when, during a barbecue with some friends, he discovers two huge seed pods that burst open to release a bubbly fluid and two incomplete human replicas, one of which is well on its way to looking like himself. Speculating that a bizarre alien invasion is underway, Miles and his love interest Becky (Dana Wynter) attempt a getaway as the entire town falls sway to the pods' dehumanizing effects.

A cinematic nightmare concerning the potential communist threat or an anti-McCarthyist "message" movie wrapped in the protective garb of sci-fi fantasy? *Invasion of the Body Snatchers* offers evidence to support either interpretation. And the film's open, pessimistic ending, as Miles wanders onto a highway and shouts, "You're next!" directly to the camera, will make you wonder who you're really sleeping next to at night. **SJS**

U.S. (Allied Artists, Walter Wanger) 80m BW **Producer** Walter Wanger **Screenplay** Daniel Mainwaring, from the novel *The Body Snatchers* by Jack Finney **Photography** Ellsworth Fredericks **Music** Carmen Dragon **Cast** Kevin McCarthy, Dana Wynter, Larry Gates, King Donovan, Carolyn Jones, Jean Willes, Ralph Dumke, Virginia Christine, Tom Fadden, Kenneth Patterson, Guy Way, Eileen Stevens, Beatrice Maude, Jean Andren, Bobby Clark

i

Don Siegel made a cameo as a taxi driver in the 1978 remake of the movie, starring Donald Sutherland.

1956

Giant George Stevens, 1956

U.S. (Giant, Warner Bros) 197m Warnercolor
Language English / Spanish Producer Henry
Ginsberg, George Stevens Screenplay Fred
Guiol, Ivan Moffat, from novel by Edna
Ferber Photography William C. Mellor
Music Dimitri Tiomkin Cast Elizabeth Taylor,
Rock Hudson, James Dean, Carroll Baker, Jane
Withers, Chill Wills, Mercedes McCambridge,
Dennis Hopper, Sal Mineo, Rod Taylor,
Judith Evelyn, Earl Holliman, Robert Nichols,
Paul Fix Oscar George Stevens (director)
Oscar nominations George Stevens, Henry
Ginsberg (best picture), Fred Guiol, Ivan
Moffat (screenplay), James Dean (actor), Rock
Hudson (actor), Mercedes McCambridge
(actress in support role), Boris Leven, Ralph S.
Hurst (art direction), Moss Mabry, Marjorie
Best (costume), William Hornbeck, Philip W.
Anderson, Fred Bohanan (editing), Dimitri
Tiomkin (music)

i

Rock Hudson and Elizabeth Taylor
became lifelong friends after
working on *Giant* togther.

Edna Ferber specialized in writing sprawling family sagas, several of them set in the West. Her 1930 novel *Cimarron* was twice filmed by Hollywood, as was the 1926 film *Show Boat*, set in the Deep South.

In *Giant*, written in 1950, Bick Benedict (Rock Hudson) is a Texas cattle baron who marries a spirited Maryland belle, Leslie (Elizabeth Taylor). Bick's sister has left some of the property to Jett Rink (James Dean), a former employee. Rink discovers oil and grows immensely rich, but his personal life is a disappointment—he carries a torch for Leslie— and he declines into alcoholism. As Bick and Leslie grow older, they are concerned with who will run the ranch after they have gone. Their daughter (Carroll Baker) wants to take over, but Leslie doesn't approve. To Bick's disappointment, their son (Dennis Hopper, who also appeared with Dean in *Rebel Without a Cause*) has married a Latina woman and become a doctor. Eventually Bick and Leslie come to terms with life.

At well over three hours, *Giant* certainly lives up to its title. But the performances are outstanding, not least that of the twenty-four-year-old James Dean, who was tragically killed in a car crash shortly after completing his part. Director George Stevens does justice to the immensity of the Texas landscape, and, unusually for the time, the film deals interestingly with both racial and class differences. **EB**

The Wrong Man Alfred Hitchcock, 1956

U.S. (First National, Warner Bros.) 105m BW
Producer Herbert Coleman, Alfred Hitchcock
Screenplay Angus MacPhail, Maxwell
Anderson, from the novel *The True Story
of Christopher Emmanuel Balestrero* by
Maxwell Anderson **Photography** Robert
Burks **Music** Bernard Herrmann **Cast** Henry
Fonda, Vera Miles, Anthony Quayle, Harold
Stone, John Heldabrand, Doreen Lang,
Norma Connolly, Lola D'Annunzio, Robert
Essen, Dayton Lummis, Charles Cooper,
Esther Minciotti, Laurinda Barrett,
Nehemiah Persoff, Kippy Campbell

The Wrong Man is one of the bleakest pictures Hitchcock ever directed. Henry Fonda plays Manny Balestrero, a jazz musician who is mistakenly identified as the man who held up an insurance office. Although he is released on bail, the worry and disgrace begin to affect his wife Rose (Vera Miles). They try to find the people who can confirm Manny's alibi, but fail. Rose has a breakdown before the trial and is confined to an asylum. Eventually, quite by chance, the real hold-up man is discovered, but this has little effect on her state of mind.

Shot in black and white, with an almost documentary-style realism, *The Wrong Man* is based on a real case, as stated by Hitchcock himself in a short prologue. "This is a true story, every word of it," he notes. "And yet it contains elements that are stranger than all the fiction that has gone into many of the thrillers that I've made before." It explores one of his perennial themes: that of the man accused of a crime he did not commit (1959's *North by Northwest* has a similar situation). The director brilliantly conveys how readily the procedures of indictment and incarceration conspire to impart a sensation of guilt even in the innocent. In a masterly sequence making use of a subjective camera, we see Manny suffer the humiliation of being booked, searched, and fingerprinted, the dirty ink on his hands seeming like a confirmation of his guilt. **EB**

High Society Charles Walters, 1956

U.S. (Bing Crosby, MGM, Sol C. Siegel) 107m
Technicolor **Producer** Sol C. Siegel
Screenplay John Patrick, from the play *The
Philadelphia Story* by Philip Barry
Photography Paul Vogel **Music** Saul
Chaplin, Cole Porter **Cast** Bing Crosby, Grace
Kelly, Frank Sinatra, Celeste Holm, John
Lund, Louis Calhern, Sidney Blackmer, Louis
Armstrong, Margalo Gillmore **Oscar
nominations** Edward Bernds, Elwood
Ullman (screenplay)*, Johnny Green, Saul
Chaplin (music), Cole Porter (song)

* nomination declined when the Academy
realized it had confused Bernds and Ullman's
1955 film *High Society* with this one

A musical update of George Cukor's romantic farce *The Philadelphia Story* (1940), *High Society* unites the unbeatable melodic talents of Bing Crosby, Frank Sinatra, and Louis Armstrong with the beauty of Grace Kelly in her final film role before she became Princess Grace of Monaco.

Icy, spoiled Tracy (Kelly) is due to marry dull, dependable beau George (John Lund)—but, on the eve of her nuptials, her ex-husband Dexter (Crosby) returns to try and put a stop to the wedding. On hand to report on the shenanigans behind the social event of the year are journalists Liz (Celeste Holm) and Mike (Sinatra), with jazz great Armstrong (playing himself) providing something of a Greek chorus, bringing the audience up to speed with Dexter and Tracy's complicated entanglements.

Following endless Hollywood musicals of the 1940s and early 1950s that were packed with elaborate song and dance numbers, director Charles Walters seamlessly fits nine simple renditions of Cole Porter songs into the proceedings, rather than have them take over the film. Armstrong begins by singing the plot-explaining "High Society" from the back of a cramped limousine shared with his band, while the classic "Who Wants To Be a Millionaire?" is spiritedly sung by Sinatra and Holm alone in a room filled with Tracy's many extravagant wedding gifts. A light, frothy, and timeless piece of musical comedy. **JB**

Kumonosu jo Akira Kurosawa, 1957
Throne of Blood

Japan (Toho) 105m BW **Language** Japanese **Producer** Akira Kurosawa, Sojiro Motoki **Screenplay** Shinobu Hashimoto, Ryuzo Kikushima, Akira Kurosawa, Hideo Oguni, from the play *Macbeth* by William Shakespeare **Photography** Asakazu Nakai **Music** Masaru Satô **Cast** Toshirô Mifune, Isuzu Yamada, Takashi Shimura, Akira Kubo, Hiroshi Tachikawa, Minoru Chiaki, Takamaru Sasaki, Kokuten Kodo, Kichijiro Ueda, Eiko Miyoshi, Chieko Naniwa, Nakajiro Tomita, Yu Fujiki, Sachio Sakai, Shin Otomo **Venice Film Festival** Akira Kurosawa nomination (Golden Lion)

Quite rightly, Akira Kurosawa's artfully chilling, formal, and extremely close adaptation of *Macbeth* is regarded as one of the most breathtaking screen versions of the play. "My aim was to transform Shakespeare…," he said, "by borrowing freely from Japanese art forms." Both the plot and psychology translate beautifully to feudal Japan, where samurai warrior General Washizu (Toshirô Mifune) and his fiendish wife Lady Asaji (Isuzu Yamada), driven by ruthless ambition and inspired by a witch's prophecy, murder their warlord, seize a kingdom, and damn themselves to an inescapable, ritual finality of bloodshed, paranoia, madness, and ruin.

The wonderful Mifune—Kurosawa's favorite leading man in a long-running collaboration (more than sixteen films) that is as notable as that of Martin Scorsese's with Robert De Niro—furthered his reputation as Japan's preeminent international star with this performance. Washizu's brilliantly staged death scene, transfixed in a hail of arrows, is one of the great iconic images of world cinema. Elements of Noh theater, traditional Japanese battle art, historical realism, and contemporary thinking on the nature of good and evil are fused in a confined, mist-shrouded world of sinister and magical portents in forest and castle (set in locations high up Mount Fuji, where the castle was built with the brawny assistance of a U.S. Marine battalion stationed nearby). **AE**

Paths of Glory Stanley Kubrick, 1957

U.S. (Bryna, Harris-Kubrick) 87m BW **Language** English / German **Producer** Kirk Douglas, James B. Harris, Stanley Kubrick **Screenplay** Stanley Kubrick, Calder Willingham, Jim Thompson, from novel by Humphrey Cobb **Photography** Georg Krause **Music** Gerald Fried **Cast** Kirk Douglas, Ralph Meeker, Adolphe Menjou, George Macready, Wayne Morris, Richard Anderson, Joe Turkel, Christiane Kubrick, Jerry Hausner, Peter Capell, Emile Meyer, Bert Freed, Kem Dibbs, Timothy Carey, Fred Bell

"Nobody in Hollywood wanted to do [*Paths of Glory*] at all," Stanley Kubrick remembered. Yet, with Calder Willingham and Jim Thompson, he adapted Humphrey Cobb's novel, about an actual shameful incident that took place in the French army in World War I, into a powerful film—one that's all the more effective for the director's matter-of-fact coolness in dealing with the unthinkably horrible.

A pair of ruthless but inept generals (Adolphe Menjou and George Macready) order their men to hurl themselves suicidally at the German positions; when a few survivors limp back after being practically wiped out, the regiment is accused of cowardice, and a randomly selected trio of foot soldiers are put on trial. Committed Colonel Dax (Kirk Douglas) mounts a defense, but politics decree that the three humble, innocent soldiers—absolutely the bravest imaginable—go to the wall.

Grim, intelligent, and wonderfully acted, this is the best type of war movie: It makes its audience angry. It also climaxes, after the executions, with the most emotional scene Kubrick ever directed, in which a roomful of jeering soldiers force a captured German girl (Susanne Christian, later Christiane Kubrick) to entertain them by singing a song, only to be moved to silence by her awkward, sincere, melancholy performance. **KN**

U.S. (Fox) 119m DeLuxe
Producer Leo McCarey, Jerry Wald
Screenplay Leo McCarey, Mildred Cram,
Delmer Daves, Donald Ogden Stewart
Photography Milton R. Krasner **Music** Hugo
Friedhofer, Harry Warren **Cast** Cary Grant,
Deborah Kerr, Richard Denning, Neva
Patterson, Cathleen Nesbitt, Robert Q Lewis,
Charles Watts, Fortunio Bonanova, George
Winslow **Oscar nominations** Milton R.
Krasner (photography), Charles Le Maire
(costume), Hugo Friedhofer (music),
Harry Warren, Harold Adamson, Leo
McCarey (song)

*"Winter must be
cold for those with
no warm memories . . .
We've already missed
the spring."*

Terry McKay
(Deborah Kerr)

i

Marni Nixon dubbed Deborah Kerr's
singing voice in both *An Affair to
Remember* and *The King and I* (1956).

An Affair to Remember Leo McCarey, 1957

"Darling, if you can paint, I can walk again!" For years, Cary Grant's and Deborah Kerr's thorny path in *An Affair to Remember* was almost illicitly adored. Then it was outed, by its prominent part in the 1993 film *Sleepless in Seattle*, as one of the definitive chicks'-night-in flicks, ideally viewed with abundant chocolate and a box of tissues at hand.

The film—a remake of his own 1939 comedy-drama starring Irene Dunne and Charles Boyer, *Love Affair*—reflects two competing sides of producer-writer-director Leo McCarey. In his prime, the comedy mastermind teamed Laurel with Hardy, directed the Marx Brothers in *Duck Soup*, and won his first Oscar directing Grant in the 1930s screwball classic *The Awful Truth*. But McCarey also had a shameless sentimentality that oozed in his 1940s favorite *Going My Way* (for which he won Academy Awards for Best Picture, Director, and Writer).

Grant's witty playboy Nickie Ferrante, a failed artist, and Kerr's wary nightclub singer Terry McKay (her vocals dubbed by premiere studio singer Marnie Nixon, who also voiced Kerr in *The King and I*) meet aboard a luxury liner and surrender—amid much worldly good humor—to their attraction. Unfortunately, both are encumbered with betrotheds and pasts. They make a romantic pact. In six months, if they have turned their lives around, they will meet atop the Empire State Building and live happily ever after. In due course, the reformed Grant puts his paintbrushes away and happily paces the skyscraper's observation deck, but Kerr, running excitedly to him, is hit by a car.

What follows is almost inconceivable to the cell phone generation. Believing he's been stood up, Grant succumbs to embittered cynicism, unaware Kerr is bravely coming to terms with paralysis, too proud to let him know her situation. Comedy is abandoned in the hanky-wringing second half of the film, as the audience is kept in a deliciously protracted will-they-or-won't-they agony. McCarey overdoes it with songs, but even Kerr coaching a choir of overly cute urchins can't spoil the reunion, the revelation, and the big-clinch climax. **AE**

Det sjunde inseglet Ingmar Bergman, 1957
The Seventh Seal

The image of a black-robed, white-faced Death (Bengt Ekerot) playing chess on the beach with a weary, questioning crusader (Max von Sydow) is as ingrained in the memory of moviegoers as King Kong atop the Empire State Building, Humphrey Bogart spurning Ingrid Bergman at the airport, Janet Leigh stabbed in the shower, or the Imperial Cruiser passing over the camera. This one scene from Swedish arthouse gem *The Seventh Seal* epitomizes the momentousness, excitement, and impact new types of cinema had at a point when Hollywood certainties were in recession. How else to explain the parodies or references in films as varied as Roger Corman's *Masque of the Red Death* (1964), Woody Allen's *Love and Death*, John McTiernan's *Last Action Hero* (1993), and Peter Hewitt's *Bill & Ted's Bogus Journey* (1991), in the last of which Death plays Twister?

But it's a shame this scene has come to represent the whole of the film in popular imagination. There's an unfair sense that writer-director Ingmar Bergman was being overly solemn, making something that could stand as an archetype of seriousness or artiness. Actually, *The Seventh Seal*, although rooted in the big themes of Bergman's great period, is a very playful, frequently comic picture: a medieval fable influenced by his enthusiasm for the samurai movies of Akira Kurosawa and as concerned with celebrating simple pleasures as indicting complicated torments.

Antonius Block (Sydow), returning after ten years on a bloody crusade that was started by a con man who now makes a living robbing corpses, feels that his faith in God is a disease that mankind should root out. With his squire (Gunnar Björnstrand), as much a debating partner as sidekick, Block encounters death in the form of a plague-ridden corpse before he meets the literal Grim Reaper. The game of chess played throughout the film between Death and the knight is not merely for the crusader's life but for his feelings about God, religion, and humanity. In the end, hope comes from an alternative Holy Family—a jolly juggler (Nils Poppe), his earthy sensual wife (Gunnel Lindblom), and their lively, innocent toddler—whom Block saves from the plague by willingly joining the dance of death that claims more venal, corrupted characters.

The knight, constantly tormented by curiosities about God and the void (he even visits an accused witch about to be burned to ask her what the Devil knows about God), represents one side of Bergman. The simple showman gently upbraided by his practical wife ("You and your dreams and visions," she says in the film's closing line) represents another seeking redemption through honest entertainment and appalled when his innocent show is upstaged by the horrible, Church-approved spectacle of a crowd of penitents being lashed and tortured. Bergman is angry and saddened by human evils, especially when sanctioned by supposed religion, but the film also celebrates physical and spiritual love, communal artistic expression, food and drink, and natural beauty. **KN**

Sweden (Svensk) 96m BW
Language Swedish **Producer** Allan Ekelund
Screenplay Ingmar Bergman, from the play *Trämålning* by Ingmar Bergman
Photography Gunnar Fischer **Music** Erik Nordgren **Cast** Gunnar Björnstrand, Bengt Ekerot, Nils Poppe, Max von Sydow, Bibi Andersson, Inga Gill, Maud Hansson, Inga Landgré, Gunnel Lindblom, Bertil Anderberg, Anders Ek, Åke Fridell, Gunnar Olsson, Erik Strandmark **Cannes Film Festival** Ingmar Bergman, tied with Andrzej Wajda's *Kanal* (special jury prize)

> *"Bergman longed for the possibility of religious phenomenon . . . But in the end he was a great entertainer.* The Seventh Seal, *all those films, they grip you. It's not like doing homework."*

Woody Allen, 2007

ⓘ

The Seventh Seal was shot in thirty-five days, said Bergman in 1971, "in the woods right outside the studio."

LIFE IS IN
THEIR HANDS— DEATH IS ON
THEIR MINDS!

IT
EXPLODES
LIKE
12
HENRY FONDA STICKS
OF
DYNAMITE!

12 Angry Men Sidney Lumet, 1957

Sidney Lumet's courtroom drama enjoys enduring popularity because it is a hothouse for smart performances, sudden twists, and impassioned monologues. Uniquely, the brilliantly economical and riveting drama of *12 Angry Men* does not actually take place in the courtroom—except for a brief prologue as the jury is sent out with the judge's instructions—but during a single, sweltering afternoon in the jury room.

Henry Fonda plays Juror No. 8, the holdout whose reasonable doubt and well-reasoned resistance gradually bring eleven other jury members around from their first swift verdict of guilty in the case of a youth prosecuted for the murder of his father. Fonda was impressed by the power in Reginald Rose's ingeniously contrived teleplay, broadcast live on CBS in 1954 (and believed lost until 2003, when a tape was found). Recognizing a role that perfectly suited his calm sincerity and seeing the opportunity for a gripping feature, he put his own money into producing the film. He gave the assignment to Lumet, a dynamic veteran of live TV drama whose expertise enabled him and director of photography Boris Kaufman—another expert at working in restricted spaces and in black and white—to mine the mounting tension from Rose's tightly structured script and to wrap the film in under twenty days.

Lumet's engrossing debut film makes no apologies for its theatricality but makes a virtue of its claustrophobic, sweaty intensity. And each actor makes his mark in this showcase of superb characterizations and ensemble dynamics, from Martin Balsam's insecure foreman to a leonine Lee J. Cobb's belligerent, embittered Juror No. 3. Interestingly, two of the men, Joseph Sweeney as elderly, insightful Juror No. 9 and George Voskovic as methodically minded Juror No. 11, had been in the original television production. Class and ethnic prejudices, private assumptions, and personalities all come out in a colossal struggle for unclouded judgment. The film won the Golden Bear at the Berlin Film Festival, but its greatest accolade is that after seeing this picture, no one ever enters into jury duty without fantasizing about becoming a dogged champion of justice à la Fonda, whatever the case at hand. **AE**

U.S. (Orion-Nova) 96m BW
Producer Henry Fonda, Reginald
Rose **Screenplay** Reginald Rose
Photography Boris Kaufman **Music** Kenyon
Hopkins **Cast** Henry Fonda, Lee J. Cobb, Ed
Begley, E.G. Marshall, Jack Warden, Martin
Balsam, John Fiedler, Jack Klugman, Ed
Binns, Joseph Sweeney, George Voskovec,
Robert Webber **Oscar nominations** Henry
Fonda, Reginald Rose (best picture), Sidney
Lumet (director), Reginald Rose (screenplay)
Berlin International Film Festival Sidney
Lumet (Golden Bear, OCIC award)

"We were going to be in one room. Let's use it dramatically!"

Sidney Lumet, 1997

i

The film lost all three of the Academy
Awards for which it was nominated
to *The Bridge Over the River Kwai.*

Smultronstället Ingmar Bergman, 1957
Wild Strawberries

Sweden (Svensk) 91m BW
Language Swedish / Latin Producer Allan
Eklund Screenplay Ingmar Bergman
Photography Gunnar Fischer Music Erik
Nordgren Cast Victor Sjöström, Bibi
Andersson, Ingrid Thulin, Gunnar
Björnstrand, Jullan Kindahl, Folke Sundquist,
Björn Bjelfvenstam, Naima Wifstrand, Gunnel
Broström, Gertrud Fridh, Sif Ruud, Gunnar
Sjöberg, Max von Sydow, Åke Fridell, Yngve
Nordwall Oscar nomination Ingmar
Bergman (screenplay) Berlin International
Film Festival Victor Sjöström (FIPRESCI
award), Ingmar Bergman (Golden Bear)
Venice Film Festival Ingmar Bergman
(Italian film critics award)

*"I'm not sure if it's
so much about me.
Of course, I'm in it
somewhere, but the basic
character in Isak Borg is
very much my dad."*

Ingmar Bergman, 2003

ℹ

Victor Sjöström's own film *Körkalen*
(*The Phantom Carriage*, 1921) was a
key influence on Ingmar Bergman.

Arguably the warmest of Bergman's masterpieces, *Wild Strawberries* charts the geographical and spiritual odyssey of the elderly Professor Isak Borg (played by Victor Sjöström), whose name in Swedish more or less means "icy fortress." With his daughter-in-law Marianne (Ingrid Thulin), Borg drives from Stockholm to the University of Lund to receive an honorary degree. En route he gives a ride to three young hitchhikers—including the vivacious Sara (Bibi Andersson), who in name and nature reminds him of the love of his life—and a middle-aged couple. He visits his now-ancient mother, before finally trying to have a heart-to-heart talk with his son Evald (Gunnar Björnstrand), a cynical misanthrope whom Marianne has planned to leave. The conversation with Evald is crucial because it might save his son's marriage and because it shows the professor's journey has brought a degree of self-knowledge. He has become aware of his mortality and emotional reticence—inherited from his parents, consolidated by life's disappointments and his immersion in work, and unwittingly passed on, like a virus, to Evald.

The strength of Bergman's account of this day in the life is the assured manner in which he combines the realities of Borg's life. The inner and external details throw light upon the man. His dreams and memories illuminate our understanding of him (and his understanding of himself), as do his various encounters and conversations. Marianne, though tactful and affectionate, explicitly alludes to Borg's failings. Sara reminds him of his more passionate youth. The arguing couple call to mind both his own grouchiness and the future Marianne may face with Evald.

Borg's redemptive acquisition of self-knowledge affects those around him, too, yet Bergman never inflects this conclusion with sentimentality. Blessed with a radiant yet courageously uningratiating performance from Sjöström—himself Sweden's greatest filmmaker before Bergman—this remarkable, much-imitated film has an emotional honesty entirely in keeping with the voyage undergone by its protagonist. **GA**

The Incredible Shrinking Man Jack Arnold, 1957

U.S. (Universal) 81m BW **Screenplay** Richard
Matheson, Richard Alan Simmons, from the
novel *The Shrinking Man* by Richard
Matheson **Photography** Ellis W. Carter
Music Foster Carling, Earl E. Lawrence
Cast Grant Williams, Randy Stuart, April Kent,
Paul Langton, Raymond Bailey, William
Schallert, Frank J. Scannell, Helene Marshall,
Diana Darrin, Billy Curtis

Exposed to a mysterious, probably radioactive cloud while on a cruise, Scott Carey (Grant Williams) finds himself gradually shrinking. Director Jack Arnold's visual flatness is perfectly suited to the absurdity and ambiguity of the premise of Richard Matheson's story. The first half of *The Incredible Shrinking Man*—portraying the hero's predicament as alternately a medical, a domestic, and a socioeconomic problem—is a worthy companion piece to Nicholas Ray's *Bigger Than Life* (1956) and Douglas Sirk's *Written on the Wind* (1956), in its ironic and terrifying depiction of American middle-class life turned inside out.

But it's in the second half of the film—Scott, now smaller than the heel of a shoe, is marooned in his basement and must cope with various natural threats—that *The Incredible Shrinking Man* really takes off. "I had complete freedom, because the studio knew nothing about the making of science-fiction films," said Arnold. The inspirational conclusion—"to God, there is no zero"—is a rare example of popular cinema explicitly dealing with metaphysics.

Much of the film's force comes from its psychological incisiveness and from its vivid and precise use of objects—its architecture of stairs, crates, matchboxes, and paint cans. For Matheson and Arnold, Scott Carey is an atomic-age Everyman: His adventure is an object lesson in the hostility of the built-up environment and in the indestructible propensity of humankind to make itself the measure of all things. **CFu**

Gunfight at the OK Corral John Sturges, 1957

U.S. (Paramount) 122m Technicolor
Producer Joseph H. Hazen, Paul Nathan,
Hal B. Wallis **Screenplay** George Scullin,
Leon Uris, from the article "The Killer" by
George Scullin **Photography** Charles Lang
Music Dimitri Tiomkin **Cast** Burt Lancaster,
Kirk Douglas, Rhonda Fleming, Jo Van Fleet,
John Ireland, Lyle Bettger, Frank Faylen, Earl
Holliman, Ted de Corsia, Dennis Hopper,
Whit Bissell, George Mathews, John
Hudson, DeForest Kelley, Martin Milner
Oscar nominations Warren Low (editing),
George Dutton (sound)

John Sturges's staging of the famous battle between Wyatt Earp and the Clanton gang in Tombstone, Arizona, on October 26, 1881, was not the first film version. But Sturges's film is a little more accurate than John Ford's *My Darling Clementine* (1946). Ford, for example, has Earp's associate Doc Holliday killed in the battle; in fact, he survived six more years. *Gunfight at the OK Corral* is a slick production, technically excellent and with a big budget, and it benefits from a fine cast. Burt Lancaster is full of authority as Earp, at times chilling in his determination. By contrast, Kirk Douglas has great fun with the consumptive Holliday, flashing a ready smile but deadly as a snake. There is also strong support from Jo Van Fleet as "Big Nose" Kate, Doc's put-upon woman, and John Ireland as gunslinger Johnny Ringo.

The melodious score, by Dimitri Tiomkin, who also did the music for other town-taming Westerns such as *High Noon* and *Rio Bravo*, made a considerable contribution, and Frankie Laine's theme song was a big hit. However, those wanting a more realistically downbeat treatment of the Wyatt Earp story should watch Sturges's 1967 sequel, *Hour of the Gun*, in which the incident at the OK Corral is just the start. **EB**

Le notti di Cabiria Federico Fellini, 1957
Nights of Cabiria

The Cabiria of the title in Fellini's classic is played by the filmmaker's wife, Giulietta Masina, who justifiably won the Best Actress award at Cannes for her portrayal of a naïve prostitute. Shamed by her profession, the feisty Cabiria hopelessly searches for a wealthy sugar daddy to take her away, but deep down what she's actually looking for is lasting love.

After its Cannes premiere, a controversial segment involving a good Samaritan with a sackful of good will was excised following the protest of the Catholic Church. Apparently spontaneous generosity is a provincial trait, but fortunately the footage was eventually returned. Indeed, the issue of goodness is paramount in Fellini's film, where beneath a worldly facade Cabiria just wishes to be happy, like anybody else. Yet Cabiria is the ultimate hooker with a heart of gold, never so glum that a good mambo or a street fair can't raise her spirits.

Cabiria can't help but to spread her kindness, but it often sets her up for disappointment or, even worse, humiliation. A chance encounter with a carnival hypnotist (Aldo Silvani) who draws out her inner desires is quite moving but particularly cruel, as it erroneously suggests that her dreams and fantasies of a better life may actually come true. Her openness even leads an onlooker to exploit her emotional weakness. The equally cruel attentions of a philandering movie star (Amedeo Nazzari) also set her up with false hopes, even if Cabiria is ultimately (and literally) treated no better than a dog.

Cabiria's dreams never do come true, and in fact frequently result in casual violence as predators prey on her plucky innocence. Still, Fellini doesn't exploit Cabiria's story for easy sympathy. She's a strong, proud woman who gets into fights, responding to every setback by picking herself up, brushing herself off, and starting her march to a new, better life all over again. *Nights of Cabiria* is—like another of Fellini's masterpieces, *La Dolce Vita* (1960)—told from the perspective of the underclass, a glimpse at the proverbial other half gilded with optimistic joy but ultimately steeped in sadness. **JKl**

Italy/France (De Laurentiis/Marceau) 110m BW **Language** Italian **Producer** Dino De Laurentiis **Screenplay** Federico Fellini, Ennio Flaiano, Tullio Pinelli, Pier Paolo Pasolini **Photography** Aldo Tonti, Otello Martelli **Music** Nino Rota **Cast** Giuletta Masina, François Périer, Amedeo Nazzari, Aldo Silvani, Franca Marzi, Dorian Gray **Oscars** Best Foreign Language Film (Italy) **Cannes Film Festival** Giuletta Masina (Best Actress), Federico Fellini (OCIC – Special Mention)

1957

> *"I think it would be immoral to present a ready-made solution at the end of a movie."*
>
> **Federico Fellini, 1961**

ℹ

The story was turned by Neil Simon into the play *Sweet Charity*, under which title it was filmed in 1969.

Letjat zhuravli Mikhail Kalatozov, 1957
The Cranes Are Flying

In the last years of Stalin and Stalinism, Soviet cinema almost vanished. The continuing economic devastation wrought by World War II, as well as the pervasive fear that defined everyday life, caused the once-thriving Soviet studios to practically close shop. After Stalin's death in 1953, a reborn Soviet cinema slowly began to emerge, and the film that came to symbolize that rebirth was Mikhail Kalatozov's *The Cranes Are Flying*.

Ostensibly a wartime romance about lovers—Boris (Aleksei Batalov) and Veronika (Tatiana Samojlova), who are separated soon after the start of the conflict—the film boldly defied just about every cliché of the genre. Rather than celebrating the glorious victories of the Red Army, *Cranes* focuses on some of the war's darkest moments, when the highly efficient and terrifying German war machine was easily routing the poorly organized and equipped (if heroic) Russian army.

On the home front there is little but despair and a sense that one has to look out for number one. Admirably, Soviet audiences heartily embraced this reflection of their wartime experiences; tired perhaps of propaganda, they knew only too well that the war had in truth produced few heroes of any sort. As the young lovers, Batalov and Samojlova are wonderfully affecting, sexy, and endearing, yet the true star of the film is cinematographer Sergei Urusevsky's voluptuous camera work. With his breathtaking crane shots, sweeping pans, and vibrant handheld work, Urusevsky (who had worked with Dovzhenko on the brilliant wartime documentary *The Battle for the Soviet Ukraine*) makes tangible the sense of a world that has lost its moorings or even any fixed point of reference—moral, political, or otherwise.

Urusevsky would go on to make with Kalatozov the infamous, if much admired, *I Am Cuba* (1964). Although that film for some feels overwhelmed by its baroque stylization, *Cranes* never indulges in visual effects for their own sake. It also became the first Cold War–era Soviet film to receive wide distribution (by Warner) in the United States. **RP**

U.S.S.R. (Mosfilm) 97m BW
Language Russian **Producer** Mikhail Kalatozov **Screenplay** Viktor Rozov, from his play **Photography** Sergei Urusevsky **Music** Moisej Vajnberg **Cast** Tatyana Samojlova, Aleksei Batalov, Vasili Merkuryev, Aleksandr Shvorin, Svetlana Kharitonova, Konstantin Nikitin, Valentin Zubkov, Antonina Bogdanova, Boris Kokovkin, Yekaterina Kupriyanova **Cannes Film Festival** Mikhal Kalatozishvili (Golden Palm), Tatyana Samojlova (special mention)

"The graphic side of the picture depended on me, and Kalatozov attached great importance to that."

Sergei Urusevsky

ℹ️

A decade after this film, Samojlova found fame once more in Aleksandr Zarkhi's version of *Anna Karenina*.

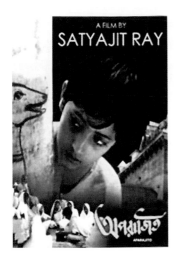

India (Epic) 127m BW **Language** Bengali
Producer Satyajit Ray **Screenplay** Satyajit
Ray, from novel by Bibhutibhushan
Bandyopadhyay **Photography** Subrata
Mitra **Music** Ravi Shankar **Cast** Kanu
Bannerjee, Karuna Bannerjee, Pinaki
Sengupta, Smaran Ghosal, Santi Gupta,
Ramani Sengupta, Ranibala, Sudipta Roy,
Ajay Mitra, Charuprakash Ghosh, Subodh
Ganguli, Mani Srimani, Hemanta Chatterjee,
Kali Bannerjee, Kalicharan Roy **Venice Film
Festival** Satyajit Ray (Golden Lion)

"If you're able to
portray universal
feelings, universal
relations, emotions, and
characters, you can cross
certain barriers and
reach out to others."

Satyajit Ray, 1982

ℹ️

The Unvanquished was the only Indian
film to win the Golden Lion until Mira
Nair's *Monsoon Wedding* in 2001.

Aparajito   Satyajit Ray, 1957
The Unvanquished

Aparajito is the second film in Satjyajit Ray's great *Apu* trilogy. Following the death of his sister in *Pather Panchali* (1955), the young Apu (Pinaki Sengupta) and his parents have moved to Benares. While his father Harihar (Kanu Bannerjee) earns his priestly living on the banks of the Ganges, the boy roams the city, fascinated and delighted by the rich ferment of sights and sounds it affords. But Harihar contracts a fever and dies, and Apu's mother Sarbojaya (Karuna Bannerjee), unable to survive on her own, takes her son back to the country to her father-in-law's household. Apu, having tasted the wider world, is no longer satisfied with the simple village life he grew up with, and the local schoolmaster encourages the lad in his ambition and curiosity. At sixteen he wins a scholarship to study in Calcutta. Caught up in the excitement of the city, Apu (now played by Smaran Ghosal) returns home rarely and reluctantly. Sarbojaya, lonely and desperately sick, refuses to appeal to her son's sympathy for fear of hampering his education. Finally a letter from Apu's uncle brings him home—a day too late. After the funeral, refusing to follow his father into the priesthood, he leaves again for Calcutta.

As befits its midway status, Aparajito forms the bridge in Ray's trilogy. It opens up the timeless, self-contained life of Pather Panchali's Bengali village to the disruptive influence of the city, showing Ray's young hero torn between the two worlds, gradually and inevitably growing away from his parents. As always, Ray doesn't load the dice in favor of one character or another. We understand why Apu feels compelled to seek the wider world; we share his delight in learning, his sense of personal achievement. At the same time, however, we see Sarbojaya's pain; she's lost her daughter to an early death, now she's losing her son. In the film's most poignant moment, Sarbojaya, near death, waits at night for the train that she hopes will bring Apu back to her one last time. In the distance a train arrives; she stumbles eagerly to her feet, gazing into the darkness. Nothing—only silence and the dance of the fireflies. **PK**

1957

The Bridge on the River Kwai David Lean, 1957

G.B. (Columbia, Horizon) 161m Technicolor
Language English / Japanese / Thai
Producer Sam Spiegel **Screenplay** Carl
Foreman, Michael Wilson, from the novel *Le
pont de la rivière Kwai* by Pierre Boulle
Photography Jack Hildyard **Music** Malcolm
Arnold **Cast** William Holden, Alec Guinness,
Jack Hawkins, Sessue Hayakawa, James
Donald, Geoffrey Horne, André Morell, Peter
Williams, John Boxer, Percy Herbert, Harold
Goodwin, Ann Sears, Heihachiro Okawa,
Keiichiro Katsumoto, M.R.B. Chakrabandhu
Oscars Sam Spiegel (best picture), David
Lean (director), Pierre Boulle, Carl Foreman,
Michael Wilson (screenplay)*, Alec Guinness
(actor), Jack Hildyard (photography), Peter
Taylor (editing), Malcolm Arnold (music)
* Then-blacklisted writers Carl Foreman
and Michael Wilson were posthumously
awarded Oscars in 1984 **Oscar nomination**
Sessue Hayakawa (actor in support role)

There may be no honor among thieves, but wartime enemies are a different matter. At least that's the belief of Alec Guinness's Colonel Nicholson in *The Bridge on the River Kwai*, who insists that the Japanese overseers of their sweltering Burmese prison camp treat his men and him with decency. But as this consummate commander and paragon of English pragmatism organizes the construction of an enemy railroad bridge, a team of Americans led by escaped prisoner of war Major Shears (William Holden) is on its way to blow it to bits.

Director David Lean plays the looming conflict for maximum irony, setting Guinness up as the tragic counterpart to Holden's unsentimental Yank. As usual, Lean loads his film with details, filling the widescreen image with elaborate action and immaculately constructed sets. But holding this epic World War II film together are the performances of its three iconic leads: the stiff and traditional Guinness, the loose and cynical Holden, and Sessue Hayakawa as the Japanese colonel unknowingly stuck in the middle of a battle of cross-Atlantic wills.

The final scenes of destruction are justly lauded for their stunt work, choreography, and editing, but one of the most memorable elements of *River Kwai* remains English composer Malcolm Arnold's whimsical, whistled "The Colonel Bogey March." **JKI**

Sweet Smell of Success Alexander Mackendrick, 1957

U.S. (Hecht, Hill & Lancaster, Norma–
Curtleigh) 96m BW **Producer** Tony Curtis,
Harold Hecht, James Hill, Burt Lancaster
Screenplay Clifford Odets, Ernest Lehman,
Alexander Mackendrick, from novella by
Ernest Lehman **Photography** James Wong
Howe **Music** Elmer Bernstein **Cast** Burt
Lancaster, Tony Curtis, Susan Harrison,
Martin Milner, Sam Levene, Barbara Nichols,
Jeff Donnell, Sally, Joe Frisco, Emile Meyer,
Edith Atwater, Chico Hamilton

A wonderfully bitter satire on the celebrity biz, with smarmy press agent Sidney Falco (Tony Curtis) toadying to monstrous newspaper columnist J.J. Hunsecker (Burt Lancaster), but clearly on the road to wrecking his own life through his devotion to getting ahead. *Sweet Smell of Success* has a great smoky jazz score from Chico Hamilton and reeks of New York circa 1957—taking us through the buzzing night spots where the desperate pay court to the demented and souls are sold for column inches, to the rainswept streets where brutally crooked cops plant dope on jazz musicians or beat J.J.'s enemies half to death.

Director Alexander Mackendrick more than makes the transfer from Ealing comedy (*Whisky Galore!*, *The Man in the White Suit*, *The Ladykillers*) to ferocious frenzy. He picks up on the cynical, observational attitude of Ernest Lehmann's hardboiled newsprint script and adds gothic shadows: The monumental Lancaster, lit like the Frankenstein monster, is amazingly hateful ("match me, Sidney"). Meanwhile, Curtis does his best screen work as the quivering minion, eating himself up from the inside as he tries to do J.J. a favor—one that rebounds dreadfully by breaking up the romance between a square jazzman (Marty Milner) and the fragile little sister (the sadly unprolific Susan Harrison) that J.J. is smothering with a palpably incestuous love. **KN**

Bharat Mata Mehboob Khan, 1957
Mother India

India (Mehboob) 172m Technicolor
Language Hindi Producer Mehboob Khan
Screenplay Mehboob Khan, Wajahat Mirza,
S. Ali Raza Photography Faredoon A. Irani
Music Naushad Ali Cast Nargis, Sunil Dutt,
Raaj Kumar, Rajendra Kumar, Kanhaiyalal,
Kumkum, Master Sajid, Sitara Devi, Mukri,
Sajid Khan, Azra, Chanchal, Kanan Kaushal,
Sheela Naik Oscar nomination India (best
foreign language film)

"India's Gone With the Wind."

Eastern Eye review,
quoted on poster

Mebhoob Khan's *Mother India* remains the quintessential Indian film over fifty years after its release. The picture depicts the struggle of a woman, Radha (Nargis), to reconcile traditional values and village life with a promised modern utopia. An international success with audiences across much of Asia and Africa—who regarded India as a role model in the struggle for decolonization—*Mother India* also gained recognition in Europe and America as one of the few Indian films ever nominated for an Oscar.

Mehboob Khan, one of the first directors in India to use color to great effect, had worked on an epic scale in his historical films, and he brought these skills to bear in this study of village life. In the process, he forged a national epic: a new story for a new nation. *Mother India* has a powerful storyline, following the heroine from marriage to old age, and is dense in mythological references, as characters' names associate them with key figures in the Hindu pantheon.

The film features the top stars of its day, notably Nargis, Raaj Kumar, and Sunil Dutt. A frisson occurred when Nargis, who had been romantically linked to the legendary Raj Kapoor, married Sunil Dutt after the film's completion, not least because he played her son on-screen. *Mother India*'s perennially popular music is by Naushad Ali, a blend of folk tunes and classical ragas (melodies) orchestrated in a Western style with the hundred-piece orchestra—a byword of Hindi film style that Ali is said to have introduced. *Mother India* also has spectacular visuals; its shots of the heroine dragging a plow like a beast of burden, and the happy faces of Radha and her sons after the harvest, looking out to a bright future in the style of Soviet realism, have become iconic.

The complexities of *Mother India* and the host of different readings it has generated make it one of the few films that can still draw audiences to theaters whenever it is screened. It is the first Indian movie to which anyone with an interest in world cinema should turn. **RDw**

1957

i

Bharat Mata was the first
Indian film to be nominated
for an Oscar.

Touch of Evil Orson Welles, 1958

For decades, filmmakers have paid homage to Orson Welles's 1950s noir *Touch of Evil*. It's a lurid tale of corruption and conscience, played out in the strip joints and motels of a sleazy border town, with honorable Mexican narcotics official Charlton Heston and degenerate American cop Welles at odds over a murder whose jurisdiction is in dispute while Janet Leigh becomes a terrorized pawn in their battle of wills.

Heston strong-armed Universal into hiring Hollywood pariah Welles to direct as well as play the role of Hank Quinlan. Welles immediately threw away the script and wrote his own adaptation of Whit Masterson's pulp novel *Badge of Evil*, transforming a cheap little thriller into great art. Steeped in sinister atmosphere, the film is celebrated for its remarkable single tracking-shot opening, a dazzling three minutes in which the camera crane swoops through the busy night scene as Miguel "Mike" Vargas (Heston) and his pert blonde American bride Susan (Leigh) stroll across into the United States for an ice-cream soda. An unidentifiable man plants a bomb in a convertible, pedestrians scurry around, the driver's floozy companion complains she's "got this ticking noise in my head," the newlyweds and a border patrol guard exchange enough small talk to establish their back story, and kaboom, the honeymoon is over.

Police chief Quinlan arrives from the American side of the border to control the investigation while Susan is waylaid by the Mexican drug dealers Vargas has been working to shut down. Within minutes the cards have been dealt in a malevolent, deeply perverse game. To prevent Vargas from exposing him as a criminal, Quinlan will have Susan abducted and drugged (by Mercedes McCambridge's lesbian in leather and her reefer-maddened thugs). Quinlan is one of the giant film noir psychopaths, a bloated figure whose abuse of power has turned him into a monster (the already hefty Welles expanded with padding and false nose). Heston as a Mexican seems a preposterous idea, but his performance is interesting, his confidence sufficient to prevent the satiric Welles from crushing him. But the most affecting character is the tragic, belatedly ennobled figure of Quinlan's adoring lackey, Pete Menzies (Joseph Calleia).

Rivaling the opening are a series of bold, complex set pieces that have given *Touch of Evil* its reputation as film noir's epitaph, Welles theatrically exaggerating stylistic elements while achieving a hyperrealism with Russell Means's sharp black-and-white cinematography and Henry Mancini's Latino/jazz/rock 'n' roll score.

Welles disliked Universal's editing, and in 1998 a restoration meticulously made from his notes was released. A few minutes longer, its most satisfying alterations are the removal of credits over the famous opening sequence and more intricate cutting between Susan's motel ordeal and Vargas's disturbing journey with Quinlan. Whether the before or after version, *Touch of Evil* endures as a superbly kinky masterpiece of technique, imagination, and audacity. **AE**

U.S. (Universal) 95m BW **Producer** Albert Zugsmith **Screenplay** Orson Welles, from the novel *Badge of Evil* by Whit Masterson **Photography** Russell Metty **Music** Henry Mancini **Cast** Charlton Heston, Janet Leigh, Orson Welles, Joseph Calleia, Akim Tamiroff, Joanna Cook Moore, Ray Collins, Dennis Weaver, Valentin de Vargas, Mort Mills, Victor Millan, Lalo Rios, Risto, Michael Sargent, Phil Harvey, Joi Lansing, Marlene Dietrich

"He was some kind of a man."

Tanya (Marlene Dietrich)

i

Welles shot predominantly at night in order to avoid interference from studio bosses.

1958

Gigi Vincente Minnelli, 1958

U.S. (MGM) 119m Metrocolor
Producer Arthur Freed **Screenplay** Alan Jay
Lerner, Anita Loos, from novel by Colette
Photography Joseph Ruttenberg
Music Frederick Loewe **Cast** Leslie Caron,
Maurice Chevalier, Louis Jourdan, Hermione
Gingold, Eva Gabor, Jacques Bergerac, Isabel
Jeans, John Abbott **Oscars** Arthur Freed
(best picture), Vincente Minnelli (director),
Alan Jay Lerner (screenplay), William A.
Horning, E. Preston Ames, Henry Grace, F.
Keogh Gleason (art direction), Joseph
Ruttenberg (photography), Cecil Beaton
(costume), Adrienne Fazan (editing),
André Previn (music), Frederick Loewe,
Alan Jay Lerner (song)

Finally breaking the record number of Academy Awards won by *Gone with the Wind* (1939), Vincente Minnelli's scrumptious MGM musical took home nine Oscars, including Best Picture and Director. Based on Colette's short story of a petite Parisienne groomed by her grandmother and great aunt to be a courtesan in the family tradition, *Gigi* was created for the screen with a witty songbook commissioned from Alan Jay Lerner and Frederick Loewe. Favorites include "Thank Heaven for Little Girls" and "I'm Glad I'm Not Young Anymore" (both sung by the ultimate boulevardier, Maurice Chevalier, in a career rebirth), and the droll Chevalier–Hermione Gingold duet shakily recollecting a long-ago liaison, "I Remember it Well."

Leslie Caron is a perfect delight as the coltish child, suffering lessons in etiquette, coquetry, seduction, and gem valuation before her sudden, inevitable transformation into a poised and desirable young woman. Louis Jordan is just divine as the bored man-about-town tunefully perplexed by the depth of his feelings for her. Fin de siècle Paris never looked lovelier (authentic locations include the Bois de Boulogne, the Tuileries, and swank mecca Maxim's), and Cecil Beaton's costumes rival his work on Lerner and Loewe's *My Fair Lady* (1964). *Gigi* is forever charming. **AE**

The Defiant Ones Stanley Kramer, 1958

U.S. (Curtleigh, Lomitas) 97m BW
Producer Stanley Kramer
Screenplay Nedrick Young, Harold Jacob
Smith **Photography** Sam Leavitt
Music Ernest Gold **Cast** Tony Curtis, Sidney
Poitier, Theodore Bikel, Charles McGraw, Lon
Chaney Jr., King Donovan, Claude Akins,
Lawrence Dobkin, Whit Bissell, Carl "Alfalfa"
Switzer, Kevin Coughlin, Cara Williams
Oscars Nedrick Young, Harold Jacob Smith
(screenplay), Sam Leavitt (photography)
Oscar nominations Stanley Kramer (best
picture), Stanley Kramer (director), Tony
Curtis (actor), Sidney Poitier (actor),
Theodore Bikel (actor in support role), Cara
Williams (actress in support role), Frederic
Knudtson (editing) **Berlin International
Film Festival** Sidney Poitier (Silver Bear)

A self-avowed "message" picture, Stanley Kramer's *The Defiant Ones* deploys a potent symbol of American race relations: two convicts, one white and one black (Tony Curtis and Sidney Poitier), are chained together when the truck taking them to prison turns over. Both men harbor racist feelings, and at first they want only to separate—but, appropriately enough in this allegory of American history, they cannot. Their unavoidable closeness makes them reach beyond stereotypes and angry words to get to know each other as individuals.

A robbery to get food goes wrong, and the pair, much to the white man's chagrin, are pursued by a mob eager to lynch them both. Arriving at a farmhouse presided over by a lonely white woman, they finally get the means to break the chain. Yet they do not then go their own ways, even though the white woman tries to separate them. A final dash for freedom through a swamp and then onto a freight train fails, and the men are recaptured.

Fine acting from both Curtis and Poitier gives life and intellectual force to the narrative, which could easily have descended into ineffective melodrama. *The Defiant Ones* is perhaps the film that best captures the agenda of "realist" liberals in the 1950s, as American society attempted to come to terms with the fact of the African-American presence. **BP**

Man of the West Anthony Mann, 1958

After making a series of exemplary Westerns starring James Stewart during the 1950s, Anthony Mann cast an aging Gary Cooper as a man forced to confront a past which he thought he had left behind him. As is usual in Mann's Westerns, personal history exerts a grip on the characters that only death can loosen. Cooper plays Link Jones, an apparently respectable citizen on his way to hire a schoolteacher for his town. After the train he's traveling on is robbed, Link finds himself marooned in the middle of nowhere with a saloon girl named Billie (Julie London), and in desperation he decides to seek help from some former associates nearby. But Link is revealed to have a criminal past, and his one-time friends are a gang of menacing grotesques, played by Western stalwarts Royal Dano, Robert Wilke, and John Dehner. It soon becomes evident that there are scores to be settled, and the gang tries to force Link to help them with a robbery, threatening Billie with rape. Their behavior in turn calls up a murderous rage in the hitherto mild-mannered Link, who hands out a brutal beating to one of the gang.

The leader of the gang is Dock Tobin (a barn-storming performance by Lee J. Cobb). In Mann's Westerns, family ties always prove stronger than any sense of the wider community, and Tobin's gang functions as a monstrous parody of kith and kin. Dock indeed regards Link as a surrogate son. In the final confrontation, beautifully staged by Mann in an old ghost town, Dock, having finally raped Billie as a direct provocation, incites Link into what amounts to an act of parricide. In finally laying to rest the threat of his menacing "father," however, Link reveals in himself a savage violence only barely under control.

Unusually for a Mann Western, a lot of the action takes place in dark and gloomy interiors, as the tensions between Link and the gang play out. But Mann's camerawork is as assured as ever. Make sure you see this film in the full CinemaScope ratio! **EB**

U.S. (Ashton) 100m Color **Producer** Walter Mirisch **Screenplay** Reginald Rose, from the novel *The Border Jumpers* by Will C. Brown **Photography** Ernest Haller **Music** Leigh Harline **Cast** Gary Cooper, Julie London, Lee J. Cobb, Arthur O'Connell, Jack Lord, John Dehner, Royal Dano, Robert J. Wilke

"Mann's direction is immaculate."

The Guardian, 2000

i

Jean-Luc Godard named *Man of the West* one of the best films of 1958, saying that it reinvented the Western.

Vertigo Alfred Hitchcock, 1958

Although director Alfred Hitchcock was then at the height of his critical success and commercial fame, *Vertigo* was not a well-liked film at the time of its release. Most criticism focused on the intricate and unlikely plot dependent on a fiendishly implausible murder scheme on the part of a thinly characterized villain, whose exposure is about as much of a surprise as the ending of your average Scooby Doo episode. The climax is so concerned with something else that the killer seems to get away with it—though Hitchcock shot an unnecessary tag, in the spirit of his TV narrations, to reveal that he was brought to justice. Closer to the mark, there was a genuine feeling of discomfort at the nasty little relationship between Jimmy Stewart and Kim Novak around which the film turns. But during a lengthy period in which *Vertigo* was unavailable for copyright reasons, the film was critically reassessed. Now it is held to be one of the Master's greatest works.

John "Scottie" Ferguson (Stewart) is a San Francisco cop who quits the force after a prologue in which his fear of heights prevents him saving the life of a colleague. Working casually as a private eye, he is hired by old friend Gavin Elster (Tom Elmore) to tail his wife Madeleine (Novak), an icy blonde in a severe suit who is apparently obsessed with a look-alike ancestress who drowned in the nineteenth century. The first half of the film is almost a ghost story, as Scottie is drawn to the neurotic Madeleine, with the suggestion that her reincarnation is ironically going to lead to her death. Here, you get the Hitchcock who was a master of atmosphere as well as suspense, and a genuine evocation of the unearthly. After Madeleine's fatal plunge from a bell tower, the film changes tack and becomes more intense, with Scottie going even further beyond Stewart's aw-shucks mannerisms into mania as he comes across Judy Barton (Novak again), a brassy, brunette shopgirl who resembles the lost Madeleine, and enters into a relationship with her. Few mainstream Hollywood movies dare to be as unsettling as *Vertigo* is in the scenes where Scottie tries to force a new reincarnation of his lost love by manipulating the new girl as she is transformed by a new hairstyle and wardrobe into the elusive Madeleine. For many, the scene in which Judy is finally transformed and embraces Scottie with a vampirish hunger is as emotionally devastating as the shower scene in *Psycho* is physically shocking.

Like several other Hitchcock greats (Rear Window [1954], North by Northwest [1959], Psycho [1960]), *Vertigo* has been endlessly imitated, homaged, and reworked. Movies like Brian De Palma's *Obsession* (1976) are feature-length footnotes to the original. Technical tricks—the simultaneous zoom-in and track-back used to convey Stewart's vertigo—have been added to the repertoire (Steven Spielberg used it in *Jaws* [1975]). In all, Vertigo is a gorgeous, disturbing, icily romantic film, with steel gray Technicolor images, evocative moments of close-up surrealism, and an insistent, probing Bernard Herrmann score. **KN**

U.S. (Alfred J. Hitchcock, Paramount) 128m
Technicolor **Producer** Alfred Hitchcock
Screenplay Samuel A. Taylor, Alec Coppel, from the novel *The Living and the Dead* by Pierre Bolleau and Thomas Narcejac
Photography Robert Burks **Music** Bernard Herrmann **Cast** James Stewart, Kim Novak, Barbara Bel Geddes, Tom Helmore, Henry Jones, Raymond Bailey, Ellen Corby, Konstantin Shayne, Lee Patrick
Oscar nominations Hal Pereira, Henry Bumstead, Sam Comer, Frank R. McKelvy (art direction), George Dutton (sound)

i

Clips from *Vertigo* have been used to add mood to other movies, such as Terry Gilliam's *Twelve Monkeys* (1995).

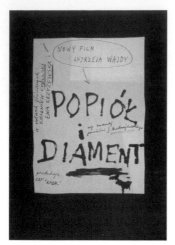

Popiól i diament Andrzej Wajda, 1958
Ashes and Diamonds

For a few years at the end the 1950s, after Italian Neorealism waned and before the French New Wave rolled in, Polish cinema was the art cinema. With their complex, often ambiguous tales of wartime solidarity, sacrifice, and commitment, the Poles offered the most cogent example yet of socialism with a human face. Films by Aleksandr Ford, Andrzej Munk, Jerzy Kawalerowicz, and others won a slew of festival prizes and attracted international audiences. Perhaps the finest of all the Polish films of this era, the one that came to stand for an emerging generation of East European artists and intellectuals, was Andrzej Wajda's *Ashes and Diamonds*.

Based on the controversial novel by Jerzy Andrzejewski, Wajda's masterpiece unspools on the last day of World War II. The enemy has surrendered, but the winners aren't sure what they've won: both Communists and Nationalists can already sense that their fragile wartime alliance is unraveling. Enter Maciek (Zbigniew Cybulski), a young hothead attached to the Nationalist underground in a provincial town; assigned to kill the recently arrived Communist district leader, he holes up in a hotel for the night. But this is just about the first night of peace that Maciek has known in his adult life, and he's eager to see what else life might offer. He meets and falls for a pretty young woman, and his attention to her threatens to get in the way of his mission.

Throughout *Ashes and Diamonds*, Wajda employs a looming deep focus, so that disparate characters as well as opposing political agendas take on equal weight in the frame. Yet the real show is Wajda's revelation of Polish actor Cybulski as Maciek. With his eyes perpetually hidden behind shades and his slightly gawky but endearing manner, Cybulski was hailed as the "James Dean of the East," the symbol for a generation that wanted to look past political labels to focus on an individual's human qualities. Within the space of a few shots, he can go from dementia to helplessness to anger; his final "death dance," with his chilling laughter as he staggers through a field after being fatally shot, is surely one of the most powerful—and often quoted—endings in film history. **RP**

Poland (Polski, ZRF) 105m BW
Language Polish **Producer** Stanislaw Adler
Screenplay Jerzy Andrzejewski, Andrzej Wajda, from the novel *Popiól i diament* by Jerzy Andrzejewski **Photography** Jerzy Wójcik **Music** Jan Krenz, Filip Nowak
Cast Zbigniew Cybulski, Ewa Krzyzewska, Waclaw Zastrzezynski, Adam Pawlikowski, Bogumil Kobiela, Jan Ciecierski, Stanislaw Milski, Artur Mlodnicki, Halina Kwiatkowska, Ignacy Machowski, Zbigniew Skowronski, Barbara Krafftówna, Aleksander Sewruk, Zofia Czerwinska, Wiktor Grotowicz
Venice Film Festival Andrzej Wajda (FIPRESCI award)

"[Wajda's] sharply etched black-and-white action has the pictorial snap and quality of some of the old Soviet pictures of Pudovkin and Eisenstein."

Bosley Crowther,
***The New York Times*, 1961**

🛈

The film is reportedly a favorite of Martin Scorsese, who used it as inspiration for *The Departed* (2006).

Bab el hadid Youssef Chahine, 1958
Cairo Station

Egypt (Gabriel Talhami) 95m BW
Language Arabic Producer Gabriel Talhami
Screenplay Mohamed Abu Youssef, Abdel
Hay Adib Photography Alevise Orfanelli
Music Fouad El-Zahry Cast Farid Shawqi,
Hind Rostom, Youssef Chahine, Hassan el
Baroudi, Abdel Aziz Khalil, Naima Wasfy, Said
Khalil, Abdel Ghani Nagdi, Loutfi El Hakim,
Abdel Hamid Bodaoha, F. El Demerdache,
Said El Araby, Ahmed Abaza, Hana Abdel
Fallah, Safia Sarwat

With the arrival of *Cairo Station*, it was as if cinema had been reborn. The product of a healthy tradition of Egyptian, Arab, and African filmmaking—though few movies produced in the region were ever seen outside of It—this new cinema had learned from Hollywood and Italian Neorealism to build a form of its own. It was filled with humor, wisdom, and anguish; paid attention to the minute details of everyday life of the city; portrayed the primal powers of lust and desire; and delved into classical and oriental iconography—all presented in a mix of fantasy and reality. *Cairo Station* is vivid and moving, precise in its portrayals, original both as the creation of a single individual and as the embodiment of a secular culture, one that is so close and yet so different to that of the West.

And who is responsible for it? Youssef Chahine, a "crazy" little guy filled with longing and despair. Bringing disturbing revelations about himself and life to the screen, he plays a crippled newspaper vendor named Kenaoui who bears an unrequited desire for a voluptuous lemonade seller (Hind Rostom). Although the plot components are simple enough, the world depicted here is both dangerous and complex. The way events turn out opens up dark abysses in the city's life, made the more unexpected by the initial friendly codes the film uses. Panned by Egyptian viewers upon its initial release, *Cairo Station* has justly been hailed as a masterpiece on its rediscovery. **J-MF**

i

Hind Rostom was famous for her seductive roles, and was described as the "Marilyn Monroe of Arabia."

India (Aurora) 100m BW **Language** Bengali
Producer Satyajit Ray **Screenplay** Satyajit
Ray, from novel by Tarashankar Banerjee
Photography Subrata Mitra **Music** Ustad
Vilayat Khan, Asis Kumar, Robin Majumder,
Dakhin Mohan Takhur **Cast** Chhabi Biswas,
Padma Devi, Pinaki Sen Gupta, Gangapada
Basu, Tulsi Lahiri, Kali Sarkar, Waheed
Khan, Roshan Kumari, Sardar Akhtar,
Tulsi Chakraborty, Bismillah Khan,
Salamat Ali Khan

*"I am . . . interested in
a way of life that
is passing and the
representatives of that
way of life . . . There's a
quality of pathos in that
which interests me."*

Satyajit Ray, 1982

🛈

Ray did not think that the film would
be successful in foreign markets, but
it proved a critical and financial hit.

Jalsaghar Satyajit Ray, 1958
The Music Room

Satyajit Ray is best known for his "Apu" trilogy, a set of three films that
together chronicle the life of a poor Bengali villager from childhood
through adulthood. These films introduced Indian art cinema to a
world that previously was familiar only with the fantasy and spectacle
of the Bollywood musical. Through them, Ray revealed a different India,
the life of a traditional village, the ravages of famine and drought, and
of poverty. Greatly influenced by Italian Neorealism, Ray's beautiful and
moving pictures sought to explore moral and social injustices.
Exquisitely shot in the countryside, they made every attempt to be
authentic documents of Indian life. In *The Music Room*, however, Ray's
style and intentions change. This moody, atmospheric, and elegiac film
will be a great surprise to those expecting the Ray of the Apu trilogy
and *Distant Thunder* (1973). With this tremendous tour de force, Ray
transcends our typical notions of national cinema, particularly in the
Third World context.

The Music Room tells the Chekhovian story of a fading lord, Huzur
Roy, in the 1920s. The character is played with a sad eyed gravity and
impressive nobility by one of Ray's most beloved actors, Chhabi Biswas.
Roy's power and fortune have slowly faded away to nothing, his palace
is crumbling, his staff of servants has dwindled down, and he spends
his days sitting on his roof in silent reveries of past glory looking out on
a barren landscape. Mahim Ganguly (Gangapada Basu) is a money
lender, one whose crass manners do not betray his rising power and
status. Ganguly represents all that Roy has lost and threatens his very
existence. When Ganguly announces that he is going to hold a concert,
Roy decides that he will hold a concert on the same night, pitting the
old and the new against one another for a final confrontation. Roy's
opulent music room is his great love, and the film flashes back to earlier
concerts held in the room in better times. This last concert will be his
final grand gesture, although it will wipe out Roy's treasury completely.
It is his chance to live as he was once accustomed to doing, and to keep
his inevitable end at bay for one last night of music and beauty.

The film's atmosphere of decay and melancholy is almost
intoxicating. We feel the end of Roy's world viscerally and yet, like him,
wish impossibly that it will not end. The close observation and careful
evocation of a time and place that characterized Ray's Neorealist films
work well in this picture, but to more Expressionist ends. We see that
the two remaining servants are losing their battle with the elements as
plants and insects are taking over the palace. The bare plains over
which Roy looks out mirror his creeping demise. Satyajit Ray is
exploring new ideas and techniques in this film, and it is fascinating to
watch his style expand. *The Music Room* is a sensual delight and an
essential masterpiece of world cinema. **RH**

Mon oncle Jacques Tati, 1958
My Uncle

France / Italy (Alter, Centauro, Gray, Specta)
110m Eastmancolor **Language** French
Producer Louis Dolivet, Jacques Tati, Alain
Terouanne **Screenplay** Jacques Lagrange,
Jean L'Hôte, Jacques Tati **Photography** Jean
Bourgoin **Music** Franck Barcellini, Alain
Romans **Cast** Jean-Pierre Zola, Adrienne
Servantie, Lucien Frégis, Betty Schneider,
Jean-François Martial, Dominique Marie,
Yvonne Arnaud, Adelaide Danieli, Alain
Bécourt, Régis Fontenay, Claude Badolle,
Max Martel, Nicolas Bataille, Jacques Tati
Oscar France (best foreign language film)
Cannes Film Festival Jacques Tati
(special jury prize)

i

An English version of the film, nine
minutes shorter than the original,
was filmed alongside the French one.

In his first two features, *The Big Day* (1948) and *Mr. Hulot's Holiday* (1953), Jacques Tati lovingly celebrated the charms of the provincial, random, and dilapidated. In *My Uncle*, he directs his satire against the mania for mechanization that threatens those easygoing old ways of life.

Tati's perennial screen persona, the gangling, near-wordless Monsieur Hulot, lives in a rickety old *quartier* of Paris. Not far away live the Arpels, his sister and brother-in-law (Adrienne Servantie and Jean-Pierre Zola), in a trendily ultramodern house packed with gadgets. Inevitably, most of these gadgets malfunction—especially when the well-meaning Hulot is around.

As always with Tati, the humor is almost entirely visual—and aural. Few comedians have made such creative use of the soundtrack, and the clickings, buzzings, hissings, and sputterings of the Arpels's assorted gizmos and of the machinery in the factory where Arpel ill-advisedly gives his brother-in-law a job, often reach a pitch of controlled lunacy. Tati takes mischievous delight in showing how automation, supposedly designed to improve the quality of life, works against comfort, relaxation, and pleasure. But the human element, represented by the walking disaster area that is Hulot, can never be excluded. There is a melancholy undertow to *My Uncle*—pneumatic drills rattle ominously over the credits—but a wistful optimism too. **PK**

Some Came Running Vincente Minnelli, 1958

U.S. (MGM) 137m Color
Producer Sol C. Siegel **Screenplay** John
Patrick, Arthur Sheekman, from novel by
James Jones **Photography** William H.
Daniels **Music** Elmer Bernstein **Cast** Frank
Sinatra, Dean Martin, Shirley MacLaine,
Martha Hyer, Arthur Kennedy, Nancy Gates,
Leora Dana, Betty Lou Klein, Larry Gates,
Steve Peck, Connie Gilchrist, Ned Weaver
Oscar nominations Arthur Kennedy (actor),
Shirley MacLaine (actress), Martha Hyer
(actress), Walter Plunkett (costume design),
Jimmy Van Heusen, Sammy Cahn
(original song)

Gloriously shot in CinemaScope, *Some Came Running* is an exemplary Hollywood melodrama that ranks alongside Nic Ray's *Bigger Than Life* (1956) and the color features of Douglas Sirk in its dissection of small-town American life. Frank Sinatra is sublime as the solitary, one-time novelist Dave Hirsh who, having been drunkenly put on a bus, along with party girl Ginny (Shirley MacLaine), returns home after years in the army.

Dave's presence threatens to undermine his elder brother's position as a pillar of respectable society, particularly when he takes up with gambling drunk Bama (Dean Martin). As his sibling desperately attempts to reform him, Dave finds himself caught between the affections of Ginny and Gwen (Martha Hyer), a schoolteacher and ardent admirer of Dave's single published work, who is desperate to see him return to writing.

Like Frankie Machine, Sinatra's character in *The Man with the Golden Arm* (1955), Dave is a good man challenged by forces that seek to lead him astray. The revelation of Bama's medical condition and the arrival of Ginny's violent ex both spell the worst for Dave, eroding any hope of redemption and creating a gulf between him and his one beacon of hope, Gwen. **IHS**

Dracula Terence Fisher, 1958

G.B. (Hammer) 82m Technicolor
Producer Michael Carreras, Anthony Hinds,
Anthony Nelson Keys **Screenplay** Jimmy
Sangster, from novel by Bram Stoker
Photography Jack Asher **Music** James
Bernard **Cast** Peter Cushing, Christopher
Lee, Michael Gough, Melissa Stribling,
Carol Marsh, Olga Dickie, John Van Eyssen,
Valerie Gaunt, Janina Faye, Barbara Archer,
Charles Lloyd Pack, George Merritt,
George Woodbridge, George Benson,
Miles Malleson

Hammer Films's revision of Bram Stoker's famous novel is one of the great horror films. Director Terence Fisher, who combines a cutter's eye for bold contrast with a delight in the logical unfolding of space, demonstrates a complete mastery of melodramatic modes. He's aided by Jack Asher's vibrant cinematography, James Bernard's unabashedly lurid and exciting score, and two career-defining performances: Peter Cushing's intellectual, refined, and athletic Van Helsing and Christopher Lee's icy, imperious, handsome Count.

Like Hammer's previous film *The Curse of Frankenstein* (1957), *Dracula* came as quite a shock to its first viewers and reviewers, and as late as the early 1970s, Hammer's emphasis on the physical aspects of horror was generally recognized both as a turning point in genre history and as the trademark of a legendary production company. Even today, sensitive viewers can appreciate the boldness with which *Dracula* oversteps the boundaries defined by earlier cinematic horrors. This is seen most clearly in Dracula's feral eyes and fangs, the blood welling up from the hearts of staked vampire women, and the unmistakable sexuality of the relationship between the vampire and his victims. At one point, Dracula enters his victim's bedroom and shuts the door on the camera, positioned in the corridor. The tactful and expected approach would have been to end the scene there, but Fisher cuts directly inside the room, as Dracula backs the young woman toward her bed. The cut itself conveys inexorability, violation, and dread. **CFu**

Some Like It Hot Billy Wilder, 1959

U.S. (Ashton, Mirisch) 120m BW
Producer I.A.L. Diamond, Doane Harrison,
Billy Wilder **Screenplay** I.A.L. Diamond, Billy
Wilder **Photography** Charles Lang
Music Adolph Deutsch, Gus Kahn, Bert
Kalmar, Leo Wood **Cast** Marilyn Monroe,
Tony Curtis, Jack Lemmon, George Raft, Pat
O'Brien, Joe E. Brown, Nehemiah Persoff,
Joan Shawlee, Billy Gray, George E. Stone,
Dave Barry, Mike Mazurki, Harry Wilson,
Beverly Wills, Barbara Drew **Oscar** Orry-Kelly
(costume) **Oscar nominations** Billy Wilder
(director), I.A.L. Diamond, Billy Wilder
(screenplay), Jack Lemmon (actor), Ted
Haworth, Edward G. Boyle (art direction),
Charles Lang (photography)

*"Will you look at that!
Look how she moves!
It's like Jell-O on springs."*

Jerry (Jack Lemmon)

Some Like It Hot was selected by
the American Film Institute as the
Best Comedy of All Time.

Down-on-their-luck jazz musicians Joe (Tony Curtis) and Jerry (Jack Lemmon) witness the 1929 St. Valentine's Day Massacre and flee Chicago with an all-girl band bound for Miami, posing as "Josephine" and "Daphne." Both are taken with Sugar Kane Kowalczyk (Marilyn Monroe), a vulnerable, boozy singer. But Daphne attracts the persistent attentions of lecherous playboy Osgood Fielding III (Joe E. Brown), and things get even more complicated when the very gangsters the boys want to avoid, Chicago mob boss Spats Columbo (George Raft) and his henchmen, arrive at the Florida hotel for a gangland summit.

This legendary drag comedy is sensationally funny, fizzing with cleverly crafted gags, breakneck timing, and terrific performances. The 1950s top sex goddess at her most enchanting, Monroe's forlorn-funny turn, maddening though it was for her costars and director to capture, is mythic. Curtis's self-consciousness in drag gave him an aloof control that is in superb contrast to the uninhibited, priceless Lemmon.

Some Like It Hot was independently produced and directed by Billy Wilder in his second screenwriting collaboration with I.A.L. "Iz" Diamond, and was sparked by the German farce *Fanfaren der Liebe* (1951), in which two unemployed musicians join an all-girl band, take a train journey, and go in for some quick-change romancing with the band's singer. Wilder didn't want his two heroes to be camp; they had to be heatedly heterosexual so that their escapade aboard the train surrounded by temptation was comically excruciating. Therefore, they had to have a desperately good reason to masquerade as women. Running for their lives from ruthless killers provided strong motivation. And although the gangsters have their own good jokes, they are effectively played straight for a note of delicious menace, with Wilder's neat noir touch of shooting Raft's key entrances from his distinctive footwear up.

The film's famous last line was written the night before shooting finished by Diamond, who insisted to the dubious Wilder that it was funny because it's so unexpected; the last reaction the audience expects to Jerry's revelation "I'm a MAN!" is Osgood's philosophical shrug, "Nobody's perfect." The other most fondly recalled moment is Daphne's engagement announcement. Lemmon shaking his maracas in absurd ecstasy is a masterpiece of comic timing, Wilder insisting on joyous fits of gourd rattling to leave space for audience laughter between lines. He also overrode objections to filming in black-and-white, not only to enhance the period setting but, shrewdly, to mute the men's makeup. Their transformation is startlingly amusing, but imagined in Technicolor it would be too grotesque. Industry mavens predicted the film would be a disaster because it broke several traditional rules of film comedy (the story springs from a grisly mass murder, the script was only half-written when shooting began, and the picture runs two hours, to cite a few), but audiences went crazy and still do. **AE**

North by Northwest Alfred Hitchcock, 1959

U.S. (MGM) 136m Technicolor
Producer Alfred Hitchcock
Screenplay Ernest Lehman
Photography Robert Burks **Music** Bernard
Herrmann **Cast** Cary Grant, Eva Marie
Saint, James Mason, Jessie Royce Landis,
Leo G. Carroll, Josephine Hutchinson, Philip
Ober, Martin Landau, Adam Williams,
Edward Platt, Robert Ellenstein, Les
Tremayne, Philip Coolidge, Patrick McVey,
Ed Binns **Oscar nominations** Ernest
Lehman (screenplay), William A. Horning,
Robert F. Boyle, Merrill Pye, Henry Grace,
Frank R. McKelvy (art direction), George
Tomasini (editing)

Alfred Hitchcock's most entertaining film, *North by Northwest* is pure funhouse: mistaken for a spy and suspected for the murder of a U.N. diplomat, Roger O. Thornhill (Cary Grant, armed only with vast stores of charm and witty rejoinders) flees across the country, pursued by villains (led by James Mason and a creepy Martin Landau) and shadowed by government agents. Somewhere in between is the stunningly beautiful and shamelessly sensual Eve Kendall (Eva Marie Saint), whose allegiances wobble warily between the twin poles of good guys and bad guys.

Working from one of the all-time great scripts by Ernest Lehman, and featuring several of cinema's greatest action sequences—the crop duster attack, the chase across the face(s) of Mount Rushmore—Hitchcock ended his golden period on the highest of notes with *North by Northwest*. Even the title sequences, designed by Saul Bass, are memorable, and Bernard Herrmann's score is equal to his iconic themes from *Psycho* (1960) and *Vertigo* (1958).

Saint is one of Hitchcock's more vulnerable female leads, and from their first encounter it is clear that she and Grant are meant for each other. It's the perennial bachelor's ultimate trial by fire on the way to wedded bliss. Therefore, the question becomes not whether but how the pair ends up together. Grant is made to surmount various threats not just for his life but implicitly for his and Saint's future life together, and Hitchcock—ever the romantic sadist—has a hoot putting up the roadblocks. **JKl**

ℹ

The suit that Cary Grant wore has become iconic, even inspiring a story that tells the film from its viewpoint.

Les quatre cents coups François Truffaut, 1959
The 400 Blows

François Truffaut's debut feature, *The 400 Blows* earned the prize for Best Director at the Cannes International Film Festival in 1959. In an instant its young maker was on the map of international film culture—and smoothing the way for such New Wave colleagues as Jean-Luc Godard and Eric Rohmer, already immersed in cutting-edge projects of their own.

Like the other New Wave filmmakers, Truffaut cultivated his key ideas writing articles for *Cahiers de Cinéma*, the literate film magazine edited by André Bazin, who encouraged his critics to pursue their convictions often far from his own distinctive blend of aesthetic and philosophical concerns. Truffaut was the most aggressive writer of the group, fiercely criticizing French cinema's "tradition of quality" while formulating the *politique des auteurs* that saw strongly creative directors as the primary authors of their films.

The 400 Blows abounds with the spirit of personal filmmaking that Truffaut had celebrated as a critic. The hero, Antoine Doinel (Jean-Pierre Léaud), is a thinly fictionalized version of the auteur himself, and Truffaut later revealed that he boosted the intensity of the fifteen-year-old actor's performance by joining him in a private conspiracy against the rest of the cast and crew. Master cinematographer Henri Decaë shot the picture in real Paris locations, and Truffaut never hesitated to stray from the story for moments of poignantly conveyed emotional detail. One such sequence comes when Antoine rides in an amusement-park centrifuge, twisting his body into wry contortions that express his rather weak impulse to rebel against society's constricting norms. Another comes at the end of the film, when Truffaut's camera escapes from a detention camp with Antoine, tracking on and on as he runs breathlessly toward nowhere, then zooming toward his face to capture a freeze-frame portrait of existential angst that is arguably the most powerful single moment in New Wave cinema.

Truffaut and Léaud continued Antoine's adventures in four more films, ending the series with *Love on the Run* in 1979, four years before Truffaut's untimely death. While these sequels have their charm, *The 400 Blows* remains unsurpassed as a distillation of the New Wave's most exuberant creative instincts. **DS**

France (Carrosse, Sédif) 94m BW
Language French Director François Truffaut Producer François Truffaut Screenplay François Truffaut Photography Henri Decaë Music Jean Constantin Cast Jean-Pierre Léaud, Claire Maurier, Albert Rémy, Guy Decomble, Georges Flamant, Patrick Auffray, Daniel Couturier, François Nocher, Richard Kanayan, Renaud Fontanarosa, Michel Girard, Henry Moati, Bernard Abbou, Jean-François Bergouignan, Michel Lesignor Oscar nomination François Truffaut, Marcel Moussy (screenplay) Cannes Film Festival François Truffaut (director, OCIC award)

1959

"A cornerstone of the French New Wave, and one of the greatest movies about childhood, from anywhere, ever."

Anthony Quinn,
Independent, 2009

ℹ️

The title of the film comes from the French phrase *"faire les quatre cents coups,"* which means "to raise hell."

Pickpocket Robert Bresson, 1959

Robert Bresson uses film to express the spiritual inferiority of life in a uniquely paradoxical way: by revealing the indescribable through an intense concentration on concrete images and sounds. Every detail and every nuance of the physical world is exposed by Bresson's intently focused camera. Eschewing traditional dramatization in the form of emoting actors, melodramatic situations, or intricate plots, Bresson allows the action to tell the story. Deadpan voice-over is used to nominally explain the motivations and feelings of characters. Bresson often used nonprofessional actors, whom he tellingly called "models," and directed them to strenuously avoid any theatricality and to simply move through his films. He uses music sparingly as well, allowing it be heard only during key moments of the story, to express something that cannot be verbally articulated. His films are pared down to their essential elements. This simplicity and lack of manipulation allow the audience a great deal of freedom to interpret the actions on screen, so viewer and character alike are involved in the same process of questioning and trying to understand the dilemmas posed by the picture in question.

Pickpocket is among the most perfect examples of Bresson's style. It tells the story of Michel (Martin LaSalle), a disaffected young intellectual who becomes obsessed with picking pockets. At first he sees it simply as a means to further his own ends, but he soon comes to view it as an end in itself and as a creative act. After an amateurish attempt at the crime, which gets him caught almost immediately, he apprentices himself to a professional thief to really learn the craft. The scenes of pickpocketing are breathtaking and rival any in cinema for their excitement and sheer cinematic virtuosity. Although Michel has contact with his sick mother and is involved with a girlfriend, Jeanne (Marika Green), the pickpocketing provides him with his most emotionally and sensually satisfying human connections. This becomes more and more obvious as Michel no longer steals for financial gain. He even seems indifferent about being caught by the end.

Although Bresson avoids the typical tools of drama, *Pickpocket* is completely engrossing and Michel's moral questioning and sense of displacement are deeply affecting. This is one of those pictures that completely changes one's understanding of what cinema is or can be. Bresson is one of the most novelistic of filmmakers, in that he is able to depict the inner world of characters and abstract philosophical concepts that are more easily expressed in language. His achievement here is all the more ingenious because he uses the literal quality of the cinema to achieve his ends, using and shaping the very specific material of the real world. *Pickpocket* expands the vocabulary of the movies. Watching a Bresson film is a demanding but extremely satisfying and enjoyable experience. **RH**

1959

France (Lux) 75m BW **Language** French
Producer Agnès Delahaie **Screenplay**
Robert Bresson **Photography** Léonce-Henri
Burel **Music** Jean-Baptiste Lully **Cast** Martin
LaSalle, Marika Green, Jean Pélégri, Dolly
Scal, Pierre Leymarie, Kassagi, Pierre Étaix,
César Gattegno **Berlin International Film
Festival** Robert Bresson nomination
(Golden Bear)

"Robert Bresson is French cinema, as Dostoyevsky is the Russian novel and Mozart is German music."

Jean-Luc Godard,
Cahiers du Cinéma, **1957**

In a career that spanned fifty years, Robert Bresson made only thirteen feature-length films.

Hiroshima mon amour Alain Resnais, 1959

In his first feature, Alain Resnais draws on the experience of his documentary short films. A Frenchwoman (Emmanuelle Riva) is having an affair with a Japanese architect (Eiji Okada) in Hiroshima, where she has come to shoot a film. Resnais uses documentary footage of the 1945 nuclear attack on the city together with shots of the museum and the rebuilt city. (In fact the film began as a documentary about Hiroshima and the bomb, which Resnais then decided to turn into a feature.) These are interspersed with lyrical scenes of the couple's love affair. The juxtaposition of the tenderness of love and the horrors of war cause the woman to remember her own past in the French town of Nevers. During the war she had an affair with a German soldier and was planning to leave the town with him when, on the last day of fighting, he was killed. Sweet and painful memories of this episode in her life rise up with increasing intensity as her brief affair with the Japanese man takes its course. At the end of *Hiroshima mon amour* this affair will be concluded, each returning to their marriages.

The film was specially written for the screen by Marguerite Duras, who was an important influence on French cinema, later to become a director herself, and whose work shows a preoccupation with the idea of memory and the influence of the past on the present. Memory too is a constant theme in Resnais's work; one of his documentaries, about the French National Library, is entitled *The Whole Memory of the World* (1956). In *Hiroshima mon amour*, Resnais employs a complex flashback structure, which gradually reveals more and more of the past as it intrudes on the present. This structure is held together by the haunting score of Giovanni Fusco and Georges Delerue, and is given a powerful emotional charge by the acting, particularly of Riva, whose face registers the complex emotions of her character down to the tiniest nuance. Our identities, the film seems to say, depend on our memories, but ultimately these will fade. **EB**

France / Japan (Argos, Como, Daiei, Pathé) 90m BW **Language** French / Japanese / English **Producer** Anatole Dauman, Samy Halfon, Sacha Kamenka, Takeo Shirakawa **Screenplay** Marguerite Duras **Photography** Michio Takahashi, Sacha Vierny **Music** Georges Delerue, Giovanni Fusco **Cast** Emmanuelle Riva, Eiji Okada, Stella Dassas, Pierre Barbaud, Bernard Fresson **Oscar nomination** Marguerite Duras (screenplay)

"Sometimes we have to avoid thinking about the problems life presents. Otherwise we'd suffocate."

Elle (Emmanuelle Riva)

ℹ Eiji Okada did not know any French and so had to memorize and deliver his dialogue phoenetically.

Ride Lonesome Budd Boetticher, 1959

U.S. (Columbia) 73m Eastmancolor
Producer Budd Boetticher, Harry Joe
Brown Screenplay Burt Kennedy
Photography Charles Lawton Jr.
Music Heinz Roemheld Cast Randolph
Scott, Karen Steele, Pernell Roberts, James
Best, Lee Van Cleef, James Coburn

The seven Westerns Budd Boetticher made with leading man Randolph Scott are notable for Scott's wry, laconic, weather-beaten virtuousness; colorful secondary characters; visual gracefulness; stark, abstract landscapes; and a muted but aching sense of tragedy. If *Ride Lonesome* stands out in the series, it's because of the optimism of its ending, the easygoing interplay between Pernell Roberts and James Coburn as Boetticher's two most likable villains, and the perfection of Burt Kennedy's script.

Scott plays a bounty hunter with the fabulous name of Ben Brigade, who, after capturing a notorious killer—a memorably infantile James Best—takes him across open country to collect his reward. During his trek, Brigade acquires, against his will, three companions: a station master's sexy wife (Karen Steele) and the aforementioned pair of good badmen, who plan on robbing Brigade of his captive. The latter's outlaw brother (Lee Van Cleef), meanwhile, is in hot pursuit of the group.

The characters are locked in a pattern of competing or complementary goals—no one can make a move without someone else making a countermove—and all are aware that they are headed together toward a showdown. Boetticher, shooting in CinemaScope, does full justice both to the elegance of this scenario and to his protagonist's mythic solitude. **CFu**

Orfeu negro Marcel Camus, 1959
Black Orpheus

Brazil / France / Italy (Dispat, Gemma,
Tupan Filmes) 100m Eastmancolor
Language Portuguese Producer Sacha
Gordine Screenplay Vinicius De Moraes,
Marcel Camus, Jacques Viot, from the play
Orfeu do Carnaval by Vinicius De Moraes
Photography Jean Bourgoin Music Luiz
Bonfá, Antonio Carlos Jobim Cast Breno
Mello, Marpessa Dawn, Lourdes de Oliveira,
Léa Garcia, Ademar Da Silva, Alexandro
Constantino, Waldemar De Souza, Jorge Dos
Santos, Aurino Cassiano Oscar France (best
foreign language film) Cannes Film Festival
Marcel Camus (Golden Palm)

Marcel Camus's restaging of the myth of Orpheus in Rio de Janeiro during Carnival was the surprise winner of the *Palme d'Or* at Cannes and later of the Academy Award for best foreign picture. Filmed using Neorealist techniques—an amateur cast and extensive location shooting in the teeming streets—it was highly praised for its vibrant depiction of Brazilian life and folklore. *Black Orpheus* was also championed as revolutionary for being one of the first international art films to have an entirely black cast. Adding to this acclaim and sense of authenticity is one of the movie's enduring charms: its glorious soundtrack composed by Luiz Bonfá and Antonio Carlos Jobim, two of the greatest composers of Afro-Brazilian sambas (Jobim wrote the 1967 song "The Girl from Ipanema").

Ironically, in Brazil the film is perennially criticized for exoticizing the country as an all-night dance party, populated by hot-blooded Latin caricatures. Although it is difficult to argue with these criticisms, which highlight many contemporary debates about visibility politics, the film is best appreciated on its own terms. Self-consciously a fable, *Black Orpheus* is beautifully shot and wonderfully played by Marpessa Dawn and Breno Mello. Camus's depiction of the River Styx and the Ferryman Charon as a night watchman at a government building, standing in a hallway with fluttering bits of paper blowing past his feet, is unforgettable. **RH**

1959

THE ENTERTAINMENT EXPERIENCE OF A LIFETIME!

METRO-GOLDWYN-MAYER

A Tale of the Christ

WILLIAM WYLER

CHARLTON HESTON · JACK HAWKINS
HAYA HARAREET · STEPHEN BOYD
HUGH GRIFFITH · MARTHA SCOTT · CATHY O'DONNELL · SAM JAFFE

KARL TUNBERG · SAM ZIMBALIST

Ben-Hur William Wyler, 1959

Based on a nineteenth-century novel by Civil War general Lew Wallace, William Wyler's *Ben-Hur* is the third and most famous version of a legendary tale of Christian forgiveness amid violent Roman times. It was the second adaptation of the story to be produced by MGM, who had bought the rights to the book in order to make a silent movie version in 1925 (the makers of the first film, in 1907, were sued by Wallace's family after not seeking permission to use the story). It was also, in fact, the second version of *Ben-Hur* that Wyler worked on—he had been one of thirty Assistant Directors on the 1925 movie.

Legendary for its exciting, action-packed, and myth-ridden chariot race, which cost one million dollars alone to devise, *Ben-Hur* featured 350 speaking roles with over 50,000 extras. Nominated for twelve Oscars, it set a record by winning every nomination but one, a feat only equaled twice since—by James Cameron's *Titanic* in 1997 and Peter Jackson's *The Lord of the Rings: The Return of the King* in 2003. The production's overt excesses incited some intellectual dismissiveness, such as Mort Sahl's four-word review, "Loved him, hated Hur." This was perhaps a comment on the commercialism of "Ben-His" and "Ben-Hers" towels available at the time of the film's release—one of the earliest instances of movie merchandising.

Ostensibly a film about Jesus Christ, the story actively centers on the friendship between Messala (Stephen Boyd) and Judah Ben-Hur (Charlton Heston), a young man whose life becomes a quest for revenge after being framed for an attempt on the life of a Roman governor. Condemned to the life of a galley slave, his mother and sister abducted, Ben-Hur seeks the death of Messala, who is by then an officer in the Roman legions. They have their duel in the infamous and truly dangerous chariot race where Ben-Hur wreaks vengeance on his old friend. In the end there were over forty different versions of the script; one of its many screenwriters was Gore Vidal, who insisted on a homosexual element between Messala and Ben-Hur. This can be seen in Boyd's performance if one looks for it; apparently the actor was told that Messala's relationship with Ben-Hur was mainly motivated by man-to-man love.

If *Ben-Hur*'s movie message was love, its aim was money: MGM was in dire straits financially and the studio was hoping to replicate the commercial success of Paramount's 1956 Biblical epic, *The Ten Commandments*. Despite the film's gargantuan production problems (some of them simple oversights such as not agreeing what the hippodrome should look like or that a camera was too big for a ship) and a budget that had doubled from seven million dollars to fifteen million dollars by the time that shooting began, the film's enormous appeal guaranteed box-office success. This saved the studio from bankruptcy, making a matinee idol of Heston in the process. **KK**

U.S. (MGM) 212m Technicolor
Producer Sam Zimbalist **Screenplay** Karl Tunberg, from novel by Lew Wallace
Photography Robert Surtees **Music** Miklós Rózsa **Cast** Charlton Heston, Jack Hawkins, Haya Harareet, Stephen Boyd, Hugh Griffith, Martha Scott, Cathy O'Donnell, Sam Jaffe, Finlay Currie, Frank Thring, Terence Longdon, George Relph, André Morell **Oscars** Sam Zimbalist (best picture), William Wyler (director), Charlton Heston (actor), Hugh Griffith (actor in support role), William A. Horning, Edward C. Carfagno, Hugh Hunt (art direction), Robert Surtees (photography), Elizabeth Haffenden (costume), A. Arnold Gillespie, Robert MacDonald, Milo B. Lory (special effects), Ralph E. Winters, John D. Dunning (editing), Miklós Rózsa (music), Franklin Milton (sound) **Oscar nomination** Karl Tunberg (screenplay)

"Out of this sea of celluloid . . . William Wyler has fished a whale of a picture."

Time magazine, 1959

🛈

Paul Newman was offered Heston's role, but turned it down because he didn't want to wear a tunic.

Anatomy of a Murder Otto Preminger, 1959

Otto Preminger's 1959 film of the 1957 novel by Rober Traver (a pen name for Michigan Supreme Court Justice John D. Voelker) was controversial in its day—making frank onscreen use of then-unheard words like "panties," "rape," and "spermatogenesis"—and remains a trenchant, bitter, tough, witty dissection of the American legal system.

From its striking Saul Bass title design (featured also on the poster) and jazzy Duke Ellington score, *Anatomy of a Murder* takes a sophisticated approach unusual for a Hollywood film of its vintage. Most radically, it refuses to show the murder or any of the private scenes recounted in court, leaving it up to us to decide along with the jury whether the grumpy and unconcerned Lieutenant Frederick Manion (Ben Gazzara) was or was not subject to an "irresistible impulse" tantamount to insanity when he shot dead Barney Quill, the bearlike bar owner alleged to have raped Manion's teasing trailer-trash wife Laura (Lee Remick in unfeasably tight trousers). Manion snags as his defense counsel Paul "Polly" Biegler (James Stewart), a former district attorney keen to get back into court to clash with the political dullard who replaced him in office, and Biegler calls on the skills of his snide secretary (Eve Arden) and boozy-but-brilliant research partner (Arthur O'Connell). For the prosecution, the befuddled local DA hauls in Claude Dancer (George C. Scott), a prissy legal eagle from the local big city whose sharp-suited, sly elegance makes an interesting clash with Biegler's aw-shucks "jimmystewartian" conniving. On the bench is a real-life courtroom giant: playing the judge is Joseph Welch, the attorney whose quiet persistence ("Have you no shame?") literally put an end to the career of Senator Joseph McCarthy.

Simply the best trial movie ever made, *Anatomy of a Murder* is far less contrived than the brilliant but stagey *12 Angry Men* (1957), with a real understanding on the part of Stewart and Scott (both among the film's Oscar nominees) of the way lawyers have to be not only great actors but stars, assuming personalities that exaggerate their inner selves and weighing every outburst and objection for the effect it has on the poor saps in the jury box. **KN**

U.S. (Carlyle, Columbia) 160m BW
Producer Otto Preminger
Screenplay Wendell Mayes, from novel by John D. Voelker **Photography** Sam Leavitt
Music Duke Ellington **Cast** James Stewart, Lee Remick, Ben Gazzara, Arthur O'Connell, Eve Arden, Kathryn Grant, George C. Scott, Orson Bean, Russ Brown, Murray Hamilton, Brooks West, Ken Lynch, John Qualen, Howard McNear, Alexander Campbell
Oscar nominations Otto Preminger (best picture), Wendell Mayes (screenplay), James Stewart (actor), Arthur O'Connell (actor in support role), George C. Scott (actor in support role), Sam Leavitt (photography), Louis R. Loeffler (editing) **Venice Film Festival** James Stewart (Volpi cup—actor), Otto Preminger (Golden Lion nomination)

"This is spellbinding, infused by an ambiguity about human personality and motivation that is Preminger's trademark."

Jonathan Rosenbaum,
Chicago Reader, 2007

i

Score composer Duke Ellington has a brief role in the movie as "Pie-Eye," a pianist working at a local roadhouse.

Shadows John Cassavetes, 1959

U.S. (Lion) 81m BW **Producer** Seymour
Cassel, Maurice McEndree **Screenplay** John
Cassavetes **Photography** Erich Kollmar
Music Shifi Hadi **Cast** Ben Carruthers, Lelia
Goldoni, Hugh Hurd, Anthony Ray, Dennis
Sallas, Tom Allen, David Pokitillow, Rupert
Crosse, David Jones, Pir Marini, Victoria
Vargas, Jack Ackerman, Jacqueline Walcott,
Cliff Carnell, Jay Crecco

John Cassavetes's exquisite and poignant first feature, shot in 16mm and subsequently blown up to 35mm, centers on two brothers and a sister living together in Manhattan. The oldest, a third-rate nightclub singer (Hugh Hurd), is visibly black, whereas the other two (Ben Carruthers and Lelia Goldoni) are sufficiently light skinned to pass for white. This is the only Cassavetes film made without a script in the usual sense of that term; he and Robert Alan Aurthur wrote most of it based on a workshop improvisation that was carried out under Cassavetes's supervision.

Shadows is also the only one of Cassavetes's films that focuses mainly on young people, with the actors using their own first names to increase the feeling of intimacy. Rarely has so much warmth, delicacy, subtlety, and raw feeling emerged so naturally and beautifully from performances in an American film. This movie is contemporaneous with early masterpieces of the French New Wave such as *Breathless* and *The 400 Blows*, and deserves to be ranked alongside them for the freshness and freedom of its vision. In its portrait of a now-vanished Manhattan during the beat period, it also serves as a poignant time capsule. A wonderful jazz score by Charles Mingus featuring alto saxophonist Shafi Hadi plays as essential a role in the film's emotional pitch.

i

An earlier and shorter version of the film, reportedly less bound by narrative, is apparently lost.

It's conceivable that Cassavetes made greater films, but, along with his final masterpiece, the 1984 film *Love Streams*—another picture focusing on the warmth and empathy between siblings—*Shadows* is the one to cherish. **JRos**

Apur Sansar Satyajit Ray, 1959
The World of Apu

India (Satyajit Ray) 117m BW
Language Bengali Producer Satyajit Ray
Screenplay Satyajit Ray, from the novel
Aparajito by Bibhutibhushan
Bandyopadhyay Photography Subrata
Mitra Music Ravi Shankar Cast Soumitra
Chatterjee, Sharmila Tagore, Alok
Chakravarty, Swapan Mukherjee, Dhiresh
Majumdar, Sefalika Devi, Dhiren Ghosh,
Belarani, Shanti Bhattacherjee,
Abhijit Chatterjee

"With this beautiful picture ... an impressive capstone is put not only upon a touching human drama but also upon the development of a genuine artist's skill."

Bosley Crowther,
The New York Times, 1960

🛈

Ray chose Chatterjee to play Apu after seeing him audition for the role when he was casting *Aparajito* (1956).

The World of Apu completes the "Apu" trilogy that made Satyajit Ray's name and introduced Indian cinema to the world. With both his parents now dead, the adult Apu (Soumitra Chatterjee) is living in shabby lodgings in Calcutta, trying to make his name as a writer. His friend Pulu (Swapan Mukherjee) invites him to his sister's wedding in a small Bengali village. But the festivities are blighted; the intended bridegroom proves to be mentally deficient. If the bride doesn't marry at the appointed hour, she will be utterly disgraced. Apu, protesting and bewildered, is pressed into service and takes his teenage bride back to his urban hovel. Against all the odds the marriage is a joyful success. After a year of happiness, Aparna (Sharmila Tagore) returns home to have her child. A message comes: She has died in childbirth. Shattered, Apu refuses even to see his son. Five years later Pulu finds him working in a remote coal mine and persuades him to come and take charge of the child, who has grown up wild and intractable. At first the boy savagely rejects this stranger posing as his father, but gradually a wary trust grows between them until Apu, his son riding on his shoulders, can start back for the city and the world.

This conclusion—Apu has symbolically returned to his native village and confronted his own childhood self—gives the whole trilogy the satisfying cyclical form of a myth. Each of the Apu films is structured around two deaths, although in *The World of Apu* the second death is that of Apu himself. He dies spiritually after losing Aparna, and only a chance event saves him from suicide; not until he reclaims his son is he reborn. The chosen instrument of his attempted suicide is a train; here, as throughout the trilogy, trains stand for the irresistible, impersonal forces that bring change, separation, and death.

At the heart of *The World of Apu* lies the brief marriage of Apu and Aparna. It is brief too in terms of screen time, running barely half an hour, yet it carries a powerful emotional and erotic impact. Not that Ray features any overt sexual contact; even had he wanted to, Indian moral conventions would have forbidden it. But he conveys a wealth of erotic revelation in moments like the one where Apu, waking in his formerly solitary bed and listening to Aparna cheerfully preparing breakfast, wonderingly discovers a hairpin on the pillow beside him. Ray draws from Chatterjee and Tagore, making their screen debuts, acting of astonishing depth and conviction; no wonder that both went on to become major stars of Indian cinema, as well as regular players in Ray's films. Tagore, enchantingly pretty as Aparna, was only fourteen at the time. Thanks to their performances, and the encompassing warmth and subtlety of Ray's direction, this rates as one of the most touching and intimate depictions of married love in all cinema. *The World of Apu* not only rounds off Ray's masterly trilogy, but encompasses a heartrending tale of love and loss. **PK**

Rio Bravo Howard Hawks, 1959

Fred Zinnemann's *High Noon* (1952) famously depicted one man's courageous stand against adversity in the name of the law. Howard Hawks's *Rio Bravo*, a response of sorts to *High Noon*, concerns another brave stand, also in the name of the law, but this time small-town sheriff John T. Chance (John Wayne) isn't alone. He's aided by the local drunk (Dean Martin), a gun-slinging young singing cowboy (Ricky Nelson), and a crippled old deputy nicknamed Stumpy (Walter Brennan). Together they must fend off a band of desperados who have laid siege to the town, intent on springing the villain's brother from jail.

Hawks was always one of Hollywood's most reliable and versatile directors, but after *Gentlemen Prefer Blondes* (1953) he left America for a disappointing stint in Europe. *Rio Bravo* marked a rousing return to America and to form, with Hawks offering a genre-smashing collision of everything he knows best. There's a musical number—with Martin and Nelson in the film, how could there not be?— moments of comedy, a touch of romance, thanks to stranded traveler Angie Dickenson, and plenty of action, all unified by yet another casually iconic Wayne performance as the pragmatic hero bound by a sense of duty.

The siege-scenario Hawks sets up—a motley crew of mismatched characters hole up in one place for one last stand—has become a genre-film standby, borrowed repeatedly by such Hawks worshippers as John Carpenter and George Romero. Both recognized how the limited setting of *Rio Bravo* could be applied to their own low-budget films. The Hawks touch is that the siege itself isn't as important as the interaction of the characters under siege. By sticking them all together in one place, Hawks has fun letting them play off of one another, revealing colorful little character traits as they fight back against insurmountable odds. Coming not long after John Ford's eulogy to the Western with his haunting *The Searchers* (1956), *Rio Bravo* also stands as one of the last of its kind, an old-fashioned and fun romp of a Western where the line between good guys and bad guys couldn't be more clear. **JKl**

U.S. (Armada) 141m Technicolor
Producer Howard Hawks **Screenplay** Leigh Brackett, Jules Furthman, from story by B.H. McCampbell **Photography** Russell Harlan **Music** Dimitri Tiomkin **Cast** John Wayne, Dean Martin, Ricky Nelson, Angie Dickinson, Walter Brennan, Ward Bond, John Russell, Pedro Gonzales-Gonzales, Estelita Rodriguez, Claude Akins, Malcolm Atterbury

"If I ever saw a man holdin' the bull by the tail, you're it."

**Pat Wheeler
(Ward Bond)**

ℹ️

The sets in Old Tucson are built to seven-eighths scale, so the performers look larger than life.

Ukigusa Yasujiro Ozu, 1959
Floating Weeds

Japan (Daiei) 119m Eastmancolor
Language Japanese Producer Masaichi
Nagata Screenplay Kôgo Noda, Yasujiro
Ozu Photography Kazuo Miyagawa
Music Kojun Saitô Cast Ganjiro Nakamura,
Machiko Kyô, Ayako Wakao, Hiroshi
Kawaguchi, Haruko Sugimura, Hikaru Hoshi,
Yosuke Irie, Hideo Mitsui, Hitomi Nozoe,
Chishu Ryu, Masahiko Shimazu, Haruo
Tanaka, Kumeko Urabe, Mantarô Ushio

Yasujiro Ozu's second color film, exquisitely shot by Kenji Mizoguchi's favored cinematographer, Kazuo Miyagawa, is a beautifully composed and staged late work, demonstrating the director's growing mastery of an expanded tonal palette. One of a series of explicit remakes Ozu undertook around this time, it concentrates on the activities of an itinerant acting troupe ("floating weeds") while maintaining the director's characteristic fascination with familial and generational interaction. In contrast to Ozu's 1934 film *A Story of Floating Weeds*, which was more comic and dramatic, this one has a decidedly autumnal, nostalgic, and philosophical air, a quality illustrated by many of its serenely staged compositions and "distilled" combinations of image and sound.

Although Ozu's films generally contain a surprisingly large number of shots and routinely experiment with the construction of cinematic space, the predominant impression one takes from *Floating Weeds* is of a series of interlocking still lifes, and a rhythm matched to the lulling repetition of everyday life. The film's opening shot—comparing and contrasting the volume, shape, and color of a bottle and a lighthouse—suggests no further movement, the chugging beat of a boat's motor on the soundtrack reinforcing the "completeness" or "fullness" of the image on display. In these moments the film achieves a kind of stillness, a resigned, gestalt serenity that accompanies even Ozu's most tragic work, such as 1953's *Tokyo Story*. **AD**

i

Out of Ozu's fifty-three films, *Floating Weeds* was one of only three that weren't made for the Shochiku studio.

Les yeux sans visage Georges Franju, 1960
Eyes Without a Face

Much has been written about Georges Franju's *Eyes Without a Face*—the only foray into the horror genre by the cofounder of the Paris Cinémathèque. While the film is justifiably celebrated as a masterpiece, connections are frequently made between its pulp fiction plot and the poetry of its cinematography—Jean Cocteau filming Edgar Allan Poe. The brilliant Doctor Génessier (Pierre Brasseur), experimenting with overcoming transplanted organ rejection, is dedicated to finding a young woman with a face to replace that of his daughter Christiane (Edith Scob), which was disfigured in a car accident he was responsible for.

Franju brings a sensitivity and complexity to the stock characters of the mad scientist and his assistant (here played by Alida Valli), not to mention his "monster"; he magnificently situates audience identification with the faceless Christiane early in the film. The first shot, of two headlights cutting through the dark French countryside, seen from inside the car, creates a masklike image echoing Christiane's expressionless mask. Our first encounter with the film is from within that mask, and when we finally see Christiane's face it is neither the plastic visage of her own mask nor (when it comes off) the out-of-focus exposed muscle which grabs our attention, but her eyes—which we've already seen through in that echoing first shot. This is what gives the film its meaning: we are the "monster" for whom Doctor Génessier commits his crimes.

Eyes Without a Face can be seen as Grand Guignol theater on the big screen: the film operates to give us an ever-increasing series of grotesque spectacles, beginning with Christiane's mask, a face being lifted from one young victim (among other medical horrors), the glimpses of Christiane's missing face, and finally to Doctor Génessier being torn apart by his own dogs. Franju here gives us a conflation of high and low cultural tastes, wherein we are shown beauty and poetry from inside the horror due to the director's refusal to exploit or turn away from the graphic images. If indeed we are the monster, the film seems to say, we would not necessarily see the events portrayed as horrific. **MK**

France / Italy (Champs-Élysées, Lux) 88m BW **Language** French **Producer** Jules Borkon **Screenplay** Pierre Boileau, Claude Sautet, Pierre Gascar, Thomas Narcejac, from novel by Jean Redon **Photography** Eugen Schüfftan **Music** Maurice Jarre **Cast** Pierre Brasseur, Edith Scob, Alida Valli, François Guérin, Alexandre Rignault, Béatrice Altariba, Juliette Mayniel, Charles Blavette, Claude Brasseur, Michel Etcheverry, Yvette Etiévant, René Génin, Lucien Hubert, Marcel Pérès

"[Franju] would say that the most beautiful horror film he had ever seen was a documentary about a trepanation, where you could see the brain of the patient and the patient smiling, as he did not feel anything. For Franju, this was the ultimate in fantasy."

Edith Scob, 2004

ℹ️

John Carpenter once said that Michael Myers's mask in *Halloween* (1978) was influenced by the one in this film.

Saturday Night and Sunday Morning
Karel Reisz, 1960

In the late 1950s and early 1960s, British cinema turned to social realism, usually dealing with stirrings of rebelliousness or aspirations of betterment among clever, articulate, embittered working-class youngsters. Almost all of these films were taken from works by "angry young man" playwrights and novelists like John Osborne (*Look Back in Anger* [1958]), John Braine (*Room at the Top* [1959]), and Stan Barstow (*A Kind of Loving* [1962]). Alan Sillitoe's book *Saturday Night and Sunday Morning* became the best of these films, though the direction of Karel Reisz isn't free from a sort of sentimental inclination to the picturesque that often came about when Cambridge-educated filmmakers trekked to the North to make slag-heaps look like alien landscapes and to spy on the strange behavior of pub-going factory workers in Nottingham.

The strength of the film is in Sillitoe's voice ("What I'm out for is a good time—all the rest is propaganda") and the delivery of his dialogue by Albert Finney, making a terrific first impression as Arthur Seaton, the grumbling, virile hedonist who bristles with indignation in the workplace and cuts loose in his off hours. The title implies the process of taming that has traditionally ground down Arthur's class, with the high-living of drunkenness and sexual excess on Saturday night paid for on Sunday morning with being coffined into a respectable marriage and a new home.

The film shows how Arthur's father (Frank Pettitt) has been reduced to staring at the television and how most of his slightly older friends (notably the one he cuckolds) are on their way to being trapped. Arthur comes out of a relationship with a married woman (Rachel Roberts) by being lured into an engagement with a pretty but conventional girl (Shirley Anne Field), but he is still resolving to keep throwing stones and breaking windows. Though, like many films in this cycle, *Saturday Night and Sunday Morning* tends to indulge in a proletarian machismo that verges on misogyny (for Arthur, all women are traps), Roberts—in a role similar to that taken by Simone Signoret in *Room at the Top*—expresses a real pain that provides an alternative reading of Arthur's rebellion. **KN**

1960

G.B. (Bryanston, Woodfall) 89m BW
Producer Tony Richardson, Harry Saltzman
Screenplay Alan Sillitoe, from his novel
Photography Freddie Francis **Music** John Dankworth **Cast** Albert Finney, Shirley Anne Field, Rachel Roberts, Hylda Baker, Norman Rossington, Bryan Pringle, Robert Cawdron, Edna Morris, Elsie Wagstaff, Frank Pettitt, Avis Bunnage, Colin Blakely, Irene Richmond, Louise Dunn, Anne Blake

> "I take a tip from the fishes, never bite unless the bait's good. I won't get married till I'm good and ready."
>
> **Arthur Seaton
> (Albert Finney)**

ℹ️

The shopfloor scenes were shot in a former munitions factory where Alan Sillitoe had himself worked.

La dolce vita Federico Fellini, 1960

An epic about triviality, Federico Fellini's portrait of a place and time captures perfectly the style and attitudes of Rome's fashionable party folk during the summer of 1959, all the while condemning them for being such gorgeous parasites. The enduring strength of *La dolce vita* comes from the tension between viciously attacking a world whose excesses are beyond satire and the fascination it can't help but feel for the mad parade of modern decadents.

Like *A Clockwork Orange* (1971), *Apocalypse Now* (1979), and *Wall Street* (1987), this is a film that paradoxically set as many fashion styles as it set out to demolish, encouraging people to sit about cafés on the Via Veneto in an unironic attempt to emulate the sweet life. The expression "paparazzi" comes from the film character of Paparazzo, who epitomizes the swarm of insectlike photojournalists found around every passing celebrity, snapping away and jostling for the best place and the most exploitable shot. The same camera horde who press around Marilyn Monroe-like American superstar Sylvia (Anita Ekberg) later, more disturbingly, snap away at an innocent housewife returning home. She is briefly flattered that they might think she is "some actress," only to learn that they are interested in her because her philospher husband Steiner (Alain Cuny) has shot their two children and himself.

Marcello Mastroianni, defining a generation of cool in his beetle-black sunglasses, is the character whose fall from at least potential grace we follow. Once he was a serious writer, but now he's a sleazy journalist who dances attendance on the pointlessly famous, gets no thrill at all from his various escapades and is always being humiliated as a hanger-on. *La dolce vita* is well remembered for the glorious image of Ekberg in the Trevi Fountain, but the scene is about the embarrassment, discomfort, and ultimate pain of Mastroianni's Marcello Rubini. He had scorned the star as "like a big doll" but becomes hopelessly smitten with her, joining her in the fountain against his better judgment to coo a wonderful Italian come-on speech ("You are the first woman on the first day of creation"). She doesn't understand, and his night ends getting sucker-punched by Sylvia's drunken actor lover (Lex Barker). Marcello's slide, which ends after the philosopher's shocking murder-suicide as he abandons all pretense at writing to become (shudder) a press agent, is prompted by ridiculous media farces, including a bogus miracle in the rain incited by cannily corrupt children, a ghost hunt at a haunted mansion (where Nico wears a medieval helmet), an attempted orgy that fizzles in unsettling references to Tod Browning's *Freaks* (1932) as a pinhead-like dancer wheels about while Marcello cruelly abuses and feathers a drunken girl singled out at random, and the dragging of a shark-ray monster from the seas. "By 1965, there'll be total depravity," muses a bystander, and the innocent smiling girl who represents a possible hope for Marcello can't make herself heard over the useless noise, leaving him sadly to join the doomed throng. **KN**

Italy / France (Pathé, Riama)
167m BW **Language** Italian / English
Producer Giuseppe Amato, Franco Magli,
Angelo Rizzoli **Screenplay** Federico Fellini,
Ennio Flaiano, Tullio Pinelli, Brunello Rondi
Music Nino Rota **Photography** Otello
Martelli **Cast** Marcello Mastroianni, Anita
Ekberg, Anouk Aimée, Yvonne Furneaux,
Magali Noël, Alain Cuny, Annibale Ninchi,
Walter Santesso, Valeria Ciangottini, Riccardo
Garrone, Ida Galli, Audrey McDonald, Polidor,
Alain Dijon, Enzo Cerusico **Oscar** Piero
Gherardi (costume) **Oscar nominations**
Federico Fellini (director), Federico Fellini,
Tullio Pinelli, Ennio Flaiano, Brunello Rondi
(screenplay), Piero Gherardi (art direction)
Cannes Film Festival Federico Fellini
(Golden Palm)

"Even the most miserable life is better than a sheltered existence in an organized society where everything is calculated and perfected."

Steiner (Alain Cuny)

The film was exceptionally controversial for its time and remained banned in Spain until 1981.

Le trou Jacques Becker, 1960
The Hole

The last film by the great and too-little-known director Jacques Becker, *The Hole* is based on a novel by José Giovanni, which recounts the true story of an attempted prison escape in which the author took part in 1947. Becker wrote the script with Giovanni and cast the film with nonprofessional actors, one of whom, Jean Keraudy, played the same role in real life that he plays in the film.

Becker's use of nonprofessionals is one of the elements that heighten this extraordinary film's sense of absolute authenticity. Also crucial to our experience of *The Hole* is his control of film time. The scene in which the five cell mates smash through the stone floor of their cell is done in an unbroken take of almost four minutes, making us aware that we're watching people expend the exact amount of effort required to produce the effects on the stone that we see. By making us share a collective duration with the heroes, Becker involves us more intensely in their struggle.

Our involvement is heightened by our also sharing, uneasily and never completely, the point of view of Gaspard (Marc Michel), a prisoner transferred from another cell. His arrival forces the others to decide whether to give up their plan or take him into their confidence. Although they choose the latter course, Gaspard is never fully integrated into the group. The tension his presence creates provides *The Hole's* main psychological interest and, in the film's stunning conclusion, allows it to achieve a tragic dimension.

Becker uses Gaspard's isolation as a device to help us perceive and value the others' comradeship. The bonds between the original members of the team are proved and celebrated in appreciative looks and smiles at each step of the journey. In a rare moment when Gaspard seems at one with the group, he shares his rice cake with them. Long after most directors would fade out, Becker holds the camera on the wordless scene: an example of his career-long insistence on showing his characters existing outside the framework created by the direct concerns of the plot.

The Hole has been compared with Robert Bresson's *A Man Escaped* (1956) and Jean Renoir's *The Grand Illusion* (1937), but Becker is less concerned than Bresson with transcendence or Renoir's critique of social differences. The prisoners' virtues—meticulousness, inventiveness, and the ability to form a collective—become the highest values of *The Hole*. Perhaps Becker is, of all directors, including even Howard Hawks, the one who has embodied and articulated these values most firmly.

Becker was in ill health throughout the production and editing of the film, and died leaving the sound mixing unfinished. *The Hole* was completed according to the director's wishes, but after its initial release in a 140-minute version, producer Serge Silberman had it reduced by about twenty-four minutes to enhance its commercial possibilities. The missing footage remains lost, but as it stands, *The Hole* is still a masterpiece. **CFu**

France / Italy (Filmsonor, Play Art, Titanus) 109m BW **Language** French **Producer** Serge Silberman **Screenplay** Jean Aurel, Jacques Becker, José Giovanni, from novel by José Giovanni **Photography** Ghislain Cloquet **Music** Philippe Arthuys **Cast** Michel Constantin, Jean Keraudy, Philippe Leroy, Raymond Meunier, Marc Michel, André Bervil, Jean-Paul Coquelin, Eddy Rasimi, Gérard Hernandez, Paul Pavel, Catherine Spaak, Dominique Zardi

"In Le Trou *there is nothing but the exact look, the alive movement, authentic faces against neutral walls, an utterly natural manner of speaking."*

François Truffaut, 1961

i

To capture the details of the story precisely, Becker used three of the original escapees as consultants.

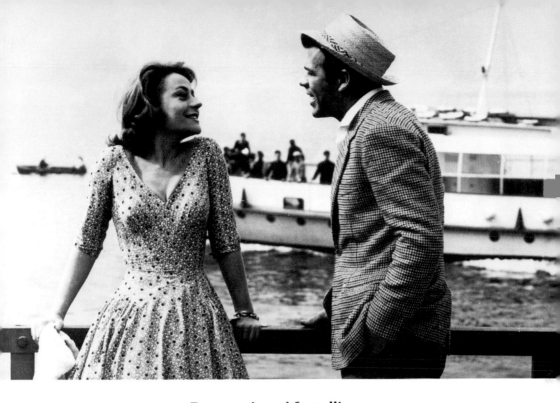

Rocco e i suoi fratelli Luchino Visconti, 1960
Rocco and His Brothers

France / Italy (Marceau-Cocinor, Titanus) 175m BW **Language** Italian **Producer** Goffredo Lombardo **Screenplay** Luchino Visconti, Suso Cecchi d'Amico, Vasco Pratolini, Pasquale Festa Campanile, Massimo Franciosa, Enrico Medioli, from the novel *Il Ponte della Ghisolfa* by Giovanni Testori **Photography** Giuseppe Rotunno **Music** Nino Rota **Cast** Alain Delon, Renato Salvatori, Annie Girardot, Katina Paxinou, Alessandra Panaro, Spiros Focás, Max Cartier, Corrado Pani, Rocco Vidolazzi, Claudia Mori, Adriana Asti, Enzo Fiermonte, Nino Castelnuovo, Rosario Borelli, Renato Terra **Venice Film Festival** Luchino Visconti (FIPRESCI award, special prize, Golden Lion nomination)

i

Francis Ford Coppola liked the film so much that he hired its composer, Nino Rota, for *The Godfather* (1972).

A key transitional film in Luchino Visconti's shift away from his initial adherence to the principles of Neorealism (admittedly already diluted by an interest in tragedy verging on the melodramatic) toward the decoratively operatic excesses of much of his later work, *Rocco and His Brothers* also remains one of his best. Giuseppe Rotunno's black-and-white camera work is tantalizingly pitched between grim, documentary-style Neorealism and the stylization of film noir, with Nino Rota's score eloquently reflecting the emotional dynamics of the story about a family newly arrived in Milan from Sicily and falling apart as the influences of money, rootlessness, and sex work their destructive magic.

It is difficult, perhaps, to be convinced by the astonishingly beautiful Alain Delon as a boxer of such saintliness that he sacrifices his happiness in the forlorn hope of keeping the family united, and Katina Paxinou's clichéd histrionics as the long-suffering matriarch are a little hard to take; however, Renato Salvatori is convincing as the brutish and irresponsible elder brother ruined by greed and obsessive jealousy, and Annie Girardot is both sexy and remarkably persuasive as the emotionally complex girl who comes between Salvatori and Delon. The final moments of her martyrlike death may be over the top, but they are nevertheless effectively cathartic. **GA**

L'avventura
Michelangelo Antonioni, 1960
The Adventure

At its premiere at the Cannes Film Festival in 1960, *L'avventura* was jeered at and booed by a predominantly hostile audience, though a large number of influential critics and filmmakers took the unprecedented step of signing a statement rejecting this reaction and hailing it as the most important film ever shown at the festival. Within two years, *L'avventura* was reckoned by the international critics' poll conducted by Britain's *Sight & Sound* magazine as the second greatest movie ever made. Although writer-director Michelangelo Antonioni had been making documentaries and features for nearly twenty years, this epic-length film was his major artistic and commercial breakthrough. Not least because it was his first proper collaboration with Monica Vitti, the actress who is the human and humane channel through which a listless, jaded, dehumanized society is viewed and who would become the focus of his subsequent films *La notte* (1961), *L'eclisse* (1962), and *Il deserto rosso* (1964).

L'avventura's premise is simple yet deeply unsettling: A small party of monied Roman characters take a cruise from Sicily and stop off at a desolate, rocky island to pass an idle afternoon that stretches into an ordeal when Anna (Lea Massari) disappears. The slightly vain, uncommitted girl has indicated to her more sensible friend Claudia (Vitti) that she knows something is not right between her and her architectural consultant lover Sandro (Gabriele Ferzetti) and has attracted attention by pretending to sight a shark while swimming. Watching the film a second time, knowing that this major character will disappear after twenty-six minutes, we might notice that there really was a shark and that a small, never-mentioned boat can be glimpsed passing the island a short fade after our last look at Anna.

A major cause of initial audience befuddlement with *L'avventura* is that Antonioni never reveals what has happened to Anna. Claudia and Sandro are drawn together as they search, but none of the other characters seem that interested in the girl's fate. The plot, presumably by coincidence, rather parallels Hitchcock's *Psycho* (1960), with the jarring absence of the character we assumed to be the heroine in the second part of the film and an uneasy relationship growing between the missing woman's lover and a woman with an equal interest in her welfare. The subject matter also parallels the same year's *La dolce vita*. Anita Ekberg's starlet has an equivalent in *L'avventura*'s flighty star-writer-whore (Dorothy De Poliolo), who is mobbed by "fans" early on when she (deliberately?) rips her tight skirt in public and pops up not so much to wreck the central couple's new relationship as to reveal it as a sham—but there is none of the ambiguous glamor of Fellini's film here. Like Marcello Mastroianni's writer who slides into the role of PR man, Ferzetti's architect-turned-rich-man's-flunky epitomizes failed promise, and Antonioni can only find a trace of hope in an eternal feminine ideal who ultimately stands apart from the corruption of new money or too-casual sex. **KN**

Italy / France (Cino Del Duca, Cinematografiche Europee, R. & R. Hakim, Lyre) 145m BW **Language** Italian **Producer** Amato Pennasilico **Screenplay** Michelangelo Antonioni, Elio Bartolini, Tonino Guerra **Photography** Aldo Scavarda **Music** Giovanni Fusco **Cast** Gabriele Ferzetti, Monica Vitti, Lea Massari, Dominique Blanchar, Renzo Ricci, James Addams, Dorothy De Poliolo, Lelio Luttazzi, Giovanni Petrucci, Esmeralda Ruspoli, Jack O'Connell, Angela Tommasi Di Lampedusa, Franco Cimino, Prof. Cucco, Giovanni Danesi **Cannes Film Festival** Michelangelo Antonioni (jury prize, tied with *Kagi*)

> "I'd like to work on design again. I used to have ideas of my own, you know."
>
> **Sandro (Gariele Ferzetti)**

i

During filming, Lea Massari suffered a heart attack that sent her into a coma for two days.

1960

À bout de souffle Jean-Luc Godard, 1960
Breathless

Michel, a petty thief who models himself on the Humphrey Bogart of Warners' 1930s gangster series, steals a car in Marseilles, but on his journey north is stopped by a policeman whom, in a moment's panic, he fatally shoots with the gun he finds in the car's glove compartment. He arrives in Paris and seeks help from his American girlfriend, a student and aspiring journalist. Ambivalent about his presence, she agrees to help. However, after discovering his crime and disappointed at his response to the news that he is the father to her unborn child, she betrays him to the authorities, then tells him what she has done. He attempts to flee, but is cornered by police. In one final mock-heroic salute to his movie idol, Michel is killed, gangster style, with gun in hand.

What remains of *Breathless* today, what speaks to a contemporary, young audience—when jump cuts figure in every other TV commercial, when its stars are long dead (Jean Seberg) or in their twilight career phase (Jean-Paul Belmondo), when "comedies of manners" pitting Americans against Europeans are commonplace, and when the mixture of a loose gangster crime plot, a smart attitude, and a hip array of high and low culture citations are more likely to be attributed to Quentin Tarantino than his genuine predecessor, Jean-Luc Godard?

Surprisingly, from an artistic iconoclast whose evolution was so rapid and ambitious, *Breathless* is a modest debut by Godard. There is the semblance of a thriller plot, complete with betrayal, tailing cops, and a final shootout. There is a lovely but conventional film noir jazz score by Martial Solal. There is an insolent, mildly outrageous rap pouring from Belmondo's punk motormouth, but even that scarcely contradicts the Chandler–Hammet–Spillane tradition of hard-boiled talk.

But the subtle, formal pleasures of *Breathless* have yet to be fully appreciated. Whether through accident or design, Godard's low-budget, on-the-fly shooting style produced remarkable innovations. Eschewing direct sound recording and using total postsynchronization not only led to an Orson Welles-style speed and inventiveness in the dialogue delivery, it also paved the way for a radical sound mix in which one can no longer spot the difference between "real" sound happening within the story and sound imposed by the filmmaker. Likewise, filming indoors in close quarters led to a new form of cinematic contemplation: the "visual study," in which a sequence of just slightly different views offers a cubist mosaic of the many moods and aspects of these extraordinary star presences.

But it is as a modern love story that *Breathless* retains its immense appeal for members of Generation X and beyond. The children of existentialist reflection, postwar affluence, Beat culture cool, and pop culture flip, these antiheroes treat love as a game, and their own identities as makeshift masks. They are stranded between traditional values that they reject, and a future way of loving that has not yet materialized. Sound familiar? **AM**

France (Impéria, Georges de Beauregard, SNC) 87m BW **Language** French **Producer** Georges de Beauregard **Screenplay** Jean-Luc Godard, François Truffaut **Photography** Raoul Coutard **Music** Martial Solal **Cast** Jean-Paul Belmondo, Jean Seberg, Daniel Boulanger, Jean-Pierre Melville, Henri-Jacques Huet, Van Doude, Claude Mansard, Jean-Luc Godard, Richard Balducci, Roger Hanin, Jean-Louis Richard, Liliane David, Jean Domarchi, Jean Douchet, Raymond Huntley, André S. Labarthe, François Moreuil, Liliane Robin **Berlin International Film Festival** Jean-Luc Godard (Silver Bear, Golden Bear nomination)

"Don't use the brakes. Cars are made to go, not to stop!"

Michel Poiccard (Jean-Paul Belmondo)

i

Neither the cast nor the production crew are credited in the movie.

Spartacus Stanley Kubrick, 1960

U.S. (Bryna) 196m Technicolor **Producer** Kirk Douglas, Edward Lewis **Screenplay** Dalton Trumbo, from novel by Howard Fast **Photography** Russell Metty, Clifford Stine **Music** Alex North **Cast** Kirk Douglas, Laurence Olivier, Jean Simmons, Charles Laughton, Peter Ustinov, John Gavin, Nina Foch, John Ireland, Herbert Lom, John Dall, Charles McGraw, Joanna Barnes, Harold Stone, Woody Strode, Peter Brocco **Oscars** Peter Ustinov (actor in support role), Alexander Golitzen, Eric Orbom, Russell A. Gausman, Julia Heron (art direction), Russell Metty (photography), Valles, Bill Thomas (costume) **Oscar nomination** Robert Lawrence (editing), Alex North (music)

🅸

During the shoot, Laurence Olivier gave Tony Curtis acting tips. In return, Curtis offered advice on bodybuilding.

This epic's first director, Anthony Mann, was fired by star Kirk Douglas not long after shooting began, although some early scenes he shot in the desert remain in the final film. It fell to a pre-*2001: A Space Odyssey* (1968) Stanley Kubrick to bring Howard Fast's tale of a slave revolt in ancient Rome to life, and he rose to the task brilliantly, mixing scenes of the power struggle in the senate with ones of brotherhood between the slaves.

Spartacus (Douglas) is the slave at the center of the action, who inspires many like him to rise up against their oppressors, including young Antoninus (Tony Curtis), a favorite of Roman Marcus Crassus (Laurence Olivier) who is none too pleased when his pretty boy goes AWOL. When the film was restored three decades after it was made, a bath scene explaining more of the relationship between the master and slave, cut in 1960 because of its homosexual references, was edited in, with Anthony Hopkins rerecording the late Olivier's lost dialogue.

Kubrick stages the slave revolt and battle sequences brilliantly, but the biggest surprise from the director not known for his emotional scenes is the way he films the final, heart-wrenching moments as Spartacus's love Varinia (Jean Simmons) holds up their child for him to see as he dies, crucified alongside the men who followed him. Superb. **JB**

U.S. (Mirisch) 125m BW **Producer** I.A.L. Diamond, Doane Harrison, Billy Wilder **Screenplay** Billy Wilder and I.A.L. Diamond **Photography** Joseph LaShelle **Music** Adolph Deutsch **Cast** Jack Lemmon, Shirley MacLaine, Fred MacMurray, Ray Walston, Jack Kruschen, David Lewis, Hope Holiday, Joan Shawlee, Naomi Stevens, Johnny Seven, Joyce Jameson, Willard Waterman, David White, Edie Adams **Oscars** Billy Wilder (best picture), Billy Wilder (director), Billy Wilder, I.A.L. Diamond (screenplay), Alexandre Trauner, Edward G. Boyle (art direction), Daniel Mandell (editing) **Oscar nominations** Jack Lemmon (actor), Shirley MacLaine (actress), Jack Kruschen (actor in support role), Joseph LaShelle (photography), Gordon Sawyer (sound) **Venice Film Festival** Shirley MacLaine (Volpi cup—actress), Billy Wilder (Golden Lion nomination)

"I was jinxed from the word go. The first time I was ever kissed was in a cemetery."

Fran Kubelik
(Shirley MacLaine)

ℹ

This was the last purely black-and-white movie to win a Best Picture Oscar until *The Artist* (2011).

The Apartment Billy Wilder, 1960

Billy Wilder used to scratch American society where it itches. Inspired by David Lean's *Brief Encounter* (1945), he had to wait ten years for the necessary slackening of censorship before being able to tell the story of the "third" man, the one who lends his apartment to the adulterous couple. Surprisingly, despite its subject matter, *The Apartment* won no fewer than five Academy Awards (including Best Picture and Director), and is now considered by many to be Wilder's last truly "realist" film.

Some have criticized the amorality of Jack Lemmon's character C.C. Baxter, who gets promoted quickly only because he helps some of the executives at the big insurance company where he works in their efforts to cheat on their wives. But Lemmon—who used to play Wilder's Everyman characters—brings to the role here a solid touch of humanity, and Baxter finally appears as nothing more than a slavish clerk unwillingly trapped in a situation that already exists at the beginning of the film and is beyond his control. Despite its humor, *The Apartment* is indeed a severe social critique, as well as an examination of contemporary American life and sexual mores. It is also a strong attack on the basic corruption of the capitalist system, in which anyone with a little influence is capable of feeding off someone else.

The Apartment skillfully blends various genres, but, by and large, it begins as a satiric comedy, transforms into a powerful drama, and finishes as a romantic comedy. Meticulously constructed, the disillusioned screenplay by Wilder and I.A.L. Diamond can in some ways be considered a kind of bitter follow-up to *The Seven Year Itch* (1955)—one that was beautifully shot in a rather gloomy black-and-white CinemaScope. After their summer vacations, when men had affairs in their wives' absence, they quickly quit their mistresses. Fran Kubelik (Shirley MacLaine) is one of these unfortunate girls, and she believes that love affairs are not just another species of consumer good. In the end, the bureaucrat is finally redeemed by love for this other lonely heart, although the film manages to avoid any syrupy feeling. Although Wilder apparently didn't think that MacLaine and Lemmon formed a great couple, viewers can legitimately hold the opposite opinion. **FL**

Hanyeo Kim Ki-young, 1960
The Housemaid

South Korea (Kuk Dong, Seki) 90m BW **Language** Korean **Producer** Kim Ki-young **Screenplay** Kim Ki-young **Photography** Kim Deok-jin **Music** Han Sang-gi **Cast** Lee Eun-shim, Ju Jeung-nyeo, Kim Jin Kyu

From the point of view of a Westerner, the discovery of a film like *The Housemaid*, more than forty years after it was made, is a marvelous feeling—marvelous not just because one finds in writer-director Kim Ki-young a truly extraordinary image maker, but in his film such an utterly unpredictable work. Who knew that Luis Buñuel had a Korean brother! Kim Ki-young is a filmmaker capable of probing deep into the human mind, its desires and impulses, while paying sarcastic attention to the details, the bad taste of contemporary colors as secret codes of one's state of being.

What makes *The Housemaid* so shocking is the intensity of the passion that the music composer and his maid experience; the fully self-conscious mechanics of the love triangle existing between the husband, his wife, and his mistress; and the way this triangle can, at any moment, be disturbed, even exploded, by the unusual length of one of the director's shots, by his pop-art use of everyday objects, or by the invading presence of the human (feminine) body. But the shocking nature of the film is both disturbing and pleasurable, as the use of seemingly trivial musical notes and the surprising mixture of sentimentality and cruelty opens the door to new sensations for the viewer, all the more amazing coming from such an unexpected source. **J-MF**

Meghe Dhaka Tara Ritwik Ghatak, 1960
The Cloud-Capped Star

India (Chitrakalpa) 134m BW **Language** Bengali **Producer** Ritwik Ghatak **Screenplay** Ritwik Ghatak, from novel by Shaktipada Rajguru **Photography** Dinen Gupta **Music** Jyotirindra Moitra, Rabindranath Tagore **Cast** Supriya Choudhury, Anil Chatterjee, Niranjan Ray, Gita Ghatak, Bijon Bhattacharya, Gita De, Dwiju Bhawal, Gyanesh Mukherjee, Ranen Ray Choudhury

"Those who suffer for others suffer forever," remarks a character in this, Ritwik Ghatak's most famous film, a melodrama that comes close to tragedy. Its heroine's tragic flaw is the sin of omission: She fails to protest at injustice, injustice to herself and her dreams, and at the hands of those she loves most dearly. Nita (Supriya Choudhury) works night and day to keep her refugee Bengali family solvent. Her father is a teacher but earns a pittance. Her elder brother wants to be a singer, and claims the artist's right to time the rest of them can ill afford. Meanwhile her mother hopes the science student who is Nita's intended may transfer his affections to her sister.

The Cloud-Capped Star is a searing piece of work, resonant and beautifully composed—and it proved a rare commercial success for its director in India. For all its implicit criticism of the harsh social conditions the refugees live under, the film is less overtly political than Ghatak's subsequent work, notably *Subarnarekha* (1965) and *A River Named Titash* (1973). "I accuse—no one," says the old man limply in a key late scene. See it for the grace of Ghatak's mise-en-scène, his Expressionist sound design, and the enormous sense of loss. **TCh**

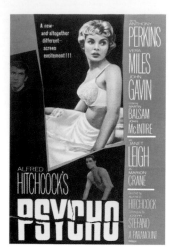

U.S. (Shamley, Alfred Hitchcock)
109m BW **Producer** Alfred Hitchcock
Screenplay Joseph Stefano, from novel by
Robert Bloch **Photography** John L. Russell
Music Bernard Herrmann **Cast** Anthony
Perkins, Vera Miles, John Gavin, Martin
Balsam, John McIntire, Simon Oakland,
Vaughn Taylor, Frank Albertson, Lurene
Tuttle, Patricia Hitchcock, John Anderson,
Mort Mills, Janet Leigh **Oscar nominations**
Alfred Hitchcock (director), Janet Leigh
(actress in support role), Joseph Hurley,
Robert Clatworthy, George Milo (art
direction), John L. Russell (photography)

*"She might have fooled
me, but she didn't
fool my mother."*

**Norman Bates
(Anthony Perkins)**

𝑖

The iconic Bates house was largely
inspired by Edward Hopper's painting
The House by the Railroad (1925).

Psycho Alfred Hitchcock, 1960

One of the most famous movies of all time, and quite possibly the most influential horror film in history, *Psycho* traded the supernatural beings of the genre's past—vampires, werewolves, zombies, and the like—for an all-too-human monster. The film made "Norman Bates" a household name and guaranteed its director's status as the master of suspense.

Adapted by Joseph Stefano from a creepy but forgettable novel by Robert Bloch, who based the character of Norman on a real-life Wisconsin serial killer, Ed Gein, *Psycho* tells the story of Marion Crane, an attractive young woman who steals $40,000 from her place of work. She leaves town without a plan, except a vague desire to shack up with her married boyfriend. Driving all night in the rain, she finally stops at a roadside motel, where the manager is an awkward but nice-enough young man named Norman (played to quirky perfection by Anthony Perkins). In a shocking twist that had audiences at the time literally screaming in the aisles, Marion is stabbed to death while taking a shower that evening by what looks like an old lady with a foot-long carving knife. Shrieking violins on the soundtrack (composed by Hitchcock regular Bernard Herrmann) punctuate the terrifying attack. Never before had the central character of a commercial movie been killed off so brutally less than halfway through the film. After an insurance detective assigned to the case, Milton Arbogast (Martin Balsam), gets snuffed out as well, Marion's sister Lila (Vera Miles) and boyfriend Sam Loomis (John Gavin) track her to the Bates family home up the road from the motel. They discover that the killer is actually Norman, a homicidal, cross-dressing schizophrenic who makes himself up just like his dead mother whenever sexual or threatening feelings arise. Although a police-employed psychologist (Simon Oakland) "explains" the cause of Norman's illness at the film's end, there can be little doubt that whatever truly motivates him lies beyond the ability of rational minds to comprehend.

When *Psycho* first opened, it received mostly lukewarm reviews from critics—though better by a mile than the venom that greeted Michael Powell's eerily similar *Peeping Tom*, also released in 1960. Public reaction to the film was staggering, however, with people lining up around the block for tickets. Generating additional buzz was Hitchcock's newly initiated "special policy" of not allowing anyone to enter the theater after *Psycho*'s opening credits had run. Clearly this British-born filmmaker had found a way of tapping directly into America's collective psyche: By making his monster so very normal, and by uniting sex, madness, and murder in one spooky and sordid tale, he effectively predicted the headlines of many of the coming decades' top news stories. The success of *Psycho* led to three forgettable "sequels," including one directed by Perkins himself in 1986 and Gus Van Sant's notorious "shot-for-shot" remake in 1998—a colorized experiment that nonetheless paled in comparison with Hitchcock's black-and-white original. **SJS**

Tirez sur le pianiste François Truffaut, 1960
Shoot the Piano Player

With his second feature, *Shoot the Piano Player*, François Truffaut set out to make a film as different as possible from his acclaimed debut, *The 400 Blows* (1959). Where *Blows* was sensitive, realistic, and autobiographical in content, *Piano Player* is zany, irreverent, and set in a lovingly pastiched B-movie world of doom-laden losers and thick-eared hoods. "I wanted to break with linear narrative," Truffaut later explained, "and make a film where all the scenes would please me. I shot without any other criteria."

The plot, adapted from a pulp crime novel, is classic noir. The hero, a once-famous concert pianist (played with sad-eyed doggy charm by singer Charles Aznavour), abandoned his career on discovering how his wife had betrayed him and now plays piano in a tawdry Paris bar. Thanks to his roughneck brothers, he finds himself, and the waitress he loves, caught up in a farcically lethal affair of kidnappings and gunplay.

Because no funding was forthcoming for a studio production, Truffaut and his crew shot on the streets, often making up the script as they went along and deciding the ending on the basis of who was still available for the final showdown. This blithely haphazard approach paid off in unpredictable mood-switches and incongruous dialogue riffs, many of which anticipate Quentin Tarantino's *Reservoir Dogs* (1992). The heavies are played as comic-strip figures, and the hero's siblings bear names recalling the Marx Brothers: Chico, Momo, and Fido. Truffaut takes mischievous delight in playing all kinds of cinematic games: when a crook swears he's telling the truth "on my mother's life," we get a quick cut to an elderly lady keeling over with a heart attack, and a nonsense song sung in the bar punctuates the action ("Avanie et framboise sont les mamelles de la vie"—"Affront and raspberry are the breasts of life").

Piano Player scored a hit in cinephile circles, but the general public was baffled by the mix of genres and the picture was a commercial disaster. Shaken, Truffaut retreated back to more conventional narrative styles; never again would he let himself have quite so much fun with a film. **PK**

France (Pléiade) 85m BW
Language French **Producer** Pierre Braunberger **Screenplay** Marcel Moussy, François Truffaut, from the novel *Down There* by David Goodis **Photography** Raoul Coutard **Music** Georges Delerue, Boby Lapointe, Félix Leclerc, Lucienne Vernay **Cast** Charles Aznavour, Marie Dubois, Nicole Berger, Michèle Mercier, Albert Rémy, Serge Davri, Claude Mansard, Richard Kanayan, Jean-Jacques Aslanian, Daniel Boulanger, Claude Heymann, Alex Joffé, Boby Lapointe, Catherine Lutz

"400 Blows... *was so French. I felt that I needed to show that I had also been influenced by the American cinema.*"

François Truffaut, 1984

i

When Truffaut met Goodis in New York, the novelist gave him a vintage camera viewfinder as a gift.

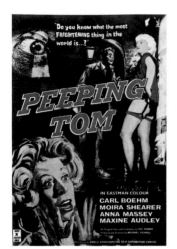

Peeping Tom Michael Powell, 1960

The invasiveness of the camera is given a disturbing twist in Michael Powell's infamous, career-destroying *Peeping Tom*. A young man named Mark Lewis (Carl Boehm) introduces himself to women as a documentary filmmaker. But attached to his camera is a metal spike with which he kills his subject as his films them. We learn this from the opening moments of *Peeping Tom*, as we witness a harrowing murder captured in the virtual crosshairs of a viewfinder.

There is no question that Mark is a monster, but Powell reveals bits and pieces of a troubled childhood that at least make him more sympathetic. His sadistic father tormented the boy while filming him for psychoanalytic experiments, shining lights in his eyes to rouse him from sleep, and dropping lizards into his bed. Later we see him posed with his dead mother, a film he combines with footage of his father's remarriage. For Mark, sex, death, love, and hate all bleed into one, and the camera is the one thing capable of capturing all those fleeting emotions. Only through the literal fusion of these feelings with his equipment is Mark able to reconcile the violent and conflicted impulses of his subconscious.

Perhaps it was its subject's ambiguous motives that turned off audiences, or maybe it was the fact that a director as beloved as Powell had turned his sights on such dark and surprising subject matter. But it just as easily could have been the film's subtle implication that the viewer, a fellow voyeur, is somehow complicit in Mark's murderous deeds, riveted by his perverse atrocities and to a degree enabling them.

Vitally, Powell presents this twisted tale with all the skill and craft he brought to his other more innocent movies. The colors of *Peeping Tom* are vibrant, often most so at the moments you wish they weren't. Even compared to the black and white of Alfred Hitchcock's somewhat likeminded shocker *Psycho* (also 1960), the vivid *Peeping Tom* comes across as more immediate and ultimately more frightening. We're shoved deep down into the recesses of a madman's brain, and Powell doesn't give us an easy way out. **JKl**

1960

G.B. (Anglo-Amalgamated, Michael Powell) 101m Eastmancolor **Producer** Michael Powell **Screenplay** Leo Marks **Photography** Otto Heller **Music** Brian Easdale, Angela Morley, Freddie Phillips **Cast** Karlheinz Böhm, Moira Shearer, Anna Massey, Maxine Audley, Brenda Bruce, Miles Malleson, Esmond Knight, Martin Miller, Bartlett Mullins, Michael Goodliffe, Nigel Davenport, Jack Watson, Shirley Anne Field, Pamela Green, Brian Wallace

"Whatever I photograph I always lose."

Mark Lewis (Carl Boehm)

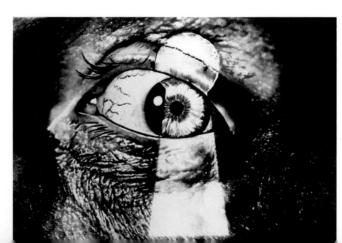

i

Michael Powell appears in a cameo role, as Mark's father, in the home-movie footage.

La maschera del demonio Mario Bava & Lee Kresel, 1960
Revenge of the Vampire / Black Sunday

Filmed in Italy as *La maschera del demonio*, this was prepared for English-language release as *The Mask of Satan* but wound up being released in a different form (with Robert Nicolosi's subtle score replaced by Les Baxter's jazzy bombast) in America as *Black Sunday* and, after a ban of some years and severe cuts, in the United Kingdom as *Revenge of the Vampire*.

Cinematographer Mario Bava had several times stepped in to complete the direction of films he was photographing, taking over both *I Vampiri* (1957) and *Caltiki, the Immortal Monster* (1959) from Riccardo Freda and doing major second-unit work on the enormously successful Steve Reeves Hercules films. Having won a shot at making his own picture, Bava turned to a Russian folk legend preserved in "The Vij," a story by Nikolai Gogol, and extrapolated a beguiling fairy tale about a young doctor (John Richardson) who finds himself stranded in a haunted Moldavian community in the nineteenth century and falls for heiress Katja Vajda (Barbara Steele), whose body becomes possessed by executed-for-witchcraft ancestress Asa (Steele again).

The plot is the usual mix of secret passages, family curses, and sudden deaths, but Bava crams every frame with fascinating, horrid detail. It opens with a marvelously grotesque execution as spiked demon masks are hammered onto the skulls of witches, and features many unforgettably eerie images as the vampires crawl from their graves to persecute the living. Beside the lavish monochrome images, the eerie music, and the touches of blood-spurting goo, *The Mask of Satan* is also your best chance to savor the unique screen presence of Steele, the most strangely sexual actress ever to star in a horror film. An unlikely graduate of the genteel Rank Charm School, a mix of finishing school and dramatic academy, the dark, huge-eyed Steele had found few roles suited to her startling looks in the British cinema and had to venture abroad. She soon became the reigning queen of 1960s Italian horror films before finding a niche parodying Sophia Loren for Federico Fellini in *8 ½* (1963). Under any of its titles, this is the greatest gothic horror movie ever made in Italy. **KN**

Italy (Galatea, Jolly) 87m BW
Language Italian Producer Samuel Z. Arkoff, Massimo De Rita Screenplay Mario Bava, Ennio De Concini, Mario Serandrei, from story by Nikolai Gogol
Photography Mario Bava Music Robert Nicolosi Cast Barbara Steele, John Richardson, Andrea Checchi, Ivo Garrani, Arturo Dominici, Enrico Olivieri, Antonio Pierfederici, Tino Bianchi, Clara Bindi, Mario Passante, Renato Terra, Germana Dominici

"You, too, can feel the joy and happiness of hating."

Katja Vajda
(Barbara Steele)

ℹ️
Barbara Steele never saw the full script, receiving only the pages of the scenes she would play that day.

Splendor in the Grass Elia Kazan, 1961

U.S. (NBI, Newton, Warner Bros.) 124m
Technicolor **Screenplay** William Inge
Producer William Inge, Elia Kazan, Charles H.
Maguire **Photography** Boris Kaufman
Music David Amram **Cast** Natalie Wood, Pat
Hingle, Audrey Christie, Barbara Loden,
Zohra Lampert, Warren Beatty, Fred Stewart,
Joanna Roos, John McGovern, Jan Norris,
Martine Bartlett, Gary Lockwood, Sandy
Dennis, Crystal Field, Marla Adams
Oscar William Inge (screenplay)
Oscar nomination Natalie Wood (actress)

From the first notes of David Amram's intense score and the opening image of Bud (first-timer Warren Beatty) and Deanie (Natalie Wood) kissing in a car by a raging waterfall, *Splendor in the Grass* sums up the appeal of Hollywood melodrama at its finest. The passions repressed by society (the setting is Kansas 1928) find a displaced expression in every explosive burst of color, sound, and gesture.

Repression is everywhere in this movie, a force that twists people in monstrous, dysfunctional directions. Men are obliged to be successful and macho, while women must choose between virginity and whorishness—as is the case for Bud's unconventional flapper sister, Ginny, indelibly incarnated by Barbara Loden.

Director Elia Kazan worked at the intersection of studio-nurtured classical narrative and the innovative, dynamic forms introduced by Method acting and the French New Wave. Here, collaborating with the dramatist William Inge, he achieved a sublime synthesis of both approaches. The film offers a lucid, concentrated analysis of the social contradictions determined by class, wealth, industry, church, and family. At the same time, *Splendor In the Grass* is a film in which the characters register as authentic individuals, acting and reacting in a register that is far from the Hollywood cliché. **AM**

1961

Viridiana Luis Buñuel, 1961

Spain / Mexico (59, Gustavo Alatriste,
UNINCI) 90m BW **Language** Spanish
Producer Gustavo Alatriste, Ricardo Muñoz
Suay, Pedro Portabella **Screenplay** Julio
Alejandro, Luis Buñuel **Photography** José F.
Aguayo **Music** Gustavo Pittaluga **Cast** Silvia
Pinal, Francisco Rabal, Fernando Rey, José
Calvo, Margarita Lozano, José Manuel
Martín, Victoria Zinny, Luis Heredia, Joaquín
Roa, Lola Gaos, María Isbert, Teresa Rabal
Cannes Film Festival Luis Buñuel
(Golden Palm), tied with Henri Colpi's
Une Aussi Longue Absence

In 1960 the new generation of Spanish filmmakers persuaded Luis Buñuel to work in his native Spain for the first time since his departure in 1936. The project he devised was an ironic drama. Viridiana (Silvia Pinal), on the eve of taking her final vows and entering a convent, visits her uncle (Fernando Rey), a rich landowner. Excited by her resemblance to his dead wife, he plots to rape her, but repents at the last moment. In his remorse he kills himself, leaving Viridiana as co-heir to his estates with his cynical natural son. Zealous in her efforts to better the world around her, Viridiana adopts a monstrous group of thieves, beggars, and whores. Inevitably her charity leads to disaster and her own undoing.

The Spanish authorities approved the script with few changes but had no opportunity to see the finished film before its competition in the 1961 Cannes Film Festival. Despite its award of the Cannes Grand Prix, *Viridiana* was instantly (and for several years) banned in Spain: Having enhanced the script in his realization, Buñuel had evidently lost none of his ability to shock and offend bigots. Full of moments of surreal observation, the film remains one of Buñuel's most perfect expositions of the irredeemable follies of human nature and the irrepressible comedy of life. **DR**

La jetée Chris Marker, 1961
The Pier

An experimental film couched in the trappings of science fiction ("remade" by Terry Gilliam in 1995 as *Twelve Monkeys*), Chris Marker's short work *La jetée* is the kind of deceptively simple project that grows in resonance and complexity as time goes on. Though the film is composed almost entirely of black-and-white still photos, Marker nonetheless infuses it with a thought-provoking narrative thrust, showing once and for all that moving pictures need not always actually move to move us.

Set in the near future after a nuclear apocalypse has sent any survivors scurrying underground for safety, *La jetée* is narrated by a man sent back in time to both discover and avert the cause of the devastating war. During his trips into the past he becomes obsessed with a violent image he recalls from his childhood—a man being shot—as well as a mysterious, beautiful woman. By the time he realizes the connection between the two it is too late, and history is doomed to repeat itself.

Marker's use of still images and spare bits of narration forces him to focus on sound design. The chatter of voices and strange noises replicates the hazy mechanics of time travel, here presented as a sort of metaphysical manipulation of memory and space. As the narrator's trips back through time progress, they also grow more lucid, leading to one of the film's most affecting moments. Picturing the beautiful woman asleep, Marker films her eyes flickering open, the one scene of *La jetée* that shows moving images.

This brief moment helps to illustrate the connection between the narrator and the woman, revealing why he would want to deviate from his compulsory mission and also setting the stage for the mind-bending (or is that time-bending?) twist at the film's conclusion. *La jetée* is short at twenty-five minutes, but Marker still manages to generate more of an impact than many films three times as long. That his intentionally cold montage achieves any sort of emotional resonance validates his creativity and ingenuity, and helps explain why such an unconventional cinematic work is revered as an influential science-fiction masterpiece. **JKl**

France (Argos) 28m BW
Language French Producer Anatole Dauman Screenplay Chris Marker Photography Jean Chiabaut, Chris Marker Music Trevor Duncan Cast Jean Négroni, Hélène Chatelain, Davos Hanich, Jacques Ledoux, André Heinrich, Jacques Branchu, Pierre Joffroy, Étienne Becker, Philbert von Lifchitz, Ligia Branice, Janine Klein, William Klein, Germano Faccetti

> *"They begin again. The man doesn't die, nor does he go mad. He suffers. They continue."*
>
> **Narrator (Jean Négroni)**

i

Marker references Hitchcock's *Vertigo* (1958) in a shot of a man and woman looking at a section of a sequoia tree.

Breakfast at Tiffany's Blake Edwards, 1961

U.S. (Jurow-Shepherd, Paramount) 115m Technicolor Producer Martin Jurow, Richard Shepherd Screenplay George Axelrod, from novella by Truman Capote Photography Franz Planer Music Henry Mancini Cast Audrey Hepburn, George Peppard, Patricia Neal, Buddy Ebsen, Martin Balsam, José Luis de Villalonga, John McGiver, Alan Reed, Dorothy Whitney, Beverly Powers, Stanley Adams, Claude Stroud, Elvia Allman, Mickey Rooney Oscars Henry Mancini (music), Henry Mancini, Johnny Mercer (song) Oscar nominations George Axelrod (screenplay), Audrey Hepburn (actress), Hal Pereira, Roland Anderson, Sam Comer, Ray Moyer (art direction)

i

To facilitate filming, Tiffany's opened on a Sunday for the first time in the twentieth century.

Truman Capote, on whose novella *Breakfast at Tiffany's* is based, originally imagined Marilyn Monroe in the lead role of good-time girl Holly Golightly, but it's now hard to imagine anyone that could have suited the part better than Audrey Hepburn. Standing outside famous Manhattan jewelry store Tiffany's in the film's memorable opening scene, the actress never looked more beautifully luminous or enchanting.

In Capote's novel, Holly is clearly a call girl, but since Blake Edwards's movie version was made in 1961, when such matters gave censors nightmares, Hepburn's Holly is depicted as a bohemian gal living off the gifts of gentlemen. Sharing the same apartment building is struggling writer Paul (George Peppard), who himself is a kept man thanks to a wealthy benefactress (Patricia Neal) with whom he is having an affair. The delicate balance of both his and Holly's relationships are placed under threat, however, when Paul falls in love with his beautiful, if sometimes maddening, neighbor.

Audrey Hepburn, her hair swept back, dressed in a chic black dress, and carrying her elegant cigarette holder, provides an unforgettable image that hasn't faded over time. Add Henry Mancini's haunting score and classic cinematic moments (Hepburn singing "Moon River," or searching for her beloved Cat in the pouring New York rain) and you have one of Hollywood's most delightful and unforgettable romantic dramas. **JB**

Lola Jacques Demy, 1961

France / Italy (EIA, Rome-Paris) 90m BW
Language French Producer Carlo Ponti,
Georges de Beauregard Screenplay Jacques
Demy Photography Raoul Coutard
Music Michel Legrand Cast Anouk Aimée,
Marc Michel, Jacques Harden, Alan Scott,
Elina Labourdette, Margo Lion, Annie
Duperoux, Catherine Lutz, Corinne
Marchand, Yvette Anziani, Dorothée Blank,
Isabelle Lunghini, Annick Noël, Ginette
Valton, Anne Zamire

Jacques Demy's magical first feature anticipates his two later masterpieces, *The Umbrellas of Cherbourg* (1964) and *The Young Girls of Rochefort* (1967), not merely in its efforts to introduce an air of fairy-tale romance into the banal world of an Atlantic port (in this case, his native Nantes) but also in its use of music and dance. While the latter elements are not yet constant in this film, they still inform plot, characterization, and mood, right from the opening sequence's use of Beethoven and Michel Legrand's jazz to accompany a white Cadillac's mysterious glide into town.

It would be wrong to write off as trivial the romantic roundelay that unravels around alluring but enigmatic cabaret-dancer and single mom Lola (Anouk Aimée), delaying a decision between several suitors while she awaits her long-gone true love's return from abroad. For all the breezy byplay, Raoul Coutard's elegantly circling camera work (the film is a delicious tribute to Max Ophüls), jaunty melodies, and far-fetched coincidences, *Lola* is imbued with a poignant awareness of the transience of happiness and the difficulties and unlikelihood of love. Formally, too, the film is more complex than it first appears, with most of the minor characters legible as telling variations on the central couple. Oh, and Anouk Aimée is unforgettable. **GA**

The Exiles Kent MacKenzie, 1961

U.S. 72m BW Producer Kent
MacKenzie Screenplay Kent MacKenzie
Photography Erik Daarstad, Robert
Kaufman, John Arthur Morrill Cast Yvonne
Williams, Homer Nish, Tom Reynolds, Rico
Rodriguez, Clifford Ray Sam, Clydean Parker,
Mary Donahue, Eddie Sunrise, Eugene Pablo

Exploited for years in Westerns as the white settler's foe, Native Americans had rarely been represented with any honesty in American cinema. Few attempts were made to explore Native American culture and traditions. Then came *The Exiles*, and its impact would ripple through the decades.

Kent MacKenzie would only complete two films, but *The Exiles* and the reputation that surrounded it cemented his position as a key director beyond the fringes of Hollywood. His film is a stark account of the lives of Native Americans living in Bunker Hill. That district of downtown Los Angeles became the locus for the many who had chosen to given up life in the confines of federally protected reservations, and it was where MacKenzie had been living for some time. His close companionship with his neighbors gave him access and permission to film their lives. Working with non-actors, MacKenzie tells the story of Yvonne (Yvonne Williams), her husband, Homer (Homer Nish), and Tommy (Tommy Reynolds), over the course of a night, offering an unvarnished portrait of his characters' lives.

Unreleased theatrically until 2008, *The Exiles* nevertheless broke down barriers in the representation of Native Americans. It preceded the shift that Hollywood witnessed with films such as *Soldier Blue* (1970) and *Little Big Man* (1970), and is a precursor to more recent—and fairer—representations of Native American life, such as *Smoke Signals* (1998). **IHS**

La notte Michelangelo Antonioni, 1961
The Night

Michelangelo Antonioni's follow-up to his groundbreaking *L'avventura* (1960) is the middle feature in a loose trilogy ending with *L'eclisse* (1962) that was made at the height of his intellectual prestige in the international film scene. Repeating many of the melancholic themes and stylistic moves of its predecessor, with particular emphasis on the boredom and atrophied emotions of the rich, *La notte* ends with a regretful recollection of former sexual desire. For better and for worse, the mainstream clichés that would circulate throughout the 1960s about Antonioni as a highbrow director making boring films about the bored rich stem largely from the excesses of this feature—despite the fact that it also showcases some of his most subtle and modulated work.

La notte's success as a structured and shapely narrative is somewhat more mixed than that of either *L'avventura* or *L'eclisse*, and the performances are generally better than those of the former and not as good as those in the latter. The minimal plot, restricted to less than twenty-four hours, involves the death of passion between a successful novelist, Giovanni Pontano (Marcello Mastroianni), and his frustrated wife, Lidia (Jeanne Moreau). The best parts of this film tend to cluster around the beginning and end, and include the novelist's brief encounter with a nymphomaniac patient at a hospital while visiting a dying friend (Bernhard Wicki) and his much longer encounter with the daughter (Monica Vitti) of an industrialist at a party, both of which foreground his shifting impulses and moods. Both these sequences show Antonioni's mise-en-scène at its most intricately plotted and emotionally subtle. By contrast, probably the weakest section is an extended walk taken by the wife around Milan, full of symbolic details meant to suggest her mental state, which arguably shows some of the ill effects that Ingmar Bergman had on certain filmmakers during the early 1960s. Yet whatever one's occasional misgivings, this feature comes from what is widely and justifiably considered to be Antonioni's richest period, and evidence of his stunning mastery is readily apparent throughout. **JRos**

Italy / France (Nepi, Silver, Sofitedip)
122m BW **Language** Italian
Screenplay Michelangelo Antonioni, Ennio Flaiano, Tonino Guerra **Photography** Gianni di Venanzo **Music** Giorgio Gaslini
Cast Marcello Mastroianni, Jeanne Moreau, Monica Vitti, Bernhard Wicki, Rosy Mazzacurati, Maria Pia Luzi, Guido A Marsan, Vittorio Bertolini, Vincenzo Corbella, Ugo Fortunati, Gitt Magrini, Giorgio Negro, Roberta Speroni
Berlin International Film Festival
Michelangelo Antonioni (Golden Bear)

1961

"Here, as in L'avventura, *it is not the situation so much as it is the intimations of personal feelings, doubts, and moods that are the substance of the film."*

The New York Times, **1962**

i

The credits of *Life of Brian* (1979) end with the line: "If you have enjoyed this film, why not go and see 'La Notte?'"

West Side Story Jerome Robbins & Robert Wise, 1961

U.S. (Mirisch, Seven Arts) 151m
Technicolor **Language** English / Spanish
Producer Robert Wise **Screenplay** Jerome
Robbins, Ernest Lehman, from play by
Arthur Laurents **Photography** Daniel L.
Fapp **Music** Leonard Bernstein, Saul Chaplin
Cast Natalie Wood, Richard Beymer, Russ
Tamblyn, Rita Moreno, George Chakiris,
Simon Oakland **Oscars** Robert Wise (best
picture), Robert Wise, Jerome Robbins
(director), George Chakiris (actor in support
role), Rita Moreno (actress in support role),
Boris Leven, Victor A. Gangelin (art direction),
Daniel L. Fapp (photography), Irene Sharaff
(costume), Thomas Stanford (editing), Saul
Chaplin, Johnny Green, Sid Ram, Irwin Kostal
(music), Fred Hynes, Gordon Sawyer (sound)
Oscar nomination Ernest Lehman
(screenplay)

The film gave rise to what was, at the time, the best-selling soundtrack LP.

An early instance of the Shakespearean approach to teen drama, getting in on the act decades before it was trendy, this Oscar-winning filming of the Broadway musical hit relocates the story of Romeo and Juliet among New York street gangs, with the Capulets and the Montagues morphed into the Puerto Rican Sharks and the Polish Jets. Stolid director Robert Wise holds the fort in the nonmusical scenes, but the film really takes off in the musical numbers by allowing the unrestrained Jerome Robbins to choreograph dances like fights and fights like dances on mostly real locations.

West Side Story stumbles by casting charisma-free Richard Beymer in the lead (the Colonel wouldn't let Elvis play Tony) and can't exactly pass the winning Natalie Wood off as Puerto Rican, but the supporting cast are perfect: Russ Tamblyn as the leader of the Jets ("Little boy you're a man, little man you're a king"), George Chakiris as his Shark opposite number, and a show-stopping Rita Moreno as the best friend who takes the lead in "America." Each and every Leonard Bernstein–Stephen Sondheim number is a classic belter: "I Feel Pretty," "When You're a Jet," "Tonight," "Gee Officer Krupke," "Maria," "Stay Cool, Boy," and "Somewhere." **KN**

The Hustler Robert Rossen, 1961

U.S. (Fox) 134m BW **Producer** Robert Rossen **Screenplay** Sidney Carroll, Robert Rossen, from novel by Walter Tevis **Photography** Eugen Schüfftan **Music** Kenyon Hopkins **Cast** Paul Newman, Jackie Gleason, Piper Laurie, George C. Scott, Myron McCormick, Murray Hamilton, Michael Constantine, Stefan Gierasch, Clifford A. Pellow, Jake LaMotta, Gordon B. Clarke, Alexander Rose **Oscars** Harry Horner, Gene Callahan (art direction), Eugen Schüfftan (photography) **Oscar nominations** Robert Rossen (best picture), Robert Rossen (director), Sidney Carroll, Robert Rossen (screenplay), Paul Newman (actor), George C. Scott (actor in support role [refused nomination]), Jackie Gleason (actor in support role), Piper Laurie (actress)

In *The Hustler*, Paul Newman plays "Fast Eddie" Felson, a cocky pool shark who spends his time shuttling from pool hall to pool hall searching for a few suckers to scam. The vulturelike middleman George C. Scott sees promise in Eddie, and tries to teach him how keeping your cool is the key to winning, but Newman discovers the hard way that keeping your cool also means excluding everything and everybody from your life save the pool table and the man you're trying to beat.

The spectacular black-and-white widescreen shots of smoky pool halls aside, *The Hustler* is a movie about people, and as such it features an array of impressive acting. Along with Newman and Scott is a laconic Jackie Gleason and a sad-sack Piper Laurie, who plays Newman's doomed, alcoholic love interest (though "love" may be too strong a word to describe what they share). Robert Rossen's film remains one of the most remarkably bitter and cynical portrayals of human nature ever made, a cold-blooded depiction of a world where loyalty only lasts as long as a winning streak, and a victory isn't always distinguishable from a loss. **JKl**

1961

The Ladies Man Jerry Lewis, 1961

U.S. (Paramount) 95m Color **Producer** Ernest D. Glucksman, Jerry Lewis **Screenplay** Jerry Lewis, Bill Richmond **Photography** W. Wallace Kelley **Music** Jack Brooks, Walter Scharf, Harry Warren **Cast** Jerry Lewis, Helen Traubel, Kathleen Freeman, Hope Holiday, Lynn Ross, Gretchen Houser, Lillian Briggs, Mary LaRoche, Madlyn Rhue, Alex Gerry, Jack Kruschen, Vicki Benet, Pat Stanley, Dee Arlen, Francesca Bellini

Jerry Lewis has never been one to be ignored. It may finally be time to admit that our movie-loving French friends know what they're talking about. Already one of the three or four most influential American screen comedians, Lewis's immense popularity as an actor did not adequately prepare the world for his talent as a director, or for the many glories of *The Ladies Man*.

In *The Ladies Man*, Lewis demonstrates a mastery of mise-en-scène that has rarely been rivaled. Very few could arrange the elements of a film frame with such skill and pitch-perfect comic timing. The proof is in, most famously, the incredible scene in which the many denizens of the women-only rooming house wake up and perform their morning rituals. In one remarkable shot, we see young women in different rooms combing their hair, exercising, and playing the French horn(!)—all while the camera cranes through the famous cutaway "dollhouse" set. Their movements are syncopated to the music, and perfectly integrated into the lavish setting. The result is a cavalcade of comic 1960s femininity that unfolds in vivid colors and psychosexual madness.

Add to this the fact that Lewis gives one of his wildest and weirdest performances, and that, as a director, he is willing to gleefully suspend reality at the drop of a hat—as in the famously bizarre "Spider Lady" sequence. *The Ladies Man* also features what is, for my money, cinema's finest "slow burn." The film is a high point not only in Jerry Lewis's comic style, but in the use of mise-en-scène in American motion pictures. **EdeS**

Såsom i en spegel Ingmar Bergman, 1961
Through a Glass Darkly

The first film in what later became known as Bergman's chamber-trilogy on the silence of God (though the director himself has here and there advised against any such formal approach to the films in question), *Through a Glass Darkly* begins somewhat misleadingly with four people—Kårin (Harriet Andersson), her husband Martin (Max von Sydow), her father David (Gunnar Björnstrand), and her teenage brother Minus (Lars Passgård)—emerging from the sea, as if out of nowhere, in peals of laughter suggestive of happiness and a sense of togetherness. They are on vacation—indeed this is the first of Bergman's films to be set on the island of Fårö, which he later made his home—and as the sun sets the mood is one of relaxed enjoyment; only gradually do we learn of the despair, doubts, and divisions within the family, as the film advances inexorably toward its dark conclusion, exactly a day later.

In that time, Kårin will learn that the mental illness she has believed she was getting over has been found to be incurable; Martin will discover that all the love he feels for her cannot prevent her hallucinations; David will confess that he has tended to put his work (he's a successful writer) before his family, and that for all his efforts he cannot change; Minus, already in teenage turmoil, will be sucked in by Kårin's spiraling madness; and she, hoping that God will show himself and help them in their need, breaks down when He reveals his cold, stony face as that of a spider. This terrifying scene (we don't see the spider, only her distraught reaction to His imagined visitation) constitutes both the dramatic climax and the logical thematic conclusion of an immaculately wrought drama virtually unmatched even by Bergman's other films for its sheer intensity.

Influenced by Strindberg, *Through a Glass Darkly*—with its handful of characters, isolated setting, brief time span, and uncluttered visuals (apart from the characters, all we seem to see are their house, the sea, sky, rocky shore, and a wrecked boat in which Kårin first experiences her breakdown)—allows nothing to dilute the force of its emotional and philosophical thrust; no wonder Bergman saw it as the first of his films to pave the way toward the masterpiece that was *Persona* (1966). **GA**

Sweden Svensk) 89m BW
Language Swedish Producer Allan Ekelund Screenplay Ingmar Bergman Photography Sven Nykvist Music Johann Sebastian Bach Cast Harriet Andersson, Gunnar Björnstrand, Max von Sydow, Lars Passgård Oscar Sweden (best foreign language film) Oscar nomination Ingmar Bergman (screenplay) Berlin International Film Festival Ingmar Bergman (OCIC award, Golden Bear nomination)

> "It's so horrible to see your own confusion and understand it."
>
> Kårin (Harriet Andersson)

i

Bergman's Best Foreign Language Film Oscar was the second of three he would receive during his career.

Chronique d'un été Edgar Morin & Jean Rouch, 1961
Chronicle of a Summer

France (Argos) 85m BW
Language French Producer Anatole
Dauman Photography Raoul Coutard,
Roger Morillière, Jean-Jacques Tarbès
Cast Marceline Loridan Ivens, Marilù
Parolini, Jean Rouch

"The people we filmed were not objects, they were subjects of the film. They were human beings."

Jean Rouch, 1991

Anthropologist Jean Rouch and sociologist Edgar Morin's *Chronicle of a Summer* is one of the most significant and quoted of all documentary films. Drawing on the traditions and techniques of several pioneers of the form—Dziga Vertov and Robert Flaherty—Rouch and Morin document the patterns and performances of everyday life in early 1960s Paris. Capitalizing on some of the key changes in 16mm filmmaking equipment and technique occurring at the time, the film demonstrates the nascent possibilities of an increasingly mobile and "objective" medium.

Although in some ways *Chronicle of a Summer* can be said to be observational in style, it constantly insists on interrogating its methodological and ethical approach. In this respect, the film extends Flaherty's practice—he insisted on showing his rushes to the Inuit subjects of *Nanook of the North* (1922)—by including a screening and critical discussion of the "finished" film within the film itself. And though *Chronicle of a Summer* "shows" us moments in the lives of its characters—sometimes talking to Morin, at others just "being" for the camera—it also self-consciously stamps itself as an ethnographic or anthropological experiment incorporating the interactive responses of its subjects.

Perhaps the most remarkable aspect of *Chronicle of a Summer* is less its ability to capture unmediated moments of reality, than its capacity to critically examine the mixture of reality and performance (and performance as reality) demanded by the presence of the camera. Unlike the documentaries of Frederick Wiseman, which painstakingly attempt to efface both the camera and the filmmaker, the presence of both in Rouch and Morin's film is constantly insisted upon. Thus, rather than being constructed as observers of everyday life, the camera and filmmaker are implicated in both its unfolding and its construction. Nevertheless, in the walk of concentration camp survivor Marcelline through the streets of Paris—accompanied by her explicitly "personal" commentary—one can glimpse the approaching "freedom" of the cinema verité form. This is a visionary work, both formative and already a critical exploration of the powers and techniques of "direct" cinema. **AD**

1961

i

Rouch and Morin built the movie around Parisian citizens' responses to the simple question "Are you happy?"

L'année dernière à Marienbad Alain Resnais, 1961
Last Year at Marienbad

Last Year at Marienbad is a touchstone of modernist cinema in general, and of postwar French film in particular. It was instantly clear in 1961 that Alain Resnais's second feature—like his first, *Hiroshima mon amour* (1959)—marked a radical departure from movies shaped by the long-dominant "tradition of quality." It wasn't just offbeat or eccentric; it mounted a full-blooded assault on ingrained assumptions of narrative film, interrogating and subverting every aspect of "correct" moviemaking from temporal structure to photographic composition to character development.

Marienbad is not the brainchild of Resnais alone. Its greatness grows organically from the dreamish poetry of Alain Robbe-Grillet's exquisitely crafted screenplay and from Sacha Vierney's majestic widescreen cinematography. Looking deeper still, one should credit the insights of the critics of the French film magazine *Cahiers du Cinéma*, developments in modernist painting, the Existentialist and Bergsonian strains of European philosophy, and other invigorating theoretical/cultural/sociopolitical innovations of this hugely fertile period in French culture.

And then there is the extraordinary cast, with legendary Delphine Seyrig as the woman called A, inimitable Giorgio Albertazzi as the inscrutable stranger called X, and subtly expressive Sacha Pitoëff as M, the perplexed husband of the tale. Their quietly restrained passion suits the elegant atmospherics to perfection.

Still, to see *Marienbad* as fundamentally a Resnais movie is both to acknowledge its kinship with his other masterpieces and to recognize his overwhelming importance to progressive cinema. With characteristic modesty, he once called *Marienbad* a "crude and primitive . . . attempt" to capture "the complexity of thought and its mechanisms." He was wrong in his choice of adjectives, but right about everything else connected with this strange and stirring film. Nowhere else in cinema have the labyrinthine workings of consciousness and memory been evoked more forcefully or explored more resonantly. **DS**

1961

France / Italy (Argos, Cineriz, Cinétel, Como, Cormoran, Tamara, Precitel, Silver, Soc. Nouvelle, Terra) 94m BW **Language** French **Director** Alain Resnais **Producer** Pierre Courau, Raymond Froment **Screenplay** Alain Robbe-Grillet, from the novel *The Invention of Morel* by Adolfo Bioy Casares **Photography** Sacha Vierny **Music** Francis Seyrig **Cast** Delphine Seyrig, Giorgio Albertazzi, Sacha Pitoëff, Françoise Bertin, Luce Garcia-Ville, Héléna Kornel, François Spira, Karin Toche-Mittler, Pierre Barbaud, Wilhelm von Deek, Jean Lanier, Gérard Lorin, Davide Montemuri, Gilles Quéant, Gabriel Werner **Oscar nomination** Alain Robbe-Grillet (screenplay) **Venice Film Festival** Alain Resnais (Golden Lion)

"Most of what happens is in the characters' imaginations, so the memory of silent film was a big influence."

Alain Resnais, 1999

🛈

In 2004, director Peter Greenaway declared *Marienbad* to have been the biggest influence on his work.

Cléo de 5 à 7 Agnès Varda, 1962
Cléo from 5 to 7

France / Italy (Rome-Paris) 90m BW / Color
Language French Producer Georges de
Beauregard Screenplay Agnès Varda
Photography Jean Rabier Music Michel
Legrand Cast Corinne Marchand,
Antoine Bourseiller, Dominique Davray,
Dorothée Blank, Michel Legrand,
José Luis de Villalonga, Loye Payen, Renée
Duchateau, Lucienne Le Marchand,
Serge Korber, Robert Postec

Precursor of the French New Wave with her debut feature *La pointe courte* (1956), in *Cléo from 5 to 7* writer-director Agnès Varda focuses on a French singer (Corinne Marchand) awaiting the results of a vital medical examination. As the film's title indicates, Varda has chosen to show Cléo's anguish virtually in real time, thereby taking into account the emergence and development of the techniques of "direct cinema." The casualness of the narrative allows fiction to merge with documentary as the young woman wanders through the left bank of Paris, mostly around Montparnasse Station, followed by dazzling tracking shots. But Varda's realism is also capable of generating powerful emotion, showing in a crescendo the slow breakdown of her lead character's face.

To a certain extent, *Cléo from 5 to 7* reflects the sociopolitical tensions of its time, with Cléo witnessing the aftermath of an attack in a bar and encountering a soldier on leave who is just about to go back to Algeria—in a way, he too can be seen as condemned. On the anecdotal side, movie buffs will appreciate the combination of a short silent film-within-the-film featuring Jean-Luc Godard with various famous actors, including Eddie Constantine, Anna Karina, and Yves Robert. **FL**

1962

Dog Star Man Stan Brakhage, 1962

U.S. (Canyon Cinema) 30m Color
Producer Stan Brakhage Screenplay Stan
Brakhage Photography Jane Brakhage,
Stan Brakhage Cast Jane Brakhage,
Stan Brakhage

Arguably the most prolific and influential figure in all of American avant-garde cinema, Stan Brakhage made films so profoundly personal that viewing them is like plunging into the tumultuous processes of thought itself. His lifelong project was to rediscover the purity and intensity of perception that people possess until education and acculturation force our unfettered mental energies into a narrow range of socially approved patterns.

Dog Star Man is exemplary Brakhage in every way, from its revolutionary aesthetic strategies to its philosophical vision of an existential hero questing for the infinite possibilities of being through a physical, psychological, and spiritual journey into inner and outer space. The narrative line is minimal: a man (Brakhage) trudges up a mountainside with his dog. By contrast, the film's structure grows ever more complex, as five discrete sections weave an escalating number of superimposed images into a rapid-fire visual tapestry so intricate that an alternate, "unraveled" version, *The Art of Vision*, runs to about four-and-a-half hours.

The title *Dog Star Man* can be taken as a nickname for the protagonist, or as an invocation of archetypal entities—the biological, the cosmological, the human—that intertwine as inextricably in this extraordinary film as in the innermost recesses of consciousness and unconsciousness themselves. **DS**

Vivre sa vie: Film en douze tableaux
My Life to Live Jean-Luc Godard, 1962

France (Pléïade, Pathé) 80m BW
Language French Producer Pierre
Braunberger Screenplay Jean-Luc
Godard, from book by Marcel Sacotte
Photography Raoul Coutard Music Michel
Legrand Cast Anna Karina, Sady Rebbot,
André S. Labarthe, Guylaine Schlumberger,
Gérard Hoffman, Monique Messine, Paul
Pavel, Dimitri Dineff, Peter Kassovitz, Eric
Schlumberger, Brice Parain, Henri Attal, Gilles
Quéant, Odile Geoffroy, Marcel Charton
Venice Film Festival Jean-Luc Godard
(Pasinetti award, special jury prize, Golden
Lion nomination)

An episodic account of the short life of a young prostitute, *My Life To Live* is the first of Jean-Luc Godard's mature masterpieces. Like much of his best work, it is both supremely analytical and supremely sensuous, achieving an austere, wintry beauty. *My Life To Live*'s primary reference points are the rigorous spirituality of filmmakers Carl Theodor Dreyer and Robert Bresson, and the lost Eden of silent cinema. Both come together most strikingly when the heroine (Anna Karina) foresees her own martyrdom at a screening of Dreyer's silent classic, *The Passion of Joan of Arc* (1928).

The Dreyer excerpt is one of several semiautonomous texts (including a jukebox ballad, a primer on prostitution, a discussion with philosopher Brice Parain, and Poe's "The Oval Portrait") punctuating the film, which additionally is divided into twelve chapters and a series of distinct formal units inscribed by the camera. Arranged into overlapping but incongruent patterns, these elements open up the narrative to juxtaposed commentaries on such topics as mainstream film style, the burden of language, and Godard's relationship with his leading lady, whose face—as riveting as those of the great silent stars—anchors *My Life To Live*'s diverse strands without subsuming them into static harmony. **MR**

Sanma no aji Yasujiro Ozu, 1962
An Autumn Afternoon

Japan (Shochiku) 112m Agfacolor
Language Japanese Producer Shizuo
Yamanouchi Screenplay Kôgo Noda,
Yasujiro Ozu Photography Yûshun Atsuta
Music Kojun Saitô Cast Chishu Ryu, Shima
Iwashita, Shinichirô Mikami, Keiji Sada,
Mariko Okada, Nobuo Nakamura, Kuniko
Miyake, Ryuji Kita, Eijirô Tono, Teruo Yoshida,
Daisuke Katô, Miseyo Tamaki, Haruko
Sugimura, Kyôko Kishida, Noriko Maki

Yasujiro Ozu's final film and only his second one in color (the other being *Good Morning* [1959]), *An Autumn Afternoon* is a marvelous testament to a career notable both for its idiosyncratic stylistic uniformity (after a few early movies, he stuck resolutely to quiet domestic dramas and comedies shot almost exclusively with a static camera positioned two or three feet above floor level) and for the extraordinary riches attained through such limited methods. He returned to the same themes—and indeed stories—again and again, and this exquisitely poignant film is to all intents and purposes a remake of the 1949 film *Late Spring*, in which the director's favorite actor, Chishu Ryu, also played a widower trying to persuade the grown-up daughter who lives with him that she should get married.

The pair's mutual awareness that such a change would leave him lonely is counterbalanced by their love of one another, creating a dilemma for each that is both banal in its everyday universality and hugely significant for the individuals involved. Ozu negotiates this precarious balancing act with his customary mastery, exercising his unerring eye for the telling detail, leavening the proceedings with gentle humor, and using the palette of colors to maintain a beautifully becalmed mood of understated melancholy. **GA**

Lolita Stanley Kubrick, 1962

U.S. / G.B. (Anya, Harris-Kubrick, Seven Arts, Transwood) 152m BW **Producer** James B. Harris **Screenplay** Vladimir Nabokov, from his novel **Photography** Oswald Morris **Music** Bob Harris, Nelson Riddle **Cast** James Mason, Shelley Winters, Sue Lyon, Peter Sellers, Gary Cockrell, Jerry Stovin, Diana Decker, Lois Maxwell, Cec Linder, Bill Greene, Shirley Douglas, Marianne Stone, Marion Mathie, James Dyrenforth, Maxine Holden, John Harrison **Oscar nomination** Vladimir Nabokov (screenplay) **Venice Film Festival** Stanley Kubrick (Golden Lion nomination)

i

Peter Sellers supposedly modeled the voice of his character Clare Quilty on that of Stanley Kubrick.

"How have they made a movie of *Lolita?*" asked a teasing trailer for Stanley Kubrick's 1962 film of Vladimir Nabokov's much-banned novel. Working from a Nabokov script, Kubrick slightly raised the age of Dolores "Lolita" Haze (Sue Lyon), from the book's twelve to somewhere around fourteen, but otherwise manages remarkably within the limits of censorship to deliver a picture exactly as erotic, absurd, obsessive, erudite, and low-comic as the book.

Shot in Britain, Kubrick's *Lolita* lacks the book's pre-road movie feel for America's tacky motels and roadside attractions but homes in on the characters, with James Mason giving a remarkable performance as the middle-aged academic Humbert Humbert, as ridiculously lusted after by Lo's leopard-print-clad mama (Shelley Winters) as he is ridiculously smitten with the underage temptress herself. Opening with the aftermath of an orgy and Humbert's murder of his pedophile rival, "genius" Clare Quilty (Peter Sellers), the film stretches from slapstick (struggling with a folding bed in a motel room) to tragedy (Humbert's affecting sobs as he realizes how incidental he has been to the girl's life). Mason's sly, careful, pointed presence is matched by Sellers in a succession of personae as a shape-shifting Satan accompanied by Marianne Stone as his silent, Morticia-like muse, Vivian Darkbloom (an anagram of Vladimir Nabokov). **KN**

The Man Who Shot Liberty Valance

John Ford, 1962

U.S. (John Ford, Paramount) 123m BW **Producer** Willis Goldbeck **Screenplay** James Warner Bellah, Willis Goldbeck, Dorothy M. Johnson **Photography** William H. Clothier **Music** Cyril J. Mockridge **Cast** John Wayne, James Stewart, Vera Miles, Lee Marvin, Edmond O'Brien, Andy Devine, Ken Murray, John Carradine, Jeanette Nolan, John Qualen, Willis Bouchey, Carleton Young, Woody Strode, Denver Pyle, Strother Martin **Oscar nomination** Edith Head (costume)

As if explaining away the beautiful evasions and downright lies of his earlier Westerns, *The Man Who Shot Liberty Valance* finds John Ford concluding that if the legend is better than the truth, then you should "print the legend." Lawyer Ransom Stoddard (James Stewart) poaches the credit for ridding the territory of a subhuman outlaw (Lee Marvin) and riding on to political success in the twentieth century while the real man who shot Liberty Valance (John Wayne) dies broke and drunk. There's further irony in that the ultimate Western hero is here a back shooter who plugs Liberty from the shadows while the supposedly unmanly politico stands suicidally out in the open playing it fair.

Shot in black and white on a soundstage to avoid the lyricism of Ford's Monument Valley epics, this revisits the cleaning-up-the-town theme of *My Darling Clementine* (1946) with a cynical insight into the whole process of civilizing the wilderness. Wayne, like Stewart too old for his role but nevertheless perfect, represents the cowboy heroism and integrity that Stewart's lawyer-teacher-congressman will whittle away as he comes to run the West. **KN**

Heaven and Earth Magic Harry Smith, 1962

U.S. 66m BW

Harry Smith is perhaps the least known major figure of American avant-garde cinema. His films reflect a fascination with alchemy and the occult, as well as a technique of incorporating the rediscovery of the cultural debris of previous eras. On his death in 1991, Smith left behind an eclectic body of "work," the landmark *The Anthology of American Folk Music* and a small number of films, mostly incomplete. *Heaven and Earth Magic*, his magnum opus, was "completed," off and on, throughout the 1950s.

The film's narrative is deliberately oblique, and its mostly cut-out-based animation predominantly "abstract" or symbolist in form. *Heaven and Earth Magic* does have a story of sorts. The spectator can grasp onto the graphic and associational links that exist between the objects and shapes that dance across the frame. In preparing his film, Smith attempted to short-circuit the processes of logic and explicit linearity, entering into the realm of the subconscious, automatic, and symbolic.

Like Joseph Cornell, Smith is concerned with placing objects, images, and sounds in new contexts and associations. *Heaven and Earth Magic* resembles both the hypnotic, trancelike juxtaposition of image and sound in *Rose Hobart* (1936), and the intricate, hand-crafted, indirectly personal qualities of Cornell's display boxes. It is totally in keeping with Smith's own broader artistic practice. Incomplete, deeply idiosyncratic, rearranged from materials taken largely from an earlier period—a Victorian-era catalogue—it is explicitly "folk" in nature. **AD**

Lawrence of Arabia David Lean, 1962

One of the greatest epics of all time, *Lawrence of Arabia* epitomizes all that motion pictures can be. Ambitious in every sense of the word, David Lean's Oscar-grabbing masterpiece, based loosely on the life of the eccentric British officer T.E. Lawrence and his campaign against the Turks in World War I, makes most movies pale in comparison and has served as an inspiration for countless filmmakers, most notably technical masters like George Lucas and Steven Spielberg. The latter eventually helped restore *Lawrence of Arabia* to its proper length and luster alongside fellow enthusiast Martin Scorsese. From Maurice Jarre's sweeping score to Robert Bolt's literary script to Freddie Young's gorgeous desert cinematography to the literal cast of thousands, the film deserves and demands to be seen and heard on the big screen.

Designed for 70mm projection, the format enhances the film's minute details, from star Peter O'Toole's piercing blue eyes to the sun beaming down on the constantly shifting sand. *Lawrence of Arabia*'s famous images and set pieces, such as Omar Sharif's appearance out of a desert mirage, the famed cut from a lit match to the sunrise, and the mind-boggling assault on Akaba, look spectacular and, indeed, unrepeatable. They were especially impressive for a picture made in the days before computer-generated special effects. Spielberg, for one, estimates the cost of making *Lawrence of Arabia* today at around $285 million, and he would know, but the truth of the matter is that no filmmaker would dare attempt to outdo Lean, a superb director and storyteller at the top of his game.

That substance runs parallel to the spectacle only enhances the stature of *Lawrence of Arabia* and the reputation of Lean. The follies of colonialism and the hypocrisies of war are cast into stark relief, as Colonel Lawrence lets the success of his Arab-fought campaign against the Turks go to his head. Yet his larger-than-life persona is cut down to size once he realizes that bloodlust has replaced honor and arrogance has replaced courage. It's a sad fall from grace shown with subtley, literacy, and craft—a true epic with the scope and scale of great literature. **JKl**

G.B. (Horizon) 216m Technicolor
Producer Sam Spiegel **Screenplay** Robert Bolt, from memoir by T.E. Lawrence
Photography Freddie Young **Music** Maurice Jarre **Cast** Peter O'Toole, Alec Guinness, Anthony Quinn, Jack Hawkins, Omar Sharif, José Ferrer, Anthony Quayle, Claude Rains, Arthur Kennedy, Donald Wolfit, I.S. Johar, Gamil Ratib, Michel Ray, John Dimech, Zia Mohyeddin **Oscars** Sam Spiegel (best picture), David Lean (director), John Box, John Stoll, Dario Simoni (art direction), Freddie Young (photography), Anne V. Coates (editing), Maurice Jarre (music), John Cox (best sound) **Oscar nominations** Robert Bolt (screenplay), Peter O'Toole (actor), Omar Sharif (actor in support role)

> *"I walked out of the theater stunned and speechless . . . it just pulverized me."*
>
> **Steven Spielberg, 2008**

ⓘ
A.W. Lawrence, T.E.'s younger brother who had sold the rights to the story, was an outspoken critic of the film.

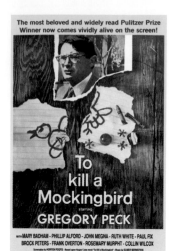

To Kill a Mockingbird Robert Mulligan, 1962

Harper Lee's beloved, Pulitzer Prize–winning novel of childhood in the Deep South during the Depression received a rare, superlative translation to the screen by the new, independent, and socially conscious production partnership of Alan J. Pakula, who produced, and Robert Mulligan, who directed this first of six films they made together in the 1960s. The adaptation was written by playwright Horton Foote, who won his first Academy Award for a screenplay that typified his feel for authentic rural Americana and real people.

Although the story is seen through the eyes of a little girl (whose adult viewpoint as narrator is voiced by Method luminary Kim Stanley), the film has a strong center in the Oscar-winning performance of Gregory Peck as the *ne plus ultra* of all the decent men he embodied, Atticus Finch. A widowed, kindly Alabama lawyer, Finch's passionate defense of a black man (Brock Peters) falsely accused of raping a white woman exposes Southern small-town bigotry at its worst and teaches his young children a painful lesson in moral courage. *To Kill a Mockingbird* is a model for literary adaptations, retaining seemingly inconsequential details along with major, heartbreaking, or deadly events—whether the children's games, a hungry farm boy drowning his dinner in syrup, Finch shooting a rabid dog, the lynch mob outside the jailhouse shamed to their senses by a child, or the black community tensely following the trial in the stifling balcony—as Mulligan brings his experience in live TV production to craft a discreetly atmospheric, intimate character drama.

The children are terrifically natural in important roles, particularly the ingenuous Scout Finch played by nine-year-old Alabaman Mary Badham (whose brother John, then at Yale, would go on to direct *Saturday Night Fever* [1977] and *WarGames* [1983]). *To Kill a Mockingbird* also boasts the feature debut of Robert Duvall as the children's elusive neighbor, bogeyman of their fantasies, and ultimately their savior, Boo Radley. Duvall would receive his own Academy Award twenty years later in another Oscar-winning screenplay by Foote, *Tender Mercies*. The melodious score by Elmer Bernstein is another asset in this tender, heartfelt film. **AE**

U.S. (Pakula-Mulligan, Brentwood, Universal) 129m BW **Producer** Alan J. Pakula **Screenplay** Horton Foote, from novel by Harper Lee **Photography** Russell Harlan **Music** Elmer Bernstein, Mack David **Cast** Gregory Peck, Mary Badham, John Megna, Frank Overton, Rosemary Murphy, Ruth White, Brock Peters, Estelle Evans, Paul Fix, Collin Wilcox Paxton, James Anderson, Alice Ghostley, Robert Duvall, William Windom, Crahan Denton, Richard Hale **Oscar** Horton Foote (screenplay), Gregory Peck (actor), Alexander Golitzen, Henry Bumstead, Oliver Emert (art direction) **Oscar nomination** Alan J. Pakula (best picture), Robert Mulligan (director), Mary Badham (actress in support role), Russell Harlan (photography), Elmer Bernstein (music) **Cannes Film Festival** Robert Mulligan (Gary Cooper award)

"You never really understand a person until you consider things from his point of view."

Atticus Finch (Gregory Peck)

i

According to comic book lore, *To Kill a Mockingbird* is the favorite movie of Clark Kent (a.k.a Superman).

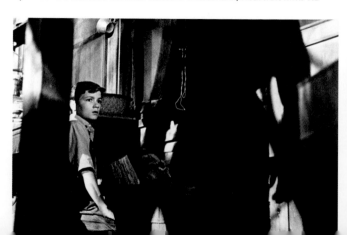

O pagador de promessas Anselmo Duarte, 1962
Keeper of Promises

Brazil / Portugal (Cinedistri, Francisco de Castro) 98m BW Language Portuguese Producer Francisco de Castro, Anselmo Duarte, Oswaldo Massaini Screenplay Anselmo Duarte, from play by Alfredo Dias Gomes Photography H.F. Fowle Music Gabriel Migliori Cast Leonardo Villar, Glória Menezes, Dionísio Azevedo, Norma Bengell, Geraldo Del Rey, Roberto Ferreira, Othon Bastos, Canjiquinha, Américo Colmbra, Walter da Silveira, Veveldo Diniz, João Di Sordi, Napoleao Lopes Filho, Milton Gaucho, Alair Liguori, Gilberto Marques, Garibaldo Matos, Jurema Penna, Antonio Pitanga, Cecília Rabelo, Conceição Senna, Irenio Simoes, Carlos Torres, Enoch Torres Oscar nomination Brazil (best foreign language film) Cannes Film Festival Anselmo Duarte (Golden Palm)

Based on the play by Brazilian playwright Alfredo Dias Gomes, *Keeper of Promises* is a parable about unconditional faith in the face of adversity. The plot revolves around Zé do Burro (Leonardo Villar), a simple-minded farmer trying to fulfill a promise to a spirit he believes saved the life of his donkey. Zé and his wife Rosa (Glória Menezes) live on a farm about thirty miles from Salvador. In the context of Brazilian spirtuality, Salvador symbolizes a religious space where Catholic and African pagan rituals blend together into a positive whole.

After the donkey's miraculous recovery, Zé sets out on the pilgrimage carrying a huge cross on his back, which he wants to place inside the church of Saint Barbara. His wish clashes with the imperviousness of priest Olavo (Dionísio Azevedo), who bans him from the church. Zé's naïveté is further exploited by unscrupulous characters. So cruel is the portrayal of the human race in the film that it is easy to understand why Zé's best friend is a donkey.

Keeper of Promises is an indictment against the intolerance of the Catholic Church, and it has a tragic ending that is cruel, sad, and extremely beautiful. Nominated for Best Foreign Language Film at the Academy Awards, it won the Golden Palm at the 1962 Cannes Film Festival. **RDe**

L'eclisse Michelangelo Antonioni, 1962
The Eclipse

Italy / France (Cineriz, Interopa, Paris) 118m BW Language French / Italian Producer Raymond Hakim, Robert Hakim, Danilo Marciani Screenplay Michelangelo Antonioni, Elio Bartolini, Tonino Guerra, Ottlero Ollieri Photography Gianni Di Venanzo Music Giovanni Fusco Cast Alain Delon, Monica Vitti, Francisco Rabal, Louis Seigner, Lilla Brignone, Rosanna Rory, Mirella Ricciardi Cannes Film Festival Michelangelo Antonioni (special jury prize), tied with *Procès de Jeanne d'Arc*

The conclusion of Michelangelo Antonioni's loose trilogy about modern life (preceded by *L'avventura* [1960] and *La notte* [1961]), *The Eclipse* is conceivably the greatest film of his career, but perhaps significantly it has the least consequential plot. A translator (Monica Vitti) recovering from an unhappy love affair links up with a stockbroker (Alain Delon) in Rome, though the stunning final sequence—perhaps Antonioni's most powerful accomplishment—does without these characters entirely. And because the two leads arguably give the most nuanced and charismatic performances of their careers here, the shock of losing them before the end of the picture is central to the film's devastating final effect.

Alternately an essay and a prose poem about the contemporary world in which the "love story" figures as one of many motifs, *The Eclipse* is remarkable both for its visual/atmospheric richness and its polyphonic and polyrhythmic mise-en-scène. Antonioni's handling of crowds at the Roman stock exchange is never less than amazing, recalling the use of deep focus in the early features of Orson Welles, where foreground and background details are brilliantly juxtaposed. But it is probably the final sequence, which depends on editing rather than mise-en-scène, that best sums up the hope and despair of the filmmaker's vision. **JRos**

1962

A QUESTO "MONDO CANE" CHE TANTO CI PIACE E NEL QUALE CI TROVIAMO TUTTI BENISSIMO

GUALTIERO JACOPETTI
PAOLO CAVARA
FRANCO PROSPERI

CINERIZ TECHNICOLOR

Italy (Cineriz) 105m Technicolor
Language Italian **Producer** Gualtiero
Jacopetti **Screenplay** Paolo Cavara,
Gualtiero Jacopetti **Photography** Antonio
Climati, Benito Frattari **Music** Nino Oliviero,
Riz Ortolani **Cast** Rossano Brazzi, Stefano
Sibaldi **Oscar nomination** Riz Ortolan, Nino
Oliviero, Norman Newell (song)

"The strangest commercially successful film in the history of cinema."

The Guardian, 2011

🛈

The theme song for *Mondo cane,*
"More," won a Grammy Award as well
as an Oscar nomination.

Mondo cane Paolo Cavara, Gualtiero Jacopetti, & A Dog's Life Franco E. Prosperi, 1962

An immensely popular documentary that problematizes the boundaries separating fiction from nonfiction filmmaking practices, *Mondo cane* initiated its own subgenre of "mondo films" (or "shockumentaries"). It also created a wave of imitators and has proved formative for such diverse pop and pseudodocumentary traditions as "mockumentaries," "snuff" films, hard-core pornography, execution videos, and reality television.

Purporting to subscribe to the adage that "truth can be stranger than fiction," all the while betraying its own principles by presenting often misleading voice-over commentary and manipulated (if not wholly faked) footage, Gualtiero Jacopetti's sensationalist travelogue-cum-nature film set out to shock viewers with its exposé of bizarre cultural behavior.

A onetime journalist and war correspondent, Jacopetti was hired to write the voice-over narration for two compilation films of popular nightclub acts. This gave him the initial idea for *Mondo cane;* only his documentary would showcase all that was lurid and sensational by contemporary Western standards. Jacopetti traveled the world with his associates, collecting assorted footage of tribal ceremonies, extreme cruelty to animals, religious rituals involving cross-dressing and self-flagellation, and environmental catastrophes. This more-or-less random material was then assembled into a 105-minute episodic whole, the various segments connected by the thinnest of associative links.

Along with its bloated orchestral score, the film's pretentious and heavily ironized voice-over became a key ingredient of the mondo cycle to follow. The privileged opening words of *Mondo cane* were both spoken and appeared as text on the screen: "All the scenes you will see in this film are true and are taken only from life. If often they are shocking, it is because there are many shocking things in this world. Besides, the duty of the chronicler is not to sweeten the truth but to report it objectively." Even if the scenes then presented were "true," in the sense of being detached and unbiased recordings of actual events—which they clearly are not; the only question concerns precisely which footage is real, which is reconstructed, and which is completely staged—*Mondo cane* still breaks its promise, as the film's reportage is anything but "objective." Besides dishing out the occasional piece of gross misinformation, Stefano Sibaldi's voice-over is haughty and condescending, and sometimes even takes on racist overtones.

Complicating any straightforwardly xenophobic reading of the film are its segments ridiculing Western cultural practices, like the tour with a gaggle of American senior citizens eager to waste their retirement savings on a Hawaiian vacation package. In this respect, *Mondo cane's* creators come across as equal-opportunity exploiters. By the end, and as the film's alternative title declares, it does seem like we are watching "a dog's life" ("mondo cane" translates as "world of dogs"). **SJS**

El ángel exterminador Luis Buñuel, 1962
The Exterminating Angel

Mexico (Producciones Gustavo Alatriste)
95m BW **Producer** Gustavo Alatriste
Screenplay Luis Buñuel, from play by José
Bergamin **Photography** Gabriel Figueroa
Music Raúl Lavista **Cast** Silvia Pinal, Enrique
Rambal, Claudio Brook, José Baviera, Agusto
Benedico, Antonio Bravo, Jaqueline Andere,
César del Campo, Rosa Elena Durgel, Lucy
Gallardo, Enrique Garciá Alvarez,
Ofelia Guilmáin

In *Midnight in Paris* (2010), Woody Allen has Luis Buñuel ask Owen Wilson's aspiring writer why the characters in his yet-to-be-made surrealist masterpiece cannot leave a room. It is a delicious moment, for it is the same enigma faced by anyone watching *The Exterminating Angel*.

One of Buñuel's most celebrated Mexican films, *The Exterminating Angel* appears to wear its political satire lightly, but beneath the banter, the director's sardonic hand delivers one of its most powerful blows. This group represents the hypocrites who believe they have raised themselves above the morass of the lower classes and beyond whatever judgment should be passed on them for their deeds. They are the Spanish elite, the supporters of Franco, whose duplicity Buñuel despised.

The drama unfolds at speed. The wealthy arrive, twice, for we see them walk through the entrance from two different perspectives. Does this make it harder for them to leave? Then most of the staff resigns. Small details suggest the increasing oddness of the guests' predicament, even before finding themselves unable to leave the drawing room. The presence of animals suggests the primacy of the behavior that ensues, when the veneer of respectability evaporates and Buñuel's scalpel reveals the venality of these crude and selfish creatures. **IHS**

i

The appearance of a bear and sheep at the dinner party was inspired by a real party that Buñuel once attended.

Jules et Jim François Truffaut, 1962
Jules and Jim

France (Carrosse, Sédif) 100m BW
Language French Producer Marcel Berbert
Screenplay Jean Gruault, François Truffaut,
from novel by Henri-Pierre Roché,
Photography Raoul Coutard Music Georges
Delerue Cast Jeanne Moreau, Oskar Werner,
Henri Serre, Vanna Urbino, Boris Bassiak,
Anny Nelsen, Sabine Haudepin, Marie
Dubois, Christiane Wagner, Michel Subor

*"Through me, François
learned about women,
and through him, I
learned about cinema."*

Jeanne Moreau, 1990

i

Truffaut also directed a film
adaptation of Roché's 1956 novel,
Les deux anglaises et le continent.

She wore rings on every finger. She sang the song. She wore a mustache and a thug cap, and she loved two men—one French, the other German—as the war was coming. She would love many more men, before, after, and during that time, and bicycles were running fast on the curved roads of happiness. In the end there was death. Mr. Jules (Oskar Werner) and Mr. Jim (Henri Serre) opened the door to the magical summer of cinema's modernity, but they came from the summer of another modernity, one that occurred way back at the beginning of the twentieth century—when Henri-Pierre Roché lived this story and then wrote it as a diary. They opened the door, and Catherine (Jeanne Moreau) ran right through it, shining with grace and strength and faith in being human. She would win all the races on the bridge—even the one where the bridge ends in the middle. It would be a tragedy, but it was shown as slapstick.

Never see *Jules and Jim* in a dubbed version; François Truffaut's voice-over is the sound of a wind that caresses and makes one world disappear, and another world appear. The beauty of the black-and-white CinemaScope is hardly large enough, delicate and nuanced enough, rooted in the origin and contemporary enough, contrasted enough to convey the vivid and subtle energy the film is made out of. Look at Moreau! Look how beautiful she is! Truffaut was in love with her (how could he not be?). *Jules and Jim* was created from this love—it would have been impossible to make this movie without the obvious happiness of the director filming his actress, the strength they gave to each other. A shadow of sadness can be felt each time she leaves the frame, a thrill of joy and desire each time she enters it again.

Cinema is essentially the art of recording—not only the recording of objects but also visual forms and sounds. It is also the recording of that distorted reality produced by experiencing powerful emotions. *Jules and Jim* records just such a distorted reality, and to an extraordinary extent. War was to come, and it would bring with it delusion and death. The film knew it, its black and white monochrome the colors of mourning.

Jules and Jim was Truffaut's third film, still made in the original impulse of the New Wave. And yet, after the autobiographical and child-centered *The 400 Blows* (1959) and the avant-garde, virtuoso game of *Shoot the Piano Player* (1960), *Jules and Jim* signaled a more adult and middle-of-the-road effort without losing any of the young and disruptive energy of the revolution Truffaut and his accomplices had just launched in world cinema. And, at least during this brief moment, that is exactly what happened. Truffaut's third film kept alive a moment of turbulence that would never come again—a jump into the future, with love. **J-MF**

The Manchurian Candidate

John Frankenheimer, 1962

U.S. (M.C. Productions) 126m BW
Producer George Axelrod, John Frankenheimer, Howard W. Koch **Screenplay** George Axelrod, from novel by Richard Condon **Photography** Lionel Lindon **Music** David Amram **Cast** Frank Sinatra, Laurence Harvey, Janet Leigh, Angela Lansbury, Henry Silva, James Gregory, Leslie Parrish, John McGiver, Khigh Dhiegh, James Edwards, Douglas Henderson, Albert Paulsen, Barry Kelley, Lloyd Corrigan, Madame Spivy **Oscar nominations** Angela Lansbury (actress in support role), Ferris Webster (editing)

One of the strangest and most mercurial movies ever made in Hollywood, adapted from Richard Condon's novel, *The Manchurian Candidate* was originally released in 1962 and then unseen for years after its star, Frank Sinatra, purchased the rights in the 1970s and withdrew the film from circulation. A salad of mixed genres and emotional textures, this political thriller runs more than two hours and never flags for an instant. The film got the green light with the active encouragement of President John F. Kennedy, a fan of the novel and a friend of Sinatra.

It's possibly the only commercial American film that deserves to be linked with the French New Wave. Early on, there's a virtuoso 360-degree shot around a lady's garden club meeting that gradually turns into a demonstration of brainwashing by Chinese communists. The politically incorrect audacity only expands from there, widening to include irreverent satire, ghoulish black humor, surrealist nonsense, and incest.

Angela Lansbury and Laurence Harvey, both brilliantly cast as evil mother and masochistically subservient son, have never been better and Sinatra and Janet Leigh have never been used as weirdly. The talented secondary cast is never less than effective. It is a powerful film, alternately corrosive with dark humor, suspenseful, moving, and terrifying. **JRos**

What Ever Happened to Baby Jane?

Robert Aldrich, 1962

U.S. (Aldrich, Seven Arts, Warner Bros.) 134m BW **Producer** Robert Aldrich, Kenneth Hyman **Screenplay** Lukas Heller, from novel by Henry Farrell **Photography** Ernest Haller **Music** Frank De Vol **Cast** Bette Davis, Joan Crawford, Victor Buono, Wesley Addy, Julie Allred, Anne Barton, Marjorie Bennett, Bert Freed, Anna Lee, Maidie Norman, Dave Willock, William Aldrich, Ernest Anderson, Russ Conway, Maxine Cooper **Oscar** Norma Koch (costume) **Oscar nominations** Bette Davis (actress), Victor Buono (actor in support role), Ernest Haller (photography), Joseph D. Kelly (sound)

An epic slice of Hollywood Grand Guignol, *What Ever Happened to Baby Jane?* considerably ups the grotesquerie of *Sunset Boulevard* (1950) as two aging grandes dames of the cinema tear each other to metaphoric shreds in a decaying movie-star mansion.

Based on a novel by Henry Farrell and directed with black glee by Robert Aldrich, the film is a remarkable vehicle for Joan Crawford, as the wheelchair-bound ex-1930s superstar at the mercy of her mad sister, and Bette Davis, in the title role as a middle-aged child star who insists on dressing in her old stage outfit, singing her one hit song ("I've Written a Letter to Daddy"), and dreaming of a big comeback. The plot is wound around the long-ago accident that crippled Blanche (Crawford) at the height of her fame and hinges on some genuinely unexpected revelations, but the nasty fun comes from the spectacle of these two screen queens—who evidently hated each other—pouring venom on one another. The supporting cast includes Davis's daughter Barbara (who later wrote a vicious biography about her mother, trying to degrade her) and the enormously creepy Victor Buono as an opportunist who takes the job as piano player for Jane's act. Best moment: Bette serving Joan a cooked rat under a platter for dinner. **KN**

1962

8 ½ Federico Fellini, 1963

Marcello Mastroianni with hat and cigar in a bathtub, immemorial white walls and the black line of a whip, impressive women and fantasies—the images of Federico Fellini's *8½* remain, and the sounds as well (a pity for those who have never heard the film in its original, though so artificial, Italian). The picture stands as a testimony to an icon of the European Baroque at the midpoint of the twentieth century. It is also one of the most brilliant, imaginative, and funny movies of its time. But that's not all. A turning point in the career of one of the greatest filmmakers of his era, who succeeded in transforming a personal crisis into a work of art, Fellini here paved the road for such subsequent classics as *Satyricon* (1969), *Roma* (1972), *Amarcord* (1973), *Casanova* (1976), *La città delle donne* (1980), and *E la nave va* (1983).

After his first eight features, Fellini had received all the recognition a director could possibly wish for (including, beyond the success, awards, and critical acclaim, scandal and even excommunication for *La dolce vita* [1960]), paid tribute, and flew away from his masters (Rossellini, Visconti, and De Sica, among others). Somehow, though only forty-three years old, he had managed to achieve a completeness in his work. *8 ½* stands as the bridge between this early period of fulfillment and a new adventure—one which, though probably his most original and creative, turns out to be only the second of three (there is also a third, and wonderful, period of Fellini's late works).

But there is even more to *8 ½*. The film represents a major step forward in cinema's march toward modernity, one of the most inventive constructions of a mirror reflection on the creative act itself. Its mental processes as well as its material, psychological, and libidinal obligations are enacted in a Pirandellian extravaganza to be cherished by anyone who cares about the exploration of artistic mechanisms and psychic labyrinths. But even this is not sufficient. Not beyond but inside all these good reasons to treasure *8 ½* lies the main one, which (it should be said) is also the most modest one.

This story about the anguish of a director having to make a film, about an artist having to make a work, about a man having to deal with women, about a human having to face life and death, is a very simple and touching tale. Through its inventive visions and disturbing situations, playing on the frontier between reality and dreams with humor and fear, it interrogates everyone's relationship with the world, with our parents, our children, the people we work with, the difficulties of getting old, or getting lost, or returning to childhood terrors. With its magnificent black-and-white look, its geometric and non-realistic framing, and its suggestive use of sounds and images, *8 ½* does not elaborate a thesis on the state of the art or engage in psychoanalytic investigation. Instead, it opens a window inside each and every one of us, artist or not, man or woman. **J-MF**

Italy / France (Cineriz, Francinex) 145m BW
Language Italian / English / French
Producer Angelo Rizzoli **Screenplay**
Federico Fellini, Ennio Flaiano, Tullio Pinelli,
Brunello Rondi **Photography** Gianni Di
Venanzo **Music** Nino Rota **Cast** Marcello
Mastroianni, Claudia Cardinale, Anouk
Aimée, Sandra Milo, Rossella Falk, Barbara
Steele, Madeleine LeBeau, Caterina Boratto,
Eddra Gale, Guido Alberti, Mario Conocchia,
Bruno Agostini, Cesarino Miceli Picardi, Jean
Rougeul, Mario Pisu **Oscars** Piero Gherardi
(costume), Italy (best foreign language film)
Oscar nominations Federico Fellini
(director), Federico Fellini, Ennio Flaiano,
Tullio Pinelli, Brunello Rondi (screenplay),
Piero Gherardi (art direction)

"Happiness consists of being able to tell the truth without hurting anyone."

Guido
(Marcello Mastroianni)

ℹ

At the start of the shoot, Fellini stuck a memo near his camera eyepiece that read: "Remember, this is a comic film."

"It could be the most terrifying motion picture I have ever made!"—

NOTHING YOU HAVE EVER WITNESSED BEFORE HAS PREPARED YOU FOR SUCH SHEER, STABBING SHOCK!

ALFRED HITCHCOCK'S "The Birds"

TECHNICOLOR

STARRING

ROD TAYLOR · JESSICA TANDY
SUZANNE PLESHETTE
And Introducing 'TIPPI' HEDREN

A Fascinating New Personality

Based on Daphne Du Maurier's Classic Suspense Story !

U.S. (Alfred J. Hitchcock, Universal) 119m
Technicolor **Producer** Alfred Hitchcock
Screenplay Evan Hunter, from story by
Daphne Du Maurier **Photography** Robert
Burks **Music** Bernard Herrmann **Cast** Tippi
Hedren, Rod Taylor, Jessica Tandy, Suzanne
Pleshette, Veronica Cartwright, Ethel Griffies,
Charles McGraw, Ruth McDevitt, Lonny
Chapman, Joe Mantell, Doodles Weaver,
Malcolm Atterbury, John McGovern,
Karl Swenson, Richard Deacon
Oscar nomination Ub Iwerks
(special visual effects)

i

Hedren wears the same green suit
throughout. Six separate suits, created
by Edith Head, were made for her.

The Birds Alfred Hitchcock, 1963

The Birds stands out as an anomaly among Alfred Hitchcock's films for many reasons. For one, it's the closest the director ever came to a conventional horror movie. But it's also perhaps the most enigmatic of all his films. *The Birds* invites many interpretations, yet Hitchcock never tips his hand. If he intended any single specific meaning to be gleaned from it, he tantalizingly (and teasingly) presents few explanations for the terror that transpires.

Tippi Hedren (hand-picked by Hitchcock as the latest in a long line of blonde leads) arrives in the small, sleepy coastal town of Bodega Bay, where she bumps into Rod Taylor at a pet store. After she later decides to drop by at his house to surprise him, she's attacked by a seagull, foreshadowing the fate of the entire town: With little warning, Bodega Bay comes under attack by flocks of frenzied birds. No explanation is ever given for the onslaught, and no one is safe. All the characters can do is board themselves up inside and wait out the mysterious, deadly invasion.

Hitchcock infamously nearly led Hedren to a nervous breakdown, his increasingly sadistic work ethic (perhaps misplaced aggression following the retirement of his favored star Grace Kelly) too intense for her to handle. In fact, coming after *Psycho* (1960), with its numerous references to "birds"—both the animal and the slang term for women)—*The Birds* (Hitchcock's third film based on a Daphne Du Maurier work) may have been intended as a vaguely misogynistic sexual allegory, with Taylor the sole male amid several women vying for his attention.

But again, the theme of the film remains oblique at best, with Hitchcock instead stressing the horror and horrific effects. *The Birds* features some pioneering uses of matte work, which, combined with a few mechanical birds and several of the real thing, makes each attack a harrowing experience. The tension is increased with the groundbreaking electronic score (overseen by Bernard Herrmann), a mix of strange sounds that often blurs ominously with the sounds of the cooing birds and the menacing flap of their wings. **JKl**

Pasazerka Witold Lesiewicz & Andrzej Munk, 1963
Passenger

Poland (P.P., WFF) 62m BW
Language Polish Screenplay Andrzej Munk, Zofia Posmysz-Piasecka
Photography Krzysztof Winiewicz
Music Tadeusz Baird, Johann Sebastian Bach Cast Aleksandra Slaska, Anna Ciepielewska, Jan Kreczmar, Marek Walczewski, Maria Koscialkowska, Irena Malkiewicz, Leon Pietraszkiewicz, Janusz Bylczynski, A. Golebiowska Cannes Film Festival Andrzej Munk (special mention)
Venice Film Festival Andrzej Munk (Italian film critics award)

Andrzej Munk's most famous film was also his last. The Polish director's death during the movie's production left *Passenger* unfinished; it was reconstructed in 1963 in the form of a speculation that compounds the questions Munk posed of his story and of his characters with questions about where he would have taken them had he survived. The interrogatory form proves apt for this stark and relentless work.

The central character, Liza (Aleksandra Slaska), recounts two versions of her past as an SS overseer at Auschwitz: in the first, sanitized version, which she gives her husband aboard a luxury liner on which she returns to Germany for the first time since the end of the war, Liza benevolently reunites two lovers among the prisoners but is powerless to intervene further in their destinies. In the second, more detailed version, which Liza remembers in solitude, her own motives are tangled and obscure, and her relationship with the female prisoner appears obsessive.

As much as for the psychological interest of this relationship, *Passenger* is extraordinary for its terrifying exactness of tone and for its indelible representation of brutalities enacted in the background, or on the periphery, of the main character's consciousness. This fragmentary film is no less painful and abrupt than Munk's short but brilliant career. **CFu**

The Servant Joseph Losey, 1963

G.B. (Elstree, Sprinukok) 112m BW
Producer Joseph Losey, Norman Priggen
Screenplay Harold Pinter, from novel by Robin Maugham Photography Douglas Slocombe Music John Dankworth
Cast Dirk Bogarde, Sarah Miles, Wendy Craig, James Fox, Catherine Lacey, Richard Vernon, Anne Firbank, Doris Knox, Patrick Magee, Jill Melford, Alun Owen, Harold Pinter, Derek Tansley, Brian Phelan, Hazel Terry
Venice Film Festival Joseph Losey (Golden Lion nomination)

As an expatriate American in Britain, Joseph Losey had always brought a cool, disenchanted eye to bear on the customs of his adopted country. But in *The Servant*, the first of his three collaborations with Harold Pinter, his gaze came still more sharply into focus. Pinter's script, typically elliptical and oblique, and Losey's crisp, astringent direction offer a sardonic analysis of class, sex, and power relationships in 1960s London. An effete, young, upper-class bachelor, Tony (James Fox in his first starring role), hires a manservant, Barrett (Dirk Bogarde), who gradually takes over his employer's life, undermines, and destroys him.

Bogarde, at last casting off the matinee-idol image that so long dogged him, gives one of his finest performances, his flickering, contemptuous smile and insinuating, off-Cockney accent embodying a whole history of festering class resentment. But Losey and Pinter create a sense of entrapment that extends to both men. Their roles may be gradually reversed, but they're still bound together in mutual exploitation—a feeling abetted by Douglas Slocombe's camera as it sinuously explores the claustrophobic spaces of the terraced house, turning it into an elegantly appointed cage and observing its residents from unsettling angles. Funny, sinister, and unnerving, *The Servant* still retains the power of unease. **PK**

1963

Flaming Creatures Jack Smith, 1963

U.S. 45m BW
Producer Jack Smith
Music Tony Conrad
Cast Joel Markman,
Mario Montez

Originally intended as a comedy, Jack Smith's stunning *Flaming Creatures* paradoxically became the greatest scandal of an increasingly notorious underground cinema scene. The film's distinctive beauty is due largely to Smith's nimble use of the handheld camera. His unexpected framings yield dense images of fabrics, body parts, and heavily made-up faces.

Shot on black-and-white film stock, *Flaming Creatures* is a gorgeous, flickering series of cloudy images, featuring Smith's friends in various forms of exotic, low-budget drag. Eschewing narrative continuity, the film instead presents a number of sequences and disconnected tableaux that recall the aesthetic indulgences of Josef von Sternberg and the exotic fantasy world of Smith's muse, the 1940s "Queen of Technicolor," Maria Montez. Beginning with a lengthy introduction to the creatures, the film moves on to a coy scene of flirtation and a hilarious, beautiful lipstick sequence. When the butch yet demure Francis Francine chases and begins to ravish the enticing Delicious Dolores (Sheila Bick), all the creatures join in and fall into rapture. Their frenzy is interrupted by the falling plaster caused by a seeming earthquake, which calms or kills them until Our Lady of the Docks (a mesmerizing Joel Markman) emerges from a coffin, breathes life into the creatures, and arouses them into a final, joyous dance. **MS**

Khaneh Siah Ast Forugh Farrokhzad, 1963
The House is Black

Iran (Golestan) 20m BW
Language Farsi Producer Ebrahim
Golestan Screenplay Forugh Farrokhzad
Photography Soleiman Minasian
Cast (narration) Ebrahim Golestan,
Forugh Farrokhzad

Forugh Farrokhzad's twenty-minute black-and-white documentary about a leper colony in northern Iran is one of the most powerful films to have come out of this country—the most poetic as well as the most radically humanist. Farrokhzad (1935–1967) is commonly regarded as the greatest Persian poet of the twentieth century, and one of her poems can be heard recited by the hero in Abbas Kiarostami's *The Wind Will Carry Us* (1999), whose title is that of the poem. Her only film—which reflects the probable influence of silent Soviet cinema without being in any way obviously derivative of it—seamlessly adapts the techniques of poetry to its framing, editing, sound, and narration. The latter is split between two voices, male and female. The male voice, belonging to Ebrahim Golestan—the film's producer, Farrokhzad's lover, and a considerable filmmaker in his own right—is mainly objective and factual; the female voice is Farrokhzad's, offering a poetic and highly emotional reverie about her subject that incorporates passages from the Old Testament.

At once lyrical and extremely matter-of-fact, devoid of sentimentality or voyeurism yet profoundly humanist, *The House Is Black* offers a view of life in the colony—people eating, various medical treatments, children at school and at play—that is spiritual, unflinching, and beautiful in ways that have no apparent Western counterparts; it registers like a prayer. **JRos**

Hud Martin Ritt, 1963

U.S. (Paramount, Salem-Dover) 112m BW
Producer Irving Ravetch, Martin Ritt
Screenplay Harriet Frank Jr., Irving Ravetch,
from the novel *Horseman Pass By* by Larry
McMurtry Photography James Wong Howe
Music Elmer Bernstein Cast Paul Newman,
Melvyn Douglas, Patricia Neal, Brandon De
Wilde, Whit Bissell, Crahan Denton, John
Ashley, Val Avery, George Petrie, Curt
Conway Oscars Patricia Neal (actress),
Melvyn Douglas (actor in support role),
James Wong Howe (photography) Oscar
nominations Martin Ritt (director), Irving
Ravetch, Harriet Frank Jr. (screenplay), Paul
Newman (actor), Hal Pereira, Tambi Larsen,
Sam Comer, Robert R. Benton (art direction)
Venice Film Festival Martin Ritt (OCIC
award, Golden Lion nomination)

🛈

To prepare for the role, Newman
worked on a cattle ranch in Texas.

This modern Western directed by Martin Ritt is set in the featureless landscape of West Texas. Paul Newman is Hud Bannon, who cares for little in life besides drinking and chasing women. His view of life is undiluted cynicism: "You take the sinners away from the saints, you're lucky to end up with Abraham Lincoln." Yet Hud is looked up to by Lonnie (Brandon De Wilde), his dead brother's son, who at seventeen admires his uncle's easy charm. There is bad blood between Hud and his father (Melvyn Douglas), a rancher of the old school. Hud wants to drill for oil, but his father refuses: "I don't want that kind of money." Their housekeeper is Alma (Patricia Neal), divorced and approaching middle age, but too much her own woman to accept Hud's advances.

When the father's precious herd of cattle is suspected of having foot-and-mouth disease, Hud proposes selling them before the disease is confirmed. The old man won't hear of it, but the slaughter of the herd removes his will to live. By the end, Lonnie and Alma have gone too, leaving Hud to nurse his beer. It's a brilliantly acted film that catches much of the feel for the dusty locale of Larry McMurtry's original novel, *Horseman Pass By*. **EB**

Il gattopardo Luchino Visconti, 1963
The Leopard

A cult classic, Luchino Visconti's adaptation from the novel of Giuseppe Tomasi Di Lampedusa, set in Sicily in the 1860s, is a sumptuous fresco of a world that's active at twilight. It accounts for the major social changes in Italy after the Risorgimento movement through the story of the prince Fabrizio di Salina (Burt Lancaster). Trying to avoid a confrontation with Garibaldi's army, the aristocrat has to move, together with his family, to their retreat at Donnafugata. He is one of the few of his caste to understand that the world is irreversibly changing and is disposed to make a pact with the representatives of the bourgeoisie. Following his personal motto ("If we want everything to stay the same, everything must change"), he decides to marry his nephew, Tancredi Falconeri (Alain Delon), to the daughter of the local mayor. The alliance between "the Leopard" and "the Jackal" will be celebrated in the marriage scene, which covers the third part of the movie.

Brightly directed and photographed, this segment of the film is where the central metaphor comes to life. The amazing camera work of Giuseppe Rotunno provides an unforgettable sense of the palace's magnificence. Beyond the splendor of the settings and costumes, however, one can feel the imminence of extinction. By way of contrast, the camera's eye also makes us attend to the vitality and rudeness of the newly rich.

Tons of ink has been spilled analyzing the ideological and stylistic features of this masterpiece, one of the best adaptations in the history of cinema. Some critics have pointed out the autobiographical suggestions of *The Leopard*, as Visconti himself was an aristocrat who flirted with the Communist Party. The analogies between the author and main character can also be extended to a deeper, more psychological level; both men are obsessed with death and perceive its premonitory signs everywhere. Visconti would return to this theme in several of his subsequent pictures, including *The Damned* (1969), *Death in Venice* (1971), *Ludwig* (1972), and 1975's *Conversation Piece*, in which "the Leopard" Burt Lancaster again plays the director's alter ego. No other filmmaker handled Lancaster the way Visconti did, making him look so aristocratic, so distinguished, but also so human. His wonderful performance made Prince Salina one of the emblematic noble characters in movie history, but one should not ignore the splendid roles played by Delon and Claudia Cardinale, whose beauty here is truly breathtaking.

The film's refined chromatic and visual style, based on Visconti's competence in the fine arts, became his signature. One of the most expensive, sumptuous movies ever produced in Europe, *The Leopard* was accused by some critics of being "a monumental production in the first person." Perhaps this charge is accurate, but that is hardly a bad thing. A film that mesmerizes huge audiences and is also highly personal—a film d'auteur—must be the dream of directors everywhere. **DD**

Italy / France (S.G.C., Nouvelle Pathé, Titanus) 205m Technicolor **Language** Italian / English **Producer** Goffredo Lombardo **Screenplay** Suso Cecchi d'Amico, Pasquale Festa Campanile, Massimo Franciosa, Enrico Medioli, Luchino Visconti, from novel by Giuseppe Tomasi Di Lampedusa **Photography** Giuseppe Rotunno **Music** Nino Rota, Vincenzo Bellini, Giuseppe Verdi **Cast** Burt Lancaster, Claudia Cardinale, Alain Delon, Paolo Stoppa, Rina Morelli, Romolo Valli, Terence Hill, Pierre Clémenti, Lucilla Morlacchi, Giuliano Gemma, Ida Galli, Ottavia Piccolo, Carlo Valenzano, Brook Fuller, Anna Maria Bottini **Oscar nomination** Piero Tosi (costume) **Cannes Film Festival** Luchino Visconti (Golden Palm)

"I belong to an unlucky generation, astride two worlds and ill-at-ease in both."

**Fabrizio di Salina
(Burt Lancaster)**

🛈

Visconti's initial choice for the Prince was Soviet actor Nikolai Cherkasov, followed by Laurence Olivier.

herbert richers apresenta

VIDAS SÉCAS
DE GRACILIANO RAMOS

direção   nelson pereira dos santos
produção   herbert richers
luiz carlos barreto
danilo trelles
maria ribeiro   atila iorio

Brazil (Sino) 103m BW
Language Portuguese **Producer** Luiz
Carlos Barreto, Herbert Richers, Danilo
Trelles **Screenplay** Nelson Pereira dos
Santos, from novel by Graciliano Ramos
Photography Luiz Carlos Barreto, José Rosa
Music Leonardo Alencar **Cast** Genivaldo,
Gilvan, Átila Iório, Orlando Macedo, Maria
Ribeiro, Jofre Soares **Cannes Film Festival**
Nelson Pereira dos Santos (OCIC award), tied
with *Les Parapluies de Cherbourg*

> *"The battered dignity etched on the characters' faces attests to their unity as both family and culture, endlessly roaming for survival, mirroring neocolonial Brazil's search for an identity and cinema of its own."*
>
> **Slant Magazine, 2006**

🛈

The film was nominated
for the coveted Palme d'Or
at Cannes in 1964.

Vidas secas Nelson Pereira dos Santos, 1963
Barren Lives

It is hard to imagine just how enormous the impact of Italian Neorealism was on world cinema; by the mid-1950s, long after the movement had ceased to exist in Italy, one could find Neorealist advocates and practitioners on every continent. In Brazil, Alex Viany's 1953 film *A Needle in a Haystack*, a gentle comedy shot on real locations in Rio, was the clear precursor of Neorealism there. Viany's chief assistant on that film, former law student Nelson Pereira dos Santos, would go on in 1955 to make *Rio, 40 Degrees*, a daring "group portrait" of Rio that follows a number of different storylines all happening on the same day. The harsh, strikingly unsentimental depiction of the Rio favelas (slums), as well as the vibrant, documentary-flavored camera work, made that film a kind of manifesto for a new cinema in Brazil.

This New Cinema, or Cinema Novo as it became known, was finally acknowledged as a major cultural movement in 1963 with the release of dos Santos's fifth feature film, *Barren Lives*. An extraordinary adaptation of the homonymous novel by Graciliano Ramos, one of the unquestionable masterpieces of Brazilian literature, *Barren Lives* tells the story of a family of retirantes, migrant laborers in the drought-stricken northeast. Often compared to Faulkner, Ramos's novel, written in 1938, is divided into brief chapters, each one offering an intensely sensual, individual point of view of one of the family members over the course of two years. Dos Santos renders this literary device exquisitely, even giving us, in one of the film's most heart-breaking scenes, the "mind" of the family dog in its dying moments. A collection of incidents and encounters, rather than a clear narrative, *Barren Lives* ends as it began, with the family once again on the road. Dos Santos's film has an effect similar to that of Luis Buñuel's *Land Without Bread* (1933): You feel that you've passed through "realism" to arrive at something else, something abstract but powerful nonetheless. A final conversation between husband and wife hints at the possibility of change, but by this point we've seen too much to dare imagine any easy solutions. **RP**

Shock Corridor Samuel Fuller, 1963

U.S. (Allied Artists, F & F) 101m BW / Technicolor **Producer** Sam Firks, Leon Fromkess, Samuel Fuller **Screenplay** Samuel Fuller **Photography** Stanley Cortez **Music** Paul Dunlap **Cast** Peter Breck, Constance Towers, Gene Evans, James Best, Hari Rhodes, Larry Tucker, Paul Dubov, Chuck Roberson, Neyle Morrow, John Matthews, Bill Zuckert, John Craig, Philip Ahn, Frank Gerstle, Rachel Romen

Working in the world of exploitation films and B-movies, with shoestring budgets and no studio expectations beyond profitability, Samuel Fuller ironically found a great deal more freedom to explore controversial ideas and new cinematic techniques than many of his higher-profile peers. *Shock Corridor* hinges on what has become a hoary cliché: A hotshot reporter has himself committed to an insane asylum to investigate a murder. He finds more than he bargained for, of course, and just the same Fuller offers more than a simple exploitation film.

Shock Corridor's camerawork, by Stanley Cortez (*The Magnificent Ambersons* [1942], *The Night of the Hunter* [1955]), is every bit as nuts as the colorful cast of characters populating the asylum, lurching, looming, and leaping from black and white into color. The acting is likewise all over the place, with the cast obviously encouraged to give voice to their inner psychotic. A fat man claims to be a famous opera singer, a pack of nymphomaniacs roam the ward like wild animals, and a black man preaches racism. Fuller doesn't always arrange the film like he knows exactly where it's going, and its inherent trashiness never belies its B-movie origins—but he does imbue *Shock Corridor* with a crazed energy more than befitting its striking name. **JKl**

Le mépris Jean-Luc Godard, 1963
Contempt

France / Italy (Compagnia, Concordia, Rome-Paris) 103m Technicolor **Language** French / English / German / Italian **Producer** Carlo Ponti, Georges de Beauregard **Screenplay** Jean-Luc Godard, from the novel *Il Disprezzo* by Alberto Moravia **Photography** Raoul Coutard **Music** Georges Delerue **Cast** Brigitte Bardot, Michel Piccoli, Jack Palance, Giorgia Moll, Fritz Lang

The sixth feature to be directed by Jean-Luc Godard, most daring of the New Wave filmmakers of the 1960s, *Contempt* combines the portrait of a marriage with a story about making a film. Camille (Brigitte Bardot) is married to screenwriter Paul (Michel Piccoli). In the first sequence she makes an inventory of her naked body, asking him which bit he likes best. Then he takes her to meet Hollywood producer Jeremy Prokosch (Jack Palance). Prokosch is making a movie of Homer's *Odyssey*, to be directed by veteran German filmmaker Fritz Lang, playing himself. Palance plays his role to the hilt, intoning, "I like gods. I know exactly how they feel." Lang replies with some gnomic observations on cinema ("CinemaScope is fine for shooting snakes and coffins").

Contempt is packed with cinematic references to Chaplin and Griffith, and to Hawks, Ray, Minnelli, and other heroes of the French film magazine *Cahiers du Cinéma*, for whom Godard was a critic. Paul's contribution is to remark that, show a woman a camera and she immediately bares her bottom—ironic, given that Bardot's naked behind is frequently in view.

And contempt? It's what Camille has come to feel for her husband, whom she accuses of trying to pimp her to Prokosch and of selling out his principles for money. A clever, elegant film with a shocking ending. **EB**

1963

Blonde Cobra Ken Jacobs, 1963

U.S. 33m
Cast Ken Jacobs, Jack Smith

Generally considered one of the masterpieces of the New York underground film scene, Ken Jacobs's *Blonde Cobra* is perhaps first and foremost a fascinating audio-visual testament to the tragicomic performance of the inimitable Jack Smith. Smith, who died of AIDS in 1989, was a photographer, writer, filmmaker, performer, and queer muse for the New York avant-garde arts scene in the 1960s and 1970s. *Blonde Cobra*, which Jacobs edited from material Smith shot with collaborator Bob Fleischner, is comprised of sequences of Smith clowning around with co-performer Jerry Sims, juxtaposed with long stretches of black leader.

During the imageless black sequences, we are treated to the hilarious and perverse stories that Smith delivers in his characteristic nasal drone on the soundtrack. These at times confessional tales of a little boy's "frustrated longings" and an older nun's dreams of lesbianism, for example, are interspersed with other Smithian ruminations ("Why shave ... when I can't even think of a reason for living?"), as well as with bits from the radio, a German tango, and a Fred Astaire–Ginger Rogers song. Though perhaps a bit "heavy," as Smith described it, Jacobs's *Blonde Cobra* provides an alluring portrait of the improvisational talents of a great experimental performer. **MS**

The Cool World Shirley Clarke, 1963

U.S. (Wiseman) 125m BW
Producer Frederick Wiseman
Screenplay Shirley Clarke, Carl Lee, Robert
Rossen, from novel and play by
Warren Miller Photography Baird Bryant
Music Mal Waldron Cast Hampton Clanton,
Yolanda Rodríguez, Bostic Felton,
Gary Bolling, Carl Lee, Clarence Williams,
Gloria Foster, Georgia Burke

"When I got to Hollywood, all the movie moguls claimed to be astounded by the reality of my films. How did I do it? And I'd say, 'Well, it wasn't hard to make Harlem look like Harlem.'" This was how writer and director Shirley Clarke described the response of mainstream Hollywood moviemakers to her independently made "fictional documentary," *The Cool World*. A radical and rarely screened classic of 1960s American experimental cinema, the film combines real locations, a loose narrative, naturalistic acting, and highly expressive editing and cinematography in a raw, unflinching look at the power struggles and casual violence of Harlem's street gangs.

Based on a play by Warren Miller and Robert Rossen (which was in turn adapted from Miller's best-selling novel), and produced by acclaimed documentary filmmaker Frederick Wiseman (four years before his own directorial debut, the 1967 film *Titticut Follies*), *The Cool World* boasts a powerful jazz soundtrack by one-time Billie Holiday accompanist Mal Waldon. The starkness of the music serves to make the already depressed living conditions seem all the more rough and unkind. Along with the score, it is *The Cool World*'s unforgettable images that led film critic Judith Christ to describe it as a "loud, long and powerful cry of outrage at the world society has created for Harlem youngsters, and at the human condition in the slum ghetto." Find a copy somewhere, somehow—you won't regret it. **SJS**

☞Please do not reveal the middle of this picture! *Jerry's a measley chemistry prof who invents the greatest drink since Dracula discovered bloody marys.*

PRODUCED PICTURES presents **JERRY LEWIS** as
'THE NUTTY PROFESSOR'
(A Jerry Lewis Production)

☞ ☞ What does he become? What kind of monster? ☜ ☜

STELLA STEVENS DEL MOORE · KATHLEEN FREEMAN · ERNEST D. GLUCKSMAN
JERRY LEWIS · BILL RICHMOND · JERRY LEWIS · A Paramount Release

U.S. (Jerry Lewis, Paramount) 107m
Technicolor **Producer** Ernest D. Glucksman,
Arthur P. Schmidt **Screenplay** Jerry Lewis
and Bill Richmond **Photography** W. Wallace
Kelley **Music** Louis Y. Brown, Walter Scharf
Cast Jerry Lewis, Stella Stevens, Del Moore,
Kathleen Freeman, Med Flory,
Norman Alden, Howard Morris, Elvia Allman,
Milton Frome, Buddy Lester, Marvin Kaplan,
David Landfield, Skip Ward,
Julie Parrish, Henry Gibson

*"If a man with an ulcer
and a splinter in his
finger and a nail in his
foot was then struck by
lightning, if you could
say that man was not
hurt, then yes, you could
say I'm not hurt."*

Julius Kelp
(Jerry Lewis)

i

In 2003, Lewis voiced the part of the
father of Professor John I.Q. Frink, Jr.,
The Simpsons' own nutty professor.

The Nutty Professor Jerry Lewis, 1963

A skit on the Dr. Jekyll/Mr. Hyde story, *The Nutty Professor* (as Eddie Murphy later discovered) could only be made by someone who wasn't as secure in the affections of the audience as he had been in the previous decade. In 1963, it was read as a strange summation of the Martin-and-Lewis films, with infantile comic Jerry Lewis proving that he didn't need a smooth straight man because he could play both roles, and the Hyde figure of swinger "Buddy Love" seen as a nasty caricature of Dino. Actually, Buddy plays more like Dean Martin's Rat Pack padrone, Frank Sinatra, and what Lewis was really doing was presenting his own showbiz dark side, emerging from the cocoon of his sweet, child-pleasing but adult-irritating comic persona. The Jekyll equivalent, Julius Kelp, is buck-toothed in an ironic nod to Fredric March's 1932 Hyde makeup, and speaks with the strangled Lewis whine that makes nonfans want to kill him. Allowing for a near-masochist series of humiliations, Kelp is picked on by the dean, football players, muscle men at a gym (Richard Kiel, another human cartoon, has a tiny cameo), and his students, exciting the sympathy only of lovely blonde student Stella Purdy (Stella Stevens).

Murphy's Buddy Love avenges wrongs done to his Sherman Klump, but Lewis's Buddy despises his alter ego and makes a play for Stella in such an unpleasant manner that he becomes the worst of the series of bullies who have picked on Kelp. From the wonderfully colored expressionist parody of the traditional Jekyll-and-Hyde transformation, in which Kelp turns into a series of ever more grotesque Hyde types before becoming the "swingingest" Buddy, through to Buddy's rise to power at the local happening place, the Purple Pit, *The Nutty Professor* is among the most uncomfortable of American comedies. Unlike Jekyll, Kelp learns his lesson, but not before he has had to accept that he has a monster inside him. The finale, in which Love transforms into Kelp in front of the whole campus, is dead serious, and as devastating as Cliff Robertson's regression to imbecility in the last reel of *Charly* (1968). **KN**

The Great Escape John Sturges, 1963

U.S. (Mirisch) 172m Color DeLuxe
Producer John Sturges Screenplay James
Clavell, W.R. Burnett, from book by Paul
Brickhill Photography Daniel L. Fapp
Music Elmer Bernstein Cast Steve
McQueen, James Garner, Richard
Attenborough, James Donald, Charles
Bronson, Donald Pleasence, James Coburn,
Hannes Messemer, David McCallum, Gordon
Jackson, John Leyton, Angus Lennie, Nigel
Stock, Robert Graf, Jud Taylor Oscar
nomination Ferris Webster (editing)

A terrific war film boasting an all-star cast from director John Sturges, *The Great Escape* remains as entertaining, moving, and thrilling now as when it was first released in 1963.

Nearly every scene is a classic, as the American and British prisoners of war plot to escape from their camp using three tunnels they have dug named Tom, Dick, and Harry. The potential escapees include: Richard Attenborough and Gordon Jackson as two of the British "stiff upper lip" officers planning the getaway; Charles Bronson, the tunneler afraid of enclosed spaces; Donald Pleasance, the forger with diminishing eyesight; James Garner, the man who can scrounge just about anything from the guards and fellow prisoners; and, of course, Steve McQueen as Hilts, a seasoned escapee dubbed "the cooler king" following his solitary confinement every time his escape attempts fail and he is recaptured.

An epic much like Sturges's picture from 1960, *The Magnificent Seven*, (three of that film's cast also appear here: McQueen, Bronson, and James Coburn), this heroic adventure, based on the novel by Paul Brickhill, is backed by a memorable score by Elmer Bernstein that beautifully punctuates every fantastic moment. **JB**

ℹ

Charles Bronson genuinely suffered from claustrophobia—an affliction that dated to his time as a coal miner.

Méditerranée Jean-Daniel Pollet & Volker Schlöndorff, 1963

France (Les Films du Losange) 45m Color
Language French Producer Barbet
Schroeder Screenplay Philippe Sollers
Photography Jean-Daniel Pollet, Jean-
Jacques Rochut Music Antoine Duhamel

Jean-Daniel Pollet's forty-five-minute *Méditerranée*, shot in 1963 and first shown publicly four years later, is the most influential of his experimental films. Its impact on Jean-Luc Godard's 1963 film *Contempt* is striking, and one reason why it remains so impressive as a minimalist tour de force is that Pollet was able to spend so much time editing it. Accompanied by an evocative text written by Philippe Sollers and a haunting score by Antoine Duhamel, who also wrote the music for Godard's 1965 film *Pierrot le Fou*, the footage shot in various countries and of various subjects around the Mediterranean—a Sicilian garden, a Greek temple, a fisherman, a young girl on an operating table—reappears throughout the film, each time in a separate order and for different durations.

Méditerranée inspired one of Godard's most poetic critical texts for the French film journal *Cahiers du Cinéma*, written in 1964 but published in 1967, in which he wrote, "In this banal series of 16mm images over which breathes the ineffable spirit of 70mm, it is up to us to discover the space which only the cinema can transform into lost time . . . or rather the contrary. . . . [F]or here are smooth, round shots abandoned on the screen like pebbles on the beach." **JRos**

1963

Yukinojo henge Kon Ichikawa, 1963
An Actor's Revenge

Japan (Daiei) 113m Eastmancolor
Language Japanese Producer Masaichi
Nagata Screenplay Daisuke Itô, Teinosuke
Kinugasa, Natto Wada, from novel by
Otokichi Mikami Photography Setsuo
Kobayashi Music Yasushi Akutagawa
Cast Kazuo Hasegawa, Fujiko Yamamoto,
Ayako Wakao, Eiji Funakoshi, Narutoshi
Hayashi, Eijirô Yanagi, Chûsha Ichikawa,
Ganjiro Nakamura, Saburo Date, Jun
Hamamura, Kikue Môri, Masayoshi Kikuno,
Raizô Ichikawa, Shintarô Katsu,
Yutaka Nakayama

An Actor's Revenge is one of the most outrageously entertaining Japanese films ever produced. At the time it was made, director Kon Ichikawa was out of favor with his studio, as his last two films had lost money. By way of punishment he was assigned the task of making a film to mark the 300th screen role of legendary actor Kazuo Hasegawa. This was to be a remake of Hasegawa's most popular film, a creaky old melodrama called *The Revenge of Yukinojo*—and Hasegawa would reprise his double role as a transvestite kabuki actor who avenges the death of his parents, and as the thief who helps him. When Hasegawa first played this swashbuckling double role he was twenty-seven; at the time of the remake, he was fifty-five.

Far from trying to tone down the project's improbabilities and absurdities, Ichikawa gleefully plays up everything artificial and theatrical about the story, unpredictably switching tone and idiom, drawing on his cartoonist's background to throw in thought bubbles, blatantly fake sets, anomalous music, and distorted visuals. The conventions of kabuki theater are affectionately parodied, with ultrastylized lighting and horizontal wipes across the CinemaScope screen. And Ichikawa makes the most of the plot's rich opportunities for sexual ambiguity: At one point Hasegawa as a man watches himself as a man-playing-a-woman making love to a woman. **PK**

The Haunting Robert Wise, 1963

In 1959, acclaimed American novelist Shirley Jackson published *The Haunting of Hill House*. Since then it has been widely praised as one of the most frightening tales ever committed to paper. Three years later, while he was wrapping up his work on *West Side Story* (1961), director Robert Wise chose this story as the one he would adapt for the big screen to honor the memory of his former mentor, Val Lewton—producer on such memorable low-budget horror flicks as *Cat People* (1942), *The Seventh Victim*, and *I Walked with a Zombie* (both 1943). The result, *The Haunting*, is considered by a great many critics, aficionados, and casual fans of the horror genre to be one of the scariest films of all time—if not the scariest. In 2009, Martin Scorsese was asked to compile a list of his favorite horror films; *The Haunting* came out on top.

In an extremely creepy prologue we learn the troubled history of Hill House—built by a stern, heartless man named Hugh Crain eighty years earlier, the residence saw the mysterious deaths of no fewer than four women since that time. We then meet Eleanor Lance (Julie Harris), a lonely and repressed woman in her mid-thirties who jumps at the chance to partake in a psychic experiment arranged by one Dr. John Markway (Richard Johnson), an anthropologist who seeks scientific evidence of paranormal activity. After arriving at Hill House, Eleanor meets Dr. Markway (to whom she is instantly attracted), Luke Sanderson (Russ Tamblyn), skeptical nephew of the current landlord, and Theodora—"just Theodora" (Claire Bloom)—an artist, psychic, and (it is strongly suggested) lesbian with an apparent interest in getting her new roommate to open up.

Shortly thereafter, the house begins making its presence felt—strange banging noises in the middle of the night, inexplicable cold spots, and a famously frightening scene in which Eleanor discovers that she has been holding hands with no one. As Mrs. Sanderson [Fay Compton], Luke's aunt, observes, with chilling understatement, "The dead are not quiet in Hill House."

It becomes increasingly clear that Eleanor is the primary target of Hill House's attention—either that or she herself is somehow responsible for the haunting. ("Supposing it is in my imagination," she asks Dr. Markway at one point. "The knocking, the voices. Everything! Every cursed bit of the haunting.") When Dr. Markway's wife shows up unexpectedly, Eleanor's anticipated breakdown (chillingly conveyed through Harris's running internal monologue) becomes a reality. Sent away by the others, who fear her complete collapse, she loses control of her car to unseen forces and crashes headlong into a tree, where she dies in the same spot as Hugh Crain's first wife did years earlier.

Making brilliant use of canted frames, mirror reflections, fish-eye lenses, and uncanny sound and image editing, Wise succeeds both in bringing Hill House to life and in making ambiguous the true source of the threat. Do not watch this one alone! **SJS**

G.B. (Argyle, MGM) 112m BW
Producer Denis Johnson, Robert Wise
Screenplay Nelson Gidding, from novel by
Shirley Jackson **Photography** Davis Boulton
Music Humphrey Searle **Cast** Julie Harris,
Claire Bloom, Richard Johnson, Russ
Tamblyn, Fay Compton, Rosalie Crutchley,
Lois Maxwell, Valentine Dyall, Diane Clare,
Ronald Adam

"It was an evil house from the beginning— a house that was born bad."

**Dr. John Markway
(Richard Johnson)**

i

Theodora's distinctive bohemian attire was created by British fashion guru Mary Quant.

G.B. (Danjaq, Eon) 112m Technicolor **Producer** Albert R. Broccoli, Harry Saltzman **Screenplay** Richard Maibaum, Paul Dehn, from novel by Ian Fleming **Photography** Ted Moore **Music** John Barry, Monty Norman **Cast** Sean Connery, Honor Blackman, Gert Fröbe, Shirley Eaton, Tania Mallet, Harold Sakata, Bernard Lee, Martin Benson, Cec Linder, Austin Willis, Lois Maxwell, Bill Nagy, Michael Mellinger, Peter Cranwell, Nadja Regin **Oscar** Norman Wanstall (special sound effects)

James Bond: *"Do you expect me to talk?"*

Goldfinger: *"No, Mr. Bond. I expect you to die."*

James Bond (Sean Connery) and Auric Goldfinger (Gert Fröbe)

i

Although many of the locations in the film are American, Sean Connery did not set foot in the U.S. during filming.

Goldfinger Guy Hamilton, 1964

If *Dr. No* (1962) was a sputnik-era Fu Manchu picture and *From Russia with Love* (1963) a Cold War Eric Ambler adventure, *Goldfinger*—the third entry in the Harry Saltzman–Albert Broccoli 007 series—marked the point when the James Bond films became their own genre. The rather brutal wit of the earlier movies is modified in the precredits sequence: Sean Connery's super-agent is first seen wearing a decoy duck on his head, then removes his wetsuit to reveal a perfect tuxedo and disposes of a villain through the old electric-heater-tossed-in-the-bath gambit, delivering another of his pointed epitaph epithets ("shocking").

With a megalomaniac millionaire, Auric Goldfinger (Gert Fröbe), as the chief villain rather than the Soviet SMERSH of the books or the communist-affiliated SPECTRE of the first films, *Goldfinger* spins away from geopolitical realities into a comic-book world, albeit one where the Chinese will lend a nuclear weapon to a bad guy in order to cripple the West's economy. Included in the mix are gold-plated murder victims, impeccably-dressed Korean wrestler minions (Harold Sakata as the bowler-throwing Oddjob), improbably-named heroines (Honor Blackman as Pussy Galore), high-tech torture by laser beam, and a scheme not to rob Fort Knox but to irradiate it for centuries—thus increasing the net value of the villain's own gold stocks. All of the vintage 007 ingredients are shaken not stirred here: a belting John Barry theme tune delivered by Shirley Bassey ("Go-o-o-o-ldfinger . . . he's the man, the man with the Midas touch, a spider's touch . . ."), the gadget-packed Aston Martin with its bulletproof shield and passenger-side ejector seat (inspiration for the first great best-selling movie tie-in toy), and the vast Ken Adam sets (note Goldfinger's lair with the model of Fort Knox under glass as a huge coffee table, and the poison gas vents—a big room designed to be used only once). In addition, one finds the residual Ian Fleming suspicion that a person is contemptible if he has a foreign accent and cheats at golf, and the touchingly macho notion that a clinch in the hay with Sean Connery is enough to persuade Pussy to change not only sides but sexual orientation. Ever since, the series has been recycling. **KN**

My Fair Lady George Cukor, 1964

U.S. (Warner Bros.) 170m Technicolor
Producer Jack L. Warner Screenplay Alan
Jay Lerner, from the play Pygmalion by
George Bernard Shaw Photography Harry
Stradling Sr. Music Frederick Loewe
Cast Audrey Hepburn, Rex Harrison, Stanley
Holloway, Wilfrid Hyde-White, Gladys
Cooper, Jeremy Brett, Theodore Bikel, Mona
Washbourne Oscars Jack L. Warner (best
picture), George Cukor (director), Rex
Harrison (actor), Gene Allen, Cecil Beaton,
George James Hopkins (art direction), Harry
Stradling Sr. (photography), Cecil Beaton
(costume), André Previn (music), George
Groves (sound) Oscar nominations Alan Jay
Lerner (screenplay), Stanley Holloway (actor
in support role), Gladys Cooper (actress in
support role), William H. Ziegler (editing)

My Fair Lady is a lumbering, airy musical, a strange compromise between Broadway and Hollywood spectacle—and a true artifact of the mid-1960s, when the studio system and its veteran professionals were floundering in the face of a new world and new ways of making movies. Yet, for all its dead time and cavernous space—André Téchiné, then a young Cahiers du Cinéma modernist, admired its "astonishing vacuum"—the basic story (from George Bernard Shaw's Pygmalion) is so undeniably affecting as to constitute a veritable modern myth.

At its center is a hate-turned-to-love match that is hard to beat: Rex Harrison as the grumpy linguist Henry Higgins and Audrey Hepburn as Eliza Dolittle, the street urchin whom he picks for his "social experiment." We empathize with Eliza at every step of her trial—when she is a pauper resisting Higgins's brutal training, when she is a collaborator slowly falling in love, and finally when she has become a resplendent "lady" fighting off superficial suitors.

George Cukor's gay sensibility was attuned to the unlikely alchemy of this star duo, as well as the reserves of glamor at his disposal (Cecil Beaton worked on costumes and art direction). And the songs are irresistible. **AM**

Il deserto rosso Michelangelo Antonioni, 1964
The Red Desert

Italy / France (Federiz, Duemila, Franco Riz)
120m Technicolor Language Italian
Producer Tonino Cervi, Angelo Rizzoli
Screenplay Michelangelo Antonioni, Tonino
Guerra Photography Carlo Di Palma
Music Giovanni Fusco, Vittorio Gelmetti
(electronic music) Cast Monica Vitti, Richard
Harris, Carlo Chionetti, Xenia Valderi, Rita
Renoir, Lili Rheims, Aldo Grotti, Valerio
Bartoleschi, Emanuela Paola Carboni,
Bruno Borghi, Beppe Conti, Julio
Cotignoli, Giovanni Lolli, Hiram Mino
Madonia, Giuliano Missirini Venice Film
Festival Michelangelo Antonioni (FIPRESCI
award, Golden Lion)

Michelangelo Antonioni's first feature in color remains a high-water mark for using color. To get the precise hues he wanted, Antonioni had entire fields painted. Restored prints make it clear why audiences were so excited by his innovations, not only for his expressive use of color, but also his striking editing. Red Desert comes at the tail end of Antonioni's most fertile period, immediately after his remarkable trilogy The Adventure (1960), The Night (1961), and The Eclipse (1962). Although Red Desert may fall somewhat short of the first and last of these earlier classics, the film's ecological concerns look a lot more prescient today than they seemed at the time of its initial release.

Monica Vitti plays a neurotic married woman (Giuliana) attracted to industrialist Richard Harris. Antonioni does eerie, memorable work with the industrial shapes and colors that surround her, shown alternately as threatening and beautiful. Like any self-respecting Antonioni heroine, she is looking for love and meaning—and finds sex. In one sequence a postcoital melancholy is strikingly conveyed via an expressionist use of color, following Giuliana's shifting moods.

The film's most spellbinding sequence depicts a pantheistic, utopian fantasy of innocence, which the heroine recounts to her ailing son, implicitly offering a beautiful girl and a beautiful sea as an alternative to the troubled woman and the industrial red desert of the title. **JRos**

1964

Suna no onna Hiroshi Teshigahara, 1964
Woman in the Dunes

Japan (Teshigahara, Toho) 123m BW
Language Japanese Producer Kiichi
Ichikawa, Tadashi Oono Screenplay Kôbô
Abe, from his novel Photography Hiroshi
Segawa Music Tôru Takemitsu Cast Eiji
Okada, Kyôko Kishida, Hiroko Ito, Koji
Mitsui, Sen Yano, Kinzo Sekiguchi
Oscar nominations Japan (best foreign
language film), Hiroshi Teshigahara (director)
Cannes Film Festival Hiroshi Teshigahara
(special jury prize)

Hiroshi Teshigahara's strange existential parable *Woman in the Dunes* strikes an unusual balance between realism and metaphor. An entomologist (Eiji Okada) gathering insects on the beach accepts an invitation of hospitality from a mysterious woman (Kyôko Kishida). But he quickly finds himself trapped like one of his collections in the woman's home, built at the bottom of a sandpit, where the incessantly creeping crystals of sand can only be slowed through constant shoveling.

Part neofeminist exercise, part political treatise, part survival tale, *Woman in the Dunes* adds up to both more and less than its premise. Okada can't escape the pit without inviting disaster, but why build a home in a sandpit in the first place? Kishida offers sexual rewards for Okada's labor, but how much of this is just her method of staving off loneliness? Does *Woman in the Dunes* mock domesticity, praise it, or depict it as a Sisiphisian horror? Teshigahara's film doesn't offer answers. It does, however, offer some remarkable sand photography. Like the film itself, the dunes captured by Hiroshi Segawa's cinematography frequently shift, slide, sink, and sift to where you least expect it. JKl

Tini zabutykh predkiv Sergei Parajanov, 1964
Shadows of Forgotten Ancestors

U.S.S.R. (Dovzhenko) 97m Sovcolor
Language Ukrainian Screenplay Ivan
Chendej, from story by Mikhaylo
Mikhaylovich Koysyubinskiy
Photography Viktor Bestayev, Yuri Ilyenko
Music Miroslav Skorik Cast Ivan
Mikolajchuk, Larisa Kadochnikova, Tatyana
Bestayeva, Spartak Bagashvili, Nikolai Grinko,
Leonid Yengibarov, Nina Alisova, Aleksandr
Gaj, Neonila Gnepovskaya, A. Raydanov,
I. Dzyura, V. Glyanko

Adapted from Mikhaylo Koysyubinskiy's novel, Sergei Paradjanov's merging of myth, history, poetry, ethnography, dance, and ritual is one of the supreme works of the Soviet sound cinema, and even subsequent Paradjanov features have failed to dim its intoxicating splendors.

Set in the harsh and beautiful Carpathian Mountains, the film tells of a doomed love between a couple belonging to feuding families, Ivan (Ivan Mikolajchuk) and Marichka (Larisa Kadochnikova), and of Ivan's life and marriage after Marichka's death. The plot is affecting, but it serves Paradjanov mainly as an armature to support the exhilarating rush of his lyrical camera movements (executed by master cinematographer Yuri Ilyenko), his innovative use of nature and interiors, his deft juggling of folklore and fancy in relation to pagan and Christian rituals, and his astonishing handling of color and music.

A film worthy of Aleksandr Dovzhenko, whose poetic vision of Ukrainian life is frequently alluded to, *Shadows of Our Forgotten Ancestors* also evokes fairy tales in general and even at times some of Walt Disney's animated representations of their settings, such as the cottage in *Snow White and the Seven Dwarfs* (1937). The visceral physicality of many other shots is no less unmistakable, exemplified by a startling one early on which places the camera on top of a just-chopped tree—taking the viewer with it on its vertiginous plunge toward the ground. JRos

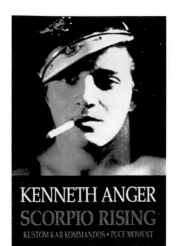

Scorpio Rising Kenneth Anger, 1964

One of the most influential of all "underground" films, this half-hour epic spells out its title and director's name in studs on the back of a black leather biker jacket, then plays a jukebox-worth of pop hits from the late 1950s and early 1960s (such as Elvis Presley's "Devil in Disguise," the Angels'"My Boyfriend's Back," and Ray Charles's "Hit the Road, Jack") over images mostly shot in a Brooklyn biker garage. Objects of romantic fetishization fill the camera screen: black leather, hair and oil grease, naked torsos, gleaming chrome, toys and motorbikes, images from comic books and movies (stills of James Dean, TV snips of Marlon Brando in the 1953 film *The Wild One*), rings and insignia, and muscular Tom-of-Finland-look youths lolling pinup style in tight jeans and peaked caps.

Without *Scorpio Rising*, Martin Scorsese would not use pop music the way he does in *Mean Streets* (1973), David Lynch couldn't have found the disturbing undercurrents in Bobby Vinton's song "Blue Velvet" (which is also used here), and action movies wouldn't include homoerotic strapping-on-the-weapons montages. Most controversial, to the extent of prompting legal action, is the witty but deliberately provocative juxtaposition of the Crystals'"He's a Rebel" with found footage from some Sunday school version of *The Life of Christ* intercut, putting forward the heretical if not sacrilegious notion of the Disciples as a strutting, gay-tinged youth gang out to overthrow the established order even as the lyrics provide a surprisingly sermonly reading ("That's no reason why I shouldn't give him all my love").

The passion play continues under Claudine Clark's "Party Lights" as Christ's life is intercut with the sort of swastika-swathed biker Walpurgis Night (the eve of May Day) later hymned by Roger Corman's *The Wild Angels* (1966). As with all of Kenneth Anger's films, the magical is never far away, with a purple-veiled skeleton representing Death.

However, this is a far less impervious piece than most of his works, oddly accessible on an MTV level in its demonstration that songs don't have to be performed on camera (as in the classical Hollywood musical) to work in the context of cinema. They can be illustrated, undercut, and lent greater depth by apt or even wildly inapt images. **KN**

U.S. (Puck) 30m Color **Screenplay** Kenneth Anger **Photography** Kenneth Anger **Cast** Bruce Byron

"I compare my films to poems—I consider myself a poet of films."

Kenneth Anger, 2012

1964

i

Kenneth Anger's $8,000 budget for the film had to be doubled in order to pay for the rights to all the songs.

Marnie Alfred Hitchcock, 1964

U.S. (Geoffrey-Stanley, Universal) 130m
Technicolor **Producer** Alfred Hitchcock
Screenplay Jay Presson Allen, from novel by
Winston Graham **Photography** Robert
Burks **Music** Bernard Herrmann **Cast** Tippi
Hedren, Sean Connery, Diane Baker, Martin
Gabel, Louise Latham, Bob Sweeney, Milton
Selzer, Mariette Hartley, Alan Napier, Bruce
Dern, Henry Beckman, S. John Launer,
Edith Evanson, Meg Wyllie

"I would say Marnie *isn't so much successful as a thriller, but as a tender and unconventional love story . . . on this level, it makes compelling viewing."*

Pauline Richardson,
New Daily, 1964

🛈

Hitchcock and Hedren fell out so badly it was rumored that he ended up directing her via intermediaries.

After her debut in the 1963 film *The Birds,* Hitchcock once again cast Tippi Hedren, this time as a beautiful kleptomaniac whom we first see striding down a railroad station platform. In a hotel she washes her hair, rinsing out the black dye to become blonde again. We discover that Marnie has recently robbed her employer, and gradually we realize something is deeply wrong with her. She gets hysterical attacks when she sees the color red, and a visit to her mother reveals an unloving relationship. Then Marnie is hired by handsome businessman Mark Rutland (Sean Connery). In a brilliantly suspenseful scene, Marnie robs his safe while a cleaning woman mops the floor. Marnie sees the woman before she can be discovered, and creeps past her in stockinged feet, only for a shoe to drop out of her pocket. But the cleaning woman doesn't turn round; at the end of the scene we discover she is deaf.

Mark soon tracks Marnie down and offers her a choice: marriage or the police. On their honeymoon cruise Marnie tells him she can't bear men touching her, but in an uncomfortable scene he forces himself upon her. Mark tries to psychoanalyze his bride, educating himself from a book entitled *Sexual Abberations of the Criminal Female,* but Marnie's response is to try and rob him again. This time Mark forces her to go with him on a visit to her mother, and there the secret of Marnie's condition is traced back to a childhood trauma.

Though full of deft and seductive Hitchcockian touches, *Marnie* is a strange and unsettling film, in part because of Mark's character. He professes love of Marnie and tries to help her overcome her neurosis, yet his conduct is full of barely suppressed sadism and he treats her like a caged animal. As Marnie says, "I'm just something you caught." The scene in which he in effect rapes her on the honeymoon caused discord between Hitchcock and his writer, Evan Hunter, who wanted to drop it on the grounds that it made Mark unsympathetic. Hitchcock refused and the script was finished by Jay Presson Allen. **EB**

The Masque of the Red Death Roger Corman, 1964

G.B. (Alta Vista, AIP, Anglo-Amalgamated) 89m Pathécolor **Producer** Roger Corman **Screenplay** Charles Beaumont, R. Wright Campbell, from the stories "The Masque of the Red Death" and "Hop-Frog" by Edgar Allan Poe **Photography** Nicolas Roeg **Music** David Lee **Cast** Vincent Price, Hazel Court, Jane Asher, David Weston, Nigel Green, Patrick Magee, Paul Whitsun-Jones, Robert Brown, Julian Burton, David Davies, Skip Martin, Gaye Brown, Verina Greenlaw, Doreen Dawn, Brian Hewlett

As Roger Corman's series of Vincent Price–starring, Edgar Allan Poe–based widescreen gothics advanced in America from T*he Fall of the House of Usher* (1960) to *The Raven* (1963), each installment became more self-referential and comic in tone. However, when production of the series shifted in 1964 to Britain, the tone changed radically for two final masterpieces, the baroque *Masque of the Red Death* and the chilling *Tomb of Ligeia* (1965).

Masque casts Price ideally as Prince Prospero, an Italian Satanist who hosts a decadent masked ball as the plague ravages the countryside. There's a youth-themed plot about an innocent abducted girl (Jane Asher) and her revolutionary love interest, but here the emphasis is on corrupt luxury, with Price twitching his mustache and eyebrows with elegant, weary cynicism even as Death itself invades his ball and spreads the contagion in a Bergmanesque dance of death. Cinematographer Nicolas Roeg is encouraged to add his own flourishes, including long tracks through a succession of differently colored rooms (an image from the story), with the shock effects having a daring sensuality. Patrick Magee is dressed as an ape and burned alive by a dwarf jester (an import from Poe's "Hop-Frog") and Hazel Court brands her swanny cleavage in tribute to Satan before being murdered by a swooping falcon. **KN**

1964

Prima della rivoluzione Bernardo Bertolucci, 1964
Before the Revolution

Italy (Cincriz, Iride) 115m BW **Language** Italian **Screenplay** Gianni Amico, Bernardo Bertolucci **Photography** Aldo Scavarda **Music** Ennio Morricone, Gino Paoli, Aldo Scavarda, Giuseppe Verdi **Cast** Evelina Alpi, Gianni Amico, Adriana Asti, Cecrope Barilli, Francesco Barilli, Amelia Bordi, Salvatore Enrico, Guido Fanti, Iole Lunardi, Antonio Maghenzani, Allen Midgette, Morando Morandini, Goliardo Padova, Cristina Pariset, Ida Pellegri

Bernardo Bertolucci's *Before the Revolution* is an astonishing film. When one realizes that the director was only twenty-two years old at the time it was made, it becomes miraculous. A transposition of Stendhal's *La Chartreuse de Parme* to the modern day, this is the story of a young man, Fabrizio (Francesco Barilli), and his hopeless love for his aunt Gina (Adriana Asti), who is ten years his senior.

This is not, as the title might lead you to expect, a militant story of heroic revolutionary struggle, but an elegy for those bourgeois lives doomed because they take place before the revolution. The story is simple: Fabrizio, on the edge of adulthood, has a life mapped out according to the middle-class norms of his city. Then the death by drowning of his friend Agostino (Allen Midgette) causes him to call his future into doubt as he starts a tempestuous affair with Gina. The final section of the film, which contrasts the future sketched by Fabrizio's Communist teacher and Gina's friend who is about to lose his hereditary estate, makes clear that Fabrizio himself can live neither in the future nor in the past, but only in an uneasy present. *Before the Revolution* is a perfect portrait of the generation who were to embrace revolt in the late 1960s, and a stunning portrait of Parma—Bertolucci's own city. **CM**

Dr. Strangelove or: How I Learned to Stop Worrying and Love the Bomb Stanley Kubrick, 1964

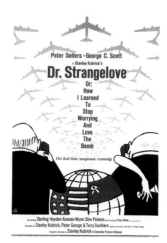

G.B. (Hawk) 93m BW
Producer Stanley Kubrick, Victor Lyndon
Screenplay Terry Southern, Stanley Kubrick,
from the novel *Red Alert* by Peter George
Photography Gilbert Taylor **Music** Laurie
Johnson **Cast** Peter Sellers, George C. Scott,
Sterling Hayden, Keenan Wynn, Slim Pickens,
Peter Bull, James Earl Jones, Tracy Reed, Jack
Creley, Frank Berry, Robert O'Neil, Glenn
Beck, Roy Stephens, Shane Rimmer, Hal Galili
Oscar nominations Stanley Kubrick
(director), Stanley Kubrick (best picture),
Stanley Kubrick, Peter George, Terry
Southern (screenplay) Peter Sellers (actor)

"Gentlemen, you can't fight in here! This is the War Room!"

**President Merkin Muffley
(Peter Sellers)**

ℹ

Sellers's fee was $1 million, 55 percent of the budget—leading Kubrick to quip: "I got three for the price of six."

Dr. Strangelove is a brilliant black comedy that works as political satire, suspense farce, and cautionary tale of technology running away with us. When a fanatical U.S. general launches a nuclear attack on the U.S.S.R. the President has his hands full recalling bombers and calming Russians while contending with his advisers and a twisted scientist. The plot came from a serious novel by Peter George, published in the United States as *Red Alert* and in the United Kingdom as *Two Hours to Doom*. Kubrick loved it but thought people were so overwhelmed by the threat of annihilation that they were in denial, apathetic to nuclear documentary or drama. So he would surprise audiences into reacting to the prospect of global extermination with outrageously funny and provocative cartoon tactics.

Kubrick and cowriter Terry Southern created a cast of grotesques whose absurd fixations, by their incongruity, play up the realism against which they are set (and which is enhanced by Gilbert Taylor's outstanding black-and-white cinematography). The information about a doomsday device is factual, as are the Strategic Air Command operations and the B-52 crew's procedures. The computers that take the situation beyond human intervention have only become more capable. Be afraid. Be very afraid.

There are just three locations, each suffering a failure to communicate. At Burpelson Air Force Base, maniacal General Jack D. Ripper (Sterling Hayden) circumvents fail-safe protocol and orders a bomber wing to nuke the "Russkies," taking appalled RAF officer Lionel Mandrake (Peter Sellers) captive. Aboard the B-52 code-named Leper Colony, dogged Major T.J. "King" Kong (Slim Pickens) and his crew suffer radio failure and are oblivious to frantic efforts to recall them. In the War Room at The Pentagon—an awesome set by production designer Ken Adam—President Merkin Muffley (Sellers), rampant General Buck Turgidson (George C. Scott), Soviet Ambassador de Sadesky (Peter Bull), and demented Dr. Strangelove (Sellers again, in a nod to *Metropolis*'s mad scientist Rotwang) are gathered in a futile attempt to stop Armageddon.

Sellers's sidesplitting three performances are legend but the entire ensemble gives a masterclass in exaggerated, perfectly timed posturing. Two images are unforgettable—Kong astride the H-bomb, yee-hawing all the way down, and demented Dr. Strangelove, unable to stop his mechanical arm from flying into the Nazi salute and throttling himself. Every viewing is a reminder the film is stuffed with hilarious dialogue, and President Muffley on the hot line to Moscow breaking it to the Soviet Premier that one of his base commanders "went and did a silly thing" remains a classic monologue. Kubrick would return to the potential menace of computer dependency in *2001: A Space Odyssey* (1968), to institutional and political violence in *A Clockwork Orange* (1971), and to the savage, surreal madness of war in *Full Metal Jacket* (1987). But he never made us laugh this much in any other film. **AE**

Deus e o diabo na terra do sol

Black God, White Devil Glauber Rocha, 1964

After attending an early screening of Glauber Rocha's *Black God, White Devil*, one Brazilian film critic was overheard marveling, "Oh my God, Eisenstein's been reborn . . . and he's Brazilian!" Born in Bahia, the Brazilian state known as ground zero for Afro-Brazilian culture, Glauber grew up fascinated by mysticism and American Westerns. In his early twenties, he moved to Rio de Janeiro, where he quickly fell in with a core of young cinephiles who would found the influential *Cinema Novo* movement.

Drawn like so many of his generation to radical politics, Rocha in *Black God, White Devil* sought to explore the connections between historical change and violence. Here, he focuses on examples of popular rebellion in Brazil's backlands. After killing his abusive employer, Manoel (Geraldo Del Rey) flees with his wife Rosa (Yoná Magalhães) into the arid backlands known as the *sertao*. They first meet up with Sebastiao (Lidio Silva), a black mystic who preaches that a millennial upheaval is coming that will "turn the sea into the land and the land into the sea." Sebastiao is eventually killed by Rosa, and his followers are dispatched by the rifle of Antonio das Mortes (Maurício do Valle), a mysterious figure hired by the Church and large landowners. Next, Manoel and Rosa meet up with Corisco (Othon Bastos), the blond "devil" who's the last surviving *cangaceiro*, wildly dressed bandits who took on a certain Robin Hood aura in popular consciousness. Eventually, das Mortes catches up with him too, but Manoel and Rosa keep running, still rebellious but now aware that neither banditry nor mysticism can truly address their needs.

Shot in a harsh black and white that practically makes the screen glow from heat, *Black God, White Devil* alternates frenetic camera movements with dynamic montage sequences, while juxtaposing Villa Lobos with wind, screams, and gunshots. The ultimate effect is a feeling that the film, and the country it's depicting, is about to burst apart; perhaps not unexpectedly, between the completion of the film and its commercial release the Brazilian military staged a coup, establishing a dictatorship that would continue for over twenty years. **RP**

Brazil (New Cinema, Copacabana, Luiz Augusto Mendes) 110m BW **Language** Portuguese **Producer** Luiz Paulino Dos Santos, Luiz Augusto Mendes **Screenplay** Walter Lima Jr., Glauber Rocha, Paulo Gil Soares **Photography** Waldemar Lima **Music** Sérgio Ricardo, Glauber Rocha **Cast** Othon Bastos, Billy Davis, Geraldo Del Rey, Sonia Dos Humildes, Maurício do Valle, João Gama, Mário Gusmão, Yoná Magalhães, Marrom, Antonio Pinto, Maria Olívia Rebouças, Milton Rosa, Regina Rosenburgo, Roque Santos, Lidio Silva

> *"The fusion of European and Afro-Brazilian elements . . . is startlingly original and poetical in conveying the hope and despair of the oppressed."*
>
> Ted Shen,
> *Chicago Reader*, 1985

i

Glauber Rocha was named after the German scientist Johann Rudolf Glauber, discoverer of Sodium Sulfate.

G.B. (Proscenium) 87m BW
Producer Walter Shenson Screenplay Alun
Owen Photography Gilbert Taylor
Music George Harrison, John Lennon,
George Martin, Paul McCartney Cast John
Lennon, Paul McCartney, George Harrison,
Ringo Starr, Wilfrid Brambell, Norman
Rossington, John Junkin, Victor Spinetti,
Anna Quayle, Deryck Guyler, Richard Vernon,
Edward Malin, Robin Ray, Lionel Blair,
Alison Seebohm Oscar nominations Alun
Owen (screenplay), George Martin (music)

"None of us think we're good actors, but we're quite happy with the film considering it's our first. It could have been a lot worse."

George Harrison, 1964

ℹ

The band's name is never actually
mentioned in the film—even though
its working title was *The Beatles*.

A Hard Day's Night Richard Lester, 1964

Famously described by an over-excited *Village Voice* as "the *Citizen Kane* of jukebox movies," Richard Lester's 1964 comedy starring The Beatles and their music may not be quite that (although it is funnier), but it did change the shape of pop music films forever. With a witty, social-realist script by Liverpudlian playwright Alun Owen and traces of Lester's British surrealist influences (he had worked with The Beatles' 1950s comic idols, The Goons), *A Hard Day's Night* takes a day in the life of a hugely successful teen group sensation and turns it into something thrilling. The camera follows The Beatles—who play a recognizable version of themselves—through a typical day of being chased by fans, hanging around, fielding idiotic press questions, and, at the end, actually playing. Lester gave the four members of the band just enough to do, most notably Ringo Starr, whose affecting scene on a canal towpath with a young boy was enhanced by the fact that Starr was monumentally hungover.

Lennon, McCartney, Harrison, and Starr come across as likeable, slightly rebellious, intelligent young men, who, in the tradition of realistic northern England dramas, are down-to-earth, unpretentious, and prone to seeing through the falseness of others ("I fought the war for the likes of you," says a derby-hatted old-timer to Starr, who replies, "I bet you're sorry you won"). This constant rejection of just about everything—TV producers, admen, authority in general—might have aged badly were it not contrasted with the astonishing force and glamor of the band's music. This combination acted exactly as it was intended, as a blast of propaganda not only for The Beatles, but also for the much-vaunted "younger generation." While *A Hard Day's Night* cannot be held directly responsible for inventing the counterculture, ousting old Hollywood, and ending the Vietnam War, it was seen, absorbed, and revered by a host of future artistic talent, particularly in the United States, where that younger generation found the movie genuinely liberating. The songs are great, too. **KK**

1964

Les parapluies de Cherbourg Jacques Demy, 1964
The Umbrellas of Cherbourg

Movie audiences have long turned to musicals as the ultimate form of escapism. Imagine, emotions so strong that mere words can't express them, inspiring characters to burst into song and dance. The characters of Jacques Demy's musical *The Umbrellas of Cherbourg* are no exception, but with this most rapturous of melodramas Demy incorporates song and dance in the service not of escape but of realism. The effect is as riveting as it is profoundly moving.

Yet *The Umbrellas of Cherbourg* further deviates from most musicals in the sense that all its dialogue is sung, matched to Michel Legrand's wall-to-wall score. The effect is both hypnotic and beautiful. The nonstop music draws us even deeper into the devastating story, and the incessant singing elicits wonderfully open and direct performances from the cast. Catherine Deneuve plays Geneviève Emery, a young girl in love with a mechanic named Guy (Nino Castelnuovo). They pledge their undying affection for one another. Then Guy heads off to war and Geneviève discovers she's pregnant. She is persuaded to accept the marriage proposal of a wealthy gem-dealer patron (Marc Michel) of her mother's shop, whose love for Geneviève is so strong he promises to raise the child as his own.

Geneviève's emotional dilemma is, of course, played for maximum pathos, and when she only hears back once from her true love Guy your heart breaks along with hers. Yet Demy never lets the film lapse into easy sentimentality. The final scene is immensely moving, but not manipulatively so, and although the music does its job, directing and reflecting the feelings of the characters, it never comes across as overly sentimental. The sad sense of inevitability that pervades *The Umbrellas of Cherbourg* at least partly accounts for its immense appeal. Demy, like most people, understood that in the real world not all stories have happy endings, and thanks to his great cast (especially the beautiful and extremely convincing Deneuve) he was deft enough to convey that realization with immense emotional honesty, magic, and maturity. **JKl**

France / West Germany (Beta, Madeleine, Parc) 87m Eastmancolor **Language** French **Producer** Mag Bodard **Screenplay** Jacques Demy **Photography** Jean Rabier **Music** Michel Legrand **Cast** Catherine Deneuve, Nino Castelnuovo, Anne Vernon, Marc Michel, Ellen Farner, Mireille Perrey, Jean Champion, Pierre Caden, Jean-Pierre Dorat, Bernard Fradet, Michel Benoist, Philippe Dumat, Dorothée Blank, Jane Carat, Harald Wolff **Oscar nominations** France (best foreign language film), Jacques Demy (screenplay), Michel Legrand, Jacques Demy (music), Michel Legrand (music), Michel Legrand, Jacques Demy (song) **Cannes Film Festival** Jacques Demy (Golden Palm and OCIC award, tied with *Vidas secas*)

> *"I think I will always feel a special relationship with* The Umbrellas of Cherbourg, *because for me it was something very, very special."*

Catherine Deneuve, on her favorite film of her career, 2005

ℹ

Umbrellas forms a romantic trilogy of Demy films with *Lola* (1961) and *The Young Girls of Rochefort* (1967).

Gertrud Carl Theodor Dreyer, 1964

Denmark (Palladium) 119m BW
Language Danish Producer Jørgen
Nielsen Screenplay Carl Theodor
Dreyer, from play by Hjalmar Söderberg
Photography Henning Bendtsen
Music Jørgen Jersild, Grethe Risbjerg
Thomsens Cast Nina Pens Rode, Bendt
Rothe, Ebbe Rode, Baard Owe, Axel Strøbye,
Karl Gustav Ahlefeldt, Vera Gebuhr, Lars
Knutzon, Anna Malberg, Edouard Mielche
Cannes Film Festival Carl Theodor Dreyer
(FIPRESCI award)

In *Gertrud*, his final film, Carl Dreyer brings to its logical culmination the process of fining down, of attenuation, that he had been pursuing for some forty years. It is an old man's film in its sense of quiet renunciation, yet at the same time a very modern one.

Gertrud is adapted from a 1906 play by the Swedish playwright Hjalmar Söderberg, whose heroine is closely based on a woman with whom he'd had a passionate affair. Dreyer's adaptation presents Gertrud as an erotic idealist, a woman who will accept love only on her own exacting, single-minded terms. Three men—her husband, a poet, and a young musician—love her, but because none of them will put his love for her before everything else in his life, she rejects them all, preferring to live celibate in Paris and devote herself to the life of the mind.

Dreyer shoots his film with mesmerizing restraint. Nearly two hours long, it consists of less than ninety shots. For long periods the camera remains motionless in medium shot, observing two people as they talk. The characters, though driven by strong passions, love, and despair, rarely raise their voices. There are few sets and only one exterior scene; decors are pared down to basics. At its premiere in Paris, *Gertrud* was received with uncomprehending hostility by press and public alike. Since then, it has come to be recognized as the last lapidary statement of one of the most individual of filmmakers—a film, like its heroine, to be approached on its own terms. **PK**

i

While the film is largely faithful to the original play, the epilogue was written by Dreyer.

Mary Poppins Robert Stevenson, 1964

U.S. / G.B (Walt Disney) 139m Color
Producer Bill Walsh, Walt Disney
Screenplay Stirling Bill Walsh, Don
DaGradi, from the novel by P.L. Travers
Photography Edward Colman
Music Richard M Sherman, Robert B
Sherman Cast Steve Julie Andrews, Dick Van
Dyke, David Tomlinson, Glynis Johns,
Hermione Baddeley, Reta Shaw, Karen
Dotrice, Matthew Garber, Elsa Lanchester,
Arthur Treacher, Reginald Owen, Ed Wynn,
Jane Darwell Oscars Julie Andrews (actress),
Peter Ellenshaw, Hamilton Luske, Eustace
Lycett (effects), Cotton Warbutton (editing),
Richard M Sherman, Robert B Sherman
(original song), Richard M Sherman,
Robert B Sherman (original music)
Oscar nominations Caroll Clark, William H
Tuntke, Emile Kuri, Hal Gausman
(art direction), Edward Colman
(cinematography), Tony Walton (costume
design), Robert Stevenson (director), Irwin
Kostal (scoring of music), Walt Disney, Bill
Walsh (picture), Robert O Cook (sound), Bill
Walsh, Don DaGradi (adaptation)

As far back as 1938, Walt Disney had been trying to buy the rights to the *Mary Poppins* books. Its author, P.L. Travers, had repeatedly refused his overtures, but Disney persisted—as good an indication as any of Disney's sharp commercial instincts. Having finally secured Travers's permission—with the author retaining script approval rights—Disney turned her work into one of his studio's best-loved classics, and one of its biggest hits.

Set in a stylized version of Edwardian England—and including some groundbreaking sequences combining live action and cell animation—the film features Julie Andrews as the eponymous nanny employed by the affluent Banks family. With the action interspersed with the Sherman Brothers' infectiously catchy songs, it ultimately sees Mary Poppins bring the Banks children closer to their well-meaning but negligent parents, with the help of friends that include the happy-go-lucky chimney sweep Bert (the much maligned, cockney-accented Dick Van Dyke).

Mary Poppins's success lay in attracting the "family audience," a demographic that Hollywood studios feared they had lost to the emergence of television. It was an audience that Julie Andrews would go on to enchant with *The Sound of Music* (1965), which cemented her reputation for wholesome, old-fashioned entertainment. **EL**

Onibaba Kaneto Shindô, 1964
The Demon

Japan (Kindai Eiga Kyokai, Toho,
Tokyo Eiga) 103m BW Language Japanese
Producer Hisao Itoya, Tamotsu Minato,
Setsuo Noto Screenplay Kaneto Shindô
Photography Kiyomi Kuroda Music Hikaru
Hayashi Cast Nobuko Otowa, Jitsuko
Yoshimura, Kei Sato, Jukichi Uno, Taiji
Tonoyama, Someshu Matsumoto,
Kentaro Kaji, Hosui Araya

Kaneto Shindô's *Onibaba* portrays history as a tale of unmitigated horror from the perspective of its losers. In so doing, he makes an allegorical statement about life amid both scarcity and class and gender antagonism, and also reveals the ideological impulses behind the horror genre itself.

The plot centers on two peasants, a mother (Nobuko Otowa) and her daughter-in-law (Jitsuko Yoshimura), who survive a medieval war by killing lost samurai and selling their armor for food. One day a samurai with a frightening mask enters the old woman's hut and asks her to lead him through the surrounding reeds. Obsessed with the desire to see his face, she kills him and, in one of the film's most stunning moments, she removes the mask to see the face of a Japanese A-bomb victim (*hibakusha*).

The old woman begins to wear the mask herself, and in a terrifying scene finds it permanently affixed to her face. The younger woman breaks open the mask with an axe and uncovers the bleeding, tortured face of an alive *hibakusha*, from whom she flees in revulsion. The film ends with the old woman crying, "I am not a demon, I am a human being."

By transforming the demonic mask into a cover for the disfigured face of the *hibakusha*—a group of people who were stigmatized in Japan after World War II—Shindô brilliantly connects generic convention with the all-too-real horrors of his home country. **JKe**

Il vangelo secondo Matteo Pier Paolo Pasolini, 1964
The Gospel According to St. Matthew

This early work by Pier Paolo Pasolini, drawing freely from religious, Marxist, and Neorealist traditions, will forever change your conception of a biblical epic. Pasolini was a film critic, writer, and political theorist before he started making movies, and many of his productions bear the weight of his intellectual ambitions. In this relatively straightforward film set in the landscape of southern Italy, Pasolini uses minimal sets and simple camera setups to create a convincing portrait of the biblical era. Pasolini cast nonprofessional actors—Enrique Irazoqui, who plays Jesus, was a student before getting the part—depicting the disciples as a group of socially committed young men, acting in a revolutionary cause. The youth and inexperience of the actors gives a sense of the tenuous nature of the fledgling Christian movement, as something unsure and as yet unformed; it is as though Pasolini wants to erase 2,000 years of dogma and tradition to examine the gospels anew.

Pasolini draws on other arts to elevate this simply told and acted story into a spiritual realm. Using little dialogue, he places his characters in iconic close-ups that recall medieval religious portraiture. Alternating with the close-ups are medium and long shots that recall the works of Peter Breugel, placing the story of Christ in a teeming, immediate context. Music, ranging from masses by Bach and Mozart to blues recordings, imparts extra meaning—a canny technique to handle the untried cast, which at times seems to be underemoting.

Pasolini succeeds in creating a moving and convincing film of the gospel as well as mounting a Marxist critique of Christianity. Without viscerally and intellectually assaulting the viewer as in his later films, *Gospel* contains many of the ideas of his later works and is a fine introduction to his work. **RH**

France / Italy (Arco, Lux) 137 m BW Language Italian Producer Alfredo Bini Screenplay Pier Paolo Pasolini Photography Tonino Delli Colli Music Luis Enríquez Bacalov Cast Enrique Irazoqui, Margherita Caruso, Susanna Pasolini, Marcello Morante, Mario Socrate, Settimio Di Porto, Alfonso Gatto, Luigi Barbini, Giacomo Morante, Giorgio Agamben, Guido Cerretani, Rosario Migale, Ferruccio Nuzzo, Marcello Galdini, Elio Spaziani Oscar nominations Luigi Scaccianoce (art direction), Danilo Donati (costume), Luis Enríquez Bacalov (music) Venice Film Festival Pier Paolo Pasolini (OCIC award, special jury prize, tied with *Gamlet*, Golden Lion nomination)

1964

"It grips the historical and psychological imagination like no other religious film I have seen."

Alexander Walker,
Evening Standard

ℹ

The movie was filmed in the city of Matera, later used by Mel Gibson for *The Passion of the Christ* (2004).

Obchod na korze Ján Kadár & Elmar Klos, 1965
The Shop on Main Street

Perhaps the most moving drama ever made about the Holocaust, Ján Kadár and Elmar Klos's *The Shop on Main Street* deals with individual morality and responsibility in the context of a "total" society, a theme whose provocation was not lost on official Czech censors. Though it addresses the irreducible human questions raised by the relationship between Jew and Gentile in German-occupied Czechoslovakia, the film discovers a utopian hope for collective happiness in the midst of profound despair. The protagonist, Tono (Jozef Kroner), is a carpenter in a small town whose worst problem is his nagging wife Evelyna (Hana Slivková), who is always pushing him to make more money by collaborating with the Germans like his reptilian brother-in-law Marcus (Frantisek Zvarík).

Finding such hopes of advancement a little appealing, Tono eventually agrees to be appointed "Aryan controller" of a small Jewish shop presided over by a quite old and somewhat senile woman, Mrs. Lautmann (Ida Kaminska). Tono discovers that the shop makes no money and that the widow is supported by the other Jews of the town, who soon hire Tono to look after her. For the first time in his life, Tono must spend time with a Jew, and the odd couple soon become quite close. Then the order goes out for the Jews to pack their belongings for transport to a "labor" camp. At first, Tono tries to force the uncomprehending woman outside to join the other Jews. But she resists, and Tono, confused and panicked, decides to lock her into a closet until the deportation has ended, hoping in the end that they will both be saved. His rough handling of the old woman, however, has killed her. Discovering Mrs. Lautmann's lifeless body, Tono is overwhelmed by guilt. He puts a noose around his head and hangs himself.

Tono is a kind of Everyman who, uninterested in the play of ideologies around him, discovers that circumstances force him to both choose and act. As he acts, he assumes responsibility and, feeling guilt, also has a vision of a community beyond ideology and sectarianism. Beautifully acted and staged, *The Shop on Main Street* is one of the masterpieces of the Czech renaissance. **RBP**

Czechoslovakia (Barrandov) 128m BW **Language** Czech / Slovak **Producer** Jordan Balurov, M. Broz, Frantisek Daniel, Karel Feix, Jaromír Lukás **Screenplay** Ladislav Grosman, Ján Kadár, Elmar Klos **Cast** Ida Kaminska, Jozef Kroner, Hana Slivková, Martin Holly, Adám Matejka, Frantisek Zvarík, Mikulas Ladizinsky, Martin Gregor, Alojz Kramar, Gita Misurova, Frantisek Papp, Helena Zvaríková, Tibor Vadas, Eugen Senaj, Luise Grossova **Oscar** Czechoslovakia (best foreign language film) **Oscar nomination** Ida Kaminska (actress) **Cannes Film Festival** Jozef Kroner, Ida Kaminska (special mention—acting)

"What can I do? What? I'm nobody. A zero."

Tono (Jozef Kroner)

i

The Shop on Main Street was the first Czech/Slovak film to win an Oscar.

U.S. (MGM, Sostar) 197m Metrocolor
Producer Arvid Griffen, David Lean, Carlo
Ponti Screenplay Robert Bolt, from novel by
Boris Pasternak Photography Freddie
Young Music Maurice Jarre Cast Omar
Sharif, Julie Christie, Geraldine Chaplin, Rod
Steiger, Alec Guinness, Tom Courtenay,
Siobhan McKenna, Ralph Richardson, Rita
Tushingham, Jeffrey Rockland, Tarek Sharif,
Bernard Kay, Klaus Kinski, Gérard Tichy, Noel
Willman Oscars Robert Bolt (screenplay),
John Box, Terence Marsh, Dario Simoni (art
direction), Freddie Young (photography),
Phyllis Dalton (costume), Maurice Jarre
(music) Oscar nominations Carlo Ponti
(best picture), David Lean (director), Tom
Courtenay (actor in support role), Norman
Savage (editing), A.W. Watkins, Franklin
Milton (sound) Cannes Film Festival David
Lean, nomination (Golden Palm)

"If people love poetry, they love poets. And nobody loves poetry like a Russian."

Yevgraf Zhivago (Alec Guinness)

🛈

Although panned by critics, the film went on to gross more than all of David Lean's other movies combined.

Doctor Zhivago David Lean, 1965

Perhaps the greatest screen epic ever produced, David Lean's film of Boris Pasternak's novel chronicles the discontents of early twentieth-century Russian society: the disastrous effects of World War I on the country, as well as the revolution that destroyed the old order only to deliver Russia to the agonies of a civil war followed by continuing political turmoil.

Robert Bolt's screenplay judiciously compresses *Doctor Zhivago*'s sprawling story, which is told in flashback from the perspective of the 1930s and a time of continuing economic and social transformation. Yuri Zhivago (Omar Sharif) is a well-born doctor whose avocation is poetry. He marries his childhood sweetheart Tonya (Geraldine Chaplin) before departing for service in the war. There he meets Lara (Julie Christie), the great love of his life, who is married to a prominent revolutionary. After the revolution, Zhivago's family suffers, and he is forced to work as the medical officer for a Bolshevik band in the civil war. Eventually, however, he escapes, only to learn his family has fled to Paris to avoid imprisonment or worse. Finding Lara, the two live together, during which time he writes his best poetry. But the lovers must part, never to see one another again.

Though a poignant love story, with Christie and Sharif effective as an ill-starred couple, *Doctor Zhivago* is perhaps most memorable for its magnificent set pieces—the assault by sword-wielding Cossacks on a group of protestors, the interminable journey by train across the country endured by Zhivago's family, the wintry landscape through which Zhivago must trudge to rejoin Lara in a deserted country estate. Lean expertly handled the international ensemble of well-known actors, with the performances by Rod Steiger and Tom Courtenay in supporting character roles particularly effective. Freddie Young's cinematography evokes the expansiveness and raw beauty of the Russian landscape, and Maurice Jarre's score complements the story admirably.

Doctor Zhivago proved hugely profitable at the box office and has continued to draw many viewers in subsequent television exhibition, with its memorable characters, riveting action, and moving depiction of important historical events. **RBP**

The War Game Peter Watkins, 1965

G.B. (BBC) 48m BW
Producer Peter Watkins Screenplay Peter
Watkins Photography Peter Bartlett
Cast Michael Aspel, Peter Graham
Oscar Peter Watkins (documentary)
Venice Film Festival Peter Watkins
(special prize)

A hypothesis about the aftermath of a nuclear attack on England, *The War Game* was banned by BBC television, which produced it, ostensibly because (among other reasons stated or hinted at) "it was too horrific for the medium of broadcasting." *The War Game* fast became a cause célèbre and won an Oscar, and remains the most widely known of Peter Watkins's films.

The film mixes scenes seemingly shot by a newsreel crew with others filmed in a documentary style (handheld, single-camera, available-lit) in situations that contradict the presence of a camera. The offscreen narrator (using a bland BBC voice) sometimes speaks as if the events shown have already taken place, giving dates and times and using the past tense, and then switches without warning to an informational mode or to the what-if ("If evacuation plans were carried out, scenes like this would be inevitable"; "This could be the way the last two minutes of peace in Britain would look"). Watkins's free play with narrative strategies gives the film a surging restlessness that's as compelling as his imagery of devastation. *The War Game* is a tour de force that has lost none of its power to horrify since its initial release. **CFu**

Tokyo Orimpikku Kon Ichikawa, 1965
Tokyo Olympiad

Japan (Organizing Committee for the XVIII
Olympiad, Toho) 170m Eastmancolor
Language Japanese Producer Suketaru
Taguchi Screenplay Kon Ichikawa, Yoshio
Shirasaka, Shuntaro Tanikawa, Natto Wada
Photography Shigeo Hayashida, Kazuo
Miyagawa, Shigeichi Nagano, Kenichi
Nakamura, Tadashi Tanaka Music Toshirō
Mayuzumi Cast Abebe Bikila, Jack Douglas

Kon Ichikawa's record of the 1964 Tokyo Olympiad raised the stakes of epic documentary and achieved a level of artistic reportage subsequent sports programming has been clamoring to mimic ever since. It begins with a rising sun and closes the same way with occasional amplification by Japanocentric flag ceremonies. In the mix are both famous and little-known events, with occasional asides to spy on riveted spectators or tour Tokyo's hotspots.

Putting action to image, however, is Ichikawa's strength. Bodies are synecdochically represented with feet, buttocks, or straining neck, turning physical achievement into the very grace of existence. Purposefulness is found both in preparing and executing athletic achievements and, as is often the case in documentary, historicity itself remains indelible.

The obsolete scissors-kick high-jump technique stings with an imprecise physics. A side-armed volleyball serve seems out of place, and the grunt-and-throw shot put, rather than a spin, defies modern excellence. Even so, the human element shows through in *Tokyo Olympiad*, perhaps most sensually during the women's 80-meter hurdles final when all ambient sound and accompanying music stops for slow-motion movement. Kneecaps scrape by. Faces grimace. Muscles loosen and pound. In short, it is the essence and root cause of sport transformed into movie magic. **GC-Q**

Giulietta degli spiriti Federico Fellini, 1965
Juliet of the Spirits

Today, the excellence of color work in cinematography and film design is judged on the achievement of an overall, carefully modulated palette. In Federico Fellini's *Juliet of the Spirits*, color is the occasion to create an aesthetic riot between and within shots: a frame that is all red and green, for instance, intercut with one that is gleaming white.

In his first color film, Fellini explored the possibilities with glee. Conceived as a companion piece to *8 ½* (1963), it delves into the psyche of Juliet, played by Fellini's famous wife Giulietta Masina. Faced with an uncertain marriage and a philandering husband (the film is lightly autobiographical), Juliet strays into a highly eroticized world of spiritual mediums, high-class whores, and affluent acquaintances. Soon, the spirit-visions come, tormenting Juliet with the gap between her oppressive, religious upbringing and the liberation or contentment she seeks.

One of the most extraordinary aspects of this movie today is its absolute modernity. The faces, costumes, and attitudes do not seem dated. The film is uniquely prescient: Already Fellini had absorbed, and lovingly exaggerated, the pop-mystical fads that were to explode in "New Age" culture, especially concerning "body and mind" philosophies—for this is truly a movie about body and mind as surrealistic "communicating vessels."

Although Fellini was reproached for using women as the ground for his narcissistic projections, Juliet is in fact his finest female character—Masina bringing to the outlandish proceedings both a childlike wonder and a down-to-earth hesitation and skepticism that make her a natural figure of identification for the viewer. Stylistically, Fellini here began marrying his dream-fed visions with the technological bric-a-brac of the modern world (telephones, movie projectors, screens), simultaneously making sublime things mundane, and mundane things sublime. His camera is a roving eye, sometimes seemingly lost: The relentless entries and exits from the frame, the artful shuttling of multiple bodies, the sudden moments when an image is revealed as Juliet's point of view—all these devices, swinging to the rhythm of Nino Rota's rich, carnival-style score, evoke a heady plunge into the realm of the unconscious. **AM**

Italy / France / West Germany (Eichberg, Federiz, Francoriz, Rizzoli) 148m Technicolor **Language** Italian **Producer** Angelo Rizzoli **Screenplay** Federico Fellini, Ennio Flaiano, Tullio Pinelli, Brunello Rondi **Photography** Gianni Di Venanzo **Music** Nino Rota **Cast** Giulietta Masina, Sandra Milo, Mario Pisu, Valentina Cortese, José Luis de Villalonga, Caterina Boratto, Sylva Koscina, Frederick Ledebur, Luisa Della Noce, Valeska Gert, Lou Gilbert, Silvana Jachino, Milena Vukotic, Fred Williams, Dany Parìs **Oscar nominations** Piero Gherardi (best art direction, best costume)

"I don't care about the clemency you offer me but the salvation of my soul."

Juliet (Giulietta Masina)

🛈
The movie went on to win a Golden Globe for Best Foreign Language Film in 1966.

La Battaglia di Algeri Gillo Pontecorvo, 1965
The Battle of Algiers

Algeria / Italy (Casbah, Igor) 117m BW
Language French Producer Antonio Musu,
Yacef Saadi Screenplay Gillo Pontecorvo,
Franco Solinas Photography Marcello Gatti
Music Ennio Morricone, Gillo Pontecorvo
Cast Jean Martin, Yacef Saadi, Brahim
Haggiag, Samia Kerbash, Tommaso Neri,
Michele Kerbash, Ugo Paletti, Fusia El Kader,
Franco Morici Oscar nominations Italy (best
foreign language film), Gillo Pontecorvo
(director), Franco Solinas, Gillo Pontecorvo
(screenplay) Venice Film Festival
Gillo Pontecorvo (FIPRESCI award,
Golden Lion nomination)

A chemistry graduate turned journalist who became a youthful leader of the partisans' antifascist Resistance in Italy through World War II, Gillo Pontecorvo entered the world of cinema as a documentary filmmaker. He brought his intellect, fierce political beliefs, and personal experience to this seminal, electrifying, political thriller, which recounts the bloody Algerian struggle for independence from France. The action takes place between 1954 and 1962 in gritty, authentic drama-documentary style, cast largely with nonprofessional actors and shot and narrated in the manner of a newsreel. Winner of the prestigious Golden Lion at the Venice Film Festival, *The Battle of Algiers* was one of the most influential films to come out of Italy in the 1960s, and it has lost none of its passionate power.

Although Pontecorvo had financial assistance from the Algerian government—and the film wears its anticolonialist heart on its sleeve—horrifying and heartrending scenes of atrocities and reprisals are laudably evenhanded, depicting both sides of the conflict and its awful human cost. It is gripping from start to finish. A particularly uncompromising tour de force is a nail-biting sequence that follows women of the Algiers casbah slipping through checkpoints and planting primitive bombs—in an airport lounge, in a milk bar—where oblivious French teens are gyrating to pop songs, to an inevitably grievous aftermath. The really superb, emotive score was co-composed by Pontecorvo himself and the great Ennio Morricone. **AE**

🛈

Uniquely, the film was nominated for Oscars twice in nonconsecutive years—first in 1966, then 1968.

The Sound of Music Robert Wise, 1965

U.S. (Fox, Argyle) 174m Color Deluxe
Producer Robert Wise **Screenplay** Ernest
Lehman, Richard Rodgers, Oscar
Hammerstein (from stage musical) and from
libretto by Howard Lindsay and Russel
Crouse **Music** Richard Rodgers, Irwin Kostal
Cast Julie Andrews, Christopher Plummer,
Eleanor Parker, Richard Haydn, Peggy Wood,
Charmian Carr, Heather Menzies, Nicholas
Hammond, Duane Chase, Angela Cartwright
Oscars Robert Wise (best picture), Robert
Wise (director), William Reynolds (editing),
Irwin Kostal (music), James Corcoran, Fred
Hynes (sound) **Oscar nominations** Julie
Andrews (actress), Peggy Wood (actress in
support role), Boris Leven, Walter M. Scott,
Ruby R. Levitt (art direction), Ted D. McCord
(photography), Dorothy Jeakins (costume)

It is all too easy to knock Robert Wise's enormously successful screen adaptation of Rodgers and Hammerstein's musical hit, what with singing nuns and a kind-of-cute clutch of seven kids coping with the double trouble of an absurdly disciplinarian widower father and the rise of the Nazi regime in 1930s Salzburg. But one should never underestimate the effectiveness of the lead performances—Julie Andrews as the eccentrically vivacious nun-turned-governess and Christopher Plummer as the strict, buttoned-up patriarch whose heart she melts. There is also the unsentimental precision of Ernest Lehman's script, and the solid, unshowy expertise of Wise's direction, in which his editor's sensitivity to structure, rhythm, and rhyming juxtapositions is always evident.

That exhilarating opening helicopter shot across the mountaintops—finally alighting on Andrews running exuberantly as she bursts into "The hills are alive" may now seem hackneyed, but that's only because its efficiency in establishing mood (and, indeed, meaning, since *The Sound of Music* is a film in which music and the life force are inextricably linked) has meant that it has been much imitated. And let us not forget: like it or not, those tunes really are unforgettable. **GA**

1965

De man die zijn haar kort liet knippen
The Man Who Had His Hair Cut Short
André Delvaux, 1965

Belgium BRT, Ministerie van
Nationale Opvoeding en Kultuur) 94m BW
Language Dutch **Producer** Paul Louyet,
Jos Op De Beeck **Screenplay** Anna De
Pagter, from novel by Johan Daisne
Photography Ghislain Cloquet
Music Frédéric Devreese **Cast** Senne
Rouffaer, Beata Tyszkiewicz,
Hector Camerlynck, Hilde Uytterlinden,
Annemarie Van Dijk, Hilda Van Roose,
François Beukelaers, Arlette Emmery, Paul
S'Jongers, Luc Philips, François Bernard,
Vic Moeremans, Maurits Goossens

The Man Who Had His Hair Cut Short is the film through which Belgian cinema entered modernism. The feature debut of André Delvaux, it also marks the arrival of Belgium's own national cinematic style, magic realism—a unique blend of reality and eerie fantasy, addressing the surreal melancholy of everyday life.

Delvaux's film follows a curious narrative, from love story to mystery-thriller, over to an exploration of the thin line between sanity and madness. Govert Miereveld (Senne Rouffaer) is a teacher who falls in love with a pupil who soon disappears, leaving us—and Govert—to wonder whether or not he has killed her. Much more than a mere detective tale, *The Man Who Had His Hair Cut Short* is a quest into the protagonist's identity crisis; together with Govert we gradually realize we can no longer trust what we see or hear, as reality itself becomes a dream. A crucial scene in the film is a countryside autopsy, mixing realism, revulsion, and dreamlike alienation.

Stylistically, *The Man Who Had His Hair Cut Short* is a very subtle movie. Minute details in the language, visuals, and behavior of the characters cast doubts upon the veracity of the very realistic settings in which Govert lives and travels, until, in the end, we give up looking for truth, settling, with Govert, for quiet contemplation—a surrender to strangeness. **EM**

Alphaville, une étrange aventure de Lemmy Caution
Alphaville Jean-Luc Godard, 1965

In the future, secret agent Lemmy Caution (Eddie Constantine) cruises into Alphaville, which is either a city or a planet, in his Ford Galaxie, which is either a car or a spaceship. His mission is to find and perhaps liquidate the missing Professor von Braun (Howard Vernon). First, Caution runs into Henri Dickson (Akim Tamiroff), an agent who has gone native, and then the mad scientist's daughter Natacha (Anna Karina), who has never heard the words "love" or "conscience." Alphaville is run by a croaking super-computer that has made honest emotion a capital crime, insisting on mass executions carried out in an eerie swimming pool. Caution naturally sets out to destroy the computer (by feeding it poetry), and incidentally woos the fragile Natacha, awakening her dormant emotions.

Godard set out to create a science-fiction film without expensive sets or special effects. Shooting in cleverly selected Paris locations, he discovers the seeds of a totalitarian future in contemporary hotel lobbies, neon signage, office buildings, and bureaucratic waiting rooms. *Alphaville*'s relationship with science fiction was initially parodic, as is Godard's affectionate borrowing of trench-coat characters and gun-pulling poses from hard-boiled Franco-American pulp (Constantine had played author Peter Cheyney's Mike Hammer-ish sleuth Lemmy Caution in a run of thick-ear thrillers). However, considered as a product of the times—when Philip K. Dick was exploring similar themes in ever-more-ambitious novels—*Alphaville* now looks a lot like proper sci-fi, to the extent of influencing a run of adaptations (from François Truffaut's take on Ray Bradbury's *Fahrenheit 451* [1966] to Ridley Scott's Dick-derived *Blade Runner* [1982]).

Like many Godard films, *Alphaville* deliberately runs out of plot after an hour and has two characters sitting in a hotel room arguing for minutes. As in *Breathless* (1959) and *Contempt* (1963), this free-ranging conversation, with Caution shaking Natacha out of zombiehood, is a highlight, confirming Godard as almost the equal of Joseph L. Mankiewicz in the cinema of conversation. A rare futurist vision that simply does not date. **KN**

France / Italy (Athos, Chaumiane, Filmstudio) 99m BW **Language** French **Producer** André Michelin **Screenplay** Jean-Luc Godard, from the novel *La capitale de la douleur* by Paul Éluard **Photography** Raoul Coutard **Music** Paul Misraki **Cast** Eddie Constantine, Anna Karina, Akim Tamiroff **Berlin Film Festival** Jean-Luc Godard (Golden Bear)

"Yes, I am afraid of death. But for a humble secret agent, it's an everyday thing, like whiskey. And I've been drinking all my life."

Lemmy Caution (Eddie Constantine)

ℹ️ Professor von Braun's original name is Leonard Nosferatu—a reference to F.W. Murnau's famous film of 1922.

Campanadas a medianoche Orson Welles, 1965
Chimes at Midnight

Orson Welles was always fascinated by Shakespeare and filmed both an *Othello* and a *Macbeth* as well as a television version of *The Merchant of Venice*. There is no doubt, however, that his greatest achievement in this vein is his adaptation of the *Henry IV* plays, *Chimes at Midnight*. But don't go looking for a faithful Shakespeare adaptation here. Scholarly opinion divides between those who think that the young Prince Hal is merely sowing his wild oats with the drunk reprobate Falstaff and is justified in abandoning him when he comes to the throne, and those who feel that the abandonment of the fat knight shows that Hal is a Machiavellian prince with no human feeling. Welles does not bother to balance his opinions. This is *Henry IV* Parts 1 and 2 told from Falstaff's point of view. His drinking and thieving, his cowardice and his greed are not faults but foibles. Falstaff is fat and Welles glories in his physical embodiment of the corpulent knight. The comic scenes in Eastcheap, particularly after the failed robbery at Gadhill, are masterful.

Shakespeare's repartee has never been so gloriously performed as it is by Welles. Even more affecting are the battle scenes shot without nobility or honor, wretched fields on which men die to serve the crooked purpose of their masters. But the real triumph of *Chimes at Midnight* is the scenes from which the film takes its title, Falstaff's encounter with Justice Shallow (Alan Webb), the acquaintance of his riotous youth who has become a country magistrate. The pathos of these encounters, which go well beyond the Shakespearean play, are truly affecting—particularly as we are in no doubt of the tragic emotional fate that awaits Falstaff as he is banished by the love of his life, young Prince Hal now become King Henry V. The cast is magnificent, with John Gielgud as Henry IV, Norman Rodway as Hotspur, Keith Baxter as Hal, and even Jeanne Moreau showing up as Doll Tearsheet and Marina Vlady as Hotspur's wife. One warning: the postsynchronization of the dialogue is truly appalling—it has to be heard to be believed. Otherwise it is a masterpiece. **CM**

Spain / Switzerland (Alpine, Española) 113m BW **Producer** Ángel Escolano, Emiliano Piedra, Harry Saltzman, Alessandro Tasca **Screenplay** Orson Welles, from plays by William Shakespeare and chronicles by Raphael Holinshed **Photography** Edmond Richard **Music** Angelo Francesco Lavagnino **Cast** Orson Welles, Jeanne Moreau, Margaret Rutherford, John Gielgud, Marina Vlady, Walter Chiari, Michael Aldridge, Julio Peña, Tony Beckley, Andrés Mejuto, Keith Pyott, Jeremy Rowe, Alan Webb, Fernando Rey, Keith Baxter **Cannes Film Festival** Orson Welles (20th anniversary prize), (grand technical prize, tied with Skaterdater, Golden Palm nomination)

> *"We have heard the chimes at midnight, Master Robert Shallow."*
>
> Falstaff (Orson Welles)

1965

The part of Falstaff's page went to Welles's youngest daughter, Beatrice, who resembled Welles as a boy.

Faster, Pussycat! Kill! Kill! Russ Meyer, 1965

U.S. (Eve) 83m BW **Producer** George
Costello, Eve Meyer, Russ Meyer, Fred Owens
Screenplay Russ Meyer, Jack Moran
Photography Walter Schenk **Music** Paul
Sawtell, Bert Shefter **Cast** Tura Satana,
Haji, Rosie, Lori Williams, Sue Bernard,
Stuart Lancaster, Paul Trinka, Dennis Busch,
Ray Barlow, Michael Finn

The title was inspired by Meyer's
belief that the ideal film should
contain speed, sex, and violence.

What can you say about Russ Meyer? His movies are, to paraphrase a
well-known saying about life itself, nasty, brutish, and short. Arguments
have been made in favor of his occasional artistry and sometimes we
are asked to reconsider the troublesome sexual politics of his films.
And although both arguments (and many of the films themselves)
should be approached with caution, *Faster, Pussycat! Kill! Kill!* remains
a favorite—and not just for John Waters, who likes to claim that it's the
best movie ever made.

Faster, Pussycat! Kill! Kill! traces the exploits (an especially significant
term in this context) of its three curvy and violent drag-racing female
protagonists: Varla (Tura Satana), Rosie (Haji), and Billie (Lori Williams).
After a racing-related murder, the crew hides out at a nearby ranch where
they spend the rest of the picture scheming to liberate the rancher of
his finances. The film enjoys its place at the top of many cult lists in part
because of its several inherent delights—creative and flashy editing,
smart black-and-white cinematography, a jazzy score, and plenty of
innuendo—and in part because it is a fascinating barometer of the shifts
occurring during the 1960s, especially with respect to cinema itself. **DO**

Vinyl Andy Warhol, 1965

U.S. (Andy Warhol) 70m BW
Screenplay Ronald Tavel, from the novel
A Clockwork Orange by Anthony Burgess
Photography Andy Warhol
Cast Edie Sedgwick, Tosh Carillo,
Gerard Malanga, J.D. McDermott,
Ondine, Jacques Potin

Andy Warhol's 1965 film, consisting of two unedited thirty-five-minute black-and-white reels, is a fascinating, sexy, pre-Stanley Kubrick rendering of Anthony Burgess's novel *A Clockwork Orange*. In *Vinyl* the homoerotics of sadomasochism take center stage, as the juvenile delinquent (or JD) Victor, played by a deliciously wooden Gerard Malanga, receives his "reeducation" at the hands of the police. The clever scenario by Warhol's frequent collaborator Ronald Tavel calls for Victor to rough up some guy, get roughed up by the police in return, watch some "flickers" of JD violence, wear an SM leather mask, sniff poppers, and dance wildly to The Supremes' song, "Nowhere to Run." This story of Victor's reeducation is juxtaposed with a sadomasochism scene led by the Doc (a sexy Tosh Carillo in tight white jeans) who slowly taunts his willingly restrained, bare-chested accomplice.

Vinyl's brilliance is largely due to Warhol's framing of the action. His use of a static camera setup condenses all the scenes into the cramped but dynamic space of the single frame: Victor's reeducation in the foreground; Doc's SM session in the background; the queeny Ondine in the middle; and, perhaps, most striking of all, a silent Edie Sedgwick sparkling at the right corner of the screen. **MS**

Rekopis znaleziony w saragossie
The Saragossa Manuscript Wojciech Has, 1965

Poland (Kamera) 124m BW
Language Polish Screenplay Tadeusz
Kwiatkowski, from novel by Jan Potocki
Photography Mieczyslaw Jahoda
Music Krzysztof Penderecki Cast Zbigniew
Cybulski, Kazimierz Opalinski, Iga
Cembrzynska, Joanna Jedryka, Slawomir
Lindner, Miroslawa Lombardo, Aleksander
Fogiel, Franciszek Pieczka, Ludwik Benoit,
Barbara Krafftówna, Pola Raksa, August
Kowalczyk, Adam Pawlikowski, Beata
Tyszkiewicz, Gustaw Holoubek

Jerry Garcia proclaimed this 1965 Polish feature his favorite movie, having seen a pared-down version in San Francisco's North Beach during the 1960s, and a few years back he, Martin Scorsese, and Francis Ford Coppola helped to restore it to its original three-hour length. It's easy to see how *The Saragossa Manuscript* became a cult film. Toward the end of the Spanish Inquisition a Napoleonic military officer— Zbigniew Cybulski, the Polish James Dean, though pudgier than usual here—is morally tested by two seductive Muslim princesses, incestuous sisters from Tunisia, and no less than nine interconnected flashbacks recounted by various characters figure in the labyrinthine plot, its tales within tales imparting some of the flavor of *The Arabian Nights* and occasional echoes of Kafka (mainly in the eroticism).

Krzysztof Penderecki's score runs the gamut from classical music to flamenco to modernist electronic noodling, and the stark, rocky settings are elegantly filmed in black-and-white CinemaScope. The late Wojciech Has was a fine journeyman director, though a film of this kind really calls for someone more obsessive, like Roman Polanski. Adapted by Tadeusz Kwiatkowski from Jan Potocki's 1813 novel, it is certainly an intriguing fantasy and a haunting reflection on the processes of storytelling. **JRos**

Repulsion Roman Polanski, 1965

Roman Polanski's first film in English is still his scariest and most disturbing—not only for its evocations of sexual panic but also because his masterful use of sound puts the audience's imagination to work in numerous ways. It is also the most expressionistic of his early black-and-white features, using wide angles that become increasingly wider and deep focus, along with other visual strategies, to convey subjective states of mind in which dreams, imagination, and everyday reality are worked into the same continuum. One result of such an expressionist style is that the conventional apartment in which most of the action takes place gradually assumes the shape and form of a tortured consciousness.

Catherine Deneuve gives one of her most impressive performances here as Carole Ledoux, a quiet and quietly mad Belgian manicurist terrified of men and living with her older sister in London. When the sister and her boyfriend, whose lovemaking in an adjacent room already disturbs and frightens her, take off on a holiday, Carole's fears and isolation in the apartment begin to fester along with the uncooked food—including a sinister-looking skinned rabbit. The results are increasingly violent and macabre, with Carole's madness becoming more and more apparent.

As narrative the film works only part of the time, and as case study it may occasionally seem too obvious, but as subjective nightmare *Repulsion* is a stunning piece of filmmaking. Put together with expertly calibrated shocks and a gradually developing sense of dread, in many respects, this thriller became something of a template for many of Polanski's subsequent ventures into horror. His films are of isolation and claustrophobia and include such disparate works as *The Tenant* in 1976 (in which Polanski played the starring role) and *The Pianist* over a quarter of a century later. Yet ironically, in his 1984 autobiography, Polanski wrote that he and his cowriter Gérard Brach regarded *Repulsion* mainly as "a means to an end"—namely, a commercial success to enable them to finance *Cul-de-sac* (1966), a much more personal, if less commercial, film in English that would star Deneuve's sister Françoise Dorléac. **JRos**

G.B. (Compton) 104m BW
Producer Gene Gutowski, Michael Klinger, Robert Sterne, Tony Tenser, Sam Waynberg **Screenplay** Gérard Brach, Roman Polanski, David Stone **Photography** Gilbert Taylor **Music** Chico Hamilton **Cast** Catherine Deneuve, Ian Hendry, John Fraser, Yvonne Furneaux, Patrick Wymark, Renee Houston, Valerie Taylor, James Villiers, Helen Fraser, Hugh Futcher, Monica Merlin, Imogen Graham, Mike Pratt, Roman Polanski **Berlin Film Festival** Roman Polanski (FIPRESCI award, Silver Bear—special jury prize, Golden Bear nomination)

"I must get this crack mended."

**Carole Ledoux
(Catherine Deneuve)**

1965

i

Polanski makes a cameo appearance as a spoons player in a group of street musicians.

Pierrot le fou Jean-Luc Godard, 1965
Pierrot Goes wild

Jean-Luc Godard's masterpiece *Pierrot le fou* is an important milestone in the director's long and brilliant career. A turning point of sorts, the film straddles the experimental élan of Godard works such as *Breathless* (1960) and *My Life to Live* (1962) and the highly politicized, cynical, and bitterly funny films like *Week End* (1967) and *Wind from the East* (1969). *Pierrot le fou* contains elements of both, and is a rich viewing experience for this reason alone. But one thing the film also possesses, in spades, is a sense of true beauty. Critics tend to forget that Godard, for all his polemicism, made some exquisitely beautiful films. *Pierrot le fou* must surely be considered alongside *Contempt* (1963) in this regard.

Godard always had a love-hate relationship with Hollywood. For him, American films are at once the most beautiful and honest, but also the most crass and ugly. As in many of his works, Godard uses American "low" culture and genre filmmaking as his launching pad: *Pierrot le fou* is (extremely) loosely based on pulp novelist Lionel White's *Obsession*, and it features an extended cameo by underappreciated Hollywood maverick and Godard favorite Samuel Fuller. The very fact that the film was shot in Techniscope by the great Raoul Coutard is a comment on the manufactured grandeur of so many Hollywood prestige pictures of the 1950s and 1960s. If you know Hollywood cinema from this era, watching *Pierrot le fou* can be an immensely rewarding, if confounding, experience, for satire in Godard is never quite as plain as one might expect.

Pierrot is bitter, satirical, humorous, and beautiful—but perhaps its most charming (and arresting) feature is its sheer outrageousness. Ferdinand/Pierrot and Marianne (Godard's regulars Jean-Paul Belmondo and Anna Karina) move deliriously from one ridiculous situation to another—be it the world's most insufferable party, a free-for-all with gas station attendants, or a bizarrely uplifting self-immolation. Almost anything is possible in this film, yet it still manages to surprise, even upon repeated viewings. The potency of Godard's imagery and satire has not diminished with age. If anything, it is even more relevant today. **EdeS**

France / Italy (De Laurentiis, Rome-Paris, SNC) 110m Eastmancolor **Language** French **Producer** Georges de Beauregard **Screenplay** Jean-Luc Godard **Photography** Raoul Coutard **Music** Antoine Duhamel **Cast** Jean-Paul Belmondo, Ferdinand Griffon, Anna Karina, Marianne Renoir **Venice Film Festival** Jean-Luc Godard nomination (Golden Lion)

1965

"A film is like a battleground. It's love, hate, action, violence, and death. In one word: emotions."

Samuel Fuller (as himself)

ℹ️

At one point, Godard considered Richard Burton for the role of Ferdinand.

Subarnarekha Ritwik Ghatak, 1965
Golden River

India (J.J. Films) 143m BW
Language Bengali Screenplay Ritwik
Ghatak, from novel by Radheshyam
Jhunjhunwala Photography Dilip Ranjan
Mukhopadhyay Music Ustad Bahadur Khan,
Nino Rota (from Fellini's *La dolce vita* [1960])
Cast Abhi Bhattacharya, Madhabi
Mukherjee, Satindra Bhattacharya, Bijon
Bhattacharya, Indrani Chakrabarty, Sriman
Tarun, Jahar Ray, Pitambar, Sriman Ashok
Bhattacharya, Sita Mukherjee, Radha
Govinda Ghosh, Abinash Bannerjee, Gita De,
Umanath Bhattacharya, Arun Chowdhury

A native of Dhaka, East Bengal (now Bangladesh), Ghatak was twenty-two at the time of the Partition, the trauma that defined him as an artist. *Golden River* begins in a colony of impoverished Bengali refugees in Calcutta with news of Gandhi's assassination. Ishwar Chakraborty (Abhi Bhattacharya) is rearing a young daughter and an abandoned boy—so when an affluent college friend offers him a post in a provincial factory, he accepts it to secure their future, at the cost of his broader aspirations.

Years pass. When the boy, Abhiram (Satindra Bhattacharya), returns from college an aspiring writer, it emerges that he is in love with his half-sister Shita (Madhabi Mukherjee), and she with him. The declaration of love is a haunting example of Ghatak's innovative experiments with sound: The words are drawn out of the young man in a whisper that seems to bypass his mouth entirely—passion straight from the heart. Of course Ishwar opposes his children's union, though this is complicated by the revelation that Abhiram is of low caste, and unworthy of his daughter. A good man watches appalled as everything his life has stood for unravels.

The American filmmaker has not been born who can match Ghatak for the cinematic expression of utter, unadulterated anguish. He is especially sensitive to the fate of the marginalized: women, the young, the old, and the insane. From the ruins of these lives, Ghatak unearths a shimmering mirage of hope. **TCh**

Hold Me While I'm Naked George Kuchar, 1966

U.S. 17m Color
Cast Donna Kerness, George Kuchar,
Andrea Lunin, Hope Morris, Steve Packard

George Kuchar's first 16mm color film is a charming and melodramatic tour de force of underground invention. The most popular of the hundreds of films Kuchar has made since the late 1950s, this 1966 low-budget short tells the story of an endearing loser of a filmmaker (Kuchar) who battles bouts of depression and loneliness in his attempt to make a film. When his voluptuous starlet (the tantalizing Donna Kerness) finds passion in the shower, Kuchar's self-pity and alienation achieve even greater depths.

Like many of George and twin brother Mike's Bronx-made Hollywood epics, *Hold Me While I'm Naked* attains a level of emotional seriousness that makes it stand out among the camp and trash Hollywood parodies to which it is inevitably compared. This is due in large part to Kuchar's technical and creative skills: his stunning title and production design; his ingenious inventory of odd, unflattering camera angles; and his insatiable talent at adapting the glamorous concerns and emotional extremes of Hollywood flicks to the banal realities and human proportions of his neighborhood friends. A colorful example of Kuchar's resourcefulness, *Hold Me While I'm Naked* has incited many a viewer—John Waters among them—to mobilize friends for their own glorious screen epics. **MS**

Who's Afraid of Virginia Woolf? Mike Nichols, 1966

You are cordially invited
to George and Martha's
for an evening of fun and games°

ELIZABETH TAYLOR
RICHARD BURTON
EDWARD ALBEE'S **WHO'S AFRAID OF VIRGINIA WOOLF?**

GEORGE SEGAL, SANDY DENNIS ERNEST LEHMAN MIKE NICHOLS PRESENTED BY WARNER BROS.

U.S. (Chenault, Warner Bros.) 134m BW
Producer Ernest Lehman **Screenplay** Ernest
Lehman, from play by Edward Albee
Photography Haskell Wexler **Music** Alex
North **Cast** Elizabeth Taylor, Richard Burton,
George Segal, Sandy Dennis, Frank Flanagan
Oscars Elizabeth Taylor (actress), Sandy
Dennis (actress in support role), Richard
Sylbert, George James Hopkins (art
direction), Haskell Wexler (photography),
Irene Sharaff (costume) **Oscar nominations**
Ernest Lehman (best picture), Mike Nichols
(director), Ernest Lehman (screenplay),
Richard Burton (actor), George Segal (actor
in support role), Sam O'Steen (editing), Alex
North (music), George Groves (sound)

*"I'm loud and I'm vulgar,
and I wear the pants
in the house because
somebody's got to, but
I am not a monster."*

**Martha
(Elizabeth Taylor)**

ℹ️

Elizabeth Taylor put on
around 30 pounds in weight
to play the part of Martha.

With its unremitting portrait of an older married couple who draw a young husband and wife into their destructive love/hate games, Edward Albee's Broadway smash of the early 1960s was at first considered too brutal in terms of language and theme to be brought to the screen because of Production Code restrictions. But by the middle of the decade, Hollywood was abandoning the code in favor of a ratings system that would permit the exhibition of more adult dramas, and Mike Nichols's adaptation of Albee's play was among the first to appear on screens (theater owners were asked not to admit anyone under eighteen, as the new ratings categories had not yet been finalized).

Nichols's version of *Who's Afraid of Virginia Woolf?* is an important part of another trend—the move, in part, away from traditional entertainment toward a greater seriousness that would characterize the "Hollywood Renaissance" of the late 1960s and 1970s. Filmed in black and white and based on a fine screenplay by Ernest Lehman that keeps much of the play's dialogue, Nichols, who came to Hollywood from stage directing, preserves the essence of Albee's original. The casting was an extraordinary coup, with Richard Burton and Elizabeth Taylor, cast as George and Martha, whose unremitting verbal and mental fencing constitutes the main action. George is a history professor at the local college and Martha the daughter of its president; they invite a younger faculty member (George Segal) and his wife (Sandy Dennis) for a late evening of mental games: first "Humiliate the Host," but then, more destructively, "Get the Guests." In this unequal contest, the young couple comes off second best, with the less-than-honorable aspects of their marriage laid bare and the young man's confidence in himself severely shaken. Of the many attempts to use the Burtons effectively in a film, *Who's Afraid of Virginia Woolf?* is by far the most successful, as Nichols elicited the best performance of the actress's career and Burton is effective as a weak man possessed of enormous emotional strength and an inexhaustible capacity to love. The film richly deserved its five Academy Awards; it is certainly one of the finest adaptations of a stage play ever produced. **RBP**

1966

Blowup Michelangelo Antonioni, 1966

After a run of masterpieces—from *L'avventura* (1960) to *Il deserto rosso* (1964)—revolving around jaded Italian upper-class ennui and Monica Vitti, Michelangelo Antonioni became an international filmmaker with this 1966 picture. Based on a short story by Julio Cortazar, *Blowup* follows *L'avventura* in offering a mystery with no solution but goes even further by wondering, after a great deal of obsessive investigation, whether there even was a mystery outside the protagonist's mind. Turning his outsider's eye on a London that was just beginning to swing, Antonioni captures precisely a time and a place that seemed culturally significant. As with Fellini's *La dolce vita* (1960), a film intended as a satirical attack on a certain type of modern sophistication and emptiness emerges almost as a celebration of the fashions, mores, music, sexuality, and strangeness of a world it would like to disapprove of.

The central character is Thomas (David Hemmings), a photographer who—perhaps like Antonioni—divides his time between assault-like sessions with vapidly lovely fashion models and vérité work among down-and-outs. Snapping away in an eerily unpopulated park in the hopes of finding a peaceful image to conclude his latest book, Thomas gets some shots that seem to show an older man and a younger woman (Vanessa Redgrave) having an innocent, quiet moment. However, the woman pursues Thomas and demands he hand over the film, then turns up at his studio to press her case with a jittery, neurotic flirtatiousness that further piques the terminally cool Thomas's interest. He palms her off with the wrong film and develops his photographs; under extreme analysis, he seems to find a man with a gun lurking in the undergrowth catching the woman's panicky or complicit eye. Another photograph shows a vague form that might be a body, and another visit to the park reveals an actual corpse—but then all the evidence is taken away and Thomas loses his conviction that he has latched onto a murder and surrenders to the distractions that clutter his life.

Despite its thriller-style hook (often hommaged in straighter suspense films like Coppola's *The Conversation* [1974] or De Palma's *Blow Out* [1981]), this is less a mystery than a portrait of swinging alienation. In 1966, when nudity in English-language films wasn't commonplace, there was a real charge to Redgrave taking off her blouse and lounging around the studio with her arms crossed over her breasts, not to mention the notorious (and actually rather tactful) sequence in which Thomas grapples on the floor with a pair of gawky, giggling groupies. Most of all, this is a film about an alien world: the creepily unvisited park, a concert (featuring The Yardbirds) where the audience stand impassive until a guitar is smashed and they erupt into a feeding frenzy, a pot party where Thomas searches for someone he is then unable to explain anything to, and a game of tennis between student mimes that leads to an ambiguous finish as Thomas is drawn into the game by returning a lost "ball." **KN**

G.B. (Bridge) 111m Metrocolor
Producer Carlo Ponti, Pierre Rouve
Screenplay Michelangelo Antonioni, Tonino Guerra, Edward Bond, from story by Julio Cortázar **Photography** Carlo Di Palma **Music** Herbie Hancock **Cast** David Hemmings, Vanessa Redgrave, Peter Bowles, Sarah Miles, John Castle, Jane Birkin, Gillian Hills, Veruschka von Lehndorff, Julian Chagrin, Claude Chagrin **Oscar nominations** Michelangelo Antonioni (director), Michelangelo Antonioni, Tonino Guerra, Edward Bond (screenplay) **Cannes Film Festival** Michelangelo Antonioni (Golden Palm)

"Just as an actor ... must arrive on the set in a state of mental virginity, so, too, must I. I force myself not to overintellectualize."

Michelangelo Antonioni, 1978

Julio Cortázar, who wrote the short story on which *Blowup* is based, has a brief cameo as a homeless man.

Sedmikrasky Vera Chytilová, 1966
Daisies

Czechoslovakia (Ceskoslovensky Státní, Barrandov) 74m Eastmancolor Language Czech Producer Ladislav Fikar, Bohumil Smída Screenplay Vera Chytilová, Ester Krumbachová Photography Jaroslav Kucera Music Jirí Slitr, Jirí Sust Cast Julius Albert, Jitka Cerhová, Marie Cesková, Ivana Karbanová, Jan Klusák

Surely one of the most exhilarating stylistic and psychedelic cinematic explosions of the 1960s, Vera Chytilová's *Daisies* is a madcap and aggressive feminist farce that explodes in any number of directions. Although many American and Western European filmmakers during this period prided themselves on their subversiveness, it is possible that the most radical film of the decade, ideologically as well as formally, came from the East—from the liberating ferment building toward the short-lived political reforms of 1968's Prague Spring in Czechoslovakia.

Daisies features two uninhibited seventeen-year-olds named Marie (Jitka Cerhová and Ivana Karbanová) whose various escapades, which add up less to a plot than to a string of outrageous set pieces, include several antiphallic gags (such as slicing up cucumbers and bananas), a penchant for exploiting dirty old men, and a free-for-all with fancy food (rivaling Laurel and Hardy) that got Chytilová in trouble with the authorities. This disturbing yet liberating tour de force shows what this talented director can do with freedom. A major influence on Jacques Rivette's *Celine and Julie Go Boating* (1974), *Daisies* is chock-full of female giggling, which might be interpreted in context as what critic Ruby Rich has called the laughter of Medusa: subversive, bracing, energizing, and rather off-putting (if challenging) to most male spectators. **JRos**

🛈

Czech authorities banned *Daisies*, and Chytilová was not allowed to work in her homeland again until 1975.

Da zui xia King Hu, 1966
Come Drink With Me

Hong Kong (Shaw Brothers)
95m Color **Language** Mandarin
Producer Run Run Shaw **Screenplay** Ye
Yang **Photography** Tadashi Nishimoto
Music Lan-Ping Chow **Cast** Cheng Pei-pei,
Hua Yueh, Chen Hung Lieh, Biao Yuen,
Jackie Chan

Long before there was *Crouching Tiger, Hidden Dragon* (2000) there was the great King Hu, a master director who, beginning with his *Come Drink with Me*, helped revolutionize the martial arts costume drama by introducing a female lead. After a young official is kidnapped, the authorities send a magnificent but mysterious swordswoman named Golden Swallow (Cheng Pei-pei) to rescue him. Aided by Drunken Cat, a kung fu master disguised as a beggar, Golden Swallow hatches a daring plan to assault the corrupt monastery where the official is being held.

The film is a visual tour de force, each sequence meticulously designed by King Hu into a feast of color, movement, and high-flying action. Yet despite its great charm, this is still early King Hu; his mastery of all aspects of the medium, especially his inimitable approach to editing, would only be perfected in later masterworks such as *A Touch of Zen* (1971). Young star Cheng Pei-pei, who wields a sword like nobody before or perhaps after her, perfectly combines steely determination with a kind of touching fragility; despite her prowess, there's always a hint that each battle may be her last. She would go on to a successful career in Hong Kong cinema and would win great acclaim for her return to the screen as the evil Nanny in Ang Lee's *Crouching Tiger*. **RP**

1966

Seconds John Frankenheimer, 1966

U.S. (Joel, John Frankenheimer, Paramount)
100m BW **Producer** John Frankenheimer,
Edward Lewis **Screenplay** Lewis John
Carlino, from novel by David Ely
Photography James Wong Howe
Music Jerry Goldsmith **Cast** Rock Hudson,
Salome Jens, John Randolph, Will Geer, Jeff
Corey, Richard Anderson, Murray Hamilton,
Karl Swenson, Khigh Dhiegh, Frances Reid,
Wesley Addy, John Lawrence, Elisabeth
Fraser, Dodie Heath, Robert Brubaker
Oscar nomination James Wong Howe
(photography) **Cannes Film Festival** John
Frankenheimer (Golden Palm nomination)

Thomas Wolfe once said, "You can't go home again," and anyone familiar with John Frankenheimer's Faustian vision of alienation in suburban America would understand this only too well. Long ignored in mainstream criticism, *Seconds* has achieved the status of a cult classic.

Arthur Hamilton (John Randolph) is offered a chance to leave his middle-class emotional isolation for a new life, provided he undergoes radical surgery and lets go of his past. This miracle is offered by a sinister organization known simply as the company, populated by blacklisted character actors who all but steal the film, including Will Greer as the old man with all the answers and Jeff Corey as the salesman from hell who zestfully explains how Hamilton will become the handsome and talented painter Tony Wilson (Rock Hudson). Once the transformation is effected, *Seconds* becomes a Kafkaesque nightmare as our reborn protagonist fails to adjust to the bohemian lifestyle provided by the company.

The real star here is seasoned cinematographer James Wong Howe, whose distorted lenses and offbeat camera angles earned him an Oscar nomination and made *Seconds* one of the great black-and-white films of the late 1960s. Jerry Goldsmith created one of the most unsettling scores ever used in a psychodrama, creating a surreal mood from the opening credits to the paranoid ending. **DDV**

Il buono, il brutto, il cattivo Sergio Leone, 1966
The Good, the Bad, and the Ugly

By the mid-1960s, Hollywood had grown largely tired of the Western, which was increasingly viewed as a stodgy and hokey relic of another era. Sure, the films remained essential elements of movie history, but the times were changing and Westerns no longer appeared to have a firm place in popular culture. Sergio Leone thought differently. The Italian director sensed that the moribund genre was ripe for reinvention, and the enduring influence of his so-called spaghetti Westerns (nicknamed for both the Italian location shoots as well as the copious blood) demonstrates that he was right.

Leone had worked on a handful of films before inviting then relative unknown Clint Eastwood over to Italy to remake Akira Kurosawa's *Yojimbo* (1961)—itself based on Dashiell Hammett's novel *Red Harvest*—into the first of his iconic "man with no name" Westerns, *A Fistful of Dollars* (1964). Shot on a shoestring budget, the stylish, innovative film became a huge success, and Leone followed it with *For a Few Dollars More* (1965), which also starred Eastwood as another laconic and anonymous antihero.

The third part of his "man with no name" trilogy, *The Good, the Bad, and the Ugly*, is what really confirmed Leone's reputation in cinematic legend. Set during the American Civil War, the film follows three rogues who, although clearly identified as each of the title's categories, really blur the line between them. Eastwood returns, this time as a crooked bounty hunter (ostensibly the Good) who repeatedly captures (and then releases) outlaw Eli Wallach (the Ugly) in order to drive up the price on his head. Following a sadistic falling out, the erstwhile partners team up again in search of stolen Confederate gold, but the opportunistic, amoral Lee Van Cleef (the Bad) complicates their quest.

Leone isn't terribly interested in plot—*The Good, the Bad, and the Ugly* embraces purely cinematic elements of filmmaking. He carefully composes each widescreen image like he's painting a great landscape, frequently indulging himself in extreme close-ups—sometimes little more than a character's eyes. Leone propels the story forward with radical editing techniques, often cut to the rhythms of Ennio Morricone's famous score, pairing odd instrumentation and electric guitars to more traditional orchestration. Style drips from each frame like the sweat pouring down his stars' faces.

The Good, the Bad, and the Ugly literally comes down to the faces of Eastwood, Wallach, and Van Cleef, as the mutual antagonists perform a three-way duel in an old graveyard. The scene has since become one of the most imitated and parodied in motion picture history. Morricone's hypnotic score intensifies with quickening film cuts from face to face, capturing each set of squinting eyes, each hand reaching for a gun. Camp and kitsch and utterly entrancing, the work is of a master rewriting the rules of the Western to suit Leone's own unique vision. **JKl**

Italy / Spain (Arturo González, PEA)
161m Technicolor **Language** Italian
Producer Alberto Grimaldi
Screenplay Luciano Vincenzoni, Sergio Leone, Agenore Incrocci, Furio Scarpelli
Photography Tonino Delli Colli **Music** Ennio Morricone **Cast** Clint Eastwood, Lee Van Cleef, Eli Wallach, Aldo Giuffrè, Luigi Pistilli, Rada Rassimov, Enzo Petito, Claudio Scarchilli, John Bartha, Livio Lorenzon, Antonio Casale, Sandro Scarchilli, Benito Stefanelli, Angelo Novi, Antonio Casas

"If you miss you had better · miss very well. Whoever double-crosses me and leaves me alive, he understands nothing about Tuco. Nothing!"

Tuco (Eli Wallach)

i

Clint Eastwood usually gets top billing for the film, but Eli Wallach has the most screen time during it.

1966

Sweden (Svensk) 85m BW
Language Swedish **Producer** Ingmar Bergman **Screenplay** Ingmar Bergman **Photography** Sven Nykvist **Music** Lars Johan Werle **Cast** Bibi Andersson, Liv Ullmann, Margaretha Krook, Gunnar Björnstrand

"At some time or other, I said that Persona *saved my life—that is no exaggeration. If I had not found the strength to make that film, I would probably have been all washed up . . . for the first time I did not care in the least whether the result would be a commercial success."*

Ingmar Bergman, 1990

ℹ

Woody Allen pays homage to *Persona's* famous scene at the end of *Love and Death* (1975).

Persona Ingmar Bergman, 1966

As with other prominent examples of 1960s European art-cinema narration, much of the critical discussion of Ingmar Bergman's *Persona* has portrayed it as obscure and beyond words. True, the director wanted his film to be a visual poem, and he composed the famous opening credit sequence to underline this. However, even in this dense, associative montage, most of the images are recognizable as references to familiar Bergman motifs: the Spider-God (spider), the Christian legacy (crucifixion, lamb to slaughter), art/illusion as construction (the film's title, details of a film projector, the film-within-the-film from the 1949 film *Prison*), the cold womb (a morgue interior with the young boy from the 1964 film *The Silence* naked and reaching toward a cold and distant "mom"). This sequence functions as a prelude summing up Bergman's artistic profile, as if he wished to take stock and then clear the slate for a fresh artistic start. Indeed, the whole film can be seen as a journey to an existential and aesthetic dead end, one where identity, meaning, and language finally collapse, destroying Bergman's art itself as the film strip stops in its tracks, melts, and breaks before starting again.

Superficially the plot of *Persona* is constructed as a variation of the female power game in August Strindberg's chamber play *The Stronger*. Initially, the stronger of the two women in the film appears to be psychiatric nurse Alma (Bibi Andersson), especially because she appears certain of herself and does all the talking. But faced with this enigmatic patient, famous actress Elisabet Vogler (Liv Ullmann), in an isolated summer cottage on a remote island, Alma's own seemingly stable, down-to-earth world-view begins to crumble. Her therapeutic talks turn into confessions of her own hidden secrets and desires. Gradually she is stripped of her own persona, the mask of lies and self-deception that makes up her identity and provides her life with a sense of meaning.

Persona's climax comes in the famous scene where the two women sit opposite each other dressed in identical black clothes. Alma begins to talk about Elisabet's rejection of motherhood and marriage, but soon finds herself talking about her own doubts concerning the family life she previously envisioned. Realizing this, she struggles to regain control with new words of certainty, but her construction of language breaks down and she can only utter incoherent phrases. It is at this point that Bergman uses the optical effect of fusing the two women's faces into one haunting image, a horrific vision of identity in a total state of decomposition.

The film logically ends with Alma doing the only thing she can to reconstruct her sense of self: She returns to the ordinary world that defines her and rejects Elisabet as the Other. In their final scene together we are back at the hospital from the opening of the drama. Alma, now back in her old uniform and persona, forces Elisabet to repeat the word "nothing." Cut back to the boy at the morgue—Elisabet's unwanted child? Alma's aborted fetus?—and then the projector stops. Darkness. **MT**

Au hasard Balthazar Robert Bresson, 1966
Balthazar

France / Sweden (Argos, Athos, Parc, Svensk, Svenska) 95m BW **Language** French **Producer** Mag Bodard **Screenplay** Robert Bresson **Photography** Ghislain Cloquet **Music** Jean Wiener **Cast** Anne Wiazemsky, François Lafarge, Philippe Asselin, Nathalie Joyaut, Walter Green, Jean-Claude Guilbert, Pierre Klossowski, François Sullerot, M.C. Fremont, Jean Rémignard **Venice Film Festival** Robert Bresson (OCIC award)

i

Jean-Luc Godard praised the film for its achievement of depicting "the world in an hour and half."

Robert Bresson's penultimate black-and-white film—a companion piece to the 1967 film *Mouchette*—is a study in saintliness, a powerful and poignant tale of wickedness and suffering, and a grim look at the innate cruelty and destructive impulses of man. By treating the eponymous donkey as a symbol of purity, virtue, and salvation, and by giving his picture a simple yet effective episodic structure, Bresson invests *Balthazar* with a remarkable intensity that is only enhanced by the stark visual style.

Balthazar is an oft-exploited donkey who gets passed from owner to owner, in the process experiencing and observing all manner of human good and evil. His harsh and sorrowful existence is paralleled by that of Marie (Anne Wiazemsky), a reserved young woman who becomes involved with a cruel and sadistic man, Gerard (François Lafarge), who eventually rejects her. Toward the end of his difficult life, however, the former children's pet, circus attraction, and beast of burden becomes the property of a gentle old miller who views him as a reincarnated saint.

Bresson's film has been labeled by at least one critic as "the zenith of purity in the cinema." But the highest praise of all comes from Andrew Sarris in his *Village Voice* review: "[*Balthazar*] stands alone atop one of the loftiest pinnacles of artistically-realized emotional experiences." **SJS**

Masculin, féminin Jean-Luc Godard, 1966
Masculine-Feminine

France / Sweden (Anouchka, Argos Films, Sandrews, Svensk) 103m BW **Language** French / Swedish **Producer** Anatole Dauman **Screenplay** Jean-Luc Godard, from the stories "La Femme de Paul" and "Le Signe" by Guy de Maupassant **Photography** Willy Kurant **Music** Jean-Jacques Debout **Cast** Jean-Pierre Léaud, Chantal Goya, Marlène Jobert, Michel Debord, Catherine-Isabelle Duport, Eva-Britt Strandberg, Birger Malmsten **Berlin International Film Festival** Jean-Luc Godard (Interfilm award—honorable mention, youth film award, best feature for young people, Golden Bear nomination), Jean-Pierre Léaud (Silver Bear—actor)

From the start of his career, there has been scarcely anything resembling conventional dialogue in the films of Jean-Luc Godard; back-and-forth banter between characters takes the form of interviews or inquisitions. By the time of *Masculine-Feminine*, this was a rigorous principle. What gives the film its bleakness is the sense that people cannot even talk to each other anymore except through pop-quizzes, aggressive interrogations, or "celebrity" profiling. And Godard's clean, reportage way of filming such exchanges—this is the least lyrical of his black-and-white works—increases the isolation of the characters in their existential cells.

Godard conceived this film—much to the chagrin of youth audiences then—as an unempathetic, sociological investigation. Its view of gender roles verges on the misanthropic: Girls are empty glamor-bunnies, would-be pop stars, pawns of a consumerist society; boys are posturing, graceless, wannabe revolutionaries. All their stated ideals seem as empty and transient as their intimate relationships; here, Godard anticipated Jean Eustache's *The Mother and the Whore* (1973).

And yet there remains something affecting, the fleeting residue of Godardian poetry: Amid the public confusion there is private reverie, the melancholy of solitude, given immortal expression in the darting eyes of Jean-Pierre Léaud and his inner thoughts while transfixed at the movies. **AM**

Report Bruce Conner, 1967

U.S. (Canyon) 13m BW 16mm

On the day that John F. Kennedy was shot, Bruce Conner started recording images of the assassination off his TV set onto Super 8. Four years of obsessive reworking and reediting of the found footage resulted in the thirteen-minute *Report*, an avant-garde classic.

On the soundtrack, we hear the television and radio commentaries of that day, relating the event with rising hysteria. On the image track, however, Conner withholds the violence. At the point of death we see a white screen and then a violent, flickering alternation of black-and-white frames. Hundreds of representational images return, from newsreels, ads, cartoons, and fiction films, montaged in a frantic free association.

It is as if Conner had instantly intuited, from that first TV moment, that henceforth our entire relation to this event would be through images and sounds recorded and disseminated by the mass media—and that our obsession with making sense of it would happen through an endless replay of that footage. *Report* correctly predicted two polarized responses to the Kennedy assassination: either to be frustrated by the lack of anything to truthfully see in the audiovisual archive; or to see too much, imagining one conspiracy after another, Oliver Stone-style. **AM**

1967

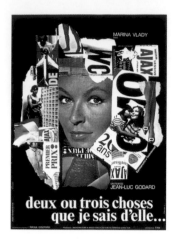

deux ou trois choses
que je sais d'elle...

France (Anouchka, Argos, Carrosse, Parc)
90m Eastmancolor **Language** French
Producer Anatole Dauman, Raoul Lévy
Screenplay Jean-Luc Godard, from letter by
Catherine Vimenet **Photography** Raoul
Coutard **Music** Ludwig van Beethoven
Cast Joseph Gehrard, Marina Vlady, Anny
Duperey, Roger Montsoret, Raoul Lévy,
Jean Narboni

*"Objects exist, and if we
pay them more attention
than we do people, it
is because they exist
more than those people.
Dead objects live on.
Living people are often
dead already."*

**Narrator
(Jean-Luc Godard)**

ℹ

Godard shot *Two or Three Things* in
the morning while simultaneously
filming *Made in USA* in the afternoon.

Deux ou trois choses que je sais d'elle
Two or Three Things I Know About Her
Jean-Luc Godard, 1967

Two or Three Things I Know About Her is one of several Jean-Luc Godard films that take prostitution as a metaphor for life in the modern capitalist state. For Godard, a woman selling herself for money provides a perfect image of how what is most personal and life-enhancing—the sexual act—becomes, like everything else, a commodity. The human being becomes alienated from herself, a mere thing to be bought and sold.

My Life to Live (1962) had been an earlier essay on this theme by Godard, in which the heroine becomes a full-time prostitute, with tragic results. *Two or Three Things* was sparked off by some articles in a French magazine that investigated the phenomenon of suburban housewives who engage in part-time prostitution to make ends meet. The film begins by presenting a shot of a woman at the window of her flat. Godard's own voice on the soundtrack informs us that she is Marina Vlady. "She is an actress. She's wearing a sweater with yellow stripes. She is of Russian origin. She has got fair hair, or maybe light brown. I'm not quite sure." The sequence thus announces a number of characteristic motifs. First, the Brechtian technique of separating the actor from the role, to make the audience question the nature of the fiction being narrated. Godard repeats the shot from another angle, this time describing the character, not the actress: "She is Juliette Janson. She lives here. She is wearing a sweater. . . ." Second, direct address by the director is another Godardian technique for distancing the spectator from the action, preventing a too-close identification with the fiction. Third, the hesitancy ("I'm not quite sure") raises a doubt about the accuracy of what we see. The film uses some of the techniques of the documentary, but constantly intervenes to create a gap between images and their meaning.

The sequence described above is not quite the opening of the film, which starts with views of the city of Paris. It is Paris who is the "Her" referred to in the title. Not for the first or last time, Godard investigates the nature of modern urban living. One of his targets is consumerism and the artificial stimulation of the desire for material goods, which produces the need for more and more money and hence leads to prostitution. Godard fills the screen with colorful images of objects (cups of coffee, cars, tins of food), rendering them at once alluring and absurd.

Overlaid on the brightly colored surface of the film, part documentary, part fiction, is another discourse, about world events. Juliette's husband (Roger Montsoret) is a radio ham, who sits at home listening to news of the Vietnam War, and her small son has a dream in which North and South Vietnam are united. Godard's revolutionary politics, at this stage marked by a kind of knee-jerk anti-Americanism, would soon turn to fully fledged Maoism, but his intellectual playfulness and curiosity about the nature of cinema endow *Two or Three Things* with enduring appeal. **EB**

Belle de jour Luis Buñuel, 1967

Luis Buñuel unfussily described *Belle de jour* as "pornographic," but added that it explored "chaste eroticism." Indeed, it is probably the last great sex film of the 1960s before greater permissiveness and (temporarily) relaxed censorship regulations created a new graphicness in erotic portrayals.

Belle de jour is a prime 1960s artifact in another way too: Alongside such movies as *Breathless* and *La dolce vita* (both 1960) that have enjoyed worldwide re-releases since the 1990s, it captures a certain "style" of the era in its smallest details of speech, gesture, dress, and attitude.

Belle de jour is a sublimely fetishistic movie. Buñuel cares not for Catherine Deneuve's nakedness, but for the clothes and veils that cover it, and for her polished and glazed feminine surface. Although the film revolves around a high-class brothel, sex is never shown. Taking place behind closed doors, within secret nooks, and even in one hilarious scene under a coffin, the sexual perversions hinted at defy the imagination.

Deneuve plays Séverine Serizy, a bourgeois wife who is frigid (perhaps even virginal) with her husband Pierre (Jean Sorel). She eventually assumes a double life on weekday afternoons as a prostitute. Here she feels safe, it seems, to explore her prodigious, masochistic sexual fantasies. However, the neatness of her system is overturned when a flamboyantly seedy gangster (Pierre Clementi) both wins her heart and intrudes into her respectable life.

Summarized like this, *Belle de jour* may seem a schematic, preposterous male fantasy. In fact, it is one of the most mysterious, poetic, complex, and beguiling films ever made. No character's psychology is ever rendered simply or clearly. Nor is the nature of the everyday world they inhabit.

Quietly but surely, Buñuel leads us into a strange territory poised perfectly between dream and reality. Hallucinatory effects that are both funny and disturbing fill the film—such as different characters referring ominously to "letting in the cats" that we hear but never see. Well before the extraordinary final scene, viewers who are open to this seductive, dreamlike texture will no longer expect to know what is really happening—a sweet liberation indeed. **AM**

France / Italy (Five, Paris) 101m
Eastmancolor **Language** French
Producer Henri Baum, Raymond Hakim,
Robert Hakim **Screenplay** Luis Buñuel,
Jean-Claude Carrière, from novel by
Joseph Kessel **Photography** Sacha Vierny
Cast Catherine Deneuve, Jean Sorel, Michel
Piccoli, Geneviève Page, Pierre Clémenti,
Françoise Fabian, Macha Méril, Muni,
Pallas, Maria Latour, Claude Cerval, Michel
Charrel, Iska Khan, Bernard Musson, Marcel
Charvey, François Maistre, Francisco Rabal,
Georges Marchal, Francis Blanch
Venice Film Festival Luis Buñuel (Golden
Lion, Pasinetti award—best film)

1967

> *"One of Buñuel's talents was the complexity he conveyed through ancillary detail: a doorway or a shot of someone's leg often spoke wonders about their social condition."*
>
> Ed Gonzalez,
> *Slant Magazine*, 2003

🛈

Many of Catherine Deneuve's costumes in *Belle de jour* were designed by Yves Saint Laurent.

Cool Hand Luke Stuart Rosenberg, 1967

THE MAN...AND THE MOTION PICTURE THAT SIMPLY DO NOT CONFORM.

PAUL NEWMAN AS COOL HAND LUKE

GEORGE KENNEDY·J. D. CANNON······ JO VAN FLEET [Stuart Rosenberg]···
DONN PEARCE and FRANK R. PIERSON·GORDON CARROLL·TECHNICOLOR® PANAVISION® FROM WARNER BROS.-SEVEN ARTS

U.S. (Jalem, Warner Bros.) 126m Technicolor
Producer Gordon Carroll, Carter De Haven Jr. **Screenplay** Donn Pearce and Frank Pierson, from novel by Donn Pearce **Photography** Conrad L. Hall **Music** Lalo Schifrin **Cast** Paul Newman, George Kennedy, J.D. Cannon, Lou Antonio, Robert Drivas, Strother Martin, Jo Van Fleet, Clifton James, Morgan Woodward, Luke Askew, Marc Cavell, Richard Davalos, Robert Donner, Warren Finnerty, Dennis Hopper, Harry Dean Stanton **Oscar** George Kennedy (actor) **Oscar nominations** Donn Pearce, Frank Pierson (screenplay), Paul Newman (actor), Lalo Schifrin (music)

> *"That's my darling Luke. He grins like a baby but bites like a gator."*
>
> **Dragline**
> **(George Kennedy)**

i

Lalo Schifrin, who was Oscar nominated for the film's score, also wrote the *Mission Impossible* theme.

There are stars and then there are actors like Paul Newman, whose iconic presence and piercing blue eyes regularly transcend even the best material in which he works. The cocky gait of *Cool Hand Luke* may wobble from time to time, but Newman's magnetic personality lends the film the weight its relatively simple story struggles nobly to support. Shot in stunning widescreen by Conrad Hall (all the better to capture the glint of the high noon sun and the glistening, shirtless prisoners of a chain gang), Stuart Rosenberg's film ambitiously vacillates from a straightforward antiauthoritarian story to a macho tall tale and winds up ultimately as a somewhat curious and incomplete Christ allegory.

That it falls awkwardly somewhere in between should surprise no one, but *Cool Hand Luke* remains thoroughly engaging all the same. Newman plays an enigmatically recalcitrant everyday guy, Lucas "Cool Hand" Jackson, thrown into prison for rebelliously cutting the tops off parking meters. Once incarcerated, he unsurprisingly butts against an even more stubborn system of rules, and as his trouble-making stoicism grows more disruptive, the punishments doled out to him grow more severe. Filled with quotable lines and memorable scenes, *Cool Hand Luke* exists as an iconic work in and of itself, deceptively light in meaning but definitely full of cultural (and countercultural) significance.

Indeed, several lines from the film have entered the cinema lexicon (the menacing understatement "What we have here is failure to communicate," for one), whereas scenes like the egg-eating bet and a prison yard fistfight are the stuff of movie legend. A great deal of *Cool Hand Luke*'s considerable charm stems from its colorful cast of supporting actors, a contingent of notable faces that include a young Dennis Hopper, Harry Dean Stanton, and George Kennedy as Newman's rival turned right-hand man.

Kennedy took home the Academy Award for Best Supporting Actor for his portrayal of the ultimately naive tough guy Dragline. But at the heart of the film is Newman's quietly charismatic performance, which showcased the actor at the top of his game and propelled him toward the peak of his popularity. Compared to Jack Nicholson's scenery-chewing performance in the oddly similar *One Flew Over the Cuckoo's Nest* (1975), Newman in *Cool Hand Luke* is all subtle, knowing smiles and beaming confidence. Short on soliloquies, Newman's Luke doesn't telegraph his every move or even clarify his motives. He seems almost to have sought out prison as an arbitrary challenge, inviting a conflict with the system just to see if he can win. In fact, it isn't until close to the film's conclusion that the toll imprisonment has taken on the free-spirited Luke becomes clearer. Unlike the rest of the prisoners, Luke steadfastly rejects the institutional conformity that comes with confinement, and his uncooperative stance ultimately leads to tragedy. If *Cool Hand Luke* is partly about how far one man can push the system, it's also about what happens when that same system pushes back. **JKl**

un film de jacques tati

France / Italy (Jolly, Specta) 155m
Eastmancolor **Language** French /
English / German **Producer** René Silvera
Screenplay Jacques Lagrange, Jacques Tati,
Art Buchwald **Photography** Jean Badal,
Andréas Winding **Music** Francis Lemarque ,
James Campbell **Cast** Jacques Tati, Barbara
Dennek, Rita Maiden, France Rumilly, France
Delahalle, Valérie Camille, Erika Dentzler,
Nicole Ray, Yvette Ducreux, Nathalie Jem,
Jacqueline Lecomte, Oliva Poli, Alice Field,
Sophie Wennek, Evy Cavallaro

*"The images are
designed so that after
you see the picture two
or three times, it's no
longer my film, it starts
to be your film. You
recognize the people,
you know them, and you
don't even know who
directed the picture."*

Jacques Tati, 1972

𝑖

In order to cut production costs,
cardboard cutouts were used as
extras in the background of the film.

Playtime Jacques Tati, 1967

Playtime is less a film than one man's successful attempt to encourage us to see with new eyes. Indeed, director Jacques Tati's timeless masterpiece is concerned, from start to finish, with imbuing the viewer with a totally new set of sensory experiences. Like no other movie, *Playtime* has the power to make us question our very faculties of eyes and ears.

Known for years as the bumbling Monsieur Hulot in such great works as *Mr. Hulot's Holiday* (1953) and *My Uncle* (1958), Tati was far more than a clown, though he played that role with aplomb. Tati's comic work is a bridge between silent and sound film, between vaudeville and the modern era. But it is for his visual sensibilities that he is best remembered. The gags in his films aren't really gags at all, but odd little moments that add up to an overall tone of a world being slightly askew. When there are enough such moments—and they are crammed into literally every corner of *Playtime*'s unbelievably dense mise-en-scène—we begin to realize that they are not there to make us laugh so much as to make us consider our roles as viewers.

Playtime takes place in a cold, clinical version of a futuristic city, and the fiercely rectilinear sets were built from the ground up, at great expense. *Playtime* was an immensely costly film and its box-office returns were minuscule, which kept Tati in hock for a decade after its release. "Tativille" is one of the great achievements of set design—or of megalomania, depending on your perspective. The set had its own roads, electrical systems, and one of the office buildings even had a working elevator. And not since the days of German Expressionism had a director achieved so much with forced perspective, carefully building to scale in order to make something look much farther away than it is.

The world of Tativille is clinical, harsh, and sterile, but Hulot, who wanders through it all with bemused detachment, occasionally finds little patches of organic matter. He finds a flower vendor, for example, who brings a little color to this gray city; and Hulot alone is able to make sense of the bizarrely designed streetlights by likening their shape to that of a tiny bouquet. *Playtime* has much to say about clinical modernity impinging upon older, more earthy ways of life. On one level, the film is about how modern city living has the potential to crush any shred of individuality one may still possess.

Playtime's elaborate visual jokes are far, far too numerous to recount here. Suffice it to say that almost every single object of modern existence—televisions, cars, supermarkets, airports, vacuum cleaners—is given new life and new form here as a comic object.

All the patterns in *Playtime* come to a head in the incredible restaurant scene, which lasts forty-five minutes and which is so visually and sonically dense that repeated viewings are absolutely essential. But repeated viewings are simply more occasions for pleasure. No film offers so rich a viewing experience as *Playtime*. **EdeS**

Csillagosok, katonák Miklós Jancsó, 1967
The Red and the White

This 1967 feature was one of the first by Hungarian filmmaker Miklós Jancsó to have some impact in the United States, and the stylistic virtuosity, ritualistic power, and sheer beauty of his work are already fully apparent here. In this black-and-white pageant, set during the aftermath of the Russian Revolution, the reds are the revolutionaries and the whites are the government forces ordered to crush them. Working in elaborately choreographed long takes with often spectacular vistas, Jancsó invites us to study the mechanisms of power almost abstractly, with a cold eroticism that may glancingly suggest some of the subsequent work of Stanley Kubrick. But this shouldn't mislead one into concluding that Jancsó is any way detached from either politics or emotions.

For one thing, the markedly nationalistic elements in *The Red and the White* could be, and were, interpreted as anti-Russian, especially if one considers that the film was made less than a decade after the Soviet repression of the Hungarian Revolution. And significantly, although the film was a Hungarian–Russian coproduction, the Russian authorities refused to show the film in the Soviet Union.

Jancsó's preference for long shots can't be translated into any sort of disdain for his actors. József Madaras, one of Jancsó's regular actors, has explained that "with him, the actor's face plays a subordinate role: He will formulate and express the psyche through the movements of human masses. That's what audiences, accustomed to conventional representations, may find strange. But he insists on fully creative collaboration from his actors—only in a manner departing from the conventional. He'll never psychologize, never analyze. He makes you move. And from the way he keeps you moving I can figure out what he wants me to do, how he visualizes a character. He thinks in terms of music and sees in terms of rhythm."

If you have never encountered Jancsó's work, this is an ideal place to start. He may well be the key Hungarian filmmaker of the sound era, and later figures such as Béla Tarr would be inconceivable without him. **JRos**

Hungary / U.S.S.R. (Mafilm, Mosfilm)
90m BW **Language** Hungarian / Russian
Producer Jenoe Goetz, András Németh,
Kirill Sirjajev **Screenplay** Gyula Hernádi,
Miklós Jancsó, Luca Karall, Valeri Karen,
Giorgi Mdivani **Photography** Tamás Somló
Cast József Madaras, Tibor Molnár, András
Kozák, Jácint Juhász, Anatoli Yabbarov,
Sergei Nikonenko, Mikhail Kozakov, Bolot
Bejshenaliyev, Tatyana Konyukhova,
Krystyna Mikolajewska, Viktor Avdyushko,
Gleb Strizhenov, Nikita Mikhalkov,
Vladimir Prokofyev, Valentin Bryleyev

"In each Jancsó film, in the interests of the acerbic re-education to which the director has committed us, we are teased and irritated into thought."

Bryan Burns,
World Cinema: Hungary, **1996**

1967

🛈

The film was originally commissioned
to celebrate the fiftieth anniversary
of the October Revolution in Russia.

The Graduate Mike Nichols, 1967

As unlikely as it sounds today, *The Graduate* struck many moviegoers as daring, even a bit scandalous when it opened in 1967. Never before had a high-profile Hollywood film taken such a candid look at sex in the suburbs or focused on a more unlikely romantic trio: a college grad with too much time on his hands, an alcoholic housewife who's determined to get into his pants, and her daughter, a quintessentially nice girl who has no idea her main sexual rival is her own predatory parent. If any mainstream movie hammered the last nail into the coffin of midcentury "momism," this was it. Neither motherhood, suburbia, nor the suffocating fog of postwar middle-class mores would ever seem quite the same.

The creative team behind *The Graduate* was as fresh as its subject and style. Mike Nichols had made a strong impression with his only previous picture, the screen adaptation of Edward Albee's play *Who's Afraid of Virginia Woolf?* (1966). *The Graduate* offered him an even better opportunity to fuse his eye for sardonic details with the ear for razor-sharp verbal wit that he'd honed with Elaine May in the innovative comedy act that had made them synonymous with urban hipness. One of his most original ideas was to supplement a small amount of newly composed Simon and Garfunkel music (most notably "Mrs. Robinson") with previously recorded songs by the duo ("The Sounds of Silence," "Scarborough Fair/ Canticle") that were already loved by millions of teen and twenty-something fans. He used their popularity as an additional selling point and, equally important, a signal that this film would plug into youth-culture sensibilities more directly and sympathetically than any other of its time. The gambit worked aesthetically and commercially, influencing the music tracks of countless Hollywood pictures in years to come.

Dustin Hoffman became a star via his portrayal of Benjamin Braddock, the recently returned graduate stirred by a nebulous dread of his parents' empty-headed materialism. It's part of the movie's legend that Nichols instructed Hoffman to play the part without acting, and the unforced awkwardness of Ben's mannerisms is a key reason for the film's enduring emotional appeal. In a movie with many mythical moments, perhaps the one that has burrowed most deeply under America's pop-culture skin comes when Ben hears a family friend's one-word prescription for financial and professional happiness—"Plastics!"—and reacts with a blend of fear, loathing, and perplexity that's as understated as it is indelible.

The creatively chosen supporting cast includes Anne Bancroft as Mrs. Robinson, Katharine Ross as her daughter, Norman Fell as a landlord with a paranoid fear of what 1960s conservatives called "outside agitators," an uncredited Richard Dreyfuss as a roomer in his boarding house, and Buck Henry as a hotel clerk. Then a newcomer to feature films, Henry co-wrote the screenplay with Calder Willingham, based on Charles Webb's novel. Nichols turned their script into a key achievement of 1960s cinema. **DS**

U.S. (Embassy, Lawrence Turman) 105m Technicolor **Producer** Joseph E. Levine, Lawrence Turman **Screenplay** Buck Henry, Calder Willingham, from novel by Charles Webb **Photography** Robert Surtees **Music** Dave Grusin, Paul Simon **Cast** Anne Bancroft, Dustin Hoffman, Katharine Ross, William Daniels, Murray Hamilton, Elizabeth Wilson, Buck Henry, Brian Avery, Walter Brooke, Norman Fell, Alice Ghostley, Marion Lorne, Eddra Gale **Oscar** Mike Nichols (director) **Oscar nominations** Lawrence Turman (best picture), Calder Willingham, Buck Henry (screenplay), Dustin Hoffman (actor), Anne Bancroft (actress), Katharine Ross (actress in support role), Robert Surtees (photography)

"Hoffman's virginal panic when the leggy Anne Bancroft ... bullies him into bed is ... almost Harold Lloyd-like in its portrayal of courage barely conquering fear of the unknown."

The New Yorker, 2010

i

Despite the onscreen age difference, there were only six years between Bancroft and Hoffman in real life.

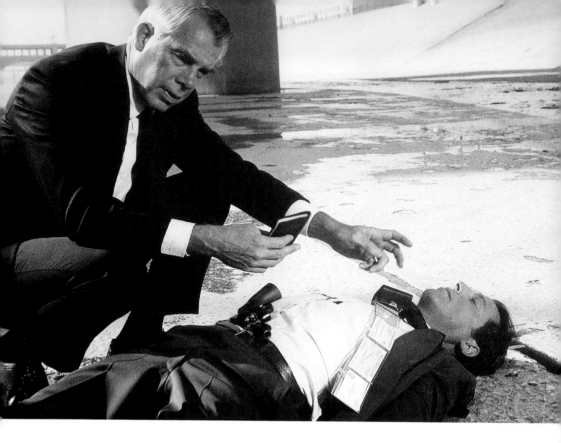

Point Blank John Boorman, 1967

U.S. (MGM) 92m Metrocolor
Producer Judd Bernard, Robert Chartoff
Screenplay Alexander Jacobs, David
Newhouse, Rafe Newhouse, from the novel
The Hunter by Donald E. Westlake
Photography Philip H. Lathrop **Music** Stu
Gardner, Johnny Mandel **Cast** Lee Marvin,
Angie Dickinson, Keenan Wynn, Carroll
O'Connor, Lloyd Bochner, Michael Strong,
John Vernon, Sharon Acker, James Sikking,
Sandra Warner, Roberta Haynes, Kathleen
Freeman, Victor Creatore, Lawrence Hauben,
Susan Holloway

Point Blank was the first movie to film
on location at Alcatraz Island after
the closure of the prison in 1963.

Based on Donald E. Westlake's 1964 novel *The Hunter*, John Boorman's thriller is as arrestingly and unselfconsciously stylish as the day it was released. Beginning with the trick of apparently killing off its main character, the two bullets that pierce Walker (Lee Marvin) set this masculine film—full of tough action and even tougher sexual circumstances—into action.

Walker is left for dead after being betrayed by his friend, gangster Mal Reese (the pock-marked John Vernon). Reese turns out to be the lover of Walker's wife. The bullet wounds healed, Walker wants the $93,000 Reese stole from him, as well as vengeance on his wife Lynne (Sharon Acker), Reese, and all his accomplices. Walker's scheme draws into its vortex Lynne's sister Chris (Angie Dickinson), who is bedded, abused, then abandoned. The long moment where she seduces Reese for Walker's revenge remains an agonizing and perversely sexual love scene, erotic yet gut-wrenchingly distasteful.

The perfect thriller in both form and vision, Boorman's use of widescreen to full effect—urban horizons appear bleak and wide; characters are thrown from one long end of the frame to another—means that *Point Blank* works as well on television as it does in the cinema. **KK**

Les demoiselles de Rochefort
The Young Girls of Rochefort
Jacques Demy & Agnès Varda, 1967

France (Madeleine, Parc) 120m Eastmancolor **Language** English / French **Producer** Mag Bodard, Gilbert de Goldschmidt **Screenplay** Jacques Demy **Photography** Ghislain Cloquet **Music** Michel Legrand **Cast** Catherine Deneuve, George Chakiris, Françoise Dorléac, Jacques Perrin, Michel Piccoli, Jacques Riberolles, Grover Dale, Véronique Duval, Geneviève Thénier, Henri Crémieux, Pamela Hart, Leslie North, Patrick Jeantet, Gene Kelly, Danielle Darrieux **Oscar nomination** Michel Legrand, Jacques Demy (music)

The Young Girls of Rochefort, Jacques Demy's companion piece to his marvelous *The Umbrellas of Cherbourg* (1964), accomplishes a goal that few other films have achieved, or even strived to attain. For two hours, it maintains a tone of unmitigated joy and exuberance.

Everything in this movie connotes happiness, buoyancy, and a joie de vivre that is unmatched in cinema. Even *Umbrellas*, which has an almost unrivaled capacity to amaze and impress, has plenty of moments where the sadness of the story runs counter to the vivaciousness of the imagery. Here there is no such tension. The colors leap from the frame and head right for the pleasure centers of the brain. Working once again with music maestro Michel Legrand, Demy conjures up a magical land where identically garbed sisters sing about the joys of being sisters, where a weekend-long local street fair becomes the apotheosis of love and happiness, and where the mundane act of crossing a bridge inspires carefully choreographed displays of frivolity.

Put simply, *Young Girls* will make you happier than almost any other film you can imagine. And this is no small achievement. **EdeS**

1967

Week End Jean-Luc Godard, 1967

France / Italy (Ascot, Comacico, Copernic, Lira) 105m Eastmancolor **Language** French **Screenplay** Jean-Luc Godard **Photography** Raoul Coutard **Music** Antoine Duhamel, Guy Béart, Wolfgang Amadeus Mozart **Cast** Mireille Darc, Jean Yanne, Jean-Pierre Kalfon, Valérie Lagrange, Jean-Pierre Léaud, Yves Beneyton, Paul Gégauff, Daniel Pommereulle, Virginie Vignon, Yves Afonso, Blandine Jeanson, Ernest Menzer, Georges Staquet, Juliet Berto, Helen Scott **Berlin International Film Festival** Jean-Luc Godard (Golden Bear nomination)

Week End might be the wildest and wooliest of all of Jean-Luc Godard's films—which is saying something. It's also one of his most audacious.

This is a film in which anything goes: A mundane phone conversation becomes an absurdly charming musical number, our heroes encounter fairy-tale characters in the woods, and main characters can meet grisly ends at, really, any time at all. Godard's decision to move from episode to bizarre episode was bold and highly influential. Radical filmmakers of all stripes and colors owe a great debt to *Week End*.

But "radical" is a somewhat unfortunate label for the film, for it connotes dire politicization and humorlessness. Rest assured that *Week End* suffers from neither of these problems. In fact, it's a deeply funny film, in part because of its political attitudes. The ability to blend the serious, the comic, the beautiful, and the absurd was but one of Godard's many gifts.

No discussion of *Week End* is complete without mention of its most famous shot—one of the most famous shots in cinema. Perhaps the film's centerpiece is the ten-minute or so tracking shot of the world's nastiest traffic jam—interrupted by Godard's irrepressible penchant for didactic, elliptical intertitles. This is no ordinary gridlock—Godard's nightmarish but hilarious version includes zoo animals, boats, the occasional picnic, and a hell of a lot of blood. But, as the director once famously said, it's nothing to worry about: It's really only red paint. **EdeS**

Le samouraï Jean-Pierre Melville, 1967
The Godson

Jean-Pierre Melville had the flair to invent a quotation from the "Bushido Book of the Samurai" as an on-screen preface: "There is no greater solitude than the samurai's, unless it is that of the tiger in the jungle . . . perhaps. . . ." No further allusion to Japanese culture is required: That's enough to give *Le samouraï* an abstract, mythic, timeless air. It is a breathtaking work, stylized to the point of asphyxiation, in which the imaginary world of cinema beats reality hands down. No wonder filmmakers from John Woo to Paul Thomas Anderson via Quentin Tarantino and Walter Hill have plundered it as the veritable Bible of cool moves.

Jef Costello (Alain Delon) is a steely hit man for whom the adjective "hard-boiled" is an understatement. Methodical, asexual, and apparently amoral in his willingness to kill on command, Jef finds himself set up and pursued—like his namesake played by Robert Mitchum in *Out of the Past* (1947), he's "in a frame" and needs to go in and "look at the picture." His ultimate confrontation with the witness who could incriminate him exposes the enigma of his inner motivations throughout.

Melville's vision of Paris is filtered through his love of American film noir: jazz nightclubs with black singers, dark and rainy streets. The cops function as in a Fritz Lang film, mapping the city through intricate surveillance and tracking this elusive human blip. Yet the heady atmosphere of movie fantasy is balanced by Melville's legendary, maniacal attention to detail, which itself borders on the obsessiveness of a police procedural: The logistics of every gesture, of every movement around the city, are impeccably plotted and recorded.

It is hard to watch *Le samouraï*—largely without dialogue, in which every sound (such as the chirping bird in Jef's apartment, the roar of a car engine, or the clanking of a key ring) is isolated and heightened, in which actors pose like gorgeous mannequins (Delon here as porcelain as Catherine Deneuve in *Belle de jour* [1967])—without remembering Robert Bresson. Melville rejected the comparison, but it's true: Jef is almost an ascetic priest, animated by an inner calling. **AM**

France / Italy (CICC, Fida, Filmel, TC) 105m Eastmancolor **Language** French **Producer** Raymond Borderie, Eugène Lépicier **Screenplay** Jean-Pierre Melville, Georges Pellegrin, from the novel *The Ronin* by Joan McLeod **Photography** Henri Decaë **Music** François de Roubaix **Cast** Alain Delon, François Périer, Nathalie Delon, Cathy Rosier, Jacques Leroy, Michel Boisrond, Robert Favart, Jean-Pierre Posier, Catherine Jourdan, Roger Fradet, Carlo Nell, Robert Rondo, André Salgues, André Thorent, Jacques Deschamps

"It is difficult to see how this story could be better accomplished. It has all the best virtues of American film noir but with a European sensibility."

Derek Malcolm,
***The Guardian*, 2000**

i

Jean-Pierre Melville changed his name from Grumbach after reading Herman Melville's novel *Moby Dick*.

Wavelength Michael Snow, 1967

U.S. / Canada (Canyon)
45min 16mm Color **Producer** Michael
Snow **Screenplay** Michael Snow
Photography Michael Snow **Cast** Hollis
Frampton, Joyce Wieland, Amy Yadrin, Lyne
Grossman, Maoto Nakagawa, Roswell Rudd

Ostensibly an archetype of minimalism, *Wavelength* is actually action-packed. An experimental movie that acknowledges the conventions of mystery and narrative inherent in all cinema, it was designed to change the relationship the viewer has with the screen, forcing audiences to think through processes and factors that most films take for granted.

Director Michael Snow presents the whole film in a single shot, a forty-five minute tracking shot across a large urban room to focus on a detail of a photograph (of waves) fixed to the far wall. It's a relentless film, witty at its own expense as it forces you to deal with physical space and the intrusions of the tiniest elements of human narrative. There's even an apparent murder as a man (Hollis Frampton) walks on during a commotion and falls dead, with a woman later showing up to discover the corpse and make a phone call and police sirens indicating the ripples of this event spreading, but by the time this melodrama is in swing, the camera has tracked in so far that the big picture is no longer available. We are too close to the wall to comprehend what has taken place.

Though *Wavelength* consists of a single shot, it is not a single take: On the voyage across the room, filmstock, color processes, and lighting change; meanwhile, a sine wave on the soundtrack progresses from its lowest note (50 cycles per second) to its highest (12,000 cycles) with snatches of The Beatles ("Strawberry Fields Forever") mixed in. Like much underground and experimental cinema, *Wavelength* is easy to parody as pretentious, but it is still a vital, important, and necessary work. **KN**

i

In 2003, Snow condensed the film into the short *WVLNT* (or *Wavelength For Those Who Don't Have the Time*).

Ostre sledované vlaky Jiří Menzel, 1967
Closely Watched Trains

With its bittersweet humor, lovingly observed detail, and ruefully affectionate humanism, *Closely Watched Trains* stands as the epitome of the cinema of the Czech New Wave. It was Jiří Menzel's first full-length feature and, like much of his early work, was adapted from the writings of the Czech novelist Bohumil Hrabal. The relationship between the writer and the director, who collaborated together on the script, was exceptionally close and cordial; Menzel, accepting his Oscar for Best Foreign Language Film, attributed all the credit to the novelist, whereas Hrabal always maintained he preferred the film to the original.

Trains takes as its main narrative thread the sentimental education of a timid, sensitive adolescent lad. Miloš, played by Václav Neckář, with a wondering gaze that often recalls Buster Keaton, is touchingly proud of his new uniform as a station guard that will allow him "to stand on a platform and avoid hard work." Yearningly in love with a conductress on a local train, he plunges into despair when nervousness causes his failure to consummate. His role model is his older colleague, the cynical and tirelessly randy Hubička (Josef Somr), who spends his time either quietly undermining authority or pursuing every female who crosses his path.

This theme—though freshly and beguilingly observed—would be conventional enough were it not for the setting: a sleepy backwater railroad station during the last years of World War II. The war, ever present but at first largely disregarded, gradually comes to overshadow events, adding layers of complexity and tragedy to Miloš's story. By approaching this period from an oblique angle, Menzel's intention was to deconstruct the heroic myth of war, "because most films, whether they mean to or not, glamorize the war." *Trains* doesn't deal in heroes: Hubička is far more concerned with his amorous adventures than with his contribution to the Resistance, for example, and Miloš gets involved largely by accident.

Likewise, nobody is demonized: A group of German soldiers, wistfully eyeing a train-load of pretty nurses, are not strutting, fascist beasts but homesick youngsters; and the pro-Nazi Czech collaborator, Counselor Zedníček (Vlastimil Brodský), is more fool than villain. A side-glance at the Soviet domination of Czechoslovakia is never insisted upon, but would have been picked up by domestic audiences at the time.

The spirit of *The Good Soldier Švejk*, embodiment of the Czech genius for smiling insubordination and dumb insolence, hovers over the film—never more so than in the station staff's straight-faced response to Zedníček's explanation of how the Wehrmacht's retreat on all fronts is in fact a brilliant tactic to ensure victory. Like Hašek's classic novel, *Closely Watched Trains* blends comedy, tragedy, and farce, eroticism and satire, naturalism and absurdity, into a highly idiosyncratic and beguiling mix. And, thanks to Hrabal, Menzel let himself be persuaded not to soften the novel's tragic ending. **PK**

Czechoslovakia (Barrandov) 92m BW / Color **Language** Czech / German **Producer** Zdenek Oves **Screenplay** Jiří Menzel, from novel by Bohumil Hrabal **Photography** Jaromír Sofr **Music** Jiří Pavlik, Jiří Sust **Cast** Václav Neckář, Josef Somr, Vlastimil Brodský, Vladimír Valenta, Alois Vachek, Ferdinand Kruta, Jitka Bendová, Jitka Zelenohorská, Nada Urbánková, Libuše Havelková, Kveta Fialová, Pavla Maršálková, Marie Ježková, Zuzana Minichová, Václav Fišer **Oscar** Czechoslovakia (best foreign language film)

> "Good comedy should be about serious things. If you start to talk about serious things too seriously, you end up being ridiculous."
>
> **Jiří Menzel, 2008**

ℹ

At one point Menzel considered playing the role of Miloš himself, but in the end concluded he was too old.

Terra em transe Glauber Rocha, 1967
Earth Entranced

On April 1, 1964, a military coup took over Brazil, ushering in a twenty-five-year-long dictatorship. For the very active and vocal Brazilian Left, the biggest shock of the takeover was not that it happened, but how quickly and bloodlessly the civilian government fell. This gnawing combination of rage, guilt, and depression curiously led to a number of remarkable cinematic meditations on politics, violence, and the role of intellectuals in both. Glauber Rocha's *Earth Entranced* was perhaps the finest example of this impressive crop.

In a land called Eldorado, the poet and filmmaker Paulo Martins (Jardel Filho) decides to abandon the patronage of the political patriarch Porfirio Diaz (Paulo Autran) to throw his support behind populist Felipe Vieira (José Lewgoy) for governor. Vieira is elected, but soon reneges on his campaign promises; Vieira brutally puts down a peasant revolt, causing Paulo to leave him and return to the wild, orgiastic life he knew so well. But led by Sara (Glauce Rocha), Paulo's former lover, a group of "radicals" who support Vieira convince Paulo it's his duty to use his connections to destroy his former patron Diaz. Paulo obliges, but the experience leaves him disgusted with all politics. Learning later that he's been betrayed, and that martial law has been declared, Paulo opts for armed, militant resistance, but he's gunned down by the police.

That's the story; what emerges while watching the film is something quite different. Told in flashback, Rocha's film is a wild mélange of grand opera and cinema verité, Villa Lobos and Afro-Brazilian exorcisms. The personal and political turmoil personified by Paulo Martins is rendered viscerally by a visual style that alternates rapid-fire jump cuts with long, daredevil handheld camera sequences. Rocha creates a galaxy of archetypes that adroitly capture the spectrum of Latin American politics in the 1950s and 1960s, experiences that by the early 1970s led to military dictatorship throughout the region. Few films were as insightful, nor as universally criticized. Yet seen today it seems not only Rocha's masterpiece, but also that of the new Latin American cinema. **RP**

Brazil (Mapa) 106m BW
Language Portuguese **Producer** Luiz Carlos Barreto, Carlos Diegues , Raymundo Wanderley Reis, Glauber Rocha, Zelito Viana **Screenplay** Glauber Rocha **Photography** Luiz Carlos Barreto **Music** Sérgio Ricardo **Cast** Jardel Filho, Paulo Autran, José Lewgoy, Glauce Rocha, Paulo Gracindo, Hugo Carvana, Danuza Leão, Jofre Soares, Modesto De Souza, Mário Lago, Flávio Migliaccio, Telma Reston, José Marinho, Francisco Milani, Paulo César Peréio **Cannes Film Festival** Glauber Rocha (FIPRESCI award, Golden Palm nomination)

> *"Wherever there is a filmmaker prepared to film the truth and to oppose the hypocrisy and repression of intellectual censorship, there will be the living spirit of Cinema Novo."*
>
> **Glauber Rocha,**
> ***The Aesthetic of Hunger*, 1965**

ℹ

It has been noted that the subject and structure of *Earth Entranced* have similarities with *Citizen Kane* (1941).

In the Heat of the Night Norman Jewison, 1967

U.S. (Mirisch Company) 109m Color
Producer Walter Mirisch Screenplay Stirling
Silliphant, from novel by John Ball
Photography Haskell Wexler Music Quincy
Jones Cast Sidney Poitier, Rod Steiger,
Warren Oates, Lee Grant, Larry Gates, James
Patterson, William Schallert, Beah Richards,
Peter Whitney, Kermit Murdock, Larry D.
Mann, Matt Clark, Arthur Malet, Fred
Stewart, Quentin Dean Oscars Walter
Mirisch (best picture), Stirling Silliphant
(screenplay), Rod Steiger (actor), Hal Ashby
(editing), (sound) Oscar nominations
Norman Jewison (director), James Richard
(special sound effects)

"They call me Mister Tibbs." Racism was still underexplored on screen when independent producer Walter Mirisch and director Norman Jewison had John Ball's novel In the Heat of the Night adapted specifically for Sidney Poitier. The result was in the vanguard of new social crime thrillers elevating what earlier would have been B-movie fare into important pictures.

Virgil Tibbs (Poitier) is arrested simply because he is a black man with money passing through segregated Sparta, Mississippi, the night of a northern industrialist's murder. To the bigoted police chief's (Rod Steiger) chagrin, Tibbs is a Philadelphia homicide detective, and the inimical odd couple are forced to cooperate in the investigation. The crime element and atmosphere are strong (enhanced by a memorable Quincy Jones score), but the film's enduring impact results from the fascinating relationship developed between the men. Poitier commands his top billing with princely disdain for the white trash who beset him while he unravels a Chandleresque tangle, but Steiger's gum-snapping, hot-tempered, huge but subtle performance claimed the Academy Award for Best Actor. The film also won Oscars for Best Picture, Screenplay, Sound, and Editing. Poitier reprised the role of Tibbs in two sequels. **AE**

Marketa Lazarová Frantisek Vlácil, 1967

Czechoslovakia (Barrandov) 162m BW
Language Czech Producer Josef Ouzky
Screenplay Frantisek Pavlicek, Frantisek
Vlácil, from novel by Vladislav Vancura
Photography Bedrich Batka Music Zdenek
Liska Cast Josef Kemr, Magda Vásáryová,
Nada Hejna, Jaroslav Moucka, Frantisek
Velecky, Karel Vasicek, Ivan Palúch, Martin
Mrazek, Václav Sloup, Pavla Polaskova, Alena
Pavlíková, Michal Kozuch, Zdenek Lipovcan,
Harry Studt, Vlastimil Harapes

Set in the thirteenth-century Bohemian forests, Frantisek Vlácil's ambitious and multilayered medieval epic thematizes the transition from paganism to Christianity through the abduction and brutal rape by a fierce pagan warrior, Mikolás Kozlík (Frantisek Veleck), of the eponymous female lead (Magda Vásáryová), the innocent, convent-bound daughter of a clan leader.

Upon its initial release (after six years in the making), Variety magazine declared Marketa Lazarová, with its nearly three hour length, elliptical narrative, and emphasis on symbol and metaphor, "a stunning work—unsuitable for general commercial release." Eventually given its due, this black-and-white Gothic masterpiece—based on a prewar avant-garde novel and visually evocative of Carl Theodor Dreyer, Akira Kurosawa, and Ingmar Bergman—was voted the best Czech film of all time by a panel of the country's critics and industry leaders in 1998.

Rather than reduce the story to an action-filled but superficial adventure, Vlácil—known for his poetic lyricism and historical films (his 1961 film The Devil's Trap was set during the counter-Reformation, and his 1967 film Valley of the Bees has its Czech hero brought up as a member of the Teutonic Knights)—here makes use of haunting cinematography and period details to delve into the psychological and spiritual state of his characters. As such, Marketa Lazarová stands as "an atavistic nightmare, a cinematic poem difficult to categorize in terms of genre or fear." **SJS**

Horí, má panenko Milos Forman, 1967
The Fireman's Ball

Czechoslovakia / **Italy** (Carlo Ponti, Barrandov) 71m Eastmancolor **Language** Czech **Producer** Rudolf Hájek, Carlo Ponti **Screenplay** Milos Forman, Jaroslav Papousek, Ivan Passer, Václav Sasek **Photography** Miroslav Ondrícek **Music** Karel Mares **Cast** Jan Vostrcil, Josef Sebanek, Josef Valnoha, Frantisek Debelka, Josef Kolb, Jan Stöckl, Vratislav Cermák, Josef Rehorek, Václav Novotny, Frantisek Reinstein, Frantisek Paska, Stanislav Holubec, Josef Kutálek, Frantisek Svet, Ladislav Adam **Oscar nomination** Czechoslovakia (best foreign language film)

"The movie is just plain funny. And as a parable it is timeless, with relevance at many times in many lands."

Roger Ebert, critic, 2002

ℹ

The idea for the film arose after Milos Forman and Ivan Passer attended a fireman's ball in a small town.

Although Milos Forman never aspired to produce an allegory, his *The Fireman's Ball* is nevertheless a potent black comedy about the evils of a Soviet-style society. Also an award-winning movie and part of the reason why Forman defected to the West, the film was lambasted for its political subtext by coproducer Carlo Ponti despite being a smash hit that debuted precisely when tanks invaded Prague to extend the Iron Curtain.

Set in a small Czechoslovakian village, this film has several points of interest: the namesake party, a ceremony to honor the volunteer fire department's retired leader, a raffle for valuable foodstuffs, a beauty contest, and a fire that breaks out toward evening's end to tragicomic result.

Not compelling for its plot alone, *The Fireman's Ball* is a must-see title featuring a motley ensemble of laypeople discovered in the town where the film was shot. Episodic in structure, naturalistic in style, and interested in the broadest possible humor, the picture skillfully develops its careful observations about group behavior within confined circumstances.

Opening as the well-intentioned committee members of a volunteer fire department commission a trophy to honor their outgoing chief, the town's meeting hall holds fine goods for a raffle. As the hall fills with guests and the committee is consumed with an effort to find pretty young women for the "Miss" contest—an opportunity for members to ogle bared flesh—the raffle prizes are stolen, one by one. Everyone present is therefore suspect of burgling the goods because of the obvious scarcity that makes taking fine products like meat and expensive liquors extremely tempting for all.

The "Miss" contest subsequently spins out of control and then a fire breaks out across town. Despite all efforts by the now-drunken committee to tame the angry flames, an old man is left to watch his home burn down in the snow. By film's end the committee's members are left with a threefold failure to hold a raffle, promote a beauty contest, or put out a fire with but one remaining grace. Celebrating their retired leader, regardless of implicit cynicism about committees, comrades, and optimism for a better tomorrow—all core values of the predominant communist rhetoric—the bestowal of respect on one's elders appears as nothing more than empty pomp and circumstance.

Written by Forman, Jaroslav Papousek, and Ivan Passer, *The Fireman's Ball* demonstrates a critical awareness of Soviet society. Without overemphasizing that condition and the consequent want and deprivation everywhere part of Czechoslovakian life in 1967, the film further suggests how moral fortitude fails in the face of corrupt leadership benefiting the few at the expense of the many. Of course this tendency stems from a lack of everyday staples like good food and water, but it easily extends to an overall breakdown in civilized behavior, which seems like the film's allegorical resonance no matter Forman's intentions. **GC-Q**

The Jungle Book Wolfgang Reitherman, 1967

U.S.(Walt Disney) 78m Technicolor
Producer Walt Disney **Screenplay** Larry Clemmons, Ralph Wright, Ken Anderson, Vance Gerry, from novel by Rudyard Kipling **Music** George Bruns, Terry Gilkyson, Richard M. Sherman **Cast** Phil Harris, Sebastian Cabot, Louis Prima, George Sanders, Sterling Holloway, J Pat O'Malley, Bruce Reitherman, Verna Felton, Clint Howard, Chad Stuart, Lord Tim Hudson, John Abbott, Ben Wright, Darleen Carr **Oscar nomination** Terry Gilkyson (song)

i

The four vultures were based on The Beatles, who they were originally intended to be voiced by.

Perhaps the best loved of all the Disney animated features, *The Jungle Book* kicks off from Rudyard Kipling's story of a boy raised in the jungle by wolves. Unlike the live-action versions by Zoltan Korda (1942) and Stephen Sommers (1994), which focus on the boy's experiences on returning to civilization, the cartoon is about Mowgli's last days in the wild; the return of the ferocious tiger Shere Khan means it's no longer safe for him here. Mowgli demurs, but like Pinocchio before him, he is easily led astray, and only saved from the clutches of Kaa (the snake)and King Louie (the ape), by his friends Bagheera (a panther), and Baloo (the bear).

Although it's a slight story and the animation is unexceptional, the characterization and score give the picture distinction. The last animated feature to be overseen by Walt Disney himself, *The Jungle Book* was the first to use stars for the voice talent: An unmistakeable George Sanders is the insidious Shere Khan, Louis Prima sings "I'm the King of the Swingers," and Phil Harris has a ball as the beatnik dropout, Baloo, with his signature song "The Bear Necessities." A belated sequel, *Jungle Book 2*, followed in 2003. **TCh**

Bonnie and Clyde Arthur Penn, 1967

Arthur Penn's attempt to make an American "outlaw" film with French New Wave style and youthful exuberance proved an outstanding success with audiences, who appreciated its antiestablishment politics. Critics, too, eventually applauded the director's effort to infuse American cinema with a new energy and seriousness. However, *Bonnie and Clyde* was roundly condemned on its release for its graphic depiction of violence. Technological developments had made it possible to show gunshot wounds more realistically, and Penn's camera often lingers on the effects of bodies being torn apart and on the pain and suffering that results. Previous American films, of course, had often centered on violence, but *Bonnie and Clyde* was the first Hollywood picture to make the spectator strongly experience its horror and, even, mesmerizing beauty.

Initial reviews of the film were dismissive, even condemnatory, but the tide of critical opinion soon dramatically turned. Alternating effectively between scenes of terror, brutal realism, and almost slapstick comedy, *Bonnie and Clyde* is loosely biographical and has a very realistic feel due to meticulous art design and location shooting in northeast Texas. With some historical inaccuracies, it traces the exploits and eventual tragic end of the Depression era's most famous bank-robbing duo, who in their own time were celebrated as folk heroes. Warren Beatty and Faye Dunaway are scintillating as the criminal couple, while terrific support is provided by Gene Hackman, Estelle Parsons, and Michael J. Pollard. After a successful early spree, the gang is cornered by police in Iowa, where Clyde's brother Buck (Hackman) is killed and his wife Blanche (Parsons) is blinded and captured. The other three elude police pursuit, but eventually Bonnie and Clyde are lured into an ambush where they are riddled with machine-gun bullets in a slow-motion ballet of death.

The film's frank treatment of sex, particularly the unusual relationship between the impotent Clyde and the aggressive Bonnie, also broke new ground. By the late 1960s, Hollywood had abandoned Production Code restrictions for a ratings system that permitted greater freedom in the portrayal of sex and violence. *Bonnie and Clyde* is among the first and most successful films made under this new system. It earned ten Academy Award nominations, and its immense drawing power at the box office helped put American cinema into a newfound profitability.

Bonnie and Clyde is a powerfully ambiguous statement about the place of violence and the individual in American society. In movie history, however, its importance is much greater. The film's popular and critical success showed the Hollywood establishment that pictures combining European stylization and seriousness with traditional American themes (mediated by conventional genres) could be successful. *Bonnie and Clyde* paved the way for the "Hollywood Renaissance" of the 1970s, with masterpieces like Francis Ford Coppola's *The Godfather* (1972) paying Penn's film the sincere praise of close imitation. **RBP**

U.S. (Tatira-Hiller, Warner Bros./Seven Arts) 111m Technicolor **Producer** Warren Beatty **Screenplay** David Newman, Robert Benton **Photography** Burnett Guffey **Music** Charles Strouse **Cast** Warren Beatty, Faye Dunaway, Michael J. Pollard, Gene Hackman, Estelle Parsons, Denver Pyle, Dub Taylor, Evans Evans, Gene Wilder **Oscars** Estelle Parsons (actress in support role), Burnett Guffey (photography) **Oscar nominations** Warren Beatty (best picture), Arthur Penn (director), David Newman, Robert Benton (screenplay), Warren Beatty (actor), Faye Dunaway (actress), Michael J. Pollard (actor in support role), Gene Hackman (actor in support role), Theadora Van Runkle (costume)

> "This here's Miss Bonnie Parker. I'm Clyde Barrow. We rob banks."
>
> **Clyde Barrow**
> **(Warren Beatty)**

i

Blanche Barrow complained that Estelle Parsons's portrayal of her made her "look like a screaming horse's ass."

Viy Georgi Kropachyov & Konstantin Yershov, 1967

U.S.S.R. (Mosfilm) 78m Color
Language Russian Screenplay Georgi
Kropachyov, Aleksandr Ptushko, Konstantin
Yershov, from story by Nikolai Gogol
Photography Viktor Pishchalnikov, Fyodor
Provorov Music Karen Khachaturyan
Cast Leonid Kuravlyov, Natalya Varley,
Aleksei Glazyrin, Vadim Zakharchenko,
Nikolai Kutuzov, Pyotr Vesklyarov, Dmitri
Kapka, Stepan Shkurat, G. Sochevko, Nikolai
Yakovchenko, Nikolai Panasyev,
Vladimir Salnikov

Based on the same short story by famed nineteenth-century Russian author Nikolai Gogol that inspired Mario Bava's Italian horror classic *The Mask of Satan* (1960), Georgi Kropachyov and Konstantin Yershov's *Viy* is a colorful, entertaining, and genuinely frightening film of demons and witchcraft that boasts some remarkable special-effects work by Russia's master of cinematic fantasy, Aleksandr Ptushko.

Ill-fated seminary student Khoma Brutus (Leonid Kuravlyov) gets lost in some fields while on holiday, and ends up staying the night in an old crone's barn. The woman soon reveals herself to be a witch, using Khoma as a living broomstick. After beating her unconscious, Khoma watches with a mix of guilt and awe as the hag transforms into a beautiful young lady. Following this, Khoma is summoned to a remote village, where he has been specially selected to preside over the wake of a young woman in an ancient church. This entails spending three nights alone with the eerily familiar-looking corpse, with only his faltering faith to protect him.

It is here that the film truly amazes, as nightmarish creatures from beyond begin a parade across the screen. They culminate with the appearance of the demon Vly, who, in the words of one reviewer, "makes his entrance against a backdrop of one of the finest collections of ghoulies, ghosties, and long-leggity beasties" ever to appear in the movies. **SJS**

Gaav Dariush Mehrju, 1968
The Cow

Iran (Iranian Ministry of Culture) 100m BW
Language Farsi Producer Dariush
Mehrjui Screenplay Dariush Mehrjui,
from play by Gholam-Hossein Saedi
Photography Fereduyn Ghovanlu
Music Hormoz Farhat Cast Ezzatolah
Entezami, Mahmoud Dowlatabadi, Parviz
Fanizadeh, Jamshid Mashayekhi, Ali
Nassirian, Esmat Safavi, Khosrow Shojazadeh,
Jafar Vali Berlin International Film
Festival Dariush Mehrjui (OCIC award—
recommendation, forum of new film)

Rumor has it that after seeing *The Cow*, the Ayatollah Khomeini opined that perhaps there might be a place for filmmaking in the Islamic Republic, thus creating at least the theoretical possibility for the Iranian cinema of Abbas Kiarostami, Mohsen Makhmalbaf, Jafar Panahi, and others. The first Iranian feature film to attract significant international attention, *The Cow* was the second feature by the UCLA-educated Dariush Mehrjui, who returned to Iran determined to create a new kind of filmmaking comparable to the new Third World cinema then just emerging.

Based on a play by Gholam-Hossein Saedi, who also contributed to the screenplay, *The Cow* is the story of Masht Hassan (Ezzatolah Entezami), proud owner of the only cow in a poor village. One day, when he is away on business, the cow unexpectedly dies; rather than reveal the truth to him, the other villagers pretend the cow has merely strayed. With so much of his identity and status wrapped up in that cow, Hassan grows increasingly obsessed with finding it, to the point of madness. Financed largely by the Shah's government, the movie's image of Iranian backwardness and poverty so outraged its producers that they forced the filmmakers to tack on a disclaimer stating that the events depicted occurred long before the current regime. **RP**

C'era una volta il west Sergio Leone, 1968
Once Upon a Time in the West

U.S. (Paramount, Rafran, San Marco)
165m Technicolor **Language** Italian
Producer Bino Cicogna, Fulvio Morsella
Screenplay Dario Argento, Bernardo
Bertolucci, Sergio Donati, Mickey Knox,
Sergio Leone **Photography** Tonino Delli
Colli **Music** Ennio Morricone **Cast** Henry
Fonda, Claudia Cardinale, Jason Robards,
Charles Bronson, Gabriele Ferzetti, Paolo
Stoppa, Woody Strode, Jack Elam, Snaky,
Keenan Wynn, Frank Wolff, Lionel Stander

i

The Flagstone set reportedly cost as
much as the entire budget for
Leone's *A Fistful of Dollars* (1964).

Sergio Leone's Western masterpiece finds Charles Bronson stepping into the "No Name" role as the vengeance-seeking Harmonica and Henry Fonda trashing his Wyatt Earp image as the dead-faced, blue-eyed killer, Frank. The opening—Woody Strode, Al Mulock, and Jack Elam waiting for a train and bothered by a fly and dripping water—is masterful bravura, homing in on tiny details for a fascinating but eventless length of time before Bronson arrives for the shoot-out that gets the film going.

Once Upon a Time in the West is the first Leone film to place violence in a truly political context, indicting the corrupt (and crippled) railroad tycoon who "leaves two shiny, slimy tracks like a snail" as he bulldozes across the landscape, employing outlaw flunkeys to dispose of inconvenient settlers who won't unsettle easily. Rapacious civilization taints the wide open spaces as Harmonica quests to track down the sadist who hanged his brother, widow-whore-earth mother Claudia Cardinale tries to fulfill her murdered husband's dream of a real community out West, and bandido Jason Robards just wants to be left in a natural state of childish abandon. With striking widescreen compositions and epic running time, this is truly a Western that wins points for both length and width. **KN**

Faces John Cassavetes, 1968

Laughter, because it is so hard to act, often comes across as phony when depicted onscreen. But in *Faces*, every kind of laughter—lunatic, lusty, nervous, hysterical, defensive—is rendered with absolute authenticity, even when prescripted or postsynchronized.

What was John Cassavetes's secret? His rapport with actors was so total, his work with them so intensely detailed, that he was able to capture lived reality like no other American director. After the experiment of *Shadows* (1959) and bad experiences within the Hollywood system, *Faces* confidently marked the beginning of the Cassavetes "signature." Filmed in his home, it records vivid scenes in the lives of people who are at once hopelessly yearning and furiously alienated—stranded, like all Cassavetes characters, between the difficult responsibilities of daily routine and the reckless intoxications of nightlife.

Cassavetes shows his brilliant ensemble cast—John Marley and Lynn Carlin are especially memorable—always *in media res*, their bodies off-center in the frame, their words and gestures truncated by the editing. Each scene is based on an unpredictable and often terrifying "turn," a sudden change in a character's mood or manner toward another. *Faces* invents a new way of experiencing time in cinema, where sudden pauses register as (in Cassavetes's words) "like stepping off a fast train."

Sometimes taken as the condemnation of a soulless, materialist middle class, the film is, rather, a painfully intimate and compassionate account of everyday suffering. Cassavetes stakes out the terrain he would often revisit—marital crisis, casual sex, hedonistic abandon, family ties—within a narrative that constantly shuffles and compares character's journey through a long night and its aftermath.

Is *Faces* the first film in cinema history where characters talk (indeed, laugh themselves stupid) about cunnilingus? Several decades later, directors including Neil LaBute and Lars von Trier are still trying to catch up to Cassavetes's astonishing ability to show the messy complexity of adult relationships. **AM**

U.S. (Castle Hill) 130m BW
Producer John Cassavetes, Maurice McEndree **Screenplay** John Cassavetes
Photography Maurice McEndree, Al Ruban
Music Jack Ackerman, Charlie Smalls
Cast John Marley, Gena Rowlands, Lynn Carlin, Seymour Cassel, Fred Draper, Val Avery, Dorothy Gulliver, Jerry Howard, Carolyn Fleming, Don Kraatz, John Hale, Midge Ware, Kay Michaels, Laurie Mock, Christina Crawford
Oscar nominations John Cassavetes (screenplay), Seymour Cassel (actor in support role), Lynn Carlin (actress in support role) **Venice Film Festival** John Marley (Volpi Cup—actor), John Cassavetes (Golden Lion nomination)

"Why did the man throw the clock out of the window, huh? He wanted to see time fly."

**Richard Forst
(John Marley)**

i

Steven Spielberg worked as an uncredited production assistant on *Faces* for two weeks.

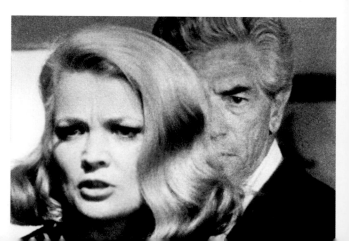

Planet of the Apes Franklin J. Schaffner, 1968

A classic science-fiction adventure that remains as powerful today as when it was first released, *Planet of the Apes* was a project that had the potential to go horribly wrong—the 2001 Tim Burton remake being an example of just how. Even if the $100 million budget was still two decades away, it was still a risky proposition to make a movie of Pierre Boulle's novel *La planète des singes*. So many actors in ape suits was surely a recipe for audiences sniggering rather than cowering behind their hands.

Before the film went into production, makeup supremo John Chambers allayed the fears of studio bosses by shooting a test scene with Charlton Heston (playing the human character, Taylor) and Edward G. Robinson (as apeman Dr. Zaius). Once the ape makeup was proved convincing, Chambers was given $50,000 to develop the simian effects in the film—Robinson, fearing hours in makeup chair would threaten his already failing health, pulled out and was replaced by Maurice Evans.

It was money well spent. The apes that Taylor and his two fellow astronauts encounter when their spaceship crashes on a desolate planet are scary indeed, especially when we and Taylor realize that they rule and humans are the mute animals in this strange place. The casting is perfect—Heston, running around in little more than a leather handkerchief, is butch and gruff, and Roddy McDowall and Kim Hunter, as "friendly" apes Cornelius and Zira, manage to escape the confines of their impressive makeup to deliver heartfelt performances.

Punctuated by memorable set pieces—Taylor's first glimpse of this new planet, his capture, and, of course, the unforgettable ending, and Rod Serling and Michael Wilson's witty script packed with killer lines ("Get your stinking paws off me, you damned dirty ape!")—this classic piece of cinema was followed by three sequels, a television series, the aforementioned disappointing remake, and even a hilarious spoof in an episode of *The Simpsons*. **JB**

U.S. (Fox, APJAC) 112m Color
Producer Mort Abrahams, Arthur P. Jacobs
Screenplay Michael Wilson, Rod Serling, from the novel *La planète des singes* by Pierre Boulle **Photography** Leon Shamroy **Music** Jerry Goldsmith **Cast** Charlton Heston, Roddy McDowall, Kim Hunter, Maurice Evans, James Whitmore, James Daly, Linda Harrison, Robert Gunner, Lou Wagner, Woodrow Parfrey, Jeff Burton, Buck Kartalian, Norman Burton, Wright King, Paul Lambert **Oscar** John Chambers (honorary award—makeup) **Oscar nominations** Morton Haack (costume), Jerry Goldsmith (music)

1968

> "If you only condescend to see an adventure thriller on rare occasions, condescend this time. You have nothing to lower but your brow."
>
> **Roger Ebert, critic, 1968**

i

Legend has it that Jerry Goldsmith wore a gorilla mask while composing the music for the movie.

U.S. (Paramount) 136m Technicolor
Producer William Castle, Dona Holloway
Screenplay Roman Polanski, from novel by
Ira Levin **Photography** William A. Fraker
Music Christopher Komeda **Cast** Mia
Farrow, John Cassavetes, Ruth Gordon,
Sidney Blackmer, Maurice Evans, Ralph
Bellamy, Victoria Vetri, Patsy Kelly, Elisha
Cook, Jr., Emmaline Henry, Charles Grodin,
Hanna Landy, Phil Leeds, D'Urville Martin,
Hope Summers **Oscar** Ruth Gordon (actress
in support role) **Oscar nomination** Roman
Polanski (screenplay)

"Some of my most praised films— Rosemary's Baby, Repulsion, The Tenant —were largely matters of convenience ... I wouldn't have chosen them."

Roman Polanski, 1979

𝒊

New York's Dakota building, outside
which John Lennon was later shot,
was used for the apartment exteriors.

Rosemary's Baby Roman Polanski, 1968

When a gaunt, hollow-eyed Rosemary Woodhouse (Mia Farrow) exclaims with relief, "It's alive," about a third of the way into the film, the baby growing in her womb finally kicking, her insides before that eerily still, her husband Guy (John Cassavetes) recoils in horror touching her belly. In her excitement, Rosemary doesn't notice his response. Even more important, she quells both her better instincts and her growing suspicion that her husband, their new apartment and neighbors, and even her pregnancy are all somehow mysteriously and darkly linked. In doing so, she stays the course for what is, arguably, one of the finest horror films ever made.

Crystallized in that one scene are many of the familiar and defining concerns of director Roman Polanski—betrayal, corruption, the boundaries of sanity, and the "mysteries" of woman. Polanski's magnificent weaving together of these elements elevates the mildly pulp source (Ira Levin's hugely successful novel) into a cinematic classic. Time has done nothing to diminish the film's taut, focused, building sense of dread, and familiarity with the movie only keeps one that much more in awe of Polanski's detail, his rhythm and pacing, his skill with his actors, and the fine script he adapted for the screen. Revisiting the film uncovers humor that is sly and intentional. The casting of the now-iconic Cassavetes—an ever-glowing symbol of the pure artist in life at the time—playing a man who has sold his soul to the devil for showbiz success. The humor that has been layered on over the years and after the fact; Mia Farrow's desperation to be a mother now inspires uneasy giggles in its own right, thanks to her midlife tabloid travails.

Scenes and characters from Rosemary's Baby are etched into memory: Farrow hunched over a kitchen sink, her mouth bloody as she gnaws raw animal flesh, catching herself in shock; the dreamscape rape/consummation of Rosemary far more unsettling for what is suggested than actually shown; Ruth Gordon's dithering senior citizen slowly evolving into something much more sinister; Rosemary, near the film's end, entering the gathering of the tribe with a knife, desperate to see the baby that she's been told is dead. Still, it isn't only the Satanic aspect of the film that makes your skin crawl. Predicated on the abuse of marital trust, on the idea that the security of family and friends might all be an illusion, a force to be used against rather than for you, Rosemary's Baby taps into visceral fears. We can't really know the people around us. We can't trust anyone, not even ourselves. There is no sure protection. Polanski's masterful manipulation of these existential fears gives the film its power. And who among viewers can help but feel that Rosemary is their proxy as she watches the good people around her fall dead or ill, all while discovering just how pervasive the evil is around her? **EH**

PARAMOUNT présente UN FILM MEMORIAL ENTERPRISES
MALCOLM McDOWELL·CHRISTINE NOONAN·RICHARD WARWICK
DAVID WOOD·ROBERT SWANN
Scénario de DAVID SHERWIN·Réalisé par LINDSAY ANDERSON
Produit par MICHAEL MEDWIN et LINDSAY ANDERSON **COULEURS**

G.B. (Memorial) 111m BW / Eastmancolor
Producer Lindsay Anderson, Michael
Medwin **Screenplay** David Sherwin, John
Howlett **Photography** Miroslav Ondrícek
Music Marc Wilkinson **Cast** Malcolm
McDowell, David Wood, Richard Warwick,
Christine Noonan, Rupert Webster, Robert
Swann, Hugh Thomas, Michael Cadman,
Peter Sproule, Peter Jeffrey, Anthony
Nicholls, Arthur Lowe, Mona Washbourne,
Mary MacLeod, Geoffrey Chater
Cannes Film Festival Lindsay Anderson
(Golden Palm)

*"I lucked out that my
first film [If....] was with a
master . . . I learned
so much from him.
I think it might have
been something like
John Wayne had with
John Ford, or Lillian Gish
with Griffith."*

Malcolm McDowell, 2007

ℹ

A British ambassador at the time
reportedly described *If....* as
"an insult to the nation."

If.... Lindsay Anderson, 1968

Modeled on Jean Vigo's brief hymn to schoolboy anarchy *Zéro de Conduite* (1933), Lindsay Anderson's follow-up to his *This Sporting Life* (1963) gets away from the realism and working-class rebellion that characterized the "kitchen sink" cinema movement and embraces a satiric style that now seems like a link between the classic surrealists and the Monty Python troupe.

Whereas the earlier film required that Anderson, who came from a respectable upper-class background, make an ethnographic study of Northern rugby-playing louts, *If....* is also paradoxically a more genuinely realist film, in that it was made by someone who actually came from the public school system it so rigorously attacks. The opening section of the film follows sixteen-year-old Mick Travis (Malcolm McDowell) and his few equally "antisocial" friends as they are bored by masters and bullied by prefects, bristling against a system that imposes punishments at once farcical and cruel like floggings in the gym administered with all the ceremony of a nineteenth-century execution. Alternating between color and black-and-white film stock, allegedly not for any significant reason but because the budget for color ran out before the film was finished, *If....* breaks out of the rigid confines of the school, with its crusty character actors and licensed homosexual predation, as Mick begins a perhaps-imaginary affair with a voluptuous waitress (Christine Noonan). The sex scene, explicit for 1969, is unusual in the area of taboo-breaking in that it depicts not a rape or self-hating promiscuity with morality rammed home afterward but a couple enjoying physical love.

While Vigo overturned his school's shabby dignity with a pillow fight, Anderson—working after the student risings of 1968 and the growth of the protest movement—has Mick and his friends don guerrilla chic outfits and stage an attack on the school's Speech Day, gunning down the patronizing headmaster (Peter Jeffrey) and other establishment figures. Although shot in a fantastical manner, with odd gags such as a speaking corpse in a filing cabinet, there is no return to "reality" to blunt the revolutionary wish-fulfillment fervor. Anderson, writer David Sherwin, and star McDowell brought the character of Mick Travis back for two further, wildly different satires, *O Lucky Man!* (1973) and *Britannia Hospital* (1982). **KN**

1968

David Holzman's Diary Jim McBride, 1968

U.S. (Paradigm) 74m BW
Producer Jim McBride Screenplay Jim
McBride Photography Michael Wadleigh
Cast L.M. Kit Carson, Eileen Dietz, Lorenzo
Mans, Louise Levine, Fern McBride, Michel
Lévine, Robert Lesser, Jack Baran

In his early twenties, on the staggeringly small budget of $2,500, Jim McBride began making *David Holzman's Diary* from three ideas: the image of a man filming himself in a mirror, the banality of daily life, and how the oppressiveness of New York affects people's perceptions and behavior.

David (screenwriter L.M. Kit Carson) is a schmuck. He decides to film the smallest details of his daily life to "find the truth." But his approach, by turns obsessive, voyeuristic, and paranoiac, swiftly alienates everyone around him. Far from a standard "mockumentary," McBride's recreation of the stages of this audiovisual diary is peppered with dramatic ellipses, emotional suspense, and a pleasing, always surprising set of variations. The result is remarkably prescient. The cinema-verité obsessions of the 1960s targeted here were to reach their full flowering much later, in the eras of video and digital.

David Holzman's Diary has aged well. Not only has it been paid elaborate homage—in Roman Coppola's *CQ* (2001)—but its formal inventions (static long takes, black screen, fish-eye distortion, lateral traveling shots, and single-frame pixilations) have prefigured many other experiments. McBride had already synthesized, and critiqued, the legacies of Godard, Mekas, and "direct cinema." **AM**

Memorias del subdesarrollo
Memories of Underdevelopment
Tomás Gutiérrez Alea, 1968

Cuba (Cuban State Film, ICAIC) 97m BW
Language Spanish Producer Miguel
Mendoza Screenplay Edmundo Desnoes,
Tomás Gutiérrez Alea, from the novel
Memorias del subdesarrollo by Edmundo
Desnoes Photography Ramón F. Suárez
Music Leo Brouwer Cast Sergio Corrieri,
Daisy Granados, Eslinda Núñez, Omar Valdés,
René de la Cruz, Yolanda Farr, Ofelia
González, Jose Gil Abad, Daniel Jordan,
Luis López, Rafael Sosa

Part documentary, part feature film, Tomás Gutiérrez Alea's *Memories of Underdevelopment* portrays an important segment of Cuban life during the period 1961–62. Centered on Sergio (Sergio Corrieri), a wealthy former businessman-turned-aspiring-writer, the movie considers his relationship to the transformation of Havana into a communist dictatorship organized around a police state.

Layered with voice-over narration, Alea peppers the account of Sergio's life with discourses on various subjects. There is an illuminating monologue about the Marxist dialectic, curiosity about the struggles of aging in a tropical climate, the general theme of underdevelopment, and social inconsistency during the early days of Fidel Castro's reign.

Perhaps Cuba's most internationally famous film, *Memories of Underdevelopment* is a trenchant critique of capitalism and the Communist Revolution. Within its simple story of one man in crisis are elements of fantasy, rolls of newsreel footage, and poignant bits of situational drama to express simultaneous wonder and contempt at the upheaval of the Cold War. Elegant and powerful, it's a tribute to Cuban creative influence in a moment of acute cultural suppression as the mask for a better tomorrow. **GC-Q**

High School Frederick Wiseman, 1968

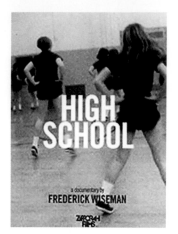

U.S. (Osti) 75m BW **Producer** Frederick Wiseman **Screenplay** Frederick Wiseman **Photography** Richard Leiterman

"I have an obligation to the people who have given me permission [to film them] not to simplify the material in the service of some personal ideology which they may not share."

Frederick Wiseman, 2012

Frederick Wiseman's second film is one of the most horrifying and ambiguous of his institutional studies. The film is a documentary view of Northeast High School in Philadelphia, apparently a public school serving a largely white, middle-class community. From the start, Wiseman makes it clear that his focus is on the authoritarianism of the teachers and administrators, the failure of the school to foster self-expression and critical thinking, and the emphasis on meaningless rituals and forms.

A Spanish teacher makes her students repeat the words "Jean-Paul Sartre" and "existentialista," with apparently no discussion of who Sartre is or what existential philosophy is about. An English teacher recites the poem "Casey at the Bat" to a room of sixteen-year-olds and is later heard to offer the inspirational wisdom, "The dictionary is the only place where success comes before work." A student protesting an imposed detention is told that unquestioning acceptance of punishment is a mark of maturity.

A college counselor advises one of her charges to prepare for the worst by applying to an inexpensive school with low academic standards. A gynecologist giving a sex education lecture to an auditorium full of boys refers to the hymen as a "cherry" and reaps applause for joking that he gets paid to put his finger into vaginas. Female students must endure an inane calisthenics session in gym class (to the accompaniment of the 1910 Fruitgum Company's mind-numbing "Simon Says") and a fashion-show rehearsal in which a teacher (who must have graduated from the same modeling school as the millionaire's wife on Gilligan's Island) blithely describes a girl, in the latter's presence and in front of her peers, as having "a weight problem."

In the film's blood-freezing ending, a principal reads a letter she received from a recent graduate of the school, now serving in Vietnam, where he has volunteered for a dangerous mission. Thanking the school for the lessons he learned there, the student calls himself "only a body doing a job." In the last sounds heard in the film, the woman reading the letter claims that it proves that "we are very successful at Northeast High School." No filmmaker has ever cut to black with more stunning effect. Wiseman allows the principal's words, and the world view behind them, to stand out naked against the film's slatelike silence.

The portrait isn't entirely negative. Never a heavy-handed slagging of obvious problems, Wisemanian social criticism is based on a detailed and ironic exposition of situational and behavioral facts. Above all, Wiseman's filmmaking, sensitive to how his subjects reveal themselves, respects the humanity of even the most reprehensible among them. Thus he challenges the antipathies, no less than the complicities, of the viewer. Like Renoir, Wiseman reminds us that "everyone has his reasons"—a message that is no more reassuring in *High School* than it is in *La règle du jeu* (1939). **CFu**

i

In 1994 Wiseman made *High School II*, about a successful alternative high school in New York's Spanish Harlem.

Vargtimmen Ingmar Bergman, 1968
Hour of the Wolf

Hour of the Wolf's original 1964 script was entitled *The Cannibals* and was conceived as an expensive, monumental film. But due to a serious bout of pneumonia and the decision upon hospital recovery to make the low-budget project *Persona* (1966), writer-director Ingmar Bergman reworked the scenario into a companion piece to the latter film on a much smaller scale than originally intended. In *Hour of the Wolf* the artist's spiritual torment is not witnessed as an enigma from the outside, as in *Persona*, but conveyed to us directly from the artist's own thoughts by way of the film's staging of texts from his diary. Clearly inspired by the uncanny writings of E.T.A. Hoffmann—even down to the names of characters—this is an all-out horror film about a sensitive (if not sympathetic) artist spiritually torn to pieces by his demonic critics and audience.

Reversing the vampire metaphor from *Persona*, in which nurse Alma (Bibi Andersson) dreams about actress Elisabet Vogler (Liv Ullmann) sucking her blood, painter Johan Borg (Max von Sydow) in *Hour of the Wolf* sees his feudal and bourgeois benefactors at Baron von Merkens's (Erland Josephson) castle as living-dead creatures of the night in vampiric need of an artist to prey on. For their sadistic amusement, they invite him to a party only to treat him like a court jester. His pretensions to artistic freedom are openly mocked as the tormentors adoringly present a toy theater version of Mozart's *The Magic Flute* (later to be staged and filmed by Bergman) and then praise it as a commodity, suggesting that its value stems from the fact that it was a commissioned piece. The ultimate humiliation comes in a scene where Johan finds himself wearing clown/female makeup and being teased by his mistress Veronica Vogler (Ingrid Thulin) while his tormentors laughingly watch in the dark.

However, Bergman also hints that Johan as a narrator is not to be trusted. His tormentors possess supernatural qualities and an uncanny insight into his psyche that ultimately reveal them as projections of destructive forces from within himself. This makes the film yet another variation of Bergman's recurring motif concerning the predatory relationship between the artist and his audience. **MT**

Sweden (Svensk) 90m BW
Language Swedish Producer Lars-Owe Carlberg Screenplay Ingmar Bergman Photography Sven Nykvist Music Lars Johan Werle Cast Max von Sydow, Liv Ullmann, Gertrud Fridh, Georg Rydeberg, Erland Josephson, Naima Wifstrand, Ulf Johansson, Gudrun Brost, Bertil Anderberg, Ingrid Thulin

1968

"The old ones called it 'the hour of the wolf.' It is the hour when the most people die, and the most are born. At this time, nightmares come to us. And when we awake, we are afraid."

**Johan Borg
(Max von Sydow)**

i

Bergman and von Sydow made thirteen films together in total, including *Shame*, also in 1968.

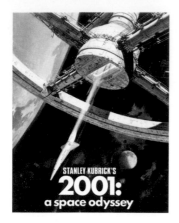

2001: A Space Odyssey Stanley Kubrick, 1968

An artifact of evidently extraterrestrial origin triggers and monitors key stages on man's journey from ape to star child. At the dawn of man a mysterious monolith is the catalyst for an evolutionary leap in primates, from scavenger and gatherer to tool-wielding hunter and killer. Many millennia later a monolith uncovered by a geological team stationed on the moon alarmingly emits a short radio signal toward Jupiter. A manned expedition to investigate (impassively shepherded by Keir Dullea and Gary Lockwood while mission specialists slumber in stasis) is sabotaged by the spaceship Discovery's psychologically disturbed computer HAL (voiced by Douglas Rain), but surviving astronaut Bowman's (Dullea) contact with another monolith in Jupiter's orbit hurtles him though a gateway "full of stars"—through time and space, to age, die, and be reborn into a new phase of existence. That's one summary of a film that has enjoyed an enduring reputation for unfathomability.

Influential but still unique, coolly detached, obsessional, pretentious, contentious, bewildering, forever fascinating—*2001* is all of these. Certainly it deviates from director Stanley Kubrick's stated intention to make the "proverbial good science-fiction movie" from his coscreenwriter Arthur C. Clarke's intriguing story "The Sentinel," as his film defies genre convention and is unlike any science-fiction movie before it. Visually, *2001* is undeniably awesome. Oscar-winning, ground-breaking special effects are a dazzling mix of imagination and science. Meticulous mime work and 1960s state-of-the-art prosthetics makeup in the first of the film's four distinct acts create the best ape impersonations by humans ever seen at the time (and still highly effective, though arguably topped by John Chambers's creations for *Planet of the Apes* [also 1968]). And the movie is strewn with unforgettable images: the unexpected, stunning cut from a bone brandished by an ape-man and thrown aloft to a satellite; the magnificent alignment of sun and moon directly above the rim of the monolith; the orbital waltz of the space station and a docking shuttle; the circular crew habitat of the Discovery.

The sound is equally rich, with its experimental choral music, the classical themes (Richard Strauss's "Thus Spoke Zarathustra," Johann Strauss's "Blue Danube Waltz") that forever bring the film to mind, and its snippets of minimalist dialogue ("Open the pod bay doors, Hal") that recur in wide-ranging homages and cultural references.

2001 can be taken as a mysterious adventure, sermon, or vision, but even viewed simply as a haunting spectacle it is unsurpassed, demanding to be seen on a big screen to be fully appreciated. Its faults—its overblown abstraction and its sketchy narrative of scarcely articulated, unresolved speculation on the origins and destiny of human life—are more than compensated for by its gripping engagement between man and machine, its visual starkness and serenity, and, above all, its rhapsodic wonder at heaven and earth and the infinite beyond. **AE**

G.B. (MGM, Polaris) 141m Metrocolor **Language** English / Russian **Producer** Stanley Kubrick **Screenplay** Stanley Kubrick, Arthur C. Clarke, from the story "The Sentinel" by Arthur C. Clarke **Photography** Geoffrey Unsworth **Music** Aram Khachaturyan, György Ligeti, Richard Strauss, Johann Strauss **Cast** Keir Dullea, Gary Lockwood, William Sylvester, Daniel Richter, Leonard Rossiter, Margaret Tyzack, Robert Beatty, Sean Sullivan, Douglas Rain, Frank Miller, Bill Weston, Ed Bishop, Glenn Beck, Alan Gifford, Ann Gillis **Oscar** Stanley Kubrick (special visual effects) **Oscar nominations** Stanley Kubrick (director), Stanley Kubrick, Arthur C. Clarke (screenplay), Anthony Masters, Harry Lange, Ernest Archer (art direction)

> *"[2001] avoids intellectual verbalization and reaches the viewer's subconscious in a way that is essentially poetic and philosophic."*
>
> **Stanley Kubrick, 1969**

The special effects were created by Kubrick and Douglas Trumbull, who also worked on *Blade Runner* (1982).

1968

Night of the Living Dead George A. Romero, 1968

Night of the Living Dead looks cheaply shot and starts out seeming like it might turn into a comedy: A brother and sister visit their mother's grave to pay their respects and the brother tries to scare his sibling by pretending to be a ghoul out to get her. Minutes later, however, he is killed and the young woman finds herself holed up in an abandoned farmhouse with an assortment of people as they are attacked by a mindless mob made up of the dead, newly risen, mindless, and craving the taste of human flesh.

Slowly, through emergency broadcasts on radio and television, the refugees begin to piece together what is happening. Corpses are getting up across the land, possibly even the world, and attacking the living in order to eat their flesh. Tensions arise among the heroes as they argue over what course of action to take. Should they try to escape or should they hold up and wait for help that may never arrive? Who should be taking the lead and giving the orders: the calm, rational black man or the impulsive family man? As the number of walking dead increases outside, the farmhouse may not hold for much longer, and drastic action will have to be taken. Before long, all bets are off. Every glimmer of hope and expectation you might have in a story is undercut by a wrong decision, bad luck, a cruel twist of fate, and all we are left with is the horror of despair.

This is the horror movie that raised the bar on the genre in the second half of the twentieth century, dragging the stories away from the antiquated gothic conventions of yesteryear and into the cold, merciless light of the present. George Romero's *Night of the Living Dead*, with its matter-of-fact, almost documentary-style approach, touches upon the issues that preoccupied America in the late 1960s: civil unrest, racism, the breakdown of the nuclear family, fear of the mob, and Armageddon itself. Nothing can be taken for granted. Good does not always triumph. And for the first time, a horror movie reflected the sense of unease that permeated contemporary society with no offer of comfort or reassurance. **AT**

U.S. (Image Ten, Laurel, Market Square) 96m BW **Producer** Karl Hardman, Russell Streiner, Karen L. Wolf **Screenplay** George A. Romero, John A. Russo **Photography** George A. Romero **Music** Scott Vladimir Licina **Cast** Duane Jones, Judith O'Dea, Karl Hardman, Marilyn Eastman, Keith Wayne, Judith Ridley, Kyra Schon, Charles Craig, S. William Hinzman, George Kosana, Frank Doak, Bill Cardille, A.C. McDonald, Samuel R. Solito, Mark Ricci

"My stories are about humans and how they react, or fail to react, or react stupidly. I'm pointing the finger at us, not at the zombies. I try to respect and sympathize with the zombies as much as possible."

George A. Romero, 2010

The word "zombie" is never used in the film. Instead, the living dead are referred to as ghouls or "those things."

U.S. (Saticoy) 90 m Pathécolor
Producer Peter Bogdanovich,
Daniel Selznick **Screenplay** Polly Platt,
Peter Bogdanovich, Orson Welles
Photography László Kovács **Music** Ronald
Stein **Cast** Tim O'Kelly, Boris Karloff, Arthur
Peterson, Monte Landis, Nancy Hsueh, Peter
Bogdanovich, Daniel Ades, Stafford Morgan,
James Brown, Mary Jackson, Tanya Morgan,
Timothy Burns, Warren White, Mark Dennis,
Sandy Baron

"Everybody's dead.
I feel like a dinosaur. Oh,
I know how people feel
about me these days—
old-fashioned, outmoded
... "Mr Boogeyman, King
of Blood" they used
to call me."

**Byron Orlok
(Boris Karloff)**

🛈

The script so impressed Karloff that
he refused pay for any shooting time
over his contracted two days.

Targets Peter Bogdanovich, 1968

The story goes that Peter Bogdanovich got his chance to direct when producer Roger Corman realized Boris Karloff owed him two shooting days. He also had about twenty minutes of unused footage from *The Terror* (1963), which he told Bogdanovich to use. But instead of the Edgar Allan Poe rip-off Corman had been expecting, Bogdanovich came up with a brilliant original scenario: Karloff in effect plays himself (his character is an old horror movie star called Byron Orlok), and Bogdanovich costars as the earnest young director trying to coax him into one last performance. This is cross-cut with a parallel story in which the apparently all-American "boy next door," Bobby Thompson (Tim O'Kelly), murders his wife and mother, then embarks on a random shooting spree, first from a water tower overlooking a highway, then from behind the screen at a drive-in cinema—where Orlok is making a personal guest appearance (and where Bogdanovich works in the footage from *The Terror* [1963], including shots of a young Jack Nicholson).

Targets is an American counterpart to the French New Wave films by directors like François Truffaut and Claude Chabrol. Like them, Bogdanovich was an auteurist film critic, and *Targets* features direct or coded references to Howard Hawks's *The Criminal Code* (1931—a film that starred Karloff), Orson Welles's *Touch of Evil* (1958), and Alfred Hitchcock's *Psycho* (1960). This postmodernist aesthetic extends to the film's self reflexivity: "I'm an anachronism," says Orlok. "My kind of horror isn't horror anymore." His point is chillingly underlined by Thompson's motiveless crimes. Obviously based on the Texas tower sniper Charles Whitman—the ex-marine who murdered his mother, then shot fourteen strangers on August 1, 1966—Thomson is clean-cut, a "normal, healthy boy," who is nevertheless fascinated with guns (he carries a small arsenal around with him in the back of his car). The film plays on this same fixation, putting the camera behind Thomson's sight lines, asking us, like Harry Lime (Orson Welles) in *The Third Man* (1949), how much we really care about those dots in the distance. Coolly dissociative and intelligently mounted, *Targets* is a sharp snapshot of America falling to a new, violent age. **TCh**

Skammen Ingmar Bergman, 1968
Shame

Of the films Ingmar Bergman made in the mid-to-late 1960s with Max von Sydow and Liv Ullmann on his beloved island of Faro, *Shame* is perhaps the greatest. Not that Bergman, reconsidering the film in his book *Images: My Life in Film*, was too happy with it. He felt that the script was uneven, resulting in a poor first half and a better second half. He also felt that he had perhaps taken on too much in attempting to depict war. Such an assessment seems far too harsh. This study of the devastating effects of war on a couple is one of the most persuasive accounts of a relationship transformed by forces over which it has little or no control. Bergman may not have had Hollywood's resources on hand to stage spectacular destruction and carnage, but he more than compensated for such material constraints with the boldness, assurance, and conviction of his drama and the acuity of his psychological, emotional, and social insights.

Ullmann and von Sydow play a couple, their love flawed by weakness and complacency but able to sustain itself. But when the war they have managed more or less to ignore finally turns up on their doorstep, it forces them to look at themselves, each other, and their relationship with a new, cruel honesty. The violence, death, and betrayals around them are both arbitrary and terrifying, but perhaps no more so than these more intimate and, indeed, more shocking revelations. All par for the course, perhaps, in Bergman's corrosive chamber dramas. But here they are lent added force by the wider context of a world in conflagration. Sven Nykvist's typically magnificent black-and-white cinematography—as eloquent in its close-ups of faces as in its shots of trundling tanks, burning trees, and scarred landscapes—and the performances do ample justice to Bergman's magisterial conception. The two leads are memorable in the justly famous scene of a last, brief moment of sunny, domestic happiness just before the conflict arrives at their farm. But also is Gunnar Björnstrand, as a well-connected friend who helps them out, only to abuse his privileged position later on. Grim, hauntingly beautiful, and still scarily relevant. **GA**

Sweden (AB, Svensk) 103m BW
Language Swedish **Director** Ingmar Bergman **Producer** Lars-Owe Carlberg **Screenplay** Ingmar Bergman **Photography** Sven Nykvist **Cast** Liv Ullmann, Max von Sydow, Sigge Fürst, Gunnar Björnstrand, Birgitta Valberg, Hans Alfredson, Ingvar Kjellson, Frank Sundström, Ulf Johansson, Vilgot Sjöman, Bengt Eklund, Gösta Prüzelius, Willy Peters, Barbro Hiort af Ornäs, Agda Helin

"It ends with one of the cinema's most awesomely apocalyptic visions: not the cheeriest of films, but a masterpiece."

Time Out Film Guide

🛈

Footage from *Shame*—as well as its lead actors—are used in Bergman's later film, *The Passion of Anna* (1969).

488

The Producers Mel Brooks, 1968

U.S. (Crossbow, MGM, Springtime) 88m Pathécolor **Producer** Sidney Glazier, Jack Grossberg **Screenplay** Mel Brooks **Photography** Joseph F. Coffey **Music** Norman Blagman, Mel Brooks, John Morris **Cast** Zero Mostel, Gene Wilder, Kenneth Mars, Estelle Winwood, Renée Taylor, Christopher Hewett, Lee Meredith, William Hickey, Andréas Voutsinas, David Patch, Dick Shawn, Barney Martin, Madelyn Cates, Shimen Ruskin, Frank Campanella **Oscar** Mel Brooks (screenplay) **Oscar nomination** Gene Wilder (actor in support role)

"Will the dancing Hitlers please wait in the wings!" The first feature by writer-director-producer Mel Brooks is his gem. Less vulgar and more dangerous than anything else in his oeuvre, *The Producers* won the Oscar for his screenplay, a classic farce with gasp-inducing irony: a New York showbiz Jew, however deviously, staging a musical, however detestable, about Hitler.

The biggest joy of the film is the incomparable Zero Mostel, a Broadway titan returning after blacklisting blighted his film career and finding immortality as irrepressible scoundrel Max Bialystock. His foil is uptight accountant Leo Bloom (Gene Wilder), who innocently observes that a dishonest man could make a fortune if he knew a show would fail. Raise a million dollars to produce it for a fraction of that amount, and when it closes no one expects their money back. Electrified, Max perpetrates the fraud with a surefire flop, *Springtime For Hitler*, authored by a demented Nazi (Kenneth Mars). Absurdly, the show is a smash, leading to an opening at Leavenworth for Max's penitentiary opus "Prisoners of Love."

The film's beloved production number "Springtime for Hitler" gives new meaning to the term "showstopper," with its Busby Berkeley homage of dancers in swastika formation. Beautifully acted and staged lunacy, *The Producers* gets better on each viewing. **AE**

1969

Z Costa-Gavras, 1969

Algeria / France (Office National pour le Commerce et l'Industrie Cinématographique, Reggane, Valoria) 127m Eastmancolor **Language** French **Producer** Jacques Perrin, Ahmed Rachedi, Eric Schlumberger, Philippe d'Argila **Screenplay** Jorge Semprún, from novel by Vassilis Vassilikos **Photography** Raoul Coutard **Music** Mikis Theodorakis **Cast** Yves Montand, Irene Papas, Jean-Louis Trintignant, Jacques Perrin, Charles Denner, François Périer, Pierre Dux, Georges Géret, Bernard Fresson, Marcel Bozzuffi, Julien Guiomar, Magali Noël, Renato Salvatori, Habib Reda, Clotilde Joano **Oscars** Algeria (best foreign language film), Françoise Bonnot (editing) **Oscar nominations** Jacques Perrin, Ahmed Rachedi (best picture), Costa-Gavras (director), Jorge Semprún, Costa-Gavras (screenplay) **Cannes Film Festival** Jean-Louis Trintignant (actor), Costa-Gavras (jury prize, Golden Palm nomination)

Costa-Gavras's fast-paced political drama confirmed its director's high standing in the international film community while bringing attention to the plight of Greek democratic rule, which was ousted following the shocking assassination of left-leaning professor and legislator Gregorios Lambrakis in Salonika in 1963.

Although *Z* is in French and stars mostly French actors, Costa-Gavras's (a Greek émigré) film is based on Vassili Vassilikos's fictionalized account of the Lambrakis affair. After a liberal politician (Yves Montand) is brutally murdered following a speech at a peace demonstration, the subsequent investigation brings to light a degree of corruption that threatens to bring down the entire military establishment. The sense of anxiety is heightened by the director's use of discontinuous, staccato editing techniques, balanced by the sharp cinematography of Raoul Coutard. In the words of critic Pauline Kael, "Z is almost intolerably exciting—a political thriller that builds up so much tension that you'll probably feel all knotted up by the time it's over." In addition to its stylistic accomplishments, the film boasts fine performances from Jean-Louis Trintignant as the examining magistrate and Irene Papas as Montand's wife. **SJS**

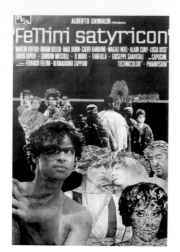

Satyricon Federico Fellini, 1969

The popularity of the European art film with American audiences began with the Italian Neorealist films of the 1940s, and expanded with the engaged and visionary films of that movement's most influential successor, Federico Fellini. More famous, perhaps, for productions that examine the mores and difficulties of contemporary society, the director also, like many in the Italian film industry, showed an interest in historical reconstructions. *Satyricon* is an epic reimagining of Petronius's novella about life in the time of Nero. Fellini's sprawling film—the action ranges far and wide throughout the Roman world—was an immediate success with art-house audiences. Shocking scenes of debauchery, grotesquerie, and black comedy fully earned an R rating from the recently installed ratings system, taking advantage of the new freedom of expression offered with the demise of the Production Code.

At once a quite faithful depiction of ancient Rome in the tradition of the Italian historical film and an evocation of the sexual revolution of the 1960s, *Satyricon* has much in common with the director's earlier films, particularly *La Dolce Vita* (1960). However, many reviewers felt it lacked the intellectual themes and meaningful stylizations of the director's earlier efforts. Certainly an emphasis on nudity and sex issued an appeal to certain segments within the "art cinema" audience of the period. Following his fragmentary source closely, Fellini offers a narrative of twenty-five distinct episodes, only loosely connected by the presence of the young and cynical Encolpio (Martin Potter). In the manner of Odysseus, Encolpio finds himself embarked on a continual series of adventures that threaten death and disaster, but from which he always manages to escape.

Encolpio's friendship with Ascilto (Hiram Keller), and their joint attraction to a handsome young slave boy (Max Born), is placed at the center of the film whose twists and turns are often difficult to follow. One thing is certain, however—Encolpio, much like the viewer, finds great difficulty understanding the morals and behavior of the many strange characters he encounters. The movie is filled with memorable sequences: a whorehouse filled with obese customers and prostitutes, animal sacrifices replete with rivers of blood, an earthquake that knocks down the building where Encolpio is staying, a nymphomaniac met in the desert whom Encolpio is called upon to satisfy, an encounter with a minotaur in the tradition of Theseus's famous adventure, and the startling richness of Trimalcione's (Mario Romagnoli) feast, whose guests, in the tradition of the nouveau riche, display an amazing vulgarity.

In the picaresque tradition, *Satyricon* ends not with some establishment of social stability, but with the hero's departure for even further adventures. A comment, perhaps, on the hedonism and unrepentant materialism of modern society, the film is more memorable as a feast of surprising, even shocking images, with visual rhymes and repeated motifs imposing a kind of unity on the continuing flow. **RBP**

1969

Italy / France (PEA) 138m Technicolor
Language Italian **Producer** Alberto Grimaldi **Screenplay** Federico Fellini, Brunello Rondi, Bernardino Zapponi, from book by Petronius **Photography** Giuseppe Rotunno **Music** Tod Dockstader, Ilhan Mimaroglu, Nino Rota, Andrew Rudin **Cast** Martin Potter, Hiram Keller, Max Born, Salvo Randone, Mario Romagnoli, Magali Noël, Capucine, Alain Cuny, Fanfulla, Danica La Loggia, Giuseppe Sanvitale, Genius, Lucia Bosé, Joseph Wheeler, Hylette Adolphe **Oscar nomination** Federico Fellini (director)

"[Fellini] arrives, if not at understanding, then at a magnificently realized movie of his own—and our—wildest dreams."

Vincent Canby,
The New York Times, 1970

ℹ

Fellini's *Roma* (1972) was a kind of sequel to *Satyricon*, but it was unable to recapture the original's magic.

Andrei Rublyov Andrei Tarkovsky, 1969
Andrei Rublev

U.S.S.R. (Mosfilm) 181m BW / Color
Language Russian / Italian
Producer Tamara Ogorodnikova
Screenplay Andrei Konchalovsky, Andrei
Tarkovsky **Photography** Vadim Yusov
Music Vyacheslav Ovchinnikov **Cast** Anatoli
Solonitsyn, Ivan Lapikov, Nikolai Grinko,
Nikolai Sergeyev, Irma Raush, Nikolai
Burlyayev, Yuri Nazarov, Yuri Nikulin, Rolan
Bykov, Nikolai Grabbe, Mikhail Kononov,
Stepan Krylov, Irina Miroshnichenko, Bolot
Bejshenaliyev **Cannes Film Festival** Andrei
Tarkovsky (FIPRESCI award)

It's a mystery. Not a whispered mystery, but a mystery sung by the strong voice of gigantic bells, shouted by the storms, illuminated by the bonfires of war, of faith, of love. The origin of this powerful mystery is perfectly obvious: Andrei films Andrei. Evoking the similarities between Andrei Rublev (played here by Anatoli Solonitsyn), the fifteenth-century monk who became the master of icon painting, and Andrei Tarkovsky, the great twentieth-century Soviet filmmaker, is not the goal. It is more like the huge caldron in which fear and hope, personal dedication (bordering on madness), and mass impulse can be heated up together.

Certainly, the film concerns the relationships between man and God, man and nature, the artist and the people, the artist and the art form, and the Russian and his land as a physical and mystical element. But as rich as *Andrei Rublev* might be on the thematic level, Tarkovsky's fresco is not made out of ideas. It is made out of light and darkness, of noise and silence, of human faces and rough material. It is a telluric move and a magical stay, suspended above the void. Dark, sensual, and deeply moving, the film is a mystery, in the best sense of the word. **J-MF**

Sayat nova Sergei Parajanov & Sergei Yutkevich, 1969
The Color of Pomegranates

U.S.S.R. / Armenia (Armenfilm) 73m Color
Language Armenian **Screenplay** Sergei
Parajanov, from the poetry of Sayat Nova
Photography A. Samvelyan, Martyn
Shakhbazyan, Suren Shakhbazyan
Music Tigran Mansuryan **Cast** Sofiko
Chiaureli, Melkon Aleksanyan, Vilen Galstyan,
Giorgi Gegechkori, Spartak Bagashvili,
Medea Djaparidze, Onik Minasyan

Sergei Paradjanov's greatest film is also his most radical and obscure. It inaugurated the most serious difficulties he had with Russian authorities that culminated in his being sent to prison in 1973, for homosexuality and other charges—after having already been attacked as a formalist, a Ukrainian nationalist, and an ideological deviant. This groundbreaking masterpiece remains the most extreme expression of his eccentric vision.

A mystical and historical mosaic about the life and work of eighteenth-century Armenian poet Aruthin Sayadin, popularly known as Sayat Nova (the "King of Song"), *The Color of Pomegranates* was previously available only in an ethnically "dry-cleaned" Russian version. The superior original version, found in an Armenian studio in the early 1990s, can't be regarded as definitive, but it's certainly the finest available: some shots and sequences are new, some are positioned differently, and, of particular advantage to Western viewers, much more of the poetry is subtitled.

In both versions, the striking use of tableau-like framing recalls the shallow space of movies made roughly a century ago, whereas the gorgeous uses of color and the wild poetic and metaphoric conceits seem to derive from some utopian cinema of the future. But we don't have to decode the images in any systematic way to experience their haunting power—at once "difficult" and immediate, cryptic and ravishing, they resemble Persian miniatures infused with ecstasy. **JRos**

1969

Midnight Cowboy John Schlesinger, 1969

"I'm WALKIN' here!" Texan dishwasher Joe Buck (Jon Voight in a star-making performance) heads for New York City, to the infectious lament "Everybody's Talkin' at Me" sung by Harry Nilsson, believing wealthy women will be eager to pay a strapping stud for sex (the film's title is slang for a hustler). His tragicomic progress of the naive newcomer is punctuated by sad, disturbing flashbacks, particularly a horrific assault on Joe and his girl Crazy Annie, played by the screenwriter Waldo Salt's daughter Jennifer. His "career path" in New York is a string of dispiriting encounters, unforgettably one with Sylvia Miles as a drab blonde whose pitiful insistence she is "a gorgeous chick" sees the credulous Joe paying her.

Destitute and lonesome, Joe bonds with the crippled, consumptive con man Enrico "Ratso" Rizzo (Dustin Hoffman, a compelling study of "street weasel"), who invites him to share his squat. Joe's hopes dim as his sordid failures mount, while as Ratso's chronic physical condition worsens his fantasies of a new life in Florida soar. Although the film is often called cynical and bleak, director John Schlesinger's view that it is ultimately a story of hope is justified by Joe's abandonment of his gigolo fantasy just when it seems attainable, for the sake of a real, human relationship. The British Schlesinger brought an acute eye to his American debut, finding a harsh vitality in the city that emphasized the characters' desperate isolation, and filming on location enhanced the seedy verisimilitude.

Arguably the bravest choice ever made by Academy Award voters, *Midnight Cowboy* is the only X-rated movie to have won the Academy Award for Best Picture. The film also won Oscars for direction and Salt's adaptation of the James Leo Herlihy novel. The distinction prompted a rethink, and despite its then-thorny subject matter of homosexuality and prostitution the film's U.S. rating was changed to an R, its commercial success proving audiences were ready to embrace its maturity, frank realism, and the compassionate power of its performances. And despite the film's visual nods to 1960s fashion—most obviously in the Warhol circle's psychedelic loft party sequence—Schlesinger's focus on the relationship rather than style endures, and is always affecting. **AE**

U.S. (Florin, Jerome Hellman) 113m Color **Producer** Jerome Hellman, Kenneth Utt **Screenplay** Waldo Salt, from novel by James Leo Herlihy **Photography** Adam Holender **Music** John Barry, Floyd Huddleston, Fred Neil **Cast** Dustin Hoffman, Jon Voight, Sylvia Miles, John McGiver, Brenda Vaccaro, Barnard Hughes, Ruth White, Jennifer Salt, Gilman Rankin, Gary Owens, T. Tom Marlow, George Eppersen, Al Scott, Linda Davis, J.T. Masters **Oscars** Jerome Hellman (best picture), John Schlesinger (director), Waldo Salt (screenplay) **Oscar nominations** Dustin Hoffman (actor), Jon Voight (actor), Sylvia Miles (actress in support role), Hugh A. Robertson (editing) **Berlin International Film Festival** John Schlesinger (OCIC award, Golden Bear nomination)

"I was privileged to make films at a time when cinema dared to deal with people and their relationships to each other and society."

John Schlesinger, 2002

ℹ

Bob Dylan wrote the song "Lay, Lady, Lay" for the film, but didn't finish it in time to make the soundtrack.

1969

Butch Cassidy and the Sundance Kid

George Roy Hill, 1969

U.S. (Fox, Campanile)
110m BW (Sepiatone) / Color
Language English / Spanish **Producer** John
Foreman **Screenplay** William Goldman
Photography Conrad L. Hall **Music** Burt
Bacharach **Cast** Paul Newman, Robert
Redford, Katharine Ross, Strother Martin,
Henry Jones, Jeff Corey, George Furth, Cloris
Leachman, Ted Cassidy, Kenneth Mars,
Donnelly Rhodes, Jody Gilbert, Timothy
Scott, Don Keefer, Charles Dierkop
Oscars William Goldman (screenplay),
Conrad L. Hall (photography), Burt
Bacharach (music), Burt Bacharach, Hal
David (song) **Oscar nominations** John
Foreman (best picture), George Roy Hill
(director), William E. Edmondson, David
Dockendorf (sound)

*"If he'd just pay me what
he's spending to make
me stop robbing him,
I'd stop robbing him."*

**Butch Cassidy
(Paul Newman)**

i

Robert Redford later named his Utah
estate and film institute "Sundance,"
after his character in the film.

"What do you mean, you can't swim? The fall'll probably kill ya!" The
iconic teaming of Paul Newman and Robert Redford was so magical—
and so profitable, scoring the year's biggest hit—that this offbeat
character study/action comedy in Western trappings and bathed in
cinematographer Conrad Hall's Oscar-winning sepia hues has been a
touchstone for bickering buddy pictures ever since.

Outlaws Butch (Newman) and The Kid (Redford) belong to the
notorious Hole in the Wall Gang, but an over-the-top train robbery makes
things too hot, with a tireless posse pursuit prompting the recurring
question from Butch that became a catchphrase—"Who ARE those
guys?"—and the decision to relaunch their career of crime abroad with
The Kid's mistress Etta Place (Katharine Ross) in tow. The famous last act
has its share of humor—memorably practicing "This is a robbery; back
against the wall!" in Spanish to become the bandito scourge of Bolivia.
But the film is immortal for its final image of the pair, freeze-framed as
they run out into a shoot-'em-up with an army.

Butch Cassidy and the Sundance Kid is an utterly disarming
combination of smart, original screenwriting, handsome visual treatment,
and star power. With all the jokes and poses, there is still real interest in
the well-defined, contrasting characters. Butch, the brains, is a smooth
talker with vision, carried away by his enthusiasms, The Kid a golden boy
with darkness within, cool and sardonic, ashamed to admit any weakness.

William Goldman's Oscar-winning screenplay is exciting, funny, and
romantic, both slyly satirizing and embracing Western legend (the real
Butch and Sundance were far from Newman's and Redford's charismatic
charmers). It also has audacious nerve, as when The Kid accosts "teacher
lady" Etta and orders her to undress at gunpoint. After the initial shock in
a thus-far genial movie, it is a relief, a big laugh, and a turn-on when it
becomes clear they are already well acquainted. The Burt Bacharach song
interlude, "Raindrops Keep Falling on My Head," is the only dated element.
Movies just don't come more attractive and likeable than this one. **AE**

Hsia nu King Hu, 1969
A Touch of Zen

Taiwan (International, Lian Bang, Union) 200m Eastmancolor Language Mandarin Producer Jung-Feng Sha, Shiqing Yang Screenplay King Hu, Songling Pu Photography Yeh-hsing Chou, Hui ying Hua Music Tai Kong Ng, Dajiang Wu Cast Billy Chan, Ping Yu Chang, Roy Chiao, Shih Chun, Hsue Han, Yin-Chieh Han, Feng Hsu, Ching-Ying Lam, Tien Miao, Hong Qiao, Peng Tien, Cien Tsao, Pai Ying Cannes Film Festival King Hu (grand technical prize), nomination (Golden Palm)

There's a reason *A Touch of Zen* is considered a benchmark in Chinese cinema: It's like a Rosetta Stone of the *wuxia*, or swords-and-sorcery, genre. The story begins simply, centering on the life of a daydreaming scholar (Shih Chun), whose mother despairs of his ever marrying and siring children. Then he becomes smitten with the mysterious woman (Feng Hsu) who has moved into the abandoned mansion, long rumored to be haunted, and the intimations of a ghost story come to the fore. The revelation that she is in fact a princess fleeing from imperial enemies who slaughtered her family throws the story into even greater relief. Each plot twist opens the narrative up into something bigger, and before the end, Buddhist monks with supernatural powers and metaphysical fantasy are added to the mix as well. At more than three hours long, the pace is surprisingly brisk because this is a movie that's genuinely unpredictable.

King Hu is rightly regarded as the pioneering director of the *wuxia* film, in spite of the genre's existence in film history since the silent era. Granted, *wuxia* novels may already have possessed great richness and complexity, but it was Hu who brought these traits to the cinema, combining them with the acrobatics and pageantry of Peking Opera and the underpinnings of Zen Buddhism. Hu understood that films were experienced with the senses, and he fills the CinemaScope frame with a constant swirl of color and movement. Honing his craft on several previous *wuxia* films, *A Touch of Zen* stands as the zenith of Hu's career. **AT**

The literal English translation of *A Touch of Zen*'s Chinese title is "Warrior Woman."

A man went looking for America.
And couldn't find it anywhere...

easy RiDeR

PETER FONDA · DENNIS HOPPER · JACK NICHOLSON

U.S. (BBS, Columbia, Pando, Raybert) 94m
Technicolor **Language** English / Spanish
Producer Peter Fonda, William Hayward, Bert
Schneider **Screenplay** Peter Fonda, Dennis
Hopper, Terry Southern **Photography** László
Kovács **Music** Hoyt Axton, Mars Bonfire,
Roger McGuinn, Jimi Hendrix **Cast** Peter
Fonda, Dennis Hopper, Antonio Mendoza,
Jack Nicholson, Phil Spector, Mac
Mashourian, Warren Finnerty, Tita Colorado,
Luke Askew, Luana Anders, Sabrina Scharf,
Robert Walker Jr., Sandy Wyeth, Robert Ball,
Carmen Phillips, Ellie Wood Walker
Oscar nominations Peter Fonda, Dennis
Hopper, Terry Southern (screenplay), Jack
Nicholson (actor in support role) **Cannes
Film Festival** Dennis Hopper (best first work,
Golden Palm nomination)

> ### "This used to be a helluva good country. I can't understand what's gone wrong with it."
>
> **George Hanson
> (Jack Nicholson)**

ℹ

Four police bikes were customized
for the film, three of which were
stolen before shooting finished.

Easy Rider Dennis Hopper, 1969

Easy Rider is one of those movies whose importance goes far beyond its status as a work of art. The story is slight. Two young men, nicknamed Captain America (Peter Fonda) and Billy (Dennis Hopper), make a lot of money on some drugs that they buy in Mexico. Feeling rich, they decide to realize a long-standing ambition to visit New Orleans during Mardi Gras. They buy a couple of motorbikes and set off across country. On the way, they pass by some celebrated icons of the American West, including Monument Valley and Taos Pueblo. They drop in on a commune, run into an engaging small-town lawyer who helps them get out of jail, and go on a drug trip with a couple of hookers in a New Orleans graveyard—all of which leads to the shock ending.

This seemingly inconsequential narrative proved to be one of the seminal films of the post-1968 generation in Hollywood, one of the first to put "the alternative society" on the screen. The two bikers are iconic figures, Hopper with his long hair, shades, and Indian necklace, Fonda with his stars and stripes helmet and bike. There is plentiful drug consumption (reputedly among cast and crew, as well as in the film itself). The two heroes go skinny-dipping with a couple of accommodating hippie girls and engage in marijuana-fueled campfire philosophizing with their lawyer friend George. Played by Jack Nicholson in his first big break, George is a rich man's son who rejects straight society, articulating most of what passes as the film's ideological position. In his view the country has gone to the dogs, terrified of the unconventional: "It's real hard to be free when you're bought and sold in the marketplace."

Easy Rider challenged much of the conventional Hollywood wisdom. It's a film by and for the young (Hopper was only thirty-two when he directed it), with music by such stalwarts of the counterculture as Steppenwolf, Jimi Hendrix, and Bob Dylan. None of the principals (Nicholson, Hopper, and Fonda) were big stars. The narrative is as freewheeling as the characters. There's no conventional love story, and the film has a brutally unhappy ending. Made for very little money, *Easy Rider* was a huge box-office success. It helped pave the way for works that challenged conventional Hollywood ideas, including further Jack Nicholson vehicles such as *Five Easy Pieces* (1970) and *The King of Marvin Gardens* (1972).

Subsequently, there has been a lively disagreement as to who did exactly what on the film. Hopper has laid claim to being its "auteur," not only directing and starring but also in his view responsible for the script. Others see it differently, contending that the most articulate scenes in the film—for example the conversations involving George—were carefully scripted in advance by Terry Southern, whose previous screen credits included Stanley Kubrick's *Dr. Strangelove, or How I Learned to Stop Worrying and Love the Bomb* (1964). All agree on one thing, though—that the title was Southern's invention. **EB**

Kes Ken Loach, 1969

G.B. (Kestrel, Woodfall) 110m Technicolor
Producer Tony Garnett **Screenplay** Tony Garnett, Ken Loach, from the novel *A Kestrel for a Knave* by Barry Hines **Photography** Chris Menges **Music** John Cameron **Cast** David Bradley, Freddie Fletcher, Lynne Perrie, Colin Welland, Brian Glover, Bob Bowes, Bernard Atha, Laurence Bould, Joey Kaye, Ted Carroll, Robert Naylor, Agnes Drumgoon, George Speed, Desmond Guthrie, Zoe Sutherland

With *Kes*, the director's first feature, Ken Loach essentially transferred the realist methodology he'd been using in his television work and proffered a statement of intent for his future films. Working with Barry Hines on an adaptation of the latter's novel, Loach depicts the brief opportunity of escape that opens up when a young Barnsley boy (David Bradley) finds and trains a kestrel (falcon). His growing interest in the art of falconry, coupled with his admiration for the bird's own hunting skills and proud independence, allows him at least to glimpse an alternative to the tediously oppressive present and uninvitingly constricted future of his life in the working-class English town.

Loach avoids the sentimental clichés of many earlier films set in Britain's industrial north by focusing not on grim, grimy streets and chimneys but on how human relationships and aspirations are stunted and twisted by a continuous diet of economic and cultural deprivation. Hence the emotional force of those scenes in which the lad's enthusiasm—long-neglected rather than nourished by family, friends, and all but one teacher—is betrayed and, finally, extinguished. And Chris Menges's typically fine camerawork catches the power of the falcon in flight, perfectly balancing the bird's very real agility with its value as a symbol of intuitive freedom. **GA**

Lucía Humberto Solás, 1969

Cuba (ICAIC) 160m BW **Language** Spanish **Screenplay** Julio García Espinosa, Nelson Rodríguez, Humberto Solás **Photography** Jorge Herrero **Music** Leo Brouwer **Cast** Raquel Revuelta, Eslinda Núñez, Adela Legrá, Eduardo Moure, Ramón Brito, Adolfo Llauradó, Idalia Anreus, Silvia Planas, Flora Lauten, Rogelio Blain, Maria Elena Molinet, Aramís Delgado, Teté Vergara, Flavio Calderín

Humerto Solás's *Lucía* is undoubtedly one of the landmark works of modern, postrevolutionary Cuban cinema. In many ways, it can be said to offer a kind of summation of many of the key tenets of the cinema of this decade. This exhilarating mix of styles and tones is partly accommodated by the film's three-part structure, following the fate—and love stories—of three characters named Lucía at pivotal moments in "modern" Cuban history.

From a contemporary perspective, the most remarkable aspect of *Lucía* is its ability to move dynamically between various modes of cinema and present eye-popping tableaux of equal beauty and horror. In this respect, the film's opening segment is probably the most commented upon and remembered. In particular, the battle sequences—featuring naked black riders slaughtering government troops—have a visceral ferocity akin to Orson Welles's *Chimes at Midnight* (1965). In its mixture of various styles of performance, its fatalistic staging of history, and its dynamic movement between proximity and distance, the extreme close-up and the long shot, it can also be said to resemble the equally operatic work of Sergio Leone. In its clashing of perspectives and approaches, *Lucía* explores the consciousness-raising possibilities of film as well as the link between postrevolutionary Cuban cinema and the new waves of Europe and South America. **AD**

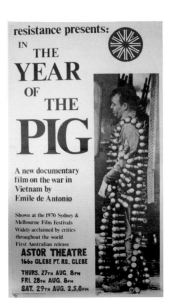

resistance presents:

IN
THE
YEAR
OF
THE
PIG

A new documentary
film on the war in
Vietnam by
Emile de Antonio

Shown at the 1970 Sydney &
Melbourne Film Festivals
Widely acclaimed by critics
throughout the world
First Australian release

ASTOR THEATRE
166b GLEBE PT. RD. GLEBE

THURS. 27TH AUG. 8PM
FRI. 28TH AUG. 8PM
SAT. 29TH AUG. 2,5,8PM

U.S. (Pathé) 101m BW
Producer Vincent Hanlon, Emile
de Antonio **Photography** Jean-Jacques
Rochut **Music** Steve Addiss **Cast** Harry S.
Ashmore, Daniel Berrigan, Joseph Buttinger,
William R. Corson, Philippe Devillers, David
Halberstam, Roger Hillsman, Jean Lacouture,
Kenneth P. Landon, Thruston B. Morton, Paul
Mus, Charlton Osburn, Harrison Salisbury,
Ilya Todd, John Toller, David K. Tuck, David
Werfel, John White **Oscar nomination** Emile
de Antonio (documentary)

"*[In the Year of the Pig]*
now plays as priceless
found footage, a
record of history that
would otherwise be
lost—or suppressed."

Glenn Erickson,
DVD Savant, **2008**

ℹ

There was such hostility toward the
film that movie theaters showing it
suffered bomb threats and vandalism.

In the Year of the Pig Emile de Antonio, 1969

Argued through indirect means, Emile de Antonio's *In the Year of the Pig* mounts an impressive attack on American foreign policy and the war in Vietnam. One result is an extraordinarily provocative documentary. Another is a textbook example of flaws within the American sensibility that are most easily identified as simple arrogance.

Opening with images of protest, the film sketches a backdrop for American involvement in Southeast Asia, ostensibly to defend the world from communist infiltration, necessitating a digression into the history of colonialism. First up is China, then various European powers before France's expulsion at Dien Bien Phu in 1954. Throughout these sequences, interesting as they may be, de Antonio's film wastes precious little time getting to a point. Namely, that all Vietnam wars have been in no way inevitable, humane, or helpful in assisting the indigenous population form a sovereign nation when this much has always seemed to be their purpose.

Zeroing in on found footage or else relying on carefully edited interviews, the film manipulates talking heads into its argument without overtly stating its point. In this way, de Antonio and his production staff remain carefully off screen even though their imprint is everywhere present. Thus the included historical figures produce discursive positions along the twin axes of fame and context.

Expanding the former are a "who's who" collection of important leaders, writers, and critics. Naturally certain of these are better known, such as American presidents Dwight Eisenhower, John Kennedy, Lyndon Johnson, Richard Nixon, and Gerald Ford, Vietnamese hero Ho Chi Minh, red-baiter Joseph McCarthy, and war hawk Robert McNamara. Yet the weight of gold is supplied by those figures providing context rather than political drumbeats, among them David Halberstam, Jean de Lattre de Tassigny, Harry S. Ashmore, Hubert Humphrey, and even George S. Patton III. Of course, some of these figures have since become synonymous with establishment thinking. In 1969, however, their views formed the basis of this treatise and one of the more successful antiwar, if at times anti-American, diatribes on the evils of political expediency. **GC-Q**

The Wild Bunch Sam Peckinpah, 1969

A Hemingwayesque answer to the Erich Segal-ish Western revisionism of *Butch Cassidy and the Sundance Kid* (1969), *The Wild Bunch* is at once disgusting and romantic, investigating the thesis that "even the worst of us" want to be children again—"perhaps the worst of us most of all." Director Sam Peckinpah, in his breakthrough picture, opens with innocent children pouring ants onto scorpions and setting fire to the nest as the Bunch ride into town disguised as the U.S. Army. Continually cutting away to kids watching the action, they imitate the grown-up bang-bang games and finally take part. Even the repulsive General Mapache (Emilio Fernandez) is hero-worshipped by a boy who picks up a gun to avenge his death. The opening bank raid is a complete botch as the corrupt railroad tycoon lures the Bunch into town with bags of washers disguised as payroll—"silver rings," gasps a hopeful idiot when the ruse is revealed. A shoot-out between the bandits and a crew of degenerate bounty hunters leads to the deaths of many innocents as a temperance parade marches into the gunfire.

Violent but honorable badman Pike Bishop (William Holden) is pursued by his former friend Deke Thornton (Robert Ryan). Pike is admired by his sidekick Dutch (Ernest Borgnine) and tagalong Mexican (Jaime Sánchez), tolerated by the fractious, grumpy, childish Gorch brothers (Warren Oates, Ben Johnson), and looked over by father figure Freddy Sykes (Edmond O'Brien), though he abandoned the old man's crazy grandson (Bo Hopkins) during the initial raid. With the American frontier closing down, the Bunch find themselves appalled by the tyranny of pre-Revolutionary Mexico as Mapache, with his German advisors, represents a legitimate government but acts far worse than the most evil outlaws. In a classic "last stand," the grizzled heroes opt to take on Mapache's whole town in order to stick up for their fallen comrade. Peckinpah realized that the shots of four gunmen walking through the streets to the showdown are the necessary setup for the brilliantly edited, semi-slow-motion orgy of mass destruction that climaxes the picture as the Bunch die, taking an entire army with them, spurting blood like burst firehoses.

Set in 1913, at the end of the era of the Western outlaw, *The Wild Bunch* drags the cowboy movie myth into an age of mass-produced murder symbolized aptly by the Gatling gun and the Model T Ford. Shot through with whiskey Western eccentricity, including a hilarious double act from L.Q. Jones and Strother Martin as human vultures ("This one's got gold in his teeth") and a great deal of picturesque dialogue ("Well, kiss my sister's black cat's ass"), this was the film that reclaimed the American tradition of the Western back from the Italians and proved that Peckinpah could pop more blood capsules than Sergio Leone. Famous at first for its gory violence, *The Wild Bunch* has lasted for its elegiac lyricism ("It ain't like it used to be, but it'll do"), strong performances, and sense of dead-end honor. **KN**

U.S. (Warner Bros./Seven Arts) 145m
Technicolor **Language** English / Spanish
Producer Phil Feldman, Roy N. Sickner
Screenplay Walon Green, Roy N. Sickner, Sam Peckinpah **Photography** Lucien Ballard
Music Jerry Fielding **Cast** William Holden, Ernest Borgnine, Robert Ryan, Edmond O'Brien, Warren Oates, Jaime Sánchez, Ben Johnson, Emilio Fernández, Strother Martin, L.Q. Jones, Albert Dekker, Bo Hopkins, Dub Taylor, Paul Harper, Jorge Russek
Oscar nominations Walon Green, Roy N Sickner, Sam Peckinpah (screenplay), Jerry Fielding (music)

> *"In purely cinematic terms, the film is a savagely beautiful spectacle, Lucien Ballard's superb cinematography complementing Peckinpah's darkly elegiac vision."*
>
> *Time Out Film Guide*

🛈

Ernest Borgnine's limp was real—he had broken his foot and had to wear a cast throughout the shoot.

Ma nuit chez Maud Eric Rohmer, 1969
My Night at Maud's

France (FFD, Pléiade, Deux Mondes, Carrosse, Losange, Guéville, Renn, Simar, SFP, Two World) 110m BW **Language** French **Producer** Pierre Cottrell, Barbet Schroeder **Screenplay** Eric Rohmer **Photography** Néstor Almendros **Cast** Jean-Louis Trintignant, Françoise Fabian, Marie-Christine Barrault, Antoine Vitez, Léonide Kogan, Guy Léger, Anne Dubot **Oscar nomination** France (best foreign language film), Eric Rohmer (screenplay) **Cannes Film Festival** Eric Rohmer nomination (Golden Palm)

1970

My Night at Maud's, the third of Eric Rohmer's six "Moral Tales" and often considered the best, takes place over a few days one winter in the provincial city of Clermont, France. Jean-Louis Trintignant plays an engineer, a practicing Jesuit, who decides to marry a student, Françoise (Marie-Christine Barrault), whom he has seen at Mass but never met. By chance, he runs into an old school friend (Antoine Vitez) who takes him to the apartment of the witty, intelligent Maud (Françoise Fabian), a divorced doctor. Over the course of a long conversation that forms the centerpiece of the film, the hero and Maud discover an affinity for each other.

In no other filmmaker's work are place and season more important. In *My Night at Maud's*, the falling snow cools the air in the long scene in Maud's apartment, provides a pretext for the hero's spending the night there, and later makes it possible for him to meet and spend the night with the student. The film's complexity and poignancy owe as much to Néstor Almendros's black-and-white cinematography as it does to the vigorous and brilliant dialogue. An atmosphere of uneasy détente prevails, linked emotionally to the hero's agreeable alienation. Despite Trintignant's great likeability (this is one of this best performances), the film is not, finally, on the hero's side, and it views his decisions with a sadness that lingers with the viewer long after the film is over. **CFu**

Tristana Luis Buñuel, 1970

France / Italy / Spain (Corona, Selenia, Talía, Época) 95m Eastmancolor **Language** Spanish **Producer** Luis Buñuel, Robert Dorfmann **Screenplay** Julio Alejandro, Luis Buñuel, from novel by Benito Pérez Galdós **Photography** José F. Aguayo **Music** Frédéric Chopin **Cast** Catherine Deneuve, Fernando Rey, Franco Nero, Lola Gaos, Antonio Casas, Jesús Fernández, Vicente Solar, José Calvo, Fernando Cebrián, Antonio Ferrandis, José María Caffarel, Cándida Losada, Joaquín Pamplona, Mary Paz Pondal, Juanjo Menéndez **Oscar nomination** Spain (best foreign language film)

It is often said that the defining characteristic of classicists from John Ford to Clint Eastwood is the invisibility of their style. But even their films look ostentatious and contrived next to the late work of Luis Buñuel. What makes *Tristana* so disquieting is the seeming simplicity of its manner and the sense of it unfolding, with rigorous and brutal logic, into an inevitable tragedy.

Buñuel had nursed this adaptation of Benito Pérez Galdós's classic novel since 1963. It tackles one of his favorite topics: the seduction and corruption of an innocent, Tristana (Catherine Deneuve), by the much older Don Lope (Fernando Rey), a gentleman whose stated political ideals are far more radical than his treatment of women. Tristana survives this oppression, after the loss of one leg, by doubling its viciousness and spreading its effects—as in the disturbing scene where she exhibits her body to the young servant, Saturno (Jesús Fernández).

Is *Tristana* a surrealist film? Not obviously, but profoundly: A subterranean world of unconscious drives, a parallel dimension, seems to lurk just beneath the surface of everything Buñuel presents—peeking out only in the final glimpse of how this sad story could have headed in another direction altogether. **AM**

Il conformista Bernardo Bertolucci, 1970
The Conformist

The title of Bernardo Bertolucci's film refers to Marcello Clerici (Jean-Louis Trintignant), who readily embraces Mussolini's Fascist government. He joins the secret police and is set up with a new life, including a new wife (Stefania Sandrelli), but his honeymoon has an ulterior motive. He is to assassinate an old college professor (Enzo Tarascio), a leader of the anti-Fascist movement. However he begins to have doubts about the validity of his mission, provoked in part from repressed childhood memories.

Has there ever been a movie so utterly at odds with its title as *The Conformist*? Bertolucci's film couldn't be more conspicuously immodest in its audacious use of style; conformity appears to be the furthest element from its intent. The film features a nonlinear narrative, leaping back and forth across time with flashbacks to paint a more detailed portrait of Trintignant's complicated protagonist. Even more impressive is Vittorio Storaro's astounding cinematography. *The Conformist* makes such good use of color, camera placement, and design that the story often seems subservient to the images.

This is eye candy of the highest order, as undercover assassins and political intrigue have never looked so stylish. Yet the politics of Bertolucci's film never fade entirely to the background. *The Conformist* is, after all, a damning indictment of Fascist collaborators. Trintignant is depicted as a weak-willed follower who ultimately pays the price for basing his life on the strong (and wrong) convictions of others.

Curiously, Bertolucci clouds the story with a bit of dubious psychology. Trintignant's behavior, it seems, can be traced back to a sexual encounter in his childhood, a literal link between violence and sex at the root of his desire for order. It's as if his decision to join the Fascist Party will in some way keep his homosexuality in check. Like much of the film itself, the psychoanalysis is mostly surface and introduces little substance. But Bertolucci takes advantage of the muddy psychology by introducing copious symbolic references and images, some of them obvious, some of them oblique, but all never less than entrancing to watch. **JKl**

Italy / France / West Germany (Maran, Marianne, Mars) 115m Technicolor **Language** Italian **Producer** Giovanni Bertolucci, Maurizio Lodi-Fe **Screenplay** Bernardo Bertolucci, from novel by Alberto Moravia **Photography** Vittorio Storaro **Music** Georges Delerue **Cast** Jean-Louis Trintignant, Stefania Sandrelli, Gastone Moschin, Enzo Tarascio, Fosco Giachetti, José Quaglio, Dominique Sanda, Pierre Clémenti, Yvonne Sanson, Giuseppe Addobbati, Christian Aligny, Carlo Gaddi, Umberto Silvestri, Furio Pellerani **Oscar nomination** Bernardo Bertolucci (screenplay) **Berlin International Film Festival** Bernardo Bertolucci (interfilm award, journalists' special award, Golden Bear nomination)

"A fascinated perplexity is the mood you bring away from The Conformist."

Tim Parks, *The Guardian*, **2008**

1970

ℹ️

Francis Ford Coppola, Martin Scorsese, and Steven Spielberg have all cited *The Conformist* as a major influence.

Le boucher Claude Chabrol, 1970
The Butcher

It is unusual for a single film to reshape the whole perception of the work of a major filmmaker. Claude Chabrol was seen as the cruel portraitist of the French bourgeoisie, drawing with dark ink and a ferocious sense of humor the complexities lying beyond the moral common law, the conformism of manners, the clichés of "good" and "bad" that mask the reality of impulses, the narrative conventions that destroy the possibility of apprehending the depths of human nature. And he certainly was all that, which is saying quite a lot. But he was not just that.

In 1969, during the boiling point of an ideological heating-up of the entire French society, when Chabrol seemed to be quite obviously in the grip of History, he took an incredible step back, to get a larger view, a broader comprehension of the world as a cosmic whole, beyond good and evil. The resulting film, *The Butcher*, is a love story with a serial killer. This is what filmmaking can do: allow for the peaceful merging of two genres that seem to exclude one another, the murder story and the romance. Taking place in a remote portion of the Garden of Eden in southern France, Chabrol allows the intensity of his wonderful actors, Jean Yanne and Stéphane Audran, to burn slowly. The pair underplay their absurd parts—this absurdity is the flesh and bone of the terrestrial (not only human) condition—and let everything go to catastrophe.

He loved her, she was quite fond of him, and he killed young girls. The butcher Popaul (Yanne) is the flesh, the school headmistress (Audran) the mind. This is the state of things, water and blood and dark forces separate them, but that isn't a reason not to pay attention to each other, not to care for someone so different from yourself—quite the opposite, in fact. But Paradise is lost forever, and this too is what Chabrol's subtle cinema is about. Don't bother to question the director on this point: he is far too elegant and smart to admit it, and prefers instead to hide behind his social tales and genre games. Just enter the smooth sadness of *Le boucher*. **J-MF**

France / Italy (Euro International, La Boétie) 93m Eastmancolor **Language** French **Producer** André Génovès **Screenplay** Claude Chabrol **Photography** Jean Rabier **Music** Pierre Jansen **Cast** Stéphane Audran, Jean Yanne, Anthony Pass, Pascal Ferone, Mario Beccara, William Guérault, Roger Rudel

"I know about blood."

**Popaul
(Jean Yanne)**

i

At the time that *The Butcher* was filmed, lead actress Stéphane Audran was Chabrol's wife.

1970

El Topo Alejandro Jodorowsky, 1970

Mexico (Panicas) 125m Color
Language Spanish **Producer** Juan López
Moctezuma, Moshe Rosemberg, Roberto
Viskin **Screenplay** Alejandro Jodorowsky
Photography Rafael Corkidi
Music Alejandro Jodorowsky, Nacho
Méndez **Cast** Alejandro Jodorowsky, Brontis
Jodorowsky, José Legarreta, Man Alfonso
Arau, José Luis Fernández, Alf Junco,
Gerardo Cepeda, René Barrera, René Alís,
Federico Gonzáles, Pablo Leder, Giuliano
Girini Sasseroli, Cristian Merkel, Aldo
Grumelli, Mara Lorenzio

Taking his cue from Fellini, writer-director-star Alejandro Jodorowsky takes the simple story of a gunfighter who sets out to defeat the greatest gunslingers of the land and turns it into an allegory for man's quest for enlightenment. El Topo the gunslinger journeys across a desert filled with brutal gangs and grotesque, surreal warriors, each symbolizing a different stage in the hero's journey. There's an endless parade of biblical references, Freudian motifs, and Jungian symbols. El Topo starts out vain and selfish, eager to attain power and glory, only to find himself bereft and empty once he achieves his goal. Realizing the futility of his mission, he renounces his worldly ambitions. He undergoes a symbolic death before returning from the desert a cleansed, empty vessel with the weight of the world's suffering on his shoulders, trying to protect a band of cripples and deformed, childlike freaks. Faced with a world as uncaring as the one he left, and a vengeful son he abandoned, he has no choice but to make one last sacrifice, an act of self-immolation that evokes the image of the monk who burned himself to death to protest against War and Destruction.

Unlike other Westerns, *El Topo* makes no pretense at naturalism or historical accuracy. The world depicted is a highly personal landscape, a setting for the cycle of Life, Death, and Rebirth. Granted, it could be said that Jodorowsky lays it on a bit thick, that his casting himself as the lead is the height of hubris and narcissism. But *El Topo* is fascinating for being a product of its time, a document of the lessons and philosophies people were then studying, and their fears, both conscious and unconscious. **AT**

𝑖

The rights to *El Topo* were bought by Allen Klein, at the time John Lennon's manager, on Lennon's advice.

Five Easy Pieces Bob Rafelson, 1970

U.S. (BBS, Columbia, Raybert) 96m Technicolor **Producer** Bob Rafelson, Richard Wechsler **Screenplay** Carole Eastman, Bob Rafelson **Photography** László Kovács **Music** Bach, Chopin, Mozart **Cast** Jack Nicholson, Karen Black, Billy Green Bush, Fannie Flagg, Sally Struthers, Marlena MacGuire, Richard Stahl, Lois Smith, Helena Kallianiotes, Toni Basil, Lorna Thayer, Susan Anspach, Ralph Waite, William Challee, John P. Ryan **Oscar nominations** Bob Rafelson, Richard Wechsler (best picture), Bob Rafelson, Carole Eastman (screenplay), Jack Nicholson (actor), Karen Black (actress in support role)

🛈

The movie's title is a reference to a book of piano lessons for beginners. Nicholson's character is a pianist.

If for nothing else, Bob Rafelson's *Five Easy Pieces* is worth seeing for the pleasure of watching Jack Nicholson unable to get an order of toast. Nicholson's first star turn after gaining notoriety in his supporting role as the lawyer in *Easy Rider* (1969) is as Robert Dupea, an oil rigger living in a trailer park with his waitress girlfriend, Rayette (Karen Black). Robert decides to take a road trip up the West Coast to reconcile with his sick father. Structured around the road trip and Robert's return home, the film has a meandering, capricious style ideally suited to the revelation of character and savoring the actors' nuanced performances in a series of set pieces.

It is fascinating to see the beginnings of Nicholson's persona here, as a charismatic antihero with an edge of violence and vulnerability. Black is outstanding as a good-time girl, a little past her prime, who must slowly watch as she loses Robert to his past. The film is a thoughtful, meticulous character study that is ultimately extremely moving and surprising. *Five Easy Pieces* comes at the beginning of an innovative and fruitful period of American filmmaking, and is an excellent introduction to it. **RH**

Deep End Jerzy Skolimowski, 1970

G.B. / Poland / West Germany (Bavaria Atelier, COKG, Kettledrum, Maran) 88m Eastmancolor Producer Helmut Jedele Screenplay Jerzy Gruza, Jerzy Skolimowski, Boleslaw Sulik Photography Charly Steinberger Music Can, Cat Stevens Cast Jane Asher, Sean Barry-Weske, Erica Beer, Will Danin, Diana Dors, Dieter Eppler, Cheryl Hall, Anne-Marie Kuster, Burt Kwouk, Karl Ludwig Lindt, Eduard Linkers, Anita Lochner, Louise Martini, Peter Martin, Ursula Mellin, John Moulder-Brown, Christina Paul, Gerald Rowland, Christopher Sandford, Jerzy Skolimowski, Uli Steigberg, Karl Michael Vogler, Erika Wackernagel

Jerzy Skolimowski's first English-language film after writing Roman Polanski's *Knife in the Water* (1962) is a remarkable excursion into the mind of a sexually frustrated fifteen-year-old boy. *Deep End* functions as both a black sex comedy and a rite-of-passage tale with tragic consequences for all involved.

John Moulder-Brown plays the youth with a comedic sensitivity that darkens as the object of his desire rebuffs his advances, while Jane Asher plays the young woman who is his obsession with great insight, her performance as Susan semi-improvised to great effect. Both young people are trapped in the seedy world of the Newford Bathhouse, filled with unhappy people who live for sex and soccer. Susan uses her looks to make extra money with the clients and suggests the same to Brown. He is disgusted with her lifestyle and longs to take her away from it all.

Skolimowski shows an astute insight into the eccentricities of the British, and captures a side of the so-called swinging London that is both ugly and faded with a real sense of impending spiritual breakdown. The film attains a voyeuristic tone as Moulder-Brown searches though Soho's seedy strip joints until he steals a cardboard cutout of Susan for a final fantasy of his mental deep end. A date film to see before you die! **DDV**

La strategia del ragno Bernardo Bertolucci, 1970
The Spider's Stratagem

Italy (RAI, Red Film) 100m Eastmancolor Language Italian Producer Giovanni Bertolucci Screenplay Bernardo Bertolucci, Eduardo de Gregorio, Marilù Parolini, from the story *Theme of the Traitor and Hero* by Jorge Luis Borges Photography Franco Di Giacomo, Vittorio Storaro Music Arnold Schönberg, Giuseppe Verdi Cast Giulio Brogi, Alida Valli, Pippo Campanini, Franco Giovanelli, Tino Scotti

Bertolucci's *The Spider's Stratagem* is, for many, the definitive European art film. The narrative is fragmented, the characters behave inconsistently, it's nearly impossible to keep track of time and place, and viewers are left with an overall impression of uncertainty. All of this, of course, is there by design. Bertolucci, like Michelangelo Antonioni, Alain Resnais, and others, was interested in having us question even those elements of film comprehension that we normally take for granted: story, plot, time, space, action. This is the cinema of the anti-Hollywood.

But don't let this keep you away from the film. *The Spider's Stratagem* (a title that is never explained) is challenging, but few pictures encourage such delightful aesthetic consternation: if you go into it not expecting to have any questions answered, you will be richly rewarded.

The story concerns a man's (Giulio Brogi) journey to his father's hometown, where he intends to uncover the circumstances of his questionable political activities. But this simple quest soon takes over the protagonist's life; in fact, Bertolucci hints that he begins not only to fall in love with his father's former lover but also to become his own father. Through clever, innovative editing and framing, Bertolucci consistently toys with our narrative expectations. *The Spider's Stratagem* is a baffling film, to be sure, but we are being manipulated by the hands of a master. **EdeS**

1970

Ucho Karel Kachyna, 1970
The Ear

Shot under the watchful eyes of the Soviet occupying forces, Karel Kachyna's daring political drama was withheld from circulation immediately upon completion. Although *The Ear*'s direct criticism of the rule of right-wing party leader Gustave Husák distinguishes Kachyna from other former New Wave Czech directors, the film's back-to-basics look and hard-won insights into the not-so-private life of a passionate yet embittered married couple are the two main reasons for its enduring interest.

Ludvik (Radoslav Brzobohaty) is a senior official in the bureaucracy of Prague's ruling Communist Party. Anna (Jirina Bohdalova) is his alcoholic wife, daughter of a small-town pub owner. The couple has a young son and lives in a comfortable home. At first, the cruel insults, nasty looks, and open hostility they direct toward one another strike the viewer as little more than character development in the film—Ludvik and Anna coming across as the characteristically depoliticized citizens of Czech society at the time. Later we realize that their complex marital relationship is at the very center of *The Ear*'s concerns, at once allegorizing and distinguishing itself from the equally complex relationship between a ruthless, oppressive political regime and its justifiably paranoid populace.

The film's action takes place over the course of one long evening. Returning from a political function, Ludvik and Anna find their front gate open and the spare set of house keys missing. Initially dismissing this as of no consequence, gradually other strange occurrences—including a power outage and dead phone lines—make them wonder whether they are not under surveillance by suspicious and unethical Communist authorities. In his mind's eye, Ludvik replays scenes from earlier that night. What initially seemed innocuous now takes on the surreal quality of a nightmare, as every sentence spoken to Ludvik—"Sorry, the comrades are listening"; "All that counts is whether they accept socialist goals"; "Didn't they speak to you?"—seems now to signify that he is in great danger. Connecting the dots, Ludvik comes to believe that he is a target of the Communist Party and that his arrest is imminent.

Desperate to destroy materials that could be cited as evidence against him, Ludvik burns his correspondence. Anna needles him about the deteriorating state of their relationship and his lack of interest in her both sexually and emotionally. But as dawn approaches, a submerged dynamic in their relationship rises to the surface. Expressing tenderness, protectiveness, and depth of feeling, they discuss how to proceed once the authorities come to take Ludvik away. Anna weeps hysterically. Ludvik tries to comfort her, the psychological warfare at an end as Big Brother closes in. The analogies established earlier between marriage and citizenship diminish. Instead we become sensitive to the dis-analogies: the limitless capacity of those in power to plot, conspire, and use advanced technology to terrorize, manipulate, and control a population. **SJS**

Czechoslovakia (Barrandov) 94m BW
Language Czech **Producer** Karel Vejrík
Screenplay Karel Kachyna, Jan Procházka,
Ladislav Winkelhöfer **Photography** Josef
Illig **Music** Svatopluk Havelka **Cast** Jirina
Bohdalová, Radoslav Brzobohaty, Jirí Císler,
Miroslav Holub, Borivoj Navrátil,
Gustav Opocensky, Lubor Tokos
Cannes Film Festival Karel Kachyna
nomination (Golden Palm)

"*Mr. Kachyna's direction is remarkably agile in balancing its portrait of a marriage with the larger terrors of life in a police state.*"

The New York Times, 1992

ℹ️

The film was banned until 1989, when it was finally shown at a film festival in the Czech town of Písek.

1970

Little Big Man Arthur Penn, 1970

U.S. (Cinema Center 100
Productions, Stockbridge-Hiller
Productions) 147m Technicolor
Producer Gene Lasko, Stuart Millar
Screenplay Calder Willingham, from novel
by Thomas Berger **Photography** Harry
Stradling Jr. **Music** John Hammond
Cast Dustin Hoffman, Faye Dunaway, Chief
Dan George, Martin Balsam, Richard
Mulligan, Jeff Corey, Aimée Eccles, Kelly Jean
Peters, Carole Androsky, Robert Little Star,
Cal Bellini, Ruben Moreno, Steve Shemayne,
William Hickey, James Anderson
Oscar nomination Chief Dan George
(actor in support role)

ℹ️

Hoffman yelled in his dressing room
for an hour prior to filming to acquire
a croaky rasp befitting a very old man.

Thomas Berger's novel (published in 1964), on which Arthur Penn's *Little Big Man* is based, is one of the funniest and most original works of Western fiction. It relates the picaresque adventures of Jack Crabb, in the course of which he is several times captured by Indians, becomes a Western gunfighter, meets Wild Bill Hickok, and joins General Custer at the Battle of the Little Big Horn. In the movie, Jack is played by Dustin Hoffman, and is first encountered at the advanced age of 111 by an earnest researcher who swallows whole his unlikely tale.

What follows is a thoroughly entertaining debunking of the Western myth, showing Custer to be a vainglorious bully and Hickok an anxious neurotic. By contrast, the Cheyenne, who adopt Jack into the tribe, are a courteous and life-loving people, especially in the person of Old Lodge Skins, wonderfully played by Chief Dan George. The depiction of an attack on a Cheyenne camp by Custer's Seventh Cavalry (based on the 1868 Massacre of the Washita) hardly bothers to disguise its obvious reference to the Vietnam War, which was raging at the time the film was made, and in particular to the infamous My Lai Massacre. **EB**

Patton Franklin J. Schaffner, 1970

U.S. (Fox) 170m Color **Producer** Frank McCarthy **Screenplay** Francis Ford Coppola, Edmund H. North **Photography** Fred J. Koenekamp **Music** Jerry Goldsmith **Cast** George C. Scott, Karl Malden, Stephen Young, Michael Strong, Carey Loftin, Albert Dumortier **Oscars** Frank McCarthy (best picture), Franklin J. Schaffner (director), Francis Ford Coppola, Edmund H. North (screenplay), George C. Scott (actor), Urie McCleary, Gil Parrondo, Antonio Mateos, Pierre-Louis Thévenet (art direction), Hugh S. Fowler (editing), Douglas O. Williams, Don J. Bassman (sound) **Oscar nominations** Fred J. Koenekamp (photography), Alex Weldon, (special effects), Jerry Goldsmith (music)

"Now I want you to remember that no bastard ever won a war by dying for his country. He won it by making the other poor dumb bastard die for his country." So begins the prologue of Franklin J. Schaffner's *Patton*.

After such a vivid monologue, the picture trails George C. Scott's eponymous lead in a race to fulfill his destiny. First up is Tunisia, then Sicily, some tongue-lashing for raucous insubordination, various real-life vignettes, much German preoccupation with his whereabouts, and a snowy race to the Battle of the Bulge. Concluding with Patton's demotion, the film's detail-rich canvas enlivens a fascinating personality during a moment of historic importance.

Scott's General is both nursemaid to dying men and terror to his foe. He's also conflicted about being a modern warrior put-upon by the political exigencies of his day. As a poet, trained killer, and acolyte of reincarnation, he is an enigma whose maverick sensibilities appealed to Vietnam War-era protestors and hawks alike.

His story consists of realistic battle sequences and was born from a Francis Ford Coppola cowritten script. Thus *Patton* valorizes a bureaucratic war machine while sanctifying individuality through the gravelly voice of a career soldier in what may well be the definitive biopic of the 1970s. **GC-Q**

1970

L'uccello dalle piume di cristallo
The Bird with the Crystal Plumage Dario Argento, 1970

Italy / West Germany (CCC Filmkunst, Glazier, Seda Spettacoli) 98m Eastmancolor **Language** Italian **Producer** Salvatore Argento **Screenplay** Dario Argento, from the novel *The Screaming Mimi* by Fredric Brown **Photography** Vittorio Storaro **Music** Ennio Morricone **Cast** Tony Musante, Suzy Kendall, Enrico Maria Salerno, Eva Renzi, Umberto Raho, Renato Romano, Giuseppe Castellano, Mario Adorf, Pino Patti, Gildo Di Marco, Rosita Torosh, Omar Bonaro, Fulvio Mingozzi, Werner Peters, Karen Valenti

An unauthorized version of Fredric Brown's novel *The Screaming Mimi*—and far closer to the plot of the original than the "official" 1958 Gerd Oswald film—Dario Argento's *The Bird with the Crystal Plumage* took the guidelines for a particularly Italianate spin on the Hitchcockian thriller, laid down by Mario Bava in *The Evil Eye* (1963) and *Blood and Black Lace* (1964). In so doing, the director mapped out his own subgenre with this, his first feature.

Sam Dalmas (Tony Musante), an American writer in Rome, is walking late at night past a modern art gallery and is alerted by a struggle within. Trapped between two glass doors, he sees a man struggling with a woman and is helpless as the woman is stabbed. The victim survives and the hero is told that her attacker was a serial murderer at large in the city, but Musante becomes obsessed with the idea that he saw something during the incident that doesn't make sense. As his puzzled girlfriend (Suzy Kendall) inevitably catches the killer's interest and the cops follow up a bizarre audio clue connected with the title, Musante has a brush with the unforgettable skull-faced hit man (Reggie Nalder) from Hitchcock's *The Man Who Knew Too Much* (1956), and realizes in an ironic-horrific finale that he has always been The Man Who Didn't Realize What He Knew. **KN**

M*A*S*H Robert Altman, 1970

U.S. (Fox, Aspen, Ingo Preminger) 116m Color **Producer** Leon Ericksen, Ingo Preminger **Screenplay** Ring Lardner Jr., from novel by Richard Hooker **Photography** Harold E. Stine **Music** Mike Altman, Ahmad Jamal, Johnny Mandel **Cast** Donald Sutherland, Elliott Gould, Tom Skerritt, Sally Kellerman, Robert Duvall, Roger Bowen, Rene Auberjonois, David Arkin **Oscar** Ring Lardner Jr. (screenplay) **Oscar nominations** Ingo Preminger (best picture), Robert Altman (director), Sally Kellerman (actress in support role), Danford B. Greene (editing) **Cannes Film Festival** Robert Altman (Golden Palm)

It didn't take long before the innovations of Robert Altman's Korean War comedy M*A*S*H appeared almost quaint in their simplicity and obviousness, especially after Altman himself later compounded his achievements with the even more ambitious *Nashville* (1975). Yet the use of chaotically overlapping dialogue within widescreen ensemble acting scenes proved as surprising and shocking, at the time of the film's release, as Altman's use of gory makeshift operating theaters as a vehicle for droll black comedy.

Altman's technique captured his actor's improvisations by zooming in from a distance, resulting in some playful thespian anarchy. The specter of the Vietnam War loomed large at the time. M*A*S*H's antiestablishment streak in many ways reflected the mood of the antiwar movement, which increasingly viewed the folly of Vietnam as a black comedy itself. In fact, Altman created much of M*A*S*H on the sly, tricking the studio into thinking he was making a patriotic war film. The studio was ready to shelve the film until test audiences reacted favorably. Release led to a wave of acclaim cresting with a number of Academy Award nominations, and a successful television spin-off, immediately cementing Altman's reputation. **JKl**

Zabriskie Point Michelangelo Antonioni, 1970

U.S. (MGM, Trianon) 110m Metrocolor **Producer** Carlo Ponti, Harrison Starr **Screenplay** Michelangelo Antonioni, Franco Rossetti, Sam Shepard, Tonino Guerra, Clare Peploe **Photography** Alfio Contini **Music** Jerry Garcia, David Gilmour, Nick Mason, Roger Waters, Richard Wright, Roy Orbison **Cast** Mark Frechette, Daria Halprin, Paul Fix, G.D. Spradlin, Bill Garaway, Kathleen Cleaver, Rod Taylor

Although Michelangelo Antonioni's only American film was poorly received when it was released in 1969, time has in some ways been kinder to *Zabriskie Point* than to *La Notte*, made a decade earlier. The director's boldly nonrealistic and poetic approach to American counterculture myths, and his loose and deliberately slow approach to narrative, may still put some people off. He also cast two young unknowns as his romantic leads—a carpenter (Mark Frechette) and a college student (Daria Halprin), neither of whom has been seen since—along with a relatively wooden professional, Rod Taylor. Antonioni was at the height of his commercial prestige at the time, having just made his only international hit in England (*Blowup* [1966]), and expectations that he would bring off something similar in relation to countercultural America were undoubtedly overblown.

But his beautiful handling of widescreen compositions, Pop Art colors and subject matter (largely derived from southern California billboards), and wistful moods have many lingering aftereffects, and the grand and beautiful apocalyptic finale is downright spectacular. Some of Antonioni's other pictures—most notably, *Red Desert* (1964), *Eclipse* (1962), and *The Passenger* (1975)—end or almost end with passages of stylistic bravura that drastically recast as well as summarize everything in the pictures preceding them, and in this case, Antonioni doesn't disappoint. **JRos**

Vice. And Versa.

Mick Jagger.   And Mick Jagger.

James Fox.   And James Fox.

See them all in a film about fantasy. And reality. Vice. And versa.

performance.

James Fox/Mick Jagger/Anita Pallenberg/Michele Breton

G.B. (Goodtimes) 105m BW / Technicolor
Producer David Cammell, Sanford
Lieberson **Screenplay** Donald Cammell
Photography Nicolas Roeg **Music** Jack
Nitzsche **Cast** James Fox, Mick Jagger, Anita
Pallenberg, Michèle Breton, Ann Sidney,
John Bindon, Stanley Meadows, Allan
Cuthbertson, Anthony Morton, Johnny
Shannon, Anthony Valentine, Kenneth
Colley, John Sterland, Laraine Wickens

*"The only performance
that makes it, that makes
it all the way, is the one
that achieves madness."*

Turner
(Mick Jagger)

Performance Donald Cammell & Nicolas Roeg, 1970

Not so much a reflection of the 1960s counterculture as an outright affront to the Summer of Love, *Performance* (codirected by Donald Cammell and Nicolas Roeg) marked changing mores and attitudes with a confrontational and audacious sense of style. Although completed in 1967, the film sat on the shelf for two years as the studio scratched its head. What to do with such a unique and unusual film?

Yet the long wait actually worked to the film's advantage. By the time *Performance* appeared, hippie idealism was on the wane, and the utopia of Woodstock had given way to the hell of the Rolling Stones' Altamont debacle—captured in the 1970 concert film *Gimme Shelter*. *Performance*, starring Stones singer Mick Jagger as a debauched aging rock star, only heightened its cultural impact ("You'll look funny when you're forty," remarks James Fox's Chas to Jagger's Turner).

The story itself is relatively simple. Chas is a gangster (a "performer") who decides to give up his life of crime and goes on the lam. Searching for a place to secretly wait out his violent pursuers, he discovers a reclusive rock star, Turner, who lives a sex-and-drug-filled lifestyle in a fun house-like home. Chas realizes this is the last place anyone would ever look for him, so he rents a room and bunkers down with Turner and his two female housemates (Anita Pallenberg and Michèle Breton). But after changing his looks and lifestyle, and with Turner and his Sapphic crew as catalysts, Chas begins to change as well.

By the time the story plays out, nothing (and no one) we've seen is necessarily what we thought it was. Cammell's script and Roeg's camera keep everything off-kilter, not just through skewed drug logic but also through overtly and intentionally confusing editing, punctuated with startling bursts of violence. Frequent drug-fueled hallucinations drive *Performance* toward its mind-bending conclusion, when art and identity intersect and the line between fantasy and reality finally blurs into oblivion. **JKl**

i

To prepare for his role in
Performance, James Fox spent time
with real-life London gangsters.

Woodstock Michael Wadleigh, 1970

U.S. (Wadleigh-Maurice, Warner Bros.)
184m Technicolor **Producer** Bob Maurice
Photography Don Lenzer, David Myers,
Richard Pearce, Michael Wadleigh,
Al Wertheimer **Cast** Richie Havens, Joan
Baez, Roger Daltrey, John Entwistle, Keith
Moon, Pete Townshend, Joe Cocker, Country
Joe McDonald, Arlo Guthrie, David Crosby,
Graham Nash, Stephen Stills, Alvin Lee, John
Sebastian, Carlos Santana, Sly Stone, Jimi
Hendrix, 10 Years After, Richard Alvarez,
Lennie Baker, Jon Bauman, Canned Heat,
Jack Casady, Chick Churchill, Johnny
Contardo, Crosby Stills Nash & Young,
Spencer Dryden, Lawrence Ferlinghetti,
Jerry Garcia, Bill Graham, Frederick Greene,
Bob Harvey, Bob Hite, Jefferson Airplane,
Janis Joplin, Jorma Kaukonen, Michael Lang,
Ric Lee, Leo Lyons, Jocko Marcellino, Hugh
Romney, Sha-Na-Na, Group, Screamin' Scott
Simon, Grace Slick, The Who, Johnny Winter,
Max Yasgur, Donald York, Swami
Satchidananda, Sidney Westerfield
Oscar Bob Maurice (documentary)
Oscar nominations Thelma Schoonmaker
(editing), Dan Wallin, Larry Johnson (sound)

i

Financially, the concert was a disaster
for its promoters, who failed to invest
in the lucrative movie and soundtrack.

The 1960s generation crashed headlong into unchecked idealism and the pressures of practical reality when the last baby boomers reached majority age at the end of the decade. Thereafter the United States was increasingly embroiled in varied generational conflicts, not least of which centered on popular music and growing ambivalence about the overall American project. Summer 1969 was therefore a turning point and a ripple in time. Although boomers had already splintered into factions pursuing an array of cultural values from strictest patriotism to hallucinogenic drugs, what was needed was a milestone event to convey the fractured spirit of innocence on the cusp of experience. The three-day Woodstock Music and Art Festival of Bethel, New York, provided just such a punctuation mark and became a historical keynote. Its cultural currency has since been co-opted to sell soft drinks and new musical acts, although it continues to be the mirror through which the state of 1960s youth is displayed in a flash of celebration and song.

As captured by documentarian Michael Wadleigh, who employed, among others, Martin Scorsese, George Lucas, and Thelma Schoonmaker on the picture, the best-laid plans of Woodstock's concert promoters are seen failing the realities of the event. Set in a paddock some distance from East Coast urban centers and with few approaching surface roads, a storm turns the Woodstock fields into a big mud puddle. Concert-goers show up in the thousands, way over estimates, to be serenaded by the best of R&B, rock, folk, and funk. Flooded and inconvenienced as they are, they become the most famous massed music audience for one of the greatest performance events ever staged.

The music, the atmosphere, the mythology, all of it together now symbolizes everything lost in the 1970s and the resulting baby boomlet. The point is made most forcefully in the brilliant, nearly four-hour long director's cut of Wadleigh's film, since mimicked by innumerable music-oriented movies and media spectacles. *Woodstock's* split-screen techniques, stereophonic sound recording, simultaneous and multiple-coverage of events, and detached viewpoint fill the screen with absolutely accurate observations. The attitude of reportage further contributes to the film's value as a snapshot of the times without imposing too much of an authorial point of view, but still looking on with wonder now lost but once gloriously true.

Vignettes center on concert-goers dealing with festival discomforts and townies reacting to the waves of outsiders streaming into their village. Bad acid makes its way through the crowd. Marriage proposals are matched. Food is airlifted in to help relieve a state of emergency. People skinny-dip, clean outhouses, smoke pot, smile, and sleep, all in the midst of many musical highlights, including an outstanding acoustic set by Crosby, Stills, and Nash, an appearance by Janis Joplin, the garage-band style of Canned Heat, and an improvised riff by Santana. **GC-Q**

1970

515

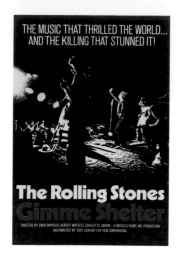

THE MUSIC THAT THRILLED THE WORLD...
AND THE KILLING THAT STUNNED IT!

The Rolling Stones
Gimme Shelter

DIRECTED BY DAVID MAYSLES, ALBERT MAYSLES, CHARLOTTE ZWERIN · A MAYSLES FILMS, INC. PRODUCTION
DISTRIBUTED BY 20TH CENTURY-FOX FILM CORPORATION

U.S. (Maysles Films) 91m Color
Producer Ronald Schneider
Photography Ron Dorfman, George Lucas,
Albert Maysles, David Maysles, McKinney
Music Mick Jagger, Keith Richards, the
Rolling Stones **Cast** Mick Jagger, Keith
Richards, Mick Taylor, Charlie Watts, Bill
Wyman, Marty Balin, Melvin Belli, Dick Carter,
Jerry Garcia, Meredith Hunter, Paul Kantner,
Michael Lang, Phil Lesh, Ronald Schneider,
Grace Slick, Ike Turner, Tina Turner, Bob Weir

*"Think I've busted
a button on my trousers
. . . You don't want my
trousers to fall down
now, do ya?"*

Mick Jagger

Gimme Shelter
Albert Maysles, David Maysles, & Charlotte Zwerin, 1970

Rock documentaries are generally prosaic affairs, at best good extended promotional films for their subjects, at worst overlong pop videos with bad interviews. There are noble exceptions, the most famous being D.A. Pennebaker's Bob Dylan documentary *Don't Look Back* (1967), but even that is only a heightened diary, a fly-on-the-wall character study. The most alarming and dramatically satisfying rock documentary must surely be the Maysles Brothers' *Gimme Shelter*, a film of the Rolling Stones' 1969 U.S. tour.

With its narrative structure (partially imposed rather than cinema verité-style inherent) and its climax, the disastrous, tragic free concert at Altamont Speedway on December 6, 1969, *Gimme Shelter* is a harrowing, exciting social commentary and rock 'n' roll all at the same time. The film begins conventionally enough, with the Stones performing at Madison Square Garden, but then cuts to an editing room, some months later, where the band are listening to a radio report on the aftermath of Altamont. This is a directed narrative, product of Albert and David Maysles's (and editor/codirector Charlotte Zwerin's) belief in direct cinema, which used techniques drawn from "fictional" moviemaking and applied them to nonfiction works. Thus the Altamont concert is "reedited" to increase dramatic tension; sticklers for realism may carp at the fact that the murder of black concert-goer Meredith Hunter takes place during the wrong Stones song, but the Maysles were editing for dramatic effect, not for rock history books. *Gimme Shelter* ends with the Rolling Stones watching the murder (committed by one of the Hells Angels hired by the band for "security" purposes) in their editing suite. It's a unique moment, rock stars confronted by the consequences of their own actions.

The movie helped seal the image both of the Stones as rock devils and, more importantly, of Altamont as the anti-Woodstock, as negative closure to the 1960s. It suggested that the counterculture was really a lot of drugged fools who thought murder was a "bummer" and that the 1960s dream was well and truly over. That may be debatable, but the force and drama of this documentary are not. **KK**

ℹ️
George Lucas worked as
a cameraman on the film, although
his footage was not used in the end.

Il giardino dei Finzi-Contini Vittorio De Sica, 1970
The Garden of the Finzi-Continis

Italy / West Germany (CCC Filmkunst, Documento) 94m Eastmancolor Language Italian Producer Artur Brauner, Arthur Cohn, Gianni Hecht Lucari Screenplay Vittorio Bonicelli, from novel by Giorgio Bassani Photography Ennio Guarnieri Music Bill Conti, Manuel De Sica Cast Lino Capolicchio, Dominique Sanda, Fabio Testi, Romolo Valli, Helmut Berger, Camillo Cesarei, Inna Alexeieff, Katina Morisani, Barbara Pilavin, Michael Berger, Ettore Geri Oscar Italy (best foreign language film) Oscar nomination Ugo Pirro, Vittorio Bonicelli (screenplay) Berlin International Film Festival Vittorio De Sica (Golden Bear, Otto Dibelius film award)

Vittorio De Sica's *The Garden of the Finzi-Continis* marked an international comeback for a director who had never stopped working, but whose star had fallen since the days of Neorealist masterpieces like *Umberto D* (1952). Its story, derived from Giorgio Bassani's novel of Italian Jews slowly adapting to the coming Fascist oppression, compellingly spoke to a 1970s audience appreciating the resurgence of such political-historical themes in art-house cinema.

The story holds off its tragic punchline until the end, meanwhile intimating it as a dark shadow while the characters obliviously enjoy their last revelries. The beautiful young things who gather in their high-bourgeois paradise are caught in an agonizing daisy chain of mismatched desires—no one, straight or gay, is loved by the person they want.

Stylistically, the film is no masterpiece. But it comes alive in those moments when De Sica rivets his camera in close-up on his glamorous stars (Dominique Sanda and Helmut Berger especially), in order to observe the furtive darting of their soulfully expressive eyes. *The Garden of Finzi-Continis* is a keen, touching parable about the interrelation of personal and political, private, and public drama. The encroaching social tragedy renders the romantic palpitations by turns petty, desperate, absurd, and poignant. **AM**

1971

Dirty Harry Don Siegel, 1971

U.S. (Malpaso, Warner Bros) 102m Technicolor Producer Don Siegel Screenplay Harry Julian Fink, Rita M. Fink, Dean Riesner Photography Bruce Surtees Music Lalo Schifrin Cast Clint Eastwood, Harry Guardino, Reni Santoni, John Vernon, Andrew Robinson, John Larch, John Mitchum, Mae Mercer, Lyn Edgington, Ruth Kobart, Woodrow Parfrey, Josef Sommer, William Paterson, James Nolan, Maurice Argent

One of the most influential and controversial police movies ever made, *Dirty Harry* is a canny mix of the simple and the sophisticated. The characters, notably supercop Harry Callahan (Clint Eastwood) and superpsycho Scorpio (Andy Robinson), are vivid, hyperbolic cartoons. They gain definition not through psychological depth and nuance but through their interaction with the film's intricate, richly articulated environments.

Brilliantly exploiting San Francisco locations, director Don Siegel gets a high-low motif going in the first shots, zooming back to reveal a woman swimming in a sky-blue pool on a high-rise roof while a sniper draws a bead on her from the top of another, taller building. From then on, the film soars and plunges in roller-coaster contours to delineate a multileveled metropolis where a precarious Sky City of helicopters, hilltops, rooftops, glass towers, and enveloping fog perches over a primitive underworld of burrows, tunnels, alleys, and quarries. No mere backdrop to the action, this formidable labyrinth molds and tests the characters as they twist and fight their way through it. This is vividly depicted in the tour de force sequence in which Scorpio runs Harry ragged from one end of town to the other as part of an evasive scheme to receive a bundle of ransom money. **MR**

A Clockwork Orange Stanley Kubrick, 1971

A Stanley Kubrick Production "A CLOCKWORK ORANGE" Starring Malcom McDowell · Patrick Magee
Adrienne Corri and Miriam Karlin · Screenplay by Stanley Kubrick · Based on the novel by Anthony Burgess
Produced and · Directed by Stanley Kubrick · Executive Producers Max L. Raab and Si Litvinoff

From Warner Bros. ⬤ A Kinney Communications Company

1971

G.B. (Hawk, Polaris, Warner Bros.) 137m
BW / Color **Producer** Stanley Kubrick
Screenplay Stanley Kubrick, from novel by
Anthony Burgess **Photography** John Alcott
Music Nacio Herb Brown, Walter Carlos,
Rachel Elkind, Edward Elgar, Gioacchino
Rossini, Ludwig van Beethoven, Henry
Purcell, Nikolai Rimsky-Korsakov
Cast Malcolm McDowell, Patrick Magee,
Michael Bates, Warren Clarke, John Clive,
Adrienne Corri, Carl Duering, Paul Farrell,
Clive Francis, Michael Gover, Miriam Karlin,
James Marcus, Aubrey Morris, Godfrey
Quigley, Sheila Raynor **Oscar nominations**
Stanley Kubrick (best picture), Stanley
Kubrick (director), Stanley Kubrick
(screenplay), William Butler (editing)

> *"I think it'd be impossible
> if you took that script
> into a studio and tried to
> pitch it today..."*
>
> **Malcolm McDowell, 2009**

ℹ

Alex's snake was introduced to the
story after Kubrick found out that
McDowell had a fear of reptiles.

Stanley Kubrick's most controversial film, a social sci-fi fable made in
1971, was withdrawn in the United Kindom by the director himself for
nearly thirty years despite its initial, phenomenally successful but heavily
criticized release. It resurfaced, enveloped in mystique, not long after his
death. *A Clockwork Orange* is still electrifying, a bold translation of the
dystopian Anthony Burgess novel that was itself published to a mixture
of acclaim and notoriety in 1959 and was long believed unfilmable.

Delinquent but clever, smart-aleck youth Alex De Large (Malcolm
McDowell) gets his kicks from pornography, Beethoven, and leading his
bowler-hatted, white overall–clad gang of "Droogs" (including a baby-
faced Warren Clark) on hectic vivid rampages of "ultra-violence" in which
they speak a distinctive argot, a hybrid of Russian and London Cockney
rhyming slang. The most disturbing scene in this first, twenty-minute
section of the film is one that comes back to haunt Alex when he is
helpless. After breaking into a futuristic luxury home, they cripple the
husband (Patrick Magee) and rape the wife (Adrienne Corri) while Alex
bellows "Singin' in the Rain," aiming vicious blows of his Doc Marten boots
to the rhythm of the song. Although it is interesting that the rape looms
large in memories as particularly nasty, Kubrick cuts away from the
woman's ordeal just as Alex finishes cutting away her skin-tight red
jumpsuit. Another thrill-seeking outing culminates in Alex bashing in a
woman's brains with a giant phallic sculpture, the crime for which he is
eventually apprehended.

But the institutionalized brutality that ensues in Alex's punishment
and his "rehabilitation" into a craven, boot-licking victim is just as scary as
the Droogs' misdeeds, and more thought provoking, in this scathing satire
of society's hypocrisy, corruption, and sadism. Seeing a way out of prison,
Alex cockily volunteers for a politically showcased, experimental aversion
therapy and is subjected to dire behaviorist "cure"—strapped down, his
eyes clamped wide open—that suppresses his violent tendencies but
also robs him of his essential humanity. Stripped of his capacity to commit
evil, he is an enfeebled individual. Back in the world, he doesn't enjoy
his "freedom." Betrayed by former thug-comrades, who, ironically,
have become policemen, he ultimately gets a hilariously unnerving
comeuppance in an encounter with one of his damaged victims.

Kubrick's arresting vision of the not-too-distant future is amusingly
dated in some details (vinyl records, Alex's IBM typewriter), and the
violence for which it was so castigated on its release is discreet by
contemporary standards. But the picture of aimless louts alleviating their
boredom in mindless viciousness is chillingly topical, as is the real issue
at the picture's center—the fragility of individuality and personal rights
when they do not conform to the desires of the state. Stylish and often
startlingly funny, with a delirious soundtrack, *A Clockwork Orange* still
packs far more punch than its many blatantly derivative descendants. **AE**

The story of a gambling man and a hustling lady and the empire they fashioned from the wilderness.

WARREN & JULIE
BEATTY CHRISTIE
McCABE &
Mrs. MILLER

U.S. (Warner Bros.) 120m Technicolor
Producer Mitchell Brower,
Robert Eggenweiler, David Foster
Screenplay Robert Altman, Brian McKay,
Edmund Naughton **Photography** Vilmos
Zsigmond **Music** Leonard Cohen
Cast Warren Beatty, Julie Christie, Rene
Auberjonois, William Devane, John Schuck,
Corey Fischer, Bert Remsen, Shelley Duvall,
Keith Carradine, Michael Murphy, Antony
Holland, Hugh Millais, Manfred Schulz,
Jace Van Der Veen, Jackie Crossland
Oscar nomination Julie Christie (actress)

> *"If not the greatest Western ever made, McCabe & Mrs. Miller could be the most authentic representation of wilderness life ever put on screen."*
>
> **Ed Gonzalez,**
> *Slant Magazine,* **2002**

🛈

Altman's initial choice for the role of McCabe was Elliot Gould, but the studio producing the film disagreed.

McCabe and Mrs. Miller Robert Altman, 1971

At the peak of his 1970s powers, director Robert Altman seemed capable of anything. Even so, *McCabe and Mrs. Miller*, arriving between *M*A*S*H* (1970) and *Nashville* (1975), is something special, an elegiac tale of the Old West imbued with a sense of contemporary filmmaking adventure. Set in the Pacific Northwest in the early 1900s, the film stars a quiet Warren Beatty as the titular braggart, a cowardly but charismatic man who has lucked into a position of power. But the nature of the country is changing around him, and Beatty can't see the inevitable, violent consequences of progress for all his narcissistic pipe dreams.

Altman wanted his film to capture the feeling of an old photograph, so he instructed cinematographer Vilmos Zsigmond to flash-expose the film, resulting in a heavy haze that hangs over the image. Another brilliant decision was the use of Leonard Cohen for the film's anachronistic soundtrack, as the singer-songwriter's gloomy folk music perfectly suits the somber mood and darkly lit, snowy scenery. But best of all may be the casting of Julie Christie as an opium-addicted madam. She lends the role an ethereal quality at odds with Beatty's more natural performance as a bearded buffoon in a big fur coat, and hers is a ghostly presence that portends bad things to come.

McCabe and Mrs. Miller mourns the death of the Wild West even as it signals the fertile start of the 1970s filmmaking renaissance. The picture is filled with striking widescreen imagery as well as Altman's usual roving camerawork, but the exercise exudes a palpable sadness here. *McCabe and Mrs. Miller's* message seems to be that progress and capitalism go hand in hand, and not always for the better. The flourishing success of Beatty's frontier town initially draws workers, then well-wishers, but his hard work and vision mean nothing to the men who ultimately want to take it away. Altman's view of America as an experiment in Darwinism (accelerated with guns) might strike some as cynical, but the spectral visuals lend the film a palpable sadness that supplants any specific message. **JKl**

Le chagrin et la pitié Marcel Ophüls, 1971
The Sorrow and the Pity

France / West Germany / Switzerland (NDR, Télévision Rencontre, TSR) 262m BW
Language French / German / English
Producer André Harris, Alain de Sedouy
Screenplay André Harris, Marcel Ophüls
Photography André Gazut, Jürgen Thieme
Cast Georges Bidault, Matheus Bleibinger, Charles Braun, Maurice Buckmaster, Emile Coulaudon, Emmanuel d'Astier de la Vigerie, René de Chambrun, Anthony Eden, Marcel Ophüls, Denis Rake, Henri Rochat, Paul Schmidt, Mme. Solange, Edward Spears, Helmut Tausend, Roger Tounze, Marcel Verdier **Oscar nomination** Marcel Ophüls (documentary)

For over two decades, French society seemed unwilling to examine the moral questions raised by the German occupation, but the disturbances of May 1968 led to a new openness. Marcel Ophüls's documentary *The Sorrow and the Pity* focuses on events in the town of Clermont-Ferrand. Though receiving initial support from French national television, Ophüls was not allowed to broadcast it. Instead, the film opened in art houses, quickly becoming the year's most controversial production. Worldwide distribution followed, and this four-hour recording of the reminiscences of survivors of the period, interspersed with archival footage, quickly became one of world cinema's most acclaimed documentaries.

Ophüls picked a town in the "free zone" of Vichy France so that he could explore the ways in which the collaborationist government operated. His informants ranged from members of the nobility to peasants to former German soldiers. With a minimum of narration and distorting generalizations, *The Sorrow and the Pity* captures the ambiguities and contradictions of the period. The sense of the film, however, is the *chagrin* (sorrow, but also shame) of its title, established by the insistent questions of the interviewer and the lies or distortions that become obvious across the different forms of testimony and the unrehearsed reactions of the interviewees to difficult inquiries. **RBP**

Willy Wonka and the Chocolate Factory
Mel Stuart, 1971

U.S. (David L. Wolper, Quaker Oats, Warner Bros.) 100m Technicolor
Producer Stan Margulies, David L. Wolper
Screenplay Roald Dahl, from his book *Charlie and the Chocolate Factory*
Photography Arthur Ibbetson **Music** Leslie Bricusse, Anthony Newley **Cast** Gene Wilder, Jack Albertson, Peter Ostrum, Roy Kinnear, Julie Dawn Cole, Leonard Stone, Denise Nickerson, Nora Denney, Paris Themmen, Ursula Reit, Michael Bollner, Diana Sowle, Aubrey Woods, David Battley, Günter Meisner **Oscar nomination** Leslie Bricusse, Anthony Newley, Walter Scharf (music)

Although most children's movies are saccharine, if not silly, Mel Stuart's adaptation of Roald Dahl's popular children's novel is a happy exception. *Willy Wonka and the Chocolate Factory* is a juvenile black comedy replete with flash visuals, engaging songs, and an over-the-top performance by Gene Wilder as the title character, whose claim to fame is being the world's greatest candy maker.

Wonka has hidden five golden tickets in his candy bars, and those who find them get to tour the factory and receive a lifetime supply of sweets. The factory offers a gallery of marvels, including a river of chocolate. The catch for the lucky winners is that they must obey Wonka's difficult and capricious rules. The point of the exercise, however, is to identify the one child who is truly honest (it turns out, of course, to be the most charming and irascible of the group). His reward is to be the inheritor of Wonka's factory; one day he will become the chocolate maker whose duty is not only cater to children but also to provide the proper rite of passage into the adult world. Like *The Wizard of Oz* (1939), *Willy Wonka* is full of strange creatures, artificial sets, and lively song and dance numbers. A film to entertain the young and set their elders to thinking. **RBP**

The Devils Ken Russell, 1971

G.B. (Warner Bros.) 111m Technicolor
Producer Ken Russell, Robert
H. Solo **Screenplay** Ken Russell
Photography David Watkin **Music** Peter
Maxwell Davis **Cast** Oliver Reed, Vanessa
Redgrave, Dudley Sutton, Max Adrian,
Gemma Jones, Murray Melvin, Michael
Gothard, Georgina Hale, Brian Murphy,
Christopher Logue, Graham Armitage,
John Woodvine

Ken Russell's film ("my most, indeed my only, political film," he insisted) was inspired by Aldous Huxley's "non-fiction novel" *The Devils of Loudun*. In the 1630s Louis XIII of France was leveling the fortifications of any town that might resist his rule. Loudun held out, led by its parish priest, Father Urbain Grandier. Conveniently, a local convent of Ursuline nuns began exhibiting hysterical symptoms, cavorting naked and screaming that Grandier had seduced them with the help of devils. Grandier was tried, found guilty, and burnt alive. The walls of Loudun were demolished.

To Russell, the story's mix of religion, sex, and politics proved irresistible. As Grandier, Oliver Reed gives a career-best performance, moving from a preening libertine to something gentler in his love for the widowed Madeleine (Gemma Jones), as the shadows of his fate darken around him. He's matched by Vanessa Redgrave as the hunchbacked Sister Jeanne of the Angels, lusting vengefully over the priest's tortured body.

The film caused outrage; both the British and American censors demanded extensive cuts. The film's backers, Warner Bros., were horrified upon seeing it, and insisted on a sanitized version. Today it looks less shocking, and Russell's trademark visual flamboyance perfectly suits his sensational story of nudity, masturbation, blasphemy, torture, and blackest political skulduggery. **PK**

The Hired Hand Peter Fonda, 1971

U.S. (Universal Pictures)
92m Color **Producer** William Hayward,
Stanley A. Weiss, Frank Mazzola (2002
restoration) **Screenplay** Alan Sharp
Photography Vilmos Zsigmond
Music Bruce Langhorne **Cast** Peter Fonda,
Warren Oates, Verna Bloom, Robert Pratt,
Severn Darden

Following the phenomenal success of *Easy Rider* (1969), leading man Peter Fonda was given the green light by Universal to direct any project of his choosing. The result, and the first of the three films Fonda would direct, was *The Hired Hand*, an elegiac and under-appreciated Western whose stature only came to light with an astonishing 2002 restoration.

Chasing their dream of a better life, Harry (Fonda) and his good friend Archie (Warren Oates) have drifted across the plains of America together. However, Harry has grown weary of his transient existence and has decided to return to the home and wife, Hannah (Verna Bloom), he had abandoned many years before. At first refuting acceptance, Hannah orders him to sleep in the barn and work the farm as a hired hand. After confessing that she has taken former help as lovers, the romance slowly rekindles. However, when news reaches Harry that Archie has run intro trouble in a seedy town, he is forced to make a fateful choice.

Eschewing action in favor of a more melancholic tone, *The Hired Hand* is remarkable for its trio of excellent performances, Vilmos Zsigmond's astonishing cinematography, and its radical feminist overtones. Set to a mournful score by Dylan cohort Bruce Langhorne, the film's final shot of Hannah accepting her loss and abandonment is among the most remarkable of any closing image in the genre. **JWo**

W.R.: Misterije organizma Dusan Makavejev, 1971
W.R.: Mysteries of the Organism

Yugoslavia / West Germany (Neoplanta, Telepool) 85m BW **Language** Serbo-Croatian **Screenplay** Dusan Makavejev **Photography** Aleksandar Petkovic, Predrag Popovic **Music** Bojana Marijan **Cast** Miodrag Andric, Jim Buckley, Jackie Curtis, Betty Dodson, Milena Dravic, Nancy Godfrey, Dragoljub Ivkov, Milan Jelic, Jagoda Kaloper, Tuli Kupferberg, Zivka Matic, Nikola Milic, Zoran Radmilovic, Wilhelm Reich, Ivica Vidovic **Berlin International Film Festival** Dusan Makavejev (FIPRESCI award—special mention, Interfilm award—recommendation forum of new cinema)

Dusan Makavejev's most critically acclaimed film, *W.R: Mysteries of the Organism*, is a magnificently obscene parody of Cold War politics and social mores. It tells the story of three warring cultures in the late 1960s: old-fashioned Soviet-style communism, U.S. bourgeois militarism, and the sexual revolutionaries whose values put them at odds with both.

These cultures are explored through interlocked narratives whose juxtaposition is utterly silly and disturbing by turns. A documentary look at the life of radical psychiatrist Wilhelm Reich is intercut with a goofy fictional spoof of communist Yugoslavia, in which the sexually liberated, feminist-communist Milena tries to seduce an old-fashioned Russian "People's artist." We also follow The Fugs's singer Tuli Kupferberg around Manhattan and see footage of Stalin from a 1946 Soviet propaganda flick, as well as medical films of people getting electroshock therapy. Occasionally we are treated to interviews with American sexual subversives.

The cumulative effect of these story fragments is a growing sense that the world is in chaos because politics try—and fail—to constrain sexual desire. Makavejev is famous for saying that his collage-style filmmaking represents the true embodiment of Eisenstein's ideal of dialectical montage because Eisenstein himself just didn't have a good enough sense of humor to do it right. *W.R.* may be the only avant-garde slapstick communist documentary sex romp ever made. That alone makes it a must-see. **AN**

𝑖

W.R. has a terrific soundtrack, featuring the song "Kill for Peace" by New York protest band The Fugs.

Walkabout Nicolas Roeg, 1971

Nicolas Roeg's second feature as director (and first solo effort) is deceptively simple: a bowler-hatted office worker (John Meillon) drives into the empty heart of Australia with his sixteen year-old daughter (Jenny Agutter) and much younger son (Luc Roeg). The father sets fire to the car and shoots himself, stranding the siblings in the desert. At a dried-out waterhole, they meet an Aborigine youth (David Gulpilil) who is on his "walkabout," a time apart from the tribe when he must commune with nature. Of course, the city kids' spell in the wild also serves as a walkabout of their own, during which they learn something that is muted when they return to their lives, leaving behind a devastation that only the doomed Aborigine understands.

Walkabout is a deep film, but it's also elusive: constantly forcing you to think for yourself, or accept that some mysteries should never be solved. The story begins and ends with suicides that we don't have enough information to "understand." If the story (from a novel by James Vance Marshall) were to be remade conventionally, the film would be full of exciting wilderness perils and go heavy on the kind of love affair between the repressed miss and the nature boy that you get in *Blue Lagoon* (1980). Instead, a drama of transformation and tragedy is played out through apparently throwaway dialogue. Flashes of cinematic trickery, footnote-like scenes, provide a "civilized" contrast with wilderness behavior—Gulpilil's spearing and bludgeoning of a kangaroo is intercut with shots of a butcher knife impersonally chopping cuts of meat—combined with documentary footage of crawling lizards and swarming insects.

The normal skills associated with "acting" aren't required here, and Roeg cast two of the major roles with players who had never acted before, the Aborigine Gulpilil—later a fixture in Australian cinema—and his own son Luc. *Walkabout* lives in the fantasies of a generation because Agutter, in and out of school uniform (she has a famous nude swim), emerged from her prim *Railway Children* television series image to be strikingly sensual as the girl who takes a "memory" of something that never happened back to the city. **KN**

G.B. (Fox, Litvinoff) 95m Eastmancolor
Producer Si Litvinoff, Max L. Raab
Screenplay Edward Bond, from novel by James Vance Marshall **Photography** Nicolas Roeg **Music** John Barry, Warren Marley, Billy Mitchell, Rod Stewart, Karlheinz Stockhausen **Cast** Jenny Agutter, Luc Roeg, David Gulpilil, John Meillon, Robert McDarra, Peter Carver, John Illingsworth, Hilary Bamberger, Barry Donnelly, Noeline Brown, Carlo Manchini **Cannes Film Festival** Nicolas Roeg (Golden Palm nomination)

> *"People usually arrive to see something with an open mind. I want to make them feel something emotionally, but not by planning how to get them there."*
>
> **Nicolas Roeg, 2005**

1971

i

Edward Bond's script for the film consisted of just fifteen pages of handwritten notes.

Lots of guys swing with a call girl like Bree.

One guy just wants to kill her.

'klute'

U.S. (Gus, Warner Bros.) 114m Technicolor
Producer C. Kenneth Deland, David Lange,
Alan J. Pakula Screenplay Andy Lewis,
Dave Lewis Photography Gordon Willis
Music Michael Small Cast Jane Fonda,
Donald Sutherland, Charles Cioffi, Roy
Scheider, Dorothy Tristan, Rita Gam, Nathan
George, Vivian Nathan, Morris Strassberg,
Barry Snider, Betty Murray, Jane White,
Shirley Stoler, Robert Milli, Anthony
Holland Oscar Jane Fonda (actress)
Oscar nomination Andy Lewis, David P.
Lewis (screenplay)

"After spending a week with prostitutes, I asked Alan Pakula to let me out of my contract. I said, 'I can't do it, hire Faye Dunaway. I can't do it.' And then I figured out a way to get into it—but I didn't think I could do it."

Jane Fonda, 2011

i

Jane Fonda's acceptance speech for her Best Actress Oscar for *Klute* was one of the shortest in movie history.

Klute Alan J. Pakula, 1971

The post-Vietnam/Watergate sensibilities of 1970s cinema were never more evident than in Alan Pakula's classic neonoir *Klute*. From the fetishized phone conversation of the opening credits, the director makes us aware of the surveillance age that would culminate so strikingly in Francis Coppola's *The Conversation* (1974). *Klute* is an unconventional film that is both detective thriller and character-driven mood piece, one rife with subtexts of urban decay and a claustrophobic sense of helplessness.

Despite the title, this is Bree Daniels's (Jane Fonda) story, and its success relies on the complex inner life of Fonda's call girl, who is neither your typical tramp with a heart of gold nor a total bitch. Fonda's turn is the crowning achievement of her career. Bree wants to be an actress and model, and Pakula's depiction of New York makes it understandable that she would need to turn tricks to survive, as it is all just another acting job.

Enter John Klute (Donald Sutherland), a small-town detective out of his depth in the underbelly of New York vice and fraud, and an enigma for Bree as he seems beyond corruption. Sutherland's morally uptight investigator fascinates her enough to allow him into a world he could never hope to enter on his own. Much like Paul Schrader's *Hardcore* (1979), a small-town innocent is drawn into the shadowland of urban wickedness only to find it pathetic, and reaches out to a damaged soul in hopes of salvation, even if a relationship is out of the question.

As a mystery, *Klute* has no real suspense because the killer's identity is made known early on. The dynamic between the two leads is what keeps the film on target. The real joy is Fonda's acting virtuosity, and her ability to register so many edges and contradictions on camera. Pakula's aesthetic centers on the voyeuristic pleasure of watching Bree develop into a nonhero as fear envelopes her world and her tough veneer starts to crumble when she must trust a man, perhaps for the first time.

As for Pakula, his three masterworks (*Klute*, *The Parallax View* [1974], and *All the President's Men* [1976]) more than justify his place among the great directors of the 1970s or any other decade. His style remained unique to the last. **DDV**

Harold and Maude Hal Ashby, 1971

His hangups are Hilarious

From the creator of "Silver Streak" and "Foul Play"

Paramount Pictures Presents

HAROLD and MAUDE
RUTH GORDON
BUD CORT

"A very funny comedy of the absurd"
-Charles Champlin
LA Times

Written by Colin Higgins
Directed by Hal Ashby
Produced by Colin Higgins and Charles & Mulvehill
Executive Producer Mildred Lewis
Songs by Cat Stevens
A Paramount Pictures Re-release

Color by TECHNICOLOR

U.S. (Paramount) 91m Technicolor
Producer Colin Higgins, Mildred Lewis,
Charles Mulvehill **Screenplay** Colin Higgins
Photography John A. Alonzo **Music** Cat
Stevens, Johann Strauss, Tchaikovsky
Cast Ruth Gordon, Bud Cort, Vivian Pickles,
Cyril Cusack, Charles Tyner, Ellen Geer, Eric
Christmas, G. Wood, Judy Engles, Shari
Summers, Tom Skerritt, Susan Madigan, Ray
K. Goman, Gordon Devol, Harvey Brumfield

> *"A lot of people enjoy being dead. But they're not dead, really. They're just . . . backing away from life. Reach out. Take a chance. Get hurt, even!"*
>
> **Maude**
> **(Ruth Gordon)**

🛈

A cinema in Minnesota showed
Harold and Maude a record-breaking
1,957 times between 1972 and 1974.

The label of "cult film" is commonly used today as a marketing stunt for quasi-independent or mainstream films flirting with various subcultures. *Harold and Maude*, however, is the genuine thing, combining the directorial talents of former editor Hal Ashby with the oddball personas of main actors Bud Cort and Ruth Gordon. Cort, age twenty-one, had just done his first leading part as a flight-obsessed kid in Robert Altman's *Brewster McCloud* (1970). Ex-screenwriter Gordon, age seventy-six, had a string of memorable supporting roles behind her in the 1960s, the most well known being her Manhattan witch in *Rosemary's Baby* (1968), for which she won an Academy Award. In *Harold and Maude*, their peculiar chemistry made them an engaging, unforgettable romantic couple, challenging taboos of youth, aging, sex, death, and happiness.

Most interesting, perhaps, is that this challenge not only is a run-of-the-mill counterculture pose against traditional patriarchal society, but is even more aggressively directed against the contemporary youth-quake. This is primarily made by reversing the 1960s concept of youth as the vital, mold-breaking counterforce to the inevitable physical and spiritual deadness affecting everybody over age thirty. Here the young and rich Harold is a living corpse because of his inability to break free from an oedipal fixation with his cold mother (Vivian Pickles), whose attention he tries to get in vain through a series of hilarious fake suicide attempts. It is only when he meets the old but vital and anarchic Maude that he comes to life. Thus Harold's fear of life is equated with a fear of growing up and aging. Maude, on the other hand, is not afraid of death, having survived the Nazi prison camps (implied by the number tattooed on her arm flashing by in a shot). Rather, we learn at the end of the film that she longs for it.

Ironically, this strange love story grows out of their obsessive habit of attending funerals, which—for different reasons, as we have seen—have a therapeutic value for them both. And it is to Ashby's credit that he doesn't turn this into a sentimental story of platonic friendship, in which the old and wise gives the young and reckless life lessons. Instead, Maude is the reckless one, impulsively acting out all her fantasies even to the point of stealing cars and seducing boys sixty years younger than herself. And it is their sexual liaison that is the key to this film, revolting as it seems to several of the characters and possibly to many in the audience—even to those who think of themselves as "liberated." The words of Eric Christmas's preaching priest that the thought of Harold's young body having intercourse with Maude's aging flesh "makes me want to puke," brings to mind acts of necromancy or a gothic horror film in which the old monster feeds on the young victim. Triumphantly, though, *Harold and Maude* rids us of all such cultural preconceptions. In the final scene, in which Maude prepares to die on her eightieth birthday, this bias toward youth is replaced with the existential insight that death is ultimately what gives life meaning. **MT**

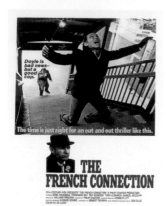

The French Connection William Friedkin, 1971

Together with *Bullitt* (1968) and *Dirty Harry* (1971), *The French Connection* spearheaded the cop-movie revival that took place around 1970. Loosely based on fact, it centers on the fanatical efforts of New York City police detective "Popeye" Doyle (Gene Hackman) to intercept a heroin shipment engineered by the urbane Marseilles entrepreneur Charnier (Fernando Rey). Although its view of the war on drugs as a class struggle waged by street cops against establishment fat cats now seems dated, *The French Connection* remains a tremendously exciting and powerful movie.

The editing—its rough-edged energy enhanced by jagged, truncated scene transitions—conveys both off-balance disorientation and reckless forward propulsion. The celebrated chase scene, in which Doyle's car hurtles down a busy avenue in pursuit of an elevated train, never seems an overblown set piece, because it simply extends the kinetic, careering, tunnel-vision effect sustained throughout the film.

The French Connection's view of the embattled "drugopolis" goes beyond its impressively squalid locations to encompass a resonant interplay between different cityscapes. Gritty, grungy New York is at first ironically contrasted with spacious, gracious Marseilles and then split into two of its boroughs: Manhattan, citadel of the rich and powerful, and Brooklyn, cockpit of junkies, small-time hoods, and street cops. An added twist is provided by a brief scene in Washington, D.C.—shown as a lifeless White City, detached from the real urban battlegrounds.

Has there ever been a Best Picture Oscar winner with such a downbeat ending? After chasing Charnier into a hideously decayed building, Doyle not only loses his man but also gets swallowed up by his obsession. Too demented to acknowledge that he has just fragged an FBI agent, Doyle disappears in futile pursuit. The final scene can be read as an apocalyptic vision of the city's future, the ruined building as a relic of a lost civilization, the doorway through which Doyle vanishes as the gate of hell. The awesome bleakness of this conclusion is what lifts *The French Connection* above the level of middlebrow award winners and into the ranks of truly gripping films. **MR**

U.S. (Fox, D'Antoni, Schine-Moore) 104m Color **Language** English / French **Producer** Philip D'Antoni, G. David Schine, Kenneth Utt **Screenplay** Ernest Tidyman, from novel by Robin Moore **Photography** Owen Roizman **Music** Don Ellis **Cast** Gene Hackman, Fernando Rey, Roy Scheider, Tony Lo Bianco, Marcel Bozzuffi, Frédéric de Pasquale, Bill Hickman, Ann Rebbot, Harold Gary, Arlene Farber, Eddie Egan, André Ernotte, Sonny Grosso, Ben Marino, Patrick McDermott **Oscars** Philip D'Antoni (best picture), William Friedkin (director), Ernest Tidyman (screenplay), Gene Hackman (actor), Gerald B. Greenberg (editing) **Oscar nominations** Roy Scheider (actor in support role), Owen Roizman (photography), Theodore Soderberg, Christopher Newman (sound)

"The way that film was cast, it was like the Movie God took care of it."

William Friedkin, 1997

i

Fernando Rey was cast after being mistaken for the gangster in *Belle de jour* (actually Francisco Rabal).

Még kér a nép Miklós Jancsó, 1971
Red Psalm

Hungary (Mafilm) 88m Eastmancolor
Language Hungarian Producer Ottó Föld
Screenplay Yvette Biro, Gyula Hernádi
Photography János Kende Music Tamás
Cseh Cast Lajos Balázsovits, András Bálint,
Gyöngyi Bürös, Erzsi Cserhalmi, Mari
Csomós, László Csurka, Andrea Drahota,
Zsuzsa Ferdinándy, Ilona Gurnik, Péter
Haumann, Jácint Juhász, János Koltai, József
Madaras, Tibor Molnár, Elemér Ragályi,
Bertalan Solti, Éva Spányik, Frantisek Velecky,
Márk Zala Cannes Film Festival Miklós
Jancsó (director, Golden Palm nomination)

The 1997 documentary *East Side Story* assumes that Eastern-Bloc directors were just itching to make Hollywood extravaganzas that invariably looked strained, square, and ill equipped. But *Red Psalm*, Miklós Jancsó's dazzling, open-air revolutionary pageant, is a sensual communist musical that employs occasional nudity as lyrically as the singing, dancing, and nature.

Set in the nineteenth century, when a group of peasants have demanded basic rights from a landowner and soldiers arrive on horseback, *Red Psalm* consists of only twenty-six shots, each one an intricate choreography of panning camera, landscape, and clustered bodies. Jancsó's awesome fusion of form with content, politics with poetry, equals the exciting innovations of the French New Wave.

The picture may well be the greatest Hungarian film of its time, summing up an entire strain in his work that lamentably has been forgotten in the United States. One of Jancsó's characteristic achievements is to create a striking continuum between past and present, a sense of immediacy about history found in few other period films. This suggests that the charge of formalism frequently leveled against him stems from an inability to fully comprehend his historical and political meanings—combined with an understandable effort to become intoxicated by the stylistic virtuosity and beauty. **JRos**

Get Carter Mike Hodges, 1971

G.B. (MGM) 112m Metrocolor
Producer Michael Klinger Screenplay Mike
Hodges, from the novel *Jack's Return Home*
by Ted Lewis Photography Wolfgang
Suschitzky Music Roy Budd Cast Michael
Caine, Ian Hendry, Britt Ekland, John
Osborne, Tony Beckley, George Sewell,
Geraldine Moffat, Dorothy White, Rosemarie
Dunham, Petra Markham, Alun Armstrong,
Bryan Mosley, Glynn Edwards, Bernard
Hepton, Terence Rigby

Gangster Jack Carter (Michael Caine), who works as strong-arm man for a London mob, returns to his northern hometown of Newcastle to avenge the death of his brother. While there, he finds himself genocidally involved in a complicated series of faction fights between local crooks, and is set up to take a fall because he has unwisely been fooling around with his boss's girlfriend Anna (Britt Ekland).

Among *Get Carter*'s interestingly cast provincial hoodlums are playwright John Osborne—surprisingly convincing as an effete gangland figure—and reliable hardhead Ian Hendry, memorably described as having eyes "like pissholes in the snow." Blunt and forceful, with effective use of location, Mike Hodges's film makes no concessions to morality and yet hardly condones the brutalities of its characters, with Caine getting a couple of shocks as he discovers that his niece (who might be his daughter) has starred in a credibly amateur porno movie, then coming to a bad end after he extracts rough justice on a deserted beach. Memorable scenes include a stark-naked Caine with a shotgun ejecting a couple of thugs from his bed-and-breakfast; the car going into the docks with an unnoticed passenger in the trunk; and a mob boss taking a dive from a multistory parking garage. **KN**

Shaft Gordon Parks, 1971

The mob wanted Harlem back. They got Shaft... up to here.

SHAFT's his name. SHAFT's his game.

U.S. (MGM) 100m Metrocolor
Producer Joel Freeman, David Golden
Screenplay Ernest Tidyman, John D.F. Black, from novel by Ernest Tidyman
Photography Urs Furrer **Music** Isaac Hayes, J.J. Johnson **Cast** Richard Roundtree, Moses Gunn, Charles Cioffi, Christopher St. John, Gwenn Mitchell, Lawrence Pressman, Victor Arnold, Sherri Brewer, Rex Robbins, Camille Yarbrough, Margaret Warncke, Joseph Leon, Arnold Johnson, Dominic Barto, George Strus **Oscar** Isaac Hayes (song) **Oscar nomination** Isaac Hayes (music)a

"You knew we had something really exciting, but we had no idea how big this thing was going to be."

Richard Roundtree, 2000

ℹ

Shaft was followed by two sequels, *Shaft's Big Score!* (1972) and *Shaft in Africa* (1973), plus a remake in 2000.

"He's cool and tough. He's a black private dick who's a sex machine with all the chicks. He doesn't take orders from anybody, black or white, but he'd risk his neck for his brother man. I'm talkin' about Shaft. Can you dig it?" These lines, from Isaac Hayes's Oscar-winning theme, serve as the perfect introduction to Richard Roundtree's African-American hero/rebel/icon John Shaft, eponymous star of the wildly successful feature directed by Gordon Parks. *Shaft* followed directly on the heels of Melvin Van Peebles's *Sweet Sweetback's Baadasssss Song* (1971) and is widely acknowledged as the film that initiated the short-lived (but fondly remembered) blaxploitation cinema explosion of the 1970s.

The screenplay was written by Ernest Tidyman, author of a series of popular detective novels featuring the movie's protagonist. After the success of *Sweetback*, MGM gave Parks—an esteemed African-American photographer, writer, composer, and filmmaker—the go-ahead for a project that would hopefully capitalize on the fast-emerging black market. Parks wanted a fresh face to play the lead, and found exactly what he was looking for in Roundtree, a former *Ebony* model and occasional theater actor whose physical presence and acting chops provided just the right combination of machismo, virility, and confidence for the part.

The film's convoluted plot is fairly standard hard-boiled detective fare. After inadvertently causing the death of a gangster who shows up at his office, Shaft is coerced by a pair of white police inspectors to help them gather information about a gang war rumored to be taking place in Harlem. Meanwhile, a drug-dealing black godfather hires Shaft to save his daughter from the men who have recently kidnapped her. This turns out to be the Italian Mafia, so with the help of a former comrade and his cadre of black nationalist followers, Shaft undertakes a dangerous but ultimately successful rescue mission. The mostly nonstop action is interrupted twice by romantic interludes. Shaft has no qualms about cheating on his girlfriend, and proves himself an equal-opportunity lover.

If ever there was a film in which the narrative is simply a vehicle for showcasing a particular character, *Shaft* is it. Together, Tidyman, Parks, and Roundtree create a strong black protagonist who—for the first time in Hollywood cinema—makes his own rules, listens to no one, gives the orders instead of taking them, and is not the least bit afraid of making jokes at the expense of white authority figures. Despite (perhaps because of) its subversive lead and militant undertones, *Shaft* did remarkable business among both black and white audiences, grossing over $23 million at U.S. box offices alone. Such broad-ranging success is partly explained by the fact that *Shaft* is perfectly comfortable in any situation, with people of every stripe (including a blatantly homosexual bartender, who feels compelled to pinch his butt), and that his magnetism and coolness under fire transcend mere color boundaries. **SJS**

Sweet Sweetback's Baadasssss Song

Melvin Van Peebles, 1971

"This film is dedicated to all the Brothers and Sisters who have had enough of the Man." With the $70,000 he earned from his 1970 race-reversal comedy *Watermelon Man*, plus additional funds (including a $50,000 loan from Bill Cosby), Melvin Van Peebles—one of the first African-American directors to work in Hollywood—financed his new project, *Sweet Sweetback's Baadasssss Song*. Van Peebles wrote, directed, scored, and starred in the film, which not only was a sound economic decision but also ensured his creative control over every facet of production. Early in 1971, *Sweetback* opened in the only two theaters that would agree to show it on a first-run basis. By the end of the year the film had become the most profitable independent production in history. A sleeper hit across the nation, it ended up grossing over $15 million.

Sweetback is a film so original in both conception and realization that it defied all expectations, providing a popular alternative to the dominant Hollywood paradigm. But it is also a film that borrows narrative threads and conventions from an assortment of different genres, including the chase film, the gangster movie, the biker flick, and the soft-core porno. Finally, *Sweetback* is a film whose huge and unanticipated commercial success ensured its place at the head of an explosion in black-marketed, black-cast, and black-directed productions—an explosion that soon went by the ambivalent name of "blaxploitation cinema."

The shocking first scene finds a preteen Sweetback (played by Melvin's son, Mario) working in a whorehouse, where a grateful call girl screams out his nickname during orgasm. We next observe the grown-up Sweetback performing as a stud in a sex show in South Central Los Angeles. Watching as two white cops proceed to beat a young black activist (Hubert Scales) within an inch of his life, Sweetback jumps the officers and nearly kills them. The rest of the film tracks our hero's progress as he rides, runs, and hitches in a desperate effort at avoiding capture. At one point, Sweetback has his life threatened by a motorcycle gang, and only survives by winning a public sex duel with the female leader. And that's just the beginning—as one reviewer describes it, Sweetback "evades the police by raping a black woman at knifepoint, spears a cop with a pool cue, kills a number of dogs tracking him, heals himself with his own urine, and bites off the head of a lizard before escaping across the Mexican border into the desert." The film concludes with the words "A Baadasssss nigger is coming to collect some dues" flashing across the screen.

Whatever one makes of *Sweetback*'s sociopolitical "message," the energy and innovativeness of Van Peeble's directorial style can hardly be denied. By making creative use of such techniques as montage, superimposition, freeze-frames, jump cuts, zoom ins, split-screen editing, stylized dialogue, multiply exposed scenes, and a soulful musical score, Van Peebles broke new ground and challenged viewers of all colors. **SJS**

U.S. (Yeah) 97m Color **Producer** Jerry Gross, Melvin Van Peebles **Screenplay** Melvin Van Peebles **Photography** Robert Maxwell **Music** Earth Wind and Fire, Melvin Van Peebles **Cast** Simon Chuckster, Melvin Van Peebles, Hubert Scales, John Dullaghan, West Gale, Niva Rochelle, Rhetta Hughes, Nick Ferrari, Ed Rue, John Amos, Lavelle Roby, Ted Hayden, Mario Van Peebles, Sonja Dunson, Michael Agustus

"[Blaxploitation is] not my term. I don't consider myself a sociologist, I consider myself a filmmaker, among other things. Maybe an asshole, but a filmmaker."

Melvin Van Peebles, 2005

ℹ

Van Peebles pretended to be making a porn film to save money, as it allowed him to hire black and nonunion crew.

The Last Picture Show Peter Bogdanovich, 1971

U.S. (BBS, Columbia) 118m BW
Producer Stephen J. Friedman
Screenplay Peter Bogdanovich, James Lee Barrett, from novel by Larry McMurtry
Photography Robert Surtees **Music** Hank Williams, John Philip Sousa **Cast** Timothy Bottoms, Jeff Bridges, Cybill Shepherd, Ben Johnson, Cloris Leachman, Ellen Burstyn, Eileen Brennan, Clu Gulager, Sam Bottoms, Sharon Ullrick, Randy Quaid **Oscars** Ben Johnson (actor in support role), Cloris Leachman (actress in support role)
Oscar nominations Stephen J. Friedman (best picture), Peter Bogdanovich (director), James Lee Barrett, Peter Bogdanovich (screenplay), Jeff Bridges (actor in support role), Ellen Burstyn (actress in support role), Robert Surtees (photography)

🛈

All but one of the film's shots are taken at eye-level.

An ardent formalist at a time when his early 1970s peers were spending their time breaking rules, Peter Bogdanovich doggedly stuck to old-fashioned ideals and ideas when directing *The Last Picture Show*. In this sense, his adaptation of Larry McMurtry's novel stands as a eulogy for the previous generation of master filmmakers (like Howard Hawks or John Ford) as a new generation of youthful pioneers steered filmmaking in a looser, more visceral direction.

A coming-of-age story set in a small, dusty Texas town, *The Last Picture Show* bids adieu to the 1950s, capturing the nation's shifting mores and interests. A superb cast of newcomers (including Jeff Bridges, Cybill Sheppard, Randy Quaid, and Timothy Bottoms) plays against such veterans as Cloris Leachman and Ben Johnson as they all try to find their place in a changing world. Bogdanovich's vision is bleak but honest, and he captures (in stark but striking black and white) the awkward moments when innocence lurches into experience, without judgment and without pat nostalgia. The film is like a wake for an entire era, ripe with tragedy and exuding a heavy pall of unmistakable sadness. **JKl**

Wanda Barbara Loden, 1971

U.S. (Foundation for Filmakers) 102m Color
Producer Harry Shuster **Screenplay** Barbara
Loden **Photography** Nicholas T. Proferes
Cast Barbara Loden, Michael Higgins,
Dorothy Shupenes, Peter Shupenes,
Jerome Thier, Marian Thier, Anthony Rotell,
M.L. Kennedy, Gerald Grippo, Milton
Gittleman, Lila Gittleman, Arnold Kanig, Joe
Dennis, Charles Dosinan, Jack Ford

The heartbreaking final image of *Wanda*—a freeze-frame snapshot of the eponymous character sadly drifting through a life of small-town bars and quiet misery—is given further tragic resonance through the knowledge that this masterpiece of American independent cinema remained the only film ever directed by its star, Barbara Loden, before she succumbed to cancer in 1980. The wife of Elia Kazan (and actress in Kazan's *Wild River* [1960] and *Splendor in the Grass* [1961]), Loden derived inspiration from the improvisational cinema verité rhythms of the burgeoning independent film movement of the late 1960s with this raw, naturalistic portrait of a destitute, uneducated young woman in a Pennsylvania steel town who abandons her husband and children with the same degree of apathy that guides her subsequent entanglement with a bullying bank robber (Michael Higgins).

Loden admirably refuses to transform her protagonist into a symbolic martyr for feminist causes, just as she also never shies from depicting Wanda's complicity in making poor choices—and yet one can't help but retain great empathy for Wanda and her shattered self-esteem. Expertly coaxing authentic performances from a cast mixing professionals with local nonactors, Loden has chronicled a type of character rarely glimpsed in American film—and in the process, she also created one of the greatest "one-shot" directing achievements in this country's cinema. **TCr**

Le souffle au coeur Louis Malle, 1971
Murmur of the Heart

France / Italy / West Germany (Franz Seitz,
Marianne, NEF, Vides) 118m Eastmancolor
Language French **Producer** Vincent
Malle, Claude Nedjar **Screenplay** Louis
Malle **Photography** Ricardo Aronovich
Music Sidney Bechet, Gaston Frèche, Charlie
Parker, Henri Renaud **Cast** Lea Massari,
Benoît Ferreux, Daniel Gélin, Michael
Lonsdale, Ave Ninchi, Gila von
Weitershausen, Fabien Ferreux, Marc
Winocourt, Micheline Bona, Henri Poirier,
Liliane Sorval, Corinne Kersten, Eric
Walter, François Werner, René Bouloc
Oscar nomination Louis Malle (screenplay)
Cannes Film Festival Louis Malle (Golden
Palm nomination)

Louis Malle liked to call *Murmur of the Heart* "my first film." In fact it was his eighth feature, but the first one he scripted on his own. It was also, he felt, his "first happy, optimistic film." Loosely based on Malle's own adolescent memories, it is set in a world seen entirely through the eyes of its hero, the fifteen-year-old Laurent Chevalier (Benoît Ferreux). The episodic plot springs few surprises: Laurent resents his father, adores his pretty young mother, veers unpredictably between childhood and adulthood, and is fascinated and disconcerted by his own rampant sexuality. The film's freshness lies in its evocative re-creation of bourgeois, provincial, French society of the early 1950s—and in the physical immediacy of family life, shown as a rich, lively mixture of jokes, fights, embarrassment, horseplay, feuds, and alliances.

The film's key moment—which ran it into major problems with the French government—is the act of incest between Laurent and his mother, filmed by Malle with great subtlety and discretion. Audaciously, he treats it not as a source of guilt and trauma, but as a loving, liberating event, to be recalled (as Laurent's mother tells him) "not with remorse, but with tenderness . . . as something beautiful." **PK**

Straw Dogs Sam Peckinpah, 1971

G.B. (ABC, Amerbroco, Talent) 118m
Eastmancolor **Producer** Daniel Melnick
Screenplay David Zelag Goodman, Sam
Peckinpah, from the novel *The Siege of
Trencher's Farm* by Gordon M. Williams
Photography John Coquillon **Music** Jerry
Fielding **Cast** Dustin Hoffman, Susan
George, Peter Vaughan, T.P. McKenna, Del
Henney, Jim Norton, Donald Webster, Ken
Hutchison, Len Jones, Sally Thomsett, Robert
Keegan, Peter Arne, Cherina Schaer, Colin
Welland **Oscar nomination** Jerry Fielding
(music)

> "Nihilism leaches from every frame. Peckinpah's Cornwall resembles the Old West reimagined as Hammer horror."
>
> Simon Kinnear,
> *Total Film*, **2011**

Sam Peckinpah was not a director known for his delicacy, and indeed *Straw Dogs* remains his most divisive and galvanizing film, especially following the more stylized Western violence of the 1969 film *The Wild Bunch*. Dustin Hoffman plays a timid mathematician who moves with his wife Susan George to her childhood village in the United Kingdom. There she flaunts her success and beauty before the insular townsfolk, who treat the arrival of Hoffman and her as an intrusion, and it's clear that their already rocky marriage may collapse under the strain. Hoffman, for his part, grows more and more uncomfortable, and the townsfolk more and more bold in their contempt for the couple—but it is only when his wife is raped that Hoffman explodes with violence.

More than just implicitly supporting vigilantism—the apparently inevitable outcome when one man is pushed too far—*Straw Dogs* proves equally ambiguous when it comes to George's character. She parades around in tight sweaters and flirts shamelessly with old flames, so when she is finally assaulted, Peckinpah initially makes it appear as if she'd invited the horrific invasion, both as an affront to her bookish husband and also as a provocative response to his inaction. But that ambiguity quickly passes as Peckinpah plays up the terror of the infamous rape scene, and by the time it's over the viewer is almost as shaken as George's character.

Given the brutal lead-up, Peckinpah hardly lets the audience off easy when it comes to *Straw Dogs*'s willfully barbaric conclusion. Having kept the film brilliantly off-balance with his disorienting editing and the steady, audacious ratcheting of intensity, Peckinpah further strains and exploits the viewer's emotions by stacking the deck against the brutish antagonists. But the disturbing, bloody outcome hardly results in any real catharsis or satisfaction. Rather, it leaves you feeling even more stunned and unsure of what you've seen than ever before. The uncertain morality of *Straw Dogs* sparked a great deal of controversy, which ironically validates Peckinpah's instincts. We may not like what we see, but we're compelled to watch it anyway. **JKl**

1971

ℹ️

Straw Dogs was banned on video and DVD in Britain from 1984 to 2002, due to its portrayal of rape.

Two-Lane Blacktop Monte Hellman, 1971

U.S. (Michael Laughlin, Universal) 102m Technicolor **Producer** Gary Kurtz, Michael Laughlin **Screenplay** Will Corry, Rudy Wurlitzer **Photography** Jack Deerson **Music** Billy James **Cast** James Taylor, Warren Oates, Laurie Bird, Dennis Wilson, David Drake, Richard Ruth, Rudy Wurlitzer, Jaclyn Hellman, Bill Keller, Harry Dean Stanton, Don Samuels, Charles Moore, Tom Green, W.H. Harrison, Alan Vint

Monte Hellman's *Two-Lane Blacktop* is probably the best film to come out of the post–*Easy Rider* (1969) craze in Hollywood for greenlighting hippie-era road movies that studio executives (and sadly most audiences) didn't understand.

Having made a pair of remarkable existentialist Westerns, *Ride in the Whirlwind* (1965) and *The Shooting* (1967), Hellman set out to strip away the longhaired glamor of *Easy Rider* (1969). *Two-Lane Blacktop* is a deliberately paced story about an absurd race between a pair of black-car cultists in a 1955 Chevrolet played by musicians (James Taylor, Dennis Wilson) and a fast-spieling, grinning neurotic in a yellow GTO (Hellman regular Warren Oates), with glum tagalong chick Laurie Bird passed between them and pink slips put up as the prize.

Whereas *Easy Rider* and *Vanishing Point* (1971) zoom down the highways toward apocalypse, *Two-Lane Blacktop* depicts a race with no end, the film burning up in the projector before any resolution has been reached. A depiction of a country in a profound state of bad faith, the film has a lot of on-the-road detail, with sharp little cameos from the likes of Harry Dean Stanton (as a gay hitchhiker), but presents a central set of relationships between uncommunicative folks who are as stuck in their cars and on their courses as toys on a boy's racing game. **KN**

Wake in Fright Ted Kotchef, 1971

Australia (Group W, NLT Productions) 108m Color **Producer** George Willoughby **Screenplay** Kenneth Cook (novel), Evan Jones **Photography** Brian West **Music** John Scott **Cast** Gary Bond, Donald Pleasance, Chips Rafferty, Sylvia Kay, Jack Thompson, Peter Whittle, Al Thomas, John Meillon

Released to critical acclaim but met with extreme caution by the public, *Wake In Fright* (released in Europe and the United States as *Outback*) was neglected and in fact believed lost, until it was painstakingly restored by Australia's National Film and Sound Archive. Screened in competition at Cannes in 1971, it returned as part of the Cannes Classics selection in 2009.

Both brutal and awe-inspring, *Wake in Fright* is the story of John Grant (Gary Bond), a teacher who arrives in the rough outback mining town of Bundanyabba, only planning to stay overnight before catching the plane to Sydney. But his one night stretches to five and, accompanied by a motley crew of locals (among them Donald Pleasance's quietly sinister Doc), he plunges headlong toward his own destruction. When the alcohol-induced mist lifts, Grant is left a self-loathing man in a desolate wasteland, dirty, red-eyed, and looking down the barrel of a rifle.

Based on the novel by Kenneth Cook and marketed under the tagline "Sweat, Dust, and Beer . . . There's Nothing Else Out Here Mate!," *Wake In Fright* is one of the key works in the New Australian Cinema movement. A glimpse into a tortured psyche that manages to be both stark, tough, and, at times, surprisingly tender, the film has been acknowledged as an influence on contemporary Australian directors, including John Hillcoat (*The Proposition*, 2005) and Justin Kurzal (*Snowtown*, 2010). **JWo**

What did happen on the Cahulawassee River?

Deliverance

U.S. (Elmer, Warner Bros.) 109m
Technicolor **Producer** John Boorman
Screenplay James Dickey, from his novel
Photography Vilmos Zsigmond **Music** Eric
Weissberg **Cast** Jon Voight, Burt Reynolds,
Ned Beatty, Ronny Cox, Ed Ramey, Billy
Redden, Seamon Glass, Randall Deal, Bill
McKinney, Herbert Coward, Lewis Crone,
Ken Keener, Johnny Popwell, John Fowler,
Kathy Rickman **Oscar nominations** John
Boorman (best picture), John Boorman
(director), Tom Priestley (editing)

> "Sometimes you have
> to lose yourself 'fore you
> can find anything."
>
> **Lewis
> (Burt Reynolds)**

Deliverance John Boorman, 1972

Like Sam Peckinpah's *Straw Dogs* (1971) and Wes Craven's *Last House on the Left* (1972), John Boorman's *Deliverance* deals with complacent, middle-class folk faced with unreasoning, disturbingly sexualized violence in the wilds away from civilization, only to discover in themselves that they are "natural-born killers." Ironically, while the American Peckinpah, who had considered making *Deliverance*, was in Britain filming *Straw Dogs*, British director Boorman was in Georgia, using the Chattooga River to sub for poet-novelist James Dickey's fictional Cahulawassee River, shooting his own journey into the heart of darkness.

The film opens with four suburban types—quiet Ed (Jon Voight), survivalist Lewis (Burt Reynolds), bluff Bobby (Ned Beatty), and sensitive Drew (Ronny Cox)—traveling into woodland about to be destroyed by a dam that will create a new lake, opting to take a canoe trip downriver rather than play golf. When Ed and Bobby are waylaid by a pair of frightening, irrational hillbillies, Bobby is stripped, made to "squeal like a pig," and raped while Ed is tethered to a tree with his own belt, absurdly hanging on to his pipe through the ordeal. Archer Lewis intervenes, killing the rapist (Bill McKinney), and the quartet, with deeply mixed feelings, opts to cover up the incident and get out of the region, pitted against the surviving hillbilly rifleman (Herbert Coward) and the hostile landscape.

Most other directors would have made a standard he-man adventure movie, but Boorman, working from Dickey's screenplay, goes for a more disturbing approach, always questioning what the characters' heroism really means. The film eventually concludes that Voight's sad-eyed Ed, finding in himself the bestiality to survive, has lost rather than won. Reynolds, given a chance to rethink his "good ol' boy" screen persona, gives as generously self-critical a performance as John Wayne's in *The Searchers* (1956). Among the highlights: the unforgettable "feudin' banjos" scene as Drew plays a duet with a withered, porch-sitting manchild who turns out to be an amazing musician, and an oft-imitated last-minute horror twist (as in *Carrie* [1976]), as Ed's sleep is troubled by dreams of a hand emerging from the waters of the new lake. **KN**

1972

🛈

James Dickey, on whose novel the film was based, appears in a cameo as the sheriff at the end of the film.

Aguirre, der Zorn Gottes Werner Herzog, 1972
Aguirre, The Wrath of God

Werner Herzog had a remarkable run of important films in the radical German New Cinema. But his epic adventures featuring his maniacal tormentor and impulsive, inspired interpreter, Klaus Kinski, are the best known. And *Aguirre, the Wrath of God*—the first of Herzog's features widely seen internationally—is the most spellbinding. Supposedly narrated from the diary of the Spanish monk Gaspar de Carvajal, the film is a disturbing parable that encapsulates Herzog's flair for allegory, metaphor, dark humor, and the grotesque; his interest in alienation, obsession, and social decay; and his sense of the landscape taking on awful, human aspects.

Don Lope de Aguirre (Kinski) is one of Pizarro's pillaging conquistadors cutting a swathe across sixteenth-century South America. Having overwhelmed the Incas, Pizarro's soldiers are greedy for conquest and gold, but the expedition reaches an impasse in difficult terrain. What is supposed to be a one-week foraging and scouting trip by a party sent up the Amazon basin by raft quickly begins to suffer disasters. Soldiers and slaves are picked off by Indians, disease, and hunger; Aguirre leads a revolt against his commander; and the desperate journey degenerates into a homicidal power trip driven on by Aguirre's increasingly demented obsession with reaching the fabled city of gold, El Dorado.

Shooting on remote locations in Peru on a tiny budget was sufficiently problematic and arduous, but Herzog's account (particularly vivid in his documentary *My Best Fiend* [1999]) of a frequently raving Kinski adds appalling and entertaining background to the film. Toward the end of filming, Herzog prevented Kinski from walking out by threatening to shoot him. Clearly the real-life struggles enhanced the film's heated intensity, its tragic inevitability signaled by the murdered commander's graceful wife, dressed in her (improbably clean) best, determinedly walking away into the jungle. By the end, a mad Aguirre rules a floating bier strewn with corpses and swarming with squealing monkeys. Kinski's fascinating presence may dominate the film, but it is Herzog's uncompromising vision and control that keeps it on its hallucinatory, hypnotic course. **AE**

West Germany / Peru / Mexico (Werner Herzog) 100m Eastmancolor **Language** German **Producer** Werner Herzog **Screenplay** Werner Herzog **Photography** Thomas Mauch **Music** Popol Vuh **Cast** Klaus Kinski, Daniel Ades, Peter Berling, Daniel Farfán, Justo González, Ruy Guerra, Julio E. Martínez, Del Negro, Armando Polanah, Alejandro Repulles, Cecilia Rivera, Helena Rojo, Edward Roland

"I am the great traitor ... I am the wrath of God."

Don Lope de Aguirre (Klaus Kinski)

1972

i

Werner Herzog wrote the entire screenplay for the movie in just two-and-a-half days.

Cabaret Bob Fosse, 1972

U.S. (ABC) 124m Technicolor
Producer Cy Feuer **Screenplay** Jay Presson
Allen, from the book *Berlin Stories* by
Christopher Isherwood, from the play *I Am a
Camera* by John Van Druten and musical by
Joe Masteroff **Photography** Geoffrey
Unsworth **Music** John Kander **Cast** Liza
Minnelli, Michael York, Helmut Griem, Joel
Grey, Fritz Wepper, Marisa Berenson,
Elisabeth Neumann-Viertel, Helen Vita
Oscars Bob Fosse (director), Liza Minnelli
(actress), Joel Grey (actor in support role),
Rolf Zehetbauer, Hans Jürgen Kiebach,
Herbert Strabel (art direction), Geoffrey
Unsworth (photography), David Bretherton
(editing), Ralph Burns (music), Robert
Knudson, David Hildyard (sound)
Oscar nominations Cy Feuer (best picture),
Jay Presson Allen (screenplay)

ⓘ

No other film has ever won so many
Oscars without also winning the
award for Best Picture.

What was just the second film of director, dancer, choreographer, and Broadway giant Bob Fosse took home eight Academy Awards, including Best Director over Francis Ford Coppola for *The Godfather*. *Cabaret* was the only truly great musical made in the 1970s, despite prophecies that it would be Fosse's *Springtime For Hitler* ("Who wants to see a musical with Nazis?").

The answer was anybody who cares to be dazzled. Fosse was a cynic, brought up in vaudeville, who came of age in burlesque and sleazy nightclubs. No one else could have taken the John Kander–Fred Ebb musical (based on John Van Druten's play *I Am a Camera*, itself based on Christopher Isherwood's *Berlin Stories*) and cast such a cold, glittering eye on its sinful, soulless denizens of 1930s Berlin. The film's sharp, shiny musical numbers and incisive cuts between the cabaret and the world outside chillingly counterpoint the doom-laden tale of misconceived love and ambition amid the rise of Nazism, while Joel Grey's sinister club emcee is brilliant. But ultimately the film belongs to Liza Minnelli, who brought desperate-to-please nervous energy to sad, wild-eyed Sally Bowles with her feverish vitality and feigned depravity, giving warmth and frailty to a masterpiece of menace and show-stopping tunes. **AE**

Solyaris Andrei Tarkovsky, 1972
Solaris

U.S.S.R. (Creative Unit of Writers & Cinema Workers, Mosfilm, Unit Four) 165m BW / Sovcolor **Language** Russian **Producer** Viacheslav Tarasov **Screenplay** Fridrikh Gorenshtein, Andrei Tarkovsky, from novel by Stanislaw Lem **Photography** Vadim Yusov **Music** Eduard Artemyev, Johann Sebastian Bach **Cast** Natalya Bondarchuk, Donatas Banionis, Jüri Järvet, Vladislav Dvorzhetsky, Nikolai Grinko, Anatoli Solonitsyn **Cannes Film Festival** Andrei Tarkovsky (FIPRESCI award, grand prize of the jury, Golden Palm nomination)

"Whenever we show pity, we empty our souls."

Kris Kelvin (Donatas Banionis)

i

Tarkovsky's film is more than an hour longer than the 2002 remake directed by Steven Soderbergh.

Adapted from the best seller by Stanislaw Lem, Andrei Tarkovsky's *Solaris* meditates on an imaginary planet and Stanley Kubrick's *2001: A Space Odyssey* (1968). A sci-fi masterpiece, the film is equally an epic performed without a budget. Instead of offering innovative special effects or mind-blowing spectacle, it's confined to the experience of a character through whom fantasy and everyday life merge into one.

When psychologist Kris Kelvin (Donatas Banionis) is asked to evaluate the usefulness of a space station orbiting Solaris, he is confronted with the unsettling story of astronaut Berton (Vladislav Dvorzhetsky). Some years earlier, when there was hope to unravel the secrets of the new world's swirling oceans of consciousness, all turned for the worse when Berton became the lone survivor of a mishap that killed several explorers. Intrigued, Kris visits the space station and meets Dr. Snauth (Jüri Järvet), Dr. Sartorius (Anatoli Solonitsyn), and the suicide case Dr. Gibaryan (Sos Sarkisyan). They advise him to take his time and adjust. Meanwhile strange sights and sounds assault him, including the appearance of his long-dead wife Khari (Natalya Bondarchuk). Thus he begins realizing the ability of Solaris to recreate the memories of visitors.

In fear of Khari's seeming reality, Kris destroys, or aids the destruction of, several different Kharis, only to discover other truths about Solaris. Namely, that its illusions are materially real, emotionally as needy as he is, and that he's the first person to form a lasting relationship with the planet's sentience. Finally unable to perform his duty, Kris joins with Khari and all she represents. Snauth and Sartorius recognize his fall and accept the burden of ending Solaris, although the film's final image is of the planet fashioning itself into Kris's imagined redemption.

Through Kris's journey from indifferent outsider to being literally the center of a world created just for him, we see the unmaking of a rational mind by sheer desire. As such, Tarkovsky's film uses the widescreen frame and lengthy takes to organize truly beautiful imagery. In this fashion, *Solaris* externalizes interior states to embody the mood of its protagonist.

Banionis's Kris Kelvin is a sad, middle-aged man. His shock of white hair on an otherwise brunette scalp suggests tragic experience and orients his first attempts to categorize Solaris before submitting to its dream logic. The irresolvable conflict of the planet—both soothing and all consuming—is then perfectly expressed in various sequences shot in circular patterns. While a stationary camera spins slowly on a central pivot, the actors and sets change to reveal new layers of possibility from what existed only moments before.

A mind game in the same way 2001 was a head film, *Solaris* was produced in the heart of Soviet pogroms against free expression, and certainly without benefit of a large budget. Tarkovsky's film is a touchstone of the cinematic impetus to unravel what it is to be alive. **GC-Q**

Viskningar och rop Ingmar Bergman, 1972
Cries and Whispers

One of Ingmar Bergman's most exquisitely executed achievements, *Cries and Whispers* begins with early-morning shots of a country estate, Sven Nykvist's camerawork capturing the play of sunlight through trees and mist to ravishing effect. By the time we have entered the house itself, where antique clocks tick inexorably on as a woman is awakened from her slumbers by the agony of the cancer consuming her from within, it's clear we are witnessing a filmmaker at the peak of his artistry, so assured are the measured rhythms of his editing, the placement of the camera, and the telling use of sound and color. Indeed, it is perhaps color that sticks most vividly in the mind after viewing this autumnal masterpiece: the rich red so unnaturally predominant both in the furnishings and on the walls of most of the mansion's rooms, in sharp contrast to the graceful white gowns favored by the four women whose lives we glimpse therein.

Bergman explained that he'd imagined the human soul to be this shade of red; certainly, its brooding presence intensifies his study of death and its influence on the living. The four women are the mansion's dying owner (Harriet Andersson), her devoted maid (Kari Sylwan), and the two sisters (Ingrid Thulin and Liv Ullmann) who have come to tend to her during her final days. The former is emotionally and physically reticent thanks in part to a loveless marriage, the latter is superficially warmer but given to flightiness and insecurity. As the sisters and maid try first to comfort the sick woman and then to come to terms with her death, Bergman provides a glimpse into the inner life of each, tracing their fears, frustrations, anxieties, and regrets by means of memories and, at least for the maid, nightmarish fantasy. Such is his dramatic expertise that he blends the stuff of horror movies—vampirish kisses, the nightmarish prospect of a corpse returning to life—with chamber drama evocative of Chekhov or Strindberg, and makes it not only coherent and compelling but recognizable as part of his own artistic universe. Bergman is helped in this, of course, by extraordinary performances by actresses he'd worked with for many years, but then what a gift to them was his screenplay! **GA**

Sweden (Cinematograph AB, Svenska) 106m Eastmancolor **Language** Swedish **Producer** Lars-Owe Carlberg **Screenplay** Ingmar Bergman **Photography** Sven Nykvist **Music** Johann Sebastian Bach, Frédéric Chopin **Cast** Harriet Andersson, Kari Sylwan, Ingrid Thulin, Liv Ullmann, Anders Ek, Inga Gill, Erland Josephson, Henning Moritzen, Georg Årlin, Fredrik **Oscar** Sven Nykvist (photography) **Oscar nominations** Ingmar Bergman (best picture), Ingmar Bergman (director), Ingmar Bergman (screenplay), Marik Vos-Lundh (costume) **Cannes Film Festival** Ingmar Bergman (grand technical prize)

"How have I managed to tolerate you so long and not say anything? I know of what you're made—with your empty caresses and your false laughter."

Karin (Ingrid Thulin) to Maria (Liv Ullmann)

The lead actresses and the cinematographer loaned their salaries to help finance the film.

Le charme discret de la bourgeoisie
The Discreet Charm of the Bourgeoisie Luis Buñuel, 1972

France / Italy / Spain (Dean, Greenwich, Jet) 105m Eastmancolor **Language** French / Spanish **Producer** Serge Silberman **Screenplay** Luis Buñuel, Jean Claude Carrière **Photography** Edmond Richard **Cast** Fernando Rey, Paul Frankeur, Delphine Seyrig, Bulle Ogier, Stéphane Audran, Jean-Pierre Cassel, Julien Bertheau, Milena Vukotic, Maria Gabriella Maione, Claude Piéplu, Muni, Pierre Maquelon, François Maistre, Michel Piccoli, Ellen Bahl **Oscar** France (best foreign language film) **Oscar nomination** Luis Buñuel, Jean-Claude Carrière (screenplay)

The Discreet Charm of the Bourgeoisie, Luis Buñuel's comic masterpiece, about three well-to-do couples who try, but fail, to sit down and have a meal together, is perhaps the most perfectly achieved and executed of all his late French films. The film proceeds with diverse interruptions, digressions, and interpolations that identify the characters, their class, and their seeming indestructibility with the very processes of narrative illusion and narrative continuity.

One thing that makes *The Discreet Charm of the Bourgeoisie* as charming as it is, despite its radicalism, and helped Buñuel to win his only Oscar, is the perfect cast, many of whom bring along nearly mythic associations acquired in previous films. Thus Delphine Seyrig makes us think of *Last Year at Marienbad* (1961), Stéphane Audran summons up the high bourgeoisie of Claude Chabrol's middle period, Bulle Ogier's neurotic is like a light-comic version of the mad character she played in *L'amour fou* (1969), and even Rey unmistakably calls to mind *The French Connection* (1971) when he brandishes some cocaine.

Shortly after this film was nominated for an Oscar, Buñuel was interviewed by reporters in a Mexican restaurant, and when they asked if he expected to win, his reply was immediate: "Of course. I've already paid the $25,000 they wanted. Americans may have their weaknesses, but they do keep their promises." **JRos**

i

Buñuel credited himself with creating the sound effects, even though he was practically deaf by this time.

The Godfather Francis Ford Coppola, 1972

U.S. (Paramount) 175m Technicolor
Language English / Italian **Producer** Albert S. Ruddy **Screenplay** Francis Ford Coppola, Mario Puzo, from novel by Mario Puzo **Photography** Gordon Willis **Music** Carmine Coppola, Nino Rota **Cast** Marlon Brando, Al Pacino, Diane Keaton, Richard S. Castellano, Robert Duvall, James Caan, Sterling Hayden, Talia Shire, John Marley, Richard Conte, Al Lettieri, Abe Vigoda, Gianni Russo, John Cazale, Rudy Bond **Oscars** Albert S. Ruddy (best picture), Mario Puzo, Francis Ford Coppola (screenplay), Marlon Brando (actor—refused award) **Oscar nominations** Francis Ford Coppola (director), James Caan (actor in support role), Al Pacino (actor in support role), Robert Duvall (actor in support role), Anna Hill Johnstone (costume), William Reynolds, Peter Zinner (editing), Nino Rota (music— ineligible because he reused Fortunella score), Charles Grenzbach, Richard Portman, Christopher Newman (sound)

The youngest son, Michael Corleone (Al Pacino), returns from World War II outside the family business, organized crime. When his father, Don Corleone (Marlon Brando), is gunned down, however, Michael is driven to commit a revenge murder, bound by blood and "honor" to a violent course (or curse) of underworld power and survival. Eventually Michael inherits the role as family head, closing the door on his uncomprehending WASP wife (Diane Keaton) as he receives the homage as the new "Godfather."

The dialogue and characters of *The Godfather* instantly entered the collective consciousness of filmgoers. It made stars of Pacino and James Caan (hot-headed elder brother Sonny) and won Oscars for Best Picture, Screenplay, and Best Actor for Brando, in a triumphant comeback. Adapting Mario Puzo's best seller, writer-director Francis Ford Coppola made a pulp fiction gangster opera, an epic of patriarchy, family, and of America itself. Original protests by Italian-Americans citing defamation were swept away in the film's staggering popularity. All descendants of immigrants viewed with nostalgic yearning the Corleone clan pounding the pasta, celebrating and sorrowing together. Anecdotes, footnotes, and postscripts are part of film folklore: Brando did not stuff his cheeks with cotton, but had resin blobs clipped to his back teeth; he sent a fake Indian "Satcheen Littlefeather" to the Academy Awards ceremony to reject his Oscar.

Coppola laid much of the groundwork of 1970s cinema with his commanding technique. The audacious, visceral, and stately set pieces are legend—the horse's head in the bed, Sonny's slaughter, the intercutting of a sunny wedding party in the garden with Don Corleone's court indoors, and the dazzling finale of assassinations carried out during the christening of a new Corleone (in effect the sacramental rites for Michael as he assumes the role of Godfather). The film's finest qualities reveal Coppola's fluency in classics, pulp, noir, and social dramas, but an enduring criticism of *The Godfather* is that it glorifies the Mafia. Pacino's Michael is the film's hero, and Michael is not a good guy. But its mythic exploration of familial ties, be it one cursed in blood and ambition, still entices viewers with the idea that Family is better than no family at all. **AE**

"I'm going to make him an offer he can't refuse."

**Don Corleone
(Marlon Brando)**

i

The baby baptized in the film is Sofia Coppola, the director's daughter, who was three weeks old at the time.

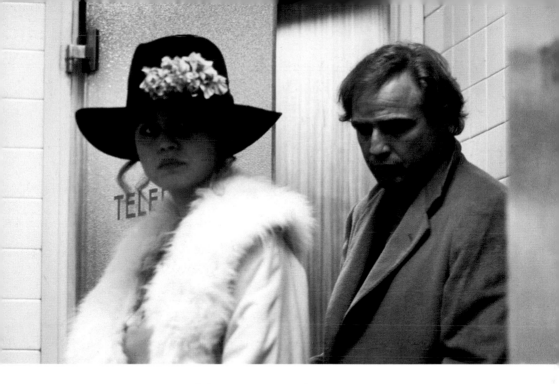

Ultimo tango a Parigi Bernardo Bertolucci, 1972
Last Tango in Paris

Italy / France (Artistes Associés, PEA) 129m Technicolor **Language** English / French **Screenplay** Bernardo Bertolucci, Franco Arcalli, Agnès Varda **Photography** Vittorio Storaro **Music** Gato Barbieri **Cast** Marlon Brando, Maria Schneider, Maria Michi, Giovanna Galletti, Gitt Magrini, Catherine Allégret, Luce Marquand, Marie-Hélène Breillat, Catherine Breillat, Dan Diament, Catherine Sola, Mauro Marchetti, Jean-Pierre Léaud, Massimo Girotti **Oscar nominations** Bernardo Bertolucci (director), Marlon Brando (actor)

🄸

The opening sequence of cast and crew credits was inspired by the art of Francis Bacon.

Bernardo Bertolucci's *Last Tango in Paris* started a trend in art-house erotica that has endured to this day—films including *Intimacy* (2001) continue its premise of a "no questions asked" sexual affair that gives way to difficult familiarity; while writer-director Catherine Breillat (*Romance* [1999]), who appears in it, updates its themes of Eros and Thanatos.

Would *Last Tango in Paris* have mattered without Brando? His remarkable performance alludes to many previous, iconic roles. His obscene, scatological monologues, replete with Bertolucci's allusions to theories of Reich and Bataille, still have the power to startle. And the emotions of this middle-aged, despairing man are palpable.

A casting coup set the relatively inexperienced Maria Schneider against Brando. Her scenes with Jean-Pierre Léaud are deliberately superficial, contrasting with the central, primal, relationship and its stripping away of illusions. Yet *Last Tango in Paris* is more than the sum of its big ideas. Bertolucci's hyper-baroque style takes us into a subterranean, fractured, psychic space. Partitions, mirror reflections, incongruous props, and off-center framings multiply, disorienting the viewer at every turn, perfectly accompanied by Gato Barbieri's surging saxophone waltzes. A film of obstinate bloodstains and empty walls, inarticulate cries and bodily convulsions, *Last Tango in Paris* vigorously enacts its descent into the "womb of death." **AM**

Die Bitteren Tränen der Petra von Kant
The Bitter Tears of Petra von Kant
Rainer Werner Fassbinder, 1972

West Germany (Autoren, Tango)
124m Color **Language** German
Director Rainer Werner Fassbinder
Producer Rainer Werner Fassbinder,
Michael Fengler **Screenplay** Rainer
Werner Fassbinder, from his play
Photography Michael Ballhaus
Music Giuseppe Verdi **Cast** Margit
Carstensen, Hanna Schygulla, Katrin
Schaake, Eva Mattes, Gisela Fackeldey,
Irm Hermann **Berlin International Film
Festival** Rainer Werner Fassbinder
nomination (Golden Bear)

ℹ️

Fassbinder completed the entire
screenplay during the course of
a flight from Berlin to Los Angeles.

For many prominent gay artists, George Cukor's *The Women* (1939) has proved an irresistible model for cinematic storytelling in a queer mode: a group of women stuck together in a house, their destinies nominally defined and dominated by off-screen males, but lived through the melodramatic intensity of same-sex exchanges.

The Bitter Tears of Petra von Kant—cheekily subtitled "a case history"—is Rainer Werner Fassbinder's lesbian variation on this model. Preserving and indeed exaggerating the claustrophobic theatricality of his play, Fassbinder offers a parade of chic women who visit Petra (Margit Carstensen), a fashion designer, and her mute and ever-obedient servant Marlene (Irm Hermann). Psychological domination and expert game playing are Petra's forte (she gives good phone) and, in her lair, transactions are a dance in and around her bed—while the seethingly jealous Marlene types and sketches forever in the background.

The possibilities that arise for camp humor are many, such as the ironically contrapuntal use of old pop hits, but Fassbinder keeps it cool. His film builds to a simple but valuable life lesson for those embroiled in emotionally sadomasochistic relations, which for Fassbinder means everyone: "The weaker" in any situation has one ultimate, devastating weapon—the power to walk away. **AM**

Fat City John Huston, 1972

U.S. (Columbia, Rastar) 100 min Technicolor
Producer John Huston, Ray Stark
Screenplay Leonard Gardner, from his novel
Photography Conrad L. Hall Music Kris
Kristofferson Cast Stacy Keach, Jeff Bridges,
Susan Tyrrell, Candy Clark, Nicholas
Colasanto, Art Aragon, Curtis Cokes, Sixto
Rodriguez, Billy Walker, Wayne Mahan,
Ruben Navarro Oscar nomination Susan
Tyrrell (actress in support role)

John Huston's most effective "small film," *Fat City* tells the story of an over-the-hill boxer (Stacy Keach) who, conforming to Hollywood stereotypes, launches a comeback that inevitably fails, even as his gritty determination in defeat offers him a kind of transcendence. Like most Hustonian heroes, Tully (Keach) has missed his main chance, but is tendered yet another opportunity by chance to reclaim his self-respect. He connects with a younger boxer named Ernie (Jeff Bridges), becoming his mentor and rival as the pair seek to "make it big." Ernie may be talented enough to make a success of boxing, but he too becomes trapped by circumstances, forced to marry his girlfriend and enter a life of unending responsibility. Paradoxically, perhaps, Tully's romantic interest, the psychotic and self-destructive Oma (Susan Tyrrell), abandons him for a former lover, a man who abuses and mistreats her.

At the end of the film, Tully is not so much "free" to live the life of masculine accomplishment, as he is confirmed in his isolation and failure. There is, Huston suggests, no easy path to the "fat city" that is the American dream. With its authentic boxing sequences, drab California locations, and fine, understated acting from a talented ensemble, *Fat City* offers a realistic, yet poetic portrait of the all-too-human obsession to realize unrealizable dreams of self-transformation and transcendence. **RBP**

The Heartbreak Kid Elaine May, 1972

U.S. (Palomar) 106m Color
Producer Michael Hausman, Erik Lee
Preminger, Edgar J. Scherick
Screenplay Neil Simon, from the story "A
Change of Plan" by Bruce Jay Friedman
Photography Owen Roizman Music Cy
Coleman, Sheldon Harnick, Garry Sherman
Cast Charles Grodin, Cybill Shepherd,
Jeannie Berlin, Audra Lindley, Eddie Albert,
Mitchell Jason, William Prince, Augusta
Dabney, Doris Roberts, Marilyn Putnam,
Jack Hausman, Erik Lee Preminger, Art
Metrano, Tim Browne, Jean Scoppa
Oscar nominations Eddie Albert
(actor in support role), Jeannie Berlin
(actress in support role)

Elaine May is the most underrated director in American cinema. *The Heartbreak Kid* is the closest she has yet come to mainstream success, but it stays true to her corrosive, uncompromising vision. While remaining essentially faithful to Neil Simon's script (with its echoes of the 1967 film *The Graduate*), May manages to slaughter the sentimental, feel-good aura of that writer's baleful contribution to popular movies, by emphasizing the unpalatable facts of cruelty, humiliation, and embarrassment.

"Black comedy" here wears a mundane face. Lenny (Charles Grodin in his best role), a gormless salesman, is on his honeymoon with the nightmarish but good-hearted Lila (Jeannie Berlin—has ever a mother directed her daughter in such a brave, extreme part?). Feeling trapped and suffocated, Lenny's rather shallow fantasies turn to the all-American ideal, perky Kelly (Cybill Shepherd). Every consequence of this triangle is a disaster.

Few films plunge us so mercilessly into the tawdriness of romantic and sexual dreaming. May's focus on this material is pure John Cassavetes: an unflinching documentation of discomfort; real pain played out in real time. Our laughter—so brilliantly elicited by May's fractured mise-en-scène—turns hysterical in the psychoanalytic sense, a way of momentarily fleeing horror. **AM**

Frenzy Alfred Hitchcock, 1972

Alfred Hitchcock returned to Britain in 1972 to collaborate with Anthony Shaffer on a film version of Arthur La Bern's novel *Goodbye Piccadilly, Farewell Leicester Square*, which resurrects many of the conventions of the director's first hit, *The Lodger* (1926). Here again, London is plagued by a Jack the Ripper-like serial murderer, and the leading man does himself no favors by acting so suspiciously that he becomes the prime suspect.

Hitchcock evokes a precise mix of prurient fascination and genuine horror in the English attitude to murder that is also a great part of his own obsession. Embittered ex-RAF officer Richard Blaney (Jon Finch) is an alcoholic working as a bartender in a Covent Garden pub, reduced to sponging off his sensible ex-wife Brenda (Barbara Leigh-Hunt), who in an ironic stroke runs a successful matchmaking agency. In one of the creepiest, most explicit scenes the Master of Suspense ever directed, Brenda is visited by cheery cockney fruit-market trader Bob Rusk (Barry Foster), whose unstated but perverse special requirements she doesn't want to fulfill professionally; Rusk then reveals himself as the notorious Necktie Murderer by raping Brenda and strangling her with his paisley tie.

Frenzy proceeds by cutting between the antisocial, degraded hero and the charming, successful villain, who further inconveniences Blaney by murdering his sometime-girlfriend (Anna Massey), a chirrupy barmaid. As in *Psycho* (1960) and *Strangers on a Train* (1951), Hitchcock manages a suspense sequence by enlisting our sympathies in a murderer's attempt to cover up his crime, showing Rusk fumbling about with a nude corpse in a potato sack in the back of a van to get back his incriminating tie clip. Hitchcock takes advantage of the period's more relaxed censorship regulations to be more explicit with the sex and violence, though he also knows when a long, slow pull-back away from a murder will convey more horror than another close-up of plunder and strangulation. There is a streak of Mike Leigh-style comedy of social embarrassment in the subplot of a police inspector (Alec McCowen) whose wife (Vivien Merchant) keeps confronting him with hideous gourmet meals. **KN**

G.B. (Universal) 116m Technicolor
Producer William Hill, Alfred Hitchcock
Screenplay Anthony Shaffer, from the novel *Goodbye Piccadilly, Farewell Leicester Square* by Arthur La Bern
Photography Gilbert Taylor **Music** Ron Goodwin **Cast** Jon Finch, Alec McCowen, Barry Foster, Billie Whitelaw, Anna Massey, Barbara Leigh-Hunt, Bernard Cribbins, Vivien Merchant, Michael Bates, Jean Marsh, Clive Swift, John Boxer, Madge Ryan, George Tovey, Elsie Randolph

"Can you imagine me creeping around London, strangling all those women with ties? That's ridiculous . . . For a start, I only own two."

**Bob Rusk
(Barry Foster)**

i

This was Alfred Hitchcock's penultimate film, and the first of his movies to feature nude scenes.

Pink Flamingos John Waters, 1972

Quite possibly the best worst movie ever made—certainly one of the most notorious and beloved (if that's the right word) pieces of trash cinema to come out of the American underground—John Waters's 1972 feature offers a virtual manual on the aesthetics of "pure" gross-out moviemaking.

Shot around Waters's beloved hometown of Baltimore, Maryland, *Pink Flamingos* traces the victory of the writer-director's transvestite diva Divine, who lives in a trailer with her equally eccentric family—including her retarded hippie son, Crackers (Danny Mills), and her obese, egg-obsessed, playpen-residing mama, Edie (Edith Massey, truly unforgettable). The battle is to outdo the twisted and antisocial Marbles (Waters regulars Mink Stole and David Lochary) in disgusting and immoral behavior to become nothing less, or more, than "The Filthiest People Alive." Whereas the Marbles pose a strong challenge by abducting and impregnating female hitchhikers, selling their babies to lesbian couples, and using the money to finance schoolyard heroin schemes, Divine's Babs Johnson is not to be denied in her mission to maintain her family's throne.

The gritty, home-movie feel of *Pink Flamingos* (with its occasionally off-centered and out-of-focus cinematography, seemingly random zooms and cutaways, and uneven sound quality) only adds to the trash-and cult-movie watching experience. After all, we're dealing here with a film that gives extended screen time to butthole lip-synching, bowel movements delivered by post, and sex with chickens. In the notorious epilogue, Divine stops on a street in downtown Baltimore to pick up the freshly laid turd of a small dog. She puts it in her mouth, chews for a moment, then gags a bit and gives what can only be called a shit-eating grin to the camera. Critic Justin Frank hardly exaggerates when he identifies this scene as "the most famous . . . in all underground cinema—the underground equivalent of the shower scene in *Psycho*." Although Waters would go on to make several other memorable exercises in bad taste, including *Female Trouble* (1974) and *Desperate Living* (1977), none of his movies so perfectly combine humor and vulgarity as this one. **SJS**

U.S. (Dreamland) 93m Color
Producer John Waters **Screenplay** John Waters **Photography** John Waters **Cast** Divine, David Lochary, Mary Vivian Pearce, Mink Stole, Danny Mills, Edith Massey, Channing Wilroy, Cookie Mueller, Paul Swift, Susan Walsh, Pat Moran, Pat Lefaiver, Jack Walsh, Bob Skidmore, Jackie Sidel

"Oh my God Almighty! Someone has sent me a bowel movement!"

Babs Johnson (Divine)

1972

ℹ

Waters filmed only on weekends, as he had to spend weekdays trying to raise money to make the movie.

Sleuth Joseph L. Mankiewicz, 1972

G.B. (Palomar) 138m Color
Producer Morton Gottlieb
Screenplay Anthony Shaffer, from his play
Photography Oswald Morris Music John
Addison, Cole Porter Cast Laurence Olivier,
Michael Caine, Alec Cawthorne, John
Matthews, Eve Channing, Teddy Martin
Oscar nominations Joseph L. Mankiewicz
(director), Michael Caine (actor), Laurence
Olivier (actor), John Addison (music)

ℹ

Laurence Olivier's own laughter is
used for the chortles that emit from
Jolly Jack Tar, the sailor dummy.

Given Joseph L. Mankiewicz's reputation as the most conversational of filmmakers, a man who always prized high-quality talk over visual flash, he was a perfect choice to direct the film version of Anthony Shaffer's long-running Broadway and West End stage hit *Sleuth*. Though a few scenes "open out" the setting by venturing into the garden of mystery writer Andrew Wyke's prop-filled stately home, the piece remains essentially confined to the drawing room as two actors from different generations clash in style, temperament, and method.

Sir Laurence Olivier, reclaiming the status of movie star after more "serious" theater work, plays the role of Wyke, a mischievous sadist with a childish delight in nasty trickery ("that's a puzzle jug") and an addiction to complex games (an all-white jigsaw). Michael Caine is Milo Tindle, hairdresser and lover of Wyke's neglected wife. At first apparently outclassed in every way by his opponent, Tindle reveals a surprising emotional range in the first act climax. He pulls a coup de théâtre in the second act that really works even if you see it coming—invited over to be ensnared in a plot that has many twists and turns before it ends unhappily but justly for all concerned. **KN**

Superfly Gordon Parks Jr., 1972

U.S. (Superfly, Warner Bros.) 93m Technicolor
Producer Sig Shore Screenplay Phillip
Fenty Photography James Signorelli
Music Curtis Mayfield Cast Ron O'Neal, Carl
Lee, Sheila Frazier, Julius Harris, Charles
McGregor, Nate Adams, Polly Niles, Yvonne
Delaine, Henry Shapiro, K.C., James G.
Richardson, Make Bray, Al Kiggins, Bob
Bonds, Fred Rolaf

One of the most beloved and oft-quoted films of the blaxploitation cycle, boasting a sizzling funk soundtrack by Curtis Mayfield, a macho, drug-dealing antihero, and pimpin' 1970s streetware, Superfly is simply unforgettable. Directed by Gordon Parks Jr., the hard-boiled action/crime drama was financed by a group of independent African-American businessmen (making it the first to achieve this honor), with a crew that was nearly all black as well. Superfly tells the saga of a hip Harlem drug pusher, Youngblood Priest (Ron O'Neal), who hopes to make one last deal, converting all his coke to cash before starting a new, crime-free life for himself. It makes a strong statement about the continuous supply of drugs to the ghetto begetting pain, suffering, and an endless cycle of violence. It also makes Priest the richest, and most admired dude in the 'hood, glamorizing the era's "machismo-cocaine consciousness," and rendering black political consciousness inconsequential and ineffectual.

It's damn near impossible to criticize Superfly for its lack of a coherent, politically correct message. The dialogue is so crisp, the still-frame montage to the tune of "Pusherman" so unselfconsciously affecting, O'Neal's character so quietly charismatic, that audiences can hardly help feeling the rush that comes from watching the film unfold. Or as one review puts it, Superfly perfectly captures "the essence of that which is the life of a Playa." **SJS**

The Sting George Roy Hill, 1973

U.S. (Universal) 129m Technicolor
Producer Tony Bill, Robert L. Crawford, Julia
Phillips, Michael Phillips Screenplay David S.
Ward Photography Robert Surtees
Music Scott Joplin Cast Paul Newman,
Robert Redford, Robert Shaw, Charles
Durning, Ray Walston, Eileen Brennan,
Harold Gould, John Heffernan, Dana Elcar,
Jack Kehoe, Dimitra Arliss Oscars Tony Bill,
Michael Phillips, Julia Phillips (best picture),
George Roy Hill (director), David S. Ward
(screenplay), Henry Bumstead, James Payne
(art direction), Edith Head (costume), William
Reynolds (editing), Marvin Hamlisch (music)
Oscar nominations Robert Redford (actor),
Robert Surtees (photography), Ronald
Pierce, Robert R. Bertrand (sound)

George Roy Hill first directed Paul Newman and Robert Redford in Butch Cassidy and the Sundance Kid (1969). The results were far-reaching inasmuch as the film affirmed viewers' interest in Westerns while demonstrating the commercial attraction of Newman and Redford. Assembled again four years later in the caper pic The Sting, Hill gave the actors more room to play, though this time without any tragic resonance.

Set in post-Depression Chicago, Henry Gondorff (Newman) and Johnny Hooker (Redford) are two con men with ambition. After mobster Doyle Lonnegan (Robert Shaw) kills one of their friends, they set out for revenge. The subsequent effort, built on smoke, mirrors, and a number of situational reversals, also depends on a dense network within Chicago's criminal underworld.

Sparkling wit abounds as a strong supporting cast of smart men pitch personal style to other smart men. The timelessness of Scott Joplin's rags ring throughout the soundtrack and, in the end, the long con defeats the most intimidating bad guy.

Perhaps not high art, The Sting is nonetheless a luscious meringue. Blue-eyed Newman and dusty-haired Redford look great, and into their friendship is entrenched the joy of screen masters jousting in a comic adventure centered on loyalty and deception. **GC-Q**

France (Ciné Qua Non, Elite, Losange, Simar Films, V.M) 219m BW **Language** French **Producer** Pierre Cottrell, Vincent Malle **Screenplay** Jean Eustache **Photography** Pierre Lhomme **Music** Mozart, Offenbach **Cast** Bernadette Lafont, Jean-Pierre Léaud, Françoise Lebrun, Isabelle Weingarten, Jacques Renard, Jean-Noël Picq, Jessa Darrieux, Geneviève Mnich, Marinka Matuszewski

"Films teach you how to live."

Alexandre
(Jean-Pierre Léaud)

La maman et la putain Jean Eustache, 1973
The Mother and the Whore

In this autobiographical feature, Jean Eustache spends 220 minutes depicting an intense ménage à trois: Alexandre (Jean-Pierre Léaud) lives with Marie (Bernadette Lafont) but falls in love with Veronika (Françoise Lebrun). Shot in 16mm and black and white, *The Mother and the Whore* deploys the aesthetics of the New Wave to offer a trenchant portrait of post-May '68 disillusionment. The mobile camera work (by the distinguished Pierre Lhomme) charts a seductive Parisian cityscape: old apartments, boulevards, and cafés in which the characters conduct a dizzying flow of conversation. While Eustache's extraordinary dialogues merge high literature, slang, and obscenities, Lhomme's camera stretches duration in extreme long takes and real-time scenes.

Like many New Wave films, *The Mother and the Whore* inhabits a Parisian intellectual world in which real-life film critics and filmmakers appear as secondary characters, including Eustache himself. But most evocative of the New Wave, apart from Lafont, is Léaud, François Truffaut's alter ego. The boy wonder of *The 400 Blows* (1959) and whimsical young man of *Stolen Kisses* (1969) has grown into the manic, obsessive, exasperating, yet spellbinding Alexandre. As he discusses the meaning of life, love, and art, Léaud/Alexandre merges the anomic New Wave male with the May '68 libertarian; *The Mother and the Whore* is at once narcissistic portrayal and scathing exposé of this figure, and thus deeply of its time.

What of the "mother" and the "whore" of the title? Like Alexandre, the film wavers between them and swaps the two female stereotypes in the process. Both women, who have jobs while he is idle, emerge as stronger than the immature Alexandre. Yet the film turns them into "tragic" but ultimately marginal figures, subservient to his (and the director's) existential angst, despite stunning performances by Lafont and newcomer Lebrun. In this respect too, *The Mother and the Whore* is of its time, a monument to the confused, "liberated," and yet still oppressively patriarchal sexual politics of 1970s France. Eustache (who committed suicide in 1981) had enough talent to make it also deeply moving. **GV**

ℹ️
Renowned French magazine *Cahiers du Cinéma* declared the movie to be the best film of the 1970s.

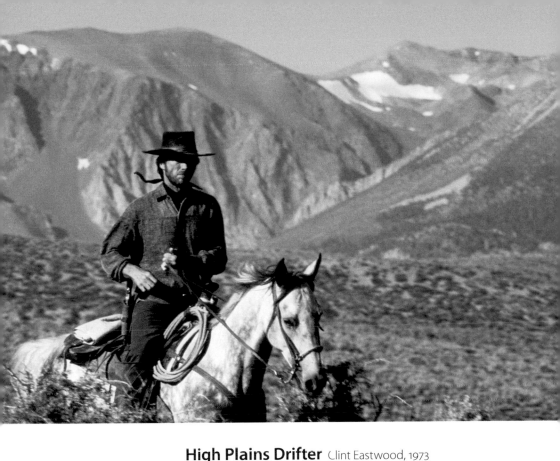

High Plains Drifter Clint Eastwood, 1973

U.S. (Malpaso) 105m Technicolor
Producer Robert Daley Screenplay Ernest
Tidyman Photography Bruce Surtees
Music Dee Barton Cast Clint Eastwood,
Verna Bloom, Marianna Hill, Mitch Ryan, Jack
Ging, Stefan Gierasch, Ted Hartley, Billy
Curtis, Geoffrey Lewis, Scott Walker, Walter
Barnes, Paul Brinegar, Richard Bull, Alex
Tinne, John Hillerman

Clint Eastwood's second film as director-star (after *Play Misty for Me* [1971]) relocates his spaghetti Western persona into an American gothic morality tale. An unshaven saddle tramp rides out of a desert haze into Lago, where the townsfolk once stood by as a marshal was whipped to death. In a surreal rerun of *High Noon* (1952), Eastwood—who might be the murdered man's ghost, or more prosaically his brother—is begged to stand up to three outlaws just released from territorial prison and on their way home for violent revenge.

The mystery man demonstrates his powers not only by meting out the kind of gunplay and abuse expected of a grungy cowboy antihero circa 1972, but also by forcing everyone to take part in a bizarre fiesta. The latter involves making a dwarf into the combined Sheriff and Mayor, literally painting the town red, and renaming it "Hell." Recalling the Vietnam slogan "We destroyed the village in order to save it," the stranger finally burns down the town. With at least as much borrowed from Luis Buñuel as Sergio Leone, this is a funny, brutal, scary movie, daringly weird in its mixture of Western and horror themes, and shot through with acid self-analysis. **KN**

ℹ

The name of spaghetti Western director Sergio Leone appears on one of the tombstones in the graveyard.

Badlands Terrence Malick, 1973

"I can't deny we've had fun . . . and that's more than some can say." Harvard graduate, Rhodes scholar, sometime journalist and philosophy teacher at MIT, Terrence Malick is a true artist, utterly indifferent to the conventions and commercialism of the American film industry. He wrote, produced, and directed only two films in the 1970s before withdrawing from the fray for a reclusive twenty years (when he returned to make his long-mooted World War II project *The Thin Red Line* [1998]), becoming both a revered legend and a terrible loss to American cinema in the process. *Days Of Heaven* (1979) derives its power from its exquisite beauty and evocation of mood. But it is *Badlands*, a disturbing, fatalistic study of a mindlessly violent odyssey, that is the more arresting and influential cult favorite. Far from dating, the film has a timeless quality and has become increasingly relevant in an age with little innocence but a mass hankering for celebrity.

In the roles of Kit and Holly, *Badlands'* two about-to-be stars are extraordinary. In his early thirties but looking much younger, wild, and edgy, Martin Sheen is explosive as the aimless and alienated Midwestern misfit eager for notoriety, a garbage man who fancies himself a James Dean look-alike outlaw. Sissy Spacek, twenty-four but utterly believable as a fifteen-year-old, is unnerving as his blank, freckle-faced, passive nymphet moll. Inspired by the real, shocking 1950s case of the delinquent teenaged Bonnie and Clyde, Charles Starkweather and Carol Fugate, there is a horrible fascination in this narrative of a bad boy and his baton-twirling baby doll. The casual disposing of the girl's dour father (Warren Oates), the building of a tree house love-nest refuge in a cotton grove, and a cross-country killing spree and chase are all reminiscent of Bonnie and Clyde.

Badlands is cool, bleak, and scary in its awareness that the seemingly ordinary adolescent girl has thrown in her lot compliantly with a sociopath because she doesn't have any other ideas. It is also singularly literate, with Malick finding a dispassionate, humorless distance from the violent psychodrama through clever writing. A brilliant device has Spacek gauchely reading her character's romanticized but banal diary entries—in the style of the trashy 1950s movie fan magazines she reads—for a voice-over that adds odd pathos to the duo's nihilistic progress. The details, using the iconography of the era, are both disarming (the couple, heedless of their situation, dancing outdoors like any carefree kids to Mickey and Sylvia's "Love Is Strange" or dreamily in the beam of their headlights to Nat King Cole) and eloquent (Kit checking his hair in the mirror during a car chase when the police are all but on top of him, or cheerfully tossing souvenirs to his captors). The contrasts—of the American heartland landscapes with their run-down dwellings, tedious lives, and tawdry dreams; of the bright, vibrant musical score with recurring images of death—are continually striking. And the echoes of Malick's majestically brooding, moody style continue to reverberate in the love-on-the-run genre to this day. **AE**

U.S. (Badlands, Pressman-Williams) 95m Color **Producer** Jill Jakes, Terrence Malick, Edward R. Pressman, Louis A. Stroller **Screenplay** Terrence Malick **Photography** Tak Fujimoto, Stevan Larner, Brian Probyn **Music** Gunild Keetman, James Taylor, George Aliceson Tipton, Carl Orff, Erik Satie **Cast** Martin Sheen, Sissy Spacek, Warren Oates, Ramon Bieri, Alan Vint, Gary Littlejohn, John Carter, Bryan Montgomery, Gail Threlgeld, Charles Fitzpatrick, Howard Ragsdale, John Womack Jr., Dona Baldwin, Ben Bravoa

"Suppose I shot you. How'd that be?"

Kit Carruthers (Martin Sheen)

i

In a 1999 interview Martin Sheen said that Malick's script for *Badlands* was still the best script he'd ever read.

American Graffiti George Lucas, 1973

Produced by Francis Ford Coppola and directed by his protégé and former assistant George Lucas, who also cowrote the autobiographically flavored screenplay, this hugely entertaining, perceptive coming-of-age ensemble piece of high school graduates cruising through one eventful summer's night in 1962 was inspired by 1950s teen pics but set the style—often imitated, never surpassed in hilarity, penetration, or technical virtuosity—for a hundred and one rites of passage comedies played out in classic cars to a vintage rocking soundtrack. It was also the clear inspiration for such wholesome, nostalgic television sitcoms as *Happy Days* and *Laverne and Shirley*, featuring some of the same players and fancifully revisiting that supposedly more carefree youth era before Vietnam.

Marvel at that *Graffiti* ensemble: Richard Dreyfuss and Ron Howard when he was still Ronny as the college-bound boys, Paul "whatever happened to?" LeMat as the Brylcreemed bad boy, Cindy Williams, Candy Clark, Charles Martin Smith, legendary rock-'n'-roll disc jockey Wolfman Jack, and, in humbler roles, Joe Spano, Suzanne Somers, Kathy before she became Kathleen Quinlan, and a not-so-very-young hopeful named Harrison Ford as drag racer Bob Falfa. The confluence of young talents brought energy, comedy, insight, and craft, superbly captured by cinematographer Haskell Wexler, one of Lucas's early mentors. *American Graffiti* was shot on location in Modesto and San Rafael, California— where the time-honored tradition of "dragging the main" was long a strictly observed ritual of mooning, foam spraying, flirtatious pursuit, and furtively obtained liquor in paper bags, and where Lucas was to build the center of his filmmaking empire, the Skywalker Ranch complex.

In what was only his second feature, Lucas demonstrated a charm and warmth not found in his cool, futuristic debut, the Orwellian *THX 1138* (1971). Shot in just twenty-eight nights for well under a million dollars, *American Graffiti* not only became a box-office smash, one of the most profitable pictures of all time, but it also received critical kudos and five Academy Award nominations, including Best Picture and Director, a triumph that enabled Lucas to make an even more phenomenal mark with his next film, *Star Wars* (1977). **AE**

U.S. (Lucasfilm, Coppola, Universal) 110m Technicolor **Producer** Francis Ford Coppola, Gary Kurtz **Screenplay** George Lucas, Gloria Katz, Willard Huyck **Photography** Jan D'Alquen, Ron Eveslage **Music** Sherman Edwards, Chuck Berry, Buddy Holly, Booker T. Jones **Cast** Richard Dreyfuss, Ron Howard, Paul Le Mat, Charles Martin Smith, Cindy Williams, Candy Clark, Mackenzie Phillips, Wolfman Jack, Bo Hopkins, Manuel Padilla Jr., Beau Gentry, Harrison Ford, Jim Bohan, Jana Bellan, Deby Celiz, Johnny Weissmuller Jr., Suzanne Somers **Oscar nominations** Francis Ford Coppola, Gary Kurtz (best picture), George Lucas (director), George Lucas, Gloria Katz, Willard Huyck (screenplay), Candy Clark (actress in support role), Verna Fields, Marcia Lucas (editing)

> *"That can't be your car. It must be your mama's car! I'm sorta' embarrassed to be this close to ya!"*
>
> **Bob Falfa**
> **(Harrison Ford)**

i

Falfa drives the same 1955 Chevrolet that features in cult road-trip movie *Two Lane Blacktop* (1971).

Papillon Franklin J. Schaffner, 1973

U.S. / France (Allied Artists, Corona-General, Solar) 150m Technicolor **Producer** Robert Dorfmann, Ted Richmond, Franklin J. Schaffner **Screenplay** Dalton Trumbo, Lorenzo Semple Jr., from the novel by Henri Charrière **Photography** Fred J. Koenekamp **Music** Jerry Goldsmith **Cast** Steve McQueen, Dustin Hoffman, Victor Jory, Don Gordon, Anthony Zerbe, Robert Deman, Woodrow Parfrey, Bill Mumy, George Coulouris, Ratna Assan, William Smithers, Val Avery, Gregory Sierra, Vic Tayback, Mills Watson, Ron Soble, Barbara Morrison, Don Hanmer, E.J. André, Richard Angarola, Jack Denbo, Len Lesser, John Quade, Fred Sadoff, Allen Jaffe, Liam Dunn **Oscar nomination** Jerry Goldsmith (music)

Tagged, "Two men with nothing in common but a will to live and a place to die," Franklin J. Schaffner's *Papillon* is a male love-story-turned-adventure tale. It opens with Papillon (Steve McQueen) being sent to a French Guyana prison for a crime he didn't commit. There he meets Dega (Dustin Hoffman), another convict. Afterward the film concerns their respective misadventures trying to escape until Papillon finally succeeds.

Accompanying this eye candy, Jerry Goldsmith's score echoes off tropical backdrops to make *Papillon* less an action vehicle and more a confrontation between man and nature. McQueen is therefore the foil for exploring individual loyalty and pain—the long-suffering hero. Attentive viewers will be struck by how little dialogue is spoken. Instead, *Papillon*'s impact comes from bits of actor's business and the sheer force of imprisonment. Perhaps the finest example is the lead's solitary confinement; although he speaks nary a word, McQueen still comes across as a powerful screen presence and star.

Yet the point of the film shines through in a nightmare. "I accuse you of a wasted life," Papillon is told, but the movie becomes a counter-argument because his triumph is that of an insignificant man defeating a system designed to break him. **GC-Q**

1973

The Long Goodbye Robert Altman, 1973

U.S. (E-K-Corp., Lions Gate) 112m Technicolor **Producer** Jerry Bick, Robert Eggenweiler **Screenplay** Leigh Brackett, from novel by Raymond Chandler **Photography** Vilmos Zsigmond **Music** John Williams **Cast** Elliott Gould, Nina Van Pallandt, Sterling Hayden, Mark Rydell, Henry Gibson, David Arkin, Jim Bouton, Warren Berlinger, Jo Ann Brody, Stephen Coit, Jack Knight, Pepe Callahan, Vincent Palmieri, Pancho Córdova, Enrique Lucero

The Long Goodbye, Robert Altman's languid, free-form version of Raymond Chandler's last great novel, relocates the 1953 story to 1973, subtly critiquing the out-of-time values of Philip Marlowe. Elliott Gould's slobby, unshaven, chain-smoking private eye is an all-time loser, introduced in a brilliant sequence that has him try to pass off inferior pet food on his supercilious cat. Shambling through the remains of Chandler's plot, Gould tries to help an alcoholic Hemingwayesque writer (Sterling Hayden, who wrote his own scenes) and clear his only friend (Jim Bouton) of a murder rap.

John Williams's brilliant score plays endless variations on a title tune, and many sequences are astonishing: violent gangster Jark Rydell making a point by smashing a coke bottle in his mistress's face ("That's someone I love, you I don't even like"), Hayden's stumbling suicide on the beach, and an invigoratingly cynical punch line ("and I lost my cat") that turns Marlowe into some sort of winner after all. Arnold Schwarzenegger, no less, has an unbilled cameo as a minor thug. Altman makes sure a lot of the vital action happens almost unnoticed in the corners of the frame and loves highlighting tiny moments of visual and aural impact in a sun-struck tapestry of Los Angeles sleaze. **KN**

The Wicker Man Robin Hardy, 1973

G.B. (British Lion) 102m Eastmancolor **Producer** Peter Snell **Screenplay** Anthony Shaffer **Photography** Harry Waxman **Music** Paul Giovanni **Cast** Edward Woodward, Christopher Lee, Diane Cilento, Britt Ekland, Ingrid Pitt, Lindsay Kemp, Russell Waters, Aubrey Morris, Irene Sunters, Walter Carr, Ian Campbell, Leslie Blackater, Roy Boyd, Peter Brewis, Barbara Rafferty

Repressed Scots policeman Howie (Edward Woodward), "a Christian copper," investigates the disappearance of a little girl on Summerisle, where the charming but fiendish local laird (Christopher Lee) is taking extreme measures to ensure the success of the next harvest. Written by Anthony Shaffer (*Sleuth* [1972]), *The Wicker Man* is a highly original combination of horror movie, murder mystery, pagan ethnography, and folk musical that stood as an auspicious debut for its sadly unprolific director, Robin Hardy. It manages an audacious combination of the sexy and the sinister, leading to a shock ending that still has an impact, even though audiences coming fresh to the film tend now to know how things will turn out at the festival where a holy virgin fool is led to a giant man-shaped bonfire on the cliffs.

A bizarre cast includes a dubbed and body-doubled Britt Ekland as the landlord's seductive daughter, cult starlet Ingrid Pitt as the naked librarian, mime Lindsay Kemp as a slyly camp publican, and Diane Cilento as the headmistress-like high priestess. Although edited significantly for its original release, the version generally available now restores much (if not all) the trimmed footage—in some ways, the shorter cut plays a little better because the expanded version is at times heavy-handed in leading viewers to the final twist. **KN**

Enter the Dragon Robert Clouse, 1973

Hong Kong / U.S. (Concord, Sequoia, Warner Bros.) 98m Technicolor **Producer** Raymond Chow, Paul M. Heller, Bruce Lee, Fred Weintraub **Screenplay** Michael Allin **Photography** Gil Hubbs **Music** Lalo Schifrin **Cast** Bruce Lee, John Saxon, Kien Shih, Jim Kelly, Ahna Capri, Robert Wall, Angela Mao, Bolo Yeung, Betty Chung, Geoffrey Weeks, Peter Archer, Ho Lee Yan, Marlene Clark, Allan Kent, William Keller

Having established his action movie superstar credentials with rough-hewn Hong Kong vehicles like *Fist of Fury* (1972) and *The Big Boss* (1971), former cha-cha champion and American TV sidekick Bruce Lee only had one shot at completing a movie with Hollywood production values. Lee, a martial artist whose physical skills have attained a spiritual level, infiltrates a master-baddie's island enclave (along with sidekicks John Saxon and Jim Kelly) and sees off hordes and hordes of junior villains (Jackie Chan gets a walk-on necksnap).

Director Robert Clouse has the style you'd expect of someone directing a Brock Landers adventure (lots of zooms and flares), and Lee, whose real-life Hong Kong English was heavily-accented but fluent and distinctive, is stuck with Charlie Chan dialogue consisting of enigmatically wise pronouncements. But the action still delivers nonstop astonishment as, without the aid of the wires or effects used in the likes of *Crouching Tiger Hidden Dragon* (2000), Lee goes magnificently through the motions, twirling his signature nunchaku, flexing his oiled torso. Influential on an entire genre of subsequent martial arts movies and a template for every beat-'em-up computer game, *Enter the Dragon* wins its place in film history purely on the strength of Lee's charismatic presence and literally inimitable fighting moves. **KN**

Serpico Sidney Lumet, 1973

U.S. / Italy (Paramount, De Laurentis)
129m Technicolor **Producer** Martin
Bregman **Screenplay** Waldo Salt, Norman
Wexler, from book by Peter Maas
Photography Arthur J. Ornitz **Music** Mikis
Theodorakis **Cast** Al Pacino, John Randolph,
Jack Kehoe, Biff McGuire, Barbara Eda Young,
Cornelia Sharpe, Tony Roberts, John Medici,
Allan Rich, Norman Ornellas, Edward Grover,
Albert Henderson, Hank Garrett, Damien
Leake, Joseph Bova **Oscar nominations**
Waldo Salt, Norman Wexler (screenplay),
Al Pacino (actor)

ℹ

Serpico was filmed in reverse order,
with Pacino's hair starting long and
then being trimmed for each scene.

Maverick cops rooting out departmental corruption is now a familiar theme in many of TV's law enforcement drama series. In 1973, however, this was exciting cinematic territory fully exploited by director Sidney Lumet in *Serpico*, featuring a sizzling performance by Al Pacino. Based on Peter Maas's 1972 biography, this is the gripping story of New York cop Frank Serpico. The real-life Serpico refused to take paybacks, a decision which made him massively unpopular in the many departments he was transferred to. Receiving personal threats from fellow officers, he was mysteriously shot in the face on duty—yet lived to testify at an important police-corruption hearing.

Fresh off his groundbreaking role in the 1972 film *The Godfather*, Pacino's Serpico is a high-energy but low-key performance that won him the Golden Globe and the second of his many Oscar nominations. *Serpico* staves off being a mere cop cliché film because of its balanced view of the main character—a man in the right who becomes an embittered martyr. The only jarring element is Mikis Theodorakis's heavy-handed Mediterranean-themed soundtrack. Judd Hirsch and F. Murray Abraham appear in cameos. **KK**

559

Daphne du Maurier's shattering psychic thriller.

Julie Christie

Donald Sutherland

"DON'T LOOK NOW"

Directed by
NICOLAS ROEG
Produced by
PETER KATZ

Executive Producer
ANTHONY B. UNGER
Screenplay by
ALLAN SCOTT
and CHRIS BRYANT

Lion International Films of London   Technicolor ·

G.B. / Italy (Casey, Eldorado)
110m Technicolor **Producer** Peter
Katz, Frederick Muller, Anthony B. Unger
Screenplay Allan Scott, Chris Bryant,
from story by Daphne Du Maurier
Photography Anthony B. Richmond
Music Pino Donaggio (as Pino Donnagio)
Cast Julie Christie, Donald Sutherland,
Hilary Mason, Clelia Matania, Massimo
Serato, Renato Scarpa, Giorgio Trestini,
Leopoldo Trieste, David Tree, Ann Rye,
Nicholas Salter, Sharon Williams, Bruno
Cattaneo, Adelina Poerio

*"Nothing is what
it seems."*

**John Baxter
(Donald Sutherland)**

Don't Look Now Nicolas Roeg, 1973

Based on a short story by Daphne du Maurier, Nicholas Roeg's *Don't Look Now* showcases the British director's characteristically nonlinear style of storytelling, in which temporal ellipses and frenetic crosscuts serve to reflect and enhance the already palpable atmosphere of psychological disturbance and dread.

Shortly after their young daughter dies in a drowning accident, art restorer John Baxter (Donald Sutherland) and his wife Laura (Julie Christie) travel to Venice in the off-season to work on an old church and recover from their traumatic loss. Instead what they find is a creepy city filled with lonely canals and eccentric characters, including a pair of strange old sisters (Hilary Mason and Clelia Matania), one of them a blind psychic who insists that she can communicate with their late child and who warns them of impending danger. John is initially skeptical but starts to come around after catching random glimpses of his daughter darting through the streets wearing the same red raincoat she had on when she died.

In the film's unforgettable conclusion, John races through the Venice alleys at night in pursuit of the mysterious red-garbed figure—who he now believes is the ghost of his deceased child—only to catch up with her in a dark passageway, her back toward him. The figure then turns around, revealing an ambiguously gendered dwarf, and John can only stand there stunned as the little person (who is quite real, and quite deadly, having been on a killing spree in the city for some time) walks up to him and slashes his throat with a straight razor. It is no exaggeration to say that few scenes in the history of cinema have proven as effective at sending chills up the spines of viewers as this one.

But *Don't Look Now*'s terrifying finale is not even the best-known scene in the film. That honor goes to the lengthy sex scene between John and Laura, mixed with quiet shots of the married couple impassively dressing for dinner. Rumor spread that the remarkable passion on display during this lovemaking session resulted from an off-screen affair between Christie and Sutherland. Whatever the case, it is this same passion that suffuses the entire picture. **SJS**

i

Christie and Sutherland met for
the first time on this movie. Their first
scene together was the sex scene.

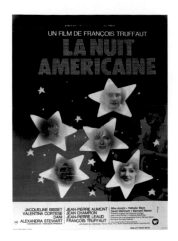

La nuit américaine François Truffaut, 1973
Day for Night

In a typical scene of *Day for Night*, the director Ferrand (François Truffaut) throws down a pile of his latest film-book acquisitions (on Bresson, Rossellini, Hitchcock), while Georges Delerue's musical theme is piped through a tinny telephone speaker. The mixture of everyday detail with an unexpected, restrained surge of poetic lyricism is quintessential Truffaut.

Day for Night is Truffaut's valentine to the process of moviemaking. Controversially for the post-1968 period, he chose classical, studio-bound, generic cinema as his premise, not the New Wave. The emphasis of the film is on filmmaking as craft rather than art (no one pretends that Ferrand's middlebrow diversion *Meet Pamela* is a masterpiece). And, ultimately, it is less about the "product" than the collective process leading to it. Truffaut paints an affectionate portrait of good-natured "family" relations among cast and crew in place of the vicious power plays usually presented, making *Day for Night* the polar opposite to Jean-Luc Godard's *Contempt* (1963) or Rainer Werner Fassbinder's *Beware of a Holy Whore* (1970).

Gentle, bittersweet wisdom is the keynote here, as a rich ensemble of performers (from smooth Jean-Pierre Aumont to firecracker Jean-Pierre Léaud) share fleeting lessons in life, love, and loss. The film deftly sketches a wide range of characters, cleverly compared on certain points: for example, their attitudes to casual sex (tragic and histrionic for Jacqueline Bisset's happily married character once Léaud makes their liaison public, flippant for Natalie Baye as a no-nonsense assistant director).

Truffaut stresses the transience, fragility, and unreality of life on a set—even allowing, in one hilarious scene, an outsider to finally explode and criticize these film people for their rampant immorality. *Day for Night* gently exposes the many illusions of the filmmaking process, but also maintains our awe over the magic of movies. Characteristically for Truffaut, the brisk montage scenes—devoted to the frenzy of the editing room, or an elaborate scene filmed in artificial snow—express a deep affection for, and appreciation of, the mundane practicalities of his trade.

As such strangely exhilarating scenes serve to show, Truffaut's cinema is essentially unspectacular. There is no melodramatic underlining in *Day for Night*, no ostentatious, point-making rhetoric in his mise-en-scène. Truffaut's obsession is with maintaining a lightness of tone, maximizing narrative flow, and conveying incidents with the utmost economy: In this he truly married the tautness of Hitchcock or Lang with the observational grace of Renoir or Becker.

Amid the whimsical succession of ordinary situations, the rare, strong moments of drama occur as sudden interruptions (such as Alexander's death) that switch the mood. The sadness of these "punctual" events enhances the keenness of the characters' fleeting pleasures: secret moments of intimacy or complicity, joyful epiphanies, chance eruptions of comedy, and stolen kisses. **AM**

France / Italy (Carrosse, PECF, PIC) 115m BW / Eastmancolor **Language** English / French **Producer** Marcel Berbert **Screenplay** Jean-Louis Richard, Suzanne Schiffman, François Truffaut **Photography** Pierre-William Glenn **Music** Georges Delerue **Cast** Jacqueline Bisset, Valentina Cortese, Dani, Alexandra Stewart, Jean-Pierre Aumont, Jean Champion, Jean-Pierre Léaud, François Truffaut, Nike Arrighi, Nathalie Baye, Maurice Seveno, David Markham, Bernard Menez, Gaston Joly, Zenaide Rossi **Oscar** France (best foreign language film) **Oscar nominations** François Truffaut (director), François Truffaut, Jean-Louis Richard, Suzanne Schiffman (screenplay), Valentina Cortese (actress in support role)

> *"Making a film is like a stagecoach ride in the old West. When you start, you are hoping for a pleasant trip. By the halfway point, you just hope to survive."*
>
> **Ferrand (François Truffaut)**

i

The movie's title refers to the practice of treating scenes shot by day to appear as if they were shot at night.

1973

Mean Streets Martin Scorsese, 1973

Scorsese's breakthrough movie was an instant declaration of the themes he's been elaborating ever since and of his showy talent. Set in his home turf of New York City's Little Italy, though shot mostly in Los Angeles with some spliced-in footage of the San Gennaro religious festival, *Mean Streets* is about hustlers in the midlevel of organized crime. It explores the exhilaration and destructiveness of extended adolescence and a peculiar search for redemption that continues throughout his filmography.

A young, smooth Harvey Keitel stars as Charlie Cappa, Scorsese's semiautobiographical stand-in (the director actually uses his own voice for the character's narration), a minor mob hanger-on who believes "you pay for your sins on the street not in church" but is still willing to hold his hand to a votive candle to atone for his crimes. So concerned with presenting an impressive face to the world that he fetishistically grooms himself like a knight donning armor, Charlie believes it is possible to have an old-fashioned sense of honor and loyalty and still prosper in a business run by gentlemanly elders. However, his cousin-girlfriend (Amy Robinson) undercuts his man-of-integrity attitudes by reminding him "St. Francis didn't run numbers."

Charlie spends his time palling around with his friends in Little Italy, exchanging Hope-and-Crosby wisecracks with his dangerously irresponsible cousin Johnny Boy (Robert De Niro), going to the movies (cue cinephile clips from John Ford's *The Searchers* (1956) and Roger Corman's *Tomb of Ligeia* (1964), to show you where Marty is coming from), running minor scams, wondering which girl to settle with, and hoping to advance himself in the rackets. However, his sense of what he must be seen to be leads him to get out of a relationship with his epileptic cousin because he is worried that he'll be tainted as a flake, and then to duck out on a possible liaison with an obviously wonderful woman he has been flirting with just because she's black. Meanwhile, his loyalty to Johnny Boy is clearly dragging him toward disaster as the irresponsible rebel, who simply doesn't care what anyone thinks, ticks off a powerful local loan shark (Richard Romanus) by not only not paying him back but by making a point of being contemptuous of him in public.

The intense, interior, earnest, considered Charlie and the explosive, free-associating, impulsive smart-ass Johnny Boy (first seen bombing a mailbox) are key characters in 1970s cinema, establishing personae the stars would explore in a run of outstanding work for Scorsese and others. It ends in a bloody apotheosis, a shoot-out-cum-car-crash that leaves some of the characters bleeding and others dead (though it isn't entirely clear which is which). Along the way, there is a joyous energy as Keitel struts into neon-lit bars in his sharp suits, the camera prowling along with him, while Scorsese's unparalleled record collection plays on the soundtrack. David Carradine, star of Scorsese's earlier *Boxcar Bertha* (1972), has a funny cameo as a drunken murder victim. **KN**

U.S. (Taplin, Perry, Scorsese) 110m Technicolor **Producer** E. Lee Perry, Martin Scorsese, Jonathan T. Taplin **Screenplay** Martin Scorsese, Mardik Martin **Photography** Kent L. Wakeford **Music** Eric Clapton, Bert Holland, Mick Jagger and Keith Richards **Cast** Robert De Niro, Harvey Keitel, David Proval, Amy Robinson, Richard Romanus, Cesare Danova, Victor Argo, George Memmoli, Lenny Scaletta, Jeannie Bell, Murray Moston, David Carradine, Robert Carradine, Lois Walden, Harry Northup, Catherine Scorsese, Martin Scorsese

"It's all bullshit except the pain. The pain of hell. The burn from a lighted match increased a million times. Infinite."

Charlie
(Harvey Keitel)

🛈

The film's last shot is of Scorsese's mother, Catherine, closing a window and pulling down a blind.

Sleeper Woody Allen, 1973

U.S. (Rollins-Joffe Productions)
89m Color **Producer** Jack Grossberg
Screenplay Woody Allen, Marshall
Brickman **Photography** David M. Walsh
Music Woody Allen **Cast** Woody Allen,
Diane Keaton, John Beck, Mary Gregory,
Don Keefer, John McLiam, Bartlett
Robinson, Chris Forbes, Mews Small, Peter
Hobbs, Susan Miller, Lou Picetti, Jessica
Rains, Brian Avery, Spencer Millig

i

Luna's rebel song is the same as
Esposito's rebel song in Allen's
earlier comedy *Bananas* (1971).

One of Woody Allen's self-described "early, funny films," this is a Bob Hope-style comedy vehicle for Allen's whiny neurotic Jewish character, set loose in a 1973 vision of the future informed by films like *2001: A Space Odyssey* (1968), *A Clockwork Orange* (1971), *THX 1138* (1971), and *Z.P.G.* (1972).

Miles Monroe (Allen), jazzman and proprietor of a Greenwich Village health food store, is defrosted 200 hundred years into the future after being cryofrozen in tinfoil when complications set in during a routine ulcer surgery. As in *Bananas* (1971) and *Love and Death* (1975), Allen's character is a foul-up who gets drawn into revolutionary activity that seems doomed to exchange one tyranny for another. There are some barbed philosophical bits about doomed romantic relationships, but the main focus of the picture is the comedy. It ranges from satiric jabs at contemporary mores seen from a skewed futurist perspective (it has been proved that fatty foods and cigarettes are better for you than health foods), through silent cinema-style slapstick (a giant banana naturally leads to a giant banana-skin gag), to left-field surrealism like a mental deprogramming session that kicks into a rerun of *A Streetcar Named Desire* (1951) with Diane Keaton and Allen doing Marlon Brando and Vivien Leigh. **KN**

The Exorcist William Friedkin, 1973

The first major blockbuster in horror movie history, this film has exerted a powerful influence on the development of the genre. Never before had a horror film been the subject of so much prerelease hype, so much gossip about postproduction strife, so much speculation as to why people of all ages would stand in line for hours to watch something reputed to induce fits of vomiting, fainting, even temporary psychosis. The cultural impact of *The Exorcist* can hardly be overestimated. The film stole U.S. newspaper headlines away from the ongoing Watergate scandal, at least for a while, led to a detectable increase in the number of "real-life" spiritual possessions reported, and, as one critic wrote, "established . . . disgust as mass entertainment for a large audience."

Inspired by newspaper reports of a thirteen-year-old Maryland boy whose body was said to have been taken over by demonic forces, novelist William Peter Blatty made the possessee a girl. He sensationalized many details, adding heavy doses of philosophical-theological speculation on the nature of evil, and came out with the *The Exorcist* in 1971. Correctly anticipating a best seller, Warner Brothers purchased the film rights and, after numerous rewrites of the original script, Blatty finally came up with a version of *The Exorcist* that managed to meet Friedkin's exacting demands.

Regan MacNeil (Linda Blair) is the adorable, almost-pubescent daughter of divorcee and well known movie star Chris MacNeil (Ellen Burstyn). But when she prophesies the death of her mother's acquaintance and urinates in front of a roomful of dinner guests, Chris starts to wonder what has "gotten into" her daughter. More odd behavior, and a wildly shaking bed, lands Regan in the hospital, where she is subjected to a battery of extremely invasive procedures best described as medical pornography. A brain lesion is suspected, but the tests prove nothing. When Regan, supposedly under hypnosis, responds to the smug questions of a hospital shrink by grabbing his scrotum, it is recommended that Chris seek the Church's help. She does, pleading with doubt-ridden Jesuit priest Damien Karras (Jason Miller) to perform an exorcism. The film's second half culminates in an intense battle between Karras and Regan's demonic possessor, after the more experienced exorcist on the scene, Father Merrin (Max von Sydow), dies in the struggle. Karras finally saves Regan by accepting the demon into his own body, only to throw himself, or let himself be thrown, out of a window to his death.

In an era of student protest, experimental drug use, and questioning of authority, *The Exorcist* allowed viewers to take pleasure in the terrible punishments inflicted on the rebellious Regan. But by making Regan-the-demon so fascinating to watch, so filled with nasty surprises, *The Exorcist* also allowed viewers to take pleasure in that rebelliousness. The film not only gave rise to a slew of lesser-quality sequels, imitations, and variants on the possession theme, it also made the child with malevolent powers a dominant motif in horror cinema. **SJS**

U.S. (Hoya Productions, Warner Bros.) 122m Metrocolor **Language** English / Latin / Greek / French / German / Arabic **Producer** William Peter Blatty **Screenplay** William Peter Blatty, from his novel **Photography** Owen Roizman, Billy Williams **Music** Jack Nitzsche, David Borden, George Crumb, Hans Werner Henze, Mike Oldfield, Krzysztof Penderecki, Anton Webern **Cast** Ellen Burstyn, Max von Sydow, Lee J. Cobb, Kitty Winn, Jack MacGowran, Jason Miller, Linda Blair, Reverend William O'Malley, Barton Heyman, Peter Masterson, Rudolf Schündler, Gina Petrushka, Robert Symonds, Arthur Storch, Reverend Thomas Bermingham **Oscars** William Peter Blatty (screenplay), Robert Knudson, Christopher Newman (sound) **Oscar nominations** William Peter Blatty (best picture), William Friedkin (director), Ellen Burstyn (actress), Jason Miller (actor in support role), Linda Blair (actress in support role), Bill Malley, Jerry Wunderlich (art direction), Owen Roizman (photography), John C. Broderick, Bud S. Smith, Evan A. Lottman, Norman Gay (editing)

i

The Exorcist was the first horror movie to be nominated for Best Picture at the Academy Awards.

1973

Vérités et mensonges Orson Welles, 1973
F for Fake

France/Iran/West Germany
(Astrophore/Saco/Janus) 85m Color
Producer Dominique Antoine
Screenplay Orson Welles, Oja Kodar
Photography François Reichenbach
Music Michel Legrand **Cast** Orson Welles,
Oja Kodar, Elmyr de Hory, Clifford Irving,
François Reichenbach, Joseph Cotten, Paul
Stewart, Richard Wilson, Laurence Harvey,
Nina van Pallandt

From the start Orson Welles's last completed feature film, *F for Fake*, teases us with questions. Is it a feature? A documentary? A film-essay? Maybe the best term would be a "jeu d'esprit." A loose-limbed meditation on trickery and fraud, on fakery, lies, magic, and illusion, it borrows footage shot by Welles's friend, French documentarist François Reichenbach, about Hungarian art forger Elmyr de Hory. We see Elmyr on Ibiza, chatting to Clifford Irving, who's writing a book about him entitled *Fake!* Subsequently, Irving himself proves to be no less a fraud when he publishes a supposed book-length interview with the reclusive Howard Hughes.

Interwoven with this are scenes of Welles wandering around Paris and Ibiza, ruminating on art as confidence trick, and footage of a beautiful young woman—Oja Kodar, Welles's companion for the last twenty years of his life—being ogled by every man she passes.

F for Fake has been called "Welles's happiest film." Yet it's possible to detect in it that undertow of melancholy that tinges all his work. At one point he muses on Chartres Cathedral, a towering masterpiece without a signature. "Maybe," he adds, "a man's name doesn't matter all that much." Early on, he promises us: "During the next hour, everything you'll hear from us is really true." As you might guess, there's a sting in that particular tale. Yet the ultimate message is one of affirmation. In the long run, says Welles, "Our songs will all be silenced. But what of it? Go on singing." **PK**

Pat Garrett and Billy the Kid Sam Peckinpah, 1973

U.S. (MGM) 122m Metrocolor
Producer Gordon Carroll **Screenplay** Rudy
Wurlitzer **Photography** John Coquillon
Music Bob Dylan **Cast** James Coburn, Kris
Kristofferson, Richard Jaeckel, Katy Jurado,
Chill Wills, Barry Sullivan, Jason Robards,
Bob Dylan, R.G. Armstrong, Luke Askew,
John Beck, Richard Bright, Matt Clark,
Rita Coolidge, Jack Dodson

Truncated and neglected on its original release, Sam Peckinpah's final true Western has been restored to something like his original vision and can be hailed as one of the director's greatest films. It opens (in the restored version) with Pat Garrett (James Coburn, in the performance of his career) being shot dead and flashing back to the days when he gave up being an outlaw and pinned on a badge to hunt down his former friend Billy (Kris Kristofferson) because "this country's getting old, and I intend to get old with it." Along the way, Garrett loses every shred of integrity and Peckinpah shows us a West decaying in an almost gothic manner, as a succession of familiar genre faces crop up and mainly get bloodily shot.

On parade here are Slim Pickens, Katy Jurado, Jack Elam, Richard Jaeckel, L.Q. Jones, Harry Dean Stanton, Chill Wills, Matt Clark, Elisha Cook Jr., Denver Pyle, and Barry Sullivan. It would be hard to find a great Western that didn't include one of these players; collectively they provide a roll call of the form's greatness, and each cameo adds to the elegiac, melancholy, and wistful tapestry of Western and genre history, shot through with dollops of blood and poetry, plus original music by Bob Dylan. **KN**

Netherlands (VNF) 112m Color
Language Dutch **Producer** Rob Houwer
Screenplay Gerard Soeteman, from the
novel *Turks Fruit* by Jan Wolkers
Photography Jan de Bont **Music** Rogier van
Otterloo **Cast** Monique van de Ven, Rutger
Hauer, Tonny Huurdeman, Wim van den
Brink, Hans Boskamp, Dolf de Vries, Manfred
de Graaf, Dick Scheffer, Marjol Flore, Bert
Dijkstra, Bert André, Jon Bluming,
Paul Brandenburg, Suze Broks, David
Conyers **Oscar nomination** Netherlands
(best foreign language film)

"*This film, it ran in
Europe in a ton of
cinemas for a year,
outrunning* Cabaret *and*
Last Tango in Paris.
It was incredible."

Rutger Hauer, 2011

ℹ

The movie was given the accolade of
"Best Dutch Film of the Century" at
the 1999 Nederlands Film Festival.

Turks fruit Paul Verhoeven, 1973
Turkish Delight

1973

Turkish Delight is Dutch director Paul Verhoeven's outrageous precursor to his cycle of big-budget Hollywood movies probing human sexuality, such as *Basic Instinct* (1992), *Showgirls* (1995), and *Starship Troopers* (1997). Often criticized for his use of extreme violence and sexual explicitness, Verhoeven has always maintained that his films mirror life rather than influence it. *Turkish Delight* stars Rutger Hauer as Eric Vonk, a promiscuous sculptor who gets involved with the beautiful Olga (Monique van de Ven), whose sexual appetite matches his own. As the affair progresses, they decide to marry, but differences between Eric's and his in-laws' value systems bring about the end of their romance. Years later, Eric and Olga meet again and finally achieve some closure to their turbulent relationship. The film is constructed as a series of flashbacks through which Eric's inner world and sensibility are slowly revealed.

The film opens with Eric bludgeoning a man to death before putting a bullet between the eyes of a young woman. There is a panning shot of Eric's room until the camera freezes on him lying on his bed, with these fantasies still fresh in his mind. He leafs through a box of photographs of the same woman, who we later learn is Olga. The next sequence follows at a frenetic pace with Eric's seduction of a series of random women, and his obsessive collecting of sexual souvenirs. In an interesting narrative composition, halfway through *Turkish Delight* we are brought back to the present, and the latter section picks up from where the film started. The mood of the final third is vastly different from that of the beginning, almost as if it were another film. It is transformed into a moving tale of love and loss, of ecstasy and despair; while there is a fair degree of erotic content, it is tempered with extreme doses of both fantasy and reality.

The free-spirited sexuality that drives Verhoeven's films is at the heart of *Turkish Delight*, here presented as the ultimate assault on bourgeois values. Sustained by the extreme behavior of the protagonist, this unconventional romance never fails to provoke, its effect enhanced by the explosive chemistry between Hauer and van de Ven. **RDe**

El espíritu de la colmena Víctor Erice, 1973
The Spirit of the Beehive

Spain (Elías Querejeta) 97m
Eastmancolor **Language** Spanish
Producer Elías Querejeta **Screenplay** Víctor
Erice, Ángel Fernández Santos, Francisco J.
Querejeta **Photography** Luis Cuadrado
Music Luis de Pablo **Cast** Fernando Fernán
Gómez, Teresa Gimpera, Ana Torrent, Isabel
Tellería, Ketty de la Cámara, Estanis González,
José Villasante, Juan Francisco Margallo,
Laly Soldevila, Miguel Picazoa

Victor Erice's *The Spirit of the Beehive* takes almost twenty minutes to establish a few, basic facts—that there is a family comprising a father (Fernando Fernán Gómez), a mother (Teresa Gimpera), and two girls (Isabel Tellería as Isabel, Ana Torrent as Ana). Erice shows us the man with his bees, and in his study; the woman writing, riding, and passing a letter into a train; the girls in a crowd at a makeshift movie hall screening James Whale's *Frankenstein* (1931). These introductory portraits figure as studies in haunted solitude, the windows of the character's rooms resembling the cell-structures of the father's beehive.

This is a mysterious, unforgettable film, touching on many bases but refusing to congeal into any one genre or intention. As elsewhere in Erice's sadly unprolific career, the family unit is seen as the site of psychic trauma, and celebrated as the one place where intimate community seems possible.

Erice evokes with breathtaking delicacy the ambience of this small Castilian town. The characters dream of an elsewhere until reality comes crashing into an abandoned farmhouse—a political fugitive whom the impressionable, frightened but fascinated Ana takes to be the wandering "spirit" of the Frankenstein monster incarnated. This movie that begins as a fairy tale ("Once upon a time . . .") ends with a stirring declaration addressed to the spirits of the wind: "I am Ana." **AM**

ℹ

There is not a single shot of the entire family all together at one time in the entire movie.

The Harder They Come Perry Henzell, 1973

Jamaica (International) 120m Metrocolor
Producer Perry Henzell Screenplay Perry
Henzell, Trevor D. Rhone Photography Peter
Jessop, David McDonald, Franklyn St. Juste
Music Jimmy Cliff, Desmond Dekker, The
Slickers Cast Jimmy Cliff, Janet Barkley, Carl
Bradshaw, Ras Daniel Hartman, Basil Keane,
Bobby Charlton, Winston Stona, Lucia White,
Volair Johnson, Beverly Anderson, Clover
Lewis, Elijah Chambers, Prince Buster,
Ed "Bum" Lewis, Bobby Loban

A slice-of-life film set in Jamaica's slums, Perry Henzell's *The Harder They Come* features a pretty shopworn scenario: A country boy comes to the city and butts heads with local baddies. But as a low-budget homage to gangster films, *The Harder They Come* works great.

Thanks to the rough locations and unpolished acting, the film speeds along with a raw verisimilitude. Jimmy Cliff plays the naive country boy who finds himself diving headfirst into a fight between corrupt cops and gangs that have infiltrated the reggae industry. Indeed, as impressive a mark as *The Harder They Come* may have made on the midnight movie circuit, its most lasting effect was the introduction of reggae to non-Jamaican ears. The soundtrack (a character in and of itself) features stellar work from the likes of Toots and the Maytals, and Cliff himself, whose "Many Rivers to Cross" remains one of the most soulful songs ever recorded. The soundtrack immediately set the stage for the ascent of superstar Bob Marley, but from the perspective of Jamaicans reggae was, of course, old news. They embraced the film as a vivid portrait of their meager everyday lives, a gritty postcard sent from the Caribbean to the world at large. **JKl**

1973

La planète sauvage René Laloux, 1973
Fantastic Planet

Czechoslovakia / France (Ceskoslovensky
Filmexport, Krátky Film Praha,
Les Films Armorial) 72m Eastmancolor
Language French Producer Roger Corman,
S. Damiani, Anatole Dauman, A. Valio-
Cavaglione Screenplay Steve Hayes,
René Laloux, Roland Topor, from the
novel *Oms en serie* by Stefan Wul
Photography Boris Baromykin, Lubomir
Rejthar Music Alain Goraguer Cannes
Film Festival René Laloux (special award
and Golden Palm nomination)

Animation became big business again in the late 1980s, and ever since then, it's become less and less likely that there will be another full-length animated feature quite as weird as René Laloux's underground French classic *Fantastic Planet*. Drawn with sharp details in warm pastel colors, the movie is just the kind of hippie allegory—and trippy visual experience—that many filmmakers of the 1960s produced.

Adapted from a novel by Stefan Wul, *Fantastic Planet* was inspired by the invasion of Czechoslovakia by the Russians in the late 1960s. On the planet Ygam lives a race of giant, alien beings called Traags. These Traags keep the oddly humanlike Oms as pets, often treating them with the sadism and perverse maternalism humans frequently inflict upon their own pets. When one Om absconds with one of the Traags's knowledge devices, he uses the tool to foment a wild Om uprising. Laloux's film, which won the 1973 Cannes Grand Prix Prize, is a welcome respite from slick animated marketing vehicles and countless shoddy imitators.

Started in Prague but completed in Paris because of political pressure, *Fantastic Planet* uses an accessible medium to show the evils of propaganda and express the need for individuality. Laloux's vision of a Dalí-meets-Krazy Kat alien landscape populated by twisted creatures is quite striking, even if the film's psychedelic elements haven't exactly aged well. **JKl**

FRANCO CRISTALDI presenta

FEDERICO FELLINI
AMARCORD

scritto e sceneggiato da
FEDERICO FELLINI . TONINO GUERRA
F.C. (Roma) - P.E.C.F. (Paris) TECHNICOLOR UNA ESCLUSIVITA' P.I.C.

1973

Italy / France (F.C., PECF) 127m Technicolor
Language Italian **Producer** Franco Cristaldi
Screenplay Federico Fellini, Tonino
Guerra **Photography** Giuseppe Rotunno
Music Nino Rota **Cast** Pupella Maggio,
Armando Brancia, Magali Noël, Ciccio
Ingrassia, Nando Orfei, Luigi Rossi, Bruno
Zanin, Gianfilippo Carcano, Josiane Tanzilli,
Maria Antonietta Beluzzi, Giuseppe Ianigro,
Ferruccio Brembilla, Antonino Faa Di Bruno,
Mauro Misul, Ferdinando Villella, Antonio
Spaccatini, Aristide Caporale, Gennaro
Ombra, Domenico Pertica, Marcello Di Falco,
Stefano Proietti, Alvaro Vitali, Bruno
Scagnetti, Fernando De Felice, Bruno Lenzi,
Gianfranco Marrocco, Francesco Vona,
Donatella Gambini **Oscar** Italy (best foreign
language film) **Oscar nominations** Federico
Fellini (director), Federico Fellini, Tonino
Guerra (screenplay)

i

The movie was to become
the last significant commercial
success of Fellini's career.

Amarcord Federico Fellini, 1973

Federico Fellini is at his gloomiest when dealing with individuals (as in *8 1/2* [1963]), and at his happiest when dealing with gangs, packs, and crowds. A magnificent scene in *Amarcord* is devoted to recording the diverse movements of every member of a community toward a beach. Propelled by Nino Rota's music, the entire world flows and sings in rhythmic fusion. And ultimately, Fellini will mark the end of a day and of a wedding ceremony—as well as the end of his reminiscence (and thus his film) and even the end of an era—by slowly emptying a long shot of its formerly teeming mass of humanity.

Amarcord ("I remember") is the least grandiose and most immediate of the maestro's later films and deserves to be rated among the finest screen memoirs of the twentieth century. It offers an extraordinarily lyrical and vivid succession of vignettes, inside the most subtly rigorous narrative structure of Fellini's career.

It is the least obviously modernist of Fellini's films of the 1960s and beyond, eschewing the sorts of self-reflexive games that fill *Roma* (1972) or *Ginger and Fred* (1986). Although the figure of the boy Titta is obviously his alter ego, Fellini builds a generously fractured mosaic that belongs to no one central character or even the on-screen narrator (the old, amateur historian who is a typically Felliniesque figure of fun)—a palpable influence on Scorsese's epic chronicles of criminal life, *Goodfellas* (1990) and *Casino* (1996). *Amarcord* uses certain time-honored, classical devices, such as a progression through the seasons, to great effect to wheel through a various modes, from the comic to the melancholic.

Like many autobiographical tales written or filmed, this one weaves the innocent, limited viewpoint of children into its wider social context, which here heralds the reign of Fascism in Italy in the 1930s. Poignant indeed is the gap, gradually revealed to the viewer, between the hints of violence and social exclusion to come (especially in relation to the Jewish population), and the life-affirming antics of youth. But children are not the only ones duped, for the politics of Fascism comes to the adoring masses as showbiz—a giant head of Mussolini is paraded through the streets in an especially brilliant sequence poised between comedy and mordant social commentary—and mixed up with the glamorous images of the silver screen, as shown in a fantasy sequence imagined by town belle La Gradisca.

Fellini's comedy, refreshingly, goes to the outer limits of vulgarity in a number of hilarious scenes centered on urination, masturbation, and breast worship, revisiting the peculiarly Italian form of the "teen movie" genre, which he vigorously pioneered in *I Vitelloni* (1953).

Fellini's style, sometimes too baroque for its own good in works such as *Casanova* (1976), is streamlined here into a pure, exalted poetry of mist, flowing camera movements, pastel colors, and lightly artificial set design. A triumph of artistic form, its emotions are direct and affecting. **AM**

The Towering Inferno John Guillermin, 1974

U.S. (20th Century Fox, Warner Bros.) 165m Color **Producer** Irwin Allen **Screenplay** Stirling Silliphant, from novels by Richard Martin Stern, Thomas N. Scortia and Frank M. Robinson **Photography** Fred Koenekamp, Joseph F. Biroc **Music** John Williams **Cast** Steve McQueen, Paul Newman, William Holden, Faye Dunaway, Fred Astaire, Susan Blakely, Richard Chamberlain, Jennifer Jones, O.J. Simpson, Robert Vaughan, Robert Wagner, Susan Flannery **Oscars** Fred Koenekamp, Joseph F. Biroc (cinematography), Harold F. Kress, Carl Kress (editing), Al Kasha, Joel Hirschhorn (original song) **Oscar nominations** Irwin Allen (picture), Fred Astaire (actor), William J. Creber, Ward Preston, Raphael Bretton (art direction), John Williams (score), Theodore Soderberg, Herman Kress (sound)

The Towering Inferno was the film that helped define the disaster movie genre. Like *Airport* (1970) and *Earthquake* (1974), it assembled a group of A-list stars and visited on them a spectacular catastrophe that left only a few alive. It was a formula studios would repeat throughout the 1970s.

The setting is San Francisco. On the eve of the opening of a new skyscraper, its architect Doug Roberts (Paul Newman) worries about the safety of the electrics. Despite his concerns, the opening goes ahead, with an exclusive party near the top floor. When a fire eventually breaks out below, the guests are stranded, prompting Roberts and fire chief O'Hallorhan (Steve McQueen) to take desperate measures to save them.

The Towering Inferno boasted some high-profile on-screen talent. Newman and McQueen—both exponents of the cooler, more naturalistic performance style that emerged from the 1950s—were joined by stars of the "classical" Hollywood era like Fred Astaire. But all were second to the movie's main attraction: its state-of-the-art action scenes depicting the skyscraper's fiery demise, overseen by "Master of Disaster" Irwin Allen.

In a footnote arguably more dramatic than the onscreen action, stars Newman and McQueen argued over who was to get top billing, a conflict ultimately resolved by placing their names diagonally on the credits. **EL**

Bring Me the Head of Alfredo Garcia
Sam Peckinpah, 1974

U.S. / **Mexico** (Churubusco Azteca, Optimus) 112m Color **Producer** Martin Baum, Helmut Dantine, Gordon T. Dawson **Screenplay** Gordon T. Dawson, Frank Kowalski, Sam Peckinpah **Photography** Álex Phillips Jr. **Music** Jerry Fielding **Cast** Warren Oates, Isela Vega, Robert Webber, Gig Young, Helmut Dantine, Emilio Fernández, Kris Kristofferson, Chano Urueta, Jorge Russek, Don Levy, Donnie Fritts, Chalo González, Enrique Lucero, Janine Maldonado, Tamara Garina

Bring Me the Head of Alfredo Garcia is one of those rare films that divides audiences into those who rate it a five-star classic and those who see it as a one-star dog. Sam Peckinpah's most brutal, nihilistic vision follows seedy piano player Benny (Warren Oates) through a modern-day Mexico made as infernal as the nightmare Western world of the director's earlier classic, *The Wild Bunch* (1969).

Because his daughter has been impregnated by the now-dead Alfredo, El Jefe (Emilio Fernandez, reincarnating his *Wild Bunch* evil patriarch) puts a bounty on the eponymous relic and Benny hopes to collect. Toting the fly-blown head across the desert in a sack, Oates tangles with mob hit-men and crazed bikers, hooks up with earth-mother whore Isela Vega, and arrives at the hacienda for one of the director's trademarked bullet-strewn apocalypse finales. *Bring Me the Head of Alfredo Garcia* is the quintessence of "cinema grunge," with an unshaven and weaselly antihero and a parade of amazingly corrupt supporting characters. Peckinpah goes out of his way to make the settings sleazy and repulsive, with a trace of blood-streaked pretension that suggests Ernest Hemingway at the point his brain exploded. Obviously the work of an alcoholic genius, with moments of affecting melancholy and beauty even during the rapes and gunfights. **KN**

Dersu Uzala Akira Kurosawa, 1974

Dersu Uzala is a spectacular epic, made in screen-filling 70mm in the Soviet Union during a period when the great Japanese director Akira Kurosawa was surprisingly out of favor in his homeland. *Dersu Uzala's* international success and Best Foreign Language Film Oscar were factors in restoring the filmmaker's reputation, but its understated approach also served as a reminder that Kurosawa was a genuine master, not just a skilled maker of action-oriented samurai entertainments. This vast movie, dominated by awesomely empty landscapes, is also an intimate two-character piece built on tiny gestures and a simple evocation of deep love between apparent opposites.

Set in Siberia at the turn of the century and based on a story by Vladimir Arseniev, the film revolves around the relationship between an officer (Yuri Solomin) on a mapmaking expedition and Dersu (Maksim Munzuk), an elderly, bow-legged peasant woodsman recruited as a guide for the survey. Through minor brushes with bandits and a major struggle with the elements, Dersu shows his strength and knowledge of his environment. In the film's most tense sequence, a threatening storm gathers as the heroes use a theodolite and some grass to rig up life-saving shelter in the wilderness. It's about the vulnerability and hardiness of man in the vastness of creation, but it gets to its huge theme through a buildup of little details.

At first, the officer's associates think Dersu is a comical character, but it soon becomes apparent that his natural wisdom makes him far better suited than they are to endure in the amazingly harsh and unpredictably dangerous landscape. Five years after the initial expedition, the officer returns to Siberia to finish the job and rejoices in his reunion with Dersu, only to realize that the old man's health is failing—Dersu worries that he is going blind and that all the region's tigers are stalking him to avenge a big cat he has killed. In a poignant stretch, the well-intentioned mapmaker tries to take Dersu into his home back in more civilized regions but realizes that although the old man could help him survive in Siberia, he can't repay the service by fitting Dersu into society. **KN**

U.S.S.R. / Japan (Atelier 41, Daiei Studios, Mosfilm, Satra) 137m Color Language Russian Producer Yoichi Matsue, Nikolai Sizov Screenplay Akira Kurosawa, Yuri Nagibin, from journals by Vladimir Arseniev Photography Fyodor Dobronravov, Yuri Gantman, Asakazu Nakai Music Isaak Shvarts Cast Yuri Solomin, Maksim Munzuk, Suimenkul Chokmorov, Svetlana Danilchenko, Dima Kortitschew, Vladimir Kremena, Aleksandr Pyatkov Oscar Soviet Union (best foreign language film)

1974

> *"I think people should be more humble toward nature because we are a part of it and we must become harmonized with it . . . we can learn a lot from Dersu."*
>
> **Akira Kurosawa, 1991**

ℹ️

Kurosawa had planned a Japanese film version of the story back in the 1940s but was unable to realize it.

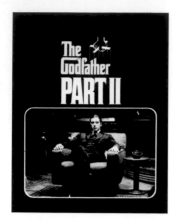

The Godfather: Part II Francis Ford Coppola, 1974

"Keep your friends close but your enemies closer." Time and two more pictures would highlight the despair and nihilism in *The Godfather* saga. This follow-up to the 1972 landmark original is an essential companion piece, "haunted," as writer-director Francis Ford Coppola intended, by "the specter" of the first film. Ironically, considering that Coppola was nearly fired from the first movie—and was so worried about his financial situation that he was holed up in a hotel room scripting *The Great Gatsby* (1974) as *The Godfather* opened. After the film's enormous success Paramount wanted a sequel from him so badly they made him an offer he couldn't refuse. Besides receiving a hefty portion of the profits, he would also have complete artistic control.

The Godfather: Part II took six Oscars and is darker, more profound, and arguably even more compelling for its elaboration of power's corruption into complete moral decay. Scenes, patterns, and motifs deliberately mirror the original, but *Part II* is more elegiac and rueful and on a far grander scale, with its complex interweaving of time periods and its parallels and contrasts between the two Corleone dons, Vito (Robert De Niro) and Michael (Al Pacino). This time unequivocally down on the mob, Coppola explores two generations as Michael ascends in power and control as he descends into melancholy, ruthlessness, and betrayal. Family celebrations are again central to the cycle, the film opening in the 1950s on the overblown party at Michael's and Kay's (Diane Keaton) Lake Tahoe estate in honor of their son Anthony's confirmation. We learn that the master plan to legitimatize the Corleone family business is ongoing as Michael pursues his criminal interests from Nevada to Cuba. Michael is beset by problems at home, government scrutiny, and the threats posed by rivals and associates—including the highly influential Actors Studio director Lee Strasberg making his film debut, aged seventy-one, as Hyman Roth—who take a dim view of Michael's expansionism.

Twinned with Michael's progress is the sepia-toned story of his father, born Vito Andolini in turn-of-the-century Corleone, Sicily, where a bloody vendetta makes him an orphan, a fugitive emigrant, and a bewildered detainee on Ellis Island. Years later, on New York's Lower East Side as a grocery clerk and family man, quiet Vito—De Niro, hot off Martin Scorsese's *Mean Streets* (1973), brilliantly reimagining Brando's characterization in the first film as a young man and winning his first Oscar—observes the power wielded by the feared local crime boss and stealthily, remorselessly, usurps it. Respected and prosperous, he returns to Corleone to settle old scores while nurturing a heritage for his sons.

Again, the film is full of richly drawn characters and superb set pieces—the festa in Little Italy, the New Year's revolution in Havana. It is the last shot in *The Godfather: Part II* that continues to satisfy, however, with its chilling image of Michael, his sins accrued beyond redemption, alone. **AE**

U.S. (Paramount, Coppola) 200m
Technicolor **Language** English / Italian
Producer Francis Ford Coppola, Gray Frederickson, Fred Roos **Screenplay** Francis Ford Coppola, Mario Puzo, from novel by Mario Puzo **Photography** Gordon Willis **Music** Carmine Coppola, C. Curet Alonso, Nino Rota **Cast** Al Pacino, Robert Duvall, Diane Keaton, Robert De Niro, John Cazale, Talia Shire, Lee Strasberg, Michael V. Gazzo, G.D. Spradlin, Richard Bright, Gastone Moschin, Tom Rosqui, Bruno Kirby, Frank Sivero, Francesca De Sapio **Oscars** Francis Ford Coppola, Gray Frederickson, Fred Roos (best picture), Francis Ford Coppola (director), Francis Ford Coppola, Mario Puzo (screenplay), Robert De Niro (actor in support role), Dean Tavoularis, Angelo P. Graham, George R. Nelson (art direction), Nino Rota, Carmine Coppola (music) **Oscar nominations** Al Pacino (actor), Michael V. Gazzo (actor in support role), Lee Strasberg (actor in support role), Talia Shire (actress in support role), Theadora Van Runkle (costume)

> "If anything in this life is certain, if history has taught us anything, it's that you can kill anyone."
>
> **Michael Corleone (Al Pacino)**

i

The Godfather: Part II was the only sequel to win a Best Picture Oscar until *The Return of the King* (2003).

1974

The Conversation Francis Ford Coppola, 1974

Riding a crest of creative energy, Francis Ford Coppola was always looking ahead to his next project even as he was still finishing the last. *The Conversation* appeared between the bookends of *Godfather I* and *Godfather II* (1972 and 1974), and it may seem small compared to those dual epics. But small does not mean slight, and *The Conversation* is every bit as provocative as the *Godfather* movies in its take on America's crumbling morals.

Gene Hackman, in a remarkably reserved and internalized performance, plays a surveillance expert who feels more at ease eavesdropping on strangers from hundreds of feet away than interacting with friends in the same room. He's a sad, shy, and inevitably lonely man of many secrets who prefers to sit in his spartan apartment playing the saxophone, at least until a snippet of conversation gleaned from a jumble of static and noise he picked up piques his interest. Troubled by the distance professionalism imposes, Hackman personalizes the investigation. Sensing an imminent tragedy, he attempts to solve the mystery hidden in his scrambled surveillance tapes before time runs out, only to discover that the two things he trusts in the world—his eyes and ears—have deceived him.

As sad as it is cynical, *The Conversation* arrived shortly before the Watergate break-in and subsequent investigation, when surveillance and dishonesty rose to the fore of public consciousness, and in this way the film was eerily prescient. But Coppola also presents a postmodern study of voyeurism. As Hackman's Harry Caul uncovers more and more about his discovery, assembling some horrible truth out of bits and pieces of discussion fueled by his own imagination, we discover more and more about him. By the time Caul's obsessive investigation falls apart around him, he's left with virtually nothing: no friends, no belongings, no life, and no freedom in the face of rapidly encroaching and enveloping paranoia. Revered by his colleagues for his skills, we see Caul as something of a fraud, a broken shell of a man whose uncertainty about the world around him has effectively robbed him of any identity. **JKl**

U.S. (Zoetrope, Paramount, Coppola Co., Directors Co.) 113m Technicolor
Producer Francis Ford Coppola
Screenplay Francis Ford Coppola
Photography Rill Butler **Music** David Shire, Duke Ellington **Cast** Gene Hackman, John Cazale, Allen Garfield, Frederic Forrest, Cindy Williams, Michael Higgins, Elizabeth MacRae, Teri Garr, Harrison Ford, Mark Wheeler, Robert Shields, Phoebe Alexander
Oscar nominations Francis Ford Coppola (best picture), Francis Ford Coppola (screenplay), Walter Murch, Art Rochester (sound) **Cannes Film Festival** Francis Ford Coppola (Golden Palm, prize of the ecumenical jury—special mention)

> *"Coppola's cerebral classic of paranoia and surveillance still looks outstanding, and [is] more relevant than ever in the age of CCTV."*
>
> Peter Bradshaw,
> *The Guardian*, 2002

i

Shots from the film are used in *Enemy of the State* (1998), in which Hackman also plays a surveillance expert.

Zerkalo Andrei Tarkovsky, 1974
The Mirror

U.S.S.R. (Mosfilm) 108m BW / Color
Language Russian / Spanish **Producer** Erik
Waisberg **Screenplay** Aleksandr Misharin,
Andrei Tarkovsky **Photography** Georgi
Rerberg **Music** Eduard Artemyev
Cast Margarita Terekhova, Ignat Daniltsev,
Larisa Tarkovskaya, Alla Demidova, Anatoli
Solonitsyn, Tamara Ogorodnikova, Yuri
Nazarov, Oleg Yankovsky, Filipp Yankovsky, S.
Sventikov, Tamara Reshetnikova, Innokenti
Smoktunovsky, Arseni Tarkovsky

𝑖

The poems that can be periodically
heard throughout the movie were
written by Tarkovsky's father.

The Mirror is a beguiling and remarkable film—full of the pregnant mysteriousness of places, people, and gestures. This fugitive self-portrait by Andrei Tarkovsky is an intergenerational affair, in which the terse melancholy of his mother's situation—abandoned in the 1940s by her husband and left to raise a son—is mirrored by his own adult relationships (Margarita Terekhova plays both the mother in the past and the present-day wife). Men, largely absent from the story as from the image, appear as voices, and are poignantly identified with the making of art and poetry.

The Mirror is constructed as a collage, in which recreated vignettes that blur past and present are freely mingled with archival footage and disconnected quotations from classical music. The ambience is dreamlike, secretive, elliptical. Yet there is also a beautiful simplicity in Tarkovsky, aligning him with Terrence Malick: the movement of natural elements, the bottomless landscapes of the human face, and a sense of time passing, all conspire to give a sense of the world itself "breathing."

Tarkovsky, like Robert Bresson, is a master of the precisely chosen image and sound. The economy of his camera movements and the gradual revealing of the disparate parts of any scene create an aura and an effect that overflow the material reality of what we see and hear, opening a portal to another world. His is a cinema of texture, of aura, and the senses. *Mirror* is all at once an intimate confession, a summoning of history, and a cryptic poem. **AM**

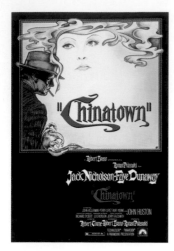

Chinatown Roman Polanski, 1974

"It seems like half the city is trying to cover it all up, which is fine by me. But, Mrs. Mulwray, I goddamn near lost my nose. And I like it. I like breathing through it." Robert Towne wrote *Chinatown* specifically for his friend Jack Nicholson and won the film's only Oscar in a year dominated by *The Godfather: Part II*. It is a conspiracy and a hard-boiled detective mystery in the Raymond Chandler/Dashiell Hammett line. It is also a highly sophisticated film that covered everyone involved in glory, including audiences who responded appreciatively to the compelling, complex puzzle and colossal performances.

Private eye Jake Gittes is more dapper, humorous, prosperous, and alienated than Chandler's Philip Marlowe or Hammett's Sam Spade. Jake is a former cop haunted by the past when his beat was Los Angeles's Chinatown. This is intriguingly alluded to, suggesting it represents failure and being out of his depth in something he doesn't understand, and hinting at the disaster he brings down back in Chinatown at the film's fateful climax. Jake is hired by a dolled-up broad (Diane Ladd) to spy on her allegedly philandering husband, prominent chief engineer for the city's water and power department. He gets the dirt but a rude awakening when the real and outraged Mrs. Mulwray (Faye Dunaway) appears. Jake, who doesn't like being made a fool of, persists in investigating further as intimidation and corpses mount. This leads him to bluff tycoon and chief villain Noah Cross (John Huston) into a catastrophe of greed, murder, and incest in the mean streets and orange groves of 1930s Los Angeles.

It was Roman Polanski's genius that made the film not merely an intelligent and intricate narrative but a great, disturbing vision. With his tragically intimate experience of evil, Polanski toughened up the script, most crucially by changing Towne's ending to the bitter but unforgettable conclusion which leaves Jake pole-axed. It was also Polanski who observed with humane and sharp perception the collected oddballs, victims, and miscreants (including the little weasel who slits Jake's nose, played by the director himself). That it is ultimately his film was verified by the unfathomable 1990 sequel *The Two Jakes*, scripted by Towne and directed by Nicholson revisiting his Gittes in 1948. It, too, is well acted, complicated, and polished-looking, but sadly lacking in unifying magic.

Faye Dunaway, whose neurasthenic quality has never been exploited to better advantage, is the cool, elegant Evelyn, whose birthmark—"a flaw in the iris"—represents the film's heart of darkness. She is presented as a high-class femme fatale and indeed her suspect motives enhance the menace and jeopardy until both her anxiousness and her glowing seduction scene are suddenly cast in a different light by the most shocking of *Chinatown*'s revelations. It is still Nicholson's show, though, his fatalistic glamor and presence as the cynical, wisecracking, impulsively decent snoop unspoiled by the ignominy of sporting a bandage over his nose for much of the film's running time. **AE**

U.S. (Long Road, Paramount, Penthouse) 131m Technicolor **Producer** Robert Evans **Screenplay** Robert Towne **Photography** John A. Alonzo **Music** Jerry Goldsmith **Cast** Jack Nicholson, Faye Dunaway, John Huston, Perry Lopez, John Hillerman, Darrell Zwerling, Diane Ladd, Roy Jenson, Roman Polanski, Richard Bakalyan, Joe Mantell, Bruce Glover, Nandu Hinds, James O'Rear, James Hong **Oscar** Robert Towne (screenplay) **Oscar nominations** Robert Evans (best picture), Roman Polanski (director), Jack Nicholson (actor), Faye Dunaway (actress), Richard Sylbert, W. Stewart Campbell, Ruby R. Levitt (art direction), John A. Alonzo (photography), Anthea Sylbert (costume), Sam O'Steen (editing), Jerry Goldsmith (music), Charles Grenzbach, Larry Jost (sound)

"Forget Hitchcock. We've got Polanski!"

Tom Burke,
Rolling Stone review of
Chinatown, 1974

i

Chinatown was intended as the first of a trilogy of films about Jake Gittes, but the third was never made.

A Woman Under the Influence John Cassavetes, 1974

U.S. (Faces) 155m Color
Producer Sam Shaw **Screenplay** John
Cassavetes **Photography** Mitch Breit, Caleb
Deschanel **Music** Bo Harwood **Cast** Peter
Falk, Gena Rowlands, Fred Draper,
Lady Rowlands, Katherine Cassavetes,
Matthew Laborteaux, Matthew Cassel,
Christina Grisanti, O.G. Dunn, Mario Gallo,
Eddie Shaw, Angelo Grisanti, Charles
Horvath, James Joyce, John Finnegan
Oscar nominations Gena Rowlands
(actress), John Cassavetes (director)

John Cassavetes and his wife Gena Rowlands collaborated on a number of challenging and risky projects, but it was Rowlands's exhausting portrayal of a housewife's impending nervous breakdown in *A Woman Under the Influence* that remains the apotheosis of their improvisation-fueled method. Full of ticks, strange noises, and unpredictable mannerisms, Rowlands's descent into madness eventually gives way to the realization that her frustrating behavior may not be as spontaneous or debilitating as it seems. Similarly, her rock of a husband (Peter Falk) may not be as sane as he initially appears to be, and the same could be said for his support network of friends and acquaintances.

Stuck in the middle are the couple's three children, a steady reminder that amidst the confusion is a surprisingly operational (if decidedly unconventional) nuclear family. In fact, *A Woman Under the Influence* may best be considered an unflinching depiction of what it sometimes takes to keep a family together, though Cassavetes never injects the film with such blatant moralizing. Rather, he prefers to leave the action ambiguous and relentless, united by Rowlands's unhinged and kinetic performance, and a strangely touching sentimentalism that achieves its emotional force honestly—mostly free from standard-issue plot conventions. **JKl**

Young Frankenstein Mel Brooks, 1974

U.S. (Fox, Crossbow, Gruskoff / Venture,
Jouer) 108m BW **Language** English /
German **Producer** Michael Gruskoff
Screenplay Gene Wilder, Mel Brooks, from
the novel *Frankenstein* by Mary Shelley
Photography Gerald Hirschfeld **Music** John
Morris **Cast** Gene Wilder, Peter Boyle, Marty
Feldman, Madeline Kahn, Cloris Leachman,
Teri Garr, Kenneth Mars, Richard Haydn, Liam
Dunn, Danny Goldman, Oscar Beregi Jr.,
Arthur Malet, Richard A. Roth, Monte Landis,
Rusty Blitz **Oscar nominations** Mel Brooks,
Gene Wilder (screenplay), Richard Portman,
Gene S. Cantamessa (sound)

Mel Brooks's 1974 black-and-white horror spoof of Mary Shelley's classic novel is the prolific writer-director's most balanced comedy in his overegged oeuvre. Having yet to come to terms with being the grandson of the famous Victor Frankenstein, Gene Wilder's modern young brain surgeon Dr. Frederick Frankenstein (pronounced, we are told, "Fronkunshteen") returns to the family castle in Transylvania. Assisted by trusty hunchback Igor (bulbous-eyed Marty Feldman), pretty village girl Inga (Teri Garr), and housekeeper Frau Bleucher (Cloris Leachman, so gloriously sinister that she went on to play similar roles in two more Brooks films), he sets out to recreate his grandfather's pioneering work in human reanimation. Who could predict the reaction between Frederick's overcoifed (and later oversexed) fiancée Elizabeth (Madeline Kahn) and the Monster (Peter Boyle)?

Gene Hackman has a show-stealing cameo as the lonely blind man who makes the mistake of offering hot soup and a cigar to the fire-shy untamed creature. Shot in the same castle and featuring lab equipment originally used in the 1931 James Whale classic, the film's overall reverential feel is marred (in a good way) by the singing and dancing "Puttin' on the Ritz" sequence featuring the monster and the doctor. A silly take and a serious homage, *Young Frankenstein* earned Academy Award nominations for Best Sound and Best Adapted Screenplay. **KK**

Who will survive and what will be left of them?

"THE TEXAS CHAINSAW MASSACRE"

America's most bizarre and brutal crimes!...

What happened is true. Now the motion picture that's just as real.

U.S. (Vortex) 83m Color **Producer** Tobe Hooper, Lou Peraino **Screenplay** Kim Henkel, Tobe Hooper **Photography** Daniel Pearl **Music** Wayne Bell, Tobe Hooper, John Lennon **Cast** Marilyn Burns, Allen Danziger, Paul A. Partain, William Vail, Teri McMinn, Edwin Neal, Jim Siedow, Gunnar Hansen, John Dugan, Robert Courtin, William Creamer, John Henry Faulk, Jerry Green, Ed Guinn, Joe Bill Hogana

"There are horror films which . . . deal with the psychological, the suggested . . . and then there are the sheer, in-your-face, terrifying horrors which threaten to drain your body of sweat and lock your jaw shut forever. This is one of the latter."

Time Out London, 2012

i

Tobe Hooper hoped to get a PG rating for the film by keeping most of the violence implied offscreen.

The Texas Chain Saw Massacre Tobe Hooper, 1974

Loosely inspired by the real-life story of Wisconsin serial killer Ed Gein—as was *Psycho* (1960) before it and *The Silence of the Lambs* (1991) after it—Tobe Hooper's ultra-low-budget shock-horror classic *The Texas Chain Saw Massacre* opened to a firestorm of controversy, and since then has continued to generate heated debate over its aesthetic merits and potentially damaging effects on viewers.

The film, which begins with some voice-over by a young (and then unknown) John Laroquette, follows five hippieish teenagers on a road trip through 1970s Texas who have the grave misfortune of bunking down next to an all-male clan of cannibalistic ex-slaughterhouse workers. The most memorable baddie is Leatherface (Gunnar Hansen in the role of a lifetime), he of the eponymous chain saw and gruesome mask made from the facial skin of several of his victims. After an unforgettable family dinner in which she is served as dessert to the ancient, vampiric patriarch who can barely move his lips enough to suck the blood from her finger, Sally Hardesty (Marilyn Burns)—the one teen still alive—manages an escape from this chamber of horrors by jumping through a second-story window. After a seemingly endless run through the woods at night, with Leatherface's motorized saw (which incredibly never runs out of gas) literally inches away from her back, Sally finally hops on the back of a conveniently situated pickup truck and drives away as Leatherface angrily waves his phallic weapon in the morning light.

Upon viewing this intense picture, with its relentless pace and quasi-documentary style, critic Rex Reed declared it one of the most frightening movies ever made. Shortly after its release, the Museum of Modern Art purchased a print for its permanent collection, and the film was honored in the "Directors' Fortnight" at Cannes. The accolades continued to pour in—the prestigious London Film Festival even went so far as to name it "Outstanding Film of the Year" in 1974. Eventually grossing close to $31 million at U.S. box offices alone, and spawning three sequels (plus a remake), Hooper's warped labor of love stood for a time as one of the most profitable independent films in motion picture history. **SJS**

1974

Blazing Saddles Mel Brooks, 1974

Though it may not be the peak of Mel Brooks's cinematic output—*The Producers* is still more shocking and pointed—with its mixture of surrealism, slapstick, and (then groundbreaking) vulgarity, *Blazing Saddles* is certainly his most influential film. Despite both its hackneyed setting—the old West—and its 1970s veneer—hip gags about race and sex—it stands as one of the more brilliant works in the career of a great 1950s comedy writer.

For all Brooks's much-publicized nods to the zany comedy of the Marx Brothers and the Three Stooges, *Blazing Saddles* owes a great deal to the deranged, parodic, reference-obsessed humor of early *MAD* magazine. Brooks's film takes on that tradition—sight gags where Klansmen and Nazis wait in line to join an 1870s lynch mob, oxen with YES and NO painted on them, verbal references to other movies ("You'd do it for Randolph Scott!")—and puts it into the cinema for the first time. In doing so, it preempted and influenced the Zucker Brothers and their imitators, and hence invented a genre (there's also some Monty Python in the ending, which mirrors that of *Holy Grail* [1975]).

Blazing Saddles may, essentially, be an extended riff on *High Noon* (1952), but its genius lies in being more than just a parody. While other, later Brooks movies waver by just being straight pastiches of one particular film, *Blazing Saddles* adds additional layers, most notable of which is the twist that the new sheriff is black. Cleavon Little (whose career sadly peaked with this film, and who died of colon cancer at fifty-three) beat Richard Pryor for the role of Sheriff Bart, largely because the studio believed that Pryor was an insane drug addict; and he is superbly supported by an almost restrained Gene Wilder. The movie is laced with the "n" word to an extent that anyone not familiar with modern rap records may find alarming, but is in fact constantly hilarious. While hardly a political film about color, *Blazing Saddles*' constant glee in using the word and mocking white prejudice makes the whole concept of racism seem absurd. **KK**

U.S. (Crossbow, Warner Bros.) 93m Technicolor **Producer** Michael Hertzberg **Screenplay** Andrew Bergman, Mel Brooks, Richard Pryor, Norman Steinberg, Alan Uger **Photography** Joseph F. Biroc **Music** Mel Brooks, Vernon Duke, John Morris **Cast** Cleavon Little, Gene Wilder, Slim Pickens, David Huddleston, Liam Dunn, Alex Karras, John Hillerman, George Furth, Jack Starrett, Mel Brooks, Harvey Korman, Carol DeLuise, Richard Collier, Charles McGregor **Oscar nominations** Madeline Kahn (actress in support role), John C. Howard, Danford B. Greene (editing), John Morris, Mel Brooks (song)

"I watched so many westerns when I was a kid ... And I always wondered: How many beans could you eat and how much black coffee could you drink out of those tin cups without letting one go?"

Mel Brooks, 2007

i

The film was almost never released after no-one laughed when it was screened for Warner Bros. executives.

Céline et Julie vont en bateau Jacques Rivette, 1974
Celine and Julie Go Boating

France (Action, Christian Fechner, Le Films 7, Losange, Renn, Saga, Simar, V.M. Prod.) 193m Eastmancolor **Language** French **Producer** Barbet Schroeder **Screenplay** Juliet Berto, Eduardo de Gregorio, Dominique Labourier, Bulle Ogier, Marie-France Pisier, Jacques Rivette **Photography** Jacques Renard **Music** Jean-Marie Sénia **Cast** Juliet Berto, Dominique Labourier, Bulle Ogier, Marie-France Pisier, Barbet Schroeder, Nathalie Asnar, Marie-Thérèse Saussure, Philippe Clévenot, Anne Zamire, Jean Douchet, Adèle Taffetas, Monique Clément, Jérôme Richard, Michael Graham, Jean-Marie Sénia

i

Juliet Berto and Dominique Labourier were cast in their roles because they were friends in real life.

English-speaking viewers will never taste the real flavor of this film. It starts with the title, which means nothing in translation but, in its original version and for French-speaking people, opens wide the doors toward tales, jokes, and children's stories. *Celine and Julie Go Boating* is a password to a realm where sinuous roads travel the fringe between the exterior world and intimate dreams, between present and past, and between reality and fiction.

This is a movie by one of the most demanding and delicate of film critics, Jacques Rivette, who became a remarkable explorer of the nature of cinema through the questioning of its relations with the real world and with other forms of art. Rivette's magnificent work has always been made with a joyful taste for telling tales, watching pretty women, listening to songs and stories, and sharing love and admiration for actors. Never, perhaps, was it designed in such a free and inventive way than at this moment, when he created *Celine and Julie Go Boating*'s narrative labyrinths with the film's actresses. Along with writer Eduardo di Gregorio, Celine (Juliet Berto), Julie (Dominique Labourier), Camille (Bulle Ogier), and Sophie (Marie-France Pisier) gave birth to this sunny inner travel, this diving into mirrors with a funny splash, a dance with specters so light. Ghosts and smiles followed the silent music, Jacques Rivette seemed to conduct without moving, and the world was spinning round—magic. **J-MF**

Angst essen Seele auf Rainer Werner Fassbinder, 1974
Ali: Fear Eats the Soul

Rainer Werner Fassbinder had the plot germ in mind for this film—the unlikely love affair between a sixty-something German cleaning lady in Munich and a Moroccan guest worker twenty years her junior—at least since *The American Soldier* (1970), in which the chambermaid Margarethe von Trotta recounts the story of Emmi and her husband Ali. What he produced with it in 1974 combines poignant melodrama and occasionally over-the-top social satire. *Ali: Fear Eats the Soul* takes its visual style from Fassbinder's patient camera work, lingering on motionless faces or retreating through a doorway to a respectful distance. The film's texture is created from the details of working-class life, including the songs played on the local jukebox, and its heart from the acting of Brigitte Mira as Emmi and El Hedi ben Salem as Ali.

It starts out as a joke. Ali, challenged by a German girl in the bar he frequents to dance with the old lady sitting alone at the table. He finds a woman kind enough to invite him in for coffee, and actually interested in the man hidden behind the all-purpose "Ali"—with which Germans replace unpronounceable (and to them irrelevant) Arab names. Both are lonely and the love affair blossoms against and despite a backdrop of near-universal mockery and hostility from neighbors and family. Emmi doesn't want to care, and pretends not to, but other people make up her world and she cannot help but care.

Gradually, though, external pressure lessens, not out of real acceptance but because everyone wants something from Emmi. Fassbinder falters when inner tensions mount in inverse proportion: the Emmi we have come to know would happily prepare couscous, not spurn it as foreign, and would never objectify Ali, showing off his muscles to her colleagues from work. But neither this nor the caricatured racist grocer and gossiping women (a homage to F.W. Murnau's great 1924 silent film *The Last Laugh*) detract from the indomitable and moving connection forged between these two people—and finding happiness with each other against all odds they are wise enough to know how lucky they are. **JW**

1974

West Germany (Autoren, Tango) 93m
Eastmancolor **Language** German
Producer Christian Hohoff
Screenplay Rainer Werner Fassbinder
Photography Jürgen Jürges **Music** Rainer Werner Fassbinder **Cast** Brigitte Mira, El Hedi ben Salem, Barbara Valentin, Irm Hermann, Elma Karlowa, Anita Bucher, Gusti Kreissl, Doris Mattes, Margit Symo, Katharina Herberg, Lilo Pempeit, Peter Gauhe, Marquard Bohm, Walter Sedlmayr, Hannes Gromball **Cannes Film Festival** Rainer Werner Fassbinder (FIPRESCI award, prize of the ecumenical jury, Golden Palm nomination)

"Technically flawless, deceptively simple, and avoiding excesses, it is about problems that are timely and timeless in implications."

Variety, 1974

ℹ

Fassbinder shot the film in just fifteen days, reportedly to fill time between making *Martha* and *Effi Briest*.

Barry Lyndon Stanley Kubrick, 1975

Perhaps Stanley Kubrick's most underrated film, *Barry Lyndon*—adapted from William Makepeace Thackeray's 1844 picaresque novel *The Memoirs of Barry Lyndon, Esq., As Told By Himself*—inhabits the eighteenth century the way *A Clockwork Orange* (1971) and *2001: A Space Odyssey* (1968) inhabit the future, with perfect sets, costumes, and cinematography trapping characters whose rises and falls are at once deeply tragic and absurdly comical.

Narrated in avuncular form by Michael Hordern, who replaces Thackeray's ironically self-serving first-person hero with wise third-person melancholia, the film follows the fortunes of Redmond Barry (Ryan O'Neal), a handsome Irish youth forced to flee his hometown after a duel with a cowardly English officer (Leonard Rossiter). Stripped of his small fortune by a deferential highwayman, Barry joins the British army and fights in the Seven Years' War, attempting a desertion that leads him into the Prussian army. A position as a spy on an exquisitely painted con man (Patrick Magee) leads to a life of gambling around the courts of Europe, and just before the intermission our hero achieves all he could want by marrying the wealthy, titled, beautiful widow Lady Lyndon (Marisa Berenson). A sign of Barry's willingness to humiliate himself for worldly advancement is that he takes his married name from his wife's titled first husband. However, Part Two reveals that Barry can no more be a clockwork orange than the protagonist of Kubrick's previous film, and his spendthrift ways, foolhardy pursuit of social advancement, and unwise treatment of his new family lead to several disasters, climaxing in another horrific (yet farcical) duel.

Shot by John Alcott almost entirely in the "magic hour," that point of the day when the light is mistily perfect, with innovative use of candlelight for interiors, *Barry Lyndon* looks ravishing, but the perfection of its images is matched by the inner turmoil of seemingly frozen characters. Kubrick is often accused of being unemotional, but his restraint here is all the more affecting, as when Barry is struck by the deaths of those close to him, his wife writhes into madness, or his stepson (Leon Vitali) vomits before he can stand his ground in a duel. **KN**

G.B. (Hawk, Peregrine) 184m Eastmancolor
Language English / German / French
Producer Stanley Kubrick, Bernard Williams
Screenplay Stanley Kubrick, from novel by William Makepeace Thackeray
Photography John Alcott **Music** Leonard Rosenman **Music** The Chieftains, Johann Sebastian Bach, Georg Friedrich Händel, Wolfgang Amadeus Mozart, Giovanni Paisiello, Franz Schubert, Frederick The Great, Antonio Vivaldi **Cast** Ryan O'Neal, Marisa Berenson, Patrick Magee, Hardy Krüger, Steven Berkoff, Gay Hamilton, Marie Kean, Belle, Diana Körner, Murray Melvin, Frank Middlemass, André Morell, Arthur O'Sullivan, Godfrey Quigley, Leonard Rossiter, Philip Stone **Oscars** Ken Adam, Roy Walker, Vernon Dixon (art direction), John Alcott (photography), Ulla-Britt Söderlund, Milena Canonero (costume), Leonard Rosenman (music) **Oscar nominations** Stanley Kubrick (best picture), Stanley Kubrick (director), Stanley Kubrick (screenplay)

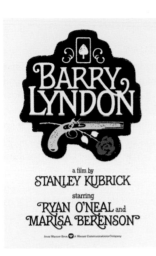

> *"I'm not sorry. And I'll not apologize. And I'd as soon go to Dublin as to hell."*
>
> **Redmond Barry
> (Ryan O'Neal)**

ℹ

Some of the costumes were genuine antiques, bought at auction by costume designer Milena Canonero.

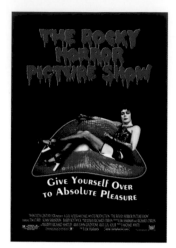

The Rocky Horror Picture Show Jim Sharman, 1975

Richard O'Brien's unusual stage musical was translated onto the big screen in 1975, and on its initial release it flopped. However, when a New York cinema began to show it at midnight screenings word soon spread about the odd spoof sci-fi/horror film. It became cult viewing and now holds the record for the longest theatrical run of any movie, having been shown in the same Munich, Germany cinema each week for more than twenty-seven years.

A very young Susan Sarandon and Barry Bostwick star as Janet and Brad, an innocent couple whose car breaks down on a stormy night forcing them to seek refuge in a nearby castle, unaware that it belongs to stocking-and-suspender-clad transvestite Frank N. Furter (Tim Curry, in a role he played on stage) and his Transylvanian pals, including sinister Riff Raff (Richard O'Brien) and Magenta (Patricia Quinn). Also living at the mansion are biker Eddie (Meat Loaf), a botched creation (think Frankenstein's monster) of Frank N. Furter's, and Rocky (Peter Hinwood), his buff and tanned improvement/replacement.

Narrated by "the Criminologist" (Charles Gray), the film is a glam rock celebration of sexuality as Frank N. Furter and his clan try to seduce the virginal Brad and Janet to the tune of memorable songs like "Touch-a Touch-a Touch Me," "Sweet Transvestite," and, of course, "Time Warp." The mixture of brazen sexuality, tongue-in-cheek humor, outrageous clothing, and double entendres are not quite like anything else ever committed to film. It is easy to see why the easy-to-remember songs and quotable dialogue have been such a hit with fans—the most devoted of whom dress up like the various characters, act out portions of the movie at screenings, and bring props for certain parts of the film (for example, they throw rice during the wedding scene). *The Rocky Horror Picture Show* may not be one to watch with Grandma, perhaps, but it's a terrific exercise in kitsch fun nonetheless. **JB**

G.B. (Fox) 100m Eastmancolor **Producer** Michael White **Screenplay** Jim Sharman, Richard O'Brien, from the play *The Rocky Horror Show* by Richard O'Brien **Photography** Peter Suschitzky, Richard O'Brien **Music** Richard O'Brien **Cast** Tim Curry, Susan Sarandon, Barry Bostwick, Richard O'Brien, Patricia Quinn, Nell Campbell, Jonathan Adams, Peter Hinwood, Meat Loaf, Charles Gray, Jeremy Newson, Hilary Labow, Perry Bedden, Christopher Biggins, Gaye Brown

"Do you think I made a mistake splitting his brain between the two of them?"

**Frank N. Furter
(Tim Curry)**

🛈

Mick Jagger reportedly expressed an interest in playing Frank N. Furter, and Steve Martin auditioned for Brad.

JEANNE DIELMAN
23, quai du Commerce
1080 Bruxelles

Un Film de Chantal Akerman
avec Jan Decorte, Henri Storck, Jacques Doniol-Valcroze, Yves Bical, Images de Babette Mangolte

Belgium / France (Paradise Unité Trois)
225m Color **Language** French
Producer Corinne Jénart, Evelyne Paul
Screenplay Chantal Akerman
Photography Babette Mangolte
Cast Chantal Akerman, Yves Bical,
Jan Decorte, Jacques Doniol-Valcroze,
Delphine Seyrig, Henri Storck

"I sometimes think I should have made it after many other films, at the end of my career. I remember saying to myself, how can I make a better film? But it was also exactly the film I had to make then."

Chantal Akerman, 2009

ℹ

The film wasn't released in the United States until 1983, and only became available on home video in 2009.

Jeanne Dielman, 23 quai du Commerce, 1080 Bruxelles Chantal Akerman, 1975

One of the key works of feminist filmmaking, not to mention one of the most important European films of the 1970s, Belgian director Chantal Akerman's minimalist masterwork *Jeanne Dielman* is admittedly demanding viewing, and this undoubtedly contributes to the film's marginalized status four decades later. The film offers a view of bourgeois ennui so spare and bleak that it makes *L'Avventura* (1960) look like a Frank Tashlin picture. With a degree of aesthetic rigor unusual even within that era's European auteur cinema, *Jeanne Dielman* is a three-hour documentation of alienation, and the methodical precision of Akerman's approach inarguably defeats all but the most patient of filmgoers.

The film chronicles three days in the life of its eponymous protagonist, a widowed homemaker who supports the comfortable existence she shares with her adolescent son through occasional prostitution. The bulk of the picture simply observes Jeanne (Delphine Seyrig) in the minutiae of her daily life. Using static long shots, Akerman allows the monotonous domestic tasks to unfold in real time. However, the film is largely a bravura conceptual exercise ultimately defined by its final two shots. It concludes as Jeanne, after servicing one of her clients, calmly stabs him to death with a pair of scissors. Then she sits serenely alone in the darkness of the family dining room. Whereas the writer-director's other films are similarly meditative and deliberate in their style of pacing, they are largely also mesmerizing and hypnotic experiments in narrative. This film, however, is arguably Akerman's coldest, most difficult and remote work, and many will be left wondering if the film's expansive running time was truly necessary to relate the slim character study.

Although the film is taxing, its rewards are great and often linked to the work's length. For one, Akerman's feminist thesis is conveyed with a cogent urgency as a result of her decision to depict Jeanne's life in such unsparing detail. It isn't enough for Akerman to suggest the tedium of her protagonist's selfless existence, but rather, by explicitly presenting the drab banality of her routine in real time, Akerman expertly conveys the stifling emptiness that ultimately drives Jeanne to her tragic final act.

The film also triumphs as a study in performance. Seyrig's perfectly realized portrayal provides subtle glimpses into Jeanne's psychological unraveling, with slight gradations of behavior that would likely be imperceptible if contained within a film of more compact structure and traditional dramatic emphasis. By the three-hour mark, the microscopic tightening of facial muscles and increased brusqueness of gesture that accompany the boiling of coffee or the overcooking of potatoes assume the heft of epic melodrama. It may be the kind of picture that's better to contemplate in theory rather than as a vehicle for viewing pleasure, but for the spectator attuned to Akerman's austere approach, her film remains, in many respects, an unforgettable achievement. **TCr**

1975

MIA TAINIA TOY ΘΟΔΩΡΟΥ ΑΓΓΕΛΟΠΟΥΛΟΥ

Greece (Papalios) 230m Color
Language Greek Producer Giorgis
Samiotis Screenplay Theo Angelopoulos
Photography Yorgos Arvanitis
Music Loukianos Kilaidonis Cast Eva
Kotamanidou, Aliki Georgouli, Stratos Pahis,
Maria Vassiliou, Petros Zarkadis, Kiriakos
Katrivanos, Yannis Firios, Nina
Papazaphiropoulou, Alekos Boubis, Kosta
Stiliaris, Greg Evaghelathos, Vangelis Kazan
Berlin International Film Festival Theo
Angelopoulos (Interfilm award, forum of
new cinema) Cannes Film Festival Theo
Angelopoulos (FIPRESCI award,
parallel sections)

"A masterpiece in a dozen different ways, The Traveling Players is so complex that a critic attempting to explain it is in the same quandary as the proverbial blind men discovering an elephant."

Henry Sheehan, critic, 1990

i

The troupe make a phantasmal reappearance in Angelopoulos's 1988 film, *Landscape in the Mist*.

O Thiassos   Theo Angelopoulos, 1975
The Traveling Players

Since the early 1970s, Greek director Theo Angelopoulos has tirelessly explored a landscape that has largely remained unseen in cinema. His subject is Greece—not the sunny land of the travel brochures, but a northern wintry one, situated in a Balkan geography and bounded both by its classical and modern past and by geographic borders. Formerly a critic for a socialist newspaper, Angelopoulos claimed that the colonels' Junta provided his subject matter and made him want to understand the historic roots of dictatorship. He made *The Traveling Players* more or less surreptitiously, telling the authorities that he was working on a version of the Orestes myth, set in the time of the German occupation. This is not inaccurate: in Angelopoulos's film, a troupe of traveling actors moves around Greece between 1939 and 1952, attempting to perform a nineteenth-century popular play, *Golfo the Shepherdess*. But they are always interrupted by history—from the German occupation, through the Civil War, to the rise of the Papagos government—and their attempts at performing are invariably interrupted by gunfire, flight, or death.

The members of the troupe themselves reincarnate figures from the *Oresteia*—Aegisthus (Vangelis Kazan) is a Nazi collaborator, Orestes (Petros Zarkadis) a communist partisan, Agamemnon (Stratos Pachis) the troupe's betrayed leader. They are less characters, conventionally speaking, than archetypes or even ghosts. Time and space in the film have much the same uncertain quality that character does, and a single shot can drift seamlessly from one period to another.

Angelopoulos is one of cinema's great landscape artists, a specialist in those moments where space turns into the stage for a vast dramatic panorama. But he is also a filmmaker of motion, who makes films about travel—on trains, cars, buses, on foot, and above all in the imagination. Claiming Orson Welles and Kenji Mizoguchi as his primary influences, Angelopoulos is known—together with his long-time cameraman Giorgos Arvanitis—as a specialist of flowing, precisely choreographed long takes. *The Traveling Players* is a prime example of that, a four-hour film containing only eighty shots. In the most distinctive of these, the camera and the actors move in such a way that time and space seem to turn inside out, to achieve a Möbius-strip elasticity.

Angelopoulos is a masterful director of crowd movements and set pieces: a characteristic shot that recurs throughout *The Traveling Players* has a group of figures walking through a town and emerging, as the camera tracks through the streets, in another year, perhaps crossing the path of another, larger grouping. His films suggest a theory of history as a sort of parade—at once funeral procession and political demonstration, continually crossing its own tracks, changing its direction and ideological colors. In *The Traveling Players*, movement itself becomes a formidably acute and supple tool for historical analysis. **JRom**

Monty Python and the Holy Grail
Terry Gilliam & Terry Jones, 1975

"You can't expect to wield supreme executive power just because some watery tart threw a sword at you."

Dennis (Michael Palin)

It all started with a TV show called *Monty Python's Flying Circus*, featuring the verbal and visual antics of a comedy team comprising five British wits—John Cleese, Michael Palin, Eric Idle, Terry Jones, and Graham Chapman—and an American named Terry Gilliam, whose cutout animations stitched the program's flyaway episodes together.

Produced by the British Broadcasting Corporation, which seemed a tad surprised by the anarchic nature of the capers it had unleashed, the show ran more or less continuously from 1969 to 1974. A shot at widescreen success seemed an obvious next step, especially because the compilation film *And Now for Something Completely Different* had been well received in 1971. These things combined led to the 1975 production of *Monty Python and the Holy Grail*, written by the whole Python crew and codirected by Gilliam and Jones.

The process of making the movie had aspects as darkly comical as a typical Python sketch. For one thing, the two directors didn't make a compatible duo; they had different visions of the movie's style, and Gilliam resented Jones's tendency to reduce the grandeur of his set designs with cramped camera setups. For another, Chapman's alcoholism was in full flower, sometimes rendering the star of the production—in the key role of King Arthur—unable to enunciate his lines while the camera rolled.

But hey, you can't keep a good Python down. The troupe triumphed over these problems as readily as they overcame the production's dauntingly low funding. Like much of Monty Python's best work, *Holy Grail* is a keen-minded parody with a political edge, debunking a foundational myth of Western power while playing Brechtian havoc with traditionalist ideas ranging from benevolent despotism to chivalric masculinity. And oh yes—it's a laugh riot, too. **DS**

i

Clicking coconuts were used to signify horses because the budget was too low to stretch to real ones.

Deewaar Yash Chopra, 1975
The Wall

India (Trimurti) 174m Color
Language Hindi Producer Gulshan Rai
Screenplay Javed Akhtar, Salim Khan
Photography Kay Gee Music Rahul Dev
Burman Cast Parveen Babi, Amitabh
Bachchan, Iftekhar, Shashi Kapoor, Satyen
Kappu, Yunus Parvez, Nirupa Roy,
Neetu Singh

Yash Chopra had his own production house where he established his trademark style of romance among the wealthy urban bourgeoisie. But *Deewaar*, produced by Gulshan Rai's Trimurti Films, is more of an action movie, driven by one of the best scripts in Hindi film history, written by the major screenwriters of the 1970s, Salim Khan and Javed Akhtar.

India's greatest-ever superstar, Amitabh Bachchan, plays the career-defining role of Vijay Verma—an innocent child whose family is wronged taking the law into his own hands in search of justice. Bombay provides a spectacular setting, with scenes shot in its docks, busy streets, and its glamorous hotels and mansions. One of the most famous dialogues in Hindi film history is the exchange between Vijay and his brother Ravi (Shashi Kapoor), who has become a policeman in his own search for justice. Vijay argues that he has riches and Ravi has nothing. Ravi's reply: "Mere paas maa hai" ("I have Mummy"). Vijay's relationship with a call girl, shown in unusually explicit detail, is overshadowed by his devotion to his mother. At the end of the film, this avowed atheist dies in his mother's arms in a temple, saying he could never sleep away from her, in one of the most celebrated and symbolic death scenes in the history of Hindi film. **RDw**

Dog Day Afternoon Sidney Lumet, 1975

U.S. (Artists Entertainment Complex) 124m
Technicolor Producer Martin Bregman,
Martin Elfand Screenplay Frank Pierson,
from article by P.F. Kluge and Thomas
Moore Photography Victor J. Kemper
Cast Penelope Allen, Al Pacino, Sully Boyar,
John Cazale, Beulah Garrick, Carol Kane,
Sandra Kazan, Marcia Jean Kurtz, Amy Levitt,
John Marriott, Estelle Omens, Gary Springer,
James Broderick, Charles Durning, Carmine
Foresta Oscars Martin Bregman, Martin
Elfand (best picture), Frank Pierson
(screenplay) Oscar nominations Sidney
Lumet (director), Al Pacino (actor), Chris
Sarandon (actor in support role),
Dede Allen (editing)

Sidney Lumet's taut film of the true story of a bank robbery turned hostage crisis in Brooklyn is as quintessentially New York as anything by Woody Allen or Martin Scorsese. Al Pacino and John Cazale play hapless would-be bankrobbers (Sonny and Sal respectively), who are forced through circumstances into an impossible situation. Before the robbers can make their getaway, the bank is surrounded by police and Sonny decides to hold the bank employees and try to negotiate an escape. Abandoned before the robbery by their third accomplice, Sonny and Sal are outnumbered by the increasingly unruly employees. As the situation continues and Sonny's loud discussions with the police over a bullhorn are heard throughout the streets, a crowd gathers and begins to cheer Sonny on. For a few brief moments during the social unrest of the early 1970s, Sonny becomes a counterculture hero.

Dog Day Afternoon moves between moments of hyperbolic absurdity and scenes of real tragedy. Perhaps the most poignant character in the film is Cazale's Sal, whose limitations are revealed by his answer, "Wyoming," when Sonny asks him what country he'd like to visit if they are able to get their demands met. The film captures the swirling passions of a moment in its characters' lives and in history, with a brilliant immediacy. **RH**

One Flew Over the Cuckoo's Nest
Milos Forman, 1975

A project of actor Kirk Douglas's for years (he owned the rights, but by the time the film made it to production he believed he was too old to star in it), *One Flew Over the Cuckoo's Nest* won his son Michael Douglas his first Oscar—not as an actor, but as the film's producer.

Based on Ken Kesey's best-selling novel, which he wrote after his experiences working in a California Veterans Hospital, the film is set in a state mental home where antiestablishment wiseguy Randle P. McMurphy (Jack Nicholson) is sent for rehabilitation. While there he falls under the watchful eye of the sadistic Nurse Ratched (Louise Fletcher, a role turned down by several top Hollywood actresses, including Jane Fonda, Anne Bancroft, Ellen Burstyn, and Faye Dunaway), and soon stirs up a rebellion against her with the help of some of the other patients.

A groundbreaking film that Kesey apparently never wanted to see—he was upset that the story isn't told from the perspective of Chief Bromden (Will Sampson), as in his book—*One Flew Over the Cuckoo's Nest* made Oscar-night history when it became only the second film to win five major awards. Each award was well deserved, with Czech director Forman (*The Loves of a Blonde* [1965], *The Firemen's Ball* [1967], and later *Amadeus* [1984] and *The People vs. Larry Flynt* [1996]) delivering a hypnotic and humanistic movie filled with eccentric characters (among the actors making their film debuts are Brad Dourif and Christopher Lloyd) and garnering a career-best performance from Fletcher. Nicholson, of course, is mesmerizing as the incarcerated but free-spirited McMurphy, and the scenes between him and Fletcher's contemptible Nurse Ratched are the most electric of this modern classic of American cinema. **JB**

1975

U.S. (Fantasy, N.V. Zvaluw) 133m Color **Producer** Michael Douglas, Saul Zaentz **Screenplay** Bo Goldman, Lawrence Hauben, from novel by Ken Kesey **Photography** Haskell Wexler **Music** Jack Nitzsche **Cast** Jack Nicholson, Louise Fletcher, William Redfield, Michael Berrayman, Peter Brocco, Dean R. Brooks, Alonzo Brown, Scatman Crothers, Mwako Cumbuka, Danny DeVito, William Duell, Josip Elic, Lan Fendors, Nathan George, Ken Kenny **Oscars** Saul Zaentz, Michael Douglas (best picture), Milos Forman (director), Lawrence Hauben, Bo Goldman (screenplay), Jack Nicholson (actor), Louise Fletcher (actress) **Oscar nominations** Brad Dourif (actor in support role), Haskell Wexler, Bill Butler (photography), Richard Chew, Lynzee Klingman, Sheldon Kahn (editing), Jack Nitzsche (music)

> *"Which one of you nuts has got any guts?"*
>
> **Randle P. McMurphy
> (Jack Nicholson)**

i

One Flew Over the Cuckoo's Nest was shot in sequence, except for the fishing scene, which was shot last.

Maynila: Sa mga kuko ng liwanag
Manila in the Claws of Brightness Lino Brocka, 1975

Philippines 125m Color **Producer** Severino Manotok **Screenplay** Clodualdo Del Mundo Jr. **Photography** Mike De Leon **Music** Max Jocson **Cast** Bembol Roco, Hilda Koronel, Lou Salvador, Princess Reymundo, Juling Bagabaldo

Lino Brocka's low-budget hit was a breakthrough for Filipino cinema and is still often regarded as the best Filipino film of all time. Julio (Bembol Roco), a poor fisherman from the country, comes to Manila to look for his lost love, Ligaya (Hilda Koronel). Working at a construction site, he encounters unfair labor practices, dangerous working conditions, and a range of attitudes and politics among his fellow workers. He also becomes involved with a male-prostitution ring. Finally, he finds that Ligaya has been recruited by a brothel. Julio's attempt to free her and himself from the hell of Manila ends in tragedy.

Manila in the Claws of Brightness captures the harshness of urban poverty through an assaulting soundtrack in which industrial noises, traffic sounds, and crowd hubbub are prominent, the crudeness of the recording and mixing contributing to an overwhelming tension, not lessened by the faux-Ennio Morricone songs and synthesizer music. The images of urban entrapment and pain are sharply contrasted with intermittent flashbacks to the lovers' coastal idyll, demonstrating Brocka's commitment to melodrama. The surprisingly strong quotient of homoeroticism anticipates Brocka's later *Macho Dancer* (1988). **CFu**

i

The film is based on a story written by Edgardo Reyes that was serialized in *Liwayway* magazine over 1966–67.

Faustrecht der Freiheit Rainer Werner Fassbinder, 1975
Fox and His Friends

This Rainer Werner Fassbinder classic has often been portrayed as the bisexual director-writer-actor's study in homophobic self-hatred. However, the plot of *Fox and His Friends*—about gay, low-life crook Franz "Fox" Biberkopf's (Fassbinder) self-delusion of being elevated to the land of the rich and beautiful after he wins 500,000 marks in a lottery and suddenly becomes the love interest of handsome bourgeois Eugen Thiess (Peter Chatel)—is less about sexuality than it is about class. At first Fox, with his impulsive energy, insatiable libido, and cunning street smarts, seems to have the upper hand in the relationship, putting him in stark contrast to Eugen and his circle of friends' lifeless world of etiquette. Gradually, however, his brute force is worn down by Eugen's condescending treatment, transference of guilt, and manipulation. Fox might be a successful predator in the world of hoodlums and whores on the street, but in the salon world of capitalists (even small-time ones) he is no match for cold-hearted vampires like Eugen.

Fassbinder makes Fox's fateful journey all the more painful by inviting us to witness the telling signs of his doom early on, the first and most fateful one being his infatuation with and reverence of Eugen's lifestyle. The film poignantly dramatizes the ways in which the mass media has marketed desire for social status and wealth to the postwar working class through commercials, glossy magazines, and soap operas. The unforgettable final shot of Fox deprived by Eugen of all his money as well as his human dignity, collapsing or maybe dying of a broken heart in the subway only to be robbed of his last belongings by some boys, has been criticized as a melodramatic gimmick. But Fox's fate bears a connection to other men named Franz—mainly played by Fassbinder—for instance in his *Love Is Colder Than Death* (1969). However, the most significant reference is, of course, to the tragic death of another Franz Biberkopf, the protagonist of the Alfred Döblin novel *Berlin Alexanderplatz* (adapted five years later for TV by the director)—one of the most powerful descriptions of death in a society where human value has a price tag. **MT**

West Germany (City, Tango) 123m
Eastmancolor **Language** German
Producer Rainer Werner Fassbinder
Screenplay Rainer Werner Fassbinder,
Christian Hohoff **Photography** Michael
Ballhaus **Music** Peer Raben **Cast** Peter
Chatel, Rainer Werner Fassbinder, Adrian
Hoven, Christiane Maybach, Hans Zander,
Kurt Raab, Rudolf Lenz, Karl Scheydt,
Peter Kern, Karl-Heinz Staudenmeyer,
Walter Sedlmayr, Bruce Low, Brigitte Mira,
Evelyn Künneke, Barbara Valentin

"Fassbinder's precision,
assured sense of milieu,
and cool but human
compassion for his
characters, make it
a work of brilliant
intelligence."

Time Out Film Guide

i

The film is partly based on the plight of Fassbinder's then lover Armin Meier, to whom the film is dedicated.

Nashville Robert Altman, 1975

U.S. (ABC, Paramount) 159m Metrocolor
Producer Robert Altman **Screenplay** Joan
Tewkesbury **Photography** Paul Lohmann
Music Arlene Barnett, Jonnie Barnett, Karen
Black, Ronee Blakley, Gary Busey, Keith
Carradine, Juan Grizzle, Allan F. Nicholls,
Dave Peel, Joe Raposo **Cast** David Arkin,
Barbara Baxley, Ned Beatty, Karen Black,
Ronee Blakley, Timothy Brown, Keith
Carradine, Geraldine Chaplin, Robert DoQui,
Shelley Duvall, Allen Garfield, Henry
Gibson, Scott Glenn, Jeff Goldblum,
Barbara Harris **Oscar** Keith Carradine (song)
Oscar nominations Robert Altman (best
picture), Robert Altman (director), Ronee
Blakley (actress in support role), Lily Tomlin
(actress in support role)

"Sure, it's only a movie. But after I saw it I felt more alive, I felt I understood more about people, I felt somehow wiser. It's that good . . ."

Roger Ebert, critic, 1975

i

Original footage was so long, it was almost released as two movies: *Nashville Red* and *Nashville Blue*.

Robert Altman's *Nashville* arrived at the intersection of two important periods in American history. It followed the combined scandals of Watergate and Vietnam, which diminished America's faith in its government and gave rise to a cynical national malaise, but preceded the country's bicentennial celebration, meant to honor the values and beliefs that gave birth to the United States. Altman recognized the hypocrisy of celebrating the roots of a faltering nation and in essence twisted the knife, setting his epic in the gaudy, populist heart of show business itself: *Nashville*, the home of country music.

With so much going on culturally, Altman tried to replicate that confusion cinematically. *Nashville* includes two dozen main characters and numerous storylines, all apparently colliding chaotically but actually controlled carefully by Altman's acute filmmaking instincts. Over the course of five days, a music festival and a political campaign cross paths (and cross fates), with Altman equating the folly of politics with the sleaze and dishonesty of the entertainment industry.

But populating Altman's mosaic is a richly drawn variety of characters, some blindly ambitious but others barely holding on in a world caving in around them. It's these smaller characters that stick out from the vast cast and rambling story, and you root for their success and happiness. But all of *Nashville*'s characters bob up and down like buoys in a sea of failure and denial. This effect is heightened by Altman's famous overlapping dialogue, which constantly shifts your attention to the least expected corners of the wide-screen frame and to that barely familiar face in the crowd, who may or may not play an important role in the story.

Instead of a straight narrative, Altman works with various themes, but he never stresses one over the other. Instead, he uses country music (written and performed by his actors) as his Greek chorus, directing the flow of the film with their songs of banal populism and passivity. By the time the film is over it is unclear exactly what *Nashville* is about, but there's no question something has been conveyed by its colorful characters. The film is a portrait of life during wartime, a fight for national identity at a time when things like that seemed to matter the least. **JKl**

1975

ALBERTO GRIMALDI

PIER PAOLO PASOLINI

SALÒ
O LE 120 GIORNATE DI SODOMA

PAOLO BONACELLI · GIORGIO CATALDI
UMBERTO P. QUINTAVALLE · ALDO VALLETTI
CATERINA BORATTO · ELSA DE' GIORGI
HÉLÈNE SURGÈRE · SONIA SAVIANGE
Regia di
PIER PAOLO PASOLINI

Italy / France (Artistes Associés, PEA)
117m Eastmancolor **Language** Italian
Producer Alberto De Stefanis, Antonio
Girasante, Alberto Grimaldi **Screenplay** Pier
Paolo Pasolini, Roland Barthes, Maurice
Blanchot, Sergio Citti, Pierre Klossowski,
from the novel *Salo ou les 120 Journées
de Sodome* by the Marquis de Sade
Photography Tonino Delli Colli **Music** Ennio
Morricone **Cast** Paolo Bonacelli, Giorgio
Cataldi, Umberto Paolo Quintavalle, Aldo
Valletti, Caterina Boratto, Hélène Surgère,
Sonia Saviange, Elsa De Giorgi, Ines
Pellegrini, Rinaldo Missaglia, Giuseppe
Patruno, Guido Galletti, Efisio Etzi, Claudio
Troccoli, Fabrizio Menichini

*"This may not be an
enjoyable experience
but it is definitely
an experience."*

Kim Newman,
Empire Magazine, **2001**

ℹ

Despite the film's grim subject,
actress Hélène Surgère said that the
mood on set was quite jovial.

Salò o le centoventi giornate di sodoma
Salò, or the 120 Days of Sodom Pier Paolo Pasolini, 1975

Salò is notionally based on *The 120 Days of Sodom*, a work by the
Marquis de Sade, who gave his name to the form of sexual perversion
that the film explores. Though the story makes many departures from
de Sade's work, it retains much of the spirit of it. De Sade's project was
in part political, one that satirized the established forces of the day, in
particular the Catholic church. Pasolini too was fervently anticlerical, but
relates *Salò* directly to Italian history.

The film is set in the short-lived Republic of Salò, where Mussolini
made a last stand at the end of World War II. Pasolini was caught up in
these events, and his brother was killed in Salò. In Pasolini's fantasy of
this wartime episode, four Fascist libertines have total power over a
group of attractive young captives of both sexes and subject them to a
series of sexual tortures and humiliations. These are presented by the
director in a series of bleakly formal scenes that are curiously devoid
of erotic passion. There is scant attempt at characterization; even the
libertines have little in the way of personality and seem to derive no
real pleasure from their debaucheries, whereas their victims are largely
anonymous, simply bodies to be abused and penetrated.

Pasolini's intent was to use the unbridled use of power, taken to the
ultimate of sexual degradation, as a metaphor for Fascism itself, seen as
a philosophy that worships power for its own sake. But there are other
messages. One libertine is identified as a bishop, and at one point two
of the victims are put through a form of marriage ceremony, though
the consummation is interrupted by the libertines, who interject their
own bodies into the coupling of the newlyweds. And in a particularly
notorious scene, a naked young woman is forced to eat excrement,
which Pasolini maintained was a metaphor for consumer capitalism and
its production of junk food.

The end of the film is an orgy of cruelty as victims are strangled
and scalped, and have their tongues cut out and their nipples burned.
All is set to the music of Carl Orff's *Carmina Burana*, which Pasolini
considered Fascist music, and a reading of the *Cantos* of Ezra Pound, the
American poet who supported Mussolini. Yet though the obscenities
the film presents have an undeniable power to shock, perhaps what is
ultimately most disturbing is the sense that by this point in his career
Pasolini had at best an ambiguous attitude toward the body and
sexuality. If the object of pornography is to excite sexual desire, *Salò*
would not fit the definition, because its effect, and presumably its
purpose, is to arouse disgust.

Shortly after this powerful and disturbing film was completed, and
before it was released, Pasolini was murdered. His film was prosecuted
or banned in many countries and has only recently become generally
available in Britain and the United States. **EB**

Cría cuervos Carlos Saura, 1975
Cria!

Spain (Elías Querejeta, Querejeta y Gárate, Elías) 110m Eastmancolor
Language Spanish **Producer** Carlos Saura **Screenplay** Carlos Saura
Photography Teodoro Escamilla **Music** Federico Mompou **Cast** Geraldine Chaplin, Mónica Randall, Florinda Chico, Ana Torrent, Héctor Alterio, Germán Cobos, Mirta Miller, Josefina Díaz, Conchita Pérez, Juan Sánchez Almendros, Mayte Sanchez
Cannes Film Festival Carlos Saura (grand prize of the jury), tied with *Die Marquise von O*, nomination (Golden Palm)

i

Geraldine Chaplin's voice as the adult Ana was dubbed by the Spanish actress Julieta Serrano.

"Raise ravens and they'll pluck out your eyes!" So goes the Spanish adage—equivalent perhaps to "You reap what you sow"—that gave Saura's best-loved film its title. Young Ana, played by the extraordinary Ana Torrent, awakes one night and goes downstairs; strange sounds seem to be emanating from her widowed father's bedroom. Suddenly a woman bursts out the door and flees the house. Her father, a Franco military man, is dead, and somehow Ana is sure she's to blame. After this haunting opening, *Cria!* becomes a chronicle of Ana and her two sisters as they negotiate the shoals of growing up, learning bit by bit what freedom might be.

Made literally as Franco lay dying, the film follows the metaphor of life under fascism as a kind of stunted childhood seen in several other Spanish movies of the period, yet handles it with a refreshing sensitivity and grace. Geraldine Chaplin, Saura's constant muse in these years, is wonderful in a dual role as Ana's cancer-stricken mother and the adult Ana reflecting back on all these events. Her assured presence as the adult Ana seems to imply that fascism is already a thing of the past, something painfully endured but in the end conquered. **RP**

Picnic at Hanging Rock Peter Weir, 1975

Australia (AFC, BEF, McElroy & McElroy, SAFC) 115m Eastmancolor **Producer** A. John Graves, Patricia Lovell, Hal McElroy, Jim McElroy **Screenplay** Cliff Green, from novel by Joan Lindsay **Photography** Russell Boyd **Music** Bruce Smeaton **Cast** Rachel Roberts, Vivean Gray, Helen Morse, Kirsty Child, Tony Llewellyn-Jones, Jacki Weaver, Frank Gunnell, Anne-Louise Lambert, Karen Robson, Jane Vallis, Christine Schuler, Margaret Nelson, Ingrid Mason, Jenny Lovell, Janet Murray

A ghost story without the ghosts, a puzzle without a solution, and a story of sexual repression without the sex, Peter Weir's enigmatic *Picnic at Hanging Rock* remains maddeningly elliptical.

The story itself is deceptively simple: a group of students from an all-girl Australian prep school go on a picnic in the Outback. But following a delirious hike to the top of the titular landmark, three girls and a teacher vanish, leaving behind no clues and the growing suspicion that something more dreadful than mere foul play was at work that day. With his sharp understanding that fear of the unknown often trumps the usual bogeymen, Weir bravely refuses to clarify the many lingering mysteries at the center of his brilliant film. When one student does show up, her mind is a complete blank.

As depicted, the excursion itself plays out like a fever dream or hallucination, a wobbly mirage provoked by the shimmering desert heat, and the remainder of the film drips with queasy menace even as Weir avoids enlisting overly familiar means of ratcheting up the suspense. One conspicuous exception is Bruce Smeaton's haunting, otherworldly electronic score, humming like a call from some other dimension. **JKl**

1975

India Song Marguerite Duras, 1975

France (Armorial, Sunchild) 120m Eastmancolor **Language** French **Producer** Stéphane Tchalgadjieff **Screenplay** Marguerite Duras **Photography** Bruno Nuytten **Music** Carlos d'Alessio **Cast** Delphine Seyrig, Michael Lonsdale, Claude Mann, Mathieu Carrière, Didier Flamand, Vernon Dobtcheff, Claude Juan, Satasinh Manila, Nicole Hiss, Monique Simonet, Viviane Forrester, Dionys Mascolo, Marguerite Duras, Françoise Lebrun, Benoît Jacquot

There is no room for middle ground when viewing the films of Marguerite Duras—one either finds the work to be hypnotically seductive or maddeningly pretentious, which is not to imply that those two reactions are mutually exclusive. Her films are largely an extension of her literature, and viewers attuned to experimental European filmmaking of the 1960s and 1970s will likely recognize affinities with the cinema of directors Alain Resnais (a Duras collaborator) and Alain Robbe-Grillet, both thematically (explorations of the effects that time's passing has on the memory and identity of enigmatic characters) and formally (a languorous tone aided by slow tracking shots).

India Song is Duras's most renowned achievement, a trance-inducing evocation of 1937 Calcutta (filmed entirely near Paris), with Delphine Seyrig as the wealthy wife of a French diplomat, collapsing under the weight of boredom and mental distress. Duras has crafted an elliptical dream poem rather than a linear narrative, but *India Song* is most fascinating in its use of language and sound as a contrast to the images on display. She creates aural disorientation through jarring off-screen cries and shrieks, overlapping and discordant dialogue, and deceptively displaced narration, providing a jagged counterpoint to the somnolent visuals.

Duras's follow-up to this film, *Son nom de venise dans Calcutta Désert* (1976), uses *India Song*'s complete soundtrack, accompanied by different visuals. *India Song* is demanding but fascinating viewing. **TCr**

The terrifying motion picture from the terrifying No. 1 best seller.

JAWS

ROBERT
SHAW
ROY   RICHARD
SCHEIDER   DREYFUSS

JAWS

Co-starring LORRAINE GARY · MURRAY HAMILTON · A ZANUCK/BROWN PRODUCTION
Screenplay by PETER BENCHLEY and CARL GOTTLIEB · Based on the novel by PETER BENCHLEY · Music by JOHN WILLIAMS
Directed by STEVEN SPIELBERG · Produced by RICHARD D. ZANUCK and DAVID BROWN · A UNIVERSAL PICTURE ·
TECHNICOLOR® PANAVISION® PG

U.S. (Universal, Zanuck/Brown) 124m
Technicolor **Producer** David Brown, Richard
D. Zanuck **Screenplay** Carl Gottlieb, from
novel by Peter Benchley **Photography** Bill
Butler **Music** John Williams **Cast** Roy
Scheider, Robert Shaw, Richard Dreyfuss,
Lorraine Gary, Murray Hamilton, Carl
Gottlieb, Jeffrey Kramer, Susan Backlinie,
Jonathan Filley, Ted Grossman, Chris Rebello,
Jay Mello, Lee Fierro, Jeffrey Voorhees, Craig
Kingsbury **Oscars** Verna Fields (editing),
John Williams (music), Robert L. Hoyt, Roger
Heman Jr., Earl Mabery, John R. Carter
(sound) **Oscar nomination** Richard D.
Zanuck, David Brown (best picture)

> *"I was too young to know I was being foolhardy when I demanded that we shoot the film in the Atlantic Ocean and not in a North Hollywood tank."*
>
> **Steven Spielberg, 2011**

ℹ️

The shark was never tested in water
before filming, and the first time it
was put in the ocean it sank.

Jaws Steven Spielberg, 1975

Throughout his career, be it with Michael Crichton's monster adventure *Jurassic Park* (1993) or Thomas Keneally's Holocaust drama *Schindler's List* (1993), Steven Spielberg has been adept at translating novels onto the screen—and none with greater effect than his first hit movie, an adaptation of Peter Benchley's *Jaws*.

Essentially a piece of pulp fiction about a killer shark terrorizing the East Coast resort of Amity Island, Spielberg (with the help of a lot of studio marketing money) created the first big summer "event" movie. Word of mouth was built up by advertising before the film was even released, and lines grew around the block once the movie came out and people saw it, told their friends, and then went to see it again.

One of the many joys of this adventure thriller is the cast. Roy Scheider is perfect as the Amity cop who first realizes that chewed torsos washing up on the local beach may be a good reason to keep bathers out of the water, but who fails to convince the mayor that there is anything to worry about. Luckily he has expert Matt Hooper (Richard Dreyfuss) and old sea dog Quint (the wonderful Robert Shaw) on his side, and soon it's three men against the aquatic munching machine, leading to a Captain Ahab/Moby Dick–style showdown that's just as tense the tenth time you watch it as the first.

It's Spielberg, of course, who deserves the credit for being the man who made a whole generation of people think twice before dipping their big toe in the sea. Playing on our fear of the unknown, he builds up the tension by slowly revealing the shark to the strains of John Williams's unforgettable score, partly to keep us on the edge of our seats and partly because he knew the rubber shark (named Bruce) used in the film looked more like the real thing the less we saw of it. His Hitchcockian sleights of hand clearly worked, as this cleverly scripted (by Benchley and Carl Gottlieb, while Shaw's infamous "Indianapolis" speech has been attributed to John Milius), tautly directed tale remains the scariest ocean-set movie ever made. **JB**

The Man Who Fell to Earth Nicolas Roeg, 1976

G.B. (British Lion) 140m Color
Producer Michael Deeley, Barry Spikings
Screenplay Paul Mayersberg, from the novel
by Walter Tevis Photography Anthony B.
Richmond Music John Phillips, Stomu
Yamashta Cast David Bowie, Rip Torn,
Candy Clark, Buck Henry, Bernie Casey,
Jackson D. Kane, Rick Riccardo, Tony Mascia,
Linda Hutton, Hilary Holland, Adrienne
Larussa, Lilybelle Crawford, Richard
Breeding, Albert Nelson, Peter Prouse
Berlin International Film Festival Nicolas
Roeg (Golden Bear nomination)

𝑖

Thomas Jerome Newton is named
after Isaac Newton, the English
scientist who discovered gravity.

An adaptation of the Walter Tevis novel of the same name, Nicholas Roeg's 1976 science-fiction story was and is often misunderstood. Directed in Roeg's trademark nervy style, *The Man Who Fell to Earth* is a visually challenging tale of an alien's doomed visit to our planet. Told in cross-edits with unexplained chronological and location jumps, this ultrasophisticated take on American culture, love, and homesickness was also a major technical achievement.

Early on, Peter O'Toole was considered for the role of the alien Thomas Jerome Newton, but the part ultimately went to David Bowie, an internationally renowned pop star with limited acting experience. Newton comes to earth seeking water for his dying world, and along the way becomes immensely wealthy by introducing lucrative new technologies to our world. Newton falls prey to human vices, alcohol in particular, and to human pursuers; his mission fails, the years roll away, and the vulnerable alien is milked for his advanced technical knowledge and then abandoned.

The later success of *Memento* (2000) and *Mulholland Dr.* (2001), two films that similarly displace time and place, show that *The Man Who Fell to Earth* was not only ahead of its time but also ahead of its audience. **KK**

All the President's Men Alan J. Pakula, 1976

U.S. (Warner Bros, Wildwood) 138m
Technicolor **Producer** Walter Coblenz
Screenplay William Goldman, from book by
Carl Bernstein and Bob Woodward
Photography Gordon Willis **Music** David
Shire **Cast** Dustin Hoffman, Robert Redford,
Jack Warden, Martin Balsam, Hal Holbrook,
Jason Robards, Jane Alexander, Meredith
Baxter, Ned Beatty, Stephen Collins, Penny
Fuller, John McMartin, Robert Walden, Frank
Wills, F. Murray Abraham **Oscars** Alan J.
Pakula (director), William Goldman
(screenplay), Jason Robards (actor in support
role), George Jenkins, George Gaines (art
direction), Arthur Piantadosi, Les Fresholtz,
Rick Alexander, James E. Webb (sound)
Oscar nominations Walter Coblenz
(best picture), Jane Alexander (actress in
support role), Robert L. Wolfe (editing)

ℹ

Frank Wills, the security guard who
discovered the break-in at the
Watergate complex, plays himself.

The ultimate in investigative journalism pictures, the scoop of the
century—as written by William Goldman and directed by Alan J. Pakula—
continually pleases for the entertaining intelligence at work. It is among
the most gripping, deft, and utterly compelling of thrillers, and this despite
being based on well-known facts whose conclusion is never in doubt.

Following a break-in at the Watergate complex, *Washington Post*
newspaper reporter Bob Woodward (Robert Redford) attends the low-
key arraignment of the burglars and sniffs a mystery. Defying men in the
corridors of power, with the support of editor Ben Bradlee (Jason Robards,
winning the first of his two consecutive Oscars) and the melodramatic
tipster Deep Throat (Hal Holbrook), Woodward and his thrusting colleague
Carl Bernstein (Dustin Hoffman) doggedly get the goods on dirty tricks
electioneering and its shameful cover-up conspiracy, ultimately leading
them all the way to the White House and the ignominious resignation of
President Richard Nixon. A satirist couldn't have concocted better villains
than CREEP (The Committee to Re-Elect the President) and its schemers
in this sorry story turned into a hopeful, heroic crusade, the real
Woodward and Bernstein benefiting ever after from their identification
with the decidedly more lustrous Redford and Hoffman. **AE**

The Outlaw Josey Wales Clint Eastwood, 1976

U.S. (Malpaso) 135m Color
Producer Robert Daley **Screenplay** Sonia
Chernus, Philip Kaufman, from the novel
Gone to Texas by Forrest Carter
Photography Bruce Surtees **Music** Jerry
Fielding **Cast** Clint Eastwood, Chief Dan
George, Sondra Locke, Bill McKinney, John
Vernon, Paula Trueman, Sam Bottoms,
Geraldine Keams, Woodrow Parfrey, Joyce
Jameson, Sheb Wooley, Royal Dano,
Matt Clark, John Verros, Will Sampson
Oscar nomination Jerry Fielding (music)

A truly great Western, and probably director-star Clint Eastwood's all-round best picture. Josey Wales is the typical Eastwood character—a scarred, vengeance-crazed, super-skilled die-hard gunman who refuses to surrender after the Civil War is over and heads for Texas with hordes of scurvy bounty killers on his trail. Though the film racks up a genocidal body count as Josey guns down assorted human filth, it develops a surprising warm streak as the grim hero gradually loses his loner status by collecting a retinue of waifs and strays who finally form a community in the West that enables him to set aside his guns and settle down.

The most moving moment in *The Outlaw Josey Wales* comes when Josey faces an Indian chief (Will Sampson) set on massacring him, and—delivering the longest speech Eastwood has ever learned—makes a plea to set aside murder and get on with life. This speech not only constitutes a personal change on the part of Eastwood the star but also represents a major turning point in the Western genre as a whole. Chief Dan George is wonderful as the hero's wry Indian sidekick, and even the often irritating Sondra Locke is winning as a pioneer lass. *Unforgiven* (1992), in which a reformed Clint becomes a killer again, is a despairing thematic sequel. **KN**

The Killing of a Chinese Bookie
John Cassavetes, 1976

U.S. (John Cassavetes) 108m Color
Producer Al Ruban **Screenplay** John
Cassavetes **Photography** Mitch Breit, Al
Ruban **Music** Bo Harwood **Cast** Ben
Gazzara, Timothy Carey, Seymour Cassel,
Robert Phillips, Alice Friedland, Soto Joe
Hugh, Al Ruban, Azizi Johari, Virginia
Carrington, Meade Roberts

John Cassavetes's first crime thriller, a postnoir masterpiece, failed miserably at the box office when first released, and a recut, shorter version released two years later didn't fare much better. The first, longer, and in some ways better of the two versions is easier to follow, despite reports that—or maybe because—Cassavetes had less to do with the editing (though he certainly approved it). A personal, deeply felt character study rather than a routine action picture, *The Killing of a Chinese Bookie* follows Cosmo Vitelli (Ben Gazzara at his best), the charismatic owner of an Los Angeles strip joint—simultaneously a jerk and a saint—who recklessly gambles his way into debt and has to bump off a Chinese bookie to settle his accounts.

In many respects the film serves as a personal testament. What makes the tragicomic character of Cosmo so moving is its alter-ego relation to the filmmaker—the proud impresario and father figure of a tattered showbiz collective (read Cassavetes's actors and filmmaking crew) who must compromise his ethics to keep his little family afloat (read Cassavetes's career as a Hollywood actor). Peter Bogdanovich used Gazzara in a similar part in *Saint Jack* (1979), but as good as that film is, it doesn't catch the exquisite warmth and delicacy of feeling of Cassavetes's doom-ridden comedy drama. **JRos**

Network Sidney Lumet, 1976

U.S. (MGM, United Artists) 120m
Metrocolor **Producer** Fred C. Caruso, Howard
Gottfried **Screenplay** Paddy Chayefsky
Photography Owen Roizman **Music** Elliot
Lawrence **Cast** Faye Dunaway, William
Holden, Peter Finch, Robert Duvall, Wesley
Addy, Ned Beatty, Arthur Burghardt, Bill
Burrows, John Carpenter, Jordan Charney,
Kathy Cronkite, Ed Crowley, Jerome Dempsey,
Conchata Ferrell, Gene Gross **Oscars** Paddy
Chayefsky (screenplay), Peter Finch (actor),
Faye Dunaway (actress), Beatrice Straight
(actress in support role) **Oscar nominations**
Howard Gottfried (best picture), Sidney
Lumet (director), William Holden (actor), Ned
Beatty (actor in support role), Owen Roizman
(photography), Alan Heim (editing)

> "Network *can be faulted
> both for going too far and
> not far enough, but it's
> also something that very
> few commercial films are
> these days. It's alive.*"
>
> **Vincent Canby,**
> *The New York Times, 1976*

ℹ

Beatrice Straight's performance is the
briefest one ever to win an Oscar, at
just five minutes and forty seconds.

Do television producers and executives bear any responsibility to the millions of people glued to the boob tube, or are they merely beholden to the bottom line? Sidney Lumet's cynical treatise on the moral and ethical decline of television hinges on the somewhat naive belief that things were ever run differently. Even so, *Network* remains a biting satire of the lurid lengths television will go to appease its corporate overseers as well as the complicity of its vast, passive viewership.

In *Network*, ratings rule, and vice president of programming Diana Christensen (Faye Dunaway) will do anything to boost the numbers. That anything includes putting the messianic blathering of a suicidal Howard Beale (Peter Finch, subsequently the first posthumous recipient of an Academy Award for acting) on prime time, despite the delusional bent of his paranoid rants. His line, "I'm mad as hell and I'm not going to take it anymore," becomes his mantra and the mantra of his audience, yet Christensen doesn't see the danger of her runaway success. Max Schumacher (William Holden), head of the nightly news, does, and he grows increasingly disaffected when he sees what Christensen and fellow executive Frank Hackett (Robert Duvall) are doing to his profession.

Network could have come across as hypocritical and patronizing had Sidney Lumet and writer Paddy Chayefsky not done such a sharp job of depicting the world of television as a particularly sleazy and destructive social parasite. They keep the bitter, desperate acts and darkly comic perversities coming at such a brisk clip that you barely realize the film is a damning portrayal of not just the television providers but us, the compulsive television viewers. It's enough to make you want to unplug your set and toss it out into the street, but one of the film's major points is that we can't. The sensationalism and tawdriness of TV is exactly what keeps us coming back to it: it's all about the numbers, which is what we are. **JKl**

Carrie Brian De Palma, 1976

U.S. (Redbank) 98m Color
Producer Brian De Palma, Paul Monash
Screenplay Lawrence D. Cohen, from novel
by Stephen King **Photography** Mario Tosi
Music Pino Donaggio **Cast** Sissy Spacek,
Piper Laurie, Amy Irving, William Katt, Betty
Buckley, Nancy Allen, John Travolta, P.J. Soles,
Priscilla Pointer, Sydney Lassick, Stefan
Gierasch, Michael Talbott, Doug Cox, Harry
Gold, Noelle North **Oscar nominations** Sissy
Spacek (actress), Piper Laurie (actress in
support role)

By the mid-1970s, Brian De Palma had already spent over a decade honing his diverse influences, including Alfred Hitchcock, rock music, and political satire. But *Carrie* marked his breakthrough. It is an operatic horror melodrama blending the family gothic, supernaturalism, and teen movie. It remains the cinema's best adaptation of a Stephen King novel.

The film inaugurated De Palma's penchant for surprise switches between fantasy and reality, as in the opening, which segues from a soft-core porn fantasia of girls showering to the fact of Carrie's menstruation—the first sign of "otherness" that will set her apart as a monster from her small-minded community.

All the oppression that Carrie suffers both at home (with her religious fanatic mother played by Piper Laurie) and at school creates a smoldering tension that takes the form of telekinetic power. We watch with ambivalence as Carrie's revenge fantasies cross the line into uncontrolled mass murder in the climactic prom scene (a De Palma tour de force).

Sissy Spacek is astonishing in the title role. Her face and body contort like a living special effect to express the unbearable contradictions of Carrie's experience, as well as the character's startling passage from wallflower to Queen of Death. **AM**

i

The name of the high school is Bates High, a reference to Norman Bates from Hitchcock's *Psycho* (1960).

The 20th Anniversary Presentation

Newly Restored Picture
First Time Anywhere in True Stereo

COLUMBIA PICTURES
ROBERT DE NIRO
TAXI DRIVER
A BILL/PHILLIPS Production of a MARTIN SCORSESE Film

JODIE FOSTER ALBERT BROOKS as "Tom" HARVEY KEITEL
LEONARD HARRIS PETER BOYLE as "Wizard" and
CYBILL SHEPHERD as "Betsy"

Written by PAUL SCHRADER Music BERNARD HERRMANN Produced by MICHAEL PHILLIPS

U.S. (Bill/Phillips, Italo/Judeo, Columbia)
113m Metrocolor **Producer** Julia Phillips,
Michael Phillips **Screenplay** Paul Schrader
Photography Michael Chapman
Music Bernard Herrmann **Cast** Robert De
Niro, Cybill Shepherd, Peter Boyle, Jodie
Foster, Harvey Keitel, Leonard Harris, Albert
Brooks, Diahnne Abbott, Frank Adu, Victor
Argo, Gino Ardito, Garth Avery, Harry Cohn,
Copper Cunningham, Brenda Dickson-
Weinberg **Oscar nominations** Michael
Phillips, Julia Phillips (best picture), Robert
De Niro (actor), Jodie Foster (actress in
support role), Bernard Herrmann (music)
Cannes Film Festival Martin Scorsese
(Golden Palm)

"I don't believe that one should devote his life to morbid self-attention. I believe that one should become a person like other people."

**Travis Bickle
(Robert De Niro)**

i

The scene where Travis Bickle is talking to himself in the mirror was completely ad-libbed by De Niro.

Taxi Driver Martin Scorsese, 1976

"Some day a real rain will come and wash all this scum off the street." So mutters tormented taxi driver malcontent Travis Bickle, played with maximum intensity by Robert De Niro in the first of his lauded lead turns for Martin Scorsese. Bickle's job shuttling back and forth across New York City—"anytime, anywhere," he boasts—provides him an insomniac's view of the city's underbelly, all those things on dark backstreets that most people never witness. But he's become so inured to the world around him that he feels numb, invisible, and ultimately impotent.

Yet Bickle is not so much outraged at the signs of social and physical decay around him as he is frustrated that he no longer knows anything else. He's also conflicted, attracted to the very things he purports to despise. Sick of himself and what he sees, he embarks on a final, desperate quest to reintegrate himself into society. But in Paul Schrader's bleak, hell-on-earth script, there's no way out. Bickle is already too far gone.

Bickle's descent is at first painful to watch, then nerve-racking and ultimately pitiful. He begins by wooing beautiful campaign aid Betsy (Cybill Shepherd), and when his awkward romantic advances are inevitably rebuffed, his alienation grows more intense. After trying to rejoin society, Bickle's next goal is to destroy it, beginning with the planned assassination of a popular presidential candidate. When this plan also fails he then tries to redeem society, with the suicide-mission rescue of an underage prostitute (Jodie Foster) from her abusive pimp.

Portraits of urban malaise and anomie don't come any darker, bleaker, or more claustrophobic than *Taxi Driver*. The film has some noirish elements—Bickle's voice-over, Bernard Herrmann's haunting, jazzy score—but veers sharply when it comes to the actual storytelling. *Taxi Driver* proceeds like a film noir told from the perspective of an anonymous stranger standing at the corner of a murder scene, peering over the police tape at the shrouded body splayed out on the street. What's going through that person's head? How will he react when confronted with such a vivid display of violence?

Scorsese, Schrader, and De Niro seem to be asking that of us as well. For the film's duration we're stuck viewing the city from Bickle's relentlessly isolated perspective, with few peripheral glimmers of hope taking us out of his deranged head. He's Dostoyevsky's *Underground Man* surfacing with a gun and a death wish, a vigilante antihero with a hands-on approach to cleaning up the city. "Here is a man who would not take it anymore," he announces triumphantly. "A man who stood up against the scum, the cunts, the dogs, the filth, the shit. Here is a man who stood up."

But is this what we want? In an ironic ends-justifying-the-means twist, Bickle is ultimately praised as a crusading hero, and it's hard to say if Bickle's inadvertent triumph is actually a tragedy. Because the film has done such a successful job wobbling the moral compass, we're left desperately grappling for impossible answers. **JKl**

1976

His whole life was a million-to-one shot.

ROCKY

Rocky John G. Avildsen, 1976

Short on brains, long on brawn—and heart. John G. Avildsen's *Rocky* catapulted the floundering career of Sylvester Stallone into the stratosphere. At the same time, it reaped unprecedented box-office sales, established a movie franchise, and landed a one-two punch of jock stereotypes as rich with caricature today as they were riveting performances in 1976.

The story centers on Rocky Balboa (Stallone), a boxer beyond his prime. He falls in love with Adrian (Talia Shire), the sister of his friend Paulie (Burt Young), and then works to earn the respect of his trainer Mickey (Burgess Meredith). On the receiving end of a publicity stunt, he eventually gets a chance to unseat Apollo Creed (Carl Weathers), the heavyweight boxing champion of the world.

Scored with Bill Conti's pulsing trumpet blasts and percussive rumble, *Rocky* is an immensely entertaining drama about struggling for satisfaction in an indifferent world. As the combined story work of former Muhammad Ali opponent Chuck Wepner and "Italian Stallion" Sylvester Stallone, the now famous actor-writer proved versatile and tenacious. Writing the script, he connected its sale to his participation in the lead role, despite being virtually unknown at the time. Desperate or inspired bid, he hit a grand slam and became one of Hollywood's biggest superstars.

The film is often overlooked as schmaltz, especially considering Stallone's subsequent career, yet *Rocky* lovingly details the white working class. Rocky, Paulie, Adrian, and Mickey respectively work as a debt collector, meat packer, pet store clerk, and gym proprietor; the only upward mobility each has are wishes and dreams. This "biopic" returns to a world of folklore where underdogs get their well-deserved chance after working hard.

Important in *Rocky* are the values of honor and courage, so often questioned in movies throughout the late 1960s and early 1970s. Such reassurance was well received, if gross receipts are any indication, and Avildsen's film walked off with Best Picture honors at the Academy Awards to make it one for the record books. **GC-Q**

U.S. (Chartoff-Winkler) 119m Technicolor **Producer** Robert Chartoff, Irwin Winkler **Screenplay** Sylvester Stallone **Photography** James Crabe **Music** Bill Conti **Cast** Sylvester Stallone, Talia Shire, Burt Young, Carl Weathers, Burgess Meredith, Thayer David, Joe Spinell, Jimmy Gambina, Bill Baldwin Sr., Al Silvani, George Memmoli, Jodi Letizia, Diana Lewis, George O'Hanlon, Larry Carroll **Oscars** Irwin Winkler, Robert Chartoff (best picture), John G. Avildsen (director), Richard Halsey, Scott Conrad (editing) **Oscar nominations** Sylvester Stallone (screenplay), Sylvester Stallone (actor), Burt Young (actor in support role), Burgess Meredith (actor in support role), Talia Shire (actress), Bill Conti, Carol Connors, Ayn Robbins (song), Harry W. Tetrick, William L. McCaughey, Lyle J. Burbridge, Bud Alper (sound)

"I don't look at Rocky *as a boxing movie. It was a love story. That's why I think it worked."*

Sylvester Stallone, 2012

🛈

Parts of the famous scene where Rocky runs up the stairs in training are played backward.

1976

Ai no corrida Nagisa Oshima, 1976
In the Realm of the Senses

Japan / France (Argos, Oshima, Shibata) 105m Eastmancolor **Language** Japanese **Producer** Anatole Dauman **Screenplay** Nagisa Oshima **Photography** Hideo Itoh **Music** Minoru Miki **Cast** Tatsuya Fuji, Eiko Matsuda, Aoi Nakajima, Yasuko Matsui, Meika Seri, Kanae Kobayashi, Taiji Tonoyama, Kyôji Kokonoe, Naomi Shiraishi, Shinkichi Noda, Komikichi Hori, Kikuhei Matsunoya, Akiko Koyama, Yuriko Azuma, Rei Minami

Japan, 1936. A young prostitute, Sada (Eiko Matsuda), begins an affair with Kichi-zo (Tatsuya Fuji), the husband of the brothel madam. The relationship is intense and highly physical. They have sex in a series of explicit scenes, often watched by third parties: geishas, serving women, other prostitutes. They play sex games, Sada putting items of food in her vagina before feeding them to her lover, and encouraging Kichi-zo to have sex with other partners, including an old woman who comes to sing for them. But Sada eventually grows jealous of Kichi-zo's continuing sexual relations with his wife, and threatens to cut off his penis. They begin to play asphyxiation games during sexual intercourse, and at last, with his encouragement, Sada strangles her lover, then castrates him.

Oshima's film achieves an extraordinary level of erotic intimacy and physical frankness. For the first time in a picture not intended for the pornographic circuit there are frequent shots of the erect male penis and scenes of fellatio. But Oshima also manages to convince us that this story of crazy love (*amour fou*) is a true manifestation of passion, taken to the ultimate extreme. The elegance of the director's mise-en-scène is a cool counterpoint to the sexual frenzy of the lovers. **EB**

1977

Voskhozhdeniye Larisa Shepitko, 1977
Ascent

U.S.S.R. (Mosfilm) 111m BW **Language** Russian **Screenplay** Yuri Klepikov, Larisa Shepitko, from the novel *Sotnikov* by Vasili Bykov **Photography** Vladimir Chukhnov, Pavel Lebeshev **Music** Alfred Shnitke **Cast** Boris Plotnikov, Vladimir Gostyukhin, Sergei Yakovlev, Lyudmila Polyakova, Viktoriya Goldentul, Anatoli Solonitsyn, Mariya Vinogradova, Nikolai Sektimenko **Berlin International Film Festival** Larisa Shepitko (FIPRESCI award, Golden Bear, Interfilm award—special mention, OCIC award)

In 1942, Russian partisans and peasants run afoul of German invaders and Russian collaborators. The style Lariso Shepitko adopts for *Ascent* seems at first harsh, unadorned, and off-putting: flat lighting, shallow focus, jarring rhythms. Much of the action takes place in snowy landscapes in which the characters are relentlessly exposed and overlit. The visual flatness matches Shepitko's approach to the characters, who are less introduced than thrust before us. Although it attends to the details of faces and captures with special vividness the nervous expressiveness of eyes, the film avoids psychological depth in its characterizations. The three main characters exist less as fully realized individuals than as the starkly drawn symbolic figures of a morality play: the intellectual, self-sacrificing partisan Sotnikov (Boris Plotnikov); his frightened, wavering comrade (Vladimir Gostyukhin); and their Satanic interrogator (played by Tarkovsky regular Anatoli Solonitsyn).

The intensity of Shepitko's film, which culminates in a feverish and protracted calvary, is heightened through elemental imagery (fire, snow, steam, wood, metal), Alfred Shnitke's shimmering, harrowing score, and Vladimir Chukhnov's lighting, which etherealizes an experience that would otherwise have been oppressive and hopeless. *Ascent* is one of the most powerful of all films that have war as their background. **CFu**

Close Encounters of the Third Kind
Steven Spielberg, 1977

A sci-fi mystery in which an Everyman's search for its meaning climaxes in contact with extraterrestrials, *Close Encounters* incorporates themes that recur throughout Steven Spielberg's work. There are his staple characters (the individual on a quest, sympathetic mother, lost boy, and untrustworthy authorities), and a transforming experience. There are rescue, redemption, and affirmation of an individual's worth. Take away the spectacular special effects, and what remains is a compassionate human story of an ordinary man in extraordinary circumstances.

Richard Dreyfuss's appealing Roy Neary is Joe Six-Pack having an epiphany. When his UFO encounter is dismissed he becomes obsessed with discovering what his experience means, alienating his family in the process. The only person who understands is Melinda Dillon's Jillian Guiler, driven by her own search for her son (Cary Guffey), who was taken in a terrifying visitation at her home. It becomes clear they are among "implantees" privileged with a shared connection. Parallel with these intimate experiences of frustration and fear of the unknown, of courage and joy in confronting it (and finding something wonderful in the childlike aliens), are the efforts of François Truffaut's hopeful Claude Lacombe, head of the project to investigate and respond to alien contact.

Close Encounters shows all the sensibilities of the suburban baby boomer nurtured on Disney and 1950s sci-fi, and was indeed an adult, professional rethink of Spielberg's adolescent, homemade epic, *Firelight* (1964). While *E.T.* (1982) may be even more revealing of his psyche, *Close Encounters* is a definitive Spielberg film in both style and substance. It is also one he can't leave alone, reediting it into the 1980 Special Edition (tightened middle section of Neary's crisis, extended alien climax) and the 1997 Collector's Edition (digitally remastered, snippets reinstated, the unnecessary "afterthought" sequence inside the mothership deleted).

Released six months after his friend George Lucas's *Star Wars* (1977), *Close Encounters* was another instantly iconic event film. The five-tone musical motif by John Williams and the mashed potato mountain both entered popular culture, and the collective gasp of awe at the mothership serves as yet another testimonial to Spielberg's gift for wonder. **AE**

U.S. (Columbia, EMI) 135m Metrocolor **Language** English / French **Producer** Julia Phillips, Michael Phillips **Screenplay** Steven Spielberg **Photography** Vilmos Zsigmond **Music** John Williams **Cast** Richard Dreyfuss, François Truffaut, Teri Garr, Melinda Dillon, Bob Balaban, J. Patrick McNamara, Warren J. Kemmerling, Roberts Blossom, Philip Dodds, Cary Guffey, Shawn Bishop, Adrienne Campbell, Justin Dreyfuss, Lance Henriksen, Merrill Connally **Oscars** Vilmos Zsigmond (photography), Frank Warner (special sound effects) **Oscar nominations** Steven Spielberg (director), Melinda Dillon (actress in support role), Joe Alves, Daniel A. Lomino, Phil Abramson (art direction), Roy Arbogast, Douglas Trumbull, Matthew Yuricich, Gregory Jein, Richard Yuricich (special visual effects), Michael Kahn (editing), John Williams (music), Robert Knudson, Robert J. Glass, Don MacDougall, Gene S. Cantamessa (sound)

"Some people go to the wood shop and make bowling-pin lamps ... I tell stories about aliens."

Steven Spielberg, 2004

ℹ

George Lucas lost a bet to Spielberg that *Close Encounters* would be a bigger hit than *Star Wars*.

The Last Wave Peter Weir, 1977

Australia (Ayer, McElroy & McElroy) 106m
Color **Producer** Hal McElroy, Jim McElroy
Screenplay Peter Weir, Tony Morphett,
Petru Popescu **Photography** Russell Boyd
Music Charles Wain **Cast** Richard
Chamberlain, Olivia Hamnett, David Gulpilil,
Frederick Parslow, Vivean Gray, Nandjiwarra
Amagula, Walter Amagula, Roy Bara, Cedrick
Lalara, Morris Lalara, Peter Carroll, Athol
Compton, Hedley Cullen, Michael Duffield,
Wallas Eaton

Where Peter Weir's *Picnic at Hanging Rock* (1975) appears to be about man's adversarial relationship with nature, the director's enigmatic *The Last Wave* seems to be about man's symbiotic relationship with nature. Richard Chamberlain—enlisted to boost the Australian film's fortunes in the U.S.—plays attorney David Burton, hired to defend an Aborigine accused of murder. The problem is, no one will talk about the murder, and Burton begins to believe that something more mysterious (and possibly nefarious) is at work. The murder may have been an Aborigine ritual, strange weather formations are befalling Sydney, and Burton is beset by frightening visions of an impending apocalypse. As his physical and spiritual journey takes him deeper into the realm of the mystical and the feeling of impending doom weighs heavier and heavier on his subconscious, Chamberlain begins to lose faith in reality.

Weir plays *The Last Wave* (titled *Black Rain* in the U.S.) as a detective story steeped in the mythology of the Aborigines, whose profound (and perhaps supernatural) relationship with the land precedes and exceeds the laws and rules of the Anglo civilization around them. Increasing the tension with a hallucinatory intensity, Weir seems intent on leaving us as confused as his protagonist, leading to a perplexing conclusion that may or may not belie everything we have been made to believe. **JKl**

i

Chamberlain's costar Olivia Hamnett reappeared in the popular Australian TV drama *Prisoner: Cell Block H*.

Star Wars George Lucas, 1977

U.S. (Lucasfilm) 121m Technicolor
Producer Gary Kurtz, George
Lucas **Screenplay** George Lucas
Photography Gilbert Taylor **Music** John
Willlams **Cast** Mark I lamill, Harrison Ford,
Carrie Fisher, Peter Cushing, Alec Guinness,
Anthony Daniels, Kenny Baker, Peter
Mayhew, David Prowse, James Earl Jones,
Phil Brown, Shelagh Fraser, Jack Purvis, Alex
McCrindle, Eddie Byrne **Oscars** John Barry,
Norman Reynolds, Leslie Dilley, Roger
Christian (art direction), John Mollo
(costume), John Stears, John Dykstra,
Richard Edlund, Grant McCune, Robert
Blalack (special visual effects), Paul Hirsch,
Marcia Lucas, Richard Chew (editing), John
Williams (music), Don MacDougall, Ray West,
Bob Minkler, Derek Ball (sound), Ben Burtt
(special sound effects) **Oscar nominations**
Gary Kurtz (best picture), George Lucas
(director), George Lucas (screenplay), Alec
Guinness (actor in support role)

*"[Hollywood] opened
a Pandora's Box when
they made* Star Wars.*"*

Woody Allen, 1985

ℹ️

Scenes set on Tatooine were filmed
on sets in Tunisia, reused when Lucas
filmed *The Phantom Menace* (1999).

Writer-director George Lucas's film was not expected to be a success. Studio bosses were so convinced the movie—a "sci-fi Western" with a virtually unknown principal cast (Harrison Ford, Mark Hamill, and Carrie Fisher)—would flop that they happily gave Lucas the merchandising rights to any *Star Wars* products for free. They obviously never expected that it would lead to two sequels, three prequels, an Ewok spin-off, cartoons, computer games, toys, soundtracks, books, huge video and DVD sales, clothes, bed linen, and even food. (And innumerable parodies, notably three *Star Wars*-specific editions of the cartoon *Family Guy*.)

The movie cost $11 million, and went on to make over $460 million, but probably didn't sound like a potential blockbuster, let alone one of the most successful films ever made. After the death of the aunt and uncle who raised him, the headstrong young Luke Skywalker (Hamill) teams up with an old Jedi Knight, Ben "Obi-Wan" Kenobi (Alec Guinness), two creaky robots, a cocky spaceship pilot named Han Solo (a star-making performance from Ford), and Solo's furry Wookie pal Chewbacca (Peter Mayhew) to rescue a princess (Fisher) from an evil guy wearing robes and a big plastic helmet. *Star Wars* could have turned out a bit silly. (Even Lucas was plagued by doubt. "George came back from *Star Wars* a nervous wreck," recalled friend Steven Spielberg. He didn't feel [it] came up to the vision he initially had. He felt he had just made this little kids' movie.")

But Lucas had big dreams. A couple of decades before computer-generated images could be used to create fantastical worlds and distant planets, the visionary director—using incredibly detailed models, clever photography, and well-chosen locations—tells the story of another universe. In it, the evil Empire—led by Darth Vader (David Prowse, with voice supplied by James Earl Jones)—rules, but rebel forces are gathering to bring down the bad guys.

Lucas created a mythology that has been embraced by young and old alike. As well as creating various creatures from his galaxy far, far away, his good-versus-evil storyline introduces us to people, phrases, and concepts that have since become part of the English language: the Millennium Falcon (Solo's spaceship, which Lucas originally imagined would look like a flying hamburger), light sabers (the swordlike weapon with its own recognizable "swoosh" sound), Imperial Stormtroopers, "May the Force be with you," and, of course, the Jedi Knights (now so much a part of our collective consciousness that an online campaign suggesting people enter "Jedi" under the religion section of a United Kingdom census form proved hugely successful).

In giving the world *Star Wars*, Lucas succeeded in making much more than just a movie (one that would eventually get its own exhibit at the Smithsonian, no less). He made a world, a new style of cinema, and an unforgettable outer space opera that has been many times imitated but never bettered. And you never can see the strings. **JB**

Stroszek Werner Herzog, 1977

In 1974, German director Werner Herzog made *The Enigma of Kaspar Hauser*, based on the nineteenth-century case of a man suddenly thrust into the world after years living in a cell. In the lead he cast Bruno S., a street musician and real-life social outsider who—with his strange tics and oddly histrionic speech rhythms—proved an inspired choice.

If *Kaspar Hauser* felt like an indirect portrait of Bruno S., that is even more true of *Stroszek*, in which he plays a street musician and drinker newly released from prison. Finding German life unmanageably brutal, he teams up with a prostitute (Eva Mattes) and a borderline-crazy father figure (Clemens Scheitz). Together they set out for a new life in America, but end up in a barren, banal nowhere. Inevitably ending up alone and at bay, Bruno stages an elaborate gesture of despair. The final sequence—involving a ski lift, a pick-up truck, and a colony of performing animals in a roadside attraction—is one of the most savage and unforgiving endings on film.

Herzog's 1970s films are often lyrical, steeped in mystical German romanticism. *Stroszek* is a stark exception. This is a brutally lucid view of the dream of freedom; America is entirely stripped of mystique, presented as a spiritual wasteland and a trap for the unwary. And the final image of the chicken, dancing manically to a cacophony of harmonica and hillbilly whooping, is as unbearably cruel an image of the human condition—obsessive and out of control—as any filmmaker has asked an audience to watch. (The crew disliked it so much that Herzog filmed it singlehanded.)

What makes the picture phenomenal, however, is the way Bruno S. commands the screen, with indomitable charm and verve. In the role of holy fool, he embodies one of the distinctively strange intelligences of modern cinema. Its naturalistic approach and minor-key subject matter mean *Stroszek* is less celebrated than Herzog's great visionary follies of the 1970s—but it is among his best films and certainly one of the most unpitying dramas ever made about Europe's dreams of America. **JRom**

West Germany (Skellig, Werner Herzog, ZDF) 108m Color **Language** English / German **Screenplay** Werner Herzog **Photography** Stefano Guidi, Wolfgang Knigge, Edward Lachman, Thomas Mauch **Music** Chet Atkins, Sonny Terry **Cast** Pit Bedewitz, Burkhard Driest, Alfred Edel, Michael Gahr, Eva Mattes, Scott McKain, Ely Rodriguez, Bruno S., Clemens Scheitz, Clayton Szalpinski, Yuecsel Topcuguerler, Vaclav Vojta, Wilhelm von Homburg, Ralph Wade

> *"We do have to create ... images for our civilization. If we do not do that, we die out like dinosaurs."*
>
> **Werner Herzog, 2004**

ℹ

This was the last film that Ian Curtis, singer with British band Joy Division, watched before committing suicide.

Ceddo Ousmane Sembene, 1977

Senegal (Domireew, Sembene) 120m
Eastmancolor **Language** French / Wolof
Screenplay Ousmane Sembene
Photography Georges Caristan
Music Manu Dibango **Cast** Tabata Ndiaye,
Moustapha Yade, Ismaila Diagne, Matoura
Dia, Omar Gueye, Mamadou Dioumé, Nar
Modou, Ousmane Camara, Ousmane
Sembene **Berlin International Film Festival**
Ousmane Sembene (Interfilm award,
forum of new cinema)

In Ousmane Sembene's complex meditation on African history, the king of an African nation has converted to Islam, while members of the warrior class (the ceddo) retain the traditional religion. In protest at the religious constraints they are made to endure, a ceddo kidnaps the monarch's daughter. Successive men try and fail to rescue her, until civil war erupts.

Limpid, elegant, and direct, the film eliminates inessentials, showing people only as they appear while engaging in acts and debates of high political importance, establishing an equivalence between speech and action. In scenes of ritualized council meetings in public spaces, Sembene presents arguments, counter-arguments, and accusations through contrasting styles of speech and movement (the sour imam and his followers with their rote formulae and the king's childhood friend with his springy, expressive hand gestures).

Sembene's use of African-American spirituals, one of his most daring and brilliant strokes, widens the film's context to include the African diaspora and the future of the villagers, whom we see herded together and branded with a hot iron, waiting to be transported to slavery. Intercutting these scenes with the main narrative, *Ceddo* establishes a scathing tone and a crisp, intellectual atmosphere all its own. **CFu**

1977

Der Amerikanische Freund Wim Wenders, 1977
The American Friend

West Germany / France (Autoren,
Losange, Moli Films, Road Movies, WDR,
Wim Wenders) 127m Eastmancolor
Language German / English
Producer Renée Gundelach, Wim Wenders
Screenplay Wim Wenders, from the novel
Ripley's Game by Patricia Highsmith
Photography Robby Müller **Music** Jürgen
Knieper **Cast** Dennis Hopper, Bruno Ganz,
Lisa Kreuzer, Gérard Blain, Nicholas Ray,
Samuel Fuller, Peter Lilienthal, Daniel
Schmid, Jean Eustache, Rudolf Schündler,
Sandy Whitelaw, Lou Castel **Cannes
Film Festival** Wim Wenders (Golden
Palm nomination)

A brilliant adaptation of Patricia Highsmith's 1974 novel *Ripley's Game* and one of the most eloquent expressions of Wim Wenders's existential universe, *The American Friend* casts Dennis Hopper as an American expatriate in Europe, luring a Hamburg picture framer (Bruno Ganz) who has a possibly fatal illness into committing a murder. The financial reward will help out the man's wife and son.

The film works effectively as a thriller, with the muted expressionist colors of Robby Müller's wondrous camerawork and Jürgen Knieper's subtly urgent score contributing to the air of paranoid suspense. But it is also a marvelously astute psychological study, deftly delineating the fear, envy, wariness, and finally friendship that defines the relationship between the two men, each doomed in different ways. (Hopper himself was still two years away from a career-reviving turn in *Apocalypse Now*.)

Typically for Wenders at this highly productive stage in his career, the movie also speaks volumes about the symbiotic but troubled cultural relationship between America and Europe. In some respects similar to a Jean-Pierre Melville film in its juxtaposition of Hollywood and European art-movie tropes and motifs, *The American Friend* pays tribute to those traditions with pleasing cameos by U.S. directors Nicholas Ray and Samuel Fuller, and Frenchmen Jean Eustache and Gérard Blain. **GA**

U.S. (Rollins-Joffe) 93m Color
Producer Charles H. Joffe, Jack Rollins
Screenplay Woody Allen, Marshall Brickman
Photography Gordon Willis **Cast** Woody
Allen, Diane Keaton, Tony Roberts, Carol
Kane, Paul Simon, Shelley Duvall, Janet
Margolin, Colleen Dewhurst, Christopher
Walken, Donald Symington, Helen Ludlam,
Mordecai Lawner, Joan Neuman, Jonathan
Munk, Ruth Volner **Oscars** Charles H. Joffe
(best picture), Woody Allen (director),
Woody Allen, Marshall Brickman
(screenplay), Diane Keaton (actress)
Oscar nominations Woody Allen (actor)

*"There's one clear
autobiographical
fact in the picture:
I've thought about sex
since my first intimation
of consciousness."*

Woody Allen, 1977

ℹ

An abandoned opening sequence
featured Alvy descending into hell,
where he encounters Richard Nixon.

Annie Hall Woody Allen, 1977

Woody Allen's most celebrated film began when the director and his cowriter Marshall Brickman embarked on a comedy set in Allen's mind, with flashbacks to the main male character's previous marriages and childhood crushes, and the addition of a murder mystery. It was reshaped in development and production, with casualties including the removal of a scene featuring an eleven-year-old Brooke Shields. This streamlined version—now focused on the romance between Alvy, a neurotic, over-sexed comedian (played, inevitably, by Allen) and the eponymous Annie Hall (Diane Keaton)—was a modern screwball comedy colored with doubt, indecision, and pop psychology.

Nominated for five Academy Awards, the film won four, including Best Picture of 1978, and was a critical and commercial hit. In fact, *Annie Hall*'s popularity was so great that parts of the dialogue lodged in the vernacular; some years had to pass before spiders were not typically described by ordinary people as being "the size of a Buick." It was the director's coming of age: a film that marked a turning point in his career as well as the way his talent was perceived. Until then, Allen's work comprised pure comedies like *Bananas* (1971) and *Sleeper* (1973). While both are still extremely funny, neither has the emotional resonance or the zeitgeist-catching relevance of *Annie Hall*.

After a surreal, and severely edited, opening monologue, the story begins on a street in New York City, as Alvy and his friend Rob (Tony Roberts) reflect on the nature of life. Rob brought Annie into Alvy's life via a tennis match where Alvy's main concern was being allowed into the club because he was Jewish. (Allen insists that the character of Alvy is nonautobiographical, but the similarities between Alvy and Allen are too many to be coincidental; as well as the fact that Keaton, his former girlfriend, was born Diane Hall and nicknamed Annie.)

The film then becomes the story of Annie and Alvy's affair, weaving in stand-up comedy, postmodern pieces to camera, Jewish humor, barbed observations about sex, love, and the differences between New York and Los Angeles, and a very funny scene with lobsters. Arguably Allen's most honest film, it is also (ironically, given its theme of emotional immaturity), his most emotionally mature one.

Originally titled *Anhedonia* (the incapacity for pleasure), the film was changed to *Annie Hall* only after several test screenings. There was no sequel, but aspects of its original storyline and the pairing of Keaton and Allen were echoed in the director's *Manhattan Murder Mystery* (1993).

Annie Hall is also notable for early acting appearances from Jeff Goldblum, Christopher Walken, Beverly D'Angelo, Paul Simon, and (in a nonspeaking role at the end) Sigourney Weaver. More bizarrely, author Truman Capote and philosopher Marshall McLuhan make appearances. The former plays "a Truman Capote look-alike," and the latter was a last-minute (and reluctantly made) substitution for Federico Fellini. **KK**

Suspiria Dario Argento, 1977

Suspiria begins as if it were an Italian *giallo* (pulp thriller): a series of spectacular murders staged with the baroque quality of a musical. But director Dario Argento soon switches gears, revealing a world not of masked or gloved human killers, but of supernatural forces, black magic, and malignant witches. ("I went all round Europe trying to find witches and sorceresses," he told *Bizarre*. "But they're not so easy to find.")

However, *Suspiria* is not only a late-ish entry in a European horror subgenre. It is also a product of the stylistic influence of Argento's mentor, Mario Bava, a pioneer in multiple Italian genres whose highly visual effects were created with amazing intelligence and economy. Perhaps the most enduring legacy of Bava's style was a relentless tracking shot that Argento makes outrageously his own, and which now, thanks to directors ranging from Martin Scorsese to Sam Raimi, has become a basic part of contemporary film language.

Suspiria takes place in a classically gothic setting—an old dance academy. The true nature of the instruction offered there is revealed in a rain of maggots that showers the girls one evening. In this pure gross-out lies a kind of key, as the big, spectacular scenes themselves become tests of endurance. While the audience and the student-protagonist, Susy Banyon (Jessica Harper), are drawn along by traces of mysterious and esoteric revelations, the intense array of audiovisual shocks and effects teeter on the very edge of unbearableness. This is the texture of the whole film, not only in its grand surreal deaths but even its smallest gestures, as when a malevolent dance instructor pours water straight into Susy's mouth, the heavy glass pitcher rattling against her teeth.

Argento's film stands out for the sheer intensity of watching—and hearing—it, the latter due to an almost overpowering score by the director and the Italian rock group Goblin. From beginning to end, this is a nightmarish fairy tale, culminating in a grotesque confrontation with the hideous elder of a witches coven. Finally, *Suspiria* reveals the horror film to be a kind of initiation ritual for protagonist and spectator alike— the horror genre itself as a kind of secular mystery religion. **AS**

Italy / West Germany (Seda Spettacoli) 98m Technicolor **Language** Italian / Russian / English / German / Latin **Producer** Claudio Argento, Salvatore Argento **Screenplay** Dario Argento, Daria Nicolodi, from the book *Suspiria de Profundis* by Thomas De Quincey **Photography** Luciano Tovoli **Music** Dario Argento, Agostino Marangolo, Massimo Morante, Fabio Pignatelli, Claudio Simonetti **Cast** Jessica Harper, Stefania Casini, Flavio Bucci, Miguel Bosé, Barbara Magnolfi, Susanna Javicoli, Eva Axén, Rudolf Schündler, Udo Kier, Alida Valli, Joan Bennett, Margherita Horowitz, Jacopo Mariani, Fulvio Mingozzi, Franca Scagnetti

> *"I was not prepared for how beautiful the film would ultimately look. And who knew how important [it] would be?"*
>
> **Jessica Harper, 2011**

i

It was reported in 2012 that David Gordon Green (*Pineapple Express* [2000]) was remaking *Suspiria*.

Sleeping Dogs Roger Donaldson, 1977

New Zealand (Aardvark Films, Broadbank Films, New Zealand Film Commission, QE2) 107m Color **Producer** Roger Donaldson **Screenplay** Ian Mune, Arthur Baysting, from novel by Karl Stead **Photography** Michael Seresin **Music** Matthew Brown, David Calder, Murray Grindlay **Cast** Sam Neill, Warren Oates, Ian Mune, Nevan Rowe, Ian Watkin, Clyde Scott, Donna Akersten, William Johnson, Don Selwyn, Davina Whitehouse, Melissa Donaldson, Dougal Stevenson, Bernard Kearns

Set one day in the future, this political thriller details how a democratic state can slip into autocracy, via the gradual erosion of individual rights and personal freedom. Sam Neill plays Smith, an ordinary citizen who, following the breakdown of his marriage, chooses to pursue a solitary life in the country. Mistaken for a terrorist, he is arrested, escapes, and becomes involved with an underground movement. But state forces, too, powerful and all pervasive, soon catch up with him.

Neill's charisma makes an ambiguous and unmotivated character more appealing than he should be. In fact, no one in the film is likable —especially Warren Oates's U.S. officer, brought in to bolster the state's strength (and to support the filmmakers' view of American imperialism overseas; Vietnam had only recently come to an end). Jack Nicholson was the producer's first choice, but his agent laughed at the amount on offer. Oates is better. His character is tired and seems unconvinced of the role he has to play, preferring the pleasures of women and alcohol.

A stylish and confident yet underrated feature debut, *Sleeping Dogs* was the first New Zealand film to be widely released in the U.S. **IHS**

1977

Last Chants for a Slow Dance Jon Jost, 1977

U.S. 90m Color **Screenplay** Jon Jost **Photography** Jon Jost **Cast** Tom Blair, Wayne Crouse, Jessica St. John, Steve Voorheis

Before indie cinema made a fetish of serial killers, shattered masculinity, long takes, and songs-as-commentary, *Last Chants for a Slow Dance*, handmade on a ridiculously small budget, culminated in an endless shot of a murderer driving down a highway to the haunting "Fixin' to Die."

The images, the cuts, even the song and its performance, come from Jon Jost. *Last Chants* inaugurated the "Tom Blair" trilogy (named after the astonishing lead actor) and, with *Sure Fire* (1990) and *The Bed You Sleep In* (1993), created a milestone of contemporary American cinema.

Last Chants is a despairing document of social breakdown: Its antihero wanders through the landscape raving, screwing, and killing. Jost weaves an avant-garde structure around his actions, which renders them both fascinating and horrifying. The film eschews easy spectacle but still goes to extremes—the slaughter of an animal, for instance, standing in for the killer's equally indifferent disposal of human life.

Loosely inspired by the Gary Gilmore case, the film takes pride of place—alongside John McNaughton's *Henry: Portrait of a Serial Killer* (1990)—among cinema's most intelligent explorations of a difficult subject. Its distancing effects—color filters, words printed on-screen, stretched-out durations—push us not to judge but to understand an American culture nurtured on aggression, violence, and the hateful exclusion of anyone "other." The best index of its ambivalent sensitivity to the real world it traverses are its songs, simultaneously soulful and ironic ("Hank Williams wrote it long ago," runs one chorus). **AM**

Czlowiek z marmuru Andrzej Wajda, 1977
Man of Marble

One of the best movies ever made in Poland, *Man of Marble* is also an important testimony to the power of cinema. Recalling the puzzling structure of Orson Welles's *Citizen Kane* (1941), it concerns an ambitious film student, Agnieszka (the remarkably convincing Krystyna Janda). Her diploma film is dedicated to a forgotten "worker-hero of the state" of the 1950s, bricklayer Birkut (Jerzy Radziwilowicz), transformed by the communist propaganda machine into a national myth. Despite her difficulties tracking down the witnesses of Birkut's "sanctification" two decades later, the stubborn young woman manages to meet with some of them and gets them to talk about the naive worker.

It turns out that after being victimized by an act of sabotage, when someone placed a burning brick in his hands, the young Birkut lost his innocence. Realizing just how cynical was the idea of having been turned into a legend, he began to experience an awakening of social conscience, though not in the revolutionary sense. After starting to ask the authorities challenging questions, Birkut was eliminated. This is the conclusion suggested by the movie's finale (though it was censured)—a daring exposé of the communist state's tendency to "devour its beloved sons."

In the course of her investigations, Agnieszka meets Jerzy Burski (Tadeusz Lomnicki), a film director who participated in the creation of Birkut's heroic image: fragments of his "documentaries" are important pieces in the narrative puzzle. Andrzej Wajda depicts with admiration the young woman's battle, convincing us that it is the filmmaker's duty to reveal the truth. This moral upshot to the story intensifies the film's importance, as was the case with Wajda's 1969 film, *Wszystko na sprzedaz* (Everything for Sale), a parable about truth and falsity in the cinema.

A meditation on cinema, *Man of Marble* is also is a complex depiction of a horrid period in the history of its country. It also anticipated social change, portraying the beginning of an implacable process: the fall of communism. The film's sequel, *Man of Iron* (1981), focuses on the workers' strikes in Gdansk and other Polish cities in 1980, casting the excellent Radziwilowicz once again, now in the role of Birkut's son.

Man of Marble consolidated Wajda's international status, sometimes unjustly judged as "academic." Together with Krzysztof Kielsowski and Krzysztof Zanussi, he became a protagonist of the so-called "cinema of moral anxiety," which held an enormous prestige and a subversive reputation in Poland. This film also confirms an assertion made by another important Polish director, Janusz Zaorski, who noted near the beginning of the 1990s that, "We did our best films against the state with the state's money." This paradoxical situation is what allowed for the appearance of masterpieces such as *Man of Marble*. An absolute must, especially for those perplexed as to why Wajda was honored with a special Oscar in 2000. **DD**

Poland Polski, Zespol) 165m BW / Color **Language** Polish **Screenplay** Aleksander Scibor-Rylski **Photography** Edward Klosinski **Music** Andrzej Korzynski **Cast** Jerzy Radziwilowicz, Krystyna Janda, Tadeusz Lomnicki, Jacek Lomnicki, Michal Tarkowski, Piotr Cieslak, Wieslaw Wójcik, Krystyna Zachwatowicz, Magda Teresa Wójcik, Boguslaw Sobczuk, Leonard Zajaczkowski, Jacek Domanski, Irena Laskowska, Zdzislaw Kozien, Wieslaw Drzewicz **Cannes Film Festival** Andrzej Wajda (FIPRESCI award), tied with Miris Poljskog Cveca

"I was lucky to have stayed in Poland. I belong here, and I reached my international position while working here. I believe in my mission of creating the Polish school in film."

Andrzej Wajda, 2002

🛈

Among the actresses in this film and several others by the same director is Wajda's wife Krystyna Zachwatowicz.

1977

Saturday Night Fever John Badham, 1977

U.S. (Paramount, RSO) 118m Color
Producer Milt Felsen, Kevin McCormick,
Robert Stigwood Screenplay Norman
Wexler, from the magazine article "Tribal
Rites of the New Saturday Night" by Nik
Cohn Photography Ralf D. Bode Music The
Bee Gees Cast John Travolta, Karen Lynn
Gorney, Barry Miller, Joseph Cali, Paul Pape,
Donna Pescow, Bruce Ornstein, Julie
Bovasso, Martin Shakar, Sam Coppola,
Nina Hansen, Lisa Peluso, Denny Dillon,
Bert Michaels, Robert Costanzo
Oscar nomination John Travolta (actor)

i

First rated R, the film was edited and
reissued as a PG in 1979 to cash in on
Travolta's youth-based *Grease* fame.

Saturday Night Fever is a movie phenomenon based on a magazine article, "Tribal Rites of the New Saturday Night," that author Nik Cohn has since admitted was fabricated. But whether discos in New York, or anywhere else in the world for that matter, were full of young people experiencing life, love, and the Hustle before the article came out isn't really the point. They took to the floor in droves after the film's success helped make disco the dance style of the late 1970s.

John Travolta, previously a TV star in the series *Welcome Back, Kotter*, became the man to mob in the streets after he donned his white suit as Brooklyn boy Tony Manero, king of the local dancehall. Backed by the infectious Bee Gees song "Stayin' Alive," his opening scene walk down the street became the strut to emulate. His dance moves—on which Travolta spent so long that he persuaded director John Badham to film his whole body rather than in close-up as originally planned—have been copied on many a dance floor and parodied in many a movie since. **JB**

Killer of Sheep Charles Burnett, 1977

KILLER OF SHEEP

U.S. 83m BW **Producer** Charles Burnett **Screenplay** Charles Burnett **Photography** Charles Burnett **Cast** Henry G. Sanders, Kaycee Moore, Charles Bracy, Angela Burnett, Eugene Cherry, Jack Drummond

"This man works to support his family and he works hard . . . There are a lot of people around like that. They never make the newspapers or TV as a character, but they are there."

Charles Burnett, 1979

i

Henry G. Sanders went on to enjoy a prolific TV career, including a lengthy stint on *Dr Quinn, Medicine Woman*.

Charles Burnett's *Killer of Sheep* slid into the world between two popular waves of Black American cinema: the blaxploitation period of the early to mid-1970s and the Spike Lee–led charge of revitalized Black film of the 1980s. *Killer of Sheep* fits in neither camp, being both more daring and more quietly revolutionary than anything from those eras.

Writer-director Burnett anchored his exploration of black American, inner-city life on the story of Stan (Henry G. Sanders, "a last-minute replacement after my main character failed to get his parole in time," said the director), a quiet, unexceptional man who works in a slaughterhouse to support his young family. They live in 1970 Watts, Los Angeles, when urban struggle wasn't yet synonymous with the soul-crushing despair of drugs, drive-by shootings, and an unbreakable cycle of poverty.

Although the bloody, backbreaking work that Stan does is what gives the film its title, the real thrust of the picture is in its nostalgia for a kind of innocence that was already fading by the time the film was made in the mid-1970s. (Though copyrighted 1977, and garlanded at the Berlin International Film Festival in 1981, the film was never widely distributed, owing to the expense of clearing rights for songs on the soundtrack.) Children play in worn-down yards, making toys out of whatever they find; a picnic is planned, and goes hilariously astray; Stan crawls under a sink to fix a pipe, and the camera lingers on his soft, curled body. It sounds unremarkable, but it's in that simplicity that the film sings.

Shot in raw black-and-white stock that imbues it with a gilded grace, *Killer of Sheep* is astonishing for being an American film in which black characters are not metaphors for something or someone else. They're not simply some variation of stereotype, or merely passive victims of or snarling reactors to racism, class struggle, or the crush of American life. Burnett's camera pierces behind facades and public personas of American blackness to show the human beings beneath them. He paces the film leisurely so that we get to linger on faces and expressions. He captures intimacy—between husband and wife, parent and child, and friends—with a documentarian's skill, so we feel as if we are privy to secrets, to sides of a black self that are not often displayed in cinema.

So much film about African-Americans is filtered through both a horrible real-life history and an insidiously racist film industry that what is produced, more often than not, is ciphers with attitude who swagger, make wisecracks, and gun blast through one contrived scene after another. Burnett slows things down, peels back layers, creates settings that are purposefully banal, and illuminates the spirit behind the flesh and bone. He takes your breath away by not trying to take your breath away, by not trying to dazzle or overwhelm the viewer with a weighty political treatise—and yet his film is an example of the most radical, subversive art. It forces you to question all else you've seen or heard about blackness; it forces you to see and hear in all new ways. **EH**

Eraserhead David Lynch, 1977

The remarkable product of more than five years' worth of intermittent shooting and postproduction editing, *Eraserhead* was David Lynch's feature debut after several promising but rarely seen shorts. A popular "midnight movie" and cult film phenomenon, this "dream of dark and troubling things," as Lynch described it, assured a passionate fan base for the budding auteur. It anticipated the remarkable visuals of *The Elephant Man* (1980), *Dune* (1984), and *Wild at Heart* (1990), as well as the twisting, twisted narratives of *Twin Peaks: Fire Walk with Me* (1992), *Lost Highway* (1997), and Mulholland Drive. (2001).

With its unconventional plot, postindustrial wasteland setting, and black-and-white imagery seemingly extracted from the subconscious of a neurotic nebbish, *Eraserhead* has been compared to the Expressionist mise-en-scènes of *The Cabinet of Dr. Caligari* (1919), the futuristic urban decay of *Metropolis* (1926), and the absurdist/surrealist dreamscape of *Un Chien Andalou* (1929)—all with some justification, despite Lynch's insistence that none of these was a direct influence. Commentators often note that the question "What is this movie about?" is misplaced if not irrelevant, then argue that, despite its idiosyncrasies, Eraserhead is a narrative film with dialogue, a protagonist, and a more-or-less linear plot.

This last claim isn't easy to support. *Eraserhead* opens with a strange-looking man (Jack Fisk) pulling levers inside a jagged planet, while out of the mouth of our floating "hero" Henry Spencer (Jack Nance) appears a wormlike creature, perhaps implying conception and birth. Arriving at his squalid apartment building, in a desolate urban landscape, a neighbor informs him that his girlfriend Mary (Charlotte Stewart) wants him over to her parents' house for dinner. Over a meal that includes a miniature hen that hemorrhages blood and moves its legs up and down after he sticks a fork in it, Henry learns he's the father of a premature baby still at the hospital. Mary moves in with Henry, but leaves when the malformed and apparently quadriplegic baby's crying keeps her awake.

The baby, which looks like a cross between an animatronic reptile and a calf fetus, becomes increasingly repulsive and disease-ridden. After fantasizing about a chipmunk-cheeked blonde singer (Laurel Near) who stomps on umbilical worms inside his radiator, and having a one-night stand with his seductive neighbor (Judith Anna Roberts), Henry imagines his own head popping off—replaced by that of his baby—and taken to a factory to be converted into pencil-top erasers. Finally Henry cuts open his baby's full-body bandage, killing it and releasing mountains of foamy innards in the process. In a blinding flash of white, Henry embraces the Lady in the Radiator in what could be the afterlife.

No mere summation of the plot, however, can possibly convey the tone (and, indeed, sound) of this unique and challenging film. The feelings of unease, even horror, that result from watching it and that only increase in intensity on repeated viewings are simply unforgettable. **SJS**

U.S. (AFI) 90m BW **Producer** David Lynch **Screenplay** David Lynch **Photography** Herbert Cardwell, Frederick Elmes **Music** Peter Ivers, David Lynch, Fats Waller **Cast** Jack Nance, Charlotte Stewart, Allen Joseph, Jeanne Bates, Judith Anna Roberts, Laurel Near, V. Phipps-Wilson, Jack Fisk, Joan Lange, Thomas Coulson, John Monez, Darwin Joston, Neil Moran, Hal Landon Jr., Brad Keeler

"We only worked at night. Sometimes I would be building a set or something in the daytime, but on the set . . . the so-called 'real world' outside disappeared completely."

David Lynch, 2012

i

A rundown area in Philadelphia, where Lynch lived when he became a father, inspired the film.

Soldaat van Oranje Paul Verhoeven, 1977
Soldier of Orange

Belgium / Netherlands (Excelsior, Holland, Rank, Rob Houwer) 167m Fastmancolor **Language** Dutch / English **Producer** Rob Houwer **Screenplay** Kees Holierhoek, Gerard Soeteman, Paul Verhoeven, from the book *Soldaat van Oranje '40–'45* by Erik Hazelhoff Roelfzema **Photography** Jost Vacano **Music** Rogier van Otterloo **Cast** Rutger Hauer, Jeroen Krabbé, Susan Penhaligon, Edward Fox, Lex van Delden, Derek de Lint, Huib Rooymans, Dolf de Vries, Eddy Habbema, Belinda Meuldijk, Peter Faber, Rijk de Gooyer, Paul Brandenburg, Ward de Ravet, Bert Struys

With *Black Books* (2006), Verhoeven wrested back the accolade of having made Holland's most expensive film.

Paul Verhoeven's most elaborate Dutch film—and the most spectacular and expensive film from Holland at the time—announced themes that the director would return to later on when he was working in Hollywood (notably in 2006's *Black Books*).

Soldier of Orange sketches the experiences of a group of Dutch students during World War II. Initially reacting with a shrugging "a bit of war would be nice," they soon find themselves forced to make choices—joining the Germans, the resistance movement, or going underground. Throughout the film, Erik Lanshof (Rutger Hauer) is at the center of things. While others around him are compelled to choose between different paths, Erik enjoys the freedom of letting chance make his decisions for him, jumping from one adventure to another.

The movie is at its best when it addresses, in minute detail, the social issues dominating wartime Holland. Each character is a microcosm of Dutch society during the war. They are made human by connecting them to real people (among the film's characters is Dutch monarch Queen Wilhelmina), but also used as a detailed reflection on how war changes people and their opinions—as if the film is asking us not to judge but to understand the motives of friend and foe. **EM**

The Hills Have Eyes Wes Craven, 1977

U.S. (Blood Relations) 89m Color
Producer Peter Locke **Screenplay** Wes
Craven **Photography** Eric Saarinen
Music Don Peake **Cast** Susan Lanier,
Robert Houston, Martin Speer, Dee Wallace-
Stone, Russ Grieve, John Steadman, James
Whitworth, Virginia Vincent, Lance Gordon,
Michael Berryman, Janus Blythe, Cordy Clark,
Brenda Marinoff, Peter Locke

"It was a hard shoot. It was hot in the daytime and cold at night. We were stuck out in the desert but everyone got along well."

Susan Lanier, 2012

i

Having retained rights to the film, Craven himself chose the 2006 remake's director, Alexandre Aja.

Between his notorious debut *The Last House on the Left* (1972) and supernatural slasher *A Nightmare on Elm Street* (1984), Wes Craven's *The Hills Have Eyes* tends to get lost in discussion of America's reigning horror auteur. This may be truer today than ever, considering Craven's meteoric rise to mainstream respectability with the staggering success of his *Scream* series (1996–2011). A relentless chronicle of violence against and within a bourgeois family unit, *Hills* usually occupies the role of Craven's "cult classic"—celebrated by the director's hard core fans, appreciated for its low-budget aesthetic, generating semi-ironic readings which praise its archetypal allusions as well as its exploitation movie themes. Arguably, however, *Hills* warrants consideration as one of the richest and most perfectly realized films of Craven's career.

A structural correspondence is established between two families who face off in a battle to the death on the desolate site of a U.S. bomb-testing range. In one corner are the suburban middle-class Carters, headed for Los Angeles by car but making an unwise detour through the Yucca Flat to locate a silver mine willed to Ethel (Virginia Vincent) and her husband "Big Bob" (Russ Grieve) by a deceased aunt. In the other corner is a clan of scavengers who live in the surrounding hills and are ruled with an iron fist by mutated monster-patriarch Jupiter (James Whitworth). These cannibalistic guerillas—standing for oppressed and embattled minority/social/ethnic groups—eke out a squalid existence by using discarded army surplus tools and weapons to commit petty thievery.

When their car crashes in the desert, the Carter family reveal their ideologically inherited arrogance, repression, and capacity for denial, all of which make them prime targets for victimization by their ruthless, unscrupulous enemies. Big Bob is crucified and eventually immolated by his counterpart Papa Jupiter in a highly symbolic act signifying utter repudiation of Judeo-Christian values—values which Big Bob himself hypocritically cites in an earlier racist diatribe. Two of Jupiter's sons raid the Carter's RV trailer, where they rape younger daughter Brenda (Susan Lanier) and murder her sister and mother. Stripped of all pretensions, desperate for survival, the remaining members of the Carter clan finally find within themselves the courage, craftiness, and rage to kill off their enemies. The film closes with a powerful, red-filtered freeze-frame of son-in-law Doug (Martin Speer) in full fury, set to stab Jupiter's son Mars (Lance Gordon) in the chest—though Mars is surely already dead.

Craven's creativity is especially evident in his mixing and matching of genres, including the horror film, the Western, the road movie, and the siege film. Stylistically, Craven makes innovative use of shock tactics and startle effects to keep the anxiety level high throughout. And the varied use of handheld camerawork, masked point-of-view shots, night photography, and rapid-fire editing is all endowed with a strong sense of purpose, serving to sustain pace and tension in the narrative. **SJS**

Days of Heaven Terrence Malick, 1978

Terrence Malick is the most unusual member of the generation of American directors usually termed the Hollywood Renaissance, with a strong interest in visual cinema that recalls the directors of classic Hollywood, particularly John Ford, whose fascination with symmetrical compositions and landscape vistas Malick shares. His first two feature films, *Badlands* and *Days of Heaven*, both follow very much in the tradition of outlaw couple narratives such as Arthur Penn's *Bonnie and Clyde*. But the crime narrative at the heart of each film—especially the complex love triangle in *Days of Heaven* between Richard Gere, Brooke Adams, and Sam Shepard—is hardly what is most memorable. Malick's interest in cinema as an intense, pictorial experience, is nowhere better illustrated than in this, his third film, which is memorable for its images of 19th-century American life. The misery and squalor of Eastern cities overpopulated by immigrants contrast with the vast, open spaces of the American prairie, the two settings linked by the inescapable fact of social class.

In the East, the upper class is represented impersonally by the factory system, but on the prairie, the house of the landowner, who hires workers directly and presides over them in the field, dominates the landscape, the one visible sign of human industry and wealth. Malick energizes this environment by putting a woman in the middle between two men, both of whom she loves, with the ultimate tragedy caused by their bitter rivalry. Instead of relying on sequences heavy with dialogue to advance the story, Malick uses what are essentially silent-film techniques: well-designed images whose meaning can be fixed, as needed, by a memorable voiceover commentary that replaces the earlier device of title cards. Here, as in Badlands, the narrator is a female (17-year-old Linda Manz), called upon to describe and explain the behavior of men, especially their embracing of violence which seems so contrary to their better nature. Despite its beauty and pastoral evocation of an accommodating environment, *Days of Heaven* is filled with struggle, destruction, and ruminations on the vagaries of the human condition, much like the director's more recent The Thin Red Line. **RBP**

U.S. (Paramount) 95m Metrocolor
Producer Bert Schneider, Harold Schneider **Screenplay** Terrence Malick **Photography** Néstor Almendros **Music** Ennio Morricone **Cast** Richard Gere, Brooke Adams, Sam Shepard, Linda Manz, Robert J. Wilke, Jackie Shultis, Stuart Margolin, Tim Scott, Gene Bell, Doug Kershaw, Richard Libertini, Frenchie Lemond, Sahbra Markus, Bob Wilson, Muriel Jolliffe **Oscar** Néstor Almendros (photography) **Oscar nominations** Patricia Norris (costume), Ennio Morricone (music), John Wilkinson, Robert W. Glass Jr., John T. Reitz, Barry Thomas (sound)

"You know how people are. You tell them something, they start talking."

Linda
(Linda Manz)

ℹ️
Most of the film was shot at dawn or dusk, using a new, ultra light-sensitive film developed by Eastman.

Halloween John Carpenter, 1978

No director since Alfred Hitchcock has captured the delicious voyeurism of horror as well as John Carpenter in *Halloween*, a film so entrenched with our primordial anxieties that it continues to define the genre several decades later. Indeed, the comparison between Hitchcock and Carpenter is no stretch; *Halloween* is saturated with Carpenter's tribute to Hitchcock, from character names—Sam Loomis and Tom Doyle, from *Psycho* (1960) and *Rear Window* (1954), respectively—to the casting of Jamie Lee Curtis, daughter of Janet Leigh, the ill-fated shower victim in *Psycho*.

Halloween's plot is simple enough: a masked psychopath, Michael Myers, stabs and strangles his way through a group of teenage friends as they drink beer and pursue sexual encounters, until he finally comes up against the one pure force in the movie, the virginal babysitter Laurie Strode (Curtis). Despite its minimalism, the pronounced societal anxieties of *Halloween*'s good-versus-evil plot are left unresolved, a strategy repeated consistently in slasher films from *Friday the 13th* (1980) to *Scream* (1996). The intensity of Carpenter and Debra Hill's screenplay lies in situating the terror in the calm visage of suburbia, where one would (or at least used to) assume children were safe and sound.

Deconstructing notions of the protective homestead, *Halloween*'s camera work violates the fictitious town of Haddonfield with the roving point-of-view shot. The film's opening is itself a radiantly executed point-of-view take, peering through the eyes of the then-six-year-old killer. Carpenter constructs a purely aesthetic fear, separating *Halloween* from its own drudgingly expository progeny. Throughout the film, someone is always watching, be it predator or prey, and as the film unravels we are left to peek around corners, over shoulders, through windows, and out of closets at what we are sure is impending doom.

The brilliant pacing and excruciatingly long takes manage to keep the adrenaline pumping, as Michael slinks in the shadows, rising from death again and again to chase the clever Laurie. In the end, we are left to wonder uncomfortably about the thread of separation between fact and fiction. **KB**

U.S. (Compass, Falcon) 91m Metrocolor
Producer Debra Hill, Kool Lusby
Screenplay John Carpenter, Debra Hill
Photography Dean Cundey **Music** John Carpenter **Cast** Donald Pleasence, Jamie Lee Curtis, Nancy Kyes, P.J. Soles, Charles Cyphers, Kyle Richards, Brian Andrews, John Michael Graham, Nancy Stephens, Arthur Malet, Mickey Yablans, Brent Le Page, Adam Hollander, Robert Phalen, Tony Moran

> "It's Halloween, everyone's entitled to one good scare."
>
> **Sheriff Leigh Brackett (Charles Cyphers)**

1978

🛈

Many props in the film were adapted or reused—the mask was originally worn by William Shatner in *Star Trek*.

L'albero degli zoccoli Ermanno Olmi, 1978
The Tree of Wooden Clogs

In this elegiac recreation of the lives of Lombardy peasants, Ermanno Olmi offers a corrective to the anxiety of his earlier portraits of contemporary Italy: *The Job* (1961), *The Fiancés* (1962), *One Fine Day* (1968), and *The Circumstance* (1973).

Several stories emerge out of the details of the peasants' work and communal life: the courtship and marriage of a modest young couple; a father cutting down his landlord's tree to make shoes for his son to wear on his walk to school; an old man fertilizing tomatoes with chicken manure so they'll ripen more quickly. The soft lighting, apparently almost entirely from "natural" sources, and, above all, the discrete, precise soundtrack give us the sense of assisting at an almost unmediated reality. The shortness of shots is a directorial statement, not letting us become involved for long in any one activity or point of view, allowing the film to expand, calmly, in multiple directions.

In a privileged sequence, a woman prays while walking, fills a wine bottle from a stream, and is finally seen silhouetted in the doorway of a church. It is here, perhaps (or in the use of Bach at several points of the film), that an unsympathetic viewer might accuse Olmi of aestheticism. But such criticism would miss the director's point about the positive role of religious faith in the peasants' lives. Its restrained treatment of this theme makes *The Tree of Wooden Clogs* one of the most touching and compelling of all films about religion.

If the cumulative emotional effect of *The Tree of Wooden Clogs* is close to that of *The Fiancés*, an earlier Olmi masterpiece set in an alienating, modern-day, industrial world, it shows how useless words like "humanism" (often invoked in reference to the director) are in trying to account for it. The combination of deep uncertainty and fervent idealism at the end of *The Fiancés* is extremely moving. This is also what we are left with after the more outwardly pessimistic ending of *The Tree of Wooden Clogs*, and this may be what, above all, stamps Olmi's work with its poignancy and urgency. **CFu**

Italy / France (Gaumont, Gruppo Produzione Cinema, Italnoleggio, RAI, SACIS) 170m Gevacolor
Language Italian **Screenplay** Ermanno Olmi **Photography** Ermanno Olmi
Music Johann Sebastian Bach **Cast** Luigi Ornaghi, Francesca Moriggi, Omar Brignoli, Antonio Ferrari, Teresa Brescianini, Giuseppe Brignoli, Carlo Rota, Pasqualina Brolis, Massimo Fratus, Francesca Villa, Maria Grazia Caroli, Battista Trevaini, Giuseppina Langalelli, Lorenzo Pedroni, Felice Cessi
Cannes Film Festival Ermanno Olmi (Golden Palm, Prize of the ecumenical jury)

> *"Many think this three-hour epic about the lives of peasants in turn-of-the-century Bergamo is [Olmi's] masterwork."*
>
> *The Guardian*, 1999

ℹ️

The characters were all played by peasants from the Bergamo area; none was a professional actor.

The Chant of Jimmie Blacksmith Fred Schepisi, 1978

Australia (Film House, VFC) 120m Eastmancolor **Producer** Fred Schepisi, Roy Stevens **Screenplay** Fred Schepisi, from novel by Thomas Keneally **Photography** Ian Baker **Music** Bruce Smeaton **Cast** Tommy Lewis, Freddy Reynolds, Ray Barrett, Jack Thompson, Angela Punch McGregor, Steve Dodds, Peter Carroll, Ruth Cracknell, Don Crosby, Elizabeth Alexander, Peter Sumner, Tim Robertson, Ray Meagher, Brian Anderson, Jane Harders **Cannes Film Festival** Fred Schepisi (Golden Palm nomination)

i

Tommy Lewis had no acting experience before being cast in the lead role of Jimmie Blacksmith.

Fred Schepisi's adaptation of Thomas Keneally's sensational novel about the plight of the Aborigine in late nineteenth-century Australia, as questions of federation and independence for the nation are coming to the fore, juxtaposes the marginalization, even destruction of the native peoples as the modern nation of white settlers is taking place.

The Chant of Jimmie Blacksmith traces the tragic situation of the half-caste main character (Tommy Lewis), who suffers ill treatment from white employers, even as his connection to his people weakens. Finally, he takes a job with a more brutal family, who try to starve him into submitting to their decision that his wife should leave him. Always patient and humble, Jimmie now explodes into a murderous rage. Crippled by a horrific gunshot, he is eventually captured and killed.

At the time, this was the most expensive picture made by the nascent Australian film industry. Despite praiseworthy reviews, it did not find much of an audience in its own country, though it was exhibited successfully abroad. Australian filmgoers perhaps found the subject matter too uncomfortable; its depiction of violence is shocking. It remains one of the cinema's most moving and effective treatments of racism and its horrific consequences. **RBP**

631

The Deer Hunter Michael Cimino, 1978

THE DEER HUNTER

ROBERT DE NIRO ... MICHAEL CIMINO ... THE DEER HUNTER

JOHN CAZALE · JOHN SAVAGE · MERYL STREEP · CHRISTOPHER WALKEN

... MICHAEL CIMINO

U.S. (EMI, Universal) 183m Technicolor
Language English / Russian / Vietnamese /
French **Producer** Michael Cimino, Michael
Deeley, John Peverall, Barry Spikings
Screenplay Michael Cimino, Louis Garfinkle,
Quinn K. Redeker, Deric Washburn
Photography Vilmos Zsigmond
Music Stanley Myers **Cast** Robert De Niro,
John Cazale, John Savage, Christopher
Walken, Meryl Streep, George Dzundza,
Chuck Aspegren, Shirley Stoler, Rutanya
Alda, Pierre Segui, Mady Kaplan, Amy Wright,
Mary Ann Haenel, Richard Kuss, Joe Grifasi
Oscars Barry Spikings, Michael Deeley,
Michael Cimino, John Peverall (best picture),
Michael Cimino (director), Christopher
Walken (actor in support role), Peter Zinner
(editing), Richard Portman, William L.
McCaughey, Aaron Rochin, C. Darin Knight
(sound) **Oscar nominations** Michael
Cimino, Deric Washburn, Louis Garfinkle,
Quinn K. Redeker (screenplay), Robert De
Niro (actor), Meryl Streep (actress in support
role), Vilmos Zsigmond (photography)

*"You wanna play games?
All right, I'll play your
fucking games."*

Michael (Robert De Niro)

ℹ

The realism of the Russian roulette
scenes was heightened by the actors'
agitation at the authentic slapping.

The second picture by Michael Cimino, originally a noted Hollywood
screenwriter, *The Deer Hunter* was immediately declared both a cinematic
masterwork and a hate film of gross historical distortion. Somewhere
between these two extremes it also became a commercial hit despite
being focused on the loss of American innocence during the Vietnam War.

Opening in a Pennsylvania steel town, three mill workers, Michael
(Robert De Niro), Steven (John Savage), and Nick (Christopher Walken),
are drafted for war. Before leaving their friends behind, however, Steven
gets married, with his wedding ceremony and ensuing reception
doubling as a send-off party for the new recruits.

Jump cut in country. All three are made prisoners of war who finally
escape their torment, albeit with several complications. Steven ends up
a paraplegic, Nick flounders in Southeast Asia, an emotional cripple, and
Michael returns home guilt-ridden for letting his friends fall in harm's
way. His lot is further complicated when he falls in love with Linda (Meryl
Streep), once Nick's betrothed, while struggling to live as a civilian.

Over more than three hours of screen time, *The Deer Hunter* presents
strong performances and a group of remarkably intense set pieces. First
up the wedding, later supplanted by the now much discussed POW
Russian roulette game. In between are various depictions of a collapsing
community in the Pennsylvania hills.

Ironically and with an odd note of corny patriotism, the film's cast
sing "God Bless America" just before the closing credits roll. The sequence
provides a broken-hearted, conciliatory commentary on the sad state of
affairs that views the United States as the source of incredible heroism,
cowardice, ignorance, and blind celebration. Sounding the false hope of
a new day, *The Deer Hunter* is therefore a negative American classic.

Hindsight and distance from this 1978 reflection on the Vietnam war
also demonstrate how the film is a provocative domestic melodrama. It
offers a bravura depiction of the Vietnam experience channeled through
individual men without concern for a wider social context. Most critics
hold to this point, citing the film's simplistic, if not racist, depiction of
Asians and the distorted use of Russian roulette in no less than two
different narrative pivots. Still others focus on the homosocial, even
homosexual, subtext concerning the warrior class and its assimilation of
civilian life, read as the feminine sphere of influence.

The point may be most poignantly put, however, when recognizing
The Deer Hunter was among the first mainstream American movies to
focus on Vietnam. Simultaneously important for helping massage release
patterns for so-called prestige pictures that screen only at the end of the
year to qualify for Academy Award recognition, it provided indelible
images for the pop imagination before earning a Best Picture Oscar. All
this for presenting the seemingly banal story of working stiffs called up
to their civic duty. **GC-Q**

Dawn of the Dead George A. Romero, 1978

George Romero understands the metaphoric social impact of the horror film like no other writer-director. With his directorial debut, *Night of the Living Dead* (1968), he engaged race relations in the 1960s at an almost documentary level. Ten years later, *Dawn of the Dead* continued Romero's trend of refracting collective issues in the most unexpected of places. Within the vessel of the disturbing "living dead," Romero here explores the uncanny relationship between the zombie and the culture of capitalism, setting his flesh-eating horror in, of all places, a suburban shopping mall.

Four escapees of inner-city violence, zombie and otherwise, decide to take off in a helicopter for less dangerous surroundings. Running low on gas and supplies, they land on the roof of a mall inhabited by a mass of flesh-eating zombies. After securing a storage area, two members of the escape party decide to do a little looting. After their pleasant shopping experience, the group decides to remain in the mall, securing the exits, ridding themselves of the undead, and living out the American dream.

Dawn of the Dead provides a cunning critique of the American consumer: arms outstretched, feet shuffling to the mellow pop of Muzak, the zombies wander stupidly around the mall, with only the most basic need for survival. Beyond these automatons, however, the mall's four human inhabitants add a complexity to Romero's assessment of capitalism. Spending months there, the survivors convert their storage area into a plush apartment, taking all they need and want. Nevertheless, the omnipresent views of the cavernous and deserted mall are a constant reminder that this excess of consumerism is only a distraction from the danger that exists just beyond the door, danger borne from humanity's own violence.

Romero's horror films have an enduring and eerie quality, perpetually jarring us from the fantasy of graphic zombie horror to remind us that real life is just as frightening. The mortal concerns of *Dawn of the Dead* unsettle us even after the living dead are left behind. **KB**

U.S. / Italy (Target, Laurel) 126m
Technicolor **Producer** Claudio Argento, Dario Argento, Alfredo Cuomo, Richard P. Rubinstein **Screenplay** George A. Romero **Photography** Michael Gornick **Music** Dario Argento, Agostino Marangolo, Massimo Morante, Fabio Pignatelli, Claudio Simonetti **Cast** David Emge, Ken Foree, Scott H. Reiniger, Gaylen Ross, David Crawford, David Early, Richard France, Howard Smith, Daniel Dietrich, Fred Baker, James A. Baffico, Rod Stouffer, Jesse Del Gre, Clayton McKinnon, John Rice

"When the dead walk, señores, we must stop the killing . . . or lose the war."

Old Priest
(Jesse Del Gre)

🛈

The location for much of the action was Monroeville Mall, at the time one of the largest malls in the U.S.

Up in Smoke Lou Adler & Tommy Chong, 1978

U.S. (Paramount) 86m Metrocolor
Language English / Spanish **Producer** Lou
Adler, John Beug, Lou Lombardo
Screenplay Tommy Chong, Cheech Marin
Photography Gene Polito **Music** Tommy
Chong, Danny Kortchmar, Cheech Marin,
Waddy Wachtel **Cast** Cheech Marin, Tommy
Chong, Strother Martin, Edie Adams, Harold
Fong, Richard Novo, Jane Moder, Pam Bille,
Arthur Roberts, Marian Beeler, Donald
Hotton, John Ian Jacobs, Christopher Joy,
Ray Vitte, Michael Caldwell

ⅈ

Denied traditional advertising
outlets, the film was promoted by
putting comic strips on bus benches.

It would be easy to dismiss *Up in Smoke* as a stoner comedy whose
appeal is limited to midnight tokers and carefree college kids—and,
surely, these groups remain the film's most ardent devotees—but to do
so would be to ignore the inspired blend of improvisational comedy,
absurdism, and free-wheeling nuttiness that makes the film far greater
than the sum of its parts.

The first and best of the cinematic excursions of the wildly popular
comedy duo, Cheech Marin and Tommy Chong, *Up in Smoke* boasts
some of the most colorful characters in 1970s American comedy. Pedro
(Cheech) is one of those rare protagonists who are played for both
sympathy and mockery: he's a down-on-his-luck Mexican-American who
lives in poverty but buys outrageous accoutrements for his beloved car.
Man (Chong) is a burnout of the highest order, for whom a sausage-sized
joint is but an appetizer. But the greatest performance is surely Stacy
Keach as Sergeant Stedenko, the tightly wound, tic-ridden policeman
whose determination is matched only by his incompetence.

One of *Up in Smoke*'s surprising pleasures is its use of the widescreen
frame; one wouldn't expect such a low-budget effort to be so careful in its
compositions. Not only is the film a hoot, it is also pretty well made. **EdeS**

AN ALL-TIME MOVIE BLOCKBUSTER!

GREASE

IS THE WORD
FOR THE HAPPIEST MOVIE OF THE SEASON!
John Travolta Olivia Newton-John
Stockard Channing Jeff Conaway

U.S. (Paramount) 110m Metrocolor
Producer Allan Carr, Neil A. Machlis, Robert
Stigwood **Screenplay** Bronte Woodard,
Allan Carr, from musical by Jim Jacobs and
Warren Casey **Photography** Bill Butler
Music John Farrar, Barry Gibb, Sylvester
Bradford, Warren Casey, Sammy Fain, Jim
Jacobs, Al Lewis, Richard Rodgers, Louis St.
Louis, Mike Stoller, Ritchie Valens, David
White **Cast** John Travolta, Olivia Newton-
John, Stockard Channing, Jeff Conaway,
Barry Pearl, Michael Tucci, Kelly Ward, Didi
Conn, Jamie Donnelly, Dinah Manoff, Eve
Arden, Frankie Avalon, Joan Blondell, Edd
Byrnes, Sid Caesar **Oscar nomination**
John Farrar (song)

"It doesn't matter if
you win or lose, it's
what you do with
your dancin' shoes."

Vince Fontaine
(Edd Byrnes)

i

Several numbers from the broadway
show were cut for the film, but they
can be heard as background music.

636

Grease Randal Kleiser, 1978

A kitsch classic, *Grease* was to pubescent girls of the late 1970s what *Star Wars* was to young boys. Snake-hipped, slick-haired John Travolta shines as Danny Zuko, hip leader of the T-Birds at Rydell High in the 1950s. He falls for sugary sweet out-of-town gal Sandy Olsson (Olivia Newton-John) during the holidays and is then mortified when she turns up at his school, her virginal image threatening to cramp his style.

Based on the Broadway musical by Jim Jacobs and Warren Casey, the film has an old-as-the-hills plot: cool boy won't date goody-two-shoes girl, boy gets jealous when she dates someone else. There are various misunderstandings thanks to their interfering friends, and then he realizes love is more important than being cool and it all ends happily ever after. However, the point here isn't the story—it's all the other ingredients that director Randal Kleiser throws into the mix that make this one of the best film musicals ever made. As well as finding two perfect leads in Travolta (who was hotter than hot, especially with teenage girls, in 1978 following the megasuccess of *Saturday Night Fever*) and Newton-John (in a role originally offered to Marie Osmond), each supporting cast member is well chosen, from Didi Conn as beauty-school dropout Frenchy to Stockard Channing as school tart Rizzo to Frankie Avalon as Frenchy's heavenly advisor.

There are also some great set pieces: the Thunder Road car race in the style of *Ben-Hur* (1959), Travolta pouring his aching heart out at the drive-in while animated hot dogs dance on the screen behind him, and, best of all, the toe-tappin', hand-jivin' song-and-dance numbers. Every one of them is a classic, from the sad songs of love, "Hopelessly Devoted to You" and "Sandy," to the sexy "You're the One that I Want" (in which Newton-John went from cutesy girl next door to black spray-on-trouser-clad vamp, a transformation some of her fans never quite got over), to the bouncy "Summer Nights." Best of all, of course, is "Greased Lightnin'"—the dance moves practiced in a million teenagers' homes in the decades ever since the film's release. **JB**

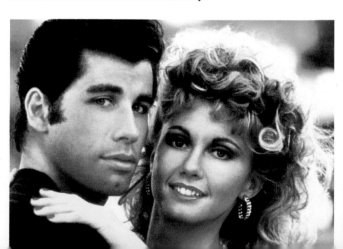

Shao Lin san shi liu fang Chia-Liang Liu, 1978
Shaolin Master Killer

Hong Kong (Shaw Brothers) 115m Color
Language Cantonese / English
Producer Mona Fong, Run Run Shaw
Screenplay Kuang Ni Photography Yeh tai
Huang, Arthur Wong Music Yung-Yu Chen
Cast Lung Chan, John Cheung, Norman
Chu, Hou Hsiao, Hoi San Lee, Chia Hui Liu,
Chia Yung Liu, Lieh Lo, Casanova Wong, Yue
Wong, Siu Tien Yuen

Chia-Liang Liu is nothing less than the best fight choreographer ever to work in the Hong Kong film industry. After cutting his teeth as the martial arts director for many of Chang Cheh's best films, he made the move to the director's chair, bringing his unparalleled kinetic sense with him.

Nowhere are Liu's visual gifts more apparent than in Shaolin Master Killer. Like so many other martial arts movies, this is a simple revenge story, but one that is broken into three unusually discrete chunks. In the first, San Te's (Gordon Liu) family is killed by the Manchus, and he swears revenge; in the third, he exacts that revenge. But the second section is where the story, the action, and the visuals all come together in glorious fashion.

The middle hour is devoted entirely to San Te's laborious training sessions within the thirty-six chambers of the legendary Shaolin Temple, where he develops his mind as well as his body. Most memorably, San Te must haul heavy buckets of water up a steep incline with daggers strapped to his biceps: lower the arms, stab yourself in the brisket.

The film's star is the famously bald Gordon Liu. The intensity he brings to his performance serves to make Shaolin Master Killer stand out in yet another way. And this isn't even to mention the fight scenes. Suffice it to say, they can't possibly leave you disappointed. **EdeS**

My Brilliant Career Gillian Armstrong, 1979

Australia (GUO, Margaret Fink, NSWFC)
100m Eastmancolor Producer Margaret
Fink Screenplay Eleanor Witcombe,
from novel by Miles Franklin
Photography Donald McAlpine
Music Nathan Waks, Robert Schumann
(from "Kinderszenen") Cast Judy Davis, Sam
Neill, Wendy Hughes, Robert Grubb, Max
Cullen, Aileen Britton, Peter Whitford, Patricia
Kennedy, Alan Hopgood, Julia Blake, David
Franklin, Marion Shad, Aaron Wood, Sue
Davies, Gordon Piper Oscar nomination
Anna Senior (costume)

One of a series of international hits to come from Australia in the late 1970s and early 1980s, My Brilliant Career also reflects the feminist movement of that era. Based on a novel by an Australian female writer (Miles Franklin), and with prominent women serving as director, screenwriter, and producer, the film traces the coming of age of Sybylla (Judy Davis), an adolescent who lives in the outback near the turn of the century.

Sybylla, determined on a "brilliant career," pays little respect to the more restricted life that her parents and society expect her to lead. A bit of a tomboy, she is out of place at her grandmother's house, where the women are elegant and finely mannered. Courted by two interesting suitors, Sybylla is well matched with Harry Beecham (Sam Neill). In the end, however, she decides against marriage, knowing that she will not be able to endure life as the wife of a country farmer—even one who offers her the opportunity to pursue her interest in writing. The film ends with Sybylla mailing off the manuscript that will be published as My Brilliant Career. Excellent acting from a fine ensemble cast and an interesting presentation of early twentieth-century sexual politics. **RBP**

West Germany (Albatros, Fengler, Autoren, Tango Film, Trio Film, WDR) 120m Fujicolor
Language German Producer Michael Fengler Screenplay Rainer Werner Fassbinder, Pea Fröhlich, Peter Märthesheimer Photography Michael Ballhaus Music Peer Raben Cast Hanna Schygulla, Klaus Löwitsch, Ivan Desny, Gisela Uhlen, Elisabeth Trissenaar, Gottfried John, Hark Bohm, George Byrd, Claus Holm, Günter Lamprecht, Anton Schiersner, Sonja Neudorfer, Volker Spengler, Isolde Barth, Bruce Low, Günther Kaufmann, Karl-Heinz von Hassel, Kristine De Loup, Hannes Kaetner Berlin International Film Festival Rainer Werner Fassbinder (reader jury of the Berliner Morgenpost, Golden Bear nomination), Hanna Schygulla (Silver Bear—actress), the whole team (outstanding single achievement—the whole team)

"I'm a master of deceit: a capitalist tool by day, and by night an agent of the proletarian masses."

Maria Braun
(Hanna Schygulla)

i

Actor and singer Schygulla was a major figure in the New German Cinema of the 1970s and '80s.

Die Ehe der Maria Braun Rainer Werner Fassbinder, 1979
The Marriage of Maria Braun

Like many of Rainer Werner Fassbinder's other films, *The Marriage of Maria Braun* focuses on a female character whose fate reflects the history of the German director's country. Married to a soldier, Hermann (Klaus Löwitsch), during World War II, Maria (Hanna Schygulla) believes her husband has died in battle; when peace is declared, she begins to work in a cabaret. Attacked by an American soldier who tries to rape her, she accidentally kills him during the struggle, which occurs on the very same night her husband returns. He takes responsibility for the crime, and while he remains in jail Maria works desperately to achieve redemption and to prepare a safe life for the days to come after his release. A decade of restless efforts turns her into a successful career woman, but happiness still seems impossible to attain because, though liberated, Hermann feels uncomfortable in her presence. He leaves for South America to make his own fortune, and finally comes back near the end of the film. But Maria's fate again proves to be cruel as, on the night of their reconciliation, a gas line blows up and kills them both.

The melodramatic premises in no way diminish the force of this remarkable film, which analyzes, through a particular case, the "German miracle." Paid for with huge sacrifices, Germany's reconstruction rested mostly on the fragile shoulders of its women. Not unanimously accepted, Fassbinder's idea about this postwar boom was that, "If the walls were reconstructed, the hearts remained broken." *The Marriage of Maria Braun* speaks about the loss of the soul in a society exalting prosperity. Brightly performed by Schygulla, Maria is forced to suffer for seeking self-respect and dignity by inhuman means. Fascinated by money, she loses her feminine charm.

Convinced by Danish-German director Douglas Sirk that melodrama always works, Fassbinder managed to avoid sentimentalism by being rigorous and efficient: His unmistakable "cold look" is still in place here. With *The Marriage of Maria Braun*, Fassbinder once again proves to be a master of the feminine portrait. **DD**

West Germany / France (Gaumont, Werner Herzog) 107m Eastmancolor **Language** German **Producer** Michael Gruskoff, Werner Herzog, Daniel Toscan du Plantier **Screenplay** Werner Herzog, from the novel *Dracula* by Bram Stoker **Photography** Jörg Schmidt-Reitwein **Music** Popol Vuh **Cast** Klaus Kinski, Isabelle Adjani, Bruno Ganz, Roland Topor, Walter Ladengast, Dan van Husen, Jan Groth, Carsten Bodinus, Martje Grohmann, Rijk de Gooyer, Clemens Scheitz, Lo van Hensbergen, John Leddy, Margiet van Hartingsveld, Tim Beekman **Berlin International Film Festival** Henning von Gierke (Silver Bear—production design), Werner Herzog nomination (Golden Bear)

*"Death is not the worst
... Can you imagine
enduring centuries,
experiencing each day
the same futilities."*

**Count Dracula
(Klaus Kinski)**

Nosferatu: Phantom der Nacht
Nosferatu: Phantom of the Night Werner Herzog, 1979

Werner Herzog's remake of F.W. Murnau's 1922 adaptation of *Dracula* is at once an effective and touching tribute to the German silent classic and a remarkable work in its own right. Arriving almost simultaneously with John Badham's *Dracula* and the George Hamilton vampire comedy *Love at First Bite* (both 1979), *Nosferatu: Phantom of the Night* retells Bram Stoker's story in a steady, almost hypnotic manner. Jonathan Harker (Bruno Ganz) travels through mistily beautiful yet threatening Carpathian mountainscapes to arrange for the relocation of the rat-faced, repulsive but melancholy Count Dracula (Klaus Kinski) from his castle fastness to the thriving city of Bremen. When his boat drifts into dock, the vampire unleashes a horde of white rats who bring plague to the community and cause far more death and devastation than his few petty predations.

In this version of the tale, Dr. Van Helsing (Walter Ladengast) is a petty irrelevance who is carried away by the police after Dracula's death, and—as for Murnau—humanity is represented by the heroine, the porcelain-fragile Lucy (Isabelle Adjani), whose self-sacrifice tempts the creature to linger beyond sunrise. Adding in themes perhaps drawn from other vampire films, the coda has Jonathan transformed into Dracula reborn and galloping across a beach to spread the contagion further.

Opening with footage of Mexican mummies and slow-motion bats, Herzog's film is misty and suggestive, recreating famous images of the long-fingered, hollow-eyed bloodsucker from the original film as Kinski's slightly whiny, self-pitying, nevertheless vicious Dracula elaborates on the inhumanity of Max Schreck's Graf von Orlok. With the novelist Roland Topor (The Tenant) as a giggling Renfield and very strange, portrait-like readings of the traditional hero and heroine roles from Ganz and Adjani, this is unconventional as a horror movie—with scare scenes that are paced slowly, struck by magical or black-comic business rather than anything like action or even plot. If the original *Nosferatu* remains the most frightening screen version of *Dracula*, then this transformative rethinking is certainly the most mystic and mysterious. **KN**

1979

[i]

Klaus Kinski's makeup took some four hours each day, with new latex ears having to be molded daily.

Stalker Andrei Tarkovsky, 1979

Like Andrei Tarkovsky's earlier *Solaris* (1972), *Stalker* is adapted from a popular Eastern bloc science-fiction novel (*The Roadside Picnic*, by Arkadi and Boris Strugatsky) and uses genre trappings—again a mysterious, possibly alien phenomenon that debatably materializes the innermost wishes of flawed investigators—to ask fundamental questions about humanity, memory, desire, and desolation.

In an unnamed small country, a Zone has appeared where the laws of physics and geography are suspended. Though the authorities police the borders of the Zone for the "protection" of the unwary, the title character, Stalker, (Aleksandr Kajdanovsky) is one of a small group of wounded sensitives who smuggle people past the barriers and guide them through the treacherous but magical space. Against the wishes of his wife (Alisa Frejndlikh), who has to care for their physically challenged but psychically gifted daughter, the Stalker takes two men—a writer in search of inspiration (Anatoli Solonitsyn) and a scientist with a covert mission (Nikolai Grinko)—into the Zone, past the rusting remains of a former military expedition, through perilous and often-changeable pathways, to "the Room," where wishes may come true.

It is not unthinkable that the Strugatskys' original novel could be remade one day as an action movie, but Tarkovky's version might more properly be tagged a reflection film: in the Zone, forward movement as often as not means doubling back, and we far more frequently see the travelers at rest; long periods of speechlessness, marked by haunting music and a natural soundscape, are punctuated by intense, challenging, possibly futile debate among the characters. The Zone is one of cinema's great magical places: damp green and sylvan above-ground giving way to watery, muddy, uninhabited recent ruins as the party nears the perhaps-mythical Room. Like MGM's Oz, the Zone is colored amid drab, monochrome reality, though the Stalker's daughter has her own color, notably in a breathtaking final shot that conveys her telekinetic powers with a simplicity as affecting in its own way as the bloody shocks of Brian De Palma in *Carrie* (1976) and *The Fury* (1978). **KN**

West Germany / Soviet Union (Mosfilm, ZDF) 163m BW / Eastmancolor **Language** Russian **Producer** Aleksandra Demidova **Screenplay** Arkadi Strugatsky, Boris Strugatsky, from the novel *The Roadside Picnic* by Arkadi and Boris Strugatsky **Photography** Aleksandr Knyazhinsky **Music** Eduard Artemyev **Cast** Aleksandr Kajdanovsky, Alisa Frejndlikh, Anatoli Solonitsyn, Nikolai Grinko, Natasha Abramova **Cannes Film Festival** Andrei Tarkovsky (prize of the ecumenical jury—special award)

"While I am digging for the truth . . . instead of discovering the truth I dig up a heap of, pardon . . . I'd better not name it."

Pistatel [the writer]
(Anatolly Solonitsyn)

i

The Zone of the film was inspired by a nuclear disaster in 1957 in the Russian province of Chelyabinsk.

Life of Brian Terry Jones, 1979

G.B. (HandMade, Python) 94m
Eastmancolor **Producer** John Goldstone
Screenplay Graham Chapman, John Cleese,
Terry Gilliam, Eric Idle, Terry Jones,
Michael Palin **Photography** Peter Biziou
Music Geoffrey Burgon, Eric Idle, Michael
Palin **Cast** Graham Chapman, John Cleese,
Terry Gilliam, Eric Idle, Terry Jones, Michael
Palin, Terence Bayler, Carol Cleveland,
Kenneth Colley, Neil Innes, Charles
McKeown, John Young, Gwen Taylor, Sue
Jones-Davies, Peter Brett

🛈

The script is dedicated to Keith
Moon of The Who, who died in 1978;
he had been cast as a street prophet.

Beginning its life as a joke (when asked what the next Python movie would be, cast member Eric Idle said, "Jesus Christ: Lust For Glory"), *Life of Brian* evolved into a subtler vehicle. Well, subtle for the Monty Python team, that is.

While trying (unsuccessfully) to avoid accusations of blasphemy by clearly establishing that Graham Chapman's Brian is "not the Messiah, he's a very naughty boy," *Life of Brian* plays fast and loose with New Testament characters, and along the way makes both satirical and moral points. Although the movie, like all the other Python films, is essentially a collection of surreal, violent, and very funny sketches held together with a loose narrative thread, this one has—for obvious reasons—a strong story. The final scene, with a crucified Idle singing "Always look on the bright side of life," as Brian dies on the cross, deserted by family, supporters, and friends, was arguably the bleakest of any comedy since Stanley Kubrick's *Dr. Strangelove* (1964). A huge international hit, *Life of Brian* nevertheless nearly failed to get made, only going into production courtesy of money from ex-Beatle George Harrison's nascent production company, HandMade Films. **KK**

Real Life Albert Brooks, 1979

U.S. (Paramount) 99m Color
Producer Penelope Spheeris
Screenplay Albert Brooks, Monica Mcgowan
Johnson, Harry Shearer **Photography** Eric
Saarinen **Music** Mort Lindsey **Cast** Dick
Haynes, Albert Brooks, Matthew Tobin, J.A.
Preston, Joseph Schaffler, Phyllis Quinn,
James Ritz, Clifford Einstein, Harry Einstein,
Mandy Einstein, Karen Einstein, James L.
Brooks, Zeke Manners, Charles Grodin,
Frances Lee McCain

Albert Brooks's debut feature, *Real Life*, has enjoyed a long life as a cult movie. Conceived in its day as a comedy inspired by a single, famous media event, the American "television verité" series *An American Family*, it has turned out to be an even more far-reaching satire of the entire, international phenomenon now known as "reality TV."

Developing the acerbic tone of his sketches for *Saturday Night Live*, Brooks here again casts himself as the entirely unlovable center of a hilariously misanthropic, modern fable. Once he moves himself and a crew (whose cameras are built into astronaut-like headgear) into the home of an "ordinary, typical" family, nothing remains real or sane for long. The seduction of glamorous showbiz and the lure of the almighty dollar control every single transaction in this film, giving the story its brutal logic.

Outside America, Brooks is often hailed as an idiosyncratic, radical filmmaker; Stanley Kubrick was among his biggest fans. His ruthlessly pared-down style, serving a form of comedy that lets no one off the hook, is deliberately disquieting, almost anti–Woody Allen. But if he had made only *Real Life*, his place in the annals of alternative American cinema would still be secure. **AM**

Breaking Away Peter Yates, 1979

U.S. (Fox) 100m Color **Producer** Peter
Yates **Screenplay** Steve Tesich
Photography Matthew F. Leonetti
Music Patrick Williams **Cast** Dennis
Christopher, Dennis Quaid, Daniel Stern,
Jackie Earle Haley, Barbara Barrie, Paul
Dooley, Robyn Douglass, Hart Bochner, Amy
Wright, Peter Maloney, John Ashton, Lisa
Shure, Jennifer K. Mickel, P.J. Soles, David K.
Blasé **Oscar** Steve Tesich (screenplay)
Oscar nominations Peter Yates (best
picture), Peter Yates (director), Barbara
Barrie (actress in support role),
Patrick Williams (music)

Some of the most perceptive accounts of modern America have been made by filmmakers blessed with an outsider's eye. In *Breaking Away*, British director Peter Yates manages to invest what might have been a routine coming-of-age teen movie with persuasive insights into how class functions in that allegedly classless society.

On the surface, it's simply about cycling nut and Italianophile Dave (Dennis Christopher), torn between loyalty to his likewise just-out-of-school pals, his working-class parents, and his attraction to a student at the university that sometimes seems to dominate his Indiana home-town. Will he get the girl, will he and his buddies beat the student teams in the Little Indy cycling race, will he pass—or even take—his exams? But for all the laughs and action (and the movie is very funny and very exciting), there is also a serious, intelligent, and surprisingly honest examination of how money, education, work prospects, and private aspirations combine to shape one's life and the person with whom one shares it.

Also worthy of mention are the skill in the construction of the racing sequences (Yates made *Bullitt* [1968], after all), the snappy dialogue, the Hawksian interweaving of ethics and relationships, the excellence of the cast (many of whom, like Paul Dooley as Dave's father, were never better), and the superb use of music. Huge fun. **GA**

Alien Ridley Scott, 1979

"In space no one can hear you scream." Alien's poster line was a classic come-on, but satisfyingly screams could be heard in cinemas. Defying the *Star Wars* (1977) craze, Ridley Scott resurrected the cheap genre of scary monsters from space, introduced it to exquisite, high-budget visuals, and created an arresting, nerve-wracking, adult-oriented science-fiction horror film.

Dan O'Bannon's hip screenplay is indebted to nifty 1950s schlocker *It! The Terror from Beyond Space* (1958) and follows the spooky manor formula of *The Cat and the Canary* (1939) or *Ten Little Indians* (1965), but set aboard a spacecraft and with a much more alarming yuck factor. The Nostromo is a giant deep-space tug with a minimal (and offbeat) crew led by Captain Dallas (Tom Skerrit) and including sharp Warrant Officer Ripley (Sigourney Weaver) and ship's cat Jones. Responding to a distress call, they discover a derelict alien craft and strange eggs. One hatches a face-hugging parasite that attaches itself to John Hurt's Kane and wreaks gruesome havoc once Kane collapses shrieking at breakfast and the alien bursts out of his chest. The rest of the cast reportedly didn't know what was coming, making their shock and revulsion genuine. Scott produces thrills and makes tense dramatic use of dark corridors as the dwindling crew, never having seen a teen horror flick apparently, make their ways into the beast's double set of extending jaws. What elevated anxiety into art via Oscar-winning visual effects is Alien's unique, awesome design and art direction mixing organic motifs with the metallic, and the sparingly glimpsed alien designed by artist H.R. Giger, its terrible beauty given a startling grace by statuesque Masai dancer Bolaji Badejo.

Weaver became a star and icon overnight as gutsy survivor Ripley, making her stand in skimpy vest and panties. She was actually set to film the ending naked, emphasizing the frailty of the human against the perfect killing machine, but 20th Century Fox forbade it, anxious to secure an R rating. Unusually for a horror franchise, the sequels were all assigned to directors with strong reputations for their distinctive visual styles—James Cameron, David Fincher, and Jean-Pierre Jeunet. **AE**

G.B. (Fox, Brandywine) 117m Color
Producer Gordon Carroll, David Giler, Walter Hill, Ivor Powell **Screenplay** Dan O'Bannon, Ronald Shusett, Dan O'Bannon, Walter Hill **Photography** Derek Vanlint **Music** Jerry Goldsmith **Cast** Tom Skerritt, Sigourney Weaver, Veronica Cartwright, Harry Dean Stanton, John Hurt, Ian Holm, Yaphet Kotto, Bolaji Badejo, Helen Horton **Oscar** H.R. Giger, Carlo Rambaldi, Brian Johnson, Nick Allder, Denys Ayling (special visual effects) **Oscar nomination** Michael Seymour, Leslie Dilley, Roger Christian, Ian Whittaker (art direction)

1979

> "Alien life form. Looks like it's been dead a long time. Fossilized. Looks like it's growing out of the chair."
>
> **Dallas**
> **(Tom Skerritt)**

i

Conceptual artist H.R. Giger suffered from night terrors, which inspired his design work to some extent.

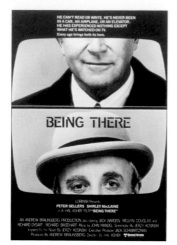

Being There Hal Ashby, 1979

While this was not actually Peter Sellers's last movie—that was the less-well-remembered *The Fiendish Plot of Doctor Fu Manchu* (1980)—*Being There* is generally accepted as the swan song to Sellers's career. Based on the 1971 novel by Jerzy Kosinski (who also wrote the screenplay), *Being There* was a labor of love for Sellers, who was obsessed with the book's central character, the simple gardener, Chance. In 1971, shortly after the book came out, Sellers sent Kosinski a telegram saying "AVAILABLE IN MY GARDEN OR OUTSIDE OF IT," followed by his telephone number.

Sellers's influence must have helped this film get made, as it is remarkably low-key and quirky even by 1970s standards. The story is, aptly, a simple one: after the death of his wealthy employer Chauncey Gardiner, the childlike Chance (Sellers) is mistaken for Gardiner. Taken in by Senator Benjamin Rand (Melvyn Douglas) and his wife (Shirley Maclaine), his every utterance is taken as a profound remark about the state of human existence. Following a series of just-about-plausible events, he is seemingly about to become President of the United States when he vanishes in a suitably Christlike manner.

In less capable hands, *Being There* might have been a clumsy parable or weak satire on human gullibility, but with carefully paced direction by Hal Ashby (who gives the film a gentle, calm, and wintry feel throughout) and a superb central performance by Sellers, the movie works beautifully. This is also thanks to its often hilarious script, which constantly plays on verbal misunderstanding (most famously, Chance's unintentional sexual innuendo when, talking about television, he tells a pair of swingers that "I like to watch").

Sellers, who once said, "I have absolutely no personality at all. I am a chameleon. When I am not playing a role, I am nobody," brought a powerful passivity to the role, playing a polar opposite to his manic comic creations. Fittingly, after a long search for a suitable voice for Chance, he found one in the cautious, flat tones of another great British movie comic, Stan Laurel. **KK**

U.S. / G.B. / West Germany / Japan (BSB, CIP, Enigma, Fujisankei, Lorimar, NatWest, Northstar) 130m Technicolor **Language** English / Russian **Producer** Andrew Braunsberg **Screenplay** Jerzy Kosinski, from his novel **Photography** Caleb Deschanel **Music** Johnny Mandel **Cast** Peter Sellers, Shirley MacLaine, Melvyn Douglas, Jack Warden, Richard A. Dysart, Richard Basehart, Ruth Attaway, David Clennon, Fran Brill, Denise DuBarry, Oteil Burbridge, Ravenell Keller, Brian Corrigan, Alfredine P. Brown, Donald Jacob **Oscar** Melvyn Douglas (actor in support role) **Oscar nomination** Peter Sellers (actor) **Cannes Film Festival** Hal Ashby (Golden Palm nomination)

"I admire your good solid sense. That's precisely what we lack on Capitol Hill."

President "Bobby" (Jack Warden)

i

Peter Sellers chose a deliberately blank style of voice to convey the character of Chance.

U.S. (Rollins & Joffe)
96m BW **Producer** Charles H. Joffe
Screenplay Woody Allen, Marshall Brickman
Photography Gordon Willis **Music** George
Gershwin **Cast** Woody Allen, Diane Keaton,
Michael Murphy, Mariel Hemingway, Meryl
Streep, Anne Byrne, Karen Ludwig, Michael
O'Donoghue, Victor Truro, Tisa Farrow, Helen
Hanft, Bella Abzug, Gary Weis, Kenny Vance,
Charles Levin **Oscar nominations** Woody
Allen, Marshall Brickman (screenplay), Mariel
Hemingway (actress in support role)

> "No, I didn't read the
> piece on China's faceless
> masses. I was checking
> out the lingerie ads."
>
> **Isaac Davis**
> **(Woody Allen)**

Manhattan Woody Allen, 1979

"Chapter One. He adored New York City. He idolized it all out of proportion." Satiric and lovely, *Manhattan* is the rapturous high point of Woody Allen's on-screen love affair with New York City and even opens like an expressive Valentine, with an affectionate montage of city images. His 1977 film *Annie Hall* won the major prizes, but this bittersweet follow-up film (also written by Allen and Marshall Brickman) is the perfect balancing act between wry, screamingly good wit ("When it comes to relationships with women, I ought to get the August Strindberg award") and well-aimed wounds. Allen's intellectual romantic Isaac Davis, a comedy writer, is hurt by Diane Keaton's pretentious WASP/Radcliffe tootsie Mary Wilke and runs back to the delightful and very fine, worryingly young Tracy (Mariel Hemingway) whom he has himself hurt.

Manhattan has some of the same Annie Hall elements that have come to be thought of as signature Woody. There are the psychoanalysis-dependent protagonists ("He's done a great job on you, you know ... your self-esteem is like a notch below Kafka's") and the confidence-sharing, wisecracking relationship with a male buddy (here Michael Murphy). Among the pleasures that are distinctive to Manhattan are an early film role for Meryl Streep (as Ike's antagonistic ex-wife Jill), atmospheric wide shots like the dawn scene of Allen and Keaton sitting on a bench below the 59th Street Bridge (the image used for the poster), or the compositions in their planetarium date, luminous black-and-white, widescreen cinematography by Gordon Willis, and a dazzlingly deployed George Gershwin score (played by the New York Philharmonic, conducted by Zubin Mehta).

There is a particularly great, revealing moment at the end of the film when Woody/Ike muses in monologue that Manhattanites create neuroses for themselves to avoid "more unsolvable, terrifying problems about the universe" and cheers himself (and the viewer) up by listing a captivating assortment of people and things—headed up by Groucho Marx, sports, music, literature, art, food, and not forgetting movies—that make life worth living. **AE**

i

Mariel Hemingway, granddaughter of the famous writer, was just sixteen during the filming of *Manhattan*.

Apocalypse Now Francis Ford Coppola, 1979

During the Vietnam War, Captain Willard (Martin Sheen) is ordered to find and "terminate with extreme prejudice" a Special Forces commander, Colonel Kurtz (Marlon Brando), who has turned renegade. Willard's journey is superficially an action adventure, but equally obviously an allegory of war's insanity and the journey of self-discovery. Finally, when Brando makes his appearance, the film becomes a philosophical search for a resolution to the insoluble mysteries of madness and evil.

Francis Coppola's epic was developed by gung-ho, prowar writer John Milius with Coppola's Zoetrope colleague and fellow antiwar guilty liberal George Lucas (originally set to direct) as a loose adaptation of Joseph Conrad's 1902 novel *Heart Of Darkness*, made pertinent to the war then being fought. The other main inspiration was Homer's *Odyssey*, prompting Coppola in a moment of levity to dub his movie "The Idiocy." The difficulties of filming are legend: A sixteen-week shoot in the Philippines became 238 days of principal photography. Sheen, only thirty-six, suffered a near-fatal heart attack on location, but returned five weeks later. Brando showed up overweight and unprepared, forcing yet another re-think of how to end the picture before it killed them all.

Flawed but staggering cinema, the set pieces are unforgettable. *Apocalypse Now* opens (to The Doors' song "The End") with an electrifying montage as the broken and wasted Willard's demons overwhelm him in a Saigon hotel room. His indispensable and highly quotable narration, an afterthought during editing, was written by Michael Herr, whose Vietnam reportage in his 1977 book *Dispatches* had provided another source for Milius. Heading upriver aboard a patrol boat, Willard and the crew rendezvous with their Air Cavalry escort, commanded by one of the great scary loonies of the screen, Colonel "I love the smell of napalm in the morning" Kilgore (Robert Duvall), a demented, charismatic surfer dude in a Stetson who orders a dawn raid on a Viet Cong–held coastal village, the film's tour de force. The unit takes off at sunrise as the bugler blows the traditional cavalry charge. Kilgore blasts Wagner's "The Ride of the Valkyries" from his chopper and dispenses "Death from Above" in fountains of smoke and fire. This is but the first of several surreal, nightmarish, stoned rock-'n'-roll encounters vividly evoking fatal culture clashes and the psychoses of war, leading up to the "Gates of Hell," an engagement at the last outpost before Cambodia and the scene of an acid-trip frenzy of flares, screams, and gunfire.

On the other side, decapitated heads and the miasma enveloping Kurtz's compound await. Even more horrifically, so do the gibbering photojournalist (Dennis Hopper) and the ranting Brando, whose butchering is feverishly intercut with the sacrificial slaughter of an ox before Coppola surrenders to an unnervingly ambiguous ending. The ultimate horror of this hypnotic trip, though, is how closely it has been said to capture the reality of 'Nam. **AE**

1979

U.S. (Omni, Zoetrope) 153m Technicolor **Language** English / French / Vietnamese / Khmer **Producer** Francis Ford Coppola, Gray Frederickson, Fred Roos, Tom Sternberg **Screenplay** John Milius, Francis Ford Coppola, from the novel *Heart of Darkness* by Joseph Conrad **Photography** Vittorio Storaro **Music** Carmine Coppola, Francis Ford Coppola, Mickey Hart, The Doors, Wagner **Cast** Marlon Brando, Robert Duvall, Martin Sheen, Frederic Forrest, Albert Hall, Sam Bottoms, Laurence Fishburne, Dennis Hopper, G.D. Spradlin, Harrison Ford, Jerry Ziesmer, Scott Glenn, Bo Byers, James Keane, Kerry Rossall **Oscars** Vittorio Storaro (photography), Walter Murch, Mark Berger, Richard Beggs, Nathan Boxer (sound) **Oscar nominations** Francis Ford Coppola, Fred Roos, Gray Frederickson, Tom Sternberg (best picture), Francis Ford Coppola (director), Robert Duvall (actor in support role), John Milius, Francis Ford Coppola (screenplay), Dean Tavoularis, Angelo P. Graham, George R. Nelson (art direction), Richard Marks, Walter Murch, Gerald B. Greenberg, Lisa Fruchtman (editing) **Cannes Film Festival** Francis Ford Coppola (FIPRESCI award, Golden Palm, tied with Die Blechtrommel)

ℹ

The sound of helicopters was created on a synthesizer to blend in with the music in some sequences.

All That Jazz Bob Fosse, 1979

"It's showtime, folks!" This fascinating, imaginative, and intimately autobiographical musical that still divides audiences is an American 8½ (1963), a startlingly candid testament from Bob Fosse, the gifted dancer, brilliant choreographer, multiple Tony award winner, and Oscar-winning director of *Cabaret* (1972). Fosse's astonishingly frank dance drama—which he conceived, co-scripted, and made shortly after he had undergone open-heart surgery—has as his alter ego the Oscar-nominated Roy Scheider's chain-smoking, womanizing, pill-popping choreographer-director Joe Gideon. Too busy rehearsing his erotically charged new show, browbeating backers, and chasing leggy showgirls to seriously heed his troubling chest pains, Joe is dying, while contemplating personal failures, professional triumphs, and great showbiz moments. Brilliant or pretentious, according to taste, *All That Jazz* is savagely witty on backstage life and thrilling in how well it conveys the obsessive, all-consuming excitement of those passionately committed and driven in their work.

Sensational dancing in the jazzy signature Fosse style and eye-popping production numbers punctuate the confessional reminiscences of the arrogant, satirical theatrical eminence. These include flashes from his seedy burlesque roots and his insufficiently remorseful view of the women he has loved, exploited, adored, and discarded in his life (one of them obviously based on Fosse's third wife, Broadway star Gwen Vernon, another played by his protégé and latter-day partner Anne Reinking).

Audaciously structured and edited as well, *All That Jazz* won four deserved Oscars and stands alongside *Cabaret* as the best two musical dramas in thirty years. As it turned out, this undeniably self-indulgent celluloid epitaph was made nearly a decade before the fact. Fosse died suddenly, if inevitably, of a heart attack in 1987, at the moment his revival of his 1960s Broadway hit *Sweet Charity* (which had provided his feature directorial debut) was opening. His legacy made itself felt in the Oscar-winning *Chicago* (2002), an old Kander–Ebb musical reworked into the dark razzmatazz danse macabre we know by Fosse in the 1970s. **AE**

U.S. (Fox, Columbia) 123m Technicolor **Producer** Robert Alan Aurthur **Screenplay** Robert Alan Aurthur, Bob Fosse **Photography** Giuseppe Rotunno **Music** Ralph Burns, Peter Allen, Barry Mann, Mike Stoller, Antonio Vivaldi **Cast** Roy Scheider, Jessica Lange, Ann Reinking, Leland Palmer, Cliff Gorman, Ben Vereen, Erzsebet Foldi, Michael Tolan, Max Wright, William LeMassena, Irene Kane, Deborah Geffner, Kathryn Doby, Anthony Holland, Robert Hitt **Oscars** Philip Rosenberg, Tony Walton, Edward Stewart, Gary J. Brink (art direction), Albert Wolsky (costume), Alan Heim (editing), Ralph Burns (music) **Oscar nominations** Robert Alan Aurthur (best picture), Bob Fosse (director), Robert Alan Aurthur, Bob Fosse (screenplay), Roy Scheider (actor), Giuseppe Rotunno (photography) **Cannes Film Festival** Bob Fosse (Golden Palm), tied with Kagemusha

"Sometimes I don't know where the bullshit ends and the truth begins."

Joe Gideon (Roy Scheider)

i

Ann Reinking had to audition several times before being cast as Kate Jagger, a part based on herself.

The Muppet Movie James Frawley, 1979

U.S. / G.B. (Henson, ITC) 97m Eastmancolor
Producer Jim Henson Screenplay Jack
Burns, Jerry Juhl Photography Isidore
Mankofsky Music Kenny Ascher, Paul
Williams Cast Jim Henson, Frank Oz, Dave
Goelz, Jerry Nelson, Richard Hunt, Charles
Durning, Austin Pendleton, Scott Walker,
Edgar Bergen, Milton Berle, Mel Brooks,
James Coburn, Dom DeLuise, Elliott Gould,
Bob Hope Oscar nominations Paul
Williams, Kenny Ascher (music), Paul
Williams, Kenny Ascher (song)

When is a road movie not a road movie? When the travelers along that road are a bunch of puppets—or, more specifically, Muppets, the creation of Jim Henson, whose eye for the absurd revolutionized children's programming. Although placing such "stars" as Kermit the Frog, Fozzy Bear, Ralph the Dog, and Miss Piggy in the real world (as opposed to the soundstage of "The Muppet Show") robs them of some of their magic, *The Muppet Movie* still has plenty of magic to go around. And, of course, silliness, because Muppets don't always agree with the laws of logic, let alone physics.

Kermit is a country frog out to make it big in Hollywood, and on the way he picks up a motley crew of companions, overcomes several obstacles, and evades capture by a villain who wants to exploit him as the mascot for his chain of Frog's Legs restaurants. But the plot comes a distant second to the songs and numerous celebrity cameos (some of them Muppets as well), culminating in an encounter with Orson Welles. The music is engaging, the voices (courtesy of the likes of Henson and Frank Oz) expressive, and the whole exercise just so much giddy fun. **JKl**

1979

Cristo si è fermato a Eboli Francesco Rosi, 1979
Christ Stopped at Eboli

Italy (RAI-Radiotelevisione Italiana - TV2,
Vides Cinematografica) 150m Color
Producer Nicola Carraro, Franco Cristaldi
Screenplay Francesco Rosi, Tonino Guerra,
Raffaele La Caprina, from novel by Carlo Levi
Photography Pasqualino De Santis
Music Piero Piccioni Cast Gian Maria
Volonté, Paolo Bonacelli, Alain Cuny, Lea
Massari, Irene Papas, François Simon, Luigi
Infantino, Antonio Allocca, Enzo Vitale

Francesco Rosi's adaptation of Carlo Levi's autobiographical novel is a stately, picturesque drama that captures the cadences of pastoral life in a small, rural village in southern Italy during the mid-1930s. Levi's anti-fascist activities led to his being banished to the region of Lucania, now known as Basilicata. The film's title comes from the local belief that "Christ stopped short of here, at Eboli," suggesting that because of the area's remoteness, even Christianity passed it by. Its people are so removed from the realities of their country as a whole that they are oblivious to the turbulence tearing Italy apart, as it heads inexorably toward war.

The town Levi resides in has no commercial center. Food is scarce and life, mostly comprised of toiling near-fallow land, is harsh. As days turn to months, Levi becomes ingrained within the small community, setting up a small medical practice, which challenges centuries of superstitious belief, but to which the locals are grateful. However, the outside world slowly creeps into the town, as Mussolini's grip on the country intensifies.

Gian Maria Volonté's one-note performance notwithstanding—nothing seems to move the actor beyond an expression of glazed bemusement throughout—Rosi's film underpins the political, cultural, and economic rift between the country's wealthy north and its struggling south. He invests his characters with dignity and, through Levi, reveals his admiration for their capacity for survival as they eek out a living upon this beautiful, yet barren, land. **IHS**

The last law in a world gone out of control. Pray that he's out there somewhere.

MAD MAX

BYRON KENNEDY · GEORGE MILLER · MEL GIBSON · BRIAN MAY
JAMES McCAUSLAND AND GEORGE MILLER

Mad Max George Miller, 1979

Australia (Crossroads, Kennedy Miller) 93m Eastmancolor **Producer** Byron Kennedy **Screenplay** James McCausland, George Miller **Photography** David Eggby **Music** Brian May **Cast** Mel Gibson, Joanne Samuel, Hugh Keays-Byrne, Steve Bisley, Tim Burns, Roger Ward, Lisa Aldenhoven, David Bracks, Bertrand Cadart, David Cameron, Robina Chaffey, Stephen Clark, Mathew Constantine, Jerry Day, Reg Evans

"I'm scared Fif... Look, any longer out on that road and I'm one of them, a terminal psychotic..."

Max Rockatansky (Mel Gibson)

Although the 1981 film *The Road Warrior*—the second installment of writer-director George Miller's postapocalyptic "trilogy" (*Mad Max Beyond Thunderdome* followed in 1985, and a fourth film is also in the works)—tends to receive most of the critical acclaim, the jaw-dropping *Mad Max*, released two years earlier, is where it all started. For it was here that Miller first brought to the screen his hellish vision of a barren, gang-ridden Australia, with the aid of a new young actor by the name of Mel Gibson.

Gibson was just twenty-three years old when he won the role of Max Rockatansky (as legend has it, Gibson auditioned the day after being in a bar fight and his distinctively black-and-blue face stuck in the mind of the casting director), and was such an unknown that when *Mad Max* was released in America, the preview trailers didn't even feature him but instead focused on the movie's explosions and car crashes. In retrospect, of course, Gibson's portrayal of a leather-jacketed antihero is an essential element of the picture.

In a desolate future Australia, Rockatansky is a motor cop trying to retain order in a quickly disintegrating society. Gangs race up and down the abandoned highways, raping and pillaging wherever they see fit, and one such group ends up at the door of Max's wife and child. When they are murdered, he seeks revenge, and so begins a violent rampage involving spectacular car chases, brutal fights, and relentless action.

What is even more impressive is the fact that the entire film cost just $400,000 to make—the budget was so tight that Miller is said to have crashed his own car for one scene—yet went on to make over $100 million, making it one of the most profitable movies of all time. *Mad Max* deservedly became a cult hit around the world (despite being dubbed into "American" in the United States, where it was thought audiences wouldn't understand the Australian accents) and remains to this day a striking, bleak, and memorable piece of cinema. **JB**

i

Director George Miller raised funds for the film by working as an emergency room doctor.

Die Blechtrommel Volker Schlöndorff, 1979
The Tin Drum

West Germany / France / Poland /
Yugoslavia (Argos, Artémis, Bioskop, Film
Polski, Franz Seitz, GGB-14, Hallelujah,
Jadran) 142m Eastmancolor
Language German / Polish / Russian
Producer Anatole Dauman, Franz Seitz
Screenplay Jean-Claude Carrière, Günter
Grass, Franz Seitz, Volker Schlöndorff, from
novel by Günter Grass **Photography** Igor
Luther **Music** Lothar Brühne, Maurice Jarre,
Friedrich Meyer **Cast** Mario Adorf, Angela
Winkler, David Bennent, Katharina Thalbach,
Daniel Olbrychski, Tina Engel, Berta Drews,
Roland Teubner, Tadeusz Kunikowski, Andréa
Ferréol, Heinz Bennent, Ilse Pagé, Werner
Rehm, Käte Jaenicke, Helmut Brasch
Oscar West Germany (best foreign
language film)

From 1997 to 2001 *The Tin Drum* was
banned in Oklahoma after being
accused of violating obscenity laws.

An allegory about infantilism, Volker Schlöndorff's *The Tin Drum* is told
through the point of view of Oskar Metzerath (David Bennent), a German
boy on the sideline of history. Omniscient before birth, his life becomes
the frame for judging adult behavior, especially with regard to
troublesome, obsessive sexuality. When he receives a tin drum for his
third birthday, Oskar refuses to grow any bigger even as he grows older.
Afterward observing the rise of Nazism, he bangs his drum and exhibits
a scream to break glass whenever he feels libidinously challenged or
disappointed. Gradually, however, Oskar's size reduces him to little more
than a freak show, simultaneously suggesting the absence of a moral
conscience among people who supported the Third Reich.

Throughout its length the picture shocks and confuses. A midget
circus act transforms into the headline of Parisian nightlife. Eels spill from
a severed horse's head. A Nazi rally transforms into "The Blue Danube."
Most disturbing, Oskar, the teenager trapped in a boy's body played by
twelve-year-old Bennent, makes love to his housemaid-turned-
stepmother, possibly conceiving his child/brother. A sensation ever since
being released in 1979, *The Tin Drum* is a fantasy turned on end with
unexpected jolts. **GC-Q**

651

The Jerk Carl Reiner, 1979

U.S. (Aspen) 94m Technicolor
Producer William E. McEuen, David V. Picker
Screenplay Steve Martin, Carl Gottlieb,
Michael Elias Photography Victor J. Kemper
Music Jack Elliott Cast Steve Martin,
Bernadette Peters, Catlin Adams, Mabel King,
Richard Ward, Dick Anthony Williams, Bill
Macy, Dick O'Neill, Maurice Evans, Helena
Carroll, Ren Woods, Pepe Serna, Sonny Terry,
Brownie McGhee, Jackie Mason

Even though largely misunderstood upon release, Carl Reiner's blissfully silly 1979 comedy turned out to be that year's third biggest box office draw. The debut feature film of comedian and writer Steve Martin, his concept of an idiot living his dream despite appearances was well ahead of its time. Years later, excessive stereotyping formed the backbone of successful comedies by the Farrelly Brothers—updating Martin only with their trademark obscene and overt sexual references for a more shock-resistant 1990s audience.

The Jerk's main character, a white-haired, thin, and pale Navin R. Johnson (Martin) was "raised a poor black child." It is funny because it is the bald and bland truth. Navin was abandoned as a baby and adopted by a black family who had love to spare. On his eighteenth birthday, shocked to learn that he isn't the Johnson's natural child, the naïf heads off to St. Louis to seek his destiny. The trip is serendipitous, leading the gullible but happy-go-lucky jerk to fame, fortune, and love. Romantically linked to Martin at the time, Bernadette Peters's quiet, creamy-limbed Gibson girl is a nifty foil to her leading man's riveting comedic skills. *The Jerk* led to a TV movie remake and a pilot for a television series, although both were unsuccessful. Hopes were high, but in vain, for the next pairing of Martin and Peters was in the grievously mistimed *Pennies from Heaven* (1981). **KK**

Kramer vs. Kramer Robert Benton, 1979

U.S. (Columbia) 105m Technicolor
Producer Stanley R. Jaffe Screenplay Robert
Benton, from novel by Avery Corman
Photography Néstor Almendros
Music Herb Harris, John Kander
Cast Dustin Hoffman, Meryl Streep, Jane
Alexander, Justin Henry, Howard Duff,
George Coe, JoBeth Williams, Bill Moor,
Howland Chamberlain, Jack Ramage, Jess
Osuna, Nicholas Hormann, Ellen Parker,
Shelby Brammer, Carol Nadell Oscar Stanley
R. Jaffe (best picture), Robert Benton
(director), Robert Benton (screenplay),
Dustin Hoffman (actor), Meryl Streep (actress
in support role) Oscar nomination Justin
Henry (actor in support role), Jane Alexander
(actress in support role), Néstor Almendros
(photography), Gerald B. Greenberg (editing)

The 1970s began with Arthur Hiller's old-fashioned weepie *Love Story*, but ended with this very modern heart-wrencher from writer-director Robert Benton. When Joanna Kramer (Meryl Streep) realizes her marriage to Ted (Dustin Hoffman) isn't working, she walks away, leaving him to bring up their young son Billy (a nice performance from eight-year-old Justin Henry, one that's not overly cute. It won him an Oscar nomination for Best Supporting Actor—making him the youngest-ever Oscar nominee). Previously a working dad who had contributed more money than time and emotion to his child, Ted has to learn by trial and error how to raise his son alone. Of course, because nothing in movie life goes smoothly, he is just getting the hang of things when Joanna returns, wanting to sue him for custody.

Both Hoffman and Streep give strong, natural performances (they won Best Actor and Best Supporting Actress Oscars, and the movie won Best Picture), especially in the tense courtroom scenes, while director Benton shows restraint during the bonding moments between Ted and his son that could easily have become overwrought and overplayed. A fascinating and moving look at the true impact—on parents as well as children—of both separation and divorce. **JB**

Ordinary People Robert Redford, 1980

U.S. (Paramount, Wildwood) 124m
Technicolor **Producer** Ronald L. Schwary
Screenplay Alvin Sargent, from novel by
Judith Guest **Photography** John Bailey
Music Marvin Hamlisch **Cast** Donald
Sutherland, Mary Tyler Moore, Judd Hirsch,
Timothy Hutton, M. Emmet Walsh, Elizabeth
McGovern, Dinah Manoff, Fredric Lehne,
James Sikking, Basil Hoffman, Scott Doebler,
Quinn K. Redeker, Mariclare Costello, Meg
Mundy, Elizabeth Hubbard **Oscars** Ronald L.
Schwary (best picture), Robert Redford
(director), Alvin Sargent (screenplay),
Timothy Hutton (actor in support role)
Oscar nominations Mary Tyler Moore
(actress), Judd Hirsch (actor in support role)

> *"We would have been
> all right if there hadn't
> been any mess. But you
> can't handle mess."*
>
> **Calvin Jarrett
> (Donald Sutherland)**

"We were going to our son's funeral and you were worrying what I wore on my feet!" It is still a source of indignation to some that Robert Redford's beautifully crafted and measured directorial debut should have bested Martin Scorsese's *Raging Bull* in the Academy Awards, taking the Oscars for Best Picture and Direction. Honors for *Ordinary People* also went to nineteen-year-old Timothy Hutton for Best Supporting Actor (making him the youngest male to win this Oscar), and to screenwriter Alvin Sargent for his sensitive, intelligent adaptation of Judith Guest's acclaimed novel about the impact of a teenage son's death on a family. But those who don't "get" this movie are missing a remarkably fine, intimate personal drama about people unable to articulate the truth of their inner lives. Understandably, its appeal proved strongest in the United States, where its impressive commercial showing reflected 1980s America's receptiveness to the subject of getting in touch with one's feelings.

Hutton plays high-school teen Conrad Jarrett, overwhelmed by guilt and suicidal depression since his popular older brother drowned in the sailing accident he survived. There is no understanding or help for him from his distant, unsympathetic mother, Beth (Mary Tyler Moore), a control freak preoccupied with neatly ordered appearances and firmly in denial of her resentment. His successful, easygoing father, Calvin (Donald Sutherland), is concerned for the boy but doesn't know how to talk to him about what matters or express his own feelings. It falls to a frank, hands-on psychiatrist (Judd Hirsch) to reach Conrad and encourage him to acknowledge his deep distress and anger. Ultimately, only his father's love can **save** the boy, when connecting with him forces a painful choice.

Set in a wealthy Chicago suburb, the calm depiction of the Jarretts' social status and privileged comfort plays up the turbulence beneath the surface. The principals are superb, cast very much against type, particularly sitcom sweetheart Moore, and there is a radiant debut from Elizabeth McGovern as Conrad's sweet, awkward girlfriend. Redford's films are uniquely American and always graceful. This sincere, restrained, signature production epitomizes his liberal humanism. **AE**

i

Aged nineteen, Tim Hutton was the
youngest actor to win an Academy
Award for Best Supporting Actor.

Star Wars: Episode V—The Empire Strikes Back Irvin Kershner, 1980

"It is a dark time for the Rebellion...." Darth Vader (David Prowse) searches obsessively for callow hero Luke Skywalker (Mark Hamill). Luke begins to discover his destiny. Roguish adventurer Han Solo (Harrison Ford) has bounty hunter Boba Fett (Jeremy Bulloch) snapping at his heels. Rebel princess Leia (Carrie Fisher) has unbraided her earmuff coiffure into a bun, and the evil Empire has a new array of techno-terrors with which to plague the gallant freedom fighters beleaguered in a galaxy far, far away.

The best picture in George Lucas's touchstone of modern cinema, the original *Star Wars* trilogy, this knockout sequel to the 1977 blockbuster and cultural phenomenon caps the first with more Oscar-winning special effects. Episode V has more personality: Romance blossoms in the lead trio, and strong new characters appear, all of them safely in the sure hands of studio workhorse Irvin Kershner. The action rages, from the spectacular ice planet Hoth to the rebels fighting their first epic land battle. The battle drives on to the cliffhanging climax in Cloud City, where Han's past catches up with him—and arch-fiend Vader reveals to Luke the shocking truth at the heart of the *Star Wars* myth. Between these assaults, Luke continues to train as a Jedi knight, experiencing the Force in the swamps of Dagobah under the tutelage of quirky mystic master Yoda—a wizened puppet sage performed with startling expressiveness and exasperation by Muppeteer Frank "Miss Piggy" Oz.

Like its predecessor, *The Empire Strikes Back* incorporates all the hectic thrills of 1930s Saturday serials. The cracking screenplay by Leigh Brackett—noted for her collaborations with Howard Hawks—and impressive newcomer Lawrence Kasdan hurtles along with a spirited sense of romantic fun. One-liners became catchphrases—"I have a baaad feeling about this." Charming comic interplay for the scene-stealing androids C-3PO and R2-D2, and ever-weirder alien creatures wowed audiences the world over. Restored by Lucas in 1997 with digitally enhanced effects and an additional three minutes, this rollicking popcorn adventure is arguably even slicker and just as entertaining today. **AE**

U.S. (Lucasfilm Ltd.) 124m Color
Producer Gary Kurtz, George Lucas
Screenplay George Lucas, Leigh Brackett, Lawrence Kasdan **Photography** Peter Suschitzky **Music** John Williams **Cast** Mark Hamill, Harrison Ford, Carrie Fisher, Billy Dee Williams, Anthony Daniels, David Prowse, Kenny Baker, Peter Mayhew, Frank Oz, Alec Guinness, Jeremy Bulloch, John Hollis, Jack Purvis, Des Webb, Kathryn Mullen **Oscars** Bill Varney, Steve Maslow, Gregg Landaker, Peter Sutton (sound), Brian Johnson, Richard Edlund, Dennis Muren, Bruce Nicholson (special visual effects) **Oscar nominations** Norman Reynolds, Leslie Dilley, Harry Lange, Alan Tomkins, Michael Ford (art direction), John Williams (music)

> "The force is with you, young Skywalker, but you are not a Jedi yet."

Darth Vader (David Prowse)

🛈

Stuart Freeborn's design for Yoda was based partly on his own face, partly on that of Albert Einstein.

Atlantic City Louis Malle, 1980

U.S. / Canada / France (Cine-Neighbor, Famous Players, International, Merchant, Paramount, Selta, CFDC) 104m Color **Language** English / French **Producer** Denis Héroux **Screenplay** John Guare **Photography** Richard Ciupka **Music** Michel Legrand **Cast** Burt Lancaster, Susan Sarandon, Kate Reid, Michel Piccoli, Hollis McLaren, Robert Joy, Al Waxman, Robert Goulet, Moses Znaimer, Angus MacInnes, Sean Sullivan, Wallace Shawn, Harvey Atkin, Norma Dell'Agnese, Louis Del Grande **Oscar nominations** Denis Héroux (best picture), Louis Malle (director), John Guare (screenplay), Burt Lancaster (actor), Susan Sarandon (actress)

A wonderfully hard-to-categorize combination of crime thriller, love story, *Beauty and the Beast*–style fairy tale, and meditation on the changes affecting an American resort over half a century, Louis Malle's wry masterpiece centers on Burt Lancaster's aging numbers-runner, a garrulous romantic given to escaping the seedy circumstances of his current life with nostalgic fabulations of the way it was when he was big-time with the likes of Capone, Siegel, et al.

Suddenly an opportunity arises to revive his fortunes and self-respect in the shape of a feckless hippie coke-dealer (Robert Joy) who just happens to be the ex of a casino croupier (Susan Sarandon) the old man fancies from afar. Wealth and a young woman might be his again; trouble is, the coke really belongs to the Mob.

Malle and writer John Guare gently explore the gulf between dreams, delusion, and reality, making superb use of the fading glories of the titular playground, notching up the suspense here and there with expertly staged action sequences, and tethering the whole feather-light confection with solidly constructed performances from all involved. It's Lancaster, however, who finally steals the laurels in *Atlantic City*, with a career-best performance rivaled only by his J.J. Hunsecker in *Sweet Smell of Success* (1957). **GA**

Le dernier métro François Truffaut, 1980
The Last Metro

France (Carrosse, SFP, Sédif, TF1) 128m Fujicolor **Language** French **Producer** François Truffaut **Screenplay** Jean-Claude Grumberg, Suzanne Schiffman, François Truffaut **Photography** Néstor Almendros **Music** Georges Delerue **Cast** Catherine Deneuve, Gérard Depardieu, Jean Poiret, Heinz Bennent, Andréa Ferréol, Maurice Risch, Paulette Dubost, Jean-Louis Richard, Sabine Haudepin, Jean-Pierre Klein, Renata, Marcel Berbert, Hénia Ziv, László Szabó, Martine Simonet **Oscar nomination** France (best foreign language film)

There have been many French films about World War II and the German occupation, but none as sumptuous as François Truffaut's *The Last Metro*. This is also Truffaut's film about the theater, the second installment in his unfinished trilogy about spectacle, after his film about filmmaking, *La Nuit Américaine* (aka *Day for Night* [1973]).

While Jewish director Lucas Steiner (Heinz Bennent) hides in the cellar for the duration of the war, his wife Marion (Catherine Deneuve) runs the theater, putting on a play with rising star Bernard Granger (Gérard Depardieu). Truffaut takes a few liberties with history, yet crams in myriad true details of everyday life in occupied France, from placating an influential fascist critic to smuggling black market ham. Above all, he vividly evokes the feel of the era through period songs, clothes, and objects, and recreates a picturesque theatrical milieu, with playful reverberations between the world of the film and the play-within-the-film.

Although Truffaut made two pictures afterward, *The Last Metro* remains his swansong before his premature death. The film's huge success, which also owed much to the romantic central star couple of Deneuve and Depardieu, crowned his brilliant career. A consensual view of a troubled period, no doubt, but a wonderful, uplifting, and glamorous movie. **GV**

1980

A MASTERPIECE
OF MODERN HORROR

THE SHINING

A STANLEY KUBRICK FILM
JACK NICHOLSON SHELLEY DUVALL "THE SHINING"
SCATMAN CROTHERS, DANNY LLOYD STEPHEN KING
STANLEY KUBRICK & DIANE JOHNSON STANLEY KUBRICK
JAN HARLAN

G.B. (Hawk, Peregrine, Producers Circle, Warner Bros.) 119m Color **Producer** Stanley Kubrick **Screenplay** Stanley Kubrick, Diane Johnson, from novel by Stephen King **Photography** John Alcott **Music** Wendy Carlos, Rachel Elkind **Cast** Jack Nicholson, Shelley Duvall, Danny Lloyd, Scatman Crothers, Barry Nelson, Philip Stone, Joe Turkel, Anne Jackson, Tony Burton, Lia Beldam, Billie Gibson, Barry Dennen, David Baxt, Manning Redwood, Lisa Burns

"I dreamed that I, that I killed you and Danny. But I didn't just kill ya. I cut you up in little pieces. Oh my God . . . I must be losing my mind."

**Jack Torrance
(Jack Nicholson)**

i

The scene near the end where Wendy runs up the stairs carrying a knife was shot thirty-five times.

The Shining Stanley Kubrick, 1980

Thanks to Stanley Kubrick's ingenious adaptation of Stephen King's novel of the same name, *The Shining* not only brought unfaltering fame to both writer and director—it also launched actor Jack Nicholson into the realm of superstardom. His eerie and blood-curdling *Tonight Show* cry "Heeeeeeeeere's Johnny!" has become one of the most memorable scenes in the history of cinema. Recovering alcoholic Jack Torrance (Jack Nicholson) takes his wife Wendy (Shelley Duvall) and young son Danny (Danny Lloyd) to live in the now empty Overlook Hotel, a palatial resort in the Colorado Rockies where he has been hired as off-season caretaker. As the weeks pass, each member of the family experiences some form of chilling hallucinatory episode. Danny, the most psychically gifted, is the first to catch glimpses of the bloody murders that occurred in the hotel many years before. Next, Jack begins a slow and inexorable plunge into madness. Though he doesn't consciously acknowledge his experiences, with each encounter his behavior becomes more erratic, violent, and abusive. Distracted by Danny's withdrawal and Jack's irrational behavior, Wendy is the last to succumb. In the end, she is painfully aware of her imminent danger and despite her near-hysteria manages to survive with her son.

In his own words, King's book is "just a little story about writer's block." Collaborating with novelist Diane Johnson, Kubrick strikes heavily upon the novel's themes of communication and isolation, reinforcing them with rich symbolism. These themes recur throughout the film, partly through the psychic ability of "shining," and partly through Jack's terrifying spiral into insanity.

The film is dark, disturbing, and claustrophobic, and Kubrick demonstrates his mastery of the art, creating an atmosphere of great dread. Carefully selecting his camera angles and rhythms, he draws us into fear. Like all masterpieces, *The Shining* transcends its status as a literary adaptation to become not only vintage Kubrick—with spectacular aerial shots, a breathtaking and symbolic use of color, and recurrent mirror and labyrinth imagery, all enhanced by a memorable music score and Roy Walker's unforgettable production design—but a classic of modern horror cinema. Curiously, Stephen King was not particularly happy with Kubrick's interpretation of his tale of the deterioration of reality and gradual descent into madness. He believed that Kubrick's religious skepticism made it impossible for him to grasp the "sheer inhuman evil of the Overlook Hotel," looking instead for evil in the characters. The result, he argued, was a film with only vaguely supernatural overtones, made by a man who thinks too much and feels too little; a domestic tragedy—one that fails to get you by the throat the way real horror should. In 1997 King collaborated with Mick Garris on a TV mini-series that follows his original novel almost to the letter. **RDe**

The Elephant Man David Lynch, 1980

G.B. / U.S. (Brooksfilms Ltd)
124m BW **Producer** Jonathan Sanger
Screenplay Christopher De Vore, Eric
Bergren, David Lynch, from the books *The
Elephant Man and Other Reminiscences* by Sir
Frederick Treves and *The Elephant Man: A
Study in Human Dignity* by Ashley Montagu
Photography Freddie Francis **Music** John
Morris **Cast** Anthony Hopkins, John Hurt,
Anne Bancroft, John Gielgud, Wendy Hiller,
Freddie Jones, Michael Elphick, Hannah
Gordon, Helen Ryan, John Standing, Dexter
Fletcher, Lesley Dunlop, Phoebe Nicholls,
Pat Gorman, Claire Davenport **Oscar
nominations** Jonathan Sanger (best
picture), David Lynch (director), Christopher
De Vore, Eric Bergren, David Lynch
(screenplay), John Hurt (actor), Stuart Craig,
Robert Cartwright, Hugh Scaife (art
direction), Patricia Norris (costume), Anne V.
Coates (editing), John Morris (music)

ℹ

John Hurt's makeup was designed
directly from casts taken of Joseph
Merrick's head, arm, and foot.

David Lynch's 1977 debut feature *Eraserhead* is a nightmarish vision of a
heavily industrialized world full of hissing steam and polluting factories,
perfect catalysts for Jack Nance's primal childbirth phobia. In *The Elephant
Man*, Lynch works in many of those same themes and images, but this
time they add up not to some weird, enigmatic metaphor but to a
moving, humanistic statement.

Mel Brooks fought for years to bring the true story of John Merrick—
cruelly nicknamed the "Elephant Man" due to his large tumors—to the
big screen. He fought equally hard to bring Lynch on board. The director,
working in beautiful widescreen black and white, depicts nineteenth-
century London as an ugly, uncomfortable collision between Victorian
sensibilities and the gritty, grungy realities of the industrial revolution.

Rescued from a sideshow by a well-intentioned surgeon (Anthony
Hopkins), Merrick (John Hurt) tries fitting into a world whose first reaction
to his deformed visage is shock and revulsion. Trained in the etiquette
and formalities of the times, the gentle Merrick cannot overcome the
prejudice and distaste of many of those around him.

Hurt plays Merrick with a sensitivity and dignity that radiates from
beneath the tons of makeup that make him unrecognizable. Equally
excellent is Hopkins, who realizes he may subconsciously be exploiting
Merrick as a medical oddity despite his initial good intentions. It's a
triumph all around but especially for Lynch, who earned numerous
accolades that helped him escape from the art film ghetto. **JKI**

The Big Red One Samuel Fuller, 1980

U.S. (Lorimar Television) 113m Metrocolor
Language English / French / Italian
Producer Gene Corman **Screenplay** Samuel
Fuller **Photography** Adam Greenberg
Music Dana Kaproff **Cast** Lee Marvin, Mark
Hamill, Robert Carradine, Bobby Di Cicco,
Kelly Ward, Stéphane Audran, Siegfried
Rauch, Serge Marquand, Charles Macaulay,
Alain Doutey, Maurice Marsac, Colin Gilbert,
Joseph Clark, Ken Campbell, Doug Werner
Cannes Film Festival Samuel Fuller
(Golden Palm nomination)

The most ambitious war film in Samuel Fuller's career, a chronicle of his own First Infantry Division in World War II, *The Big Red One* was a long time coming. When it finally made it to the screen, a wholesale reediting by the studio and a tacked-on narration (by filmmaker Jim McBride) made it something less than Fuller had intended—he originally provided the studio with four-hour and two-hour cuts, both of which were rejected. Fuller enthusiasts still hold out hope that either or both of these versions might someday be restored. Nevertheless, *The Big Red One* is a grand, idiosyncratic war epic, with wonderful poetic ideas, intense emotions, and haunting images rich in metaphysical portent.

The effective cast is headed by Lee Marvin (as the grim, hardened sergeant), with Mark Hamill, Bobby Di Cicco, and Robert Carradine (as the dogface who corresponds most closely to Fuller himself). Packed with energy and observation, the film is full of unforgettable, spellbinding moments and haunting surrealist images: an inmate in an insane asylum grabbing and using a machine gun while declaring his enthusiasm for war; a protracted focusing on a corpse's wristwatch during the Normandy landing (a sequence that Steven Spielberg was well aware of when he made *Saving Private Ryan* [1998]); and a soldier carrying a dead child after the liberation of one of the death camps—an uncanny sequence that indelibly evokes the homecoming of the hero to a ghost in Kenji Mizoguchi's *Ugetsu Monogatari* (1953). **JRos**

1980

Loulou Maurice Pialat, 1980

France (Action, Gaumont) 110m
Eastmancolor **Language** French
Producer Yves Gasser, Klaus Hellwig, Yves
Peyrot **Screenplay** Arlette Langmann,
Maurice Pialat **Photography** Pierre-William
Glenn, Jacques Loiseleux **Music** Philippe
Sarde **Cast** Isabelle Huppert, Gérard
Depardieu, Guy Marchand, Humbert Balsan,
Bernard Tronczak, Christian Boucher,
Frédérique Cerbonnet, Jacqueline Dufranne,
Willy Safar, Agnès Rosier, Patricia Coulet,
Jean-Claude Meilland, Patrick Playez, Gérald
Garnier, Catherine De Guirchitch
Cannes Film Festival Maurice Pialat
(Golden Palm nomination)

This groundbreaking drama by Arlette Langmann and French realist Maurice Pialat is a scathing criticism of French society, in the guise of a sexually frank (and possibly titillating) look at relationship dynamics. Its lasting value goes well beyond that.

The simple story provides a framework for a meandering and somewhat confusing tale which nevertheless hangs together with the utmost credibility. Nelly (Isabelle Huppert) leaves her boor of a husband (Guy Marchand) for the lazy ex-con Loulou (Gerard Depardieu—completely absorbing as a rough but sensitive rogue). He won't work but he'll steal. She works but pops back and forth to her ex for any number of reasons, very few of them clear. Seemingly improvised, the dialogue still seems fresh and real even if the quality of the English translation varies greatly. The notion that a woman would, as Nelly succinctly puts it, "prefer a loafer who fucks, to a rich guy who bugs me," was shocking for its time. Two decades later, the language is still salty and direct and extremely enjoyable because of it. Famous for its "breaking bed" scene as well as an outtake where Huppert disappears between two parked cars, *Loulou* is compelling, intelligent, and very adult entertainment. **KK**

Raging Bull Martin Scorsese, 1980

This boxing biopic was a personal project for actor Robert De Niro, who discovered the as-told-to autobiography of former middleweight champion Jake La Motta and persuaded director Martin Scorsese and writer Paul Schrader, his *Taxi Driver* (1976) collaborators, to commit to the intense, apparently unpromising material. With the *Rocky* movies (1976, 1979)—ironically also produced by Irwin Winkler and Robert Chartoff—celebrating the ring underdog who survives and triumphs standing as the most successful sports saga of all time, *Raging Bull* dares to deal with the anti-Rocky, a hungry contender who winds up a bloated has-been without really learning anything along the way.

After long years and many setbacks, *La Motta* (De Niro) wins the champion's belt, but in screen time a few minutes later he is clawing off the jewels to pawn so he can try to bribe his way out of a morals charge. *Raging Bull* is also a poetic, daring exploration of the soul of an inarticulate, violent man. It never excuses his many horrific flaws as it establishes the physical and psychological punishment he takes as well as dishes out, showing the deep-seated misogyny (and raging homophobia) that characterizes his whole Italian-American Bronx-limited world. The miracle is that De Niro, in a textbook example of masterly screen acting, can find as much sympathy as he does for La Motta, showing how a jealous streak and in-the-ring aggression have appalling consequences for himself and his family. It's a remarkable feat, with the actor equally convincing as the wolverine-sleek, uncontrollably vicious punching machine of the early bouts and the fat-bellied shambles La Motta becomes when his ring career is over and he can at last give in to his uncontrollable lust for pastrami sandwiches.

Aside from the extraordinary fights—black-and-white hallucinations of popping flashbulbs, exploding body fluids, and brutal blows caught by cinematographer Michael Chapman on rollerskates—Scorsese stages many scenes that frighten or move: La Motta's brother Joey (Joe Pesci) hugging the sobbing boxer after he has been forced to throw a fight, a vignette that makes the Budd Shulberg "coulda been a contender" speech (rehearsed later as part of La Motta's nightclub act) from *On the Waterfront* (1954) seem hollow and contrived; La Motta needling his wife (Cathy Moriarty) and becoming so ferociously abusive that anyone who loves him has to leave; a low point when he is dragged into prison and batters at the stone walls as if he were yet again matching himself against Sugar Ray Robinson; and the rambling nightclub act La Motta performs as he tries to use words as viciously as he once used his fists, only to show how verbally punchy he has become as he struggles through his terrible act to the desperate catchphrase "That's entertainment."

Raging Bull is a film about masculinity that does not flinch from the collateral damage inflicted on women at the ringside—female spectators are seen trampled in a riot or receiving a face-full of blood splatter. **KN**

1980

U.S. (Chartoff-Winkler Productions) 129m BW / Technicolor **Producer** Robert Chartoff, Irwin Winkler **Screenplay** Paul Schrader, Mardik Martin, from book by Jake La Motta, Joseph Carter, Peter Savage **Photography** Michael Chapman **Music** Pietro Mascagni **Cast** Robert De Niro, Cathy Moriarty, Joe Pesci, Frank Vincent, Nicholas Colasanto, Theresa Saldana, Mario Gallo, Frank Adonis, Joseph Bono, Frank Topham, Lori Anne Flax, Charles Scorsese, Don Dunphy, Bill Hanrahan, Rita Bennett **Oscars** Robert De Niro (actor), Thelma Schoonmaker (editing) **Oscar nominations** Irwin Winkler, Robert Chartoff (best picture), Martin Scorsese (director), Joe Pesci (actor in support role), Cathy Moriarty (actress in support role), Michael Chapman (photography), Donald O. Mitchell, Bill Nicholson, David J. Kimball, Les Lazarowitz (sound)

"I'm gonna make him suffer. I'm gonna make his mother wish she never had him."

Jake La Motta (Robert De Niro)

Robert De Niro and Joe Pesci are really punching each other in the famous "hit me" scene.

Airplane! Jim Abrahams, David Zucker, & Jerry Zucker, 1980

Airplane! was the third film credited to the producer/director/writer team of David and Jerry Zucker and Jim Abrahams, and the one that made their unique, parodic, detailed style part of the common consciousness. Essentially a parody of 1970s disaster films such as *The Towering Inferno* (1974), *Earthquake!* (1974), and *Airport* (1970), *Airplane!* was largely based on one disaster movie in particular—the 1957 film *Zero Hour*. Zuckers and Abrahams bought the rights to *Zero Hour*, and *Airplane!* follows the original's story quite closely—thereby, as the Zuckers later admitted, accidentally giving the film a structure that their other efforts like *Top Secret* (1984) and *Kentucky Fried Movie* (1977) lack—to the point of containing some of that movie's dialogue (most famously Leslie Nielsen's line, "We have to find someone that not only can fly this plane but didn't have fish for dinner!"). But *Airplane!* adds other strands as well, taking what was by then an absurdly overwrought disaster film genre and playing upon all of its familiar conventions: a strained relationship, dangerously sick children, cowards who must face their weaknesses, a nun, blaxploitation jiveass dudes, as well as a wide streak of vulgarity.

While *Airplane!* may lack the R-rated humor of debtor movies like *Dumb And Dumber* (1994) and *Scary Movie* (2000), it does have its share of close-to-the-bone moments, mostly in the form of Peter Grave's Captain Oveur, whose pedophiliac remarks to Little Joey (Rossie Harris) were, probably fortunately, toned down in the writing process. Most important of all, the film continued the trio's ruling that parody must be played straight, and while some characters—pilot Ted Striker (sitcom actor Robert Hays) being the most notable—veer from this wise path, veteran actors like Graves and Nielsen play their parts as though starring in the most serious of dramas. The exception that proves the rule here is the superb Stephen Stucker as air controller Johnny Hinshaw, who seems to inhabit his own deranged camp galaxy. The team has cited as their biggest influence *MAD* magazine's regular feature, "Scenes You'd Like to See," which parodied harrowing movie moments in a completely deadpan manner. **KK**

U.S. (Paramount) 88m Metrocolor
Producer Jon Davison, Howard W. Koch Jr.
Screenplay Jim Abrahams, David Zucker,
Jerry Zucker **Photography** Joseph F. Biroc
Music Elmer Bernstein, John Williams
Cast Robert Hays, Julie Hagerty, Lloyd
Bridges, Leslie Nielsen, Robert Stack, Peter
Graves, Lorna Patterson, Stephen Stucker,
Kareem Abdul-Jabbar, Jim Abrahams, Frank
Ashmore, Jonathan Banks, Craig Berenson,
Barbara Billingsley

> *"There's no reason to become alarmed . . . By the way, is there anyone on board who knows how to fly a plane?"*
>
> **Elaine Dickinson
> (Julie Hagerty)**

i

The Bee Gees gave permission for their song "Stayin' Alive" to be speeded up for the dance scene.

An American Werewolf in London John Landis, 1981

U.S. / G.B. (American Werewolf,
Guber-Peters, Lyncanthrope, PolyGram)
97m Technicolor **Producer** George
Folsey Jr. **Screenplay** John Landis
Photography Robert Paynter **Music** Elmer
Bernstein **Cast** David Naughton, Jenny
Agutter, Griffin Dunne, Don McKillop, Paul
Kember, John Woodvine, Joe Belcher, David
Schofield, Brian Glover, Lila Kaye, Rik Mayall,
Sean Baker, Paddy Ryan, Anne-Marie Davies,
Frank Oz **Oscar** Rick Baker (makeup)

An imaginative and witty horror-comedy—written by director John Landis when he was just nineteen years old—*An American Werewolf in London* revealed a more sinister side to England's capital city during the same year (1981) in which all news was devoted to the "fairy-tale" wedding of Charles and Diana that took place there. David Naughton and Griffin Dunne are two young American backpackers who venture onto the Yorkshire Moors one night despite being warned by the suspicious regulars of the Slaughtered Lamb pub not to, and find out why they should have listened when they are pursued by a hungry werewolf. Dunne meets a grisly end, while Naughton discovers the bite he has received has turned him into a half-wolf when he wakes up naked in London's Regents Park Zoo one morning with the taste of human flesh in his mouth.

Filled with gruesome, blackly comic scenes (most memorably, the werewolf pursuit through a subway station, and Naughton meeting his decaying—and rather annoyed—victims in a cinema), and great performances (including ex-*Railway Children* [1970] star Jenny Agutter as the nurse and Brian Glover as the grumpiest of the Slaughtered Lamb's patrons), the movie also boasts extraordinary werewolf effects from Rick Baker, which prompted Michael Jackson to hire him and Landis to work on his classic video epic *Thriller*. **JB**

1981

Diva Jean-Jacques Beineix, 1981

France (Les Films Galaxie, Antenne-2) 117m
Color **Producer** Irène Silberman, Serge
Silberman **Screenplay** Jean-Jacques
Beineix, Jean Van Hamme, from novel by
Delacorta **Photography** Philippe Rousselot
Music Vladimir Cosma **Cast** Frédéric Andréi,
Wilhelmina Wiggins Fernandez, Richard
Bohringer, Thuy An Luu, Jacques Fabbri,
Chantal Deruaz, Anny Romand, Roland
Bertin, Gérard Darmon, Dominique Pinon,
Jean-Jacques Moreau, Patrick Floersham

Jean-Jacques Beineix's ultra-stylized blend of pop culture, high art, and B-movie thrills is recognized as the first entry in the Cinema du Look "movement." These films featured intense love affairs, were cynical in their view of the police, made prominent use of the Paris Metro, and, most significantly, were seen to be more about style than substance. Critics derided them at the time of their release. It was only with the publication of Raphaël Bassan's seminal 1988 essay, "The Neo-Baroque Directors: Beineix, Besson, Carax, from Diva to Le Grand Bleu," that the films began to be taken seriously as a reflection of French society.

Two illicit recordings, of an opera singer and the wiretapped conversation of corrupt cops, are the MacGuffins that prompt a series of chases around Paris. The film's pacy narrative occasionally segues into more relaxed divertissements. Most famously, in one sequence an entire room has been designed around the color of a small pile of Gitane cigarette packs on the floor.

Like Francis Ford Coppola's *One from the Heart* (1982), *Diva* is all about the artifice of, and a passion for, the movies. Beineix draws on Jean-Pierre Melville as well as 1940's Noir to create an entertaining and visually resplendent confection, whose artfulness and dynamic gives it a vibrancy and allure that has outlasted many other films from this period. **IHS**

Raiders of the Lost Ark Steven Spielberg, 1981

An homage to rather than a spoof of the Saturday matinee serials of the 1930s, *Raiders of the Lost Ark* brought producer George Lucas (hot from *Star Wars* [1977]) together with director Steven Spielberg for a movie combining excitement, special effects, and adventure, all played with a wry sense of humor.

Harrison Ford, in the role that suited him best in all his career, stars as Indiana Jones, a tweed-wearing professor of archeology by day, who spends the rest of his time scouring the globe for treasures and artifacts—like the Lost Ark of the Covenant (the gold chest in which Moses supposedly stored the stone tablets inscribed with the Ten Commandments). Unfortunately, the Nazis are after it too, having heard that any army who carries the ark before it is indestructible.

With his trademark fedora, bullwhip, and rumpled clothes, Indy outruns a speeding boulder in a booby-trapped cavern, escapes from a pit of snakes, dodges sinister bandits in an African market, and hangs underneath a moving truck in a nail-biting chase through the desert. These are only some of the movie's impressive set pieces. Our dashing hero is no Superman, though, getting beaten and bashed up at every turn.

The film works on many levels, not only thanks to Ford's superb performance and Spielberg's skill at piling on the action and excitement, but also because Lawrence Kasdan delivers a script that is more than just an old-fashioned adventure. His hero is a complicated, less-than-perfect guy who walks the fine line between being a thief of priceless artifacts and protector of them. The villains—especially Indy's archeological rival, Belloq (Paul Freeman)—aren't really that much different from the hero, except in their motivation. The heroine, Marion (Karen Allen) isn't your archetypal girl-in-distress either, but a physically capable woman who (most of the time) can rescue herself and doesn't need the hero at all.

Raiders is a perfect package of adventure, humor, effects, escapism, and terrific performances that has been imitated but never equaled. It was followed by two sequels in the 1980s, and, after a lengthy development period, a third in 2008. **JB**

1981

U.S. (Lucasfilm, Paramount) 115m Metrocolor **Language** English / German / French / Spanish **Producer** Frank Marshall **Screenplay** Lawrence Kasdan, George Lucas, Philip Kaufman **Photography** Douglas Slocombe **Music** John Williams **Cast** Harrison Ford, Karen Allen, Paul Freeman, Ronald Lacey, John Rhys-Davies, Denholm Elliott, Alfred Molina, Wolf Kahler, Anthony Higgins, Vic Tablian, Don Fellows, William Hootkins, Bill Reimbold, Fred Sorenson, Patrick Durkin **Oscars** Norman Reynolds, Leslie Dilley, Michael Ford (art direction), Richard Edlund, Kit West, Bruce Nicholson, Joe Johnston (special visual effects), Michael Kahn (editing), Bill Varney, Steve Maslow, Gregg Landaker, Roy Charman (sound), Ben Burtt, Richard L. Anderson (special sound effects) **Oscar nominations** Frank Marshall (best picture), Steven Spielberg (director), Douglas Slocombe (photography), John Williams (music)

"An Army that carries the Ark before it . . . is invincible."

**Dr. Marcus Brody
(Denholm Elliott)**

i

Indy's hat, from a shop in London's Saville Row, had to be twisted and sat on to make it look lived-in.

Das Boot Wolfgang Petersen, 1981
The Boat

Wolfgang Petersen's 1981 World War II drama *Das Boot* was nominated for six Academy Awards, a "mission impossible" for any foreign film. Capturing in authentic claustrophobic detail the sights and sounds of underwater warfare, the film sidelines issues of nationalism to focus on the dangerous task of manning a submarine in war-torn waters.

Following a single mission to hunt down Allied ships in the North Atlantic, the action takes place mostly in the filthy, mold-ridden stench of the cramped U96 submarine. In charge is Captain Lieutenant Henrich Lehmann-Willenbrock, a veteran submariner at the age of thirty. Blue-eyed leading man Jürgen Prochnow, until then unknown outside Germany, tempers the captain's expected ironclad professionalism with subtle, believable humanity. Although he acts as he must—letting enemy sailors drown rather than picking up prisoners, barking for clear reports even as his vessel sinks far below its depth capacity as the cabin rivets pop like gunfire—he is not without heart. The emotional truth of the terrible events lies between the lines of his daily diary entries. Prochnow, later embraced by Hollywood with appearances in *The Keep* (1983), *The English Patient* (1996), and others, so embodies the captain that it is unimaginable to think that both Robert Redford and Paul Newman were slated for this vital role when the film was a German-American concern. Within the superb supporting cast, Herbert Grönemeyer, now a well-known German rock musician, plays Lieutenant Werner, a character drawn from Lothar-Gunther Buchheim, the war correspondent whose best-selling 1973 memoirs form the basis of the script for *Das Boot*.

Much of the film's nerve-shattering realism is due to the three scale-model U-boats built for the production, which took up a large portion of the film's $14 million budget. As much a sonic as a visual experience, the entire film was shot silent; it was impossible to record live in the submarine interiors. The subtitled version is considered definitive, with all German and English dialogue added later—many of the German actors dubbing their own voices for the spoken English version. **KK**

West Germany (Bavaria, Radiant, SDR, WDR)
149m Technicolor **Language** German / English **Producer** Günter Rohrbach, Michael Bittins **Screenplay** Wolfgang Petersen, from novel by Lothar G. Buchheim **Photography** Jost Vacano **Music** Klaus Doldinger **Cast** Jürgen Prochnow, Herbert Grönemeyer, Klaus Wennemann, Hubertus Bengsch, Martin Semmelrogge, Bernd Tauber, Erwin Leder, Martin May, Heinz Hoenig, Uwe Ochsenknecht, Claude-Oliver Rudolph, Jan Fedder, Ralf Richter, Joachim Bernhard, Oliver Stritzel **Oscar nominations** Wolfgang Petersen (director), Wolfgang Petersen (screenplay), Jost Vacano (photography), Mike Le Mare (special sound effects), Hannes Nikel (editing), Milan Bor, Trevor Pyke, Mike Le Mare (sound)

1981

"They made us all train for this day. 'To be fearless and proud and alone.' The only thing I feel is afraid."

Lt. Werner
(Herbert Grönemeyer)

ℹ

The submarine models built for *Das Boot* were also used in Spielberg's *Raiders of the Lost Ark* (1981).

Gallipoli Peter Weir, 1981

Australia (AFC, R & R, SAFC) 110m Eastmancolor **Producer** Patricia Lovell, Robert Stigwood **Screenplay** David Williamson, Peter Weir **Photography** Russell Boyd **Music** Brian May, Tomaso Albinoni, Georges Bizet, Jean Michel Jarre **Cast** Mark Lee, Bill Kerr, Harold Hopkins, Charles Lathalu Yunipingli, Heath Harris, Ron Graham, Gerda Nicolson, Mel Gibson, Robert Grubb, Tim McKenzie, David Argue, Brian Anderson, Reg Evans, Jack Giddy, Dane Peterson

Australian filmmaker Peter Weir re-created the tragic and notorious World War I debacle of Gallipoli—a blundered campaign that sent thousands of Anzac soldiers to slaughter in 1915—with atmosphere and harrowing action, producing one of the classic films on war's folly and waste. Sporting rivals and pals, two fleet-footed young Australian runners—Frank Dunne (Mel Gibson) the rough charmer, Archy Hamilton (Mark Lee) the sensitive idealist—enlist in the Great War and journey across the world for the British Empire, finding comradeship, courage, and horror in the trenches in the Dardanelles.

Weir distinguishes himself by creating a strong sense of time, place, culture clash, and intimate human drama while imbuing even simple acts with beauty and mystery, finding magical images that evoke excitement, high spirits, fear, and grief. Like much of Weir's work, Gallipoli radiates intelligence, humanity, and warmth through many such small moments. Charismatic Gibson, of course, is the one who went on to international superstardom, Gallipoli persuading Hollywood that Mad Max was not just a tough guy but one who looked like a romantic leading man. But the film's haunting last image is a freeze-frame of Lee—Weir's homage to a famous photograph taken by Robert Capa during the Spanish Civil War. **AE**

Chariots of Fire Hugh Hudson, 1981

G.B. (Allied Stars, Enigma, Goldcrest, Warner Bros.) 123m Color **Producer** David Puttnam **Screenplay** Colin Welland **Photography** David Watkin **Music** Vangelis **Cast** Nicholas Farrell, Nigel Havers, Ian Charleson, Ben Cross, Daniel Gerroll, Ian Holm, John Gielgud, Lindsay Anderson, Nigel Davenport, Cheryl Campbell, Alice Krige, Dennis Christopher, Brad Davis, Patrick Magee, Peter Egan **Oscars** David Puttnam (best picture), Hugh Hudson (director), Colin Welland (screenplay), Milena Canonero (costume), Vangelis (music) **Oscar nominations** Ian Holm (actor in support role), Terry Rawlings (editing) **Cannes Film Festival** Hugh Hudson (prize of the ecumenical Jury—special mention, Golden Palm nomination), Ian Holm (supporting actor)

Opening on a beach with a group of barefoot runners, Hugh Hudson's *Chariots of Fire* made Vangelis a household name as his electronic score became synonymous with sporting excellence. Telling the story of two English runners, the film also won the Best Picture Academy Award despite being a British production.

The film centers on Harold Abrahams (Ben Cross), a Jewish sprinter, and Eric Liddell (Ian Charleson), his devoutly Christian rival, as the men struggle for national and personal honor following Word War I. As they train for the 1924 Summer Olympics, the values of sacrifice and fair play pepper their tale, although an ample reserve is set aside to exalt the brilliance of physical grace. Over the course of this journey, Abrahams hires Arab-Italian trainer Mussabini (Ian Holm), both sprinters confound their Cambridge Masters (played by John Gielgud and Lindsay Anderson), and the respective competition sparks the success of their teammates.

Ultimately concluded with triumph and redemption, *Chariots of Fire* equates athleticism with religious conviction, although Abrahams and Liddel are no mere figureheads. Instead they engage their times, wherein anti-Semitism, British classicism, and the lack of Hollywood high-concept technique mark this simple drama about seeking glory on the world's greatest stage for peaceful competition. **GC-Q**

1981

Body Heat Lawrence Kasdan, 1981

The controversial directorial debut of *The Empire Strikes Back* (1980) and *Raiders of the Lost Ark* (1981) writer Lawrence Kasdan, *Body Heat* generated powerful and divergent reactions upon its initial release. David Chute called it "perhaps the most stunning debut movie ever," whereas Pauline Kael wrote a famously scathing review, deriding the film for its self-consciousness and neonoir pretensions.

Body Heat makes no effort to hide its indebtedness to noir tradition. Ned Racine (William Hurt) is a lazy, womanizing lawyer who works in a small town in Florida. In the midst of a terrible heat wave, he accidentally meets Matty Walker (Kathleen Turner), a rich married woman from a nearby suburb. A steamy affair quickly develops. Soon enough, Matty has convinced Ned to murder her husband so they can be together (and rich) forever—and to think it's his idea. After the murder, Ned gets double-crossed in various ways, discovering he was picked out and set up by Matty from the very beginning. After Matty fakes her own death, Ned is sent to jail, where he does some research and learns that she had actually taken on another woman's identity. But it's too late to do anything. The last shot shows Matty sunbathing on an anonymous tropical island.

Besides the archetypal noir plot, in which a sexy mystery woman embroils a likeable, attractive but immoral male protagonist and brings him down, *Body Heat* is characteristically noirish in its rapid and super-snappy dialogue, and in its depiction of a femme fatale who is untrustworthy but enchanting nonetheless. Over time, positive response to Kasdan's film has won out, with subsequent neonoirs (such as *Blood Simple* [1984] and *The Last Seduction* [1994]) paying homage to *Body Heat*, much as *Body Heat* pays tribute to noirs such as *Double Indemnity* (1944) and *Out of the Past* (1947).

But there is also a subversive quality to *Body Heat*, which moves it away from classical noir. It is closer to the so-called erotic thriller. What was left implicit and suggestive in the earlier films is here foregrounded and made the visual focus. The extended soft-core sex scenes between Hurt and Turner are shocking and risqué even by today's more promiscuous standards. **SJS**

U.S. (Ladd) 113m Technicolor **Producer** Fred T. Gallo **Screenplay** Lawrence Kasdan **Photography** Richard H. Kline **Music** John Barry **Cast** William Hurt, Kathleen Turner, Richard Crenna, Ted Danson, J.A. Preston, Mickey Rourke, Kim Zimmer, Jane Hallaren, Lanna Saunders, Carola McGuinness, Michael Ryan, Larry Marko, Deborah Lucchesi, Lynn Hallowell, Thom Sharp

> *"You better take me up on this quick. In about 45 minutes, I'm going to give up and go away."*
>
> **Ned Racine (William Hurt)**

i

To help the crew feel comfortable filming the love scenes, Turner and Hurt introduced themselves naked.

Czlowiek z zelaza Andrzej Wajda, 1981
Man of Iron

Poland (Film Polski, Zespol Filmowy X)
153m BW / Color **Language** Polish
Screenplay Aleksander Scibor-Rylski
Photography Janusz Kalicinski, Edward
Kloslnskl **Music** Andrzej Korzynski
Cast Jerzy Radziwilowicz, Krystyna Janda,
Marian Opania, Boguslaw Linda, Wieslawa
Kosmalska, Andrzej Seweryn, Krzysztof
Janczar, Boguslaw Sobczuk, Franciszek
Trzeciak **Oscar nominations** Poland (best
foreign language film) **Cannes Film Festival**
Andrzej Wajda (Golden Palm, prize of the
ecumenical jury)

*"I trust you will be a
democratic couple,
so let me share these
flowers democratically."*

**Lech Walesa [to Maciek and
Agnieszka at their wedding]**

This sequel to the 1977 film *Man of Marble* confirmed director Andrzej Wajda's concern never to miss an opportunity to account for the major events in Poland's history. If the first film dealt mostly with the Stalinist era and its crimes, *Man of Iron* deals with the rousing of the Solidarity Movement, the strong union organization whose actions succeeded in blowing up the communist regime at the end of the 1980s.

Here again we meet documentary filmmaker Agnieszka (Krystyna Janda), who is now married to Mateusz (Jerzy Radziwilowicz), the son of former Polish worker-hero Birkut. Deeply involved in the organization of the 1980 strike in Gdansk, Mateusz is one of the Solidarity Movement's founders, and he tries to convince the intellectuals to join the union, too. A series of flashbacks shows us what was only suggested in the previous film: that Birkut was killed during the earlier strike in Gdansk in 1970, an insurrection that was savagely repressed by the communist Special Forces. However, this parallel between the events of the recent past and the new strike in Gdansk allows for the optimistic anticipation of a final victory.

Less intricately structured than *Man of Marble*, the sequel nevertheless provides worthy testimony of a decade that brought a surprising turn in the history of communism. The amazing documentary sequences shot in 1970 and then in 1980 intensify the film's national and international echoes. Western audiences, who were not too interested in movies coming from Eastern Europe, were especially shocked by what they saw: That is one reason why *Man of Iron* was awarded the Golden Palm at the 1981 Cannes Film Festival. A brief appearance in the film by Lech Walesa, leader of the Solidarity Movement, as himself, also speaks to Wajda's sense of history and his uncanny ability to anticipate the future.

Determined to make a political movie with a strong impact, Wajda insisted on foregrounding the ideological message through dialogue—excessively so, in the opinion of some critics. Despite such remarks, however, his film is a moving tribute to the Polish citizens whose struggle enabled the freedom so cherished in this part of Europe. **DD**

ℹ️
Andrzej Wajda was one of the
leading figures in the Polish Film
School, active from 1955 to 1963.

Reds Warren Beatty, 1981

The commercial acceptability of the title alone signaled the end of Hollywood's fear of engaging meaningfully with leftist politics. Warren Beatty's tribute to journalist John Reed provides an intriguing look into American political radicals of the early twentieth century and their fascination with the Bolshevik Revolution in Russia, and the improbable foundation of a communist state.

Beatty worked for years on *Reds*. He is credited, in the tradition of Orson Welles, as producer, director, screenwriter, and featured performer. The film was a daring venture, mostly because Reed, its central focus, was virtually unknown to the cinema public of the late twentieth century. Limited by Hollywood conventions, Beatty is able only to suggest the complex and frenetic aspects of Reed's meteoric career: front-line reporting from Europe; a fascination with Pancho Villa; involvement in union politics and World War I; his experiences at Harvard as a dandy and cheerleader; and his Byronic compulsion to seek out the unusual and the forbidden. The first half of *Reds* is devoted to Reed's love affair with feminist intellectual Louise Bryant (Diane Keaton). This part of the film is enlivened by some fine performances from secondary characters.

Once Reed leaves for Russia, *Reds* does an excellent job of delineating the epic events of the developing revolution, with its riotous parades and unruly mass meetings. Especially in the Russian scenes, Beatty conveys Reed's messianic enthusiasm and his deep commitment to political change after a period of self-absorbed adventurism (Beatty was especially suited to this role, given his own conversion to activism after a misspent youth). Wisely, Beatty gives the film a documentary flair by interspersing fictional sequences with short interviews featuring eyewitnesses of the period, including such luminaries as Will Durant and Henry Miller. These interviews not only provide a good deal of information about Reed but also argue for his importance in American history, which is the film's overall project. *Reds*, despite its concessions to entertainment cinema, is arguably Hollywood's most effective presentation of politics and ideological conflict in twentieth-century America. **BP**

U.S. (Barclays, JRS, Paramount) 194m Technicolor **Language** English / Russian / German **Producer** Warren Beatty **Screenplay** Warren Beatty, Trevor Griffiths, from the book *Ten Days That Shook the World* by John Reed **Photography** Vittorio Storaro **Music** Stephen Sondheim, Dave Grusin, Pierre Degeyter **Cast** Warren Beatty, Diane Keaton, Edward Herrmann, Jerzy Kosinski, Jack Nicholson, Paul Sorvino, Maureen Stapleton, Nicolas Coster, M. Emmet Walsh, Ian Wolfe, Bessie Love, MacIntyre Dixon, Pat Starr, Eleanor D. Wilson, Max Wright, George Plimpton, Harry Ditson, Leigh Curran, Kathryn Grody, Brenda Currin, Nancy Duiguid, Norman Chancer, Dolph Sweet, Ramon Bieri, Jack O'Leary, Gene Hackman, Gerald Hiken, William Daniels, Dave King, Joseph Buloff, Stefan Gryff, Denis Pekarev, Roger Sloman, Stuart Richman, Oleg Kerensky **Oscars** Warren Beatty (director), Maureen Stapleton (actress in support role), Vittorio Storaro (photography) **Oscar nominations** Warren Beatty (best picture), Warren Beatty, Trevor Griffiths (screenplay), Warren Beatty (actor), Diane Keaton (actress), Jack Nicholson (actor in support role), Richard Sylbert, Michael Seirton (art direction), Shirley Russell (costume), Dede Allen, Craig McKay (editing), Dick Vorisek, Tom Fleischman, Simon Kaye (sound)

1981

i

Reds broke records by receiving Academy Award nominations in all four acting categories.

U.S. (Amblin, Universal) 115m Technicolor
Producer Kathleen Kennedy, Steven
Spielberg **Screenplay** Melissa Mathison
Photography Allen Daviau **Music** John
Williams **Cast** Henry Thomas, Dee Wallace-
Stone, Robert MacNaughton, Drew
Barrymore, Peter Coyote, K.C. Martel, Sean
Frye, C. Thomas Howell, David M. O'Dell,
Richard Swingler, Frank Toth, Robert Barton,
Michael Durrell **Oscars** Charles L. Campbell,
Ben Burtt (special sound effects), Carlo
Rambaldi, Dennis Muren, Kenneth Smith
(special visual effects), John Williams (music),
Robert Knudson, Robert J. Glass, Don
Digirolamo, Gene S. Cantamessa (sound)
Oscar nominations Steven Spielberg,
Kathleen Kennedy (best picture), Steven
Spielberg (director), Melissa Mathison
(screenplay), Allen Daviau (photography),
Carol Littleton (editing)

*"Everyone has a hobby
and mine is aliens."*

Steven Spielberg, 2004

E.T.: The Extra-Terrestrial Steven Spielberg, 1982

Despite Ridley Scott's *Alien* having convinced us that beings from outer space were something to be wary of, three years later Steven Spielberg showed that they could be cute and cuddly too, especially if they came in the form of pot-bellied creatures like E.T. His adorable, wide-eyed appearance was supposedly imagined after Spielberg's team superimposed Einstein's eyes and forehead onto the face of a baby.

A sci-fi adventure for the whole family, this was Spielberg's homage to childhood. A lonely little boy, Elliott (Henry Thomas), befriends the outer space being (played in many scenes by a small person in an E.T. suit) left behind by his pals. He introduces him to Earth customs such as how to communicate, drink beer, eat candy, and dress up in his little sister Gertie's (Drew Barrymore) clothes. Of course their secret friendship can't last for long, and soon the boy and his alien are under threat from government men wanting to experiment on the intergalactic traveler.

Based on an idea Spielberg had nurtured for a while and related to screenwriter Melissa Mathison after shooting *Raiders of the Lost Ark* (1981), *E.T.* works as a delightful adventure that appeals to the child in all of us, also delivering enough sentimental moments to have the hardest viewer reduced to a blubbering mess before the end credits. That it doesn't become too sugary sweet comes from Spielberg's pacing and the mixture of humor and sadness in Mathison's script, coupled with Debra Winger and Pat Welsh's raspy vocalizations for E.T. and superb performances by the mainly young cast. Thomas—as the lucky boy whose imaginary friend is actually real—virtually carries the film on his own small shoulders, while Robert MacNaughton (as older brother Michael) and seven-year-old Drew Barrymore give terrific turns as the initially hesitant siblings won over by E.T.'s considerable charm.

Twenty years after the movie's original release, Spielberg brought out a special anniversary edition, featuring some computer alterations to E.T.'s facial expressions that he was unable to accomplish in 1982. The other notable change was the digital replacement of guns from the hands of the government agents (something Spielberg had never been comfortable with) with walkie-talkie radios. **JB**

i

Foley artist John Roesch said he used
a wet T-shirt filled with jello to create
the noise of E.T.'s walk.

The Evil Dead Sam Raimi, 1982

U.S. (Renaissance) 85m
Color **Producer** Robert G. Tapert
Screenplay Sam Raimi **Photography** Tim
Philo **Music** Joseph LoDuca **Cast** Bruce
Campbell, Ellen Sandweiss, Hal Delrich, Betsy
Baker, Theresa Tilly, Philip A. Gillis, Dorothy
Tapert, Cheryl Guttridge, Barbara Carey,
David Horton, Wendall Thomas, Don Long,
Stu Smith, Kurt Rauf, Ted Raimi

This "ultimate experience in grueling horror," as it immodestly bills itself in the end credits, changed the history of its genre. Sam Raimi took the gore of Italian horror movies and mixed it with a proudly juvenile sense of humor—making its teenage heroes so vapidly wholesome that we cannot wait, once they are holed up in a remote country shack, for them to die or be zombiefied. Such self-consciousness would subsequently come to dominate screen horror.

It is the ultimate "movie nerd" success story, flagrantly amateurish in many of its effects, but powered by a full-on soundtrack and ubiquitous, rapid, low-to-the-ground point of view shots. Raimi absorbed lessons from the 1970s generation of William Friedkin, Wes Craven, George Romero, and Brian De Palma, but added a down-home surrealism, somewhere between Jean Cocteau and Tex Avery. And in Bruce Campbell, Raimi found a sympathetically cartoonish star.

Today, it is hard to see anything but comedy in *The Evil Dead*, especially in the light of its sequels, *Evil Dead II* (1987) and *Army of Darkness* (1993). But we must remember that in 1982 the film had the same terrifying effect on audiences as *The Blair Witch Project* seventeen years later—taking them, momentarily, out of their comfort zone. **AM**

Fast Times at Ridgemont High Amy Heckerling, 1982

U.S. (Refugee, Universal) 90m Technicolor
Producer Irving Azoff, Art Linson
Screenplay Cameron Crowe, from his
novel **Photography** Matthew F. Leonetti
Music Jackson Browne, Jimmy Buffett,
Charlotte Caffey, Danny Elfman, Rob Fahey,
Louise Goffin, Sammy Hagar, Don Henley,
Danny Kortchmar, Giorgio Moroder, Graham
Nash, Stevie Nicks, Tom Petty, Marv Ross,
Billy Squier, Joe Walsh, Rusty Young,
Charlotte Caffey, Jane Wiedlin **Cast** Sean
Penn, Jennifer Jason Leigh, Judge Reinhold,
Robert Romanus, Brian Backer, Phoebe
Cates, Ray Walston, Scott Thomson, Vincent
Schiavelli, Amanda Wyss, D.W. Brown,
Forest Whitaker, Zoe Kelli Simon, Tom Nolan,
Blair Ashleigh

Just one year after Bob Clark's gross-out classic *Porky's* set new (albeit short-lived) lows for Hollywood humor, Amy Heckerling's *Fast Times at Ridgemont High* brilliantly melded the teen comedy with the coming-of-age tale in this surprisingly sensitive take on suburban high school life. Featuring a bevy of young actors, *Fast Times* holds up extraordinarily well under repeat viewings (spot the star!) and possesses strong nostalgic appeal for those who caught it on its initial release. In fact, a sweet sense of melancholy underlies this look at an adolescent American present fading all too quickly into the past—not surprising for a movie scripted by the future writer-director of such Gen-X hits as *Say Anything* (1989) and *Almost Famous* (2000), ex-*Rolling Stone* reporter Cameron Crowe.

But Heckerling deserves as much credit as Crowe for seamlessly weaving together *Fast Times*'s multiple narratives, and for bringing out the humor in a story that sounds far more depressing than funny. Anticipating the touch she would later show in *Clueless* (1995), Heckerling mines the melodramatic material for laughs, avoids oversentimentality, and provides happy endings for everyone. Best line: "All I need are some tasty waves, a cool buzz, and I'm fine," spoken by perennially stoned surfer dude Jeff Spicoli (Penn, who almost steals the whole film from his peers) in an ultra-lazy Southern California accent that predates *Bill & Ted's Excellent Adventure* (1989) by more than half a decade. **SJS**

Zu früh, zu spät Danièle Huillet & Jean-Marie Straub, 1982
Too Early, Too Late

France 100m 16mm Eastmancolor **Language** German **Screenplay** Friedrich Engels, Danièle Huillet, Mahmoud Hussein, Jean-Marie Straub **Photography** Robert Alazraki, Caroline Champetier, William Lubtchansky, Marguerite Perlado **Music** Beethoven

This color documentary by Jean-Marie Straub and Danièle Huillet, one of their few works in 16mm, is one of the best landscape films. There are no "characters" in this 105-minute feature about places, yet paradoxically it's the most densely populated work that they made. The first part shows a series of locations in contemporary France, accompanied by Huillet reading part of a letter Friedrich Engels wrote to Karl Kautsky describing the impoverished state of French peasants, and excerpts from the "Notebooks of Grievances," compiled in 1789 by the village mayors of those same locales in response to plans for further taxation.

The especially fine second section, roughly twice as long, does the same thing with a more recent Marxist text by Mahmoud Hussein about Egyptian peasants' resistance to English occupation before the "petit-bourgeois" revolution of Neguib in 1952. Both sections suggest that the peasants revolted too soon and succeeded too late. One of the film's formal inspirations is Beethoven's late quartets, and its slow rhythm is central to the experience it yields; what is so remarkable about Straub and Huillet's beautiful long takes is how their rigorous attention to both sound and image seems to open up an entire universe, whether in front of a large urban factory or out on a country road. **JRos**

Poltergeist Tobe Hooper, 1982

U.S. (MGM) 114m Metrocolor **Producer** Steven Spielberg **Screenplay** Steven Spielberg, Michael Grais, Mark Victor **Photography** Mathew F. Leonetti **Music** Jerry Goldsmith **Cast** JoBeth Williams, Craig T. Nelson, Beatrice Straight, Dominique Dunne, Oliver Robins, Heather O'Rourke, Michael McManus, Virginia Kiser, Martin Casella, Richard Lawson, Zelda Rubinstein, Lou Perry, Clair E. Leucart, James Karen, Dirk Blocker **Oscar nominations** Stephen Hunter Flick, Richard L. Anderson (special sound effects), Richard Edlund, Michael Wood, Bruce Nicholson (special visual effects), Jerry Goldsmith (music)

Texas Chain Saw Massacre (1974) helmsman Tobe Hooper gets on-screen credit for directing *Poltergeist*, but by all accounts producer Steven Spielberg played a more-than-supporting role in the film's creation. Indeed, the story of a suburban family disrupted and threatened by the increasingly malevolent unknown jibes with many of Spielberg's past and future scenarios, as does the somewhat playful casting of that modern bogeyman the television as the film's proxy villain, through which the malevolent spirits first make contact.

What begins as a wondrous encounter with the supernatural soon turns horrific, as the spooks manifest themselves in increasingly nasty ways (and via increasingly elaborate special effects). Copious movie magic and southern California family dynamics aside, *Poltergeist* proves far more terrifying than most of Spielberg's projects. This swings the see-saw of credit back to Hooper, who knows a thing or two about scaring audiences out of their wits: Skeletons start bobbing in the swimming pool, a boy is eaten by a tree, and a paranormal investigator tears off his own face. While anyone would be forgiven for asking why the family doesn't just pack their bags and leave, Hooper keeps the shocks and surprises coming at such a deviously steady pace that common sense plays second fiddle here to suspense and outright horror. **JKl**

Yol Serif Gören & Yilmaz Güney, 1982

The story surrounding *Yol* is nearly as fascinating as the film itself. Director and writer Yilmaz Güney realized the film from prison. It was shot and overseen by Güney's assistant, Serif Gören, who worked from detailed notes and instructions written by Güney in his cell. The director subsequently escaped from jail and was present for the editing and postproduction. *Yol* went on to win the grand prize at the Cannes Film Festival and brought the world's attention to the violation of political prisoners' human rights in Turkey's right-wing dictatorship. Sadly, Güney died of cancer of a few years later after completing just one more film, *The Wall* (1983).

Yol is a deeply political film with an overt message and purpose that subordinates all the other elements. In each of the five prisoners' stories, hidebound traditions, religion, or the repression of the state are exposed. One of the prisoners must go back right away because of a petty rule. Another prisoner is cowed by his family, who want him to perform an honor killing on his unfaithful wife. A third convict who is happy to come home to his fiancée is soon disappointed because his family has selected a different woman for him to marry. A Kurdish prisoner returns to his native village after a long trip that takes nearly half of his leave, only to find that the Turkish army has completely wiped it out. Only one prisoner's story is hopeful, although he too suffers many setbacks and faces similar problems to the others.

The film is deeply pessimistic and pulses with a palpable rage, making this otherwise fairly conventionally structured film stirring and fresh. Güney's eye for detail and his desire to expose the reactionary forces in his society together provide a more intimate look into the life of a country than do most foreign films. Although *Yol*'s perspective is ultimately searing and critical, Güney takes pains to humanize his characters and make us care for them as individuals as well. Much of the credit for this must also go to the actors, who are uniformly excellent. Few better examples of engaged, political filmmaking exist. **RH**

Turkey / Switzerland / France
(Cactus, Films A2, Güney Film, Maran Film, Schweizer Fernsehen DRS) 114m Fujicolor **Language** Turkish / Kurdish **Producer** Edi Hubschmid, Yilmaz Güney **Screenplay** Yilmaz Güney **Photography** Erdogan Engin **Music** Sebastian Argol, Zülfü Livaneli **Cast** Tarik Akan, Serif Sezer, Halil Ergün, Meral Orhonsay, Necmettin Çobanoglu, Semra Uçar, Hikmet Celik, Sevda Aktolga, Tuncay Akça, Hale Akinli, Turgut Savas, Engin Çelike, Hikmet Tasdemir, Osman Bardakçi, Enver Güney **Cannes Film Festival** Serif Gören, Yilmaz Güney (FIPRESCI award, prize of the ecumenical jury—special mention, Golden Palm, tied with *Missing*)

"The film's poetry, its combination of sound and image especially, has an unconscious innocence no longer available to most European and American narratives."

Time Out Film Guide

i

Güney's five protagonists in *Yol* were inspired by some of the men that he shared his cell in prison with.

1982

Blade Runner Ridley Scott, 1982

U.S. (Blade Runner, Ladd) 117m
Technicolor **Language** English / Japanese /
Cantonese **Producer** Michael Deeley
Screenplay Hampton Fancher, David Webb
Peoples, Roland Kibbee, from the novel *Do
Androids Dream of Electric Sheep?* by Philip K.
Dick **Photography** Jordan Cronenweth
Music Vangelis **Cast** Harrison Ford, Rutger
Hauer, Sean Young, Edward James Olmos,
M. Emmet Walsh, Daryl Hannah, William
Sanderson, Brion James, Joe Turkel, Joanna
Cassidy, James Hong, Morgan Paull, Kevin
Thompson, John Edward Allen, Hy Pyke
Oscar nominations Lawrence G. Paull, David
L. Snyder, Linda DeScenna (art direction),
Douglas Trumbull, Richard Yuricich, David
Dryer (special visual effects)

*"Replicants are like
any other machine.
They're either a benefit
or a hazard. If they're
a benefit, it's not
my problem."*

**Rick Deckard
(Harrison Ford)**

ℹ

The film's title came from an unrelated
novella by William Burroughs, called,
oddly enough, *Blade Runner (a movie)*.

Written in 1968, sci-fi author Philip K. Dick's *Do Androids Dream of Electric Sheep?* took fourteen years to make it to the big screen, and it was another decade after that before Ridley Scott's jaw-dropping cinematic version—*Blade Runner*—was finally recognized as a masterpiece of science-fiction filmmaking. The $28 million movie was not well received on its original release and was a financial flop; only after the Director's Cut version was released in 1992 did critics and audiences fully embrace it.

Books have been devoted to the story behind the film itself. A tough production by all accounts, there were numerous reports of on-set bad feeling—star Harrison Ford reportedly didn't like costar Sean Young, the crew had T-shirts made to express their irritation at the punishing shooting schedule, and, most notably, Ford and Scott didn't get along. Ford has rarely commented on the movie since its initial release, only remarking that it was the toughest movie he has ever worked on.

But what a movie it is. Justly acclaimed for its astonishing production design, Scott's vision of 2019 Los Angeles as bleak and neon-lit, with overcrowded streets and continual acid rain, has often been copied but never bettered. It is through this world that detective Rick Deckard (Ford) wanders, searching out "replicants"—mutinous androids masquerading as humans—while inadvertently falling for one such robot (Young). Packed with symbolism, *Blade Runner* has generated much debate over the years, with some fans arguing that the movie is subliminally about religion, citing examples such as replicant Roy Batty (Rutger Hauer) piercing his hand with a nail to possibly represent crucifixion, and Tyrell (Joe Turkel), creator of the replicants, serving as a God figure.

It is hard to imagine the film having the same impact with a different director (before Scott, Adrian Lyne, Michael Apted, and Robert Mulligan were all approached, and Martin Scorsese was interested in optioning the novel in 1969). As for the lead role, names mooted included Christopher Walken and even Dustin Hoffman. Scott's superb mix of twenty-first-century sci-fi and 1940s detective film noir makes for a stunning dystopia, while Ford, as the man sent to "retire" (that is, execute) human-looking androids who have come to Earth in search of their maker, may not have liked to "stand around and give some focus to Ridley's sets," as he told a journalist in 1991, but his bemusement works perfectly with the storyline.

One of the reasons *Blade Runner* has had such a cult following is the existence of more than one version of the film—the Director's Cut has added scenes, and leaves out Ford's voice-over narration along with the feel-good ending imposed by the studio. Another reason is the ongoing debate as to whether Deckard is actually a replicant himself. Whatever the answer—Scott has, on one occasion at least, hinted that Deckard may be an android—*Blade Runner* remains one of the most beautifully art-directed and visually stunning science-fiction movies ever made. **JB**

1982

Diner Barry Levinson, 1982

U.S. (MGM) 110m Metrocolor
Producer Jerry Weintraub **Screenplay** Barry
Levinson **Photography** Peter Sova
Music Bruce Brody, Ivan Kral **Cast** Steve
Guttenberg, Daniel Stern, Mickey Rourke,
Kevin Bacon, Timothy Daly, Ellen Barkin, Paul
Reiser, Kathryn Dowling, Michael Tucker,
Jessica James, Colette Blonigan, Kelle Kipp,
John Aquino, Richard Pierson, Claudia Cron
Oscar nomination Barry Levinson
(screenplay)

"Diner's groundbreaking
evocation of male
friendship changed the
way men interact, not
just in comedies and
buddy movies, but in
fictional Mob settings, in
fictional police and fire
stations, in commercials,
on the radio . . ."

Vanity Fair, 2012

i

In 2012 Levinson developed a
Broadway musical version of *Diner*,
with songs by Sheryl Crow.

After George Lucas's landmark *American Graffiti* (1973), the movieland
zeitgeist preferred optimistic nostalgia for its maturing baby boomer
audience. Responding to this theme, Barry Levinson wrote and directed
the Baltimore-based comedy classic *Diner* with a cast of unknowns,
several of whom would move on to remarkable showbiz success.

Diner opens on Christmas night, 1959. It tells the story of six twenty-
somethings grappling with their intermingled friendship and the closing
decade, all of which is interposed over the preparation for the marriage
of one of their own on New Year's Eve. Interrupting these activities, the
film's eponymous restaurant becomes the group's home-away-from-
home, their surrogate womb. Within its walls, ensconced among leather
booths and eating off polished tabletops, they talk, talk, talk to retard
the demands of the outside world and revel in one another's company.

Eddie (Steve Guttenberg) is an insecure loudmouth counting the
days to his pending nuptials. Shrevie (Daniel Stern) is the hometown
Everyman beholden to a steady job and a wife named Beth (Ellen Barkin),
with whom he lacks an adult friendship. Boogie (Mickey Rourke) is a
night-school law student, womanizer, and hairdresser with a gambling
problem. Fenwick (Kevin Bacon) is the rich-kid dropout on the cusp of
alcoholism, and Billy (Timothy Daly) is a graduate student with a longtime friendship-turned-pregnancy by way of his old friend Barbara
(Kathryn Dowling). The last of the six is Modell (Paul Reiser), a hanger-on,
but someone with an acute sense of comic timing.

Well remembered for a few outstanding scenes, *Diner* is a bittersweet
coming-of-age story set beyond the confines of Los Angeles or New York
City. The very act of filming in Baltimore gives the picture a more general
sensibility and expands the horizon of such screen tales beyond
cosmopolitan city centers. Yet the humor of *Diner* is found in the set
pieces, constructed around an aspiring cast exhibiting a great deal of
camaraderie, and the production design elements that provide enough
period details to seem utterly authentic. The cars are of the moment, and
the music is too. A nascent sense of female political empowerment is in
the air, but so is the queasiness of these young men on the verge of
either conforming to society's general consensus or else striking out on
their own in stunningly new directions.

Laugh-out-loud moments appear alongside dramatic vignettes. There
is a spirited debate about Frank Sinatra and Johnny Mercer, for example,
an unpleasant brotherly confrontation, and a penis in a popcorn bag.

Ending not with a bang but a question mark, the structuring absence
of the piece is undoubtedly Eddie's fiancée. She looms large and
represents the entanglements of family and domesticity—in short, the
final acceptance of adult responsibility. Altogether, these are the values
all six characters in *Diner* seem to loathe but simultaneously long for in
their last gasp of innocence at the end of 1959. **GC-Q**

Tootsie Sydney Pollack, 1982

U.S. (Columbia, Mirage, Punch) 119m Color
Producer Sydney Pollack, Dick Richards
Screenplay Larry Gelbart, Don McGuire,
Murray Schisgal Music Dave Grusin
Cast Dustin Hoffman, Jessica Lange, Teri
Garr, Dabney Coleman, Charles Durning, Bill
Murray, Sydney Pollack, George Gaynes,
Geena Davis Oscar Jessica Lange (actress in
support role) Oscar nominations Sydney
Pollack, Dick Richards (best picture), Sydney
Pollack (director), Larry Gelbart, Murray
Schisgal, Don McGuire (screenplay), Dustin
Hoffman (actor), Teri Garr (actress in support
role), Owen Roizman (photography), Fredric
Steinkamp, William Steinkamp (editing), Dave
Grusin, Alan Bergman, Marilyn Bergman
(song), Arthur Piantadosi, Les Fresholtz, Rick
Alexander, Les Lazarowitz (sound)

i

The crew would reportedly only give
bad news to Hoffman when he was
in drag, as he was "nicer as a woman."

British critic Judith Williamson once disparaged the "Tootsie Syndrome"
in contemporary culture—the device that decrees it only takes a few
days in the shoes of your social "other" in order to completely understand
and sympathize with their plight. The syndrome began with this film
about a frustrated actor (Dustin Hoffman in a wonderful performance)
who lands a role in a successful television soap opera by secretly
impersonating a woman (who, these days, seems to resemble a Southern
version of Dame Edna Everage).

The complications that follow for Tootsie the frantic effort to
maintain this masquerade, and the difficult attempt to romance a costar
(Jessica Lange), including a mild lesbian complication—evoke the days
of screwball sex-and-identity farce in the 1930s and 1940s. But director
Sydney Pollack (who also plays Tootsie's agent) has a keen sense of his
contemporary moment, both in behavioral detail and aesthetics.

Tootsie, alongside the work of James L. Brooks, pioneered a new style
in mainstream cinema: intensely busy, bristling with subplots, pop
allusions (such as, here, a cameo from Andy Warhol), and jazzy montage
sequences—raising dramatic complications and hinting at subversive
implications while skating gracefully past them to a happy ending. **AM**

West Germany / Peru (Autoren, Pro-ject, Werner Herzog, Wildlife, ZDF) 158m Color Language English / German Producer Werner Herzog, Lucki Stipetic Screenplay Werner Herzog Photography Thomas Mauch Music Popol Vuh, Vincenzo Bellini, Giacomo Puccini, Richard Strauss, Giuseppe Verdi Cast Klaus Kinski, José Lewgoy, Miguel Ángel Fuentes, Paul Hittscher, Huerequeque Enrique Bohorquez, Grande Otelo, Peter Berling, David Pérez Espinosa, Milton Nascimento, Ruy Polanah, Salvador Godínez, Dieter Milz, William L. Rose, Leoncio Bueno, Claudia Cardinale Cannes Film Festival Werner Herzog (director, Golden Palm nomination)

> "As a document of a quest and a dream, and as the record of man's audacity and foolish, visionary heroism, there has never been another movie like it."
>
> Roger Ebert, critic, 1982

i

The difficult process of making *Fitzcarraldo* is shown in Les Blank's 1982 documentary *Burden of Dreams*.

Fitzcarraldo Werner Herzog, 1982

It is difficult to address *Fitzcarraldo* without first examining the obsessive bent of its director Werner Herzog, as well as his perplexing collaboration with frequent (and frequently inscrutable) star Klaus Kinski. Their working relationship was predicated on mutual antagonism and outright aggression tempered by a mutual admiration, and that contradiction regularly manifested itself in their confrontational efforts. Needless to say, despite his unpredictable behavior Kinski often served as Herzog's first choice when it came time for casting. Or was it just that Herzog could rarely convince anyone else to commit to his infamous grueling projects?

Indeed, both Jason Robards and Mick Jagger were originally signed to the role, and it was only after both bowed out that Herzog contacted Kinski. And no wonder: The film's plot epitomizes both Herzog's and Kinski's legendary tenacity. Opera lover Brian Sweeney Fitzgerald (Kinski) vows to bring opera to remote Peru. But first he must make a fortune to fund the quixotic goal, and his plan involves hauling a huge steamboat over a mountain ridge to an isolated plot of land where he might harvest the rubber trees.

Fittingly, or perhaps typically, making a film depicting such a near-impossible feat encumbered by almost insurmountable obstacles indeed turned out to be an ordeal itself. It didn't help that Herzog approached the project with every bit the stubborn madness of his titular character. Injury, insanity, pain, illness, and even death in Herzog's quest to realize such a uniquely impressive vision in fact marred *Fitzcarraldo*'s production.

Herzog actually filmed deep in the jungles of Ecuador and Peru, dealing directly with all their inherent challenges, from mosquitoes to mudslides. To capture footage of a raft expedition threatened by tumultuous rapids, Herzog and a small crew ran the tumultuous rapids themselves. Most famously, to show the steamboat being transported over the mountain, Herzog did just that, depicting the effort with a documentary-like verisimilitude.

Yet *Fitzcarraldo*, the finished film, hardly comes across like Joseph Conrad's *Heart of Darkness*, let alone Francis Ford Coppola's *Apocalypse Now* (1979), and Kinski is no Kurtz-like invader. Compared with Herzog and Kinski's bleak conquistador tale *Aguirre: The Wrath of God* (1972), *Fitzcarraldo* is downright innocent. Kinski's optimistic opera lover, nicknamed "Fitzcarraldo" by the Peruvian locals, is driven by idealism as much as intransigence. The curious natives help him bring his dream to fruition in part because of his innocence, exuberance, and total passion for opera, which he plays on an old Victrola record player that he carries with him. As the steamboat is dragged uphill, against all odds, Kinski's Fitzcarraldo stands on the top deck, beaming, as his Victrola blasts opera singer Enrico Caruso. It's a sight as surreal as it is inspiring, simultaneously announcing an accomplishment that is both dramatic (in terms of the narrative) and impressively tactile (in terms of filmmaking). **JKl**

Gandhi Richard Attenborough, 1982

G.B. / India (Carolina Bank, Goldcrest, Indo-British, International, NFDC) 188m Technicolor **Producer** Richard Attenborough **Screenplay** John Briley **Photography** Ronnie Taylor, Billy Williams **Music** Ravi Shankar, George Fenton **Cast** Ben Kingsley, Candice Bergen, Edward Fox, John Gielgud, Trevor Howard, John Mills, Martin Sheen, Ian Charleson, Athol Fugard, Günther Maria Halmer, Saeed Jaffrey, Geraldine James, Alyque Padamsee, Amrish Puri, Roshan Seth **Oscars** Richard Attenborough (best picture), Richard Attenborough (director), John Briley (screenplay), Ben Kingsley (actor), Stuart Craig, Robert W. Laing, Michael Seirton (art direction), Billy Williams, Ronnie Taylor (photography), John Mollo, Bhanu Athaiya (costume), John Bloom (editing) **Oscar nominations** Tom Smith (makeup), Ravi Shankar, George Fenton (music), Gerry Humphreys, Robin O'Donoghue, Jonathan Bates, Simon Kaye (sound)

"An eye for an eye only ends up making the whole world blind."

Mohandas Gandhi (Ben Kingsley)

🛈

Ben Kingsley looked so much like Mohandas Gandhi that many locals thought him to be Gandhi's ghost.

"The truth," Richard Attenborough said, "is that I never wanted to be a director at all. I just wanted to direct that film." For him, therefore, *Gandhi* represented a mission: Attenborough survived twenty years of delays, frustrations, ridicule, and personal financial risk to achieve his dream of recreating the life and times of Mohandas Kharamchand Gandhi (1869–1948), in a way that would touch audiences of East and West alike.

Attenborough first conceived the project in 1962: His particular inspiration was Gandhi's dictum, "It has always been a mystery to me how men can feel themselves honored by the humiliation of their fellow beings." Already a producer, Attenborough was not to embark as a director until 1969, with *Oh! What a Lovely War*, and at various stages of his eighteen-year struggle to raise finances for *Gandhi*, Fred Zinnemann and David Lean were proposed as more likely and more marketable directors. Various writers, including Gerald Hanley, Donald Ogden Stuart, and Robert Bolt, tried their hand before John Briley's script masterfully captured the essence of Gandhi's life and achievement.

Over the years, generations of actors—including Alec Guinness, Dirk Bogarde, Peter Finch, Albert Finney, Tom Courtenay, Robert De Niro, Dustin Hoffman, John Hurt, and Richard Burton—were considered for the leading role. In the end the choice was the practically unknown Ben Kingsley, who had the advantage of facial features inherited from his Indian father. Kingsley dedicated himself to the role, shedding weight, taking up yoga, learning to spin cotton, and making a brave attempt to live life by Gandhi's example. The huge supporting cast included a remarkable display of stage and screen luminaries of the time.

Briley's script opens with the assassination and state funeral of Gandhi in 1948, and then flashes back to his beginnings as a young lawyer, protesting against racial discrimination in South Africa in 1893. From this it traces the main biographical landmarks of his battle against British imperial domination, and for an integrated Indian society and culture. Ironically, Gandhi's passionate commitment to peaceful protest often leads to violence and death, as well as his own lengthy imprisonment. Much of the action was filmed on the actual historic locations. The funeral scene, shot on the Rajpath using eleven camera crews, assembled an estimated 400,000 extras.

Gandhi triumphantly disproved the general tenet that films that are long in the making usually fall short of their ambition. *Gandhi* found an instant response in critical acclaim and a worldwide audience. Its eight Academy Awards marked a record, surpassed only by *Ben-Hur* (1959). For Attenborough a greater personal satisfaction was evidently the certainty that at least some of his audience felt themselves enriched by the encounter with Gandhi, through his screen portrait. For better or worse, *Gandhi* was to mark his future career as a director of inspirational film biographies. **JRos**

The Thing John Carpenter, 1982

U.S. (Turman-Foster, Universal) 109m
Technicolor **Language** English / Norwegian
Producer David Foster, Lawrence Turman
Screenplay Bill Lancaster, from the story
"Who Goes There?" by John W. Campbell Jr.
Photography Dean Cundey **Music** Ennio
Morricone **Cast** Kurt Russell, Wilford Brimley,
T.K. Carter, David Clennon, Keith David,
Richard A. Dysart, Charles Hallahan, Peter
Maloney, Richard Masur, Donald Moffat, Joel
Polis, Thomas G. Waites, Norbert Weisser,
Larry J. Franco, Nate Irwin

𝓲

The movie was shot in the middle of
summer in Los Angeles, on artificially
cooled sound stages.

A group of scientists (including Kurt Russell's protagonist) at an isolated outpost in Antarctica find themselves under siege by an alien lifeform that can take over their bodies. Cut off from the outside world, the men grow increasingly paranoid as they suspect each other of being taken over by the alien, and realize that they can't afford to let it venture beyond the outpost, lest it infect the entire world.

Based on the classic science-fiction story "Who Goes There?" by John W. Campbell, and having originally been adapted by Howard Hawks in 1951 as *The Thing from Another World*, this 1982 version by John Carpenter eschews the Boy's Own adventure of the Hawks film and goes straight for claustrophobia and existential dread. Carpenter's *The Thing* proved to be one of the most influential horror movies of the 1980s, much imitated but rarely bettered.

Along with the films of David Cronenberg, *The Thing* is one of the prime texts to explore the themes of bodily invasion that pervade horror and sci-fi movies of that decade. It is one of the first films to unflinchingly show the rupture and warp of flesh and bone into grotesque tableaus of surreal beauty, forever raising the bar on cinematic horror. **AT**

Fanny och Alexander Ingmar Bergman, 1982
Fanny and Alexander

Swedish director Ingmar Bergman's large body of work is so distinctive that it is frequently spoofed by comedians as well as imitated and cited by lesser filmmakers. Showing the deeper, darker side of the human spirit without flinching or resorting to melodrama, Bergman's dreamy, allegorical films present life as it is rather than how we wish it would be.

Announced as the director's penultimate film (afterwards he worked primarily in television), the autobiographical tale of *Fanny and Alexander* came as a jolt to fans of his brooding earlier films. Written by Bergman, and featuring many of Bergman's most talented, seasoned actors, including Erland Josephson, Harriet Andersson, and Gunnar Björnstrand, *Fanny* is considered his most accessible movie—it won four of its six Academy Award nominations, including Best Foreign Language Film.

This part-autobiography spans a stormy year in the life of a brother and sister (Pernilla Allwin and Bertil Guve) born into an aristocratic family in turn-of-the-century Sweden. Filmed with an energy unseen in previous Bergman productions, the story is part Dickensian drama, part mystical fairy tale. Beginning at a luxurious family Christmas told from the boy's point of view, it switches to their miserable life after the death of the children's much-loved theater-owning father. By then, the usual Bergmanesque sense of foreboding has descended on the story, settling on life during the deeply unfortunate and terrifying remarriage of their mother to an awful bishop—Jan Malmsjö in a suitably hateful role.

Fanny and Alexander's length and languorous, careful pace may put modern action viewers off, but Bergman's famous cinematographer Sven Nykvist uses lustrous lighting to make each frame a delight. The entire film has a dreamy sense of the unreal, a relief during its more tragic moments. Bergman, ever the master, wisely structures the tale to have its most horrific and most satisfying moment just when the story demands a resolution. By then the viewer is left breathless and waiting for the good times to return. Despite his life's work analyzing the frightening world of the living, Bergman here allows his audience some comfort—albeit with certain philosophical provisions. **KK**

Sweden / France / West Germany (Cin. AB, Gaumont, Persona, Swedish Film Inst., Sandrews, Svenska, TVI, Tobis) 188m Eastmancolor **Language** Swedish / German / Yiddish / English **Producer** Jörn Donner **Screenplay** Ingmar Bergman **Photography** Sven Nykvist **Music** Daniel Bell **Cast** Erland Josephson, Jarl Kulle, Pernilla Allwin, Allan Edwall, Bertil Guve, Gunn Walgren, Ewa Fröling **Oscars** Sweden (best foreign language film), Anna Asp, Susanne Lingheim (art direction), Sven Nykvist (photography), Marik Vos-Lundh (costume) **Oscar nominations** Ingmar Bergman (director), Ingmar Bergman (screenplay) **Venice Film Festival** Ingmar Bergman (FIPRESCI award)

"One of those masterpieces that plainly presents itself as a work that transcends even the long career of a great artist."

Chris Cabin,
Slant Magazine, 2011

ℹ

There are two versions of *Fanny and Alexander*: a three-hour cinematic one and a five-hour television one.

La notte di San Lorenzo
The Night of the Shooting Stars
Paolo Taviani & Vittorio Taviani, 1982

Italy (Ager, RAI) 105m Eastmancolor
Language Italian Producer Giuliani G.
De Negri Screenplay Paolo Taviani, Vittorio
Taviani, Giuliani G. De Negri, Tonino Guerra
Photography Franco Di Giacomo
Music Nicola Piovani Cast Omero Antonutti,
Margarita Lozano, Claudio Bigagli, Miriam
Guidelli, Massimo Bonetti, Enrica Maria
Modugno, Sabina Vannucchi, Giorgio Naddi,
Renata Zamengo, Micol Guidelli, Massimo
Sarchielli, Giovanni Guidelli, Mario Spallino,
Paolo Hendel Cannes Film Festival Paolo
Taviani, Vittorio Taviani (grand prize of the
jury, prize of the ecumenical jury,
Golden Palm nomination)

The Night of the Shooting Stars is the masterwork of the Taviani Brothers, Paolo and Vittorio, and takes place on the Night of San Lorenzo when all dreams come true. Narrated by a mother speaking to her sleeping baby, the story returns to 1944 when the narrator was six years old and German invaders and Fascist Italian collaborators controlled her village. With her hometown split between Nazi regulations and eventual liberation, a group of her townsfolk cross the Tuscan countryside seeking salvation.

Without either ignoring or dwelling on wartime terrors, this journey expresses civilian resistance. Daily struggles for food take priority over bullets or tactical advantage. Periodically the narrator's childhood perspective even shines through with tragicomically surreal images that discount the fearful quality of their odyssey.

Notable for its ensemble cast, The Night of the Shooting Stars also offers indelible images to salve the etched memory of unwanted conflict. A cathedral is bombed to kill worshippers. Wild watermelon is feasted upon in a field. Friends on opposite sides of a political divide murder one another. Two older people consummate a love affair decades in the making. Together these moments signify the gravity of World War II while remembering the dignity of everyday life. **GC-Q**

1982

De stilte rond Christine M. Marleen Gorris, 1982
A Question of Silence

Netherlands (Sigma) 92m Color
Language Dutch / English
Producer Matthijs van Heijningen
Screenplay Marleen Gorris
Photography Frans Bromet Music Lodewijk
de Boer, Martijn Iasebos Cast Edda
Barends, Nelly Frijda, Henriëtte Tol, Cox
Habbema, Eddie Brugman, Hans Croiset,
Erik Plooyer, Anna van Beers, Noa Cohen,
Kees Coolen, Edgar Danz, Diana Dobbelman,
Miranda Frijda, Frederik de Groot,
Noortje Jansen

A key moment in women's filmmaking, Marleen Gorris's A Question of Silence charged and polarized audiences. It addressed women's submerged rage, reconnecting feminists with the anger that fueled the movements of the 1960s and 1970s while sparking accusations of reverse stereotyping.

Provoked by a news story about a working-class woman's arrest for shoplifting, A Question of Silence centers on three women, strangers to each other, who spontaneously kill a boutique manager as he confronts a frazzled housewife in the act. A unique mix of thriller, courtroom drama, black comedy, quasi-documentary, and political allegory, A Question of Silence is alternately riveting and distancing, mortifying and electrifying. The murder itself is heard rather than seen and embedded in a series of three flashbacks sequences, subverting the visual imperative.

In the film's courtroom climax, as the women are pronounced the sane, their act becomes politically charged. The concluding scene must be experienced rather than described—other than to say that the picture ends not in a bang or a whimper but in waves of laughter, and finishes in silence. Although Gorris's recent films are mellower and more popular, A Question of Silence makes ideology visceral and is a true shocker. **LB**

The Draughtsman's Contract Peter Greenaway, 1982

G.B. (Channel Four Television, British Film Institute) 108m Color **Producer** David Payne **Screenplay** Peter Greenaway **Photography** Curtis Clark **Music** Michael Nyman **Cast** Anthony Higgins, Janet Suzman, Anne-Louise Lambert, Hugh Fraser, Neil Cunningham, Dave Hill, David Grant, David Meyer, Tony Myer, Nicolas Amer, Suzan Crowley, Lynda La Plante, Michael Feast

In late seventeenth-century England, Mrs. Herbert, a wealthy aristocrat (Janet Suzman), hires Mr. Neville, an ambitious and arrogant young artist (Anthony Higgins), to produce twelve drawings of her husband's grand Wiltshire estate. The artist agrees, but his terms require certain sexual favors from his employer. Meanwhile, Mrs. Herbert's husband remains absent, quite possibly murdered, with clues pointing to the nature of his disappearance appearing in the artist's sketches.

Having worked for the previous few years in experimental cinema and faux documentaries, Peter Greenaway made his fiction feature debut with this beguiling puzzle-piece of a film. The film still retains the formal challenge of his earlier work: The compositions are geometrically exact, the dialogue is anachronistic and avowedly non-naturalistic, and the narrative confounds rather than clarifies. But there is a sparkling wit and pleasing theatrical playfulness to the film, which made it an unexpected British hit. The grand country-estate setting is exquisitely captured by Curtis Clark's cinematography, while Michael Nyman's music, which uses motifs from Purcell, is a joy. One of the most striking directorial debuts of recent British cinema, *The Draughtsman's Contract* remains Greenaway's most accessible film. **EL**

A Christmas Story Bob Clark, 1983

U.S. / Canada (Christmas Tree, MGM) 94m Metrocolor **Producer** Bob Clark, René Dupont **Screenplay** Leigh Brown, Bob Clark, Jean Shepherd, from the novel *In God We Trust, All Others Pay Cash* by Jean Shepherd **Photography** Reginald H. Morris **Music** Paul Zaza, Carl Zittrer **Cast** Melinda Dillon, Darren McGavin, Peter Billingsley, Ian Petrella, Scott Schwartz, R.D. Robb, Tedde Moore, Yano Anaya, Zack Ward, Jeff Gillen, Colin Fox, Paul Hubbard, Leslie Carlson, Jim Hunter, Patty Johnson

It's the 1940s, a time when American families still eat dinner together, children walk long distances to school in well-bundled packs, and everyone knows their neighbors. For young Ralphie (Peter Billingsley) in *A Christmas Story*, life is good but not quite complete. Christmas is fast approaching and all he wants is a Red Ryder BB gun. Despite the opposition of his family and teacher, he's determined to come up with a scheme that will secure the toy by Christmas day.

This simple set-up gives director Bob Clark more than enough ammunition to lovingly but bitingly send up Christmas, family values, nostalgia for bygone eras, and the consumerism that has come to define the holiday season. Both droll and laugh-out-loud funny, this modern holiday classic resonates so deeply because it never becomes cruel or dismissive as it tackles its targets.

School bullies, a cantankerous dad and overworked mom, an odd younger sibling, and a posse of misfit friends all come to life in the voice-over by a grown-up Ralphie. Classic scenes (a schoolmate getting his tongue frozen to the flagpole, Christmas dinner at a Chinese restaurant) manage to be both uproarious and touching without ever sliding into schmaltz or sentimentality. For those who loathe the saccharine aspects of the holidays, but don't actually want to be Scrooge, *A Christmas Story* is a perfect fit. **EH**

L'argent Robert Bresson, 1983
Money

An hour into *Money*, a sudden burst of whiteness introduces a new turn in the narrative. A gray-haired woman (Sylvie Van den Elsen) walks by, with a subtle glance passing between her and a criminal fugitive, Yvon (Christian Patey). A few moments later, everything is green and natural for the first time in the film.

Mystery is a watchword in the cinema of Robert Bresson, but the relationship that begins here between Yvon and his benefactress is the most mysterious of all. The woman seems to realize that she has a murderer on her hands. Her submission to him is masochistic, spiritual, and sexual all at once—not to mention, eventually, suicidal.

Is this woman a fool doomed by her code of misplaced goodness, or a saint who brings momentary grace to a damned soul? And what is Yvon by this stage of his harrowing journey—the premise, borrowed from Leo Tolstoy, of a 500-franc note forged by a trio of schoolboys triggering the inexorable dissolution of every structure in his life—an alienated madman, a cold manipulator, or a victim in search of his lost innocence?

The world of *Money* is barren and bare. The cold architecture of middle-class shops, courtrooms, and prisons is matched by an equally harsh sound-collage of sirens, cars, and machinery. Bodies are frequently pinned within the lines of doorways and windows.

Is *Money* Bresson's most secular, materialist work a logical culmination of the despair about modern industrialized life enacted in *The Devil Probably* (1977), or is there a glimmer of hope buried somewhere in its bleak vision? Some poignant details escape the determinist grid, like the shots of Yvon collecting hazelnuts from tree leaves and sharing them with the woman, as white sheets gently blow in the breeze—one of the simplest yet most beautiful passages in any Bresson film. Here we intuit the profound mystery of beings who move through landscapes of dehumanizing violence with their capacities for evil and goodness locked silently inside them—and we witness fleeting moments of absolute, natural purity in a world gone to hell. **AM**

1983

France / Switzerland (EOS-Film, France 3 Cinéma, Marion's Films) 85m Eastmancolor **Language** French **Producer** Jean-Marc Henchoz, Daniel Toscan du Plantier **Screenplay** Robert Bresson, from the novella *The Forged Coupon* by Leo Tolstoy **Photography** Pasqualino De Santis, Emmanuel Machuel **Music** Johann Sebastian Bach **Cast** Christian Patey, Vincent Risterucci, Caroline Lang, Sylvie Van den Elsen, Béatrice Tabourin, Didier Baussy, Marc Ernest Fourneau, Bruno Lapeyre, François-Marie Banier, Alain Aptekman, Jeanne Aptekman, Dominique Mullier, Jacques Behr, Gilles Durieux, Alain Bourguignon **Cannes Film Festival** Robert Bresson (director, tied with Andrei Tarkovsky for *Nostalghia*, Golden Palm nomination)

"I love the cinema because I know it's perishable . . . I don't believe in the immortality of works of art."

Robert Bresson, 1983

ℹ️

Money was Bresson's final movie. He once described it as the film of his that gave him the "most pleasure."

U.S. (The Ladd Co.) 193m Technicolor
Producer Robert Chartoff, Irwin Winkler
Screenplay Philip Kaufman, from book by
Tom Wolfe **Photography** Caleb Deschanel
Music Bill Conti, Gustave Holst **Cast** Sam
Shepard, Scott Glenn, Ed Harris, Dennis
Quaid, Fred Ward, Barbara Hershey, Kim
Stanley, Veronica Cartwright, Pamela Reed,
Scott Paulin, Charles Frank, Lance Henriksen,
Donald Moffat, Levon Helm, Mary Jo
Deschanel **Oscars** Jay Boekelheide (special
sound effects), Glenn Farr, Lisa Fruchtman,
Stephen A. Rotter, Douglas Stewart, Tom Rolf
(editing), Bill Conti (music), Mark Berger,
Thomas Scott, Randy Thom, David
MacMillan (sound) **Oscar nominations**
Irwin Winkler, Robert Chartoff (best picture),
Sam Shepard (actor in support role),
Geoffrey Kirkland, Richard Lawrence,
W. Stewart Campbell, Peter R. Romero, Jim
Poynter, George R. Nelson (art direction),
Caleb Deschanel (photography)

*"Who was the best pilot
I ever saw? Well, uh,
you're lookin' at 'im."*

**Gordon Cooper
(Dennis Quaid)**

i

Ironically for an actor playing
the part of an aviator, Sam Shepard
has a phobia of flying.

The Right Stuff Philip Kaufman, 1983

High expectations for this celebratory, epic three-hour drama of America's early manned space program, with its ensemble of actors on the verge of stardom (Ed Harris, Dennis Quaid, and, in a small comic-relief role, Jeff Goldblum among them), were disappointed by its modest box-office return against a hefty budget. But writer-director Philip Kaufman's offbeat take on the heroics and striking treatment of the visuals saw *The Right Stuff* rewarded with eight Academy Award nominations (including Best Picture) and four wins, and an appreciative cult of admirers for whom the film's aerial and Earth-orbiting space sequences remain sheer bliss.

Adapted from Tom Wolfe's best-selling, tough, touching, and tale-telling nonfiction chronicle of the Mercury astronauts, the film contrasts the courageous but comparatively unsung exploits of sound-barrier-breaking test pilot Chuck Yeager (Sam Shepard perfectly cast as the laid-back, ruggedly individualistic fly boy) with the selection, training, and media parading of more competitive, crewcut-wearing jocks into an elite, all-American cadre with "the right stuff." The admiring but good-humored and realistic, warts-and-all portrayals of the pilots is set against a distinctly satiric view of the Cold War's space race, with politicians desperate to minimize the Soviets' aerospace achievements by endangering and aggrandizing a batch of instant apple pie heroes.

There are many memorable moments: A race to find the crashed Yeager has a searcher point to a speck and ask, "Is that a man?" before cutting to the charred figure striding manfully from the smoking wreckage and then back to Yeager's buddy (The Band's Levon Helm, also the film's narrator) exulting, "You're damn right it is!"; Alan Shepard (Scott Glenn), equally anxious to pee and to make history while his vigil in the capsule atop a Saturn rocket is torturously protracted, John Glenn's (Harris) orbital flight graced with a mystical slant and a nail-biting reentry that explodes into his triumphal ticker-tape parade; Quaid's cocky, grinning Gordon Cooper awed by the "heavenly light" glowing across his helmet. The picture is consistently thrilling, including its use of Gustav Holst's powerful work *The Planets* with Bill Conti's exhilarating, Oscar-winning score. **AE**

The Big Chill Lawrence Kasdan, 1983

U.S. (Carson, Columbia) 105m
Metrocolor **Producer** Michael Shamberg
Screenplay Barbara Benedek, Lawrence
Kasdan **Photography** John Bailey
Music Mick Jagger, Smokey Robinson, John
Williams **Cast** Tom Berenger, Glenn Close,
Jeff Goldblum, William Hurt, Kevin Kline,
Mary Kay Place, Meg Tilly, JoBeth Williams,
Don Galloway, James Gillis, Ken Place, Jon
Kasdan, Ira Stiltner, Jake Kasdan, Muriel
Moore **Oscar nominations** Michael
Shamberg (best picture), Lawrence Kasdan,
Barbara Benedek (screenplay), Glenn Close
(actress in support role)

Much imitated but never bettered—it is unlikely the television series *thirtysomething* would have existed without this movie—Lawrence Kasdan's nostalgic film about a handful of 1960s college friends, reunited in middle age for a funeral, manages to be both sharply witty and achingly moving.

Following the suicide of Alex—played by Kevin Costner, though only a scene in which he is already deceased and being prepared for his coffin remain in the final version—seven of his friends gather for a weekend to remember him. Sam (Tom Berenger), Michael (Jeff Goldblum), Nick (William Hurt), Karen (JoBeth Williams), and Meg (Mary Kay Place) are the pals, all dealing with their own midlife crises, who descend on married couple Sarah (Glenn Close) and Harold's (Kevin Kline) house, to reminisce, bicker, and open old wounds to a suitably 1960s soundtrack.

Kasdan and Barbara Benedek's observant script captures all the idealistic feelings and disappointments of a '60s generation stuck in the far more materialistic '80s, while *The Big Chill*'s ensemble cast delivers just the right combination of sadness and humor, never lapsing into sentimentality. **JB**

Sans soleil Chris Marker, 1983
Sunless

France (Argos Film) 100m Color
Language French **Screenplay** Chris Marker
Photography Chris Marker **Music** Isao
Tomita, Modest Mussorgsky, Jean Sibelius
Cast Florence Delay, Arielle Dombasle,
Riyoko Ikeda, Charlotte Kerr, Alexandra
Stewart **Berlin International Film Festival**
Chris Marker (OCIC award—honorable
mention, new cinema)

Chris Marker's masterpiece is one of the key nonfiction films of our time: a personal philosophical essay that concentrates mainly on contemporary Tokyo but also includes footage shot in Iceland, Guinea-Bissau, and San Francisco, where the filmmaker tracks down all the original locations in Hitchcock's *Vertigo* (1958), one of Marker's key cinematic obsessions. Difficult to describe and almost impossible to summarize, this poetic journal of a major French filmmaker and video artist radiates in all directions, exploring and reflecting on decades of experience all over the world.

A film about subjectivity, death, photography, social custom, and consciousness itself, *Sans soleil* registers like a poem one might find in a time capsule. Characteristically, it is a film of second thoughts by a photographer, a leftist, and a compulsive globe-trotter who remains haunted and transfixed by some of his own images. Significantly, as in his other films and videos, Marker refuses to take a directorial credit. It also seems pertinent that he assigns his own narration to an American woman (Alexandria Stewart) in the film's English-language version—he is quoted only in the third person and past tense—marking him as a master of indirection. The wit and beauty of Marker's highly original form of discourse leave a profound aftertaste. **JRos**

Star Wars: Episode VI—Return of the Jedi

Richard Marquand, 1983

U.S. (Lucasfilm) 134m Color **Producer** Howard G. Kazanjian **Screenplay** George Lucas, Lawrence Kasdan **Photography** Alan Hume **Music** John Williams, Joseph Williams **Cast** Mark Hamill, Harrison Ford, Carrie Fisher, Billy Dee Williams, Anthony Daniels, Peter Mayhew, Sebastian Shaw, Ian McDiarmid, Frank Oz, James Earl Jones, David Prowse, Alec Guinness, Kenny Baker, Michael Pennington, Kenneth Colley **Oscars** Richard Edlund, Dennis Muren, Ken Ralston, Phil Tippett (special visual effects) **Oscar nominations** Ben Burtt (special sound effects), Norman Reynolds, Fred Hole, James L. Schoppe, Michael Ford (art direction), John Williams (music), Ben Burtt, Gary Summers, Randy Thom, Tony Dawe (sound)

The third installment of George Lucas's original Star Wars trilogy (otherwise known as *Episode VI—Return of the Jedi*) picks up some time after the cliffhanger events of *The Empire Strikes Back* (1980). Luke Skywalker (Mark Hamill), an eager young Jedi trainee in the first installment, is now a brooding warrior (hence the black clothing). Skilled in the ways of the Force, he returns to his home planet of Tatooine to help his friends—Princess Leia (Carrie Fisher, clad in a sci-fi bikini male fans still rave about today), Lando Calrissian (Billy Dee Williams), and Chewbacca the wookie—rescue their frozen-in-carbonite pal Han Solo (Harrison Ford) from the clutches of Jabba the Hutt.

The main strand of the plot covers similar ground to *Star Wars* (1977). The evil Empire is constructing another Death Star, which our heroes have to destroy. Executive producer Lucas (who cowrote the script with Lawrence Kasdan) and director Richard Marquand introduce a new race of teddy-bear-like creatures, the Ewoks, to entertain younger members of the audience. The stars, meanwhile, are never eclipsed by cuddly muppets and impressive special effects, and skillfully bring Lucas's vision of intergalactic good-versus-evil to a close. **JB**

Narayama bushi-ko Shohei Imamura, 1983
The Ballad of Narayama

Japan (Toei) 130m Color **Language** Japanese **Producer** Goro Kusakabe, Jiro Tomoda **Screenplay** Shohei Imamura, from the novel *Narayama Bushi-Ko* by Shichirô Fukazawa **Photography** Masao Tochizawa **Music** Shinichirô Ikebe **Cast** Ken Ogata, Sumiko Sakamoto, Takejo Aki, Tonpei Hidari, Seiji Kurasaki, Kaoru Shimamori, Ryutaro Tatsumi, Junko Takada, Nijiko Kiyokawa, Mitsuko Baisho **Cannes Film Festival** Shohei Imamura (Golden Palm)

This strange film chronicles the lives and deaths of the inhabitants of a remote village, hidden in a mountainous region of nineteenth-century Japan. At age seventy, each villager must be carried on a male relative's back over a rugged mountain path to the burial ground at Narayama, and left there to die.

The Ballad of Narayama centers on one family headed by a matriarch, Orin (Sumiko Sakamoto), who is approaching her seventieth birthday. Director Shohei Imamura portrays village life both unsparingly and surrealistically, revealing the unvarnished desires and hardships that drive the villagers. In a time of famine, when a family takes more than their fair share of the food, they are buried alive. A sexually frustrated young man, unable to get a woman, finds relief with a neighbor's dog. The village and Orin's family are revealed like this, vividly existing in a brutal hand-to-mouth existence.

In the film's last segment, Orin reaches her seventieth birthday and her oldest son, Tatsuhei (Ken Ogata), must carry her to Narayama. The trip over steep mountain passes is even more difficult than life in the village. As the journey continues Tatsuhei doggedly perseveres, and Orin gracefully faces her mortality. We come to realize that the fulfillment of this extravagantly useless ritual is what makes the villagers human. **RH**

Terms of Endearment James L. Brooks, 1983

U.S. (Paramount) 132m
Metrocolor **Producer** James L. Brooks
Screenplay James L. Brooks, from novel by
Larry McMurtry **Photography** Andrzej
Bartkowiak **Music** Michael Gore
Cast Shirley MacLaine, Debra Winger, Jack
Nicholson, Danny DeVito, Jeff Daniels, John
Lithgow, Lisa Hart Carroll, Betty King,
Huckleberry Fox, Troy Bishop, Shane Serwin,
Megan Morris, Tara Yeakey, Norman Bennett,
Jennifer Josey **Oscars** James L. Brooks (best
picture), James L. Brooks (director), James L.
Brooks (screenplay), Shirley MacLaine
(actress), Jack Nicholson (actor in support
role) **Oscar nominations** Debra Winger
(actress), John Lithgow (actor in support
role), Polly Platt, Tom Pedigo (art direction),
Richard Marks (editing), Michael Gore
(music), Donald O. Mitchell, Rick Kline, Kevin
O'Connell, James R. Alexander (sound)

"Don't worship me
until I've earned it."

**Aurora Greenway
(Shirley MacLaine)**

i

Shirley MacLaine passed on
the role of Diane Freeling in
Poltergeist (1982) to play Aurora.

From the author of *The Last Picture Show*, *Lonesome Dove*, and *Horseman Pass By* (upon which Martin Ritt's classic 1963 film *Hud* was based), Larry McMurty's novel of a strained, emotional, and difficult relationship between a mother and daughter was translated into a successful, award-winning Hollywood movie by screenwriter-director James L. Brooks. It remains a textbook example of how to make a successful mainstream American weepie.

Debra Winger, at the height of her career in the 1980s, stars as Emma, the stubborn daughter of possessive, often smothering mother Aurora (Shirley MacLaine). *Terms of Endearment* follows their relationship over a series of years, from Emma trying to extricate herself from her mother by marrying the laid-back (and ultimately unfaithful) Flap Horton (Jeff Daniels), to mother and daughter reaching some sort of truce when Emma is dying of cancer. Although the film is a tearjerker of the highest order, Brooks manages to keep sickly sentiment at bay and in doing so helps his cast deliver one of the most moving deathbed scenes in recent cinema history.

The light relief—away from the mother/daughter harsh words and tears—is delivered in scenes by MacLaine, in an Oscar-winning turn, and Jack Nicholson, as astronaut Garrett Breedlove. It is during the moments between these two experienced actors that the film really sizzles, most notably as Garrett, displaying his devil-may-care attitude, drives himself and Aurora along the beach at the edge of the waves.

Subtly played by Winger, Daniels, John Lithgow (as the man Emma has an affair with following Flap's infidelity), and Danny DeVito (as another of Aurora's suitors), *Terms of Endearment* features scene-stealing performances from Nicholson and MacLaine that threaten to overtake the entire film. However, former television director Brooks (who reunited with Nicholson for the Oscar-winning *As Good as It Gets* in 1997) paces the movie in such a manner—cleverly mixing the humor and the tragedy—that their star turns only enhance this melancholy look at modern family relationships. **JB**

El Norte Gregory Nava, 1983

U.S. / G.B. (American Playhouse, Channel Four, Independent, Island Alive, PBS) 139m Color **Language** English / Spanish **Producer** Trevor Black, Bertha Navarro, Anna Thomas **Screenplay** Gregory Nava, Anna Thomas **Photography** James Glennon **Music** The Folkloristas, Malecio Martinez, Linda O'Brien, Emil Richards **Cast** Zaide Silvia Gutiérrez, David Villalpando, Ernesto Gómez Cruz, Lupe Ontiveros, Trinidad Silva, Alicia del Lago, Abel Franco, Enrique Castillo, Tony Plana, Diane Civita, Mike Gomez **Oscar nomination** Gregory Nava, Anna Thomas (screenplay)

Exploring illegal passage into the United States, *El Norte* brilliantly confronts the fantasy of First World comfort with the reality of Third World people. Written by the husband–wife team of Gregory Nava and Anna Thomas and directed by Nava, the film is significant for exposing the porous nature of national borders and the exploitation of nomadic workers. Praising the humanity of illegal immigrants eking out an existence beneath the American dream, *El Norte* further recognizes the context of such experience.

For Guatemalan siblings Enrique (David Villalpando) and Rosa (Zaide Silvia Gutiérrez), the issue is much simpler than geopolitics. When their father is murdered for organizing bean pickers and their mother "disappeared" by paramilitary functionaries, they flee for their lives. In Tijuana they struggle with that city's poverty and capture a coyote before arriving in Los Angeles. Realizing the rampant racism of their Northern employers, though now with the advantages of indoor plumbing and electricity, they work as day laborers with an insecure future.

Guatemala is herein characterized by green and yellow, Tijuana with tan, and the United States with blues and white. Music also cues the siblings' journey, but finally it's the total effect of their migration that registers the force of modern economic disparity. **GC-Q**

De Vierde Man Paul Verhoeven, 1983
The Fourth Man

Netherlands (De Verenigde Nederlandsche) 105m Color **Language** Dutch **Producer** Rob Houwer **Screenplay** Gerard Soeteman, from novel by Gerard Reve **Photography** Jan de Bont **Music** Loek Dikker **Cast** Jeroen Krabbé, Renée Soutendijk, Thom Hoffman, Dolf de Vries, Geert de Jong, Hans Veerman, Hero Muller, Caroline de Beus, Reinout Bussemaker, Erik J. Meijer, Ursul de Geer, Filip Bolluyt, Hedda Lornie, Paul Nygaard, Guus van der Made

Wrapping up his auspicious European period before heading to the fertile fields of Hollywood, Dutch director Paul Verhoeven reached some sort of trashy apotheosis in black comedy with *The Fourth Man*. Essentially a Hitchcock film had Hitchcock made more explicit his fear of female sexuality, *The Fourth Man* stars Jeroen Krabbé as a semicloseted, alcoholic gay writer who suspects his wealthy bisexual meal ticket Renée Soutendijk may have killed her previous three husbands. Krabbé hates his homosexuality yet can't resist seducing Soutendijk's boy toy, and leeches off her even as he thinks he could be murder victim number four.

Confused by self-loathing, Krabbé's suspicions deepen, but Verhoeven keeps the truth intentionally vague. He packs the film with overtly Catholic symbolism and premonitions of death, perversely toying with expectations. In fact, Verhoeven has since claimed that he and screenwriter Gerard Soeteman intentionally added superfluous and utterly extraneous symbolism just to throw off critics, and indeed the movie proceeds unpredictably. Verhoeven would later revisit essentially the same scenario with his Hollywood smash *Basic Instinct* (1992), but that far glossier film failed to recapture the humor and twisted energy of *The Fourth Man*. **JKl**

Videodrome David Cronenberg, 1983

U.S. / Canada (Famous Players, Filmplan, Guardian, CFDC, Universal) 87m Color **Producer** Claude Héroux **Screenplay** David Cronenberg **Photography** Mark Irwin **Music** Howard Shore **Cast** James Woods, Sonja Smits, Deborah Harry, Peter Dvorsky, Leslie Carlson, Jack Creley, Lynne Gorman, Julie Khaner, Reiner Schwartz, David Bolt, Lally Cadeau, Henry Gomez, Harvey Chao, David Tsubouchi, Kay Hawtrey

A groundbreaking film of the commercial/independent movement of 1980s Hollywood, David Cronenberg's story about the horrible transformations wrought by exposure to televised violence wittily thematizes the very problems that the director's exploration of violent sexual imagery in his previous productions had caused with censors, Hollywood distributors, and feminist groups. Max Renn (James Woods) is a cable-station operator whose cynical marketing of sex and violence backfires on him when his abdomen suddenly grows a vagina-like opening into which, among other objects, audiocassettes can be inserted. The film, in which such sado-masochistic fantasy and transgendering play key roles, ends tragically, with Max's self-destruction.

In many ways the most audacious formal incarnation of Cronenberg's characteristic themes, *Videodrome* begins as a fairly standard commercial thriller, only to be transformed, at midpoint, into subjective fantasy of the most outrageous and unusual kind. Visually rich, *Videodrome* is also thought-provoking in its startling meditation on both polymorphous perversity and the interpenetration between the public and subjective realms of experience. Cronenberg has been both praised and condemned for his fluid treatment of gender (a closing sequence in which two female characters grow penises in a kind of riposte to Max's "vagination" was cut from the release print as too disturbing). Even in its edited form, *Videodrome* remains one of Hollywood's most unusual films, too shocking and idiosyncratic to be anything but a commercial failure. **RBP**

i

Andy Warhol described *Videodrome* as "A *Clockwork Orange* for the Eighties."

Koyaanisqatsi Godfrey Reggio, 1983

As if a movie like *Koyaanisqatsi* weren't adventurous enough in its own right—an avant-garde feature with no story, nonstop minimalist music, and a serious sociopolitical message—director Godfrey Reggio announced from the start that this 1983 production was only the initial phase of a *qatsi* trilogy, all of which would be shot on commercial-grade 35mm film and aimed at mainstream theatrical release.

The series didn't continue until *Powaqqatsi* opened in 1988, and funding problems prevented Reggio from finishing it until 2002, when *Naqoyqatsi* finally arrived. Although all three installments have admirers, *Koyaanisqatsi* is easily the most fully realized of the bunch, retaining its power to tease the mind, tantalize the eye, and enchant the ear.

The film is rooted in three bold ideas. One is Reggio's wish to devise a new kind of sensuous, alluring cinema in which all the key creative partners—cinematographer Ron Fricke, composer Philip Glass, and himself as director—would be equal partners, making equal contributions to the finished film. Another is his conviction that general audiences will support nonnarrative cinema if it presents important ideas in an appealing, unpretentious manner. The third is his commitment to the message at the heart of the trilogy: that nature and culture have lost their ancient equilibrium in the modern era, and may spin out of control if humanity doesn't wake up to the dangers generated by its technological hubris.

True to its title—a word meaning "life out of balance" in the Hopi Indian language—the kaleidoscopic *Koyaanisqatsi* presents images of a world rendered incipiently unstable by all manner of human activities. The most memorable sequences use a diverse array of cinematic devices, from anamorphic lenses and freewheeling montage to time-lapse photography and varying camera speeds, to portray the world in fresh, original terms meant to spark fresh, original thinking about ecological and environmental issues. Reggio's vision borrows important elements from earlier experimental filmmakers—the influences of Stan Brakhage and Hilary Harris are especially hard to miss—while reaching out to a wider audience than any avant-gardist had previously attracted. The ongoing appeal of *Koyaanisqatsi* shows how well he succeeded. **DS**

U.S. (Institute for Regional Education, Santa Fe) 87m Color **Language** English /Hopi **Director** Godfrey Reggio **Producer** Godfrey Reggio **Screenplay** Ron Fricke, Michael Hoenig, Godfrey Reggio, Alton Walpole **Photography** Ron Fricke **Music** Philip Glass, Michael Hoenig **Berlin International Film Festival** Godfrey Reggio (Golden Bear nomination)

"The film's role is to provoke, to raise questions that only the audience can answer. This is the highest value of any work of art, not predetermined meaning, but meaning gleaned from the experience of the encounter."

Godfrey Reggio, 2005

ℹ️

The movie drew on several sources for its visuals, including unused footage from *The Shining* (1980).

SAY GOODNIGHT TO THE **BAD GUY**

MAKE WAY FOR THE **GOOD GUY**

Scarface Brian De Palma, 1983

Brian De Palma's updated remake of Howard Hawks's 1932 gangster classic *Scarface* is bloody, excessive, outrageous, and brilliantly crafted—and it sports an unforgettably histrionic performance from Al Pacino. When it first appeared, the film seemed like a striking departure for De Palma, away from Hitchcockian games with voyeurs, rear windows, and doppelgängers. Seen today, *Scarface* is quintessential De Palma, a treatise on the fragile conditions of male selfhood and power politics.

The film begins with documentary footage detailing the wave of Cuban refugees flooding into North America—adding a political dimension that completely transforms the template provided by Hawks's original. Tony Montana (Pacino) quickly realizes that crime and murder are his best ways out of the immigrant ghetto. His rise and fall as a modern gangster is rendered in a spectacular, garish style: De Palma takes every opportunity to heighten the fashions and musical crazes of the 1970s as a counterpoint to all the bloodshed and betrayal.

Commentators rushed to dub this take on Hawks's original (scripted by Oliver Stone) the first "postmodern" gangster epic. Montana even talks about himself in terms that recall Robert Warshow's classic essay "The Gangster as Tragic Hero"—"You need me, I'm the bad guy!" Yet, for all its dazzling self-consciousness, this is a grand narrative in the old style—and its cathartic, apocalyptic kick is tremendous.

De Palma takes to a new, melodramatic extreme one of the classic themes of the gangster genre: The hero's obsession with territorial control and the inexorable loss of this power. Tony dreams of absolute command—over his own body, over the hearts and allegiances of those close to him, and over the turf of his criminal empire. But after snorting mountains of cocaine, he cannot even see, on his own security cameras, those who come to kill him.

More than any disaster film made since the 1970s, De Palma's controversial masterpiece gives us the subversive thrill of seeing a social microcosm explode into a thousand fragments—and all the while, a blimp flies above, heralding a bitterly mocking slogan in neon: "The World is Yours." **AM**

U.S. (Universal) 170m Technicolor
Language English / Spanish
Producer Martin Bregman
Screenplay Oliver Stone, from the novel
Armitage Trail and 1932 screenplay *Scarface*
by Howard Hawks Photography John A.
Alonzo Music Giorgio Moroder
Cast Al Pacino, Steven Bauer, Michelle
Pfeiffer, Mary Elizabeth Mastrantonio, Robert
Loggia, Miriam Colon, F. Murray Abraham,
Paul Shenar, Harris Yulin, Ángel Salazar,
Arnaldo Santana, Pepe Serna, Michael P.
Moran, Al Israel, Dennis Holahan

"The last time you gonna see a bad guy like this again, let me tell you. Come on. Make way for the bad guy. There's a bad guy comin' through!"

**Tony Montana
(Al Pacino)**

i

De Palma had been in line to direct
Flashdance (1983) but switched to
Scarface on the strength of the script.

1983

The King of Comedy Martin Scorsese, 1983

U.S. (Fox, Embassy) 101m Technicolor **Producer** Arnon Milchan **Screenplay** Paul D. Zimmermann **Photography** Fred Schuler **Music** Robbie Robertson **Cast** Robert De Niro, Jerry Lewis, Diahnne Abbott, Sandra Bernhard, Shelley Hack, Ed Herlihy, Lou Brown, Loretta Tupper, Peter Potulski, Vinnie Gonzales, Whitey Ryan, Doc Lawless, Marta Heflin, Katherine Wallach, Charles Kaleina **Cannes Film Festival** Martin Scorsese (Golden Palm nomination)

Coming after *Taxi Driver* (1976) and especially *Raging Bull* (1980), Martin Scorsese's *The King of Comedy* might initially seem comparatively light. But while Scorsese does play the strange tale of loser Rupert Pupkin (Robert De Niro), who is obsessed with becoming a television host, for laughs, there's a queasy uneasiness to the film.

De Niro's confident smile packs as much menace as his far more imposing creations, while his unpredictable stalker associate Masha (Sandra Bernhard) comes across as so disconnected from reality that her appearances exude an aura of anxiety. Both are colorful reminders of the lonely and perhaps dangerous characters that exist in the periphery of any urban center. Still, the crucial key to *The King of Comedy* is Jerry Lewis as TV host Jerry Langford, playing, after all those years as a patsy, more or less an arrogant, bitter, and jaded version of himself. Lewis's dramatic break from his goofy public persona blurs the difference between fact and fiction, further highlighting the delusions of Pupkin and Masha. But Scorsese seems equally interested in the power and pitfalls of fame in general, offering *The King of Comedy* as a scathing indictment of the way our society overvalues celebrity. **JKl**

Local Hero Bill Forsyth, 1983

G.B. (Warner Bros) 111m Technicolor **Producer** David Puttnam **Screenplay** Bill Forsyth **Photography** Chris Menges **Music** Mark Knopfler **Cast** Burt Lancaster, Peter Riegert, Fulton Mackay, Denis Lawson, Peter Capaldi, Jenny Seagrove, Jennifer Black, Rikki Fulton, Norman Chancer

A gentle Scottish-set culture-clash comedy in the tradition of *Whisky Galore!* (1949) and *The Maggie* (1954)—though without quite the undertow of malice that Mackendrick brought to his films—Bill Forsyth's *Local Hero* pits native Scots guile against the forces of global big business. An eccentric Texan oil tycoon (Burt Lancaster in the warmest of his latter-day performances) plans to site a giant refinery on an unspoiled stretch of Scottish coastline and sends a bewildered young executive (Peter Riegert) to clinch the deal, along with a Scots-based company rep (Peter Capaldi). Most of the locals seem eager to sell out, apart from the aged recluse (Fulton McKay) who owns the crucial beach. But before they can persuade him, the two oilmen start succumbing to the romance of the place. And then the tycoon arrives in person . . .

Forsyth's near-mystical sense of place and his affection for all his characters (not least a visiting and highly convivial Russian sea captain) play into his low-key, quirky humor. Riegert, as the hopelessly fish-out-of-water Yank (his surname of MacIntyre, he explains, was chosen by his Hungarian immigrant forebears because they thought it sounded American), is touchingly bemused, and there's a delectable turn from Jenny Seagrove as a seductive water-nymph; but the film's almost stolen by Denis Lawson as the shrewd, uxorious innkeeper, unofficial leader of the village community. And the ending, though seemingly happy, brings a final touch of wistful melancholy. **PK**

Once Upon a Time in America Sergio Leone, 1983

Sergio Leone spent so much time luring actors to Italy for his spectacular string of Westerns that the setting of *Once Upon a Time in America* marked a radical change. Rather than the wide open spaces of the desert, Leone constructed an elaborate reproduction of New York's Lower East Side, the setting of his multigenerational story of Jewish gangsters (a wholly different kind of gunslinger) crossing paths and clashing over the years.

Beginning during Prohibition and leading up to the late 1960s, the film follows partners-in-crime Robert De Niro and James Woods as two gangland leaders whose different approaches inevitably lead to conflict. Noodles (De Niro) is quieter and prone to depression, whereas Max (Woods) is his hotheaded opposite. The film tracks the pair at three specific dates—1921, 1933, and 1968— and each time we catch up with the characters we are reminded of their inability to change.

At nearly four hours long, *Once Upon a Time in America* is Leone's longest and most languorous film. The patient narrative drifts along with the same narcotic haze of the opium den where Noodles reflects on his wayward life. As usual, Leone pays close attention to period details and composition, once again emphasizing his preference for the power of images over dialogue. His story plays out in simmering glances, scurrilous squinting, and barely concealed sneers. Helping this elegiac mood piece along is yet another brilliant score from longtime Leone collaborator Ennio Morricone, whose conspicuous use of the pan flute somehow suits the material.

Alas, Leone died shortly after the production of *Once Upon a Time in America*, but the film proved a fascinating conclusion to an iconic career. Lacking some of the force and invention of his more visceral and stylish spaghetti Westerns, it nonetheless offers a different set of distinct pleasures, slower paced, but still representative of the director's unerring good taste and confident control of filmmaking's every parameter. **JKl**

U.S. / Italy (Embassy, PSO, Rafran, Warner Bros., Wishbone) 227m Technicolor **Producer** Arnon Milchan **Screenplay** Leonardo Benvenuti, Piero De Bernardi, Enrico Medioli, Franco Arcalli, Franco Ferrini, Sergio Leone, Ernesto Gastaldi, from the novel *The Hoods* by Harry Grey **Photography** Tonino Delli Colli **Music** Ennio Morricone **Cast** Robert De Niro, James Woods, Elizabeth McGovern, Treat Williams, Tuesday Weld, Joe Pesci, Burt Young, Danny Aiello, William Forsythe, James Hayden, Darlanne Fluegel, Larry Rapp, Dutch Miller, Robert Harper, Richard Bright

> *"I like the stink of the streets. It makes me feel good. And I like the smell of it, it opens up my lungs."*
>
> **Noodles (Robert De Niro)**

1983

i

The song "God Bless America" is heard in the final scenes of this movie and in De Niro's 1978 film *The Deerhunter*.

The Terminator James Cameron, 1984

This potential kitsch candidate for the Golden Turkey Award actually became one of the surprise hits of 1984, and its popularity over the past three decades has established it as a genre classic. *The Terminator* is a triumph of style over plot, smartness over intelligence, and a combination of elements that outstrips its parts. Its circular narrative about the future trying to control the past in order to take control of itself—hence changing the very premises of its own state—is a familiar one to all fans of postwar science-fiction literature (Harlan Ellison, Philip K. Dick, and others) and TV shows (such as *The Outer Limits* and *Star Trek*).

Fresh from low-budget effects work for Roger Corman and John Carpenter, director-screenwriter James Cameron adapted the disarming humor of his mentors to deflect objections to the many plot holes. The vision of a dark, dirty, and apocalyptic future was very much in vogue at the time, as witnessed by Carpenter's *Escape from New York*, George Miller's *Mad Max 2: The Road Warrior* (both 1981), Luc Besson's *The Last Combat* (1983), and Lars von Trier's *The Element of Crime* (1984).

Cameron's assured style—tech noir, as it was called after a nightclub in the film—and his kinetic energy combined with a sparse economy of narration, keep the viewer distracted from the sheer absurdity of it all. Even Arnold Schwarzenegger—the very epitome of bad acting with his bland facial expression, heavy Austrian accent, and body language from the school of Frankenstein's monster—becomes a major asset to the film. The casting, Cameron admitted to *Wired*, "shouldn't have worked. The guy is supposed to be an infiltration unit, and there's no way you wouldn't spot a Terminator in a crowd instantly if they all looked like Arnold." All his violent acts and his ten or so lines are delivered with a mechanical dullness and a mock-grim look that charges them with an irresistible, multilayered irony. Virtually all of his dialogue consists of short, unremarkable phrases. Yet everybody who saw this sleeper phenomenon knows most of them by heart, down to Schwarzenegger's quirky pronunciation. "I'll be back" is probably the most quoted among them—frequently used as a catchphrase in radio and TV shows.

If *The Terminator*'s ability to engage the audience in such interplay is reminiscent of *The Rocky Horror Picture Show*'s (1975) ritualistic cult following, then the nudging irony points to the *Scream* quadrilogy's (1996–2011) satire of generic clichés. The same goes for the sadistic but slapstick violence and the "final girl" twist at the end. Under the surface of this mess of sci-fi elements actually lies an even less original slasher movie, complete with a (literally) mechanical killer and a tomboy (Linda Hamilton) discovering her resources to fight and overcome evil. But *The Terminator* is greater than the sum of its parts. The response to the film, like that to all great genre movies, lies not in a presumed originality. It is the way that Cameron fuses familiar elements and breathes new life into them that makes for such a memorable experience. **MT**

U.S. (Cinema 84, Euro Film Fund, Hemdale, Pacific Western) 108m Color **Language** English / Spanish **Producer** Gale Anne Hurd **Screenplay** James Cameron, Gale Anne Hurd, from the screenplays *Soldier* and *Demon with a Glass Hand* by Harlan Ellison **Photography** Adam Greenberg **Music** Brad Fiedel **Cast** Arnold Schwarzenegger, Michael Biehn, Linda Hamilton, Paul Winfield, Lance Henriksen, Rick Rossovich, Bess Motta, Earl Boen, Dick Miller, Shawn Schepps, Bruce M. Kerner, Franco Columbu, Bill Paxton, Brad Rearden, Brian Thompson

"It made no sense whatsoever. But the beauty of movies is that they don't have to be logical. They just have to have plausibility."

James Cameron, 2009

i

Arnold Schwarzenegger's famous "I'll be back" line was originally scripted as "I'll come back."

1984

The Natural Barry Levinson, 1984

U.S. (Delphi, TriStar) 134m Technicolor
Producer Mark Johnson **Screenplay** Roger
Towne, Phil Dusenberry, from novel by
Bernard Malamud **Photography** Caleb
Deschanel **Music** Randy Newman
Cast Robert Redford, Robert Duvall, Glenn
Close, Kim Basinger, Wilford Brimley, Barbara
Hershey, Robert Prosky, Richard Farnsworth,
Joe Don Baker, John Finnegan, Alan Fudge,
Paul Sullivan Jr., Rachel Hall, Robert Rich,
Michael Madsen **Oscar nominations** Glenn
Close (actress in support role), Mel Bourne,
Angelo P. Graham, Bruce Weintraub
(art direction), Caleb Deschanel
(photography), Randy Newman (music)

A baseball movie that turns America's national pastime into a heroic myth, Barry Levinson's romantic adaptation of Bernard Malamud's 1952 novel traces the career of Roy Hobbs (Robert Redford), whose "gift" for the sport shows at an early age. Like all heroes, Hobbs acquires a magic weapon, a bat he makes from a tree hit by lightning and names "Wonder Boy." Although he shows great promise, his career is almost ended when a beautiful woman in black (Barbara Hershey), who sees his considerable talent, shoots him and then kills herself.

Roy becomes separated from Iris (Glenn Close), the good woman who loves him and bears his son—then, after years of drifting, finally makes it to the major leagues at age thirty-eight. There he struggles to get into the lineup of a last place team, which he soon turns around with his talent and charisma. Tempted by Memo (Kim Basinger), a big-city woman, Roy almost loses himself again. But, in the end, he not only rescues his team from defeat but is reunited with Iris and his son (the novel ends more bleakly, with Hobbs striking out).

Levinson's style is hardly realistic—Roy's final home run destroys a light tower and starts a storm of electric sparks—but the film features subtle, restrained performances from Redford and a fine ensemble cast (including Robert Duvall and Wilford Brimley). **BP**

Ghostbusters Ivan Reitman, 1984

U.S. (Black Rhino, Columbia) 107m
Metrocolor **Producer** Ivan Reitman
Screenplay Dan Aykroyd, Harold Ramis
Photography László Kovács **Music** Elmer
Bernstein **Cast** Bill Murray, Dan Aykroyd,
Sigourney Weaver, Harold Ramis, Rick
Moranis, Annie Potts, William Atherton,
Ernie Hudson, David Margulies, Steven Tash,
Jennifer Runyon, Slavitza Jovan, Michael
Ensign, Alice Drummond, Jordan Charney
Oscar nominations Richard Edlund, John
Bruno, Mark Vargo, Chuck Gaspar (special
visual effects), Ray Parker Jr. (song)

Special effects and comedy are brilliantly interwoven in this fantasy adventure written by two of its stars, *National Lampoon*'s Harold Ramis and *Saturday Night Live*'s Dan Aykroyd. With Bill Murray they play a trio of paranormal "experts"—in reality, goofy science professors, kicked off campus for their antics—who set up a ghost-busting business from an abandoned New York City firehouse. Their timing couldn't be better, because the city is suddenly bursting with ghostly apparitions running riot, terrorizing visitors to the library, ransacking an upscale hotel, and even taking up residence in a skeptical Sigourney Weaver's refrigerator.

Ramis (the nerd of the group), Aykroyd (the bumbling dimwit), and costars Weaver and Rick Moranis (as the "Key Master") all have superb comic timing. But Murray's Dr. Peter Venkman, with his sleazy charm and cockiness, steals every scene—an impressive achievement when you consider that his special effects costars include a gigantic, stampeding marshmallow man intent on reducing Manhattan to a pile of sugary rubble that would hijack the movie from a less skilled comic talent.

Sadly, while the stars realigned for *Ghostbusters II* (1989), Murray endeavored to rule himself out of a long-mooted third installment, insisting to its makers that he would do it only "if you kill me off in the first reel." But could that mean he comes back… as a ghost? **JB**

Paris, Texas Wim Wenders, 1984

Who is that walking man? Travis (Harry Dean Stanton in his best role) emerges from the Texan desert to the haunting strains of Ry Cooder's slide guitar. Instantly the possibility of a story seizes us: Where did he come from, where is he going? It turns out that Travis is fleeing a catastrophic family breakdown that left his wife, Jane (Nastassja Kinski), who has also since disappeared, and his young son, Hunter (Hunter Carson), in the care of Travis's brother, Walt (Dean Stockwell).

Travis does not want to stop walking. Walt and others slowly bring him back to language, to sociability, to a remembrance of home and belonging. But nothing will be right until Travis finds Jane. He discovers her in a strip club where she acts as a therapist to the often troubled and lonely customers. In a touching scene, he tells her his own story through a one-way mirror—he can see Jane but she is unable to see him.

Wim Wenders's European, aesthetic vision—carried most powerfully by the landscape cinematography of Robby Müller (who also shot that year's *Repo Man*, another Harry Dean Stanton showcase)—meshed perfectly with the American sensibility of writer Sam Shepard. It is an affecting story of "otherness," a man who cannot fit into the "symbolic order." In the course of his tentative reentry into civilization, Travis naturally bonds with other outsiders, such as a Latin American maid who teaches him eccentric lessons in dress and manners, and especially Hunter, with whom he shares a charmingly childlike rapport.

Paris, Texas was pivotal for Wenders. Just as Travis negotiates gingerly his relationship with society, Wenders was slowly coming to terms with the act of storytelling in cinema—an obligation he had suspended in the wandering, episodic era of his German-language *Alice in den Städten* (1974) and *Im Lauf der Zeit* (1976). He was also bringing himself to contemplate traditional values of marriage, family, and community. For some, he subsequently went too far in his embrace of both conventional cinema and traditional values. But *Paris, Texas*, like *Wings of Desire* (1987), captures the best of both phases in Wenders's career: the longing for home and the recognition of a difficult, modern alienation from it. **AM**

G.B. / France / West Germany (Fox, Argos, Channel Four, Pro-ject, Road Movies, WDR) 147m Color **Producer** Anatole Dauman, Don Guest **Screenplay** L.M. Kit Carson, Sam Shepard **Photography** Robby Müller **Music** Ry Cooder **Cast** Harry Dean Stanton, Nastassja Kinski, Dean Stockwell, Aurore Clément, Hunter Carson, Socorro Valdez, Bernhard Wicki **Cannes Film Festival** Wim Wenders (Golden Palm, prize of the ecumenical jury, FIPRESCI award, tied with *Taxídi sta Kíthira*)

"Sam Shepard and I enjoyed ourselves immensely. As a writer and director it doesn't get much better."

Wim Wenders, 2006

1984

i

The film was shot by a crew of twenty, many risking deportation by breaching their tourist visas.

A Nightmare on Elm Street Wes Craven, 1984

A Nightmare on Elm Street creatively combined horror and humor, gothic literary motifs and slasher movie conventions, gory special effects and subtle social commentary. And it let loose a new monster in America's pop culture: the wisecracking, fedora-wearing teen killer, Freddy Krueger.

Wes Craven's *Last House on the Left* (1972) and *The Hills Have Eyes* (1977) had established the former English professor as a low-budget horror auteur along the lines of Tobe Hooper and George Romero. After his next few works failed to live up to this early potential, Craven developed the idea of a killer who claims his victims in their dreams. Made for less than $2 million, *A Nightmare on Elm Street* was cast with unknown and B-movie actors (including a twenty-one-year-old Johnny Depp in his film debut) and was completed in just thirty-two days. Not bad for a movie that would gross over $25 million at the box office, and which, as of 2010, had inspired eight further films (including a remake).

The film opens inside a basement-cum-workshop, where a hideously scarred man wearing a red-and-green sweater and crusty old hat welds razor-sharp blades to metal fingertips and attaches these to a battered leather glove. As events unfold and secrets are revealed, we learn this is Freddy Krueger (Robert Englund), a former child killer who was burned to death by a mob of furious Elm Street parents. Years later, Freddy has returned from the grave as evil incarnate, obsessed with revenge on the adolescent offspring of those who ended his mortal life. Residing in his victims' subconscious, attacking them as they sleep, Freddy rewrites the laws of physics and carries out grotesque yet creative killings. Spectacular set pieces, laden with special effects wizardry and gallons of fake blood, are balanced by an anxiety-inducing score and a gripping narrative, as we feel for the intended victims in their hopeless battle to stay awake.

Unlike earlier slasher films like *Halloween* (1978) and *Friday the 13th* (1980), *A Nightmare on Elm Street*'s monster-murderer is less a silent death machine than an archetypal "evil trickster." This gothic antihero—a vicious killer with charm, a sense of humor, and a flair for the dramatic—proved immortal in a way even Craven can scarcely have envisaged. **SJS**

U.S. (Media Home Entertainment, New Line, Smart Egg) 91m Color **Producer** Robert Shaye **Screenplay** Wes Craven **Photography** Jacques Haitkin **Music** Charles Bernstein **Cast** John Saxon, Ronee Blakley, Heather Langenkamp, Amanda Wyss, Jsu Garcia, Johnny Depp, Charles Fleischer, Joseph Whipp, Robert Englund, Lin Shaye, Joe Unger, Mimi Craven, Jack Shea, Ed Call, Sandy Lipton

> "I think that [A Nightmare on Elm Street] really is one of the best fairytales of any decade, because Craven understands the roots of those myths."

Guillermo del Toro, 2006

i

Having signed away rights in order to get the original made, Craven was powerless to stop the 2010 remake.

U.S. (Spinal Tap Prod.) 82m Color
Producer Karen Murphy
Screenplay Christopher Guest, Michael McKean, Rob Reiner, Harry Shearer
Photography Peter Smokler
Music Christopher Guest, Michael McKean, Rob Reiner, Harry Shearer
Cast Rob Reiner, Kimberly Stringer, Chazz Domingueza, Shari Hall, R.J. Parnell, David Kaff, Tony Hendra, Michael McKean, Christopher Guest, Harry Shearer, Bruno Kirby, Jean Cromie, Patrick Maher, Ed Begley Jr., Danny Kortchmar

"After watching the 'Stonehenge' scene ... I thought, why not fake the execution of a midget onstage?"

Ozzy Osbourne, 2008

i

Among the inspirations for the Tap were British metal act Saxon, whom Harry Shearer accompanied on tour.

This is Spinal Tap Rob Reiner, 1984

Rob Reiner's made-up documentary ("mockumentary," if you will) dances on that "fine line between stupid and clever," taking elements from real rock docs (*Don't Look Back* [1967], *The Last Waltz* [1978]) and creating a new genre (later examples include *The Blair Witch Project* [1999] and *Bob Roberts* [1992]). Tap fans treasure favorite routines and lines: Derek Smalls (Harry Shearer) trapped in a stage pod or setting off an airport metal detector with the foil-wrapped cucumber in his underpants; the band getting lost backstage as they try to reach an eager audience ("Hello, Cleveland!"); the undersized Stonehenge triptych descending to be "in danger of being crushed by a dwarf"; the blank looks of the band when confronted with their backlist of bad reviews or a radio DJ's classification of Spinal Tap as "currently residing in the 'Where Are They Now?' file"; the arguments over the offensive cover of the *Smell the Glove* album; Nigel's (Christopher Guest) tour of his guitar and amp collection ("These go to eleven"); "It's called 'Lick My Love Pump.'"

And it's a collection of masterly cameos, from Fran Drescher as publicist Bobbi Flekman (her clones are still working in the business) to Bruno Kirby as the Sinatra-loving limo driver, with microbits from Billy Crystal and Dana Carvey as mime waiters ("Mime is money!"). Copping the Yoko thread from the 1970 Beatles film *Let It Be*, *Spinal Tap* delivers a genuine plot as childhood friends David St. Hubbins (Michael McKean) and Nigel Tufnel fall out when David's girlfriend Jeanine Pettibone (June Chadwick) worms her way into the band as manager, displacing the long-suffering Ian Faith (Tony Hendra), who memorably characterizes the dim girl as dressing "like an Australian's nightmare."

It's an achievement that after an hour of jokes at the expense of the group's crassness and stupidity, with hideously accurate parodies of rock dinosaurs ("Big Bottoms," "Sex Farm"), the film wrings emotion out of the threat that they will break up. McKean, whose London accent is letter-perfect, has a great acting moment as he becomes so angry and hurt at his friend's betrayal that he can hardly speak—all the more remarkable given that most of the movie's dialogue was improvised. **KN**

A Passage to India David Lean, 1984

David Lean's final film found him just as obsessed with the widescreen tableau that defined *Lawrence of Arabia* (1962), *The Bridge on the River Kwai* (1957), and *Doctor Zhivago* (1965). However, *A Passage to India* (not, admittedly, shot in CinemaScope) is clearly more a movie of ideas than a movie of spectacle. More or less faithfully adapting E. M. Forster's story of class and cultural conflict in colonial India, the film by necessity loses some of the internalized thrust of the multi-perspective novel, and therefore misses some of the nuance of its characters' motivations. It also, sometimes, comes across as a story of mystery and vague sexual hysteria rather than a biting *adieu* to British colonialism. But in the hands of Lean—the consummate craftsman—*A Passage to India* blazes by. If he too often relies on frequent collaborator Alec Guinness (conspicuously cast as an Indian) for humor and James Fox to make obvious the movie's themes, Lean's respect for the script and his actors allows them to transcend the sometimes romanticized depiction of India.

Particularly strong is the wan, Academy Award-nominated Judy Davis. In her search for the "real" India—the India neither homogenized nor shunned by her fellow Brits—she gets more than she bargained for in the form of Victor Banerjee, whose obsequious and oblivious Dr. Aziz sparks in the mind of Davis's naive Ms. Quested a primal aversion to "going native." As the country's relentless heat, claustrophobia, and chattering monkeys wear down Quested's banal enthusiasm, she grows increasingly unstable, leading to an encounter in the echo-enhancing Marabar caves that results in Aziz being accused of rape.

If Forster's collision of psychology and colonialism comes across almost as an afterthought, the film's disdain for English condescension ultimately lends the trial of Dr. Aziz an ironic inevitability. *A Passage to India* ends on an appropriately and satisfyingly ambivalent note, implying that some of the film's central characters still haven't learned their lesson. It's not as forceful or thought-provoking a conclusion as it could (or should) have been, but the film remains a strong effort all the same, and a fine conclusion to an illustrious career. **JKl**

G.B. (EMI, HBO, Thorn-EMI) 163m Technicolor **Producer** John Brabourne, Richard B. Goodwin **Screenplay** David Lean, from novel by E.M. Forster **Photography** Ernest Day **Music** Maurice Jarre **Cast** Judy Davis, Victor Banerjee, Peggy Ashcroft, James Fox, Alec Guinness, Nigel Havers, Richard Wilson, Antonia Pemberton, Michael Culver, Art Malik, Saeed Jaffrey, Clive Swift, Anne Firbank, Roshan Seth, Sandra Hotz **Oscars** Peggy Ashcroft (actress in support role), Maurice Jarre (music) **Oscar nominations** John Brabourne, Richard N. Goodwin (best picture), David Lean (director), David Lean (screenplay), Judy Davis (actress), John Box, Hugh Scaife (art direction), Ernest Day (photography), Judy Moorcroft (costume), David Lean (editing), Graham V. Hartstone, Nicolas Le Messurier, Michael A. Carter, John W. Mitchell (sound)

"[Forster] keeps going off on the most wonderful sidetracks, and one is tempted to go down them with him."

David Lean, 1984

i

The scene in which Davis finds the overgrown temple, illustrating her sexual stirrings, is not in the book.

Beverly Hills Cop Martin Brest, 1984

U.S. (Paramount) 105m Technicolor
Producer Jerry Bruckheimer, Don Simpson
Screenplay Daniel Petrie Jr., Danilo Bach
Photography Bruce Surtees **Music** Harold
Faltermeyer **Cast** Eddie Murphy, Judge
Reinhold, John Ashton, Lisa Eilbacher, Ronny
Cox, Steven Berkoff, James Russo, Jonathan
Banks, Stephen Elliott, Gilbert R. Hill, Art
Kimbro, Joel Bailey, Bronson Pinchot, Paul
Reiser, Michael Champion **Oscar
nomination** Daniel Petrie Jr., Danilo
Bach (screenplay)

What a different movie *Beverly Hills Cop* would have been had Sylvester Stallone—who was originally attached to the project—been the lead actor. The action would have been far bloodier no doubt, while the film would have lacked the rapid-fire comedy of its star, Eddie Murphy (hot from 1983's *Trading Places*), that made it a worldwide smash.

Murphy is Axel Foley, a smart-talking, streetwise Detroit detective who—like all the best movie cops—doesn't play by the rules. When an old friend is murdered, he heads to Los Angeles to investigate the crime, and inevitably causes a major upset among the Beverly Hills police (who presumably spend most of their time arresting celebrities).

Backed by a pop soundtrack and Harold Faltemeyer's annoyingly infectious "Axel F" theme, director Martin Brest—later to helm *Midnight Run* (1988), *Scent of a Woman* (1992), and *Meet Joe Black* (1998)—delivers a fast-paced, fish-out-of-water action comedy that takes sharp digs at the all-style-and-no-substance L.A. lifestyle. It also makes the most of a charismatic star, who has never been better. Many police action-comedy movies have followed, including two sequels also featuring Murphy, but none have felt as fresh as this one. In 2011, the star mooted the franchise's resurrection, this time on the small screen. **JB**

1984

The Killing Fields Roland Joffé, 1984

G.B. (Enigma [First Casualty], Goldcrest,
International Film Investors, Warner Bros.)
141m Color **Language** English / French /
Khmer **Producer** David Puttnam
Screenplay Bruce Robinson
Photography Chris Menges **Music** Mike
Oldfield **Cast** Sam Waterston, Haing S. Ngor,
John Malkovich, Julian Sands, Craig T.
Nelson, Spalding Gray, Bill Paterson, Athol
Fugard, Graham Kennedy, Katherine Krapum
Chey, Oliver Pierpaoli, Edward Entero Chey,
Tom Bird, Monirak Sisowath, Lambool
Dtangpaibool **Oscars** Haing S. Ngor
(actor in support role), Chris Menges
(photography), Jim Clark (editing) **Oscar
nominations** David Puttnam (best picture),
Roland Joffé (director), Bruce Robinson
(screenplay), Sam Waterston (actor)

Roland Joffé's morally earnest film depicts the disastrous aftermath of American involvement in Cambodian politics during the Vietnam War era. Future *Law & Order* mainstay Sam Waterston offers a bravura performance as *New York Times* journalist Sydney Schanberg, whose dispatches from the country revealed the dreadful results of the U.S. bombing campaign against suspected communist bases.

The Killing Fields divides into two parts. Schanberg's brave, perhaps foolhardy decision to remain even after the Khmer Rouge take the country occupies the first part. Schanberg's Cambodian assistant, Dith Pran (Haing S. Ngor, a former medical officer in the Cambodian army), assists a small group of Western journalists as they negotiate a series of harrowing encounters with the victors, but, despite their attempts to pass him off as a U.S. citizen, he is left behind when they leave.

In the second part, Pran becomes the protagonist. With ingenuity and fortitude, he endures harsh captivity and evades death, escaping through rice paddies filled with the corpses of his countrymen—the "killing fields" of the title—until he is brought to New York, there to be reunited with Schanberg. Although the film effectively evokes the atmosphere of terror, confusion, and dislocation that war brings, it dwells on international politics, but on the damage done to human dignity by impersonal violence. **BP**

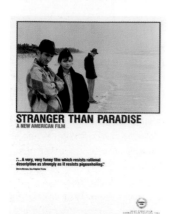

U.S. / West Germany (Cinesthesia,
Grokenberger, ZDF) 89m BW
Language English / Hungarian
Producer Sara Driver **Screenplay** Jim
Jarmusch **Photography** Tom DiCillo
Music John Lurie **Cast** John Lurie, Eszter
Balint, Richard Edson, Cecillia Stark, Danny
Rosen, Rammellzee, Tom DiCillo, Richard
Boes, Rockets Redglare, Harvey Perr, Brian J.
Burchill, Sara Driver, Paul Sloane **Cannes
Film Festival** Jim Jarmusch (Golden Camera)

*"It's easier to talk about
the style of the film than
'what it's about.'"*

Jim Jarmusch, 1984

Stranger Than Paradise Jim Jarmusch, 1984

Three decades down the line, Jim Jarmusch's modus operandi seems pretty clear. His films reveal the way different cultures intersect, overlap, and interact in the modern world, and how differences often pale compared to the traits we all have in common. At the time, however, *Stranger than Paradise* seemed as weird as it did wonderful, a striking debut from a fiercely independent filmmaker. Jarmusch described it as, "a semi-neorealist black comedy in the style of an imaginary Eastern European film director obsessed with [Japanese filmmaker] Ozu, and familiar with the 1950s American television show *The Honeymooners*."

Though it doesn't have much of a plot, *Stranger than Paradise* is anything but loose. Willie, a New York slacker (John Lurie), is surprised by a visit from his Hungarian cousin Eva (Eszter Balint). Eva, stuck in his small apartment, then heads west to Ohio to visit her aunt (Cecilia Stark). With nothing better to do, Willie and his pal Eddie (Richard Edson) follow her. All three head to Florida together for one last stab at staving off boredom, but even the ocean can't stir them from a self-imposed stupor.

Stranger than Paradise is like a parody of the American dream, with Eva's grass-is-always-greener view of the nation dashed by the harsh discovery that the States can be just as plain and uneventful as any other country. But Eva is the only one of them willing to do anything about her stifling predicament. Willie and Eddie bring with them to Ohio, and then Florida, the same sense of monotony, like roving black holes sucking the life out of wherever they end up. Faced with such a fate, Eva has nothing better to do than escape, though Willie and Eddie realize she may be their own only escape as well.

Jarmusch sets most of his movie in claustrophobic rooms, keeping the camera relatively static as he captures the strangely banal exchanges. No one seems to be friends, yet since they're all in the same situation they make the most of their companionship. Nothing is keeping them in any one place, but nothing is drawing them out of their modest environs. America seems like a vast cultural purgatory, and even the most ambitious of his characters don't seem especially eager to get out. **JKl**

i

Jarmusch used "lighting, filtration,
and composition of shots" to make
all the locations look similar.

Amadeus Milos Forman, 1984

U.S. (Saul Zaentz) 160m Color
Producer Saul Zaentz Screenplay Peter
Shaffer, from his play Photography Miroslav
Ondrícek Music Johann Sebastian Bach,
Wolfgang Amadeus Mozart, Antonio Salieri
Cast F. Murray Abraham, Tom Hulce,
Elizabeth Berridge, Simon Callow, Roy
Dotrice, Christine Ebersole, Jeffrey Jones,
Charles Kay, Kenny Baker Oscars Saul
Zaentz (best picture), Milos Forman
(director), Peter Shaffer (screenplay), F.
Murray Abraham (actor), Patrizia von
Brandenstein, Karel Cerny (art direction),
Theodor Pistek (costume), Paul LeBlanc, Dick
Smith (makeup), Mark Berger, Thomas Scott,
Todd Boekelheide, Christopher Newman
(sound) Oscar nominations Tom Hulce
(actor), Miroslav Ondrícek (photography),
Nena Danevic, Michael Chandler (editing)

🛈

When F. Murray Abraham appears in
Last Action Hero (1993), a recurring
joke is about him killing Mozart.

Milos Forman's casting of American Tom Hulce (who had spots in *Animal House* [1978] and TV series *St. Elsewhere* under his belt) as the giggling German composer Wolfgang Amadeus Mozart contrasts with the period sets and details on display throughout this epic biopic. But Hulce's over-the-top performance as the brilliant enfant terrible jibes with the theory that larger-than-life music must flow from a larger-than-life personality. He cavorts and parades around as if acknowledging the silliness of his frilly frocks and colored wigs. Nevertheless, he propels the film at such a pace that his clownish attitude and incongruous accent hardly matter.

Adapted by Peter Shaffer (in whose *Equus* Hulce had appeared on stage) from his own play, *Amadeus* sets Mozart's effortless creative strides against the simplistic compositions of his envy-ridden rival Salieri (played by an appropriately sour F. Murray Abraham). Salieri's bitterness is introduced for laughs, whereas Mozart is depicted as a womanizing fool. Yet the proof is in the latter's achievements, as revealed via the film's thunderous score and a generous staging of *Don Giovanni*. Although seeing even a portion of such a stirring work in the context of what amounts to a piece of pop art may seem strange, that may be the point. Forman seems nothing if not intent on contemporizing the life and accomplishments of one of history's greatest fonts of genius. **JKl**

Prizzi's Honor John Huston, 1985

U.S. (ABC) 130m Color **Producer** John Foreman **Screenplay** Richard Condon, Janet Roach, from novel by Richard Condon **Photography** Andrzej Bartkowiak **Music** Alex North, Gaetano Donizetti, Gioacchino Rossini **Cast** Jack Nicholson, Kathleen Turner, Robert Loggia, John Randolph, William Hickey, Lee Richardson, Michael Lombard, Anjelica Huston, George Santopietro, Lawrence Tierney, CCH Pounder, Ann Selepegno, Vic Polizos, Dick O'Neill, Sully Boyar **Oscar** Anjelica Huston (actress in support role) **Oscar nominations** John Foreman (best picture), John Huston (director), Richard Condon, Janet Roach (screenplay), Jack Nicholson (actor), William Hickey (actor in support role), Donfeld (costume), Rudi Fehr, Kaja Fehr (editing)

In 1985, director John Huston, despite waning health, embarked on his fortieth film—a black comedy that examines what might happen if two assassins fell in love. Jack Nicholson stars as Charley Partanna, a none-too-smart hitman for influential New York Mob family the Prizzis. The godfather, Don Corrado (William Hickey), treats Charley like an adopted son since the Don's granddaughter Maerose (Anjelica Huston, daughter of the director and Nicholson's paramour at the time) did him wrong. Charley falls for smoldering blonde Irene Walker (bombshell *du jour* Kathleen Turner) at a wedding, but it turns out the soon-to-be lovers have been hired to kill each other.

Unusually—and refreshingly—the ending is what the story requires, not what the audience wants. Although the film was nominated for eight Academy Awards, Anjelica Huston was the only one to win, for best supporting actress. But Hickey, who was nominated as well, is the film's stealthy dynamo. Seemingly on his last legs, he makes such lines as, "Would you like a cookie?" both threatening and hilarious. Lawrence Tierney (who played the eponymous Dillinger in Max Dosseck's 1945 film) also appears as a corrupt cop. Imperfect and ultimately depressing, *Prizzi's Honor* is nonetheless a comedic gem. **KK**

Tong nien wang shi Hsiao-hsien Hou, 1985
The Time to Live and the Time to Die

Taiwan (Central) 138m Color **Language** Mandarin **Screenplay** Chu T'ienwen, Hou Hsiao-hsien **Photography** Lee Pin Bing **Music** Wu Chuchu **Cast** Mei-Feng, Tang Yu-Yuen, Tien Feng, Xin Shufen, Yiu Ann-Shuin **Berlin International Film Festival** Hou Hsiao-hsien (FIPRESCI award—forum of new cinema)

Taiwan in the 1950s: Young Ah Xiao's life is an apparently endless and uncomplicated round of playing marbles, chasing chums, and listening to his grandmother's plans to return home to mainland China. After a first, shocking taste of death, however, life darkens and the boy turns into a brutish teenager, trapped between feelings of familial duty and the need to prove his worth among the local street gangs.

In many respects, Hsiao-hsien Hou's autobiographical coming-of-age movie marked a distinct advance upon his earlier *A Summer at Grandpa's* (1984). It paved the way for the considerably more complex narrative structure of *City of Sadness* (1989), with its deployment of an individual character study to explore the dynamics of Taiwanese society at a precise moment in time. What shapes Ah Xiao's early life is a community unsure of its own identity and future since the separation from the communist mainland, with conflicting emotions potentially leading either to delinquency and crime or, as in Hou's case, a more fulfilling adulthood. The direction is understated, reflective, and measured—in the style of Yasujirō Ozu, Hsaio-hsien Hou's acknowledged antecedent—making all the more devastatingly powerful the paroxysms of agonized emotion when they are eventually allowed to ignite the screen. The film is a work of remarkable maturity, assurance, and clarity. **GA**

The Breakfast Club John Hughes, 1985

In the 1960s, teen movies involved Frankie Avalon, Annette Funicello, lots of sand (no sex), and bouncy music. In the 1970s, being a teen was about being slaughtered in your bed in numerous horror movies. But in 1984 writer-director John Hughes revolutionized the teen genre with *Sixteen Candles*, and followed it a year later with *The Breakfast Club*, a movie credited with finally showing teens as they really speak and think.

No single film better epitomized the period, or has become more of a cult movie for teens, than The Breakfast Club. It made Hughes a name to watch—he went on to make the terrific *Ferris Bueller's Day Off* (1986) and hugely successful *Home Alone* (1990)—and brought together a skilled group of young actors (as did Francis Ford Coppola's *The Outsiders* two years before) that the media dubbed the "Brat Pack."

Five disparate teenagers are sentenced to a Saturday detention for various reasons and, despite their differences at the beginning of the day, they have formed some sort of bond by the end. There's the school jock (Emilio Estevez), the weirdo with the heavy eye-liner (Ally Sheedy), the stuck-up princess (Molly Ringwald, a teen fave and muse of Hughes following her lead role in *Sixteen Candles*), the nerd (Anthony Michael Hall), and the rebel (Judd Nelson), all trying to entertain themselves under the watchful eye of anally-retentive teacher Vernon (Paul Gleason).

A film that relies on cleverly scripted banter rather than action, *The Breakfast Club* works in large part because of the characterizations of the cast as truths are revealed, grudges are aired, and each one gets their moment to shine. Much imitated in numerous films and TV series, this ultimate teen movie has never been bettered—be it because of its perfect timing, sharp performances, quotable lines, or the 1980s time-capsule soundtrack, featuring that classic Simple Minds song (written for the film) "Don't You Forget About Me." **JB**

U.S. (A&M, Universal) 92m Technicolor
Producer John Hughes, Ned Tanen, Michelle Manning **Screenplay** John Hughes **Photography** Thomas Del Ruth **Music** Gary Chang, Wang Chung, Keith Forsey **Cast** Emilio Estevez, Paul Gleason, Anthony Michael Hall, John Kapelos, Judd Nelson, Molly Ringwald, Ally Sheedy, Perry Crawford, Mary Christian, Ron Dean, Tim Gamble, Fran Gargano, Mercedes Hall, John Hughes

1985

"I saw this movie when I was fourteen years old and, from that moment forward, I wanted to join The Breakfast Club."

Kevin Smith, 2009

i

Among the hours of footage shot but not included was a series of fantasies when the kids fall asleep.

Idi i smotri Elem Klimov, 1985
Come and See

U.S.S.R. (Belarusfilm, Mosfilm, Sovexportfilm) 142m Color **Language** Russian **Screenplay** Ales Adamovich, Elem Klimov **Photography** Aleksei Rodionov **Music** Oleg Yanchenko, Wolfgang Amadeus Mozart, Richard Wagner **Cast** Aleksei Kravchenko, Olga Mironova, Liubomiras Lauciavicius, Vladas Bagdonas, Juris Lumiste, Viktor Lorents, Kazimir Rabetsky, Yevgeni Ticheyev, Aleksandr Berda, G. Velts, V. Vasilyev, Igor Gnevashov, Vasili Domrachyov, G. Yelkin, Ye. Kryzhanovsky

It's World War II in countryside near the Polish border. A boy (Aleksei Kravchenko) leaves his village to join the partisans fighting the invading Nazis. He gets separated from his unit and has to make his way home, only to find his entire village slaughtered, the bodies piled in a haphazard heap behind a farm. Lost, alone, and deafened, things can only get worse.

No war movie matches *Come and See* for nightmarish relentlessness. There is no plot, only a terrifying picaresque journey as the boy wanders the countryside and encounters one horrific scenario after another. There are no feats of heroism or sacrifice, nor any stirring speeches exhorting people to fight. There is only death and brutality and randomness and victimhood. Survival is utterly arbitrary, and possibly a cruel, cosmic joke.

There are surrealist tableaus at once alien and strangely familiar. There are bursts of visionary weirdness that take your breath away—a partisan soldier, using mud, sticks, and a discarded Nazi uniform, constructs a totem for a mob of grieving widows and mothers to attack and tear apart in an act of catharsis; or when a field is illuminated by enemy tracer fire, leaving the young hero with no place to take cover except behind a cow. Events unfold like dream logic. There are moments when the movie switches to the boy's point of view and all sound collapses into a dull echo, duplicating his deafness after mortar shells explode around him.

Most war movies claim to be antiwar, but revel in gung-ho heroism. *Come and See* offers no such relief. It shows there are only victims. **AT**

i

Aleksei Kravchenko, the film's young star, apparently claimed that the ammunition used in it was live.

Mishima: A Life in Four Chapters

Paul Schrader, 1985

U.S. (American Zoetrope, Filmlink, Lucasfilm, M Co.) 120m BW / Color **Language** Japanese / English **Producer** Francis Ford Coppola, George Lucas, Tom Luddy, Mata Yamamoto **Screenplay** Leonard Schrader, Paul Schrader **Photography** John Bailey **Music** Philip Glass **Cast** Ken Ogata, Masayuki Shionoya, Hiroshi Mikami, Junya Fukuda, Shigeto Tachihara, Junkichi Orimoto, Naoko Otani, Gô Rijû, Masato Aizawa, Yuki Nagahara, Kyuzo Kobayashi, Yuki Kitazume, Haruko Kato, Yasosuke Bando, Hisako Manda, Roy Scheider **Cannes Film Festival** John Bailey, Eiko Ishioka, Philip Glass (best artistic contribution—photography, art direction, music), Paul Schrader (Golden Palm nomination)

Paul Schrader's extraordinary film about the Japanese writer-activist Yukio Mishima (played by Ken Ogata) is an anomaly, a lavish American art movie in the Japanese language (although Roy Scheider provides some spare English voice-over). Mishima was a narcissist, a revolutionary patriot, a samurai manqué, and arguably the most important Japanese writer of the twentieth century. The creator of Travis Bickle (from *Taxi Driver* [1976]) clearly sees himself as a kindred spirit, although the film is more than mere homage. Schrader flips through Mishima's many masks with great intelligence and clarity.

The film interweaves the events leading up to Mishima's final act of defiance—a grandstand attempt to reconcile art with action that involves kidnapping a general—with black-and-white biographical sequences showing the author's childhood, and three highly stylized, studio-bound dramatizations inspired by the writer's *Temple of the Golden Pavilion*, *Kyoko's House*, and *Runaway Horses*. Made under the auspices of executive producers Francis Ford Coppola and George Lucas (a noted sinophile), *Mishima* is a film as illuminating and coherent as it is intricate and involved, boasting breathtaking production design by Eiko Ishioka, gleaming cinematography by John Bailey, and a powerful, pulsing score by Philip Glass. **TCh**

1985

Out of Africa Sydney Pollack, 1985

U.S. (Mirage, Universal) 162m Color **Producer** Sydney Pollack **Screenplay** Kurt Luedtke, from memoirs by Isak Dinesen (Karen Blixen) **Photography** David Watkin **Music** John Barry, Mozart **Cast** Meryl Streep, Robert Redford, Klaus Maria Brandauer, Michael Kitchen, Joseph Thiaka, Stephen Kinyanjul, Michael Gough, Suzanna Hamilton, Rachel Kempson **Oscars** Sydney Pollack (best picture), Sydney Pollack (director), Kurt Luedtke (screenplay), Stephen B. Grimes, Josie MacAvin (art direction), David Watkin (photography), John Barry (music), Chris Jenkins, Gary Alexander, Larry Stensvold, Peter Handford (sound) **Oscar nominations** Meryl Streep (actress), Klaus Maria Brandauer (actor in support role), Milena Canonero (costume), Fredric Steinkamp, William Steinkamp, Pembroke J. Herring, Sheldon Kahn (editing)

Awesome landscapes nearly overpower this Best Picture winner, shot on location in Kenya. "Nearly," however, is the operative word, because Meryl Streep and Robert Redford bring to life an uncommon love story to counterbalance this absurdly beautiful spectacle.

Truly every frame is a marvel, every set piece a gem. Sydney Pollack's epic—based on the memoirs of Danish writer Karen Blixen, the author of *Babette's Feast*—is a sharply produced romance-cum-travelogue. (Nicolas Roeg planned to shoot another adaptation in the early 1970s.)

When Blixen (Streep, in a role also offered to Audrey Hepburn) is forced into a marriage of convenience with Baron Bror Finecke (Klaus Maria Brandauer, whom Pollack had admired in the 1983 Bond movie *Never Say Never Again*), her dowry affords him a farm in Kenya. Afflicted with wanderlust he disregards her, so she finds sustenance in the adventurer Denys Hatton (Redford). World War I interrupts the affair, as do other personal complications, after which the lovers continue falling in love. In the end, Bror's activities cause Karen's wealth to founder, and she is forced to bury Denys after a tragic accident.

Highlights include a safari via biplane, glimpses of naturally occurring wildlife, and the sweeping uplift of John Barry's thrilling score. **GC-Q**

Ran Akira Kurosawa, 1985

Ran was made at the time Akira Kurosawa was turning seventy-five (and losing his eyesight). It is important to understand the wisdom and artistry that those years brought to the creation of this film, quite possibly one of the greatest ever made. Of the 1001 films one must see before dying, *Ran* is certainly in the top ten. The director has called it "a series of human events viewed from Heaven."

Kurosawa is unsurpassed in his mastery of film technique, and *Ran*'s battle sequences are unequaled to this day. They are like a cinematic ballet, violent and bloody yet filled with tremendous beauty. The story is adapted from Shakespeare's *King Lear*, combined with an ancient Japanese legend of three arrows. This combination moves the Bard's tragedy into distinctly new territory. Lear's daughters are now sons and the emphasis is on revenge rather than catharsis.

The performances range from brilliant to something resembling utter perfection. The standout without question is Mieko Harada as Lady Kaede, one of Lord Hidetora's (Tatsuya Nakadai) daughters-in-law—watching her slink across the floor of her palace, her silk gowns rustling on the soundtrack, is unforgettable. Nakadai as Lord Hidetora displays a fierce defiance that melts into despair. And Lear's fool is transformed into the jester Kyoami, beautifully played by transvestite Shinnosuke Ikehata, an accomplished Noh actor—the makeup and much of *Ran*'s story is inspired by Noh drama and tradition.

Toru Takemitsu's minimalist score makes fine use of percussion and flute to accent the epic. A special emphasis is placed on silence during the battle scenes—a tactic far more effective than all the cannon roar of previous attempts at depicting war on screen.

Ran displays the wisdom of a lifetime in a "mere" two hours and forty minutes, during which time itself is simply suspended. As the jester Kyoami declares in the film's most often quoted line, "Man is born crying; when he has cried enough, he dies." **DDV**

Japan / France (Greenwich, Herald Ace, Nippon Herald) 160m Color **Language** Japanese **Producer** Masato Hara, Serge Silberman **Screenplay** Masato Ide, Akira Kurosawa, Hideo Oguni, from the play *King Lear* by William Shakespeare **Photography** Asakazu Nakai, Takao Saitô, Masaharu Ueda **Music** Tôru Takemitsu **Cast** Tatsuya Nakadai, Akira Terao, Jinpachi Nezu, Daisuke Ryu, Mieko Harada, Yoshiko Miyazaki, Takashi Nomura, Hisashi Igawa, Peter, Masayuki Yui, Kazuo Kato, Norio Matsui, Toshiya Ito, Kenji Kodama, Takashi Watanabe **Oscar** Emi Wada (costume) **Oscar nominations** Akira Kurosawa (director), Yoshirô Muraki, Shinobu Muraki (art direction), Takao Saitô, Masaharu Ueda, Asakazu Nakai (photography)

> "A reason I couldn't shoot this film for so long was that producers complained that the ending was tragic."
>
> **Akira Kurosawa, 1986**

ℹ

Kurosawa refused to discuss the film with Japanese journalists—who, he complained, asked "silly questions."

Back to the Future Robert Zemeckis, 1985

U.S. (Amblin, Universal) 116m
Technicolor **Producer** Neil Canton, Bob Gale
Screenplay Robert Zemeckis, Bob Gale
Photography Dean Cundey **Music** Alan
Silvestri **Cast** Michael J. Fox, Christopher
Lloyd, Lea Thompson, Crispin Glover,
Thomas F. Wilson, Claudia Wells, Marc
McClure, Wendie Jo Sperber, George
DiCenzo, Frances Lee McCain, James Tolkan,
J.J. Cohen, Casey Siemaszko, Billy Zane, Harry
Waters Jr. **Oscar** Charles L. Campbell, Robert
R. Rutledge (special sound effects) **Oscar
nominations** Robert Zemeckis, Bob Gale
(screenplay), Chris Hayes, Johnny Colla, Huey
Lewis (song), Bill Varney, B. Tennyson
Sebastian, Robert Thirlwell,
William B. Kaplan (sound)

i

Eric Stoltz was filmed as Marty
before the producer's original
choice—Fox—became available.

Michael J. Fox, already a TV heartthrob with the sitcom *Family Ties*, became a full-fledged movie star thanks to this time-traveling comedy adventure. He stars as Marty McFly, a seventeen-year-old who despairs of his pushover dad George (Crispin Glover), and so spends most of his time with eccentric inventor Emmett Brown (Christopher Lloyd). Doc Brown's latest invention is a time-travel machine in the shape of a DeLorean car, and soon enough Marty finds himself speeding backward in time to 1955, where his parents have barely met let alone started the relationship that will lead to Marty's very existence.

A clever premise is enlivened by quick-fire direction from Robert Zemeckis (hot property after 1984's *Romancing the Stone*) and a superb, witty script. Marty—with the help of a much younger Doc Brown—tries to get back to the present without wreaking havoc on future events by altering the past (not as easy as it sounds when your unsuspecting mother-to-be has developed a crush on you). Fox is perfect as the teen trying to unite his parents so he can one day be born, and Lloyd is suitably foolish as the nutty scientist. Meanwhile, Glover and Lea Thompson (Marty's mom) have a great time playing their characters as both middle-aged parents and teenagers. A timeless adventure. **JB**

Brazil Terry Gilliam, 1985

G.B. (Embassy, Universal) 131m Technicolor
Producer Arnon Milchan **Screenplay** Terry
Gilliam, Charles McKeown, Tom Stoppard
Photography Roger Pratt **Music** Michael
Kamen **Cast** Jonathan Pryce, Robert De
Niro, Katherine Helmond, Ian Holm, Bob
Hoskins, Michael Palin, Ian Richardson, Peter
Vaughan, Kim Greist, Jim Broadbent, Barbara
Hicks, Charles McKeown, Derrick O'Connor,
Kathryn Pogson, Bryan Pringle **Oscar
nominations** Terry Gilliam, Tom Stoppard,
Charles McKeown (screenplay), Norman
Garwood, Maggie Gray (art direction)

*"The original title of
Brazil was 1984 ¹/₂.
Fellini was one of
my great gods and it
was 1984, so let's put
them together."*

Terry Gilliam, 2003

🛈

Universal's cut of the film (its happy
ending disowned by Gilliam) is
called the "Love Conquers All" edit.

The tale of bad feeling between *Brazil* creator Terry Gilliam and distributor Universal—in which the filmmaker resisted the studio's attempts to put out a severely truncated cut and eventually prevailed in getting his challenging picture released in the United States—has tended to soak up all the interest in this movie. But it has strengths (and weaknesses) quite distinct from any status it might retain as a near-political cause.

Made in 1984, and in parallel with the Michael Radford film of George Orwell's eponymous novel, Brazil is set "somewhere in the twentieth century." Its imaginary but credible oppressive state combines the worst of 1940s British bureaucracy, 1950s American paranoia, Stalinist or fascist totalitarianism, and the ills of the 1980s (such as an obsession with plastic surgery). Whereas Orwell's Airstrip One is built on horribly effective state surveillance, the worst aspect of Gilliam's invented dystopia is that it doesn't even work: The plot is kicked off by a farcical mistake as a bug falls into a printer so an arrest warrant intended for terrorist heating engineer Tuttle (Robert De Niro) is applied to an innocent Mr. Buttle (Brian Miller). Meanwhile, the grimly utilitarian city is falling apart even without the possibly state-sponsored bombs that wreak carnage.

Like *1984*'s protagonist Winston Smith, Sam Lowry (Jonathan Pryce) is a mid-level functionary of the brutal state who comes through a romantic attachment to align himself with rebellion and winds up squashed and broken by a friendly torturer. Gilliam, however, is far more concerned with the imaginary than Orwell, and delivers a fantastical setting that is escaped from only by even more fantasy. Sam enjoys romantic flights of imagination (scored with the Latin flavored title tune) in which he is an angelic superhero knight facing up to Gilliamesque creations—who seem like Pythonesque knock-offs from Japanese giant monster movies—in order to rescue a dream girl (Kim Greist).

Perhaps thanks to the involvement of cowriter Tom Stoppard, *Brazil* is a more dramatically engaging film than most of Gilliam's cartoonish efforts. The gruesome black humor and bizarre visuals (embodied by Katherine Helmond as a surgery-obsessed matron with a succession of shoe-shaped hats) exist alongside a credible—and horribly fact-based—depiction of a regime that charges its victims for the electricity and labor that goes into their own torture, as represented by the family man specialist from "Information Retrieval" (Michael Palin) and the desperate, middle-management paper-shuffler (Ian Holm).

In one thing, at least, Universal had a point—the film does run a good reel beyond its optimum length, with a few too many slapstick routines that take it close to conventional knockabout. *Brazil*'s home stretch includes a gruesome funeral scene that addresses various subplots that have been developing in the "real" world of the film, before it is revealed to be the *Occurrence at Owl Creek Bridge*–like fantasy of a dead man, as Sam's mind snaps under torture. **KN**

713

Kiss of the Spider Woman Hector Babenco, 1985

Based on a novel by Manuel Puig, Brazilian director Hector Babenco's courageous exploration of political, psychological, and sexual issues within the confines of a high-security South American prison thanks Burt Lancaster in its ending credits. The project was initiated by Lancaster, who intended to star in the leading role that ultimately went to William Hurt. In a breakthrough performance, Hurt won an Oscar as Luis Molina, a window dresser imprisoned for homosexuality. Stagy and somewhat dated, the story itself still resonates, and Raul Julia's exceptionally believable performance is a match for the high camp of Hurt's Luis.

Tall, mannered, and effeminate, Luis shares an enormous prison cell with heterosexual political prisoner Valentin Arregui (Julia). To pass the time, Luis recounts in intricate, almost maddening detail a melodrama he saw some years before. In a series of nostalgically colored flashbacks, Sonia Braga plays a stereotypical French singer during World War II. Braga, who didn't speak English at the time, phonetically sounded out her words, lending an unreal aspect to the arch-satire. Beautifully groomed and extremely sensitive, she falls for a handsome blonde Gestapo officer. Despite being a member of the French Resistance, she is convinced by her lover that the Nazis are good people who only want to rid the world of misery. Devoted to his politics, Arregui takes exception to the story, but is gradually lulled by its telling—as long as Luis doesn't concentrate on descriptions of food or naked women. Luis is only concerned about the film's romantic details but he has his own secret. The warden is promising him early release if he can draw valuable information from his cellmate, with whom Luis has fallen in love.

Although largely of historical significance (homosexuality had rarely been portrayed in such terms in mainstream cinema), Hurt's performance goes beyond theatricality—his skill is keeping the character's real feelings hidden away under several layers of varying intensity. Even at the very end, the audience is unsure if he has betrayed Arregui or not. Considered the "gay *Casablanca*," *Kiss of the Spider Woman*'s main virtue lies in its humanization of love in all forms. **KK**

Brazil / U.S. / **Argentina** (HB, Sugarloaf) 119m Metrocolor **Language** English / Portuguese **Producer** David Weisman **Screenplay** Leonard Schrader, from the novel *Beijo da Mulher Aranha* by Manuel Puig **Photography** Rodolfo Sánchez **Music** John Neschling **Cast** William Hurt, Raul Julia, Sonia Braga, José Lewgoy, Milton Gonçalves, Míriam Pires, Nuno Leal Maia, Fernando Torres, Patricio Bisso, Herson Capri, Denise Dumont, Antônio Petrin, Wilson Grey, Miguel Falabella, Walter Breda **Oscar** William Hurt (actor) **Oscar nominations** David Weisman (best picture), Hector Babenco (director), Leonard Schrader (screenplay) **Cannes Film Festival** William Hurt (actor), Hector Babenco nomination (Golden Palm)

"I don't like the film . . . But I love the reaction of the audiences . . . So I would like to complain, but I cannot."

Manuel Puig, 1985

i

Director Babenco did not speak English, so the screenplay had to be translated into Portuguese for him.

The Quiet Earth Geoff Murphy, 1985

New Zealand (Cinepro, Mr. Yellowbeard)
91m Color **Producer** Sam Pillsbury,
Don Reynolds **Screenplay** Bill Baer, Bruno
Lawrence, Sam Pillsbury, from novel by
Craig Harrison **Photography** James Bartle
Music John Charles **Cast** Bruno Lawrence,
Alison Routledge, Pete Smith, Anzac Wallace,
Norman Fletcher, Tom Hyde

i

This was Pete Smith's first film role. He
later featured in fellow New Zealander
Jane Campion's *The Piano* (1993).

Geoff Murphy's *The Quiet Earth* is a distinctly New Zealand take on the classic last man-on-Earth narrative that sprang from *I Am Legend*. Scientist Zac Hobson (Bruno Lawrence) awakens one morning to discover that he is alone in the world following a scientific project gone awry. Lawrence's initial thirty-six-minute solo performance is superb, as Zac vacillates between euphoria and despair at his isolation. Eventually he meets another survivor, Joanne (Alison Routledge), with whom he attempts a relationship. Their idyll is disrupted by a third survivor, Api (Pete Smith), an aggressive Maori and the third point in the love triangle.

The film's subject matter places it squarely within the sci-fi genre. But its treatment of the material makes it less akin to dystopias such as *Mad Max* (1979) and closer to an investigation of human relationships and interracial concerns. What particularly sets the film apart is Murphy's depiction of the depopulated world. The entire soundtrack was redubbed in a studio to remove any trace of sound. Zac's gradual breakdown is conveyed via striking collages of images: walking around in a ladies slip; driving trains as if they were part of a toy train set; a beautiful shot of him wandering in the rain playing the sax. *The Quiet Earth* does not appeal with ostentatious special effects—instead it is an intellectually stimulating, character-driven look into the human condition. **RDe**

THE PURPLE ROSE OF CAIRO

FARROW DANIELS AIELLO
ROLLINS JOFFE HYMAN PEYSER MORSE WILLIS JOFFE GREENHUT ALLEN

The Purple Rose of Cairo Woody Allen, 1985

This sublime nostalgic comedy avoids the usual Allen formula of "goofy New Yorkers having trouble with relationships." Both Woody Allen and his famous neurotic monologue are absent this time, but fans of the writer-director needn't worry, because the hilarious one-liners and odd characters are still present. Above all, *The Purple Rose of Cairo* is about love, perhaps Allen's greatest love of all: for cinema.

A tribute to the magical powers of the screen, *The Purple Rose of Cairo* tells the story of Cecilia (Mia Farrow), a poor waitress who, during the Depression era, spends much of her time watching movies. "I forget my sorrows," confesses the young woman, who is terrorized by a rude and unemployed husband. Only by watching the brave and unbeatable heroes on screen can she resist the daily nightmare that is her life.

While Cecilia is watching, for the eighth time, a film entitled *The Purple Rose of Cairo*, the charming hero (Jeff Daniels) walks right off the screen to meet her, though the rest of the audience protests and asks for their money back. In a bid to prevent a financial fiasco, the film's Hollywood producers send the actor who performs the hero to seduce her. Although the fictitious character is gentle and romantic, the star who impersonates him is cynical and arrogant. Assuming both roles, Daniels ironically suggests the difference between the ideal and the real man. Charmed by both of them, Cecilia experiences an amazing metamorphosis from Cinderella to a beautiful princess, and Farrow's excellent performance makes us believe in a such a miraculous transformation.

The Purple Rose of Cairo—whose screenplay was Allen's fifth to be nominated for an Oscar—is a meditation on illusion. The film's conclusion is not cynical, as with his *Deconstructing Harry* (1997). Fiction can save our lives, Allen argues in *Purple Rose*, managing to convince us. Among the lines, Cecilia's unforgettable remark, "I met a wonderful man. He's imaginary, but who cares? You can't have everything you want," recalls the famous closing line, "Nobody's perfect," from *Some Like It Hot* (1959), and intensifies any belief we might have in cinema's magical powers. **DD**

1985

U.S. (Jack Rollins & Charles H. Joffe, Orion) 84m BW / Color **Producer** Robert Greenhut **Screenplay** Woody Allen **Photography** Gordon Willis **Music** Dick Hyman **Cast** Mia Farrow, Jeff Daniels, Danny Aiello, Irving Metzman, Stephanie Farrow, David Kieserman, Elaine Grollman, Victoria Zussin, Mark Hammond, Wade Barnes, Joseph G. Graham, Don Quigley, Maurice Brenner, Paul Herman, Rick Petrucelli **Oscar nomination** Woody Allen (screenplay) **Cannes Film Festival** Woody Allen (FIPRESCI award)

"Some of the reviews have said Purple Rose *is about the movies. I don't agree with that. To me, the film is strictly about reality and fantasy."*

Woody Allen, 1985

𝑖

Viggo Mortensen filmed this before his big-screen debut *Witness* (1985), but his scenes missed the final cut.

G.B. / France (Channel Four, Ciné
Tamaris, Films A2, French Ministry of
Culture and Communication) 105m
Color **Language** French **Producer** Oury
Milshtein **Screenplay** Agnès Varda
Photography Patrick Blossier **Music** Joanna
Bruzdowicz, Fred Chichin **Cast** Sandrine
Bonnaire, Setti Ramdane, Francis Balchère,
Jean-Louis Perletti, Urbain Causse,
Christophe Alçazar, Dominique Durand, Joël
Fosse, Patrick Schmit, Daniel Bos, Katy
Champaud, Raymond Roulle, Henri Fridlani,
Patrick Sokol, Pierre Imbert **Venice Film
Festival** Agnès Varda (FIPRESCI award,
Golden Lion, OCIC award)

"Harrison Ford came
to the opening of
Vagabond in Los
Angeles. Whenever we
meet he is very friendly."

Agnès Varda, 2009

Sans toit ni loi Agnès Varda, 1985
Vagabond

An erstwhile participant in the French New Wave, Agnès Varda lacked some of the credentials of her former film critic peers like François Truffaut and Jean-Luc Godard. Rather, she came from a photography background and, although she didn't initially know a great deal about filmmaking, she quickly demonstrated a style of her own. Perhaps best known for earlier films such as *Cléo de 5 à 7* (1962), a real-time wait for a woman to get the results of her cancer test, Varda actually veered back and forth between nonfiction and fiction filmmaking. *Sans toit ni loi* followed a long stretch of the former, which explains its hybrid merger of documentary style and more traditional cinematic techniques.

One morning, a farmer discovers the frozen body of a female drifter, Mona Bergeron, curled up in a field, her face blue and glazed with frost. Once the police arrive, Varda's own voice interrupts. She explains that little is known about her, then proceeds to enact a series of faux interviews and flashbacks, each revealing small facts and passing details of the doomed young woman. Nothing, of course, is really known about the drifter (played with icy disaffection by Sandrine Bonnaire). She is merely a construct of the director's elliptical narrative.

Yet Varda enlists the drifter as a metaphor for how little we ever actually know about many of the people we encounter on a day-to-day basis. Bonnaire's drifter comes across a number of people while in search of food and shelter, but she rarely makes an effort to know them. She's sullen and unthankful, slinking across the frigid French landscapes away from who knows what and toward her telegraphed tragic end. In the "interview" segments, characters recount bits and pieces of her behavior and demeanor but nobody can offer a complete picture of the enigmatic girl. Varda arranges each scene and bleak landscape with a photographer's eye, frequently placing her increasingly feral protagonist (and sometimes antagonist) at the margins of the frame—just as the mysterious Mona herself exists in the periphery of the world itself. **JKl**

i

Actress Sandrine Bonnaire made an
acclaimed directorial debut with
2007's *My Name is Sabine*.

SHOAH
A FILM BY CLAUDE LANZMANN

France (Les Films Adelph/Historia) 566m
Color **Language** English / German /
Hebrew / Polish / Yiddish / French
Photography Dominique Chapuis,
William Lubtchansky

"I still have a lot of material that I filmed and did not include... Some I've already used in other films I have done."

Claude Lanzmann, 2010

1985

Shoah Claude Lanzmann, 1985

It might seem absurd, even outrageous, to include Claude Lanzmann's *Shoah* with the other films selected here, using the regular number of words to describe and discuss it. But with all its particularities, including its nine-hour length and the authentic genius inhabiting it, it is vital to consider *Shoah* as a film among films.

Lanzmann traveled the world for nearly ten years discussing Nazi extermination camps—not the concentration camps, not the Nazi system as a whole, not antisemitism as a process, but the specific places where death reigned, the inner circle of the Inferno. He collected testimonies from some of the very few survivors, several witnesses, and even former organizers of the mass murdering. He edited together these voices and images of the present, showing the bodies, the faces, the landscapes as they look now, forever haunted by this tragic past. At the same time, he made every viewer aware of the absolute impossibility of representing what happened in such places as Auschwitz, Birkenau, Sobibor, Treblinka, and Chelmno—not because it's forbidden, just because it's impossible.

"Many years before the film reached the screens in 1985," he told *Haaretz*, "I was so stunned by the enormity of the event that in some places I was certain that whoever had been involved in it—the victims, the witnesses, even the hangmen—had long ago died. As a result, every time I discovered that one of them was still living, this was for me an amazing revelation, like that of an archeologist who uncovers a rare find after months of patient and difficult searching."

Lanzmann accomplished several things of great importance. He invented a way of bringing back memories of the Holocaust's horrors without distorting what these horrors had been. He also gave a name to this process—the "Shoah" of the film's title—which is now widely used. But Lanzmann also achieved what one might call the essence of cinema: the highest degree of presence through a total absence. Absence of the millions of dead, of the past, of any evidence of remains, carefully eliminated by the murderers, of visual or audio archives.

Shoah stands as the absolute answer to Jean-Luc Godard's plea for "not a just image, just an image." The discussion it generated confirms the importance of this extraordinary work of art. **J-MF**

🛈
Very critical of other films about the period, Lanzmann nonetheless liked Tarantino's *Inglourious Basterds* (2009).

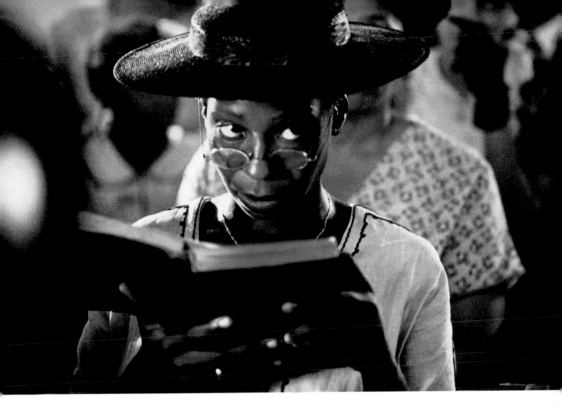

The Color Purple Steven Spielberg, 1985

U.S. (Amblin, Guber-Peters Co., Warner Bros.) 154m Color **Producer** Quincy Jones, Kathleen Kennedy, Frank Marshall, Steven Spielberg **Screenplay** Menno Meyjes, from the novel by Alice Walker **Photography** Allen Daviau **Music** Quincy Jones **Cast** Danny Glover, Whoopi Goldberg, Margaret Avery, Oprah Winfrey, Willard E. Pugh, Akosua Busia, Desreta Jackson, Adolph Caesar, Rae Dawn Chong, Dana Ivey, Leonard Jackson, Bennet Guillory, John Patton Jr., Carl Anderson, Susan Beaubian, James Tillis, Phillip Strong, Laurence Fishburne, Sonny Terry **Oscar nominations** Steven Spielberg, Kathleen Kennedy, Frank Marshall, Quincy Jones (best picture), Menno Meyjes (screenplay), Whoopi Goldberg (actress), Margaret Avery (actress in support role), Oprah Winfrey (actress in support role), J. Michael Riva, Linda DeScenna (art direction), Allen Daviau (photography), Aggie Guerard Rodgers (costume), Ken Chase (makeup), Quincy Jones, Jeremy Lubbock, Rod Temperton, Caiphus Semenya, Andraé Crouch, Chris Boardman, Jorge Calandrelli, Joel Rosenbaum, Fred Steiner, Jack Hayes, Jerry Hey, Randy Kerber (music), Quincy Jones, Rod Temperton, Lionel Richie (song)

Intent on dispelling his distorted reputation as a creator of popular youthful fantasies, Steven Spielberg chose Alice Walker's story of an impoverished rural black community in the early twentieth-century American South as his vehicle for dramatic affirmation. Oddly enough, Spielberg's established skills as a director both help and hinder the project, as his knack for wry humor and glossy technical prowess fits uneasily with the material, which he toned down from Walker's novel.

But even if he bit off more than he could chew, *The Color Purple* still proved the director's willingness to take risks. He elicits powerful performances from Oprah Winfrey (making her big screen debut) and Danny Glover (still two years from *Lethal Weapon* superstardom), but his instincts proved particularly invaluable in the casting of the then relatively unknown Whoopi Goldberg. Her Celie rarely speaks but is full of emotion, relayed through Goldberg's impressive, Oscar-nominated performance that does more with a well-timed wide smile than most actors do with a showy monologue.

Spielberg too often falls back on sentimentality, but promising glimmers of the director who would graduate to more mature works like *Empire of the Sun* (1987), *Schindler's List* (1993), and *Artificial Intelligence: A.I.* (2001) are there to be studied. **JKl**

A Room with a View James Ivory, 1985

G.B. (Channel Four, Curzon, Goldcrest, Merchant-Ivory, National Film Finance) 117m Technicolor **Producer** Ismail Merchant **Screenplay** Ruth Prawer Jhabvala, from novel by E.M. Forster **Photography** Tony Pierce-Roberts **Music** Richard Robbins **Cast** Maggie Smith, Helena Bonham Carter, Denholm Elliott, Julian Sands, Simon Callow, Patrick Godfrey, Judi Dench, Fabia Drake, Daniel Day-Lewis **Oscars** Ruth Prawer Jhabvala (screenplay), Gianni Quaranta, Brian Ackland-Snow, Brian Savegar, Elio Altramura (art direction), Jenny Beavan, John Bright (costume) **Oscar nominations** Ismail Merchant (best picture), James Ivory (director), Denholm Elliott (actor in support role), Maggie Smith (actress in support role), Tony Pierce-Roberts (photography)

Ismail Merchant and James Ivory had been working together since 1963, but it was *A Room with a View*, their 1985 adaptation of E.M. Forster's novel, that made the producing/directing team famous for a luxurious period style that would later be apparent in movies like *The Remains of the Day* (1993) and *Howards End* (1992).

Much of the credit for revitalizing the cinematic period drama should also go to the third member of their team, Ruth Prawer Jhabvala, who had previously worked with Merchant Ivory on *Heat and Dust* (1983) and here beautifully adapted the tale of a young woman's awakening from the novel to the screen. Lucy (Helena Bonham Carter) is the woman in question, who discovers much about life and love in the Tuscan countryside as she decides between prospective suitors George (Julian Sands) and Cecil (Daniel Day-Lewis).

Sands, in his best screen performance, is passionate as George, kissing the demure Lucy in a yellow-tinted field of grass, while Day-Lewis hits just the right note as priggish Cecil (complete with oiled hair and annoying affectations). But it is Maggie Smith, as Lucy's dotty companion, and Denholm Elliott, as George's forward-thinking father, who stand out the most from a cast of superb actors in this stately and picturesque setting. **JB**

Manhunter Michael Mann, 1986

U.S. (De Laurentiis Entertainment Group, Red Dragon Productions, Studio Canal) 119m Technicolor **Producer** Dino De Laurentiis, Richard A. Roth **Screenplay** Michael Mann, from the novel *Red Dragon* by Thomas Harris **Photography** Dante Spinotti **Music** Michel Rubini, Klaus Schulze **Cast** William L. Petersen, Kim Greist Joan Allen, Brian Cox, Dennis Farina, Stephen Lang, Tom Noonan, David Seaman, Benjamin Hendrickson, Michael Talbott, Dan Butler, Michele Shay, Robin Moseley, Paul Perri, Patricia Charbonneau

Based on Thomas Harris's bestseller *Red Dragon*, *Manhunter* introduced cannibalistic psychiatrist Hannibal Lecter (in the form of Brian Cox) five years before Anthony Hopkins's interpretation in the Oscar-winning *The Silence of the Lambs*.

Atmospherically and stylishly directed by Michael Mann (who at that time was best known for the television show *Miami Vice* and went on to direct *Heat* [1995]), *Manhunter* focuses on FBI man Will Graham (William Petersen), who is coaxed out of breakdown-induced retirement so that his special talent of connecting with the psyche of killers can be put to good use in tracking down a particularly gruesome serial murderer. However, in order to do that, he has to confront the last man he helped catch—Lecter—in his prison cell, even though it was Lecter's mind games that endangered Graham's sanity in the first place.

One of the most tense and disturbing thrillers of the 1980s (and obviously a template for Chris Carter's TV series *Millennium*, among others), *Manhunter* features gripping performances, not only from the chilling Cox and intense Petersen, but also from the supporting cast, which includes Kim Greist, Joan Allen, and Dennis Farina. If you thought *The Silence of the Lambs* was scary, you ain't seen nothing yet. **JB**

1986

Blue Velvet David Lynch, 1986

"It's a strange world, isn't it?" Graphic sexual violence and Dennis Hopper's shocking portrayal of a sadistic psychopath holding a singer's family hostage for her acquiescent brutalization provoked a storm of controversy around David Lynch's dark, disturbing, dreamlike mystery. Lynch's depiction of the cruelty, sickness, and horror lying just beneath the surface of nice, clean, white-picket-fenced middle America is not exactly subtle, but it is remorselessly gripping, bold, and stylish. *Blue Velvet* combines an air of twisted mystery with ironic, satiric Americana and a singular, chirpy, lightly stylized tone. The same winning mixture of the repulsively strange with the cozily familiar, the artful and the artless, made Lynch's television series *Twin Peaks* the cultural phenomenon of 1990 and strongly influenced numerous imitators.

Kyle MacLachlan and Laura Dern are engaging as Jeffrey Beaumont and Sandy Williams, the naive youngsters caught up in the macabre relationship between Hopper's crazed, oxygen-tank-dependent kidnapper-killer and brave Isabella Rossellini's bruised Dorothy Vallens, the tormented cabaret singer at his never-tender mercy while he holds her husband and little boy captive. Lumberton is a sunny, dreary American Everytown, with its neat lawns and flowerbeds, its industrial core, and the colorless diner where Jeffrey and Sandy combine forces as amateur sleuths while love blossoms. But everything is off-kilter, from curious college boy Jeffrey's discovery of a human ear in a field and his anxious, dangerous adventures as a crime-busting voyeur to his stunned arrival on a bizarre death tableau.

The scene in which Jeffrey, hiding in Dorothy's closet, witnesses Frank's frenzied rape of the blue-velvet-robed victim is most contentious but an undeniably arresting, classic example of Lynch's nerve. Clever use of innocuous pop ballads—most hauntingly the title song—laced through regular Lynch collaborator Angelo Badalamenti's creepy score heightens the atmosphere. And although he appears in only one scene, Dean Stockwell's performance as Frank's confederate Ben, with his deceptively camp bonhomie—miming to Roy Orbison's "In Dreams"—almost rivals Hopper's for spectacularly sinister weirdness. **AE**

U.S. (De Laurentiis) 120m Color
Producer Fred C. Caruso **Screenplay** David Lynch **Photography** Frederick Elmes **Music** Angelo Badalamenti, David Lynch, Roy Orbison, Bernie Wayne, Victor Young **Cast** Isabella Rossellini, Kyle MacLachlan, Dennis Hopper, Laura Dern, Hope Lange, Dean Stockwell, George Dickerson, Priscilla Pointer, Frances Bay, Jack Harvey, Ken Stovitz, Brad Dourif, Jack Nance, J. Michael Hunter, Dick Green **Oscar nomination** David Lynch (director)

> "The most brilliantly disturbing film ever to have its roots in small-town American life."
>
> **Sheila Benson,**
> *Los Angeles Times*, **1986**

ℹ️

With nobody willing to touch the movie, Dino De Laurentiis had to set up his own distribution company.

**WOODY ALLEN MICHAEL CAINE
MIA FARROW CARRIE FISHER
BARBARA HERSHEY LLOYD NOLAN
MAUREEN O'SULLIVAN DANIEL STERN
MAX VON SYDOW DIANNE WIEST**

JACK ROLLINS...CHARLES H. JOFFE..... SUSAN E. MORSE.... CARLO Di PALMA....
JACK ROLLINS...CHARLES H. JOFFE.... ROBERT GREENHUT WOODY ALLEN
.....ORION.....

U.S. (Orion, Charles H. Joffe & Jack Rollins) 103m Technicolor **Producer** Robert Greenhut **Screenplay** Woody Allen **Photography** Carlo Di Palma **Music** James V. Monaco, Johann Sebastian Bach, Giacomo Puccini **Cast** Barbara Hershey, Carrie Fisher, Michael Caine, Mia Farrow, Dianne Wiest, Maureen O'Sullivan, Lloyd Nolan, Max von Sydow, Woody Allen, Daniel Stern, Julie Kavner, Joanna Gleason, Bobby Short, Lewis Black, Julia Louis-Dreyfus **Oscars** Woody Allen (screenplay), Michael Caine (actor in support role), Dianne Wiest (actress in support role) **Oscar nominations** Robert Greenhut (best picture), Woody Allen (director), Stuart Wurtzel, Carol Joffe (art direction), Susan E. Morse (editing)

"How the hell do I know why there were Nazis? I don't know how the can opener works!"

**Mickey's Father
(Leo Postrel)**

ℹ

Woody Allen has claimed that he was inspired to write this film after re-reading Tolstoy's *Anna Karenina*.

Hannah and Her Sisters Woody Allen, 1986

The last and most expansive of the remarkably fine run of Woody Allen pictures that began with *A Midsummer Night's Sex Comedy* (1982), *Hannah and Her Sisters* is Bergmanesque in inspiration, perhaps, but Renoir-like in tone, betraying the influence of both of those masters as it traces the shifts in various tangled relationships over the space of a single year. Set, as some of his other films are, in arty, upper-crust Manhattan, the film centers on three sisters (Mia Farrow, Barbara Hershey, and Dianne Wiest), the partners of the first two (Michael Caine, Max von Sydow), the first's ex-husband (Allen), and a few other friends and colleagues brought in to complicate the romantic "roundelay." Allen himself is less to the fore than usual, his customarily neurotic hypochondriac taking up rather less time and sympathy than Caine, waivering in his fidelity to Farrow thanks to an infatuation with the younger Hershey. Indeed, one of the delights of the film is the way Allen handles this broader-than-usual canvas; the characters are if anything more rounded than previously, even as the wider focus gives us more of a sense of a world outside the rather limited one at the film's core.

In many respects, of course, it's the same old cozily predictable situations, types, even gags as before, yet there is something quite Chekhovian about the piece: the delicate poignancy of the various emotional dilemmas; the awareness of a very real pain underlying the jokes; the grim, inevitable fact of death hovering all the while just off-screen while Woody's own angst-filled jester faces a medical scare. The gags are not just one-liners, but wholly plausible in terms of character and plot—a quality done ample justice by one of the best casts Allen ever managed to put together. And unlike some of the other films, the tribute to the good things that make life just about worth living feels heartfelt in *Hannah and Her Sisters* rather than forced (even though Allen did indeed once consider a darker ending). A feel-good movie in the best sense of the word. **GA**

She's Gotta Have It Spike Lee, 1986

U.S. (40 Acres & a Mule) 84m BW / Color
Producer Spike Lee Screenplay Spike Lee
Photography Ernest R. Dickerson Music Bill
Lee Cast Tracy Camilla Johns, Tommy
Redmond Hicks, John Canada Terrell, Spike
Lee, Raye Dowell, Joie Lee, S. Epatha
Merkerson, Bill Lee, Cheryl Burr, Aaron
Dugger, Stephanie Covington, Renata
Cobbs, Cheryl Singleton, Monty Ross, Lewis
Jordan Cannes Film Festival Spike Lee
(award of youth foreign film)

Spike Lee's debut feature, *She's Gotta Have It* is an exploration of the life of Nola Darling (Tracy Camilla Johns), a young black woman living in New York City who worries that her sexual appetites make her a "freak," and who juggles relationships with three different men, none of whom can entirely satisfy her. Whereas the self-regarding male model and "buppie" Greer (John Canada Terrell) and the gangly, irresponsible, pattering Mars Blackmon (Lee) are almost one-note comical caricatures, the decent, caring, poetic Jamie (Tommy Redmond Hicks) is positioned to win the girl.

Jamie disrupts the black-and-white movie by staging a full-color musical number as a birthday present, and is the one who forces the big, expected confrontation scene that makes Nola reassess her life and commit to him. But he also, in effect, rapes her to make a point, and the smothering "happy ending" is undercut by Nola's own narration, which concludes: "I'm not a one-man woman. . . . There you have me." Usually characterized as a primarily African-American filmmaker, Lee is certainly willing to explore strata of black American life that are usually neglected in all the hood movies, but his approach to chat, insight, New York, and the human heart makes him kin also to Eric Rohmer, Martin Scorsese, and Woody Allen. **KN**

Children of a Lesser God Randa Haines, 1986

U.S. (Paramount) 119m Color
Producer Patrick J. Palmer, Burt Sugarman
Screenplay Hesper Anderson, from play by
Mark Medoff Photography John Seale
Music Michael Convertino Cast William
Hurt, Marlee Matlin, Piper Laurie, Philip
Bosco, Allison Gompf, John F. Cleary, Philip
Holmes, Georgia Ann Cline, William D. Byrd
Oscars Burt Sugarman, Patrick J. Palmer
(best picture), Hesper Anderson, Mark
Medoff (screenplay), Marlee Matlin (actress)
Oscar nominations William Hurt (actor),
Piper Laurie (actress in support role) Berlin
International Film Festival Randa Haines
(reader jury of the Berliner Morgenpost,
Silver Bear—bringing a major theme to
public attention, Golden Bear nomination)

On paper, this sounds like a disease-of-the week TV movie, but thanks to a skillful adaptation of the stage play on which it is based, and two superb central performances, *Children of a Lesser God* is instead a thought-provoking film that is also a genuinely affecting love story.

Sign-language teacher James Leeds (William Hurt) goes to work at a school for the deaf, and encounters a former pupil, Sarah Norman (Marlee Matlin), who is now employed there as a janitor. An angry young woman who had been one of the school's brightest students, Sarah is initially resistant to James's charms and methods— he encourages his deaf students to use their voices—but eventually relents and becomes his lover.

Matlin, who is hearing-impaired, gives a superb performance as Sarah (a performance that won her an Oscar), signing with such furious intensity that Hurt's translation of her sign language is often unnecessary as we can see her meaning in her face. Hurt delivers an understated turn (which is exactly what is needed to prevent the film from becoming sentimental), while director Randa Haines (who had previously won an Emmy for the 1984 television drama *Something About Amelia*) beautifully explores Sarah's world of silence, especially in a scene between James and Sarah in a swimming pool, where James can finally experience the world the way Sarah does. Lovely. **JB**

Caravaggio Derek Jarman, 1986

G.B. (BFI) 93m Technicolor **Producer** Sarah Radclyffe **Screenplay** Derek Jarman **Photography** Gabriel Beristain **Music** Simon Fisher-Turner **Cast** Noam Almaz, Dawn Archibald, Sean Bean, Jack Birkett, Sadie Corre, Una Brandon-Jones, Imogen Claire, Robbie Coltrane, Garry Cooper, Lol Coxhill, Nigel Davenport, Vernon Dobtcheff, Terry Downes, Dexter Fletcher, Michael Gough, Jonathan Hyde, Spencer Leigh, Emile Nicolaou, Gene October, Cindy Oswin, John Rogan, Zohra Sehgal, Tilda Swinton, Lucien Taylor, Nigel Terry, Simon Fisher-Turner **Berlin International Film Festival** Derek Jarman (C.I.D.A.L.C. award, Silver Bear—visual shaping, Golden Bear nomination)

In *Caravaggio*, Derek Jarman uses a studio in London and the sounds of contemporary Italy to create an astonishing portrait of the world of Renaissance art. The film opens with Caravaggio dying at Porto Ercole, looking back over his life in decadent Rome and entertaining his ruthless patrons with tales of energy and life stolen from his companions of bars and back rooms. The acting, from Nigel Terry and Tilda Swinton to Robbie Coltrane and Jonathan Hyde, is superb, Christopher Hobbs's sets are visually stunning, and Simon Fisher-Turner's music is utterly compelling. Art becomes life becomes art as Jarman breathes biographical life into Caravaggio's greatest paintings while the artist reflects without any mercy on his own life split between the braying snobbery of the art world, and the exciting danger of a universe where violence and sex intersect.

The film is remarkable for the set pieces that recreate Caravaggio's masterpieces, for the scenes of chilling hilarity as the cardinals plot their deadly strategems, and for the extraordinary triangle composed of Ranuccio (Sean Bean), the prostitute Lena (Swinton), and Caravaggio (Terry). One of the few biopics of an artist to really show what's on the end of an artist's brush. **CM**

Salvador Oliver Stone, 1986

U.S. (Hemdale) 123m Color **Language** English / Spanish **Producer** Gerald Green, Oliver Stone **Screenplay** Oliver Stone, Rick Boyle **Photography** Robert Richardson **Music** Georges Delerue **Photography** Robert Richardson **Cast** James Woods, James Belushi, Michael Murphy, John Savage, Elpidia Carrillo, Tony Plana, Colby Chester, Cynthia Gibb, Will MacMillan, Valerie Wildman, José Carlos Ruiz, Jorge Luke, Juan Fernández, Salvador Sánchez, Rosario Zúñiga **Oscar nominations** Oliver Stone, Rick Boyle (screenplay), James Woods (actor)

Oliver Stone's directorial breakthrough came after a string of screenplays—including *Midnight Express* (1978), *Scarface* (1983), and *Year of the Dragon* (1985)—that resulted in controversial box-office successes. In stark contrast to the racist and reactionary politics of these earlier films, *Salvador* is an openly leftist attack on the American support of brutal, fascist repression in Latin America. Written with shamelessly melodramatic plot points at every dramatic turn, triggering emotional responses from the audience, and directed with an engaging kinetic force from the first to the last image, it stands as a model for Stone's later films. It is also the first in his series of history lessons, where an American Everyman faces the truth behind the official lie—the American dream, governmental propaganda, and so on—and gets to a point of no return at which he must re-evaluate his world view.

Salvador follows true-life journalist Richard Boyle (James Woods) and his DJ friend Dr. Rock (James Belushi) traveling to what they expect to be a hedonistic holiday in the sun with cheap sex, drugs, and rock-'n'-roll. Once there, however, they get caught up in a civil war so ugly that they cannot look away. Though the film fails to show the full scale of brutality in El Salvador during the "events that occurred in 1980–1981" (as is claimed by the opening notice), this journey into a living hell in the U.S. backyard stands as an uncompromising, shattering testimony to American foreign policy at its worst. **MT**

Platoon Oliver Stone, 1986

U.S. (Cinema 86, Hemdale)
120m Color **Language** English /
Vietnamese **Producer** Arnold Kopelson
Screenplay Oliver Stone
Photography Robert Richardson
Music Georges Delerue **Cast** Tom
Berenger, Willem Dafoe, Charlie Sheen,
Forest Whitaker, Francesco Quinn, John C.
McGinley, Richard Edson, Kevin Dillon,
Reggie Johnson, Keith David, Johnny Depp,
David Neidorf, Mark Moses, Chris Pedersen,
Tony Todd **Oscars** Arnold Kopelson (best
picture), Oliver Stone (director), Claire
Simpson (editing), John Wilkinson, Richard
D. Rogers, Charles Grenzbach, Simon Kaye
(sound) **Oscar nominations** Oliver Stone
(screenplay), Tom Berenger (actor in support
role), Willem Dafoe (actor in support role),
Robert Richardson (photography) **Berlin
International Film Festival** Oliver Stone
(Silver Bear—director, Golden Bear
nomination)

ℹ

Sheen's narration echoes that of his
father, Martin Sheen, in the 1979
Vietnam epic *Apocalypse Now*.

A savage yet moving look at the Vietnam War, as seen through the eyes of a young soldier, *Platoon* remains one of the most powerful war movies ever made, and is one of writer-director Oliver Stone's most accomplished films.

The first of Stone's "Vietnam film trilogy"—the second and third being *Born on the Fourth of July* (1989) and *Heaven & Earth* (1993)— *Platoon* follows the experiences of nineteen-year-old Chris Taylor (Charlie Sheen), an idealistic, middle-class boy who volunteers for the army, unaware of the horrors to come. His letters home detail his relationships with fellow grunts and the two sergeants who divide the platoon—hippie Elias Grodin (Willem Dafoe), who uses drugs to escape the nightmares all around him, and dangerously violent Bob Barnes (Tom Berenger).

Platoon has a unique perspective on war in general and the Vietnam War in particular, largely because Stone himself served in the conflict and uses the film to relate his own experiences as a young soldier. In each scene he directs from every point of view, so the audience is never sure where the next attack may come from, creating a feeling of unease and discomfort as if you were really there, watching this horrific, chaotic encounter unfold around you. With the help of military advisor Dale Dye, he delivers a series of blistering, messy images of war—a war where there is no Hollywood hero but instead just a patriotic boy who slowly becomes disillusioned with all he believed he was fighting for. For Stone, it was a personal triumph after fighting for ten years to get his script made; for the audience, it is an unforgettable, authentic, modern classic. **JB**

Down by Law Jim Jarmusch, 1986

Long recognized as a leading figure of American independent cinema, writer-director Jim Jarmusch is well known for highly idiosyncratic, noncommercial films. *Down by Law*, his landmark feature from 1986, epitomizes this counter-hegemonic interest and style and unwinds inside a hermetically sealed creative universe divorced from the demands of box-office receipts or audience gratification.

The story of chance encounters and luck, *Down by Law* draws on the interrelated lives of Jack (John Lurie), a pimp; Zack (Tom Waits), an unemployed DJ; and Bob (Roberto Benigni), an Italian tourist. All end up incarcerated, with Jack and Zack fall guys for crimes they didn't commit, and Bob serving time for committing murder in self-defense. At first not particularly fond of one another, they each nevertheless undertake a friendship of circumstance, eventually escaping into the relative calm of rural America. It's as straightforward as that, with little embellishment.

Still, Jarmusch's shorthand matters because his purposes are often deceptively simple. Long takes predominate with in-depth compositions showcasing wonderfully expressive black-and-white film. Time-killing activities like card games frame and support the characters' lives. Everywhere touched by a sense of farcical adventure, the movie is nominally set in Louisiana, though it clearly reflects the world we know.

Often riding a thin line between amateur technique and professional brilliance, *Down by Law* avoids cliché-ridden expressions and the usual restrictions of space and place. In its length are domestic squabbles, the briefest of exposition to realize the prison setting, and an inexplicable escape through an underground sewer system, after which the film more or less works out a set of scenarios as if through improvisation.

For Jarmusch fans it's a must see. Even for his opponents it affirms the value of small-scale American film productions in opposition to the usual Hollywood fare. Regardless, Jarmusch draws his funding from German sources. Somehow his temperament, style, and commercial (dis)interests resonate within this looming Teutonic tradition, embellished here by the noted cinematographer Robby Müller, who transforms a relatively shapeless plot into something undeniably beautiful. **GC-Q**

U.S. / **West Germany** (Black Snake, Grokenberger, Island) 107m BW **Producer** Alan Kleinberg Tom Rothman, Jim Stark **Screenplay** Jim Jarmusch **Photography** Robby Müller **Music** John Lurie, Tom Waits **Cast** Tom Waits, John Lurie, Roberto Benigni, Nicoletta Braschi, Ellen Barkin, Billie Neal, Rockets Redglare, Vernel Bagneris, Timothea, L.C. Drane, Joy N. Houck Jr., Carrie Lindsoe, Ralph Joseph, Richard Boes, Dave Petitjean **Cannes Film Festival** Jim Jarmusch (Golden Palm nomination)

"My mama used to say that America's the big melting pot. You bring it to a boil and all the scum rises to the top."

**Bobbie
(Billie Neal)**

ℹ️

Roberto Benigni wrote and improvised his rabbit soliloquy, based on his own experiences.

Le déclin de l'empire américain Denys Arcand, 1986
The Decline of the American Empire

Canada (Corporation Image M & M, Malofilm, NFB, Société Radio Cinema, Société Général du Cinéma du Québec, Téléfilm Canada) 101m Color Language French Producer Roger Frappier, René Malo Screenplay Denys Arcand Photography Guy Dufaux Music François Dompierre Cast Dominique Michel, Dorothée Berryman, Louise Portal, Pierre Curzi, Rémy Girard, Yves Jacques, Geneviève Rioux, Daniel Brière, Gabriel Arcand, Évelyn Regimbald, Lisette Guertin, Alexandre Remy, Ariane Frédérique, Jean-Paul Bongo Oscar nomination Canada (best foreign language film) Cannes Film Festival Denys Arcand (FIPRESCI award)

The first international success of Canadian filmmaker Denys Arcand, *The Decline of the American Empire* is a sardonic study in sexual mores where the sex is much more evident in talk than in action. In a lakeside country house, four male French-Canadian academics are preparing a gourmet meal and talking about sex. Meanwhile, the four women who will be their guests meet at a health club in the city—and talk about sex. Then they all assemble for dinner where the conversations—and the revelations—continue.

Early on, in a radio interview, one of the women asks whether the "frantic drive for personal happiness" is "linked to the decline of the American empire." Arcand's film ironically explores this question. All the characters, it seems, are hell-bent on finding happiness; yet everyone is frustrated and desperate, and their relationships are disaster areas. This, Arcand hints, is the fallout of a society where sexual gratification is elevated over all other values. Interactions between the characters—especially during the dinner party—are filmed like a battle, with shot and countershot; the dialogue is witty, erudite, and oblique. *Decline* is at once bleak and funny; we may not like these people, but they're ceaselessly fascinating to watch. **PK**

1986

Do ma daan Tsui Hark, 1986
Peking Opera Blues

Hong Kong (Cinema City) 104m Color Language Cantonese Producer Claudie Chung Chun, Tsui Hark Screenplay Wai To Kwok Photography Poon Hang-Sang Music James Wong Cast Brigitte Lin, Cherie Chung, Sally Yeh, Kenneth Tsang, Wu Ma, Paul Chu, Hoi Ling Pak, Mark Cheng, Cheung Kwok Keung, Ku Feng, Lee Hoi San

When the post–New Wave Hong Kong cinema of the 1980s was embraced in the West, admirers were entranced by its ability to construct populist entertainment with imagination, wit, and intelligence—qualities largely absent from Hollywood products of the era. Perhaps no other title from the Hong Kong boom years of the '80s contains these elements in such abundance as *Peking Opera Blues*, director Tsui Hark's gloriously gravity-defying historical epic that unfolds in an opera house circa 1913.

Weaving the aspirations of three female protagonists—a general's daughter with revolutionary affiliations (Brigitte Lin), an aspiring acrobat who strives to infiltrate her father's all-male opera troupe (Sally Yeh), and a scheming mercenary on the hunt for stolen jewels (Cherie Chung), Tsui also deftly interweaves a melange of film genres to encompass historical melodrama, bedroom farce, and wirework action spectacular.

The political themes and gender issues at work within the narrative of *Peking Opera Blues* provide a fascinating subtext for this classic of contemporary Hong Kong film. One can only reflect back on such a burst of pure cinematic pleasure with bittersweet nostalgia—Tsui's recent output has been a dire mess, Peking's charming trio of leading ladies have all retired from the screen, and the early-twenty-first-century Hong Kong film industry is in a catastrophic slump. **TCr**

Aliens James Cameron, 1986

1986

U.S. / G.B. (Fox, Brandywine) 137m
Eastmancolor **Producer** Gale Anne Hurd
Screenplay James Cameron, David Giler,
Walter Hill **Photography** Adrian Biddle
Music James Horner **Cast** Sigourney
Weaver, Michael Biehn, Paul Reiser, Lance
Henriksen, Carrie Henn, Bill Paxton, William
Hope, Jenette Goldstein, Al Matthews, Mark
Rolston, Ricco Ross, Colette Hiller, Daniel
Kash, Cynthia Dale Scott, Tip Tipping
Oscars Don Sharpe (special sound effects),
Robert Skotak, Stan Winston, John
Richardson, Suzanne M. Benson (special
visual effects) **Oscar nominations**
Sigourney Weaver (actress), Peter Lamont,
Crispian Sallis (art direction), Ray Lovejoy
(editing), James Horner (music), Graham V.
Hartstone, Nicolas Le Messurier, Michael A.
Carter, Roy Charman (sound)

"Get away from her, you bitch!" Sigourney Weaver's Lt. Ellen Ripley gets madder when maternal and becomes the greatest sci-fi action heroine ever in James Cameron's sensational follow-up to *Alien* (1979). One of cinema's greatest sequels, *Aliens* picks up Ripley (and Jones the cat) being recovered in the escape craft. The snag is that it's fifty-seven years later and, besides having a trying time explaining what happened to the Nostromo, Ripley is appalled to learn that the site of their disastrous discovery (planet LV 426) has been colonized. Inevitably something bad happens there and the traumatized Ripley is sent back with an untrustworthy company man, a team of swaggering Marines (including Cameron favorites Michael Biehn, Bill "Game over!" Paxton, plus Jenette Goldstein's terrific tough cookie Vasquez), and another ambiguous android (Lance Henrikson as Bishop).

If *Alien* was a haunted-house-in-space frightener, Cameron's relentless, furiously intense thrill-ride (winning the franchise's second effects Oscar) is the fort under siege in space, with the dwindling band and resourceful orphan Newt (Carrie Henn) beset by an implacable multiplicity of H.R. Giger's formidable, acid-drooling, giant foe and the mother of the species. The Director's Cut adds about seventeen minutes without letting up. **AE**

Ferris Bueller's Day Off John Hughes, 1986

U.S. (Paramount) 102m Metrocolor
Producer John Hughes, Tom Jacobson
Screenplay John Hughes **Photography** Tak
Fujimoto **Music** Ira Newborn **Cast** Matthew
Broderick, Alan Ruck, Mia Sara, Jeffrey Jones,
Jennifer Grey, Cindy Pickett, Lyman Ward,
Edie McClurg, Charlie Sheen, Ben Stein,
Del Close, Virginia Capers, Richard Edson,
Larry Flash Jenkins, Kristy Swanson

Every male adolescent's dream—and every parent's nightmare—comes true on screen in writer-director John Hughes's teen comedy *Ferris Bueller's Day Off*, as the film's hero (Matthew Broderick) does all the things in just one day that most of us don't have the nerve to do in a lifetime.

Realizing one morning that "life moves pretty fast. If you don't stop and look around once in awhile, you could miss it," Ferris decides to skip school, and this time aims to make it count. Enlisting the help of his pal Cameron (Alan Ruck), Ferris "borrows" Cameron's father's prized Ferrari, performs "Twist and Shout" during a city parade (in one of the movie's most memorable scenes), catches a game at Chicago's Wrigley Field, and scams his way into a high-class restaurant.

Like previous Hughes movies such as *The Breakfast Club* (1985), *Pretty in Pink* (1986), and *Sixteen Candles* (1984), adults here don't understand the teenagers in their care, be it Ferris's parents or the high school dean (Jeffrey Jones) who has made it his mission in life to catch Ferris in the act of doing something he shouldn't be doing. The grown-ups are just bystanders, the film really belonging to the supporting cast of Ruck (who was thirty playing the teenage role of Cameron), Jennifer Grey (as Ferris's bitter sister, who is sick of her popular brother), Mia Sara (Ferris's girlfriend Sloane), and, most of all, Matthew Broderick (nominated for a Golden Globe) as the adorable, exuberant lead. **JB**

The Fly David Cronenberg, 1986

Even in his earliest films, director David Cronenberg imagined how advances in science, medicine, and technology (and often a fusion of the three) might alter human behavior. *The Fly* takes that fusion to its literal extreme, and while the movie exemplifies horror in the strictest sense, in actuality Cronenberg plays it like a twisted love story.

Retaining the bare-bones premise of the 1958 B-movie original with Vincent Price, *The Fly* stars Jeff Goldblum as a scientist who designs a matter transporter, a means to disassemble matter in one location and reassemble it in another. Much to the dismay of his lover, Geena Davis, one night Goldblum tests the machine on himself. Something goes wrong. Goldblum's DNA is accidentally fused with that of a common house fly, and while the genetic alteration at first enhances Goldblum's senses, it quickly results in a battle of genetic dominance between the two disparate species.

Cronenberg has never shunned visceral impact, and as Goldblum begins his transformation from human to human–fly hybrid, *The Fly* features a nonstop escalation of increasingly nasty special effects. Tough hair sprouts up in strange places. Goo oozes from every orifice. Body parts wither and fall off only to be replaced by mysterious new appendages.

Rob Bottin's array of repulsive prosthetics threatens to take center stage, and indeed his vomitous effects are played not only for shock but also for perverse humor. But as disgusting as this central transformation sounds (and is), Cronenberg and his capable cast somehow infuse it with real emotion. Davis struggles with Goldblum's gross transformation to connect with the man she once knew, while Goldblum struggles to retain his humanity as his free will is subsumed by instinct.

Alas, all of this can only end one way, as the sweet romance is destined to be squashed by fate's fly swatter. Cronenberg therefore plays his tragedy for maximum pathos, and thanks in no small part to the chemistry of its leads and the plausibility of their against-all-odds relationship, rarely has such a stomach-churning series of events resulted in so many shed tears. **JKl**

U.S. (Brooksfilms) 95m Color
Producer Stuart Cornfeld, Marc Boyman, Kip Ohman **Screenplay** David Cronenberg, George Langelaan, Charles Edward Pogue **Photography** Mark Irwin **Music** Howard Shore **Cast** Jeff Goldblum, Geena Davis, John Getz, Joy Boushel, Leslie Carlson, George Chuvalo, Michael Copeman, David Cronenberg, Carol Lazare, Shawn Hewitt **Oscar** Chris Walas, Stephan Dupuis (makeup)

"*The Fly is that rare species of movie—a remake that surpasses the original and, quite frankly, all expectations.*"

Boston Globe, **1986**

1986

i

The first and last bars of music on the soundtrack are from Puccini's tragic opera *Madame Butterfly*.

Top Gun Tony Scott, 1986

U.S. (Paramount) 110m Metrocolor **Producer** Jerry Bruckheimer, Don Simpson **Screenplay** Jim Cash, Jack Epps Jr., from article by Ehud Yonay **Photography** Jeffrey L. Kimball **Music** Harold Faltermeyer, Giorgio Moroder **Cast** Tom Cruise, Kelly McGillis, Val Kilmer, Anthony Edwards, Tom Skerritt, Michael Ironside, John Stockwell, Barry Tubb, Rick Rossovich, Tim Robbins, Clarence Gilyard Jr., Whip Hubley, James Tolkan, Meg Ryan, Adrian Pasdar **Oscar** Giorgio Moroder, Tom Whitlock (song) **Oscar nominations** Cecelia Hall, George Watters (special sound effects), Billy Weber, Chris Lebenzon (editing), Donald O. Mitchell, Kevin O'Connell, Rick Kline, William B. Kaplan (sound)

i

The film is dedicated to the memory of Hollywood stunt pilot Art Scholl, whose plane crashed during filming.

Applications to the U.S. Navy's fighter-pilot program rose considerably after the release of this testosterone-fueled homage to the men who feel the need for speed, and it isn't hard to see why. Tom Cruise, in the role that turned him from teen pinup to megastar, is Maverick, a pilot at the Top Gun school in San Diego, California. He isn't great with authority, butting heads with superior officer Michael Ironside, and has intimacy issues, which cause problems when he falls for his aeronautics instructor (Kelly McGillis).

Cruise's macho but deep-down-I'm-sensitive performance appealed to the female audience, thanks especially to his barroom serenade of "You've Lost that Lovin' Feelin'" (a 1964 number one hit by The Righteous Brothers) to a bemused McGillis. But the impressive flight scenes are the real reason to appreciate the film. Director Tony Scott, at his best when directing fast-paced action (movies like *The Last Boy Scout* [1991] and *Days Of Thunder* [1990]), spends the briefest amount of time on the somewhat predictable romance and personal conflicts to pack the film with realistic dogfights and dazzling aeronautic displays. An enjoyable example of the archetypal 1980s action flick, *Top Gun* also contains a hit rock soundtrack and a host of young actors (including Meg Ryan, Val Kilmer, and Anthony Edwards) who all went on to become big stars. **JB**

Sherman's March Ross McElwee, 1986

U.S. (First Run Features)
157m Color **Screenplay** Ross McElwee
Photography Ross McElwee **Cast** Ross
McElwee, Burt Reynolds, Charleen Swansea

Ross McElwee's *Sherman's March* could be seen as the *Citizen Kane* (1941) of the diary film genre (a genre inspired by the arrival of small, high-quality recorders in the 1970s). Like *Kane*, it was hailed as something utterly new in American cinema, but its greatest achievement lay less in its originality than in the way it perfected techniques and approaches already present in earlier film diaries. McElwee originally set out to make a film about the lingering effects of the South's defeat in the Civil War, but a break-up with his long-time girlfriend just before shooting began found his return home becoming equally an attempt to find romance.

Unlike the cinema verité films of the early 1960s, with their invisible camera crews, *Sherman's March* has McElwee constantly interacting with the subjects in front of his camera. He is remarkably talented at making people unselfconscious as he films them, never stooping to the cheap shot, or assuming an attitude of condescension.

Over the course of the film, he embarks on a few tentative attempts to create a relationship. None work out and some fail hilariously. His voice-over commentary becomes increasingly self-critical, until in an exceptionally poignant moment he finally wonders aloud whether he's filming his life or filming so he'll have a life. Yet *Sherman's March* is never heavy, and one leaves it moved at the recognition of how effectively McElwee has captured the spirit of contemporary romance. It may look "simple," a kind of glorified home movie, but what makes it art is McElwee's generous spirit, good humor, and remarkable candor. **RP**

1986

Stand by Me Rob Reiner, 1986

U.S. (Act III, Columbia, The Body) 89m
Technicolor **Producer** Bruce A. Evans,
Raynold Gideon, Andrew Scheinman
Screenplay Raynold Gideon, Bruce A. Evans,
from the novella *The Body* by Stephen King
Photography Thomas Del Ruth **Music** Jack
Nitzsche **Cast** Wil Wheaton, River Phoenix,
Corey Feldman, Jerry O'Connell, Gary Riley,
Kiefer Sutherland, Casey Siemaszko, Bradley
Gregg, Jason Oliver, Marshall Bell, Frances
Lee McCain, Bruce Kirby, William Bronder,
Scott Beach, Richard Dreyfuss
Oscar nomination Raynold Gideon,
Bruce A. Evans (screenplay)

Stephen King's short story *The Body*—a nonhorror ode to boyhood friendships—is beautifully adapted for the screen by director Rob Reiner and screenwriters Raynold Gideon and Bruce A. Evans. In *Stand by Me*, quiet Gordie (Wil Wheaton), daring Teddy (Corey Feldman), pudgy Vern (Jerry O'Connell), and group leader Chris (River Phoenix) are the four boys who spend the summer of 1959 doing nothing much more than hanging out at their treehouse until the day Vern announces that he knows where they can find a dead body. Intrigued to see what a corpse looks like, the friends set off on a long walk to find it.

A tale of friendships—related by a grown-up Gordie (an uncredited Richard Dreyfuss)—set against the beautiful Oregon scenery (standing in for the novel's Maine location), *Stand by Me* expertly depicts the fears, games, catchphrases, debates ("Mickey is a mouse, Donald is a duck, Pluto is a dog. What's Goofy?"), and secrets shared by young boys, whereas Kiefer Sutherland's older, meaner Ace gives a taste of what could be round the next corner in their lives. Beautifully played by the young cast, and lyrically directed by Reiner. **JB**

Tampopo Juzo Itami, 1986

Japan (Itami P, New Century) 114m Color
Language Japanese Producer Seigo
Hosogoe, Juzo Itami, Yasushi Tamaoki
Screenplay Juzo Itami Photography Masaki
Tamura Music Kunihiko Murai
Cast Tsutomu Yamazaki, Nobuko Miyamoto,
Ken Watanabe, Koji Yakusho, Mario Abe,
Izumi Hara, Isao Hashizume, Hisashi Igawa,
Toshimune Kato, Yoshi Kato, Yoshihiro Kato,
Fukumi Kuroda, Nobuo Nakamura, Mariko
Okada Shuji Otaki, Ryutaro Otomo, Yoshihei
Saga, Kinzoh Sakura, Setsuko Shino, Hitoshi
Takagi, Choei Takahashi, Akio Tanaka,
Masahiko Tsugawa, Rikiya Yasuoka

Juzo Itami's second comedy represents a quantum leap from his first, the 1984 *The Funeral*. Without abandoning his flair for social satire, Itami expands his scope here to encompass the kind of free-form narrative play we associate with late Luis Buñuel. His subjects are food, sex, and death, his ostensible focal point the opening of a noodle restaurant. He takes us on a wild spree through an obsession, winding his way through various digressions with a dark wit that is both hilarious and disturbing.

The title heroine (Nobuko Miyamoto) is a widowed mother determined to master the art of ramen with the aid of a mentor. Her story is interlaced with that of a nameless wealthy gangster, accompanied by a mistress, who is preoccupied with food, sex, death, and cinema. We initially see the gangster sitting down in a movie theater before a sumptuous array of food, ostensibly preparing to watch the story of Tampopo. Various digressions extend these themes to incorporate such Japanese standbys as deception, poverty, family, and guilt.

As in *The Funeral*, Itami's ultimate interest appears to be in exploring as well as ridiculing some of the paradoxes of Japanese society, including those involving class and etiquette, and he carries this off with energy and inventiveness. **JRom**

Dao ma zei Tian Zhuangzhuang, 1986
The Horse Thief

China (Xi'an) 88m Color
Language Mandarin Producer Wu Tian-
Ming Screenplay Zhang Rui
Photography Zhao Fei, Hou Yong
Music Qu Xiao-Song Cast Dan Jiji,
Gaoba, Jayang Jamco, Tseshang
Rinzim, Daiba

Tian Zhuangzhuang's second feature, set in the remote wilds of Tibet, is a breathtaking spectacle in scope and color. Tian's originality and mastery of sound and image communicate directly, beyond the immediate trappings of the film's slender plot and regional culture, expressing an environmental and ecological mysticism that suggests a new relationship between man and nature. The relatively small roles played by dialogue and story line, and the striking handling of composition and superimposition, make *The Horse Thief* evocative of certain 1920s Westerns, though it is far from being a silent film: The chants, percussion, and bells of Buddhist rituals and the beautiful music score are an essential part of the film's texture.

Tian's intention was to make the film timeless. However, government authorities insisted that the date 1923 be flashed on the screen before the first image, placing the action in a specific period. They also required the elimination of corpses from the first of the film's three "sky burials." But the story—a parable about a reluctant thief who, in order to feed his family, becomes a more methodical thief, albeit a social outcast— remains intact, and the modernist style was similarly untampered with, despite the fact that the film was barely seen in mainland China because of its focus on a minority culture and its overall eclecticism. **JRos**

Au revoir les enfants Louis Malle, 1987
Goodbye, Children

How close this avowedly autobiographical film is to the precise facts can only be gauged by the intensity of the recollected emotion and guilt that it conveys. Julien (Gaspard Manesse) is a twelve-year-old pupil in a Catholic boarding school in Nazi-occupied France. Apart from the welcome distractions of air-raid warnings, the war makes little impact on the daily routines of school life, and when three new kids arrive, they are submitted to the ritualistic antagonism of infant communities to strangers. Julien, himself something of an outsider, strikes up a friendship with one of the new boys, Jean (Raphael Fejtö). As they grow closer, he discovers that the newcomers have all adopted false names, though he only gradually and vaguely grows to understand the enormity of anti-Semitism, and that the Catholic fathers are endeavoring to shelter these endangered children. When the net grows tighter, it is an inadvertent action by Julien himself that betrays the Jewish children and sends them to an inconceivable fate. We realize that this moment will never cease to torment Julien.

Writer and director Louis Malle (*The Lovers* [1958], *Murmur of the Heart* [1971], *Atlantic City* [1980]), is not concerned with Hollywood-style war melodrama but with the life of the school—the daily drags and discoveries, the eccentric habits of schoolmasters, friendships, and suspicions. The war impinges in the air-raid warnings, and the puzzle that the occupying Nazis are, like any other group, a dangerous mix of goons and gentlemen.

Malle genuinely sees it all through the boys' own acute but still unformed vision, and the performances of Manesse and Fejto are so moving precisely because of the open honesty that compensates for technical expertise. Malle's most personal film, *Au revoir les enfants* was the recipient of a slew of international awards (among them the Golden Lion at the 1987 Venice Film Festival), and represented a triumphant swan song in a career that had faltered somewhat since its brave beginnings in the era of the New Wave cinema. **DR**

France / West Germany
(MK2, NEF, Nouvelles Éditions, Stella Films)
104m Color **Language** French / German
Producer Louis Malle **Screenplay** Louis Malle **Photography** Renato Berta
Music Camille Saint-Saëns, Franz Schubert
Cast Gaspard Manesse, Raphael Fejtö, Francine Racette, Stanislas Carré de Malberg, Philippe Morier-Genoud, François Berléand, François Négret, Peter Fitz, Pascal Rivet, Benoît Henriet, Richard Leboeuf, Xavier Legrand, Arnaud Henriet, Jean-Sébastien Chauvin, Luc Etienne **Oscar nominations** France (best foreign language film), Louis Malle screenplay) **Venice Film Festival** Louis Malle (Golden Lion, OCIC Award)

"Louis Malle's Au revoir les enfants *is more than his wartime memoir; it is an epitaph to innocence."*

Rita Kempley,
The Washington Post, 1988

1987

In the voiceover epilogue, an older Julien relates that the children died at Auschwitz concentration camp.

Raising Arizona Joel Coen, 1987

U.S. (Circle) 94m Color **Producer** Ethan
Coen **Screenplay** Ethan Coen, Joel
Coen **Photography** Barry Sonnenfeld
Music Carter Burwell **Cast** Nicolas Cage,
Holly Hunter, Trey Wilson, John Goodman,
William Forsythe, Sam McMurray, Frances
McDormand, Randall "Tex" Cobb, T.J. Kuhn,
Lynne Dumin Kitei, Peter Benedek,
Charles "Lew" Smith, Warren Keith,
Henry Kendrick, Sidney Dawson

The Coen brothers' enormously inventive second feature abandoned the
noir mood of *Blood Simple* (1984) for this larger-than-life (but likewise
intricately plotted) comedy featuring cartoon-style caricature. Nicolas
Cage is the convenience-store robber, forever in and out of jail, who falls
for and weds prison officer Holly Hunter; their somewhat improbably
blissful trailer-park marriage is blighted when they find she's infertile
and, to keep her happy, he kidnaps one of the quintuplets born to a local
unpainted-furniture tycoon. As if it weren't bad enough that the father
hires the biker from hell (Randall "Tex" Cob) to bring back his baby and
wreak vengeance on the abductors, Cage's fortunes take a turn for the
even worse. Much to his wife's anger, he is visited by escaped former
cellmates John Goodman and William Forsythe, who have plans of their
own for the famously missing infant.

The farcical improbabilities of *Raising Arizona* are as nothing to the
absurdly overpoetic voice-over the Coens brilliantly concoct for their
hapless and none-too-bright hero. The film is as fervently and intelligently
in love with tacky excess as anything dreamed up by Preston Sturges.
Indeed, some of the camera pyrotechnics may actually distract attention
away from the deliciously witty dialogue, but overall the aura of heady
hysteria is sustained with considerable expertise, not least in the perfectly
pitched performances. **GA**

i

Fifteen babies played the
quintuplets. One was fired during
production when he learned to walk.

Yeelen Souleymane Cissé, 1987
Brightness

Mali (Artificial Eye, Cissé, Souleymane) 105m Color **Language** Bambara / French **Producer** Souleymane Cissé **Screenplay** Souleymane Cissé **Photography** Jean-Noël Ferragut, Jean-Michel Humeau **Music** Salif Keita, Michel Portal **Cast** Issiaka Kane, Aoua Sangare, Niamanto Sanogo, Balla Moussa Keita, Soumba Traore, Ismaila Sarr, Youssouf Tenin Cissé, Koke Sangare **Cannes Film Festival** Souleymane Cissé (prize of the ecumenical jury—special mention, jury prize, tied with *Shinran: Shiroi michi*, Golden Palm nomination)

Brightness, an extraordinarily beautiful and mesmerizing fantasy by Souleymane Cissé, is set in the ancient Bambara culture of Mali (formerly French Sudan) long before it was invaded by Morocco in the sixteenth century. A young man named Niankoro (Issiaka Kane) sets out to discover the mysteries of nature—or komo, the science of the gods— with the help of his mother (Soumba Traore) and uncle (Ismaila Sarr). But Soma (Niamanto Sanogo), Niankoro's jealous and spiteful father, contrives to prevent him from deciphering the elements of the Bambara sacred rites and tries to kill him.

Apart from creating a dense and exciting universe that should make George Lucas green with envy, Cissé shoots his breathtaking images in Fujicolor and accompanies his story with a spare, hypnotic, percussive score. Quite possibly the greatest African film ever made, sublimely mixing the matter-of-fact with the uncanny, this wondrous work won the Jury Prize at the 1987 Cannes Film Festival. In all, *Brightness* provides an ideal introduction to a filmmaker who is, next to Ousmane Sembène, probably Africa's greatest director. **JRos**

"A" gai waak juk jaap Jackie Chan, 1987
Project A, Part II

Hong Kong (Golden Harvest) 101m Color **Language** Cantonese **Producer** Willie Chan, David Lam, Edward Tang **Screenplay** Jackie Chan **Photography** Yiu-Tsou Cheung **Music** Siu-Tin Lei **Cast** Jackie Chan, Kenny Bee, Anthony Chan, Wai-Man Chan, John Cheung, Maggie Cheung, Mui Sang Fan, Kenny Ho, Ricky Hui, Regina Kent, Hoi-Shan Kwan, Rosamund Kwan, Benny Lai, Ben Lam, David Lam, Wai Lam, Carina Lau, Siu-Ming Lau, Hoi San Lee, Siu-Tin Lei, Fong Liu, Ken Lo, Ray Lui, Sam Lui, Mars, Bozidar Smiljanic, Po Tai, Bill Tung, Lung Wei Wang

The setup is simple: Director and star Jackie Chan plays a hotshot in the Royal Hong Kong Navy at the turn of the last century. He sets out to quash a band of marauding pirates preying on ships off the South China coast. There are good guys and bad guys. Do we doubt that the hero will triumph over the bad guys? Of course not. Let's face it, we don't watch a Jackie Chan movie for the plot. The plot is only a framework, an excuse for Chan to present us with one mind-blowing set piece after another.

For Chan, his immediate environment frequently becomes both playground and endurance course. The architecture and objects at hand might help or hurt him as he ducks, dodges, rolls, and weaves to get away from the inexhaustible supply of bad guys always in pursuit. Watching him evade, jump, spin, and improvise his way out of a savage beating is to experience the joy and exhilaration of meticulous comic timing and old-fashioned slapstick. He makes it look easy, but the outtakes that run under the end credits (a tradition in Jackie Chan movies) reveal the set pieces to be painstaking, dangerous work.

But why the sequel rather than the original movie? *Project A, Part II* follows the dictum of being "the same, only bigger," and it is here that one finds Chan at the peak of his powers as a filmmaker, a choreographer, and a martial artist, when he was still young, fast, and agile, before age and broken bones inevitably began slowing him down. **AT**

West Germany / France (Argos, Road Movies, WDR) 127m BW / Color
Language German / English / French
Producer Anatole Dauman, Wim Wenders
Screenplay Peter Handke, Wim Wenders
Photography Henri Alekan **Music** Jürgen Knieper **Cast** Bruno Ganz, Solveig Dommartin, Otto Sander, Curt Bois, Peter Falk, Hans Martin Stier, Elmar Wilms, Sigurd Rachman, Beatrice Manowski, Lajos Kovács, Bruno Rosaz, Laurent Petitgand, Chick Ortega, Otto Kuhnle, Christoph Merg
Cannes Film Festival Wim Wenders (director, Golden Palm nomination)

> *"Wings [of Desire] is a soaring vision that appeals to the senses and the spirit."*
>
> **Desson Howe,**
> **The Washington Post, 1988**

i

A stocking belonging to Henri Alekan's grandmother was used as a filter for the black-and-white scenes.

Der Himmel Über Berlin Wim Wenders, 1987
Wings of Desire

Cowritten with Peter Handke, Wim Wenders's sumptuous fantasy *Wings of Desire* encompasses the division of Berlin, the effects of the Holocaust, and the ultimate beauty of life, daring to make a choice between two worlds—that of humans and that of their unseen but palpable guardian angels—via Damiel (Bruno Ganz), an angel who falls in love with a mortal. Atmospheric, elegiac, and patiently paced, the film was critically acclaimed and won honors at many film festivals, including the Best Director prize at Cannes upon its release.

As in Michael Powell and Emeric Pressburger's 1946 classic *A Matter of Life and Death*, Wenders's heaven is shown in crisp black and white, whereas the human world springs to life in vivid color, aided by the work of legendary cinematographer Henri Alekan, who also photographed Jean Cocteau's *Beauty and the Beast* (1946). High atop buildings or upon the shoulders of statues, angels are watching. Wearing trenchcoats and Mona Lisa smiles, they are invisible except to children and the occasional blind person who senses their presence. The angels see everything, feel everything, and so appear at mortals' sides at times of worry, frequenting lonely bedrooms, libraries, and accident scenes. Although unable to directly affect the actions of humans, the angels may lend a glimmer of hope where before there was only darkness.

But when the broad-faced angel Damiel goes to the aid of Marion (Solveig Dommartin), a beautiful trapeze artist who fears she will fall, he begins to long for the simple things humans take for granted: to touch, to hold, to be seen. On a dank film set around the ruins of Berlin, Peter Falk (playing himself) is a mysterious man: He is the actor famous for TV's *Columbo*, but he is also the only human who openly greets Damiel. At a coffee stand Falk extends his hand to the angel, saying "I can't see you, but I know you're here," without explaining how he knows the unknowable. Second-guessing the audience, Wenders allows Falk to be obliquely referred to twice as "Columbo," a device that amuses and jolts the viewer, making a soothing film experience suddenly less of a reverie and more of a reality. Inspired by Falk's recognition, Damiel decides "to take the plunge" and literally falls to his own mortality.

Inspired by the poetry of Rainer Maria Rilke, *Wings of Desire*'s slow heartbeat pace is essential to the feel of the story. It takes the time to fully examine questions only children ask, such as "Why am I me and not you? Why am I here and not there? When did time begin and where does space end?". Its slow tempo draws the audience inevitably into a world where priorities become clearer and life in general more hopeful. A languid, profound, and gentle "message" movie, its popularity demanded a sequel, *Faraway, So Close!* (1989), as well as an inevitable reshaping by Hollywood into the schematic romantic drama *City of Angels* (1998), starring Meg Ryan and Nicolas Cage. **KK**

Withnail and I Bruce Robinson, 1987

G.B. (Handmade) 107m Color
Producer Paul M. Heller **Screenplay** Bruce
Robinson **Photography** Peter Hannan
Music David Dundas, Rick Wentworth, Jimi
Hendrix **Cast** Richard E. Grant, Paul McGann,
Richard Griffiths, Ralph Brown, Michael
Elphick, Daragh O'Malley, Michael Wardle,
Una Brandon-Jones, Noel Johnson, Irene
Sutcliffe, Llewellyn Rees, Robert Oates,
Anthony Wise, Eddie Tagoe

i

Much of the promotional art for
Withnail and I was designed by
British cartoonist Ralph Steadman.

Bruce Robinson's subsequent films may so far have proved a disappointment, but nothing can diminish the wonderfully idiosyncratic delights of his debut, a ruefully nostalgic comic account of living in partly self-imposed poverty and squalor in late-1960s Camden Town.

Richard Grant is appropriately and hilariously acerbic and theatrical as Withnail, the upper-middle-class reprobate slumming it while (vainly and not very often) trying to find work as an actor, and Paul McGann is equally effective as his quieter, slightly more conscientious and pretty young flatmate (the "I" of the title). Leaving behind the squalor of their unwashed North London slum for a cheap holiday in the Lake District in a cottage owned by Withnail's porcine gay uncle Monty (Richard Griffiths), the impoverished, booze-and-drugs obsessed pair find themselves bemused, bewildered, and even besieged by country ways and avuncular lusts.

Withnail and I is more or less a one-off, its representation of a story ("I" eventually sees the error of Withnail's eternally irresponsible ways and moves on toward a grown-up career) taking second place to the very funny verbal and visual gags, the oh-so-slightly grotesque exaggeration that underpins the comic remembrance of things past, and reveling in (revulsion for?) the colorful characters. Amazingly, it all—even the "Camberwell Carrot" joint—rings frighteningly true. **GA**

The Princess Bride Rob Reiner, 1987

U.S. (Act III, Buttercup, Princess Bride)
98m Color **Producer** Rob Reiner, Andrew
Scheinman **Screenplay** William Goldman,
from his book **Photography** Adrian Biddle
Music Willy De Ville, Mark Knopfler
Cast Cary Elwes, Mandy Patinkin, Chris
Sarandon, Christopher Guest, Wallace
Shawn, André the Giant, Fred Savage, Robin
Wright Penn, Peter Falk, Peter Cook, Mel
Smith, Carol Kane, Billy Crystal, Anne Dyson,
Margery Mason **Oscar nomination** Willy
De Ville (song)

Rob Reiner's friendly fairy-tale adventure *The Princess Bride* delicately mines the irony inherent in its make-believe without ever undermining the effectiveness of the fantasy. The framing device is a grandfather (Peter Falk) reading a favorite book aloud to his skeptical grandson (Fred Savage), and Reiner uses the grandson's initial recalcitrance as both a challenge and a safety net. In the imaginary kingdom of Florin, the beautiful Buttercup (Robin Wright) is separated from the farmhand she loves (Cary Elwes), betrothed to the evil Prince Humperdinck (Chris Sarandon), and spirited away by the nefarious Vizzini (Wallace Shawn).

The colorful characters and adventures are, at their best, like live-action equivalents of Disney animated features, with lots of other fond Hollywood memories thrown in. Andre the Giant seems a cross between Andy Devine and Lumpjaw the Bear. Mandy Patinkin's engaging Inigo Montoya conjures up Gene Kelly in *The Pirate* (1948). Not even the crude ethnic humor—Billy Crystal's Mel Brooks-ish Miracle Max—pricks the dream bubble, and the spirited cast has a field day. The film was adapted by William Goldman from his novel of the same name, with Christopher Guest as a six-fingered sadist, Peter Cook as a lisping clergyman, and Carol Kane as Max's wife. **JRos**

Sinnui yauman Siu-Tung Ching, 1987
A Chinese Ghost Story

Hong Kong (Cinema City, Film Workshop)
98m Color **Language** Cantonese
Producer Hark Tsui **Screenplay** Kai-Chi
Yun, from novel by Songling Pu
Photography Poon Hang-Sang
Music Romeo Díaz, James Wong
Cast Leslie Cheung, Joey Wong, Wu Ma,
Wang Zuxian, Liu Zhaoming

When it comes to fantasy filmmaking, Hong Kong can make Hollywood look imaginatively bankrupt. This 1987 cult classic suggests a combination of Sam Raimi, Jean Cocteau, Georges Méliès, and Tim Burton. It's a ghost story that is also a love story, a sword-and-sorcery tale, and a comedy. Leslie Cheung stars as a naive young debt collector who falls in love with the enigmatic beauty (Joey Wong) haunting an abandoned temple. Unfortunately, she's a ghostly handmaiden for an ancient tree spirit who feeds on living souls—so, with a Taoist swordsman (Wu Ma) protecting him, Cheung ventures into the netherworld to save his love from a fate worse than death. This picture is gorgeous to look at, especially in the velvety nocturnal sequences when skeletons stir, spirits come out to play, and it seems anything can happen and probably will. The special effects are indeed extraordinary: People fly through the air, their robes flowing, blades flashing in the moonlight (these are stunts, remember, not optical process shots); an evil tongue rolls out and slicks through the room like an obscene elastic slug; while hell itself is a bravura chamber of horrors. The film's broad, amiable slapstick doesn't really play, but its surprisingly lyrical, sensual romanticism is effective, and there's so much to enjoy that overlooking the sometimes clumsy storytelling is easy. **TCh**

IN VIETNAM THE WIND DOESN'T BLOW IT SUCKS

BORN TO KILL

Stanley Kubrick's
FULL METAL JACKET

1987

Full Metal Jacket Stanley Kubrick, 1987

U.S. (Natant, Warner Bros.)
116m Color **Language** English /
Vietnamese **Producer** Stanley Kubrick
Screenplay Gustav Hasford, Michael
Herr, Stanley Kubrick, from the novel *The
Short-Timers* by Gustav Hasford
Photography Douglas Milsome
Music Abigail Mead (Vivian Kubrick)
Cast Matthew Modine, Adam Baldwin,
Vincent D'Onofrio, R. Lee Ermey, Dorian
Harewood, Arliss Howard, Kevyn Major
Howard, Ed O'Ross, John Terry, Kieron
Jecchinis, Bruce Boa, Kirk Taylor, Jon Stafford,
Tim Colceri, Ian Tyler **Oscar nomination**
Stanley Kubrick, Michael Herr, Gustav
Hasford (screenplay)

*"The most eloquent
and exacting vision
of the war to date ...
Inspired with technique
rather than overblown
with it."*

Desson Howe,
The Washington Post, 1987

🛈

The term "full metal jacket" refers to
small arms ammunition with a
copper coating around the lead core.

In Stanley Kubrick's *Barry Lyndon* (1975), the major battle scene depicts an engagement that the narrator tells us did not make the history books, "though it was memorable enough for those who took part." When he came to make a movie about Vietnam, a little after the various angst-ridden and fantastical takes by Francis Ford Coppola (*Apocalypse Now* [1979]) and Oliver Stone (*Platoon* [1986]) had established an acid/napalm-haze cinematic vocabulary for that war, Kubrick built on this approach. *Full Metal Jacket* presents a grunt-level world in which all officers, commissioned or not, are ridiculous but deadly alien beings (even hookers, we're told, are "serving officers in the Vietcong") and the trudging, heroic Marines of so many *Take the High Ground!* (1953) kind of pictures are nicknamed kids without a clue of where they are or what they're doing.

Based on *The Short-Timers*, an autobiographical novel by Gustav Hasford, with script input from Michael Herr (author of *Despatches* and the *Apocalypse Now* voice-over), *Full Metal Jacket* is ruthless, comic, horrific, and affecting in equal measure, depicting areas of the war rarely glimpsed in movies. A long opening act is set entirely on Parris Island, the induction-and-training center: After a montage in which long-haired young men are shorn to become bald drones no more distinguishable than the future folk of George Lucas's *THX 1138* (1971), the film is commandeered by the astonishing R. Lee Ermey as drill sergeant Hartman, whose obscene, inventive, relentless abuse against all the recruits ("I bet you're the kind of guy that would fuck a person in the ass and not even have the goddamned common courtesy to give him a reacharound") is designed to break down the "maggots" totally before they can be rebuilt as killing machines. In a lecture, Hartman takes pride in the fact that Lee Harvey Oswald and Charles Whitman learned to shoot in the Marines. The horrible irony of this sequence—which closely parallels the gladiator-training regime of *Spartacus* (1960)—is that the logical payoff is the transformation of a pudgy foul-up (Vincent d'Onofrio) into one of Kubrick's grotesque ape-men, with a primal glare that echoes the droogs of *A Clockwork Orange* (1971) and Jack Torrance (Jack Nicholson) of *The Shining* (1980). The first thing the new-made Marine does is murder his tormentor-creator and kill himself.

After this, the Vietnam sequences are almost a relief, as Private Joker (Matthew Modine), a journalist, unbends a little only to be confronted with even more demented individuals—when asked how he can kill women and children, a helicopter gunner gives a technical answer, while a colonel remarks, "Son, all I've ever asked of my Marines is that they obey my orders as they would the word of God." The climax is a skirmish during a battle in the rubble of Hue City, in which Joker's platoon encounter a female Vietcong sniper: Nobody wins the encounter, and the Marines troop off into the night singing the Mickey Mouse Club marching song. Only Kubrick would dare tweak Disney like this. **KN**

Broadcast News James L. Brooks, 1987

U.S. (Fox, Amercent, American Entertainment Partners, Gracie) 127m Color **Producer** James L. Brooks **Screenplay** James L. Brooks **Photography** Michael Ballhaus **Music** Bill Conti **Cast** William Hurt, Albert Brooks, Holly Hunter, Robert Prosky, Lois Chiles, Joan Cusack, Peter Hackes, Christian Clemenson, Jack Nicholson, Robert Katims, Ed Wheeler, Stephen Mendillo, Kimber Shoop, Dwayne Markee, Gennie James **Oscar nominations** James L. Brooks (best picture), James L. Brooks (screenplay), William Hurt (actor), Holly Hunter (actress), Albert Brooks (actor in support role), Michael Ballhaus (photography), Richard Marks (editing) **Berlin International Film Festival** Holly Hunter (Silver Bear—actress), James L. Brooks (Golden Bear nomination)

"I think we have the kind of friendship where if I were the devil, you'd be the only one I would tell."

Aaron Altman
(Albert Brooks)

i

James L. Brooks wrote *Broadcast News* for Debra Winger, but she had to turn it down as she was pregnant.

An invitation to the 1984 Democratic Convention inspired the hectic spirit of James L. Brooks's fast-paced 1987 media romance. A former CBS television newsman himself, Brooks puts a career twist into the classic concept of screwball comedy. This time, the story centers on the unpredictable outcome of a love triangle between three ambitious and talented people who are made more emotionally fearful within the high-pressure confines of network news. A film about love, it is also about lovers who think that the only safe love affair is the one they have with their work.

Jane Craig (Holly Hunter) is a petite and tidy news producer who comes in early to have a cry at her desk every morning. Working in the Washington bureau of a TV network, she runs her newsroom as a meritocracy. Infatuated with Jane, Aaron Altman (Albert Brooks) is a good reporter with a few strikes against him: The camera doesn't love him, nor apparently does Jane. Tom Grunick (William Hurt at his most affable and calculating) is everything Aaron is not—charming, telegenic, and not too smart. Jane, torn between both men emotionally, is forced to make a decision which lies at the heart of *Broadcast News*'s brilliance: When the going gets tough, the tough do nothing. Sometimes work is an easier option than being emotionally honest; in fact, loving work is often the most emotionally honest decision there is.

Co-starring Joan Cusack (famous for her bad hair and makeup as much as her memorably awkward, headlong dash to get a video tape to the newsroom in time), a delightfully slick Jack Nicholson appears in an uncredited supporting performance as the network's head anchorman, a professional who sees that Grunick is one of his own kind.

As "news" itself has become the show business of which Altman was so fearful, the earnestness and time devoted to TV stories seems to issue from another age. But the laughs are still there, and anyone who has ever been turned down for someone less intelligent will never forget Aaron's quip, "I say it here and it comes out there," when he calls the newsroom to update Grunick, his romantic nemesis, in an emergency broadcast. **KK**

Babbetes Gaestebud Gabriel Axel, 1987
Babette's Feast

Denmark (Det Danske, Panorama) 102m
Eastmancolor **Language** Danish / Swedish /
French **Producer** Just Betzer, Bo Christensen
Screenplay Gabriel Axel, from novel by Isak
Dinesen **Photography** Henning Kristiansen
Music Per Nørgaard **Cast** Stéphane Audran,
Birgitte Federspiel, Bodil Kjer, Jarl Kulle, Jean-
Philippe Lafont, Bibi Andersson, Ghita Nørby,
Asta Esper, Hagen Andersen, Thomas Antoni,
Gert Bastian, Viggo Bentzon, Vibeke Hastrup,
Therese Hojgaard Christensen, Pouel Kern,
Cay Kristiansen **Oscar** Denmark (best
foreign language film) **Cannes Film Festival**
Gabriel Axel (prize of the ecumenical jury—
special mention)

Those familiar with Isak Dinesen's story *Babette's Feast* will surely agree that Gabriel Axel's film—besides being a gem in many other respects—is a superb example of the art of adaptation. Relocating it from a Norwegian town to a tiny village on Denmark's windswept Jutland coast was simply a smart start to Axel's strategy of rethinking the whole relationship that exists between the austere lives led by two elderly sisters who are part of the village's devoutly religious community, and the sumptuous hedonism of the banquet cooked just once for the old folks and their fellow-believers by Babette (Stéphane Audran), the maid who ended up in Jutland as a refugee from the Paris Commune fighting.

How and why Babette came to be there forms the first half of this consistently warm, witty, and wise contemplation of love, faith, and art. The second half comprises the preparation and (initially very wary) enjoyment of the unsung wizard's cuisine. Like Babette (and Prospero, who seems to have inspired Dinesen's creation), Axel proved himself something of a magician with this modest but enormously resonant, big-hearted movie; but he was helped no end by his actors, several of them familiar from Bergman and Dreyer classics. And Audran, herself famously a gourmet, clearly savors every moment of her mouthwateringly exquisite performance. **GA**

1987

Good Morning, Vietnam Barry Levinson, 1987

U.S. (Silver Screen, Touchstone)
119m Color **Producer** Larry Brezner, Mark
Johnson **Screenplay** Mitch Markowitz
Photography Peter Sova **Music** Alex North
Cast Robin Williams, Forest Whitaker, Tung
Thanh Tran, Chintara Sukapatana, Bruno
Kirby, Robert Wuhl, J.T. Walsh, Noble
Willingham, Richard Edson, Juney Smith,
Richard Portnow, Floyd Vivino, Cu Ba
Nguyen, Dan Stanton, Don Stanton **Oscar**
nomination Robin Williams (actor)

Rapid-fire stand-up comic Robin Williams, who had been stifling his motor mouth on screen with disappointing results in movies like *Moscow on the Hudson* (1984) and *Popeye* (1980), finally got the chance to let rip in Barry Levinson's comedy drama *Good Morning, Vietnam*. Williams plays real-life U.S. Armed Forces Radio Service DJ Adrian Cronauer, who broadcasts his irreverent, wisecracking jokes (effectively Williams's stand-up routine, delivered sitting down), and Motown music from his base in Saigon to the troops fighting the Vietnam War. He also manages to annoy the military brass in the process—a process which includes a terrific turn from Bruno Kirby as a lieutenant who thinks he is funny but clearly isn't.

There are various subplots: Cronauer's butting heads with his superiors, a romance with a Vietnamese woman, and a friendship with her brother. This is one of the few American-made movies set during the Vietnam War that portrays the Vietnamese as real people. However, the real joy is in watching the inimitable Williams deliver his manic monologues. Many of them were ad-libbed, and director Levinson made the wise decision to sit back and let the camera roll to capture each and every energetic outburst. **JB**

Moonstruck Norman Jewison, 1987

U.S. (MGM) 102m Technicolor
Producer Norman Jewison, Patrick J. Palmer
Screenplay John Patrick Shanley
Photography David Watkin **Music** Dick
Hyman **Cast** Cher, Nicolas Cage, Vincent
Gardenia, Olympia Dukakis, Danny Aiello,
Julie Bovasso, John Mahoney, Louis Guss,
Feodor Chaliapin Jr., Anita Gillette, Leonardo
Cimino, Paula Trueman, Nada Despotovich,
Joe Grifasi, Gina DeAngeles **Oscars** Cher
(actress), Olympia Dukakis (actress in
support role), John Patrick Shanley
(screenplay) **Oscar nominations** Patrick J.
Palmer, Norman Jewison (best picture),
Norman Jewison (director), Vincent Gardenia
(actor in support role) **Berlin International
Film Festival** Norman Jewison (Silver Bear—
director, Golden Bear nomination)

A delightful tribute to the Italian-American family from director Norman Jewison, *Moonstruck* stars singer-turned-actress Cher as widow Loretta Castorini, who is about to be married to safe and reliable (read—dull and boring) Johnny Cammareri (Danny Aiello). While he is away tending to his ailing mother, Loretta takes it upon herself to contact Johnny's estranged brother Ronny (Nicolas Cage) and invite him to the wedding, but when they get to know each other the pair fall in love.

The central love story in this romantic comedy is fun and sparky thanks to two great central performances from Cage and especially Cher (a role for which she won an Oscar). She gets the opportunity to be a modern-day Cinderella, transforming from dowdy duckling to glamour queen after one trip to the hair salon. But it is the supporting players who add even more spice to the proceedings—especially Vincent Gardenia as Loretta's womanizing father Cosmo and Olympia Dukakis as her mother Rose—delivering scriptwriter John Patrick Shanley's words with zest. A much imitated treat that has yet to be bettered. **JB**

Wall Street Oliver Stone, 1987

U.S. (20th Century Fox, Amercent Films,
American Entertainment Partners) 126m
Color **Producer** Edward R. Pressman
Screenplay Stanley Weiser, Oliver Stone
Photography Robert Richardson
Music Stewart Copeland **Cast** Michael
Douglas, Charlie Sheen, Daryl Hannah,
Martin Sheen, Hal Holbrook, John C.
McGinley, Terence Stamp, James Spader,
Richard Dysart, Sean Young, Saul Rubinek
Oscars Michael Douglas (actor)

Michael Douglas was Hollywood royalty and its good guy: a faithful sidekick in *The Streets of San Francisco* and a socially conscious cameraman in *The China Syndrome* (1979). *Romancing the Stone* (1984) added some blemish, but we knew he would eventually do the right thing. Then Oliver Stone cast him in *Wall Street* and gave him a role, like the ones his father took in *Out of the Past* (1947), *Ace in the Hole* (1951), and *The Bad and the Beautiful* (1952), which made us love to hate him.

In an age of bombast, where the moneymen of the world's financial sectors were the rising stars of a new form of capitalism, Oliver Stone was perfectly suited to direct a story about the rot at the core of a very big apple. Charlie Sheen is a young broker, keen to break into the big game. Gordon Gekko is his target and Bud Fox has a soul to sell.

Dedicated to his father, Oliver Stone's financial drama is a guilty entertainment. It reveals little of how this world works, but feeds us enough so as not to be confused. Complexity is conveyed through the use of split screens; in this world, many deals happen at once. You don't say.

Hollywood has made better films about high finance: *Boiler Room* (2000) and *Margin Call* (2011) are two recent examples. When the economic winter of 2008 shrouded the world, Stone returned to Gekko in *Wall Street: Money Never Sleeps* (2010). The thrill was gone. Bud had become an irrelevance; the new, young turk had no fire in his eyes and age had softened the tyrant. But for a moment, as he sidled up against the heft of power and unimaginable wealth, we saw a brief glimpse of the Gordon Gekko that once lit up the screen. **IHS**

The Untouchables Brian De Palma, 1987

U.S. (Paramount) 119m Technicolor
Producer Art Linson **Screenplay** David
Mamet, from the books *The Untouchables* by
Oscar Fraley and Eliot Ness and *The Last of
the Untouchables* by Oscar Fraley and Paul
Robsky **Photography** Stephen H. Burum
Music Ennio Morricone **Cast** Kevin Costner,
Sean Connery, Charles Martin Smith, Andy
Garcia, Robert De Niro, Richard Bradford,
Jack Kehoe, Brad Sullivan, Billy Drago,
Patricia Clarkson, Vito D'Ambrosio, Steven
Goldstein, Peter Aylward, Don Harvey,
Robert Swan **Oscar** Sean Connery (actor in
support role) **Oscar nominations** Patrizia
von Brandenstein, William A. Elliott, Hal
Gausman (art direction), Marilyn Vance
(costume), Ennio Morricone (music)

🛈

Kevin Costner was coached for his
portrayal of Eliot Ness by one of the
"real" Untouchables, Albert H. Ness.

It's Prohibition-era Chicago, and someone has to sort out those pesky
gangsters running around town. That man, of course, is Eliot Ness (Kevin
Costner), a Treasury agent who sets up his own special unit, with the help
of an assortment of cops and crime fighters, to bring down the bad guys
and, most notably, the baddest of them all, Al Capone (Robert De Niro).

Director Brian De Palma's vision of the crime ridden Windy City is
bloodier than many that have gone before—including the TV drama on
which this movie is loosely based—but he doesn't let the gore detract
from the story, or from the performances of his cast. Costner successfully
holds his own against two powerhouse turns from De Niro and Sean
Connery (who won an Oscar as Best Supporting Actor). Connery, as
world-weary cop Malone, has the best of David Mamet's dialogue, most
notably the "he sends one of yours to the hospital, you send one of his
to the morgue" speech. In another "Method outing," De Niro packed on
the pounds and wore suits (and, rumor has it, underpants) made by
Capone's tailors to get a true feel for the character.

Filled with eye-widening set pieces—the Odessa Steps sequence at
the train station and Capone's meeting that ends with punishment by
baseball bat—*The Untouchables* remains a fascinating and gripping look
at a particularly bloody piece of American history. **JB**

Hong gao liang Zhang Yimou, 1987
Red Sorghum

Winner of the Golden Bear at the 1988 Berlin International Film Festival, Zhang Yimou's feature from the People's Republic of China mixes local history and legend. It follows the adventures of a young girl (Gong Li) who is sold by her father to an elderly and wealthy leper, then carried off by a chair bearer posing as a highwayman, eventually becoming the head of a sorghum-wine distillery.

Red Sorghum is the first feature directed by the cinematographer of *Yellow Earth* (1984), *The Big Parade* (1986), and *Old Well* (1986). One of the leading members of the famous "Fifth Generation" of Chinese filmmakers, Zhang has been widely considered the most versatile of the group because of his background in cinematography and acting (he was the lead in *Old Well*). Many of *Red Sorghum*'s most striking virtues are visual: handsome CinemaScope compositions of landscapes and sorghum waving in the wind, and a deft use of color filters.

Narrated offscreen by the heroine's grandson, the plot is set in the late 1920s and early 1930s and ends with the Japanese invasion. Although the action is often intriguing—lyrical in the early sections, whimsical toward the middle, and bloody and suspenseful toward the end—the overall narrative gets broken up quite a bit by the episodic structure, and the film registers mainly as detachable set pieces.

The film presents the debut of Gong Li, who went on to become one of the major actresses of mainland Chinese cinema and starred in subsequent Zhang features. Like Zhang's early features with Gong, especially *Ju Dou* (1990) and *Raise the Red Lantern* (1991), *Red Sorghum* is concerned both covertly and overtly with the persistence of feudalism in the life of mainland China. **JRos**

China (Xi'an) 91m Eastmancolor **Language** Mandarin **Producer** Tian-Ming Wu **Screenplay** Jianyu Chen, Wei Zhu, from the books *Red Sorghum* and *Sorghum Wine* by Yan Mo **Photography** Changwei Gu **Music** Jiping Zhao **Cast** Gong Li, Wen Jiang, Rujun Ten, Liu Jia, Cunhua Ji, Ming Qian, Yimou Zhang **Berlin International Film Festival** Yimou Zhang (Golden Bear)

"It wants to splash its passionate colors all over the screen . . . and the sheer visual impact of the film is voluptuous."

Roger Ebert,
Chicago Sun-Times, **1989**

1987

Born in Shenyang in 1965, Gong Li graduated from Beijing's Central Academy of Drama in 1989.

Fatal Attraction Adrian Lyne, 1987

U.S. (Paramount) 123m Technicolor
Producer Stanley R. Jaffe, Sherry
Lansing **Screenplay** James Dearden
Photography Howard Atherton
Music Maurice Jarre **Cast** Michael Douglas,
Glenn Close, Anne Archer, Ellen Hamilton
Latzen, Stuart Pankin, Ellen Foley, Fred
Gwynne, Meg Mundy, Tom Brennan, Lois
Smith, Mike Nussbaum, J.J. Johnston,
Michael Arkin, Sam Coppola, Eunice Prewitt
Oscar nominations Stanley R. Jaffe, Sherry
Lansing (best picture), Adrian Lyne (director),
James Dearden (screenplay), Glenn Close
(actress), Anne Archer (actress in support
role), Michael Kahn, Peter E. Berger (editing)

Director Adrian Lyne made men all over the world squirm in their seats, and added the term "bunny boiler" to our vocabulary with this (let's face it, misogynistic) nightmare film. Dan Gallagher (Michael Douglas) has a one-night stand with colleague Alex Forrest (Glenn Close) while his wife and kids are away. Alex wants more than a one-night stand, however, and her ever-increasing dementia about rejection finally erupts to destroy what she can never have: a proper, picket-fence, all-American family. It seems that all a high-powered independent woman in the 1980s really ever wanted was to be June Cleaver, but failing that, "June-with-a-cleaver" would do nicely.

Fatal Attraction is a wonderful example of what happens when big-budget Hollywood tries its hand at the exploitation market. With a less flashy, style-over-substance director like Lyne and without stars like Douglas and Close, this would be a typical run-of-the-mill, almost straight-to-video thriller, perhaps even marketed as a slasher film. But with typical Hollywood gloss, the film earns an aura of respectability—this appears not to be a horror movie, but a domestic drama-cum-suspense thriller, with (perhaps) erotic overtones. The ruse worked and this was one of the most successful films of 1987, winning six Oscar nominations and grossing $320,145.693 worldwide. **MK**

1987

The Dead John Huston, 1987

G.B. (Liffey, Zenith) 83m Color
Producer Wieland Schulz-Keil, Chris
Sievernich **Screenplay** Tony Huston, from
story by James Joyce **Photography** Fred
Murphy **Music** Alex North **Cast** Anjelica
Huston, Donal McCann, Dan O'Herlihy,
Donal Donnelly, Helena Carroll, Cathleen
Delany, Ingrid Craigie, Rachael Dowling,
Marie Kean, Frank Patterson, Maria
McDermottroe, Sean McClory, Kate O'Toole,
Maria Hayden, Bairbre Dowling **Oscar
nominations** Tony Huston (screenplay),
Dorothy Jeakins (costume)

The late John Huston devoted the better part of his career to a cinema predicated on the adaptation of literary works—informed by crafty casting and fluid storytelling, but often limited by the fact that his attraction to heavyweights like *The Maltese Falcon* (1941), *The Red Badge of Courage* (1951), *Moby Dick* (1956), *The Man Who Would Be King* (1975), *Wise Blood* (1979), and *Under the Volcano* (1984) guaranteed "faithful" reductions at best. His last film, *The Dead*, which adapts the final story in James Joyce's *Dubliners*—one of the greatest examples of English-language literature, by one of Huston's favorite authors—represents the apotheosis of this position: isolating the story from the rest of the collection and most of its flawlessly composed language, and then doing his best with what remains.

Working with a script by his son Tony and starring his daughter Anjelica as Gretta Conroy, Huston hews to the original and much of its dialogue with rigorous affection, and within its acknowledged restrictions, the film's concentrated simplicity and purity achieve a kind of perfection. The lilting Irish flavor is virtually decanted, and Fred Murphy's gliding camera movements are delicately executed. There is also a rather awesome directness as well as calmness about the way that Huston contemplates his own rapidly approaching death. **JRos**

Bull Durham Ron Shelton, 1988

U.S. (Mount) 108m Color **Producer** Mark Burg, Thom Mount **Screenplay** Ron Shelton **Photography** Bobby Byrne **Music** Michael Convertino **Cast** Kevin Costner, Susan Sarandon, Tim Robbins, Trey Wilson, Robert Wuhl, William O'Leary, David Neidorf, Danny Gans, Tom Silardi, Lloyd T. Williams, Rick Marzan, George Buck, Jenny Robertson, Gregory Avellone, Garland Bunting **Oscar nomination** Ron Shelton (screenplay)

Writer-director Ron Shelton brought his own experiences as a minor league baseball player to this smart, madly sexy comedy, and used his directorial debut to share his passions for baseball, lusty women, and small-timers with big hearts.

The central character in *Bull Durham* is baseball groupie, amateur philosopher, and uninhibited, well-read Annie (Susan Sarandon). She selects a player from the Durham Bulls each year to share her bed and benefit from her life wisdom (sometimes tying her partner to the bed to read him Walt Whitman). Having chosen dim-witted rookie Ebby "Nuke" LaLoosh (Tim Robbins), a pitcher with "a million dollar arm and a five cent brain," she belatedly realizes that a veteran catcher nearing the end of his career, cynical Crash Davis (Kevin Costner), would have been the classier option. Meanwhile Crash gives Nuke manlier advice, providing several of the best laughs as he wearily expounds on meeting the media and avoiding foot fungus in curt, mid-game seminars on the pitcher's mound. Naturally this is really about the big game of life, with witty, sassy dialogue, highly engaging performances, an amusing soundtrack, and absolutely sizzling sex scenes between Sarandon and Costner (although it was Robbins who became her off-screen partner). **AE**

Hôtel Terminus: Klaus Barbie et son temps
Hotel Terminus: The Life and Times of Klaus Barbie
Marcel Ophüls, 1988

France / U.S. (Samuel Goldwyn, Memory) 267m Color **Language** French / English / German / Spanish **Producer** Marcel Ophüls **Screenplay** Marcel Ophüls **Photography** Reuben Aaronson, Pierre Boffety, Daniel Chabert, Michael J. Davis, Paul Gonon, Hans Haber, Lionel Legros, Wilhelm Rösing **Cast** Klaus Barbie, Claude Lanzmann, Jeanne Moreau, Marcel Ophüls **Oscar** Marcel Ophüls (documentary) **Cannes Film Festival** Marcel Ophüls (FIPRESCI award, tied with Krótki film o zabijaniu) **Berlin International Film Festival** Marcel Ophüls (peace film award)

Marcel Ophüls devised a new kind of Holocaust documentary in *The Sorrow and the Pity* (1969), letting interviews and montages speak for themselves without the aid of voice-over narration.

He innovated further in *The Memory of Justice* (1976), bringing in more of his personal reactions to the film's subject—the Nuremberg war-crimes trials. In *Hotel Terminus*, he took the radical step of centering a four-and-a-half-hour film on a Nazi who had successfully eluded photographers throughout his career. Equally uncompromising was Ophüls's decision not to use Holocaust atrocity footage, on the grounds that it has lost some of its impact after decades of exposure.

Hotel Terminus gains more than it loses from the near-invisibility of its protagonist and from Ophüls's insistence on evoking Holocaust evils through verbal testimony rather than filmic and photographic evidence. His choices have uncommon moral clarity if one believes that the enormity of Holocaust suffering ultimately defies media representation, and that cinema's big-screen charisma inevitably risks giving historical horrors a measure of aesthetic allure. A work of art in every sense, *Hotel Terminus* is among the most rigorous as well as the most accessible documentaries about the Nazi era. **DS**

Mujeres al borde de un ataque de nervios
Women on the Verge of a Nervous Breakdown
Pedro Almodóvar, 1988

Thanks to the Oscar nomination it received for Best Foreign Language Film, *Women on the Verge of a Nervous Breakdown* confirmed Almodóvar's international status. It certainly improves on the most worthy aspects of his previous works: the radical subjectivity of feelings, the exaggeration of emotions, and the bizarre mixture of melodrama and comedy.

The story's premises belong to melodrama. Pepa Marcos (Carmen Maura) and her lover Iván (Fernando Guillén) make their living dubbing films. One day he announces that he wants to break things off. Deciding to meet him one last time for an explanation, Pepa investigates Iván's family life and discovers that his wife, recently released from a psychiatric hospital, plans on killing him. Despite his betrayal, Pepa runs to the airport, where he is about to take off with his new love, and saves his life. Iván tries to make up with Pepa but she turns him down.

Although *Women on the Verge* is full of melodramatic situations, the way Almodóvar develops it reveals his particular sense of humor, based mostly on the eccentric characters populating the film. While Pepa is on the phone investigating her missing lover, her apartment fills with all sorts of people: Candela (María Barranco), a friend who is running from the police because she had an affair with a Shiite terrorist; a stuttering young man who wants to rent the apartment after Pepa moves out; and Iván's mad wife, with a gun in her purse. Everyone is so desperate, and the sheer accumulation of such despair in one place is so exaggerated we can only roar with laughter. The quid-pro-quos and the vaudeville situations might make the movie seem like a farcical comedy, but Almodóvar's sure touch is there to make the difference, with its exaltation of kitsch, excessive colors, and hyperbole.

Women on the Verge is a moving female monologue about happiness and loneliness. Loosely inspired by Jean Cocteau's 1930 play *The Human Voice*, the film showcases the tremendous talent of Almodóvar's muse, Carmen Maura. Nor should we forget Antonio Banderas, who took an important step here toward international stardom. **DD**

Spain (El Deseo, Laurenfilm) 90m Eastmancolor **Language** Spanish **Producer** Pedro Almodóvar **Screenplay** Pedro Almodóvar **Photography** José Luis Alcaine **Music** Bernardo Bonezzi, C. Curet Alonso, Ventura Rodríguez **Cast** Carmen Maura, Antonio Banderas, Julieta Serrano, Rossy de Palma, María Barranco, Kiti Manver, Guillermo Montesinos, Chus Lampreave, Yayo Calvo, Loles León, Ángel de Andrés López, Fernando Guillén, Juan Lombardero, José Antonio Navarro, Ana Leza **Oscar nomination** Spain (best foreign language film) **Venice Film Festival** Pedro Almodóvar (Golden Osella— screenplay)

> *"All my movies have an autobiographical dimension, but that is indirectly, through the personages."*
>
> **Pedro Almodóvar**

1988

i

Almódovar was born in the Spanish province of La Mancha—a region made famous by *Don Quixote*.

De spannendste nederlandse film sinds 'De Lift'.

Genomineerd voor de Europese Oscar.

BESTE FILM VAN 1988

Bekroond met de Grote Prijs van de Nederlandse film.

SPOORLOOS

Een Film van George Sluizer
naar de roman Het Gouden Ei, van Tim Krabbé

JOHANNA TER STEEGE · GENE BERVOETS
BERNARD PIERRE DONNADIEU · GWEN ECKHAUS

Fotografie TONI KUHN Muziek HENNY VRIENTEN Uitgebracht door
THE MOVIES/METEOR FILM Shot on FUJI Lab. HAGHEFILM

Netherlands / France (Argos, Golden Egg, Ingrid, MGS, Movie Visions) 107m Color
Language Dutch / French / English
Producer George Sluizer, Anne Lordon
Screenplay Tim Krabbé, George Sluizer, from the novel *The Golden Egg* by Tim Krabbé
Photography Toni Kuhn **Music** Henny Vrienten **Cast** Bernard-Pierre Donnadieu, Gene Bervoets, Johanna ter Steege, Gwen Eckhaus, Bernadette Le Saché, Tania Latarjet, Lucille Glenn, Roger Souza, Caroline Appéré, Pierre Forget, Didier Rousset, Raphaeline, Robert Luclbello, David Bayle, Doumee

"Sometimes I imagine she's alive."

**Rex Hofman
(Gene Bervoets)**

ℹ

The Vanishing is the most well known and highly regarded example of Dutch thriller cinema.

Spoorloos George Sluizer, 1988
The Vanishing

The Golden Egg, a best-selling novel published in 1984 by Dutch journalist and author Tim Krabbé, served as the source material for director George Sluizer's highly acclaimed thriller *The Vanishing*. Like the book, the film tells the story of Rex Hofman (Gene Bervoets), a young Dutchman whose girlfriend Saskia (Johanna ter Steege) mysteriously disappears while the couple are on vacation in central France. Obsessed with finding out what happened to her, Rex single-handedly launches an international missing-persons campaign that completely takes over his life.

Years later, long after the trail has gone cold and the police have closed the case, Rex still scours the countryside out of guilt and as a tribute to Saskia, alienating and eventually losing his new girlfriend in the process. Saskia's unlikely abductor, a French chemistry teacher named Raymond Lemorne (Bernard-Pierre Donnadieu) turns up with an offer to tell all, but only if Rex agrees in advance to undergo the exact same experience as his girlfriend. Rex hesitantly agrees because the worst thing of all is "not knowing." Raymond explains that he did indeed kill Saskia, not for sexual or personal reasons, but merely because he wanted to find out if he was capable of committing such an evil act. Rex willingly takes a sedative, and in the film's penultimate scene, awakens to find himself buried alive inside a narrow coffin. *The Vanishing* ends with a slow zoom in on a newspaper headline concerning the mysterious "double vanishing" of Rex and Saskia, while Raymond sits contemplatively at his cottage, his unsuspecting wife watering the plants that mark the couple's otherwise anonymous graves.

Despite its adherence to the mystery/horror/suspense form, and its international promotion and reception as an example of contemporary Hitchcockian moviemaking, *The Vanishing*'s plaintive score, melodramatic tone, and focus on subjectivity rather than detection all serve to make the film extremely difficult to analyze in traditional generic terms. Sluizer's picture fits most comfortably as part of a cycle of distinctively Dutch "thrillers," all of which possess an essentially national, culturally specific dimension. Other entries in this cycle include Paul Verhoeven's *The Fourth Man* (1983), Dick Maas's *The Lift* (1983) and *Amsterdamned* (1987), and, to some extent, Marleen Gorris's *Broken Mirrors* (1984).

Despite their incorporation of conventions from disparate genres, and the undeniable presence of auteurist elements in each, it is possible to identify an underlying thematic preoccupation across all of these films. The male protagonists suffer an anxiety about being bound to a female partner in a normal relationship—the expectation or reality of marriage and all it legally and socially entails, namely monogamy, heterosexuality, and lifelong commitment. As with the Italian giallo, Dutch thriller cinema is not so much a genre as a body of films resisting simple generic definition. **SJS**

1988

Neco z Alenky Jan Svankmajer, 1988
Alice

Czechoslovakia / Switzerland / G.B. / Germany (Channel Four, Condor, Hessischer Rundfunk, SRG) 86m Eastmancolor Language Czech / English Producer Peter-Christian Fueter Screenplay Jan Svankmajer, from the novel *Alice in Wonderland* by Lewis Carroll Photography Svatopluk Maly Cast Kristyna Kohoutová

In his characteristically bizarre and hyperimaginative manner, Czech filmmaker, animator, and puppet maker extraordinaire Jan Svankmajer captures the feel of Lewis Carroll's children's tale *Alice in Wonderland* while still managing to convey several "adult" and culturally specific themes. The creative force behind many of his country's most celebrated shorts—including *Dimensions of Dialogue* (1982), *Down to the Cellar* (1983), and *The Pit, the Pendulum and Hope* (1983)—Svankmajer here finds ideal inspiration in the protosurrealist story of little Alice (played by young Kristyna Kohoutová, who enters a world of strange creatures and animals and constantly questions the (il)logic of all she encounters.

In Svankmajer's conception, the disposable products of domestic life (such as rulers, socks, jars, and buttons) become the raw material for gothic splendor. And Lewis's familiar characters—such as the White Rabbit, the Mad Hatter, and the March Hare—are here more creepy than charming; as one critic writes, "they're partly enchanted, partly haunted, and there's a hint of the morphologist's lab in them, a trace of formaldehyde." Finally, however, Alice is less an adaptation than an exercise in auteurism, as Svankmajer finds new ways of treating his familiar obsessions with the inhumanness of routine and the vulgarity and danger of overeating. **SJS**

Ariel Aki Kaurismäki, 1988

Finland (Villealfa) 73m Eastmancolor Language Finnish Producer Aki Kaurismäki Screenplay Aki Kaurismäki Photography Timo Salminen Music Esko Rahkonen, Rauli Somerjoki Cast Turo Pajala, Susanna Haavisto, Matti Pellonpää, Eetu Hilkamo, Erkki Pajala, Matti Jaaranen, Hannu Viholainen, Jorma Markkula, Tarja Keinänen, Eino Kuusela, Kauko Laalo, Jyrki Olsonen, Esko Nikkari, Marja Packalén, Mikko Remes

A woman (Susanna Haavisto), impulsively quitting her job and going off with a retrenched miner (Turo Pajala), remarks: "Hopefully, I won't regret this." Later, as the man enters jail for a murder he didn't commit, he declares he has no religion, no fixed address, no family or friends. One of his newfound criminal colleagues dies trying to flee the country, uttering these famous last words: "Bury my heart on a tip."

If anyone has perfected the cinematic language to express drollness, it is Finnish director Aki Kaurismaki. His films have a sardonic, deadpan, couldn't-care-less air that belies the real depth of their commitment to society's marginals. *Ariel,* one of his best works of the 1980s, is a relentless parable of hard luck befalling ordinary people. Yet these characters never lament or protest their lot; the best they expect is a ticket to somewhere, anywhere, else.

At certain moments of his career, Kaurismaki has seemed, especially in his public pronouncements, incurably flip. But *Ariel*'s bleak outlook and its determinedly minimal means (approaching the austerity of Robert Bresson) reveal a more authentic engagement with his subject matter. *Ariel* makes for hypnotic viewing, forecasting the greatness that Kaurismaki would achieve in his 2002 film *Man Without a Past*. **AM**

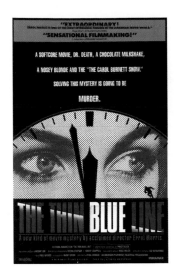

The Thin Blue Line Errol Morris, 1988

Errol Morris's third documentary feature (after *Gates of Heaven* [1978] and *Vernon, Florida* [1981]) is an absorbing if problematic reconstruction of an investigation into the 1976 murder of a Dallas policeman. As an investigative detective-journalist who spent many years working on this case, Morris uncovered a disturbing miscarriage of justice in the conviction of Randall Adams—who came very close to being executed, but was saved as a result of this film. Morris goes so far in his talking-head interview technique that he eventually goads David Harris, Adams's companion on the night of the murder in question, into something very close to a confession.

It's the latter achievement that makes *The Thin Blue Line* as memorable and as important as it is. But it is worth bearing in mind that Morris's highly selective approach also leaves a good many questions unanswered. The issue of motive is virtually untouched, and the quasi-abstract re-creations of the crime, accompanied by what is probably the first effective film score ever composed by Philip Glass, give rise to a lot of metaphysical speculations that, provocative as they are, tend nevertheless to overshadow many of the issues about what actually happened during the crime.

The results are compelling, even though they provide an object lesson in the dangers of being influenced by Werner Herzog; the larger considerations and the film noir overtones wind up distracting us from the facts of the case, and what emerges are two effective half-films, each of which is partially at odds with the other. Yet one can also see Morris honing his flair for juxtaposition and editing that would eventually bear fruit in his remarkable 1997 film *Fast, Cheap & Out of Control*, where he manages to juggle the continuities and discontinuities between four seemingly unrelated talking heads, and in the multiple achievements of his episodes in the TV series *First Person* (2000), which has already enjoyed two seasons. **JRos**

U.S. (American Playhouse) 103m Color
Producer Mark Lipson **Screenplay** Errol Morris **Photography** Robert Chappell, Stefan Czapsky **Music** Philip Glass **Cast** Randall Adams, David Harris, Gus Rose, Jackie Johnson, Marshall Touchton, Dale Holt, Sam Kittrell, Hootie Nelson, Dennis Johnson, Floyd Jackson, Edith James, Dennis White, Don Metcalfe, Emily Miller, R.L. Miller

"He don't give a damn if you're innocent, he don't give a damn if you're guilty. He's talking ... about killing you."

**Randall Adams
(playing himself)**

1988

i

In light of evidence uncovered by this film, David Harris recanted and Randall Adams was freed from prison.

1988

Akira Katsuhiro Ôtomo, 1988

Katsuhiro Ôtomo's animated masterpiece *Akira* is the pinnacle of Japanese apocalyptic science fiction. The plot is deceptively simple: in the chaotic future of Neo-Tokyo (named for its replacing the original Tokyo, destroyed by a mysterious cataclysm in the late twentieth century), Kaneda, a teenage motorcycle gang member, finds his former best friend Tetsuo transformed into a homicidal telepath with the will and the power to kill hundreds. He reluctantly joins a group of antigovernment terrorists in their search for the mysterious Akira, a telepath even more powerful than Tetsuo.

Ôtomo's genius lies in linking the apocalypse with the rage of disaffected teenagers. After all, for a teenager, every emotion is apocalyptic. So imagine if a teenager had telekinetic powers that increase exponentially with his emotions, and imagine that this teenager were the most angry, resentful little bastard you've ever met. Think about that and then think about the most epic scenes of devastation you could possibly imagine, and you have this film. The energy-rush action of Akira is more than a 200 mph adrenaline ride. It provides the sugarcoating for some serious exploration of ideas and metaphors that preoccupy the Japanese psyche, namely social collapse, malaise, and the continuing ambivalence toward military power. It's not an accident that the chief opposing forces in the story are delinquent teenage bikers, would-be revolutionaries, and the military.

Most of all, *Akira*'s story is fueled by society's fear of its youth—wild, uncontrollable, chaotic youth. Tetsuo is the ultimate pissed-off teen, one with enough power to garner himself a body count in the dozens, and there's a reason the government and the army are terrified of the enigmatic Akira, forever frozen in an arrested childhood. This is adolescence causing destruction on an epic scale, drawing on memories of the atom bombs dropped on Japan in World War II, and our continuing collective fears of annihilation. The fascination that Japanese pop culture has with the Apocalypse goes beyond mere flirtation and leaps headlong into mad, dirty, monkey sex every chance it gets, which isn't necessarily very healthy, but certainly makes for some excellent stories. **AT**

Japan (Akira, Dragon, Nakamura, Telecom Animation, Tokyo Movie) 124m Color **Language** Japanese **Producer** Shunzo Kato, Yoshimasa Mizuo, Ryohei Suzuki **Screenplay** Katsuhiro Ôtomo, Izô Hashimoto **Photography** Katsuji Misawa **Music** Shoji Yamashiro **Cast** Mitsuo Iwata, Nozomu Sasaki, Mami Koyama, Tesshô Genda, Hiroshi Ôtake, Kôichi Kitamura, Michihiro Ikemizu, Yuriko Fuchizaki, Masaaki Ôkura, Tarô Arakawa, Takeshi Kusao, Kazumi Tanaka, Masayuki Katô, Yôsuke Akimoto, Masato Hirano

"The most expensive animated feature ever made in Japan and it's easily the most impressive, as well."

Richard Harrington,
The Washington Post, **1989**

i

The production budget for *Akira* was nearly $10 million—a record sum for a Japanese animation film.

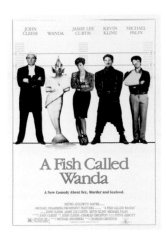

A Fish Called Wanda Charles Crichton, 1988

A Brit named George (Tom Georgeson), his American girlfriend Wanda (Jamie Lee Curtis), her Yankee lover Otto (Kevin Kline), and George's stuttering English minion Ken (Michael Palin) together rob a jewelry vault. Untrusting and untrustworthy, they're each criminal amateurs with secretly developed cross-purposes and internal alliances. So Wanda and Otto double-cross George by framing him for the crime, although Ken unwittingly intercedes and hides the ill-gotten treasure in his aquarium.

When George is brought to trial and defended by Archie (John Cleese), a frustrated lawyer, Wanda resolves to seduce the good magistrate and learn the secret of her gang's stolen booty. Complications quickly develop, perhaps none more aggressively funny than Ken's several attempts to dispatch dog owner Mrs. Coady (Patricia Hayes), the one witness connecting George with the crime. Mixed in for good measure are Otto's play-acted gay come-ons to Ken, Archie's browbeaten home life, Archie and Wanda's developing love affair interrupted at every turn by Otto's bumbling jealousy, and an airport finale with flight to a leisurely future the prize for all comers.

A caper comedy of manners and not so subtle Anglo-American cultural disconnects, the success of Charles Crichton's *A Fish Called Wanda* lay in its treatment of stereotypical gangster types. First is the absurd motif of the piece that rests on the communications skills of a man with a lifetime stutter (Ken). Then there's a psycho killer (Otto) rendered as an oversensitive nincompoop manipulated by a femme fatale (Wanda) with a debilitating erotic weakness for romance languages. Last is the straight-laced hero (Archie), no more than a cloistered man with great passions, but also someone with an almost pathological knack for receiving the butt end of bad luck situations.

Laughs aside, *A Fish Called Wanda* offers a triumphant reappraisal of one-time scream queen Curtis as a comic actress while providing a launch pad for Kline's ascent into critical circles as an awards-worthy performer. Effortlessly, but most of all humorously, the film elevated the careers of Monty Python alums John Cleese and Michael Palin and made them Hollywood stars in the genre. **GCQ**

1988

U.S. (MGM, Prominent, Star) 108m Technicolor **Language** English / Italian / Russian **Producer** Michael Shamberg **Screenplay** John Cleese, Charles Crichton **Photography** Alan Hume **Music** John Du Prez **Cast** John Cleese, Jamie Lee Curtis, Kevin Kline, Michael Palin, Maria Aitken, Tom Georgeson, Patricia Hayes, Geoffrey Palmer, Cynthia Cleese, Mark Elwes, Neville Phillips, Peter Jonfield, Ken Campbell, Al Ashton, Roger Hume **Oscar** Kevin Kline (actor in support role) **Oscar nominations** Charles Crichton (director), John Cleese, Charles Crichton (screenplay)

"To call you stupid would be an insult to stupid people! I've known sheep that could outwit you."

Wanda Gershwitz (Jamie Lee Curtis)

𝑖

The poem Archie recites in Russian to Wanda is "Molitiva," by Russian poet Mikhail Lermontov (1814–41).

Une histoire de vent Joris Ivens, 1988
A Tale of the Wind

Reading over the filmography of Joris Ivens, it's hard to believe that a single filmmaker made all his films. Here was an artist who was an active member of the first European avant-garde film movement; who filmed the first Soviet Five-Year Plan (*Komsomolsk* [1932]), the Spanish Civil War (*The Spanish Earth* [1937]), and the American New Deal (*Power and the Land* [1940]); and who made one of the first essential anticolonialist films (*Indonesia Calling* [1946]). Such a life was not without its contradictions—few artists could claim to have been awarded both the International Lenin Prize and the rank of Commander of the French Légion d'Honneur. Therefore, it's so wonderfully appropriate that his final film, *A Tale of the Wind*, which he codirected with his wife and filmmaking partner Marceline Loridan, is one of the most graceful and haunting works of self-reflection in cinema.

Having witnessed during his ninety years enough for ten lifetimes, this "flying Dutchman" turned his camera on perhaps his most elusive subject—himself. A lifelong asthmatic begins with some thoughts on the breath that sustains his and all life, and that is manifest in the world as the wind. Like Ivens himself, the wind knows no boundaries, naturally linking peoples, cultures, and continents. Ivens's exploration eventually brings him back to China, site of several of his greatest films, where he sets out to find the Dragon, mythic representative of the wind, in order to learn its secret. There are bumps along the way; some Party officials do all they can to very politely stop him from shooting, while at times nature has to be coaxed into cooperating with the filmmakers' project. Unable to film the magnificent terracotta warriors of the Qin Dynasty, Ivens and Loridan conjure up their own artifacts, even staging a Busby Berkeley–ish number with them. Moving between documentary, fiction, mythology, philosophy, and sheer whimsy, Loridan and Ivens created with their epitaph one of the most magnificently "free" films ever made, a fitting tribute to one of the cinema's true originals. **RP**

Netherlands / G.B. / France / Germany (Air France, Capi, Channel Four, La Sept, NOS, NDR, Stichting, Documentaire, TF1, WDR) 80m Color **Language** French **Screenplay** Joris Ivens, Marceline Loridan Ivens **Photography** Thierry Arbogast Jacques Loiseleux **Music** Michel Portal **Cast** Henxiang Han, Joris Ivens, Guilian Liu, Zhuang Liu, Hong Wang

"Miss Loridan said that she and Ivens were working in a 'no man's land between Lumiere and Melies."

Caryn James,
The New York Times, 1989

🛈
The movie, the Dutch filmmaker's last, premiered at the 65th Venice Film Festival in September 1988.

The Naked Gun David Zucker, 1988

U.S. (Paramount) 85m Technicolor
Producer Robert K. Weiss **Screenplay** Jerry
Zucker, Jim Abrahams, David Zucker,
Pat Proft, from television series by Jerry
Zucker, Jim Abrahams, David Zucker
Photography Robert M. Stevens **Music** Ira
Newborn **Cast** Leslie Nielsen, Priscilla
Presley, George Kennedy, Ricardo
Montalban, O.J. Simpson, Raye Birk, Susan
Beaubian, Nancy Marchand, Jeannette
Charles, Ed Williams, Tiny Ron, "Weird Al"
Yankovic, Leslie Maier, Winifred Freedman,
Joe Grifasi

David Zucker, Jim Abrahams, and Jerry Zucker, the team behind the 1980 blockbuster hit *Airplane!*, first introduced the world to bumbling cop Frank Drebin (Leslie Nielsen) with the comic TV series *Police Squad* in 1982. But it was this feature-length parody of the traditional cop show six years later that turned Nielsen's Drebin into a star, spawning two successful sequels.

The cop who always gets his man—usually by complete accident—is assigned to a new case: Investigating criminal mastermind Victor Ludwig (Ricardo Montalban), who plans to assassinate Queen Elizabeth II at a baseball game. (What, you expected the plot to make sense?!) Aiding him is the beautiful Jane (Priscilla Presley, showing a deft comic touch) and an assortment of oddballs including Police Captain Ed Hocken (George Kennedy) and Drebin's partner Nordberg (former football star O.J. Simpson, six years before his notorious trial).

The jokes are dumb and dumber, the spoofs and sight gags coming thick and fast as everything from the American National Anthem to classic movies like *Casablanca* (1942) are skewered by Zucker/Abrahams/Zucker's hilariously silly script. Stupid—but in a good way. **JB**

1988

Nuovo cinema paradiso Giuseppe Tornatore, 1988
Cinema Paradiso

Italy / France (Cristaldifilm, Ariane, RAI, TF1)
155m Color **Language** English / Italian
Producer Mino Barbera, Franco Cristaldi,
Giovanna Romagnoli **Screenplay** Giuseppe
Tornatore **Photography** Blasco Giurato
Music Andrea Morricone, Ennio Morricone
Cast Antonella Attili, Enzo Cannavale, Isa
Danieli, Leo Gullotta, Marco Leonardi,
Pupella Maggio, Agnese Nano, Leopoldo
Trieste, Salvatore Cascio, Tano Cimarosa,
Nicola Di Pinto, Roberta Lena, Nino Terzo
Oscar Italy (best foreign language film)
Cannes Film Festival Giuseppe Tornatore
(grand prize of the jury, tied with *Trop belle
pour toi*, Golden Palm nomination)

Marked by an autobiographical touch, this second movie by Italian director Giuseppe Tornatore is a nostalgic evocation of his childhood days, but also of those happy times before television when people used to go to the cinema. It tells the story of a filmmaker who, after being told by his mother that "Alfredo died," starts to remember the 1950s, when as a boy living in a small Sicilian village, he spent almost all his time in the Cinema Paradiso. While there he became friends with the projectionist Alfredo (Philippe Noiret, in one of his best roles), a father substitute who, after being blinded during a fire, continued to do his job with help from the child. Everything in their village revolves around the cinema, a place of entertainment, but also of meeting and chatter.

The personalities of the Paradiso audience are quizzically charming, especially that of the priest, Father Adelfio (played by Leopoldo Trieste), who assumes the censor's role, cutting out the "daring" scenes. In the esteemed traditions of Neorealism and Italian comedy, *Cinema Paradiso* finds an excellent balance between humor and nostalgia. Echoing François Truffaut's *The 400 Blows* (1959), the image of a happy childhood nurtured by the tones of movies reveals Tornatore's gratitude to the masters of cinema. The film is enjoyable and heartwarming, especially for the relationship between the boy and the projectionist. **DD**

Hotaru no haka Isao Takahata, 1988
Grave of the Fireflies

Japan (Ghibli) 93m Technicolor
Language Japanese **Producer** Tohru Hara
Screenplay Isao Takahata, from novel by
Akiyuki Nosaka **Music** Yoshio Mamiya
Cast Tsutomu Tatsumi, Ayano Shiraishi,
Yoshiko Shinohara, Akemi Yamaguchi,
Rhoda Chrosite, Amy Jones, J. Robert
Spencer, Veronica Taylor

With an attention to craft and design absent from so much mainstream Western animation, several Japanese animators have subverted the traditionally child-oriented nature of cartoons (at least that's how they're often perceived) into grand achievements equal to any big-budget, live-action film. In fact, as Isao Takahata's *Grave of the Fireflies* readily attests, sometimes these animated films actually surpass their live-action equivalents, finding narrative freedom, emotional honesty, and a greater sense of artistic control on the plane of a two-dimensional set.

A harrowing and painful story of the horrors of war, *Grave of the Fireflies* follows two Japanese children orphaned after the firebombing of their village during World War II. Yet the film seems less interested in accusing the military of villainy in the name of battle and more interested in showing the often-silent victims of war, the innocent children left fending for themselves as hell rains down from above. Remarkably, *Grave of the Fireflies* debuted on a double-bill with Hayao Miyazaki's much lighter *My Neighbor Totoro*, and indeed it is hard to imagine audiences of children, let alone adults, making it through this powerful and disturbing film without being overwhelmed by sadness and disappointment in the seeming inevitability of human conflict. **JKl**

Film critic Roger Ebert considers *Grave of the Fireflies* one of the most powerful war films ever made.

Big Penny Marshall, 1988

U.S. (Fox, Gracie) 104m Color
Producer James L. Brooks, Robert Greenhut
Screenplay Gary Ross, Anne Spielberg
Photography Barry Sonnenfeld
Music Howard Shore Cast Tom Hanks,
Elizabeth Perkins, Robert Loggia, John
Heard, Jared Rushton, David Moscow, Jon
Lovitz, Mercedes Ruehl, Josh Clark,
Kimberlee M. Davis, Oliver Block, Erika Katz,
Allan Wasserman, Mark Ballou, Gary Howard
Klar Oscar nominations Gary Ross, Anne
Spielberg (screenplay), Tom Hanks (actor)

When young Josh (David Moscow) is refused a ride on a fairground rollercoaster, he puts a quarter in a carnival wishing machine and wishes he were big. Next morning, it seems Josh's dream has come true—sort of—when he wakes up to find himself in the body of a thirty-something (and definitely taller) man (Tom Hanks). Fleeing his home when his mother fails to recognize him (and in fact suspects him of being her son's abductor), big Josh has to go out into the adult world on his own with only his boyish innocence to help him.

Hanks would go on to win Best Actor Academy Awards two years running for *Philadelphia* (1993) and *Forrest Gump* (1994), but this is arguably his best performance. Perfectly capturing the mannerisms of a pre-teen boy (Hanks watched his "younger self," Moscow, playing with costar Jared Rushton, and copied his behavior), Hanks portrays overgrown Josh as a gangly innocent who believably charms his way into a job—at a toy company, of course. While the ending gets a little schmaltzy, director Penny Marshall otherwise keeps the three-hanky stuff to a minimum and gets maximum humor from her cast, especially in the pairing of Hanks and Rushton (as Josh's schoolboy pal), and the casting of Robert Loggia (as the toy firm's owner) and John Heard (as Josh's conniving business rival). **JB**

1988

Who Framed Roger Rabbit Robert Zemeckis, 1988

U.S. (Amblin, Silver Screen, Touchstone)
103m Color Producer Frank Marshall,
Robert Watts Screenplay Jeffrey Price,
Peter S. Seaman, from the novel *Who
Censored Roger Rabbit?* by Gary K. Wolf
Photography Dean Cundey Music Alan
Silvestri Cast Bob Hoskins, Christopher
Lloyd, Joanna Cassidy, Charles Fleischer,
Stubby Kaye, Alan Tilvern, Richard
LeParmentier, Lou Hirsch, Betsy Brantley, Joel
Silver, Paul Springer, Richard Ridings, Edwin
Craig, Lindsay Holiday, Mike Edmonds
Oscars Charles L. Campbell, Louis L.
Edemann (special sound effects), Ken
Ralston, Richard Williams, Ed Jones, George
Gibbs (special visual effects), Arthur Schmidt
(editing), Richard Williams (special
achievement award —animation direction
and creation of the cartoon characters)
Oscar nominations Elliot Scott, Peter Howitt
(art direction), Dean Cundey (photography),
Robert Knudson, John Boyd, Don
Digirolamo, Tony Dawe (sound)

Although live action and animation had shared the screen before—most notably when animated mouse Jerry (of *Tom and Jerry* fame) danced with Gene Kelly in *Anchors Aweigh* (1945)—director Robert Zemeckis and animation director Richard Williams skillfully blended the two into this feature-length comedy thriller that still looks technically flawless decades after it was made.

Gruff, seedy-looking private eye Eddie Valiant, memorably played by Bob Hoskins at his grumpy best, doesn't like Toons, the animated characters who live in the Toontown suburb of Los Angeles. So he is less than pleased when he is hired by film studio boss Marvin Acme (Stubby Kaye) to check into the activities of his star, a sexy cartoon named Jessica Rabbit (smokily voiced by Kathleen Turner). Eddie is even less impressed by her excitable rabbit husband, Roger (voice of Charles Fleischer), especially when the mismatched pair are plunged into a hilarious tangle of murder and blackmail.

Smartly characterized, by both the human and animated cast, and wittily scripted by Jeffrey Price and Peter S. Seaman, *Who Framed Roger Rabbit* is an action comedy just like the classic Warner cartoons it pays homage to: bursting with fun, deliciously surreal, and watchable many times over. It won three well-deserved Oscars. **JB**

Dekalog, jeden Krzysztof Kieslowski, 1988
The Decalogue

Poland (Polish TV) 53m color
Language Polish **Producer** Ryszard
Chutkowski **Screenplay** Krzysztof
Kieslowski, Krzysztof Piesiewicz
Photography Wieslaw Zdort
Music Zbigniew Preisner **Cast** Henryk
Baranowski, Wojciech Klata, Maja
Komorowska, Artur Barcis, Maria
Gladkowska, Ewa Kania, Aleksandra
Kisielewska, Aleksandra Majsiuk,
Magda Sroga-Mikolajczyk

"A masterwork of modern cinema, essential viewing for anyone who cares about the movies as a serious art form."

Stephen Holden,
***The New York Times*, 2000**

i

Kieslowski was made a Fellow of the British Film Institute in 1990 for his contribution to film culture.

Polish director Krzysztof Kieslowski was that rare filmmaker who could mix politics, comedy, religion, tragedy, and metaphysics into his works without coming across as either pretentious or silly. But sadly, just as the director was finally beginning to taste the fruits of international success, he died unexpectedly in 1996 at the early age of fifty-four.

Although Kieslowski was the creator of many masterpieces, including *The Double Life of Veronique* (1991) and the *Three Colors* trilogy (*Blue* [1993], *White* [1994], and *Red* [1994]), *The Decalogue* may be his most profound and perfect work. Originally filmed for Polish television, *The Decalogue* is a collection of ten hour-long short films, each ambitiously featuring a story based loosely on one of the Ten Commandments and all set in the same bleak Warsaw apartment complex.

Many of Kieslowski's earlier works obliquely addressed the political realities of Poland at the time, but with *The Decalogue* the director aims for something grander and more universal. The collection addresses the concepts of fate, chance, and faith through the intersection of different lives—children, parents, siblings, and strangers—seeking to illuminate the invisible threads that tie us together but also the feelings and beliefs that connect us to a higher power.

In one installment a father and son ponder the place of God in a time dominated by technology. In another, a doctor deliberates the ethics of keeping a patient on life support, when his life or death will forever alter the complicated future of the patient's troubled wife. Two brothers try to honor their estranged father's memory by caring for his priceless stamp collection. A horrifying murder calls into question the ethics of the death penalty. Each installment focuses on a mostly blameless domestic situation, profound quandaries with no right or wrong way out, and Kieslowski carefully follows the different paths his characters take.

Although each of *The Decalogue*'s segments may be attached to a specific Commandment, the connection is rarely clear or obvious. Kieslowski seems more interested in how those ancient rules apply when considered in the not always cut-and-dried context of contemporary, everyday life. Each installment shares certain thematic similarities, even if they possess slightly different aesthetics. As with his later *Three Colors* trilogy, the various episodes of *The Decalogue* sometimes also share the same actors, actors whose presence helps connect the disparate (and without exception compelling) stories.

Working in close tandem with his regular screenwriter Krzysztof Piesiewicz, composer Zbigniew Preisner, and nine different cinematographers, Kieslowski achieves that rare feat: a seamlessly unified diverse anthology that gets closer than almost any other film to what it means to be human. Compelling, intelligent, and poetic, *The Decalogue* is a true work of art that teaches even as it entertains. **JKl**

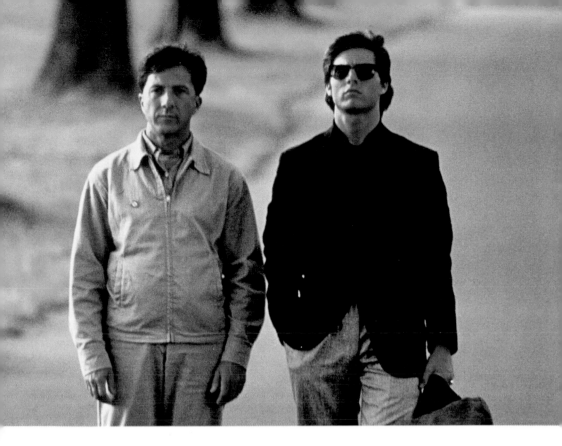

Rain Man Barry Levinson, 1988

U.S. (Mirage, Star II) 133m Color
Producer Mark Johnson **Screenplay** Ronald
Bass, Barry Morrow **Photography** John Seale
Music Ian Gillan, Roger Glover, Doc Pomus,
Hans Zimmer **Cast** Dustin Hoffman, Tom
Cruise, Valeria Golino, Gerald R. Molen, Jack
Murdock, Michael D. Roberts, Ralph Seymour,
Lucinda Jenney, Bonnie Hunt, Kim Robillard,
Beth Grant, Dolan Dougherty, Marshall
Dougherty, Patrick Dougherty, John-Michael
Dougherty **Oscars** Mark Johnson (best
picture), Barry Levinson (director), Ronald Bass,
Barry Morrow (screenplay), Dustin Hoffman
(actor) **Oscar nominations** Ida Random,
Linda DeScenna (art direction), John Seale
(photography), Stu Linder (editing), Hans
Zimmer (music) **Berlin International Film
Festival** Barry Levinson (Golden Bear, reader
jury of the *Berliner Morgenpost*)

i

Dustin Hoffman prepared for this
role by working with autistic men.

Numerous writers and directors had tinkered with the script of *Rain Man*
before director Barry Levinson came on board. Many believed the story
of a used-car salesman trying to befriend his autistic brother on a cross-
country journey so he can get his hands on the latter's multimillion
dollar inheritance just too difficult to bring to the screen. Even the film's
eventual stars, Dustin Hoffman and Tom Cruise, seemed worried about
the movie's outcome when they dubbed it "Two Schmucks in a Car"
during shooting.

Levinson luckily didn't balk at the idea of making a film with little
dramatic story, instead focusing on the human development that is at
the picture's heart. Traveling across country with the autistic Raymond
(Hoffman) because Raymond won't fly, Charlie Babbitt (Cruise) gradually
gets to understand the brother he hardly knows and in the process
develops a sense of decency he didn't have before. Hoffman captures
his character's autism without going overboard on the nervous tics, but
most impressive here is Cruise, who holds his own alongside a more
experienced actor and expertly depicts a shallow man who finally finds
some depth in his life. **JB**

40 STORIES OF SHEER ADVENTURE!

High
above
the city of L.A.
a team of terrorists
has seized a building,
taken hostages, and
declared war.

One man has managed to escape.
An off-duty cop hiding somewhere inside.

He's alone, tired.
and the only chance anyone has got.

BRUCE WILLIS

DIE HARD

U.S. (Fox, Gordon, Silver) 131m Color
Language English / German / Italian
Producer Lawrence Gordon, Joel Silver
Screenplay Jeb Stuart, Steven E. de Souza,
from the novel *Nothing Lasts Forever* by
Roderick Thorp **Photography** Jan de Bont
Music Michael Kamen **Cast** Bruce Willis,
Bonnie Bedelia, Reginald Veljohnson, Paul
Gleason, De'voreaux White, William
Atherton, Hart Bochner, James Shigeta, Alan
Rickman, Alexander Godunov, Bruno Doyon,
Andreas Wisniewski, Clarence Gilyard Jr.,
Joey Plewa, Lorenzo Caccialanza **Oscar
nominations** Stephen Hunter Flick, Richard
Shorr (special sound effects), Richard Edlund,
Al Di Sarro, Brent Boates, Thaine Morris
(special visual effects), Frank J. Urioste,
John F. Link (editing), Don J. Bassman,
Kevin F. Cleary, Richard Overton,
Al Overton Jr. (sound)

*"Nine million terrorists
in the world and I gotta
kill one with feet smaller
than my sister."*

**John McClane
(Bruce Willis)**

ℹ️

The scene where McClane falls down
a shaft was a mistake: the stuntman
was meant to grab the first vent.

Die Hard   John McTiernan, 1988

Before *Die Hard*, Bruce Willis was just an actor with one hit TV show (*Moonlighting*) and a flop movie (*Blind Date* [1987]) to his name, but following *Die Hard*'s huge success, he deservedly became one of Hollywood's hottest stars.

His cocky charm breathes life into the character of John McClane, a New York cop visiting his estranged wife Holly (Bonnie Bedelia) at her office in Los Angeles, just as the building falls into the control of a group of ruthless terrorists led by Hans Gruber (Alan Rickman). While all the office workers—staying late for the company Christmas party—are herded into one area by the bad guys, our hero (who was in the bathroom when the assault begins) is off and running around the partially incomplete tower. In his own words, he is "a fly in the ointment, a monkey in the wrench, a pain in the ass" to the terrorists who aren't quite sure who is attacking them or how he got loose.

John McTiernan—who previously helmed the Arnold Schwarzenegger alien-action movie *Predator* (1987) —packs his skyscraper adventure with explosions, fights, and relentless action, as our antihero (he smokes, curses, and bloodily despatches the bad guy) picks off the terrorists by listening in on their walkie-talkies in an attempt to figure out their nefarious plan.

McTiernan, along with writers Jeb Stuart and Steve DeSouza (adapting a Roderick Thorpe novel), effectively redefines the action movie as a one-man-army. Willis quips his way through a series of clever setups and payoffs (when McClane takes his shoes and socks off at the beginning of the movie to combat jet lag, you just know his bare feet are going to be a plot device later, and they are), his undershirt getting dirtier by the second. His only pal is a flat-footed cop (Reginald Veljohnson) whom he communicates with by radio, whereas most of the other police officers and federal agents are either too dumb or too trigger-happy to realize what's really going on.

Superbly acted by Willis as a guy who really would rather be somewhere else, McClane is a hero for the 1990s who has continued to mutter his "yippee-ki-yay motherfucker" catchphrase in three enjoyable sequels. A true rollercoaster ride of a movie. **JB**

Dangerous Liaisons Stephen Frears, 1988

U.S. / G.B. (Lorimar, NFH, Warner Bros.) 119m
Eastmancolor **Producer** Norma Heyman,
Hank Moonjean **Screenplay** Christopher
Hampton, from novel by Choderlos de
Laclos and play by Christopher Hampton
Photography Philippe Rousselot
Music George Fenton **Cast** Glenn Close,
John Malkovich, Michelle Pfeiffer, Swoosie
Kurtz, Keanu Reeves, Mildred Natwick, Uma
Thurman, Peter Capaldi, Joe Sheridan,
Valerie Gogan, Laura Benson, Joanna Pavlis,
Nicholas Hawtrey, Paulo Abel Do
Nascimento, François Lalande
Oscars Christopher Hampton (screenplay),
Stuart Craig, Gérard James (art direction),
James Acheson (costume)
Oscar nominations Norma Heyman, Hank
Moonjean (best picture), Glenn Close
(actress), Michelle Pfeiffer (actress in
support role), George Fenton (music)

Christopher Hampton translated his own acclaimed play *Les Liaisons Dangereuses* (itself based on a Choderlos de Laclos novel) into *Dangerous Liaisons*, a sumptuous, decadent drama of eighteenth-century French sexual intrigue, brought to life on screen by director Stephen Frears.

Glenn Close steals the show as the vicious and vindictive Marquise de Merteuil, whose main enjoyment in her bored, rich life is to conspire with the equally cynical Vicomte de Valmont (John Malkovich). Their latest scheme involves the virginal Cécile (Uma Thurman) and the pure Madame de Tourvel (Michelle Pfeiffer), but Valmont's attempts to ruin them both for his own pleasure is complicated when he falls for the unsuspecting Madame.

Frears leads us into the boudoirs and drawing rooms of the wealthy aristocracy, each one dripping with elegance and wickedness in equal measure. Close is perfectly acid tongued, Malkovich both seductive and slimy, and the cast rounded out by the unusual casting of Keanu Reeves (better known for more modern roles) as Chevalier Danceny, just one of the poor fellows caught up in Valmont's machinations. A handsome look at lust, betrayal, and guilt, *Dangerous Liaisons* is both lavishly mounted and beautifully portrayed. **JB**

1988

Dead Ringers David Cronenberg, 1988

Canada (Morgan Creek) 115m Color
Producer Marc Boyman, David Cronenberg
Screenplay David Cronenberg, Norman
Snider **Photography** Peter Suschitzky
Music Howard Shore **Cast** Jeremy Irons,
Geneviève Bujold, Heidi von Palleske,
Barbara Gordon, Shirley Douglas, Stephen
Lack, Nick Nichols, Lynne Cormack, Damir
Andrei, Miriam Newhouse

One of the coolest and most controlled of David Cronenberg's films, *Dead Ringers* explores his perennial theme of bodily penetration not through the visceral gore and horror of his earlier work but through the seemingly clinical medium of gynecology. Jeremy Irons plays identical twin gynecologists, Elliot and Beverly Mantle, who run a fertility clinic in Toronto. Elliot, an extrovert who is self-confident, seduces his patients and, when he's tired of them, passes them on to his shy, insecure twin. The women never know the difference. But when hedonistic junkie actress Claire Niveau (Geneviève Bujold) enters their lives, their perverse symbiotic dependency is undermined.

Inspired by a real-life event, Cronenberg creates a fragile interior world of emotional and psychological vulnerability, structured and lit in such a way as to suggest an aquarium: The outside world is held precariously at bay, and disintegration threatens the mind even more than the body. Claire's physical peculiarity foreshadows the three-way disruption that will destroy the brothers' relationship, and their lives.

With the help of split-screen techniques, Irons gives a masterly double performance, ensuring by subtle variations in stance, voice, and gesture that we're never in any doubt which twin we're seeing. His tour de force, and Cronenberg's quiet, insidious intensity, forge a film that's even more disturbing to think about in retrospect than it is to watch. **PK**

RoboCop Paul Verhoeven, 1988

U.S. (Orion Pictures) 102m
Color Producer Louis D. Lighton
Screenplay Edward Neumeier, Michael
Miner Photography Charles Lang
Music Ernst Toch Cast Peter Weller, Nancy
Allen, Dan O'Herlihy, Ronny Cox, Kurtwood
Smith, Miguel Ferrer, Robert DoQui, Ray
Wise, Felton Perry, Paul McCrane, Jesse Goins
Oscars Stephen Hunter Flick, John Pospil
(sound effects editing) Oscar nominations
Frank J. Urioste (editing), Michael J. Kohut,
Carlos Delarios, Aaron Rochin,
Robert Wald (sound)

Hollywood may be a cynical place, but it rarely welcomes cynicism in its films. All the more remarkable, then, that a studio should lavish a big budget on a Dutch filmmaker who was known in his own country for films that indulged in sex, violence, and depravity. But perhaps it recognized the brilliance in Edward Neumeier and Michael Miner's script, and understood that no Hollywood director could do it justice.

Crime has brought the America of tomorrow to its knees. In Detroit, Omni Consumer Products, which owns the city's police department, unveils its latest weapon: a half-man, half-robot cop, trained in all aspects of the justice system. However, the rot of corruption on both sides of the law leaves the new defender fighting alone in the battle to save the city.

RoboCop's strength lies in its subversiveness; the film is one of the finest satires of Western culture that Hollywood produced in the 1980s. Punctuating the action sequences, a series of advertising breaks question the values of a consumer-obsessed society. Each of them, from sunscreen that will likely cause cancer and a car security system that electrocutes thieves, to a nuclear war game for the family, are merely an exaggeration of real commercials. Likewise, the blurred line between corporate malfeasance and criminal activity is all too believable, while the notion that law enforcement could become privatized has become a reality. **IHS**

Distant Voices, Still Lives Terence Davies, 1988

G.B. 84 mins Producer Colin MacCabe,
Jennifer Howarth Screenplay Terence
Davies Photography William Diver and
Patrick Duval Music Various Cast Freda
Dowie, Pete Postlethwaite, Angela Walsh,
Lorraine Ashbourne, Dean Williams
Cannes International Critics' Prize

Distant Voices, Still Lives (1988) remains Terence Davies' masterpiece. One of the finest features ever produced in the UK, it's a highly distinctive marriage of style and content, combining the social concerns of much British cinema with formal and existential preoccupations more readily associated with European art cinema.

An autobiographical work, the film examines the life of a working-class family in Liverpool, encompassing the wedding of the elder daughter, the christening of the younger daughter's infant child, and the secondment into the armed forces of the family's son. Presiding over the family is the sadistic father (Pete Postlethwaite), who is always too quick with his fists, and the long-suffering, loving mother (Freda Dowie).

Unfolding as a series of meticulously constructed vignettes, told from the perspectives of different members of the same family, *Distant Voices, Still Lives* is rich in poetry, emotion, and performance. An affecting work, in which ordeal and sufferance are brilliantly juxtaposed with passages of intense happiness and communal spirit, it is also the film with which Davies established his ability to write incredible female characters. 1940s Liverpool is beautifully rendered by the use of a muted palette, which gives a hand-tinted look to certain scenes. The director's visual aesthetic is all the more impressive given the film's modest budget. **JWo**

When Harry Met Sally Rob Reiner, 1989

When Harry Met Sally provides indisputable proof, if it were needed, that all the right ingredients—a skilled comic director (Rob Reiner), great script (Nora Ephron), and brilliant casting (Billy Crystal, Meg Ryan)—do add up to a damn-near perfect piece of film entertainment.

Sharing a postcollege car journey from Chicago to New York in 1977, smart-mouthed Harry (Crystal) announces to snobbish Sally (Ryan) that they will never be friends because, in his often skewed logic, "men and women can't be friends because the sex part always gets in the way." At the end of the trip, the pair go their separate ways, only to cross paths a few years later in an airport and then again when she is on the verge of breaking up with her boyfriend and he has split up with his wife. Of course, they do eventually become friends, and it is inevitable that they become more than that before the movie's end—but that is half the fun.

A romantic comedy that tips its cap to Woody Allen movies like *Annie Hall* (1977), this is brought right up to date by Ephron's witty dialogue that accurately depicts the modern-day dating game. Harry learns the drawbacks of dating a younger woman when he asks a girl where she was when Kennedy was shot only to get the reply, "Ted Kennedy's been shot?" Against the backdrop of the most cinematic of cities, New York, scene upon scene is either a classic or features memorable dialogue and is played expertly by the two leads: Sally's fake orgasm in the deli, after which a woman at a neighboring table (played by Reiner's own mother) says, "I'll have what she's having," and the store karaoke session when Harry bumps into his ex-wife are just two examples. Excellent support roles include Bruno Kirby as Harry's pal and Carrie Fisher as Sally's.

A triumph for all involved—Nora Ephron (who died in 2012) didn't write another script to match this Oscar-nominated one—the film turned Ryan into a highly sought-after leading lady and made Harry Connick Jr., who performs the film's 1930s and 1940s standards (including "It Had to be You") on the soundtrack, a bona fide star (it won him his first Grammy Award, for Best Jazz Male Vocal Performance). **JB**

U.S. (Castle Rock, Columbia, Nelson) 96m Color **Producer** Rob Reiner, Andrew Scheinman **Screenplay** Nora Ephron **Photography** Barry Sonnenfeld **Music** Marc Shaiman **Cast** Billy Crystal, Meg Ryan, Carrie Fisher, Bruno Kirby, Steven Ford, Lisa Jane Persky, Michelle Nicastro, Gretchen Palmer, Robert Alan Beuth, David Burdick, Joe Viviani, Harley Jane Kozak, Joseph Hunt, Kevin Rooney, Franc Luz **Oscar nomination** Nora Ephron (screenplay)

"You know, you may be the first attractive woman I've not wanted to sleep with in my entire life."

Harry Burns
(Billy Crystal)

i

The famous orgasm scene was filmed at a real restaurant—Katz's Deli in E. Houston Street, New York.

CRIMES AND
MISDEMEANORS

CAROLINE AARON   ALAN ALDA
WOODY ALLEN   CLAIRE BLOOM
MIA FARROW   JOANNA GLEASON
ANJELICA HUSTON   MARTIN LANDAU
JENNY NICHOLS   JERRY ORBACH
SAM WATERSTON "CRIMES
AND MISDEMEANORS"

JACK ROLLINS | CHARLES H. JOFFE
JULIET TAYLOR | JEFFREY KURLAND
SUSAN E. MORSE | SANTO LOQUASTO
JACK ROLLINS   SVEN NYKVIST
CHARLES H. JOFFE   ROBERT GREENHUT
WOODY ALLEN
ORION

U.S. (Rank, Orion) 107m Color
Producer Robert Greenhut
Screenplay Woody Allen
Photography Sven Nykvist **Music** Bach,
Schubert **Cast** Bill Bernstein, Martin
Landau, Claire Bloom, Stephanie Roth,
Gregg Edelman, George J. Manos, Anjelica
Huston, Woody Allen, Jenny Nichols, Joanna
Gleason, Alan Alda, Sam Waterston, Zina
Jasper, Dolores Sutton, Joel Fogel **Oscar
nominations** Woody Allen (director), Woody
Allen (screenplay), Martin Landau
(actor in support role)

> "Crimes and
> Misdemeanors *is a
> thriller about the dark
> nights of the soul."*
>
> **Roger Ebert,**
> *Chicago Sun-Times,* **1989**

Crimes and Misdemeanors Woody Allen, 1989

Woody Allen in winning philosophical form (coming off *September* [1987] and *Another Woman* [1988], two of his bleaker dramas, made back-to-back and both coolly received) tackles life, death, truth, love, God, and all things Dostoyevskian in *Crimes and Misdemeanors*. A wonderful cast plays out a plot constructed like a set of Chinese boxes for a novel on film about close encounters of the Upper East Side kind. Handsomely shot by Ingmar Bergman's regular cinematographer Sven Nykvist, with Allen making striking use of music by Schubert and Bach as well as the jazz and swing favorites we associate with him.

Two apparently quite different stories dovetail at the last moment. Judah Rosenthal, a respected eye surgeon (played by Martin Landau in a brilliant, Oscar-nominated role), is an adulterer desperate to discard his angry mistress Dolores (Anjelica Huston) when she threatens to make a mess of his well-ordered, comfortable, and hypocritical life. Meanwhile, Allen's documentary filmmaker Cliff Stern's attempts to woo Mia Farrow's Halley are frustrated by his insufferable brother-in-law, Lester (a marvelous turn by Alan Alda), a practiced charmer who makes sitcoms and is, incidentally, the subject of Cliff's current film. The big questions are Judah's to ponder when his shady brother (Jerry Orbach) offers to take the Dolores situation in hand—homicidally. Around his dilemma a network of family, friends, and brief acquaintances expose themselves, suffer, love, struggle, and crack deathless one-liners.

Allen in his familiar existentialist, angst-ridden Manhattan intellectual nebbish persona unsurprisingly delivers the best of these in the bittersweet comedic strand: "He wants to produce something of mine," trills Farrow. "Yes," worries Allen, "your first child!" More unusually, weighty, realistic, tragic drama and comedy of manners mingle in a uniquely sophisticated, ambitious discussion of values, morality, and law. Allen, firing on all cylinders, steers through pain, profundity, and outrageous humor with his inimitable, signature style, addressing good and evil, guilt and retribution, movies versus reality, and swell cocktail parties with wit and penetration. *Crimes and Misdemeanors* is intricate and adult, dark and delightful, and right up there among his very best work. **AE**

i
Allen wrote this film after feeling he'd been "too nice" to the characters in *Hannah and Her Sisters* (1986).

Batman Tim Burton, 1989

U.S. / G.B. (PolyGram, Warner Bros.) 126m Technicolor **Producer** Peter Guber, Jon Peters **Screenplay** Sam Hamm, Warren Skaaren, Bob Kane **Photography** Roger Pratt **Music** Danny Elfman, Prince **Cast** Michael Keaton, Jack Nicholson, Kim Basinger, Robert Wuhl, Pat Hingle, Billy Dee Williams, Michael Gough, Jack Palance, Jerry Hall, Tracey Walter, Lee Wallace, William Hootkins, Richard Strange, Carl Chase, Mac McDonald **Oscar** Anton Furst, Peter Young (art direction)

In this blockbuster movie version of Bob Kane's classic comic, director Tim Burton reimagines eponymous superhero Batman (last seen on screen in a campy 1960s TV incarnation) as a dark and conflicted character.

Michael Keaton stars as tortured soul Bruce Wayne, a brooding man who as a child saw his parents killed by muggers in a darkened alleyway. Now a multimillionaire industrialist by day, at night he dons a cape, mask, and knee-high boots to become Batman and right the wrongs of bleak, gothic Gotham City. But is he a superhero or a crazed vigilante? Photojournalist Vicki Vale (Kim Basinger) and reporter Alex Knox (Robert Wuhl) are among those who want to discover Batman's secret identity and find out the truth.

While Burton gives his Caped Crusader depth, darkness, and even romance (in the form of Vicki), the show is almost stolen from his hero by the villain of the piece, the Joker, played with gusto by Jack Nicholson. Resplendent in purple suit and clown-like makeup, dancing to the Prince songs that pepper the soundtrack, he was surely the most enjoyably unlikable bad guy to hit the big screen in a long time. **JB**

1989

Field of Dreams Phil Alden Robinson, 1989

U.S. (Gordon Company, Universal Pictures) 107m Color **Producer** Brian E. Frankish, Charles Gordon, Lawrence Gordon, Lloyd Levin **Screenplay** W.P. Kinsella (writer) Phil Alden Robinson (screenplay) **Photography** John Lindley **Music** James Horner **Cast** Kevin Costner, Amy Madigan, Gaby Hoffmann, Ray Liotta, Timothy Busfield, James Earl Jones, Burt Lancaster, Frank Whaley, Dwier Brown

With the mantra "If you build it, he will come" ringing in his head, Kevin Costner's Iowa farmer acts on the voice emanating from his cornfield and, against the opposition of all those around him, ploughs through his crops to build a baseball diamond. The apparition of legendary batter "Shoeless" Joe Jackson (Ray Liotta) may be the catalyst for Ray's journey to find more players from the game's long, distant past, but his mission is merely a cover for some deeper meaning in Phil Alden Robinson's mythical family drama.

In Ray Kinsella, Kevin Costner embodies the average Joe of middle America. Ray is a more domesticated variation of the sports-obsessed everyman figure Costner played in *Bull Durham* (1988) and other sports-related characters from such films as *Tin Cup* (1996) and *For the Love of the Game* (1999). But *Field of Dreams* is about more than America's obsession with sport – it signaled the beginning of the masculinity-in-crisis era for Hollywood's white alpha male stars.

In opposition to the "hard bodies" of Stallone and Schwarzenegger, Ray's more sensitive soul nostalgically yearns for a time when patriarchal superiority was seemingly infallible, thus defining the search for a new male identity in a post-Reagan era. He is not merely on a voyage of self-discovery, but a quest to find his position in the gender revolution of late-twentieth-century America. The resulting drama perfectly encapsulates the period that witnessed America on the cusp of a new age, when the ideologies it had lived by had finally crumbled away. **JT**

Glory Edward Zwick, 1989

U.S. (TriStar) 122m Technicolor
Producer Freddie Fields **Screenplay** Kevin
Jarre, from the letters of Robert Gould Shaw,
from the books *Lay This Laurel* by Lincoln
Kirstein and *One Gallant Rush* by Peter
Burchard **Photography** Freddie Francis
Music James Horner **Cast** Matthew
Broderick, Denzel Washington, Cary Elwes,
Morgan Freeman, Jihmi Kennedy, Andre
Braugher, John Finn, Donovan Leitch, J.D.
Cullum, Alan North, Bob Gunton, Cliff De
Young, Christian Baskous **Oscars** Denzel
Washington (actor in support role), Freddie
Francis (photography), Donald O. Mitchell,
Gregg Rudloff, Elliot Tyson, Russell Williams
(sound) **Oscar nominations** Norman
Garwood, Garrett Lewis (art direction),
Steven Rosenblum (editing)

Following the bloom of American Civil Rights it became fashionable to resurrect little-known stories from the ravages of time. Edward Zwick's *Glory* is one such exercise meant to rewrite the blank slate of memory.

The film opens on a Civil War battlefield, where former slave John Rawlins (Morgan Freeman) labors to bury dead soldiers. Colonel Robert Shaw (Matthew Broderick), a liberal white blue blood, is thereafter placed in charge of the Union Army's first all-black volunteer company. Into his care are entrusted the raison d'être of the war, slaves and free blacks, each of whom is transformed into a fighting elite finally sent to their doom storming a fort.

Notable for being an inspirational alternative history, *Glory* more importantly showcased a group of outstanding young black actors. Foremost was Denzel Washington in his first Oscar-winning role as Private Trip. Other standouts include Jihmi Kennedy (Private Jupiter Sharts) and Andre Braugher (Corporal Thomas Searles), although the sign of the times is surely the picture's eulogy of sacrifices made on behalf of racial harmony as the salve for present-day racial tensions.

True, *Glory* is consumed with sentimentalism and fatal purpose. But it is equally an antidote for contemporary cynicism, with a heroic true story and a winning score by James Horner. **GC-Q**

The Cook, the Thief, His Wife & Her Lover
Peter Greenaway, 1989

France / Netherlands / G.B. (Allarts, Elsevira,
Erato, Erbograph, Films, Vendex) 124m Color
Producer Kees Kasander **Screenplay** Peter
Greenaway **Photography** Sacha Vierny
Music Michael Nyman **Cast** Richard
Bohringer, Michael Gambon, Helen Mirren,
Alan Howard, Tim Roth, Ciarán Hinds, Gary
Olsen, Ewan Stewart, Roger Ashton-Griffiths,
Ron Cook, Liz Smith, Emer Gillespie, Janet
Henfrey, Arnie Breeveld, Tony Alleff

Taking his dissatisfaction with conservative politics to the extreme, Peter Greenaway devised *The Cook, the Thief, His Wife & Her Lover* as an opulent and decadent riposte to Margaret Thatcher's England. Michael Gambon plays Albert Spica, the monstrous, obnoxious, oafish thief of the title, holding court at a trendy London restaurant, decimating a disgustingly over-the-top banquet while surrounded by numerous sycophants and lackeys. Ignored for too long, his wife Georgina (Helen Mirren) initiates a passionate affair with a quieter, bookish patron (Alan Howard), facilitated by the accommodating chef back in the kitchen. So busy consuming and humiliating his hangers-on, Gambon at first doesn't notice his wife's deception, but once he discovers her adultery he concocts a cannibalistic revenge.

Greenaway directs his film like a tapestry gone wrong, revealing all manner of depravity as he pans back and forth between the kitchen and dining room (with a different color scheme in each locale) in search of a smidgen of good will amid the savagery. *The Cook, the Thief, His Wife & Her Lover* seethes anger and disgust, most of it directed toward the upper class, whose waste and barbarism is portrayed not just as a blight on society but frankly as an affront to good taste. **JKl**

1989

My Left Foot Jim Sheridan, 1989

Despite the strong potential for maudlin depression, *My Left Foot* emerged as a surprisingly entertaining, earthy, funny, and uplifting celebration of Irishman Christy Brown, who was born imprisoned in a body horribly crippled by cerebral palsy but won recognition and respect as an artist and writer. The concept of a disabled man with a surprising intellectual gift clearly has parallels with the fictional *Rain Man* (1988), but *My Left Foot* is at least its equal in every department, not least in the principal performances. Daniel Day-Lewis is riveting in a role as far as he could get from his affected aesthete of *A Room with a View* (1986) or his gay opportunist in *My Beautiful Laundrette* (1985). Brenda Fricker is radiant as Christy's devout, careworn mother. Ray McAnally, who sadly died before the film's release, gave his last rich characterization as Christy's unpredictable, heavy-drinking father. And young Hugh O'Conor as the boy Christy conveys the nightmarish frustration of a bright child, presumed to be an idiot, struggling to communicate with his family.

First-time director Jim Sheridan and cowriter Shane Connaughton don't flinch from the tragedy and rage in Christy's life as a wheelchair-bound wit patronized and subjected to daily humiliations despite his considerable abilities. But their rounded impression of the man leaves an overwhelming sense of the miraculousness of life and of Christy's remarkable spirit. This is underlined by the magical quality injected into the smallest incidents—like the child Christy's wonder when he is borne by his brothers and sisters to their sweet, spooky Halloween street festivities.

The famous left foot is featured in running jokes and dramatic episodes as Christy saves his mother's life, scores goals, paints, fells an adversary in a pub brawl, attempts suicide, lays bricks, and types his autobiography, all with the eponymous appendage. Having mastered the physical difficulties of a rigid, twisted body and impaired speech, he conveys a man whose cleverness brings him little relief, but whose humor, lust, and single-mindedness illuminate what might otherwise have been simply harrowing. **AE**

Ireland / G.B. (Ferndale, Granada, RTE) 98m Technicolor **Producer** Noel Pearson **Screenplay** Shane Connaughton, Jim Sheridan, from book by Christy Brown **Photography** Jack Conroy **Music** Elmer Bernstein **Cast** Daniel Day-Lewis, Brenda Fricker, Alison Whelan, Kirsten Sheridan, Declan Croghan, Eanna MacLiam, Marie Conmee, Cyril Cusack, Phelim Drew, Ruth McCabe, Fiona Shaw, Ray McAnally, Patrick Laffan, Derry Power, Hugh O'Conor **Oscars** Daniel Day-Lewis (actor), Brenda Fricker (actress in support role) **Oscar nominations** Noel Pearson (best picture), Jim Sheridan (director), Shane Connaughton (screenplay)

"Jim Sheridan's My Left Foot *must be the most passionately empathetic film about a physical affliction ever made."*

Hal Hinson,
The Washington Post, 1989

1989

i

Daniel Day-Lewis, as Christy Brown, proved the out-of-left-field Oscar winner who could not be denied.

Die xue shuang xiong John Woo, 1989
The Killer

Although director John Woo, producer Tsui Hark, and star Chow Yun-Fat had worked together previously and had each amassed a body of major work, it was the international success of *The Killer* that established Hong Kong action cinema as a distinct brand. Most of the major creatives then proceeded to up-and-down Hollywood careers, while Western filmmakers like Robert Rodriguez and Quentin Tarantino began lifting elements of their distinctive style—the popular flat-on-his-back, gun-in-each-hand slide is a favorite Chow Yun-Fat move, often imitated by pretenders—to enliven their own action pictures.

The Killer is an action melodrama about an honorable, sentimental hit man (Chow) trying to save enough money from a run of assassinations to pay for an operation to restore the sight of a singer (Sally Yeh) accidentally blinded during one of his hits, while a tough cop (Danny Lee) learns to respect the murderer he's required to track down and finally joins with him for a gruesome glorification. A genocidal film with more corpses than *Total Recall* (1990) and *Die Hard 2* (1990) combined—ironic in that the plot hinges on the lack of suitable cornea donors in Hong Kong—this is a literally astonishing mix of stunts, soap, and sly humor. The comic-book gunplay and violence of the action elements are mixed with an emotional strain that owes something to Douglas Sirk, but the real love story isn't the mild triangle between cop, killer, and blind victim but the almost-gay buddyship that works up between the two male leads.

The original Chinese title translates as *Bloodshed of Two Heroes*, which represents the film rather better than the export title, emphasizing its status as a relationship movie rather than privileging one of its main characters as a solitary figure. It winds up with a scene that establishes Woo's screen personality: a shoot-out in a chapel that sees candles, bullets, and bodies flying across the screen as doves flutter (sometimes in snatches of slow motion) and liturgical music swells, with blotches of blood on bright-white clothes and tears flowing as freely as gore. **KN**

Hong Kong (Film Workshop, Golden Princess, Magnum) 111m Color
Language Cantonese / Japanese
Producer Tsui Hark **Screenplay** John Woo
Photography Peter Pau, Wing-Hung Wong
Music Lowell Lowe **Cast** Chow Yun-Fat, Danny Lee, Sally Yeh, Kong Chu, Kenneth Tsang, Fui-On Shing, Wing-Cho Yip, Fan Wei Yee, Barry Wong, Parkman Wong, Siu-Hung Ng, Sing Yeung, Siu Hung Ngan, Kwong Leung Wong

"The director's greatest gift is his talent for Dexedrine-spiked, apocalyptic action."

Hal Hinson,
The Washington Post, 1991

i

All of the action sequences were improvised on the set with the actors, stuntmen, and stunt director.

Drugstore Cowboy Gus Van Sant, 1989

U.S. (Avenue) 100m Color **Producer** Karen Murphy, Nick Wechsler **Screenplay** Gus Van Sant, Daniel Yost, from novel by James Fogle **Photography** Robert D. Yeoman **Music** Elliot Goldenthal **Cast** Matt Dillon, Kelly Lynch, James LeGros, Heather Graham, Eric Hull, Max Perlich, James Remar, John Kelly, Grace Zabriskie, George Catalano, Janet Baumhover, Ted D'Arms, Neal Thomas, Stephen Rutledge, Beah Richards **Berlin International Film Festival** Gus Van Sant (C.I.C.A.E. award—forum of new cinema)

Gus van Sant's Drugstore Cowboy is a funny and very moving account of addiction. We follow a gang of junkies led by Bob (Matt Dillon) who feed their habits by robbing drugstores in Portland, Oregon. The petty crimes and the repetitive lives of the addicts are chronicled by the director without moralizing or comment. But the fragile nature of the relationships within the gang, and particularly the doomed love of Bob and his wife Dianne (Kelly Lynch), are as well observed as they are brilliantly acted.

While the plot may seem simple—run-ins with police and other junkies—there is real tragedy as the film moves toward its denouement. When one of the gang overdoses and Bob has to smuggle the body out of a motel hosting a sherriff's convention and then bury the body in the woods, he decides that he has to go straight. In the detox hostel he meets up with an old friend, a junkie priest played by William Burroughs, and their conversations punctuate his final encounters with the world he has left. The entire film is magnificent but these final conversations between Dillon and Burroughs are sublime. **CM**

1989

Astenicheskij sindrom Kira Muratova, 1989
The Asthenic Syndrome

U.S.S.R. (Goskino, Odessa) 153m BW / Color **Language** Russian **Screenplay** Aleksandr Chernykh, Kira Muratova, Sergei Popov **Photography** Vladimir Pankov **Music** Franz Schubert **Cast** Olga Antonova, Sergei Popov, Galina Zakhurdayeva, Natalya Buzko, Aleksandra Svenskaya, Pavel Polishchuk, Natalya Ralleva, Galina Kasperovich, Viktor Aristov, Nikolai Semyonov, Oleg Shkolnik, Vera Storozheva, Aleksandr Chernykh, Leonid Kushnir, Nadya Popova **Berlin International Film Festival** Kira Muratova (Silver Bear—special jury prize, Golden Bear nomination)

A great movie about the contemporary world, but far from an easy one to take or understand, because it breaks so many rules about what films are supposed to be like. Directed in 1989 by Kira Muratova, The Asthenic Syndrome has been perhaps rightly called the only "masterpiece of glasnost." It begins with a powerful, black-and-white narrative about a woman doctor named Natasha (Olga Antonova) who is in an exploding, aggressive rage about the death of her husband. The film then turns into an even more unorthodox tale in color about a disaffected high-school English teacher named Nikolai (played by cowriter Sergei Popov) who periodically falls asleep regardless of what is happening around him. The title alludes to a form of weakness or disability that presumably encompasses both the doctor's aggressiveness and the schoolteacher's passivity. Muratova evidently regards these two forms of behavior as emblematic of what is blighted about contemporary society.

Though this epic has plenty to say about postcommunist Russia, it is also one of the few recent masterpieces that deal more generally with the demons loose in today's world. And it is interesting to add that at least two of Muratova's subsequent features, Three Stories (1987) and Chekhov's Motifs (2002), have continued the process of extreme stylization in the acting as well as the practice of squeezing together two or more fictions. Both factors sharply distinguish her late work from such relatively conventional and relatively naturalistic early features as Brief Encounters (1967), in which she acted. **JRos**

Do the Right Thing Spike Lee, 1989

U.S. (40 Acres & a Mule) 120m Color
Producer Spike Lee Screenplay Spike Lee
Photography Ernest R. Dickerson
Music Rubén Blades, Cathy Block, Chuck D,
Flavor Flav, James Weldon Johnson,
Rosamond Johnson, Raymond Jones, Bill
Lee, Sami McKinney, Michael O'Hara, Lori
Perry, Mervyn Warren, Public Enemy
Cast Danny Aiello, Ossie Davis, Ruby Dee,
Richard Edson, Giancarlo Esposito, Spike
Lee, Bill Nunn, John Turturro, Paul Benjamin,
Frankie Faison, Robin Harris, Joie Lee,
Miguel Sandoval, Rick Aiello, John Savage
Oscar nominations Spike Lee (screenplay),
Danny Aiello (actor in support role)
Cannes Film Festival Spike Lee (Golden
Palm nomination)

"Living, breathing, riveting proof of the arrival of an abundantly gifted new talent."

Vincent Canby,
The New York Times, 1989

i

The movie's title comes from a Malcolm X quote: "You've got to do the right thing."

It's sometimes hard to remember, living now on a global, pop-culture landscape that has been so thoroughly sculpted by the language, music, aesthetics, and politics of hip-hop, that there was a time when the force of that youth movement hadn't yet been tapped. At the same time, given the materialistic, shallow artistry that has come to define mainstream hip-hop and the music (rap) that is its soundtrack, it's sometimes just as hard to remember when the music was radical, subversive, and proudly revolutionary. Spike Lee's social protest film *Do the Right Thing* brilliantly captures that moment when rap was urgent and conscious; more impressively, it channels the issues of racism, race pride, class struggle, and the joys and grinds of everyday urban life into a paradoxically brightly colored snapshot. Incendiary and insightful, it's a film borne of hip-hop, when hip-hop had something to say.

The film's opening is set to the music—an assault of beats and booming voices—of hip-hop elders and icons Public Enemy. Filled with a cast of vibrant characters whose intersecting day-in-the-life stories are used to illuminate larger sociopolitical points, *Do the Right Thing* is anchored by Mookie (Lee), a pizza delivery boy who canvases the neighborhood making his deliveries. We meet his shrill, demanding girlfriend (Rosie Perez), cantankerous but lovable elders (Ruby Dee and Ossie Davis), and neighborhood youth as represented by, among others, Radio Raheem (Bil Nunn) and Buggin' Out (Giancarlo Esposito). We also meet the Italian pizzeria owner, Sal (Danny Aiello), whose ambivalence about his black clientele is forked in the differing attitudes of his racist son Pino (John Turturro) and more color-blind child Vito (Richard Edson). Rounding out the characters is a profane, hilarious Greek chorus of middle-aged and elderly black men whose scathing commentary on the day's events provides comic relief.

As the hot summer's day progresses and tempers flare, ordinary slights take on huge significance. Sexual and racial tensions that lie just below the surface of daily exchanges explode, and the resulting fiery violence is a clear metaphor for the state of late twentieth-century American race relations. Controversial and frequently misrepresented by detractors (many of whom claimed that the film was a call to riot), *Do the Right Thing* is an unapologetic, angry film. It's also filled with images of black love and camaraderie that continue to be so rare in American cinema that they're radical. Shot in bright colors that all but pop off the screen, filled with slightly skewed camera angles often suggesting the freewheeling style of comic books, and edited to reflect the energetic thrust of the most propulsive rap track, *Do the Right Thing* has become one of the most influential movies in the history of filmmaking, not only for its stylistic flourishes, but for giving filmmakers permission to draw from the experiences of lives previously ignored or distorted in both Hollywood and so-called independent film. It dares you to dismiss it. **EH**

The Unbelievable Truth Hal Hartley, 1989

U.S. (Action) 90m Color **Producer** Hal Hartley, Bruce Weiss **Screenplay** Hal Hartley **Photography** Michael Spiller **Music** Jim Coleman, Kendall Brothers, Philip Reed, Wild Blue Yonder **Cast** Adrienne Shelly, Robert John Burke, Chris Cooke, Julia McNeal, Katherine Mayfield, Gary Sauer, David Healy, Matt Malloy, Edie Falco, Jeff Howard, Kelly Reichardt, Ross Turner, Paul Schulze, Mike Brady, Bill Sage

The *Unbelievable Truth* is the highly intriguing, if not always fully successful, first feature by independent writer-director Hal Hartley. Shot in his hometown on Long Island, he gives us, among other characters, a mechanic mistaken for a priest (Robert Burke) returning from a prison sentence, a politically alienated teenager (Adrienne Shelly) who later finds work as a model for lingerie ads, and the teenager's mercenary redneck father (Christopher Cooke). Burke, Shelly, and Cooke would go on to work with Hartley again in subsequent features—Burke in *Simple Men* (1992) and *Flirt* (1993), Shelly in *Trust* (1990), and Cooke in *Trust* and *Simple Men*.

Fantasies about global annihilation obsess the teenager, fantasies about money obsess her father, and fantasies about a pair of murders apparently committed by the mechanic obsess almost everyone else in the film. The unvarnished quality of some of the acting limits this effort in spots, but the quirky originality of the story, characters, and filmmaking, and the offbeat, deadpan humor serve to keep the audience curious and alert. **JRos**

Roger & Me Michael Moore, 1989

U.S. (Dog Eat Dog, Warner Bros.) 91m Color **Producer** Michael Moore **Screenplay** Michael Moore **Photography** Chris Beaver, John Prusak, Kevin Rafferty, Bruce Schermer **Music** Buddy Kaye **Cast** James Bond, Pat Boone, Rhonda Britton, Anita Bryant, Karen Edgely, Bob Eubanks, Ben Hamper, Dinona Jackson, Timothy Jackson, Tom Kay, Michael Moore, Kaye Lani Rae Rafko, Ronald Reagan, Fred Ross, Robert Schuller, George Sells, Roger B. Smith, Steve Wilson **Berlin International Film Festival** Michael Moore (peace film award—honorable mention)

Michael Moore's black-comedy documentary about the consequences of massive layoffs by General Motors in Flint, Michigan, and the writer-director's own unsuccessful attempts to meet with Roger Smith, GM's chairman, and bring him to Flint to see what his actions have wrought, is certainly impressive, as well as bracing proof that movies can be both hugely entertaining and politically sharp at the same time. Mixed in with Moore's justifiably lethal anger, however, is a certain sense of glib superiority over Flint's victims and corporate villains, which one is invited to share, but the breezy results, many of which are exhilarating and never boring, are not exactly devoid of cheap shots and journalistic oversimplifications. These qualities could be said to carry over into Moore's second big success, *Bowling for Columbine*, thirteen years later. Thus the cheerful heartlessness of Reaganism that is the film's subject is not entirely irrelevant to its own methods, and critic Dave Kehr aptly dubbed *Roger & Me* around the time of its initial release, "the first feel-good atrocity film."

Roger & Me's rather cavalier manner of juggling certain timeframes and sequences of events led at least one reviewer at the time to dismiss Moore as a charlatan. Despite this there are irrefutable facts in his muckraking. Moore's populist desire to entertain, which ensured his commercial success and the wider reach of his ideas, also entailed some self-aggrandizement as well as a certain number of journalistic shortcuts. In the final analysis it is worth asking which is more important: corporate greed, or Moore's ego trip. **JRos**

U.S. (Outlaw, Virgin) 100m Color
Producer John Hardy Screenplay Steven
Soderbergh Photography Walt Lloyd
Music Cliff Martinez Cast James Spader,
Andie MacDowell, Peter Gallagher, Laura San
Giacomo, Ron Vawter, Steven Brill,
Alexandra Root, Earl T. Taylor, David Foil
Oscar nomination Steven Soderbergh
(screenplay) Cannes Film Festival Steven
Soderbergh (Golden Palm, FIPRESCI award)
tied with Yaaba), James Spader (actor)

"Anyway, being happy
isn't all that great. I
mean, the last time I was
really happy . . . I must
have put on 25 pounds."

Ann (Andie MacDowell)

Sex, Lies, and Videotape Steven Soderbergh, 1989

Writer-director Steven Soderbergh—now best known for *Erin Brockovich* (2000) and the Oscar-winning *Traffic* (2000)—made a striking debut with this drama that went on to win the Golden Palm and Best Actor awards at the 1989 Cannes Film Festival.

Written in just eight days and filmed in five weeks on a budget of just $1.2 million, *Sex, Lies, and Videotape* has been credited with transforming the independent movie industry, enticing mainstream audiences to see small-scale indie films they otherwise would have missed. And this film is certainly unmissable, a sly, sexy, and intelligent look at modern-day relationships set in the steamy South.

Andie MacDowell, in her first leading role following appearances in *St. Elmo's Fire* (1985) and *Greystoke: The Legend of Tarzan* (1984), stars as Ann Millaney, a perfect wife stuck in a dull, almost sexless marriage to John (Peter Gallagher), an egotistical lawyer. Unbeknownst to Ann, John is having an affair with her feisty sister Cynthia (Laura San Giacomo), but all the secrets and lies in their combined relationships are revealed when John's former school friend Graham (James Spader) drives into town and forces the others to face truths about themselves and each other. Graham, of course, has surprises of his own to be exposed—he has a trunk full of videotapes, each featuring a woman talking openly about her sexual secrets. But how did he get all these women to open up to him?

Soderbergh's dialogue is breathtakingly frank, and he fills his film with skilled actors who deliver their lines brilliantly. Former model MacDowell—who has yet to give a better performance—is terrific as the prissy Southern flower, and San Giacomo a discovery as her uninhibited sibling. But the film really belongs to Spader—a former teen actor (Pretty in Pink [1986], *Less than Zero* [1987]) who here shows an unexpected depth and sensitivity as he expertly portrays the most interesting of Soderbergh's repressed quartet. Superb. **JB**

i

Soderbergh's first big break came in 1985 when rock group Yes asked him to shoot a full-length concert film.

Taiwan (Artificial Eye, 3-H, Era) 157m Color
Language Taiwanese / Mandarin / Japanese
Producer Chiu Fu-Sheng **Screenplay** Chu
T'ien-wen, Wu Nien-Jen **Photography** Chen
Huai'en **Music** Tachikawa Naoki **Cast** Wou
Yi Fang, Nakamura Ikuyo, Jack Kao, Tony
Leung Chiu Wai, Li Tianlu, Ikuyo Nakamura,
Xin Shufen **Venice Film Festival** Hou
Hsiao-hsien (Golden Lion)

"By the end of A City
of Sadness, *you realize
Hou sees the world
as it is, in all its
contradictory glory."*

Glenn Heath Jr,
Slant Magazine, **2011**

Beiqing chengshi Hou Hsiao-hsien, 1989
A City of Sadness

There are two separate stories to tell here. One is this wonderful story that happens sometimes, most of the time unpredictably: the rise of a New Wave, of an artistic movement in a country, and of the emergence of one or two (rarely more) exceptionally talented filmmakers. This occurred in the 1980s in Taiwan with the New Cinema movement, and one of the most talented directors who appeared at the time was Hou Hsiao-hsien. He began by making personal, autobiographical films (The Boys from Fengkuei [1983], *A Summer at Grandpa's* [1984], *The Time to Live* and the *Time to Die* [1985]) that revealed his sense of pace, the physical intensity of his shots, and the suggestive strength in the apparently indifferent way he filmed even the most simple situations.

Then there is a second story, concerning that inevitable moment when a nation needs its cinema to tell itself and the world its own tale—its collective autobiography, so to speak. In 1989, the vanishing of the military dictatorship that had ruled the island for forty years presented filmmakers the opportunity to tell the recent story of Taiwan. And this is what Hou, the "subjective avant-garde auteur," decided to do (and what he continued to do with *The Puppetmaster* [1993] and *Good Men, Good Women* [1995]). *A City of Sadness*, which was clearly viewed in its own country as a huge step forward in the ability of cinema to look, finally, at Taiwan's recent past, constitutes a real turning point—a fact which also enabled the film to become a great public success.

A combination of historical fresco and modern film, the complex narrative structure of *A City of Sadness* (based on the intricate lives of four brothers) and the enormous amount of historical information it embodies convey a beautiful and emotional sense of the period, the group, the individual, the inner feelings, and the demands of the various communities each brother belongs to—willingly or not. *A City of Sadness* is not only a masterpiece, it is a model for all those films that intend to show the major events of a country, most of the time becoming boring monuments instead. **J-MF**

ℹ
This was the first Chinese-language film to win the Golden Lion award at the Venice Film Festival.

Trust Hal Hartley, 1990

U.S. / G.B. (Channel Four, Republic, True Fiction, Zenith) 90m Color **Producer** Hal Hartley, Bruce Weiss **Screenplay** Hal Hartley **Photography** Michael Spiller **Music** The Great Outdoors, Philip Reed **Cast** Adrienne Shelly, Martin Donovan, Merritt Nelson, John MacKay, Edie Falco, Gary Sauer, Matt Malloy, Suzanne Costollos, Jeff Howard, Karen Sillas, Tom Thon, Hannah Sullivan, Marko Hunt, Kathryn Mederos, Bill Sage

Hal Hartley's second feature—a decided improvement over his first, *The Unbelievable Truth* (1989)—returns to the same basic turf, a Long Island commuter town, and features the same lead actress (Adrienne Shelly) as an alienated teenager. This time around, Shelly plays a high school student who finds herself pregnant, provokes her father's fatal heart attack, gets unceremoniously dumped by her boyfriend, and kicked out of the house by her mother (Merritt Nelson). Then she is assaulted, witnesses a kidnapping, and meets an angry and disgruntled electronics whiz (Martin Donovan), all in the same day.

It's a credit to the film that this overflow of incident neither strains credibility nor becomes exploited for facile comedy. In fact, the real story in *Trust* only begins once the heroine and the electronics whiz become involved and their mutual adjustments—including the strains represented by their difficult parents—gradually transform both of them. Unpredictable while remaining honest to both its characters and its milieu, this flaky comedy drama improves as it proceeds, much as Hartley's own body of work has often done. **JRos**

1990

S'en fout la mort Claire Denis, 1990
No Fear, No Die

France / Germany (Cinéa, NEF) 97m Eastmancolor **Language** French **Producer** Francis Boespflug, Philippe Carcassonne **Screenplay** Claire Denis, Jean-Pol Fargeau **Photography** Pascal Marti **Music** Abdullah Ibrahim **Cast** Isaach De Bankolé, Alex Descas, Solveig Dommartin, Christopher Buchholz, Jean-Claude Brialy, Christa Lang, Gilbert Felmar, Daniel Bellus, François Oloa Biloa, Pipo Sarguera, Alain Banicles, Valérie Monnet **Venice Film Festival** Dominique Auvray (Silver Osella editing)

French director Claire Denis refers to her films *Chocolat* (1988), *No Fear No Die* (1990), and *I Can't Sleep* (1994) as her trilogy about colonialism and its aftermath. *No Fear, No Die* follows, in a quasidocumentary fashion, a few months in the lives of Dah (Isaach De Bankolé) and Jocelyn (Alex Descas), two black men training roosters for illegal cockfights in the basement of a shady suburban nightclub in France. Besides its underlying portrayal of exploitation of illegal immigrants, the film's claustrophobic, oppressive atmosphere is a fascinating ground for the dynamics of power, violence, desire, and cruelty enacted in this marginal world, as tensions gradually mount between Jocelyn and the nightclub owner's son Michel (Christopher Buchholz). Michel becomes jealous of the attention Jocelyn gets not only from his father, but also from his father's beautiful girlfriend Toni (Solveig Dommartin), whom both men covet.

The rivalry between Jocelyn and Michel, complicated by issues of race and power, finds its brutal resolution in a senseless murder at the end of *No Fear, No Die*, highlighting the absurdity of postcolonial violence. The close and raw filming of the ritual training of roosters, of the protagonists' faces and bodies, as well as the powerful performances of Descas and Bankolé, make this film an intense, intimate experience of a facet of human behavior triggered by circumstances in which "all men, whatever their race, color, or origins, are capable of anything and everything." **CO**

Goodfellas Martin Scorsese, 1990

With this epic, Martin Scorsese returned to the world of tough-talking (mostly) Italian-American hoods featured in *Mean Streets* (1973), following thirty years in the lives of a group of neighborhood crooks. From hanging around the taxi rank, punk kid Henry Hill (Ray Liotta) progresses to hijacking, airport robberies, extortion, grievous bodily harm, drug dealing, and, finally, informing. Along the way, he gets a Jewish wife (Lorraine Bracco) who, unlike the Corleone women, finds it impossible to keep out of the wholesale sleaze that goes along with her husband's way of life. More important, of course, are Henry's close male relationships: with Jimmy (Robert De Niro), a coolly violent heist man, and Tommy (Joe Pesci), an unstable psychopath with hopes of getting "made." In the end, Hill is turned by the FBI and informs on his few surviving friends, winding up condemned to a Federal Witness Protection limbo where if you order spaghetti with marinara sauce you get "egg noodles and ketchup."

Drawn from cowriter Nicholas Pileggi's nonfiction book *Wiseguy*, this is more matter-of-fact in its insider's chattiness than the mythmaking *The Godfather* (1972). Indeed, *Goodfellas* is almost a companion piece to the comical *Married to the Mob* (1988) as it observes the manners and fashions of the organized crime world. Underlaid by a constant barrage of cunningly selected pop singles, from Tony Bennett to Phil Spector to Sid Vicious, this panorama of illegal America stays with a group of wholly repulsive, increasingly corrupt people for nearly two and a half hours but never loses its fascination. De Niro, underplaying in a secondary role, is quietly chilling as the repressed but unpredictable robber who sometimes seems to think he'll only be safe once he has killed everyone he knows. However, the show-off monster is Pesci, who plays the maniacal Tommy as a homicidal Lou Costello, segueing instantly from foul-mouthed rat-tat-tat wisecrack routines into mortifying threats or slap-in-the-face atrocities. Without moralizing, the film manages to convey the dead-end horrors of a life not just outside the law but outside all possible law. **KN**

1990

U.S. (Warner Bros.) 145m
Technicolor **Producer** Irwin Winkler
Screenplay Nicholas Pileggi and Martin
Scorsese, from the novel *Wise Guy* by
Nicholas Pileggi **Photography** Michael
Ballhaus **Music** Various artists
Cast Robert De Niro, Ray Liotta, Joe Pesci,
Lorraine Bracco, Paul Sorvino, Frank Sivero,
Tony Darrow, Mike Starr, Frank Vincent,
Chuck Low, Frank DiLeo, Henny Youngman,
Gina Mastrogiacomo, Catherine Scorsese,
Charles Scorsese **Oscar** Joe Pesci (actor in
support role) **Oscar nominations** Irwin
Winkler (best picture), Martin Scorsese
(director), Nicholas Pileggi, Martin Scorsese
(screenplay), Lorraine Bracco (actress in
support role), Thelma Schoonmaker
(editing) **Venice Film Festival** Martin
Scorsese (Silver Lion—director)

*"As far back as
I can remember,
I always wanted to
be a gangster."*

**Henry Hill
(Ray Liotta)**

i

Martin Scorsese's parents appear in
the film—his mother as Tommy's
mother and his father as a prisoner.

Nema-ye Nazdik Abbas Kiarostami, 1990
Close-Up

Iran (Institute for the Intellectual Development of Children & Young Adults) 97m Color **Language** Farsi **Producer** Ali Reza Zarrin **Screenplay** Abbas Kiarostami **Photography** Ali Reza Zarrindast **Cast** Hossain Sabzian, Mohsen Makhmalbaf, Abolfazl Ahankhah, Mehrdad Ahankhah, Monoochehr Ahankhah, Mahrokh Ahankhah, Nayer Mohseni Zonoozi, Ahmad Reza Moayed Mohseni, Hossain Farazmand, Hooshang Shamael, Mohammad Ali Barrati, Davood Goodarzi, Haj Ali Reza Ahmadi, Hassan Komaili, Davood Mohabbat

Based on a real incident, Abbas Kiarostami's masterly film first appears to present itself as a purely documentary reconstruction of the events leading to the trial of Hossein Sabzian for attempted fraud.

Kiarostami's subtle approach to the narrative comprises a witty, illuminating, highly inventive exploration of the symbiotic relationships between truth and falsehood, appearance and reality, documentary and fiction. The characters are "played" by themselves. Some events are dramatically recreated, some simply described, others—like the trial itself (at which, strangely, Kiarostami is often allowed to take over questioning)—are presented as documentary footage. Although the narrative line, for all its flashbacks, is clear, the way in which it is presented and the status of what we're shown—is this for real, or acted out?—keep shifting, and the film becomes a multilayered investigation into that most elusive of phenomena: the Truth.

But even as he undermines our assumptions about objectivity, Kiarostami directs us toward one small, inescapable truth: that everyone, to quote Renoir, has his reasons. Besides being a funny, thought-provoking deconstruction of documentary conventions, *Close-Up* is a tribute both to the power of cinema and to the essential goodness—and imaginative capabilities—of ordinary people. **GA**

i

Directors to have praised *Close-Up* include Werner Herzog, Quentin Tarantino, and Martin Scorsese.

King of New York Abel Ferrara, 1990

U.S. / Italy (Caminito, Rank, Reteitalia, Scena) 103m Color **Producer** Augusto Caminito, Mary Kane **Screenplay** Nicholas St. John **Photography** Bojan Bazelli **Music** Joe Delia **Cast** Christopher Walken, David Caruso, Laurence Fishburne, Victor Argo, Wesley Snipes, Janet Julian, Joey Chin, Giancarlo Esposito, Paul Calderon, Steve Buscemi, Theresa Randle, Leonard L. Thomas, Roger Guenveur Smith, Carrie Nygren, Ernest Abuba

Abel Ferrara's *King of New York* is a chronicle of the downfall of New York drug kingpin Frank White (Christopher Walken), who, after years of illegal activity, decides to expiate his sins by building a hospital in an inner-city neighborhood. His attempts to give something back to the community encounter hostile resistance from every side—his Chinese drug partner (Joey Chin), the local Mafia, and an overzealous tough cop (David Caruso) ready to do anything to bring him down. Frank's futile efforts trigger an ethnically motivated gangster war that ends in a bloody showdown among the city's criminal factions.

Walken gives a tour de force performance in the lead as a ruthless killer with a twisted sense of morality, and Laurence Fishburne as White's henchman Jimmy Jump contributes to the film's frenetic energy. Like all of Ferrara's work, *King of New York* is not an easy movie to watch. It is violent and disturbing, with a high body count, further exploring the director's interest in characters who seek salvation against the backdrop of a drug-infested and violent New York City underground—depicted here as the archetypal Gotham City. Ferrara's 1992 follow-up, *Bad Lieutenant*, featuring Harvey Keitel as an unnamed cop who is as corrupt as Walken's White is devious, takes the director's bloody yet introspective examination of sin and redemption even further. **RDe**

Pretty Woman Garry Marshall, 1990

U.S. (Silver Screen, Touchstone) 119m Technicolor **Language** English / Italian **Producer** Arnon Milchan, Steven Reuther **Screenplay** J.F. Lawton **Photography** Charles Minsky **Music** James Newton Howard **Cast** Richard Gere, Julia Roberts, Ralph Bellamy, Jason Alexander, Laura San Giacomo, Hector Elizondo, Alex Hyde-White, Amy Yasbeck, Elinor Donahue, Judith Baldwin, Jason Randal, Bill Applebaum, Tracy Bjork, Gary Greene, Billy Gallo **Oscar nomination** Julia Roberts (actress)

A 1940s-style romantic comedy given a modern twist, *Pretty Woman* was a refreshing antidote to the macho wham-bam movies that dominated Hollywood's output in the late 1980s. One of the highest-grossing pictures of 1990, it succeeded in making the "date movie" popular again.

Pretty Woman also gave huge career boosts to its two stars, Richard Gere (who hadn't had a hit since the mid-1980s) and Julia Roberts, who earned an Oscar nomination for her performance. Gere is at his suave best as Edward Lewis, a business mogul on a trip to L.A. who winds up lost near Hollywood Boulevard, and asks hooker-with-a-heart-of-gold Vivian (Roberts in a miniscule miniskirt and PVC thigh boots) for directions back to his Beverly Hills hotel. Being the smart and sensible prostitute she is, Vivian offers to take him where he needs to go, and it's not long before she has charmed him into hiring her for the week to be his "beck-and-call girl." In return for her time and effort she gets unlimited use of his credit card to buy clothes and learns how to dine at a fancy restaurant (thanks to the friendly hotel concierge, played by Hector Elizondo). And, no surprise, Vivian falls in love with her benefactor.

The whole thing is highly improbable, of course. For starters, it's unlikely any Hollywood Boulevard streetwalkers look as well groomed as Vivian. The success of Roberts in the role of a hooker is politically incorrect, but the sheer charm of *Pretty Woman* never fails to shine through. **JB**

Dances with Wolves Kevin Costner, 1990

U.S. (Tig, Majestic) 183m Color
Language English / Sioux / Pawnee
Producer Kevin Costner, Jim Wilson
Screenplay Michael Blake, from his novel
Photography Dean Semler **Music** John
Barry, Peter Buffett **Cast** Kevin Costner, Mary
McDonnell, Graham Greene, Rodney A.
Grant, Floyd "Red Crow" Westerman, Tantoo
Cardinal, Robert Pastorelli, Charles Rocket,
Maury Chaykin, Jimmy Herman, Nathan Lee
Chasing His Horse, Michael Spears, Jason R.
Lone Hill, Tony Pierce, Doris Leader Charge
Oscars Jim Wilson, Kevin Costner (best
picture), Kevin Costner (director), Michael
Blake (screenplay), Dean Semler
(photography), Neil Travis (editing), John
Barry (music), Russell Williams, Jeffrey
Perkins, Bill W. Benton, Gregory H. Watkins
(sound) **Oscar nominations** Kevin Costner
(actor), Graham Greene (actor in support
role), Mary McDonnell (actress in support
role), Jeffrey Beecroft, Lisa Dean (art
direction), Elsa Zamparelli (costume)
Berlin International Film Festival Kevin
Costner (Silver Bear— outstanding single
achievement, producing/directing/acting,
Golden Bear nomination)

"I want to see the frontier . . . before it's gone." An idealistic Union soldier is rewarded for gallantry in the Civil War with his choice of assignment, an outpost in the Dakotas. There he is befriended by a tribe of Lakota Sioux and goes native, only to witness the encroachment of the white man and twilight falling on the great horse culture of the Plains.

Heartthrob Kevin Costner's directorial debut—ambitious, epic, some of it in Lakota with subtitles—*Dances with Wolves* had Hollywood wags predicting it would be another *Heaven's Gate* (1980). But Costner had the last laugh, riding away with seven Oscars including Best Picture and Best Director (over Martin Scorsese for *Goodfellas*).

"Dances with Wolves" is the name the Indians give to Costner's Lieutenant John Dunbar. He is by stages terrified, intrigued, then captivated by his feather-decked neighbors and their way of life. And the story of how he finds himself and comes by his new name is as enchanting a Western as ever was—rich, lyrical, warm, full of unlooked-for laughs, heartbreaking, and spectacularly cinematic. Costner's direction is remarkably accomplished, taking each elegiac, mystical, or romantic interlude to an exciting action payoff, with battles, buffalo, the spectacular plains of South Dakota, and the handsome cast all gifts to Australian cinematographer and *Mad Max* (1979) veteran Dean Semler. The Indians are portrayed with unprecedented respect and affectionate intimacy as proud, quick, and humorous by Native Americans who are both magnificent looking and engaging, notably Graham Greene as shaman Kicking Bird and Rodney A. Grant as warrior Wind in His Hair.

Sentiment is strong, at times exhaustingly melodramatic. But the film's eloquence and evocative beauty make it enduringly enjoyable. A year later Costner presented the special edition, with an hour of additional material which expands the hero's romance with Stands with a Fist (Mary McDonnell) and shows the fate of captured white buffalo hunters. But there is no new major action scene and the added length, lovely and involving for devotees, does slow the pace. Action fans prefer the original, utterly enjoyable three-hour version. **AE**

1990

i

In 1991, *Dances with Wolves* became the first Western to win a Best Picture Oscar for sixty years.

Henry: Portrait of a Serial Killer

John McNaughton, 1990

U.S. (Filmcat, Fourth World Media, MPI, Maljack) 83m Color
Producer Lisa Dedmond, Steven A. Jones, John McNaughton **Screenplay** Richard Fire, John McNaughton **Photography** Charlie Lieberman **Music** Mic Fabus, Ken Hale, Steven A. Jones, Robert McNaughton **Cast** Mary Demas, Michael Rooker, Anne Bartoletti, Elizabeth Kaden, Ted Kaden, Denise Sullivan, Anita Ores, Megan Ores, Cheri Jones, Monica Anne O'Malley, Bruce Quist, Erzsebet Sziky, Tracy Arnold, Tom Towles, David Katz

"I'm not going to make moral decisions for you. I'll present you with a situation. I know how I feel about it, but it's not my place to tell you how to feel about it."

John McNaughton, 1999

ℹ️

Henry was filmed in 1986, but was not released until 1990 due to a dispute with the U.S. censors.

Directed by John McNaughton, *Henry: Portrait of a Serial Killer* is loosely based on the story of real serial murderer Henry Lee Lucas. It is exceptional for its realism of style and amoral viewpoint, and it remains with the viewer as one of the most disturbing movies ever made.

Henry flouts horror-film conventions with its flat narrative, a build-up of episodes where the expected murders occur in unexpected ways. In one scene, Henry (Michael Rooker) kills two prostitutes in his car and then goes with his roommate Otis (Tom Towles) to buy a hamburger.

The plot of *Henry* (insofar as it has one) follows events that occur after Otis's sister Becky (Tracy Arnold) moves into their small Chicago apartment, disrupting this pair's somewhat repressed homosexual partnership in crime. A low-budget movie, *Henry* excels in depicting the life of drifters amid a grubby lower-class milieu. At one point the film cuts from the corpse of a woman Henry has killed to show a nasty matron in Becky's beauty salon spouting racist slurs.

Becky romanticizes about Henry when she hears how he killed his mother. Rooker brings a surly, Brandoesque appeal to the role of this psychopath, which helps to explain Becky's bad choice of love objects. The film culminates in two especially upsetting murders. First, Henry and Otis kill a suburban family. After witnessing the mayhem, we suddenly realize that we have watched this footage alongside the killers, who are sitting on the sofa reviewing their home movie of the deed. Later, Henry kills Otis, whom he has caught raping Becky. Henry and Becky leave town, but the next morning, in the film's final sequences, Henry leaves their hotel room alone, pausing to drop off a heavy suitcase by the roadside.

Henry is so understated it might seem dull to younger viewers jaded by the gory excesses of other post-1980s horror flicks. Nor does it boast a charmingly elegant killer like Hannibal Lecter. Instead, *Henry* evokes horror through gritty realism and excellent acting. The film is not fun to watch, but it is important in that it forces viewers into questioning our cultural fascination with serial killers. **CFr**

1990

Archangel Guy Maddin, 1990

Canada (Cinephile, Ordnance, Winnipeg) 90m BW **Producer** Greg Klymkiw **Screenplay** Guy Maddin, George Toles **Photography** Guy Maddin **Cast** Kyle McCulloch, Kathy Marykuca, Sarah Neville, Ari Cohen, Michael Gottli, Victor Cowie, David Falkenburg, Michael O'Sullivan, Margaret Anne MacLeod, Ihor Procak, Robert Lougheed, Stephen Snyder, Michael Powell, Sam Toles, Lloyd Weinberg

Guy Maddin, the underground cult wizard from Winnipeg, followed up *Tales from the Gimli Hospital* (1988) with *Archangel*, an even stranger black-and-white feature made on a heftier budget. The film involves amnesiac victims of mustard gas during World War I and the Russian Revolution. The hero, a Canadian soldier (Kyle McCulloch), mistakes a nurse (Kathy Marykuca) for his dead love; she's married to a Belgian aviator (Ari Cohen) who can't remember he's married, and she gets so confused that she winds up mistaking the Canadian for the Belgian.

There are other complications, some of which, like the amnesia, suggest a deranged remake of *Random Harvest* (1942), but *Archangel* often appears to be about nothing at all—except perhaps Maddin's obvious love for late silent and early talkie studio productions with kitschy pictorial effects, as well as offbeat surrealist conceits (such as a hailstorm of bunny rabbits falling into trenches). The results may not be consistently funny or affecting, but it never seems that Maddin is out to produce straight-out comedy or camp, much less serious drama. What comes across is a fascinating fetishist delirium, where memories of remote war movies get recycled into something that is alternately creepy and beautiful. **JRos**

1990

Total Recall Paul Verhoeven, 1990

U.S. (Carolco, TriStar) 109m Technicolor **Producer** Buzz Feitshans, Ronald Shusett **Screenplay** Ronald Shusett, Dan O'Bannon, Gary Goldman, from the short story "We Can Remember It for You Wholesale" by Philip K. Dick **Photography** Jost Vacano **Music** Jerry Goldsmith, Bruno Louchouarn **Cast** Arnold Schwarzenegger, Rachel Ticotin, Sharon Stone, Ronny Cox, Michael Ironside, Marshall Bell, Mel Johnson Jr., Michael Champion, Roy Brocksmith, Ray Baker, Rosemary Dunsmore, David Knell, Alexia Robinson, Dean Norris, Mark Carlton **Oscar** Eric Brevig, Rob Bottin, Tim McGovern, Alex Funke (special visual effects) **Oscar nominations** Stephen Hunter Flick (special sound effects), Nelson Stoll, Michael J. Kohut, Carlos DeLarios, Aaron Rochin (sound)

Cult science fiction author Philip K. Dick's story *We Can Remember It for You Wholesale* is impressively translated onto the screen with numerous jaw-dropping special effects and lashings of violence by Dutch director Paul Verhoeven, who had previously scored a similar sci-fi hit with the 1987 blockbuster *RoboCop*.

Arnold Schwarzenegger stars as Doug Quaid, an everyday Joe (albeit one built like Hercules) who has recurring dreams about living on Mars. His wife (Sharon Stone) dismisses his fantasies, so Doug pays a visit to a virtual reality vacation company and gets hooked up to a machine that will simulate a trip to the red planet. Unfortunately, it also gives his brain a good zapping, and Doug wakes up from his virtual trip believing he is a secret agent. He soon finds himself pursued by various human and mutant heavies while he tries to work out in his head what is fact and what is fiction.

Many of Dick's favorite themes (also explored in *Do Androids Dream of Electric Sheep?*, which became Ridley Scott's classic sci-fi film *Blade Runner* in 1982) are explored in *Total Recall*—identity, perception, memories, real and manufactured—but never at the expense of action. And action there certainly is, from a fun fight between Stone and Schwarzenegger, their sparring dialogue an added bonus, to the final, gruesome but gripping showdown. **JB**

THE DIRECTOR OF "BATMAN" & "BEETLEJUICE" INVITES YOU TO MEET HIS NEWEST CREATION:

edward SCISSORHANDS

Edward Scissorhands Tim Burton, 1990

Rather than follow the hugely successful *Batman* (1989) with another special-effects-driven bonanza, director Tim Burton instead delivered a delightfully realized movie that was about as far from a mainstream Hollywood blockbuster as it was possible to get. The result is *Edward Scissorhands*, a decidedly left-of-center fairy tale that remains the most whimsical and touching film of Burton's career so far.

The Edward of the title (Johnny Depp) is not a man at all, but the creation of The Inventor (an all-too-brief cameo performance from the marvelous Vincent Price in his last film role). Edward looks human enough, except for one detail—he has scissors instead of hands—and he lives a solitary life in a crumbling mansion high above a neighborhood of pastel-colored houses. It is only when kindly Avon lady Peg Boggs (Dianne Wiest) discovers his hiding place that Edward descends to the "real" world below, and finds himself embraced by Peg's neighbors when he displays his special talent for hairdressing, dog grooming, and hedge shaping. Life for the trusting and innocent Edward is complicated, however, when he falls for Peg's cheerleader daughter Kim (Winona Ryder) and is soon coerced by her boyfriend (Anthony Michael Hall) into committing a crime.

One of the many successes Burton pulls off in this delightfully odd film is to cast his various players against type in this eccentric dreamlike world. Hall, best known for playing the nerd in John Hughes's *The Breakfast Club* (1985), succeeds in showing a far nastier side in his role as oafish boyfriend Jim. Ryder, on the other hand, devoid of the ample cynicism she displayed in *Heathers* (1988), brings a delicate touch to her role as the nice girl on the block. It is Depp, however, who impresses the most, creating a character trapped by his incomplete body, conveying Edward's frustration with few words, his pale, scarred face showing the hurt when he discovers that even his gentlest touch with his scissor hands can cause pain. An ambitious, beautifully conceived modern-day fairy tale. **JB**

U.S. (Fox) 105m Color
Producer Tim Burton, Denise Di Novi
Screenplay Tim Burton and Caroline Thompson **Photography** Stefan Czapsky
Music Danny Elfman **Cast** Johnny Depp, Winona Ryder, Dianne Wiest, Anthony Michael Hall, Kathy Baker, Robert Oliveri, Conchata Ferrell, Caroline Aaron, Dick Anthony Williams, O-Lan Jones, Vincent Price, Alan Arkin, Susan Blommaert, Linda Perri, John Davidson **Oscar nomination** Ve Neill, Stan Winston (makeup)

"Edward Scissorhands isn't perfect. It's something better: pure magic."

Peter Travers,
***Rolling Stone*, 1990**

i

As the character of Edward, Johnny Depp said only 169 words throughout the entire movie.

Von Zeit zu Zeit gibt es Filme,
die man nie vergißt.

HITLERJUNGE SALOMON

MARCO HOFSCHNEIDER · JULIE DELPY

Hitlerjunge Salomon Agnieszka Holland, 1990
Europa Europa

Salomon Perel, played by Marco Hofschneider, changes uniforms, languages, and identities in an effort to survive the Holocaust. Renowned Polish filmmaker Agnieszka Holland refrains from passing judgment on her chameleon-like protagonist as she represents unspeakable psychological tortures and miraculous escapes from a matter-of-fact distance, not dwelling on agony or bloodbath. This is what renders this incredible story so shockingly believable and separates it from other films about the Holocaust.

Set between 1938 and 1945, *Europa Europa* is actually based on the real-life adventures of Salomon "Solly" Perel. Solly is a young Polish Jew from Germany, whose life takes a grotesque turn when the Nazis break into his family's apartment. With the family dispersed, Solly ends up alone, saved only by the Nazi uniform he puts on. This act launches his career as a performer. First, he winds up in a Russian orphanage in eastern Poland, where he receives a thorough education in communist dogma, renouncing his Jewish identity and denouncing religion as "the opiate of the masses." Hitler's troops take him back to Germany, where he is employed as a Russian interpreter, accepted as an Aryan. The irony and danger of his performance reach their epitome when he joins the Hitler Youth, where he is taught how to recognize and kill Jews.

Hiding his circumcision becomes particularly dangerous when his good looks win the hearts of a gay Nazi officer and a desirable but excessively anti-Semitic girl, played by Julie Delpy. As the only physical reminder of Solly's true identity, circumcision becomes a rich metaphor in the movie. Some of the most powerfully ambiguous moments of *Europa Europa* show Solly overidentifying with the role he is playing, suggesting that true identity might not be possible at all. Unsurprisingly, there is no catharsis or tragedy at the end; although when Solly is miraculously reunited with his lost brother Isaak (René Hofschneider), we sense that his performance is far from over. **AI**

Germany / France / Poland
(CCC Filmkunst, Losange) 112m
Eastmancolor **Language** German / Russian
Producer Artur Brauner, Margaret Ménéqoz
Screenplay Agnieszka Holland, from book
by Salomon Perel **Photography** Jacek
Petrycki, Jacek Zaleski **Music** Zbigniew
Preisner **Cast** Marco Hofschneider, Salomon
Perel, René Hofschneider, Piotr Kozlowski,
Klaus Abramowsky, Michèle Gleizer, Marta
Sandrowicz, Nathalie Schmidt, Delphine
Forest, Andrzej Mastalerz, Wlodzimierz Press,
Martin Maria Blau, Klaus Kowatsch, Holger
Hunkel, Bernhard Howe **Oscar nomination**
Agnieszka Holland (screenplay)

1990

"*There are a great many movies about the tragic experience of the Jews during the Second World War, but only a handful as passionate, as subtly intelligent, as universal as this one.*"

The Washington Post, **1991**

ℹ

The film received a lukewarm reception in Germany, but won much praise in the United States.

Boyz 'N the Hood John Singleton, 1991

U.S. (Columbia) 107m Color
Producer Steve Nicolaides **Screenplay** John
Singleton **Photography** Charles Mills
Music Stanley Clarke, Ice Cube **Cast** Hudhail
Al-Amir, Laurence Fishburne, Lloyd Avery,
Cuba Gooding Jr., Ice Cube, Mia Bell, Morris
Chestnut, Lexie Bigham, Nia Long, Angela
Bassett, Kenneth A. Brown, Nicole Brown,
Tyra Ferrell, Ceal, Desi Arnez Hines II
Oscar nominations John Singleton
(director), John Singleton (screenplay)

*"How you think
the crack rock gets into
the country? We don't
own any planes. We
don't own no ships."*

**Jason "Furious" Styles
(Laurence Fishburne)**

Singleton is the youngest nominee for
the Best Director Oscar. He was just
twenty-four years old at the time.

Given early 1970s heralds like Melvin Van Peebles and Gordon Parks, the
1980s saw a select few African-American filmmakers break into the
mainstream. Foremost among them were Robert Townsend and Spike
Lee, each crafting witty comedy-dramas about the condition of black
America. Yet it was John Singleton's autobiographical debut, *Boyz 'N the
Hood*, that fully introduced a so-called black American cinematic voice
into the critical establishment. For his efforts Singleton earned two
Academy Award nominations, and his film was a runaway hit that
provided Columbia Pictures with a monster windfall.

Opening in the aftermath of the 1984 Los Angeles Olympiad,
Singleton's drama settles on three ten-year-olds, Tre (Desi Arnez Hines II),
Doughboy (Baha Jackson), and Ricky (Donovan McCrary). Raised in
single-parent homes, their world is riven with gang violence, police
brutality, and economic hardship. When Tre's mother Reva (Angela
Bassett) deposits him at the front door of his father Jason "Furious"
(Laurence Fishburne), he gets a crash course in masculinity and
transforms into an upwardly mobile teen.

Flash forward seven years. Tre (now played by Cuba Gooding Jr.) is a
high school senior with a part-time job, an application to a historic black
college, and a girlfriend named Brandi (Nia Long). Doughboy (Ice Cube)
is a gangbanger and loafer trading on the patience of his mother,
Mrs. Baker (Tyra Ferrell), while his brother Ricky (Morris Chestnut) builds
himself up as a Division I college football draft prospect. Though trying
to escape the 'hood, Tre still remains linked to his neighborhood friends.
When Doughboy's underworld connections threaten the trio, Ricky is
killed in a drive-by shooting. Afterward Tre confronts his father's sage
training and manages to avoid the mistakes of his downtrodden world.
Through an ending scrawl we learn he escapes the trap of poverty and
violence and accompanies Brandi to college.

Pedantic but expertly orchestrated through a moving depiction of
intraracial violence in the American inner city, *Boyz 'N the Hood* is a vividly
memorable morality tale addressed to the same youth represented on
screen. After a sobering dedication reminding us of the number of young
black men killed by other young black men, it launches into a realistic,
profanity-laden, and affecting coming-of-age story.

Noteworthy for the screen debut of rapper Ice Cube, Singleton's film
evinces an awareness of Hollywood storytelling conventions and
demonstrates a real affection for the topical influence of hip-hop music.
Organized in a clear three-act structure and tending toward broad
moralizing, the picture therefore exudes a professional polish. But it is
also scored with the percussive beats and hypnotic raps of various chart-
toppers lending their sounds to Tre's escape, making *Boyz 'N the Hood*
the achievement of a career, the origin of a wave of small-scale, black-
centered inner city and ghetto dramas that flourished in the 1990s. **GC-Q**

La belle noiseuse Jacques Rivette, 1991
The Beautiful Troublemaker

France / Switzerland (CNC, France 3, George Reinhart, Canal+, Pierre Grisé, Region Languedes, Ronsillon Sofica 2, Sofica 3) 240m Eastmancolor **Producer** Martine Marignac **Screenplay** Pascal Bonitzer, Christine Laurent, Jacques Rivette, from the short story "The Unknown Masterpiece" by Honoré de Balzac **Photography** William Lubtchansky **Music** Igor Stravinsky **Cast** Michel Piccoli, Jane Birkin, Emmanuelle Béart, Marianne Denicourt, David Bursztein, Gilles Arbona, Marie Belluc, Marie-Claude Roger, Leila Remili, Daphne Goodfellow, Susan Robertson, Bernard Dufour **Cannes Film Festival** Jacques Rivette (grand prize of the jury, prize of the ecumenical jury—special mention, Golden Palm nomination)

Films about artists are risky, courting terrible clichés—romantic genius in the garret, tormented soul projected onto canvas—to show what someone goes through while shaping sensations and intuitions into pictures. Jacques Rivette accepts the challenge gleefully in *La belle noiseuse*, extrapolating from a short story by Balzac: This will be the story of an "unfinished masterpiece," produced and then hidden by a famous artist in his twilight years.

Rivette and his writers, Pascal Bonitzer and Christine Laurent, juggle many themes skillfully. On one level, the film offers a glimpse into the privileged world of art, where creators, dealers, and confidants weave a subtly erotic tangle. At the film's core, Rivette studies, with a minute attention to detail and duration, the dancelike rapport between an artist, Edouard Frenhofer (Michel Piccoli) and his mostly naked model, Marianne (Emmanuelle Béart). Their sessions wheel through many moods: Frustration, aggression, exuberance. The master–slave relationship shifts. Slowly, through many trials, an artistic work takes form.

As Frenhofer faces the disturbance in his marriage to Liz (Jane Birkin), warily watches the emergence of a new generation, and confronts the specter of his own mortality, it is hard not to see this melancholy hero as the director's own self-portrait. **AM**

The Rapture Michael Tolkin, 1991

U.S. (New Line) 100m Color **Producer** Karen Koch, Nancy Tenenbaum, Nick Wechsler **Screenplay** Michael Tolkin **Photography** Bojan Bazelli **Music** Thomas Newman **Cast** Mimi Rogers, Darwyn Carson, Patrick Bauchau, Marvin Elkins, David Duchovny, Stephanie Menuez, Sam Vlahos, Rustam Branaman, Scott Burkholder, Vince Grant, Carole Davis, Patrick Dollaghan, James LeGros, Dick Anthony Williams, DeVaughn Nixon

Few movies have treated religion seriously, and fewer still have explored evangelical Christianity on its own theological terms. This is what Michael Tolkin does in *The Rapture*, which may be viewed with equal pleasure as a spiritual melodrama, a faith-based fable, and an eccentric fairy tale with roots in a real religious subculture.

Mimi Rogers plays Sharon, a swinging single who enjoys cruising for foursomes with a sleazy male friend. Then she hears about a religious movement that emphasizes a personal relationship with God, whose day of judgment—complete with a transcendent "Rapture" that will whisk good souls to heaven—is said to be coming soon. Her newfound faith helps her weather turbulent storms, such as her husband's death. When she thinks the end of times is imminent, she takes her daughter to a lonely patch of desert, where they await God's saving hand. In the film's most audacious twist, the Rapture actually does arrive, but by now suffering has led her to reject the idea of a just and merciful deity.

At once a psychological drama, a reflection on faith and free will, and a crisp 1990s variation on what Hollywood used to call the "woman's picture," this offbeat parable offers rich rewards for the open-minded moviegoer. **DS**

baidubar CHEN CHANG

牯
嶺街
少年殺
人事件

Taiwan (ICA, Jane Balfour, Yang & His Gang)
237m Color **Language** Mandarin
Producer Yu Welyan **Screenplay** Yan
Hongya, Lai Mingtang, Yang Shunqing,
Edward Yang **Photography** Huigong Li,
Longyu Zhang **Music** Zhan Hongda
Cast Zhang Guozhu, Flaine Jin, Wang Juan,
Zhang Han, Jiang Xiuqiong, Lai Fanyun,
Lisa Yang, Zhang Zhen

*"Every event has one
best position to observe
from . . . [You] have to be
aware of the risk of using
close-ups. You might lose
important information
if you restrict the viewer's
attention to a very
focused spot."*

Edward Yang, 2000

Guling jie shaonian sha ren shijian
A Brighter Summer Day Edward Yang, 1991

Epic in scope if not always in scale, Edward Yang's subtle and rich portrait of Taiwan fits so many details into its deceptively brisk four-hour running time that it's a wonder Yang delivered the film as short as it is. Set during a single Taipei school year in the early 1960s, *A Brighter Summer Day* depicts a country still reeling from the disruptive influx of Chinese Nationalists (led by the repressive Chiang Kai-shek) in 1948. Yang's Taiwan is torn between communism and democracy, nationalism and liberality, with confusion, alienation, and uncertainty leading to a sometimes debilitating anomie.

Yet as powerful as *A Brighter Summer Day* may be, Yang infuses it with touches of humor and humanism that temper the distressing atmosphere of impending doom. The direction is patient and serene; the film is like a masterful symphony of dozens of characters whose tone and tempo are deftly orchestrated by Yang. Favoring static or slow-moving long shots over close-ups, Yang gives his cast great freedom to explore their emotions (or apparent lack thereof), acting for the story and each other and not just the camera; yet Yang clearly wants the film to be about specific places and things as much as people. That *A Brighter Summer Day* reveals facts and plot points with the care, planning, and deliberation of a great novel therefore comes as no surprise.

Neither does the emotional weight of the film's tragic conclusion, the payoff of all of Yang's rigorous narrative design (itself the product of four years of preparation), which manages to seamlessly weave together the story of Taipei street gangs, puppy love, rock and roll, lost cultural signifiers, and the search for a national identity. While often compared loosely to Nicholas Ray's moody classic *Rebel Without A Cause* (1955), *A Brighter Summer Day* is so much more. A masterpiece of the Taiwanese New Wave and a cinematic highpoint of the tail end of the twentieth century, this is a film whose grasp of period and place is masterful almost beyond the realm of mere storytelling. It's like a multifaceted photo album composed of truly moving, thought-provoking pictures. **JKl**

i

The movie is based on a real-life incident that Yang recalled from his own childhood.

KEVIN COSTNER

JFK

JFK Oliver Stone, 1991

Never a stranger to controversy, Oliver Stone followed up his powerful post-Vietnam movie *Born on the Fourth of July* (1989) with a film that angered and amazed people in equal measure—his questioning, overwhelming, urgent conspiracy movie *JFK*.

Many people believe that we don't know the whole truth about the assassination of President John F. Kennedy on November 22, 1963. Do we really think Lee Harvey Oswald acted alone? Does the Warren Commission report, which attempted to come to a conclusion, really provide the answers? Although many people have debated whether more than one person pulled a trigger that day, Stone went one further and committed some of the many theories to celluloid, and in doing so delivers a fascinating film that raises even more questions than it answers.

At the picture's heart is Jim Garrison (Kevin Costner), the real-life New Orleans district attorney who had his own theories about who shot JFK and conducted an investigation into the matter from 1966 to 1969. Stone quite rightly doesn't buy into all of Garrison's theories—some believe he was a loose cannon who couldn't distinguish real clues from crackpot conspiracy ideas. But the director uses him as a push-off point, the symbolic center of a film simply because he is the only man in America who even attempted to bring anyone to justice for what must be the most famous murder of all time (and one that remains incompletely solved, shocking when you realize how many witnesses were present).

Using documentary footage—including the infamous home movie shot by Abraham Zapruder—as well as flashbacks, reconstructions, quick editing, and a skillful use of words and music, Stone weaves many ideas and theories together using the huge mountain of evidence and witness testimony without ever confusing or hoodwinking his audience. We don't get a result by the time the end credits roll three breathtaking hours later, but we do know—as if there was any doubt in our minds previously—that it was impossible for Lee Harvey Oswald to have acted alone.

And for those who were not alive or weren't old enough to remember the events of 1963, they are all here—the shooting of Kennedy during a cavalcade through Dallas, Jack Ruby's murder of Oswald, and so on. We see them as Garrison does, and Stone cleverly shows us what would convince this ordinary man to wade through so many reports and stories to seek out conspiracies that may have involved the CIA, Castro supporters, or various fringe groups. He would not succeed in getting us to care so completely about this search for truth without a strong central performance from Costner, who holds your attention throughout the film despite the numerous heavyweight actors who stroll in and out playing small roles—from Tommy Lee Jones as suspect Clay Shaw to Joe Pesci, Gary Oldman (as Oswald), Donald Sutherland, Jack Lemmon, Walter Matthau, Kevin Bacon, and Sissy Spacek, all of whom are superb. A truly astonishing piece of filmmaking from a one-of-a-kind director. **JB**

U.S. (Alcor, Camelot, Ixtlan, Canal+, Regency, Warner Bros.) 189m BW / Color
Producer A. Kitman Ho, Oliver Stone
Screenplay Oliver Stone, Zachary Sklar, from the book *Crossfire: The Plot that Killed Kennedy* by Jim Marrs and *On the Trail of the Assassins* by Jim Garrison
Photography Robert Richardson
Music John Williams Cast Kevin Costner, Kevin Bacon, Tommy Lee Jones, Laurie Metcalf, Gary Oldman, Beata Pozniak, Michael Rooker, Jay O. Sanders, Sissy Spacek, Brian Doyle-Murray, Gary Grubbs, Wayne Knight, Jo Anderson, Vincent D'Onofrio, Pruitt Taylor Vince Oscars Robert Richardson (photography), Joe Hutshing, Pietro Scalia (editing) Oscar nominations A. Kitman Ho, Oliver Stone (best picture), Oliver Stone (director), Oliver Stone, Zachary Sklar (screenplay), Tommy Lee Jones (actor in support role), John Williams (music), Michael Minkler, Gregg Landaker, Tod A. Maitland (sound)

1991

"*Kings are killed, Mr. Garrison, politics is power, nothing more!*"

"X" (Donald Sutherland)

ℹ️

The part of Earl Warren, chairman of the Warren Commission, is played by the real-life Jim Garrison.

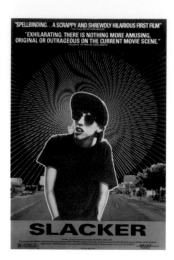

Slacker Richard Linklater, 1991

Richard Linklater's delightfully different and immensely enjoyable second feature was the first one to get any substantial distribution, after the more obscure and more obviously cinephiliac Super 8mm opus *It's Impossible to Learn to Plow by Reading Books* (1988). *Slacker* takes us on a twenty-four-hour tour of the flaky dropout culture of Austin, Texas, which has remained Linklater's headquarters throughout his multifaceted career. Unlike all his subsequent films to date, *Slacker* doesn't have anything resembling a continuous plot except in the most literal way that it moves chronologically and geographically through part of a day in Austin, but it's brimming with weird characters and wonderful talk (which often seems improvised, though it was all scripted by Linklater, apparently with the input of some of the participants, as in his 2001 animated film, *Waking Life*). The structure of dovetailing dialogues calls to mind an extremely laid-back variation of Luis Buñuel's *The Phantom of Liberty* (1974) or Jacques Tati's *Playtime* (1967), in which various events are glued together simply by virtue of appearing in proximity within the same patch of time and space. Combining a certain formal logic with an illogical drive toward spinning out gratuitous fantasies and digressions is an impulse that follows Linklater through many of his subsequent pictures, but it's likely that this combination has never been displayed quite as brazenly as it is here.

"Every thought you have fractions off and becomes its own reality," remarks Linklater himself to a poker-faced cabdriver in the first (and in some ways funniest) sequence, again anticipating *Waking Life* by spouting fanciful philosophy from the back seat of a car. And the remainder of the movie amply illustrates this notion with its diverse paranoid conspiracy and assassination theorists, serial-killer buffs, musicians, cultists, college students, pontificators, petty criminals, street people, and layabouts (around ninety in all). Even if the movie goes nowhere in terms of narrative and winds up with a somewhat arch conclusion, the highly evocative scenes give an often hilarious sense of the surviving dregs of 1960s culture and a superbly realized sense of a specific community. **JRos**

U.S. (Detour) 97m Color
Producer Richard Linklater
Screenplay Richard Linklater
Photography Lee Daniel **Cast** Richard Linklater, Rudy Basquez, Jean Caffeine, Jan Hockey, Stephan Hockey, Mark James, Samuel Dietert, Bob Boyd, Terrence Kirk, Keith McCormack, Jennifer Schaudies, Dan Kratochvil, Maris Strautmanis, Brecht Andersch, Tommy Pallotta

"Who's ever written a great work about the immense effort required in order not to create?"

**Dostoyevsky Wannabe
(Brecht Andersch)**

i

Slacker directly inspired Kevin Smith to make his own debut as a filmmaker with *Clerks* (1994).

Wong fei-hung Tsui Hark, 1991
Once Upon a Time in China

Hong Kong (Film Workshop) 134m Color
Language Cantonese / English / Mandarin
Producer Tsui Hark Screenplay Yiu Ming
Leung, Tang Pik-Yin, Tsui Hark, Yu Kai-Chi
Photography Chan Tung-Chuen, Wilson
Chan, David Chung, Andy Lam, Arthur
Wong, Bill Wong Music Romeo Díaz, James
Wong Cast Jet Li, Biao Yuen, Rosamund
Kwan, Jacky Cheung, Steve Tartalia, Kent
Cheng, Yee Kwan Yan, Mark King, Jonathan
Isgar, Shun Lau, Chi Yeung Wong, Ma Wu,
Simon Yam, Yuen Cheung-Yan, Yuen Kam-
Fai, Yuen Shun-Yee, Tony Yuen

Tsui Hark was Hong Kong's reigning filmmaker in the 1980s and early 1990s, deftly infusing his eye-popping action films with witty political commentary. *Once Upon a Time in China* finds him breathing new life into the chronicles of Chinese folk hero Wong Fei-Hung.

Wong, a legendary healer and martial artist, the subject of several of Hark's films dating back to the 1960s, is given a lavish reintroduction in this, the first episode in Tsui Hark's *Once Upon a Time* series. Set in 1875, Wong (Jet Li) faces off against British exploiters and corrupt Chinese businessmen in a wild and convoluted plot involving imperialism, the press-ganging of Chinese peasants into the building of America's railroads, arms smugglers, and disgraced martial artists forced to work as hired thugs.

This is popular Hong Kong cinema at its most breathless, aided by the superb athleticism of Li, who makes his entry into world stardom as the poised and stoical hero. He is the center of dazzling set pieces that include a gravity-defying duel fought with ladders, and a standoff between an unarmed Wong and an opponent with a gun. Underneath the twisting plot and relentless action, however, is a palpable melancholy—a lament for a China about to change forever under Western influences. **AT**

1991

Thelma & Louise Ridley Scott, 1991

U.S. (MGM, Pathé) 129m Color
Producer Mimi Polk, Ridley
Scott Screenplay Callie Khouri
Photography Adrian Biddle Music Hans
Zimmer Cast Susan Sarandon, Geena Davis,
Harvey Keitel, Michael Madsen, Christopher
McDonald, Stephen Tobolowsky, Brad Pitt,
Timothy Carhart, Lucinda Jenney, Jason
Beghe, Marco St. John, Sonny Carl Davis, Ken
Swofford, Shelly Desai, Carol Mansell
Oscar Callie Khouri (screenplay) Oscar
nominations Ridley Scott (director), Geena
Davis (actress), Susan Sarandon (actress),
Adrian Biddle (photography),
Thom Noble (editing)

To call *Thelma & Louise* a feminist road movie is both accurate and a slight disservice to the film—the latter simply because you run the risk of minimizing the picture's far demographic reach. The story of a browbeaten housewife (Geena Davis) and her sardonic, world-weary waitress best friend (Susan Sarandon) who embark on a weekend getaway and end up fleeing the law after one of them kills a would-be rapist, this film struck a deep chord in audiences across gender, racial, and class lines when it was released. It continues to resonate with viewers because it not only confidently feminized a genre previously owned by men, but it did so by supplying details about social inequities that allowed a host of spectators to see themselves in the heroines and to identify with both the fright and the flight of the women's journey.

As the titular characters, Sarandon and Davis embody everyday American women struggling against a host of obstacles (boorish men, dead-end jobs, joyless lives) while simply trying to survive. Director Ridley Scott captures a blue-skied, green-plain United States that is the stuff of myth and legend, promising freedom—but not to all. And it's the gap between that promise and the harsh reality that gives the film its punch, making it a biting commentary on America's dreams, truths, and limitations. **EH**

793

My Own Private Idaho Gus Van Sant, 1991

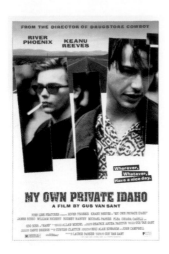

U.S. (New Line) 102m Color
Producer Laurie Parker **Screenplay** Gus
Van Sant **Photography** John J. Campbell,
Eric Alan Edwards **Music** Bill Stafford
Cast River Phoenix, Keanu Reeves, James
Russo, William Richert, Rodney Harvey,
Chiara Caselli, Michael Parker, Jessie Thomas,
Flea, Grace Zabriskie, Tom Troupe, Udo Kier,
Sally Curtice, Robert Lee Pitchlynn, Mickey
Cottrell **Venice Film Festival** River Phoenix
(Volpi cup—actor)

*"I'm a connoisseur
of roads. I've been
tasting roads my whole
life. This road will never
end. It probably goes
all around the world."*

**Mike Waters
(River Phoenix)**

i

The film's title is taken from
the B-52's song "Private Idaho,"
released in 1980.

Gus Van Sant's *My Own Private Idaho*, only his third feature and the follow-up to his 1989 breakthrough *Drugstore Cowboy* (his 1985 debut, the ultra-low-budget *Mala Noche*, is an unsung treasure), remains the writer-director's most profound, moving, and complete film—what Desson Howe has called "an exquisite, cinematic poem . . . about the eternal search to belong somewhere, and the lonely landscape of the soul." Without stifling his artistic, even avant-garde impulses for the sake of accessibility and mainstream appeal—something he would be accused of doing after his maudlin middle-of-the-road dramas *Good Will Hunting* (1997) and *Finding Forrester* (2000)—Van Sant delivers a delightfully idiosyncratic story that relies on images at least as much as words to captivate viewers.

True, the casting of teen heartthrobs Keanu Reeves (in what may be his finest performance to date) and River Phoenix (who would die tragically of a drug overdose at the age of twenty-three, right on the cusp of a brilliant career) as the leads certainly didn't hurt *My Own Private Idaho*'s commercial prospects. But in explicitly thematizing homelessness, homosexuality, and teenage prostitution; by offering up a protagonist who suffers from narcolepsy and romanticized memories of a mother who abandoned him as a child; and in paying extended homage to Orson Welles's adaptation of Shakespeare's *Henry IV* plays, *Chimes at Midnight* (1965), via a self-consciously anachronistic use of bardspeak in several key scenes, no one can claim that Van Sant was unwilling to risk alienating unsuspecting middle-American audiences. Though too unconventional at both the narrative and stylistic levels to generate blockbuster appeal, the picture was lauded by critics, cherished by Van Sant enthusiasts, and awarded prizes at several international film festivals.

The film centers on the relationship between Mike (Phoenix) and Scott (Reeves), two young hustlers living on the streets in Portland, Oregon. Members of a raucous and libidinal family of social outcasts who congregate in a condemned building, the pair sell their bodies to whomever is buying in order to survive—though we eventually learn that Scott is actually the rebellious son of a well-to-do Portland family who has chosen this lifestyle largely as a means of humiliating his father. With Mike, on the other hand, what you see is definitely what you get: a quiet, dreamy, gentle boy who is in love with his best friend, falls asleep at the drop of a hat—frequently at inopportune moments, a trait the director taps for both humor and pathos—and is obsessed with finding his long-lost mom. It is this latter quality that provides the impetus for the film's rambling (but never slow) road trip of a plot, as Scott accompanies his always-endangered buddy on excursions ranging from Idaho to Italy in search of a myth of maternal love that the audience sees as the scratchy home-video footage of Mike's mind. In this tender yet unsentimental picture, Van Sant succeeds as few other filmmakers have in conveying the subjective experience of troubled, disaffected youth. **SJS**

The Silence of the Lambs Jonathan Demme, 1991

The first horror movie to win an Academy Award for Best Picture, *The Silence of the Lambs* also has the distinction of being only the third movie in history to win the five major Oscars—after *It Happened One Night* (1934) and *One Flew Over the Cuckoo's Nest* (1975).

An adaptation of Thomas Harris's best-selling novel, the film was a deserved winner, featuring superb performances from Jodie Foster and Anthony Hopkins, with director Jonathan Demme, previously best known for comedy, delivering a continuous shiver down the spines of the audience without ever resorting to gore. Foster, as FBI recruit Clarice Starling, is asked by her superior, Jack Crawford (Scott Glenn), to visit notorious serial killer Hannibal "The Cannibal" Lecter (Hopkins, in a role originally offered to Jeremy Irons), a former psychiatrist held in a subterranean prison who may have an insight into the psyche of a murderer named Buffalo Bill (creepily brought to life by Ted Levine), which will help the FBI catch him.

Of course, the witty, cultured Hannibal is too clever to give up such information easily. He draws Clarice into an uneasy, disturbing relationship in which he demands insight into her childhood in return for his opinions. It is their exchanges, in Hannibal's dark, gothic dungeon, separated only by glass, that are at the film's heart as Foster and, most notably Hopkins, give tour de force performances, delivering Ted Tally's often quotable words—"A census taker once tried to test me. I ate his liver with some fava beans and a nice Chianti"—with delicious (if that word can be used in reference to a movie about a cannibal) verve.

Since the movie's release in 1991, Hopkins's memorable character has taken on a life of its own, appearing in the disappointing 2001 sequel *Hannibal*—with the role of Clarice played by Julianne Moore—and more enjoyable prequel *Red Dragon* (2002), based on the same Harris novel as Michael Mann's superior, stylish *Manhunter* (1986). **JB**

U.S. (Orion) 118m Color **Producer** Ronald M. Bozman, Edward Saxon, Kenneth Utt **Screenplay** Ted Tally, from novel by Thomas Harris **Photography** Tak Fujimoto **Music** Howard Shore **Cast** Jodie Foster, Anthony Hopkins, Scott Glenn, Anthony Heald, Ted Levine, Frankie Faison, Kasi Lemmons, Brooke Smith, Paul Lazar, Dan Butler, Lawrence T. Wrentz, Don Brockett, Frank Seals Jr., Stuart Rudin, Masha Skorobogatov **Oscars** Edward Saxon, Kenneth Utt, Ronald M. Bozman (best picture), Jonathan Demme (director), Ted Tally (screenplay), Anthony Hopkins (actor), Jodie Foster (actress) **Oscar nominations** Craig McKay (editing), Tom Fleischman, Christopher Newman (sound) **Berlin International Film Festival** Jonathan Demme (Silver Bear—director, tied with Ultrà; Golden Bear nomination)

> "Oh, he's a monster. Pure psychopath . . . From a research point of view, Lecter is our most prized asset."

Dr. Frederick Chilton (Anthony Heald)

i

Surprisingly for such a major role, Hopkins is only on screen for around sixteen minutes.

Terminator 2: Judgment Day James Cameron, 1991

U.S. / France (Carolco, Canal+, Lightstorm, Pacific Western) 137m Color **Language** English / Spanish **Producer** James Cameron **Screenplay** James Cameron, William Wisher Jr. **Photography** Adam Greenberg **Music** Brad Fiedel **Cast** Arnold Schwarzenegger, Linda Hamilton, Edward Furlong, Robert Patrick, Earl Boen, Joe Morton, S. Epatha Merkerson, Castulo Guerra, Danny Cooksey, Jenette Goldstein **Oscars** Gary Rydstrom, Gloria S. Borders (special sound effects), Dennis Muren, Stan Winston, Gene Warren Jr., Robert Skotak (special visual effects), Stan Winston, Jeff Dawn (makeup), Tom Johnson, Gary Rydstrom, Gary Summers, Lee Orloff (sound) **Oscar nominations** Adam Greenberg (photography), Conrad Buff, Mark Goldblatt, Richard A. Harris (editing)

Arnold Schwarzenegger got the best role of his career in director James Cameron's 1984 movie *The Terminator* as a monosyllabic killer robot sent from the future, so it was hardly surprising he decided to reprise the role seven years later in Cameron's sequel. This time, Arnie's T-800 cyborg is the good guy, sent by rebel leader of the future John Connor (Michael Biehn's character from the original movie) to protect his younger self (Edward Furlong) and his mother Sarah (Linda Hamilton), so they can lead the fight that is to come against machines that will take over the earth.

It is what the T-800 is protecting them from that really impresses here—a new breed of Terminator, the far nastier T-1000 (Robert Patrick) that, thanks to some eye-popping special effects, is made of liquid metal and can morph into any shape, taking on the guise of another human or reforming from a puddle in his quest to terminate John and Sarah. In fact, everything in this sequel is bigger and better, from Hamilton's beefed-up physique to the multiple explosions, slick direction, and fast-paced action. A spectacular treat. **JB**

Delicatessen Marc Caro & Jean-Pierre Jeunet, 1991

France (Constellation, Hachette, Sofinergie, UGC) 99m Color **Language** French **Producer** Claudie Ossard **Screenplay** Gilles Adrien, Marc Caro, Jean-Pierre Jeunet **Photography** Darius Khondji **Music** Carlos d'Alessio **Cast** Pascal Benezech, Dominique Pinon, Marie-Laure Dougnac, Jean-Claude Dreyfus, Karin Viard, Ticky Holgado, Anne-Marie Pisani, Boban Janevski, Mikael Todde, Edith Ker, Jacques Mathou, Rufus, Howard Vernon, Chick Ortega, Silvie Laguna

Creatively combining genres—postapocalyptic sci-fi, black comedy, and sweet romance—and offering audiences an impressively oddball collection of sounds, colors, actors, and images, Jean-Pierre Jeunet and Marc Caro's inspired film *Delicatessen* was the recipient of several European awards and anticipated the pair's subsequent collaboration, *The City of Lost Children* (1995). Jeunet would go on to direct *Alien: Resurrection* in 1997, which was followed by the international blockbuster *Amélie* in 2001.

Delicatessen boasts an unforgettable opening: A mysterious figure covered from head to toe in an outfit made entirely of trash anxiously attempts to sneak away from a deli (located beneath a dilapidated apartment building) by hitching a ride in a garbage truck. Suddenly the lid to his can of freedom is violently ripped open and the menacing butcher-in-charge (Jean-Claude Dreyfus) brings a huge meat cleaver down upon him. We soon learn that the butcher's specialty is human flesh, and once his new employee—the saw-playing ex-clown Louison (a beautifully smush-faced Dominique Pinon)—falls for his bespectacled cellist daughter (Marie-Laure Dougnac), the race to make Louison the special of the day is on. To save her clown boyfriend from her cannibal dad, Julie betrays the latter to a group of lentil-eating rebels who live underground. With an eccentric screenplay by comic-book writer Gilles Adrien, and a number of darkly humorous set pieces, *Delicatessen* is a feast for the eyes and ears. **SJS**

La double vie de Véronique
The Double Life of Veronique Krzysztof Kieslowski, 1991

France / Poland / Norway (Canal+, Norsk, Sidéral, Tor) 98m Color **Language** French / Polish **Producer** Leonardo De La Fuente **Screenplay** Krzysztof Kieslowski, Krzysztof Piesiewicz **Photography** Slavomir Idziak **Music** Zbigniew Preisner **Cast** Irène Jacob, Halina Gryglaszewska, Kalina Jedrusik, Aleksander Bardini, Wladyslaw Kowalski, Jerzy Gudejko, Janusz Sterninski, Philippe Volter, Sandrine Dumas, Louis Ducreux, Claude Duneton, Lorraine Evanoff, Guillaume De Tonquedec, Gilles Gaston-Dreyfus, Alain Frérot **Cannes Film Festival** Krzysztof Kieslowski (FIPRESCI award, prize of the ecumenical jury, Golden Palm nomination), Irène Jacob (actress)

The Double Life of Veronique, Krzysztof Kieslowski's first feature after his ten-part masterpiece *Decalogue* (1988)—launching the European coproduction mode of making films that would lead to his *Three Colors* trilogy (*Blue* [1993], *White* [1994], and *Red* [1994])—is an exquisite enigma following the parallel lives of two twenty-year-old women, one in Poland and one in France, both played by the beautiful Irène Jacob. As in *Three Colors*, European coproduction becomes not only a means of financing but also part of the formal and thematic conceptualization of the project.

The Polish Veronika is a talented singer with a heart condition; the French Véronique quits her voice lessons and gets involved with a puppeteer (Philippe Volter) who writes children's books. Masterfully directed, this rather dreamlike film is simultaneously an effort on Kieslowski's part to hold onto to his Polish identity and an equally determined effort to move beyond it—almost as if the filmmaker were dreaming of a resurrected artistic identity for himself as Polish state financing went the route of Polish communism. **JRos**

Tongues Untied Marlon Riggs, 1991

U.S. (Frameline) 55m Color **Producer** Brian Freeman **Cast** Essex Hemphill **Berlin International Film Festival** Marlon Riggs (Teddy—documentary)

The late Essex Hemphill's politically sparked, erotically charged poetry and defiant punk spirit deeply infuse *Tongues Untied*, the groundbreaking, controversial documentary that vogued before Madonna, brought homo-thugs to light almost a decade before homophobic rappers and an idiotic mainstream media clumsily acknowledged their existence, and gave nuance and dignity to the degraded black sissy—all with humor and pathos. Performance footage, outrageous set pieces (the famous "snap off" scene), queen-on-the-street interviews, stinging critiques of homophobia in black films (using clips from Eddie Murphy's *Raw* [1987] and Spike Lee's *School Daze* [1988]), and talking heads either reciting poetry or simply testifying about their lives, add up to a portrait of both blackness and queerness that fairly seethes with energy.

Above all, what makes the film mandatory viewing is the way it critiques socially sanctioned bigotry while celebrating art (the creation of one's self and life) and Art (the creation of culture and its artifacts) that are produced within and beyond the confines of said bigotry. The depth and heart of *Tongues Untied* exposes the failings of both the largely white, theory-driven New Queer Cinema and the narrowly defined "authenticity" of most post-Spike Lee black cinema. Taking the viewer on a tour of a doubly marginalized subculture without pandering to the tourist's expectations or preconceptions, *Tongues Untied* transforms object into self-defining subject. **EH**

Da hong deng long gao gao gua
Raise the Red Lantern Yimou Zhang, 1991

China / Hong Kong / Taiwan (Palace, Era, China Film) 125m Eastmancolor **Language** Mandarin **Producer** Fu-Sheng Chiu **Screenplay** Ni Zhen, from novel by Su Tong **Photography** Zhao Fei, Lun Yang **Music** Naoki Tachikawa, Jiping Zhao **Cast** Li Gong, Caifei He, Jingwu Ma, Cuifen Cao, Qi Zhao, Jin Shuyuan, Ding Weimin, Cao Zhengyln, Zhihgang Cui, Chu Xiao, Lin Kong **Oscar nomination** Hong Kong (best foreign language film) **Venice Film Festival** Zhang Yimou (Silver Lion, tied with *The Fisher King* and *J'entends plus la guitare*)

i

The face of Master Chen (Jingwu Ma), husband of the four wives, is never clearly seen on screen.

Completing a loose trilogy that began with *Red Sorghum* (1987) and *Ju Dou* (1990), Yimou Zhang's grim adaptation of a novel by Su Tong once again stars Li Gong as a young woman who marries a much older man. Again he tells a story that explicitly critiques Chinese feudalism and indirectly contemporary China. This time, however, the style is quite different (despite another key use of the color red) and the vision bleaker.

The heroine, a less sympathetic figure than her predecessors, is a university student in the 1920s who becomes the fourth and youngest wife of a powerful man in northern China after her stepmother can no longer afford to pay for her education. She quickly becomes involved in the various intrigues and rivalries between wives that rule her husband's world and family tradition. Each wife has her own house and courtyard within the palace, and whoever the husband chooses to sleep with on a given night receives a foot massage, several lighted red lanterns, and the right to select the following day's menu.

Raise the Red Lantern confines us throughout to this claustrophobic universe of boxes within boxes, where wives and female servants devote their lives to scheming against one another. Zhang confirms his mastery and artistry here in many ways, some relatively new (such as his striking soundtrack), though the cold, remote, and stifling world he presents here offers little emotional release. **JRos**

Hearts of Darkness: A Filmmaker's Apocalypse

Fax Bahr, Eleanor Coppola, & George Hickenlooper, 1991

THE MAGIC AND THE MADNESS OF MAKING "APOCALYPSE NOW"

"The best picture of the year."

Hearts of Darkness

A Filmmaker's Apocalypse

U.S. (American Zoetrope) 96m Color
Producer Doug Claybourne, Les Mayfield, George Zaloom **Screenplay** Fax Bahr, George Hickenlooper **Photography** Larry Carney, Igor Meglic, Steven Wacks **Music** Todd Boekelheide, Carmine Coppola, Francis Ford Coppola, Mickey Hart **Cast** Sam Bottoms, Marlon Brando, Colleen Camp, Eleanor Coppola, Francis Ford Coppola, Gia Coppola, Roman Coppola, Sofia Coppola, Robert De Niro, Robert Duvall, Laurence Fishburne, Harrison Ford, Frederic Forrest, Albert Hall, Dennis Hopper, George Lucas, John Milius, Martin Sheen, G.D. Spradlin

> "It's scary to watch someone you love go into the center of himself and confront his fears, fear of failure, fear of death, fear of going insane."
>
> **Eleanor Coppola**

ℹ️

Francis Ford Coppola disliked his portrayal in the film and did not want it released on DVD initially.

During the 238 days it took Francis Ford Coppola and company to finish principal shooting of *Apocalypse Now* in the Philippines, Coppola's wife Eleanor documented on camera and in writing the nightmarish trials experienced by the film's cast, crew, and, perhaps most profoundly its renowned director. The astounding commercial and critical success of *Apocalypse Now* following its 1979 release resulted in its attaining the almost immediate status of a contemporary American classic. Contributing mightily to the legend is *Hearts of Darkness: A Filmmaker's Apocalypse*, directed by Fax Bahr with George Hickenlooper, which chronicles the turbulent making of Coppola's film. *Hearts of Darkness* seamlessly blends together the on- and off-set footage shot by Eleanor—as well as private conversations between her and her husband that Coppola was unaware were being taped—with more standard "talking head" interviews with numerous people involved in the production (conducted by Bahr more than ten years later). Also punctuating the documentary are outtakes and scenes left on the cutting-room floor, as well as aural snippets of Orson Welles narrating Joseph Conrad's 1901 novel *Heart of Darkness* (upon which the *Apocalypse Now* screenplay was loosely based) for the Mercury Theatre radio program in 1938.

Hearts of Darkness is widely considered among the very best entries in the subgenre loosely known as "making of" documentaries, in large part because of its creators' access to primary source materials that would normally be difficult to obtain. Among the highlights (lowlights for those involved): Interruptions on set by the Filipino military; increasingly grim confessions of insecurity and despair by the director to his wife; a heart attack suffered by the film's main actor, Martin Sheen, during the middle of shooting; and heated discussions between Coppola and two key cast members, Dennis Hopper (seemingly stoned the entire time and incapable of remembering his lines) and Marlon Brando (who showed up on set grossly overweight, without having read Conrad's novel). Add to all this the sacking of the originally contracted lead, Harvey Keitel; a massive typhoon that destroyed numerous sets; Coppola's endless dissatisfaction with his film's conclusion; and the fact that a project originally scheduled for sixteen weeks of shooting ended up taking more than three years to complete, and one has to figure the creators of *Hearts of Darkness* knew they had a "making of" gold mine on their hands.

On the one hand, as *Hearts of Darkness* labors to make clear beyond the shadow of a doubt, *Apocalypse Now* could only ever have been a Coppola picture. On the other hand, it is just as clear that *Apocalypse Now* could never have been the masterpiece it turned out to be had Coppola not received such magnificent contributions from his cast and crew. Not to mention from Eleanor, who, if *Hearts of Darkness* is at all to be trusted, had much more faith in her husband than he had in himself. **SJS**

Romper Stomper Geoffrey Wright, 1992

Australia (Australian Film Commission, Film Victoria, Romper Stomper P/L, Seon) 94m Eastmancolor Language English / Vietnamese Producer Ian Pringle, Daniel Scharf Screenplay Geoffrey Wright Photography Ron Hagen Music John Clifford White Cast Russell Crowe, Daniel Pollock, Jacqueline McKenzie, Alex Scott, Leigh Russell, Daniel Wyllie, James McKenna, Eric Mueck, Frank Magree, Christopher McLean, Josephine Keen, Samantha Bladon, Tony Lee, John Brumpton, Don Bridges

Romper Stomper ignited a passionate debate in Australia about whether it was a racist or antiracist tract. The passage of time allows us to judge the qualities of Geoffrey Wright's impressive feature debut more clearly.

Set within the skinhead subculture of the Melbourne suburb of Footscray, *Romper Stomper* vividly details the disintegration of a gang led by Hando (Russell Crowe in an early role)—from bashing up Vietnamese Australians to being picked off like scared animals by the law and aggrieved citizens alike.

The central focus of the film is a violently melodramatic love triangle, involving Gabe (Jacqueline McKenzie) and her shifting intimacies with the bullish Hando and the more sensitive Davey (the remarkable Daniel Pollock). The influences of Stanley Kubrick and Martin Scorsese are palpable, especially in set pieces like the siege on a bourgeois home in *A Clockwork Orange* (1971) style.

Romper Stomper does not pretend to offer a sophisticated commentary on the complexities of multicultural Australia. These "skins" are what gangsters or juvenile delinquents so often are in cinema—a flamboyant metaphor for a life lived at the edge of society. Both Wright and Crowe strive to give these events a Shakespearean grandeur, à la Richard III, and they largely succeed. **AM**

Strictly Ballroom Baz Luhrmann, 1992

Australia (M & A, Australian Film Finance Corporation, Beyond, Rank) 94m Eastmancolor Producer Tristram Miall Screenplay Baz Luhrmann, from story by Andrew Bovell and Baz Luhrmann Photography Steve Mason Music David Hirschfelder Cast Paul Mercurio, Tara Morice, Bill Hunter, Pat Thomson, Gia Carides, Peter Whitford, Barry Otto, John Hannan, Sonia Kruger, Kris McQuade, Pip Mushin, Leonie Page, Antonio Vargas, Armonia Benedito, Jack Webster Cannes Film Festival Baz Luhrmann (award of the youth—foreign film)

Before writer-director Baz Luhrmann made the frenetic bauble *Moulin Rouge* (2001), he deftly captured the magic and power of old-fashioned Hollywood musicals with *Strictly Ballroom*. He did so by intertwining two classic themes: the rebel who eventually triumphs over adversity and naysayers, and the ugly duckling who blossoms into a swan—and gets the prince in the end.

When promising dancer Scott Hastings (a devastatingly sexy Paul Mercurio) defies the ballroom dancing community and its rules, his shrieking stage mother (Pat Thomson) nearly disowns him and resorts to all manner of trickery to rein him back in. Simultaneously, one of the mother's beginning dance students, the mousy Fran (Tara Morice, sweetly affecting) develops a crush on Scott, a man seemingly far out of her league in every way. Defying odds and doubters, the two become a couple, both on and off the dance floor. Fast-moving, romantic, funny, and full of wit, *Strictly Ballroom* is sterling escapist fare.

What makes the film work is that beneath the fast edits, swooning soundtrack, and gloriously garish costumes (and even more garish secondary characters) is an enormous heart. Its knowing evocation of what it means and costs to be both a dreamer and an outcast makes the couple's heart-stopping finale a lump-in-the-throat triumph. **EH**

The Player Robert Altman, 1992

At the start of *The Player*, two fast-talking Hollywood types amble out the front door of a studio office, trading one-liners about films that begin with spectacular "long takes." As the camera leaves these characters and picks up others, the joke becomes knowingly clear: This is the ultimate such take, a parody of modern cinema's jazzy, showy moments.

The Player was touted as Robert Altman's comeback—his recovery twelve years after the commercial disaster of *Popeye* (1980). This claim is far from correct—Altman never stopped working in film, theater, and TV. But *The Player*, displaying a breathtaking mastery and modernity, brought him back to mainstream attention. It is fabulously cynical entertainment.

The witty script (by Michael Tolkin, from his novel of the same name) resembles a more successful screen adaptation of Tom Wolfe's *The Bonfire of the Vanities* than Brian De Palma's official 1990 version. Griffin Mills, played with icy charm by Tim Robbins, is a slick studio executive. He evaluates pitches—brief verbal synopses of often absurdly high-concept film ideas (such as *The Graduate II*). Griffin is being made increasingly nervous by the power plays in his company, and especially by the death threats he is receiving from a disgruntled, ignored scriptwriter.

Here begins a thriller plot involving mysterious identity, accidental murder, deception, bluff, coincidence, physical danger, and sexual intrigue. Altman carries it all off faultlessly, yet his true interest lies elsewhere. As usual, Altman delights in the painting of a detailed mosaic, a world in miniature. The oddball minor characters, fleeting incidents, overheard conversations, strange digressions—these are what make *The Player* marvelous.

Altman effortlessly encapsulates modern Hollywood filmmaking, while providing a radical alternative to it. Against all those feel-good movies with strong heroes, clear conflicts, and clear-cut motivations, *The Player* offers a shifty hero, fuzzy situations, and ambiguous motives—sliced and diced with the purest irony. By the end, you'll wonder how the cream of Hollywood's stars—from Jack Lemmon to Julia Roberts—ever agreed to be a part of this supreme exercise in subversive mischief. **AM**

U.S. (Avenue, Guild, Spelling) 124m Color **Producer** David Brown, Michael Tolkin, Nick Wechsler **Screenplay** Michael Tolkin, from his novel **Photography** Jean Lépine **Music** Thomas Newman **Cast** Tim Robbins, Greta Scacchi, Fred Ward, Whoopi Goldberg, Peter Gallagher, Brion James, Cynthia Stevenson, Vincent D'Onofrio, Dean Stockwell, Richard E. Grant, Sydney Pollack, Lyle Lovett, Dina Merrill, Angela Hall, Leah Ayres **Oscar nominations** Robert Altman (director), Michael Tolkin (screenplay), Geraldine Peroni (editing) **Cannes Film Festival** Robert Altman (director, Golden Palm nomination), Tim Robbins (actor)

1992

> "It's not as tough in [The Player] as it really is in real life. These people are much uglier in real life than they were in that film."

Robert Altman, 1999

ℹ

The Player has more Oscar-winning actors in its cast (twelve) than any other movie in history.

Reservoir Dogs Quentin Tarantino, 1992

Self-confessed video geek Quentin Tarantino was just twenty-eight when he wrote the script for this groundbreaking—and much imitated—movie. Its title apparently came from a patron of the video store where Tarantino used to work who referred to *Au Revoir les Enfants* (1987) as "that reservoir dog movie."

Dripping with quotable dialogue and superb performances from the almost totally male cast, *Reservoir Dogs* tells the story of the bloody aftermath of a diamond heist gone wrong. In flashback, we see the criminals as they are brought together by Joe Cabot (Lawrence Tierney)—none of whom know each other's real identities (making it impossible for anyone to rat their accomplices out)—and are given new monikers: Mr. Brown (Tarantino), the jerky Mr. Pink (Steve Buscemi), young Mr. Orange (Tim Roth), world-weary Mr. White (Harvey Keitel), and violent Mr. Blonde (Michael Madsen, in a creepily mesmerizing performance); and in a series of revealing scenes we learn about the events that have led to the film's blood-soaked climax in a warehouse.

But it isn't just the clever plotting that makes this film such a 1990s classic. Like the second film that Tarantino directed, *Pulp Fiction* (1994), the movie is cleverly cast (Madsen, Keitel, and Roth all giving career-best performances) and packed with memorable scenes that have become part of cinematic history, each containing pop culture references that are now recognized as a trademark of his scripts. Whether it's a scene in which the men—convening in a coffee shop before the heist—discuss everything from the etiquette of tipping to the real meaning of Madonna's "Like a Virgin" (their conclusion being unprintable here), or the shocking "ear" tableau with Madsen (featuring the unforgettable use of Steeler's Wheel classic "Stuck in the Middle with You"), Tarantino choses his words and actions so cleverly that much is revealed about each character's personality no matter how trivial the words are that they speak. A superb debut from one of the most individual cinematic talents to come out of the 1990s. **JB**

1992

U.S. (Dog Eat Dog, Live) 99m
Eastmancolor **Producer** Lawrence
Bender **Screenplay** Quentin Tarantino
Photography Andrzej Sekula **Cast** Harvey
Keitel, Tim Roth, Michael Madsen,
Chris Penn, Steve Buscemi, Lawrence
Tierney, Randy Brooks, Kirk Baltz, Edward
Bunker, Quentin Tarantino, Rich Turner,
David Steen, Tony Cosmo, Stevo Polyi,
Michael Sottile

"[My films are] my children. I love them all, but at the end of the day I'm always going to have a soft spot for Reservoir Dogs. *That was my first, the one that changed my life."*

Quentin Tarantino, 2007

i

Tarantino's original budget was just $30,000, but with the help of Harvey Keitel it was raised to $1.5 million.

Glengarry Glen Ross James Foley, 1992

U.S. (GGR, New Line, Zupnik II) 100m Color
Producer Jerry Tokofsky, Stanley R. Zupnik
Screenplay David Mamet, from his play **Photography** Juan Ruiz Anchía **Music** James Newton Howard **Cast** Jack Lemmon, Al Pacino, Ed Harris, Alan Arkin, Kevin Spacey, Alec Baldwin, Jonathan Pryce, Bruce Altman, Jude Ciccolella, Paul Butler, Lori Tan Chinn, Neal Jones, Barry Rossen, Leigh French, George Cheung **Oscar nomination** Al Pacino (actor in support role) **Venice Film Festival** Jack Lemmon (Volpi cup—actor)

With *Glengarry Glen Ross*, James Foley crafts the ultimate black comedy about selling. Adapted for the screen by David Mamet from his own 1984 Pulitzer Prize–winning play, Mamet's trademark repeating dialogue not only keeps the story at one remove from reality but keeps the viewer in a tension-filled holding pattern as well.

In a depressingly functional real-estate office on a rainy New York night, a team of desperate salesmen are given an ultimatum: Sell dubious property to "dead leads"—people who have no history of land investment—by morning or else be fired. Those who succeed will be given the "Glengarry leads," a list of genuine buyers. As for the actors—Jack Lemmon, Al Pacino (nominated for a supporting actor Oscar here; he won it for his lead in *Scent of a Woman* the same year), Kevin Spacey, Alan Arkin, Jonathan Pryce, and Alex Baldwin—*Glengarry Glen Ross* doesn't have a cast, it has a pantheon. Baldwin in particular gives a supporting yet pivotal performance as the hardline company man, a role created expressly for the film. Director Foley makes *Glengarry Glen Ross* into more than an updated *Death of a Salesman*: It's the only film for which antacids should be taken before viewing. **KK**

1992

Conte d'hiver Eric Rohmer, 1992
A Tale of Winter

France (C.E.R., Canal+, Losange, Sofiarp, Soficas) 114m Color
Language French **Producer** Margaret Ménégoz **Screenplay** Eric Rohmer **Photography** Luc Pagès **Music** Sébastien Erms **Cast** Charlotte Véry, Frédéric van den Driessche, Michael Voletti,Hervé Furic, Ava Loraschi, Christiane Desbois, Rosette, Jean-Luc Revol, Haydée Caillot, Jean-Claude Biette, Marie Rivière, Claudine Paringaux, Roger Dumas, Danièle Lebrun, Diane Lepvrier **Berlin International Film Festival** Eric Rohmer (FIPRESCI award, prize of the ecumenical Jury—special mention, Golden Bear nomination)

The second film in Eric Rohmer's *Contes des quatre saisons* ("Tales of Four Seasons") series begins a little disconcertingly with a summer romance (featuring equally surprising explicit sex) between a young hairdresser (Charlotte Véry) and the handsome hero she meets while vacationing in Brittany (Frédéric van den Driessche). That brief prologue over, however, the rest of the film is a more familiarly cool Christmas-period conversation piece as, five years later, the heroine dithers between two stolid suitors, perversely still believing that the holiday lover—who unwittingly fathered her daughter and to whom she accidentally gave an incorrect home address with which to contact her—will reappear as if by magic out of the blue.

With its witty but wintry study of seemingly forlorn faith and lost love reminiscent of *My Night at Maud's* (1969), and the almost irritatingly indecisive and self-centered heroine recalling *The Green Ray* (1986), this is archetypal Rohmer territory, down to the beautifully judged nod to Shakespeare's play and, consequently, a miraculous but extremely satisfying ending. As ever, too, the naturalistic performances are entirely plausible, the use of place—Paris and Burgundy—evocative, and the characterizations (including an intellectual librarian and the girl's more pragmatic boss as her admirers) precisely representative of the choices she faces. Quietly brilliant, and finally very moving. **GA**

Unforgiven Clint Eastwood, 1992

Clint Eastwood's last Western is a grand one to have ridden out on. Dark, gripping, and embracing complex themes, *Unforgiven* is a saga of melancholy beauty and unflinching moral, physical, and historical realism. Eastwood received his belated due as a filmmaker with this, his sixteenth feature, winning Oscars for Best Picture and Best Director. It's a radical revision of his younger, iconic, "supercool" man with no name and few words. Graying gunmen, oppressed women, and the painful ugliness of death provide the dark matter. Debunking Western heroics, and a dime novelist rewriting and glamorizing the bloody events he witnesses, adds sardonic humor to *Unforgiven*'s mix.

Eastwood's weather-beaten William Munny is a retired killer, reformed by the love of a good woman who has died, leaving him struggling to raise two children on a failing farm. Unlike Eastwood's Josey Wales, Munny doesn't need to redeem his humanity but struggle to retain it when he teams with old sidekick Ned (Morgan Freeman) to claim a bounty offered by brothel women. Their task: to avenge a knifed whore in bleak Big Whiskey, where brutal sheriff Little Bill (Gene Hackman) is indifferent to the women's demands for justice. Meanwhile, Richard Harris's flamboyant killer English Bob arrives to take up the prostitutes' reward himself, traveling with his biographer, one of those Eastern journalists who transformed some of the scum of the earth into the libertarian outlaw heroes of penny dreadful novellas.

Unforgiven is most fascinating in its revisionist approach to the mythology of the Old West, of dashing desperados and daring deeds, juxtaposed with the realities as recalled by Munny and Ned concerning the discomfort of sleeping on the trail, the misery of riding through the rain, and the ugly actuality of shooting a man—preferably when he's down. In another sharp contrast, the settings are gorgeous (Alberta, Canada, spectacularly doubling for the Midwestern frontier). The film is punctuated with grim scenes of horror from the slashing of the young prostitute to the inevitable final showdown.

Both Hackman's and Freeman's performances stand out, but there is an interesting dichotomy in Eastwood's own. Munny's pious utterances and his professed loss of appetite for killing do not ring entirely true, and when he is at last aroused to rage the result is what Eastwood devotees have been awaiting. In the end, Munny becomes an amalgam of all the violent avenging riders Eastwood has portrayed over the years.

This is as fine a piece of craftsmanship as one would expect from Eastwood, who brings to the film all his understanding of a genre he single-handedly kept alive for twenty years when it was out of fashion. Hackman won an Oscar for his sadistic Little Bill, having turned down the script years before Eastwood bought it. Touchingly, in its final grace note the film is dedicated "to Sergio and Don"—Eastwood's late directorial mentors Leone and Siegel. He did them proud. **AE**

U.S. (Malpaso, Warner Bros) 131m Technicolor **Producer** Clint Eastwood **Screenplay** David Webb Peoples **Photography** Jack N. Green **Music** Clint Eastwood, Lennie Niehaus **Cast** Clint Eastwood, Gene Hackman, Morgan Freeman, Richard Harris, Jaimz Woolvett, Saul Rubinek, Frances Fisher, Anna Levine, David Mucci, Rob Campbell, Anthony James, Tara Dawn Frederick, Beverley Elliott, Liisa Repo-Martell, Josie Smith **Oscars** Clint Eastwood (best picture), Clint Eastwood (director), Gene Hackman (actor in support role), Joel Cox (editing) **Oscar nominations** David Webb Peoples (screenplay), Clint Eastwood (actor), Henry Bumstead, Janice Blackie-Goodine (art direction), Jack N. Green (photography), Les Fresholtz, Vern Poore, Rick Alexander, Rob Young (sound)

"*Unforgiven . . . is a masterpiece . . . and certain to take its place among the great Westerns.*"

Philip French,
The Observer, 1992

i

The script for *Unforgiven* did the rounds in Hollywood for twenty years before Eastwood seized on it.

Yuen Ling-yuk Stanley Kwan, 1992
The Actress

Stanley Kwan's 1992 masterpiece is quite possibly the greatest Hong Kong film ever; perhaps only some of the works of Wong Kar-wai, such as *Days of Being Wild* (1991) and *In the Mood for Love* (2000) are comparable in depth and intensity. Yet it must be acknowledged that the shortening of the original 167-minute running time to 126 minutes has been harmful. Adding insult to injury, the Hong Kong producers destroyed the original negative; apparently the uncut version survives only on Australian television. The story of silent film star Ruan Ling-yu (1910–1935), known as the Garbo of Chinese cinema, *The Actress* combines documentary footage with period re-creation, biopic glamor with profound curiosity, and ravishing historical clips with color simulations of the same sequences being shot—all to explore a past that seems more complex, sexy, and mysterious than the present.

Maggie Cheung won a well-deserved best actress prize at Berlin for her classy performance in the title role, despite the fact that her difference from Ruan Ling-yu as an actress is probably more important than any similarities. She was known as a comic actress in relatively lightweight Hong Kong entertainment before this film, and *The Actress* proved to be a turning point in her career toward more dramatic and often meatier parts. But the gap between her own polished star image and that of Ruan as a more unbridled tragedienne is crucial, and much of Kwan's work as a director goes into creating a kind of nimbus around Cheung's poise and grace. Kwan also creates a labyrinth of questions around who Ruan was and why she committed suicide—a labyrinth both physical (with beautiful uses of black-and-white movie sets) and metaphysical.

Highlights include the stylish beauty of an imagined Shanghai film world of the 1930s and the flat abrasiveness of Kwan chatting with Cheung on video about what all this means and coming up with damn little. Any historical movie worth its salt historicizes the present along with the past, and this movie implicitly juxtaposes our own inadequacy with those potent clips of Ling-yu herself. **JRos**

Hong Kong (Swift) 167m Color
Language Cantonese Producer Jackie Chan, Leonard Ho Screenplay Chiu Tai An-Ping Photography Poon Hang-Sang Music Huang Jin Chen Cast Maggie Cheung, Han Chin, Carina Lau, Shin Hong, Tony Leung, Lawrence Ng Berlin International Film Festival Maggie Cheung (Silver Bear—actress), Stanley Kwan nomination (Golden Bear)

"Nothing like an orthodox biopic, the result is tender, vivid, and almost overwhelmingly moving."

Time Out Film Guide

1992

i

Cheung became the first Chinese actor to win a major European film award for her performance.

C'est arrivé près de chez vous
Man Bites Dog

Rémy Belvaux, André Bonzel, & Benoît Poelvoorde, 1992

Man Bites Dog is probably the most controversial film in the history of Belgian cinema. It rose to instant fame after critics all over the world denounced its portrayal of on-screen violence, linking it to contemporary films such as *Reservoir Dogs* (1992) and *Henry: Portrait of a Serial Killer* (1990). Although *Man Bites Dog* shares some features with these other movies, it is also very different.

Shot in grainy black-and-white stock, employing handheld camera work and direct sound (there is no music), *Man Bites Dog* has the look of a cinema verité documentary. The story concerns a film crew who are following around a self-proclaimed serial killer named Ben (played by cowriter and codirector Benoît Poelvoorde). As Ben goes about his business, he slowly makes the crewmen accomplices to his crimes. He takes them out to a copious meal, they start helping him dispose of bodies, and he even helps them out financially.

Ben's running commentary—on his "craft," on his victims and their social peculiarities, and on the crew—invests *Man Bites Dog* with a surprisingly humorous tone. Here we are, enjoying a serial killer's work, because he is so funny, upbeat, and unpredictable. While murdering a man in his bathroom, Ben abruptly stops and asks the crew which French film this scene reminds them of.

Then the laughter stops. The turning point is a gruesomely explicit rape scene. Here the film stops being a black comedy, becoming instead a bleak criticism of our desire to watch everyday life tilt out of balance. The impact of the scene is so shocking that it forces us to rethink our earlier pleasures, and changes the status of the narrative.

According to the creators of *Man Bites Dog*, the idea for the film stemmed from a Belgian tabloid journalism TV series, one which blew small stories out of proportion and intruded on people's private lives. This underlying concept helped guarantee the film's success, and secured its status as an all-time cult favorite. **EM**

Belgium (Artistes Anonymes) 92m BW **Language** French **Producer** Rémy Belvaux, André Bonzel, Benoît Poelvoorde **Screenplay** Rémy Belvaux, André Bonzel, Benoît Poelvoorde, Vincent Tavier **Photography** André Bonzel **Music** Jean-Marc Chenut, Laurence Dufrene **Cast** Benoît Poelvoorde, Jacqueline Poelvoorde-Pappaert, Nelly Pappaert, Hector Pappaert, Jenny Drye, Malou Madou, Willy Vandenbroeck, Rachel Deman, André Laime, Edith Lemerdy, Sylviane Godé, Zoltan Tobolik, Valérie Parent, Alexandra Fandango, Olivier Cotica **Cannes Film Festival** Rémy Belvaux, André Bonzel, Benoît Poelvoorde (SACD award—best feature, special award of the youth)

> *"A grisly sick joke of a film that some will find funny, others simply appalling."*
>
> **Stephen Holden,**
> **The New York Times, 1992**

i

Rémy Belvaux had the idea for the film while looking for a project that could be made without any money.

The Crying Game Neil Jordan, 1992

G.B. / Japan (British Screen, Channel Four, Eurotrustees, Nippon Film Development and Finance, Palace) 112m Color Producer Stephen Woolley Screenplay Neil Jordan Photography Ian Wilson Music Simon Boswell, Anne Dudley Cast Forest Whitaker, Miranda Richardson, Stephen Rea, Adrian Dunbar, Breffni McKenna, Joe Savino, Jaye Davidson, Andrée Bernard, Jim Broadbent, Ralph Brown, Tony Slattery Oscar Neil Jordan (screenplay) Oscar nominations Stephen Woolley (best picture), Neil Jordan (director), Stephen Rea (actor), Jaye Davidson (actor in support role), Kant Pan (editing)

The Crying Game's big, infamous twist is actually far less interesting than the more radical depiction that it offers: Forest Whitaker's character, Jody, whose queerness is so removed from most people's preconceptions that few critics or viewers ever even seem to notice the slyly drawn man's tiered sexuality. Writer-director Neil Jordan crafts an often droll, frequently melodramatic essay on the unfathomable laws of desire in this layered tale of a mysterious "woman" (the aloof and beautiful Jaye Davidson, reviving the tragic mulatto), her lover who is murdered under bizarre circumstances (Whitaker), and a man involved with the murder (Stephen Rea). It's all wrapped in a bow of political intrigue that's centered on longstanding tensions between the British army and the Irish Republican Army.

As the love triangle between the deceased man, his faux widow, and his assassin deepens, all sorts of secrets come tumbling out; the movie abandons what the story first appeared to be about for a new tale altogether, this one about sexual intrigue. A landmark film for the convergence of marketing chutzpah and layered sexual subversiveness that made it a hit, The Crying Game proved that there was an audience for audacious, nervy independent cinema. With its varying takes on race, sexuality, and gender, it kicked open the doors for discussions on the complexities of attraction and erotic longing. Its extraordinary box-office success, for better or worse, helped transform independent film from a cult item to a highly profitable market share. **EH**

1993

Lan feng zheng Tian Zhuangzhuang, 1993
The Blue Kite

China / Hong Kong (Beijing Film, Longwick) 138m Color Language Mandarin Producer Luo Guiping, Cheng Yongping Screenplay Xiao Mao Photography Hou Yong Music Yoshihide Otomo Cast Yi Tian, Zhang Wenyao, Chen Xiaoman, Lu Liping, Zhong Ping, Chu Quanzhong, Song Xiaoying, Zhang Hong

Banned in China, the powerful eighth feature of Tian Zhuangzhuang (The Horse Thief [1986] and Li Lianying, The Imperial Eunuch [1991]) follows its fictional hero, Tietou, and his family in Beijing from 1953 to 1968, through the Cultural Revolution and its ensuing repercussions and purges. Tietou's father is a librarian, and in one unforgettable and disquieting postrevolution scene, the hero's father, attending a meeting for library staff, briefly leaves the room to go to the toilet. Upon his return he finds that he's been branded a reactionary, leading to his banishment to a collective farm for "reeducation" and a radical change in his entire family's fortunes.

The Blue Kite offers a sublime and often subtle look at how history and politics disrupt ordinary lives, with a memorable use of its central courtyard location and a keen feeling for everyday life within that space. One comes away from this film with a profound sense of how individuals strive to maintain a sense of ethics within a changing society that periodically confounds those ethics or makes them irrelevant. **JRos**

Philadelphia Jonathan Demme, 1993

U.S. (Clinica Estetico, TriStar)
125m Technicolor **Producer** Edward
Saxon **Screenplay** Ron Nyswaner
Photography Tak Fujimoto **Music** Howard
Shore, Bruce Springsteen, Neil Young
Cast Tom Hanks, Denzel Washington,
Antonio Banderas, Roberta Maxwell, Buzz
Kilman, Karen Finley, Daniel Chapman,
Jeffrey Williamson, Joanne Woodward, Jason
Robards **Oscars** Tom Hanks (actor), Bruce
Springsteen (song) **Oscar nominations** Ron
Nyswaner (screenplay), Carl Fullerton, Alan
D'Angerio (makeup), Neil Young (song)
Berlin International Film Festival Tom
Hanks (Silver Bear—actor), Jonathan
Demme nomination (Golden Bear)

Although AIDS had been tackled on TV, most notably in the acclaimed 1985 drama *An Early Frost,* and in independent cinema (the 1990 film *Longtime Companion*), Jonathan Demme's *Philadelphia* was the first mainstream Hollywood movie about the disease. Tom Hanks, in a role that won him his first Best Actor Oscar, stars as Andrew Beckett, a homosexual Philadelphian lawyer who is fired by his firm after they discover he has AIDS. They claim they dismissed him for incompetence at work, so he hires a hotshot lawyer to defend him in a suit against them. Of course, the lawyer he hires, Joe Miller (Denzel Washington), is homophobic and harbors misconceptions about the disease, but in the course of their fight he learns from Andrew and comes to respect him.

Demme fills his heartfelt drama with accomplished actors, from Hanks (who pulls off an opera-appreciation scene that lesser actors would have fumbled) and Washington to Jason Robards, as the firm's bigoted boss, and Antonio Banderas as Andrew's companion. Some may argue that Demme sanitizes the ravages AIDS inflicts on a person in the film, but Hanks's sympathetic, passionate performance more than makes up for any attempts at softening the subject matter for a mainstream audience. **JB**

Hsimeng jensheng Hou Hsiao-hsien, 1993
The Puppetmaster

Taiwan (ERA, Nian Dai, Qiu Fusheng) 142m
Color **Language** Mandarin / Taiwanese /
Japanese **Producer** Chiu Fu-Sheng, Zhang
Huakun **Screenplay** Chu T'ien-wen, Li
Tianlu, Wu Nien-Jen **Photography** Lee Pin
Bing **Music** Chen Ming Chang, Zhang
Hongda **Cast** Li Tianlu, Lim Giong, Lin
Chung, Bai Ming Hwa, Cheng Fue Choung,
Liou Hung, Tsai Chen-Nan, Yang Lai-Yin
Cannes Film Festival Hou Hsiao-hsien (jury
prize, Golden Palm nomination)

Part of a loosely connected trilogy on the history of Taiwan that includes *City of Sadness* (1989) and *Good Men, Good Women* (1995), *The Puppetmaster* is set during the Japanese occupation, which lasted from 1895 to 1945. Based on fact, it recounts the life story of Li Tianlu, recollected in old age, with Li himself appearing occasionally as an on-screen narrator. Li is apprenticed to a puppeteer, and as he develops his skills we witness the events of his life. The film weaves together the personal and the political, as Li gets married and acquires a mistress, as well as negotiating other family complications. At times the Japanese are presented as oppressors—in one scene they arrive to demand that the men in his grandfather's family cut their pigtails. But Li manages an accommodation with them, even working as a puppeteer for the Japanese propaganda service. At the end of the war the Japanese commander invites him to lunch and tells him how much he will miss him.

Director Hou Hsiao-hsien has an unhurried style, with long shots that calmly observe the interaction of the characters. If the narrative method, with its frequent ellipses, requires attention, audiences will be well rewarded by a deeply felt portrait of Taiwanese life. **EB**

Short Cuts Robert Altman, 1993

U.S. (Avenue, Fine Line, Spelling) 18/m Color
Producer Cary Brokaw **Screenplay** Robert
Altman, Frank Barhydt, from stories by
Raymond Carver **Photography** Walt Lloyd
Music Gavin Friday, Mark Isham, Doc Pomus
Cast Andie MacDowell, Bruce Davison, Jack
Lemmon, Julianne Moore, Matthew Modine,
Anne Archer, Jennifer Jason Leigh, Chris
Penn, Lili Taylor, Robert Downey, Jr.,
Madeleine Stowe, Tim Robbins, Peter
Gallagher, Lily Tomlin, Tom Waits, Lori Singer,
Lyle Lovett, Huey Lewis, Darnell Williams
Oscar nomination Robert Altman (director)
Venice Film Festival Robert Altman (Golden
Lion, tied with Trois couleurs: Bleu),
entire ensemble cast (Volpi cup)

i

Each of the stories was shot in
a week, the entire movie being
completed in ten weeks.

One of the shortest-seeming long movies of the 1990s, this is Robert Altman's braiding-together of a fistful of Raymond Carver stories. *Short Cuts* follows various plot and character threads through a Los Angeles blighted by insects and earthquake, where everyone is on the point of cracking up and random tragedy is always impending.

Altman assembles a once-in-a-lifetime cast, but also manages to give them all things worth doing: Jack Lemmon as an estranged father, Julianne Moore naked from the waist down, Anne Archer as a party clown, Bruce Davison and Andie MacDowell shocked by grief, Jennifer Jason Leigh as a phone-sex operator, Robert Downey, Jr. and Chris Penn as casually awful men, Tim Robbins as a callous cop, Peter Gallagher wrecking his wife's home, Lily Tomlin and Tom Waits drinking. On repeated viewings, the overlaps become more fun to spot and individual performances take the spotlight. In the end, the film is especially notable for its mosaic portrait of Altman's sparkly, haunted, corrupt Los Angeles (a very different place from Carver's drier Midwest).

An interesting counterpart to Altman's insider's vision of *The Player* (1992), *Short Cuts* gets away from the arena of the movie business (which is only a brief presence here) into the strange little lives of other involved Angelenos. **KN**

Schindler's List Steven Spielberg, 1993

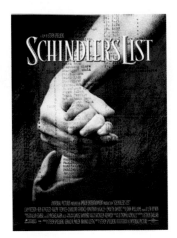

U.S. (Amblin, Universal) 197m BW / Color
Producer Branko Lustig, Gerald R. Molen,
Steven Spielberg **Screenplay** Steven
Zaillian, from the novel *Schindler's Ark* by
Thomas Keneally **Photography** Janusz
Kaminski **Music** John Williams **Cast** Liam
Neeson, Ben Kingsley, Ralph Fiennes,
Caroline Goodall, Jonathan Sagall, Embeth
Davidtz, Malgoscha Gebel, Shmulik Lev,
Mark Ivanir, Béatrice Macola, Andrzej Seweryn,
Friedrich von Thun, Krzysztof Luft, Harry
Nehring, Norbert Weisser **Oscars** Steven
Spielberg, Gerald R. Molen, Branko Lustig
(best picture), Steven Spielberg (director),
Steven Zaillian (screenplay), Allan Starski,
Ewa Braun (art direction), Janusz Kaminski
(photography), Michael Kahn (editing), John
Williams (music) **Oscar nominations** Liam
Neeson (actor), Ralph Fiennes (actor in
support role), Anna B. Sheppard (costume),
Christina Smith, Matthew W. Mungle, Judith
A. Cory (makeup), Andy Nelson, Steve
Pederson, Scott Millan, Ron Judkins (sound)

*"Stern, if this factory
ever produces a shell
that can actually be fired,
I'll be very unhappy."*

Oskar Schindler
(Liam Neeson)

i

At his own request, Spielberg
was not paid for making the film.
He felt it would be inappropriate.

Working from a well-constructed script by Steven Zaillian (*Searching for Bobby Fischer* [1993]), adapting Thomas Keneally's nonfiction novel—a fascinating account of the Nazi businessman Oskar Schindler, who saved the lives of over 1,100 Polish Jews—Spielberg does an uncommonly good job both of holding our interest over the course of 185 minutes and of showing more of the nuts and bolts of the Holocaust than we usually get from fiction films. One enormous plus is the rich and beautiful black-and-white cinematography by one-time Chicagoan Janusz Kaminski—who opted for monochrome because he wanted the movie to possess a timeless quality. Spielberg was adamant that his film should not be seen simply a period piece and should carry contemporary relevance. As he noted after completing the shoot, "I made it this year because I was so upset about what was happening in Bosnia, as well as about the attempted genocide of the whole Kurdish population." For similar reasons, much of the picture was shot using handheld cameras, in order to project an documentary-like, "cinema verité" atmosphere.

Spielberg's capacity to milk the maximal intensity out of the existential terror and pathos conveyed in Keneally's book—Polish Jews could be killed at any moment by the capriciousness of a labor camp director (Ralph Fiennes)—is complemented and even counterpointed by his capacity to milk the glamor of Nazi high life and absolute power. (In a telling phrase, the director later commented on the "sexual evil" conveyed by Fiennes's performance.) Significantly, each emotional register is generally accompanied by a different style of cinematography, and much as Liam Neeson's effective embodiment of Schindler works as our conduit to the Nazis, Ben Kingsley's subtle performance as Itzhak Stern—his Jewish accountant, right-hand man, and mainly silent conscience—provides our conduit to the Polish Jews. In 2011, Kingsley recalled that Spielberg told him at the time that he was "the witness of the film."

What are unfortunately missing, and therefore distorted, are many of the more fascinating elements in the real-life story that don't match Spielberg's pious, patriarchal scenario—such as the major role that Schindler's wife, Emilie, played in saving Jewish lives after he resumed living with her while he was establishing a mock munitions plant in Moravia, or the fact that he continued to betray her with other women. One also wonders how Spielberg might have coped with the subject of the bribes that were necessary for many of the Polish Jews to find their way onto Schindler's list—actually compiled mostly by Marcel Goldberg (played here by Mark Ivanir)—and thus survive. If he had dealt with this sort of material, though, the film would have probably lost some of its moral directness even while gaining in moral complexity. **JRos**

Trois couleurs: Bleu Krzysztof Kieslowski, 1993
Three Colors: Blue

France / Poland / Switzerland (CAB, CED, Eurimages, France 3, MK2, Tor) 100m Eastmancolor **Language** French **Producer** Marin Karmitz **Screenplay** Agnieszka Holland, Slavomir Idziak, Krzysztof Kieslowski, Krzysztof Piesiewicz, Edward Zebrowski **Photography** Slavomir Idziak **Music** Zbigniew Preisner **Cast** Juliette Binoche, Benoît Régent, Florence Pernel, Charlotte Véry, Hélène Vincent, Philippe Volter, Claude Duneton, Hugues Quester, Emmanuelle Riva, Florence Vignon, Daniel Martin, Jacek Ostaszewski, Yann Trégouët, Alain Ollivier **Venice Film Festival** Krzysztof Kieslowski (Golden Lion), tied with Short Cuts, Slavomir Idziak (Golden Osella—photography), Juliette Binoche (Volpi cup—actress)

Blue, the first film in Krzysztof Kieslowski's "Three Colors" trilogy, may be inspired by the meaning of the first color in the French flag (liberty), but the irascible director would never be so literal. Instead he keeps the movie mysterious and oblique, with both beautiful and haunting results. Juliette Binoche plays a widow who reacts to the death of her composer husband and daughter by withdrawing from the world. Yet memories of her past, as well as the secrets her husband left behind, interrupt her selfish emotional isolation, leading her to complete unfinished business.

Along with a top-tier score and evocative cinematography, *Blue* benefits most from Kieslowski's sharp eye and unerring feel for the fleeting emotions, enigmatic actions, and minute details that comprise human nature. Thanks to his perceptive script and careful control of the story, Kieslowski creates a film whose richness and honesty offer a glimpse into the enigmatic workings of the soul. He fills every frame of *Blue* with meaning, enhanced and accented in no small part by Binoche's brave and powerful performance, which hinges on subtle tics and other physical nuances in its depiction of a broken spirit slowly pulling herself back together. **JKl**

Ba wang bie ji Kaige Chen, 1993
Farewell My Concubine

China / Hong Kong (Beijing Film, China Film, Maverick, Tomson) 171m Color **Language** Mandarin **Producer** Feng Hsu **Screenplay** Wei Lu, from novel by Lillian Lee **Photography** Changwei Gu **Music** Jiping Zhao **Cast** Leslie Cheung, Fengyi Zhang, Li Gong, Qi Lu, Da Ying, You Ge, Chun Li, Han Lei, Di Tong, Mingwei Ma, Yang Fei, Zhi Yin, Hailong Zhao, Dan Li, Wenli Jiang **Oscar nominations** Hong Kong (best foreign language film), Changwei Gu (photography) **Cannes Film Festival** Kaige Chen (FIPRESCI award, Golden Palm, tied with *The Piano*)

First of the "Fifth Generation" of Chinese filmmakers to emerge onto the world scene from the Beijing Film Academy since it reopened its doors in 1978, Kaige Chen bravely invoked his own bitter memories of the Cultural Revolution with *Farewell My Concubine*. The film is an exquisite, fascinating drama of the fifty-year relationship between two male Beijing Opera singers that spans China's turbulent twentieth century through convulsive collective and personal betrayals.

Farewell My Concubine, China's first Golden Palm winner at Cannes (to the dismay of officials provoked by elements of homosexuality and recent history), is an impassioned, sumptuous epic and a stunning achievement, particularly because it was made in a troubled, censorious environment. Hong Kong pop star Leslie Cheung plays the abandoned boy sexually abused and groomed to become a star in female roles—most significantly as a tragic royal concubine in a popular classic. Fengyi Zhang is his lifelong intimate, the less artistic and less idealistic costar whose marriage to conniving prostitute Li Gong is a catalyst for jealousy, denunciation, and haunted self-preservation during upheavals in the company and society. Rare indeed is a film on this scale that balances exotic culture and thrilling spectacle (the opera, civil war, and revolutionary mobs) with intimate and universally powerful human experience. **AE**

Groundhog Day Harold Ramis, 1993

Comic actor Bill Murray gives what may be the best and warmest performance of his career in this genius comedy—arguably the best of the 1990s—from writers Harold Ramis (who also directs) and Danny Rubin. Murray plays Phil Connors, a grumpy weatherman who is dispatched with producer Rita (Andie MacDowell) and cameraman Larry (Chris Elliott) to the friendly little town of Punxsutawney, Pennsylvania, to witness the annual Groundhog Day ceremony. A groundhog named Punxsutawney Phil emerges and, depending on whether or not he sees his shadow, predicts if the town will experience a few more weeks of winter. Disparaging and self-centered, Phil doesn't want to be there at all, so when he wakes up the next morning to discover he is reliving Groundhog Day all over again, he isn't exactly thrilled. Especially when he relives it again the next day, and the next, and seems to be the only person who is experiencing, and remembering, the same events over and over (and over) again.

It's a terrific conceit (one that is never explained, which makes it even better) that first causes the scheming Phil to take advantage of the situation. He asks a woman one day what she looks for in a man, and the following day embodies all those attributes to the unwitting lady. It then drives him to attempt suicide in various ways (until he discovers that he will inevitably wake up alive again the next/same morning). Eventually he is led to improve his behavior as well as his people skills in an effort to redeem himself in the eyes of Rita, who sees him only as the grouch he has always been.

In between, there are delicious running gags including waking up to the same banter and Sonny and Cher song ("I've Got You Babe") on the radio; seeing Stephen Tobolowsky in a superb turn as irritating insurance salesman Ned Ryerson, and knowing what is going to happen before it does. Groundhog Day is both wonderfully clever and hysterically funny—comedy is rarely this perfect. **JB**

U.S. (Columbia) 101m Technicolor
Producer Trevor Albert **Screenplay** Danny Rubin, Harold Ramis **Photography** John Bailey **Music** George Fenton **Cast** Bill Murray, Andie MacDowell, Chris Elliott, Stephen Tobolowsky, Brian Doyle-Murray, Marita Geraghty, Angela Paton, Rick Ducommun, Rick Overton

"This is one time where television really fails to capture the true excitement of a large squirrel predicting the weather."

**Phil Connors
(Bill Murray)**

1993

i

Bill Murray was bitten twice by a groundhog during shooting, necessitating anti-rabies jabs.

The Piano Jane Campion, 1993

Australia / NZ / France (AFC, CiBy NSW Film & TV Office) 121m Eastmancolor **Producer** Jan Chapman **Screenplay** Jane Campion **Photography** Stuart Dryburgh **Music** Michael Nyman **Cast** Holly Hunter, Harvey Keitel, Sam Neill, Anna Paquin, Kerry Walker, Geneviève Lemon, Tungia Baker, Ian Mune, Peter Dennett, Te Whatanui Skipwith, Pete Smith, Bruce Allpress **Oscars** Jane Campion (screenplay), Holly Hunter (actress), Anna Paquin (actress in support role) **Oscar nominations** Jan Chapman (best picture), Jane Campion (director), Stuart Dryburgh (photography), Janet Patterson (costume), Veronika Jenet (editing) **Cannes Film Festival** Jane Campion (Golden Palm, tied with *Farewell My Concubine*), Holly Hunter (actress)

i

Hunter is a capable pianist and performed the majority of the piano sequences in the film herself.

Sweetie (1989) and *An Angel at My Table* (1990) taught us to expect startling as well as beautiful things from Jane Campion, and this assured and provocative third feature offers yet another lush parable about the perils and paradoxes of female self-expression.

Set during the nineteenth century, this original story by Campion—which evokes at times some of the romantic intensity of Emily Brontë—focuses on a Scottish widow (Holly Hunter) who hasn't spoken since her childhood, presumably by choice, and whose main form of self-expression is her piano playing. She arrives with her nine-year-old daughter (Anna Paquin) in the New Zealand wilds to enter into an arranged marriage, which gets off to an unhappy start when her husband-to-be (Sam Neill) refuses to transport her piano. A local white man living with the Maori natives (Harvey Keitel) buys the piano from him and, fascinated by and attracted to the mute woman, agrees to "sell" it back to her a key at a time in exchange for lessons—lessons that have ultimately traumatic consequences.

Setting out to be politically correct, erotic, and romantic at the same time, *The Piano* inevitably bites off more than it can possibly chew, but winds up stimulating passionate feelings nonetheless. **JRos**

Hsi yen Ang Lee, 1993
The Wedding Banquet

Taiwan / U.S. (Central Motion Pictures Corp., Good Machine) 106m Color Language Mandarin / English Producer Ted Hope, Ang Lee, James Schamus Screenplay Ang Lee, Neil Peng, James Schamus Photography Jong Lin Music Mader Cast Dion Birney, Jeanne Kuo Chang, Winston Chao, Paul Chen, May Chin, Chou Chung-Wei Oscar nomination Taiwan (best foreign language film) Berlin International Film Festival Ang Lee (Golden Bear, tied with The Women from the Lake of Scented Souls)

A young Taiwanese businessman living in New York and sharing an apartment with his physical therapist boyfriend decides to marry a Chinese artist who needs a green card. The next thing he knows, his parents from Taiwan, not knowing he's gay, have decided to come to the wedding, leading to a good many predictable if enjoyable comic complications. Director Ang Lee collaborated on the script for The Wedding Banquet with Neil Feng and producer James Schamus—the latter of whom has continued to work with the director ever since as both producer and cowriter.

This 1993 feature, Lee's second, is a clever and entertaining social comedy that helped to establish him as a commercial director long before such more obvious mainstream crowd-pleasers as The Ice Storm (1997) and Crouching Tiger, Hidden Dragon (2000). Satire about—yet also clearly for—the middle class, The Wedding Banquet has a lot more heart than edge, and is pitched mainly at liberal straight people, though the Chinese cultural details should be fascinating to all non-Chinese viewers. **JRos**

Thirty-Two Short Films About Glenn Gould
François Girard, 1993

Canada / Portugal / Netherlands / Finland (CBC, Glenn Gould, NOS, Rhombus, Samuel Goldwyn, Société Radio-Canada, Ontario Film Development Corporation, Téléfilm Canada, YLE) 92m Color Producer Michael Allder, Niv Fichman, Barbara Willis Sweete, Larry Weinstein Screenplay François Girard, Don McKellar Photography Alain Dostie Music Johann Sebastian Bach, Richard Wagner Cast Colm Feore, Derek Keurvorst, Katya Ladan, Devon Anderson, Joshua Greenblatt, Sean Ryan, Kate Hennig, Sean Doyle, Sharon Bernbaum, Don McKellar, David Hughes, Carlo Rota, Peter Millard, John Dolan, Allegra Fulton

Glenn Gould was the brilliant, eccentric Canadian pianist who retired from the concert stage young and spent the rest of his driven, reclusive but remarkable life making acclaimed recordings, experimental radio programs, a fortune on the commodities market, and legendarily bizarre telephone calls until his death at age fifty in 1982. An entirely appropriate acknowledgment of his other-worldly genius was the inclusion of Gould's performance of a Bach prelude in the Voyager spacecraft's message to the stars from planet Earth.

Young French-Canadian writer-director François Girard adroitly juggles dramatic fiction, documentary realism, humor, and even animation with insight into the artist's agony and ecstasy in a beguiling, dazzlingly adventurous series of vignettes—the playful structure of thirty-two short films a witty mimicking of Bach's "Goldberg Variations"—for a unique, funny, tender, and exhilarating biopic. "Diary of One Day," for example, is an X-ray film of a pianist's skeleton, musculature, and nerve endings at work; "Truck Stop" observes Gould mentally orchestrating conversations around him in a café into a pleasing rhythmic arrangement. Colm Feore gives a wonderful, commanding performance of this rare individual, suggesting all the complexities of a gifted, multifaceted, and idiosyncratic character. And the soundtrack, compiled from Gould's own repertoire, is glorious. **AE**

Jurassic Park Steven Spielberg, 1993

U.S. (Universal, Amblin) 127m Color
Producer Kathleen Kennedy, Gerald R.
Molen **Screenplay** Michael Crichton, David
Koepp, from novel by Michael Crichton
Photography Dean Cundey **Music** John
Williams **Cast** Sam Neill, Laura Dern, Jeff
Goldblum, Richard Attenborough, Bob Peck,
Martin Ferrero, B.D. Wong, Joseph Mazzello,
Ariana Richards, Samuel L. Jackson, Wayne
Knight, Gerald R. Molen, Miguel Sandoval,
Cameron Thor, Christopher John Fields
Oscars Gary Rydstrom, Richard Hymns
(special sound effects), Dennis Muren,
Stan Winston, Phil Tippett, Michael Lantieri
(special visual effects), Gary Summers,
Gary Rydstrom, Shawn Murphy,
Ron Judkins (sound)

*"Dinosaurs and man,
two species separated
by 65 million years of
evolution have just been
suddenly thrown back
into the mix together."*

Alan Grant (Sam Neill)

𝒊

Prior to *Jurassic Park*, Attenborough
had not acted in a film since
The Human Factor (1979).

The same year that saw his "grown-up" war drama *Schindler's List* win vast critical acclaim, Steven Spielberg also delivered the kind of movie we had come to expect from the director of *Raiders of the Lost Ark* (1981)—a rip-roaring adventure of dinosaurs and disaster based on Michael Crichton's best-selling novel, *Jurassic Park*.

Slightly bonkers millionaire John Hammond (Richard Attenborough) has created the ultimate theme park on a remote island, and he wants to offer a sneak preview to a few carefully selected people: paleontologists Alan Grant (Sam Neill) and Ellie Sattler (Laura Dern), mathematician Ian Malcolm (Jeff Goldblum), and Hammond's own grandchildren Tim (Joseph Mazzello) and Lex (Ariana Richards). What they find is a luscious isle populated by real-life dinosaurs recreated using DNA found in pieces of long-buried amber. A perfect sanctuary, in theory, but because the dinosaur breeds they have "made" include the infamous T. rex and some nasty, toothy creatures named velociraptors—and because one of the park's employee is secretly working for one of Hammond's rivals, and is set on stealing dinosaur embryos—it's obvious that the whole scheme is going to end in tears. And screaming and dying.

Part monster movie and part disaster movie as the island is thrashed by a storm and the assembled characters find there is nowhere to hide from giant rampaging (and, one assumes, hungry) prehistoric creatures, *Jurassic Park* is packed with so many thrills and jaw-dropping dino effects—utilizing both CGI and animatronics—it isn't hard to see why the movie went on to gross over $900 million worldwide. Indeed, it succeeded in becoming the highest-grossing movie of all time, before being overtaken by *Titanic* (1997). Spielberg cleverly builds up to the revelation of the "monsters" by stunning us with the visual treat of cuddly, friendly, vegetarian dinosaurs first—and by rationing appearances of any prehistoric beasts for most of the first half of the film, much as he did with the fearsome shark in *Jaws* (1975). So when we do finally meet the ass-kicking T. rex, it results in one of the movie's fabulous set pieces. The imperiled adults and children are stranded in the broken-down "ride" (jeeps on a track taking them through the park) as the storm hits, the electric fences malfunction, and the scariest dinosaur of them all gets loose.

There are many other impressive moments in Crichton and Spielberg's fable of science gone out of control, ranging from the raptors in the kitchen to the T. rex/raptor showdown. The actors, while realizing the true stars of the film are computer generated, have fun with their performances (especially Goldblum as the "I-told-you-so" chaos theorist) and make the most of the smart, witty dialogue. But ultimately this is Spielberg's show, and what an impressive, edge-of-the-seat show it is. **JB**

The Lion King Roger Allers & Rob Minkoff, 1994

U.S. (Walt Disney) 89m Technicolor
Language English / Swahili **Producer** Don
Hahn **Screenplay** Irene Mecchi, Jonathan
Roberts, Linda Woolverton **Music** Hans
Zimmer, Elton John, Tim Rice, Lebo M.,
Joseph Williams **Cast** (voices) Matthew
Broderick, Joseph Williams, Jonathan Taylor
Thomas, Jason Weaver, James Earl Jones,
Jeremy Irons, Moira Kelly, Niketa Calame,
Laura Williams, Ernie Sabella, Nathan Lane,
Robert Guillaume, Rowan Atkinson, Madge
Sinclair, Zoe Leader **Oscars** Hans Zimmer
(music), Elton John, Tim Rice (song)
Oscar nomination Elton John, Tim Rice
(two more nominations for song)

ℹ

The movie spawned two hits
for Elton John: "Circle of Life" and
"Can You Feel the Love Tonight."

In 1991, Disney released the magical *Beauty and the Beast*—the first animated movie to be nominated for a Best Picture Academy Award—and brought its animation right up to date with a beautiful mix of traditional and computer-generated cartooning. *The Lion King* followed three years later and not only improved on the standards set by *Beauty* but also instantly became a Disney classic.

Young Simba the lion cub (voiced by Jonathan Taylor Thomas as a cub and Matthew Broderick as an adult lion) is exiled by his evil uncle Scar—a creepily effective performance from Jeremy Irons—following his father Mufasa's (James Earl Jones) death. Forced to fend for himself, he befriends two odd characters, Pumbaa (Ernie Sabella) and Timon (Nathan Lane), and also falls for a lioness named Nala (voiced by Niketa Calane and later by Moira Kelly) before returning to regain his place as head of the pride.

This animated adventure works so well because it has all the elements of a terrific movie and plenty of action and adventure. The lion cub scenes appeal to small children and the impressive animation causes even adult jaws to drop. The film has a classic story arc as the carefree cub becomes a wise and respected lion. Backed by a catchy score by Elton John, *The Lion King* is surprisingly moving, considering that we are only relating to cartoon characters, and the ending is capable of turning even grown men into blubbering piles of mush. **JB**

The Last Seduction John Dahl, 1994

U.S. (ITC) 110m Color **Producer** Jonathan Shestack **Screenplay** Steve Barancik **Photography** Jeff Jur **Music** Joseph Vitarelli **Cast** Linda Fiorentino, Peter Berg, Bill Pullman, Michael Raysses, Bill Nunn, Zack Phifer, J.T. Walsh, Brien Varady, Dean Norris, Donna Wilson, Mik Scriba, Erik-Anders Nilsson, Patricia R. Caprio, Herb Mitchell, Renee Rogers

Made for U.S. cable TV company HBO (which broadcast it before giving the film a theatrical release, thus sadly making it ineligible for the Academy Awards), *The Last Seduction* was director John Dahl's third, and best, venture into the film noir genre.

Linda Fiorentino positively sizzles across the screen as femme fatale Bridget, whom we first meet when she cons her husband (Bill Pullman) into making a large drug deal, only to run off with the money and leave him behind. She then slithers into a small town and into the life of sweet, infatuated Mike (Peter Berg), who has no clue just what he has let himself in for.

Simmering with steamy sexuality, Dahl's thriller is deliciously bitter and twisted as Fiorentino twirls unsuspecting men around her little finger then casts them aside just as quickly. Pullman—best known for kinder roles—is a revelation as Fiorentino's almost-as-nasty-as-she-is spouse, while Berg hits exactly the right note as the poor guy who never quite realizes how deep he is being dragged in. But the true star of the film is Fiorentino, who chews up and spits out Steve Barancik's delicious dialogue, reducing men to quivering, whimpering victims in the process. **JB**

Les roseaux sauvages André Téchiné, 1994
The Wild Reeds

France (IMA, Alain Sarde, Strand) 110m Color **Language** French **Producer** Georges Benayoun, Alain Sarde **Screenplay** Olivier Massart, Gilles Taurand, André Téchiné **Photography** Jeanne Lapoirie **Cast** Élodie Bouchez, Gaël Morel, Stéphane Rideau, Frédéric Gorny, Michèle Moretti, Jacques Nolot, Eric Kreikenmayer, Nathalie Vignes, Michel Ruhl, Fatia Maite, Claudine Taulère, Elodie Soulinhac, Dominique Bovard, Monsieur Simonet, Chief Officer Carre

The Wild Reeds is a wonderful and masterful feature from Andre Téchiné (his twelfth) and one of the best movies from an excellent French television series of fiction features on teenagers from the 1960s to the early 1980s. As Téchiné's *French Provincial* (1974) evokes in some ways the Bernardo Bertolucci of *The Conformist* (1970), this account of kids living in southwest France in 1962 toward the end of the Algerian war has some of the feeling, lyricism, and sweetness of Bertolucci's *Before the Revolution* (1964). *Wild Reeds*, however, is clearly the work of someone much older and wiser.

The main characters are all completing their baccalaureate examination at a boarding school. They include a boy struggling with his homosexual desire for a close friend (Gael Morel), an older student who is a right-wing opponent of Algerian nationalism (Frédéric Gorny), and a communist daughter of one of the teachers (Élodie Bouchez), who befriends the homosexual and falls for the older student in spite of their political differences. One comes to regard these characters and others as old friends, and Téchiné's handling of pastoral settings is as exquisite as his feeling for period. *Wild Reeds* was the winner of César awards (the French equivalent of the Oscars) for best picture, director, screenplay, and "new female discovery" (for Bouchez). **JRos**

Crumb Terry Zwigoff, 1994

Anyone familiar with the work of underground comic artist R. Crumb might assume that he has a few screws loose, and indeed they might be right. But the most remarkable discovery made by Terry Zwigoff's sad, fascinating documentary is that R. Crumb is actually the least strange and best adjusted of three siblings, all of whom reveal an offhand brilliance and creativity yet channel that brilliance into radically contrasting outlets and lifestyles. One spends much of his time meditating on the streets of San Francisco. The other is a recluse, holed up at home with his mother as he battles clinical depression and madness. Both exhibit an artistic inclination and talent at least equal to R. Crumb's, and the film spends much of its time revealing how a relatively inconsequential shared childhood steered each sibling in different directions.

Crumb, of course, spends most of its duration tracking the rise of R. Crumb as an underground comic icon during the heyday of the American Haight-Ashbury hippie culture in the late 1960s. Through a series of revealing and shockingly honest interviews, Zwigoff shows Crumb to be contrary at heart. He is a rebel against seemingly arbitrary (and often infuriatingly politically correct) rules of art and behavior with a taste for vintage jazz, fashions, and affectations that existed before American culture was gripped tighter by its corporate overseers. Crumb is the quintessential rebel whose form of passive resistance—comics—ironically transformed him into an underground icon.

Crumb marked an auspicious debut for Zwigoff, a longtime fan of vintage jazz and underground comics who eventually parlayed his success as a documentary filmmaker into a feature film, directing *Ghost World* (which happened to be based on an underground comic by Daniel Clowes, another vintage jazz obsessive). Needless to say, *Crumb* has as much to say about the lifestyle and attitude of eccentrics like Zwigoff in general as it does about R. Crumb. Specifically, his portrayal of the jaded Crumb in the months before his retirement remains an invaluable document (and in some ways outcome) of the underground 1960s comics scene. **JKl**

U.S. (Superior) 119m Color
Producer David Lynch, Lynn O'Donnell, Terry Zwigoff **Photography** Maryse Alberti **Music** David Boeddinghaus **Cast** Robert Crumb, Aline Kominsky, Charles Crumb, Maxon Crumb, Robert Hughes, Martin Muller, Don Donahue, Dana Crumb, Trina Robbins, Spain Rodriguez, Deirdre English, Peggy Orenstein, Beatrice Crumb, Kathy Goodell, Dian Hanson

> *"When I listen to old music, it's one of the few times I actually have a kind of a love for humanity."*
>
> **Robert Crumb**

i

Zwigoff told critic Roger Ebert that he "called in every favor he owed me" to persuade R. Crumb to be in the film.

Heavenly Creatures Peter Jackson, 1994

G.B. / Germany / New Zealand (Fontana, Miramax , New Zealand Film Commission, Senator, WingNut) 99m Eastmancolor **Producer** Jim Booth **Screenplay** Frances Walsh, Peter Jackson **Photography** Alun Bollinger **Music** Peter Dasent **Cast** Melanie Lynskey, Kate Winslet, Sarah Peirse, Diana Kent, Clive Merrison, Simon O'Connor, Jed Brophy, Peter Elliott, Gilbert Goldie, Geoffrey Heath, Kirsti Ferry, Ben Skjellerup, Darien Takle, Elizabeth Moody, Liz Mullane **Oscar nomination** Frances Walsh, Peter Jackson (screenplay) **Venice Film Festival** Peter Jackson (Silver Lion)

i

In the 1970s, Juliet became a writer of mystery stories, publishing under the pseudonym of Anne Perry.

More often than not, filmmakers wilt into reverence or undue solemnity when they take on fact-based movies rooted in tragedy. Not Peter Jackson, who, though now famous for his *Lord of the Rings* trilogy (2001, 2002, 2003), was already hedging the lines between good and evil, innocence and sin, comedy and drama in his early film *Heavenly Creatures*: a gleefully free interpretation of a 1952 murder case in which two schoolgirls in New Zealand, Pauline Parker and Juliet Hulme, conspired to kill Pauline's mother (prophetically named Mrs. Rieper) in hopes of avoiding being separated from one another.

At once prankish and moving, the film tells the girls' story as a parable of teenage puppy love gone awry between two bookish misfits. Juliet (Kate Winslet, in the role that launched her career), a smart-mouthed poor little rich girl from England who's cursed with callously neglectful parents, bonds with the shy, dowdy but intelligent Pauline (Melanie Lynskey). The more the girls' parents, disturbed by the homoerotic intensity of their friendship, try to pry them apart, the more they retreat into a florid dream universe, driven by their journals and populated by avenging princes and princesses. Each girl jacks up the other's obsessive imagination until they have abolished the line between reality and desire—as does Jackson in gorgeous fantasy sequences filled with digitally manipulated clay figures and featuring, hilariously, the girls' idols, Mario Lanza and Orson Welles. **ET**

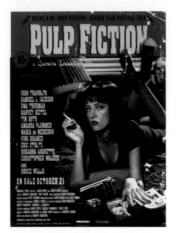

Pulp Fiction Quentin Tarantino, 1994

This clever and immensely entertaining second feature by Quentin Tarantino (after *Reservoir Dogs* [1992] and before *Jackie Brown* [1997]) is a chronologically scrambled collection of interrelated and interlocking crime stories. Apart from its ingenious structure, *Pulp Fiction* extracts nearly all its kicks from allusions to and echoes of other movies and TV shows. Despite all its thematic nudges about redemption and second chances, its true agenda is only the flip side of *Forrest Gump* (1994): to make the escapist, media-savvy viewer the real hero of the story.

Taken on its own crass terms, Tarantino's mock-tough narrative—which derives most of its titillation from farcical mayhem, drugs, deadpan macho monologues, evocations of anal penetration, and terms of racial abuse—resembles a wet dream for fourteen-year-old male closet queens (or, perhaps more accurately, the fourteen-year-old male closet queen in each of us), and his command of this smart-alecky mode is so sure and confident that this nervy movie sparkles throughout with canny twists and turns.

John Travolta, Samuel L. Jackson, Bruce Willis, and Harvey Keitel all vibrate with high-voltage star power, while the rest of the film's cast (including Uma Thurman, Ving Rhames, Maria de Medeiros, Tim Roth, Amanda Plummer, Eric Stoltz, Rosanna Arquette, Christopher Walken, Steve Buscemi, and Tarantino himself) amply fill out the remaining scenery. Only occasionally—as in an overloaded and ugly basement episode and some anemic love scenes—does Tarantino seem to be straining, though even here his overall project is evident: to evict real life and real people from the art film once and for all and replace them with generic teases and assorted homages, infused with hype and attitude, building a veritable monument to the viewer's assumed cinema connoisseurship. The references range from Douglas Sirk to Howard Hawks to *Saturday Night Fever* (1977) to kung fu by way of Godard, but one shouldn't expect any of the life experiences of the old movie sources to leak through; punchy, flamboyant surface is all. **JRos**

U.S. (Band Apart, Jersey, Miramax) 154m Color **Producer** Lawrence Bender **Screenplay** Quentin Tarantino, Roger Avary **Photography** Andrzej Sekula **Music** Dick Dale and his Del-tones, Kool and the Gang, Al Green, Tornadoes, Ricky Nelson, Dusty Springfield, Centurians, Chuck Berry, Urge Overkill, Maria McKee, Revels, Statler Brothers, Lively Ones **Cast** Tim Roth, Amanda Plummer, Laura Lovelace, John Travolta, Samuel L. Jackson, Phil LaMarr, Frank Whaley, Burr Steers, Bruce Willis, Ving Rhames, Paul Calderon, Bronagh Gallagher, Rosanna Arquette, Eric Stoltz, Uma Thurman **Oscar** Quentin Tarantino, Roger Avary (screenplay) **Oscar nominations** Lawrence Bender (best picture), Quentin Tarantino (director), John Travolta (actor), Samuel L. Jackson (actor in support role), Uma Thurman (actress in support role), Sally Menke (editing) **Cannes Film Festival** Quentin Tarantino (Golden Palm)

"If my answers frighten you, then you should cease asking scary questions."

Jules (Samuel L. Jackson)

ℹ️

Travolta was second choice for his role, after Michael Madsen—Vic Vega in Tarantino's *Reservoir Dogs* (1992).

Trois couleurs: Rouge Krzysztof Kieslowski, 1994
Three Colors: Red

France / Poland / Switzerland (CAB, France 3, Canal+, MK2, Tor, TSR) 99m Eastmancolor
Language French **Producer** Marin Karmitz
Screenplay Krzysztof Kieslowski, Krzysztof Piesiewicz **Photography** Piotr Sobocinski
Music Bertrand Lenclos, Zbigniew Preisner
Cast Irène Jacob, Jean-Louis Trintignant, Frédérique Feder, Jean-Pierre Lorit, Samuel Le Bihan, Marion Stalens, Teco Celio, Bernard Escalon, Jean Schlegel, Elzbieta Jasinska, Paul Vermeulen, Jean-Marie Daunas, Roland Carey, Brigitte Raul, Leo Ramseyer **Oscar nominations** Piotr Sobocinski (cinematography), Krzysztof Kieslowski (director), Krzysztof Piesiewicz, Krzysztof Kieslowski (screenplay) **Cannes Film Festival** Krzysztof Kieslowski (director, Golden Palm nomination)

> "Maybe you're the woman I never met."

The Judge
(Jean-Louis Trintignant)

The third color of the French flag stands for fraternity, and although the last film of Krzysztof Kieslowski's "Three Colors" trilogy again remains only loosely connected to that theme, he gets to the heart of brotherhood via the sometimes tenuous and often-impossible-to-comprehend ties that connect all of humanity. If each of the "Three Colors" films ends up much more than the sum of their ambiguous parts, then *Red* provides the grand and illuminating summation of all three entries. Like the last chapter of a great philosophical novel, *Red* parcels out its details patiently and elliptically, drawing power from the mysterious plot machinations that connect a good-natured model (the ineffable Irène Jacob) with a cynical retired judge (Jean-Louis Trintignant). Both lead empty lives yet express their loneliness in completely different ways, but the judge sees something intriguing in the model that draws him out of his shell of self-hatred.

Like many of Kieslowski's works, *Red* runs deep with chance and coincidence, and although the metaphysical director rarely addresses spirituality in his work per se, his final film (Kieslowski retired after directing *Red* and died shortly later) often seems a meditation on not just earthly bonds but also our place in the universe. In lesser hands such subject matter would no doubt have gotten bogged down in New Age musings, but Kieslowski is smarter than that. His characters develop and interact organically, as if tapping into a script made entirely of emotional cues rather than mere words. His camera captures places and moments that appear insignificant yet whose importance is inevitably born out. In *Red* he even manages to almost magically make manifest the very fabric of our existence, as the metaphors and symbolic touches of all three films—*Blue* (1993), *White* (1994), and *Red*—blur together during the challenging and undeniably moving conclusion, which casts the entire trilogy in a new light. Rarely has a film so brilliantly fused together so many ideas, images, and emotions into one masterful whole, a life primer and work of art posing as a mere movie. **JKl**

1994

i

The film features cameo appearances by the main actors and actresses in the previous two films of the trilogy.

Natural Born Killers Oliver Stone, 1994

U.S. (Alcor, Ixtlan, J D, Regency, Warner Bros.) 118m BW/ Technicolor **Producer** Jane Hamsher, Don Murphy, Clayton Townsend **Screenplay** David Veloz, Richard Rutowski, Oliver Stone, from story by Quentin Tarantino **Photography** Robert Richardson **Music** Zack De La Rocha, Peter Gabriel, Tom Hajdu, Brent Lewis, Andy Milburn, Trent Reznor, Eric Avery Weiss, Leonard Cohen, Dr. Dre, Bob Montgomery, Patti Smith **Cast** Tommy Lee Jones, Woody Harrelson, Juliette Lewis, Rodney Dangerfield, Robert Downey, Jr. **Venice Film Festival** Oliver Stone (special jury prize), Juliette Lewis (Pasinetti Award—actress)

Never one to avoid controversy with films like *Platoon* (1990) and *JFK* (1991), Oliver Stone caused his biggest storm yet with this superb, satirical comment on the relationship between the media and violence. Using diverse film techniques and styles—animation, video, back and front projection, black-and-white and color film—*Natural Born Killers* tells the story of Mickey (Woody Harrelson) and Mallory (Juliette Lewis) Knox on a cross-country murder spree. The lurid tale soon comes to the attention of the media, and is related to an eager public by sleazy TV host Wayne Gale (Robert Downey, Jr.).

The movie is graphically violent as the white-trash lovers slaughter their way across the United States, but Stone should be commended for this provocative tale rather than condemned for it. Many acclaimed actors believed in his clever, stylized, and striking movie enough to appear in it, from Tommy Lee Jones (as a particularly smarmy prison governor) to Tom Sizemore (as the dogged cop on Mickey and Mallory's trail), and lead actors Harrelson, Lewis, and Downey, Jr. all deliver searing performances that are among the best of their respective careers. **JB**

Muriel's Wedding P.J. Hogan, 1994

Australia / France (CiBy 2000, Film Victoria, House & Moorhouse) 106m Color **Producer** Lynda House, Jocelyn Moorhouse, Michael D. Aglion, Tony Mahood **Screenplay** P.J. Hogan **Photography** Martin McGrath **Music** Peter Best **Cast** Toni Collette, Rachel Griffiths, Sophie Lee, Rosalind Hammond, Belinda Jarrett, Pippa Grandison, Bill Hunter, Jeanie Drynan, Daniel Wyllie, Gabby Millgate, Gennie Nevinson, Matt Day, Chris Haywood, Daniel Lapaine

What seemed at first like a small, silly, romantic Australian comedy about a fat girl who desperately wants to get married, *Muriel's Wedding* became something of a cult classic. It also made more ripples within the rom-com community than arguably any other film of its generation. The moment Rachel Griffiths and Toni Collette appear on screen together, moviegoers know this is not going to be your average gooey-sweet romantic adventure. (Both have since gone on to receive Oscar nominations.) Collette does not play the overweight Muriel Hislop, an awkward soul from Porpoise Spit, Australia, as much as she inhabits her. She's a girl who will do anything to have a white wedding, never mind the romance or the happily ever after.

Bumping into old friend Rhonda (Rachel Griffiths), Muriel begins her transformation, renaming herself and trying to find her romantic feet. But it is not all happy endings, as her potential husband—a swinish South African Olympic swimmer—is only after an Australian passport. Writer-director P.J. Hogan's placement of unexpectedly bitter strands within what is essentially a girl's fantasy world make this comedy unique and lasting: Few films have managed to balance the sense of girlish joy with a sense of foreboding and doom. Even years after its release, it is easy to see why Griffiths and Collette made such a breakthrough duo, Abba tunes (of which this film is crammed) or not. Hogan went on to make the Julia Roberts hit *My Best Friend's Wedding* (1997), which benefitted from the director's love of the romantic underbelly. **KK**

1994

The Adventures of Priscilla, Queen of the Desert
Stephan Elliott, 1994

One of the first films to celebrate the "fabulous" nature of the drag queen, *Priscilla* shocked the cinema-going world by featuring venerable British actor Terence Stamp as Bernadette, an out-and-out boa-wearing transsexual. Teamed with newcomer Hugo Weaving (who since went onto fame, most notably in *The Matrix Trilogy* [1999, 2003]) as Teke and Guy Pearce (*Memento* [2000]), Australian director Stephan Elliot shows us a perfected, candy-colored world of the drag queen, stained somewhat by their ever-lurking fears of growing old and ugly. This is basically (and literally) a dressed-up road movie: Two gay men from Sydney are given the opportunity to put on a transvestite show in the desert. Bernadette is mourning the death of her young lover and so joins the duo as a distraction. The trio buy a bus and make a scene wherever it stops.

Homophobia, rampant in the outback, makes the journey full of danger—especially when Pearce's character Adam insists on walking the streets in full drag. What is endearing is the character portrayal of each of the drag artists. They are not merely the screaming, painted queens of *To Wong Foo, Thanks for Everything! Julie Newmar* (1995), who are caring, sharing, and catty. Each of the three has a different aspiration—one to climb Ayers Rock, another to finally meet his son, and Bernadette, whose elegant front drops and we see that she is longing to have a new love in her life. Even if you are not fascinated by drag queens (who can be a rich confection at the best of times), the visuals in *Priscilla* (which is, by the way, the name of the bus) are heavily cinematic.

The Oscar-winning costume design, complete with makeup and wigs as used by the trio in their drag act and on the street, is superb. Most memorable, however, is the shot of Pearce atop the bus as it drives through the desert, the wind trailing an enormous silver scarf behind him. For added oomph, he's lip-synching opera. Joyous and poignant, *Priscilla* gives us a rare glimpse behind the drag queen guise to see the real people within. **KK**

1994

Australia 104m Color **Producer** Al Clark, Michael Hamlyn **Screenplay** Stephan Elliott **Photography** Brian J. Breheny **Music** Guy Gross **Cast** Terence Stamp, Hugo Weaving, Guy Pearce, Rebel Russell, John Casey, June Marie Bennett, Murray Davies, Frank Cornelius, Bob Boyce, Leighton Picken, Maria Kmet, Joseph Kmet, Alan Dargin, Julia Cortez, Daniel Kellie, Hannah Corbett, Trevor Barrie, Ken Radley, Sarah Chadwick, Mark Holmes **Oscar** Lizzie Gardiner, Tim Chappel (best costume design)

"We dress up in women's clothes and parade around mouthing the words to other people's songs."

Felicia (Guy Pearce)

ℹ️

The opening and closing scenes of the movie were both filmed on the same day.

1994

U.S. (KTCA-TV, Kartemquin) 170m Color
Producer Peter Gilbert, Steve James,
Frederick Marx **Screenplay** Steve James,
Frederick Marx **Photography** Peter Gilbert
Music Ben Sidran **Cast** William Gates, Arthur
Agee, Emma Gates, Curtis Gates, Sheila
Agee, Arthur "Bo" Agee, Earl Smith, Gene
Pingatore, Isiah Thomas, Sister Marlyn
Hopewell, Bill Gleason, Patricia Weir, Marjorie
Heard, Luther Bedford, Aretha Mitchell
Oscar nomination Frederick Marx, Steve
James, William Haugse (editing)

*"Even though I love
playing basketball, you
know I want to do other
things with my life too."*

William Gates

🛈

When the electricity supply to the
Agee home was cut off at one point,
the filmmakers paid for its restoration.

Hoop Dreams Steve James, 1994

Hoop Dreams follows the true story of a pair of inner-city Chicago teens, Arthur Agee and William Gates, and their pursuit of NBA fame. Straight out of junior high school the two boys are recruited by an athletic scout, literally pulled off the streets and placed in a predominately white college preparatory school, St. Joseph High. Following in the footsteps of their basketball idol and St. Joseph's alumnus Isiah Thomas, both boys are inundated with the intense demands of maturation, academia, and, of course, athletics.

Within the first year documented by the film, only one of the boys survives the rigors of the prep school. In an attempt to continue following his basketball dreams, the other returns to the city and attends a public high school. Although separated by different basketball programs, we continue to watch the boys mature and grow into athletic powerhouses over a five-year period. Such a concentrated time span allows a personal look into these two boys' lives, showing that their pursuit of basketball glory is not just their passion, but their respective families' dream.

Keeping in step with their failures and successes, director and narrator Steve James unravels a unique story of inner-city struggles. As the film's layers become more apparent, intricate subplots make us intimately familiar with the other players in their lives. The constant ebb and flow of life plays on the boys' emotions and fate. Basketball functions not only as a game for Arthur and William, but as a way for their instructors and family members to play out their own dreams and desires. The film thus allow us to peer into the world of competitive high school basketball through the eyes of young men, torn families, and passionate coaches.

Hoop Dreams represents five years of painstaking dedication by both of the featured boys, as well as by the filmmakers. Following both Arthur and William from their boyish scrawny days of junior high to their highs and lows as prized high school basketball players, this film questions and contemplates inner-city life, family, sacrifices, success, and failure. **AK**

Sátántangó Béla Tarr, 1994

Hungary / Germany / Switzerland (Mafilm, Vega Film, Von Vietinghoff) 450m BW **Language** Hungarian **Producer** György Fehér, Ruth Waldburger, Joachim von Vietinghoff **Screenplay** Béla Tarr, from novel by László Krasznahorkai **Photography** Gábor Medvigy **Music** Mihály Vig **Cast** Mihály Vig, Putyi Horváth, László Lugossy, Éva Almássy Albert, János Derzsi, Irén Szajki, Alfréd Járai, Miklós Székely B., Erzsébet Gaál, Erika Bók **Berlin International Film Festival** Béla Tarr (Caligari film award)

ℹ

In an interview in 2000, Tarr revealed that there were only around 150 separate shots in the entire movie.

How can one do justice to this grungy seven-hour black comedy, which in many ways is among the most impressive films of the 1990s? Adapted by Hungarian director Béla Tarr and László Krasznahorkai from the latter's 1985 novel, *Sátántangó* is a diabolical piece of sarcasm about the dreams, machinations, and betrayals of a failed farm collective, set during two consecutive rainy fall days (rendered more than once from the perspectives of different characters) and later the same month. The form of the novel was inspired by the steps of the tango—six forward, six backward—an idea reflected by the film's overlapping time structure, its twelve sections, and its remarkably choreographed long takes and camera movements, which often suggest a despiritualized Andrei Tarkovsky with the hothouse intensity of a John Cassavetes. Each section ends powerfully with offscreen third-person narration—eloquent, poetic commentary on the characters and their world that comes directly from the novel.

The story may seem to comment indirectly on the collapse of communism, but it has just as much to say about the subsequent degradations of capitalism; as Tarr has pointed out, the police—and human nature—are the same everywhere. The subject of this brilliantly constructed narrative is nothing less than the world today, and its 431-minute running time is necessary not so much because Tarr has so much to say, but because he wants to say it right. **JRos**

Clerks Kevin Smith, 1994

U.S. (Miramax, View Askew) 92m BW **Producer** Scott Mosier, Kevin Smith **Screenplay** Kevin Smith **Photography** David Klein **Music** Scott Angley **Cast** Brian O'Halloran, Jeff Anderson, Marilyn Ghigliotti, Lisa Spoonhauer, Jason Mewes, Kevin Smith, Scott Mosier, Walter Flanagan, Scott Schiaffo, Al Berkowitz, Ed Hapstak, Lee Bendick, David Klein, Pattijean Csik, Ken Clark **Cannes Film Festival** Kevin Smith (award of the youth foreign film, Mercedes-Benz award)

Writer-director Kevin Smith stepped forward in 1994 as the most promising Generation-X newcomer with this impressive debut film. Set in a New Jersey convenience store, Smith's *Clerks* is a day-in-the-life tale of two shopworkers, Dante (Brian O'Halloran) and his reckless friend Randal (Jeff Anderson) who works at the video store next door. As various oddballs come into the store, Dante tries to sort out relationship problems, while Randal spends most of the day bored, insulting customers, watching porn movies, and discussing important matters like the true meaning of the destruction of the Death Star in *Return of the Jedi* (1983).

Shot in black and white, the $27,500-budget movie was filmed over twenty-one days at the QuickStop Groceries store where Smith had worked since he was nineteen, and where he edited the film each night. Anchored by a pair of great central performances, and packed with witty dialogue, the film also introduced the two hilarious characters Smith has used in his subsequent movies (*Mallrats* [1995], *Chasing Amy* [1997], *Dogma* [1999], and *Jay And Silent Bob Strike Back* [2001], all of which are at least partly set in Smith's home state of New Jersey): Stoner Jay (Jason Mewes) and his aptly named pal Silent Bob (played by Smith himself). **JB**

Four Weddings and a Funeral Mike Newell, 1994

G.B. (Channel Four, PolyGram, Working Title) 117m Eastmancolor **Producer** Duncan Kenworthy **Screenplay** Richard Curtis **Photography** Michael Coulter **Music** Richard Rodney Bennett **Cast** Hugh Grant, James Fleet, Simon Callow, John Hannah, Kristin Scott Thomas, David Bower, Charlotte Coleman, Andie MacDowell, Timothy Walker, Sara Crowe, Ronald Herdman, Elspet Gray, Philip Voss, Rupert Vansittart, Nicola Walker **Oscar nominations** Duncan Kenworthy (best picture), Richard Curtis (screenplay)

Hugh Grant is the perennial best man in this hugely successful British comedy set at various social functions from director Mike Newell and TV comedy series *Blackadder* writer Richard Curtis.

Grant—in the part that propelled him from stiff-upper-lipped roles in movies like *Bitter Moon* (1992) and *The Remains of the Day* (1993) to Hollywood megastar—is perfect as the chronically late Charles, who falls for Carrie (Andie MacDowell) at one wedding and then spends the rest of the film awkwardly attempting to woo her. In between, this richly humorous look at the British upper middle class at play features all those classic wedding nightmares (the bumbling priest, a tactless toast from the best man, a bride jilted at the altar, the awkwardness of being seated at a table with all your ex-girlfriends) dressed up in lovely hats and gowns. However, it is the funeral of the title that provides the movie with its poignant heart.

Some may argue that the rarely expressive MacDowell was miscast as the love interest (perhaps so the British filmmakers could boast a Hollywood name). However, she sensibly takes a backseat to the wonderful supporting cast of characters, including Simon Callow, John Hannah, and Kristin Scott Thomas, who provide *Four Weddings and a Funeral* with its charm and funniest moments. **JB**

Forrest Gump Robert Zemeckis, 1994

A brisk trot through events in American history from the 1950s until the 1980s as seen through the eyes of one man, *Forrest Gump* succeeds as both epic and character study. This is thanks to clever, if occasionally sentimental, direction from Robert Zemeckis and a sensitive central performance from Tom Hanks, who won his second Best Actor Academy Award in as many years for the role.

We first meet Forrest, an amiable idiot savant with an IQ of 75, sitting on a park bench, waiting for a bus to take him to meet his childhood friend Jenny (Robin Wright Penn). While lingering there, he relates his life story to a succession of people who share the bench—and what a story it is. Raised by a mother (Sally Field) who corrected his gait with leg braces but never attempted to correct his mind ("Stupid is as stupid does" being her motto), Forrest went on to experience many of America's most famous events of the twentieth century. This begins on the day he discovered that he could run (outrunning bullies, his braces fly off and he speeds into the distance) when he uses his talent to become a football star. Over the next three decades, this simple man meets John F. Kennedy, Lyndon Johnson, and Richard Nixon; becomes a Vietnam war hero (saving "Lieutenant Dan," his grumpy superior brilliantly portrayed by Gary Sinise); and later a shrimp tycoon. All the while he dreams of being reunited with Jenny, whose life takes a different path from his. Where Forrest experiences many cultural historical moments, Jenny is deep into American counterculture, protesting the war and embracing alcohol and drugs.

The love story between Jenny and Forrest is somewhat unconvincing—she seems to turn up only when she needs help, which makes her character less sympathetic. However, this adaptation of Winston Groom's novel works best as the moving story of an honest, innocent man (superbly played by Hanks, who modeled his distinctive accent on that of Michael Conner, who plays Forrest as a boy), and as a meditation on the latter half of the last century, made possible by computer trickery that places Hanks—to often hilarious effect—in old footage of notable events. **JB**

U.S. (Paramount) 142m BW / Color **Producer** Wendy Finerman, Steve Starkey, Steve Tisch **Screenplay** Eric Roth, from novel by Winston Groom **Photography** Don Burgess **Music** Alan Silvestri **Cast** Tom Hanks, Robin Wright Penn, Gary Sinise, Mykelti Williamson, Sally Field, Rebecca Williams, Michael Conner Humphreys, Harold G. Herthum, George Kelly, Bob Penny, John Randall, Sam Anderson, Margo Moorer, Ione M. Telech, Christine Seabrook **Oscars** Wendy Finerman, Steve Starkey, Steve Tisch (best picture), Robert Zemeckis (director), Eric Roth (screenplay), Tom Hanks (actor), Ken Ralston, George Murphy, Stephen Rosenbaum, Allen Hall (special visual effects), Arthur Schmidt (editing) **Oscar nominations** Gary Sinise (actor in support role), Rick Carter, Nancy Haigh (art direction), Don Burgess (cinematography), Gloria S. Borders, Randy Thom (special sound effects), Daniel C. Striepeke, Hallie D'Amore, Judith A. Cory (makeup), Alan Silvestri (music), Randy Thom, Tom Johnson, Dennis S. Sands, William B. Kaplan (sound)

1994

"Life's a box of chocolates, Forrest. You never know what you're gonna get."

Mrs. Gump (Sally Field)

i

Jim Hanks, Tom Hanks's younger brother, doubled for him in many of the running scenes in the movie.

Zire darakhatan zeyton Abbas Kiarostami, 1994
Through the Olive Trees

France / Iran (Abbas Kiarostami, CiBy 2000, Farabi, Miramax) 103m Color **Language** Farsi **Producer** Abbas Kiarostami **Screenplay** Abbas Kiarostami **Photography** Hossein Djafarian, Farhad Saba **Cast** Mohamad Ali Keshavarz, Farhad Kheradmand, Zarifeh Shiva, Hossein Rezai, Tahereh Ladanian, Hocine Redai, Zahra Nourouzi, Nasret Betri, Azim Aziz Nia, Astadouli Babani, N. Boursadiki, Kheda Barech Defai, Ali Ahmed Poor, Babek Ahmed Poor, Mahbanou Darabi **Cannes Film Festival** Abbas Kiarostami nomination (Golden Palm)

ℹ

Two key characters from the earlier parts of the "trilogy" reappear in *Through the Olive Trees*.

The social status of filmmaking among ordinary people, central to Abbas Kiarostami's wonderful movies *Close-Up* (1990) and *Life, and Nothing More* (1991) is equally operative in this entertaining and sometimes beautiful film. *Through the Olive Trees* concludes an unofficial trilogy begun with *Where Is the Friend's Home?* (1987), which focused on the adventures of a poor schoolboy in a mountainous region of northern Iran. *Through the Olive Trees* is a comedy about the making of a movie, mostly emphasizing the persistent efforts of a young actor to woo an actress who won't even speak to him. Like Kiarostami's subsequent *Taste of Cherry* (1997), all three films in the trilogy strategically leave out certain information about the characters, inviting audiences to fill in the blanks and in this case yielding a mysteriously beautiful and open-ended conclusion.

If you're unfamiliar with Kiarostami—one of the greatest filmmakers alive and certainly the greatest in Iran—this is an excellent introduction. It was the first of his European coproductions and has the only professional actor he's ever hired, Mohammad-Ali Keshavarz, as the director. Shot exclusively in exteriors, it's an especially effective showcase for Kiarostami's gifts as a landscape artist, and the beautiful ways that he interweaves conversations in cars moving through this mountainous region, and the people and sights that they pass on the road, are often breathtaking. **JRos**

The Shawshank Redemption Frank Darabont, 1994

U.S. (Castle Rock, Columbia) 142m Technicolor **Producer** Niki Marvin **Screenplay** Frank Darabont, from the novella *Rita Hayworth and the Shawshank Redemption* by Stephen King **Photography** Roger Deakins **Music** Doris Fisher, Thomas Newman, Allan Roberts **Cast** Tim Robbins, Morgan Freeman, Bob Gunton, William Sadler, Clancy Brown, Gil Bellows, Mark Rolston, James Whitmore, Jeffrey DeMunn, Larry Brandenburg, Neil Giuntoli, Brian Libby, David Proval, Joseph Ragno, Jude Ciccolella

Much of horror writer Stephen King's work has been successfully translated to the screen (including *Misery* [1990], *Carrie* [1976], and *The Shining* [1980]), but the best adaptations are arguably those of his nonhorror short stories, like *Stand by Me* (1986) and this reworking of a tale originally titled *Rita Hayworth and the Shawshank Redemption*.

In 1946, quiet young banker Andy Dufresne (Tim Robbins) is sent to Shawshank Prison for the murder of his wife and her lover. While there he slowly builds a friendship with another long-term prisoner, Red (Morgan Freeman, who narrates Andy's story). Over a period of twenty years, Andy gradually learns the prison system and wins the respect of the governor and guards by using his banking skills to do their tax returns and business dealings for them, but he never stops wishing for his freedom.

Simply and movingly played by Freeman and Robbins, and beautifully scripted by director Frank Darabont (who keeps close to the source material, the only major change being that Red was an Irishman in King's story), *Shawshank* is an intelligent, engrossing tale, rich with characterization that, although not a box-office success on its initial release in 1994, has deservedly become a must-see movie thanks to word of mouth in the years since. **JB**

Caro diario Nanni Moretti, 1994
Dear Diary

Italy / France (Banfilm, La Sept, Canal+, Rai Uno, Sacher) 100m Technicolor **Language** Italian / English / Mandarin **Producer** Nella Banfi, Angelo Barbagallo, Nanni Moretti **Screenplay** Nanni Moretti **Photography** Giuseppe Lanci **Music** Nicola Piovani, Keith Jarrett, Angélique Kidjo **Cast** Nanni Moretti, Giovanna Bozzolo, Sebastiano Nardone, Antonio Petrocelli, Giulio Base, Italo Spinelli, Carlo Mazzacurati, Jennifer Beals, Alexandre Rockwell, Renato Carpentieri, Raffaella Lebboroni, Marco Paolini, Claudia Della Seta, Lorenzo Alessandri, Antonio Neiwiller **Cannes Film Festival** Nanni Moretti (director, Golden Palm nomination)

Nanni Moretti has attracted the label of the "Italian Woody Allen," but this description is woefully inadequate. In *Dear Diary* he turns to the genre of the diary film. Yet this is not a spontaneous, cinema verité piece; everything we see is carefully scripted and staged.

The film is made up of three sections. The first and best is "On My Vespa," a glimpse at Moretti's daily travels. The second, "Islands," is the most overtly comic, showing Moretti and a friend in search of an ever elusive quiet island on which to work. The third, "Doctors," is a sobering and unforgettable account of Moretti's brush with cancer.

Dear Diary teems with marvelous digressions, reflections, and cinema quotations. Exercises in personal filmmaking can sometimes prove narcissistic and cloying, but that is not the case here. Moretti's hatred of pathos and easy spectacle serve him well. Everything in the film—from chemotherapy to a visit to the place where Pier Paolo Pasolini was murdered—is presented with utter simplicity and directness. *Dear Diary* is a glorious movie about everyday experience—about traveling, dancing, thinking, getting sick, even drinking a glass of water. Few films give such a grounded and joyous sense of what it is to live in the material world. **AM**

Chong qing sen lin Wong Kar-wai, 1994
Chungking Express

Wong Kar-wai's preference to work without a script gives his films some brilliantly off-kilter cadences. That the results are just as often as beautiful and touching as they are challenging stands as a testament to his choice of collaborators and his trust in the same. *Chungking Express* tells two unconventional (and barely related) love stories, each involving a lonely policeman and set in the bustling urban epicenter of Hong Kong. In the first, young detective Takeshi Kaneshiro pledges to find a new girlfriend before an arbitrary can of pineapples reaches its expiration date. He thinks he succeeds when he comes across Brigitte Lin, who (unbeknownst to him) happens to be a drug dealer in search of a lost shipment. Then the director suddenly shifts gears to the laconic Tony Leung, a beat cop who catches the eye of counter girl Faye Wong at his regular eating spot. Frustrated by his apparent lack of interest, Wong expresses her affection by breaking into Leung's apartment, cleaning and redecorating it, relishing the chance (however fleeting and furtive) to live in his world and absorb his essence.

Both stories are as funny as they are oddly compelling. Yet the real star of *Chungking Express* is neither the actors nor the story, but the way they are presented. Working with talented cinematographer and frequent collaborator Christopher Doyle, Wong Kar-wai transforms Hong Kong into a blur of orange neon lights and disjointed, distorted images, playing with film stock, exposure, and speed the way others might fiddle with a script. Add to this a keen understanding of the power of song—in the case of *Chungking Express*, the Mamas and the Papas' quirkily incongruous "California Dreamin'"—and Wong reveals himself as one of the more pop savvy and iconoclastic of Hong Kong's new generation of filmmakers. While other films by Wong may pack more emotional resonance, *Chungking Express* gets by and gets off on sheer innocence, exuberance, and cinematic freedom, a striking triumph of style over substance that gives life to the grunge and chaos at the heart of contemporary Hong Kong. **JKl**

Hong Kong (Jet Tone) 97m Color
Language Cantonese / Mandarin
Producer Yi-kan Chan **Screenplay** Wong Kar-wai **Photography** Christopher Doyle, Wai Keung Lau **Music** Frankie Chan, Roel A. García **Cast** Brigitte Lin, Tony Leung Chiu-wai, Faye Wong, Takeshi Kaneshiro, Valerie Chow, Chen Jinquan, Huang Zhiming, Liang Zhen, Zuo Songshen

"We're all unlucky in love sometimes. When I am, I go jogging. The body loses water when you jog, so you have none left for tears."

He Qiwu/Cop 223
(Takeshi Kaneshiro)

ℹ️
Chungking Express was shot entirely in sequence and over the course of just twenty-three days.

Riget Morten Arnfred & Lars von Trier, 1994
The Kingdom

Denmark / France / Germany / Sweden (Arte, Coproduction, DR, Greco, MEDIA, NOS, Nordic Film & TV, SVT, TV Collaboration Fund, WDR, Zentropa) 280m Color **Language** Danish / Swedish **Producer** Sven Abrahamsen, Philippe Bober, Peter Aalbæk Jensen, Ole Reim, Ib Tardini **Screenplay** Tomas Gíslason, Lars von Trier, Niels Vørsel **Photography** Eric Kress **Music** Joachim Holbek **Cast** Ernst-Hugo Järegård, Kirsten Rolffes, Holger Juul Hansen, Søren Pilmark, Ghita Nørby, Jens Okking, Otto Brandenburg, Anneviq Schelde Ebbe, Baard Owe, Birgitte Raaberg, Peter Mygind, Vita Jensen, Morten Rotne Leffers, Solbjørg Højfeldt, Udo Kier

ℹ

Stephen King's Kingdom Hospital, a thirteen-part U.S. miniseries based on the movie, was aired in 2004.

A medical horror epic, *The Kingdom* was originally a four-part TV miniseries: Sewn together into two parts for theatrical showings, it ends tantalizingly with a "To Be Continued" caption setting up the similarly inconclusive *Kingdom 2* (1997). Dr. Stig Helmer (Ernst-Hugo Järegård), an arrogant Swedish neurosurgeon in exile after plagiarizing research, is in trouble in the eponymous Copenhagen hospital because his botched brain operation has left little Mona (Laura Christensen) a babbling imbecile. Helmer's Danish nemeses are spiritualist malingerer Mrs. Drusse (Kirsten Rolffes), pompous administrator Moesgaard (Holger Juul Hansen), and Bilko-esque fixer Hook (Troels Lyby).

The Kingdom's spare, but escalating, supernatural manifestations are genuinely eerie, sometimes magical: a little quake as water eats away at the foundations; a discarnate spirit communicating with Mrs. Drusse through flickering fluorescent lights; a bloody hand waving in intense light inside a driverless ambulance. Throughout, von Trier (with codirector Morten Arnfred and longtime collaborator Niels Vørsel sharing the Mark Frost role) seamlessly blends the distinctive look of his early films (rust-colored filters, lots of water, muted or brown-toned color, suppurating unpleasantnesses) with the mock-documentary aesthetic of irony-laden 1990s soap: Jittery handheld camera work, deliberately rough edits, cross-cut subplots, catch-phrases ("Danish scum"), likably obsessive characters, and out-of-left-field plot developments. **KN**

Braveheart Mel Gibson, 1995

U.S. (Fox, B.H. Finance, Icon, Paramount, Ladd) 177m Color **Language** English / French / Latin **Producer** Bruce Davey, Mel Gibson, Alan Ladd, Jr. **Screenplay** Randall Wallace **Photography** John Toll **Music** James Horner **Cast** Mel Gibson, James Robinson, Sean Lawlor, Sandy Nelson, James Cosmo, Sean McGinley, Andrew Weir, Gerda Stevenson, Brian Cox, Patrick McGoohan, Sophie Marceau **Oscars** Mel Gibson, Alan Ladd, Jr., Bruce Davey (best picture), Mel Gibson (director), John Toll (cinematography), Lon Bender, Per Hallberg (special sound effects), Peter Frampton, Paul Pattison, Lois Burwell (makeup) **Oscar nominations** Randall Wallace (screenplay), Charles Knode (costume), Steven Rosenblum (editing), James Horner (music), Andy Nelson, Scott Millan, Anna Behlmer, Brian Simmons (sound)

Producer, director, and star Mel Gibson's gigantic historical epic combines brutal action, heaps of derring-do, and romantic tragedy so wholeheartedly that both the testosterone-crazed action crowd and women who love a good cry are pleased by at least one or the other half of its ruggedly handsome three hours.

Financed heavily by Gibson himself, whose attractions in tartan skirt and blue dye are matched by one of his most appealing and heroic performances, *Braveheart* is a panegyric for Scottish warrior William Wallace, whose loss of his love (stunning Catherine McCormack) triggers a handkerchief-wringing sequence of events in spectacular locations with a cast of thousands. Wallace's grassroots revolt against Edward I (dastardly Patrick McGoohan) at the turn of the fourteenth century climaxed with the Scots' victory at Stirling but ended in tears, betrayal, and butchery. Punctuated by battle sequences that run from thrilling to repulsively gory, the story is a good old-fashioned swashbuckler with vengeance and historical figures. Gibson took Best Picture and Best Director Oscars (among *Braveheart*'s five wins) for a film made with passionate gusto and heart that retains a sense of humor and exhibits a flair for the mythic, balancing the sadistic and partisan excesses. **AE**

Deseret James Benning, 1995

U.S. 82m BW / Color **Producer** James Benning **Writer** James Benning **Photography** James Benning **Cast** Fred Gardner (narrator)

The better-known work of experimental/structuralist filmmaker James Benning, *Deseret* became an undisputed succès d'estime when it was premiered at Sundance in 1996. The title is an allusion to the name proposed by the Mormons when applying for statehood for the territory in which they were settling—later to become Utah. The film combines ninety-two *New York Times* excerpts from 1852 to 1991 with magnificently composed static shots taken throughout the territory.

Benning recorded images at different times of the year over eighteen months with his 16mm camera, pared them down to ninety-two shots of one minute each, and then reorganized them to "match," one shot per sentence, a prerecorded soundtrack of the *New York Times* stories boiled down to a few lines. Creating sometimes mysterious ties between image and text, the film leaves viewers free to make their own connections.

The text recounts the turbulent genesis of Utah. Apart from one spectacular instance, image and sound are at odds with each other, the East Coast style of the *New York Times* seemingly missing the point of the real drama that took place there. The landscapes resist the inscription of official history, yet they are haunted by its imperfect traces. Never have Benning's images been so beautiful, so starkly composed, and so sad. Their deceptively still surface hides troubled waters, but the emotion is kept at bay. **BR**

Babe Chris Noonan, 1995

This joyous fable of a pig who becomes a champion sheep-herder makes previously unrepentant carnivores seriously contemplate vegetarianism. Babe is an innocent, irresistible piglet whisked from breeding pen to the barnyard of an eccentric man of few words, Farmer Hoggett (James Cromwell), who develops an affectionate bond with the creature. The farmer's fat, rosy wife (Magda Szubanski) unsentimentally eyes the piggy as a Christmas dinner of roast pork. But Babe has "an unprejudiced heart," unfailing courtesy, curiosity, and courage, affecting every life on the farm and reshaping his ultimately heroic destiny.

Ten years passed from the time Australian producer and cowriter George Miller—doctor, vegetarian, and creator-director of the *Mad Max* trilogy (1979, 1981, 1985)—became captivated with British farmer turned teacher and author Dick King-Smith's charming children's book *The Sheep-Pig* to the film's production. Miller waited for the development of the technology he required. Now he could seamlessly mix real livestock with uncanny animatronic doubles. Plausible dubbing of voice performances (notably those by Christine Cavanaugh as Babe and Miriam Margolyes and Hugo Weaving as Hoggett's sheepdogs) set a new standard for anthropomorphic entertainment. Within moments, the illusion that the animals are talking completely takes over, giving credibility to the impulses of human behavior they display, from generosity and selflessness to neuroses to spite, bigotry, and criminality.

Longtime Miller colleague Chris Noonan made his feature directorial debut with witty invention, delightful pace, emotive use of music from Charles Camille Saint-Saens's "Carnival of the Animals," and the serenity of a St. Francis in choreographing his four-footed and feathered company to wildly hilarious and exciting effect. The story, narrated by Roscoe Lee Browne and a zany chorus of singing mice, has sweet, touching simplicity to enchant children while operating as beautifully on a more mature level. We hear and see gentle echoes of George Orwell's *Animal Farm*, whose satire was reproduced more faithfully in the darker, underrated sequel *Babe: Pig in the City* (1998). **AE**

Australia / U.S. (Kennedy Miller, Universal) 89m Color **Producer** Bill Miller, George Miller, Doug Mitchell **Screenplay** George Miller, Chris Noonan, from the novel *The Sheep-Pig* by Dick King-Smith **Photography** Andrew Lesnie **Music** Nigel Westlake **Cast** Christine Cavanaugh, Miriam Margolyes, Danny Mann, Hugo Weaving, Miriam Flynn, Russi Taylor, Evelyn Krape, Michael Edward-Stevens, Charles Bartlett, Paul Livingston, Roscoe Lee Browne, James Cromwell, Magda Szubanski, Zoe Burton, Paul Goddard **Oscar** Scott E. Anderson, Charles Gibson, Neal Scanlan, John Cox (special visual effects) **Oscar nominations** George Miller, Doug Mitchell, Bill Miller (best picture), Chris Noonan (director), George Miller, Chris Noonan (screenplay), James Cromwell (actor in support role), Roger Ford, Kerrie Brown (art direction), Marcus D'Arcy, Jay Friedkin (editing)

1995

"The **Citizen Kane** of talking pig movies."

Dann Gire,
The Chicago Daily Herald, **1995**

i

Babe was played by a combination of forty-eight real Yorkshire pigs and an animatronic double.

Se7en David Fincher, 1995

Who would have guessed that a grisly and upsetting serial-killer police procedural costarring Brad Pitt and Morgan Freeman as detectives, written by a Tower Records cashier (Andrew Kevin Walker), and directed by David Fincher (*Alien 3* [1992]) would bear a startling resemblance to a serious work of art? One can already tell that this film is on to something special during the opening credits, which formally echo several classic American experimental films and thematically point to the eerie kinship between the serial killer (Kevin Spacey) and the police—not to mention the kinship between murder and art-making that the movie is equally concerned with. The detectives are trying to solve a series of hideous murders based on the seven deadly sins, and the sheer foulness and decay of the nameless city that surrounds them—which makes those of *Taxi Driver* (1976) and *Blade Runner* (1982) seem almost like children's theme parks—conjures up a metaphysical mood that isn't broken even when the film moves to the countryside for its climax.

Admittedly, designer unpleasantness is a hallmark of our era, and this movie may be more concerned with wallowing in it than with illuminating what it means politically. In this respect, it shares some of the duplicity of *Taxi Driver*—another film that derives much of its power from America's love-hate relationship with fundamentalism. *Se7en* is one of the only Hollywood films to have shown widely in postrevolutionary Iran (along with the *Godfather* trilogy [1972, 1974, 1990] and *Dances with Wolves* [1990]). It likely showed there in censored form; one can't account for its appeal in that country simply by noting that its highly skilled cinematographer, Darius Khondji, is Iranian.

The filmmakers stick to their vision with such dedication and persistence that something indelible comes across—something ethically and artistically superior to *The Silence of the Lambs* (1991) that refuses to exploit suffering for fun or entertainment and leaves one wondering about the world we're living in. One should note, however, that the film originally had a much grimmer ending—available now as a DVD bonus—that preview audiences resisted. **JRos**

U.S. (New Line) 127m Color
Producer Phyllis Carlyle, Arnold Kopelson
Screenplay Andrew Kevin Walker
Photography Darius Khondji **Music** Howard Shore **Cast** Morgan Freeman, Brad Pitt, Kevin Spacey, Gwyneth Paltrow, R. Lee Ermey, Andrew Kevin Walker, Daniel Zacapa, John Cassini, Bob Mack, Peter Crombie, Reg E. Cathey, George Christy, Endre Hules, Hawthorne James, William Davidson **Oscar nomination** Richard Francis-Bruce (editing)

"I thought what was amazing about what Andy prescribed in his script and what he was so adamant about was that you don't need to see stuff. He unlocks the Pandora's Box of your imagination, in a really gripping way."

David Fincher, 2009

🛈

David Fincher named the detectives in *Fight Club* (1999), Andrew, Kevin, and Walker, after *Se7en*'s screenwriter.

1995

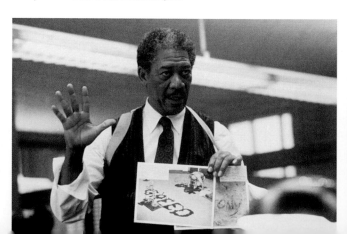

Smoke   Wayne Wang & Paul Auster, 1995

U.S. / Germany (Eurospace, Internal, Miramax, NDF, Smoke) 112m BW / Color **Producer** Kenzo Hirikoshi, Greg Johnson, Hisami Kuroiwa, Peter Newman **Screenplay** Paul Auster **Photography** Adam Holender **Music** Rachel Portman **Cast** Giancarlo Esposito, José Zúñiga, Stephen Gevedon, Harvey Keitel, Jared Harris, William Hurt, Daniel Auster, Harold Perrineau Jr., Cole/Paul Benjamin, Deirdre O'Connell, Victor Argo, Michelle Hurst, Forest Whitaker, Stockard Channing, Vincenzo Amelia, Erica Gimpel **Berlin International Film Festival** Wayne Wang, Harvey Keitel (Silver Bear—special jury prize), Wayne Wang (Golden Bear nomination)

Centered on a Brooklyn tobacco shop that also serves as a meeting place for colorful eccentrics representing a cross-section of New York society, this collaboration between director Wayne Wang and author Paul Auster wobbles intriguingly between an intricate character study and an improvisational comedy. But given the film's general emotional pay-off, punctuated with a bravura Harvey Keitel monologue, *Smoke* ultimately falls closer to the former, especially considering the heavy themes of trust, regret, and responsibility.

Keitel, William Hurt, Forest Whitaker, and Stockard Channing are all great here, and Wang weaves their interrelated tales into a single impressive tapestry. *Smoke*'s diverse plotlines are in fact all held together by tiny thematic threads: Many of the characters dwell on some significant loss in their life, others reflect on unrequited love, and still others try to restore a frayed bond between child and parent. Each thread connects one character to the other in subtle ways, and while the fabric of society may for better or worse be in constant flux or full of gaps, Wang and Auster optimistically imply that it's the inherent goodness of man which keeps it all from unraveling. **JKl**

1995

Badkonake sefid   Jafar Panahi, 1995
The White Balloon

Iran (Ferdos Films) 85m Color **Language** Farsi **Producer** Kurosh Mazkouri **Screenplay** Abbas Kiarostami **Photography** Farzad Jadat **Cast** Aida Mohammadkhani, Mohsen Kalifi, Fereshteh Sadr Orfani, Anna Borkowska, Mohammad Shahani, Mohammed Bakhtiar, Aliasghar Smadi, Hamidreza Tahery, Asghar Barzegar, Hasan Neamatolahi, Bosnali Bahary, Mohammadreza Baryar, Shaker Hayely, Homayoon Rokani, Mohammad Farakani **Cannes Film Festival** Jafar Panahi (Golden Camera)

This fresh and unpredictable comic "thriller" from Iran is the first feature of Jafar Panahi, a former assistant to the great Iranian filmmaker Abbas Kiarostami, who's credited, along with Panahi and Parviz Shahbazi, with the screenplay. *The White Balloon* describes in real time the adventures of a seven-year-old girl named Razieh (Aida Mohammadkhani) and her older brother in the streets of Tehran during the eighty-five minutes that elapse immediately before the celebration of the Iranian New Year.

After convincing her mother she needs another goldfish for the celebration, Razieh sets off to buy one, but twice en route to the store she loses the banknote she's been given. Most of the remainder of the film is devoted to her efforts to get the money back. If the plot sounds slender, the movie is both gripping and charming, with well-sketched characters and expert storytelling—and Panahi's efforts to redefine our sense of time along the way are remarkable. Bit by bit, we're drawn into this child's perception of time passing, focused on her desire for the goldfish and the various obstacles standing in the way of her acquiring it.

No less important is *The White Balloon*'s abrupt, last-minute revelation of middle-class snobbery on Razieh's part after a soldier goes to significant trouble to help her recover her money. This points one toward the more obvious ethical concerns of Panahi's next two features, *The Mirror* (1997) and *The Circle* (2000). **JRos**

Underground Emir Kusturica, 1995

France / Yugoslavia / Germany / Hungary (CiBy 2000) 192m Color **Language** Serbo-Croatian / German **Screenplay** Dusan Kovacevic, Emir Kusturica, from the novel *Bila jednom jedna zemlja* by Dusan Kovacevic and the play *Prolece u januaru* by Dusan Kovacevic and Emir Kusturica **Photography** Vilko Filac **Music** Goran Bregovic **Cast** Miki Manojlovic, Lazar Ristovski , Mirjana Jokovic, Slavko Stimac, Ernst Stötzner, Srdjan Todorovic, Mirjana Karanovic, Milena Pavlovic, Danilo "Bata" Stojkovic, Bora Todorovic, Davor Dujmovic, Dr. Nele Karajlic, Branislav Lecic, Dragan Nikolic, Erol Kadic **Cannes Film Festival** Emir Kusturica (Golden Palm)

Although slightly trimmed by director-writer Emir Kusturica for American consumption, this riotous 167-minute satiric and farcical allegory about the former Yugoslavia from World War II to the postcommunist present is still marvelously excessive. The outrageous plot of *Underground* involves a couple of anti-Nazi arms dealers and go ld traffickers who gain a reputation as communist heroes. One of them (Miki Manojlovic) installs a group of refugees in his grandfather's cellar, and on the pretext that the war is still raging upstairs he gets them to manufacture arms and other black-market items until the 1960s, meanwhile seducing the actress (Mirjana Jokovic) whom his best friend (Lazar Ristovski) hoped to marry.

Loosely based on a play by cowriter Dusan Kovacevic, this sarcastic, carnivalesque epic won the Golden Palm at Cannes in 1995 and has been at the center of a furious controversy ever since for what's been called its pro-Serbian stance. (Kusturica himself is a Bosnian Muslim.) However one chooses to take its jaundiced view of history, it is probably the best film to date by the talented filmmaker (*Time of the Gypsies* [1988], *Arizona Dream* [1993]), a triumph of mise-en-scène mated to a comic vision that keeps topping its own hyperbole. **JRos**

Dilwale Dulhaniya Le Jayenge Aditya Chopra, 1995
The Brave-Hearted Will Take the Bride

India (Eros) 192m Color **Language** Hindi **Producer** Yash Chopra **Screenplay** Aditya Chopra, Javed Siddiqi **Photography** Manmohan Singh **Music** Jatin Pandit, Lalit Pandit **Cast** Shahrukh Khan, Kajol Mukherjee, Amrish Puri, Farida Jalal, Anupam Kher, Karan Johar, Pooja Ruparel, Satish Shah, Anaita, Mandira Bedi, Arjun Sablok, Achla Sachdev, Parmeet Sethi, Himani Shivpuri, Lalit Tiwari

In the 1990s, Hindi film reinvented itself as a slicker, younger, and more stylish form, the new cable and satellite television channels setting the pace for a new look and the growth in advance music sales allowing budgets to rise. This resulted in a return to the cinema halls of the middle-class audience that had deserted it for VHS. This decade also saw more films about the Indian diaspora—people of Indian origin settled overseas—and *The Brave-Hearted Will Take the Bride* was as much a hit with this audience as in its home country, making it one of the biggest hits in Indian film history.

Londoners Raj Malhotra and Simran Singh (Shahrukh Khan and Kajol Mukherjee, respectively, one of the decade's most popular screen pairs), meet on a vacation in Switzerland but are separated when Simran's family takes her to Punjab for a marriage that was arranged at the time of her birth. Although the girl is ready to run away with her lover, Raj insists her father should give her away; so he persuades her family to accept him by showing them he knows how an Indian boy should behave. The tight script and hit music made it clear that Aditya Chopra, though very much his own director, was set to follow in the footsteps of his famous filmmaker father, Yash Chopra (known for films such as *Deewar* [1975] and *Lamhe* [1991]). **RDw**

Xich lo Tran Anh Hung, 1995
Cyclo

Vietnam / France (Entertainment, Lazannec, Lumière, La Sept, SFP) 120m Color Language Vietnamese / Italian Producer Christophe Rossignon Screenplay Trung Binh Nguyen, Tran Anh Hung Photography Benoît Delhomme, Laurence Trémolet Music Tôn-Thât Tiêt Cast Le Van Loc, Tony Leung Chiu-wai, Tran Nu Yên-Khê, Nhu Quynh Nguyen, Hoang Phuc Nguyen, Ngo Vu Quang Hal, Tuyet Ngan Nguyen, Doan Viet Ha, Bjuhoang Huy, Vo Vinh Phuc, Le Kinh Huy, Pham Ngoc Lieu, Le Tuan Anh, Le Cong Tuan Anh, Van Day Nguyen Venice Film Festival Tran Anh Hung (FIPRESCI award, Golden Lion)

ℹ️

Soundtrack composer Tôn-Thât Tiêt also collaborated with Tran Anh Hung on *The Scent of Green Papaya* (1993).

In 1990s Hanoi, a young rickshaw rider (Le Van Loc) has his bicycle stolen, which puts him in debt to the woman who rented it to him. She sends him to the silent gangster and pimp Poet (Tony Leung Chiu-wai), who puts him to work committing petty crimes to pay off his debt. What he doesn't know is that Poet has also persuaded his sister into working as a prostitute, servicing rich clients who pay with U.S. dollars. Thus two innocents are put on the path to corruption by the same man.

Cyclo's story may sound like a recipe for melodrama, but director Tran Anh Hung is after something else altogether. His approach is measured and considered. His focus is on color and silence as his camera lurks around the characters, discreetly awaiting the smallest flicker in their faces as thoughts and emotions shift and turn. The plot may take its starting point from Vittorio De Sica's *The Bicycle Thief* (1948), but it is not an exercise in Neorealism. Rather, the tone is almost magical realist, focusing on unexpected eruptions of odd beauty. There's a sense of Tran striving for a new form of storytelling, eschewing commercial genre conventions. The film could easily have been a thriller or a gangster movie, but *Cyclo* is a film in tune with the rhythms of the city it's set in, preparing to quietly reacquaint us with a place and a people we haven't seen since the news footage of the Vietnam War in the 1970s. **AT**

Sex. Clothes. Popularity.
Is There A Problem
Here?

Clueless

Opens July 19th

Clueless Amy Heckerling, 1995

When Jane Austen wrote the novel *Emma*, it is unlikely she ever imagined her tale of a nineteenth-century meddling young romantic heroine would be transplanted to late-twentieth-century Beverly Hills, but that is precisely what writer-director Amy Heckerling did with *Clueless*.

The film made a star of young Alicia Silverstone (who previously was best known as the star of the Aerosmith video "Crazy"). She plays Cher, a 90210 teen whose mother, as she tells us, "died in a freak accident during a routine liposuctioning," leaving Cher to be raised by her wealthy father (Dan Hedaya) in their vast Beverly Hills home. Although she does go to school with her pal Dionne (Stacey Dash), much of Cher's life is spent shopping on Rodeo Drive, coordinating her humongous wardrobe, and matchmaking for her friends, including school newcomer Tai (Brittany Murphy), who soon becomes something of a clone of her more savvy pal.

Like the Austen book on which it is (very loosely) based, there is a central love story. While interfering in other people's love lives, Cher barely notices her stepbrother Josh (Paul Rudd) as a possible romantic entanglement until it is almost too late. However, the film works best as a sharply funny satire on twentieth-century teens, complete with its own language (good-looking men are "Baldwins"—a nod to the handsome acting family led by Alec and Billy), blistering asides ("searching for a boy in high school is like searching for meaning in a Pauly Shore movie"), and well-aimed jabs at contemporary L.A. culture (Cher points out that she doesn't need to practice parking because everywhere she goes there is valet parking).

Heckerling keeps everything moving at a brisk pace, skewering fashion victims while making her heroine one of the most devoted, and Silverstone proves to be the perfect muse, fitting the role of the chic but dippy Cher to perfection. A funny, touching, and biting movie. **JB**

U.S. (Paramount) 97m Color
Producer Robert Lawrence, Scott Rudin **Screenplay** Amy Heckerling
Photography Bill Pope **Music** David Kitay
Cast Alicia Silverstone, Paul Rudd, Brittany Murphy, Stacey Dash, Donald Adeosun Faison, Dan Hedaya, Breckin Meyer, Justin Walker, Wallace Shawn, Jeremy Sisto, Twink Caplan, Elisa Donovan, Aida Linares, Sabastian Rashidi, Herb Hall

"Okay, so you're probably going, 'Is this like a Noxzema commercial or what?' But seriously, I actually have a way normal life for a teenage girl."

Cher
(Alicia Silverstone)

i

The scene where Cher realizes her true feelings for Josh as fountains erupt is a homage to *Gigi* (1958).

Safe Todd Haynes, 1995

U.S. / G.B. (Metro Tartan, American Playhouse, Channel Four, Chemical, Good Machine, Kardana) 119m Color **Producer** Christine Vachon, Lauren Zalaznick **Screenplay** Todd Haynes **Photography** Alex Nepomniaschy **Music** Brendan Dolan, Ed Tomney **Cast** Julianne Moore, Peter Friedman, Xander Berkeley, Susan Norman, Kate McGregor-Stewart, Mary Carver, Steven Gilborn, April Grace, Peter Crombie, Ronnie Farer, Jodie Markell, Lorna Scott, James LeGros, Dean Norris, Julie Burgess

Even though it arrived a few years early, Todd Haynes's *Safe* epitomized America's premillennial tension in the days leading toward the year 2000. Julianne Moore plays a vapid and materialistic suburban housewife who develops a severe allergic reaction to the world around her, starting with a rash and lethargy but leading ultimately to more violently disruptive responses. Desperate, she ensconces herself in a holistic retreat for people with the same problem. But is the ailment just a figment of Moore's imagination, a by-product of her tedious, banal existence? Or has her body truly revolted against modernity?

Haynes coyly keeps the exact nature of her illness ambiguous, depicting Moore's syndrome as very real while at the same time implying that her descent into sickness and subsequent embrace of New Age treatment may just be a search for something to fill a void in her life. Moore's performance is increasingly wrought with anxiety, panic, and fear, as she realizes that everything she knows—her home, her routine, her family—may have to be sacrificed for the sake of her well-being. *Safe* offers a lot of questions but few answers, bravely subverting sickness-of-the-week tropes by withholding the promise of a miracle cure. It's a thoroughly modern horror film whose threat seems to be civilization itself. **JKl**

Heat Michael Mann, 1995

U.S. (Forward Pass, Monarchy, Regency, Warner Bros.) 171m Color **Producer** Art Linson, Michael Mann **Screenplay** Michael Mann **Photography** Dante Spinotti **Music** Elliot Goldenthal **Cast** Al Pacino, Robert De Niro, Val Kilmer, Jon Voight, Tom Sizemore, Diane Venora, Amy Brenneman, Ashley Judd, Mykelti Williamson, Wes Studi, Ted Levine, Dennis Haysbert, William Fichtner, Natalie Portman, Tom Noonan

In Michael Mann's telemovie *L.A. Takedown* (1987), there is a scene in which a cop and the criminal he has been obsessively tracking happen to bump into each other while shopping. There is a tense pause, and then the criminal breaks the ice with a classic invitation: "Coffee?"

That scene reappears in Mann's *Heat*, a film whose richly deserved cult following has steadily grown since 1995. Set in Los Angeles, it takes a well-worked theme—the symbiotic relationship between cop Vincent (Al Pacino) and criminal Neil (Robert De Niro)—and meditates moodily upon it. Mann combines a flamboyant, epic style with a manic attention to realistic detail—resulting in indelible set pieces like the street shoot-out.

In its exploration of family and intimacy, *Heat* treats a founding theme of noir fiction: the danger of bonding with another person. Agonizing scenes dramatize Neil's assertion that a "professional" should be able to walk away from everything in his life within thirty seconds. These professionals are almost automatons: hard-driven, single-minded, and married to their unsavory work (rather than their teary, long-suffering companions). But they are also proud, stoic men, and in their determination lies a lofty splendor to which Mann pays immortal tribute. **AM**

1995

Toy Story Trilogy

John Lasseter, Ash Brannon, & Lee Unkrich, 1995, 1999, & 2010

Toy Story (1995) 81m
Toy Story 2 (1999) 92m
Toy Story 3 (2010) 103m

All three films U.S. (Pixar Animation Studios, Walt Disney) Color **Music** Randy Newman **Cast** (voices) Tom Hanks, Tim Allen, Don Rickles, Jim Varney (not *Toy Story 3*), Wallace Shawn, John Ratzenberger, Annie Potts, John Morris, Erik von Detten, Laurie Metcalf, R. Lee Ermey, Sarah Freeman, Penn Jillette, Jack Angel, Spencer Aste

Toy Story **Producer** Bonnie Arnold, Ralph Guggenheim **Screenplay** Joss Whedon, Andrew Stanton, Joel Cohen, Alec Sokolow, John Lasseter, Pete Docter, Joe Ranft **Oscars** John Lasseter (Special Achievement Award) **Oscar nominations** Randy Newman (music), Randy Newman (song), Joss Whedon, Andrew Stanton, Joel Cohen, Alec Sokolow, John Lasseter, Pete Docter, Joe Ranft (screenplay)

Toy Story 2 **Producer** Karen Robert Jackson, Sarah McArthur, Helene Plotkin **Screenplay** John Lasseter, Pete Docter, Ash Brannon, Andrew Stanton, Rita Hsiao, Doug Chamberlin, Chris Webb **Cast** (voices) Joan Cusack, Kelsey Grammer, Wayne Knight, Estelle Harris, Jodi Benson, Jonathan Harris, Joe Ranft, Andrew Stanton, Jeff Pidgeon **Oscar nominations** Randy Newman (music), Randy Newman (song)

Toy Story 3 **Producer** Darla K. Anderson, Nicole Paradis Grindle, John Lasseter **Screenplay** John Lasseter, Andrew Stanton, Lee Unkrich, Michael Ardnt **Cast** (voices) Joan Cusack, Wayne Knight, Estelle Harris, Jodi Benson, Michael Keaton, Ned Beatty, Emily Hahn, Blake Clark, Teddy Newton, Bud Luckey, Beatrice Miller, Javier Fernandez Pena, Timothy Dalton, Lori Alan, Charlie Bright, Kristen Schaal, Jeff Garlin, Bonnie Hunt, John Cygan, Whoopi Goldberg, Jan Rabson, Richard Kind, Erik von Detten, Amber Kroner, Brianna Maiwand, Jack Willis **Oscars** Randy Newman (music), Randy Newman (song), Lee Unkrich (animated film) **Oscar nominations** Tom Myers, Michael Silvers (sound editing), Darla K. Anderson (film), John Lasseter, Lee Unkrich, Andrew Stanton, Michael Arndt (screenplay)

i

A Pizza Planet reference has appeared in every Pixar movie so far, apart from *The Incredibles* (2004).

A Hollywood film franchise that heralded a new era in animation, the *Toy Story* trilogy irrevocably changed the cinematic landscape when the series' first installment arrived in the mid-1990s. Since then, a generation has grown up alongside Andy and his toys: Woody (Tom Hanks), Buzz (Tim Allen), and the gang, delighting at their adventures in America's suburban landscape. And if the first two films detailed the wondrous adventures and occasional travails of infancy and youth, the third installment tackled the bittersweet reality of growing up.

With each installment we witness the gradual loss of childhood innocence, with the toys placed in an increasingly urgent state of peril. In *Toy Story* it is the cruelty of the boy next door, who mutilates his own toy collection, producing a dismembered population that wouldn't look out of place in a Tim Burton film. (The author Michael Chabon finds the film's adherence to orthodoxy troubling, instead admiring the imagination of a child who puts a wrestler doll in a dress.)

In its sequel, it is an adult—up until that moment an entirely trustworthy figure—who takes on the role of the villain. It introduces the notion that value can extend beyond friendship to commerce, where feelings and comradeship are replaced by profit and greed. And through Jessie (Joan Cusack) we first encounter the possibility of a child outgrowing their most valued possessions, which becomes the dominant theme in the third film.

In *Toy Story 3* Andy is preparing to leave for college and with that he packs away his treasured toys. A comedy of errors results in Woody and his friends being accidentally donated to Sunnyside, a local day care center, whose happy exterior masks a darker, more threatening toy regime. The group's quest to return to Andy results in their being held hostage by Teddy Kingpin Lotso (Ned Beatty), a grubby, pink and white toy bear, who happens to be the center's de facto boss.

Two scenes heighten *Toy Story 3*'s gravitas and emotional heft: the near-oblivion encounter faced by the toys when they are almost pulled into a furnace, and Andy's realization that he must let go of his youth and pass on his toys to a more appreciative and understanding child. It is these moments, interspersed among the usual banter and knockabout scenes, which saw the film resonate strongly among an adult audience.

The *Toy Story* series realized the emotional depth that could be invested in animation, recalling earlier Disney successes, such as *Snow White and the Seven Dwarfs* (1937) and *Bambi* (1942), and highlighted how much had been lost among the less adventurous traditional animated features of recent decades. They are the pinnacle of Pixar's achievements and a treasure for those young enough to still play with toys, as well as the many who have long since given them up. **JT**

Dead Man Jim Jarmusch, 1995

At the beginning of Jim Jarmusch's *Dead Man*, a timid, bespectacled, hypercivilized clerk, William Blake (Johnny Depp), is heading west to take up a career in the frontier town of Machine. The journey seems endless, and once he arrives he discovers that his position was filled months ago. Feeling dejected, he beds a prostitute, only to be interrupted by her fiancé who shoots her dead, wounds William, and is shot by him in return. William flees, beginning a journey through the wilderness of the American West in which, with an enigmatic Indian named Nobody (Gary Farmer) at his side. Progressively suffering from his untreated wound, he navigates toward his death. Nobody is his guide: "Do you know how to use that weapon?" he asks. "It will replace your tongue."

An essay on contemplation, *Dead Man* charms through Robby Müller's black-and-white cinematography (influenced by Ansel Adams), the exquisitely simple guitar score by Neil Young, and Depp's gentle performance poetry—typified when he lies down to embrace a dead fawn. Bizarre support roles by John Hurt, Iggy Pop, Lance Henriksen, Gabriel Byrne, and the lanky, towering, Robert Mitchum, in his last screen appearance, a smoking cigar between his lips—persuading Blake to leave his office by pointing a double-gage shotgun into his face—fill out the almost plotless scenery.

Much of the narrative and violence in *Dead Man* is flat and unromantic, especially the perverse, almost catatonic behavior of Cole Wilson (Henriksen)—a killer not so much cold-blooded as bloodless. The pervading silences of the great Western emptiness, the silver birch gliding by as William rides through the forest, Nobody's matter-of-factness as he performs not entirely comprehensible rituals upon a man not entirely conscious, all lead to an almost meaningless evocation of person, place, and moment. When at the end Nobody pushes William off on a great lake, the spirit-canoe glides away into the other world in a vision that recalls the Death of King Arthur at Avalon. **MP**

U.S. / Germany / Japan (12 Gauge, JVC, Miramax, Newmarket, Pandora) 121m BW **Producer** Demetra J. MacBride **Screenplay** Jim Jarmusch **Photography** Robby Müller **Music** Neil Young **Cast** Johnny Depp, Gary Farmer, Lance Henriksen, Michael Wincott, Mili Avital, Iggy Pop, Crispin Glover, Eugene Byrd, Michelle Thrush, Jimmie Ray Weeks, Mark Bringleson, Gabriel Byrne, John Hurt, Alfred Molina, Robert Mitchum **Cannes Film Festival** Jim Jarmusch (Golden Palm nomination)

> "*Dead Man is likely Jim Jarmusch's most stunning achievement . . . He tears down one mythopoetic image of [the] West and in its place resurrects his own.*"
>
> **Zach Campbell,**
> *Slant Magazine*, 2004

ℹ️

Gary Farmer had a cameo as Nobody in the 1999 Jim Jarmusch film *Ghost Dog: The Way of the Samurai.*

The Usual Suspects Bryan Singer, 1995

U.S. / Germany (PolyGram, Spelling, Blue Parrot, Bad Hat Harry, Rosco) 106m Technicolor **Language** English / Hungarian / Spanish / French **Producer** Michael McDonnell, Bryan Singer **Screenplay** Christopher McQuarrie **Photography** Newton Thomas Sigel **Music** John Ottman **Cast** Gabriel Byrne, Kevin Spacey, Stephen Baldwin, Chazz Palminteri, Pete Postlethwaite, Kevin Pollak, Benicio Del Toro, Suzy Amis, Giancarlo Esposito, Dan Hedaya, Paul Bartel, Carl Bressler, Phillip Simon, Jack Shearer, Christine Estabrook **Oscars** Kevin Spacey (actor in support role), Christopher McQuarrie (screenplay)

🛈

Kevin Spacey had the fingers on his left hand glued together to make his character's disability more realistic.

With its convoluted plotting, macho repartee, and Bryan Singer's confident direction, *The Usual Suspects* is an absorbing confidence trick concerning the identification of a criminal archfiend: Who is Keyser Soze?

Spacey snatches his first Oscar as Verbal "people say I talk too much" Kint, a con man and the talkative cripple to whose narrative we cling. Five criminals are placed in a holding cell to appear in a lineup, although none were actually involved with the crime for which they have been arrested. The seemingly chance meeting, however, inspires them to team up on a heist, which sets them up for blackmail and betrayal.

A hip, urban *Rashômon* (1950) with bursts of violent, beautifully choreographed action, *The Usual Suspects* opens on a scene of carnage in which a mystery man executes Gabriel Byrne's Keaton. This sequence will recur, revised, as remembered by Verbal and as imagined by his interrogator, a federal agent (Chazz Palminteri) too fixated on his own theory of why these men came together to "stand back from it" and "look at it right." The viewer makes the same mistake, cleverly misdirected.

Singer delights in sleights of hand (like a camera dissolve into a swirling cup of coffee and a thrilling elevator shaft assassination) that make one forgetful of loose ends. The contribution of John Ottman, performing the unusual double of editing labyrinthine scenes and composing the brooding score, shouldn't be underestimated either. The ultimate accolade is that one cannot say that the film does not hold up. It may not add up, but it remains a madly intriguing puzzle. **AE**

Kjærlighetens kjøtere Hans Petter Moland, 1995
Zero Kelvin

Norway / Sweden (Norsk, Sandrews) 118m
Color **Language** Norwegian **Producer** Bent
Rognlien **Screenplay** Lars Bill Lundholm,
Hans Petter Moland, from the novel *Larsen*
by Peter Tutein **Photography** Philip Øgaard
Music Terje Rypdal **Cast** Stellan Skarsgård,
Gard B. Eidsvold, Bjørn Sundquist, Camilla
Martens, Paul-Ottar Haga, Johannes Joner,
Erik Øksnes, Lars Andreas Larssen, Juni Dahr,
Johan Rabaeus, Frank Iversen, Tinkas Qorfiq

Hans Petter Moland's *Zero Kelvin* has the crisp economy of a tough, knotty thriller by Roman Polanski. The story occurs in a grimly circumscribed setting: a shack in Greenland where three men hired as seal hunters quickly go crazy. Larsen (Garb B. Eidsvold) is a dandy; Holm (Bjørn Sundquist) is the quiet, scientific type; and Randbaek (Stellan Skarsgård) is a raging bull. For a while, dramatic tension occurs only between Larsen and Randbaek, as they seesaw between violence and boyish, petulant displays. But then Holm makes a sudden, decisive intervention—propelling the characters out of the shack and into the ice and snow. Now Moland can produce his most striking images and most ingenious narrative moves.

Although they are stranded in a landscape where all traces of civilization are absent, the characters' social values do not disappear, but instead are placed into stark relief by the monumental setting. Moland's ultimate concern is with the ethical dilemmas of human behavior under pressure. *Zero Kelvin* brilliantly examines what a

ⅈ

The Arctic island of Spitsbergen was used to stand in for Greenland on location shooting for the film.

normally civilized person will do in extreme circumstances, with all restraints removed. It asks what can separate men from beasts. And it coolly probes the constant claims of its characters to moral superiority or lofty idealism. **AM**

Trainspotting Danny Boyle, 1996

The team behind the 1994 British cult hit *Shallow Grave*—producer Andrew Macdonald, writer John Hodge, director Danny Boyle, and star Ewan McGregor—reunited for this punchy, grim look at the Edinburgh drug scene, based on offbeat writer Irvine Welsh's controversial novel.

McGregor stars as Mark "Rent Boy" Renton, an addict with a collection of misfit pals: casual dealer Sick Boy (Jonny Lee Miller); Spud (Ewen Bremner), a character who is destined to be one of life's losers; and Begbie (Robert Carlyle in a scary standout performance), a violent psycho who picks fights with anyone and everyone.

Boyle uses a clever cinematic imagination to bring these losers' lives onto the screen, from the showstopping opening moment as Renton runs down the street, to his infamous "Choose life" speech narrated as he is pursued for yet another petty crime committed to pay for his habit. Drug abuse here isn't depicted as a glamorous option—Renton's horrific hallucinations include a dive into possibly the most disgusting toilet in Scotland in an attempt to retrieve lost narcotics, and the unforgettable images of a dead baby that haunt him when he is trying to detox.

At the time of its release, some critics of the film complained that although *Trainspotting* doesn't glamorize drugs, it also doesn't pass any moral judgments on its drug-addicted characters. But Boyle and Hodge's refusal to take a moral stance is in fact one of the movie's many attributes—we are not there to judge Renton and his pals; we are just there to watch as, in a bleakly humorous fashion, their lives fizzle away to nothing. A fascinating, highly charged, and brilliantly played movie, *Trainspotting* is rightly regarded as one of the best British films of the 1990s. It features some of the country's most startling young talent: Carlyle, McGregor, writer Hodge, and director Boyle (who went on to work with McGregor again two years later in the interesting but uneven *A Life Less Ordinary*). **JB**

G.B. (Channel Four, Figment, PolyGram, Noel Gay) 94m Color **Producer** Andrew Macdonald **Screenplay** John Hodge, from novel by Irvine Welsh **Music** Johann Sebastian Bach, Georges Bizet, Brian Eno, Iggy Pop **Photography** Brian Tufano **Cast** Ewan McGregor, Ewen Bremner, Jonny Lee Miller, Kevin McKidd, Robert Carlyle, Kelly Macdonald, Peter Mullan, James Cosmo, Eileen Nicholas, Susan Vidler, Pauline Lynch, Shirley Henderson, Stuart McQuarrie, Irvine Welsh, Dale Winton **Oscar nomination** John Hodge (screenplay)

1996

> *"People think it's all about misery and desperation and death ... but what they forget is the pleasure of it."*
>
> Renton
> (Ewan McGregor)

ℹ️

The toilet-diving scene is a reference to Thomas Pynchon's postmodern novel *Gravity's Rainbow* (1973).

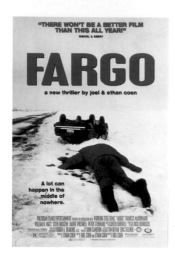

Fargo Joel Coen, 1996

One specialty of sibling partners Joel and Ethan Coen is twisting time-honored Hollywood genres into flamboyant, contemporary delights. The foremost filmmakers to emerge from America in the 1980s, their best films still look great, and the devilishly clever *Fargo* is among their very best. It's a wicked tale that provokes gasps of admiration and shock along with belly laughs. Embezzlement, abduction, deceit, misunderstanding, and murder are all in the frame, as is another regular feature of the Coenesque experience—a crime that gets totally out of control.

Fargo takes place in North Dakota, where oppressed car salesman Jerry Lundergaard (William H. Macy in the anxious performance that lifted him from ever-useful character actor to eagerly sought character actor) arranges a meeting with the two ex-cons he hires to abduct his wife. But most of the film, impishly introduced as a true story in the first of its macabre deceptions, is set in the austere, snowy landscapes of the Coens's native Minnesota (where the exaggerated regional dialect amusingly employed in hilariously banal chitchat is a flat, singsong relic of the area's Scandinavian immigrant pioneers, and at absurd odds with the heinous goings-on).

The desperately in debt Lundergaard cuts a supposedly simple, "no rough stuff" deal. His wife's ransom is to be paid by her rich, bullying father (Harve Presnell) and split between hubby and his hired thugs, with the woman going free none the wiser. Only things go horribly and grotesquely awry in the hands of the psychopath (Peter Stormare's Grimsrud) with a craving for pancakes, and the agitated bungler ("funny lookin' little fella" Steve Buscemi's Showalter) who can't control him or events. Enter Frances McDormand (Mrs. Joel Coen), absolutely fantastic as the very pregnant, comically ordinary but sharp small-town police chief, Marge Gunderson. Resolutely conducting her first triple homicide investigation with unhurried waddle and droll aplomb, Marge is easily the most engaging character ever conceived by the Coens (along with, later, Jeff Bridge's "The Dude" Lebowski).

The Coens's witty expertise results in a quirky, bizarre tragicomedy that manages to be wildly funny and violently distressing by neatly accomplished turns, the essential innocence and simplicity of some characters contrasted effectively with the depravity of others. Hapless criminals and victims are there not to be empathized with but to be cruelly toyed with for our wincing pleasure. That cold, malevolent streak that has recurred in much of their work is what prompted one detractor famously to dub them "arty nuisances." But it does not diminish their flagrant talent to dazzle, bemuse, and amuse. Against its icy visuals, *Fargo* contains some of their warmest work, full of signature Coen brothers set pieces and running jokes but also the surprisingly redemptive comfort of straightforward decency. McDormand and the Coens's screenplay won Oscars for breaking the mold in a unique case of murder. **AE**

U.S. / G.B. (Gramercy, PolyGram, Working Title) 98m Color **Producer** Ethan Coen **Screenplay** Joel Coen and Ethan Coen **Photography** Roger Deakins **Music** Carter Burwell **Cast** William H. Macy, Steve Buscemi, Frances McDormand, Peter Stormare, Kristin Rudrüd, Harve Presnell, Tony Denman, Gary Houston, Sally Wingert, Kurt Schweickhardt, Larissa Kokernot, Melissa Peterman, Steve Reevis, Warren Keith, Steve Edelman, Sharon Anderson **Oscars** Ethan Coen, Joel Coen (screenplay), Frances McDormand (actress) **Oscar nominations** Ethan Coen (best picture), Joel Coen (director), William H. Macy (actor in support role), Roger Deakins (photography), Ethan Coen, Joel Coen (editing) **Cannes Film Festival** Joel Coen (director, Golden Palm nomination)

"Deakins's darkly delicious shots create a beautiful wintry collage that turns the prosaic into cinematic poetry."

Peter Stack,
SF Chronicle, 1996

ℹ

The (false) "Based on a true story" disclaimer was added to help viewers suspend disbelief.

Gabbeh Mohsen Makhmalbaf, 1996

Iran / France (MK2, Sanaye Dasti) 75m Color
Language Farsi Producer Khalil Daroudchi,
Khalil Mahmoudi Screenplay Mohsen
Makhmalbaf Photography Mahmoud Kalari
Music Hossein Alizadeh Cast Abbas Sayah,
Shaghayeh Djodat, Hossein Moharami,
Rogheih Moharami, Parvaneh Ghalandari

Mohsen Makhmalbaf's *Gabbeh* is an overwhelmingly gorgeous film. From its first bold strokes—when a young woman (Shaghayeh Djodat) seems to spring to life from a figure in a Persian carpet—the colors, sounds, and rapid associative editing are entrancing. But *Gabbeh* is much more than another exotic exercise in the vein of, say, *Il Postino* (1994). The mournful story of deferred love that fills the film offers a profound humanist panorama of love and longing, birth and death, nature and culture, magic and loss.

These days, every film with a few red-tinted sunset shots is lazily labeled "poetic." *Gabbeh*, however, is an authentic expression of the "cinema of poetry." Every word, sight, sound, gesture, and color comes to resonate metaphorically with something else: The gesture of an animal resembles the motions of carpet makers; rapidly flowing water is like a field of grass sent dancing by the wind.

Within the context of burgeoning Western appreciation of the Iranian New Wave, *Gabbeh* has been faulted in comparison with the Neorealist films of Abbas Kiarostami, such as *Through the Olive Trees* (1994), but *Gabbeh* shows a hushed, patient, timeless aspect of Makhmalbaf's prodigious talent. The breathtaking style he adopts here fuses folk and modernist elements in a way that refuses any absolute distinction between them. This is a film that has a limpidity and directness that are truly sublime, a movie that makes its way straight into the soul. **AM**

ℹ

The film takes its title from a type of carpet woven by the Ghashghai nomads of southwest Iran.

Trois vies & une seule mort Raoul Ruiz, 1996
Three Lives and Only One Death

France / Portugal (CNC, Gémini, La Sept, Le Groupement National des Cinémas de Recherche, Canal+ Madragoa) 123m Eastmancolor **Language** French **Producer** Paulo Branco **Screenplay** Pascal Bonitzer, Raoul Ruiz **Photography** Laurent Machuel **Music** Jorge Arriagada **Cast** Marcello Mastroianni, Anna Galiena, Marisa Paredes, Melvil Poupaud, Chiara Mastroianni, Arielle Dombasle, Féodor Atkine, Jean-Yves Gautier, Jacques Pieiller, Pierre Bellemare, Smaïn, Lou Castel, Roland Topor, Jacques Delpi, Jean Badin **Cannes Film Festival** Raoul Ruiz (Golden Palm nomination)

Perhaps the most accessible movie of the Chilean-born Raul Ruiz (who has more than a hundred titles to his credit), *Three Lives and Only One Death* provides a sunny showcase for the charismatic talents of the late Marcello Mastroianni, who plays four separate roles, and stands as a testament to the filmmaker's imaginative postsurrealist talents as a yarn spinner and a weaver of magical images and ideas.

Mixing together ideas borrowed liberally and freely from stories by Nathaniel Hawthorne and Isak Dinesen with whimsical notions that could belong to no one but Ruiz (such as the tale of a millionaire who willingly and successfully turns himself into a beggar), *Three Lives and Only One Death* is a French comedy with a Paris setting, which often resembles a kind of euphoric free fall through the works and fancies of a writer like Jorge Luis Borges. Among the spirited cast members are Mastroianni's daughter Chiara, and Melvil Poupaud (who played in Ruiz's 1983 film *City of Pirates*). **JRos**

1996

Shine Scott Hicks, 1996

Australia (Australian Film Finance Corporation, Film Victoria, South Australian Feature Film Company) 105m Color **Producer** Jane Scott **Screenplay** Scott Hicks, Jan Sardi **Photography** Geoffrey Simpson **Music** David Hirschfelder **Cast** Geoffrey Rush, Justin Braine, Sonia Todd, Chris Haywood, Alex Rafalowicz, Gordon Poole, Armin Mueller-Stahl, Nicholas Bell, Danielle Cox, Rebecca Gooden, Marta Kaczmarek, John Cousins, Noah Taylor, Paul Linkson, Randall Berger **Oscar** Geoffrey Rush (best actor in a leading role) **Oscar nominations** Armin Mueller-Stahl (best actor in a supporting role), Scott Hicks (best director), Pip Karmel (best film editing), David Hirschfelder (best music, original dramatic score), Jane Scott (best picture), Jan Sardi, Scott Hicks (best writing, screenplay written directly for the screen)

David Helfgott (Geoffrey Rush) is a gifted pianist. But his promising talent as a concert pianist never reached the heights experts—his father included—expected of him. This film, by Australian director Scott Hicks, a former TV documentary maker, shows why, allowing Helfgott's story to unfold in a tragic way.

Like a slow-motion car accident, it is sometimes almost too painful to watch. As a young boy, Helgott (played as a youth by Alex Rafalowicz) was cited as possibly the best pianist of his generation and the next big thing in classic piano. This talent, however, wilted under the overwhelming pressure and presence of his father (played by Armin Mueller-Stahl). He's a man who lost his parents in the gas chambers and who certainly loves his son—but does not have a clue how to understand or manage his talent. It is the father's mistakes about his son that ultimately destroy the boy's burgeoning career.

Mentally fragile, Helfgott's prodigious skill at the piano surfaces only at the rarest times. *Shine*, for all its sadness, contains some of the most lustrous cinematic moments in memory, if only through juxtaposition with its bleaker instances. Based on a true story, this intense drama disturbingly reinforces the idea that suffering might just be the key for some artistic geniuses. Putting that cliché aside, however, *Shine* is an elegiac, nonjudgmental look at a true-life tormented prodigy who fought his own demons and finds redemption despite crippling emotional and mental odds. Much of the soundtrack features music by the real David Helfgott. John Gielgud appears as his London-based teacher. **KK**

Scream Wes Craven, 1996

In 1996, Wes Craven—director of such modern horror classics as *The Hills Have Eyes* (1978) and *A Nightmare on Elm Street* (1984)—shocked everyone who thought his career was over by initiating one of the most popular and successful horror series of all time. *Scream*, featuring a bevy of talented young actors (including Drew Barrymore, Neve Campbell, Skeet Ulrich, David Arquette, Rose McGowan, and Jamie Kennedy), took the United States by storm, bringing in over $103 million at the box office and kicking off a new wave of hip and reflexive slasher movies. *Urban Legend* (1998), *I Know What You Did Last Summer* (1997), and of course *Scream 2* (1997), *Scream 3* (2000), and the stalker parody *Scary Movie* (2000) all owe much of their success to Craven's original.

   Scream's intense ten-minute prologue is among the most talked-about horror scenes in recent memory. An anonymous caller threatens the lives of high school cutie Casey Becker (Barrymore) and her boyfriend unless she can answer such questions as "Who was the killer in *Friday the 13th*?" Like everyone else in *Scream*, Casey has seen most of the classic slasher movies: Halloween (1978), *Prom Night* (1980), and so on. But only the most hard-core horror fans have a chance to live here and even that's not always enough. The main story concerns the efforts of virginal heroine Sidney Prescott (Campbell) to survive the attacks of a slasher film fanatic with a ghost mask and a very sharp knife. Only the timely help of dirt-seeking news reporter Gale Weathers (Courteney Cox) is enough to save Sidney, who is shocked to discover that her enemy is really a pair of close male friends (including her sometimes boyfriend) who seem to get off on the fact that they kill without reason.

   Among the reasons for *Scream*'s outstanding success is an often hilarious script (written by Kevin Williamson, who would go on to create the hit teen TV show *Dawson's Creek*), the numerous jokey references to earlier horror movies, and Craven's expert direction, which manages to frighten audiences even while they're laughing. **SJS**

U.S. (Dimension, Woods) 111m Color
Producer Cathy Konrad, Cary Woods **Screenplay** Kevin Williamson **Photography** Mark Irwin **Music** Marco Beltrami **Cast** David Arquette, Neve Campbell, Courteney Cox, Skeet Ulrich, Rose McGowan, Matthew Lillard, Jamie Kennedy, W. Earl Brown, Drew Barrymore, Joseph Whipp, Lawrence Hecht, Roger L. Jackson, David Booth, Liev Schreiber, Carla Hatley

"It's so sad. Her mom and dad found her hanging from a tree limb, her insides on the outside."

Tatum (Rose McGowan)

🅸
Marco Beltrami has written the scores for seven of Wes Craven's films since this first collaboration.

Secrets & Lies Mike Leigh, 1996

France / G.B. (Channel Four, CiBy 2000, Thin Man) 142m Metrocolor **Producer** Simon Channing-Williams **Screenplay** Mike Leigh **Photography** Dick Pope **Music** Andrew Dickson **Cast** Timothy Spall, Phyllis Logan, Brenda Blethyn, Claire Rushbrook, Marianne Jean-Baptiste, Elizabeth Berrington, Michele Austin, Lee Ross, Lesley Manville, Ron Cook, Emma Amos, Brian Bovell, Trevor Laird, Claire Perkins, Elias Perkins McCook **Oscar nominations** Simon Channing-Williams (best picture), Mike Leigh (director), Mike Leigh (screenplay), Brenda Blethyn (actress), Marianne Jean-Baptiste (actress in support role) **Cannes Film Festival** Mike Leigh (Golden Palm, prize of the ecumenical jury), Brenda Blethyn (actress)

i

As with all of Mike Leigh's projects, most of the script was improvised.

Secrets & Lies, Mike Leigh's gripping, multifaceted comedy-drama, winner of the grand prize at Cannes in 1996, may well be his most accessible and optimistic film. This possibly helps to explain why it remains the most celebrated work of a writer-director for stage and screen who is often best known for his anger and merciless skewering of class differences in Thatcherite and post-Thatcher England.

Hortense, a young black optometrist (Marianne Jean-Baptiste), seeks out her white biological mother (Brenda Blethyn), a factory worker who put her up for adoption at birth. As the two become acquainted, tensions build between the mother and another illegitimate daughter (Claire Rushbrook), between the mother and her younger brother (Timothy Spall), and between him and his wife (Phyllis Logan), everything leading to a ferocious climax.

The dense, Ibsen-like plotting of family revelations in *Secrets & Lies* is dramatically satisfying in broad terms, though it leaves a few details unaccounted for. But the acting is so strong—with Spall a particular standout—that you're carried along as if by a tidal wave. **JRos**

The English Patient Anthony Minghella, 1996

U.S. (J&M, Miramax, Tiger Moth) 160m Color
Language English / German **Producer** Saul
Zaentz **Screenplay** Anthony Minghella,
from novel by Michael Ondaatje
Photography John Seale **Music** Gabriel
Yared **Cast** Ralph Fiennes, Juliette Binoche,
Willem Dafoe, Kristin Scott Thomas, Naveen
Andrews, Colin Firth, Julian Wadham, Jürgen
Prochnow, Kevin Whately, Clive Merrison,
Nino Castelnuovo, Hichem Rostom, Peter
Rühring, Geordie Johnson, Torri Higginson
Oscars Saul Zaentz (best picture), Anthony
Minghella (director), Juliette Binoche (actress
in support role), Stuart Craig, Stephanie
McMillan (art direction), John Seale
(photography), Ann Roth (costume), Walter
Murch (editing), Gabriel Yared (music), Walter
Murch, Mark Berger, David Parker, Christopher
Newman (sound) **Oscar nominations**
Anthony Minghella (screenplay), Ralph
Fiennes (actor), Kristin Scott Thomas (actress)
Berlin International Film Festival Juliette
Binoche (Silver Bear), Anthony Minghella
(Golden Bear nomination)

*"Every night I cut out my
heart. But in the morning
it was full again."*

Almásy (Ralph Fiennes)

ℹ️

Fiennes's burn makeup took five
hours each day to apply and used an
eleven piece foam prosthetic.

Anthony Minghella's epic adaptation of Michael Ondaatje's Booker
Prize–winning novel owned Oscar night, winning nine Academy Awards
in the most sweeping victory since the 1987 film *The Last Emperor*. It was
particularly remarkable for a film that the writer-director had almost
despaired of making. Having been "intoxicated" by the poetic book, he
spent over three years restructuring it, greatly expanding the doomed
love story at its heart. The independent producer Saul Zaentz (*One Flew
Over the Cuckoo's Nest* [1975], *Amadeus* [1984]) originally found backing
from 20th Century Fox. But disagreements, such as casting Kristin Scott
Thomas rather than an American actress, culminated in the studio pulling
out. Production was halted before Miramax stepped in with the finance.

A severely burned and disfigured pilot (Ralph Fiennes) is found in the
wreckage of his biplane in North Africa near the end of World War II.
Apparently amnesiac, unidentified but presumed to be English, he is
dying and in the care of French-Canadian nurse Hana (Juliette Binoche).
Taking refuge in a devastated Italian monastery, they are joined by
Willem Dafoe's vengeful Canadian torture victim and two bomb disposal
experts for intimate explorations of memory, loss, and healing. The
mystery patient—revealed as Hungarian Count Laszlo Almásy—recalls
his past gradually between the late 1930s and 1945, in Tuscany, Cairo,
and the Sahara Desert. Almásy's love affair with the married Katharine
Clifton (Kristin Scott Thomas) unfolds with tragic consequences.

The film has two strong elements to captivate. The story is convoluted
but classically, passionately romantic. And the production is meticulously
artful, repeatedly likened to the style of David Lean, from dreamlike aerial
sequences and a dramatic sandstorm to sensuous love scenes and
enchanting effects—cave paintings examined by torchlight, church
frescoes illuminated by a flare. *The English Patient*'s scale, its majesty on
big screens, and its sense of importance demanded recognition for its
artistic and technical achievements. **AE**

Lone Star John Sayles, 1996

John Sayles's wise and witty study of interconnected lives down by the Texan border with Mexico is about crossing lines, digging up the past, learning lessons, and moving on. It proffers a garrulous gallery of characters, all somehow connected with or investigated by Rio County Sheriff Sam Deeds (Chris Cooper) after a skeleton is discovered in the desert just outside of town. Deeds privately reckons it may have something to do with the ongoing battle his late dad (Matthew McConaughey)—for years a local hero—had with a notoriously corrupt and racist lawman (Kris Kristofferson) several decades previously. What happened way back then? And how has it affected the present town, with its uneasy mix of whites, Hispanics, and blacks all keen to rewrite history as well as claim the future? How does the personal affect the political, and vice versa?

On the surface, *Lone Star* might be seen as a cross between a detective story and a modern Western, but it's more pertinently the kind of kaleidoscopic survey of a society in the process of change at which Sayles has been excelling for years—ever since *Matewan* (1987) and *City of Hope* (1991), in fact. Here, however, for the first time he adds flashbacks (sometimes as private memories, sometimes as shared experience) to include time as an extra ingredient in a heady brew already made up of class, money, sex, friendship, family, and race. Inevitably, given the border setting, the last figures heavily in terms of fear, hatred, desire, immigration, job prospects, and prejudice; mercifully, Sayles never sermonizes, but simply shows us how things function (or not, as the case may be). The dialogue is witty and colorful but naturalistic, the performances are excellent throughout, the use of music is characteristically sly and expressive, and Stuart Dryburgh's camera work eloquently conveys the various allegiances and divisions in the community on view. And watch out for that quietly subversive (albeit eminently justifiable) ending—forget the Alamo, indeed! **GA**

U.S. (Castle Rock, Columbia, Rio Dulce) 135m Color **Producer** R. Paul Miller, Maggie Renzi **Screenplay** John Sayles **Photography** Stuart Dryburgh **Music** Mason Daring **Cast** Stephen Mendillo, Stephen J. Lang, Chris Cooper, Elizabeth Peña, Oni Faida Lampley, Eleese Lester, Joe Stevens, Gonzalo Castillo, Richard Coca, Clifton James, Tony Frank, Miriam Colon, Kris Kristofferson, Jeff Monahan, Matthew McConaughey **Oscar nomination** John Sayles (screenplay)

"Buddy Deeds said a thing, he damn well backed it up. Never be another one like him."

**Fenton
(Tony Frank)**

1996

i

Lone Star is regarded as director John Sayles's masterpiece. His screenplay won an Oscar nomination.

1996

Denmark / Sweden / France / Netherlands / Norway (Argus, Canal+, CoBo, Det Danske, Eurimages, European Script Fund, Finnish Film Foundation, La Sept, Liberator, Lucky Red, Media Investment Club, Nederlands Fonds voor de Film, Nordic Film & TV Fund, Northern Lights, Norwegian Film Institute, October, Philippe Bobor, SVT Drama, Swedish Film Institute, TV1000 AB, Icelandic Film Corporation, Trust Film Svenska, VPRO TV, Villealfa, YLE, Zentropa, ZDF, Arte) 159m Eastmancolor **Director** Lars von Trier **Producer** Peter Aalbæk Jensen, Vibeke Windeløv **Screenplay** Lars von Trier, Peter Asmussen **Photography** Robby Müller **Music** Joachim Holbek **Cast** Emily Watson, Stellan Skarsgård, Katrin Cartlidge, Jean-Marc Barr, Adrian Rawlins, Jonathan Hackett, Sandra Voe, Udo Kier, Mikkel Gaup, Roef Ragas, Phil McCall, Robert Robertson, Desmond Reilly, Sarah Gudgeon, Finlay Welsh **Oscar nomination** Emily Watson (actress) Cannes Film Festival Lars von Trier (grand prize of the jury, Golden Palm nomination)

"I don't make love with them, I make love with Jan and I save him from dying."

Bess (Emily Watson)

𝒊

Helena Bonham Carter was originally lined up to play Bess, but she pulled out just before shooting started.

Breaking the Waves Lars von Trier, 1996

Before issuing a manifesto that urged subscribing to a dogma, Danish filmmaker Lars von Trier made a film about the ambiguous horrors of living by dogma. Set in remote Scotland in the 1970s, *Breaking the Waves* leaves behind the slickly designed, highly wrought artifice of the often monochrome magical worlds of earlier von Trier productions (*The Element of Crime* [1984], *Europa* [1991]) to experiment with the edgy, hand-held, rough-around-the-edges look typical of his *The Idiots* (1998) and Dogme95 pictures by other directors (such as Thomas Vinterberg's *Festen* [1998] and Joren Kragh-Jacobsen's *Mifune* [1999]). However, this is by no means a dogma or dogmatic film, as scenes are set with computer-augmented haunted landscapes and deeply unfashionable 1970s pop music selections.

Von Trier was obsessed as a child with a fairy tale called *Golden Heart*, about a good little girl who gives away so much that she uses herself up—though his copy was missing a crucial happy ending. *Breaking the Waves* is the first of a trilogy, followed by *The Idiots* (1998) and *Dancer in the Dark* (2000), extrapolating from this theme. Here, the heroine is Bess (Emily Watson), a withdrawn, almost childish young woman raised in an austere, religious community in Scotland's Outer Hebrides. She begins to emerge from her shell when she impulsively marries Jan (Stellan Skarsgård), a Swede who works on an oil rig in the North Sea, but her new life is fractured when Jan is crippled by an industrial accident. Replacing her cold religion with extreme love, Bess takes a peculiar path to sainthood and martyrdom, discovering that she can reach the bedridden Jan only by recounting to him tales of sexual adventures, which leads her to comic, tragic, and ultimately fatal encounters.

Ostracized as a whore by village elders who routinely stand over the graves of women and curse them to hell for causing the fall of man, Bess is drawn out to sea to a boat captained by a Satanic Udo Kier, but the final moments of the film present her post humous influence as genuinely miraculous. The plot takes a difficult but rewarding path, and it might shade into gimmickry were it not for a startlingly real, affecting, and strange central performance from Watson. **KN**

Independence Day Roland Emmerich, 1996

U.S. (Fox, Centropolis)
145m Color Producer Dean Devlin
Screenplay Dean Devlin, Roland Emmerich
Photography Karl Walter Lindenlaub
Music David Arnold Cast Bill Pullman,
Mary McDonnell, Mae Whitman, Jeff
Goldblum, Judd Hirsch, Will Smith, Vivica A.
Fox, Ross Bagley, Margaret Colin, Robert
Loggia, James Rebhorn, Randy Quaid,
James Duval, Lisa Jakub, Giuseppe Andrews
Oscar Volker Engel, Douglas Smith, Clay
Pinney, Joe Viskocil (special visual effects)
Oscar nomination Chris Carpenter, Bill W.
Benton, Bob Beemer, Jeff Wexler (sound)

Special effects movies don't get much bigger than *Independence Day,* a sci-fi bonanza that oozes American patriotism from every frame. Jeff Goldblum is the satellite whizz who picks up a transmission from outer space that seems to be counting down to zero. He heads off to Washington D.C. to warn the president, played by Bill Pullman (a very Clintonesque leader, with Mary McDonnell his Hillary-like wife) that spaceships appearing all over the planet may not be filled with fuzzy and friendly E.T.s, but are actually hostile aliens planning to devastate Earth.

Director Roland Emmerich and producer Dean Devlin pack their movie with humorous actors—Will Smith, Robert Loggia, Judd Hirsch, Harvey Fierstein—playing the action with tongue planted firmly in cheek, though the real star here is not any of the actors, but the brilliant special effects. From alien spaceships reminiscent of cult television series *V,* to the attacks on Earth (almost too realistic), we watch in horror as once great landmarks—the Empire State Building and the White House—are reduced to piles of smoking rubble. All in all, a great example of what edgy fun a sci-fi extravaganza can be. **JB**

1997

The Ice Storm Ang Lee, 1997

U.S. (Canal+ Droits Audiovisuels,
Fox Searchlight, Good Machine) 112m
Technicolor Producer Ted Hope, Ang Lee,
James Schamus Screenplay James
Schamus, from novel by Rick Moody
Photography Frederick Elmes
Music Mychael Danna Cast Kevin Kline,
Joan Allen, Henry Czerny, Adam Hann-Byrd,
David Krumholtz, Tobey Maguire, Christina
Ricci, Jamey Sheridan, Elijah Wood,
Sigourney Weaver, Kate Burton, William
Cain, Michael Cumpsty, Maia Danziger,
Michael Egerman Cannes Film Festival
James Schamus (screenplay), Ang Lee
(Golden Palm nomination)

Novelist Rick Moody captured the mood of the 1970s with *The Ice Storm,* a mesmerizing tale of two suburban families in emotional free fall. Making a film of the book in 1997, Taiwanese director Ang Lee elicited deftly controlled performances from a stellar ensemble cast of Kevin Kline, Joan Allen, Sigourney Weaver, Christina Ricci, Elijah Wood, Adam Hann-Byrd, and Tobey Maguire. The limited plot of a story of tragedies, both small and large, is less told than felt, through the staging of a series of moody and atmospheric scenes.

Set in New Canaan, Connecticut, 1973, a suburban satellite of New York City—finally getting what the city has had for some time, a sense of being ill at ease—neighboring families the Hoods and the Carvers lead almost identical lives. The adults drink and smoke too much and talk about porn films or Watergate. Benjamin Hood (Kline) conducts a dispassionate affair with Janey Carver (Weaver, wearing the wild clothing of a 1970s suburban seductress), while Hood's wife (Allen, her hair in a controlled, precise bob), suspecting as much, is unable to coerce an admission of truth from her husband. Meanwhile, their children (Ricci, Hann-Byrd, and Wood) experiment with sex and booze in a detached manner. Paul Hood (Maguire), the film's most vibrant character, is a young man who makes sense of his family in terms of the Fantastic Four, a group of dysfunctional comic superheros. The weather, a deus ex machina so disliked by certain script theorists, works as another mysterious and deadly force the two couples can only handle after it has struck. **KK**

Hana-Bi Takeshi Kitano, 1997

U.S. (Office Kitano, TV Tokyo, Bandai Visual Company) 103m Color Producer Masayuki Mori, Yasushi Tsuge, Takio Yoshida Screenplay Takeshi Kitano Photography Hideo Yamamoto Music Joe Hisaishi Cast Takeshi Kitano, Kayoko Kishimoto, Ren Oshugi, Makoto Ashikawa, Susumu Terajima, Tetsu Watanabe, Hakuryu, Yasuei Yakushiji, Tarô Itsumi, Kan'ichi Yajima, Yûko Daike, Hitoshi Nishizawa Venice Film Festival Takeshi Kitano (Golden Lion)

Hana-Bi is a long way from Takeshi Kitano's police drama directorial debut, *Violent Cop* (1989). Kitano, simultaneously channelling Jean-Pierre Melville and Buster Keaton, plays Nishi, a cop who left the force after an incident in which one colleague was killed, another paralyzed, and the culprit ruthlessly executed by his own hand. His wife—his life—is dying, so he concocts a plan to rob a bank (witnessed on CCTV, in one of the director's most brilliantly realized comedy moments) in order to ensure a safe future for his colleague's widow and to whisk his wife off on a second honeymoon.

The tone is key to *Hana-Bi*. It is tough, but it is a film with violence in it, rather than a violent film. The brutal scenes with gangsters are contrasted with playful snapshots of the couple's journey around Japan and the paralyzed cop's tentative first steps as a painter, before the film's heartbreaking dénouement. The result is Kitano's finest work, satisfying both as a genre piece and in bringing together such disparate narrative strands.

Kitano's subsequent films have equalled only parts of this sum, and *Hana-Bi* looks more like the end of a creatively fruitful period than a beginning of a new phase. But such a blaze of glory must always offer hope of a return. **IHS**

Boogie Nights Paul Thomas Anderson, 1997

U.S. (New Line Cinema) 155m Color Producer Paul Thomas Anderson, Lloyd Levin Screenplay Paul Thomas Anderson Photography Robert Elswit Music Ernst Toch Cast Mark Wahlberg, Burt Reynolds, Julianne Moore, John C. Reilly, Heather Graham, William H. Macy, Philip Seymour Hoffman, Philip Baker Hall, Don Cheadle, Alfred Molina, Nina Hartley, Robert Ridgely Oscar nominations Burt Reynolds (actor), Julianne Moore (actress), Paul Thomas Anderson (original screenplay)

In *Boogie Nights*'s vast canvas of life in the porn industry, Paul Thomas Anderson's debt to 1970s American cinema—particularly the work of Robert Altman—is all too clear. However, the sheer scale of his sophomore feature is an astonishing achievement.

Mark Wahlberg plays Eddie Adams, whose good looks, easygoing attitude, and impressive appendage find him transformed into rising porn star Dirk Diggler. Under the tutelage of filmmaking supremo Jack Horner (Burt Reynolds) and co-star Amber Waves (Julianne Moore), Dirk attempts to raise the quality of the product he is appearing in but is soon consumed by drug abuse and undermined by the demands of an ever-changing business.

Like Altman's best work, Anderson's film features a strong ensemble cast. Hitherto known as a rap star and underwear model, Wahlberg was a revelation in the lead role, ably supported by John C. Reilly's co-star, Moore's moving turn as a mother whose work threatens her maternity rights, Heather Graham as the fun-loving roller girl, and a scene-stealing performance by Reynolds.

If the film's narrative sweep occasionally overextends itself, or Anderson's penchant for complex set-ups is a little too self-reflexive, there is no denying the ambition of the young filmmaker. **IHS**

L.A. Confidential Curtis Hanson, 1997

U.S. (Monarchy, Regency, Warner Bros.) 138m Technicolor **Producer** Curtis Hanson, Arnon Milchan, Michael G. Nathanson **Screenplay** Brian Helgeland, Curtis Hanson, from novel by James Ellroy **Photography** Dante Spinotti **Music** Jerry Goldsmith **Cast** Kevin Spacey, Russell Crowe, Guy Pearce, James Cromwell, Kim Basinger, Danny DeVito **Oscars** Brian Helgeland, Curtis Hanson (screenplay), Kim Basinger (actress in support role) **Oscar nominations** Arnon Milchan, Curtis Hanson, Michael G. Nathanson (best picture), Curtis Hanson (director), Jeannine Claudia Oppewall, Jay Hart (art direction), Dante Spinotti (photography), Peter Honess (editing), Jerry Goldsmith (music) **Cannes Film Festival** Curtis Hanson (Golden Palm nomination)

ℹ

Kevin Spacey was told to loosely base his character on Dean Martin.

Set in 1950s Los Angeles, a festering swamp of corrupt cops dallying with freshly minted mobsters and fledgling tabloids, Curtis Hanson's smart and soulful movie trims James Ellroy's heavily plotted pulp best seller to its emotional heart. Hanson's pacing is exquisite, his casting impish and inspired, as he traces the morally ambiguous alliance between three radically incompatible cops roped together in a multiple-murder investigation. Kevin Spacey cooks as a celebrity cop refusing to snitch on his mates. Russell Crowe is ardent and thuggish as a crusading policeman vying with uptight career cop Guy Pearce for the affections of a classy hooker, played by Kim Basinger (a career-making performance she subsequently failed to top).

Dressed in the sumptuous chocolate browns of warm film noir, *L.A. Confidential* is hot, funny, and sorrowful. Though it teases brash 1950s optimism with glum 1930s cynicism and tars both with the brush of the knowing 1990s, the film is also wildly romantic—perhaps the last great mounting of American film noir's feverish chase for and destruction of dreams. Dicks and dames collide in a grandiose lament for the loss of true love, moral courage, and, while we're at it, hope in our civic culture. **ET**

861

Funny Games Michael Haneke, 1997

Austria (Wega) 108m Color
Language German / French Producer Veit
Heiduschka Screenplay Michael Haneke
Photography Jürgen Jürges Music Georg
Friedrich Händel, Pietro Mascagni, Wolfgang
Amadeus Mozart Cast Susanne Lothar,
Ulrich Mühe, Arno Frisch, Frank Giering,
Stefan Clapczynski, Doris Kunstmann,
Christoph Bantzer, Wolfgang Glück,
Susanne Meneghel, Monika Zallinger
Cannes Film Festival Michael Haneke
(Golden Palm nomination)

In this brutal and provocative "home invasion" movie—a subgenre traceable as far back as D.W. Griffith and familiar today from such films as *A Clockwork Orange* (1971) and *Panic Room* (2002)—Michael Haneke pushes viewers to the limit, forcing us to contemplate the senselessness of random violence, as well as our seemingly ceaseless fascination with watching it on-screen.

A well-to-do family of three go on vacation to their lakeside cottage. Shortly after their arrival, a chubby, clean-cut young man (Frank Giering) knocks on the door, politely asking to borrow an egg. He is quickly joined by a thinner and more refined companion (Arno Frisch). Initially fooled by the young men's polished appearance and their claim to be friends of the neighboring family, wife Anna (Susanne Lothar) allows them into the house. Once inside, however, the boys proceed to disable the husband (Ulrich Mühe), force Anna to strip, and shoot the couple's young son (Stefan Clapczynski).

While the sadistic teens play not-so-funny games with their victims—all of whom end up dead by the end—the director plays games with his audience: At one point, after Anna manages to kill one of her captors, Haneke interrupts the diegesis, allowing the boy's friend to "rewind" the film, thereby saving his partner in crime. There is no happy ending here, only troubling questions and the inevitability of future mayhem. **SJS**

i

In 2008 Haneke directed a shot-for-shot English-language remake of the film, starring Naomi Watts.

Abre los ojos Alejandro Amenábar, 1997
Open Your Eyes

Spain / France / Italy (Escorpión, Alain Sarde, Lucky Red, Sogetel) 117m Color **Language** Spanish **Producer** Fernando Bovaira, José Luis Cuerda **Screenplay** Alejandro Amenábar, Mateo Gil **Photography** Hans Burman **Music** Alejandro Amenábar, Mariano Marín **Cast** Eduardo Noriega, Penélope Cruz, Chete Lera, Fele Martínez, Najwa Nimri, Gérard Barray, Jorge de Juan, Miguel Palenzuela, Pedro Miguel Martínez, Ion Gabella, Joserra Cadiñanos, Tristán Ulloa, Pepe Navarro, Jaro, Walter Prieto **Berlin International Film Festival** Alejandro Amenábar (C.I.C.A.E. Award, Panorama honorable mention)

Alejandro Amenábar's *Open Your Eyes* may be best known as the Spanish film Cameron Crowe remade with Tom Cruise as *Vanilla Sky* (2001), but it deserves to be seen for the true original it is. Intrigued with cryogenics and virtual reality, Amenábar has said he intended to make a "realistic" science-fiction movie out of mere "camera angles" instead of mind-blowing special effects. But *Open Your Eyes* transcends such easy classification unless viewed as a precursor to such films as *eXistenZ* (1999), *The Matrix* (1999), *Fight Club* (1999), *The Sixth Sense* (1999), *Memento* (2000), and *Mulholland Drive* (2001)—dark films that peel away in layers, present identity as performance or virtual experience, question the nature of time and reality, and must be seen at least twice.

The film opens as narcissistic, well-off César (Eduardo Noriega) ditches his latest one-night stand, meets his "dream girl" Sophia (Penélope Cruz), and betrays his best friend the night before he awakens, after a hideously disfiguring automobile accident, in a psychiatric prison, accused of murder. There, he projects a present and future out of remnants of his past life and previously viewed films. Breaking down, he becomes unable to distinguish life from dream—that is, until the labyrinthine series of twists and revelations leading to the conclusion, in which the "reality" of everything that has gone before is chillingly undermined. **LB**

1997

The Sweet Hereafter Atom Egoyan, 1997

Canada (Alliance, Canadian Film and Video Production Tax Credit, Ego Gort, Harold Greenberg Fund, TMN, Téléfilm Canada) 112m Color **Producer** Atom Egoyan, Camelia Frieberg **Screenplay** Atom Egoyan, from novel by Russell Banks **Photography** Paul Sarossy **Music** Mychael Danna, Sarah Polley **Cast** Ian Holm, Caerthan Banks, Sarah Polley, Tom McCamus, Gabrielle Rose, Alberta Watson, Maury Chaykin, Stephanie Morgenstern, Kirsten Kieferle **Oscar nominations** Atom Egoyan (director), Atom Egoyan (screenplay) **Cannes Film Festival** Atom Egoyan (FIPRESCI award, grand prize of the jury, prize of the ecumenical jury, Golden Palm nomination)

Truly the exception to the rule when it comes to literary adaptations, *The Sweet Hereafter* handles author Russell Banks's novel so intelligently that even Banks has conceded the film improves on the book. Toning down his trademark diced-up time lines and fascination with multimedia, director Atom Egoyan creates a stunningly direct, almost fablelike exploration of loss. In fact, Egoyan brilliantly incorporates the Pied Piper of Hamlin into his film, eventually lending the wrenching events a reflective and somber thematic unity.

When a school bus crashes and sinks below the ice, killing most of its young passengers, the residents of a small town must find ways to deal with issues of grief, exacerbated by the presence of an outsider lawyer (Ian Holm) who believes only the assignation of blame can alleviate the town's feelings of collective guilt. Egoyan reveals the tragedy itself only in bits and pieces, and as the events of that day grow clearer and clearer, so does the director's depiction of the heartbreaking accident. As Holm's drive for financial and emotional reward draws to a close, the testimony of one survivor (Sarah Polley) becomes more and more integral to his case, but he soon learns that in the face of unthinkable despair, sometimes honesty comes second to reconciliation. **JKl**

Titanic James Cameron, 1997

U.S. (Fox, Lightstorm, Paramount) 194m
Color **Producer** James Cameron, Jon
Landau **Screenplay** James Cameron
Photography Russell Carpenter
Music James Horner **Cast** Leonardo
DiCaprio, Kate Winslet, Billy Zane, Kathy
Bates, Bill Paxton, Gloria Stuart, Frances
Fisher, Bernard Hill, Jonathan Hyde, David
Warner, Victor Garber, Danny Nucci, Lewis
Abernathy, Suzy Amis, Nicholas Cascone
Oscars James Cameron, Jon Landau (best
picture), James Cameron (director), Peter
Lamont, Michael Ford (art direction), Russell
Carpenter (photography), Deborah Lynn
Scott (costume), Tom Bellfort, Christopher
Boyes (special sound effects), Robert Legato,
Mark A. Lasoff, Thomas L. Fisher, Michael
Kanfer (special visual effects), Conrad Buff,
James Cameron, Richard A. Harris (editing),
James Horner (music), James Horner, Will
Jennings (song), Gary Rydstrom, Tom
Johnson, Gary Summers, Mark Ulano
(sound) **Oscar nominations** Kate Winslet
(actress), Gloria Stuart (actress in support
role), Tina Earnshaw, Greg Cannom,
Simon Thompson (makeup)

> *"I'm the king of
> the world!"*
>
> **Jack (Leonardo DiCaprio)**

i

Her role in *Titanic* made Gloria Stuart
the oldest person ever nominated
for an Oscar. She was eighty-seven.

The story behind director James Cameron's labor of love is almost more dramatic than the tale that unfolds on screen. With a reported budget of over $200 million, even before its release *Titanic* was given the dubious honor of being the most expensive production of all time. Much of the cost went to a six-month shoot in Mexico involving a 775-foot replica of the famous boat, which sank when it hit an iceberg back in 1912. It was a shoot dogged with problems—including delays to filming when the cast and crew were poisoned by PCP-laced food in Nova Scotia. Rumors that Cameron was a crazed perfectionist emerged. His attention to detail included hiring the original companies that provided the real *Titanic*'s furnishings as supervisors so that every chandelier and plate was a perfect replica. Following the film's stupendous box-office success (more than $1 billion worldwide) and the most Academy Awards (eleven) since *Ben-Hur* (1959), however, he was rechristened a genius, and is now deservedly considered one of the most successful directors of all time.

Cameron's vision is half *Poseidon Adventure* (1972) and half *Love Boat*, as both romance and deep-sea disaster are explored in equal measure. Kate Winslet stars as Rose, the young socialite who is to marry dastardly Cal (Billy Zane) but falls for steerage passenger Jack (Leonardo DiCaprio) just before the world's most famous ship plunges into its watery grave. Their forbidden romance gives the movie its heart. Cameron piles on the special effects to truly convey the terror that is to come, forcing his actors to spend days in freezing cold water filming the scary scenes when the supposedly "unsinkable" ship begins to sink and then horrifically splits in half.

A blockbuster if ever there was one, *Titanic* made DiCaprio a superstar and teen heartthrob. The film boasts one of the biggest-selling soundtracks of all time—a number one hit for Celine Dion with the theme "My Heart Will Go On." In terms of production size and sheer epic scale, *Titanic* remains one of the most impressive films of all time. **JB**

Ta'm e guilass Abbas Kiarostami, 1997
Taste of Cherry

France / Iran (Abbas Kiarostami, CiBy 2000)
95m Color **Language** Farsi **Producer** Abbas
Kiarostami **Screenplay** Abbas Kiarostami
Photography Homayun Payvar
Cast Homayon Ershadi, Abdolrahman
Bagheri, Afshin Khorshid Bakhtiari, Safar Ali
Moradi, Mir Hossein Noori **Cannes Film
Festival** Abbas Kiarostaml (Golden Palm,
tied with *The Eel*)

A middle-aged man (Homayon Ershadi) who is contemplating suicide drives around the outskirts of Tehran, trying to find someone who will bury him if he succeeds and retrieve him if he fails. This minimalist feature by Abbas Kiarostami never explains why the man wants to end his life, and is even inconclusive about whether or not he succeeds. Yet every moment carries great poignancy and philosophical weight.

Taste of Cherry entrusts much of its meaning to the audience. Like many of Kiarostami's films, it is centered on the simultaneously private and public experience of a character in a car giving rides to others. And just as watching a movie in a theater combines private responses with public reactions, this is a film that speaks to both of these situations.

Working without a script, Kiarostami filmed his nonprofessional actors separately from either the driver's or passenger's seat, provoking their lines as if interviewing them. Thus the subject of isolation that lies at the heart of *Taste of Cherry* is integral to the way it was filmed.

Kiarostami is a master at filming landscapes and building parable-like narratives whose missing pieces solicit the viewer's active imagination. This even extends to the film's surprisingly cheerful, self-referential coda: An epilogue centered on camaraderie that follows this story about profound isolation radiates with wonder and euphoria. **JRos**

i

Despite jointly winning the Golden Palm at the 1997 Cannes Film Festival, *Taste of Cherry* divided critics.

Saving Private Ryan Steven Spielberg, 1998

U.S. (Amblin, DreamWorks, Mark Gordon, Mutual, Paramount) 170m Technicolor **Language** English / Czech / French / German **Producer** Ian Bryce, Mark Gordon, Gary Levinsohn, Steven Spielberg **Screenplay** Robert Rodat **Photography** Janusz Kaminski **Music** John Williams **Cast** Tom Hanks, Edward Burns, Tom Sizemore, Matt Damon, Jeremy Davies, Adam Goldberg, Barry Pepper, Giovanni Ribisi, Vin Diesel, Ted Danson, Max Martini, Dylan Bruno, Joerg Stadler, Paul Giamatti, Dennis Farina **Oscars** Steven Spielberg (director), Janusz Kaminski (photography), Gary Rydstrom, Richard Hymns (special sound effects), Michael Kahn (editing), Gary Rydstrom, Gary Summers, Andy Nelson, Ron Judkins (sound) **Oscar nominations** Steven Spielberg, Ian Bryce, Mark Gordon, Gary Levinsohn (best picture), Robert Rodat (screenplay), Tom Hanks (actor), Thomas E. Sanders, Lisa Dean (art direction), Lois Burwell, Conor O'Sullivan, Daniel C. Striepeke (makeup), John Williams (music)

"I could have made . . . a very safe picture . . . But my intention was to resensitize the audience."

Steven Spielberg, 2004

ℹ

The Omaha Beach scene cost $11 million to shoot and involved around 1,000 extras.

From his very first works, Steven Spielberg displayed an almost preternatural gift for filmmaking—specifically the machinations of suspense and special effects, a skill that movie audiences responded to in droves. But the massive success of such early films as *Jaws* (1975) and *Close Encounters of the Third Kind* (1977)—which helped congeal the blockbuster mentality of modern Hollywood—in some ways hurt Spielberg's reputation. Craving respect, he knew his movies would always be dismissed as merely popular entertainment and technical exercises.

Spielberg nonetheless tried to broaden his range with such mature experiments as *The Color Purple* (1985) and *Empire of the Sun* (1987), but it wasn't until the harrowing Holocaust film *Schindler's List* (1993) that he finally made a movie that satisfied both the critics and the public. With the exception of his two thrill-ride *Jurassic Park* (1993, 1997) films, Spielberg has remained more or less in serious mode ever since.

Saving Private Ryan introduced something new to the director's vocabulary: visceral, violent intensity. Spielberg had dealt with violence before, of course, but typically it was either cartoonish or carefully moderated (and then milked) as a dramatic beat punctuating moments of maximum horror. The opening battle sequence of *Saving Private Ryan*, however, is absolutely relentless. No sooner have American boats landed on the beaches of Normandy than young men are mowed down by incessant bursts of machine-gun fire, the bullets piercing their useless helmets with a sickening "ping." And it doesn't stop there. Soldiers are blown to bits. Body parts fly through the air and litter the ground. The sea turns a squeamish blood red. The camera lurches wildly, the desaturated film stock the color of death. The "new" Spielberg takes no prisoners.

Admittedly, the Spielberg of old can't always resist falling back on unabashed sentimentality. A pair of flimsy bookends start and end the film on purely manipulative notes, and Spielberg encourages his composer of choice John Williams to indulge in his worst heartstring-tugging tendencies. More uncomfortably, the same techniques Spielberg uses to depict the horrors of the war in his truly awe-inspiring opening battle scene he later enlists to propel the more traditional good-versus-evil conflict of the conclusion.

But the familiar good guy/bad guy dichotomy actually twists the antiwar message into something more challenging. War is hell, Spielberg acknowledges, except when you're winning, since victory is ultimately what accords the right to dictate the rules of morality. *Saving Private Ryan* contains just enough darkness lurking in the fog of war to stave off accusations that it supports blind patriotism. Looking over thousands of graves, a soldier asks of his wife, "Was I a good man?" That's an ambiguous way of asking not just "Was it worth it?" but "Was it justified?" These are questions that no doubt haunt all those left standing when the shooting stops, surveying the death and destruction around them. **JKl**

1998

Lola Rennt Tom Tykwer, 1998
Run Lola Run

A visually inventive, kinetically exciting movie, Tom Tykwer's *Run Lola Run* is an exercise in surprises, beginning right from the opening credits where a crowd scene turns into an aerial shot in which the assembled people spell out the movie's title.

The plot itself is simple—young, shockingly flame-haired Lola (Franka Potente) receives a telephone call from her boyfriend Manni (Moritz Bleibtreu). Manni explains that he was supposed to deliver 100,000 deutsche marks to a gangster, but he left the bag containing the loot on the subway. He has twenty minutes to find the money before the bad guys kill him, so his plan is to rob a bank—Lola's is to find the money some other way, and the film follows her high-speed adventure to save Manni as the minutes tick away.

It's the way young German director Tykwer shows us Lola's mission that is different and inventive. Her twenty-minute story is told three different times, each subtly different in a manner that delivers three different outcomes. Twyker uses animation, camera tricks, color and black-and-white film, music video effects, and instant replays to tell each adventure as Lola runs, Manni runs, and the film becomes a human obstacle course they both have to carefully maneuver in order to survive.

Potente, who would go on to appear alongside Matt Damon in the Hollywood blockbuster *The Bourne Identity* (2002), provides a striking cinematic image as she runs down the movie's various streets and avenues, arms pumping and distinctive red hair flying, but she also delivers a warm, more in-depth performance in scenes such as one between Lola and her wealthy father (Herbert Knaup), whom she visits asking for money only to learn that he plans to leave her mother and marry his mistress. *Run Lola Run* is an interesting, unusual filmmaking experiment that has humor, breathless excitement, and tremendous energy, all tightly packaged into an MTV-generation movie by the fresh talent of its writer-director. **JB**

Germany (Bavaria Film, German Independents, WDR, X-Filme, Arte) 81m Color **Language** German **Producer** Stefan Arndt **Screenplay** Tom Tykwer **Photography** Frank Griebe **Music** Reinhold Heil, Johnny Klimek, Franka Potente, Tom Tykwer **Cast** Franka Potente, Moritz Bleibtreu, Herbert Knaup, Nina Petri, Armin Rohde, Joachim Król, Ludger Pistor, Suzanne von Borsody, Sebastian Schipper, Julia Lindig, Lars Rudolph, Andreas Petri, Klaus Müller, Utz Krause, Beate Finckh **Venice Film Festival** Tom Tykwer (Golden Lion nomination)

> "*Run Lola Run could very well be the punchiest piece of concept art to ever hit the silver screen, a shock-dose of German existential cinema you can ride.*"
>
> Ed Gonzalez,
> *Slant Magazine*, 2003

🛈

The narration at the beginning is spoken by Hans Paetsch, Germany's most popular fairy tale narrator.

Rushmore Wes Anderson, 1998

U.S. (American Empirical, Touchstone) 93m Color **Producer** Barry Mendel, Paul Schiff **Screenplay** Wes Anderson, Owen Wilson **Photography** Robert D. Yeoman **Music** Mark Mothersbaugh **Cast** Jason Schwartzman, Bill Murray, Olivia Williams, Seymour Cassel, Brian Cox, Mason Gamble, Sara Tanaka, Stephen McCole, Connie Nielsen, Luke Wilson, Dipak Pallana, Andrew Wilson, Marietta Marich, Ronnie McCawley, Keith McCawley

When director Wes Anderson and cowriter Owen Wilson carved a new niche with the 1996 film *Bottle Rocket*, it single-handedly revived the then-exhausted realm of low-budget independent American comedies. Their second entry in this genre, the adorably miserable *Rushmore*, takes another look at the losers and oddballs they so adore.

Max Fischer (played by Jason Schwartzman, the son of Talia Shire and nephew to Francis Ford Coppola) is a bespectacled, intellectual geek. As a scholarship student at Rushmore Academy he is profoundly unpopular. Verging on flunking out, he manages to be president of virtually every extracurricular activity there is on campus. Doomed by his social skills, he nevertheless falls for a beautiful teacher (Olivia Williams) and finds a mentor in wealthy if depressed Herman J. Blume (Bill Murray). This slow, turn-of-the-screwball comedy is Murray's finest dramatic hour, allowing him at last to be profound, wounded, and funny, all at the same time. And the soundtrack of mostly 1960s rock music gives *Rushmore* a sense of being somewhere other than in its obviously contemporary setting. **KK**

Festen Thomas Vinterberg, 1998
The Celebration

Denmark (DR, Nimbus Film, SVT Drama) 105m Color **Language** Danish / German / English **Producer** Birgitte Hald **Screenplay** Thomas Vinterberg, Mogens Rukov **Photography** Anthony Dod Mantle **Music** Lars Bo Jensen **Cast** Ulrich Thomsen, Henning Moritzen, Thomas Bo Larsen, Paprika Steen, Birthe Neumann, Trine Dyrholm, Helle Dolleris, Therese Glahn, Klaus Bondam, Bjarne Henriksen, Gbatokai Dakinah, Lasse Lunderskov, Lars Brygmann, Lene Laub Oksen, Linda Laursen **Cannes Film Festival** Thomas Vinterberg (jury prize, tied with *La Classe de neige*, Golden Palm nomination)

On balance, Dogme95—a Danish film manifesto that calls for location shooting, handheld cameras, direct sound, and an avoidance of special effects—probably has more significance as a highly successful publicity stunt than as an ideological breakthrough, judging especially from the first two features that emerged under its ground rules, Lars von Trier's *The Idiots* (1998) and Thomas Vinterberg's *The Celebration*. Both films, in fact, are apparent acts of rebellion and daring that are virtually defined by their middle-class assumptions and dogged apoliticism. Vinterberg's work, which is even more conventional in inspiration than von Trier's—think Ibsen, Strindberg, Bergman—is genuinely explosive and powerfully executed.

Shot with the smallest and lightest digital video camera then available, *The Celebration* chronicles the acrimonious and violent family battles that ensue at a country manor house where the sixtieth birthday of the family patriarch is being observed, not long after the eldest son's twin sister has committed suicide. The extreme forms of aggressive behavior that emerge from the onset and Vinterberg's jagged style of cross-cutting disguise the fact that this is basically a very well written, acted, and directed piece of psychodrama rather than the revolutionary experiment it was proclaimed to be. But the sheer dramatic power derived from the gradual unveiling of family secrets eventually and justifiably wins one over. **JRos**

Buffalo 66 Vincent Gallo, 1998

U.S. (CFP, Lions Gate, Muse) 110m Color
Producer Chris Hanley **Screenplay** Vincent
Gallo, Alison Bagnall **Photography** Lance
Acord **Music** Vincent Gallo **Cast** Vincent
Gallo, Christina Ricci, Ben Gazzara, Mickey
Rourke, Rosanna Arquette, Jan-Michael
Vincent, Anjelica Huston, Kevin Pollak, Alex
Karras, John Sansone, Manny Fried, John
Rummel, Bob Wahl, Penny Wolfgang,
Anthony Mydcarz

Actor Vincent Gallo (*Palookaville* [1995], *The Funeral* [1996]) wrote, directed, and stars in this independent comic drama, which he has described as his masterpiece—an arrogant statement, perhaps, but one that's not too far from the truth. He plays Billy, a sleazy ex-con who kidnaps a feisty young girl (Christina Ricci, in tight skirt and fairy-tale slippers) and gets her to pretend she's his loving wife on a visit to his wacked-out parents (Anjelica Huston and Ben Gazzara), who are unaware he's been away in jail. Billy has told them his absence was because he was working as an undercover operative for the government.

Wonderfully quirky stuff, this low-budget bizarre romance boasts suitably eccentric performances from the four leads (Gazzara as Gallo's pervy dad deserves a special mention, while Huston is a hoot as his football-obsessed wife), and some neat cameos from Mickey Rourke, Jan-Michael Vincent, and Rosanna Arquette. Gallo, meanwhile, multitasks superbly (he even wrote the film's music and used his parents' Buffalo home as the main location), delivering an ironic look at relationships and disillusionment with a variety of visual styles and images. **JB**

Ring Hideo Nakata, 1998

Japan (Kadokawa Shoten, Omega)
96m BW / Color **Language** Japanese
Producer Shinya Kawai, Takenori Sento,
Takashige Ichise **Screenplay** Hiroshi
Takahashi, from the novel *Ringu* by Kôji
Suzuki **Photography** Junichirô Hayashi
Music Kenji Kawai **Cast** Nanako
Matsushima, Miki Nakatani, Hiroyuki Sanada,
Yuko Takeuchi, Hitomi Sato, Yoichi Numata,
Yutaka Matsushige, Katsumi Muramatsu,
Rikiya Otaka, Masako, Daisuke Ban, Kiyoshi
Risho, Yuurei Yanagi, Yôko Ôshima,
Kiriko Shimizu

It's a deceptively simple premise for a ghost story: A cursed videotape is being circulated. Anyone who watches it will die seven days afterward. When TV reporter Reiko Asakawa (Nanako Matsushima) discovers that her niece is one of the victims of the videotape, she sets out to find it. When she watches it, the mysterious images convince her the curse is true, and she asks her ex-husband Ryuji Takayama (Hiroyuki Sanada) for help. They have seven days to decipher the images on the video and find a way to break the curse, especially after their four-year-old son watches it as well.

Director Hideo Nakata achieves a steady sense of mounting disquiet throughout the film as Reiko and Ryuji try to unravel the mystery of the videotape's images. What they find is a decades-old tragedy involving the death of a girl with unusual psychic abilities. There are no cheap shock effects here. Instead, Nakata relies on sound and atmosphere to suggest the presence of the unquiet dead hovering over the living, poised to strike.

In movies, the popularity of genres comes in cycles. A particular genre becomes relevant when it captures the anxieties and preoccupations of the times. *Ring* singlehandedly revived the horror genre for the end of the twentieth century, spawning two sequels, a prequel, a Korean remake, and an overcooked but hugely successful Hollywood remake (directed by Gore Verbinski), not to mention influencing dozens of horror films from all over the world. **AT**

Happiness Todd Solondz, 1998

U.S. (Good Machine, Killer) 134m Color
Language English / Russian Producer Ted
Hope, Christine Vachon Screenplay Todd
Solondz Photography Maryse Alberti
Music Robbie Kondor Cast Jane Adams, Jon
Lovitz, Philip Seymour Hoffman, Dylan Baker,
Lara Flynn Boyle, Justin Elvin, Cynthia
Stevenson, Lila Glantzman-Leib, Gerry
Becker, Rufus Read, Louise Lasser, Ben
Gazzara, Camryn Manheim, Arthur J.
Nascarella, Molly Shannon Cannes Film
Festival Todd Solondz (FIPRESCI award
parallel sections)

Few filmmakers can invoke so many varied emotional responses—laughter, disgust, sympathy, just to name a few—from their audiences as contemporary American independent filmmaker Todd Solondz does with his highly controversial *Happiness*. There is no way to concisely sum up the happenings of this film, which involves a first-rate ensemble cast including audacious performances by Dylan Baker, Philip Seymour Hoffman, Ben Gazzara, Lara Flynn Boyle, Camryn Manheim, and Jon Lovitz. Suffice it to say that *Happiness* is about relationships—all of them painfully flawed—and takes us into territory few filmmakers dare (or want) to brave. One of the picture's most memorable scenes depicts a father answering, in utterly frank and matter-of-fact terms, questions from his young son about his acts of pederasty.

Happiness is perhaps best described as an indictment of the modern American family and suburban living (both on- and offscreen), suggesting that perversion lurks around every corner, inside every family's four walls. Solondz, who is evolving into a postmodern and more disturbed Woody Allen, has taken this perhaps exaggerated notion as his cinematic credo; he succeeds, in part, because he refuses to allow his flawed characters to spin off into the realm of one-dimensionality. **MO**

ℹ

Director Todd Solondz has a cameo in the film as the doorman in Allen, Helen, and Kristina's building.

The Thin Red Line Terrence Malick, 1998

After making the highly acclaimed and influential *Badlands* (1973) and *Days of Heaven* (1978), Terrence Malick did something unheard of for a prominent director—he vanished without a trace. Rumors abounded: Malick was living life as a recluse in some remote locale. Or maybe he was hiking across Texas, bird watching. Wherever he disappeared to, word of his late 1990s return to filmmaking came just as suddenly. Details of Malick's new project were closely guarded and sketchy at best, but two things were clear—it was an adaptation of James Jones's World War II novel *The Thin Red Line*, and it reportedly featured a massive cast of several prominent actors and promising newcomers alike.

Both rumors proved correct, but the film still surprised many as unexpected. Especially coming after Steven Spielberg's own World War II drama *Saving Private Ryan* (1998), Malick's *The Thin Red Line* seemed particularly cerebral. The two films couldn't have been more different, and the reactions they provoked reflected those discrepancies. Audiences left visceral *Saving Private Ryan* shaken to the core. Audiences left the more philosophical *The Thin Red Line* scratching their heads.

Yet there's no question which film leaves the stronger impression. *The Thin Red Line* addresses the madness of war from a distinctly theoretical, even theological vantage. War, the film seems to say, is more than just a conflict between two groups of men. War is depicted in *The Thin Red Line* as an affront to nature, and in turn an affront to God himself.

Malick's film delves into the collective consciousness of the troops as it struggles to reconcile the fragility of life with the recklessness of their behavior. Daringly, *The Thin Red Line* flits from soldier to soldier, getting into their heads and amplifying their thoughts as part of an ongoing internal dialogue, but otherwise retaining a sense of anonymity among the soldiers.

The men are highly aware of the exotic world around them and in particular its beauty: When the film begins, one soldier (Jim Caviezel) has gone AWOL, living a life of simplicity and innocence among a South Pacific tribe until his Eden-like existence is disrupted. Even as the soldiers slink through the forest, Malick can't resist training his camera on the colorful wildlife around them, or capturing the light streaming through the leaves of the towering trees. It's as if God and all of his creatures are watching this strange species at work destroying all that is good in the world, and wondering what free will hath wrought.

Several performances do stick out in the film—Elias Koteas's sensitive Captain; Nick Nolte's callous, career-minded colonel; Sean Penn's cynical Sergeant—but Malick keeps the narrative elliptical. *The Thin Red Line* has no real beginning or end, and although it is punctuated by dramatic beats and thrilling battle scenes, they serve as interruptions of no less a profound meditation than Malick's quest for the meaning of life. **JKl**

Canada / U.S. (Fox 2000, Geisler-Roberdeau, Phoenix) 170m Color **Producer** Robert Michael Geisler, Grant Hill, John Roberdeau **Screenplay** Terrence Malick, from novel by James Jones **Photography** John Toll **Music** Hans Zimmer **Cast** Sean Penn, Adrien Brody, James Caviezel, Ben Chaplin, George Clooney, John Cusack, Woody Harrelson, Elias Koteas, Jared Leto, Dash Mihok, Tim Blake Nelson, Nick Nolte, John C. Reilly, Larry Romano, John Savage **Oscar nominations** Robert Michael Geisler, John Roberdeau, Grant Hill (best picture), Terrence Malick (director), Terrence Malick (screenplay), John Toll (photography), Billy Weber, Leslie Jones, Saar Klein (editing), Hans Zimmer (music), Andy Nelson, Anna Behlmer, Paul Brincat (sound) **Berlin International Film Festival** Terrence Malick (Golden Bear, third place reader jury of the Berliner Morgenpost), John Toll (honorable mention)

"What difference do you think you can make, one man in all this madness?"

First Sgt. Edward Welsh (Sean Penn)

i

Gary Oldman, Martin Sheen, and Mickey Rourke all filmed scenes that were left out of the final cut.

"SCARY AS HELL."
— Peter Travers, ROLLING STONE

In October of 1994
three student filmmakers disappeared
in the woods near Burkittsville, Maryland,
while shooting a documentary...

A year later their footage was found.

THE BLAIR WITCH PROJECT
www.blairwitch.com

The Blair Witch Project

Daniel Myrick & Eduardo Sánchez, 1999

"In October of 1994, three student filmmakers disappeared in the woods near Burkittsville, Maryland while shooting a documentary… A year later their footage was found." Thus begins this shoestring-budgeted horror "mockumentary," which parlayed innovative online marketing and incredible word-of-mouth into more than $140 million in the United States alone—making it the most profitable U.S. independent film of all time (a record that stood until 2007's *Paranormal Activity*).

Led by aspiring director Heather Donahue, the three students make their way to Burkittsville (née Blair), Maryland, to shoot footage for a documentary about a local legend, the Blair Witch. Rumor has it this mysterious figure has haunted the nearby Black Hills forest since the eighteenth century and is responsible for a number of heinous murders. After conducting interviews with locals, Heather, Mike, and Josh hike into the forest to gather additional footage. None of them experienced campers, they get lost, and their cheery demeanor deteriorates into an increasingly volatile mixture of fear, blame, frustration, and panic. Ominous signs begin to appear, including piles of stones carefully positioned outside their tent and wooden effigies hanging in the trees. Then Josh silently disappears. In the film's harrowing finale, Michael and Heather stumble across a decrepit house. Hoping to find Josh, they enter; what they discover is a nightmare. Through her camcorder, we see what Heather sees: first darkness and ruins and children's handprints on the walls; then, after someone or something knocks her unconscious, just a blank ceiling, which lasts until the tape—and the film itself—runs out.

Despite criticisms of the sometimes slow pace and nausea-inducing handheld camera work, *The Blair Witch Project* clearly succeeds in its use of documentary techniques as a means of instilling terror in viewers. Myrick and Sánchez's unique production method has itself become the stuff of legend: The actors were responsible for shooting the entire film themselves (over the course of eight consecutive days and nights), had to carry their own equipment, and improvised almost all of their lines. Several times a day, the directors wrote notes to each actor, sealing them in tubes for their eyes only. By achieving such a high degree of realism, Myrick and Sánchez took their product a step beyond earlier horror films with mockumentary aspirations, such as Wes Craven's *The Last House on the Left* (1972) and Tobe Hooper's *The Texas Chain Saw Massacre* (1974).

Exploiting some of our most basic fears—the dark, the unknown, strange sounds—*The Blair Witch Project* elicits intense emotions. Some of the most terrifying moments occur when all we are able to see is a black/blank screen—what our imagination conjures up is far more frightening than anything the most sophisticated special effects or makeup can produce. It is to their credit that those involved in the making of this film were well aware of this often ignored fact. **SJS**

U.S. (Blair Witch, Haxan) 86m BW / Color
Producer Robin Cowie, Gregg Hale
Screenplay Daniel Myrick, Eduardo Sánchez
Photography Neal Fredericks **Music** Tony Cora **Cast** Heather Donahue, Joshua Leonard, Michael C. Williams, Bob Griffin, Jim King, Sandra Sánchez, Ed Swanson, Patricia DeCou, Mark Mason, Jackie Hallex **Cannes Film Festival** Daniel Myrick, Eduardo Sánchez (Award of the Youth foreign film)

"I think The Blair Witch Project *is an exceptionally well-conceived and well-made film."*

Roger Corman, producer and director, 2000

🛈

Daniel Myrick described *Cloverfield* (2008) as "very much in the spirit of the *Blair Witch*" and "very ballsy."

Being John Malkovich Spike Jonze, 1999

Acclaimed music video director turned filmmaker Spike Jonze (whose previous works included Fatboy Slim's "Weapon Of Choice" and the Beastie Boys'"Sabotage") turned one of the oddest concepts for a movie into one of the most inventive Hollywood films of the 1990s. "I had this idea that someone finds a portal into someone's head," writer Charlie Kaufman explained at a Bafta lecture in 2011, "and I had another idea… about someone having an affair with a co-worker. And neither one was going anywhere, so I just decided to combine them."

Craig Schwartz (John Cusack) is a disheveled puppeteer scraping a living with his dark (and, to children, quite traumatic) street puppet shows. His wife Lotte (an almost unrecognizable Cameron Diaz) spends what little they have on raising the menagerie of animals she has living in their small home. To earn extra cash, Craig takes a job as a filing clerk in a strange company on floor 7½ of a Manhattan office building. How an office could exist between the seventh and eighth floors is a movie in itself, but it is a door Craig discovers hidden behind a filing cabinet that sets this film's quirky events in motion. When Craig crawls through it, he discovers it is actually some sort of portal that sends him hurtling into the brain of actor John Malkovich (playing himself here). Craig experiences the things Malkovich does for just fifteen minutes before being expelled abruptly onto the side of the New Jersey Turnpike.

Kaufman weaves an intricate plot around this idea, beginning when Craig lets colleague Maxine (Catherine Keener) in on his discovery and she convinces him to charge people to try this demented ride. Jonze dazzles at every turn as he tells this smart, subversive, darkly comic tale, and the cast—Cusack and Diaz especially—beautifully translate his skewed vision to the screen. Of course, *Being John Malkovich* wouldn't have worked without the eponymous actor, who parodies his image brilliantly, especially in a scene when he tries the portal himself and ends up in a restaurant populated by Mr. Malkoviches. "It never occurred to me that anyone would actually be goofy enough to make that movie," the actor recalled. "But of course I hadn't met Spike Jonze then." **JB**

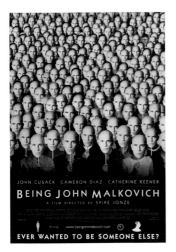

EVER WANTED TO BE SOMEONE ELSE?

U.S. (Gramercy, Propaganda, Single Cell) 112m Technicolor **Producer** Steve Golin, Vincent Landay, Sandy Stern, Michael Stipe **Screenplay** Charlie Kaufman **Photography** Lance Acord **Music** Carter Burwell **Cast** John Cusack, Cameron Diaz, Ned Bellamy, Eric Weinstein, Madison Lanc, Octavia Spencer, Mary Kay Place, Orson Bean, Catherine Keener, K.K. Dodds, Reginald C. Hayes, Byrne Piven, Judith Wetzell, John Malkovich, Kevin Carroll **Oscar nominations** Spike Jonze (director), Charlie Kaufman (screenplay), Catherine Keener (actress in support role)

> *"I wrote* Being John Malkovich *before I even knew who Spike Jonze was. He just happened to be the person who could get it made and wanted to make it."*

Charlie Kaufman, 2008

1999

ℹ️

Malkovich initially offered to direct the film if Kaufman made someone else its subject. Kaufman refused.

The Sixth Sense M. Night Shyamalan, 1999

M. Night Shyamalan, aged just twenty-nine and making only his third film, virtually reinvented the thriller with a love story/chiller infamous for its final twist. "Most movies that you see now come out of modern novels," its star, Bruce Willis, told *Reader's Digest*. "Some bestseller book immediately gets turned into a film, or you see films that are remakes of old films, or remakes of TV shows from the '60s. What Night does that makes him completely unique is he makes the stuff up out of his head… He is—and I don't use this word very often—a genius."

A year after being shot by a former patient, psychologist Malcolm Crowe (Bruce Willis) attempts to understand a troubled boy, Cole (Haley Joel Osment). Cole, it seems, can see dead people: ghosts of those who left matters unresolved before their deaths and who visit the boy searching for resolution. Meanwhile, Malcolm's own life is in disarray, his loving marriage to wife Anna (Olivia Williams) now distant and cold.

A ghost story of the highest order, *The Sixth Sense* works on many levels. The spooks are there as Cole is visited by tormented apparitions, but this is more emotional drama than scary suspense film, focusing on the relationships between boy and psychologist, Malcolm and his wife, and Cole and his mother (Toni Collette). Osment is a terrific discovery in a role that, had it been played too cute, would have wrecked the entire film, and Collette delivers the right amount of confusion and love for her unusual son. Willis, however, is the true revelation, giving a whispered, understated performance that is the heart of the film.

But it is Shyamalan who deserves the most praise. His clever use of muted colors and subtle hints of what is to come—the temperature dropping when a ghost is present, the use of the color red—and the twist in the tale are so neat that you want to reappraise the film rather than be annoyed that you have been led down a completely different path than the one you thought you were on. A modern, emotionally complex classic that is as achingly poignant as it is chillingly tense. **JB**

U.S. (Hollywood, Spyglass, Kennedy/Marshall) 107m Technicolor **Language** English / Spanish / Latin **Producer** Kathleen Kennedy, Frank Marshall, Barry Mendel **Screenplay** M. Night Shyamalan **Photography** Tak Fujimoto **Music** James Newton Howard **Cast** Bruce Willis, Haley Joel Osment, Toni Collette, Olivia Williams, Trevor Morgan, Donnie Wahlberg, Peter Anthony Tambakis, Jeffrey Zubernis, Bruce Norris, Glenn Fitzgerald, Greg Wood, Mischa Barton, Angelica Torn, Lisa Summerour, Firdous Bamji **Oscar nomination** Kathleen Kennedy, Frank Marshall, Barry Mendel (best picture), M. Night Shyamalan (director), M. Night Shyamalan (screenplay), Haley Joel Osment (actor in support role), Toni Collette (actress in support role), Andrew Mondshein (editing)

> *"Even when we were done, we still didn't quite know whether or not we were going to be able to fool the audience."*
>
> **Bruce Willis, 2002**

ℹ

Shyamalan initially shelved the idea when he heard about plans to make another ghost movie: *Casper* (1995).

Three Kings David O. Russell, 1999

U.S. (Atlas, Coast Ridge, Junger Witt, Village Roadshow, Warner Bros.) 114m Technicolor **Language** English / Arabic **Producer** Paul Junger Witt, Edward McDonnell **Screenplay** John Ridley, David O. Russell **Photography** Newton Thomas Sigel **Music** Carter Burwell **Cast** George Clooney, Mark Wahlberg, Ice Cube, Spike Jonze, Cliff Curtis, Nora Dunn, Jamie Kennedy, Saïd Taghmaoui, Mykelti Williamson, Holt McCallany, Judy Greer, Christopher Lohr, Jon Sklaroff, Liz Stauber, Marsha Horan

Three Kings is a millennium-capping antiwar film that employed what were then state-of-the-art tools (fast edits, dizzying camera work, color schemes that pop off the screen) and combined them with a helping of old-fashioned, *M*A*S*H*-style politics.

Writer-director David O. Russell tells the tale of the first Gulf War (1991) through the eyes of three American soldiers whose ignorance, greed, and naïveté is slowly wiped away as they are dragged deeper into the political and cultural trappings behind the war, forced to humanize their enemies and demystify their own country and military. In the process, the audience is exposed to a version of the war that the media was once reluctant to report—the deaths of innocents, the corruption and posturing of military officials, and the co-option of "objective" media (spiritedly represented here by Nora Dunn) to spin the story.

It's heady, even dense, stuff made accessible and urgent through a snappy script, relentlessly energetic pacing, dazzling visuals, and taut acting from the leads (George Clooney, Mark Wahlberg, Ice Cube, and Spike Jonze). An assured juggling of genre and tone shifts—it's part war story, part heist thriller, and wholly an antiwar creed—the film should fall apart at the seams but doesn't strike a single false note. **EH**

1999

Magnolia Paul Thomas Anderson, 1999

U.S. (Ghoulardi, New Line) 188m Color **Director** Paul Thomas Anderson **Producer** Paul Thomas Anderson, JoAnne Sellar **Screenplay** Paul Thomas Anderson **Photography** Robert Elswit **Music** Jon Brion **Cast** John C. Reilly, Tom Cruise, Julianne Moore, Philip Baker Hall, Jeremy Blackman, Philip Seymour Hoffman, William H. Macy, Melora Walters, Jason Robards, Melinda Dillon, Michael Bowen, Ricky Jay, Felicity Huffman, April Grace, Pat Healy **Oscar nominations** Paul Thomas Anderson (screenplay), Tom Cruise (actor in support role), Aimee Mann (song) **Berlin International Film Festival** Paul Thomas Anderson (Golden Bear, reader jury of the Berliner Morgenpost)

"As we move through life, we should try to do good." In a sprawling story of family—and the betrayal, secrets, heartaches, and disappointments within—writer-director Paul Thomas Anderson jumps back and forth between a sleazy, misogynistic television huckster (Tom Cruise); a lonely child prodigy (Jeremy Blackman); an elderly, dying misanthrope (Jason Robards) and his trophy wife (Julianne Moore); a boozing, drug-addled young woman (Melora Walters); a popular, dying quiz-show host (Philip Baker Hall); and a bumbling, lonely, big-hearted cop (John C. Reilly). The coincidences and twists of fate that link them drive this epic film.

Filled with biblical allusions, *Magnolia* makes no secret of grappling with weighty issues—the meaning of life, the nature of evil, the terms of human connection. "I thought it would be really interesting," the director told the *Guardian*, "to put this epic spin on topics that don't necessarily get the epic treatment, which is usually reserved for war movies or political topics." What makes this work so well is Anderson's ability to portray these themes by focusing on the minute details of his characters' bruised lives. Frogs fall mysteriously from the sky and people fall apart. The whole while, Anderson maintains an unwavering empathy with his broken characters, humanizing the villains while siding with the victimized and misunderstood. Magnolia seethes with anger and pain, while staggering toward hope and something like redemption. **EH**

Fight Club David Fincher, 1999

U.S. (Art Linson, Fox 2000, Regency, Taurus)
139m Color **Producer** Ross Grayson Bell,
Ceán Chaffin, Art Linson **Screenplay** Jim
Uhls, from novel by Chuck Palahniuk
Photography Jeff Cronenweth **Music** Dust
Brothers **Cast** Edward Norton, Brad Pitt,
Helena Bonham Carter, Meat Loaf, Zach
Grenier, Richmond Arquette, David Andrews,
George Maguire, Eugenie Bondurant,
Christina Cabot, Sydney Colston, Rachel
Singer, Christie Cronenweth, Tim De Zarn,
Ezra Buzzington **Oscar nomination** Ren
Klyce, Richard Hymns (special sound effects)

"The first rule about Fight Club is that you don't talk about Fight Club. The second rule about Fight Club is that you don't talk about Fight Club." Based on the novel by Chuck Palahniuk, David Fincher's film stakes out manly territory in 1999's most intriguing and angry, yet witty cinematic fantasy. *Fight Club* is as morally challenging as it is visually memorable. In a quote that a gleeful Fincher blew up and stuck on his office wall, British *Evening Standard* film critic Alexander Walker complained, "The movie is not only anti-capitalist but anti-society and, indeed, anti-God."

Edward Norton plays the mild-mannered narrator who, tortured by his empty office life, goes to group therapy just to feel something. At one of these meetings, he meets and falls for Marla (Helena Bonham Carter), then hooks up with the dangerously wild Tyler Durden (Brad Pitt). Tyler convinces Norton that his life can be better lived by learning how to fight. Soon enough, their antics attract other men, giving them all something their ordinary lives are lacking—a sort of dirty, aggressive dignity, which is eventually reorganized into a virtual terrorist cell.

With astonishing camera and special effects work, *Fight Club* moves at rocket-like pace. The result is an exciting, distressingly inspiring movie that makes even the strangest event seem normal, including Meat Loaf as a cancer patient with enormous mammary glands. **KK**

Ôdishon Takashi Miike, 1999
Audition

Japan / South Korea (АГDF,
Creators Company Connection, Omega
Project) 115m Color **Language** Japanese
Producer Satoshi Fukushima, Akemi
Suyama **Screenplay** Daisuke Tengan
Photography Hideo Yamamoto **Music** Kôji
Endô **Cast** Ryo Ishibashi, Eihi Shiina, Tetsu
Sawaki , Jun Kunimura, Renji Ishibashi,
Miyuki Matsuda, Toshie Negishi, Ren Osugi,
Shigeru Saiki, Ken Mitsuishi, Yuriko Hirooka,
Fumiyo Kohinata, Misato Nakamura, Yuuto
Arima, Ayaka Izumi

After Hideo Nakata's *Ringu* (1998) proved that contemporary Japanese horror was a force to be reckoned with, *Audition* effectively reworked the genre by masking its true intentions behind a wall of melodrama. "The directors whose films scare me the most," explained director Takashi Miike, "are the ones who carefully hide the aggression in the background and don't show it directly." The film's terrifying third act duly had many audience members hiding their eyes—if not running from the theater.

Shigeharu Aoyama (Ryo Ishibashi), the lonely, middle-aged owner of a video production company, worries about finding the right woman to replace his adolescent son's mother, who died seven years ago. A friend suggests auditioning actresses for a fake role in a made-up project so that he can review possible candidates for the role of new girlfriend. The last girl to audition is the beautiful and enigmatic Asami (Eihi Shiina). Aoyama is instantly attracted to her and they start dating. Initially, she proves as dutiful as she is beautiful, and Aoyoma proposes marriage to her during a romantic weekend away at a picturesque seaside resort.

However, Asami vanishes and *Audition* abruptly shifts from romantic drama to violent thriller. Sex is frequently depicted as a weapon as Asami's disturbing past and monstrous personality are revealed. **SJS**

American Beauty Sam Mendes, 1999

U.S. (DreamWorks SKG, Jinks/Cohen) 122m Color **Producer** Bruce Cohen, Dan Jinks **Screenplay** Alan Ball **Photography** Conrad L. Hall **Music** Thomas Newman **Cast** Kevin Spacey, Annette Bening, Thora Birch, Wes Bentley, Mena Suvari, Peter Gallagher, Allison Janney, Chris Cooper, Scott Bakula, Sam Robards, Barry Del Sherman, Ara Celi, John Cho, Fort Atkinson, Sue Casey **Oscars** Bruce Cohen, Dan Jinks (best picture), Sam Mendes (director), Alan Ball (screenplay), Kevin Spacey (actor), Conrad L. Hall (photography) **Oscar nominations** Annette Bening (actress), Tariq Anwar (editing), Thomas Newman (music)

If *Blue Velvet* (1986) peeked behind the curtains of suburbia, *American Beauty* yanked them away from the windows. "This is my neighborhood, this is my street, this is my life," says Lester Burnham (Kevin Spacey) in voice-over at the start of the film. "I'm forty-two years old. In less than a year, I'll be dead. Of course I don't know that yet. In a way, I'm dead already." Like Joe Gillis in *Sunset Boulevard* (1950), Lester and the audience know his fate from the beginning, but that is just one part of his story.

American Beauty is a bleak comedy about what life is really like for those supposedly living the American dream—people who don't lack for anything material but who are unhappy, unfulfilled, and dissatisfied. Mainly, this is Lester's story, and with Spacey in the role it is a fascinating one—that is, on the surface, a tale of midlife crisis as he tries to rediscover the freedom he has lost in the face of marital and parental responsibility.

Forced to accompany his wife to a basketball game to watch his cheerleader daughter perform, he is transfixed by the Lolita-esque Angela (Mena Suvari). He is soon having erotic visions (most memorably, her naked but for a cover of red rose petals) that lead him to completely change his life in the hope that he will be able to seduce her.

i

Before *American Beauty*, Suvari acted in a movie called *Great Falls*. It was released as *American Pie* (1999).

Written by Alan Ball—who went on to create the acclaimed HBO television series *Six Feet Under*—this is a funny, sad, wistful, and even hopeful movie that never goes quite where you think it will. **JB**

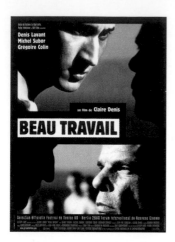

Beau Travail Claire Denis, 1999

Claire Denis is one of the world's most audacious, talented directors, and *Beau Travail* may well be her crowning glory. Based on Herman Melville's novella *Billy Budd*, the film is set in the rugged outback of Africa, where the French Foreign Legion—men of every race and hue—undergo rigorous training. The stark desert, with its endless stretch of sand and jagged rocks beneath a rolling blue sky, provides a breathtaking canvas for Denis, who captures the rituals of exercise, marching, showering, and bonding with a poet's eye. In her carefully constructed scenes, everyday routines are transformed into gracefully choreographed dances. But while this ode to masculinity and male beauty is unfolding, the jealousy of a military official, Sergeant Galoup (Denis Lavant), toward one of his underlings, Sentain (Gregoire Colin), builds toward a tragic ending.

Galoup narrates the tale in voice-over. The homoeroticism of the military experience is neither forced nor shied away from, and doesn't really qualify *Beau Travail* as an example of queer cinema, as both fans and detractors of the film declared upon its release. Denis's interests are broader than that. In brief but powerful strokes, she raises questions about the relationships of whites to blacks, especially in former European colonies. Connections between gender and racial politics are made in scenes where the men go into town on leave and mingle with local women. But the film remains steadfastly ambiguous, never taking any specific stance on these issues. Most importantly, Denis, with minimal dialogue and with a primary focus on hypnotic visuals that fill the screen in long takes, captures the beauty of ritual and repetition—as well as the power of monotony to break spirit.

In terms of sheer beauty alone, *Beau Travail* pays off frame for frame, whether it's the sight of the men in formation performing calisthenics, or the happy accident of Denis capturing a ray of sun as it's refracted in the window of a moving train—or, finally, the disgraced officer, dancing beneath a spinning disco ball. Denis tells her stories through images rather than through dialogue and plot, with a gift for color, lighting, and composition that is unsurpassed. **EH**

France (La Sept-Arte, SM, Tanaïs) 92m Color **Language** French **Producer** Patrick Grandperret **Screenplay** Claire Denis, Jean-Pol Fargeau, from the novella *Billy Budd* by Herman Melville **Photography** Agnès Godard **Music** Charles Henri de Pierrefeu, Eran Zur **Cast** Denis Lavant, Michel Subor, Grégoire Colin, Richard Courcet, Nicolas Duvauchelle, Adiatou Massudi, Mickael Ravovski, Dan Herzberg, Giuseppe Molino, Gianfranco Poddighe, Marc Veh, Thong Duy Nguyen, Jean-Yves Vivet, Bernardo Montet, Dimitri Tsiapkinis **Berlin International Film Festival** Claire Denis (reader jury of the Berliner Zeitung—special mention)

"What you're seeing is a realistic depiction . . . the French legionnaires in the desert do train under the sun half-naked."

Claire Denis, 2011

i

Not allowed into the Foreign Legion, Denis instead had to observe their training in the desert at a distance.

Spain / France (El Deseo, France 2, Renn, Vía Digital) 101m Eastmancolor
Language Spanish / Catalan / English
Producer Agustín Almodóvar, Michel Ruben **Screenplay** Pedro Almodóvar
Photography Affonso Beato **Music** Alberto Iglesias **Cast** Cecilia Roth, Marisa Paredes, Candela Peña, Antonia San Juan, Penélope Cruz, Rosa María Sardà, Fernando Fernán Gómez, Fernando Guillén, Toni Cantó, Eloy Azarín, Carlos Lozano, Manuel Morón, José Luis Torrijo, Juan José Otegui, Carmen Balagué **Oscar** Spain (best foreign language film) **Cannes Film Festival** Pedro Almodóvar (director, prize of the ecumenical jury, Golden Palm nomination)

"I read about a bunch of nuns who lived in a house and worked with transvestites and prostitutes and drug addicts, trying to help them to establish new lives for themselves."

Pedro Almodóvar, 2006

ℹ️

A stage version of the movie opened at London's Old Vic theater in 2007, with stars including Diana Rigg.

Todo sobre mi madre Pedro Almodóvar, 1999
All About My Mother

Pedro Almodóvar's 1999 film opens on a handsome boy, Esteban (Eloy Azarín), who's very close to his single mother, Manuela (Cecilia Roth). For a while (via sly references to Truman Capote and Tennessee Williams) it looks as though we're about to see a thinly disguised gay autobiopic. In a way we are, for although Esteban is killed off on his seventeenth birthday and the focus shifts to Manuela, *All About My Mother*—like many Almodóvar films—constructs femininity through the irreverent, loving gaze of a gay man who grew up surrounded by adoring women on the verge. Crazed with grief, Manuela travels to Barcelona and finds herself playing den mother to a pregnant nun with AIDS (Penélope Cruz, in one of the great Spanish roles she traded away to become a Hollywood pin-up), a beat-up transgendered prostitute (Antonia San Juan) who stage manages her every moment, and a lesbian actress (the great Marisa Paredes) who is playing Blanche Dubois in more ways than one. The plot, elaborately structured and layered with significance, is an excuse to throw together a bunch of throaty-voiced women (with or without their own breasts) to talk dirty, booze, weep, and prop each other up.

When a woman in an Almodóvar film cries, it's a heaving, gasping, aristocratic happening. Still, in his court-jester way, Almodóvar is the most enthusiastic of social levelers. A nun can fall, a hooker can rise, and, though both may rail at their fates, their suffering lacks bitterness or rage. Even the color scheme is egalitarian, and trash has its own beauty: The cars of johns trawling for hookers at night beneath a Barcelona bridge are bathed in the same moonlit loveliness as the city's old buildings.

Toward the end, the prostitute steps on stage and, having itemized her many surgeries to an appalled audience of bourgeois theatergoers, enchants them with her ad-libbed thoughts on what it takes to be real. "You are more authentic," she says, "the more you resemble the things you've dreamed of." For Almodóvar, nature is overrated, while acting—lying included—frees us to be our worst and best selves. This wonderfully seductive set piece summarizes the exuberantly humane credo that animates every movie he makes. *All About My Mother* contains scenes as candid and uproarious as any of the director's early films, but sustains the quieter, sadder, and more reflective tone that began in 1995's *The Flower of My Secret,* and continued in 2003's lovely *Talk to Her.*

As the movie closes, this alluring coven of women shakes out into fresh unions, cemented not only by Almodóvar's elastic definition of womanhood, but by his conciliatory spirit—assuring us that though anatomy may not be destiny, the kindness of female strangers is irreducible. Given the pap that is too often most studios' idea of a "women's movie," gay filmmakers like Almodóvar and Todd Haynes may be providing a last refuge for strong female roles, as well as for wholehearted melodrama in our hyper-ironic age. **ET**

1999

The Matrix Andy Wachowski & Lana Wachowski, 1999

A sci-fi blockbuster that effectively fuses pop-philosophy with skillfully choreographed action and state-of-the-art special effects, *The Matrix* was conceived of, written, and directed by siblings Andy and Lana Wachowski. The former comic book writers threw just about everything into the mix, including *The Wizard of Oz* and *The Wild Bunch*, *Alice in Wonderland* and *Hard Target*, *Sleeping Beauty* and *The Bible*.

Keanu Reeves is a dutiful company man who doubles at night as a hacker named Neo. His skepticism concerning the true nature of reality is validated after a beautiful mystery woman, Trinity (Carrie-Anne Moss), introduces him to legendary Zen-hacker Morpheus (Laurence Fishburne). Accepting Morpheus's invitation to take a mind-opening techno-drug trip, Neo discovers that the world in which he previously "existed" is nothing but a computer-generated virtual reality program controlled by artificial-intelligence machines developed by mankind years before. It seems the machines, which require endless supplies of electrical current to survive, keep the entire human population—save for a smattering of rebels and one underground city—in a state of perpetual hallucination. Lying unconscious in automated incubators, humans are deceived into believing that they are leading productive lives, while in reality vampire-like computers siphon their precious mojo. Morpheus is certain Neo is the "One," who, according to legend, will one day to save the human race from eternal subjugation. Although initially dissuaded by a surprisingly domestic soothsayer (Gloria Foster), Neo manages to summon the fortitude necessary to defeat the artificial intelligence defense squad, with the help of John Woo-style martial arts ballet, Sam Peckinpah-inspired slow-motion gunfighting, and repeated self-affirmations.

What separates *The Matrix* from other virtual reality sci-fi fare are its epic pretensions, apocalyptic overtones, and breathtaking visuals. "Bullet Time" super slo-mo photography, wire-enhanced gymnastics, and kung fu fights choreographed by Yuen Woo-Ping (*Fist of Legend* [1994], *Black Mask* [1996]) all raised the bar for Hollywood action sequences. One of the most fascinating things about the film is the manner in which it negotiates between progressive messages of nonconformity and self-realization, and the generic imperatives of Hollywood's conservative studio system. As one critic wrote, "It's cruel, really, to put tantalizing ideas on the table and then ask the audience to be satisfied with a shoot-out and a martial arts duel." Others praised the Wachowskis for beginning their film with an extended fight scene starring Trinity, only to note her relegation to "Neo's love interest" for the rest of the picture.

Such mixed messages reappear as narrative. Considering that what remains of postwar planet Earth is a bleak, inhospitable "desert of the real," and that the virtual world in which Neo grew up is not without advantages, it isn't clear what the human resistance hopes to gain by its struggles. Clearly such quandaries were not a turnoff for viewers. **SJS**

U.S. (Groucho II, Silver, Village Roadshow) 136m Technicolor **Producer** Joel Silver **Screenplay** Andy Wachowski, Lana Wachowski **Photography** Bill Pope **Music** Paul Barker, Don Davis **Cast** Keanu Reeves, Laurence Fishburne, Carrie-Anne Moss, Hugo Weaving, Gloria Foster, Joe Pantoliano, Marcus Chong, Julian Arahanga, Matt Doran, Belinda McClory, Anthony Ray Parker, Paul Goddard, Robert Taylor, David Aston, Marc Gray **Oscars** Zach Staenberg (editing), Dane A. Davis (special sound effects), John Gaeta, Janek Sirrs, Steve Courtley, Jon Thum (special visual effects), John T. Reitz, Gregg Rudloff, David E. Campbell, David Lee (sound)

"The Wachowskis really are pushers, you know. Really! In their movie, they pushed each actor, each technician to the extreme limit."

Keanu Reeves, 1999

i

The Wachowskis wanted to shoot all three of the *Matrix* movies together. "Totally crazy," noted Keanu Reeves.

CINE TAMARIS présente

LES GLANEURS
et
LA GLANEUSE

un film d'AGNES VARDA

Les glaneurs et la glaneuse Agnès Varda, 2000
The Gleaners and I

Digital technology has revolutionized filmmaking by making it more democratic and less expensive—the merits, fall-out from, and worthiness of that revolution can still be rigorously debated. What has so often been lacking in digital movies, though, is any sense of beauty or style, any eye for making movies. Even more, the "personal" films that have come out of the digital revolution have often been sophomoric and self-indulgent. Leave it to the mother of the French New Wave, Agnès Varda, to show all the upstarts how it should be done.

Unapologetically leftist in its politics, swerving from musings on life and mortality to the role of art in society, all while paying tribute to society's outcasts, *The Gleaners and I* is all over the map. Yet Varda doesn't let the film get away from her; the viewer never feels anything other than that they're in the passenger seat on an eye-opening journey that's being navigated by a master. There's a wonderful moment in the film in which Varda, picking overripe figs from a tree and eating them on the spot, launches a tirade about the greed of those who are both wealthy and selfish. Rather than spout threadbare Marxist theory, she simply observes, "They don't want to be nice." That raw truth resonates throughout the documentary, at the center of which are modern-day gleaners, people who salvage scraps after markets close, or pick through dumpsters to find food. Varda lets these marginalized people speak for themselves, and they eloquently address everything from world politics to personal tragedies, while the film shows that those two poles are not so far apart.

Tough questions of social inequity are smoothly juxtaposed against the salvelike qualities of art, and the necessity of finding beauty where you live. The result is a protest film that's part social critique, part travelogue, but always an unsentimental celebration of human resilience. Threaded throughout *The Gleaners and I* are Varda's musings on her own mortality. Rather than being pitying or sentimental, though, those moments capsulize the film's assertion that everyone who clears life's hurdles is an artist of sorts. **EH**

France (Tamaris) 82m Color
Language French Photography Didier Doussin, Stéphane Krausz, Didier Rouget, Pascal Sautelet, Agnès Varda
Screenplay Agnès Varda Music Agnès Bredel, Joanna Bruzdowicz, Richard Klugman, Isabelle Olivier Cast Bodan Litnanski, Agnès Varda, François Wertheimer

"Agnès Varda of course is a gleaner herself. She is gleaning the gleaners."

Roger Ebert,
Chicago Sun-Times, 2001

2000

Millet's *The Gleaners* (1857) is famous for its sympathetic showing of the then lowest ranks of rural society.

Fa yeung nin wa Wong Kar-wai, 2000
In the Mood for Love

In the Mood for Love takes place during the 1960s in a tiny and tightly packed tenement house in Hong Kong, where two neighbors spend so much time in close proximity that it's no wonder their lives ultimately cross. Tony Leung and Maggie Cheung suspect that their respective spouses are having an affair, but they're not sure if they should follow suit with an affair of their own. Instead they meet for quiet meals and shy discussions, passing the time together as it dawns upon them that maybe they really are meant for each other.

However, director Wong, working as usual without a script, allows the tale of infidelity to play out in an oddly reserved and unpredictable manner. Where the viewer might sense simmering romance, Wong sees sad resignation. The two potential lovers cling near one another like satellites, but they seem to understand that they may never be able to share the same orbit. This is not unrequited love but resisted love, as Leung and Cheung struggle to stay apart even though they seem destined to be together. Wong choreographs this strange relationship with the grace and rhythm of a waltz. Working with his usual director of photography Christopher Doyle, he tracks the couple in slow motion as they pass each other on the tiny staircases, fret about the weather on the shadowy streets, and cryptically act out the kind of arguments they might have were they actually lovers.

Once again Wong also makes brilliant use of music, in this case a Nat King Cole instrumental cue that grows in mysterious power the more the theme is replicated. Each scene is luminous, spilling over with carefully researched but understated period details captured in a dreamlike haze by an eavesdropping camera. Cheung, clad in a series of beautiful cheong-san dresses, is stunning, the perfect counterpart to the handsome and tasteful Leung, so in many ways you are rooting for the two to end up together. That they do not end up together doesn't come as a surprise, but the emotional power of their nonrelationship proves remarkably effective. **JKl**

France / Hong Kong (Block 2, Jet Tone, Paradis) 98m BW / Color **Language** Cantonese / French / Mandarin / Spanish **Producer** Wong Kar-wai **Screenplay** Wong Kar-wai **Photography** Christopher Doyle, Pin Bing Lee **Music** Mike Galasso, Shigeru Umebayashi **Cast** Maggie Cheung, Tony Leung Chiu-Wai, Ping Lam Siu, Tung Cho Cheung, Rebecca Pan, Lai Chen, Man-Lei Chan, Kam-wah Koo, Roy Cheung, Chi-ang Chi, Hsien Yu, Po-chun Chow, Maggie Cheung Man-yuk, Paulyn Sun, Man-lei Wong **Cannes Film Festival** Tony Leung Chiu-wai (actor), Christopher Doyle, Pin Bing Lee, William Chang (grand technical prize), Wong Kar-wai (Golden Palm nomination)

"Feelings can creep up just like that. I thought I was in control."

Chow Mo-wan

(Tony Leung Chiu-Wai)

🛈

Maggie Cheung wears a different dress in each scene. She found the close-fitted style restrictive to wear.

Gladiator Ridley Scott, 2000

G.B. / U.S. (DreamWorks SKG, Scott Free, Universal) 155m Technicolor
Producer David Franzoni, Branko Lustig, Douglas Wick **Screenplay** David Franzoni, John Logan, William Nicholson **Photography** John Mathieson **Music** Hans Zimmer **Cast** Russell Crowe, Joaquin Phoenix, Connie Nielsen, Oliver Reed, Richard Harris, Derek Jacobi, Djimon Hounsou, David Schofield, John Shrapnel, Tomas Arana, David Hemmings, Ralf Moeller, Spencer Treat Clark, Tommy Flanagan, Sven-Ole Thorsen **Oscars** David Franzoni, Branko Lustig, Douglas Wick (best picture), Russell Crowe (actor), Janty Yates (costume), John Nelson, Neil Corbould, Tim Burke, Rob Harvey (special visual effects), Scott Millan, Bob Beemer, Ken Weston (sound) **Oscar nominations** Ridley Scott (director), David Franzoni, John Logan, William Nicholson (screenplay), Joaquin Phoenix (actor in support role), Arthur Max, Crispian Sallis (art direction), John Mathieson (photography), Pietro Scalia (editing), Hans Zimmer (music)

i

To date, *Gladiator* has grossed $457,640,427 worldwide.

Hot off filming *The Insider* (1999), Russell Crowe lost forty pounds and built up his muscles to play thinking women's sex object Maximus, the Roman general turned gladiator, in *Gladiator*, Hollywood's first true Roman epic in over three decades.

Exiled when his mentor, Caesar Marcus Aurelius (Richard Harris), dies and is succeeded by his power-hungry son, Commodus (Joaquin Phoenix), Maximus, now in exile, trains as a gladiator and swears his revenge—understandable when you consider that Commodus not only kicked Maximus out of the bosom of Rome and tried to kill him, but also had his family murdered.

As you would expect from director Ridley Scott, the movie is epic not only in scale but also in imagery, as the majesty that was Rome is re-created superbly on screen (much praise is due here to Scott's cinematographer, John Mathieson). But Scott doesn't lose sight of the human side of the story amid the computer trickery, brilliantly staged battle sequences, and spectacular sets, delivering a fascinating, grisly, and heroic tale. With skilled actors, most notably Crowe, a wonderfully preening Phoenix and, in his final role, Oliver Reed, who sadly died during filming—his remaining scenes were generated using a stand-in and computer-enhanced filmwork. The film garnered five Oscars, including Best Actor in a Leading Role, for Russell Crowe. **JB**

Kippur Amos Gitai, 2000

France / Israel (Agav Hafakot, Canal+, MP, R&C, Telad, Tele Plus, Arte) 123m Color Language Hebrew Producer Amos Gitai, Michel Propper, Laurent Truchot Screenplay Amos Gitai, Marie-Jose Sanselme Photography Renato Berta Music Jan Garbarek Cast Liron Levo, Tomer Russo, Uri Ran-Klausner, Yoram Hattab, Guy Amir, Juliano Mer, Ran Kauchinsky, Kobi Livne, Liat Glick, Pini Mittleman, Meital Barda, Gidi Gov Cannes Film Festival Amos Gitai (Golden Palm nomination)

Since his debut in the early 1980s with a series of documentaries that ran afoul of Israeli television, Amos Gitai has become known as Israel's most provocative filmmaker. Despite his courage and good instincts, his films can feel somewhat clumsy and inept at times—but not *Kippur*. In this haunting remembrance of things past, Gitai conjures up a shattering vision of the 1973 Yom Kippur War, in which he himself was seriously wounded. Two friends head for the Golan Heights to join up with their unit, but are deflected into a medical team that helicopters in to rescue the wounded. From the moment the reservists begin driving out of peacetime to the front lines, literally searching for the location of war, Gitai edges us into ever more lunar landscapes where time, flesh, and the very earth, are fatally susceptible to distortion and/or disintegration.

Kippur is less about a specific struggle than it is an evocation of the hallucinatory state of war: confusion, shock, numbing fatigue, constant cacophony. There's at least one sequence that is truly the stuff from which nightmares are made: A rescue team tries to carry away a seriously wounded soldier, only to have the body keep slipping off the stretcher. In one horrifying, gruesomely funny moment, Gitai makes us experience the impact of the war—personal and cosmic, realistic and surreal. **RP**

Yi yi Edward Yang, 2000
A One and a Two

Taiwan / Japan (Atom, Nemuru Otoko Seisaku Iinkai, Omega, Pony Canyon) 173m Color Language English / Hokkien / Mandarin Producer Shinya Kawai, Osamu Kunota, Naoko Tsukeda, Wei-yen Yu Screenplay Edward Yang Photography Wei-han Yang Music Kai-li Peng Cast Wu Nien-jen, Elaine Jin, Issey Ogata, Kelly Lee, Jonathan Chang, Chen Hsi-sheng, Ko Su-yun, Michael Tao, Hsiao Shu-shen, Adrian Lin, Pang Chang Yu, Tang Ru-yun, Hsu Shu-yuan, Tseng Hsin-yi, Yiwen Chen Cannes Film Festival Edward Yang (director, Golden Palm nomination)

Edward Yang's most accessible movie—and probably his best since *A Brighter Summer Day* (1991)—this 2000 feature follows three generations of a contemporary Taipei family from a wedding to a funeral, and although it takes almost three hours to unfold, not a single moment seems gratuitous.

Working once again with nonprofessional actors, Yang coaxes a standout performance from Wu Nien-jen—a substantial writer and director in his own right—as N.J., a middle-aged partner in a failing computer company who hopes to team up with a Japanese game designer, and who has a secret rendezvous in Tokyo with a woman (Ko Su-yun) he jilted thirty years earlier. Other major characters in Yi Yi include the hero's eight-year-old son (Jonathan Chang), teenage daughter (Kelly Lee), spiritually traumatized wife (Elaine Jin), comatose mother-in-law (Tang Ru-yun), and debt-ridden brother-in-law (Chen Hsi-sheng). The son—a comic and unsentimental marvel named Yang-Yang—becomes obsessed with photographing what people can't see, like the backs of their heads, because to him it's the half of reality that's missed. He may come closest to being a mouthpiece for Yang, who seems to miss nothing as he interweaves shifting viewpoints and poignant emotional refrains, creating one of the richest family portraits in modern cinema. **JRos**

Requiem for a Dream Darren Aronofsky, 2000

Darren Aronofsky's follow-up to his acclaimed debut *Pi* (1998) is nothing short of remarkable. *Requiem for a Dream* follows four characters—Harry Goldfarb (Jared Leto), his mother Sara (Ellen Burstyn), girlfriend Marion (Jennifer Connelly), and best friend Tyrone (Marlon Wayans)—through the nightmare world of drug addiction. Each has his or her own way of handling their addiction, and they all end up in different situations, but these addictions are all caused by the same thing, the failure of the American dream. For Aronofsky, the dream is dead and his film is a nightmarish mourning for its victims.

Visually, *Requiem* owes much to both Danny Boyle's *Trainspotting* (1996) and the films of Spike Lee; but unlike Boyle, whose own drug movie included sequences of hallucinogenic subjectivity, Aronofsky resists grounding the audience in any kind of objective position. The entire film is shot within this drug-addled subjective tense. And from Lee, Aronofsky takes a hyperkinetic visual sensibility used to represent a Brooklyn state of mind, though *Requiem* makes thematic use of these elements, rather than just employing them for surface style.

The acting is uniformly magnificent, with Leto, Connelly, and Wayans giving surprisingly strong performances. But it is Ellen Burstyn's role as Harry's diet-pill addicted mom that is nothing short of astonishing, and if one had to pick a single reason to see the film it would have to be for this performance. Although nominated for a Best Actress Oscar, Burstyn lost to Julia Roberts (*Erin Brockovich*). No disrespect to either the film or Ms. Roberts, but come on! Roberts's performance was the best of her career, but the same can be said for Burstyn's Sara—and that's hardly a fair comparison.

But missing from this discussion—and the real reason to see *Requiem for a Dream*, beyond its intelligent ideas, amazing use of narcotic subjectivity, meaningful stylistics, and magnificent performances—is the film's remarkable balance of horror (the final sequences of drug madness are some of the scariest movie moments in recent years) and great Jewish comedy. Just imagine Woody Allen directing *Naked Lunch*. **MK**

U.S. (Artisan, Bandeira, Protozoa, Sibling, Industry, Thousand Words Truth & Soul) 102m Color **Producer** Eric Watson, Palmer West **Screenplay** Hubert Selby Jr., Darren Aronofsky, from novel by Hubert Selby Jr. **Photography** Matthew Libatique **Music** Clint Mansell **Cast** Ellen Burstyn, Jared Leto, Jennifer Connelly, Marlon Wayans, Christopher McDonald, Louise Lasser, Marcia Jean Kurtz, Janet Sarno, Suzanne Shepherd, Joanne Gordon, Charlotte Aronofsky, Mark Margolis, Michael Kaycheck, Jack O'Connell, Chas Mastin **Oscar nomination** Ellen Burstyn (actress)

"Purple in the morning, blue in the afternoon, orange in the evening . . . There's my three meals, Mr. Smartypants."

Sara Goldfarb
(Ellen Burstyn)

i

Burstyn's makeup included four different "necks," two different "fat suits," and nine different wigs.

Amores perros Alejandro González Iñárritu, 2000

Quentin Tarantino had such a pronounced and immediate effect on American filmmakers that it was only a matter of time before his influence stretched into other countries. *Amores Perros*—which translates roughly to "Love's a Bitch"—shows that by 2000 the Tarantino model of stylish violence and jumbled narratives had made its way south of the U.S. border, to Mexico. *Amores Perros* marked the feature debut of Mexican director Alejandro Gonzalez Iñárritu, and if the film ultimately offers nothing particularly new, his vibrant filmmaking still manages to inject the somewhat familiar scenarios with energy, humor, intelligence, and warmth.

Shot as three interlocking stories whose central characters overlap at one key juncture, *Amores Perros* remains faithful to the canine theme of its title, as each segment of the film features a dog (or dogs) in a prominent role. In the first, a boy cheats with his brother's wife while entering his prized dog into grisly (and viscerally effective) fights, hoping to raise money so that he and his sister-in-law can run off together. In the second Edgar Allan Poe by way of Luis Buñuel segment, a vain, crippled supermodel loses her dog in the crawlspace beneath the floorboards of her apartment, and is tormented by the sounds of its incessant suffering as well as her inability to alleviate it. In the final segment, a hit-man seeks redemption for the life he has led and recognition from his estranged family.

All three segments ironically illustrate man's inhumanity to man via his treatment of animals, which incidentally fare so poorly in the film that *Amores Perros* infamously sports a prominent and preemptive disclaimer at its start noting that no animals were harmed during the making of the film. In fact, the frequent dog violence (and violence to dogs) is depicted so realistically that at times it does threaten to overwhelm the picture. But Iñárritu succeeds in delivering his message of bloody disloyalty, chilling dishonesty, and class disjunction with an abundance of style, revealing in the process a strong trust for the instincts of his actors as well as the intelligence of his audience. **JKl**

Mexico (Altavista, Zeta) 153m Color **Language** Spanish **Producer** Alejandro González Iñárritu **Screenplay** Guillermo Arriaga **Photography** Rodrigo Prieto **Music** Gustavo Santaolalla **Cast** Emilio Echevarría, Gael García Bernal, Goya Toledo, Álvaro Guerrero, Vanessa Bauche, Jorge Salinas, Marco Pérez, Rodrigo Murray, Humberto Busto, Gerardo Campbell, Rosa María Bianchi, Dunia Saldívar, Adriana Barraza, José Sefami, Lourdes Echevarría **Cannes Film Festival** Alejandro González Iñárritu (critics week grand prize, young critics award, best feature)

> "Iñárritu's style contains elements of Tarantino, Peckinpah, and others, but ultimately, the synthesis is all his own."
>
> James Berardnelli, *Reelviews*, 2012

i

A disclaimer shown at the beginning of the film confirms that no animals were harmed in its production.

Memento Christopher Nolan, 2000

Based on his brother Jonathan's story *Memento Mori,* British director Christopher Nolan's second feature is a near-perfect psychological puzzle. Known to movie buffs as "the film filmed backward," this modern film noir is told in stops and starts. Scenes appear in reverse chronological order then move forward again, presenting information that is useless until another parcel of the plot is supplied. An annoying gimmick in another director's hands, Nolan makes the chronological scene shifting an effective way to unfold what is essentially a misguided murder mystery where the hero may or may not know that his facts are not "the facts." Following a long tradition of memory loss within the film noir genre—*Blue Dahlia* (1945) and *Suture* (1993)—the main character's amnesia is yet another exciting factor within a film that has many.

Australian actor Guy Pearce stars as Leonard, a nervy and smug ex-insurance investigator. He wears nice suits and drives a nice car but stays in rundown motels, an indication of the self-imposed gumshoe he has become. Suffering from a rare form of amnesia (a real condition called anterograde amnesia, the inability to make new memories), Leonard keeps track of his actions through sticky notes and Polaroids, tattooing his body with the more important "truths" of the matter. His one aim is to avenge the rape and murder of his wife, a near-impossible task considering he has the slenderest of leads and can't remember anything from the immediate past. The people around him, bedmate Natalie (Carrie-Anne Moss) or chirpy Teddy (Joe Pantoliano), could be friends or could be the killer—he has no idea.

In virtually every scene, Pearce gives a compelling, nervy performance as the man who is haplessly fanatical about his mission yet so incapable of making the decisions he needs to make. How the threads of the story are unraveled and reorganized is an impressive feat of logic minding and script continuity. This technical ploy demands the audience's vigilance yet, in true film noir form, doesn't reward it. In the end, it is the way the tale is told that is memorable, not the story itself. **KK**

U.S. (Remember, Newmarket, Todd) 113m BW / Color **Producer** Jennifer Todd, Suzanne Todd **Screenplay** Christopher Nolan, Jonathan Nolan **Photography** Wally Pfister **Music** David Julyan **Cast** Guy Pearce, Carrie-Anne Moss, Joe Pantoliano, Mark Boone Junior, Russ Fega, Jorja Fox, Stephen Tobolowsky, Harriet Sansom Harris, Thomas Lennon, Callum Keith Rennie, Kimberly Campbell, Marianne Muellerleile, Larry Holden **Oscar nominations** Christopher Nolan, Jonathan Nolan (screenplay), Dody Dorn (editing)

"I have to believe that my actions still have meaning, even if I can't remember them."

Leonard Shelby
(Guy Pearce)

2000

i

Anterograde amnesia can be caused by removing parts of the temporal lobe of the brain to treat epilepsy.

Wo hu cang long Ang Lee, 2000
Crouching Tiger, Hidden Dragon

Director Ang Lee has said that his intention with *Crouching Tiger, Hidden Dragon* was quite simply to make the best martial arts movie possible, and the artistic success and popularity of the end result indicates he achieved just that. Working from a script by his longtime collaborator James Schamus, Lee convened a cast of Asian action superstars who also possessed the requisite acting skills to deliver the story.

Lee also brought in famed fight choreographer Lee Wu-ping. Taking inspiration from the physicality of the Chinese theater, Wu-ping ignores the laws of physics by hoisting the actors up on wires so that they may fight on treetops, skip across water like stones, run up walls, and often clash in midair. For Western audiences perhaps unaccustomed to these aerial ballets, the sight of an opening foot chase over the rooftops of a village on a moonlit night proved immediately and irresistibly enticing.

Chow Yun-fat, Michelle Yeo, and relative newcomer Ziyo Zhang easily handle the supernatural physicality of their respective roles, but their acting never proves subservient to the impressive action scenes. In fact, one reason *Crouching Tiger, Hidden Dragon* became such a sensation was its attention to plot and character development, two rarities even in the most ambitious martial arts films,.

Chow Yun-fat plays a warrior in search of a stolen sword, the Green Dragon. Aided in his quest by Yeo, a former love interest, he discovers that the theft of the sword by Zhang Ziyo is connected to and clouded by longstanding issues of honor and revenge. For all the gravity-defying stunts and fitful bursts of violence, Lee keeps the focus firmly on the film's three central characters, whose philosophies on the utility of fighting and bloodshed have been shaped by their radically different experiences in life.

A strong feminist undercurrent also runs through the film, adding another layer of intelligence. The female characters fight for different reasons, but most of them seem to be fighting for respect in a man's world. The tiny Zhang, posing as a warrior, finds herself beset in a bustling way station by several unsavory fighters. Lee plays the inevitable thrashing of these few dozen would-be assailants for laughs, like a hyperkinetic variation on the old bar fight. But part of Zhang's passionate response seems to stem from simmering resentment, her understanding that were it known that she is female she would have been dismissed outright rather than respected (or feared) as a formidable opponent.

Lee modulates each scene of the movie with a similar nuance and sensitivity. His fight sequences play like psychological confrontations as much as sword fights, the clash of innocence and experience, of peace and anger. Even so, Lee leaves as much room for levity as he does or visual poetry, achieving a rare balance of thrills, beauty, humor, and smarts. **JKI**

U.S. / Hong Kong / China / Taiwan (Asia Union, China Film, Columbia, EDKO, Good Machine, Sony, United China, Zoom Hunt) 120m Technicolor **Language** Mandarin **Producer** Hsu Li-kong, William Kong, Ang Lee **Screenplay** Wang Hui-ling, James Schamus, Kuo Jung Tsai, from book by Du Lu Wang **Photography** Peter Pau **Music** Jorge Calandrelli, Yong King, Tan Dun **Cast** Chow Yun-fat, Michelle Yeo, Ziyo Zhang, Chen Chang, Sihung Lung, Cheng Pei-pei, Fa Zeng Li, Xian Gao, Yan Hai, De Ming Wang, Li Li-li, Su Ying Huang, Jin Ting Zhang, Rei Yang, Kai Li **Oscars** Taiwan (best foreign language film), Timmy Yip (art direction), Peter Pau (photography), Tan Dun (music) **Oscar nominations** William Kong, Hsu Li-kong, Ang Lee (best picture), Ang Lee (director), Wang Hui-ling, James Schamus, Kuo Jung Tsai (screenplay), Timmy Yip (costume), Tim Squyres (editing), Jorge Calandrelli, Tan Dun, James Schamus (song)

"For all the leaping action, it's the film's spirit that soars."

Peter Travers,
***Rolling Stone*, 2000**

ℹ

The movie's title is a quote from Chinese mythology. It refers to hiding your strength from others.

POWER CAN BE HELD
IN THE SMALLEST OF THINGS

THE TRILOGY BEGINS DECEMBER 2001

The Lord of the Rings Peter Jackson, 2001, 2002, & 2003

The Fellowship of the Ring (2001) 178m
The Two Towers (2002) 179m
The Return of The King (2003) 201m

All three films U.S. / New Zealand
(New Line CInema, WingNut Films, The Saul
Zaentz Company) Color **Producer** Peter
Jackson, Barrie M. Osborne, Fran Walsh,
Tim Sanders (only *The Fellowship of the Ring*)
Screenplay Fran Walsh, Philippa Boyens,
Peter Jackson, Stephen Sinclair (only *The
Two Towers*), from novels by J. R. R.
Tolkien **Photography** Andrew Lesnie
Music Howard Shore **Cast** Elijah Wood,
Ian McKellen, Liv Tyler, Viggo Mortensen,
Sean Astin, Cate Blanchett, John Rhys-
Davies, Billy Boyd, Dominic Monaghan,
Orlando Bloom, Hugo Weaving
Oscars *The Fellowship of the Ring* 4 awards,
including Andrew Lesnie (cinematography),
Howard Shore (music) *The Two Towers*
Ethan Van der Ryn, Mike Hopkins (sound
editing), Jim Rygiel, Joe Letteri, Randall
William Cook, Alex Funke (visual effects)
The Return of the King Barrie M. Osborne,
Peter Jackson, Fran Walsh (best picture),
Peter Jackson (director), Fran Walsh, Philippa
Boyens, Peter Jackson (screenplay), Jamie
Selkirk (editing), Grant Major, Dan Hennah,
Alan Lee (art direction), Ngila Dickson,
Richard Taylor (costume design), Richard
Taylor, Peter King (makeup), Fran Walsh,
Howard Shore, Annie Lennox (song),
Christopher Boyes, Michael Semanick,
Michael Hedges, Hammond Peek (sound),
Jim Rygiel, Joe Letteri, Randall William Cook,
Alex Funke, (visual effects), Howard
Shore (music)

Like J. R. R. Tolkien's original three-volume book, Peter Jackson's adaptation of *The Lord of the Rings* is best seen as a single—albeit very long—work. Watched back-to-back, the trilogy flows together almost seamlessly, from spectacular prologue to the suitably epic, record-setting closing credits.

But then, everything about this movie is record-setting, from how it was made (all three films were shot over a single sixteen-month period), to the extent of its eventual, incredible success. To date it has earned more than any other trilogy, even besting the *Star Wars* movies. By some estimates, the series has earned at least as much again on DVD sales; when you throw in merchandising, the GDP of Middle-Earth begins to rival that of actual countries. Remarkably, Jackson managed to astound not just the accountants but the critics as well. Each film topped scores of "best of" lists, and between them the three movies were nominated for a staggering thirty Academy Awards, and won seventeen.

If you've seen the movies, it will come as no surprise that all three won Oscars for visual effects. They are filled with impressive beasts and battles, the scale of each escalating from movie to movie. Despite this, it is the tragic figure of Gollum that most captured audience imagination. Based on the motion-tracked performance and vocals of actor Andy Serkis, the Gollum on-screen was totally computer-generated, yet still totally believable as a real character.

It is perhaps this that encapsulates Jackson's greatest achievement: to remember that spectacle and technical wizardry aren't enough to make a great movie. Even though *The Lord of the Rings* trilogy is filled with hobbits, elves, and wizards, the characters in his films are all very human. Gollum has regrets, tries to be good, and teases the "fat hobbit" Sam. The wizard Gandalf, played to perfection by Sir Ian McKellen, is avuncular, even mischievous, yet always retains his undeniable power and authority. And the hobbits Frodo (a wide-eyed Elijah Wood) and Sam (Sean Astin) grow from brave but naive adventurers to true heroes.

Almost as memorable as the characters is the scenery. The trilogy was shot in Jackson's native New Zealand, and little digital magic was required to create the stunning landscapes. One of the most memorable scenes from the spectacle-laden final movie is the lighting of the beacons; as the music soars, the camera simply tracks from mountaintop to mountaintop as signal fires flare up against the sky, and it is stunning.

It is remarkable that Jackson, with his scriptwriting partners Fran Walsh and Phillippa Boyens, managed to wrestle a dense and unwieldy mass of source material into a swift and engaging narrative. (Even more remarkable is the fact most hard-core fans of the book also loved the movie.) In a brief but dramatic prologue, we learn that long ago, the über-evil Sauron invested all his power into a ring, only to lose it in an epic battle against a coalition of elves and men. The ring eventually finds its way to the diminutive hobbit, Frodo Baggins. It is here that the story proper begins. Frodo agrees to destroy the ring, and so Sauron, once and for all. However, this can only be done by throwing it into the volcanic heart of Mt. Doom, which lies deep in enemy territory. He sets off on his long and dangerous journey with a fellowship of concerned hobbits, elves, dwarves, and men, including the wizard Gandalf and the mysterious Aragorn (Viggo Mortensen). Betrayals, battles, and bloodshed ensue; the fellowship ultimately splits, as Frodo and Sam (and eventually Gollum) make their way to the volcano by themselves, while the remainder prepare to take on Sauron in a final Middle Earth–shattering showdown.

Despite the vast canvas upon which Jackson was painting, at its heart his film is about people, their relationships, and the decisions they make. Friendship and self-sacrifice figure strongly, as does a sense of mortality; the final scenes make it clear that victory can be noble, and yet still come at too deep a personal cost. Tolkein spent time in the trenches during World War I, and it is hard not to draw parallels between his experiences and the tone of melancholy that surrounds the trilogy's conclusion. For many, the heart of the film lies not with a big action scene, but in a quiet moment when Gandalf comforts Frodo, who despairs that he was born to see such terrible events. "So do all who live to see such times," Gandalf says. "But that is not for us to decide. All we have to decide is what to do with the time that is given to us." It is moments like this that elevate Jackson's film from movie blockbuster to genuine masterpiece. **PH**

U.S. / Japan (Dentsu, Mitsubishi, NTV, Ghibli, Tokuma Shoten, Touhoku Shinsha Walt Disney) 125m Color **Language** Japanese **Producer** Toshio Suzuki **Screenplay** Hayao Miyazaki **Music** Jô Hisaishi **Cast** Daveigh Chase, Rumi Hiiragi, Miyu Irino, Jason Marsden, Mari Natsuki, Miyu Irino, Jason Marsden, Mari Natsuki, Suzanne Pleshette, Michael Chiklis, Takashi Naitô, Lauren Holly, Yasuko Sawaguchi, Tatsuya Gashuin, John Ratzenberger, Ryunosuke Kamiki, Tara Strong, Susan Egan **Oscar** Hayao Miyazaki (animation) **Berlin International Film Festival** Hayao Miyazaki (Golden Bear, tied with *Bloody Sunday*)

"It's not me who makes the film. The film makes itself, and I have no choice but to follow."

Hayao Miyazaki, 2002

ℹ️

Spirited Away was the first anime film to be nominated for—and win—an Academy Award.

Sen to chihiro no kamikakushi
Spirited Away Hayao Miyazaki, 2001

With every film that he makes, Hayao Miyazaki sets the standard for animated features ever higher. Yet he holds such a singular vision that it's hard to tell where to place him on the pantheon. He isn't a throwback to the past, because no one in the past made movies quite like Miyazaki's. And he certainly isn't a precursor of things to come, because it's hard to imagine anybody but Miyazaki doing what he does. He is one of a kind, and as such, his films hold a special place in the heart of movie lovers.

This is especially true in his native Japan, where each of his features exceeds the box office tally of its predecessor, with many of them eclipsing the take of even the most prominent Hollywood blockbusters. This is because Miyazaki creates fantastic worlds somehow free from the cloying characters and patronizing tone of so many mainstream animated features. Not surprisingly, his unfailingly intelligent films appeal to both children and adults, simple enough for the former to enjoy yet complex enough for the latter to appreciate on a different level.

The shy and nervous Chihiro (voiced by Daveigh Chase in the English-language version) and her parents are on their way to their new home when they take a detour through a strange tunnel. When they emerge on the other side, they discover a seemingly deserted town, but things aren't what they seem. Chihiro's parents gorge themselves on food and magically transform into a pair of pigs, and that's when Chihiro realizes they're not alone. When night falls, the town becomes populated with spirits, and Chihiro must overcome her fears to rescue her parents and find their way home. Guided by a more benevolent spirit named Haku (Jason Marsden), Chihiro sneaks her way into the inner workings of the town, where she discovers a witch named Yubaba (Suzanne Pleshette) who runs the spirit city like a booming business with an elaborate spa resort as its main draw. It's only by ingratiating herself to the enigmatic crone and her unpredictable cronies that Chihiro can hope to escape.

Spirited Away is in many ways Miyazaki's *Alice in Wonderland*. The writer-director's hand-drawn scenes burst with energy and invention, and Miyazaki takes full advantage of the fantastical story to devise dozens of unique spirits and creatures that roam this world of utterly inscrutable rules and impenetrable logic. Giant babies throw destructive temper tantrums. Evil spirits offer gifts of gold as bait before devouring everything in sight. Characters change shapes (and sometimes personalities) with no warning—one appears alternately as a boy, a dragon, and a river spirit. Chihiro reacts to each of these creatures first with confusion, then with fear, and ultimately with courage. She soon realizes that she must master this strange world if she ever hopes to get home, and just as the spirits she encounters change her outlook on life, so does Chihiro affect the behavior of the spirits. She's a stranger in a strange land whose denizens consider her the strangest of them all. **JK**

No Man's Land
Danis Tanovic, 2001

Bosnia-Herzegovina / Slovenia / Italy / France / G.B. / Belgium (Casablanca, Counihan Villiers, Eurimages, Fabrica, Fonds Slovène, Man's, Noé, Maj, Centre du Cinema et de l'Audiovisuel de la Communauté Française de Belgique, Wallons) 98m Color **Language** Serbo-Croatian / English / French **Producer** Marc Baschet, Frédérique Dumas-Zajdela, Cédomir Kolar **Screenplay** Danis Tanovic **Photography** Walther van den Ende **Music** Danis Tanovic **Cast** Branko Djuric, Rene Bitorajac, Filip Sovagovic, Georges Siatidis, Serge-Henri Valcke, Sacha Kremer, Alain Eloy, Mustafa Nadarevic, Bogdan Diklic, Simon Callow, Kathrin Cartlidge, Tanja Ribic **Oscar** Bosnia (best foreign language film)

A warrior's term associated with World War I, "no-man's-land" connotes the uninhabitable kill zone between opposing forces. Danis Tanovic's *No Man's Land* complicates the term with an absurdist drama set in the Balkans, designed around a "Mexican standoff."

It is 1993 and a relief platoon of Bosnian soldiers gets lost in the night on its way to the front. Ambushed by a Serbian patrol, the group is decimated, save for two of its number. Chiki (Branko Djuric) suffers a glancing bullet wound before finding the safety of trenches, and his friend Cera (Filip Sovagovic) is knocked unconscious. Sent to survey the trench, a Serbian veteran and his new partner Nino (Rene Bitorajac) set a mine beneath Cera's body, just before Chiki kills the veteran. When Cera wakes up, unable to move, the three are forced to cooperate to survive because they're equally cut off from both sides' rear guard and leadership.

Tanovic's film is a riveting portrait of military purposes run amuck at the very point of conflict. Chiki, Nino, and Cera bear the ravages of a much greater agenda, namely the combination of religious, political, ethnic, but most of all, nationalist impulses. *No Man's Land* is a bleak affair, indeed, but a meaningful cinematic experience can be found in its dark, dark comedy of errors wherein forthright patriots festoon one another on the symbolic bayonets of their rifles. **GC-Q**

Gangs of New York
Martin Scorsese, 2002

U.S. (Miramax Films, IEG, Alberto Grimaldi Productions) 167m Color **Producer** Alberto Grimaldi, Harvey Weinstein **Screenplay** Jay Cocks, Steven Zalian, Kenneth Lonergan **Photography** Michael Balhaus **Music** Howard Shore **Cast** Leonardo DiCaprio, Daniel Day-Lewis, Cameron Diaz, Brendan Gleeson, Henry Thomas, John C. Reilly, Jim Broadbent, Liam Neeson, Gary Lewis, Stephen Graham, Eddie Marsan, Alec McCowen, David Hemmings, Cara Seymour, Cian McCormack **Oscar nominations** Alberto Grimaldi, Harvey Weinstein (Picture), Martin Scorsese (director), Daniel Day-Lewis (actor), Jay Cocks, Steven Zalian, Kenneth Lonergan (original screenplay), Michael Balhaus (cinematography), Thelma Schoonmaker (editing), Sandy Powell (costume design), Dante Ferretti, Francesco Lo Schiavo (art direction-set decoration), Bono, The Edge, Adam Clayton, Larry Mullen Jr. (original song), Tom Fleischman, Eugene Gearty, Ivan Sharrock (sound)

Opening on a set that might not look out of place on stage at the New York Met, *Gangs of New York* could have been an opera. Leonardo DiCaprio is Amsterdam Vallon, vying to avenge his father, killed by lower Manhattan's now undisputed king, Bill Cutting (Daniel Day-Lewis). He earns the trust of Bill, who views him as a like-minded soul, until Bill finds out his real identity—thus paving the way for a fight to the death.

Scorsese's loose adaptation of Herbert Asbury's 1929 account of the low-lifes, criminals, and gangs in nineteenth-century New York makes up in energy what it loses in subtlety. Compare it to the eloquence and stateliness of the director's 1993 adaptation of Edith Wharton's *The Age of Innocence*: Though the stories are separated by mere decades, they don't seem to occupy the same universe, let alone the same streets.

Day-Lewis dominates, chewing lines and scenery with gusto, while DiCaprio looks uneasy. Brendan Gleeson, Liam Neeson, Jim Broadbent, and John C. Reilly make the most of their roles, while Cameron Diaz suffers in the only significant female role. Dante Ferretti's designs are a sight to behold. Michael Ballhaus's cinematography is crisp. And Thelma Schoonmaker's editing carries us along at a fair pace, while Scorsese's camera swoops and dives as it explores this barbaric world. It is a bold and ambitious film in an age when such enterprises are all too rare. **IHS**

Russkiy kovcheg Aleksandr Sokurov, 2002
Russian Ark

Russia (The Hermitage Bridge Studio) 99m Color **Producer** Andrey Deryabin, Jens Meurer, Karsten Stöter **Screenplay** Aleksandr Sokurov, Anatoli Nikiforov **Photography** Tilman Büttner **Music** Sergei Yevtushenko **Cast** Sergei Dontsov, Mariya Kuznetsova, Leonid Mozgovoy, Mikhail Piotrovsky

Russian Ark is a work of vaunting ambition. Set amid St. Petersburg's Hermitage Museum, the film offers an impressionistic portrait of the city's 300-year history. The narrator is a French nobleman played by Sergei Donstov, who guides us through the museum's rooms and galleries, with director Aleksandr Sokurov bringing to life fragments of St. Petersburg's eventful past. Floating in and out of scenes involving Catherine the Great and Tsar Nicholas I, and telling of the city's terrible suffering during World War II, the film transforms into a phantasmogorical tour of Russian history.

But what really makes this dreamy mix of allegory and politics so memorable is the director's visual approach. Pushing the envelope of digital technology, the entire drama unravels in a single unbroken take. It was a huge challenge, requiring 2,000 extras (all in period costume) and unfolding across thirty galleries, hallways, and rooms. Technical problems interrupted the first two attempts, but Sokurov got the shot he wanted on his third take—just as well, as there wasn't time for any more. The results are breathtaking: Sokurov's fluid camerawork evokes the continuity and flow of history like no other film. The result is one of the great technical achievements of modern cinema. **EL**

Bowling for Columbine Michael Moore, 2002

U.S. (Dog Eat Dog Films, Momentum Pictures) 120 mins Color **Producer** Michael Moore, Kathleen Glynn, Michael Donovan **Screenplay** Michael Moore **Photography** Brian Danitz, Michael McDonough **Music** Jeff Gibbs **Cast** Michael Moore, Charlton Heston, Dick Clark, Arthur Busch, Marilyn Manson, Matt Stone, Chris Rock **Oscars** Michael Moore, Michael Donovan (documentary—features) **Cannes Film Festival** Michael Moore (55th Anniversary Prize)

The film that launched Michael Moore's career internationally, as well as winning him an Oscar, *Bowling for Columbine* also showed that documentary filmmaking could be commercially successful. It placed America's predilection for gun ownership under the microscope, linking it to the escalation of violence within the country. In particular, the film focuses on the 1999 Columbine High School massacre, when two students went on a murderous rampage before committing suicide.

Adopting a style that his critics argue removes him from any claim to being a documentary filmmaker, Moore's subjectivity is never masked. His moral crusade runs the gamut, from ambushing the National Rifle Association president Charlton Heston to visiting the headquarters of Kmart with survivors of the Columbine shooting, to demand a refund on the bullets that remain lodged in the victim's bodies, which the two killers purchased from the store. Such actions saw results: Kmart would ultimately revise their sales policy for handgun ammunition.

Although the goal of the film was to hold America accountable regarding its stance on gun ownership, the sentiment was lost on some because of Moore's didactic approach. Nevertheless, it is impossible to deny the power of *Bowling for Columbine*'s thesis. Sadly, mass shootings since have shown that Moore's film ultimately failed to do little more than send ripples across the surface of the American psyche. **JT**

Cidade de deus Fernando Meirelles & Kátia Lund, 2002
City of God

Brazil / France (O2 Filmes, Video Filmes, Globo Filmes, Lereby Productions, Lumiere Productions, Studio Canal, Wild Bunch) 130m Color **Language** Portuguese **Producer** Andrea Barata Ribeiro, Mauricio Andrade Ramos **Screenplay** Bráulio Mantovani **Photography** César Charlone **Music** Ed Cortês, Antonio Pinto **Cast** Matheus Nachtergaele, Seu Jorge, Alexandre Rodrigues, Leandro Firmino da Hora, Phellipe Haagensen, Jonathan Haagensen, Douglas Silva, Roberta Rodrigues, Alice Braga, Gero Camilo, Darlan Cunha **Oscar nominations** Fernando Meirelles (director), Bráulio Mantovani (adapted screenplay) César Charlone (cinematography), Daniel Rezende (editing)

ⓘ

The story was adapted from the 1997 novel *City of God*, written by Brazilian author Paulo Lins.

There are films that capture the zeitgeist perfectly; there are films that give a peek at, if not a warning of, the world to come. *City of God* does both with aplomb. With its dizzying pace, fast edits, handheld camera, quick-shift changes in point of view, and obvious nods to Quentin Tarantino, the film is clearly rooted in both the tone and tempo of late twentieth/early twenty-first century American filmmaking.

At its core, *City of God* is about the devolution of a Brazilian housing project that is tracked from its relatively idyllic 1960s beginnings to its 1980s destination as a violent, poverty-ridden domain where each successive generation becomes less connected to the human traits of empathy, conscience, and hope. Based on a true story, *City of God* is narrated by the teenage Buscape (Alexandre Rodrigues), whose gentle disposition prevents him from becoming a gangster, but whose artistic bent leads him to become a celebrated photographer/documentarian of his surroundings. If there's a lead in the ensemble of motley characters (the cast is composed of non-actors, real-life street kids) and intertwined storylines, it's the hyper-violent Lil' Ze (Leandro Firmino da Hora), whose propensity for violence and complete lack of remorse make him a terrifying figure. It is the open-ended final minutes, in which a generation of almost feral homeless kids take over the projects, that makes the film's point crystal clear: This is a horror movie of the first order. **EH**

Hable con ella Pedro Almodóvar, 2002
Talk to Her

Spain (El Deseo S.A., Antena 3 Televisión, Good Machine, Vía Digital) 112m BW / Color **Language** Spanish **Producer** Agustín Almodóvar **Screenplay** Pedro Almodóvar **Photography** Javier Aguirresarobe **Music** Alberto Iglesias **Cast** Javier Cámara, Darío Grandinetti, Leonor Watling, Rosario Flores, Mariola Fuentes, Geraldine Chaplin **Oscar** Pedro Almodóvar (screenplay) **Oscar nomination** Pedro Almodóvar (director)

i

The character of Benigno is based on Pedro Almodóvar's close friend, actor-director Roberto Benigni.

Talk to Her provides a counterpoint to the human warmth and emotional messiness of Pedro Almodóvar's joyously cathartic previous film, *All About My Mother* (1999). Although it retains some of the Day-Glo appearances of the director's earlier, more vibrant work, *Talk to Her* is his most controlled and sustained picture. It is also his most melancholy and disconcerting film, especially in its treatment—or "silencing"—of women. Whereas Almodóvar's films generally embrace the untidiness of life and cinema, *Talk to Her* is elegant and even classical in its structure, with various motifs connecting across it.

Most of Almodóvar's previous films focus on female characters and their complex interactions with each other and the world around them. *Talk to Her* concentrates on its male protagonists and their increasingly insular dialogues with the women "in" their lives—both of whom end up in comas. One of the most remarkable aspects of Almodóvar's film is the way in which he subtly manipulates and directs the audience, shifting emphasis away from the more disturbing connotations of the actions the picture represents. In what may be the boldest move in the director's cinema, he "shows" a rape through a deft parody of a silent surrealist film called *The Shrinking Lover*. The most significant achievement of *Talk to Her* lies in the ways in which it plays with and challenges audience identification. It is a profound meditation on the way in which we talk to and through the people, objects, and texts that express our lives. **AD**

Elephant Gus Van Sant, 2003

U.S. (Fine Line Features) 81m Color
Producer Dany Wolf Screenplay Gus Van Sant Photography Harris Savides Cast Alex Frost, Eric Deulen, John Robinson, Elias McConnel, Jordan Taylor, Carrie Finklea, Nicole George, Brittany Mountain, Alicia Miles, Kristen Hicks, Benny Dixon Cannes Film Festival Gus Van Sant (Palme d'Or, director, Cinema Prize of the French National Education System)

Gus Van Sant's career has run the gamut, from indie features to Oscar winners. After the critical drubbing of his shot-for-shot remake of *Psycho* (1998) and the creative nadir of *Finding Forrester* (2000), Van Sant chose a radical new minimalist direction. Following *Gerry* (2002), he found the perfect balance between subject and style in *Elephant*.

How do you convey the horror that unfolded at the Columbine High School on April 20, 1999? Van Sant's film eschews realism; at least, it refuses a blow-by-blow account of what happened. He also steers clear of specifics by suggesting the setting could be anywhere. The film is glacial in detailing the banality of a normal school day. In one sequence, we follow a student from the playing fields and into a class, to the strains of Beethoven's "Moonlight Sonata." It is beautiful yet unsettling.

Van Sant's camera maintains an emotional distance. Then the killers arrive and the tone shifts toward terror, accentuated by the directorial style. There is no simple answer for their actions, but we are given a sense of how they reached their decision. It makes *Elephant* one of the key American films of the last decade—a coruscating appraisal of the numbing effect of modern life upon a younger generation. **IHS**

2003

Aileen Wuornos: The Life and Death of a Serial Killer Nick Broomfield & Joan Churchill, 2003

G.B. (Lafayette Films) 89m Color
Producer Jo Human Photography Joan Churchill Music Robert Lane Cast Aileen Wuornos, Nick Broomfield

A project that began ten years earlier with *Aileen Wuornos: The Selling of a Serial Killer* (1993), Broomfield and Churchill's follow-up is a powerful and profound statement against the death penalty, and raises disturbing questions about executing the mentally incapacitated.

Broomfield's first film focused on Aileen Wuornos, a prostitute charged with murdering seven of her clients (despite strong evidence to suggest that she acted in self-defense in at least one of the cases). After Aileen was coerced into entering a plea of no-contest by Arlene Pralle (a born-again Christian and her adoptive mother) and Steve Glazer (an inexperienced lawyer in charge of her defense), multiple death sentences soon followed.

Having kept in touch with Wuornos in the intervening years, Broomfield found himself subpoenaed to appear at Aileen's final appeal. Announcing that she had in fact killed all the men in cold blood, Aileen was sped toward her execution. Broomfield's resulting film examines her wretched childhood, which was filled with unrelenting abuse and violence that continued into her years as a hitchhiking prostitute. In an unguarded moment Aileen admits that she acted in self-defense, but wishes to die to escape the tortuous conditions imposed by Death Row.

A resolutely non-sensationalist work, *Aileen Wuornos* calls to account the travesties of the American justice system and provides a sympathetic insight into a deeply troubled soul. **JWo**

Oldeuboi Park Chan-wook, 2003
Oldboy

Mysticism, poetry, school days, and a futuristic bedroom are only some of the wonders found in *Oldboy*. A thriller that hinges on oedipal taboos and blind destiny, hypnotism, and fate, this breakthrough film—part action, part drama, part psychological thriller—has introduced Korean cinema to more viewers than any other film. The story is more direct and compelling than director Park Chan-wook's popular previous film, *Sympathy for Mr. Vengeance* (2002), and features an explosive beginning. A man is imprisoned for fifteen years without an explanation. Upon escape, he must find his kidnapper in only five days.

This violent, elegiac masterpiece is based on a Japanese manga cartoon by Garon Tsuchiya. Actor Min-sik Choi, who performed his own stunts, trained rigorously for his role as hapless kidnap victim Dae-su, a man who tries to escape his windowless prison by ingeniously digging through a skyscraper wall into thin air but is released before he can try his tunnel. Once free, he vows revenge, Monte Cristo–style, against the kidnapper who has effectively robbed him of his daughter, his wife, and his life. Now a ragged fighting machine who resembles a Korean Charles Bronson in a fright wig, Dae-su is befriended by a beautiful sushi chef (Hye-jeong Kang) whom he engages by eating a live squid and then passing out on the counter. Such is the knockdown, drag-out style of *Oldboy*. However complex the tale, it is underpinned by a logic that unfolds clearly, easily incorporating the film's various flashbacks. Progressing at a pace that sometimes leaves one breathless but also leaves room for thought, *Oldboy*'s choreographed fight scenes are both innovative and surprising—and all of the violence serves the plot. Despite its brutality, it is ultimately a black comedy that deftly rolls elements of mob thriller and vengeance mystery into one. After winning the Grand Prix at Cannes in 2004, the director stunned the audience by thanking the cast and crew, then thanking the four squid who gave up their lives for the vivid sushi bar scene. **KK**

South Korea (Egg Films, Show East) 120m Color **Language** Korean **Producer** Dong-ju Kim, Seung-yong Lim **Screenplay** Jo-yun Hwang, Chun-hyeong Lim, Joon-hyung Lim, Chan-wook Park, Garon Tsuchiya **Photography** Jeong-hun Jeong **Music** Yeong-wook Jo, Antonio Vivaldi **Cast** Min-sik Choi, Ji-tae Yu, Hye-jeong Kang, Dae-han Ji, Dal-su Oh, Byeong-ok Kim, Seung-Shin Lee, Jin-seo Yun, Dae-yeon Lee, Kwang-rok Oh, Tae-kyung Oh **Cannes Film Festival** Chan-wook Park (Grand Prize; Golden Palm nomination)

"It's a movie that you feel you're not so much watching on screen as having beamed directly into your skull from some malign, alien planet of horror."

Peter Bradshaw,
The Guardian, 2004

i

The final scenes of the movie (with snow and footsteps) were filmed in New Zealand.

Good Bye Lenin! Wolfgang Becker, 2003

Although it seems like ancient history—the collapse of the Berlin Wall, East and West Germans thronging the streets, and those hilarious Trabants heralding the reunification of Germany—it all happened in only 1989. This coming together of two nations brought many things to the German people, but Wolfgang Becker's *Good Bye Lenin!* showed that among the pain, angst, and unemployment there was also a lot of humor. *Good Bye Lenin!* is set in East Germany, just before the Wall came down.

Alex (Daniel Brühl) is a personable young man whose mother (Katrin Saß) is a politically active fighter for the East German socialist future. When she sees Alex arrested at a riot, she collapses and goes into a coma, which lasts right through until the early days of reunification. Alex is told by his mother's doctor that any shock could kill her, and he reasons that the end of communism and the disappearance of the German Democratic Republic might count as just such a fatal surprise. Alex decides on a simple plan—he will re-create the old East Germany for his mother. In a touching and funny series of moments, Alex manages to convince his bedridden mother that the old order has survived. Pioneer Scouts visit her to sing socialist anthems. Alex becomes an expert at sourcing vile and now-unavailable East German foodstuffs, and, in one of the film's highlights, actually re-creates her favorite news programs.

Good Bye Lenin! also manages levels of poignancy. It doesn't for one moment suggest that East Germany was a nice place to live, but it does show what has been lost in the new capitalist wave, as socialist ideals vanish and are replaced by hard cash and commerce. As the film progresses, a different, equally edgy reunification takes place as Alex's father—once an escapee from the East, now just another German—appears again, and we see that Alex's obsession with protecting his mother from reality is in some ways a way of protecting himself from other, less comfortable realities. **KK**

2003

Germany (X-Filme Creative Pool, WDR, Arte) 121m BW / Color
Language German **Producer** Stefan Arndt, Marcos Kantis, Manuela Stehr
Screenplay Wolfgang Becker, Bernd Lichtenberg **Photography** Martin Kukula
Music Yann Tiersen **Cast** Daniel Brühl, Katrin Saß, Chulpan Khamatova, Maria Simon, Florian Lukas, Alexander Beyer, Burghart Klaußner, Michael Gwisdek, Christine Schorn, Jürgen Holtz, Jochen Stern, Stefan Walz, Eberhard Kirchberg, Hans-Uwe Bauer, Nico Ledermueller, Jelena Kratz
Berlin Film Festival Wolfgang Becker (Blue Angel)

"A remarkable film that makes you laugh and leaves you thinking. It's the work of people who have a great sense of humour."

Philip French,
The Observer, 2003

i

The building in the "Coca Cola news bulletin" was also used by Billy Wilder for *One, Two, Three* (1961).

Osama Siddiq Barmak, 2003

Afghanistan (Hubert Bals Fund, NHK, Barmak Film) 83m Color **Producer** Siddiq Barmak, Julia Fraser, Julie LeBrocquay, Makoto Ueda **Screenplay** Siddiq Barmak **Photography** Ebrahim Ghafori **Music** Mohammad Reza Darvishi **Cast** Marina Golbahari, Arif Herati, Zubaida Sahar, Mohamad Nader Khadjeh, Mohamad Haref Harati **Cannes Film Festival** Siddiq Barmak (AFCAE Award, Cannes Junior Award)

A chilling account of life for a young girl under the Taliban's rule in Afghanistan, *Osama* features a cast of local non-actors and was shot in Kabul shortly after the arrival of American and allied troops in June 2002. A family of women whose men have all been killed in conflicts decide to dress up a young girl as a boy, in order for her to make a living. Only the milkman who employs her and the girl's friend, who names her Osama, know her real identity. Things become difficult when all young boys are recruited for military training. Part of their routine involves learning how to conduct ablutions. Osama's teacher becomes suspicious of her reserve, which is her undoing. Though escaping execution, her hellish fate is arguably worse, imposed by an oppressive, violently misogynistic regime.

One of the first films to be made in Afghanistan following the fall of the Taliban, *Osama* is an important and disturbing work. The film's end is a damning indictment of a society in which women were subjugated to a brutalized form of domestic slavery. The rights and wrongs over the response of America and its supporters to the September 11, 2001 attacks are still being debated, but, as this film shows, there is no doubt that the Taliban should have been removed from power. **IHS**

Gegen die Wand Fatih Akin, 2004
Head-On

Germany / Turkey (Bavaria Film International, Corazón International, Norddeutscher Rundfunk (NDR), Panfilm, Wüste Filmproduktion) 121m Color **Language** German / Turkish / English **Producer** Andreas Schreitmüller, Stefan Schubert, Ralph Schwingel **Screenplay** Fatih Akin **Photography** Rainer Klausmann **Music** Alexander Hacke, Maceo Parker **Cast** Birol Ünel, Sibel Kekilli, Catrin Striebeck, Meltem Cumbul, Zarah McKenzie, Stefan Gebelhoff **Berlin Film Festival** Fatih Akin (Golden Berlin Bear and FIPRESCI Prize)

It has been called, a little crudely, the "nuts in love" genre: two mentally disabled, drug-addicted, or alcoholic people whose sudden, explosive encounter and subsequent relationship adds up to a true tale of surrealist-style amour fou. It is a very modern genre, one that passes through Robert Rossen's *Lilith* (1964) and the Australian film *Angel Baby* (1995)—but Fatih Akin's *Head-On* stirs a particularly potent brew by adding extra ingredients to the formula. First, the union starts on a decidedly mock, non-fou note, as a marriage of convenience between two people on the bottom rung of society: Cahit (Birol Ünel) has smashed his car; Sibel (Sibel Kekilli) has slashed her wrists. Yet, as Sibel asserts her desires by prowling the local clubs and bars, Cahit becomes increasingly jealous and violent—and then love, in however perverse or clumsy a way, asserts itself. Second, Akin complicates everything by making this the story of Turkish immigrants in Germany, suffering racism and abuse in the course of their negotiation of two very different cultures.

Yet *Head-On* is not, in any strict sense, a "social realist" film. A nervy, unsettling, sometimes bleak drama of two outsiders (vividly played, with unwavering intensity and conviction, by the two leads), the film in fact continues a vital strand of provocative, post-punk creativity in contemporary European cinema—a vitality from which even Akin's subsequent films have shied away. **AM**

Le conseguenze dell'amore Paolo Sorrentino, 2004
The Consequences of Love

Italy (Lafayette Films) 104m Color
Producer Domenico Procacci,
Nicola Giuliano, Francesca Cima, Angelo
Curti Screenplay Paolo Sorrentino
Photography Luca Bigazzi Music Pasquale
Catalano Cast Toni Servillo, Olivia Magnani,
Adriano Giannini, Raffaele Pisu, Angela
Goodwin, Diego Ribon, Giselda Volodi,
Giovanni Vettorazzo.

Paolo Sorrentino's breakthrough feature, *The Consequences of Love*, was inspired by the ritualistic behavior of a businessman encountered by the director while visiting Sao Paolo. It was also influenced by his desire to show a different perspective of the mafia, representing its ferocity as well as its mechanisms and rules. It established Sorrentino as a supreme visual stylist and a significant voice in contemporary European cinema.

A former stockbroker from Southern Italy, Titta di Girolamo (Toni Servillo) resides in an anonymous hotel in a Swiss–Italian town. He seems to be a man without identity and with little to do, spending his time smoking and coldly observing the hotel's denizens, particularly the beautiful barmaid Sofia (Olivia Magnani). Girolamo once lost money owned by the mafia on the stock market and has been punished in a gruesome way: He is to deliver the mafia's money to the bank once a week and is allowed no life for himself. But as he becomes growingly aware of Sofia's presence, his neatly organized world turns upside down.

A quietly gripping psychological thriller, *Consequences* also offers a potent mediation on the discovery of love. Toni Servillo gives a masterly performance, and Luca Bigazzi's crisply composed cinematography vividly maps out the empty spaces of Girolamo's self-enclosed world. The inventive use of music is highly atmospheric, suggesting the welter of emotion that lurks beneath Girolamo's icy surface. **JWo**

i

Consequences won five David di Donatello awards, including Best Film, Best Director, and Best Actor.

Moolaadé Ousmane Sembene, 2004

Senegal (Filmi Doomireew) 119m Color
Producer Ousmane Sembene, Thierry
Lenouvel Screenplay Ousmane Sembene
Photography Dominique Gentil
Music Boncana Maiga Cast Fatoumata
Coulibaly, Maimouna Hélène Diarra,
Salimata Traoré, Dominique Zeïda, Mah
Compraoré, Aminata Dao, Rasmane
Ouedraogo, Ousmane Konaté,
Bakaramoto Sanogo

Senegalese-born director Ousmane Sembene never shrank from tackling taboos—and in his final film, *Moolaadé*, he took on one of the most sensitive: the widely practiced custom of female genital mutilation.

Sembene's films are subtle and ambivalent, acknowledging the value of traditions and regretting their erosion while still exposing the system of oppression and injustice they often upheld. His heroine, the formidable Mama Collé (Fatoumata Coulibaly), can turn tradition to her own ends. When four village girls who have fled the cutting ceremony come begging for refuge, she grants them impregnable sanctuary simply by stringing a cord across the entrance to her courtyard. This flimsy barrier is the *moolaadé* (protection) of the title.

Solemnity rarely taints Sembene's films; his anger and indignation are tempered by his warmth, humor, and generosity of spirit. The opening of *Moolaadé* shows his affectionate, intimate view of African village life at its warmest, offering a useful corrective to Western ideas of Africa as a starved, helpless continent, devoid of dignity and self-sufficiency. The film's climax is perhaps its weakest point, but the sheer liberating exhilaration of Sembene's ending is all but impossible to resist. **PK**

Der Untergang Oliver Hirschbiegel, 2004
Downfall

Germany / Italy / Austria (Constantin) 156m
Color Language German Producer Bernd
Eichinger Screenplay Bernd Eichinger
Photography Rainer Klausmann
Music Stephan Zacharias Cast Bruno Ganz,
Alexandra Maria Lara, Corinna Harfouch,
Ulrich Matthes, Juliane Köhler, Heino Ferch
Oscar nomination Germany (best
foreign language film)

A fair amount of critical hand-wringing attended the American opening of *Downfall*, the first German movie to portray Adolf Hitler in a conventional narrative. There was concern that the film—a fast-paced, doggedly straightforward account of the final days of Hitler (Bruno Ganz) and his inner circle—humanizes the Third Reich and its delusional draftsmen and thereby plays down their ghastly deeds. Hitler, Eva Braun (Juliane Köhler), Joseph Goebbels (Ulrich Matthes), and the rest are assuredly human here; but the point is that the truly monstrous usually are. And so we are left with an uncomfortable feeling of familiarity as we watch the various factions of the winding-down Nazi machine work utterly at cross-purposes, as the psychopath-romantic who was once at its hub raves, cajoles, rationalizes, and bemoans the failure of his sci-fi utopia—while disavowing his part in the annihilation of a culture.

This disorienting matter-of-factness is the key to *Downfall*'s brilliance. Hitler is routinely pushed to the edge of the frame by Oliver Hirschbiegel's camera and Ganz's grandly withered performance. Meanwhile, other modes of behavior are allowed to surface via the surrounding characters: compassion, pity, bravery, avarice, careerism, and, in the case of the German people Hitler despises, bewildering devotion. This fascinating, subtly radical exegesis of how empires crumble from within reveals the many ways in which they had it coming. **MH**

Tsotsi Gavin Hood, 2005

After several years of promise, South African cinema seemed poised for a breakthrough. *Tsotsi* duly became the country's first offering to win an Academy Award for Foreign Language Film. As often is the case with emergent cinemas, it plucks its story from the city streets and tells it in a realist style with non-professional or untried actors. The Tsotsi of the title (Presley Chweneyagae), is a small-time hoodlum who, with three hangers-on, commits the mugging of a middle-aged businessman on a train. In the course of the robbery, he stabs and kills the man. Back in the shantytown where they live, one of the gang is overcome with remorse—but Tsotsi despises him for his weakness and gives him a beating. Now working on his own, he hijacks the car of a wealthy woman, wounding her in the process. Then, having made his escape, Tsotsi discovers the woman's baby in the back of the car.

Tsotsi's instinct is to abandon the child, but something prevents him from doing so. He takes it back to his shack and tries to feed and care for it. But the child needs milk, and so Tsotsi forces a young single mother in a neighboring shack to breast-feed it. Miriam (Terry Pheto) cares for the child and tries to persuade Tsotsi to return it to its mother. At last, having failed to defend himself to Miriam, Tsotsi is forced to confront the nature of his life and the direction it is taking.

Chweneyagae and Pheto give remarkable performances in a film that powerfully conveys the brutality and squalor of the urban slums of Johannesburg—while maintaining a strong belief in the human spirit, which resists being crushed under the oppressive weight of poverty. If at times the direction seems overly theatrical—with heavy pauses while we absorb the significance of a scene—this is a small price to pay for the film's powerful insights. **EB**

G.B. / South Africa (IDC of S.A., NFVF of S.A., Moviworld, U.K. Film and TV) 94m Color **Language** Zulu / Xhosa / Afrikaans **Producer** Peter Fudakowski **Screenplay** Gavin Hood, from the novel *Tsotsi* by Athol Fugard **Photography** Lance Gewer **Music** Paul Hepker, Mark Kilian **Cast** Presley Chweneyagae, Mothusi Magano, Israel Makoe, Terry Pheto, Percy Matsemela, Jerry Mofokeng, Benny Moshe, Owen Sejake, Zola **Oscar** South Africa (best foreign language film)

"One of the privileges of being a writer is to poke your nose around and learn about worlds you don't know."

Gavin Hood, 2006

i

Of South Africa's various languages, Hood chose Tsotsi-Taal—"which," he reported, "means 'gangster speak.'"

Brokeback Mountain Ang Lee, 2005

Ang Lee's *Brokeback Mountain* got a lot of attention for being one of the first gay Westerns to hit mainstream theaters. In fact, Andy Warhol had hit the mark more than three decades earlier with his pioneering *Lonesome Cowboys* (1969), which was shot on location at Old Tucson Studios in Arizona. But while Warhol's film was a genre spoof, Lee's work is deadly serious, and directed with an air of precision and solid craftsmanship that harks back to the Westerns of Budd Boetticher, John Ford, and Howard Hawks.

Working from a screenplay by Larry McMurtry and Diana Ossana, Lee's film tells the tale of Ennis Del Mar (Heath Ledger) and Jack Twist (Jake Gyllenhaal). While working on a lonesome job watching sheep in the back country of Wyoming in the summer of 1963, they meet and fall in love. At first, the two are simply buddies at home on the range—but, as the summer wears on, their relationship deepens into what will become a lifelong love affair; albeit one that is resolutely forbidden by contemporary society, and mediated by failed marriages that neither man really cares about. While Gyllenhaal does excellent work in his role, Ledger is a revelation. Taciturn, shy, and keeping his own counsel, he hides his emotions behind a rough exterior of macho horseplay. His untimely death in 2008 at the age of twenty-eight lends an even greater poignancy to his performance. Lee's camerawork brings out the beauty and the harshness of the landscape, and the supporting cast—including Randy Quaid, Anne Hathaway, and Michelle Williams—back up the two leads with impeccably timed performances.

"Blending the macho western genre, western life, with a gay love story... that's hard to do," observed Ang Lee. Nonetheless, *Brokeback Mountain* was an instant classic, that altered the conventions of the Western to tell a wholly convincing love story that resonated in the mind long after the last image had faded. And one that is heartbreaking, honest, and refreshingly matter-of-fact about its subject matter. **WWD**

U.S. (Alberta, Focus Features, Good Machine, Paramount, River Road, This Is That Productions) 134m Color **Producer** Diana Ossana, James Schamus **Screenplay** Larry McMurtry and Diana Ossana, from a short story by Annie Proulx **Photography** Rodrigo Prieto **Music** Gustavo Santaolalla **Cast** Heath Ledger, Jake Gyllenhaal, Randy Quaid, Anne Hathaway, Michelle Williams, Valerie Planche, Graham Beckel, David Harbour, Kate Mara, Roberta Maxwell, Peter McRobbie, Anna Faris, Linda Cardellini, Scott Michael Campbell, David Trimble **Oscar** Ang Lee (director), Gustavo Santaolalla (music), Larry McMurtry, Diana Ossana (screenplay) **Oscar nominations** Rodrigo Prieto (cinematography), Diana Ossana, James Schamus (best picture), Heath Ledger (actor), Jake Gyllenhaal (actor in support role), Michelle Williams (actress in support role)

"In this year, 2005, I can't understand why anyone ... would even question any actor taking any gay role."

Heath Ledger, 2005

ℹ️

Gus Van Sant had attempted to make the film five years previously. "I dropped the ball," he admitted.

El laberinto del fauno Guillermo del Toro, 2006
Pan's Labyrinth

Mexico / Spain / U.S. (Warner Bros., Tequila Gang, Esperanto Filmoj, Estudios Picasso, OMM, Sententia, Telecinco) 112m Color **Language** Spanish **Producer** Álvaro Augustín, Alfonso Cuarón, Bertha Navarro, Guillermo del Toro, Frida Torresblanco **Screenplay** Guillermo del Toro **Photography** Guillermo Navarro **Music** Javier Navarrete **Cast** Álex Angulo, Ivana Baquero, Roger Casamajor, Ariadna Gil, Doug Jones, Sergi López, César Vea, Maribel Verdú **Oscars** Guillermo Navarro (cinematography), Eugenio Caballero, Pilar Revuelta (art direction), David Martí, Montse Ribé (makeup)

i

This was American actor Doug Jones's third del Toro movie, after 1997's *Mimic* and 2004's *Hellboy*.

Pan's Labyrinth is something of a summative film from Mexican director Guillermo del Toro. Having worked on projects that offered a high level of special effects, such as *Hellboy* (2004), as well as those that created an unnervingly otherworldly atmosphere (for example, 2001's *The Devil's Backbone*), here, in perhaps his most mature picture, the director brings the two strands together. The result is a film that is both eerie and built around effects technology (hence its three visual-related Oscars).

Set in 1944, *Pan's Labyrinth* tells the story of Ofelia, a young girl who discovers a fantastical world of woodland creatures when her mother takes her to northern Spain to join her stepfather, a brutish and bitter member of General Franco's Fascist army. Del Toro gathers together a roster of top-line Spanish actors, including Sergi López, Ariadna Gil, and Maribel Verdú, alongside Ivana Baquero as the young girl.

Set against a backdrop of post–civil war Spain, the film's startling beauty and the strength of its performances offer much to admire. "Shooting *Pan's Labyrinth* was very painful," del Toro told *Sight & Sound*, "but it also became a war about me not compromising. I gave back my entire salary in order to get the film made the way I wanted it." If the story fails to fully unite the reality and fantasy elements—*Pan's Labyrinth* remains two outstanding halves rather than one spectacular whole—this does not make del Toro's accomplishment any less extraordinary. **AW**

Das Leben der Anderen
The Lives of Others
Florian Henckel von Donnersmarck, 2006

Germany (Bayerischer Rundfunk, Creado Film, Wiedemann & Berg, Arte) 137m Color **Language** German **Producer** Quirin Berg, Max Wiedemann **Screenplay** Florian Henckel von Donnersmarck **Photography** Hagen Bogdanski **Music** Stéphane Moucha, Gabriel Yared **Cast** Hans-Uwe Bauer, Matthias Brenner, Martina Gedeck, Charly Hübner, Volkmar Kleinert, Sebastian Koch, Ulrich Mühe, Ulrich Tukur, Thomas Thieme **Oscar** Germany (best foreign language film)

2007

By turns horrifying and humorous, *The Lives of Others* is debut director von Donnersmarck's story of the East German government's obsession with tracking the populace's every move.

It's 1984 and "glasnost is nowhere in sight" as Stasi hardliner Captain Gerd Wiesler (Ulrich Mühe) decides to keep playwright Georg Dreyman (Sebastian Koch) under surveillance. When a bug planted in his Berlin apartment reveals the writer genuinely believes in the socialist state, Wiesler grows fascinated by Dreyman's life with his lover Christa-Maria (Martina Gedeck). Things are further complicated when his superior— culture minister Hempf (Thomas Thieme)—fancies Christa-Maria for himself and instructs Wiesler to clear the way by framing Dreyman. Pushed out of the comfort zone of government-sanctioned spying, Wiesler is shunted in directions with which he is profoundly unfamiliar.

The callousness of Cold War East Germany is chillingly conveyed, but when events threaten to grow overwhelmingly dark, von Donnersmarck reins back with a dose of black humor. A Kafkaesque spin on Francis Ford Coppola's *The Conversation* (1974), this was a deserved Oscar winner. **TE**

Paranormal Activity Oren Peli, 2007

U.S. (Blumhouse Productions) 86m Color **Producer** Steven Jay Schneider, Amir Zbeba, Jason Blun, Oren Peli **Screenplay** Oren Peli **Photography** Oren Peli **Cast** Katie Featherston, Micah Sloat, Mark Fredrichs, Amber Armstrong, Ashley Palmer

Paranormal Activity is proof positive that you do not need a huge budget to make a terrifying and wildly profitable film (to date, it is the most profitable movie of all time). You just need someone with true imagination. That someone is Oren Peli, a first-time filmmaker who shot the film in his own home for around $15,000.

The story is simple yet riveting. Young couple Katie (Katie Featherston) and Micah (Micah Sloat) realize something weird is happening in their new home and set up a camera to record what happens while they sleep. For the first few nights, the camera records almost nothing: a door moves, the blankets flutter. We are lulled into a false sense of security, so that when chandeliers start swinging and Ouija boards ignite, the impact is genuinely shocking. The night-vision scope through which most of the movie is seen adds an interesting depth. With no color to distract, our eyes are drawn immediately to even the slightest movement.

Peli submitted *Paranormal Activity* to Screamfest 2007, at Mann's Chinese Theater in Hollywood. It was the hit of the festival, and bloggers immediately began writing about it. It was bought by Dreamworks/ Paramount, originally with the intention of turning it into a big-budget movie. The studio realized, however, that a Hollywood movie would never be able to beat the suspense of the film Peli had made at home. Anybody who likes being scared silly will love *Paranormal Activity*. **CP**

There Will Be Blood Paul Thomas Anderson, 2007

U.S. (Ghoulardi Film Company, Paramount Vantage, Miramax Films) 158m Color **Producer** Paul Thomas Anderson, JoAnne Sellar, Daniel Lupi **Screenplay** Paul Thomas Anderson, from the novel *Oil!* by Upton Sinclair **Photography** Robert Elswit **Music** Jonny Greenwood **Cast** Daniel Day-Lewis, Paul Dano, Kevin J. O'Connor, Kevin Breznahan **Oscars** Daniel Day-Lewis (actor), Robert Elswit (cinematography) **Oscar nominations** Daniel Lupi, JoAnne Sellar, Paul Thomas Anderson (best picture), Paul Thomas Anderson (director), Paul Thomas Anderson (adapted screenplay), Jack Fisk, Jim Erickson (art direction), Dylan Tichenor (editing), Matthew Wood, Christopher Scarabosio (sound editing)

Paul Thomas Anderson grew up on the fringes of show business and Hollywood. *There Will Be Blood*, his excoriating study of greed—and the both constructive and destructive powers of competitiveness and ambition   is a stunning achievement by the still-young writer-director.

Using Upton Sinclair's satirical 1927 novel *Oil!* as a jumping-off point, Anderson creates a dark tale of a prospector seemingly without a single redemptive characteristic. Concentrating on long, almost silent passages and huge panoramas, *There Will Be Blood* delves to the painful depths of a man who, by many measures, would have been considered both a success and a genius, but in Anderson's hands is a charismatic sociopath.

The notoriously selective and methodical Daniel Day-Lewis gives an indelible performance as antihero Daniel Plainview—who turns nature's resources into his own bounty, regardless of the cost to him and the world. The picture provided 2007 audiences with a painfully resonant condemnation of so much that was then hurting America and the world: oil-based greed and violence, the madness behind such aggression, the corruption of religious fervor, the paranoia behind much foreign policy, and the betrayal of our children by capitalism. But instead of couching these themes in the overt terms of the "Iraq War pictures" of the time, Anderson makes an intimate yet epic period piece set around another boom-or-bust era, and evokes the universal truths behind his story. **JP**

ℹ

Anderson wrote the movie for Day-Lewis after learning the actor had liked his *Punch-Drunk Love* (2002).

909

The Hurt Locker Kathryn Bigelow, 2008

The Hurt Locker is Kathryn Bigelow's greatest film yet. Like the following year's *District 9, Inglourious Basterds*, and *Avatar* (by Bigelow's ex-husband and ex-collaborator James Cameron), it taps back into the sentiment of the "good war" that audiences clearly craved after an onslaught of dreary films such as *Rendition* (2007), *Stop Loss* (2008), and *Lions for Lambs* (2007): "unjustified war" stories that had kept theaters empty for years. In 2010, Bigelow made history as the first female director ever to win an Oscar—only three female directors had previously been nominated.

Her fascination with violence and our relationships to it (audience and characters alike) here gets its most distilled and most visceral treatment. Action in movies excites, she has always proclaimed, and the lives of the violent, who choose to live with danger, are the most worthy of her attention. With the steady hand of screenwriter and ex-journalist Mark Boal, she creates almost unbearable suspense, with Jeremy Renner in an Oscar-nominated turn as Staff Sergeant William James.

Set during the Iraq War, *The Hurt Locker* skillfully pulls us into the chaos of an elite U.S. bomb deactivation unit by concentrating on authenticity and character, while avoiding politics and polemics. Through escalating set pieces and dollops of personal information, Bigelow presents not the nature of war, but rather the nature of the warrior.

The soldiers' compulsions for danger, heroics, mental and physical challenge, and glory are what make them seem damaged in peacetime, but it is these very addictions that fill them with a terrible absoluteness during conflict. War may be hell, but it's the closest thing to heaven for William James. Renner is ably assisted by Anthony Mackie as J. T. Sanborn, Brian Geraghty as Owen Eldridge, and Guy Pearce as Matt Thompson.

The pleasure Renner's character gives us by challenging himself through impossible situations as the archetypal "movie hero" seems almost addictive by the fade-out. We come to see, through vicarious experience and calibrated observation, how heroism and madness can be one and the same, and to remember—thanks to Kathryn Bigelow— just how much fun men of danger are in the movies. **JP**

U.S. (Voltage Pictures, Grosvenor Park Media, FCEF, First Light Production, Kingsgate Films) 131m Color **Producer** Kathryn Bigelow, Mark Boal, Nicolas Chartier, Greg Shapiro **Screenplay** Mark Boal **Photography** Barry Ackroyd **Music** Marco Beltrami, Buck Sanders **Cast** Jeremy Renner, Anthony Mackie, Brian Geraghty, Guy Pearce, Ralph Fiennes, David Morse, Evangeline Lilly, Christian Camargo, Suhail Aldabbahc, Christopher Sayegh, Nabil Koni, Sam Spruell, Sam Redford, Feisal Sadoun, Barrie Rice, Imad Dadudi **Oscars** Kathryn Bigelow (director), Kathryn Bigelow, Mark Boal, Nicholas Chartier, Greg Shapiro (best picture), Mark Boal (screenplay), Bob Murawski, Chris Ennis (editing), Paul N. J. Ottosson, Ray Beckett (sound), Paul N. J. Ottosson (sound editing) **Oscar nominations** Jeremy Renner (actor), Barry Ackroyd (cinematography), Marco Beltrami, Buck Sanders (music)

"I'd like to dedicate this [Oscar] to the women and men in the military who risk their lives on a daily basis."

Kathryn Bigelow, 2010

i

The film was shot in and around Amman in Jordan, owing to the risk of snipers across the border in Iraq.

Slumdog Millionaire

Danny Boyle & Loveleen Tandan (co-director, India), 2008

G.B. / U.S. (Celador Films)
85m Color **Language** English /
Hindi **Producer** Christian Colson
Screenplay Simon Beaufoy, from the
novel *Q and A* by Vikas Swarup
Photography Anthony Dod Mantle
Music A.R. Rahman **Cast** Dev Patel, Freida
Pinto, Anil Kapoor, Irrfan Khan, Ayush
Mahesh Khedekar, Tanay Chheda, Saurabh
Shukla, Mahesh Manjrekar **Oscars** Christian
Colson (best picture), Danny Boyle (director),
Anthony Dod Mantle (cinematography),
Chris Dickens (editing), A.R. Rahman (music),
A.R. Rahman, Gulzar (song), Ian Tapp, Richard
Pryke, Resul Pookutty (sound), Simon
Beaufoy (screenplay) **Oscar nominations**
A.R. Rahman, Maya Arulpragasam (song),
Tom Sayers, Glenn Freemantle
(sound editing)

𝒊

Danny Boyle has described *Who
Wants to Be a Millionaire* as both
"compulsive viewing" and "vile."

Director Danny Boyle and co-director Loveleen Tandan fuse Bollywood with Hollywood in their brutal, heartbreaking, and wildly colorful movie. Written by Simon Beaufoy (*The Full Monty* [1997]) and based on the Indian novel *Q and A* by Vikas Swarup, this exciting tale brings to the screen the universals of all human life: love, success, peace, and truth.

Filmed in Mumbai, it tells of two brothers who defy the worst odds to emerge as survivors: Jamal Malik (Dev Patel) becomes a contestant in India's version of the TV game show *Who Wants to Be a Millionaire*, while Salim (Madhur Mittal) attains status as a criminal. The pair—orphans working for a Fagin-like character who creates blind, singing beggars from healthy, sighted children—befriend young Latika (Freida Pinto). As she matures into a beautiful woman, she becomes a bone to pick over, splintering the brothers' loyalty to each other.

The story arc is shaped by Jamal answering the toughest questions of *Millionaire*'s antagonistic host. The reason he knows this information forms the spine of the story and a history of his remarkable life. Just as he gets to his final question, though, Jamal is accused of cheating.

With impressive visuals and direction, *Slumdog Millionaire*'s Western narrative and Indian soul mesh to tell a story worthy of all its many awards. The Bollywood dance routine finale should not be missed. **KK**

The Dark Knight Christopher Nolan, 2008

U.S. (Warner Bros.) 152m Color
Producer Christopher Nolan, Charles Roven,
Emma Thomas **Screenplay** Christopher
Nolan, Jonathan Nolan, David S. Goyer
Photography Wally Pfister **Music** Hans
Zimmer, James Newton Howard
Cast Christian Bale, Michael Caine, Heath
Ledger, Gary Oldman, Aaron Eckhart,
Maggie Gyllenhaal, Morgan Freeman
Oscars Heath Ledger (actor in support
role), Richard King (sound editing)
Oscar nominations Nathan Crowley,
Peter Lando (art direction), Wally Pfister
(cinematography), Lee Smith (editing), John
Caglione, Jr., Conor O'Sullivan (makeup),
Lora Hirschberg, Gary Rizzo, Ed Novick
(sound), Nick Davis, Chris Corbould, Timothy
Webber, Paul J. Franklin (visual effects)

i

Asked what distinguished Nolan
from other directors, Heath Ledger
said, "He drinks a lot more tea."

A Hollywood blockbuster long and dark, *The Dark Knight* is Christopher Nolan's sequel to his *Batman Begins* (2005). Highly anticipated for its script (co-written by Nolan and his brother), its high-profile cast, and its tone, this is—with all due respect to the first and third of the director's trilogy—the most arresting and alarming installment of the Batman oeuvre, but also the richest in character and emotion.

Christian Bale returns as the millionaire Bruce Wayne/superhero Batman who finds himself trapped—with heroic District Attorney Harvey Dent (Aaron Eckhart), his assistant Rachel Dawes (Maggie Gyllenhaal), and Commissioner Gordon (Gary Oldman)—in the diabolical hands of the Joker (Heath Ledger). As the highly disturbed and disturbing villain, Ledger gives an indelible performance that richly merits his posthumous Oscar. Michael Caine and Morgan Freeman appear as Alfred and Lucius Fox, respectively, two heralds of an old world where evil knew its place.

Filmed primarily in a darkly gleaming Chicago, the story pivots on the escalation of evil and how good can be tainted in its attempts to triumph. Particularly shocking is the Joker's setup of putting people on two ships, each with a detonator for the other, in the hopes of a massacre.

Emotionally and morally complicated, *The Dark Knight* sees Batman facing the problem he has always battled: Can a vigilante be ethically sound? The answers are ambiguous but the film is astonishing. **KK**

Låt den rätte komma in Tomas Alfredson, 2008
Let the Right One In

Sweden (EFTI, Sandrew Metronome, Filmpool Nord, SVT, WAG, Canal+, The Chimney Pot, Fido Film AB, Ljudligan) 115m Color **Language** Swedish **Producer** Carl Molinder, John Nordling **Screenplay** John Ajvide Lindqvist, from his novel **Photography** Hoyte Von Hoytema **Music** Johan Söderqvist **Cast** Kåre Hedebrant, Lina Leandersson, Per Ragnar, Henrik Dahl, Karin Bergquist, Peter Carlberg, Ika Nord, Mikael Rahm

At face value, this Swedish vampire film follows the trend of prudish predators: the vampire as your abstaining friend. Any languishing for sex is thoroughly suppressed. Of course, it helps that the protagonists—blond and angelic Oskar (Kåre Hedebrant) and the enigmatic Eli (Lina Leandersson)—are (or seem to be) children. Oskar is bullied by his classmates and, though he dreams of getting even, he remains passive. Eli teaches him to stand up for himself. "Be me a little," she tells him. He does, but his actions come back with a vengeance in a bloodbath climax.

Throughout the film, pale white palettes abound, and punctured spots of red intervene in this snowy, sleepy, and dreamy design. Set in the early 1980s, there is no social media, no frantic chatter to relieve the sense of isolation. Into this constellation comes the dark, brooding Eli; she is a guest, but it is not clear how welcome she is.

The title refers to the fact that, according to folklore, vampires must be invited in by their victims. Oskar initially refuses; only after Eli almost bleeds to death from his rudeness does he give in. *Let the Right One In* thus asks the uncomfortable question whether hospitality means that one has to accept the bad with the good. A pointed commentary on immigration, perhaps; an enchanting fairytale, for sure. **EM**

2009

District 9 Neill Blomkamp, 2009

U.S. / New Zealand / Canada / South Africa (TriStar Pictures, Block / Hanson, WingNut Films) 112m Color **Language** English / Nyanja / Afrikaans / Zulu / Xhosa / Sotho **Producer** Peter Jackson, Carolynne Cunningham **Screenplay** Neill Blomkamp, Terri Tatchell **Photography** Trent Opaloch **Music** Clinton Shorter **Cast** Sharlto Copley, Jason Cope, David James, Eugene Khumbanyiwa, Mandla Gaduka, Vanessa Haywood, Louis Minnaar, John Sumner **Oscar nominations** Julian Clarke (editing), Peter Jackson, Carolynne Cunningham (best picture), Neill Blomkamp, Terri Tatchell (screenplay), Dan Kaufman, Peter Muyzers, Robert Habros, Matt Aitken (visual effects)

This acclaimed science-fiction invasion thriller was inspired by events that took place in District Six, Cape Town, during apartheid. Centering on themes of xenophobia and segregation, it tells of a spaceship that stalls over South Africa. When a group ventures up, they find hundreds of sick and malnourished aliens, or "Prawns." Earth steps in to help and places the aliens in a shantytown called District 9, forbidding them from mixing with the general populace. Two decades later, overpopulation has become a concern for the government. A plan to relocate some of the Prawns is put in place, led by kindhearted Wikus Van de Merwe (Sharlto Copley). Documentary style filmmaking gives the movie an air of authenticity that helps the audience connect on a human level with the plight of the alien population. As our hero Wikus is infected with a disease and slowly starts to turn alien himself, our empathy grows.

District 9 is a smart political allegory that puts emotion, humor, and incredible visuals to fluid and accomplished use. The special effects of the Prawns mark one of the most seamless examples of CGI thus far. Director Neill Blomkamp dictated that the species had to be insectlike but also bipedal, saying, "Unfortunately, they had to be human-esque because our psychology doesn't allow us to really empathize with something unless it has a face and an anthropomorphic shape." **SJS**

Avatar James Cameron, 2009

U.S. / G.B. (Twentieth Century-Fox Film Corporation, Dune Entertainment, Giant Studios, Ingenious Film Partners, Lightstorm Entertainment) 162m Color **Producer** James Cameron, Jon Landau, Colin Wilson, Laeta Kalogridis, Janace Tashjian **Screenplay** James Cameron **Photography** Mauro Fiore **Music** James Horner **Cast** Sam Worthington, Zoe Saldana, Sigourney Weaver, Stephen Lang, Joel Moore, Giovanni Ribisi, Michelle Rodriguez, Laz Alonso **Oscars** Rick Carter, Robert Stromberg, Kim Sinclair (art direction), Mauro Fiore (cinematography), Joe Letteri, Stephen Rosenbaum, Richard Baneham, Andy Jones (visual effects) **Oscar nominations** James Cameron, Jon Landau (best picture), James Cameron (director), James Horner (music)

𝑖

Cameron hesitated to cast Sigourney Weaver, owing to her role in his other extraterrestrial military epic, *Aliens*.

The culmination of a master filmmaker's career, *Avatar* marks a decade's worth of work and millions of dollars of investment. Though no *Gone with the Wind* in complexity of character or event, it is of the same monumental ambition and singularity of vision. Only D. W. Griffith, Cecil B. DeMille, George Lucas, and Steven Spielberg attained such heights of technical achievement in stories of such grand scope while still reaping box-office success. Like these greats, James Cameron raises the bar.

The story has been told many times, in films like *Dances with Wolves* (1990) and *The Thin Red Line* (1998), but it's still a classic. A soldier tries to find inner peace during wartime by going native, finding a more grounded, loving existence among the peoples he has been taught are his enemy. Inevitably, the cultures clash, and he finds himself in the middle, fighting for the side of right and love against his former allies.

Using state-of-the-art technologies, Jake Sully (Sam Worthington) is able to run free in his "avatar," a genetically engineered body that allows him to survive in the hostile atmosphere of the moon Pandora. Similarly, Cameron uses state-of-the-art film techniques to submerge us in the flora and fauna of a new world; much as *King Kong* did in 1933, *Star Wars* did in 1977, and *Jurassic Park* did in 1993. Like those films, *Avatar*—hailed as a game changer, a masterwork, and a box-office record breaker—will someday, no doubt, look antiquated but, hopefully, remain beloved. **JP**

Nostalgia de la luz Patricio Guzmán, 2010
Nostalgia for the Light

Chile (Atacamer Productions, Blinker Filmproduction, Westdeutscher Rundfunk) 90m Color Producer Jutta Krug, Renate Sachse Photography Katell Djian Music Miguel Miranda José Miguel Tobar

On the high plains of the Atacama Desert, as astronomers look to the skies in the hope of mapping distant galaxies, relatives of the victims of a brutal dictatorship search through the earth in the hope of uncovering the remains of loved ones. In his youth Patricio Guzmán wanted to be an astronomer, but when General Augusto Pinochet toppled the democratically-elected Allende government in 1973, he turned to filmmaking. The result has been a career dedicated to recording both the atrocities committed by Pinochet against all who opposed him and the years since, as a nation has attempted to come to terms with its past.

Guzmán's film contemplates a world in which science has mapped so much of the universe yet still bears witness to our unbridled capacity for cruelty. He weaves a fascinating narrative out of the interplay between science and history. A political prisoner describes his escape from a concentration camp and out of the Atacama Desert, using the stars as a compass. And in the film's most powerful scene, a woman gazes at a collection of observatories and wonders if such technology would be better employed looking into the ground and finding the remains of her son. Guzmán's film celebrates mankind's scientific advances, but suggests that such progression is redundant if we fail in our humanity. **IHS**

2010

Black Swan Darren Aronofsky, 2010

U.S. (Fox Searchlight Pictures, Protozoa Pictures, Phoenix Pictures, Cross Creek Pictures) 108m Color Language English / French Producer Scott Franklin, Mike Medavoy, Arnold Messer, Brian Oliver Screenplay Mark Heyman, Andres Heinz, John McLaughlin Photography Matthew Libatique Music Clint Mansell Cast Natalie Portman, Vincent Cassel, Mila Kunis, Barbara Hershey, Winona Ryder, Benjamin Millepied, Ksenia Solo, Kristina Anapau, Janet Montgomery, Sebastian Stan, Toby Hemingway, Sergio Torrado Oscar Natalie Portman (actress) Oscar nominations Darren Aronofsky (director), Matthew Libatique (cinematography), Mike Medavoy, Brian Oliver, Scott Franklin (best picture), Andrew Weisblum (editing)

Darren Aronofsky's award-winning psychological thriller is the study of a young woman's all-consuming ambition and the transformation she must undergo to achieve success. *Black Swan* tells the story of ballet dancer Nina (a superbly committed Natalie Portman) as she struggles with the dual leads in a production of *Swan Lake*. Her fragile disposition is perfect for the role of the White Swan, but director Thomas (Vincent Cassel) is doubtful of her ability to embody the more sensual, dark role of the Black Swan. Nina battles a rival dancer (Mila Kunis), her overbearing mother (Barbara Hershey), and her innermost demons in order to achieve a perfect performance.

Aronofsky's unique vision implies that there can be no true greatness without touching the darkest parts of existence, and he makes this all too clear through highly subjective storytelling reminiscent of Roman Polanski's *Rosemary's Baby* (1968). Lines of reality and hallucination blur as we follow Nina's spiraling hysteria. Her simple injuries fester into debilitating conditions, and the manifestations of her subconscious threaten to overpower her completely as she risks her sanity and soul to access the darkness and danger that lurks beneath her innocent surface. *Black Swan*'s mix of psychological torments and classic horror elements will be sure to haunt you long after the curtains close. **SJS**

Inception Christopher Nolan, 2010

Writer-director Christopher Nolan is a mastermind filmic architect, and *Inception* is a feat of complicated construction. Dom Cobb (Leonardo DiCaprio) and his partner Arthur (Joseph Gordon-Levitt) are corporate spies specializing in "extraction," the art of going into someone's subconscious to extract their deepest secrets, or at least the ones they are being paid to discover. Computer hacking is a thing of the past, and one's mind is now the most vulnerable target. Cobb has been forced to leave his children, after being exiled for espionage, and is desperate to return to them. When he is approached by Saito (Ken Watanabe) and guaranteed safe passage back to the United States upon completion of a new job, he will stop at nothing to accomplish the task.

The job is unlike any other: it is not an extraction but an "inception," the implantation of an idea so deep in one's subconscious that it is believed to be one's own. Cobb puts together a crack team to travel inside the darkest recesses of the mind of their mark, Robert Fischer (Cillian Murphy), and implement an idea that will make their bosses incredibly rich. As the team members plant the idea, they battle Fischer's subconscious barriers while fighting off their own demons. Cobb battles with the manifestation of his dead wife, Mal (Marion Cotillard), who tempts him to stay in the dream world where they can be together.

Inception works on many levels: not only is it an entirely original and fresh idea, but it also manages to be a smart action thriller, a poignant and grief-filled drama, and an examination of the deeply hidden recesses of our minds that are completely unknown. This allows viewers to enjoy the film for its superficial beauty and quality performances, while letting the cerebral plot wash over them, to be examined more closely upon a second or third viewing. Although *Inception* plays well on the popcorn-movie premise, its twisted mind-game undercurrents will set it apart in cinematic history. **SJS**

U.S. / G.B. (Warner Bros., Legendary Pictures, Syncopy) 148m Color **Producer** Christopher Nolan, Emma Thomas **Screenplay** Christopher Nolan **Photography** Wally Pfister **Music** Hans Zimmer **Cast** Leonardo DiCaprio, Ken Watanabe, Joseph Gordon-Levitt, Marion Cotillard, Ellen Page, Cillian Murphy, Tom Hardy, Dileep Rao, Tom Berenger, Michael Caine **Oscars** Wally Pfister (cinematography), Chris Corbould, Andrew Lockley, Pete Bebb, Paul J. Franklin (visual effects), Richard King (sound editing), Lora Hirschberg, Gary Rizzo, Ed Novick (sound mixing) **Oscar nominations** Christopher Nolan, Emma Thomas (best picture), Christopher Nolan (writing), Hans Zimmer (original score), Guy Hendrix Dyas, Larry Dias, Douglas A. Mowat (art direction)

2010

> "The movie is a perplexing labyrinth without a simple through-line."

Roger Ebert,
Chicago Sun-Times, 2010

i

Ariadne is a character in Greek mythology who helped Theseus find his way out of the labyrinth.

The Social Network David Fincher, 2010

U.S. (Columbia Pictures, Relativity Media, Trigger Street Productions) 120m Color **Producer** Scott Rudin, Dana Brunetti, Michael De Luca, Ceán Chaffin **Screenplay** Aaron Sorkin **Photography** Jeff Cronenweth **Music** Trent Reznor, Atticus Ross **Cast** Jesse Eisenberg, Andrew Garfield, Justin Timberlake, Brenda Song, Armie Hammer, Max Minghella, Rashida Jones, Joseph Mazzello, Rooney Mara **Oscars** Aaron Sorkin (writing), Trent Reznor, Atticus Ross (original score), Kirk Baxter, Angus Wall (editing) **Oscar nominations** Jesse Eisenberg (actor), David Fincher (director), Scott Rudin, Dana Brunetti, Michael De Luca, Ceán Chaffin (best picture), Jeff Cronenweth (cinematography), Ren Klyce, David Parker, Michael Semanick, Mark Weingarten (sound mixing)

🛈

The script was adapted from a book about Facebook, *The Accidental Billionaires* (2009) by Ben Mezrich.

More than 1 billion people log on to Facebook every day, and it is no wonder a movie about the beginning of the phenomenon became a huge hit. What is surprising is just how good a film it is. The script is brutally funny and helps to expose the ego-driven and narcissistic profiles we have created for ourselves. It is also terribly depressing.

No one is more self-obsessed than lead character Mark Zuckerberg (Jesse Eisenberg). After his girlfriend dumps him, he writes a scathing blog entry about her and is further inspired to create a webpage where male students can rate the attractiveness of their female classmates. From there, Zuckerberg takes his computer skills, the wild popularity of his webpage, and early funding from his best friend Eduardo Saverin (Andrew Garfield) to jump-start the most popular social networking site of all time. The rest, as they say, is history.

Eisenberg is exceptional, but his costars also shine. Garfield portrays Saverin with a heart-tugging vulnerability, Justin Timberlake easily captures the arrogant swagger of Napster founder Sean Parker, and Armie Hammer nails the double duty of playing rowing-star brothers the Winklevoss twins. Director David Fincher adds his subtle beautiful visual prowess to Sorkin's quick script, and the resulting film is a never-ending debate on who did what and who owes whom. As the movie closes on a shot of Zuckerberg alone at his computer, the audience cannot help but ask: Has Facebook made us feel more connected or more alone? **SJS**

The Artist Michel Hazanavicius, 2011

France (La Petite Reine, La Classe Américaine, JD Prod, France 3 Cinéma, Jouror Productions, uFilm) 100 m Color **Producer** Thomas Langmann **Screenplay** Michel Hazanavicius **Photography** Guillaume Schiffman **Music** Ludovic Bource **Cast** Jean Dujardin, Berenice Bejo, John Goodman, James Cromwell, Penelope Ann Miller **Oscars** Thomas Langmann (best picture), Jean Dujardin (actor), Michel Hazanavicius (director), Ludovic Bource (original score), Mark Bridges (costume) **Oscar nominations** Berenice Bejo (actress in support role), Michel Hazanvicius (screenplay) **Cannes Film Festival** Jean Dujardin (actor)

It is 1927 and Hollywood is at its peak. The most famous silent film star is George Valentin (Jean Dujardin), riding high from his newest success. At the premiere he meets Peppy Miller (Berenice Bejo), a flapper who is trying to break into show business. George gets her a part in his next film, and not long after a technological breakthrough changes the industry forever: the arrival of sound. "Talkies" take over, and while Peppy's career skyrockets, George's plummets.

The Artist is a black-and-white, silent film and was shot in 1:33:1, the same ratio that many 1920s films used. Dialogue is expressed using intertitles, and Ludovic Bource's jazzy score guides you through the narrative. The film is thoroughly rooted in the classics of the silent period and is filled with references to the early years of Hollywoodland.

The actors tap back into the forgotten art of silent movie acting, expressing themselves through their facial expressions and mannerisms. Bejo, meanwhile, lights up any frame she is in—equally at home dancing the Charleston or weeping for the man she secretly loves.

Crucially, *The Artist* does not spoof silent movies, nor does it wink at the audience. It wins the viewer around with its perfectly judged tone and an engaging story that shifts from light and frothy to some unexpectedly harrowing moments. As a loving tribute to the days when actions spoke louder than words, *The Artist* is charming and irresistible. And it features the best performance by a dog since Toto. **SW**

ℹ

The role of Jack the dog was played by three matching Jack Russell Terriers: Uggie, Dash, and Dude.

Jodai-e Nader az Simin Asghar Farhadi, 2011
A Separation

In a middle-class Tehran that Western audiences might be surprised to recognize from their own lives, writer-director Asghar Farhadi boils up a domestic drama with the suspense of a Hitchcock thriller. Simin (Leila Hatami) is refused a divorce by Nader (Peyman Moadi) because she intends to leave Iran with their daughter (Sarina Farhadi, the director's daughter), and so they separate and Simin moves out. Nader hires a pregnant woman to care for his sick father while he is at work, and, after a dispute, the woman falls and loses her child, holding Nader responsible. Events quickly spiral out of control, with accusations turning to threats and leading to impossible decisions from which nobody comes away a winner.

Eschewing the realist aesthetic of the Iranian cinema that found Western audiences in the 1990s, Farhadi constructs a tightly woven narrative and masterfully handles escalating deceptions that lead to his characters being dragged through Iran's Byzantine legal system, all the time encouraging empathy with each of them (even the judge's position is not without sympathy). Without explicitly articulating any criticism of Iranian government or culture, the portrayal of the daily tensions of living in a theocracy slowly builds a powerful subtext. The human condition is such that, without a villain, decent people can be compelled to lie, hindering the search for justice even as they stand up for their own principles.

The cast is uniformly brilliant, and Asghar Farhadi's intelligent script dissects the divisions that emerge not only between husband and wife but also between parent and child, lower and middle class, and state and citizen. The narrative is explored from all perspectives, and the Oscar-winning film's brilliance lies in asking the audience ultimately to examine it through their own anxieties. **DN**

Iran (Asghar Farhadi) 123m Color
Language Persian **Producer** Asghar Farhadi **Screenplay** Asghar Farhadi **Photography** Mahmoud Kalari **Music** Sattar Oraki **Cast** Leila Hatami, Peyman Moadi, Shahab Hosseini, Sareh Bayat, Sarina Farhadi **Berlin International Film Festival awards** Asghar Farhadi (Golden Bear best picture), female ensemble (Silver Bear best actress), male ensemble (Silver Bear best actor) **Oscar** Iran (best foreign language film) **Oscar nominations** Asghar Farhadi (screenplay)

> "With rare subtlety and transforming art . . . Asghar Farhadi takes us into the emotional heart of modern Iran."
>
> **Peter Travers,**
> **Rolling Stone, 2011**

2011

i

The movie was the first film ever to win three Bears from the Berlin International Film Festival.

The Cabin in the Woods Drew Godard, 2011

U.S. (Lionsgate, Mutant Enemy) 95m Color
Producer Joss Whedon **Screenplay** Joss
Whedon and Drew Godard **Photography**
Peter Deming **Music** David Julyan
Cast Kristen Connolly, Chris Hemsworth,
Anna Hutchison, Fran Kranz, Jesse Williams,
Richard Jenkins, Bradley Whitford,
Brian White

Joss Whedon's *The Cabin in the Woods* is a fiendishly clever horror with an unexpected plot development that's one of the great surprises in recent cinema. The film begins predictably, with a group of attractive-looking college students retreating to a secluded rural hideaway. Meanwhile, in an initially undisclosed location, two white-collar middle-management types next to a bank of TV screens are seemingly involved in a surveillance job. Their connection to the teenage revellers isn't immediately clear, but as the party in the cabin turns into a gruelling bloodbath, the film grips with its shocking, unfolding sense of revelation.

Directed with merciless efficiency by Drew Godard, who made the home-movie-style monster movie *Cloverfield* (2008), *The Cabin in the Woods* is co-written and produced by *Buffy* creator and *Avengers* (2012) director Joss Whedon. Like *Buffy*, it is at once a knowing pastiche of horror conventions and a horror film in its own right. With its bloody exploration of ideas of sacrifice, the movie prompts difficult questions about the audience's need for and enjoyment of onscreen violence and fear. But for the movie's ironic reference to other horror films, *The Cabin in the Woods* works in wholly visceral terms: it is at once a clever experiment in genre and a scary experience in itself. **EL**

𝒊

The movie's opening was deliberately intended to make audiences think they were watching the wrong film.

Life of Pi Ang Lee, 2012

Since its publication in 2001, filmmakers such as Alfonso Cuarón, M. Night Shyamalan and Jean-Pierre Jeunet have all attempted to bring Yann Martel's award-winning fable *Life of Pi* to the big screen. It was finally Taiwanese-American filmmaker Ang Lee, employing remarkable use of CGI, who brought this rewarding tale to life.

The story is told mostly in flashback by an adult Piscine (Irrfan Khan)—nicknamed "Pi"—who relates it to an aspiring author (Rafe Spall), telling him it is a tale to make him "believe in God." It begins in India, with Pi (played as a child by Ayush Tandon) growing up in the family zoo and finding himself drawn toward the mysteries of religious faith. Economic and political upheavals force the family to leave India and while en route to Canada the ship they and their animal cargo are traveling on is sunk in a raging storm. Pi (now a teenager, played by Suraj Sharma) is the only human survivor, but is joined on a life raft by a zebra, hyena, orangutan, and a tiger named Richard Parker. Soon it is just Pi and Richard Parker in the middle of the Pacific Ocean, finding a way to survive together on the tiny craft and with limited resources. Their journey back to civilization is a stirring and often awe-inspiring tale.

Lee works with breathtaking versatility as he employs all wonder of 3D CGI technology to flesh out the narrative vignettes that punctuate Pi and Richard Parker's desperate journey. Few films have so completely immersed the viewer in such composed, painterly photography and stunning set pieces, including a diving luminous whale and a shoal of flying fish. Most impressive is the creation of Pi's lone companion. This virtual 400-pound tiger is every bit as real as Pi.

What is real and what is not, the disparity between actual events and how we choose to remember them, is key to the story and the grander theme of what we, as an audience, believe in. It may convert few, but *Life of Pi* passionately underpins Martel's idea that spiritual faith lies at the very core of our being. **SW**

U.S. (Fox, Haishang Films) 127m Color
Producer Ang Lee, Gil Netter, David Womark
Screenplay David Magee **Photography**
Claudio Miranda **Music** Mychael Danna
Cast Suraj Sharma, Irrfan Khan, Adil Hussain,
Rafe Spall, Tabu, Gerard Depardieu
Oscars Ang Lee (best director), Claudio
Miranda (cinematography), Mychael Danna
(original score), Bill Westenhofer, Guillaume
Rocheron, Erik De Boer, Donald Elliott (visual
effects) **Oscar nominations** Ang Lee, Gil
Netter, David Womack (best picture), David
Magee (screenplay), Tim Squyres (editing),
Bombay Jayashri, Mychael Danna (original
song), Anna Pinnock, David Gropman
(production design), Eugene Gearty, Philip
Stockton (sound editing), Ron Bartlett, Doug
Hemphill, Drew Kunin (sound mixing)

2012

"Doubt is useful, it keeps faith a living thing. After all, you cannot know the strength of your faith until it is tested."

Adult Pi Patel (Irrfan Khan)

i

Ang Lee won the Oscar for Best Director without also winning Best Picture for both *Life of Pi* and *Brokeback Mountain*.

Lincoln Steven Spielberg, 2012

The Washington of Steven Spielberg's *Lincoln* is a world of collusion, compromise, and self-interest. The political sparring is brutal, with the lower chamber of Congress resembling a gladiatorial ring where legends are forged and vacillation can destroy a career. One doesn't have to look too hard to find the parallels with contemporary America.

Tony Kushner's screenplay, drawing on Doris Kearns Goodwin's impressive *Team of Rivals: The Political Genius of Abraham Lincoln*, is less a biopic of one man than an account of the machinations that led to the passing of the Thirteenth Amendment, which abolished slavery. In tone it resembles a densely plotted political thriller as the legislation undergoes its precarious journey through a fractious and ideologically-divided House of Representatives.

Daniel Day-Lewis is astonishing as the sixteenth President of the United States. Like Oskar Schindler in Spielberg's 1993 Holocaust drama, we first see him from behind, hearing his voice before seeing his face. By the time we see him in close-up, any trace of Day-Lewis is gone. Lincoln here is both a man of the people and a skilled debater, at ease in any company. As a statesman he is not immune to deception or playing the Washington game. He is shown engaging the services of lobbyists, and gambles with soldiers' lives as he tactically courts peace with the enemy, whose arrival in Washington he delays in order to see his amendment passed. The impact of one term in office and the grueling toll of a drawn-out civil war is visible in his face and physique, but when countering opposition to his plans he erupts with passion and fire.

Lincoln is Spielberg's third film to deal with race in America, after *The Color Purple* (1985) and *Amistad* (1997). It is also the best. Aided by Kushner's impressive script and Day-Lewis's towering performance, along with a strong cast that includes Sally Field, Tommy Lee Jones, and David Strathairn, Spielberg's consummate drama is a reminder of why Abraham Lincoln is among the most revered figures in U.S. political history. **IHS**

U.S. (Dreamworks SKG, 20th Century Fox, Reliance Entertainment) 150m Color **Producer** Kathleen Kennedy, Steven Spielberg **Screenplay** Tony Kushner from book by Doris Kearns Goodwin **Photography** Janusz Kaminski **Music** John Williams **Cast** Daniel Day-Lewis, Sally Field, Tommy Lee Jones, David Strathairn, Joseph Gordon-Levitt, James Spader, Hal Holbrook, John Hawkes, Jackie Earle Haley, Bruce McGill, Tim Blake Nelson, Lee Pace, Michael Stuhlbarg, Walton Goggins, David Oyelowo, Lukas Haas **Oscars** Daniel Day-Lewis (actor), Jim Erickson, Rick Carter (production design) **Oscar nominations** Kathleen Kennedy, Steven Spielberg (best picture), Steven Spielberg (director), Tony Kushner (screenplay), Sally Filed (supporting actress), Tommy Lee Jones (supporting actor), Janusz Kaminski (photography), John Williams (original score), Michael Kahn (editing), Joanna Johnston (costume design), Andy Nelson, Gary Rydstrom, Ron Judkins (sound mixing)

"No one is loved as much as you by the people. Don't waste that power."

Mary Todd Lincoln (Sally Field)

ℹ

Spielberg wore a suit and tie every day to work while directing in order to better blend in with the actors.

Wadjda Haifaa Al-Mansour, 2012

Saudi Arabia / Germany (Razor Film Produktion, Highlook Communications Group, Rotana Film Production) 98m Color **Producer** Gerhard Meixner, Roman Paul **Screenplay** Haifaa Al-Mansour **Photography** Lutz Reitemeier **Music** Max Richter **Cast** Waad Mohammed, Reem Abdullah, Abdullahraman Al Gohani, Ahd, Sultan Al Assaf, Alanoud Sajini, Rafa Al Sanea, Dana Abdullilah, Rehab Ahmed **Venice Film Festival** Haifaa Al-Mansour ("CinemAvvenire" Award, C.I.C.A.E. Award, Interfilm Award)

Trumpeted as the "first" film from a female Saudi filmmaker (although the claim is not quite true, the achievement is nonetheless a rare one), *Wadjda* is the deceptively simple tale of a young girl who wants a bicycle. However, this is contemporary Saudi Arabia and young girls do not often get what they want, not least permission to ride, let alone own, a bicycle.

Haifaa Al-Mansour's debut is a remarkable achievement in a society where women cannot vote and cinemas themselves are banned. It is a beguilingly simple story that chooses not to tackle politics or human rights issues head on. Instead it employs a subtle and often charming approach to make a very clear statement. Effortlessly told, this character-driven piece focuses on the eponymous heroine, a spiky, straight-talking 10-year-old, whose competitive streak with the neighborhood boys leads her on a quest to acquire her heart's desire: a green bicycle. Along the way we discover a family torn apart by a father bowing to pressure to take a second wife, and we delight in the subversion of Wadjda raising the money she needs by thrashing the opposition in a school Qur'an recitation competition. Funny and smart, *Wadjda* offers a window into another world—one where the realities of life for young women are harsh, but where personality can shine through. **BHa**

ℹ

Haifaa Al-Mansour had to direct some of the street scenes from inside a van, for fear of sparking protests.

923

Gravity Alfonso Cuarón, 2013

A rare commercial success that attracted almost universal critical acclaim, *Gravity* fires a Robinson Crusoe narrative into orbit thanks to state-of-the-art 3D technology. Sandra Bullock plays Dr. Ryan Stone, whose mission on a space shuttle is cut short when the wreckage from a destroyed Russian satellite creates a chain reaction and sends a cloud of debris hurtling toward her at the speed of a bullet.

As filmed by Alfonso Cuarón, this 3D disaster movie works not in spite of his intelligence as a filmmaker but because of it. Employing the same style used in his earlier films (*Y Tu Mamá También* [2001] and *Children of Men* [2006]), as evinced by the long opening shot of the orbiting shuttle coming in to view, Cuarón envelops us in the spectacle of space before unleashing the metallic tsunami that destroys everything in its wake. Throughout the groundbreaking shoot, during which Bullock spent most of her time encased in a light box that allowed the visual and special effects team to capture the weightlessness of spaceflight, Cuarón steers clear of the rapid editing style of most action movies. Instead we have time to contemplate Stone's predicament and feel the tension rise as the metal tide once again makes its way toward her.

If the film's script is a little insubstantial, George Clooney's charming captain and Bullock's scientist more than compensate for it. Though not as fully realized as Sigourney Weaver's Ripley, Bullock brings enough humanity to her character to make Stone a convincing sci-fi heroine. She is at her best in the film's quieter moments, particularly a revealing scene that suggests why she may have originally opted to travel into space.

In a later conversation, Stone manages to contact someone on Earth. Unaware who the man is, her spirits lift at the sound of a baby crying and a dog barking. In Jonás Cuarón's short *Aningaaq* (2013), we are on the other end of the line, in Greenland, as an Inuit fisherman is facing his own, potentially serious, dilemma. It is a moving and elegiac companion piece to this, the grander feature he co-wrote with his father. **IHS**

G.B. / U.S. (Warner Bros., Heyday Films, Esperanto Filmoj) 91m Color **Producer** David Heyman, Alfonso Cuarón **Screenplay** Alfonso Cuarón, Jonás Cuarón **Photography** Emmanuel Lubezki **Music** Steven Price **Cast** Sandra Bullock, George Clooney, Phaldut Sharma, Ed Harris, Orto Ignatiussen **Oscars** Emmanuel Lubezki (cinematography), Alfonso Cuarón (director), Alfonso Cuarón, Mark Sanger (editing), Steven Price (original score), Glenn Freemantle (sound editing), Skip Lievsay, Niv Adiri, Christopher Benstead, Chris Munro (sound mixing), Timothy Webber, Chris Lawrence, David Shirk, Neil Corbould (visual effects) **Oscar nominations** Alfonso Cuarón, David Heyman (best picture), Sandra Bullock (actress), Andy Nicholson, Rosie Goodwin, Joanne Woollard (production design)

"Half of North America just lost their Facebook."

Matt Kowalski
(George Clooney)

ℹ The offscreen voice of Mission Control is Ed Harris, who previously played a mission director in *Apollo 13* (1995).

La grande bellezza Paolo Sorrentino, 2013
The Great Beauty

After his uneven excursion to America with *This Must Be the Place* (2011), Paolo Sorrentino returned to Italy to continue his examination of the country's privileged class. But whereas *Il Divo* (2008) offered a scathing account of corruption among Italy's political ranks, as embodied by Guilio Andreotti, *The Great Beauty* shines a light on Rome's cultural elite.

In his youth, Jep Gambardella penned a highly praised novella and a glittering literary career awaited him. Instead, he chose to take center stage among the cream of Rome's aristocrats and wealthy, coming to life at night and partying until dawn. Now, celebrating his sixty-fifth birthday, he looks back on his life and ponders its worth.

From the curious prologue, in which a Japanese tourist dies at one of the city's many religious sites, Rome lies at the heart of Sorrentino's film. His camera prowls through gardens, glides across sculptures, and is enraptured by the city skyline, particularly the view from Jep's magnificent apartment. It is a marked contrast to the ghouls and grotesques that populate the interminable parties. The dances they perform are pathetic rituals—a desperate attempt to evade the passage of time and proximity of death. This is the Berlusconi generation, and what a sorry, self-deluded, and inelegantly wasted bunch they are.

Sorrentino's breathtaking direction is matched by the stunning performance of Toni Servillo, the director's leading man in four of his six films. In choosing to echo the themes of Felinni's *La Dolce Vita* (1960), it is perfect that Sorrentino has his own Marcello Mastroianni. Servillo, one of the finest actors in contemporary cinema, brings Jep to life with a balance of wit, cynicism, and weariness with a lifestyle he knows is contemptible, but indulges in nonetheless. Witnessing his journey through this world is like watching a car crash—we know it's wrong but we just can't look away. **IHS**

Italy / France (Indigo Film, Medusa Film, Babe Film) 142m Color **Producer** Francesca Cima, Nicola Giulliano **Screenplay** Paolo Sorrentino **Photography** Luca Bigazzi **Music** Lele Marchitelli **Cast** Toni Servillo, Carlo Verdone, Sabrina Ferilli, Carlo Bruccirosso, Galatea Ranzi, Giovanna Vignola **Oscars** Italy (best foreign language film) **Cannes Film Festival** Paolo Sorrentino (Golden Palm nomination)

"A shimmering coup de cinema to make your heart burst, your mind swim, and your soul roar."

Robbie Collin,
The Telegraph, **2014**

🛈

Sorrentino considered calling the film "L'Apparato Umano," after the title of the fictional novel by Jep.

La vie d'Adèle—Chapitres 1 et 2
Blue is the Warmest Color Abdellatif Kechiche, 2013

France / Belgium / Spain (Qaut'sous Films, Wild Bunch, France 2 Cinéma) 179m Color
Producer Brahim Chioua, Abdellatif Kechiche, Vincent Maraval
Screenplay Abdellatif Kechiche, Ghalia Kechiche **Photography** Sofian El Fani
Cast Léa Seydoux, Adele Exarchopoulos, Salim Kechiouche, Catherine Salée, Auélien Recoing, Benjamin Siksou, Mona Walravens, Alma Jodorowsky, Jérémie Laheurte, Anna Loiret, Benoît Pilot, Sandor Funtek
Cannes Film Festival Abdellatif Kechiche (FIPRESCI Prize), Abdellatif Kechiche, Adèle Exarchopoulos, Léa Seydoux (Golden Palm)

i

Initially planned to be shot in two months, the movie took nearly five-and-a-half months to film.

Seemingly coming out of nowhere to win the Golden Palm at the 2013 Cannes Film Festival, *Blue is the Warmest Color* left a fluster of over-awed reviewers trailing in its wake, smashed taboos at every turn, and rapidly disintegrated into a circus of "he said/she said" scrapping between its director and one of its stars on release. Featuring a graphic and much discussed lesbian sex scene, the film unprecedentedly saw its Golden Palm divided between its director, Abdellatif Kechiche, and two stars.

To focus on the sex scenes is to betray the extraordinary strength of a writer/director who understands the nature of drama, from how long to show a scene to when to cut. At its heart, the film is, quite simply, about love—of which sex is but a part—about the trauma of growing up, and the subtleties of class. The latter is never more perfectly observed than when watching the girls' two families at mealtimes—Adele's huddled around the TV, messily slurping simple spaghetti; Emma's enjoying a sophisticated fruits de mer, complete with oysters and riveting middle class chat. But above all else it's a study of the complexity of romantic and sexual obsession—sometimes murky, almost always inevitably doomed, but utterly irresistible all the same. Kechiche's confidence to hold our gaze with sex scenes, breakup scenes, and all the seemingly insignificant moments in between, results in a riveting film that demands and rewards our attention. **BHa**

12 Years a Slave Steve McQueen, 2013

U.S. / G.B. (Regency Enterprises, River Road Entertainment, Plan B Entertainment) 134m Color **Producer** Brad Pitt, Dede Gardner, Jeremy Kleiner, Steve McQueen, Anthony Katagas **Screenplay** John Ridley **Photography** Sean Bobbitt **Music** Hans Zimmer **Cast** Chiwetel Ejiofor, Michael Fassbender, Lupita Nyong'o, Dwight Henry, Scoot McNairy, Paul Giamatti, Sarah Paulson, Paul Dano, Benedict Cumberbatch, Brad Pitt, Adepero Oduye, Michael Kenneth Williams, Kelsey Acott, Quvenzhané Wallis **Oscars** Brad Pitt, Dede Gardner, Jeremy Kleiner, Steve McQueen, Anthony Katagas (best picture), Lupita Nyong'o (actress in support role), John Ridley (adapted screenplay) **Oscar nominations** Steve McQueen (director), Chiwetel Ejiofor (actor), Michael Fassbender (actor in support role), Patricia Norris (costume design), Joe Walker (editing), Adam Stockhausen, Alice Baker (production design)

"It is pitched pretty near perfectly in terms of sheer narrative craftsmanship."

Mark Kermode,
The Observer, 2014

ℹ

12 Years a Slave is the first film from a black director to win the Academy Award for Best Picture.

The year is 1841. Solomon Northup is a free black man who works as a violinist and lives in upstate New York with his wife and children. Tempted by the offer of a few days work in Washington, he travels there only for his supposed employers to drug and kidnap him. He wakes in rags and chains, and is beaten by two strangers when he protests. Rechristened "Platt," he is transported to the Southern states and sold as a slave.

Based on Northup's memoir, Steve McQueen's film is seen by many as mainstream U.S. cinema's most challenging account of slavery. Recounting Solomon's time under different owners and his desperate attempts to return to his family, the film never panders to easy emotion or exploits the brutality of his existence. Its power lies in the gradual degradation of daily life, which contrasts sharply with the world that Solomon knew. In one flashback, as Solomon and his wife are shopping for clothes, a slave wanders into the shop they are in and stares in disbelief as Solomon samples the tailoring.

Despite shocking scenes of violence, McQueen has crafted a beautiful film: trees droop under the weight of the Spanish moss, sunrise colors the gently flowing rivers, and the Southern landscape as a whole resembles a lush Eden. Beatings and whippings play out against this idyllic backdrop.

Yet throughout this ordeal Solomon clings to his humanity, his face taut with desperation and his eyes deep wells of sadness. It is to both McQueen and lead actor Chiwetel Ejiofor's credit that Solomon remains a fully rounded character and not merely the conduit for our sympathy and horror.

By focusing on one man's story, McQueen has laid down a challenge for future representations of this period. Upon hearing Solomon's terrible journey, Brad Pitt's character Bass comments, "Your story is amazing, and in no good way." This is an important film and long overdue. **SW**

2013

Ida Pawel Pawlikowski, 2013

Not until this, his fifth feature, did U.K.-based Polish director Pawel Pawlikowski make a narrative film in his native country and his native language. It was worth waiting for. Shot in cool, spare monochrome, *Ida* is set in Poland in 1962—and could almost have been made there in that austere, repressed era. Within its quiet confines are played out all the main currents of recent Polish history: Catholicism and Communism, the Nazi occupation, and the fate of Poland's Jews. Little is openly stated—this is a film of meaningful silences, of intercepted glances—but much is obliquely implied.

Anna (Agata Trzebuchowska), a convent-raised orphan, is about to take her vows as a nun. The mother superior tells her that first she should visit her only surviving relative, her aunt Wanda (Agata Kulesza), whom she has never met. Wanda, an embittered and burnt-out Party apparatchik, a former state prosecutor with a fearsome reputation for severity, reveals that Anna's real name is in fact Ida—and that she's Jewish. Together, the two ill-matched women set out to discover what became of Ida's parents. It is a quest that digs deep into Polish war-guilt.

Given the younger woman's gentle idealism, it would have been easy for Pawlikowski to set up a simplistic dichotomy: the false god of communism versus the true faith of the church. The director has nothing so comforting in mind. Leading the audience through featureless landscapes and stark concrete hotels, into scrubby woodlands and peasant farmhouses where poverty has settled into dull mistrust, *Ida* poses questions and raises uncertainties, but provides no answers. Sole respite from the all-pervading bleakness comes with the jazz played by a young saxophonist the women meet on the road. In 1960s Poland, jazz always represented freedom—and so it does here. **PK**

Poland / Denmark / France / G.B. (Opus Film, Phoenix Film, Portobello Pictures) 82m BW **Producers** Eric Abraham, Piotr Dzieciol, Ewa Puszczynska **Screenplay** Pawel Pawlikowski, Rebecca Lenkiewicz **Photography** Lukasz Zal, Ryszard Lenczewski **Music** Kristian Selin, Eidnes Andersen **Cast** Agata Kulesza, Agata Trzebuchowska, Dawid Ogrodnik, Jerzy Trela, Adam Szyszkowski, Joanna Kulig **Oscars** Poland (best foreign language film) **Oscar nominations** Lukasz Zal, Ryszard Lenczewski (cinematography)

"This compact masterpiece has the curt definition and the finality of a reckoning."

David Denby,
The New Yorker, 2014

𝑖

Agata Trzebuchowska had no previous acting experience—she was discovered in a cafe by a friend of Pawlikowski.

2013

Under the Skin Jonathan Glazer, 2013

G.B. (Nick Wechsler Productions, JW Films, Scottish Screen, UK Film Council) 108m Color **Producer** Nick Wechsler, James Wilson **Screenplay** Jonathan Glazer, Walter Campbell **Photography** Daniel Landin **Music** Mica Levi **Cast** Scarlett Johansson, Jeremy McWilliams, Dougie McConnell, Adam Pearson

i

It took Glazer ten years to bring the story to the screen, and at one point Brad Pitt was attached to the project.

The term "visionary," like "masterpiece," is used far too often; yet here it defines not just the cinematic power of Jonathan Glazer's third feature but its actual modus operandi: paring down and re-focusing Michel Faber's 2000 source novel about a predatory extra-terrestrial/femme fatale stalking unsuspecting men, to re-envision our species and world anew, through the eyes of a creature whose alienation is all-too literal.

Almost everything explicit in Faber's book—from its protagonist's name to why she/it cruises Scotland harvesting humans for her home planet's nutrition—is withheld. Instead, Glazer and his team prioritize rhythm and texture over narrative clarity, immersing us in a hypnotic mix of shape-shifting, sinuous visuals and eerie, discordant soundscapes— Mica Levi's score and Johnnie Burn's sound design are outstanding—all merged with a lo-fi aesthetic that set star Scarlett Johansson loose in everyday locations, covertly filming her interaction with unaware locals. The result, part Lynchian surrealist horror, part Loachian vérité realism, is uniquely disorientating. Johansson's near-mute alien, her eyes dispassionately assessing her prey's strange customs, is a marvel.

This is an allusive and elusive film, one that seeps under your skin and into your consciousness. Seeing it is to have a close encounter with a visionary masterpiece utterly of its own kind. **LS**

Leviathan Andrey Zvyagintsev, 2014

Russia (Non-Stop Productions) 142m Color
Producer Sergey Melkumov, Andrey
Zvyagintsev **Screenplay** Oleg Negin, Andrey
Zvyagintsev **Photography** Mikhail Krichman
Music Philip Glass **Cast** Aleksey Serebryakov,
Elena Lyadova, Roman Madyanov **Oscar
nominations** Russia (best foreign language
film) **Cannes Film Festival** Andrey
Zvyagintsev, Oleg Negin (screenplay),
Andrey Zvyagintsev (Golden Palm
nomination)

i

The movie was inspired by the story
of Marvin Heemeyer, who went on a
rampage with a bulldozer in 2004.

The opening credits to *Leviathan* state that the movie was made "With support from the Russian Ministry of Culture." It's difficult to imagine any member of that department signing off on the film, as Andrey Zvyagintsev's satirical drama is a coruscating attack on Russia's political elite.

A variation on the trials of Job, the movie's title alludes to the Bible, as well as to philosopher Thomas Hobbes's 1651 treatise of the same name. The story unfolds in a small town on Russia's Kola Peninsula. Kolya (Aleksey Serebryakov), a law-abiding Everyman, is being forced out of his family home because the mayor—an avaricious bureaucrat—wants to develop the land with a local businessman. The court rejects Kolya's pleas and a lawyer friend is threatened with violence for attempting to intercede. A local cleric is even less help, having been paid off handsomely.

Kolya and his friends ultimately know the score. In one scene they go shooting, using the framed images of previous Russian leaders as targets. Someone suggests they should find a more up-to-date target, but no one actually speaks the name of the current political incumbent.

Kolya's plight may be tragic, but *Leviathan* is often very funny, albeit bleakly so. Zvyagintsev peels away layer upon layer of corruption, permeating every area of civic life. It seems the only crime that doesn't pay is to oppose the system. **IHS**

Boyhood Richard Linklater, 2014

By virtue of its unusual production history, Richard Linklater's *Boyhood* gives us two films in one: a work of fiction spanning twelve years in the life of a young boy growing up in Texas; and a shadow-documentary that escorts its fictional counterpart each step of the way. How could it be otherwise, given Linklater's singular decision to shoot the film over a corresponding period of time, and with the same cast? The actors age before us, though it is the evolution of Ellar Coltrane (who plays the boy, Mason) and Lorelei Linklater (the director's daughter, playing Mason's sister) that has the most resonance.

Like François Truffaut's Antoine Doinel films (beginning with *The 400 Blows* [1959] and ending with *Love on the Run* [1979) and Michael Apted's *Up* series, *Boyhood*'s power is accumulative. However, Linklater's longitudinal study is also a lesson in compression—he gives us the incremental bloom of Mason's life, and all of its attendant experience, in less than three hours. The seamless and unannounced transitions that introduce each phase of his development elicit in the viewer a commensurate gasp of delayed recognition: look how he has grown! But underpinning it all is a feeling of concern and even suspense, no doubt encouraged by our awareness of the cast's deep investment, as well as the onset of time: what will become of Mason/Ellar?

As we follow Mason through the commonplace rituals of an American adolescence, we begin to see that one of Linklater's achievements is to have created something at once both unerringly specific (a Texas childhood in the early twenty-first century) and universal. And while the film is something of a paean to parenthood (Ethan Hawke and Patricia Arquette are both subtle and true as the boy's divorced parents), *Boyhood*'s real subject is time, unfolding as it does in a perpetual present tense. **MM**

U.S. (IFC Productions, Detour Films) 165m Color **Producer** Richard Linklater, Cathleen Sutherland, Jonathan Sehring, John Sloss **Screenplay** Richard Linklater **Photography** Shane Kelly, Lee Daniel **Cast** Patricia Arquette, Ellar Coltrane, Lorelei Linklater, Ethan Hawke **Oscars** Patricia Arquette (actress in support role) **Oscar nominations** Richard Linklater, Cathleen Sutherland (best picture), Ethan Hawke (actor in support role), Richard Linklater (director, original screenplay), Sandra Adair (editing) **Berlin Film Festival** Richard Linklater (director, Golden Bear nomination)

> "The achievement of a lifetime. Linklater has shown, perhaps with more heart-piercing acuity than any other director, how a child grows into an adult."
>
> Robbie Collin,
> *The Telegraph*, 2014

🛈

Partway through filming, Lorelei Linklater asked for her character to be killed off, but her father refused.

U.S. / Canada (Fox Searchlight) 119m Color
Producer Alejandro González Iñárritu, John
Lesher, Arnon Milchan, James W. Skotchdopole
Screenplay Alejandro González Iñárritu,
Nicolás Giacobone, Alexander Dinelaris,
Armando Bo Photography Emmanuel
Lubezki Cast Michael Keaton, Edward Norton,
Emma Stone, Naomi Watts, Andrea
Riseborough, Zach Galifianakis, Amy Ryan
Oscars Alejandro González Iñárritu, John
Lesher, James W. Skotchdopole (best picture),
Alejandro González Iñárritu (director),
Alejandro González Iñárritu, Nicolás
Giacobone, Alexander Dinelaris, Armando Bo
(original screenplay), Emmanuel Lubezki
(cinematography) Oscar nominations Michael
Keaton (actor), Edward Norton (actor in
support role), Emma Stone (actress in support
role), Jon Taylor, Frank A. Montaño, Thomas
Varga (sound mixing), Aaron Glascock, Martín
Hernández (sound editing) Venice Film
Festival Alejandro González Iñárritu (Future
Film Festival Digital Award, Leoncino d'Oro
Agiscuola Award, Nazareno Taddei Award,
Golden Lion nomination)

"Popularity is the slutty little cousin of prestige."

Mike Shiner (Edward Norton)

i

The carpet in the backstage corridor
scenes shares the same pattern as the
one in the hotel in *The Shining* (1980).

Birdman Alejandro González Iñárritu, 2014

Like Alfred Hitchcock's *Rope* (1948), Alejandro González Iñárritu's *Birdman or (The Unexpected Virtue of Ignorance)*—to give the movie its full title—will have us believe that the film unfolds as one single shot. Digital trickery has replaced someone standing in front of a camera while a fresh reel of film is loaded, but the effect remains the same— although now we're no longer confined to a single room. Iñárritu's camera swoops and swerves, first in the Broadway theater where former screen superhero Riggan Thomson is preparing to make his debut with an adaptation of a Raymond Carver story he has written, directed, and is starring in, before following him out onto the street. It's already clear that he is teetering on the edge of sanity. Throughout the film he converses with his alter ego, Birdman, the comic crusader-turned-movie character he played twice on the screen before retiring from the role in 1992. That was the same year that Michael Keaton, who plays Riggan, stopped playing Batman. What we are meant to draw from this association, Iñárritu and his star leave to us.

Hollywood loves a comeback as much it does movies about itself. As such, Iñárritu's film strikes a double whammy, offering up a brilliant satire of both the theater and film world, and giving Michael Keaton his best role since he played Ray Nicolette in the adaptations of Elmore Leonard's *Jackie Brown* (1997) and *Out of Sight* (1998). Not that the actor does anything we haven't seen before. His nervous energy is what made his Bruce Wayne such a livewire and his villains so compelling. However, more than any other director he has worked with in the last decade, Iñárritu understands how to channel that energy into a portrait of a man plagued by demons—an actor with an over-inflated ego who is nevertheless crippled by a fear of failure.

With its pounding percussive score by Antonio Sanchez, *Birdman* is a frenzied, often brilliant comedy that, unlike some of Iñárritu's previous films, never takes itself too seriously. If only Riggan would do the same. **IHS**

Whiplash Damien Chazelle, 2014

U.S. (Bold Films, Blumhouse Productions, Right of Way Films) 107m Color
Producer Jason Blum, Helen Estabrook, David Lancaster, Michel Litvak
Screenplay Damien Chazelle
Photography Sharone Meir
Music Justin Hurwitz
Cast Miles Teller, J.K. Simmons, Paul Reiser, Melissa Benoist, Austin Stowell
Oscars J.K. Simmons (actor in support role), Tom Cross (film editing), Craig Mann, Ben Wilkins, Thomas Curley (sound mixing)
Oscar nominations Jason Blum, Helen Estabrook, David Lancaster (best picture), Damien Chazelle (adapted screenplay)

i

Both actors have a musical background: Simmons has a music degree and Teller has played drums since he was fifteen.

The pouring sweat, dripping blood, and relentless emotional battering of *Whiplash*'s gladiatorial combat takes place in an esteemed New York music academy. If the setting suggests highbrow refinement, Damien Chazelle's dazzling sophomore effort generates the adrenaline of an extreme sports face-off and the pulse-pounding tension of a thriller.

Nineteen-year-old jazz drummer Andrew Neimann (Miles Teller) enrolls in the country's finest conservatory with dreams of emulating the great Buddy Rich, so he's thrilled to pique the interest of celebrated conductor Terence Fletcher (J.K. Simmons). But rather than take Andy under his wing, Fletcher homes in like a bird of prey, raining down a campaign of abuse as verbally creative as it is mentally destructive. For Fletcher, talent isn't nurtured; it must be dragged forth, kicking and screaming.

Though Fletcher convinces Andrew of his warped Darwinism, Chazelle isn't so easily swayed, laying bare both men's macho arrogance and power games. He's rewarded with two standout performances. Simmons's sadistic Fletcher is a career peak for this consistently fine character actor. He's matched beat for beat by Teller, regularly performing his own drumming. With a climactic crescendo, *Whiplash* exploits jazz drumming the way *Raging Bull* (1980) did boxing: as an arena to viscerally explore and explode male vanity, insecurity, and obsession. **LS**

The Grand Budapest Hotel Wes Anderson, 2014

The twin spirits of Ernst Lubitsch and Stefan Zweig preside benevolently over *The Grand Budapest Hotel*, Wes Anderson's intricately baroque vision of the world of Middle Europe as it probably never was before at least one, and possibly both, world wars. Anderson has always striven to devise alternative universes of his own; this is his most complete fabrication yet, a fanatically and fantastically detailed, sugar-iced, calorie-stuffed, gleefully overripe Sachertorte of a film.

The action centers around the eponymous mountain-set luxury hotel and its presiding genius, urbane omni-competent concierge Monsieur Gustave (Ralph Fiennes). The narrative jumps backward through four time-zones, the mood is stylized comedy undercut with melancholia, and the joyously melodramatic plot takes in murdered aristocrats, contested wills, purloined paintings, jailbreaks, high-speed pursuit down a ski-slope, defenestrated cats, lovelorn widows, gourmet patisserie, and a secret fraternity of hotel concierges.

It's a rich mixture—perhaps too rich for some. But those not indissolubly wedded to hard-edged realism, and prepared to succumb to the charm of Anderson's filmmaking, with its acute sense of design, its playful tone, and exhilarating pace, will find *The Grand Budapest Hotel* a delectable and unexpectedly moving experience. Shooting in three different ratios—2.35:1, 1.85:1, and the classic 1.33:1—to differentiate the movie's three main timelines, Anderson deploys a cast that, even by his standards, is bewilderingly star-studded, with many of the famous names onscreen for barely more than a minute or two. But above all, this is Fiennes's film. Gifted a rare chance to play comedy, he demonstrates an impeccable comic timing that makes his performance as Monsieur Gustave, informed as it is by an evident affection for the character, a constant joy to watch. **PK**

U.S. / Germany (Fox Searchlight, Indian Paintbrush, Studio Babelsberg) 100m Color **Producer** Wes Anderson, Scott Rudin, Steven Rales, Jeremy Dawson **Screenplay** Wes Anderson **Photography** Robert Yeoman **Music** Alexandre Desplat **Cast** Ralph Fiennes, F. Murray Abraham, Mathieu Amalric, Adrien Brody, Willem Dafoe, Jeff Goldblum, Harvey Keitel, Jude Law, Bill Murray, Edward Norton, Saoirse Ronan, Jason Schwartzmann, Tilda Swinton, Tom Wilkinson, Owen Wilson, Tony Revolori **Oscars** Milena Canonero (costume), Frances Hannon, Mark Coulier (makeup and hairstyling), Alexandre Desplat (original score), Adam Stockhausen, Anna Pinnock (production design) **Oscar nominations** Wes Anderson, Scott Rudin, Steven M. Rales, Jeremy Dawson (best picture), Wes Anderson (director), Robert D. Yeoman (cinematography), Barney Pilling (film editing), Wes Anderson, Hugo Guinness (original screenplay) **Berlin Film Festival** Wes Anderson (Grand Jury Prize, Golden Bear nomination)

"As intricately layered as a Dobos torte and nearly as rich."

Justin Chang, *Variety*, 2014

ℹ️

The name of the fictional Republic of Zubrowka comes from the Polish vodka Zubrówka.

The Look of Silence Joshua Oppenheimer, 2014

Denmark / Indonesia / Norway / G.B.
(Anonymous, Final Cut for Real,
Making Movies Oy) 103m Color
Producer Signe Byrge Sørensen
Photography Lars Skree **Oscar nomination**
Joshua Oppenheimer, Signe Byrge
Sørensen (documentary feature)
Berlin International Film Festival Joshua
Oppenheimer (Peace Film Award)
Venice Film Festival Joshua Oppenheimer
(FIPRESCI Prize, Fedeora Award, Golden
Mouse, Grand Special Jury Prize, Human
Rights Film Network Award, Golden
Lion nomination)

ℹ

The Look of Silence was shot after
The Act of Killing had been edited,
but before it was released.

In *The Act of Killing* (2012), Joshua Oppenheimer exposed the consequences of building our everyday reality on terror and lies by filming perpetrators of the Indonesian Genocide reenacting their crimes. Its companion piece, *The Look of Silence*, returns to Indonesia, with the director following a family of survivors as they discover how their son was murdered and uncover the identity of the men who killed him. Adi Rukun, whose brother Ramli was killed in a manner of unimaginable cruelty on suspicion of being a subversive, is determined to break the spell of silence and fear under which the survivors live. Confronting the men responsible for his brother's murder remains a dangerous act in a country where the killers still retain power.

Determined to avoid a simplistic Manichean view of the world, where the good are saintly and wrongdoers evil, Oppenheimer is more subtle in his exploration of what is means to live a life shattered by mass violence and abject terror. Executive produced by Werner Herzog and described by Errol Morris as "a profound comment on the human condition," *The Look of Silence* is already being discussed as one of the pivotal documentaries in film history. It's a work of total and utter integrity and reflects with both sensitivity and vitality on the almost unspeakable horrors of which humanity is frequently capable. **JWo**

Star Wars: The Force Awakens J.J. Abrams, 2015

Set thirty years after the events of *Return of the Jedi* (1983), the Skywalker saga continues with *Episode VII*. Picking up the characters from the original trilogy, *The Force Awakens* thrusts them through hyperspace and into a new adventure, along with a collection of boisterous new heroes and villains.

The Empire has fallen, but the First Order has risen in its wake, determined to quash the New Republic and bring the galaxy under its shadow. The Resistance, led by General Leia (Carrie Fisher), launches a desperate search for the missing and last remaining Jedi, Luke Skywalker (Mark Hamil), who is now little more than a myth. A penitent stormtrooper (John Boyega), hotshot pilot (Oscar Isaac), and lonely scavenger (Daisy Ridley) become embroiled in the quest and soon find their destinies intertwined with that of the entire galaxy.

Though technologically the most sophisticated movie in the series, there is debatably too much reverence to what came before. Having a climactic father-son moment upon a bridge, a planet-size superweapon, and a well-spoken villain in General Hux—whom Domhnall Gleeson struggles to delineate from previous roguish thesps—doesn't help. But when it follows its own path the film soars, such as Rey's flight from the planet Jakku and her brutal duel with the wonderfully maladjusted Kylo Ren, played with delicious malevolence by Adam Driver.

The Force Awakens oozes charm and likeability from every old-fashioned pore, from the new fan-favorite robot BB-8 and an engaged and enthusiastic Harrison Ford reprising the role of Han Solo to the use of special, rather than visual, effects to bring the creatures and sets to life. Grossing $1 billion within twelve days of opening, *Star Wars* has, once again, established itself as the dominant blockbuster franchise for a long time to come. **SW**

U.S. (Lucasfilm, Bad Robot, Truenorth Productions) 135m Color **Producer** Kathleen Kennedy, J.J. Abrams, Bryan Burk **Screenplay** Lawrence Kasdan, J.J. Abrams, Michael Arndt **Photography** Dan Mindel Photography Daniel Mindel **Music** John Williams **Cast** Harrison Ford, Carrie Fisher, Adam Driver, Daisy Ridley, John Boyega, Oscar Isaac, Lupita Nyong'o, Domhnall Gleeson, Anthony Daniels, Peter Mayhew, Andy Serkis, Max von Sydow, Mark Hamill **Oscar nominations** Maryann Brandon, Mary Jo Markey (film editing), John Williams (original score), Andy Nelson, Christopher Scarabosio, Stuart Wilson (sound mixing) Matthew Wood, David Acord (sound editing), Roger Guyett, Pat Tubach, Neal Scanlan, Chris Corbould (visual effects)

> "Star Wars *has now gone beyond the sci-fi genre to its own kind of intergalactic quasi-Arthurian romance.*"
>
> **Peter Bradshaw,**
> ***The Guardian*, 2015**

i

Daniel Craig has a cameo as a Stormtrooper with the number JB-007—James Bond 007.

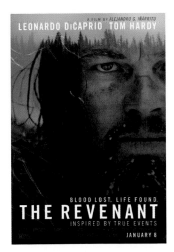

USA / Hong Kong / Taiwan (20th Century-Fox) 156m Color **Producer** Arnon Milchan, Steve Golin, Alejandro González Iñárritu, Mary Parent, Keith Redmon, James W. Scotchdopole **Screenplay** Mark L. Smith, Alejandro González Iñárritu **Photography** Emmanuel Lubezki **Music** Ryuichi Sakamoto, Alva Noto **Cast** Leonardo DiCaprio, Tom Hardy, Domnhall Gleeson, Will Poulter, Forrest Goodluck **Oscars** Leonardo DiCaprio (actor), Alejandro González Iñárritu (director), Emmanuel Lubezki (cinematography) **Oscar nominations** Arnon Milchan, Steve Golin, Alejandro González Iñárritu, Mary Parent, Keith Redmon (best picture), Tom Hardy (supporting actor), Stephen Mirrione (editing), Jacqueline West (costume design), Sian Grigg, Duncan Jarman, Robert A. Pandini (makeup), Jon Taylor, Frank A. Montaño, Randy Thom, Chris Duesterdick (sound mixing), Martín Hernández, Lon Bender (sound editing), Richard McBride, Matt Shumway, Jason Smith, Cameron Waldbauer (visual effects), Jack Fisk, Hamish Purdy (production design)

> *"As long as you can still grab a breath, you fight."*
>
> **Hugh Glass,**
> **(Leonardo DiCaprio)**

ℹ

The movie was shot in twelve locations in three countries: Canada, the United States, and Argentina.

The Revenant Alejandro González Iñárritu, 2015

Reputedly nearly as much of an ordeal for its cast and crew as for its protagonist, Alejandro González Iñárritu's film is inspired by the legend of Hugh Glass. In 1823, the American frontiersman was left for dead by his companions after being mauled by a bear, but managed to haul his battered body across 200 miles (320 km) of wilderness to the nearest settlement. Given that Glass's story has been much embellished over the years, it hardly matters if the film plays fast and loose with it. (The previous Hollywood treatment of the tale, Richard Sarafian's 1971 *Man in the Wilderness*, starring Richard Harris, took even more liberties.)

Iñárritu's purist insistence on shooting in natural light for only ninety minutes a day, and in the most remote and rugged sub-zero locations, pays off. The visual intensity of his landscapes, shot in moody near-monochrome by acclaimed cinematographer Emmanuel Lubezki, brings out all the icy indifference—and paradoxical beauty—of the stark desolation Glass has to struggle through and underlines his dogged determination to survive. Leonardo DiCaprio, rarely off-screen throughout the film's two-and-half-hour-plus running-time, has relatively little dialogue, but his expression of clenched, vengeful fury speaks volumes. (This committed performance finally won DiCaprio an Academy Award after four previous nominations.)

There's an eerie, almost mystical tone to the film, which with its theme of resurrection—Glass, seemingly dead, clambers up out of his own grave—at times seems to hint at Christian or perhaps shamanistic symbolism, a reading abetted by a scene in a ruined church. Iñárritu has created a grim epic of survival, a tale that with its extremes of violence and suffering isn't always easy to watch, but one that hooks itself relentlessly into the memory. **PK**

Saul fia László Nemes, 2015
Son of Saul

Hungary (Laokoon Filmgroup, Hungarian National Film Fund) 107m Color **Producer** Gábor Sipos, Gábor Rajna **Screenplay** László Nemes, Clara Royer **Photography** Mátyás Erdély **Music** László Melis **Cast** Géza Röhrig, Sándor Zsótér, Levente Molnár, Urs Rechn **Oscar** Hungary (foreign language film) Cannes Film Festival László Nemes (FIPRESCI Prize, François Chalais Award, Grand Prize of the Jury, Vulcain Prize for the Technical Artist, Golden Camera nomination, Palme d'Or nomination)

October 1944, Auschwitz-Birkenau. Saul Ausländer (the sensational Géza Röhrig) is a Hungarian member of the Sonderkommando, a group of Jewish prisoners isolated from the camp and forced to assist the Nazis in the machinery of large-scale exterminations. While working in one of the crematoriums, Saul discovers the corpse of a boy he takes for his son. As the Sonderkommando plans a rebellion, Saul decides to carry out an impossible task: save the child's body from the flames, find a rabbi to recite the mourner's Kaddish, and offer the boy a proper burial.

Son of Saul is an extraordinary work exhibiting courage, focus, and a clear-eyed sensibility concerning the atrocity of genocide and inhumanity. That it is the work of a director making his debut further accentuates its towering achievement. Shot on 35mm, it's a terrifying glimpse into hell, suffering, and cruelty, in which no shot is extraneous and no horror is spared. There is, however, more to the film than an endless parade of torture. The use of close up is intrinsic, making the spectator in some way a complicit witness in the horror. The sense of claustrohobia is intense and at times overpowering. Claude Lanzmann's *Shoah* (1985)is rightly regarded as the benchmark in terms of cinema dealing with the Holocaust. *Son of Saul* is perhaps the first fictional work that deserves to be spoken of in similarly reverential tones. **JWo**

Tangerine Sean Baker, 2015

U.S. (Duplass Brothers Productions, Through Films) 88m Color **Producer** Sean Baker, Karrie Cox, Marcus Cox, Darren Dean, Shih-Ching Tsou **Screenplay** Sean Baker, Chris Bergoch **Photography** Sean Baker, Radium Cheung **Cast** Kitana Kiki Rodriguez, Mya Taylor, Karren Karagulian, Mickey O'Hagan, James Ransone

Positioned in the press as either "the transgender prostitute movie" or "that film shot on an iPhone," Sean Baker's mischievous twenty-four-hour odyssey through the pulsating streets of Los Angeles is a far cry from the novelty piece such soundbites might imply. Instead, this richly emotional and imaginative Christmas Eve in the life of two sex workers on Santa Monica Boulevard is no mere gimmick. This is the real deal.

Baker's decision to shoot on three iPhone 5s (borne out of budgetary necessity) certainly informs the look and frenetic pace of the film, allowing for a sense of energy and unrestrained movement that could only be achievable with such lightweight equipment. But technique always takes a back seat to the real stars of the show: trans non-actors Kitana Kiki Rodriguez and Mya Taylor, who give two extraordinary performances as the hypnotic heroines Sin-Dee Rella and Alexandra.

With vivid colors and tart dialogue, *Tangerine* has much to offer, both from an artistic and cultural perspective. Although perhaps what is ultimately most fascinating about the film is in fact what it is not. It is not another lesson in transgender identity told through cisgender eyes. Nor is it a didactic commentary on sex work, or a simplistic portrayal of marginalized characters. It is a dizzying, crackling, and authentic celebration of female friendship and solidarity. **MB**

Bridge of Spies Steven Spielberg, 2015

In 1960, a US U-2 spy plane piloted by Francis Gary Powers was shot down over Soviet airspace. Arrested by the Russian secret service and put on trial for espionage, he was sentenced to ten years in prison. Such a story could have been the fodder of a thrilling, action-laden blockbuster. Instead, Steven Spielberg's entertaining Cold-War thriller chooses to focus on a protagonist who appears far more prosaic—the lawyer who secured the release of Powers and a young American student.

Prior to 1960, James B. Donovan's only high-profile role was as an assistant at the Nuremberg trials. (After his involvement in the U-2 prisoner exchange, he went on to secure the release of the 1,113 prisoners captured after the failed Bay of Pigs invasion of Cuba.) As played by Tom Hanks, Donovan is an everyday family man. Yet he soon realises the murkiness of the world he has been thrown into and uses his position to jockey for a deal. His bargaining chip is a Soviet spy, caught after a thrilling chase around the streets and subway platforms of Brooklyn. As played by Mark Rylance, who deservedly won a Best Supporting Actor Oscar, he is the perfect foil to Donovan. Wily as a fox, Rudolf Abel permanently lives in a world where nothing is what it seems.

Some critics have pointed out that Hanks's performance is in the mould of the roles that James Stewart played in Frank Capra's films, most notably *Mr. Smith Goes to Washington* (1939). However, Donovan's politics—and Hanks's own leanings—would better suit the Henry Fonda or Spencer Tracey mould, whose characters were no less noble but espoused a particular form of liberalism. As for the film, *Bridge of Spies* is an intelligent courtroom drama than transforms into a taut thriller. But ultimately, it is a portrait of a remarkable individual who was anything but ordinary. **IHS**

US / Germany / India (Amblin Entertainment, Dreamworks SKG, Fox 2000 Pictures, Marc Platt Productions, Participant Media, Reliance Entertainment, TSG Entertainment) 142m Color **Producer** Kristie Macosko Krieger, Marc Platt, Steven Spielberg **Screenplay** Matt Charman, Ethan Coen, Joel Coen **Photography** Janusz Kaminski **Music** Thomas Newman **Cast** Tom Hanks, Mark Rylance, Alan Alda, Amy Ryan, Sebastian Koch, Eve I lewson, Austin Stowell **Oscars** Mark Rylance (supporting actor) **Oscar nominations** Steven Spielberg, Marc Platt, Kristie Macosko Krieger (best picture) Matt Charman, Ethan Coen, Joel Coen (original screenplay), Thomas Newman (original score), Andy Nelson, Gary Rydstrom, Drew Kunin (sound mixing), Adam Stockhausen, Rena DeAngelo, Bernhard Henrich (production design)

> "We have to have the conversations our governments can't."
>
> **James Donovan (Tom Hanks)**

i

Gregory Peck tried to film the story in 1965, with himself in the role of Donovan and Alec Guiness as Abel.

The Big Short Adam McKay, 2015

The work of Michael Lewis is at once a logical yet perplexing choice for cinematic adaptation. While the financial journalist and non-fiction author is adept at finding human-interest stories to elucidate complex economic issues, his writing doesn't immediately suggest mainstream filmmaking. Despite this apparent barrier, *The Big Short* marks the second attempt by Brad Pitt's production company Plan B to adapt one of Lewis's books. Unlike their first effort, *Moneyball* (2011), which focused on a redemption story with an inspirational end goal, *The Big Short*'s strategy is more diffuse.

With the 2008 global financial crash serving as its ultimate destination, *The Big Short* focuses on "a few outsiders and weirdos" who correctly predicted the subprime mortgage market collapse and attempted to profit from it. This creates a morally complicated dilemma that is dealt with explicitly: for the protagonists to win, the audience must lose. Their success is predicated upon the worst economic crisis since the Great Depression, caused by ruinous greed. The characters are merely exploiting a calamity they can't prevent, but the unusual effect is like watching a heist movie where you're rooting for the heroes to rob your own home.

The choice of Adam McKay—best known for *Anchorman: The Legend of Ron Burgundy* (2004)—to write and direct the movie could seem anomalous unless you stayed for the end credits of *The Other Guys* (2010), which listed bonuses paid to executives at finance companies that took government bailouts. McKay reserves contempt not for his oddballs but for the system which is criminally deaf to its imminent disintegration. His righteous objective is to inform, using irreverent humor and a range of metaphysical gimmicks to do so: where Lewis employed colorful real life characters to explain daunting financial complexities, McKay uses jokes. **JW**

U.S. (Plan B Entertainment, Regency Enterprises) 130m Color **Producer** Dede Gardner, Jeremy Kleiner, Arnon Milchan, Brad Pitt **Screenplay** Adam McKay, Charles Randolph **Photography** Barry Ackroyd **Music** Nicholas Britell **Cast** Christian Bale, Steve Carrell, Ryan Gosling, Brad Pitt, John Magaro, Finn Wittrock, Hamish Linklater, Rafe Spall, Jeremy Strong, Adepero Oduye, Marisa Tomei, Melissa Leo **Oscars** Charles Randolph, Adam McKay (adapted screenplay) **Oscar nominations** Brad Pitt, Dede Gardner, Jeremy Kleiner (best picture), Christian Bale (supporting actor), Adam McKay (director), Hank Corwin (editing)

"The movie is built around having a conversation with the audiences."

Adam McKay, 2015

i

Christian Bale learnt to play drums for the movie in just two weeks.

Spotlight Tom McCarthy, 2015

U.S. / **Canada** (Anonymous Content, First Look Media, Participant Media, Rocklin / Faust) 128m Color **Producer** Blye Pagon Faust, Steve Golin, Nicole Rocklin, Michael Sugar **Screenplay** Tom McCarthy, Josh Singer **Photography** Masanobu Takayanagi **Cast** Mark Ruffalo, Michael Keaton, Rachel McAdams, Liev Schreiber, John Slattery, Brian d'Arcy James, Stanley Tucci, Jamey Sheridan, Billy Crudup **Oscars** Michael Sugar, Steve Golin, Nicole Rocklin, Blye Pagon Faust (best picture), Josh Singer, Tom McCarthy (original screenplay) Oscar nominations Mark Ruffalo (supporting actor), Rachel McAdams (supporting actress), Tom McCarthy (director), Tom McArdle (editing) **Venice Film Festival** Tom McCarthy (Brian Award, Silver Mouse)

𝑖

The credits and title cards are set in Miller, the typeface that the *Boston Globe* uses for most of its headlines and body copy.

Journalism is much like law or international spying in that the individuals practising it in movies are inevitably having a more exciting time than their real life counterparts. That *Spotlight*, which follows a small team of newspaper reporters in 2001 as they uncover widespread sexual abuse within the Boston Archdiocese, avoids the temptation to add drama where there was none is a testament to its quiet daring. Tom McCarthy draws strength from restraint, demonstrating confidence that his film can be engrossing and moving without having to squeeze in artificial conflicts and character arcs.

Spotlight is so involving precisely because it observes professionals doing a job well. It is significant that we never see the team receive the Pulitzer Prize for their efforts. (The film followed suit, winning the Oscar for Best Picture.) Instead, the focus is exactly where it should be: on the task at hand. McCarthy spends an appreciable amount of time depicting the sort of unglamorous reporting that films typically ignore, as the journalists, powered by moral horror, chase multiple sources, trawl through parish directories, and request court reports. While *Spotlight* is deeply compassionate about the well over 1,000 estimated abuse survivors, it is fundamentally a celebration of investigative journalism and the decent, ordinary people committed to it. **JW**

Straight Outta Compton F. Gary Gray, 2015

U.S. (Cube Vision, Legendary Pictures)147m Colour **Producers** Ice Cube, Dr. Dre, Tomica Woods-Wright, Matt Alvarez, Scott Bernstein, F. Gary Gray **Screenplay** Jonathan Herman, Andrea Berloff, S. Leigh Savidge, Alan Wenkus **Music** Joseph Trapanese **Photography** Matthew Libatique **Cast** Jason Mitchell, O'Shea Jackson Jr., Corey Hawkins, Paul Giamatti **Oscar nominations** Andrea Berloff, Jonathan Herman, S. Leigh Savidge, Alan Wenkus (original screenplay)

i

The actors re-recorded N.W.A's entire *Straight Outta Compton* album to help them get into character.

How do you tell the story of a gangsta rap group who, inspired by the troubled world they lived in, told us to "F**k tha police"? It helps if your director is friends with original N.W.A band members Ice Cube and Dr. Dre, and the widow of front man Eazy E, Tomica Woods-Wright.

Straight Outta Compton's tale isn't original: dodgy manager rips off naive group whose ascent involves fighting and youthful rebellion, lots of women, and rap parties. But unavoidable biopic clichés aside, the film successfully details the formation of N.W.A, their rise to fame, how they fell apart, and the tragedy that stopped them from punching the reset button. And the Compton that appears in this drama is a far cry from the ghetto ruled by gun-toting drug dealers. It's an understated backdrop, allowing the focus to fall completely on the band's emotional rollercoaster and the short-lived reign they had over the music industry.

The film also profits from the inspired casting of the leads and real-life characters, with newcomer Jason Mitchell startling as Eazy E, Corey Hawkins stolid as Dr. Dre, and O'Shea Jackson Jr. offering up an impressive characterization of his father. Veteran actor Paul Giamatti also convinces as the band's corrupt manager Jerry Heller. Then there's the soundtrack—a combination of classic N.W.A hits and a slew of popular R&B and rap songs from that era. **AG**

Mad Max: Fury Road George Miller, 2015

Long before *The Fast and the Furious* franchise tore up the world's freeways and petrolheads guzzled themselves on the antics of the *Top Gear* team, an ex-cop called Max Rockatansky ruled the barren wastelands of the open road. After Ned Kelly, Max is arguably Australia's most famous pop culture icon. Neither an outlaw nor a hero in any classic sense, he is molded by the world around him—a land that has descended into chaos, with rival factions vying for whatever remains of the Earth's natural resources.

In the frenetic *Mad Max: Fury Road*, Mel Gibson has been replaced as Max by Tom Hardy, whose more introspective road warrior allows Charlize Theron's Imperator Furiosa to steal the show. The one-armed driver of a huge eighteen-wheel war rig, she takes advantage of a fuel run to escape the clutches of the insane leader of the War Boys, Immortan Joe, taking with her his coterie of wives. With Max and Furiosa's singular talents combined, they manage to ward off an army of assailants, and the resulting vehicular mash-ups dwarf even the previous films' record-setting levels of carnage. Driving the action, which includes a vertiginous hurricane of fire, is Junkie XL's pulsating score—more than a match for Brian May's pounding accompaniment to the first two instalments.

The landscape has changed a little, too. Australia was used as the backdrop for the first three *Mad Max* films, whereas *Fury Road*'s action was mostly shot across the vast red plains of the Namib Desert. But the gothic feel of the film, both in the design of vehicles and the characters who drive them, remains the same. It's B-movie heaven filmed as a big-budget blockbuster, with an Oscar-winning team of technicians and designers ensuring the ride is a fabulous to look at as it is thrilling to experience. **IHS**

Australia / U.S. (Warner Bros., Kennedy Miller Productions, Village Roadshow Pictures) 120m Color **Producers** George Miller, Doug Mitchell, P.J. Voeten **Screenplay** George Miller, Brendan McCarthy, Nico Lathouris **Photography** John Seale **Music** Junkie XL **Cast** Tom Hardy, Charlize Theron, Nicholas Hoult, Hugh Keays-Byrne, Josh Helman, Nathan Jones, Zoë Kravitz, Rosie Huntington-Whiteley **Oscars** Margaret Sixel (editing), Jenny Beavan (costume), Lesley Vanderwalt, Elka Wardega, Damian Martin (makeup), Chris Jenkins, Gregg Rudloff, Ben Osmo (sound mixing), Mark A. Mangini, David White (sound editing), Colin Gibson, Lisa Thompson (production design) **Oscar nominations** Doug Mitchell, George Miller (best picture), George Miller (director), John Seale (cinematography), Andrew Jackson, Tom Wood, Dan Oliver, Andy Williams (visual effects)

> *"If I'm gonna die, I'm gonna die historic on the Fury Road!"*
>
> **Nux (Nicholas Hoult)**

ℹ️

The majority of the effects in the movie are real practical effects, stunts, make-up, and sets.

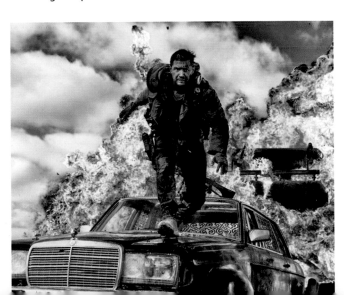

Contributors

Geoff Andrew (GA) is Senior Film Editor of *Time Out London*, Head of Programming at the National Film Theatre, and the author of numerous books on film, including studies of Nicholas Ray and Krzysztof Kieslowski's *Three Colors Trilogy*.

Linda Badley (LB) is Professor of English at Middle Tennessee State University, where she also teaches film studies. She is the author of *Film, Horror, and the Body Fantastic* and has published essays on fantasy, science-fiction, film, and TV.

Kathryn Bergeron (KB) is a graduate student in Media Arts at the University of Arizona. Her work focuses primarily on the representation of race and marginalization in film.

Joanna Berry (JB) worked as a film critic for *Time Out* before becoming reviews editor for *Empire* magazine. She has written for a number of magazines and newspapers including the *Observer*, *Maxim*, and *Radio Times*.

Edward Buscombe (EB) was formerly Head of Publishing at the British Film Institute. He is the author of books on *Stagecoach* and *The Searchers*. *Cinema Today*, his history of World Cinema since 1970, was published in 2003.

Garrett Chaffin-Quiray (GC-Q) has sponsored film festivals, taught TV and cinema history, and published book, movie, video, and event reviews, several scholarly essays and book chapters, and one short story.

Tom Charity (TCh) is Film Editor of *Time Out London* magazine. He is the author of *John Cassavetes: Life Works* and *The Right Stuff*.

Mark Cousins (MC) writes for *Sight and Sound*, is Honorary Professor of Film at the University of Glasgow, and co-founded the 8 ½ Foundation with Tilda Swinton. His films include *The First Movie* and *The Story of Film: An Odyssey*; his books include *Imagining Reality: The Faber Book of Documentary*.

Travis Crawford (TCr) is a curator for the Philadelphia Film Festival. His festival programs, "New Korean Cinema" and "Danger After Dark," highlight the best in Asian genre filmmaking. He is a regular contributor to *Filmmaker* and *Moviemaker* magazines.

Adrian Danks (AD) is the Head of Cinema Studies in the School of Applied Communication, RMIT University (Australia). He is currently President and co-curator of the Melbourne Cinémathèque, and co-editor of the journal supplement *Cteq*.

Ethan de Seife (EdeS) is a Ph.D. candidate at the University of Wisconsin-Madison. He is currently at work on a dissertation about the films of Frank Tashlin.

David Del Valle (DDV) has been Hollywood correspondent for *Films and Filming* (U.K.) and *L'Ecran Fantastique* (France). He has written for *Video Watchdog*, *Psychotronic*, *Films in Review*, and *Scarlett Street* among others.

Roumiana Deltcheva (RDe), Ph.D., is a scholar in new media technology in Montreal, Canada. She engages in interdisciplinary research in literature, film, and print media, focusing on the cultural paradigms defining post-totalitarian East Central Europe.

Wheeler Winston Dixon (WWD) is the James Ryan Endowed Professor of Film Studies, Professor of English at the University of Nebraska, Lincoln, and Co-Editor-in-Chief of the *Quarterly Review of Film and Video*. His books as author or editor include *Film and Television After 9/11*.

Dana Duma (DD) teaches film history at Hyperion University and the National University of Cinema and Theatre in Bucharest. She has written the books *Self-Portraits of the Movie*, *Gopo*, and many articles for film periodicals.

Rachel Dwyer (RDw) is Senior Lecturer in Indian Studies at SOAS, University of London. Her publications include *Yash Chopra* and *Cinema India: The Visual Culture of Hindi Film*.

Angela Errigo (AE) studied film and journalism at San Francisco State University. She is a freelance writer and broadcaster, a contributing editor on *Empire*, and film critic for the BBC Radio 2 Arts Programme.

Tim Evans (TE) is reviews editor for Skymovies. com. Born in London, he has worked for newspapers in the Midlands as well as ITN.

Chiara Ferrari (CFe) is a Doctoral candidate in the Department of Film, Television, and Digital Media at the University of California, Los Angeles. Her research includes culture, media, and society, and Latin American cinema.

Ailsa Ferrier (AF) is a London-based programmer, currently curating for the Curzon Home Cinema platform. She previously worked for Artificial Eye Film Distributors.

Cynthia Freeland (CFr) is Associate Professor of Philosophy and Director of Women's Studies at the University of Houston. She has published widely on both ancient philosophy and aesthetics.

Jean-Michel Frodon (J-MF) is the Senior Editor on cinema at *Le Monde* and teaches at the Institut de Sciences Politiques. He created L'Exception, a think tank about cinema, and has published several books.

Chris Fujiwara (CFu) is the author of *Jacques Tourneur: The Cinema of Nightfall*. He is a contributing editor of *Hermenaut*.

Tom Gunning (TG) is a professor in the Department of Art History and the Committee on Cinema and Media at the University of Chicago. He is the author of *Fritz Lang: Allegories of Vision and Modernity*.

Philip Hall (PH) studied law, literature, and film at Victoria University in Wellington, New Zealand. He now lives and writes in London.

Rahul Hamid (RH) is a Doctoral candidate in the Department of Cinema Studies at New York University, writing his thesis on Iranian film. He has written on contemporary international film in publications such as *Cineaste* magazine.

Briony Hanson (BHa) is the British Council's Director of Film and also an occasional film critic and broadcaster. She has previously run the BFI Programme Unit, programmed the London Lesbian and Gay Film Festival and been Director of The Script Factory.

Ernest Hardy (EH) is a film/music critic and poet. He is a Sundance Fellow whose work has appeared in the *New York Times*, *LA Times*, *Village Voice*, *Rolling Stone*, and *Vibe*. He is a member of LAFCA (Los Angeles Film Critics Association).

Ian Haydn Smith (IHS) is the update editor for *1001 Movies You Must See Before You Die*. He is a London-based writer and the editor of *Curzon Magazine*.

Bernd Herzogenrath (BH) is the author of *An Art of Desire: Reading Paul Auster* and editor of *From Virgin Land to Disney World: Nature and Its Discontents in the USA of Yesterday and Today*

Mark Holcomb (MH) writes about film for *The Village Voice* and other publications. He lives in Brooklyn, New York.

Anikó Imre (AI) teaches film studies in the Department of Interdisciplinary Arts and Sciences of the University of Washington, Tacoma, and has published on race and gender in cinema, violence, and postcoloniality.

Philip Kemp (PK) is a writer and film historian, and is a regular contributor to *Sight and Sound*, *Total Film*, and *International Film Guide*, among others.

James Kendrick (JKe) is an associate instructor in the Department of Communication and Culture at Indiana University, Bloomington. His research interests include violence in the media and postclassical Hollywood film history.

Joshua Klein (JKl) is a freelance writer whose work has appeared in the *Chicago Tribune*, *Washington Post*, and *The Onion*.

Laura Kloss (LK) is a writer, film workshop developer, and programmer. She is currently developing Lightbox Cinema, which combines cinema heritage and workshops for children.

Mikel J. Koven (MK) is a lecturer in Film and Television Studies at the University of Wales, Aberystwyth. He is the author of the *Pocket Essentials series: Blaxploitation Films.*

Karen Krizanovich (KK) has reviewed films for a variety of publications, including *Empire, NME, Word* magazine, and *Cosmopolitan UK.*

Andrea F. Kulas (AK) obtained her MA in Media Arts from the University of Arizona and is the coeditor of *Ridley Scott: Interviews.*

Frank Lafond (FL) has written essays on horror and film noir and has edited a book on the modern American horror film.

Edward Lawrenson (EL) is a freelance writer based in London.

Colin MacCabe (CM) is Distinguished Professor of English and Film at the University of Pittsburgh, and writer of *Godard: A Portrait of the Artist at 70.*

Adrian Martin (AM) is the author of *The Mad Max Movies, Once Upon a Time in America,* and *Phantasms,* and coeditor of *Movie Mutations.*

Ernest Mathijs (EM) is a lecturer in film at the University of Wales, Aberystwyth. He has recently researched the reception of David Cronenberg, Low Countries cinema, and the cross-cultural impact of *The Lord of the Rings.*

Mick McAloon (MM) has been writing about film for fifteen years. He also curates films and events.

Jay McRoy (JM) is Associate Professor of English and Film Studies at the University of Wisconsin-Parkside. He is the editor of *Japanese Horror Cinema.*

Spencer Medof (SM) is an independent producer with several feature and television projects in various stages of development.

Annalee Newitz (AN) is founder of the webzine Bad Subjects and has written *White Trash: Race and Class in America.*

Kim Newman (KN) is a novelist, critic, and broadcaster and the author of *Nightmare Movies, Wild West Movies,* and *Apocalypse Movies.*

Dom Nolan (DN) is a novelist and critic.

Devin Orgeron (DO) is Assistant Professor of Film Studies at North Carolina State University. His writing has appeared in a number of publications, including *CineAction.*

Marsha Orgeron (MO) is Assistant Professor of Film Studies at North Carolina State University. She has been published in *Cinema Journal, American Literature,* and *Quarterly Review of Film & Video.*

Corinne Oster (CO) completed a dissertation on new representations of marginality in contemporary French women's cinema, for the Department of Comparative Literature at the University of Massachusetts.

R. Barton Palmer (RBP) holds Ph.D.s from Yale University (Medieval Studies) and New York University (Cinema Studies). He is Professor of Literature at Clemson University and Director of the South Carolina Film Institute.

Richard Peña (RP) is Associate Professor of Film Studies at Columbia University and the Program Director of the Film Society of Lincoln Center.

Cooper Penner (CP) is a Los Angeles–based writer and lover of film. He recently completed his first novel.

Jonathan Penner (JP) is a Los Angeles multi-hyphenate. An Oscar nominee and proud father, his book *Horror Cinema,* is co-authored with Steven Schneider.

Murray Pomerance (MP) is Professor and Chair of the Department of Sociology at Ryerson University. His books include *Sugar, Spice, and Everything Nice: Cinemas of Girlhood.*

Phil Powrie (PP) is Director of the Centre for Research into Film and Media, University of Newcastle upon Tyne.

Bérénice Reynaud (BR) is the author of *Nouvelles Chines, nouveaux cinémas* and *A City of Sadness.* She teaches at the California Institute of the Arts.

David Robinson (DR) is the former film critic of *The Times* (London), a film historian, and Director of the Giornate del Cinema Muto. His publications include *From Peepshow to Palace: The Birth of American Film.*

Jonathan Romney (JRom) is the *Independent on Sunday* film critic and writes for *Sight and Sound* and *Film Comment.* His books include *Atom Egoyan* and *Short Orders.*

Jonathan Rosenbaum (JRos) is film critic for the *Chicago Reader.* His books include *Abbas Kiarostami* and *Dead Man.*

Martin Rubin (MR) programs films at the Gene Siskel Film Center in Chicago. He has written on Busby Berkeley and thrillers.

Steven Jay Schneider (SJS) is a film critic, scholar, and producer, with M.A. degrees in Philosophy and Cinema Studies from Harvard University and New York University, respectively. He is the author and editor of a number of books on movies.

Marc Siegel (MS) writes about queer theory and experimental film. He is a Visiting Lecturer in Film Studies at the Free University in Berlin.

Adam Simon (AS) is a writer and director whose work includes *Braindead, The Typewriter, The Rifle and the Movie Camera,* and *The American Nightmare.*

Leigh Singer (LS) is a freelance film journalist, programmer and filmmaker whose writing and video essays appear in print and online.

Peter Stanfield (PS) is Senior Lecturer in Media Arts at Southampton Institute, England. His books include *Hollywood, Westerns and the 1930s: The Lost Trail.*

David Sterritt (DS) is film critic of *The Christian Science Monitor,* Professor of Theater and Film at Long Island University, and a member of the Film Studies Faculty at Columbia University.

Adisakdi Tantimedh (AT) is a writer and filmmaker. He has written radio plays and television scripts for the BBC and various screenplays, including the BAFTA award winner *Zinky Boys Go Underground.*

Michael Tapper (MT) is editor of *Film International.* He has contributed to various publications including *Lars von Trier: Interviews.*

Ella Taylor (ET) is a film critic for *LA Weekly.* She has also written about film for many newspapers and magazines.

Jo Taylor (JT) graduated from Kingston University. Her Masters focused on the myth of the Hollywood Hero in modern day society.

Stacy Title (ST) is an Oscar-nominated writer-director. Her credits include *The Last Supper* and *Let the Devil Wear Black,* and she has written for *Harper's Bazaar* and *Premier.*

Ginette Vincendeau (GV) is Professor of Film Studies at the University of Warwick. Among her recent books on French cinema is *Jean-Pierre Melville: An American in Paris.*

Jason Ward (JWa) is the associate editor of *Oh Comely* magazine and a freelance film journalist.

Simon Ward (SW) is the author of *The Art and Making of Independence Day: Resurgence* and *Aliens: The Set Photography.* His work has appeared in numerous publications, including *The Greatest Movies You'll Never See.*

Andy Willis (AW) teaches film and media studies at the University of Salford. His publications include *The Cinema of Alex de la Iglesia.*

Josephine Woll (JW) teaches at Howard University. Her work includes *Real Images: Soviet Cinema and Thaw.*

Jason Wood (JWo) is the Director of Programming for Curzon Cinemas. He is also the author of numerous books on cinema.

Genre Index

Action

"A" gai waak juk jaap 735
Adventures of Robin Hood, The 140
Akira 754
Alien 643
Aliens 728
Apocalypse Now 646
Avatar 914
Batman 767
Ben-Hur 354
Beverly Hills Cop 703
Big Red One, The 659
Blade Runner 675
Braveheart 836
Captain Blood 123
Captains Courageous 137
Cidade de deus 895
City of God 895
Come Drink with Me 447
Crouching Tiger, Hidden Dragon 890
Da zui xia 447
Dark Knight, The 912
Die Hard 762
Die xue shuang xiong 770
Do ma daan 727
Eagle, The 48
Easy Rider 497
Empire Strikes Back, The 654
Enter the Dragon 558
Faster, Pussycat! Kill! Kill! 438
Fight Club 878
Full Metal Jacket 740
Get Carter 529
Gladiator 885
Goldfinger 416
Grand Budapest Hotel, The 934
Great Train Robbery, The 23
Harder They Come, The 569
Heat 843
Hsia nu 495
Inception 916
Independence Day 859
Jaws 600
Killer, The 770
King of New York 780
Lola Rennt 868
Lord of the Rings, The 892
Mad Max 650
Mad Max: Fury Road 943
Matrix, The 882
Natural Born Killers 826
Oldboy 898
Oldeuboi 898
Once Upon a Time in China 793
Peking Opera Blues 727
Planet of the Apes 477
Potomok Chingis-Khana 70
Project A, Part II 735
Public Enemy, The 89
Pulp Fiction 824
Raiders of the Lost Ark 664

Reservoir Dogs 804
Return of the Jedi 688
Rio Bravo 360
RoboCop 764
Rocky 608
Romper Stomper 802
Run Lola Run 868
Saving Private Ryan 866
Seven Samurai, The 293
Shaft 531
Shao Lin san shi liu fang 637
Shaolin Master Killer 637
Shichinin no samurai 293
Sleeping Dogs 619
Spartacus 371
Star Wars 612
Star Wars: The Force Awakens 936
Storm over Asia 70
Superfly 551
Terminator 2: Judgement Day 797
Terminator, The 697
Thelma & Louise 793
Thief of Bagdad, The 48
Thin Red Line, The 872
Three Kings 877
Top Gun 730
Total Recall 783
Touch of Zen, A 495
Towering Inferno, The 572
Untouchables, The 745
Wo hu cang long 890
Wong fei-hung 793

Adventure

2001: A Space Odyssey 484
Adventures of Prince Achmed, The 55
Adventures of Robin Hood, The 140
African Queen, The 257
Aguirre, der Zorn Gottes 538
Aguirre, the Wrath of God 538
Akira 754
Back to the Future 711
Beauty and the Beast 210
Ben-Hur 354
Black Cat, The 117
Bridge on the River Kwai, The 334
Captain Blood 123
Captains Courageous 137
Close Encounters of the Third Kind 610
Crouching Tiger, Hidden Dragon 890
Deliverance 537
Dersu uzala 573
Die Abenteuer des Prinzen Achmed 55
E.T.: The Extra-Terrestrial 670
Easy Rider 497
Empire Strikes Back, The 654

Fitzcarraldo 679
Goldfinger 416
Great Escape, The 412
Gunga Din 153
Hill 24 Doesn't Answer 304
Hsia nu 495
It Happened One Night 115
Jaws 600
Jurassic Park 818
La belle et la bête 210
Lawrence of Arabia 393
Le salaire de la peur 274
Life of Pi 921
Lion King, The 820
Lord of the Rings, The 892
Monty Python and the Holy Grail 590
Mutiny on the Bounty 119
North by Northwest 349
Prapancha Pash 71
Princess Bride, The 739
Raiders of the Lost Ark 664
Return of the Jedi 688
Right Stuff, The 686
Sen to chihiro no kamikakushi 892
Shanghai Express 95
Spirited Away 892
Stand by Me 731
Star Wars 612
Sullivan's Travels 172
Thief of Bagdad, The 48
Throw of Dice, A 71
Total Recall 783
Touch of Zen, A 495
Treasure of the Sierra Madre, The 234
Wages of Fear 274
Wizard of Oz, The 154
Wo hu cang long 890

Animation

Adventures of Prince Achmed, The 55
Akira 754
Alice 752
Die Abenteuer des Prinzen Achmed 55
Dumbo 175
Fantasia 159
Fantastic Planet 569
Grave of the Fireflies 758
Heaven and Earth Magic 392
Hotaru no haka 758
Jungle Book, The 471
La planète sauvage 569
Lion King, The 820
Neco z alenky 752
Pinocchio 165
Sen to chihiro no kamikakushi 892
Snow White and the Seven Dwarfs 136
Spirited Away 892

Toy Story trilogy 844
Who Framed Roger Rabbit 759

Avant-Garde

Blonde Cobra 410
Deseret 836
Flaming Creatures 404
Hold Me While I'm Naked 442
Koyaanisqatsi 692
Még kér a nép 529
Meshes of the Afternoon 187
Red Psalm 529
Report 453
Scorpio Rising 419
Too Early, Too Late 672
Vinyl 439
Wavelength 465
Zu Früh, Zu Spät 672

Comedy

"A" gai waak juk jaap 735
À nous la liberté 83
Adam's Rib 238
Adventures of Priscilla, Queen of the Desert, The 827
Age of Gold, The 80
Airplane! 662
All About My Mother 881
Amarcord 570
American Graffiti 556
American Werewolf in London, An 663
Annie Hall 616
Apartment, The 372
Archangel 783
Ariel 752
Artist, The 918
Artists and Models 301
Awful Truth, The 138
Bab el hadid 343
Babbetes Gaestebud 743
Babe 837
Babette's Feast 743
Back to the Future 711
Baker's Wife, The 141
Band Wagon, The 271
Bank Dick, The 164
Being John Malkovich 875
Being There 644
Beverly Hills Cop 703
Big 759
Big Chill, The 687
Big Short, The 940
Birdman 932
Blazing Saddles 582
Boudu sauvé des eaux 93
Boudu Saved from Drowning 93
Brave-Hearted Will Take the Bride, The 840
Brazil 713
Breakfast at Tiffany's 381
Breakfast Club, The 707

Breaking Away 642
Bringing Up Baby 142
Broadcast News 742
Buffalo 66 870
Bull Durham 748
C'est arrivé près de chez vous 808
Cairo Station 343
Campanadas a medianoche 437
Caro diario 833
Chimes at Midnight 437
Christmas Story, A 684
City Lights 85
Clerks 830
Closely Watched Trains 466
Clueless 842
Crimes and Misdemeanors 766
Daisies 446
Dear Diary 833
Decline of the American Empire, The 727
Delicatessen 797
Destry Rides Again 149
Dilwale Dulhania le Jayenge 840
Diner 676
Discreet Charm of the Bourgeoisie, The 543
Do ma daan 727
Do the Right Thing 772
Down by Law 726
Dr. Strangelove 422
Draughtsman's Contract, The 684
Duck Soup 105
Eagle, The 48
El ángel exterminador 397
Exterminating Angel, The 397
Fargo 850
Fast Times at Ridgemont High 671
Ferris Bueller's Day Off 728
Fireman's Ball, The 470
Fish Called Wanda, A 755
Forrest Gump 831
Four Weddings and a Funeral 830
Freedom for Us 83
General, The 60
Gentlemen Prefer Blondes 281
Ghostbusters 698
Gigi 338
Giulietta degli spiriti 433
Gold Rush, The 53
Golden Coach, The 269
Good Bye Lenin! 899
Good Morning, Vietnam 743
Graduate, The 460
Grand Budapest Hotel, The 934
Grease 636
Great Beauty, The 925
Groundhog Day 815
Gunga Din 153
Hannah and Her Sisters 722
Hanyeo 373

Happiness 871
Hard Day's Night, A 425
Harold and Maude 526
Heartbreak Kid, The 547
High Society 323
His Girl Friday 158
Horí, má panenko 470
Housemaid, The 373
Hsi yen 817
It Happened One Night 115
Jerk, The 652
Juliet of the Spirits 433
Jungle Book, The 471
Kid Brother, The 65
Kind Hearts and Coronets 242
King of Comedy, The 694
Kingdom, The 835
L'âge d'or 80
L'Atalante 116
La femme du boulanger 141
La grande bellezza 925
La règle du jeu 157
Ladies Man, The 385
Lady Eve, The 169
Lady Vanishes, The 144
Ladykillers, The 311
Lavender Hill Mob, The 259
Le carosse d'or 269
Le charme discret de la bourgeoisie 543
Le déclin de l'empire américain 727
Le roman d'un tricheur 129
Le souffle au coeur 534
Les demoiselles de Rochefort 463
Les vacances de M. Hulot 272
Little Big Man 510
Local Hero 694
Lucía 498
M*A*S*H 512
Man Bites Dog 808
Manhattan 645
Mary Poppins 428
Modern Times 125
Mon oncle 346
Monsieur Verdoux 222
Monty Python and the Holy Grail 590
Monty Python's Life of Brian 641
Moonstruck 744
Mr. Deeds Goes to Town 127
Mr. Hulot's Holiday 272
Mujeres al borde de un ataque de nervios 749
Muppet Movie, The 649
Muriel's Wedding 826
Murmur of the Heart 534
My Fair Lady 417
My Man Godfrey 128
My Uncle 346
Naked Gun, The 757
Network 604
Night at the Opera, A 121

Ninotchka 153
No Man's Land 893
Nutty Professor, The 411
Once Upon a Time in China 793
One Flew Over the Cuckoo's Nest 592
Ostre sledované vlaky 466
Our Hospitality 41
Paleface, The 229
Palm Beach Story, The 176
Peking Opera Blues 727
Philadelphia Story, The 161
Pink Flamingos 549
Player, The 803
Playtime 458
Pretty Woman 780
Princess Bride, The 739
Prizzi's Honor 706
Producers, The 489
Project A, Part II 735
Purple Rose of Cairo, The 716
Quiet Man, The 261
Rain Man 761
Raising Arizona 734
Real Life 642
Riget 835
Rocky Horror Picture Show, The 586
Roger & Me 774
Roman Holiday 282
Room with a View, A 720
Rules of the Game, The 157
Rushmore 869
Saturday Night and Sunday Morning 363
Sedmikrasky 446
She Done Him Wrong 103
She's Gotta Have It 723
Sherlock, Jr. 44
Singin' in the Rain 264
Slacker 792
Sleeper 563
Smiles of a Summer Night 312
Smoke 839
Some Like it Hot 348
Sommarnattens leende 312
Sons of the Desert 109
Steamboat Bill, Jr. 70
Sting, The 551
Story of a Cheat, The 129
Stranger than Paradise 704
Strictly Ballroom 802
Sullivan's Travels 172
Sunset Blvd. 251
Swing Time 126
Tampopo 732
Tangerine 938
Terms of Endearment 689
Thin Man, The 118
This Is Spinal Tap 701
Three Kings 877
Three Lives and Only One Death 853

To Be or Not to Be 177
Todo sobre mi madre 881
Tootsie 677
Top Hat 124
Toy Story trilogy 844
Trainspotting 849
Trois vies & une seule mort 853
Trouble in Paradise 96
Trust 777
Unbelievable Truth, The 774
Underground 840
Up in Smoke 635
W.R.: Misterije organizma 523
W.R.: Mysteries of the Organism 523
Wedding Banquet, The 817
When Harry Met Sally 765
Whisky Galore! 243
Who Framed Roger Rabbit 759
Willy Wonka and the Chocolate Factory 521
Withnail and I 738
Women on the Verge of a Nervous Breakdown 749
Wong fei-hung 793
Young Frankenstein 580
Young Girls of Rochefort, The 463
Zéro de conduite 106
Zero for Conduct 106

Crime
12 Angry Men 328
400 Blows, The 350
À bout de souffle 370
Aileen Wuornos: The Life and Death of a Serial Killer 897
All the President's Men 602
American Friend, The 615
Angels with Dirty Faces 140
Ariel 752
Asphalt Jungle, The 245
Atlantic City 655
Badlands 554
Big Heat, The 280
Bird with the Crystal Plumage, The 511
Black Cat, The 117
Blue Velvet 721
Bob le flambeur 313
Bob the Gambler 313
Body Heat 667
Bonnie and Clyde 473
Boyz 'n the Hood 787
Breathless 370
Bring Me the Head of Alfredo Garcia 572
C'est arrivé près de chez vous 808
Chinatown 578
Clockwork Orange, A 518
Come Drink With Me 447
Conformist, The 503
Consequences of Love, The 901

Conversation, The 576
Cyclo 841
Da zui xia 447
Dark Knight, The 914
Daybreak 152
De Stilte Rond Christine M. 683
Der Amerikanische Freund 615
Detour 201
Die xue shuang xiong 770
Dirty Harry 517
Dog Day Afternoon 591
Double Indemnity 196
Dr. Mabuse, der Spieler 35
Dr. Mabuse, Parts 1 and 2 35
Drugstore Cowboy 771
Elephant 897
Enter the Dragon 558
Farewell, My Lovely 198
Fargo 850
Fish Called Wanda, A 755
Force of Evil 227
French Connection, The 528
Gangs of New York 893
Get Carter 529
Godfather, The 544
Godfather: Part II, The 574
Goodfellas 778
Great Train Robbery, The 23
Gun Crazy 236
Hana-Bi 860
Harder They Come, The 569
Heat 843
Heavenly Creatures 823
Henry: Portrait of a Serial
    Killer 782
Hole, The 366
I Am a Fugitive from a Chain
    Gang 93
Il conformista 503
JFK 791
Killer, The 770
Killers, The 211
King of New York 780
Klute 525
L.A. Confidential 861
L'argent 685
L'uccello dalle piume di cristallo
    511
Lady from Shanghai, The 230
Ladykillers, The 311
Last Seduction, The 821
Lavender Hill Mob, The 259
Le consequenze dell'amore 901
Le jour se lève 152
Le trou 366
Les quatre cents coups 350
Les vampires 27
Little Caesar 77
Lone Star 857
Long Goodbye, The 557
M 90
Man Bites Dog 808
Manchurian Candidate, The 399

Mean Streets 562
Memento 889
Money 685
Murder, My Sweet 198
Natural Born Killers 826
Odd Man Out 222
On the Waterfront 284
Once Upon a Time in America
    695
Out of the Past 221
Pépé le Moko 132
Pickpocket 351
Pink Flamingos 549
Point Blank 462
Postman Always Rings Twice,
    The 209
Prizzi's Honor 706
Public Enemy, The 89
Pulp Fiction 824
Question of Silence, A 683
Rashomon 246
Reservoir Dogs 804
RoboCop 764
Rope 231
Scarface 693
Scarface: The Shame of a
    Nation 98
Serpico 559
Shaft 531
Slumdog Millionaire 911
Sting, The 551
Straw Dogs 535
Superfly 551
Targets 487
Taxi Driver 606
Thelma & Louise 793
Touch of Evil 337
Untouchables, The 745
Usual Suspects, The 847
Wall Street 744
White Heat 237
Wrong Man, The 323
Xich lo 841

Docu-Drama
Close-Up 779
Louisiana Story 235
Nema-ye nazdik 779
W.R.: Misterije organizma 523
W.R.: Mysteries of the Organism
    523

Documentary
Aileen Wuornos: The Life and
    Death of a Serial Killer 897
Battle of San Pietro, The 205
Bowling for Columbine 894
Chelovek s kinoapparatom 72
Chronicle of a Summer 387
Chronique d'un été 387
Crumb 822
Deseret 836
Dog's Life, A 396
F for Fake 566

Fires Were Started 185
Gimme Shelter 516
Gleaners and I, The 883
Great White Silence, The 45
Häxan 40
Hearts of Darkness: A
    Filmmaker's Apocalypse 801
High School 482
Hoop Dreams 828
Hôtel Terminus: Klaus Barbie et
    son temps 748
Hotel Terminus: The Life and
    Times of Klaus Barbie 748
House is Black, The 404
In the Year of the Pig 499
Khaneh Siah Ast 404
Koyaanisqatsi 692
Land Without Bread 108
Las hurdes 108
Le chagrin et la pitié 521
Les glaneurs et la glaneuse 883
Les maîtres fous 304
Look of Silence, The 935
Mad Masters, The 304
Man with a Movie Camera,
    The 72
Méditerranée 413
Mondo cane 396
Nanook of the North 36
Night and Fog 306
Nostalgia de la luz 915
Nostalgia for the Light 915
Nuit et brouillard 306
Olympia 143
Roger & Me 774
Sans soleil 687
Sherman's March 731
Shoah 718
Sorrow and the Pity, The 521
Sunless 687
Tale of the Wind, A 756
Thin Blue Line, The 753
Tokyo Olympiad 432
Tokyo Orimpikku 432
Tongues Untied 798
Triumph des Willens 111
Triumph of the Will 111
Une histoire de vent 756
Vérités et mensonges 566
Woodstock 515

Drama
8 ½ 400
12 Years a Slave 927
39 Steps, The 120
Actor's Revenge, An 413
Actress, The 807
Adventures of Priscilla, Queen of
    the Desert, The 827
Affair to Remember, An 325
Aguirre, der Zorn Gottes 538
Aguirre, the Wrath of God 538
Ai no corrida 609
Ali: Fear Eats the Soul 584

All About Eve 248
All About My Mother 881
All Quiet on the Western
    Front 79
All That Heaven Allows 314
All That Jazz 648
Alphaville 436
Alphaville, une étrange aventure
    de Lemmy Caution 436
Amadeus 705
American Beauty 879
American Friend, The 615
American Graffiti 556
Amores perros 888
Anatomy of a Murder 356
Andrei Rublev 492
Andrei Rublyov 492
Angst Essen Seele Auf 584
Aparajito 333
Apartment, The 372
Apocalypse Now 646
Apur Sansar 359
Ariel 752
Ascent 609
Ashes and Diamonds 342
Astenicheskij sindrom 771
Asthenic Syndrome, The 771
Au hasard Balthazar 452
Au revoir les enfants 733
Autumn Afternoon, An 390
Ba wang bie jie 814
Bab el hadid 343
Babbetes Gaestebud 743
Babe 837
Babette's Feast 743
Bad and the Beautiful, The 266
Badkonake sefid 839
Badlands 354
Ballad of Narayama, The 688
Balthazar 452
Barefoot Contessa, The 291
Barren Lives 408
Barry Lyndon 585
Battle of Algiers, The 434
Battleship Potemkin, The 51
Beau Travail 880
Beautiful Troublemaker, The 788
Beauty and the Beast 210
Before the Revolution 421
Being There 644
Beiqing chengshi 776
Belle de jour 455
Ben-Hur 354
Bharat Mata 335
Bicycle Thief, The 223
Big Chill, The 687
Big Red One, The 659
Big Short, The 940
Bigamist, The 275
Bigger Than Life 320
Birdman 932
Birth of a Nation, The 24
Biruma no tategoto 318